SIXTH EDITION

BUSINESS AND ITS ENVIRONMENT

David P. Baron

Stanford University

Prentice Hall
Upper Saddle River, New Jersey 07458

Cataloging for this publication can be obtained from the Library of Congress.

Acquisitions Editor: Kim Norbuta
Editorial Director: Sally Yagan
Product Development Manager: Ashley Santora
Editorial Assistant: Liz Davis
Editorial Project Manager: Claudia Fernandes
Marketing Manager: Nikki Jones
Marketing Assistant: Ian Gold
Permissions Project Manager: Charles Morris
Senior Managing Editor: Judy Leale
Production Project Manager: Kelly Warsak
Senior Operations Specialist: Arnold Vila
Operations Specialist: Ben Smith
Manager of Central Design: Jayne Conte
Cover Designer: Lisbeth Axell
Cover Illustration: Getty Images
Manager, Cover Visual Research & Permissions: Karen Sanatar
Composition: Aptara Corp.
Full-Service Project Management: Thistle Hill Publishing Services, LLC
Printer/Binder: R.R. Donnelley/Willard
Cover Printer: Lehigh-Phoenix Color/Hagerstown
Typeface: 10/12 Times Ten Roman

Credits and acknowledgments borrowed from other sources and reproduced, with permission, in this textbook appear on appropriate page within text.

Pearson Education Ltd., London
Pearson Education Singapore, Pte. Ltd
Pearson Education, Canada, Inc.
Pearson Education–Japan
Pearson Education Australia PTY, Limited

Pearson Education North Asia, Ltd., Hong Kong
Pearson Educación de Mexico, S.A. de C.V.
Pearson Education Malaysia, Pte. Ltd
Pearson Education Upper Saddle River, New Jersey

Prentice Hall
is an imprint of

www.pearsonhighered.com

10 9 8 7 6 5 4 3 2 1
ISBN-13: 978-0-13-608392-4
ISBN-10:   0-13-608392-7

To Mary

Brief Contents

PART I   STRATEGY AND THE NONMARKET ENVIRONMENT   1

Chapter 1   Market and Nonmarket Environments   1

Chapter 2   Integrated Strategy   33

Chapter 3   The News Media and Nonmarket Issues   66

Chapter 4   Private Politics   90

Chapter 5   Crisis Management   120

PART II   PUBLIC POLITICS AND NONMARKET STRATEGY   153

Chapter 6   Nonmarket Analysis for Business   153

Chapter 7   Nonmarket Strategies for Government Arenas   185

Chapter 8   Implementing Nonmarket Strategies in Government Arenas   220

PART III   GOVERNMENT AND MARKETS   265

Chapter 9   Antitrust: Economics, Law, and Politics   265

Chapter 10   Regulation: Law, Economics, and Politics   302

Chapter 11   Environmental Management and Sustainability   337

Chapter 12   Law and Markets   374

Chapter 13   Information Industries and Nonmarket Issues   413

PART IV   GLOBAL NONMARKET STRATEGY   451

Chapter 14   The Political Economy of Japan   451

Chapter 15   The Political Economy of the European Union   481

Chapter 16   China: History, Culture, and Political Economy   517

Chapter 17   Emerging Markets   549

Chapter 18   The Political Economy of International Trade Policy   574

PART V   ETHICS AND CORPORATE SOCIAL RESPONSIBILITY   619

Chapter 19   Corporate Social Responsibility   619

Chapter 20   Ethics Systems: Utilitarianism   653

Chapter 21   Ethics Systems: Rights and Justice   681

Chapter 22   Implementing Ethics Systems   720

Chapter 23   Ethics Issues in International Business   749

Contents

List of Cases   xvi

Preface   xix

PART I: STRATEGY AND THE NONMARKET ENVIRONMENT   1

CHAPTER 1   Market and Nonmarket Environments   1

Introduction   1

The Environment of Business   2

The Role of Management   3

Market and Nonmarket Environments   4

Analysis of the Nonmarket Environment: The Four I's   5

The Nonmarket Environment of the Automobile Industry   5

    Issues 5 ■ Interests 8 ■ Institutions 9 ■ Information 10

Change in the Nonmarket Environment   11

Anticipating Change in the Nonmarket Environment   13

The Nonmarket Issue Life Cycle   13

    EXAMPLE: GRADUATION CARDS   14

Summary   16

Cases   17

    The Nonmarket Environment of the Pharmaceutical Industry   17

    The Nonmarket Environment of McDonald's   20

    The Nonmarket Environment of Google   25

CHAPTER 2   Integrated Strategy   33

Introduction   33

Strategy in the Nonmarket Environment   33

    The Importance of Nonmarket Strategy 33 ■ Competition and Change in the Nonmarket Environment 35

    ■ Strategy and the Nonmarket Issue Life Cycle 36 ■ Strategies and Borders 36

Integrated Strategy   37

    Google and the Spectrum Auction 38

    EXAMPLE: DIRECT-TO-CONSUMER ADVERTISING AND INTEGRATED STRATEGY IN THE

        PHARMACEUTICAL INDUSTRY   40

    Approaches to Integrating Market and Nonmarket Strategies 41

Nonmarket Positioning   42

    Nonmarket Positioning and Market Strategies 43

    EXAMPLE: eBAY'S POSITIONING IN LEGAL SPACE   44

    Positioning Spaces 46 ■ The Perils of Positioning 47

Nonmarket Capabilities and Reputation   48

A Framework for the Analysis of Nonmarket Issues   49

    EXAMPLE: CITIBANK AND CREDIT CARDS FOR UNDERGRADUATES   51

Organization of the Nonmarket Strategy Function   52

Summary   53

Cases   54

    Exclusive Resorts: Entrepreneurial Positioning and Nonmarket Defense   54

    Envirotest Systems Corporation (A)   57

    Molecular Insight Pharmaceuticals: Integrated Strategy for a Development Stage Molecular

        Medicine Company   61

CHAPTER 3   The News Media and Nonmarket Issues   66

Introduction   66

The Role of the News Media in Nonmarket Issues   66

Messages and Their Interpretation   68

A Theory of News Media Coverage and Treatment   69
Intrinsic Audience Interest 69   ■   Societal Significance 70   ■   Combining the Perspectives 70

Extending the Theory   72
Newsworthiness 72   ■   The Cost of Coverage 73   ■   Balance and Fairness 73

The Nature of the News Media   74
News Organizations as Businesses 74   ■   The Profession 74   ■   Does the News Media Treat Issues Selectively? 75
■   Bias, Accuracy, and Fairness 76   ■   The Internet and Citizen Journalism 77

Business Interactions with the News Media   78
The Need for Information 78   ■   Media Strategies 78   ■   Responses and Media Vacuums 79
■   Media Interviews 79   ■   Anticipating Issues 80   ■   Unanticipated Events 81

Recourse in Disputes with the Media   81
Private Recourse 81
EXAMPLE: PROCTER & GAMBLE AND NEIGHBOR TO NEIGHBOR   82
Recourse to the Law: Defamation and Libel 83   ■   Political Recourse 84

Summary   85
Cases   86
General Motors: Like a Rock? (A)   *86*
Illinois Power Company (A)   *88*

CHAPTER 4   Private Politics   90

Introduction   90

Campaigns   91
EXAMPLE: PIZZA HUT AND HEALTH INSURANCE REFORM   93

Private or Public Politics?   95

Activist Strategies   96
Advocacy Science 98   ■   Target Selection 98
EXAMPLE: FISH FARM ACTIVISM   99
A Generic Strategy of Activists 100

Activist Organizations   101
Activists and Their Organizations 101   ■   Greenpeace 102

Interacting with Activist Organizations   103
Assessment 103   ■   Strategy and Negotiations 104
EXAMPLE: NEGOTIATING WITH ACTIVISTS: ONBANK   106
Challenging the Activists 106

Summary   107
Cases   109
Shell, Greenpeace, and Brent Spar   *109*
Nike in Southeast Asia   *112*
Anatomy of a Corporate Campaign: Rainforest Action Network and Citigroup (A)   *115*
Anatomy of a Corporate Campaign: Rainforest Action Network and Citigroup (B)   *118*

CHAPTER 5   Crisis Management   120

Introduction   120

The Nature and Causes of Crises   120

The Pattern of Crisis Development   121
EXAMPLE: PEPSICO AND THE SYRINGE EPISODE   124

Components of a Crisis Management Program   125
Avoidance 126   ■   Crisis Preparedness 127   ■   Root Cause Analysis 128   ■   Response 129   ■   Resolution 132

Summary   133

Cases   135
    Buffalo Savings Bank (A)   135
    Mattel: Crisis Management or Management Crisis   136
    Merck and Vioxx   140

PART I   Integrative Case: ***Wal-Mart: Nonmarket Pressure and Reputation Risk (A)   144***

PART II: PUBLIC POLITICS AND NONMARKET STRATEGY   153
CHAPTER 6   Nonmarket Analysis for Business   153
    Introduction   153
    A Framework for the Analysis of Nonmarket Action in Public Politics   154
        Interests and Interest Groups 154 ■ The Amount of Nonmarket Action 155 ■ The Demand for
        Nonmarket Action 155 ■ The Costs and Effectiveness of Nonmarket Action 156
        ■ The Distributive Politics Spreadsheet 158
    The Nature of Political Competition   159
        EXAMPLE: INTERNET WINE SALES   161
        Institutions and Institutional Officeholders 162
    Moral Determinants of Collective Action   162
    Boeing in a Pickle   162
    Analysis of Boeing in a Pickle   164
        The Nonmarket Issue 164 ■ Distributive Consequences 165 ■ Boeing's Nonmarket Agenda and
        Objectives 166 ■ The Nature of the Politics 167 ■ Interests and the Demand for Nonmarket Action 167
        ■ The Supply Side 167 ■ The Distributive Politics Spreadsheet 168 ■ Institutions and Institutional
        Officeholders 168 ■ Nonmarket Strategy Formulation 170 ■ The Outcome 171
    Summary   171
    Appendix A: Nonmarket Action and the Free-Rider Problem   173
    Appendix B: The Organization of Congress   175
    Cases   181
        Tobacco Politics   181
        Scrubbers and Environmental Politics   183
        Repeal of the Luxury Tax   184

CHAPTER 7   Nonmarket Strategies for Government Arenas   185
    Introduction   185
    Responsible Nonmarket Action   186
        Criticisms of Business Nonmarket Action 186
    Nonmarket Strategy Formulation   189
        Managers and Nonmarket Strategies 189 ■ Implementation 194
    Understanding Outcomes   195
    Generic Nonmarket Strategies   196
        Representation Strategies 196
        EXAMPLE: TOSHIBA AND TRADE SANCTIONS   197
        Majority-Building Strategies 199 ■ Informational Strategies 202 ■ Public Officeholders as Targets of
        Nonmarket Strategies 203
        EXAMPLE: CHINA AND MOST FAVORED NATION STATUS   204
    Institutions, Interests, and Strategy Choice   205
        Institutions and Responsiveness 205 ■ Interests: Client and Interest Group Politics 205
    Summary   206
    Appendix: The Politics of the Extension of Daylight Saving Time   208
    Cases   212
        Federal Express and Labor Organization   212
        Carried Interest Taxation   213
        Wal-Mart and Its Urban Expansion Strategy   217

CHAPTER 8   Implementing Nonmarket Strategies in Government Arenas   220

Introduction   220

Lobbying   220

EXAMPLE: PACIFICARE'S NONMARKET PORTFOLIO   221

The Nature of Lobbying 222 ■ Technical and Political Information 223 ■ Credibility and Relevance of Information 224 ■ Access 225 ■ Timing and Focus 226 ■ Government Allies 226 ■ Controls on Lobbying 226

Electoral Support   227

Myths and Realities of Campaign Financing 228 ■ Election Financing Laws 228 ■ The Pattern of Campaign Contributions 229 ■ Purposes of Campaign Contributions 230

Grassroots and Constituency Campaigns   231

Mobilization 231 ■ Business Grassroots Campaigns 232 ■ The Effectiveness of Grassroots Programs 232

Coalition Building   233

Peak Associations 233 ■ Trade Associations 234 ■ Ad Hoc Coalitions 235 ■ Coalitions and Consensus 235

EXAMPLE: PHARMACEUTICAL POLITICS   236

Testimony   236

Public Advocacy   237

Judicial Actions   238

Organizing for Nonmarket Effectiveness   239

Developing Nonmarket Capabilities   239

Summary   240

Cases   242

Responsible Lobbying?   242

Internet Taxation   247

Pharmaceutical Switching   252

PART II   Integrative Case: *Fuel Economy Standards 2007*   259

PART III: GOVERNMENT AND MARKETS   265

CHAPTER 9   Antitrust: Economics, Law, and Politics   265

Introduction   265

Antitrust Law   267

The Antitrust Statutes 267

EXAMPLE: MONOPOLY   269

Exemptions 269

Enforcement of the Antitrust Laws   270

Government Enforcement 270 ■ Private Enforcement 272 ■ Per Se Violations and the Rule of Reason 273

Antitrust Thought   274

The Structural Approach 275 ■ The Chicago School 277 ■ The New IO Approach 278

Examples of the Differences in Antitrust Thought   280

Vertical Arrangements 280 ■ Predatory Pricing and Entry Deterrence 282 ■ Collusion and Price-Fixing 283 ■ Mergers and Merger Guidelines 284

Compliance   286

The Politics of Antitrust   287

Summary   288

Cases   289

Price Fixing in the Airways   289

The Staples–Office Depot Merger?   290

The Microsoft Antitrust Case   294

CHAPTER 10   Regulation: Law, Economics, and Politics   302

Introduction   302

Periods of Regulatory Change   303

The Constitutional Basis for Regulation   304
Regulatory Commissions and Agencies   305
Delegation, Rule Making, Due Process, and Discretion   306
The Nonmarket Environment of Regulatory Agencies   307
    EXAMPLE: REGULATORY RULE MAKING IN THE BUSH ADMINISTRATION   309
Explanations for Regulation   310
Market Imperfections   310
    Natural Monopoly 310 ■ Externalities 312 ■ Public Goods 313 ■ Asymmetric Information 313
    ■ Moral Hazard 314 ■ Government Imperfections 315
The Political Economy of Regulation   316
    Capture and Rent-Seeking Theories 316 ■ Fairness 316 ■ Other Public Purposes: Media Ownership
    Rules 317 ■ Preemption 318
A Nonmarket Theory of Regulation   318
    EXAMPLE: THE POLITICAL ECONOMY OF REGULATION: ATVs   319
    Redistribution and Cross-Subsidization 320
Cost-of-Service Regulation   320
Deregulation   321
    Telecommunications 321 ■ Electric Power 323 ■ Auctions 324
Summary   325
Cases   326
    The FCC and Broadband Regulation   326
    Enron Power Marketing, Inc., and the California Market   330
    The FCC Media Ownership Rules   332

CHAPTER 11   Environmental Management and Sustainability   337
Introduction   337
The Environment and Sustainability   337
    Goals and Actions 337 ■ Global Climate Change 338 ■ Policy 338 ■ Tradeoffs 339
Socially Efficient Control of Externalities   340
    The Coase Theorem 340
    EXAMPLE: THE COASE THEOREM   342
    Transactions Costs and the Limits of the Coase Theorem 343
Cap-and-Trade Systems   344
    Cap-and-Trade Systems to Address Acid Rain 345
Global Climate Change and Emissions Trading Systems   346
    The United States and Carbon Emissions 347 ■ Emissions Trading in the European Union 347
    ■ Emissions Trading Within BP plc (British Petroleum) 348
Regulation as Opportunity   348
Government Policy: The EPA   349
    Enforcement 350 ■ Standards Setting and Engineering Controls 351 ■ Incentive Approaches 351
    EXAMPLE: INTEL AND THE PROJECT XL   352
    Superfund 352 ■ State Policy Initiatives 353
The Political Economy of Environmental Protection   353
    The Nature of Environmental Politics 353 ■ Judicial Politics 354 ■ Advocacy Science 354
    ■ Distributive Politics 355 ■ Private and Public Politics 356
    EXAMPLE: THE EQUATOR PRINCIPLES   357
    NIMBY and Private Politics 358
Management of Environmental Protection Issues   359
    EXAMPLE: DOW CHEMICAL AND LOCAL ENVIRONMENTALISTS   361
    EXAMPLE: MCDONALD'S AND WASTE REDUCTION   362
    EXAMPLE: ENVIRONMENTAL ACTIVISM AT HOME DEPOT   363
Voluntary Collective Environmental Programs   364
Summary   365

Cases   366
>   *Regulation as Opportunity: Cummins Inc.*   *366*
>   *Emerging Nanotechnology Regulation: Samsung's SilverCare Washing Machine*   *368*
>   *Environmental Justice and Pollution Credits Trading Systems*   *370*

CHAPTER 12   Law and Markets   374
Introduction   374
The Common Law   375
Property   376
>   Bargaining 376   ■   Incentives and Appropriability 377
Intellectual Property   377
>   Intellectual Property Protection 378
>   EXAMPLE: INTELLECTUAL PROPERTY ENFORCEMENT AND DIGITAL PIRACY   379
>   EXAMPLE: MICKEY MOUSE POLITICS AND LAW   381
Contracts   383
>   EXAMPLE: GENENTECH AND CITY OF HOPE   384
>   Enforceability 385   ■   Breach 385   ■   Remedies 385
Torts   386
The Product Safety Problem and Social Efficiency   387
Entitlements, Liability, and Social Efficiency   389
>   Entitlements and Their Protection 389   ■   The Assignment of Social Costs and the Choice Between Liability and Regulation 391
Products Liability   392
>   The Development of Products Liability Law 392   ■   Allowable Defenses Under Strict Liability 395   ■   Preemption 396   ■   Damages 397   ■   The Politics of Products Liability 398
Imperfections in the Liability System   399
>   EXAMPLE: SILICONE BREAST IMPLANTS   401
Summary   403
Cases   404
>   *California Space Heaters, Inc.*   *404*
>   *Patent Games: Plavix*   *406*
>   *Obesity and McLawsuits*   *408*

CHAPTER 13   Information Industries and Nonmarket Issues   413
Introduction   413
The Economics of Online Markets   414
Internet Privacy   417
>   EXAMPLE: GOOGLE: GMAIL AND PRIVACY   419
The Internet and Tax Policy   423
Online Communities   425
Summary   427
Cases   428
>   *DoubleClick and Internet Privacy*   *428*
>   *eBay and Database Protection*   *433*
>   *eBay: Private Ordering for an Online Community*   *438*

PART III   Integrative Case: *Credit Card Regulation*   445

PART IV: GLOBAL NONMARKET STRATEGY   451
CHAPTER 14   The Political Economy of Japan   451
Introduction   451
Issues   452
Interests   454

Institutions   455
The Diet 455 ■ Political Parties and the Electoral System 456 ■ The Bureaucracy 458
■ Political Reform 460

The Judicial System and the Antimonopoly Law   462

Cultural Foundations   462

Tying the Components Together: A Framework of Political Exchange   464
Political Exchange 464

Characteristics of Business   466

Business–Government Interactions   467
The Organization of Business for Nonmarket Action 467 ■ Nonmarket Strategies 468
■ Relationships with the Bureaucracy 469 ■ Lobbying and Points of Access 470
■ Information 471 ■ Corporate Nonmarket Styles 471

Summary   472

Cases   474
The Breakup of Nippon Telephone and Telegraph?   *474*
The Privatization of Japan Post   *476*
Uniqlo: Success Breeds Nonmarket Challenges   *479*

CHAPTER 15   The Political Economy of the European Union   481

Introduction   481

The European Union   481
The Single European Act 482 ■ The Maastricht Treaty 483

The Institutions of the European Union   484
The European Commission 484 ■ The Council of Ministers 485 ■ The European Parliament 486
■ The Court of Justice 487 ■ The European Economic and Social Committee 487 ■ The EU Legislative
Process 488 ■ Economic and Monetary Union 488 ■ The EU Constitutional
Treaty 490 ■ Competition Policy 490
EXAMPLE: MICROSOFT AND EU COMPETITION POLICY   493
State Aids and the Common Agricultural Policy 494 ■ The Social Charter, Social Democracy, and Labor
Markets 494

Nonmarket Issues   496

Interests and Their Organization   498

Nonmarket Strategies in the European Union   499
EXAMPLE: PRONUPTIA AND FRANCHISING   504

Summary   505

Cases   506
The European Union Carbon Tax   *506*
The European Union Data Protection Directive   *509*
Aldeasa and the EU Duty Free Abolition (A)   *511*

CHAPTER 16   China: History, Culture, and Political Economy   517

Introduction   517

Historical Background   518
Pre-Republican 518 ■ The Communist Era 520 ■ The Reform Era 521

Confucianism and Social Explanations   523
Applications in Society, Politics, and Business 525

The Nonmarket Environment and the Four I's   527
Institutions and Government 528 ■ State Institutions 530 ■ Provincial and Local Governments 531

Business: State-Owned Enterprises, Foreign Direct Investment, and International Trade   532
State-Owned Enterprises 532 ■ Foreign Direct Investment 533 ■ International Trade Policy and
WTO Membership 534 ■ Regulation 535

Continuing Issues   535
Human Rights 535
EXAMPLE: AN INTELLECTUAL PROPERTY CHALLENGE   537
Energy and the Environment 539

Summary   540

Cases   541

Wugang and the Reform of State-Owned Enterprises   *541*

Direct Selling in China   *543*

Google in China   *545*

CHAPTER 17   Emerging Markets   **549**

Introduction   549

Country Assessment   549

Individual Freedoms 550   ■   Economic Freedom 550   ■   Corruption 550   ■   Political Risk 551
■   Competitiveness 551   ■   Culture 551

Opportunities   551

EXAMPLE: INDIA   552

Opportunity at the Bottom of the Pyramid? 553   ■   River Blindness 553   ■   Fair Trade 554
■   Microfinance 556   ■   Underdeveloped Markets and Business Groups 557

Risk Assessment   558

Causes and Types of Risks 559

Management in the Nonmarket Environment   562

Summary   563

Cases   564

Tesco PLC in India?   *564*

Social Entrepreneurship: Banco Compartamos   *567*

Social Entrepreneurship: Kiva   *568*

MTN Group Limited   *570*

CHAPTER 18   The Political Economy of International Trade Policy   **574**

Introduction   574

The Economics of International Trade   575

Competitive Theory 575   ■   Strategic Trade Theory 578

The Political Economy of International Trade Policy   579

The Dual Nature of the Politics of International Trade 579   ■   Asymmetries in the Politics 580

International Trade Agreements   581

The World Trade Organization 581   ■   General Agreement on Trade in Services (GATS) 582   ■   Trade-Related Aspects of Intellectual Property Rights (TRIPS) 582   ■   Agriculture 583   ■   Government Procurement 584   ■   Antidumping, Countervailing Duties, and Safeguards 584   ■   Dispute Settlement 584
■   The Doha Round of WTO Negotiations 587   ■   Other Trade Agreements 588

U.S. Trade Policy   588

The Structure of U.S. Trade Policy 588   ■   U.S. Trade Law and Its Administration 589

The Political Economy of Protectionism   590

Formal Policies 590   ■   Channels of Protection 591

EXAMPLE: STEEL IMPORTS AND THE NONMARKET CAMPAIGN   592

The Political Economy of Market Opening   594

The North American Free Trade Agreement 594   ■   Market Opening Under the Threat of Retaliation 595

Summary   596

Cases   597

Cemex and Antidumping   *597*

Compulsory Licensing, Thailand, and Abbott Laboratories   *602*

Sophis Networks and Encryption Export Controls (A)   *607*

PART IV   **Integrative *Case: Toys 'Я' Us and Globalization***   **614**

PART V: **ETHICS AND CORPORATE SOCIAL RESPONSIBILITY**   **619**

CHAPTER 19   Corporate Social Responsibility   **619**

Introduction   619

The Trust Gap   620

What Is Corporate Social Responsibility?   621
Milton Friedman's Profit Maximization 621

Compliance with the Law   625

Stakeholder Theory   626

The Business Roundtable Statement on Social Responsibility   628
Discussion 629

Corporate Social Responsibility and Corporate Social Performance   630
EXAMPLE: TUNA AND DOLPHINS   631

A Framework for Corporate Social Performance   632
Terminology 632 ■ The Setting 632 ■ Motivations for CSP 633 ■ Rewards 634
■ Summary 635 ■ Empirical Research 635

Corporate Governance   637
Social Accountability 637 ■ The Duties of Boards of Directors 638 ■ Sarbanes-Oxley 639
■ The Market for Control 640

Summary   641

Cases   642
The Collapse of Enron: Governance and Responsibility   642
*Wal-Mart: Nonmarket Pressure and Reputation Risk (B): A New Nonmarket
    Strategy   647*
Playing by the Rules?   650

CHAPTER 20   Ethics Systems: Utilitarianism   653

Introduction   653

The Managerial Role of Ethics   653

What Ethics Is and Is Not   654

Personal and Business Ethics   655

Ethics and Private Interests   655

Ethics, Politics, and Change   655

Casuistry   656
EXAMPLE: SAVING THE DIVISION   657

The Methodology of Ethics   657

The Relationships Among Moral Philosophy, Ethics, and Political Philosophy   659

Utilitarianism: A Consequentialist System   660
Utilitarianism and Self-Interest 661 ■ Aligning Self-Interest with Societal Well-Being 661 ■ Utilitarianism,
Distribution, and Altruism 662 ■ Summary of the Components of Utilitarianism 662

Utilitarian Duty and the Calabresi and Melamed Principles   662

Act and Rule Utilitarianism   664
Jointly Determined Consequences 665 ■ Decision Making in the Face of a Moral Transgression 666

Utilitarianism and Rights   666

Criticisms of Utilitarianism   667
Philosophical Criticisms 667 ■ Interpersonal Comparisons of Utility 668 ■ Identifying Costs and
Benefits 668 ■ The Measurement Problem 668 ■ The Information Problem 669

Utilitarianism in Application   670
Categories of Situations 670 ■ Methodology 670
EXAMPLE: LIVING BENEFITS   671
EXAMPLE: INTEGRITY TESTS   672
EXAMPLE: LIFE INSURANCE SCREENING FOR PREEXISTING CONDITIONS   673
EXAMPLE: REDLINING   673

Summary   674

Cases   675
Pricing the Norplant System   675
Tax Shelters   677
Pfizer and Celebrex   679

CHAPTER 21 Ethics Systems: Rights and Justice 681

Introduction 681

Classification of Ethics Systems 681

Classes of Rights 682

Kantian Maxims or Moral Rules 683
EXAMPLE: LIVING BENEFITS 684
The Relationship between Maxims and Rights 684 ■ Intrinsic and Instrumental Rights 685
■ Criticisms of Kantian Rights 687
EXAMPLE: PRIVACY 688

Applied Rights Analysis 689
Claimed and Granted Rights 689
EXAMPLE: LIFE INSURANCE SCREENING FOR PREEXISTING CONDITIONS 691
A Methodology for Rights Analysis 691

Conflicts Among Rights 691
Rights and Interests 692 ■ Prioritization 692
EXAMPLE: INTEGRITY TESTS 693

Equal Employment Opportunity 694

Disabilities and Rights 696

Neoclassical Liberalism 697

Categories of Justice Theories 698
Distributive Justice 698 ■ Compensatory Justice 699 ■ Injustice 700

Rawls's Theory of Justice 700
The Framework for Justice as Fairness 700 ■ The Principles of Justice 702 ■ The Role of Incentives 703
EXAMPLE: LIVING BENEFITS 704
Duty in Rawls's Theory 704
EXAMPLE: CLINICAL TRIAL OBLIGATIONS 705
Criticisms of Rawls's Theory 705 ■ Applying the Principles of Justice 706
EXAMPLE: AFFIRMATIVE ACTION 707
EXAMPLE: INTEGRITY TESTS 709
EXAMPLE: REDLINING 709
EXAMPLE: LIFE INSURANCE SCREENING FOR PREEXISTING CONDITIONS 710

Higher Order Standards for Evaluating Ethics Systems 710

Summary 710

Cases 712
Genetic Testing in the Workplace 712
Citigroup and Subprime Lending 714
Consumer Awareness or Disease Mongering? GlaxoSmithKline and the Restless Legs Syndrome 716

CHAPTER 22 Implementing Ethics Systems 720

Introduction 720
EXAMPLE: LEVI STRAUSS & COMPANY AND GLOBAL SOURCING 721

Moral Determinants of Nonmarket Action 722
EXAMPLE: CIRCLE K'S HEALTH CARE POLICY 723

The Challenge of Corporate Social Responsibility 724

Corporate Social Responsibility and Ethics in Practice 726
EXAMPLE: UNOCAL CORPORATION AND THE DIRTY CAR BOUNTY 726
EXAMPLE: SOUTH SHORE BANK AND COMMUNITY DEVELOPMENT 727
EXAMPLE: BP AND SOCIAL RESPONSIBILITY 727
EXAMPLE: WAL-MART: REPUTATION AND STAKEHOLDER MANAGEMENT 728
EXAMPLE: CITIGROUP: RESPONSIBILITY UNDER FIRE? 730
EXAMPLE: JOHNSON & JOHNSON'S "OUR CREDO" 731
Core Principles and Their Evolution 731 ■ The Body Shop and the Social Audit 732 ■ Codes of Conduct 733 ■ Competitive and Proprietary Information 734 ■ Principles and Reasoning 734

Tensions in the Implementation of Ethic Principles   735
  Paternalism 735 ■ Nonmarket Action and Restraint 736
Sources of Unethical Behavior   738
Summary   739
Cases   740
  Denny's and Customer Service   740
  Gilead Sciences (A): The Gilead Access Program for HIV Drugs   742
  Advanced Technology Laboratories, Inc.   746

CHAPTER 23   Ethics Issues in International Business   749
Introduction   749
International Law and Institutions   750
Cultural Relativism   751
Human Rights and Justice   754
  Slave Labor in Saipan? 754
Operating in Developing Countries   755
AIDS and Developing Countries   756
  EXAMPLE: GLAXOSMITHKLINE AND NONMARKET SPILLOVERS   757
Responsibility for Working Conditions in Suppliers' Factories   758
  Sweatshops 758 ■ Private Governance and Self-Regulation: The Fair Labor Association 759
  ■ Company Responses 759
International Codes   761
Questionable Foreign Payments and Corruption   761
  Questionable Payments and Ethics Principles 762 ■ The Lockheed Case 763 ■ A Utilitarian Analysis
  of Bribery 764 ■ The Foreign Corrupt Practices Act 766 ■ Company Codes 767 ■ Cummins's
  Practice 768 ■ The OECD Anti-Bribery Convention 769
Summary   770
Cases   772
  Complications in Marnera   772
  De Beers and Conflict Diamonds   773
  Siemens: Anatomy of Bribery   774

PART V   Integrative Case: *GlaxoSmithKline and AIDS Drugs Policy*   778

References   784

Index   796

List of Cases

PART I

Chapter 1

The Nonmarket Environment of the Pharmaceutical Industry   17

The Nonmarket Environment of McDonald's   20

The Nonmarket Environment of Google   25

Chapter 2

Exclusive Resorts: Entrepreneurial Positioning and Nonmarket Defense   54

Envirotest Systems Corporation (A)   57

Molecular Insight Pharmaceuticals: Integrated Strategy for a Development Stage
Molecular Medicine Company   61

Chapter 3

General Motors: Like a Rock? (A)   86

Illinois Power Company (A)   88

Chapter 4

Shell, Greenpeace, and Brent Spar   109

Nike in Southeast Asia   112

Anatomy of a Corporate Campaign: Rainforest Action Network and Citigroup (A)   115

Anatomy of a Corporate Campaign: Rainforest Action Network and Citigroup (B)   118

Chapter 5

Buffalo Savings Bank (A)   135

Mattel: Crisis Management or Management Crisis   136

Merck and Vioxx   140

Part I Integrative Case

Wal-Mart: Nonmarket Pressure and Reputation Risk (A)   144

PART II

Chapter 6

Tobacco Politics   181

Scrubbers and Environmental Politics   183

Repeal of the Luxury Tax   184

Chapter 7

Federal Express and Labor Organization   212

Carried Interest Taxation   213

Wal-Mart and Its Urban Expansion Strategy   217

Chapter 8

Responsible Lobbying?   242

Internet Taxation   247

Pharmaceutical Switching   252

Part II Integrative Case

Fuel Economy Standards 2007   259

PART III

Chapter 9

Price Fixing in the Airways 289

The Staples–Office Depot Merger? 290

The Microsoft Antitrust Case 294

Chapter 10

The FCC and Broadband Regulation 326

Enron Power Marketing, Inc., and the California Market 330

The FCC Media Ownership Rules 332

Chapter 11

Regulation as Opportunity: Cummins, Inc. 366

Emerging Nanotechnology Regulation: Samsung's SilverCare Washing Machine 368

Environmental Justice and Pollution Credits Trading Systems 370

Chapter 12

California Space Heaters, Inc. 404

Patent Games: Plavix 406

Obesity and McLawsuits 408

Chapter 13

DoubleClick and Internet Privacy 428

eBay and Database Protection 433

eBay: Private Ordering for an Online Community 438

Part III Integrative Case

Credit Card Regulation 445

PART IV

Chapter 14

The Breakup of Nippon Telephone and Telegraph? 474

The Privatization of Japan Post 476

Uniqlo: Success Breeds Nonmarket Challenges 479

Chapter 15

The European Union Carbon Tax 506

The European Union Data Protection Directive 509

Aldeasa and the EU Duty Free Abolition (A) 511

Chapter 16

Wugang and the Reform of State-Owned Enterprises 541

Direct Selling in China 543

Google in China 545

Chapter 17

Tesco PLC in India? 564

Social Entrepreneurship: Banco Compartamos 567

Social Entrepreneurship: Kiva 568

MTN Group Limited 570

Chapter 18

Cemex and Antidumping 597

Compulsory Licensing, Thailand, and Abbott Laboratories 602

Sophis Networks and Encryption Export Controls (A) 607

Part IV Integrative Case

Toys 'Я' Us and Globalization   614

PART V

Chapter 19

The Collapse of Enron: Governance and Responsibility   642

Wal-Mart: Nonmarket Pressure and Reputation Risk (B): A New Nonmarket Strategy   647

Playing by the Rules?   650

Chapter 20

Pricing the Norplant System   675

Tax Shelters   677

Pfizer and Celebrex   679

Chapter 21

Genetic Testing in the Workplace   712

Citigroup and Subprime Lending   714

Consumer Awareness or Disease Mongering? GlaxoSmithKline
and the Restless Legs Syndrome   716

Chapter 22

Denny's and Customer Service   740

Gilead Sciences (A): The Gilead Access Program for HIV Drugs   742

Advanced Technology Laboratories, Inc.   746

Chapter 23

Complications in Marnera   772

De Beers and Conflict Diamonds   773

Siemens: Anatomy of Bribery   774

Part V Integrative Case

GlaxoSmithKline and AIDS Drugs Policy   778

Preface

The environment of business has interrelated market and nonmarket components. The market environment is characterized by the structure of the markets in which a firm operates and the rules that govern market competition. The nonmarket environment is characterized by the legal, political, and social arrangements in which the firm is embedded. The nonmarket environment determines the rules of the game for the market environment through government policies and public expectations. Just as firms compete in their market environment, they also compete in their nonmarket environment. Nonmarket competition is more complex, however, because that competition includes not only other firms but also activists, interest groups, the public, and government. *Business and Its Environment* is concerned with the interrelationships among the market and nonmarket environments and the effective management of the issues therein. In contrast to a public policy perspective, the approach taken is managerial. That is, it takes the perspective of firms and managers, not of government or the public. It focuses on issues central to the performance of firms, as measured by both shareholder value and conduct in accord with ethics principles and social responsibilities.

The emphasis in the book is on strategy—nonmarket strategy and its integration with the market strategy of a firm. A nonmarket strategy is composed of objectives and a course of action for participating effectively and responsibly in the nonmarket competition on issues arising in the environment of business. The approach taken in the book emphasizes frameworks, principles, and analysis as the foundations for formulating effective and responsible strategies.

The sixth edition of *Business and Its Environment* represents continuity and change. It retains the structure, much of the subject matter, and the conceptual frameworks of the fifth edition. It also retains the strategy orientation and the guidance provided by the normative subjects of ethics and social responsibility. The sixth edition includes chapter cases for class discussion of managerial issues and applications of the conceptual frameworks and institutional material. At the end of each of the five parts of the book are integrative cases on an activist challenge to Wal-Mart, fuel economy legislation, credit card regulation, globalization, and the pricing of AIDS drugs for developing countries. The sixth edition continues the focus on strategies for improving performance by addressing the challenges in the nonmarket environment and their effects on the market environment. The approach draws on the disciplines of economics, political science, law, and ethics to provide a foundation for strategy formulation and a deeper understanding of the environment of business and nonmarket issues. An integrated perspective strengthens the managerial orientation of the book and also enhances the usefulness of the conceptual materials for other parts of the business curriculum.

The sixth edition includes two new chapters on crisis management and emerging markets. This edition also provides an expanded emphasis on the environment and sustainability and a new framework for corporate social responsibility. The other chapters are updated with new conceptual materials and applications. The new material includes crisis management strategies, social entrepreneurship, global warming and cap-and-trade systems, a framework for understanding corporate social performance and social pressure and operating in emerging markets.

The sixth edition contains 74 cases, including 24 new cases on Google, Gilead Sciences, Tesco, Mattel, Cummins, Molecular Insight, Merck, GlaxoSmithKline, Banco Compartamos, Kiva, MTN Group, Samsung, and Siemens as well as on industry-wide issues including fuel economy standards, credit card regulation, carried interest taxation, nanotechnology regulation, compulsory licensing, tax shelters, and price fixing. The new cases address issues in antitrust and regulation, pharmaceuticals, information technology, environmental protection, international business, social entrepreneurship, and business ethics and responsibility. Twenty-four of the cases concern global and international nonmarket issues, and 19 deal with environmental and health issues. Each case poses a managerial problem that requires analysis and strategy formulation.

The book is organized in five parts. Part I introduces the nonmarket environment and nonmarket strategy with a focus on issues involving the public, activists, the news media, and crises. Part II is concerned with issues addressed in the context of government institutions and with nonmarket strategies for dealing with those issues. The frameworks developed in this part provide a foundation for Parts III and IV. Part III focuses on the interactions between firms and markets as regulated by government with an emphasis on antitrust, regulation, the environment and sustainability, the law of intellectual property, contracts, and torts, and the economics and politics of information industries. Part IV is explicitly international and provides frameworks for understanding the political economy of countries and the relationships between business and government as a foundation for formulating effective strategies. Japan, the European Union, China, and emerging markets are considered, and international trade policy is used to bring the policy and strategy issues together. Part V is normative and focuses on ethics and corporate social responsibility. The complexities involved in operating internationally are considered both through conceptual frameworks and cases.

I would like to thank David Brady, Daniel Diermeier, Timothy Feddersen, Thomas Gilligan, Kirk Hanson, Daniel Kessler, Keith Krehbiel, and Romian Wacziarg for contributing cases to the sixth edition. The Graduate School of Business of Stanford University provided institutional support for the work underpinning this book.

David P. Baron
Stanford, California

C H A P T E R

1

Market and Nonmarket Environments

INTRODUCTION

Some companies are successful in both their market environment and the social, political, and legal nonmarket environment in which they operate. Google, McDonald's, and Toyota have had continuing success in their markets and also have generally conducted themselves in a manner that has earned the respect of the public and the government. Other companies have had great success in their markets but stumbled before the public and government. Nike became synonymous with athletic footwear, but public concerns about the working conditions in its suppliers' factories in Asia tarnished its image and affected its market performance. Wal-Mart, the world's largest company, was targeted by activists, unions, and politicians for its work practices, depressing wages in the labor market, driving small merchants out of business, and weakening the culture of small towns. Microsoft is one of the great successes in the history of business, but its market conduct has resulted in recurring antitrust judgments in the United States and in the European Union where it was fined €1.7 billion for antitrust violations and failure to comply with rulings. BP had earned a reputation for its environmental programs, but in 2005–6 the company experienced a refinery explosion that killed 15 workers and resulted in criminal fines and spilled oil in Prudhoe Bay, Alaska and on the tundra. BP pleaded guilty to price fixing, paying $303 million in fines. Citigroup, the world's largest financial institution, was hit with a series of costly scandals. As a result of its $31 billion acquisition of subprime lender Associates First Capital, Citigroup faced private lawsuits for abusive practices, state legislation restricting subprime lending, and fines of $285 million imposed by the Federal Reserve and the Federal Trade Commission. Citigroup also paid $2.8 billion to settle lawsuits for its role in structuring financial instruments for Enron and WorldCom and $735 million for biased securities research. Japan ordered Citigroup to close its private banking business in the country. In addition to the fines and settlements and the damage to its reputation, Citigroup was targeted by activists for its financing of environmentally destructive projects in developing countries. Citigroup repeated its problems with subprime mortgages resulting in write-downs of $40 billion in 2007–8, the firing of its CEO, and more stringent regulations for mortgage lending.

The problems encountered by Nike, Wal-Mart, BP, Microsoft, and Citigroup originated in their market environments, but the challenges to their operations came from the nonmarket environment. That is, the challenges resulted not from the actions of competitors but instead from the public, interest groups, the legal system, and government. These companies underappreciated the importance of the nonmarket environment and have paid a price for doing so. Even companies that are generally successful in managing in their nonmarket environment face challenges. Google received criticism for tolerating the government-imposed censorship on its Web site in China; McDonald's was criticized for contributing to the obesity crisis; Toyota was criticized for introducing large, fuel inefficient pickup trucks. Some companies have changed their strategies as a result of nonmarket pressure. Nike has become a leader in improving the working conditions in its suppliers' factories, and Wal-Mart has implemented an aggressive environmental program.

Firms have more control over their fate in the markets in which they operate than they have in their nonmarket environment, but successful companies understand that if they do not manage their nonmarket environment, it will manage them. The long-run sustainability of competitive advantage requires managing effectively in the nonmarket environment. Companies like Google, McDonald's, and Toyota have learned that they can participate both responsibly and effectively in influencing developments in their nonmarket environment.

This book is about managing successfully in the nonmarket environment. The perspective taken is that of strategy—nonmarket strategy—and its implementation. That strategy is considered not in isolation but in conjunction with the firm's market or competitive strategy.

This chapter introduces the environment of business, identifies the role of management in the nonmarket environment, and presents a framework for analyzing that environment. The framework is illustrated using the automobile industry as an example. The sources of change in the nonmarket environment are then considered, and a framework for assessing the development of nonmarket issues is presented.

THE ENVIRONMENT OF BUSINESS

The environment of business consists of market and nonmarket components. The market environment includes those interactions between firms, suppliers, and customers that are governed by markets and contracts. These interactions typically involve voluntary economic transactions and the exchange of property. To achieve superior performance, firms must operate effectively in their market environment. They must be efficient in production and responsive to consumer demand. They must anticipate and adapt to change, innovate through research and development, and develop new products and services. Effective management in the market environment is a necessary condition for superior performance, but it is not sufficient.

The performance of a firm, and of its management, also depends on its activities in its nonmarket environment. The nonmarket environment is composed of the social, political, and legal arrangements that structure interactions outside of, but in conjunction with, markets and contracts. The nonmarket environment encompasses those interactions between the firm and individuals, interest groups, government entities, and the public that are intermediated not by markets but by public and private institutions. Public institutions differ from markets because of characteristics such as majority rule, due process, broad enfranchisement, collective action, and access by the public. Activities in the nonmarket environment may be voluntary, as when the firm cooperates with government officials or an environmental group, or involuntary, as in the case of government regulation or a boycott of a firm's product led by an activist group. Effective management in the nonmarket environment has become a necessary condition for superior performance just as has effective management in the market environment.

The nonmarket environment has grown in importance and complexity over time and commands increased managerial attention. Nonmarket issues high on firms' agendas include environmental protection, health and safety, regulation and deregulation, intellectual property protection, human rights, international trade policy, antitrust, pressures from nongovernment organizations (NGOs) and social activists, media coverage of business, corporate social responsibility, and ethics. Although the saliency of particular issues ebbs and flows, nonmarket issues arise sufficiently often to have important consequences for managerial and firm performance. Nonmarket issues, the forces that influence their development, and the strategies for addressing them are the focus of the field of business and its environment. The managerial objective is to achieve superior overall performance by effectively addressing nonmarket issues and the forces associated with them.

Developments in the nonmarket environment affect performance on a number of dimensions. In the automobile industry, emissions and fuel economy standards affect research and development, design, production, pricing, and marketing. Safety regulation and liability standards have similar broad effects. Import competition and access to international markets affect competitive strategies involving product design, pricing, and capacity planning. Each of these examples has two components—an underlying issue and its impact on performance. The fuel economy issue, for example, is related to global climate change and security and has broad implications for performance. The focus for management in the nonmarket environment is on how an automobile company can participate effectively and responsibly in the public and private processes addressing these issues. Activity in the nonmarket environment is generally organized around specific issues and is motivated by the impacts of those issues. The legislative process, for example, focuses on bills to address a specific issue, such as fuel economy standards. Managerial attention thus focuses on specific issues affecting performance, the forces driving those issues, the institutions in whose arenas the issues are addressed, and the participation of firms in shaping the resolution of those issues.

THE ROLE OF MANAGEMENT

Because of its importance for managerial and organizational performance, nonmarket strategy is the responsibility of managers. As illustrated in Figure 1-1, firms operate in both the market and the nonmarket environments. Managers are in the best position to assess the impact of their firm's market activities on its nonmarket environment and the impact of developments in the nonmarket environment on market opportunities and performance. Management thus is responsible for formulating and implementing nonmarket as well as market strategies.

Firms typically deal with nonmarket issues in proportion to their potential impacts on performance. Managers are in the best position to assess those impacts and, with the assistance of specialists, to formulate strategies to address the underlying issues. The implementation of nonmarket strategies also involves the active participation of managers. They may address the public on issues, communicate with the media, testify in regulatory and congressional proceedings, lobby government, participate in coalitions and associations, serve on government advisory panels, meet with activists, negotiate with interest groups, partner with NGOs, build relationships with stakeholders, and participate in constituency programs.

Successful management requires frameworks for analyzing nonmarket issues, principles for reasoning about them, and strategies for addressing them. These frameworks, principles, and strategies enable managers to address issues in a systematic manner and guide their firms successfully and responsibly in their nonmarket environments. In formulating nonmarket strategies, managers may draw on the expertise of lawyers, communications specialists, Washington representatives, and community relations specialists. Managers, however, ultimately must evaluate the quality of the advice they receive and combine it with their own knowledge of the market and nonmarket environments. Most firms have found that managers must be involved in all stages of their efforts to address nonmarket issues.

FIGURE 1-1   The Environment of Business

MARKET AND NONMARKET ENVIRONMENTS

As illustrated in Figure 1-1, the market and nonmarket environments of business are interrelated. A firm's activities in its market environment can generate nonmarket issues and change in its nonmarket environment. That change may take the form of actions by government, such as legislation, regulation, antitrust lawsuits, and international trade policies. Similarly, the actions of interest groups and activists may force a firm to change its market practices. As an example of the market origins of nonmarket issues, in the 1990s lower real gasoline prices and changing consumer demand resulted in sport utility vehicles (SUVs) and light trucks capturing half the light-vehicle market. This reduced average fuel economy and, in conjunction with the global climate change and security issues, generated pressure to increase fuel economy standards. Moreover, the size and weight of SUVs raised concerns about the safety of the occupants of other vehicles in the event of a collision.

Nonmarket issues and actions also shape the market environment. Higher fuel economy standards affect virtually all aspects of automobile design and manufacturing. Similarly, political action against Microsoft's alleged anticompetitive practices in the software industry put pressure on the Department of Justice and state attorneys general to file an antitrust lawsuit. Complaints by competitors led the European Union to impose antitrust fines and constraints on Microsoft for restricting the opportunities of other firms. The market environment is also shaped by the actions of interest and activist groups and the public sentiment for their causes. The *Exxon Valdez* oil spill increased environmental pressure on firms through liability for damages, more stringent regulations, and direct public pressure.

Both the market and nonmarket environments of business are competitive. In the market environment, performance is determined by competition among firms as directed by their market or competitive strategies. In the nonmarket environment, legislation, regulation, administrative decisions, and public pressure are the result of competition involving individuals, activists, interest groups, and firms. In the market environment, strategies are intermediated by markets, whereas in the nonmarket environment, strategies are intermediated by public and private institutions, including legislatures, courts, regulatory agencies, and public sentiment. Just as the market environment of business changes and competitive advantage evolves, the nonmarket environment changes and the issues on a firm's nonmarket agenda evolve.

The nonmarket environment should thus be thought of as responsive to the strategies of firms and other interested parties. Those strategies can affect market opportunities. Robert Galvin (1992), who led Motorola for over three decades, described the company's approach to its nonmarket environment as "writing the rules of the game."[1]

> The first step in any defined strategy is writing the rules of the game honorably and fairly in a manner that gives everyone a chance with predictable rules. Our company has started industries. We have helped write standards. We have helped write trade rules. We have helped influence policies. We have helped write national laws of countries where we have engaged, always in a respectful way. We have never taken for granted that the rules of the game would just evolve in a fashion that would make for the greatest opportunity.... With the right rules of the game, one's opportunity for success is enhanced.

Galvin's point is not that companies dictate the rules of the game but rather that those rules are shaped by the strategies of firms and other interested parties and by the governing institutions. Companies and their leaders can shape those rules by participating responsibly in the public and private processes that address market and nonmarket issues. This participation can affect the market environment of firms and the opportunities available to them as well as the nonmarket environment and the issues firms will face in the future.

---

[1] See Yoffie (1988a, 1988b) for analysis of aspects of this strategy.

ANALYSIS OF THE NONMARKET ENVIRONMENT: THE FOUR I'S

The nonmarket environment of a firm is characterized by four I's:

- Issues
- Interests
- Institutions
- Information

Issues are the basic unit of analysis and the focus of nonmarket action. Using the agricultural biotechnology industry as an example, the central nonmarket issues have been the formulation of regulatory policies for bioengineered foods and the public reaction to those foods. Interests include the individuals and groups with preferences about, or a stake in, the issue. The principal interests are the agricultural biotechnology companies, the interest groups and activists concerned about biotechnology issues, and the public. Institutions are defined by Douglass North (1990) as "the rules of the game in a society . . . that shape human interactions," and these institutions provide arenas in which interests seek to influence the outcomes on issues. Government institutions include entities such as legislatures and regulatory agencies. Nongovernmental institutions include those such as the media that provide information to society as well as public sentiment composed of societal expectations and norms of behavior that arise from ethics and culture. The Environmental Protection Agency, the Department of Agriculture, the Food and Drug Administration, and Congress are the principal public institutions in whose arenas agricultural biotechnology issues are addressed. The public sentiment about bioengineered foods is influenced by market forces as well. As the prices of agricultural products and foods rose in the late 2000s, some consumers and firms that had shunned bioengineered foods began to change their policies in response to their lower prices resulting from higher productivity and resistance to crop damage.

Information pertains to what the interests and institutional officeholders know or believe about the issues and the forces affecting their development. In the case of agricultural biotechnology, information pertains to the risks associated with individual products and with the technology itself. The public acceptance of bioengineered crops and animals is influenced by both scientific knowledge and concerns about the unknown. Information is provided by firms, activists, government institutions, and the media.

The task for management is to formulate and implement strategies that effectively address the nonmarket issues in competition with the strategies of other interests in the context of institutions in which information plays an important role. Each firm and industry has a set of issues that it must address, and these issues constitute its nonmarket issue agenda. Associated with each issue are the institutional arenas in which the issue will be addressed, the interests likely to be involved, and the information available. Many issues on a firm's nonmarket agenda require issue-specific strategies, and the analysis of the associated interests, institutions, and information provides a foundation for strategy formulation, as considered in Chapter 2. To illustrate the four I's framework, the remainder of this chapter considers the nonmarket environment of the automobile industry and then considers the origin and development of nonmarket issues.

THE NONMARKET ENVIRONMENT OF THE AUTOMOBILE INDUSTRY

This section identifies selected issues facing the automobile industry and then examines the associated interests, institutions, and information.

Issues

Fuel Economy Legislation   In 2007 Congress enacted and the president signed a bill increasing fuel economy standards by 40 percent. The Alliance of Automobile Manufacturers had initially opposed the legislation, but when it became apparent that higher standards were inevitable, it sought credits for vehicles that could run on ethanol and the opportunity to buy and sell credits for meeting and exceeding the standards.

Fuel Economy Exception In 2004 the National Highway Traffic Safety Administration (NHTSA) granted Nissan an exception from the two-fleet rule that automakers meet standards on both their domestic and imported fleets. Otherwise, Nissan said it would have to move production from its plants in Tennessee and Mississippi to its plant in Mexico, which Nissan had built as a result of the North American Free Trade Agreement (NAFTA). In 2007 Nissan supported higher fuel economy standards and lobbied for an extension of the exception with senators from Tennessee and Mississippi leading the effort.

Fuel Economy Regulation (China) In 2003 the State Council of China chose a weight-based system for fuel economy standards for automobiles, vans, and SUVs. The 2008 standards were somewhat higher than the standards in the United States.

Fuel Economy Regulation (European Union) As part of its Kyoto Treaty obligations, the European Union (EU) had adopted a voluntary fuel economy standard of 140 grams of carbon dioxide per kilometer, but the industry failed to meet the standard. Under strong pressure from environmental groups, the European Commission proposed a mandatory standard of 120 grams for 2012. The European Parliament asked for a less aggressive standard to ease the burden on automakers, and the Commission relented, setting the standard at 130 grams for automobiles with an additional 10 grams to be achieved through more efficient tires, improved air conditioners, and cleaner fuels. The European Automobile Manufacturers Association warned that the requirements would "lead to a loss of jobs and relocation of production outside the EU."[2]

State CO_2 Regulations The Clean Air Act authorized the EPA to grant California a waiver allowing it to set more stringent auto pollution standards than federal standards. In 2002 the California legislature added carbon dioxide to its list of pollutants and required by 2016 a 30 percent reduction in global-warming gases from cars and light trucks. The EPA denied the waiver application because global warming was not a localized externality and the federal government had just enacted sharply higher fuel economy standards. The Natural Resources Defense Council (NRDC) and other environmental groups strongly disagreed.

In 2008 General Motors CEO Rick Waggoner urged the 10,000 members of the National Automobile Dealers Association to oppose state efforts to set their own limits on greenhouse gases emission. Waggoner explained, "Dealers are very effective in the political process because we don't have a plant in every state. We have dealers in every state."[3]

Automobile Access (India) Tata Motors announced its $2,500 Nano people's car in 2008 to make the automobile more broadly accessible in India. The car would have few safety features but would be far safer than a motor scooter, which many people used to transport families and goods. Emissions standards posed a risk, however, because major cities planned to adopt the Euro IV standards that required a 35-fold reduction in sulfur dioxide emissions.

Battery Safety and Liability New generation hybrid and plug-in electric vehicles anticipated using lithium-ion batteries, which were quick to charge and capable of operating in all weather conditions.[4] The batteries, however, posed a risk of explosion and fire in the event of manufacturing problems or damage to the battery and hence represented a liability risk for automakers. Batteries were expensive, and automakers sought tax credits for buyers of plug-in vehicles, as provided for certain hybrid vehicles.

Federal Fuel Taxes Since 1993 federal fuel taxes had remained fixed at 18.4 cents and 24.4 cents per gallon for gasoline and diesel, respectively. In 2008 a commission authorized by Congress recommended increasing taxes by as much as 40 cents a gallon over 5 years to fund infrastructure improvements. Taxpayer resistance was expected.

---

[2]*New York Times*, February 8, 2007.
[3]*San Jose Mercury News*, February 10, 2008.
[4]The Prius used nickel-metal-hydride batteries.

Safety Standards   NHTSA had responsibility for setting mandatory safety standards for motor vehicles. A major cause of vehicle deaths was single-vehicle rollover accidents, many of which were caused when a vehicle left the roadway. Automobile manufacturers had begun to use electronic stability control (ESC) systems and planned to equip 71 percent of their model year 2011 vehicles with the systems. NHTSA issued a new federal standard requiring all model year 2012 vehicles to be equipped with ESC.

Drunk Driving   Safety standards did little to address drunk driving, which was estimated to result in 13,000 deaths a year. Mothers Against Drunk Driving (MADD), the Alliance of Automobile Manufacturers, and a state highway officials association launched a campaign to change state drunk driving laws to require convicted drunk drivers to have ignition interlocks triggered by alcohol detection devices.

Union Representation   The United Auto Workers (UAW), whose membership had fallen by 50 percent over the past 20 years as the big-three automakers had lost market share, had been unable to enlist sufficient support to hold a representation election at any Toyota plant. When a leaked document revealed that Toyota planned to reduce its North American labor costs by $300 million in the next 4 years, the UAW launched a new drive to unionize its Georgetown, Kentucky plant.

Worker Safety   The UAW had located its Resource Center half a mile from Toyota's Georgetown plant and used data reported to the Occupational Safety and Health Administration (OSHA) to identify 1,800 injured workers who were no longer employed by Toyota. Toyota stated that in its 22 years the Georgetown plant had only once been cited for a safety violation.

Antitrust   In 2007 four Canadians filed a $2 billion lawsuit in U.S. courts complaining that they were restrained by U.S. car dealers from purchasing vehicles in the United States where prices were thousands of dollars lower as a result of the appreciation of the Canadian dollar.

Free Trade Agreements (Korea)   In 2007 Korea and the United States approved a free trade agreement in which Korea would immediately eliminate its 8 percent tariff on automobile imports from the United States and change the nontariff barrier of taxing cars based on engine size. The United States agreed to eliminate immediately its 2.5 percent tariff on small cars and eliminate the tariff on larger vehicles over 3 years. Congress, however, had to ratify the agreement. Canada and the European Union also began negotiating free trade agreements with Korea.

Tariffs (China)   In 2006 the European Union (EU) and the United States filed a formal complaint with the World Trade Organization (WTO) regarding China's average 30 percent tariff on whole vehicle imports and 15 percent tariff on automobile parts.

Diversity   In 2006 Toyota had rejected demands that it provide statistical and regional information on the ethnicity of its U.S. dealers and executives. The demand was made by the National Minority Automotive Advocacy Coalition (NMAAC), composed of 10 minority business groups. Toyota said that of its 1,430 Toyota and Lexus dealers, 32 were African American, 26 Asian American, 25 Hispanic, and 11 Native American, or 6.6 percent compared to the national average of 4.93 percent.[5]

Human Rights   General Motors received a perfect score for 2007 from the Human Rights Campaign, a gay rights organization.

Environmental Pressure   At the New York auto show protesters from the Freedom From Oil campaign unfurled a banner reading "Toyota: The Truck That's Changing the Climate." Sarah Connolly explained, "Building the Prius does not give Toyota license to mass-produce the Tundra."[6] The campaign included demonstrations at Toyota dealerships and full-page newspaper ads criticizing Toyota. Activists were also upset that

[5]*Automotive News*, July 3, 2006.
[6]*New York Times*, April 7, 2007.

Toyota had opposed higher fuel economy standards, and the NRDC launched a Web site, http://www.truthabouttoyota.com/video-nrdc-and-prius-owners-changing-minds.html.

Corporate Social Responsibility   The criticism Toyota received led it to launch an extensive corporate advertising campaign emphasizing its support for the environment and its social responsibility, in addition to its traditional theme of highlighting the economic investment and employment it provided in the United States. One advertisement on the environment asked, "Can you have an impact by making none at all?"

Capacity Constraints (China)   To control the growth of auto production capacity spurred by local tax incentives, China's National Development and Reform Commission issued guidelines restricting new construction permits. The new guidelines required companies to sell at least 80 percent of their capacity before a new permit could be issued.

Recalls   General Motors recalled 1.3 million trucks in 2005, and in 2006 NHTSA detected a fire risk in a two-inch-long speed control deactivation switch on 6.7 million Ford vehicles with cruise control. Recalls in 2007 were the lowest in four years, and the auto industry credited their efforts to reduce defects.

Recalls (China)   In 2004 China issued auto recall regulations, and in 2006 22 automakers recalled 283,536 vehicles. In 2007 Honda's joint venture with Guangzhou Automobile Corporation recalled 500,000 vehicles because of possible power steering and oil pump problems, and Honda's other joint venture with Dongfeng Motor Corporation recalled 45,000 CR-V SUVs because of shock absorber problems.

Recalls (Japan)   In 2006 police in Japan charged that Toyota had covered up a defective steering mechanism in an SUV. The company recalled the vehicles after Mitsubishi Motors executives were arrested for covering up vehicle defects.

Products Liability   A products liability lawsuit against Ford for an alleged defective roof on Expeditions went to trial in a California state court. CEO Tom LaSorda of Chrysler said, "The cost of lawsuits adds at least $500 to the price of every vehicle." A study by Tillinghast-Towers Perrin estimated that the cost of tort cases in 2004 was $260 billion, which represented 2.23 percent of GDP or $886 per person in the United States. Plaintiff lawyers and their Trial Lawyers Association had consistently succeeded in stopping federal tort reform.

Intellectual Property (China)   In 2007 China Automobile Deutschland began selling in Europe the Jonway UFO, an SUV built in China that was a copy of a Toyota RAV4, the best-selling SUV in Europe. Toyota had failed to patent the design of the RAV4 in Europe. Toyota filed for patent protection for its next-generation RAV4.

Media Coverage   An activist with the Rainforest Action Network obtained a badge of a Mercedes Benz executive and attended the media day preceding the North American auto show. The activist asked a Toyota executive hostile questions while filming with a video camera. Noticing the false badge, the executive knocked the camera to the ground. The episode including the camera falling to the ground was filmed by other media and quickly appeared on YouTube.

Interests

Interests include those who have a stake in an issue and the organizations they form. U.S., Asian, and European automobile companies have interests that are opposed on some issues, such as the unionization of the plants of Japanese companies, but are aligned on others such as the state regulation of carbon dioxide emissions. Other interests with direct economic stakes in these issues are car buyers and employees. Some interests are well organized, as in the case of workers represented by the UAW, and others, such as car buyers, are unorganized.

Interests include special interest, activist, and advocacy groups and other NGOs. Special interest groups pursue issues because of the benefits that accrue to their members, as in the case of the trial lawyers' association. Watchdog groups monitor the activities of firms and call those activities to the attention of the media, government, and public. Advocacy groups, such as the NRDC, represent the interests of individuals, such as those affected by pollution. Activist groups, such as the Rainforest Action Network, take direct action against firms to force them to change their policies.

The organized and unorganized interests include:[7]

Organized Interests

Alliance of Automobile Manufacturers

European Automobile Manufacturers

Mothers Against Drunk Driving

National Automobile Dealers Association

National Minority Automotive Advocacy Coalition

Natural Resources Defense Council

United Auto Workers

Rainforest Action Network

Trial lawyers

Unorganized Interests

Car buyers

Citizens affected by global warming

Nonunion workers (Toyota)

Taxpayers

Institutions

The market and nonmarket environments in Figure 1-1 include activities that take place both within and outside formal institutions. The principal government institutions are legislatures, the executive branch, the judiciary, administrative agencies, regulatory agencies, and international institutions such as the World Trade Organization (WTO). These institutions both establish rules and serve as arenas in which interests compete to influence those rules. The nonmarket environment includes the set of laws, such as a fuel economy standard of 35 mpg, established by these institutions, as well as regulations, such as safety standards, established by administrative and regulatory agencies. The nonmarket environment also includes the common, or judge-made, law of torts, which governs the liability system.

Institutions can also be established by private means. Such institutions include markets, the insurance system, and voluntary agreements such as those pertaining to carbon dioxide emissions in the European Union. The nonmarket environment also includes nongovernmental institutions such as the news media and public sentiment. As considered in Chapter 3, the news media plays an important role in informing those in the nonmarket environment about issues, but it also serves as an institution. That is, firms and other interests attempt to communicate to the public through the news media. The NRDC and other NGOs and activist organizations attempt to influence companies such as Toyota through public sentiment.

Institutions are not unitary bodies. Congress is composed of two chambers and 535 members who represent constituencies with varied interests. Institutions also have internal structures that affect how nonmarket issues are addressed. Congress acts by majority rule, has a committee system, and follows a complex set of procedures for enacting legislation. Understanding the workings of these institutions, their procedures, and the forces that operate within them is essential for successful management in the nonmarket environment. Managers must also be familiar with the mandates, agendas, and procedures of regulatory agencies, such as NHTSA and EPA, and the standards used by the courts in rendering judgments about their actions.

---

[7]Not all relevant interests are listed.

Government officeholders may be active on nonmarket issues, and their actions to some extent reflect their personal interests. Their actions, however, are usually constrained by the mandates, procedures, and policies of the institutions in which they hold office and by the preferences of their political principals. The head of the EPA, for example, is accountable to the president, Congress, and the public. Legislators not only must follow legislative procedures and respect committee jurisdictions, but they also must be attentive to the preferences of their electoral constituents. Regulators must respect the mandates in their enabling legislation and follow a complex set of administrative procedures, both of which provide bases for judicial review. In addition, regulators must be attentive to their political principals in Congress and the office of the president. For these reasons, institutional officeholders, such as members of Congress and the administrator of NHTSA, are considered part of the institution rather than as an interest.[8]

Some institutions are specific to an individual country, whereas others represent a set of countries. The institutions in whose arenas the nonmarket issues for the automobile industry are addressed can be categorized as follows:

United States
> Congress
> Presidency
> NHTSA
> Courts—federal
> Courts—state
> OSHA
> California legislature
> EPA
> Torts—liability

International
> European Commission
> European Parliament
> NAFTA
> Environmental regulatory agencies (India)
> National Development and Reform Commission (China)
> State Council (China)

Global
> WTO
> Kyoto Treaty
> News media
> Public sentiment

Information

Information refers to what interests and institutional officeholders know about an issue, the consequences of alternative courses of action, and the preferences of those concerned with the issue. Issues are often contested because interests have conflicting preferences regarding their resolution, as in the case of the proponents and opponents of a CO_2 emissions standard of 120 grams per kilometer in the European Union. Issues can also be contested because interests have different information. Auto companies have superior information about the preferences of car buyers for higher fuel economy, and environmentalists may have superior information about the extent of public concern about climate change. Organizations such as the National Academy of

---

[8]The exception is when the jobs of officeholders, the budget, or the status of the office is at stake.

Sciences as well as universities play an important role in providing scientific assessments of issues such as fuel economy and auto safety.

Information is also frequently at the heart of strategies for addressing nonmarket issues. Lobbying, for example, involves providing information to officeholders about the likely consequences of policy alternatives as in the case of Nissan and the dual fleet exception. Information provision is also important in regulatory rule making because of the complexity of most regulatory issues and because agencies are required to develop a record supporting their actions. Information can also be an instrument of nonmarket competition. On the issue of California's law to reduce CO_2 emissions, the Union of Concerned Scientists estimated that compliance would increase the cost of a Ford Explorer by $1,960, whereas the Alliance of Automobile Manufacturers estimated that the cost increase would be $4,361.

Information can be important to the progress of issues. The experience with NAFTA and the impact of imports from China on jobs in the United States and Europe generated opposition to further trade liberalization and threatened the free trade agreement with Korea. Information can also lead to resolution of an issue. Mounting evidence and growing public concern about climate change led automakers in the United States to stop opposing higher fuel efficiency standards, and the environmental groups' campaigns targeting Toyota sought to mobilize the public to pressure Toyota to do all it could to reduce CO_2 emissions.

The chapter cases on the pharmaceutical industry, McDonald's, and Google provide opportunities to characterize the issues, interests, institutions, and information in their nonmarket environments and to consider the progress of the issues.[9]

CHANGE IN THE NONMARKET ENVIRONMENT

The nonmarket environment changes as issues are resolved, current issues progress, and new issues arise. This section focuses on the origins of issues and the forces that give rise to them. The following sections address the anticipation of nonmarket issues and their progression and resolution.

Nonmarket issues originate from both external forces and a firm's own actions. Most changes in the tax law originate in response to ideas that capture a degree of political support. However, the issue of eliminating the investment tax credit, which had been a component of U.S. tax policy for over 20 years, arose in part because of political action by service industries that viewed the credit as a subsidy to capital-intensive industries. The issue of automobile safety regulation arose from an automobile accident and articles by two young policy activists. The issue of a possible health risk from the electromagnetic field generated by high-voltage electricity transmission lines arose from a small-scale inferential study linking power lines to leukemia in children. As the varied origins of these issues indicate, managers must be sensitive to the sources of nonmarket issues—even those such as possible health risks from the electromagnetic field generated by transmission lines—that initially seem remote or even far-fetched.

Nonmarket issues have five basic sources:

- Scientific discovery and technological advancement
- New understandings
- Institutional change
- Interest group activity
- Moral concerns

Scientific discovery and technological advancement can produce fundamental changes in both the market and nonmarket environments. In the market environment, they create opportunities for new products and processes, new applications of existing knowledge, and the foundations for future discoveries. They also give rise to nonmarket issues. Measurements suggesting that the earth was warming spawned issues ranging

---

[9]The fuel economy issue in the United States is considered in the Part II integrative case, *Fuel Economy Standards 2007*.

from higher fuel economy standards to the deforestation of tropical rain forests. The discovery of an ozone hole above the Antarctic confirmed theories of ozone depletion and propelled a number of nonmarket issues ranging from the elimination of CFCs to measures to reduce the incidence of skin cancer. When the theory of ozone depletion was initially advanced, DuPont came under pressure to stop producing CFCs. DuPont argued that there was yet no evidence that CFCs actually caused ozone depletion and pledged in a public advertisement that it would cease production if scientific evidence showed a relationship. When a National Academy of Sciences study concluded that there was a causal link, DuPont announced the next day that it would cease production.

Nonmarket issues can also arise from new technology and scientific uncertainty. The spectacular success of the cellular telephone industry was interrupted one day when a man called the *Larry King Live* television talk show and claimed that his wife had died from brain cancer caused by extensive use of a cellular telephone. Earlier in the day a CEO of a major corporation had announced that he had brain cancer, and the previous day a CEO of another major corporation had died of brain cancer. The call and speculation that the CEOs might have been heavy users of cellular telephones caused a panic. The stock prices of McCaw Communications, the nation's largest cellular telephone company, and Motorola, the largest manufacturer of cellular telephones, dropped by over 5 percent. Fears were calmed by statements of government officials that there was no scientific evidence linking cellular telephones to cancer. The industry pledged to conduct additional research into whether radio-frequency radiation emitted by the telephones was harmful. The Cellular Telecommunications Industry Association earmarked $25 million for research and established a Scientific Advisory Group on Cellular Telephone Research to oversee the research program. The promise of research to fill the gap in scientific information reassured cellular telephone users, and the growth in demand resumed.

Nonmarket issues also arise from changes in understandings. The environmental movement brought to the attention of the public damage to the natural environment and the associated health risks. Renewed confidence in markets and the failure of socialist economic systems spurred a wave of privatization in both developed and developing countries. Increasing evidence of the economic benefits of international trade led not only to further reductions in trade barriers through the World Trade Organization but also to market integration in North America through NAFTA and in the European Union through the Single European Act. Antitrust policy and enforcement changed substantially during the 1980s as a consequence of new understandings about the effects of the competitive practices of firms. Changes in the membership of the Supreme Court during the 1980s and the understandings the new members brought with them resulted in changes in affirmative action policies. A Bangladesh economist, Muhammed Yunis, recognized that the lives of poor people would be improved by providing small loans at modest interest rates to replace borrowing from money lenders.

Issues also become salient because groups organize to advance their own interests. Interest groups formed around the issue of extending the period of daylight saving time and worked for nearly a decade to obtain an extension by Congress. A less visible campaign led to a further extension in 2007. The growth and developing effectiveness of the American Association of Retired Persons led it to push for congressional enactment of a catastrophic illness insurance plan, only to have a grassroots revolt among its members lead to repeal of the act before it had taken effect. Consumer groups have similarly organized to take political action to stem the increases in pharmaceutical prices. Interest groups can also block change, as in the case of the auto industry and higher fuel economy standards, which remained unchanged for more than two decades.

Nonmarket issues also arise because of institutional actions. A Supreme Court decision in 1988 supported a new theory of "fraud on the market," under which a firm could be held liable if its stock price fell significantly when the firm's projections of future earnings had been favorable. This provided incentives for trial lawyers to file class action lawsuits against high-technology companies when their naturally volatile stock price fell. No evidence of fraud was required to file a lawsuit, and filing allowed the lawyers to conduct discovery and depose company executives. To avoid the costs and disruptions of discovery and depositions, and the subsequent costs of a trial, many companies were willing to settle the lawsuits even if they expected to win. Settlements totaled nearly $7 billion. Viewing the practice as extortionary and the lawsuits as frivolous, companies backed federal legislation granting a safe harbor for forward-looking projections, and Congress enacted the statute over President Clinton's veto. In response, the trial lawyers brought their cases under state laws and backed a ballot initiative in California to increase their likelihood of extracting settlements. The high-tech companies and other targets of the lawsuits then successfully backed new federal legislation to require such cases to be filed in federal courts.

Change in the nonmarket environment also comes from market forces. In the mid-1990s, new markets associated with the Internet, wireless systems, and integrated services resulted in a restructuring of the telecommunications industry, including mergers, acquisitions, and strategic alliances. Congress then struggled with legislation to lift the archaic restrictions on competition left over from the era of regulation.

Nonmarket issues also arise because of heightened moral concerns. The increased saliency of personal privacy resulted in a ban on the use of polygraph tests by employers, who responded with a variety of pencil and paper tests, including some designed to test for honesty and loyalty. These tests ultimately became a nonmarket issue. Privacy concerns associated with the Internet resulted in both self-regulation by Internet service providers and Web sites and calls for new legislation. In the European Union, privacy concerns led to strong legislation on the handling and use of personal information on the Internet. Moral concerns were also raised about subprime lending to borrowers who did not qualify for bank loans, leading to charges of predatory lending. Moral concerns about the spread of AIDS in developing countries and the suffering of its victims resulted in pressure on pharmaceutical firms to lower their prices to the level of production costs.

ANTICIPATING CHANGE IN THE NONMARKET ENVIRONMENT

The effectiveness with which a firm and its managers address nonmarket issues depends on their approach to the nonmarket environment. One approach is to respond to nonmarket issues only when they are strong enough to force the firm to act. A second approach emphasizes limiting the extent of the damage once the firm has been challenged by an issue. A third approach is anticipatory and is intended to prepare the firm to take advantage of opportunities as they arise and address issues before they become problems. A fourth approach is proactive with the firm and its managers not only anticipating nonmarket issues but also acting to affect which issues arise and how they will be framed. This approach recognizes that nonmarket issues and their development are affected by the way business is conducted. The fourth approach is the most effective, but it requires considerable sensitivity to the sources of nonmarket issues and how they progress.

Proactive managers attempt to identify potential issues and act to reduce their adverse, or enhance their beneficial, impacts. A fundamental step in anticipating nonmarket issues is to view the potential issue or business practice from the perspective of others who might be concerned about it. The graduation cards example illustrates this point.

THE NONMARKET ISSUE LIFE CYCLE

The progression of nonmarket issues can be understood in terms of a life cycle. The nonmarket issue life cycle relates the stage of development of an issue to its impact on a firm and its management.[10] This is not a theory, since it does not provide an explanation for how or why an issue develops or a basis for predicting its likely development. In particular, it does not identify the causal factors that govern an issue's progress. The life cycle concept is useful, however, because it identifies a pattern and serves as a reminder that issues with simple origins can garner support, propelling them through a series of stages and resulting in significant impacts. Issues do not, however, have a life

---

[10]The life cycle concept was originated by Ian Wilson while at General Electric.

EXAMPLE

Graduation Cards

Graduation represents an important market for the greeting card industry. In its preparation for the college graduation season, Hallmark Cards was considering the array of cards it would market. Cards could reflect a variety of themes, but two traditionally popular ones were transition and celebration. One transition was coming of legal drinking age, and Hallmark was considering cards featuring alcoholic beverages. Alcoholic beverages were also associated with celebration, so the cards would draw on two themes. One card being considered had a photo of a Budweiser can with a small cherubic character saying, "You're graduating?" Another card portrayed a beer and eggs breakfast on graduation day, and a third suggested a robe large enough to cover two champagne bottles.

Graduation cards are bought by friends and relatives of the graduate, and it is from their perspective that the cards must be considered—for both their market and nonmarket potentials. The proposed cards were intended for the college graduation market, and virtually all those recipients would be of legal drinking age. College students, however, were not the only ones graduating. Twice as many students graduate from high school each year, and they are not of

legal drinking age. Some parents and relatives could view the cards as promoting alcoholic beverages and contributing to underage drinking and driving, a major cause of accidents and deaths. Parents and others concerned about underage drinking provide the potential for a nonmarket reaction to the cards.

The next step is to assess whether people concerned about the cards are likely to act in the nonmarket environment. Some parents and relatives will be concerned about the cards, but they are dispersed and most have limited means of generating a nonmarket issue. Some, however, participate in organizations such as the PTA and MADD that are experienced in dealing with nonmarket issues, know how to attract the news media to bring an issue to the attention of the public, and hence know how to put it on a firm's agenda. This does not mean that a nonmarket reaction is certain, but it certainly is possible.

Hallmark chose to market the cards, and the reaction was swift. MADD activists began to pressure store owners to stop selling the cards, and the media picked up the story. Faced with public criticism, Hallmark withdrew the cards from the market and subsequently decided not to produce graduation cards with a reference to alcoholic beverages.

of their own. Instead, their progression is governed by the attention they receive from interests and institutions.

Nonmarket issues can progress through five stages: (1) issue identification, (2) interest group formation, (3) legislation, (4) administration, and (5) enforcement. As an issue progresses through its life cycle, its impact on the firm and its management tends to increase. As the impact increases, management's range of discretion in addressing the issue correspondingly decreases. The impact may take the form of government actions such as regulation or changes in public sentiment that limit the options available to management.

To illustrate the nonmarket life cycle, consider the issue of automobile safety regulation. The progression of the issue is illustrated along the horizontal axis in Figure 1-2, and the vertical axis represents the impact on automobile manufacturers. In the 1950s, automobile safety was viewed primarily as a function of road conditions and the driver's skill. In 1957, as Congressman Kenneth Roberts of Alabama and his wife were returning from their honeymoon, their car was rear-ended. Both were injured, but their well-packaged glass and china wedding presents in the backseat were undamaged. Roberts recognized that an ignored dimension of the auto safety issue was the vehicle itself and how safely it contained its passengers.

Roberts held congressional hearings on the issue, but no action resulted. In 1959 two articles on the issue were published. A young attorney named Ralph Nader published an article on automobile safety that focused on automobile design. A young official in the Department of Labor, Daniel Patrick Moynihan, published an article arguing for a broader perspective on the automobile safety issue. Interest group activity began to develop, and the media was attracted to the issue, particularly when it was

FIGURE 1-2 Nonmarket Issue Life Cycle

Automobile Safety Regulation

Impact on Firm

| 1957 Roberts auto accident | 1959 Nader Moynihan news media | 1962–1966 GSA NHTSA | 1966–present NHTSA rule making recalls | Compliance NHTSA manufacturers interest groups |

Time

| Issue identification | Interest group formation | Legislation | Administration | Enforcement |

revealed that General Motors had hired a private detective to investigate Nader. In 1962 the issue entered the legislative stage when the General Services Administration (GSA) issued a standard for brake fluid. Legislation was introduced in Congress and, after considerable deliberation and intense politics, the Motor Vehicle Safety Act of 1966 was enacted. The act established NHTSA, which was given administrative rule-making authority to establish mandatory automobile safety standards.

The enforcement phase for auto safety regulation has been multifaceted. Auto manufacturers test their models extensively, not only for compliance with regulations but often to exceed government standards. NHTSA continues to mandate new standards such as electronic stability control, enforces the regulations, and orders recalls of vehicles. Advocacy groups such as the Center for Auto Safety monitor both the industry and the enforcement activities of NHTSA. Safety regulations are also enforced through the courts as a result of lawsuits filed by individuals and trial lawyers.

Nonmarket issues that complete their life cycles do not always result in more restrictions on business, as evidenced by the issue of airline deregulation. Economists analyzing the performance of airlines regulated by the Civil Aeronautics Board (CAB) concluded that regulation was inducing inefficiencies and increasing costs. The issue attracted attention because of the large differences between the fares of the CAB-regulated airlines and airlines such as Southwest that operated only intrastate routes and hence were not subject to CAB regulation. Regulatory oversight hearings brought additional attention to the issue and planted the seeds of legislative action. These developments coincided with increased public criticism of economic regulation and decreased confidence in government. As congressional and executive branch attention increased, the issue entered the legislative stage. When economist Alfred Kahn was appointed to head the CAB, he moved quickly to take administrative action to deregulate the industry, which spurred the legislative process. The result was legislation that eliminated the economic regulation of the domestic airline industry. After transferring some of its other functions to other government agencies, the CAB ceased to exist. Similar concerns about the economic consequences of surface transportation regulation resulted in the elimination of the Interstate Commerce Commission, the first federal regulatory agency.

Not all nonmarket issues, of course, garner enough support to pass through all five stages, and many do not survive the legislative stage. The fact that an issue does not pass through all the stages does not mean that it has no impact. The attention an issue receives can produce change even in the absence of institutional action. The consumer movement has not progressed as far as its supporters had hoped, and Congress has not passed major consumer legislation since 1976. Despite the consumer movement's failure to achieve new legislation, it has resulted in many significant changes. Furthermore, interest groups and NGOs are active in advocating for consumer interests.

SUMMARY

Firms operate in both market and nonmarket environments. The field of business and its environment is concerned with issues in the nonmarket environment that have potentially important effects on organizational and managerial performance. Managers are in the best position to understand how the firm's market activities give rise to nonmarket issues and to assess the significance of nonmarket issues for overall performance. Managers thus have the responsibility for addressing nonmarket issues and can use both nonmarket and market strategies to achieve superior performance.

The nonmarket environment of a firm is characterized by four I's: issues, interests, institutions, and information. As indicated by the example of the automobile industry, nonmarket issues have important implications for firms and their market and nonmarket performance. Nonmarket issues may be identified externally or by management and may arise from scientific discovery, new understandings, interest group activity, institutional change, and moral concerns. Because these factors change over time, the nonmarket environment and a firm's nonmarket issue agenda evolve.

Management must not only deal effectively with nonmarket issues but must also anticipate issues and take proactive steps to address them. Many nonmarket issues pass through stages—issue identification, interest group formation, legislation, administration, and enforcement. This pattern serves as a reminder that issues evolve, even seemingly minor issues can have substantial effects, and the impact increases as issues move through the stages of their life cycles. Not all nonmarket issues pass through all five stages, however, and some, such as deregulation, result in fewer rather than more restrictions. The progress of an issue is shaped by the actions of firms and other interests and by the characteristics of the institutions in whose arenas the issue is addressed.

Organization of the Book

The book is organized in five parts, and cases for discussion are provided in each chapter. An integrative case is provided at the conclusion of each part. Part I introduces the nonmarket environment, the nonmarket issues firms face, and the factors, including activist pressures and the news media and public sentiment, that affect the development of those issues. The focus is on the formulation of strategies for addressing nonmarket issues and the integration of those strategies with market strategies. Part II considers issues addressed in the context of government institutions with an emphasis on legislatures. The substantive focus is on conceptual frameworks for analyzing nonmarket issues, understanding government institutions, and formulating effective strategies for addressing those issues. The frameworks developed in this part provide a foundation for Parts III and IV. Part III focuses on the interactions between government and markets with an emphasis on antitrust, regulation, environmental protection, court-adjudicated law, and information industries. Part IV is explicitly international and provides frameworks for understanding the political economy of countries and the relationships between business and government. Japan, the European Union, China, and emerging markets are considered, and international trade policy is used to bring the policy and strategy issues together. Part V is normative and focuses on the social responsibilities of firms and the guidance that ethics provides. Ethics systems and reasoning are the centerpieces of Part V, and the applications focus on corporate social responsibility in domestic and international contexts.

-- C A S E S --

The Nonmarket Environment of the Pharmaceutical Industry

U.S. spending on pharmaceuticals increased by 19 percent to $131.9 billion in 2000, the fifth consecutive year of increases above 13 percent. Expenditures were expected to top $150 billion in 2001. The expenditures reflected the importance of drugs as health care therapies and the continuing discoveries of new treatments as a result of the industry's research and development efforts. A study by a research center supported by the pharmaceutical industry reported that the cost of developing a new drug had increased from $231 million in 1987 to $802 million in 2000 (in inflation-adjusted dollars). The expenditures also reflected high prices, heavy marketing expenditures, and high profits. These factors attracted the attention of government officials, activists, and advocacy groups.

Public Citizen, a consumer activist organization, published a report arguing that the pharmaceutical industry exaggerated the cost of developing new drugs.[11] The Pharmaceutical Research and Manufacturers Association (PhRMA) hired Ernst & Young to evaluate the Public Citizen report.[12] Ernst & Young criticized the report and concluded that the pharmaceutical industry paid a higher percentage of its revenues as taxes than all other industries in the United States. Critics responded that the tax payments were large because the industry's profit margins were so high.

In a study based on the annual reports of nine pharmaceutical companies, Families USA reported that eight of the companies spent more than twice as much on marketing as on research and development. Six of the companies had net incomes that exceeded their research and development expenditures. Families USA also reported that prices for the 50 most prescribed drugs for seniors had increased at twice the rate of inflation.

PhRMA replied, "The Families USA 'study' condemns the pharmaceutical industry for being a success at developing medicines upon which millions of patients depend. When the pharmaceutical industry does well, patients do even better. Because the pharmaceutical industry is profitable, Americans have the best chance in the world of getting the cure for Alzheimer's, cancer, diabetes or AIDS."[13]

One reason pharmaceutical profits were high was that the brand-name companies faced buyers that controlled only small shares of the market. One fear of the brand-name companies was that buyers would join together and use their bargaining power to drive prices down. Maine had passed a law empowering the state to negotiate prices and purchase prescription drugs for its citizens. PhRMA filed a lawsuit against the state, and a federal court issued a preliminary injunction preventing the state from implementing the law. The Court of Appeals, however, reversed the lower court decision.

The state of Florida passed new legislation to use its purchasing power for drugs included under Medicaid, the federal program administered by the states that funded medical care for the poor. Florida included in its formulary—the list of drugs for which reimbursement would be provided—only those drugs for which the manufacturers agreed to pay rebates to the state beyond the rebates required by Medicaid. Rather than give in to the pressure, Pfizer reached an agreement with the state under which its prescription drugs were included in the formulary without any price discount. Instead, Pfizer agreed to pay for nurses to monitor tens of thousands of patients to make sure they took their medications and had checkups on a regular basis. PhRMA had a different response to Florida's program. It filed a lawsuit arguing that federal law required that all prescription drugs be available to Medicaid recipients unless a drug had been shown to have no therapeutic benefits.

Florida also adopted a counter-detailing program in which pharmacists employed by the state visited doctors to encourage them to prescribe generic drugs rather than the more expensive brand-name drugs.[14] The pharmacists provided a "report card" to each doctor indicating the doctor's Medicaid prescriptions record.

On a regular basis the news media carried articles on developments in the pharmaceutical industry. Since the fortunes of companies depended on the results of clinical trials and the FDA's drug approval decisions, the business press covered the FDA closely. The business press also covered patent extension decisions and the progress of patent infringement cases. Congress and the Bush administration had pharmaceutical issues high on their agenda, resulting in media coverage of legislative and regulatory reform issues. The nonbusiness media also covered the industry, focusing more on the impact of drugs—and their prices—on consumers.

The media was also concerned about the sponsorship of research and clinical testing. Pharmaceutical companies financed research in universities and hospitals and retained the intellectual property rights to the resulting discoveries. The scientific and medical press had become

[11]Public Citizen, "Rx R&D Myths: The Case Against the Drug Industry's R&D 'Scare Card,'" Washington, DC, July 2001.
[12]Ernst & Young, LLP, "Pharmaceutical Industry R&D Costs: Key Findings about the Public Citizen Report," August 8, 2001.
[13]www.phrma.org.
[14]Marketing of drugs directly to doctors is referred to as detailing.

concerned about the implications of this trend for the integrity of their publications. The British journal *Nature* required authors to disclose any financial interests related to the studies they published in the journal.

Journals were also concerned about the symmetry of what was published. Pharmaceutical companies were hesitant to disclose negative research results that might undermine products. The *New England Journal of Medicine,* the *Journal of the American Medical Association,* and other journals adopted a policy to force pharmaceutical companies that sponsored clinical research to allow researchers to publish unfavorable as well as favorable results.

Judges had also become concerned about links between expert witnesses and the pharmaceutical industry. Some judges required expert witnesses to disclose their financial connections to the industry.

In an unprecedented action, Blue Cross of California, a unit of WellPoint Health Networks, filed a Citizen Petition with the FDA to switch from prescription-only to over-the-counter (OTC) status three second-generation antihistamines—Allegra, produced by Aventis; Claritin, produced by Schering-Plough; and Zyrtec, marketed in the United States by Pfizer.[15] This would benefit consumers because the second-generation antihistamines were nonsedating, whereas the 100 first-generation antihistamines sold on the OTC market were sedating. A switch would put the second-generation antihistamines under considerable price pressure.

In January 2001, Schering-Plough's third-generation antihistamine Clarinex was approved for sale in the European Union, and in the same month the FDA issued an "approvable" letter for the drug indicating that there were no outstanding clinical or scientific issues. The FDA, however, withheld approval because of quality control problems in Schering-Plough's New Jersey and Puerto Rico manufacturing facilities. Public Citizen had put pressure on the FDA by writing to the Secretary of Health and Human Services, citing consultants' reports on the production facilities and FDA warning letters to Schering-Plough.

Public Citizen also asked the Secretary of Health and Human Services to undertake criminal prosecution of Schering-Plough. A study by Public Citizen concluded that the probable cause of 17 deaths was asthma inhalers sold without the active medication albuterol. In 1999 and 2000 Schering-Plough had recalled 59 million inhalers because advocacy groups had raised concerns about them. A Schering-Plough spokesperson said that 5,000 people a year died from asthma and that there was "no evidence that a patient was ever harmed by an inhaler subject to any recalls." He added that "every inhaler returned to the company by a patient claiming injury and alleging the canister lacked active ingredient has been tested and found to contain active ingredient."[16]

The pricing and marketing of prescription drugs was of concern to state and federal law enforcement agencies. Twenty pharmaceutical companies were under investigation for price reporting practices associated with the sale of drugs to Medicaid and Medicare. One focus of the investigations was the reporting of high wholesale prices while providing deep discounts to doctors. This increased the doctor's margin, providing incentives to prescribe the drugs.

In 1997 the FDA had revised its regulations, allowing direct-to-consumer (DTC) advertising of prescription drugs. Schering-Plough and other pharmaceutical companies began to advertise directly to consumers through television, radio, and print. The advertisements gave a toll-free number to call for information, referred to magazine advertisements where warnings were given, and instructed viewers to "ask your doctor." The marketing strategy was to induce consumers to ask their doctors for the drug by brand name. The strategy proved to be quite successful, pushing Claritin sales to $2.5 billion in the United States. In 2000 Merck spent $161 million on DTC advertising for Vioxx, which was more than Budweiser spent advertising its beers. PhRMA explained that DTC advertising helped educate consumers and involve them more in their own health care.

The National Institute for Health Care Management, a research institute funded by Blue Cross Blue Shield, reported that DTC advertising had increased from $700 million in 1996 to $2.5 billion in 2000 and that the increase was concentrated in 50 drugs. The institute also reported that the increase in pharmaceutical spending was due to an increase in prescriptions written and not to price increases. PhRMA explained, "We have an epidemic of undertreatment of serious illnesses in the United States."[17]

The American Medical Association (AMA) took an interest in the DTC advertising issue. The AMA supported the objectives of educating patients and involving them in their own health care but was concerned that the doctor–patient relationship could be strained when patients asked for a drug by brand name. An AMA ethics committee stated, "Physicians should resist commercially induced pressure to prescribe drugs that may not be indicated. Physicians should deny requests for inappropriate prescriptions and educate patients as to why certain advertised drugs may not be suitable treatment options. . . ."[18] In 2001 the AMA wrote to the Senate Commerce Committee stating, "Our physician members have expressed concern about the impact that direct-to-consumer advertising has on the physician/patient relationship and on health care costs." The AMA asked the committee to direct the FDA to study the impact of DTC advertising. The FDA began a review.

[15]See the Chapter 8 case, *Pharmaceutical Switching.*
[16]*Wall Street Journal,* August 10, 2001.

[17]*New York Times,* November 11, 2001.
[18]American Medical Association, "E-5.015 Direct-to-Consumer Advertisements of Prescription Drugs," www.ama-assn.org.

DTC advertising also attracted the attention of activist and advocacy groups. The Prescription Access Litigation Project filed a lawsuit against Schering-Plough claiming that its advertising of Claritin was deceptive and boosted demand and the price of the drug. Some policy specialists observed that if DTC advertising were restricted, consumers would simply turn to the Internet for information on prescription drugs.

The Commission of the European Union (EU) proposed a fast-track approval process for new drugs. The objective was to reduce the approval time from 18 months to 9 to 12 months, which would be faster than the approval time of 14 months in the United States. The Commission also proposed a relaxation of restrictions on DTC advertisements, but not broadcast advertising, for treatments of certain diseases, including diabetes, AIDS, and asthma.

In 2001 Bayer withdrew its newly introduced and fast-selling cholesterol-lowering drug Baycol because over 50 deaths were associated with its use. The drug had been approved in the United Kingdom, and other EU member states had adopted that decision. Responsibility for monitoring the safety of the drug, however, was unclear. The European Agency for the Evaluation of Medical Products said it had little role in safety because it had not participated in the licensing. The recall brought home to the European governments the confusion in drug safety regulation and the poor communication among the member states. The Medicines Control Agency of Germany faulted Bayer for not having disclosed problems earlier.

Postmarketing monitoring of drugs was also an issue in the United States. One concern was the rapid adoption of drugs as a result of aggressive marketing by the brand-name pharmaceutical companies. This meant that if there were side effects not identified in the clinical testing, problems could be extensive.[19] *BusinessWeek* called for an independent body like the National Transportation Safety Board to investigate problems with drugs.

Many developing countries faced an AIDS crisis, and the cost of the cocktail of drugs used to treat AIDS was beyond their means. South Africa used its Medicines Act to threaten the pharmaceutical industry with compulsory licensing and parallel imports of AIDS drugs. Thirty-nine international pharmaceutical companies filed a lawsuit against the South African government but later dropped the lawsuit and agreed to substantial price reductions.[20]

PhRMA opposed the practice of deep discounts for drugs for developing countries because it contributed to "parallel trade." Parallel trade was the importation of drugs by developed countries that had been exported with deep discounts to developing countries. The industry argued that parallel trade resulted in the importation of adulterated and counterfeit drugs or drugs that had been improperly stored and handled and thus imposed a safety risk on the importing country. A bill introduced in Congress, however, would authorize pharmacies and wholesalers to purchase prescription drugs that had been exported from the United States.

Brazil faced high costs of purchasing AIDS drugs and negotiated price reductions with several drug companies, but Roche refused to offer a substantial reduction. Brazil then announced that it would issue a license to a Brazilian company to produce a generic version of Roche's drug.[21] Roche conceded and reduced the price to Brazil by an additional 40 percent.

The protection of intellectual property rights was an important issue for the brand-name pharmaceutical companies. The industry supported the World Trade Organization (WTO) and its enforcement of the TRIPS (Trade-Related Aspects of Intellectual Property Rights) Agreement. The United States filed a trade complaint with the WTO against Brazil for its law allowing compulsory licensing for drugs not manufactured in the country.

The pharmaceutical industry criticized India for restrictions on imports of pharmaceuticals and for encouraging a domestic industry that copied drugs under patent. A 1972 Indian law allowed companies to copy a patented drug if they used a different manufacturing process. Pharmacists prescribed much of the drugs in India, and the drug companies competed for their attention. Brand-name companies began offering gifts to pharmacists if they prescribed the company's drugs, and Indian companies began to provide bonuses of free drugs. GlaxoSmithKline provided color television sets to pharmacists who met certain targets.

Patents provided the most important protection for intellectual property in the pharmaceutical industry. The patent on Schering-Plough's Claritin was scheduled to expire in December 2002, and before the FDA and in Congress the company sought without success to extend the market exclusivity. To delay the entry of competitors, Schering-Plough filed a patent infringement lawsuit against 10 generic pharmaceutical companies, claiming that their versions of Claritin would, when ingested, necessarily produce a metabolite on which Schering-Plough held a patent. The courts had not upheld this "metabolite defense," but neither had they rejected it. At a minimum, the lawsuit could delay entry of the generics.

To resolve a lawsuit, Schering-Plough reached a settlement with Upsher-Smith Laboratories and American Home Products regarding their generic versions of K-Dur. Schering-Plough paid $60 million to Upsher-Smith, which then agreed not to market its drug. Upsher-Smith had received a 180-day exclusivity period as a result of being the first company to develop a generic version, so other companies could not market their

---

[19]See the Chapter 5 case, *Merck and Vioxx* and the Chapter 20 case, *Pfizer and Celebrex.*
[20]See the Part V integrative case, *GlaxoSmithKline and AIDS Drug Policy.*

[21]The Brazilian constitution allowed the country to violate a patent in the case of abusive practices.

generic drugs. In April 2001 the Federal Trade Commission voted unanimously to file civil charges challenging the agreement as a violation of the antitrust laws.

In addition to using patent infringement defenses, brand-name pharmaceutical companies used FDA rules to stave off generics. The patent on Bristol-Myers Squibb's blockbuster diabetes drug Glucophage expired in September 2000, and the company had initially been successful in staving off the generics by inducing patients to switch to two new versions of the drug that were not chemically equivalent to Glucophage. Based on new clinical tests, the FDA had approved Glucophage as safe for children, and Bristol-Myers received exclusive rights until 2004 for use by children. A 1994 FDA rule required that labels must contain dosage and use information for children, but generics could not include such information on their labels because Bristol-Myers had exclusive rights to the data. The dilemma for the FDA was that its rule technically might block all generic versions of Glucophage. The dilemma had delayed the FDA approval of 14 generic versions for months, and Bristol-Myers was prepared to file a lawsuit if the FDA allowed provision of dosage and use information.

Medicare did not provide prescription drug benefits, and only about one-third of the elderly had prescription drug insurance coverage. Congress wanted to provide prescription drug benefits under Medicare, but Democrats in Congress sought to provide roughly twice the coverage supported by the Bush administration. The pharmaceutical industry had opposed the legislation based on concerns that it would increase buyers' bargaining power relative to the pharmaceutical companies.

In response to congressional attempts to provide prescription drug coverage under Medicare, the Bush administration reached an agreement with pharmacy-benefits managers (PBMs) to negotiate drug discounts with pharmaceutical companies. The pharmaceutical companies opposed the plan because of the price pressures it would create. Two pharmacy associations, the National Association of Chain Drug Stores and the National Community Pharmacist Association (NCPA), filed a lawsuit to block the drug discount plan. The pharmacists opposed the plan because they feared being forced to shoulder the discounts.

The pharmacists were also concerned about direct competition from PBMs. In attempting to lower pharmaceutical expenditures, PBMs had begun to operate mail-order prescription refill services, making them direct competitors to the independent pharmacists. The NCPA, with 25,000 members nationwide, responded by launching a campaign to pressure state governments to increase their regulation of PBMs. The PBMs argued that the NCPA campaign was intended to increase its members' profits.

Preparation Questions

1. Characterize the issues, interests, institutions, and information in the environment of the pharmaceutical industry.

2. Which issues will be addressed in which institutional arenas, and which interests will be active on those issues?
3. Where are these issues in their life cycles?

The Nonmarket Environment of McDonald's

McDonald's, the world's largest restaurant chain with 30,000 restaurants in 118 countries serving 46 million customers daily, faced a host of nonmarket issues in the early 2000s.

Obesity

The body mass index (BMI) of Americans increased throughout the 20th century, and the proportion of people considered obese increased from 15 to 31 percent from 1980 to 2000.[22] Sixty-four percent of American adults were overweight or obese. Interest in the obesity issue intensified after the release in February 2004 of a report by the Centers for Disease Control and Prevention estimating that 400,000 deaths annually were caused by obesity-related illnesses compared to 435,000 deaths caused by tobacco. The Surgeon General estimated that health care costs resulting from obesity were $117 billion annually.

Economists studied the increase in the BMI and concluded that it was due to several factors. Calorie intake had increased about 10 percent, and the strenuousness of work had decreased. Moreover, technological change had substantially reduced the relative cost of food, leading people to eat more.

In contrast to the economists, activists blamed fast food and the failure to provide nutritional information about menu items. Trial lawyers sought a new mass tort after their success in litigation against tobacco companies and saw obesity as an opportunity. Professor John

---

[22]Cutler, Glaeser, and Shapiro concluded that demographic changes did not explain the increase in obesity. David M. Cutler, Edward L. Glaeser, and Jesse M. Shapiro, "Why Have Americans Become More Obese?" Working paper, National Bureau of Economic Research, no date.

Banzhaf, a law professor at George Washington University, who advised trial lawyers in obesity lawsuits against McDonald's, said, "A fast-food company like McDonald's may not be responsible for the entire obesity epidemic, but let's say they're 5 percent responsible. Five percent of $117 billion is still an enormous amount of money."[23] The first two obesity lawsuits had been dismissed.[24]

The Cheeseburger Bill

The restaurant and food industries argued that obesity was a matter of individual responsibility and lobbied Congress for protection from obesity lawsuits. In 2004 the House quickly passed the Personal Responsibility in Food Consumption Act, dubbed the cheeseburger bill, on a 276–139 vote. The bill provided protection from obesity and weight-based lawsuits unless the weight gain was due to the violation of a state or federal law. Author of the bill Ric Keller (R-FL) said, "We need to get back to the old-fashioned principles of common sense and personal responsibility and get away from this new culture where everybody plays the victim and blames other people for their problems."[25] James Sensenbrenner (R-WI) was more direct, stating that "fat people should 'look in the mirror' and that parents need to monitor children's eating habits to make sure that 'little Johnny' doesn't become 'big Johnny.'"[26] House Speaker Dennis Hastert (R-IL) commented, "We as Americans need to realize that suing your way to better health is not the answer. Trial lawyers need to stop encouraging consumers to blame others for the consequences of their actions just so they can profit from frivolous lawsuits against restaurants."[27]

Referring to the cheeseburger bill, Representative James McGovern (D-MA) argued, "It protects an industry that doesn't need to be protected at this particular point and we're dealing with a problem that doesn't exist. The problem that does exist is that we have an obesity problem in this country."[28] Neil Barnard, president of the Physicians Committee for Responsible Medicine, commented, "[The bill] is an unsavory attempt to protect corporate profits at the expense of American health. The bill strips the public of its right to seek any redress against food manufacturers for their contribution to the obesity crisis, and the related epidemics of heart disease and diabetes."[29]

The restaurant industry backed the Common-Sense Consumption Act, the state version of the cheeseburger bill, which would shield restaurants and food processors from obesity liability. As of mid-2004 the cheeseburger bill had been introduced in 23 state legislatures, and eight states had enacted it.

Filmmaking Activism

The news media extensively covered the fast-food and obesity issue, and the issue became the subject of films. McDonald's was the target of a 98-minute film, *Super Size Me,* by filmmaker Morgan Spurlock. Spurlock ate only at McDonald's for 30 days, gained 25 pounds, and received warnings from doctors about his health. "Spurlock's approach was undeniably extreme. He supersized his meals whenever a counter worker made the offer, and ordered everything on the menu at least once. He also stopped exercising. As a result he was often eating twice as many calories a day as he needed. And as any nutritionist will tell you, it only takes an extra 100 calories a day to gain 10 pounds a year."[30]

In response to Spurlock's film, the Competitive Enterprise Institute (CEI) supported preparation of a film by Soso Whaley in which for two 30-day periods she ate only at McDonald's. She lost 18 pounds by controlling her calorie intake. The CEI stated, "Whaley's documentary project, focusing on personal responsibility, obesity, and public health, is taking on the increasing victim mentality being fostered by public health activists and the dishonest bashing of the fast food industry."[31]

Meal and Menu Nutrition Information

The public attention to the obesity issue led to the introduction of the Menu Education and Labeling Act (MEAL) in the House and the Senate. The so-called McMenu bills applied to chains with 20 or more locations operating under one trade name. The Senate bill required disclosure "in a statement adjacent to the name of the food on any menu . . . the number of calories, grams of saturated fat plus trans fat, and milligrams of sodium contained in a serving of the food. . . ."

The participants in the news conference accompanying the bill submission were Senator Tom Harkin (D-IA), Representative Rosa DeLauro (D-CN), and Margo Wootan, nutrition policy director of the Center for Science in the Public Interest (CSPI). Harkin said, "So many people are getting suckered into these supersized gimmicks because they are led to believe that bigger is better value. But if you continue to choose supersized, the odds are you will be supersized." Wootan said, "People have good nutrition information in the supermarkets, but people can only guess what they're eating at

[23]*Time,* August 3, 2003.
[24]See the Chapter 12 case, *Obesity and McLawsuits,* for more information on the issue.
[25]The Daily Buzz, www.foodservice.com, March 11, 2004.
[26]The Daily Buzz, www.foodservice.com, March 11, 2004.
[27]Associated Press Online, March 10, 2004.
[28]Associated Press Online, March 10, 2004.
[29]The Daily Buzz, www.foodservice.com, March 9, 2004.

[30]*San Francisco Chronicle,* April 21, 2004. The film included John Banzhaf, who commented that the documentary would result in more lawsuits.
[31]Competitive Enterprise Institute, Washington, DC, April 15, 2004.

chain restaurants."[32] The National Restaurant Association, representing 870,000 restaurants with 11.7 million workers, opposed the "one-size-fits-all" and "pre-packaged" MEAL bill. The Association observed, "When Americans do dine out at one of the nation's 870,000 restaurants they find a wide variety of venues, menu items, and portion sizes—meeting customers' demands for choice, value and flexibility, as well as their tastes and dietary needs."[33]

Healthy Lifestyles

As a result of the concern about obesity, McDonald's suspended its promotion of supersize meals and developed a "healthy lifestyles" program, initially offering additional items, including fruit and salads. In April 2004 the company launched a Lifestyles Platform to address obesity and physical well-being. The Platform included new food choices and ordering options such as the "Go Active" adult Happy Meal, education and easily accessible nutrition information, and physical activity, including the distribution of 15 million Stepometers and walking/fitness booklets. In 2004 it announced that by the end of the year it would introduce a new "core menu" and phase-out supersize options.

The CSPI continued to focus on McDonald's. In response to McDonald's announcement that it would add salads and healthy meals to its menu, Executive Director Michael F. Jacobson declared, "Consumers have good reason to be skeptical about the company's latest promises, since the company broke its promise to reformulate its trans-fat-laden cooking oil. By frying in partially hydrogenated vegetable oil, McDonald's recklessly promotes heart disease among its consumers."[34]

Children's Advertising

Advertising to children had long been of concern to children's advocates and members of Congress, which had restricted advertising on children's television programs. McDonald's promoted its trademark golden arches on Barbie dolls and backpacks, and some schools had McDonald's days for lunch. McDonald's also used plastic toy promotions often timed with the release of a movie. "'It seems very clear it's a breach of duty,' says John Banzhaf. . . . 'Schools get paid a kickback for every sugary soft drink or burger sold.'"[35] Professor Walter Willett of Harvard University's School of Public Health said, "The vast majority of what they sell is junk. . . . We don't sell children guns, alcohol or drugs, but we do allow them to be exploited by food companies."[36]

Obesity in the Workplace

McDonald's also faced obesity issues in the workplace. A 6 feet 1 inch, 420-pound man was offered a job as a cook but was told that he could not begin work until his specially ordered uniform with a 54-inch waistband arrived. After waiting 4 months for the uniform he filed a lawsuit against McDonald's alleging violation of the Americans with Disabilities Act (ADA).[37] The ADA did not prohibit discrimination based on appearance, but some plaintiffs argued that they were not hired or not treated fairly because employers wrongly concluded that they had a disability. A 5 feet 1 inch, 320-pound woman had filed a lawsuit on this theory. In 1997 the U.S. Court of Appeals ruled that "obesity, except in special cases where the obesity relates to a physiological disorder, is not a 'physical impairment.'"

Acrylamide

Researchers in Sweden detected the chemical acrylamide in a variety of foods but particularly in carbohydrates cooked at high temperatures. The researchers specifically mentioned french fries from McDonald's and Burger King. Researchers in other countries, including those at the Food and Drug Administration (FDA), confirmed the findings. Activists, including the CSPI, argued that the concentrations of acrylamide exceeded the EPA and WHO standards for water. Author Steven Milloy countered that in the study on which the EPA based its drinking water standard, the lowest concentration at which rats had a significant increase in cancer was 500 micrograms per kilogram of body weight.[38] Milloy stated that for a 154-pound man this was equivalent to 35,000 micrograms, which would require eating 486 large servings of McDonald's french fries every day for life. He added, "Acrylamide hysteria is nothing more than a convenient, if not cynical, tactic of CSPI to advance its anti-fun food agenda."[39]

The issue of consumer warnings regarding acrylamide resurfaced in California in April 2004. The Safe Drinking Water and Toxic Enforcement Act required a public notice for substances "known to the state to cause cancer, birth defects or other reproductive harm." In 1990 California had declared acrylamide, which was used in treating sewage water, to be such a substance. The concern was for workers who produced or worked with acrylamide. Private attorneys filed lawsuits to force the state to require fast-food companies to warn the public. The state began conducting studies to determine if there was any danger to people.

[32]Copley News Service, November 24, 2003.
[33]U.S. Newswire, November 5, 2003.
[34]Press Release, CSPI, April 15, 2004.
[35]*New York Times,* August 3, 2004.
[36]*New York Times,* August 3, 2004.

[37]During this period, McDonald's sold the restaurant to a franchisee who was unaware of the employment offer (*New York Times,* August 4, 2003).
[38]Steven Milloy, *Junk Science Judo: Self-Defense Against Health Scares and Scams,* Washington, DC: Cato Institute, 2001.
[39]Steven Milloy, "French Fry Scare," www.cato.org. Americans ate 28 pounds of potato chips and french fries a year on average.

Mad Cow Disease

In December 2003 the first case of mad cow disease documented in the United States was detected in Washington state in a downer (immobile) cow that had been purchased from Canada.[40] The FDA immediately began an informational campaign, as did the beef industry and the food and restaurant industries, to assure the public that there was no threat to humans. The National Cattlemen's Beef Association (NCBA) had been preparing for such an event by providing information to the public on beef safety.

McDonald's, which did not buy meat from downer cattle nor cattle parts that could carry the disease, stated that the recall of beef by the federal government had "absolutely no connection whatsoever to McDonald's or our suppliers." McDonald's had dealt with the issue of mad cow disease in a number of other countries and had used that experience to prepare for such an event in the United States. McDonald's posted on its Web site a letter to its customers and also distributed copies to customers in its restaurants. McDonald's reported that its sales were not affected.

Critics of the FDA and U.S. Department of Agriculture (USDA) continued to sound the alarm, and the media reported their claims, but no one seemed to pay attention. The CSPI criticized the actions of the USDA, stating that "consumer protection has certainly fallen short." Concerned about the ban on American beef imposed by a number of countries, the USDA set up an international panel to assess the situation. The panel recommended that the United States adopt stronger standards, consistent with international standards, and stated that more cases were likely in the future and that the present case should not be viewed as an "imported case." The NCBA criticized the recommendation as not taking into account the steps the United States and Canada had taken since 1989 to reduce the likelihood of BSE.

Antibiotics and Growth Hormones

Human health concerns had been raised about the possible development of antibiotic resistance in humans as a result of the use of antibiotics in food animals. Recognizing the importance of antibiotics for both human and veterinary medicine, McDonald's developed a policy based on the principle that "All users of antibiotics, including those who supervise use in animals and those who supervise use in humans, must work to sustain the long-term efficacy of antibiotics for human and veterinary medicine."[41] McDonald's established Sustainable Use Guiding Principles to govern their use. In the absence of a specific disease or likely threat of a specific disease, "antibiotics belonging to classes of compounds approved for use in human medicine" were to be phased out.

McDonald's, the environmental group Environmental Defense, and Elanco Animal Health joined together to create the Antibiotics Coalition. "By working together, McDonald's and Environmental Defense have leveraged the company's purchasing power to reverse the trend of antibiotics overuse in animal agriculture. McDonald's new policy demonstrates that reducing antibiotic use is both feasible and affordable."[42]

In 2000 McDonald's began phasing out growth-promoting antibiotics in Europe, and by the end of 2001, it had eliminated all such antibiotics in its suppliers' chicken feed. Antibiotics in the fluoroquinolone class were discontinued in the United States in 2001. In 2003 it announced that use of growth-promoting hormones would be phased out by all its suppliers.

Animal Welfare

McDonald's was targeted by People for the Ethical Treatment of Animals (PETA) and other animal welfare groups over the treatment of food animals. In response McDonald's adopted new standards for its beef suppliers, including minimum space standards for cattle in feedlots. McDonald's market power quickly led feedlot operators to meet the standards, bringing about change in the entire industry. Standards were also set for animal transport and care.

In 2000 PETA distributed "Unhappy Meals" boxes similar to the boxes used for Happy Meals. Each box contained a doll resembling Ronald McDonald with a bloody butcher's knife in his hand. McDonald's pledged to improve the welfare of chickens, and PETA suspended its campaign.[43]

Change began when the USDA hired Dr. Temple Grandin, a professor at Colorado State University who researched animal welfare, to evaluate the conditions in 24 meat-processing plants.[44] Her report startled the government and the industry. She documented substantial, and unnecessary, animal suffering. In 1997 McDonald's decided to visit Grandin and was impressed by her scientific, quantitative approach to evaluating the slaughter of animals. "We went to Colorado State and saw her, and it was magic. She pitched her program, and we thought it was perfect."[45] Grandin demonstrated how she "measured animal behavior and conditions, how she paid attention to animal vocalizations, how she studied their responses to electric prods, how she cataloged their adaptations to various conditions."[46]

In response to pressure from McDonald's and other large customers, the United Egg Producers (UEP), which represented virtually all egg producers in the United States, developed an "animal care certified" logo

---

[40]Mad cow disease is bovine spongiform encephalopathy (BSE), and in humans it is known as variant Creutzfeldt-Jakob disease (vCJD).
[41]McDonald's Global Policy on Antibiotic Use in Food Animals, www.mcdonalds.com.

[42]PR Newswire, June 19, 2003.
[43]Associated Press Online, March 24, 2002.
[44]www.grandin.com.
[45]*International Herald Tribune,* June 26, 2003.
[46]*International Herald Tribune,* June 26, 2003.

that retailers could carry on their egg cartons. To qualify, producers had to file monthly reports and have an on-site compliance audit annually. Adele Douglass, former director of the American Humane Association, commented, "What the UEP has done is incredible. They've moved a whole industry forward." Paul Shapiro, of Compassion Over Killing, however, said, "What the UEP is trying to do is increase space minimally to prevent an inevitable legislative ban on cages. We find animal abuse is the norm in the egg industry and not the exception. These hens never see daylight, never touch earth, and never even flap their wings."[47]

Defamation

In 2001 Carmen Calderón complained to the public health agency in Chile that her son had come down with food poisoning after eating in a McDonald's restaurant. McDonald's filed a $1.25 million lawsuit against Calderón, seeking an apology for what it viewed as an unsubstantiated claim.

The Environment

McDonald's established an environmental policy pertaining to natural resources, rain forests, sustainability, and waste management. It refused to purchase beef from "rainforest or recently deforested rainforest land." McDonald's also participated in the European Union's Greenlights Programme and the U.S. Green Lights program to reduce electricity use in its restaurants. In Denmark McDonald's opened the first HFC/CFC-free restaurant. Minister of the Environment Hans Chr. Schmidt said, "Today McDonald's is showing how companies can make a difference by setting new standards for environmental performance. . . . It's a good day for the environment."[48] Greenpeace claimed credit for forcing McDonald's to open the restaurant.

Suppliers

As a result of concerns in the 1990s about the treatment of workers in overseas suppliers' factories, McDonald's developed a Code of Conduct for Suppliers. The code covered employment practices pertaining to the use of prison and forced labor, child labor, working hours, compensation, nondiscrimination, and the workplace environment. McDonald's refused to do business with suppliers that did not abide by the code and reserved the right to conduct unannounced inspections of suppliers' facilities.

Franchisees

By 2000 McDonald's was the largest employer in Brazil and was named employer of the year by *Exame* magazine. The economic downturn and the rise of the U.S. dollar, however, squeezed McDonald's franchisees. In response McDonald's purchased hundreds of franchises, and by 2003 only 184 of 582 restaurants in Brazil were owned by franchisees. The remaining franchisees filed a lawsuit against McDonald's alleging that it squeezed them by overcharging for rent and opening too many restaurants.[49]

Vegetarianism

A 2000 Roper poll commissioned by the Vegetarian Resource Group found that 6 percent of girls and 2 percent of boys between 6 and 17 years never eat meat. "Janet Carr, nutrition director at Remuda Ranch, a clinic for women with bulimia and anorexia in Wickenburg, Arizona, says about 25 percent of her teen clients classify themselves as vegetarians. 'Can someone be a healthy vegetarian? I would say yes, absolutely, but it's a difficult challenge, you have to put a lot of effort into it,' Carr says."[50] The National Cattlemen's Beef Association began a marketing campaign aimed at 8- to 12-year-old girls emphasizing beef as a source of protein, iron, and B_{12}, of which the USDA indicated young girls did not get nearly enough.

Brand Name Attractions

In April 2003 two incendiary devices failed to ignite at a Chico, California, McDonald's where Animal Liberation Front (ALF) activists had written "Meat is Murder" on the restaurant. The next day, firebombs exploded at a McDonald's and an Arby's in Albuquerque, New Mexico. The Earth Liberation Front (ELF) produced a videotape, "Igniting the Revolution," that featured McDonald's as a target. "Wherever they are, McDonald's are a legitimate target for people who want to protect the earth. McDonald's is a symbol of international animal abuse and environmental destruction," said Rodney Coronado, who had spent four years in prison for a firebombing in 1992.[51] Directions on building firebombs were available on the ALF and ELF Web sites.

Preparation Questions

1. Characterize the four I's.
2. What is the time frame of each issue?
3. Which issues should have the highest priority?
4. What overall strategy should McDonald's adopt for dealing with these nonmarket issues?

---

[47]The Business Press/California, March 31, 2003.
[48]McDonald's Corporate Press Release, January 16, 2003.
[49]*Wall Street Journal,* October 21, 2003.
[50]*Morning Call,* May 23, 2003.
[51]Associated Press State & Local Wire, April 28, 2003.

The Nonmarket Environment of Google

Google had become extraordinarily popular because of the efficiency of its search engine, and that popularity grew through its applications. The key to its financial success was the placement of advertisements tailored to the search queries of a user. Its strategy had three components: search, ads, and apps. Google's objective was "to organize the world's information and make it universally accessible." Its motto was "Don't be evil."

Accompanying Google's success and growth was an expanding set of nonmarket challenges. Some of these challenges came from competitors, some from producers of complementary products, some from content producers, and some from NGOs and the public.

Privacy

It was inevitable that Google would become public enemy number one to privacy activists. Google appointed Peter Fleischer as global privacy counsel with responsibility for encouraging Googlers to build privacy into new products early in the development process. He also worked for more uniformity in privacy laws across countries so that the company would not have to deal with differing laws and regulations.

More important, however, was the evolving concept of privacy. Fleischer observed, "The ability to retain and find information, once it's public, means that the whole concept of privacy is changing and might be irreversible."[52] In September 2007 Fleischer spoke to a United Nations audience and said, "The ultimate goal should be to create minimum standards of privacy protection that meet the expectations and demands of consumers, businesses and governments." Marc Rotenberg of EPIC commented, "Google, under investigation for violating global privacy standards, is calling for international privacy standards. It's somewhat like someone being caught for speeding saying there should be a public policy to regulate speeding."[53]

Some privacy issues were as amusing as serious. Mary Kalin-Casey of Oakland, California tried Google's Street View and went to the apartment building she lived in and managed. She zoomed in and saw her cat Monty sitting in the window of her apartment. She quickly wrote on a blog, "The issue that I have ultimately is about where you draw the line between taking public photos and zooming in on people's lives. The next step might be seeing books on my shelf. If the government was doing this, people would be outraged." The news media picked up on the story and raised the privacy issue. Google responded that "Street View only features imagery taken on public property. This imagery is no different from what any person can readily capture or see walking down the street."[54]

Google Earth was blocked by the government of Bahrain because it allowed people to see the private homes and royal palaces of the ruling Khalifa family. Mahmood al-Yousif, who had encouraged citizens to post photos of the properties, said, "Some of the palaces take up more space than three or four villages nearby and block access to the sea for fishermen. People knew this already. But they never saw it. All they saw were the surrounding walls." The Khalifa family was Sunni, and the majority Shias lived in the villages to which Yousif referred.[55]

The FTC issued draft rules on Internet privacy principles and sought comments. Pam Dixon, who headed the World Privacy Forum, campaigned for a binding "do not track" list similar to the "do not call" list that blocks telemarketers. The Network Advertising Initiative allowed consumers to opt out of data collection by the 20,000 Web sites that participated in the Initiative.[56] The FTC draft sought to cover a much broader set of Web sites and preferred that the advertising industry exercise self-regulation rather than require government regulation. Jules Polenetsky, the chief privacy officer for AOL, said, "The industry needs to get together and formally push out the appropriate set of rules." He said that the FTC action "will provide the much-needed push to help crystallize emerging best practices across the industry."[57] Shortly before the FTC action, Ask.com became the first search engine to allow users to opt out of collection of their queries. Congress announced plans for hearings on Internet privacy for early 2008.

Acquisition of DoubleClick

In 2007 Google made a $3.4 billion merger offer for DoubleClick. In 2000 DoubleClick had been involved in an explosive privacy conflict when it had acquired a company that collected data on catalog purchases and planned to combine that data with browsing data.[58] Privacy advocates and government officials complained, and bowing to both private and public political pressure, DoubleClick pledged not to combine any databases that contained personally identifiable information.

The merger required approval by the Federal Trade Commission (FTC) and also the attorneys general of the states. In addition, approval was required by other countries in which the two companies operated,

---

[52]*San Francisco Chronicle*, December 30, 2007.
[53]*Washington Post*, September 15, 2007.

[54]*New York Times*, June 1, 2007.
[55]*Financial Times*, November 25, 2006.
[56]*Los Angeles Times*, December 21, 2007.
[57]*New York Times*, December 21, 2007.
[58]See the Chapter 13 case, *DoubleClick and Internet Privacy*.

most importantly the European Union.[59] Microsoft objected to the acquisition, stating that it would "substantially reduce competition in the advertising market on the Web." Microsoft general counsel Bradford Smith stated, "By putting together a single company that will control virtually the entire market . . . Google will control the economic fuel of the Internet."[60] CEO Eric Schmidt replied, "We've studied this closely, and their claims, as stated, are not true." AT&T complained, "We think antitrust authorities should take a hard look at this deal and the implications. If any one company gets a hammerlock on the online advertising space, as Google seems to be trying to do, that is worrisome."[61] Both Microsoft and AT&T have been defendants in major antitrust cases. Scott Cleland, president of the consulting firm Precursor, established a Web site, googleopoly.net.

A subcommittee of the Senate Judiciary Committee on antitrust held hearings on the proposed acquisition in September, and David Drummond, chief legal officer for Google, said the two companies were "complementary businesses." The subcommittee chair and the ranking Republican member, however, wrote to the FTC stating that the proposed merger "raises very important competition issues in a vital sector of the economy" and "raises fundamental privacy concerns worthy of serious scrutiny." Microsoft testified in opposition to the acquisition.

DoubleClick's history tied the privacy issue to the competition issue. The New York State Consumer Protection Board urged federal regulators not to approve the merger unless the companies were prevented from tracking and storing information on Web surfing by consumers. Executive Director Mindy Bockstein warned that if data were misused it "could seriously harm the privacy rights of consumers."[62] The Electronic Privacy Information Center, the Center for Digital Democracy, and the U.S. Public Interest Research Group filed a formal request with the FTC to investigate the planned merger and its potential for privacy infringement. They complained that the merger "would impact the privacy interests of 233 million Internet users in North America." EPIC complained that combining Google's tracking search inquiries and DoubleClick's cookies that track browsing would be a privacy concern. DoubleClick explained that the cookies were owned by its clients and that would not change with an acquisition. Nicole Wong of Google said, "EPIC utterly fails to identify any practice that does not comply with accepted privacy standards. Nothing about the proposed

acquisition of DoubleClick changes our commitment to these privacy principles."[63]

Privacy was generally not an antitrust issue, however, although it was under the purview of the FTC. In December the FTC voted 4–1 to approve the acquisition. Drummond wrote, "It is telling that while our competitors tried hard to come up with theories of how our customers and partners could be harmed by the deal, those customers and partners did not agree with those theories."

Prior to filing for approval in the European Union (EU), Google declared that the merger "poses no risk to competition and should be approved." Upon filing, the European Commission conducted an initial investigation and concluded that the two companies were "the leading providers" of online advertising space and services. The commission then began an in-depth investigation and said it would render a decision in April, 2008.

European Union Privacy Regulations

Privacy concerns in the European Union led the national data-protection officers to examine Google's data storage practices. EU law required data holders to store an individual's data only as long as necessary.[64] For example, companies were allowed to store data for a limited period in case a customer returned a purchase and wanted a refund. Google also argued that retaining data was important to efforts to fight hackers. Privacy advocates, however, remained concerned. London-based Privacy International reported that of the 2,000 complaints it received in 2006, 96 percent were about Google and its data retention policies. An EU Data Retention Directive was to take effect on September 1 and would limit retention to 24 months for ISPs and telephone companies, but it was not clear whether the directive pertained to search engines.

An advisory panel for the data protection officers wrote to Google asking it to justify its retention policy, and Google entered into discussion with the data-protection officers.[65] Google pointed out that after data had been stored for a time, it made the queries anonymous. The officers as well as Internet users remained concerned, and the planned acquisition of DoubleClick added to the concern. BEUC, the largest consumer group in Europe, objected to the acquisition by writing to the European Commission advisory panel arguing that a merger threatened the privacy of EU residents. It wrote, "Never before has one single company had the market and technological power to collect and exploit so much information about what a user does on the Internet. The unprecedented and unmatched databases of user profiles . . . appear also to be clear violations of users' privacy rights."[66]

---

[59]Within weeks of Google's announcement of the deal other companies rushed to acquire ad placement companies. Yahoo paid $680 million to acquire the rest of Right Media, the advertising agency WPP paid $649 million for 24/7 Real Media, and Microsoft paid $6 billion for aQuantive, whose Atlas unit competed with DoubleClick (*New York Times*, May 29, 2007).
[60]*Los Angeles Times*, August 6, 2007.
[61]*New York Times*, April 16, 2007.
[62]*San Jose Mercury News*, May 10, 2007.

[63]*San Francisco Chronicle*, April 21, 2007.
[64]See the Chapter 15 case, *The European Union Data Protection Directive*.
[65]*New York Times*, May 26, 2007.
[66]*San Jose Mercury News*, July 5, 2007.

After additional criticism regarding its retention of search query data, Google announced in June that it would retain the data only for 18 months. Nicole Wong of Google explained, "We have decided to make this change with feedback from privacy advocates, regulators worldwide and, of course, our users."[67] Google's Peter Fleischer stated, "Retention of logs data is critical to our ability to operate and improve our services and to provide adequate security for our users. We believe we can still address our legitimate interests in security, innovation, and antifraud efforts with this shorter period."[68] London-based Privacy International had given Google the lowest privacy rating of any major company, and Fleischer replied, "We were disappointed with the report because it is full of numerous inaccuracies."[69]

In May 2008 Peter Hustinx, the EU's chief data protection officer, warned Google that if it introduced Street View in the EU it would have to comply with the data protection directive.

Spectrum Auction

Television broadcasters were required to convert their broadcasts to digital signals in 2009. Since digital broadcasting used less of the electromagnetic spectrum than analog broadcasting, the FCC planned to auction a block in the 700 megahertz (MHz) band of the spectrum. This band could be used to offer nationwide wireless broadband service.[70]

Mobile operators had restricted both the hardware devices and software that consumers could use on their networks. Google viewed a wireless service as a computer service rather than a telephone service, as current mobile services viewed it. Also, Google was developing a wireless telephone and wanted the phone to be usable on the network of whichever firm won the spectrum block. Google wanted any nationwide wireless broadband network to be open to all software applications and any compatible devices, which would be a major departure from current FCC policy.

Google launched a nonmarket campaign to influence the FCC's design of the auction. Its strategy was unconventional. It made an offer to the FCC to bid at least $4.6 billion for the C block but only if the spectrum license met four conditions. One condition was that the spectrum be open to any device. A second condition was that it be open to any software application. A third condition was that the operator of any network be required to lease portions of the spectrum at wholesale rates. The fourth was that new networks would have to be mutually compatible. Each of these conditions would reduce the

value of the spectrum to the winning bidder, which explained Google's pledge of a minimum bid.

Google's offer was supported by public interest groups as well as high-tech firms, including Yahoo, Intel, eBay's Skype, and Frontline Wireless, an investment fund headed by former FCC commissioner Reed Hundt and backed by Silicon Valley venture capitalists. The *Wall Street Journal*, however, in an editorial was critical of Google and its audacity: "[Google] wants to make sure it can continue to free-ride on your broadband subscription bills, even in the mobile world. It wants to make sure it won't have to share the proceeds of its massive search and advertising dominance with suppliers of network capacity."[71] A *Fortune* article was titled "Don't Be Arrogant. How Google is starting to act like your garden-variety monopoly."[72]

The FCC was responsive to Google's position, and its draft rule included Google's first two conditions but not the requirement to lease portions of the spectrum at wholesale rates. The FCC's final rules included a minimum auction price of $4.6 billion, and if that price were not met, the open access provisions would be dropped and another auction conducted.

When the FCC announced its draft auction rules, Google praised the rules but said that they did not go far enough. The Cellular Telecommunications Industry Association called it "Silicon Valley welfare."[73] AT&T said, "This is an attempt to pressure the U.S. government to turn the auction process on its head by ensuring only a few, if any, bidders will compete with Google. If Google is serious about introducing a competing business model into the wireless industry, Chairman Martin's compromise proposal allows them to bid in the auction, win the spectrum, and then implement every one of the conditions they seek."[74] Verizon was equally critical. "Google's filing urges the FCC to adopt rules that force all bidders to implement Google's business plan—which would reduce the incentives for other players to bid," said executive vice president Thomas J. Tauke.[75]

Intellectual Property

Google had an aggressive view of the intellectual property rights of others. Its vision of "organizing the world's information" required access to the content produced by others. Google did not use material from a media source that requested that it not do so, but in the absence of such a request it used the material. Lee Bromberg, a partner at Bromberg & Sustein, explained, "What characterizes Google is its very aggressive approach to copyright law. My own view, as someone who often defends intellectual property, is that in every area where Google

[67]*New York Times*, March 15, 2007.
[68]*New York Times*, June 13, 2007.
[69]*New York Times*, June 13, 2007.
[70]The 700 megahertz spectrum was ideally suited for wireless transmission, since signals could penetrate buildings and cover greater distances, requiring fewer towers.
[71]Editorial, *Wall Street Journal*, July 18, 2007.
[72]*Fortune*, August 20, 2007.
[73]*Fortune*, August 20, 2007.
[74]*New York Times*, July 21, 2007.
[75]*New York Times*, July 21, 2007.

has pushed it has been over the line, but it has an interesting carrot-and-stick approach. The carrot is your content gets to be displayed to Google's vast army of users, which increases rather than diminishes its commercial value to you. The stick is that it says it is just going to access your content as part of the plan to control and organize our knowledge, and that it is up to you to opt out. Well, you can't burden the copyright holder with an obligation to demand their content is not used."[76]

Google Books

Google announced that it would digitize the book collections of the University of California, Harvard University, Oxford University, the University of Michigan, Stanford University, and the New York Public Library. Google planned to provide short excerpts in response to queries about a book, and this required the company to scan and store the entire book. Google argued that since it would only provide snippets of a book in response to queries it represented fair use under the copyright laws.

Google's Book Search Library Project drew immediate fire from publishers and from the company's competitors. The Association of American Publishers and the Authors Guild filed a copyright-infringement lawsuit against Google. The president of the World Association of Newspapers, Gavin O'Reilly, said, "If you subscribe to the Ten Commandments, Google operated with only nine, leaving out 'thou shall not steal.'"[77] Google had a different view from traditional media. Eric Schmidt had said that Google had a "genuine disagreement" and that the media had to show that its content had value. "That's often a difficult conversation."[78]

Google responded by subpoenaing Amazon.com, Microsoft, and Yahoo ostensibly to obtain information on how they organized search-related projects. Yahoo immediately refused to comply with the subpoena.

Google News

In 2007 Google began to supplement its News service by inviting, on an experimental basis, individuals and organizations that had been mentioned or quoted in an article to offer comments attached as a link on the story page. Journalists and editors were also allowed to attach comments. Google individually checked and verified the identity of those providing the comments but did no editing. The company was generally praised for allowing rebuttals and comments. The executive editor of Washingtonpost.com, Jim Brady, said, "It's a typical Google idea: It's an interesting concept, and I'm not sure how they're going to do it technically, but because it's Google, it's worth watching."[79] Some news pages allowed anyone to post comments on articles or to link to blogs.

Google News found opposition in Europe. A Belgian court found Google guilty of copying copyrighted content without permission and fined the company for each day it had violated the copyright. Google said, "We believe that Google News is entirely legal. We only ever show the headlines and a few snippets of text and small thumbnail images. If people want to read the entire story they have to click through to the newspaper's Web site." The lawsuit was filed by Copiepresse, which represented 18 European publications. Copiepresse said, "Today we celebrate a victory for content producers. We showed that Google cannot make profit for free from the credibility of our newspaper brands, hard work of our journalists and skill of our photographers."[80] The decision by the Belgian court was significant because the copyright laws in European countries were quite similar, and Agence France-Presse had filed lawsuits in France and the United States against Google. Google defied the Belgian court, which had ordered it to publish the court's ruling in the case. Google announced that it would appeal both the decision and the order.

Publisher groups had developed software that would notify search engine Web crawlers that material was copyrighted and would attach the publisher's conditions for use, including requirements for payment. D. J. Collins of Google responded, "We welcome any initiative that enables search engines and publishers to work together more closely."[81]

Google also took the copyright issue to the content providers. The Computer and Communications Industry Association, which included Google and Microsoft as members, filed a complaint with the Federal Trade Commission alleging that the warnings used by content providers were misrepresenting the law. The warning for Major League Baseball was ". . . the accounts and description of this game may not be disseminated, without express written consent." The Association stated that the warnings "materially misrepresent U.S. copyright law, particularly the fundamental built-in First Amendment accommodations which serve to safeguard the public interest" and had a "chilling effect" on users who were deterred from legitimate uses.[82]

Trademarks

Merriam-Webster's Collegiate Dictionary included "to google" as a verb describing searching the Internet. Google was concerned about trademark protection and wrote letters to media organizations complaining about the use of its name. A spokesman explained, "We think it's important to make the distinction between using the word Google to describe using Google to search the Internet, and using the word Google to describe searching the Internet. It has some serious trademark issues." One

---

[76]*The Independent*, October 11, 2006.
[77]*Sunday Times*, March 11, 2007.
[78]*Sunday Times*, March 11, 2007.
[79]*Wall Street Journal*, August 8, 2007.

[80]*New York Times*, February 14, 2007.
[81]*New York Times*, September 23, 2007.
[82]*Wall Street Journal*, August 1, 2007.

example given by Google was: "Appropriate: I ran a Google search to check out the guy from the party. Inappropriate: I googled the hottie."[83] When the letters were posted on the Internet, bloggers went after Google.

American Airlines filed a lawsuit against Google for selling search terms like "American Airlines" to other firms for advertising. Google responded, "We are confident that our trademark policy strikes a proper balance between trademark owners' interests and consumer choice."[84] Other companies also complained about competitors' ads appearing when users searched on their name. In 2006 Google was successfully sued in France by Louis Vuitton and agreed to remove all ads for a Louis Vuitton search. In the United States Geico had filed a similar lawsuit, but the companies settled the lawsuit before the court had reached a final verdict. In a case filed by Perfect 10 about posting thumbnail images, the Ninth Circuit Court of Appeals ruled, "We conclude that the significantly transformative nature of Google's search engine, particularly in light of its public benefit, outweighs Google's superseding and commercial use of the thumbnails in this case."[85]

U.S. Government Enforcement

Google was also on the other side of intellectual property protection issues. The U.S. government sought to enforce the Child Online Protection Act, which was intended to stop child pornography by imposing criminal penalties on individuals with Web sites containing material harmful to minors. The government asked for data on search queries that it could use to develop filtering technology to identify predators and purveyors of child pornography. America Online, Microsoft's MSN, and Yahoo complied with the request, but Google refused and continued to do so after the government issued a subpoena for the data. It told the Department of Justice, "Google's acceding to the request would suggest that it is willing to reveal information about those who use its services. This is not a perception Google can accept. And one can envision scenarios where queries alone could reveal identifying information about a specific Google user, which is another outcome that Google cannot accept."[86]

The government had asked Google for a random sample of 1 million Web addresses and a week's search requests, with any information that could identify the user removed. The Department of Justice then took Google to court to force it to provide the information. In the court hearing the government substantially scaled back its request, and the judge ordered Google to provide 50,000 random Web addresses. The judge also ruled that providing the requested 50,000 random search queries could harm Google through a loss of goodwill among its users.[87]

Google Health

Google assigned a team to develop Google Health, which proclaimed on a prototype Web page, "At Google, we feel patients should be in charge of their health information, and they should be able to grant their health care providers, family members, or whomever they choose, access to this information. Google Health was developed to meet this need."[88] Earlier in the year Microsoft had acquired Medstory, which provided software to manage health care information.

Google Telephone

Eric Schmidt commented on the opportunities for ads on wireless telephones: "What's interesting about the ads in the mobile phone is that they are twice as profitable or more than the nonmobile phone ads because they are more personal." He also said, "We are partnering with almost all of the carriers and manufacturers to get Google search and other Google applications onto their devices."[89] Google also announced an open source mobile phone platform called Android that could be used to develop new wireless services.

YouTube

Google acquired YouTube in 2006 for $1.65 billion. YouTube was subject to intellectual property complaints because users posted pirated videos and broadcasts. Google was protected by the 1998 Millennium Copyright Act that provided a "safe harbor" to Internet sites that promptly removed copyrighted material in response to a complaint from the holder. The act, however, did not require the site operator to actively search to determine if material posted violated a copyright. Google investigated the complaints it received. Critics, however, were not satisfied.

YouTube was also subject to censorship. When a posting contained a trailer for an as-yet unreleased film by a Dutch lawmaker that was critical of Islam, Pakistan shut down YouTube by directing all traffic to a "black hole" where all content was discarded. A routing error, however, resulted in most of the world's access to YouTube to disappear for several hours.

Tolls

Google and other Internet sites feared that ISPs would begin to impose a "congestion charge" on users that occupied large amounts of capacity when using broadband services. The possibility of such charges posed a risk for

[83]*Independent on Sunday*, August 13, 2006.
[84]Reuters, August 20, 2007.
[85]*Washington Post*, May 17, 2007.
[86]*International Herald Tribune*, January 21, 2006.

[87]The judge also stated that the search queries could be within the scope of a subpoena. *San Francisco Chronicle*, March 18, 2006.
[88]*New York Times*, August 14, 2007.
[89]*Wall Street Journal*, August 2, 2007.

YouTube, where users uploaded and downloaded videos. Paul Gallant with Stanford Group Company observed, "Google sees network owners as potentially coming between it and its customers, so they realize how critical Washington was to their long-term game plan. Google is still nowhere near the Bells and cable [television] when it comes to lobbying, but it does have a real cachet that can make up some of the gap."[90]

Google advocated "net neutrality" and sought laws to require ISPs to treat all Internet traffic alike. This meant that users would not be differentiated by how much Internet capacity they used.

Discrimination

In 2004 Google fired its director of engineering, Brian Reed, because he was "slow." Reed filed a California age discrimination lawsuit against Google, but the trial judge dismissed the lawsuit. Reed appealed the dismissal, and the Sixth Circuit Court of Appeals in California ruled that sufficient evidence had been presented to justify the case going to trial. Google appealed the ruling, and in 2008 the California Supreme Court agreed to consider Google's appeal.

Corporate Social Responsibility

Environmental Practices

Google decided to influence attitudes and policy toward the environment. "We want to leverage our assets and influence the world beyond the computer. We are going to argue in public to change attitudes on a number of things. The first one is energy standards," said Urs Holzle of Google.[91]

With a motto of "Do no evil" Google was concerned about the environmental impact of the energy used by its hundreds of thousands of computers. The company pledged to become carbon neutral and announced a project backed by hundreds of millions of dollars to reduce the cost of renewable energy by 25 to 50 percent. Its objective was to produce a gigawatt of electricity at a cost below the cost of producing electricity from coal. Larry Page predicted that the goal could be reached within a matter of "years, not decades."[92]

Philanthropy

When it went public, Google pledged to contribute 1 percent of its assets, 1 percent of its profits, and employee time to philanthropy. In 2008 Google fulfilled its pledge by establishing Google.org, or DotOrg in Google-speak, that was unusual in its structure. It was established as for-profit so that it could invest in start-ups and form partnerships. For-profit status, however, meant that taxes had to be paid on contributions from Google to the organization and on any earnings. The organization selected five initiatives: helping communities identify and deal with potential pandemics before they could spread, supporting public services information in developing countries, aiding medium-sized businesses in developing countries, developing renewable energy at a cost less than coal, and speeding the commercialization of a car capable of getting 100 miles per gallon. DotOrg invested $10 million in closely held eSolar, Inc.

Indigenous Peoples

Google joined with the Surui tribe of Brazil's Amazon jungle in a project to provide satellite images of its reservation so that the tribe could identify illegal logging and mining. Megan Quinn of Google explained, "If you look at the Surui land today in Google Earth, you'll see their island of healthy green rainforest is surrounded almost completely by clear-cut, barren land. The stark contrast at their boundary is dramatic, and conveys vividly what is at stake."[93]

China

Human Rights

Using servers located in the United States, Google began offering a Chinese-language version of Google.com in 2000, but the site was frequently unavailable or slow because of censoring by the Chinese government. Google had a significant share of searches in China, but it lagged behind the market leader Baidu.com. Google concluded that it was imperative to host a Web site from within China, but Google had to decide how to deal with the censorship imposed by the Chinese government.[94]

As a result of an extensive debate within the company, cofounder Serge Brin explained, "We gradually came to the realization that we were hurting not just ourselves but the Chinese people."[95] Google decided to offer a site, Google.cn, but without features that allowed users to provide content. Google offered neither e-mail nor the ability to create blogs, since user-generated material could be seized by the Chinese government. This avoided Google putting individuals in jeopardy of being arrested. Because it would be required by Chinese law to censor search results associated with sensitive issues, Google decided to place a brief notice at the bottom of a search page when material had been censored, as it did in other countries such as France and Germany, which ban the sale of Nazi items. Google planned to exercise self-censorship and developed a list of sensitive items by consulting with third parties and by studying the results of the Chinese government's Internet filtering. Senior policy counsel Andrew McLaughlin stated, "In order to

[90]*Washington Post*, July 30, 2007.
[91]*Financial Times*, June 20, 2007.
[92]*Chicago Tribune*, November 28, 2007.
[93]*Sydney Morning Herald*, July 10, 2007.
[94]See the Chapter 16 case, *Google in China*.
[95]*San Jose Mercury News*, March 3, 2006.

operate from China, we have removed some content from the search results available on Google.cn, in response to local law, regulation or policy. While removing search results is inconsistent with Google's mission, providing no information (or a heavily degraded user experience that amounts to no information) is more inconsistent with our mission."[96] Representative Tom Lantos (D-CA) asked during a congressional hearing, "Can you say in English that you are ashamed of what you and your company . . . have done?"

New York City's comptroller, who managed the city's pension plans that held $338 million of Google shares, announced that he would submit a shareholder proposal with the SEC for voting at the company's annual shareholder meeting. The proposal stated, "Technology companies in the United States have failed to develop adequate standards by which they can conduct business with authoritarian governments while protecting human rights."[97] The New York State Pension Funds also qualified a shareholder resolution demanding that the company not host Web sites in countries that restricted Internet usage.

In its competition with Baidu.com Google invested in Tianya.cn, a Chinese Web site that allowed users to connect with each other and answer one another's questions. The Web site would use Google technology. This Web site seemed to raise new risks that Google had sought to avoid.

Schmidt said one of the company's "big projects" for 2007 was to give local managers greater autonomy. With respect to China, he said, "As (Google) China gets more established, it will have its own voice, its own expression and, I think, its own look."[98]

Online Video

China's State Administration of Radio, Film, and Television and the Ministry of Information Industry clarified its rules for video-streaming, allowing companies such as Youku and Tudou to "re-register and continue operations" if they were currently in compliance with the law. Although the regulations issued in early 2008 were not entirely clear, they appeared to require new companies to be owned or controlled by the government. This appeared to block Google's YouTube. The government reiterated its prohibition against pornography and material that "promoted violence or other serious illegal business."[99]

Music Downloads

Google continued to lag far behind Baidu in search market share, in part because Baidu offered free music downloads without licensing whereas Google did not offer music downloads. Respecting copyright law,

Google entered into a joint venture with a Chinese company to offer free licensed music downloads.

Microsoft and Vista

When Microsoft rolled out its new Vista operating system, Google recognized that it disadvantaged Google's search engine by only using Microsoft's search engine for queries entered by right clicks and pane windows.[100] Microsoft argued that it was easy to set the selection for the search engine. To get leverage over Microsoft, Google sought to intervene in the court responsible for the enforcement of the federal antitrust consent decree with Microsoft, which was to expire in November 2007.[101] The Department of Justice and Microsoft had reached a compromise regarding aspects of Vista. In an amicus brief Google told the court that it could provide information useful to the court and said that it was concerned that despite the compromise Microsoft would not eliminate its anticompetitive conduct. Google asked that the consent decree be extended. Google also lobbied in state capitals, arguing that its applications were unfairly discouraged in Vista. In 2007 Microsoft relented and made several changes that made it easier to conduct searches with non-Microsoft search engines.

Microsoft and Yahoo

In 2008 Microsoft made a $44.6 billion unsolicited offer for Yahoo. CEO Steve Ballmer argued that a merger would create a viable number two competitor to Google's advertising placement business. Google senior vice president David Drummond raised antitrust concerns in writing on the company's blog, "Could Microsoft now attempt to exert the same sort of inappropriate and illegal influence over the Internet that it did with the PC? While the Internet rewards competitive innovation, Microsoft has frequently sought to establish proprietary monopolies—and then leverage its dominance into new, adjacent markets." Google CEO Eric Schmidt reportedly called Jerry Yang of Yahoo to offer support in opposing the offer. Commentators speculated, however, that moves such as Yahoo outsourcing its advertising placement to Google could run into antitrust problems of their own by reducing competition. The antitrust subcommittees in both the House and Senate indicated they would hold hearings if Yahoo agreed to the merger, providing Google an opportunity to take its case to Congress as Microsoft had done in Google's acquisition of DoubleClick.

---

[96]*New York Times*, January 25, 2006.
[97]*San Jose Mercury News*, May 2, 2007.
[98]*Financial Times*, April 30, 2007.
[99]*Wall Street Journal*, February 6, 2008.

---

[100]In 2005 Google had outbid Microsoft to be the primary search service for AOL. Google paid $1 billion and obtained a 5 percent share of AOL.
[101]See the Chapter 9 case, *The Microsoft Antitrust Case*.

Preparation Questions

1. Identify the four I's for Google's nonmarket environment.
2. Where are the issues in their life cycles?
3. How should Google deal with the host of privacy issues associated with its applications? How should it deal with the risk of intellectual property lawsuits? How do these affect new product development and acquisitions?
4. Google now is huge. How does this affect its antitrust risk?
5. What issues are associated with the launch of Google Health?
6. What issues might arise in Google's ownership of Tianya.cn?
7. How should Google interact with Microsoft?

2

Integrated Strategy

INTRODUCTION

A business strategy guides a firm's actions in its market and nonmarket environments and has both market and nonmarket components. A market strategy is a concerted pattern of actions taken in the market environment to create value by improving the economic performance of a firm. A nonmarket strategy is a concerted pattern of actions taken in the nonmarket environment to create value by improving overall performance. A firm that decides to enter a country that has open markets relies primarily on a market strategy. A firm that decides to enter a country that has erected trade barriers needs a nonmarket strategy in addition to a market strategy. An effective business strategy integrates these two components and tailors them to the firm's market and nonmarket environments as well as to its capabilities.[1]

Market and nonmarket strategies focus on the pursuit of opportunity and advantage in the face of market and nonmarket competition with the objective of achieving superior performance. In this book, performance is considered on two dimensions. Initially, it is measured by the value created for the firm's owners. Then, in Part V the objective is broadened using concepts of corporate social responsibility and ethics.

This chapter focuses on nonmarket analysis and strategy and their integration with their market counterparts. As illustrated in Figure 2-1, effective management in the nonmarket environment requires conceptual frameworks for (1) analyzing nonmarket issues and the broader environment, (2) formulating effective strategies for addressing those issues, (3) integrating those strategies with market strategies, and (4) positioning the firm in its nonmarket environment. The strategy concept is introduced first, and the integration of market and nonmarket analysis and strategy formulation are considered using a Google example. Strategic positioning in the nonmarket environment is then considered and illustrated using the example of eBay. Nonmarket analysis is then considered, and a framework for analysis is presented and illustrated using an example involving Citibank.

STRATEGY IN THE NONMARKET ENVIRONMENT

The Importance of Nonmarket Strategy

The importance of a nonmarket strategy is related to the control of a firm's opportunities, as illustrated in Figure 2-2. Opportunities can be controlled by government at one extreme and markets at the other extreme. Nonmarket strategies are more important

---

[1]This material is adapted from Baron (1995b). Copyright © 1995 by the Board of Regents of the University of California. Reprinted from the *California Management Review*, Vol. 37, No. 2. By permission of The Regents.

FIGURE 2-1 Management and Integrated Strategy

the more opportunities are controlled by government and are less important, but often still important, when opportunities are controlled by markets. In some industries, such as consumer electronics and computer software, government exercises relatively little control over firms and their activities. In contrast, government exercises considerable control over pharmaceuticals and local telecommunications service. The automobile industry is somewhere in between. One important role of nonmarket strategy is to unlock opportunities controlled by government, as illustrated by the strategies of firms to deregulate the telecommunications industry. Another important role of nonmarket strategy is to avoid the control of opportunities by government, as in the case of self-regulation by companies on Internet privacy protection.

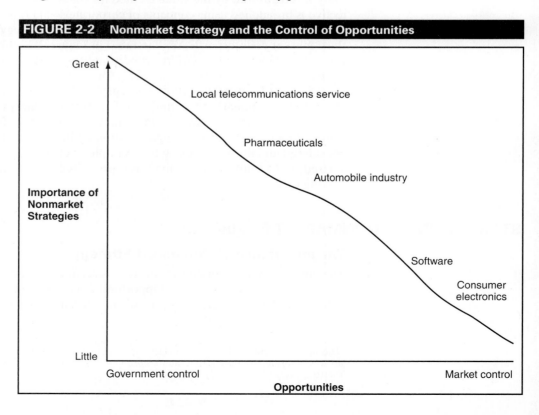

FIGURE 2-2 Nonmarket Strategy and the Control of Opportunities

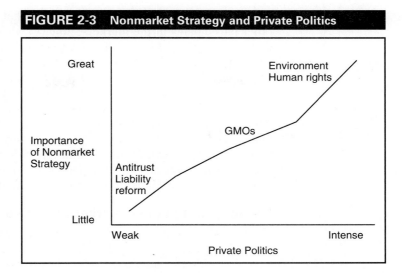

FIGURE 2-3   Nonmarket Strategy and Private Politics

Over time, industries can move along the control dimension. In many countries the government had controlled telecommunications services through ownership of a monopoly supplier. In the pursuit of improved performance, many of these countries privatized their telecommunications firms and replaced ownership with regulation and competition. In the United States the regulation of telecommunications is being replaced by market competition, with long-distance and information services being the most extensively controlled by markets and local service the least. The Internet has been at the right in Figure 2-2, but nonmarket issues such as privacy, taxation of electronic commerce, and protection of intellectual property have made nonmarket strategy more important, as considered in Chapter 13.

In addition to government and markets, two other factors affect opportunities. First, opportunities can be controlled by private politics, which includes actions such as protests, boycotts, and public criticism by activist, advocacy, and interest groups, as well as the public climate in which a firm operates. The control of opportunities typically centers on the conjunction of an issue and the practices of a firm or industry. The more intense is private politics, the more important is nonmarket strategy, as illustrated in Figure 2-3. Issues such as the environment, sustainability, human rights, privacy, health, and safety attract private politics, as considered in Chapter 4. In contrast, issues such as intellectual property protection, liability reform, and antitrust seldom attract private politics but are the subject of public politics. Issues such as the use of genetically modified organisms in food attract intense private politics in Europe but less in the United States.

Second, opportunities can be affected by moral concerns, which can require restraint in the pursuit of some opportunities. Part V of the book provides principles to guide firms and their managers in reasoning about moral concerns and broader social responsibilities and whether self-regulation on the part of a firm is required. For example, before the issue became salient, Levi Strauss & Co. used moral principles in formulating a policy governing working conditions in its overseas suppliers' factories, as considered in Chapter 22.

Competition and Change in the Nonmarket Environment

Market strategies typically take the nonmarket environment as given and focus on the competitive positions of firms in the industry, the threats from substitutes and potential entrants, and the bargaining power of suppliers and customers.[2] When a firm looks ahead, however, neither the market nor the nonmarket environments can be viewed as fixed. Moreover, change depends importantly on the strategies that firms and other interests employ to influence those environments.

---

[2]See Porter (1980); Oster (1999); Besanko, Dranove, Shanley, and Schaefer (2006); and Saloner, Shepard, and Podolny (2001).

When a firm chooses a market strategy, that strategy competes with the strategies of other participants in the market. Similarly, when a firm chooses a nonmarket strategy, that strategy competes with the strategies of others, including other firms, interest groups, and activists. That competition shapes the nonmarket environment and often the market environment as well. The nonmarket environment thus should be thought of as competitive, as is the market environment. Nonmarket competition focuses on specific issues, such as a bill to increase fuel economy standards, as well as on broader issues, such as open access to the Internet. A broader set of participants is typically present in the nonmarket environment than in the market environment, so a firm often has a more complex strategy problem in the nonmarket environment. Nonmarket strategy is essential because in its absence competitors in the nonmarket environment will influence the outcome of issues and shape the environment and the rules of the game to their advantage.

Strategy and the Nonmarket Issue Life Cycle

The timing of a nonmarket strategy can be crucial to success. Using the life cycle concept from Chapter 1, Figure 2-4 identifies strategies as a function of the stage at which a firm begins to address a nonmarket issue. The firm has more flexibility and a wider range of alternatives the earlier it addresses an issue. If an issue is addressed at the issue identification stage, strategies can be directed at affecting the development of the issue. The firm may also be able to frame the issue prior to interest group formation. Levi Strauss was one of the first companies to address the issue of working conditions in its suppliers' factories, and the policies it developed kept it out of the line of attack of activists.

If a firm addresses the issue once interest groups have formed and the issue is in the legislative stage, the firm has less flexibility and its range of alternatives is narrower. Nike was late in addressing the issue of working conditions at its suppliers' factories in Asia, and it became a target for activists and their antisweatshop campaign, as considered in Chapter 4. Nike found itself in the position of reacting to the nonmarket strategies of others rather than shaping the development of the issue. Its opportunity to participate in the resolution of the nonmarket issue was largely limited to the enforcement stage. Nike's nonmarket strategy involved damage control, followed several years later by an effort to become a leader in ensuring good working conditions.

Strategies and Borders

Bartlett and Ghoshal (1989) characterize market strategies as multidomestic (multinational), international, and global. A global market strategy is one in which "products

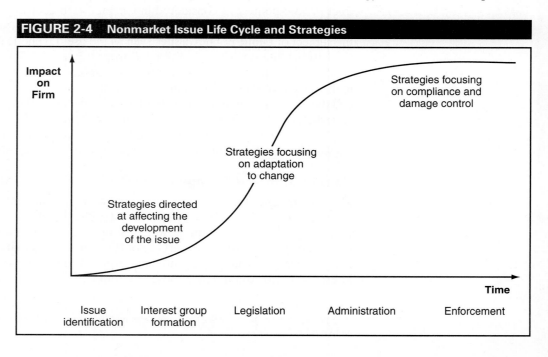

FIGURE 2-4 **Nonmarket Issue Life Cycle and Strategies**

Impact on Firm

Strategies focusing on compliance and damage control

Strategies focusing on adaptation to change

Strategies directed at affecting the development of the issue

Time

Issue identification | Interest group formation | Legislation | Administration | Enforcement and strategies are developed to exploit an integrated unitary world market." Global market strategies often focus on achieving cost advantages through global-scale operations, as exemplified by Honda's early strategy of selling the same motorcycles in all the markets it entered. In the nonmarket environment, examples of global strategies are (1) working for free trade globally, (2) applying universal ethics principles, and (3) implementing the same environmental standards in all countries.

An international strategy centers on transferring the parent's expertise to foreign markets. eBay, for example, took its online auction service to other countries, with mixed success. International strategies are specific applications of distinctive competences in other countries.

For many nonmarket issues a global or international nonmarket strategy may not be successful because strategies must take into account the institutions in whose context the issues are addressed, the organization of interests, and other country-specific factors. In France, Yahoo! was quickly met with a lawsuit because World War II Nazi items were auctioned on its U.S. Web site. French law prohibits buying or selling Nazi items, and France filed a lawsuit against Yahoo! Yahoo! refused to ban the items because it was legal to sell them in other countries, including the United States. In contrast, eBay designs its online auction venues in strict accord with the laws of each country in which it operates. Many nonmarket issues have a strong domestic component, so nonmarket strategies are more likely than market strategies to be multidomestic when issues, institutions, and interests differ across countries.

The success of a multidomestic strategy requires issue-specific action plans tailored to the institutions and the organization of interests in individual countries. Examples of nonmarket issues that require a multidomestic approach include legislation, antitrust policy, liability, safety regulation, pharmaceuticals approval, intellectual property rights, and environmental regulation. Although there are common principles, such as information provision as the key to effective lobbying, that underlie the strategies used to address these issues, differences in the institutions typically require country-specific strategies. In the United States lobbying focuses on Congress and its committees. In Japan lobbying focuses more on the bureaucracy and political parties and their leaders. In the European Union, lobbying focuses on the Commission and the Directorates-General as well as on national institutions as a means of influencing the Council of Ministers. In Germany, lobbying occurs through peak business and labor associations and their chambers, as well as directly between individual firms and the bureaucracy and political parties.

INTEGRATED STRATEGY

An effective market strategy is necessary for successful performance, but it is seldom sufficient. An effective nonmarket strategy is rarely sufficient, but for most firms it is necessary for success. Market strategies serve the objective of superior performance by developing and sustaining the competitive advantage required to take advantage of market opportunities. Nonmarket strategies serve the objective of superior performance by participating effectively and responsibly in the public processes that affect the control of opportunities. The performance of a firm also depends on how well its nonmarket strategy is integrated with its market strategy. Because firm performance is the responsibility of management, managers are responsible for both market and nonmarket strategies and for their integration, as illustrated in Figure 2-1.

Nonmarket strategies can be used to shape the market environment in which a firm operates. In the boxed example "Google and the Spectrum Auction," Google sought to open wireless communication to its applications and to reduce the bargaining power of the dominant carriers AT&T and Verizon Wireless. Google formulated a nonmarket strategy to seize an opportunity provided by the switch of television broadcasts from analog to digital transmission that freed spectrum for new uses. Its nonmarket strategy was integrated with its market strategy of providing an open access operating system for wireless communication that would accommodate applications including its AdSense advertisement placement technology, which generates the bulk of its revenue and profits.

Google and the Spectrum Auction

The Strategic Challenge

Google's core strategy centered on providing information to people, and it wanted mobile phone users to have the widest possible access to the Internet. Google's primary source of revenue was from advertising placements using its AdSense technology, and it wanted the opportunity to place ads on wireless devices. CEO Eric Schmidt explained, "There are at least 4 billion mobile phone users in the world today, and there are more mobile phones worldwide than there are Internet users of landline phones. Getting people access to information is Google's core mission and mobile phones have to be part of that."[1] He also commented on the opportunities for ads on wireless telephones: "What's interesting about the ads in the mobile phone is that they are twice as profitable or more than the nonmobile phone ads because they are more personal."

Google faced two challenges in the United States. The first was to develop a technology that allowed new applications to be developed for mobile phones. The second was the control of mobile networks by the two dominant carriers, AT&T and Verizon. Those carriers restricted the devices that ran on their networks to those they and their partners sold and also restricted the applications that could be run. For example, Verizon did allow Google's Web Search bar on its phones. Moreover, if new technology and new applications for using the Internet via mobile phones created added value for users, the mobile phone carriers were in a position to capture the rents through their charges for access to their networks. Google's goal was a nationwide network with open access for mobile phones in which users could choose their phones and applications for accessing the Internet. This required breaking the grip of the wireless carriers.

Integrated Strategy

Google's integrated strategy had market and nonmarket components. In the nonmarket environment Google had an opportunity. Television broadcasters were scheduled to end analog transmission and convert to all-digital transmission in February 2009. This would free frequencies on the so-called C block that could be used to develop a new nationwide mobile network. These frequencies were ideal for wireless service because the signals could easily penetrate buildings and carried long distances, requiring fewer transmission towers. As it had done in the past, the

Federal Communications Commission (FCC) planned to conduct an auction to allocate the frequencies.[2] Google had the resources to bid for the spectrum and develop its own mobile network, but doing so did not fit its mission or capabilities. A better outcome would be for whichever company or consortium that won the spectrum auction to build an open network. The incentives, however, for the bidders would be to put restrictions on access to increase their ability to capture value from customers, applications developers, and advertisers. Google wanted the FCC to require the winner to build an open network and better yet to require access to the network to be provided at wholesale prices to resellers. This would weaken the control of the dominant carriers.

Google made a proposal to the FCC for an open access requirement for the C block and pledged to bid at least $4.6 billion for that block if the spectrum license met four conditions. One was that the spectrum be open to any device. The second was that it be open to any software application. The third condition was that the operator of any network be required to lease portions of the spectrum at wholesale rates. The fourth was that new networks would have to be mutually compatible. Each of these conditions would reduce the value of the spectrum to the winning bidder, which explained Google's pledge of a minimum bid. Although Google pledged to bid at least $4.6 billion for the C block, its preferred outcome was that another carrier win the spectrum.

In the market environment Google prepared to deploy an operating system, named Android, for wireless devices developed in conjunction with the Open Handset Alliance (OHA) that Google had formed with 33 other companies.[3] In contrast to the wireless operating systems of Microsoft, Research in Motion, Palm, and Symbian (used by the largest handset maker, Nokia), Android was to be open with software and equipment developers developing their own applications independently of any requirements of mobile network operators or phone manufacturers. Google released Android in November 2007 to give developers an "early look" at the operating system. The key for Google was Internet access with search capabilities that could attach Google's AdSense technology. In addition, the company could produce a GPhone that would operate with Android and any applications.

---

[1] *Network World*, November 8, 2007.

[2] The C block would be made available in Europe in 2010 and in Korea in 2012.
[3] The OHA included Sprint and T-Mobile but not AT&T and Verizon Wireless. The OHA included only four device manufacturers.

(Continued)

Google refused to reveal whether it planned to introduce a GPhone, but Andy Rubin, director of mobile platforms, said, "if you were to build a GPhone, you'd build it out of this [Android] platform."[4]

Android SDK was released in a bare-bones form relying on third-party developers for specific applications. Serge Brin, Google president of technology, said, "The best applications [for the Android platform] are not here yet. That's because they're going to be written by you and by many other developers."[5] Google offered $10 million in prizes for the best applications. Fabrizio Capobianco, CEO of Funambol, speculated that Google could be contemplating capitalizing on Android's "location-aware capabilities."[6]

Dylan Schiemann, CEO of SitePen, assessed the significance of Android: "The mobile carriers always want to control everything, but they're showing signs of backing off on that. Carriers have enjoyed a long period where they've controlled what you put on a phone, and what they've charged you for what you put on your phone. If the Android platform works, it could change that dynamic."[7]

Verizon Wireless followed through with a $4.74 billion bid for the nationwide C block, topping the only other bid by Google at the FCC's reserve price of $4.71 billion. Verizon Wireless paid $9.5 billion for spectrum in the FCC auction and announced that it would launch a new wireless network in 2010.[8] Users could soon have the opportunity to choose their own devices, games, ringtones, graphics, and so on. In March 2008 Verizon released technical specifications for connection to its open access network. Commenting on Google not having to build its own wireless network, Gregory L. Rosston, a former FCC official, commented, "Now they can just spend $1 million a year on a law firm to ensure Verizon lives up to the openness requirement."[9]

Google was delighted to lose. Richard Whitt of Google said, "Although Google didn't pick up any spectrum licenses, the auction produced a major victory for American consumers. We congratulate the winners and look forward to a more open wireless world."[10]

Phase II of Its Nonmarket Strategy

On March 24, 2008 Google began the second phase of its nonmarket open access strategy. It wrote to the FCC with a proposal to unlock the white spaces—the airwaves used for television transmission. Google maintained that only 5 percent of the TV white spaces were used, and hence capacity was available for high-speed mobile services. Google further proposed that unlicensed users be allowed to use the white spaces, whereas only licensed devices were allowed on the spectrum recently auctioned. Google also proposed using spectrum-sensing technology that would allow the government to interrupt service in an emergency. Google, along with Philips Electronics, Intel, Dell, and Microsoft, was a member of the White Spaces Coalition, but the proposal was made only by Google.

---

[4]*Network World*, November 8, 2007.
[5]*Network World*, November 13, 2007.
[6]*Network World*, November 13, 2007.
[7]*Network World*, November 8, 2007.
[8]Verizon Wireless also successfully bid for a number of other licenses. Verizon Wireless was a joint venture of Verizon Communications and Vodafone Group PLC.

[9]*New York Times*, April 4, 2008.
[10]*RCR Wireless News*, March 24, 2008.

The focus of nonmarket strategy is on issues that affect the opportunities of a firm, its positioning in its market and nonmarket environments, and the sustainability of its capabilities and reputation. A nonmarket strategy consists of objectives and a plan of action to address the issues on a firm's agenda, and that strategy must be tailored to the institutions in whose arenas the issues will be addressed. That strategy must also anticipate the strategies of other interests, including those aligned with and those opposed to the objectives of the firm. Part II of this book develops these components in the context of government institutions.

Both market and nonmarket strategies have the objective of superior performance and focus on securing market opportunities and addressing threats to those opportunities. Synergies can be present between market and nonmarket strategies, and the overall business strategy is more effective the more that those synergies can be exploited. A synergy is present if a nonmarket action increases the return from a market action or, conversely, a market action increases the return from a nonmarket action.

The boxed example "Direct-to-Consumer Advertising and Integrated Strategy in the Pharmaceutical Industry" illustrates how a nonmarket strategy can unlock an

EXAMPLE

Direct-to-Consumer Advertising and Integrated Strategy in the Pharmaceutical Industry

The pharmaceutical industry had traditionally marketed patented drugs directly to doctors using detail (sales) forces, whereas over-the-counter drugs were advertised directly to consumers using the broadcast media. The industry recognized that advertising patented drugs directly to consumers through the broadcast media could generate additional demand by increasing consumer awareness of the availability of treatments. This could also generate demand for as yet unrecognized or untreated maladies and could shift some patients to patented drugs from over-the-counter drugs, as in the case of antihistamines. Since patented drugs provided margins of 90 percent or so, the opportunities for profits were huge. Although the long-run impact of direct advertising in the broadcast media was difficult to predict, the potential seemed almost unlimited. If successful, the advertising could alter the market strategies used by pharmaceutical companies. Direct advertising of patented drugs to consumers, however, was limited to the print media by Food and Drug Administration (FDA) regulations.

Unlocking this potential opportunity required an integrated strategy, the first component of which was a nonmarket strategy directed at the FDA. The industry lobbied the FDA on the direct advertising issue using the theme that consumers better informed about treatment options would improve public health. The FDA eventually concurred and in 1997 allowed direct-to-consumer (DTC) advertising of prescription drugs in the broadcast media.

The second component was to explore the potential of DTC advertising. Pharmaceutical companies began to advertise directly to consumers on television and radio. The advertisements typically gave a toll-free number to call for information, referred to magazine advertisements where warnings were required, and instructed viewers to "ask your doctor." The marketing strategy was to induce consumers to ask their doctors for the drug by brand name. This strategy proved to be quite successful. Schering-Plough reportedly spent $322 million on advertisements for Claritin in 1998 and 1999, and U.S. sales reached $2.5 billion in 2000.[1] A 2001 survey by *Prevention Magazine* found that 72 percent of the respondents recalled an advertisement for Claritin.

A complementary component of the market strategy was to set a high price, particularly for drugs

added to the formulary, which typically resulted in insurance coverage for the drugs. Drug prices in the United States were considerably higher than in most other countries. For example, the price of Claritin averaged $2.13 a tablet in the United States, whereas in Canada the price was $0.70 before taxes. As a result of the success of Claritin, Schering-Plough had profits of $2.4 billion in 2000 compared to profits of $1.2 billion in 1996 before DTC advertising on broadcast media was allowed.

The response by consumers to the advertising meant that pharmaceutical companies had new opportunities for sales of drugs for conditions that could be advertised effectively. The return on drugs with these characteristics thus was substantially higher than before DTC advertising in the broadcast media was allowed, which altered the incentives for research and development. This had several implications for market strategies. One was that the incentives for drug development were altered in favor of drugs that could be effectively advertised, as in the case of lifestyle drugs. Another implication was the reexamination of approved drugs, including those whose patents had already expired, that could be used for other indications that could be advertised. A third implication was that new "diseases" or maladies could be identified and promoted to consumers.

GlaxoSmithKline's (GSK) Requip (ropinirole) had earlier been approved for the treatment of Parkinson's disease, and when doctors began to prescribe it for patients complaining of a restless sensation in their legs, GSK recognized an opportunity. GSK obtained FDA approval for low dosages for treating the restless sensation, and upon approval began promoting the drug for a new malady—restless legs syndrome (RLS). With heavy DTC advertising, sales of Requip jumped.[2]

Criticism of DTC advertising in the broadcast media began to mount as the advertisements became pervasive. The American Medical Association was concerned that consumers would pressure doctors to obtain unneeded prescriptions. The Prescription Access Litigation Project filed a lawsuit against Schering-Plough claiming that its advertising of Claritin was deceptive, boosting demand and the price of the drug. Richard Kravitz of the University of California

---

[1]Stephen S. Hall, "Prescription for Profit," *New York Times Magazine*, March 11, 2001.

[2]See the Chapter 21 case, *Consumer Awareness or Disease Mongering? GlaxoSmithKline and the Restless Legs Syndrome.*

(*Continued*)

at Davis said of RLS, "Physicians don't know much about it and may be wanting to follow the path of least resistance and prescribe a medication for a condition that a patient might not have."[3] Referring to the promotion of drugs for an underappreciated malady, to "a growing chorus of physicians and health-care specialists, the very idea of treating the risk of a risk is wrong. They have labeled the phenomenon 'disease-mongering,' defined as the corporate-sponsored creation or exaggeration of maladies for the purpose of selling more drugs."[4] The Senate held hearings on DTC advertising.

The criticism required a nonmarket strategy by the pharmaceutical companies. The companies lobbied Congress and attempted to respond to the critics. The Pharmaceutical Research and Manufacturers of America explained the rationale and success of DTC advertising.[5]

A study released by *Prevention Magazine* . . . found DTC advertising "is an extremely effective means of promoting both the public health and prescription medicines" . . . More importantly, the survey found that DTC advertising prompted an estimated 21.2 million Americans to talk to their doctors about a medical condition or illness they had never discussed with their physicians before. In other words, millions of people who had previously suffered in silence were encouraged to seek help.

DTC advertising in the broadcast media was preserved, but the threat of restrictions remained, requiring continued monitoring of the nonmarket issue.

---

[3]*Washington Post*, May 30, 2006.
[4]*BusinessWeek*, May 8, 2006.

[5]www.phrma.org.

---

opportunity that market strategies can then exploit. The nonmarket strategy of the industry convinced the Food and Drug Administration that advertising in the broadcast media would improve public health by educating consumers about the availability of treatments. This led to products such as Claritin, Rogaine, and Viagra becoming household names. The rapid expansion of "lifestyle" drugs brought criticism of the industry, requiring a nonmarket strategy to defend the opportunity to advertise to consumers in the broadcast media.

Approaches to Integrating Market and Nonmarket Strategies

One approach to integrating market and nonmarket strategies is to incorporate both into the process of developing a market strategy. For example, regulation pertaining to who may provide services, as in telecommunications, could be incorporated into the analysis of the rivalry among existing firms and the assessment of potential new entrants and the threat of substitutes. The drawback to this approach is that the institutions in which regulatory policies are established are quite different from the institution of markets, so the nature of the analysis is different. Moreover, in markets only the parties that transact play a role, whereas in nonmarket institutions a wide range of interests is enfranchised to participate.

Market and nonmarket strategies could also be viewed as separate. Just as market analysis focuses on competitive forces, nonmarket analysis can focus on assessing threats (such as those arising from government, interest groups, and activist pressures) and on unlocking market opportunities. Viewing nonmarket issues as a separate force, however, risks missing the interrelationships between market and nonmarket issues and the synergies between strategies to address those issues.[3]

The most effective means of integrating market and nonmarket strategies is to incorporate both into the business strategy process. That is, both market and nonmarket strategies should be chosen together in addressing forces in the market and nonmarket environments.[4] The nonmarket strategy component then focuses on specific

---

[3]Gale and Buchholz (1987) discuss the relationship between political strategies and Porter's (1980) five forces. Yoffie (1987) characterizes strategies by the approach taken to political issues.
[4]Baron (1997a, 1999, 2001) provides formal models of integrated strategies and a nontechnical presentation in (1996).

nonmarket issues that affect market threats and opportunities and on nonmarket actions as complements to market actions.

For some companies, integrated market and nonmarket strategies are the principal guide to their actions and are a conscious part of everyday management. Molecular Insight Pharmaceuticals, a development stage biotherapeutic pharmaceutical company, was developing radiotherapeutic imaging and treatment drugs for heart and cancer treatment. The company developed an integrated strategy for bringing products successfully to the market. The nonmarket component of its strategy focused on gaining approval of drugs from the Food and Drug Administration (FDA), enlisting support for the firm's products, and securing intellectual property protection for its products. Its market strategy focused on research and development activities, the boundaries of the firm, and the development of capabilities for bringing products to the market. Management of the company had much experience in the pharmaceutical industry and had a deep understanding of the FDA approval process and issues of concern to the regulators. The company developed relationships with FDA personnel as well as with members of Congress. Neither of Molecular Insight's two lead drugs had patent protection, and the company had to develop a strategy for obtaining what protection was possible, as well as assess the possibility of a competitor entering the market using the same molecules. The company sought Orphan Drug approval for one of the drugs, which would give the company 7 years of market exclusivity. To strengthen its case, the company enlisted support from patient advocacy groups that would benefit from the drug. The company also sought fast-track status to speed its path through the clinical trials process. Although neither drug was under patent, the company was developing second-generation versions of the drugs that could be patented.

Another component of its market strategy focused on the boundaries of the company—which activities should be within the firm and which should be conducted by partners or contracted for in the market. The two lead products were improved versions of drugs in use in Europe and Japan but not in the United States. The company had to determine the extent to which it should develop new drugs or in-license molecules from other companies. The company had a research capability and had successfully developed a patented technology for delivering radiotherapeutics to diseased cells. Molecular Insight also had to determine whether to rely on a monopoly supplier of the isotope used in its lead imaging product or develop its own in-house production capability. The company could also develop its own sales force to market its products to doctors and hospitals or out-license the marketing to pharmaceutical companies with their own sales forces. Whether it conducted activities itself or relied on partners and the market, the activities would have to fit together and would have to be timed with the FDA approval process. The more activities that Molecular Insight decided to include within its boundaries, the greater would be its need to raise capital. It was planning an IPO, but it would need to develop a borrowing capacity if it decided to conduct its own manufacturing and marketing or to expand and extend the scope of its research and development activities. The chapter case, *Molecular Insight Pharmaceuticals: Integrated Strategy for a Development Stage Molecular Medicine Company*, provides an opportunity to formulate a detailed integrated strategy for the firm.

Because nonmarket strategies must be tailored to the specific issues, interests, institutions, and information in the nonmarket environment, there is no short list of generic nonmarket strategies. Moreover, the nonmarket agenda of a firm is in part set externally in the environment rather than by the firm, and strategies must attend to that agenda. The chapter case, *Envirotest Systems Corporation (A)*, provides an opportunity to evaluate market and nonmarket strategies and the effectiveness of their integration.

NONMARKET POSITIONING

Firms strategically position themselves in the markets in which they operate, focusing on the benefits to customers and costs to the firm.[5] They also strategically position their products in attribute space, both in an absolute sense and relative to rival products.

---

[5]See Besanko, Dranove, Shanley, and Schaefer (2007); Saloner, Shepard, and Podolny (2001); and Porter (1980, 1985).

Positioning is a foundation for market or competitive strategy because it can be a source of competitive advantage.

Just as firms position themselves strategically in their market environments, they also position themselves strategically in their nonmarket environments. Positioning provides a foundation for nonmarket strategy and can enhance a market strategy and its integration with a nonmarket strategy. Nonmarket positioning also affects the set of issues and challenges a firm faces, including challenges from activist and interest groups, governments, and competitors.[6] Market positioning also affects the set of nonmarket issues a firm encounters. Nike, the Gap, and other footwear and apparel manufacturers positioned themselves as design and marketing companies and sourced their products from independent contractors, primarily in Asia. The working conditions in the contractors' factories, however, generated a host of nonmarket issues for the firms.

Nonmarket positioning should be a conscious choice rather than dictated by a firm's market positioning or by those in its environment. Nonmarket positioning thus is a fundamental part of an integrated strategy process. Exclusive Resorts was conceived as a luxury vacation residence alternative to a second home without the hassles and expense associated with ownership. The principal form of vacation residence was a timeshare in which a consumer purchased a fraction of a year at a resort development. Timeshares had earned a bad reputation as a result of high-pressure marketing techniques, and most states closely regulated them. Exclusive Resorts faced the challenge of designing its business so that it served the market opportunity it had identified yet avoided the regulatory burden imposed on timeshares. The challenge was to position itself in its market environment to serve the demand for luxury vacation residences and to position itself in the nonmarket environment to avoid timeshare regulations. Exclusive Resorts was an instant success, and that success attracted new entrants with similar business models. The luxury vacation residence model then posed a market threat to the timeshare industry. Moreover, some of the new entrants were not as well capitalized as Exclusive Resorts, which raised the possibility that promises to consumers might not be kept. This could result in complaints that would attract the attention of regulators. The chapter case, *Exclusive Resorts: Entrepreneurial Positioning and Nonmarket Defense,* provides an opportunity to assess its positioning and formulate an integrated strategy for addressing the threats resulting from its market success.

Too often firms find themselves in a position they wish they had avoided. A firm may find itself confronted by protests over its environmental practices, disadvantaged by a regulatory action, or exposed to avoidable liabilities. Alternatively, a firm may benefit from having established a relationship of trust with a regulatory agency, joined with an environmental group to resolve a wildlife habitat problem, or provided expertise to a congressional committee addressing a complex issue in pharmaceutical patent protection. Not only is nonmarket positioning important for avoiding problems and attracting benefits, but it also provides a platform on which both market and nonmarket strategies can be constructed. Nonmarket positioning thus should be a strategic choice just as positioning a product in attribute space is a strategic choice. The eBay example illustrates this choice.

Nonmarket Positioning and Market Strategies

Nonmarket positioning is influenced by a firm's market strategy. Starbucks Coffee has cultivated a particular market segment and established an image of social awareness, concern, and action. It stated that "contributing positively to our communities and environment" is "a guiding principle of the company's mission." This positioning was appealing to a clientele of socially aware, higher income consumers and contributed to Starbucks' cachet. Starbucks backed this image with action. For example, in conjunction with Conservation International it financed Mexican farmers to grow coffee beans in the forest shade so that land would not be cleared for agricultural purposes.

---

[6]The contributors in Aggarwal (2001) consider positioning of firms in Asia, although most of the analysis focuses on market positioning.

EXAMPLE

eBay's Positioning in Legal Space

eBay, the market leader in person-to-person online auctions, had 34 million members in its trading community in 2001 and hosted 5 million auctions on a given day. eBay had carefully positioned itself relative to state and federal laws, and that positioning shielded it from certain liabilities. In turn, the scope of its activities was influenced by that shield. eBay provided a venue for online auctions, and unlike an offline auction house, it did not review the listings of items posted by sellers, see the items auctioned, or verify their authenticity. It also did not participate in the transaction, other than to charge fees for each listing and item sold. eBay did not act as an agent of either the seller or the buyer.

A critical issue for eBay was whether it could be held liable for the listings provided by sellers or for postings on its bulletin boards. The Communications Decency Act (CDA) of 1996 shielded an Internet service provider (ISP) from liability for what was said or written on an Internet site, whereas an Internet content provider could be liable for postings. eBay positioned itself as an ISP, thus receiving protection under the CDA. That positioning, however, meant that eBay had to be careful not to provide content, such as commenting on the authenticity of items listed for sale. Instead, eBay provided links to Internet sites where members could obtain opinions, authentication, and grading of items ranging from coins to Beanie Babies to comic books.

Offline auction houses were regulated by state laws, and eBay carefully avoided the jurisdiction of those and other state laws. eBay argued that it was similar to the newspaper classified ads rather than an offline auction house. eBay also positioned itself relative to violations of the law by the buyers and sellers on its site. A small number of sellers engaged in fraud, others sold items that violated copyrights, and others sold banned items. eBay monitored its site for possible fraud, as did members of its trading community. For example, eBay used shill-hunter software to identify shill bidding rings, and community members reported possible shill bidders.

Although eBay monitored for fraud, it did not monitor for copyright violations because doing so might make it liable for any infringing items it failed to find. A federal Court of Appeals decision in *Fonovisa, Inc. v. Cherry Auctions, Inc.* held that a swap meet owner was liable for copyright violations because pirated recordings were sold on its venue.[1] The Court ruled that the owner had the ability to monitor its site for illegal items and failed to do so.

eBay could monitor its site for possible copyright violations, but with nearly one million new listings a day, complete monitoring was virtually impossible.

The Digital Millennium Copyright Act of 1998 (DMCA) clarified the monitoring issue by stating that Web sites could be liable if they monitored for intellectual property infringements and failed to find an infringing item. A site, however, had a safe harbor if it did not monitor, provided that it removed violating items when notified by a copyright holder. eBay had already implemented such a program, referred to as VeRO (verified rights owners), and it continued its program. Monitoring was thus performed by the copyright holders, who asked eBay to remove infringing items. eBay assisted the copyright holders by creating a system in which VeRO members could query on key words and automatically receive e-mail notification of any listing with those key words.

This did not satisfy the Business Software Alliance (BSA), which developed a model code requiring Internet sites to prescreen listings for copyright violations. Even though Amazon.com agreed to the code, eBay refused to do so. It subsequently began restricted monitoring by examining only what was within the "Four Corners" of a seller's listing and dropping from its site items so identified as infringing a copyright. eBay believed that the CDA provided protection from liability if it relied solely on the listing provided by the seller.[2]

Intellectual property law provided little protection for eBay's database. In a 1991 decision, *Feist Publications, Inc. v. Rural Telephone Service Co.*, 499 U.S., 340, the U.S. Supreme Court held that "facts," even if collected through "sweat and effort," remained in the public domain. Earlier court decisions had held that databases were protected by copyright under the "sweat of the brow" doctrine. This doctrine prevailed despite 1976 amendments to the Copyright Act that required a degree of creativity or originality for compilations of data to receive copyright protection. In *Feist* the court affirmed the originality and creativity requirement and stated that "all facts—scientific, historical, biographical and news of the day . . . are part of the public domain available to every person."

Bidders' Edge, an auction aggregator, used a robot to copy all of eBay's auction listings and make them available to users of its Web site.[3] Bidders' Edge argued that the listings were compilations of facts and

---

[1]For the text of the ruling, see www.law.cornell.edu/copyright/cases/76_F3d_259.htm.

[2]In political space eBay attempted to obtain an amendment to the DMCA to provide a safe harbor for responsible monitoring for copyright violations.

[3]See the case *eBay and Database Protection* in Chapter 13.

(Continued)

hence under *Feist* were not protected by copyright. eBay chose not to attempt to meet the creativity test, since by doing so it would risk being viewed as an Internet content provider and being subject to other litigation. eBay was successful in protecting its database from robotic searches by relying on the law outside the realm of intellectual property.

By either good fortune or considerable foresight, eBay had also positioned itself well in another part of legal space. A competitor, BidBay, entered the online auction market with a logo and cover page that closely resembled eBay's. In addition to the similarity of its name, BidBay's cover page used the same color scheme, location of the company name and menu bar, search window, and category list as did eBay. In intellectual property law the most defensible trademarks are those that are "arbitrary and fanciful." An eBay attorney explained, "eBay is a completely coined name. It means nothing."[4] eBay filed a trademark infringement lawsuit against BidBay, which agreed to change its name.

[4]*San Jose Mercury News,* July 31, 2001.

As they do in the market environment, some firms attempt to differentiate themselves in the nonmarket environment. Starbucks has done so by its commitment to social responsibility. BP positioned itself as a green oil company. Nike experienced rapid growth in part because of aggressive marketing. Nike was in the face of the public. It was also driven by an aggressive and combative competitive attitude. That combination made Nike the largest U.S. footwear and apparel company. Its success and its in-your-face market position also made it a natural target for union activists who sought to improve the working conditions in overseas factories that supplied the footwear and apparel industries.

Frequently, firms seek cover rather than visibility in their nonmarket environment so that their positioning is obscured from the view of the public. Pharmaceutical companies often prefer the anonymity of working through the Pharmaceutical Research and Manufacturers Association (PhRMA) to taking action themselves. Moreover, in implementing nonmarket strategies pharmaceutical companies prefer to work behind the scenes, focusing on relationship building and lobbying.

One role of nonmarket strategy is to level the playing field for the implementation of a market strategy. Mattel as well as other toy companies found lead in the paint on their branded toys produced in China, resulting in a crisis in which millions of units were recalled.[7] To restore confidence in its brands, Mattel began testing all its toys for lead, putting the company at a cost disadvantage. In addition, toy manufacturers had a collective reputation for product safety that had been tarnished by the safety issue. To level the playing field and strengthen the reputation of the industry, Mattel and other leading toymakers sought government-mandated safety testing of toys. Similarly, once Nike had become a leader in improved working conditions in its suppliers' factories, it sought through nonmarket leadership to have its competitors match its performance to close the cost gap.

One benefit of nonmarket positioning can be the opportunity to work with NGOs to address nonmarket issues. A number of companies have turned to environmental groups both to find better solutions to problems and to solidify their nonmarket positioning. Conservation International (CI) works with "environment-friendly companies" to find innovative solutions to their environmental problems. In 2001 CI and Ford, which provided the $25 million funding, launched the Center for Environmental Leadership in Business to engage the private sector. The Center worked for positive environmental changes with programs in agriculture and fisheries, energy and mining, forestry, and travel and leisure. Despite funding the Center and supporting other environmental projects, Ford was targeted by several environmental activist groups demanding improved fuel economy.

Nonmarket positioning can also affect the set of issues a firm faces. As the eBay example indicates, positioning can affect the legal liabilities to which a firm is exposed. Nonmarket positioning can also affect the likelihood of targeting by activists and interest groups. BP's green stance and its demonstrated commitment reduced the risk of criticism by environmental groups. ExxonMobil had quite a different stance, opposing the Kyoto Protocol, for example. BP's positioning helped shift the environmentalists' attention toward ExxonMobil. Environmental activists launched a boycott of Esso gas stations in Europe.

[7]See the Chapter 5 case, *Mattel: Crisis Management or Management Crisis?*

Positioning Spaces

Nonmarket positioning takes place in three interrelated spaces: public sentiment, political (lawmaking and rule making), and legal (existing laws and regulation).

Positioning in the Space of Public Sentiment

Public sentiment is determined by the diverse interests, viewpoints, and preferences of the individuals in a society. These individuals may be organized or unorganized with respect to a particular nonmarket issue. Workers may be represented by a union. Those interested in the environment may be members of the Sierra Club or Greenpeace, and farmers may join organizations because they support or oppose free trade. Other individuals may be unorganized, but they may individually act, as when they participate in a boycott led by an activist group.

BP provides an example of positioning in the space of public sentiment. It withdrew from the Global Climate Coalition because of the coalition's opposition to the Kyoto Protocol and then joined the Pew Trust's climate change program—the Business Environmental Leadership Council—that requires members to implement a voluntary carbon emissions reduction program. BP also joined the International Climate Change Partnership, the World Resources Institute, the Energy and Biodiversity Initiative, the Papua Conservation Fund, and the Climate, Community, and Biodiversity Alliance. In addition, the BP Conservation Program provided conservation grants in 58 countries. More importantly, BP made substantial investments in solar energy and implemented an aggressive, voluntary CO_2 reduction program in cooperation with the environmental group Environmental Defense. To establish credibility with the public, Environmental Defense published audited inventories of the company's emissions. BP also used product design in reducing pollution. Five years before federal regulations were to take effect, BP marketed a gasoline that contained 80 percent less sulfur than ordinary premium gasoline.[8]

To solidify its positioning before the public, BP changed its corporate symbol to a starburst and adopted the slogan "Beyond Petroleum." The slogan, however, created confusion. Some activists interpreted it as a commitment to withdraw from the petroleum industry. Company officials hurriedly explained that instead it meant that the company was looking beyond the petroleum industry. BP was forced to relaunch its public positioning by taking out two-page advertisements in newspapers and magazines extolling its environmental achievements and restating its slogan as "Responsibilities Beyond Petroleum."

Positioning in Political Space

Lawmaking and rule making take place in political space, where the rules of the game are made. Positioning in political space affects the opportunity to participate effectively in lawmaking and rule-making processes.

Because of the importance of nonmarket issues to the profitability of the industry, the pharmaceutical industry has developed a position of strength in political space. The industry has positioned itself by building relationships with members of Congress and the executive branch. According to the Center for Responsive Politics, the pharmaceutical industry was twelfth in political contributions in the 2000 election cycle, contributing $26.3 million. Schering-Plough was sixth among the pharmaceutical companies, with $1.2 million in contributions. Pfizer was first, with $2.4 million.

More important than the political contributions were the lobbying and relationship-building activities of the industry. The Center for Responsive Politics reported that Schering-Plough spent $9.2 million on lobbying in 1999, of which $2.3 million went to 17 lobbying firms. Pfizer spent $3.8 million on lobbying. In addition, the companies had their own in-house lobbyists, and their managers also lobbied. The industry association PhRMA also conducted lobbying as well as positioning the industry in the space of public sentiment. The brand-name pharmaceutical companies used their positioning in political space to obtain the opportunity to market prescription drugs using direct-to-consumers advertising in the broadcast media.

---

[8]The gasoline earned BP sulfur emissions credits that it could use or sell. Emissions credits are considered in Chapter 11.

Some positioning in political space may become untenable. Automakers in the United States had successfully blocked increases in fuel economy standards for light vehicles despite growing evidence about global warming. The industry had effectively emphasized safety concerns from downsizing of automobiles that would be required by higher standards and the more limited choice as fuel-inefficient vehicles such as SUVs were removed from the market. When the Democrats became the majority party in the House and Senate in 2007, they introduced bills to increase fuel economy standards by 40 percent by 2020. The auto industry initially opposed the bills, but when it became clear that the public supported higher fuel economy standards and President Bush endorsed higher standards, the industry backed off.

Positioning in Legal Space

Positioning in legal space affects not only the liabilities to which a company is exposed but also a company's market and nonmarket strategies. eBay's positioning as an ISP provides protection under the CDA, but it also means that the company is limited in its ability to provide content on its Web site. Even though it might be able to compete profitably online with high-end offline auction houses by serving as an agent and authenticating auction items, it has been careful not to do so because that could make it an Internet content provider as well as expose it to offline auction house regulations.

In legal space, patents provide the most important protection for intellectual property for many industries, and perhaps nowhere are patents more important than in the pharmaceutical industry. The pharmaceutical industry regularly seeks patent extensions and was successful in obtaining a 6-month patent extension for approved drugs that were subsequently tested for use by children.

Microsoft has taken an aggressive approach to its markets and had largely ignored its legal environment, as considered in the Chapter 9 case, *The Microsoft Antitrust Case*. In contrast to Microsoft's approach to its antitrust environment, Cisco Systems and Intel, which both have high market shares, have sought to avoid antitrust problems and fix potential problems before they develop. Their positioning begins with respect for government officials and with a commitment to invest in relationships with antitrust enforcers so that potential problems can be fixed before they lead to a lawsuit. Cisco also works to educate antitrust enforcers about high-technology industries and stands ready to provide technical expertise to regulators. Both Cisco and Intel make regular assessments of their antitrust status and look for early warning signs of potential problems.

Part of their legal positioning is training their personnel to avoid antitrust problems and actions that might lead to problems. Sales representatives at Cisco receive antitrust training and are told to avoid aggressive competitive language that might be construed as anticompetitive. At Intel employees are trained not to use aggressive language toward competitors or partners and to avoid certain terms that might be associated with antitrust violations. For example, the word *leveraging* (i.e., leveraging from a dominant position) is not used.

The Perils of Positioning

Positioning is intended to improve overall performance by affecting the set of issues a firm faces and by providing a foundation for both market and nonmarket strategies. Positioning can at times, however, be perilous. Along with its 15,000 outlets, Starbucks' positioning in the space of public sentiment has made it a convenient arena for a variety of activists seeking to appeal to its clientele as well as to the company itself. Activists were concerned with the working conditions in coffee-producing plantations and targeted Starbucks despite its considerable efforts to support coffee-producing families and to protect the environment. Anarchists and antiglobalization activists protesting the Seattle World Trade Organization meeting laid siege to a Starbucks store.

Starbucks' positioning also created expectations about its business practices, and activists demanded more of the company than it was willing to do. In conjunction with demonstrations at the Republican national convention in 2004, several hundred demonstrators protested Starbucks' business practices, including its opposition to unionization, and also used Starbucks stores as a site for antiglobalization protests.

Starbucks was slow to adopt Fair Trade coffee because of concerns about its quality. The activist group Global Exchange sought to speed the adoption of Fair Trade coffee and had to select a target company for a campaign. It chose Starbucks rather than major coffee producers because, as a result of its positioning in the space of public sentiment, it was viewed as a soft target; that is, it was more likely to concede to demands.[9]

In addition, its positioning attracted activists who sought to promote causes with no connection to Starbucks. Local activist groups in Seattle targeted Starbucks to attract attention and media coverage to their causes with the hope that the company would take up their cause. Opponents of the use of recombinant bovine growth hormone picketed Starbucks to pressure it to stop using milk produced from cows treated with the hormone. Starbucks agreed to stop using such milk, but the protests resumed the following year to try to force Starbucks to be more aggressive in promoting the cause.

In response to a boycott intended to force Starbucks to demand reform of the Seattle police department, a Starbucks spokesperson commented, "We are not an activist or a political organization. When people say that we should do more than take money from the community, we do give back. What we are willing to do is to help invigorate the community by providing jobs, supporting educational and philanthropic programs for youth, and it hurts us when a small group of people decide that we need to be doing something else, which happens to be on their agenda."[10]

When it positioned itself as a green oil company, BP created expectations among governments and the public about how it would deal with issues. But, just as Starbucks became a symbol and target, so had BP, as activists sought to use its positioning to push the company further in pursuit of their agenda. A Greenpeace campaigner observed that BP "built their brand on how environmentally-friendly they are. This has given us the impetus to push them to fulfill the implicit promises they've made." Referring to the company's commitment to solar energy, the campaigner said, "They're one of the best-placed companies to make that change."[11]

As indicated in Chapter 1, BP's position in the space of public sentiment began to crumble in 2005 as a result of the refinery explosion that killed 15 workers, environmental damage in Alaska, and a price-fixing charge.

NONMARKET CAPABILITIES AND REPUTATION

Just as firms create value by developing market capabilities, firms develop nonmarket capabilities to add value. Nonmarket capabilities take several forms. One is expertise in dealing with government, the news media, interest and activist groups, and the public. Another is knowledge of the procedures and functioning of the institutions in whose arenas nonmarket issues are resolved. A reputation for responsible actions earned with governments, stakeholders, and the public also constitutes a nonmarket capability.

These nonmarket capabilities can give a firm a nonmarket advantage.[12] Nonmarket capabilities generate value as a function of how costly it is for market and nonmarket rivals to replicate them and for competitors, activists, and interest groups to dissipate them. As part of its business policy Wal-Mart was the largest corporate contributor to charities. Most of its contributions were made locally where its stores were located, and employees played a role in designating to whom the contributions would be made. This approach to charitable giving strengthened local communities and increased employee job satisfaction. It also helped relieve concerns about the company's impact on local competitors. This component of its overall strategy was effective in the small towns that were the focus of its market strategy, but when it came to opening stores in urban areas, the approach was insufficient.

As indicated in Chapter 1, Wal-Mart was criticized by activists, unions, and politicians for allegedly depressing wages and driving small merchants out of business. In a public referendum, voters in Inglewood, California defeated a proposal to change a

---

[9]See Argenti (2004).
[10]*Los Angeles Times,* June 26, 2001.
[11]*Wall Street Journal,* April 16, 2001.
[12]See Prahalad and Hamel (1990) for a discussion of core competencies.

zoning requirement to allow Wal-Mart to build a superstore. The criticism not only damaged its reputation but also threatened its expansion strategy, as considered in the Chapter 7 case, *Wal-Mart and Its Urban Expansion Strategy*. Wal-Mart belatedly began to develop nonmarket capabilities and improve its reputation. It began an advertising campaign featuring employees telling how happy they were working for Wal-Mart. It also opened a Washington office to develop better relationships with the federal government, sponsored PBS and NPR programs, and started a fellowship program for minority journalism students. The broader set of challenges and actions by Wal-Mart are addressed in the Part I integrative case, *Wal-Mart: Nonmarket Pressure and Reputation Risk (A)*.

Some capabilities can be developed internally, and some can be contracted for externally. Firms can hire outside legal counsel, public affairs experts, ethicists, and lobbyists. For example, Wal-Mart hired Washington lobbyists to represent its interests. The principal nonmarket capability that cannot be replicated, however, is the knowledge, expertise, and skill of managers in addressing nonmarket issues. Members of Congress are more interested in speaking with the company's CEO or local store managers than with a Washington lobbyist. The better the CEO and other managers understand the issues, interests, and institutions that comprise the nonmarket environment, the more effective they will be in developing and implementing nonmarket strategies.

The value of a nonmarket capability also depends on the effectiveness of a firm's allies in addressing nonmarket issues. On many issues, a firm's market rivals may be its nonmarket allies, as when an issue affects firms in an industry in a similar manner. Consequently, industry members frequently work through a trade association or an ad hoc coalition to implement nonmarket strategies. In markets, firms are prohibited by antitrust laws from colluding. In the nonmarket environment, the law generally allows firms to join forces to formulate and implement nonmarket strategies. Pharmaceutical companies thus work through PhRMA on issues such as patent policy that affect companies in a similar manner.

An important nonmarket asset is a reputation for responsible actions and principled behavior. In lobbying, for example, providing incorrect or strategically biased information can harm a reputation and impair future lobbying. Reputations, however, are ultimately established, and destroyed, by actions. Many firms invest in their public reputations just as they invest in their market reputations for service or quality. A reputation can be durable if sustained by actions consistent with it. Reputations, however, can be fragile and quickly tarnished. A tarnished reputation is difficult to rebuild, as BP, ExxonMobil, Nike, Wal-Mart, and others have learned.

A FRAMEWORK FOR THE ANALYSIS OF NONMARKET ISSUES

Nonmarket issues are typically complex and require conceptual frameworks to guide analysis and strategy formulation. This section presents such a framework and illustrates its use with an example involving Citibank. In this framework the unit of analysis is the nonmarket issue. The initial step involves generating strategy alternatives. Managers must exercise creativity in generating alternatives beyond those that immediately suggest themselves. For example, as an alternative to higher fuel economy standards, General Motors advocated a tax on carbon fuels as a means of addressing the global climate change issue. Subsequently, the Clinton administration tried, but failed, to have a closely related Btu tax enacted.

Once alternatives have been identified, they are to be evaluated in three stages— *screening, analysis,* and *choice,* as illustrated in Figure 2-5. In the screening stage, alternatives that are contrary to the law, widely shared ethics principles, or a well-evaluated company policy are eliminated. In the case of the automobile industry, an alternative involving noncompliance with mandatory NHTSA safety standards would be screened out. Several automobile companies, however, have routinely paid a fine, as provided for by law, for not meeting fuel economy standards.

The alternatives that remain after the screening stage are then analyzed to predict their likely consequences. The analysis stage is based on the positive methods of economics, political science, and other social sciences and focuses on predicting the actions of interests and the consequences of alternative strategies. For example, pharmaceutical

FIGURE 2-5   Framework for the Analysis of Nonmarket Issues

Screening	Analysis	Choice
Elimination of alternatives contrary to: – law – company policy – widely shared ethics principles	Interests Moral motivations Institutions and officeholders Information <u>Predictions:</u> market reactions nonmarket reactions	Evaluations of ethics claims Application of normative principles Choice and strategy formulation

Generation of Alternatives → ... → Strategy and Implementation

Policies

Refinements, reconsideration, generation of new alternatives

companies had to predict how strong the opposition to their direct-to-consumer advertising in the broadcast media might be. Prediction focuses on interests, institutions and their officeholders, and information and takes into account the likely actions of the other interested parties. The analysis stage also considers moral motivations of nonmarket behavior and thus how others evaluate the firm's actions.

The alternatives are evaluated and a choice made in the third stage. On issues that do not involve significant moral concerns, choice is based on the interests of the firm and its stakeholders. The objective is typically value creation, taking into account the impact of alternatives on stakeholders who are important to sustainable performance. If the issue involves significant moral concerns, normative principles pertaining to well-being, rights, and justice are to be applied, as considered in Part V of this book.

In the nonmarket environment, moral claims about rights are frequently made. Some rights are "granted" in the sense that the government or moral consensus has both established them and clearly assigned the associated duty to respect them. When the duty has not been clearly assigned or the right itself has not been established by government or through moral consensus, the right is said to be "claimed." Granted rights are to be used to screen out alternatives in the first stage, whereas claimed rights are to be evaluated in the choice stage. For example, there is a general consensus that firms should not exploit children. There may be disagreement, however, about what constitutes exploitation, as in the case of advertising children's toys on Saturday morning television.[13]

The process illustrated in Figure 2-5 yields specific strategies—concerted sets of actions to be taken by identified individuals or business units—and policies that guide managers in addressing market and nonmarket issues. Those policies can be stated as rules to be followed or as principles to be used in reasoning about what to do in a particular situation. For example, BP's policy for evaluating environmental protection alternatives is to take their costs into account only when the environmental impacts of alternatives are the same. Policies are to be used in the first stage to screen out alternatives that are inconsistent with the firm's business strategy.

The framework presented in Figure 2-5 is to be viewed as dynamic. The evaluations in the choice stage and the consequences of the choices made provide a basis for learning, refinement of strategies, and improved methods of analysis.

---

[13]See Hamilton (1998) for a study of the political economy of TV violence and children.

EXAMPLE

Citibank and Credit Cards for Undergraduates

In 1987 Citibank decided to offer Visa and Master-Card credit cards to undergraduate college students. Its objective was to develop an early relationship with individuals likely to be frequent users of the cards once they joined the workforce. To assess the credit-worthiness and future earnings potential of an appli-cant, Citibank used several indicators. For students who were not employed or worked only on a part-time basis, it used their undergraduate major as one measure of creditworthiness. According to Bill McGuire, a spokesman for Citibank, "using the major [is] a good indicator of future earning potential and of students' ability to pay debt."[1]

Application of the Framework

First Stage: Screening The nonmarket issue is whether it is acceptable to use students' undergraduate majors as a basis for issuing credit cards. The first stage of the framework involves determining whether use of an apli-cant's undergraduate major is contrary to the law, wide-ly shared ethics principles, or company policy. Use of un-dergraduate major as a predictor of creditworthiness is neither illegal discrimination nor a violation of the Equal Credit Opportunity Act. Similarly, individuals do not have a granted right to have a credit card, and moral consensus on using an applicant's undergraduate major is not evident. The use of undergraduate major thus passes the screening stage.

Several moral claims, however, remain to be con-sidered in the subsequent stages of the analysis. As some people claim, should everyone have a right to credit with that right withdrawn only upon failure to make the required payments? If not, which measures are acceptable predictors of creditworthiness? In-stead of resolving these difficult questions in the screening stage, the framework calls for their resolu-tion in the choice stage following the second-stage analysis.

Second Stage: Analysis The second stage of the framework focuses on predicting consequences of al-ternatives not only for Citibank but also for others, in-cluding any moral concerns that may motivate action affecting Citibank. The anticipated market conse-

quences are lower credit losses and higher usage than if Citibank did not use undergraduate major. Al-though many lower income people are good credit risks because they match their purchases to their in-come, people with higher incomes are more likely to have higher credit card usage. Based on similar con-siderations, Citibank had instituted the Citidollars program, which operated like a frequent-flyer pro-gram, providing discounts on products based on cred-it card usage.

The possible nonmarket consequences of using undergraduate major are more difficult to quantify than the market consequences, but that does not mean that they are less important or that managers cannot reason about them. Failure to anticipate the consequences of nonmarket behavior is a frequent cause of failed managerial decisions. Citibank's use of undergraduate major is a case in point.

The first question in the analysis is whether peo-ple are likely to become aware of Citibank's policy and, if so, whether they would be motivated to take action. The law requires that a person denied credit be notified of the reasons for the denial. Those de-nied will be disappointed, and some will be angry. That anger could be based on self-interest, but some students could be concerned about the principle un-derlying Citibank's policy. Some might believe on moral grounds that creditworthiness should be based on credit history and the ability to pay rather than on undergraduate major or likely future earn-ings. Others might believe that basing creditworthi-ness on undergraduate major could distort students' choices of majors and ultimately of professions. Some might be concerned that Citibank's practices could induce lying by students who might falsely re-port their majors to increase their chances of receiv-ing a credit card.

The predictive focus is on whether nonmarket action might be expected, what form that action might take, and what impact it might have. Indeed, Citibank contributed directly to the nonmarket action and to the issue becoming public. At the University of California–Berkeley, a Citibank canvasser, who had set up a table at the student union to take appli-cations, was asked by a reporter from the student newspaper if it were true that some students were being rejected as a result of their major. "The can-vasser advised her to fill in the credit application by

---

[1]*Peninsula Times Tribune*, March 20, 1988. The following is the application of the framework to the Citibank case and is not Citibank's analysis.

(Continued)

(Continued)

listing business administration or electrical engineering as her major, instead of English."[2]

The next step is to predict whether the issue will become public. Students have various means of making an issue public, ranging from bringing it before the student government to complaining to university administrators to organizing demonstrations. The most effective way to call attention to the issue, however, is to attract the news media. How likely the media is to cover this issue can be assessed using the theory presented in the next chapter. In brief, the media finds claims of discrimination and unfairness to be newsworthy. Furthermore, students know how to make the issue more newsworthy by organizing protests and taking symbolic actions. This does not imply that protests can be expected on many college campuses, but a manager should ask how many protests are necessary to attract the news media. The answer may be "one."

This analysis does not predict that the issue will inevitably become public, but it does indicate that it might. Citibank, however, need not abandon the use of undergraduate major simply because a market action might generate a nonmarket issue. Most of the public would never learn of the issue, and many of those who did might believe that Citibank's policy was appropriate. Those who view the use of undergraduate major as inappropriate, however, are the concern.

With regard to immediate effects, few students had a business relationship with Citibank that they

[2]*Peninsula Times Tribune*, March 20, 1988.

could end in protest. Nor, due to the costs of switching banks, were they likely to be able to persuade any significant number of Citibank customers to withdraw their business. The immediate market consequences were thus likely to be small. The effect on future business, however, might be more significant. Some students might choose not to deal with Citibank in the future. Furthermore, Citibank's recruiting on college campuses might be affected, either through boycotts or other direct action. At Berkeley, student protesters demanded that Citibank be barred from recruiting on campus as a result of the issue. In addition, Citibank's reputation could be affected by a controversy. Certainly, Citibank management could be embarrassed by protests and media coverage.

The Outcome

The issue became public through student protests at Berkeley, and the national media was quickly attracted to the issue. As the pressure mounted, Citibank announced that it was changing its market strategy and abandoning use of a student's undergraduate major. Had Citibank conducted a positive analysis as called for by Figure 2-5 and been sensitive to the types of concerns—in particular the moral motivations of nonmarket action—that can result from a market strategy, it could have avoided a situation that at a minimum was an embarrassment. The Chapter 21 case, *Citigroup and Subprime Lending*, provides another example.

ORGANIZATION OF THE NONMARKET STRATEGY FUNCTION

During the 1970s several companies formed strategic planning departments to assist management in developing long-range market strategies. These staff departments were typically attached to, but separate from, top management, which proved to be the cause of many failures. Similarly, several companies formed issues management groups to identify and address nonmarket issues. That experiment also produced failures, particularly when the group focused on societal issues rather than on specific issues affecting the firm's performance.[14]

Wartick and Rude (1986) analyzed the problems experienced by issues management groups in eight firms.[15] They identified four conditions necessary for success:

- Top management must support and be involved in the effort.
- Field units and relevant staff departments must be involved.
- The issues management unit must fill a void in the managerial decision-making process.
- Results must come from the effort.

[14]Littlejohn (1986) describes the issues management activities of Monsanto and Gulf Oil.
[15]Also see Sigman and McDonald (1987).

The perspective taken in this book is that there should be no void for an issues management unit to fill. That is, the responsibility for addressing nonmarket issues should reside with operating managers and not with a separate staff unit.

Management rather than staff now formulates a firm's market strategy, and the same is true for nonmarket strategies. Managers must be centrally involved because they are in the best position to assess the consequences of nonmarket factors for market strategies and overall performance. The nonmarket environment is often more complex than the market environment, however, because public institutions are complex and a larger set of interests are enfranchised to participate. Moreover, successfully addressing a nonmarket issue may require expertise in the law, government institutions, and public communication. In such cases, managers may need the advice of specialists. Managers must, however, be able to evaluate the advice they receive. To do so, they need to be as knowledgeable about the relevant nonmarket issues as they are about the markets in which the firm operates. Because managers operate continuously in their market environment and often only on an episodic basis in their nonmarket environment, frameworks such as that in Figure 2-5 can be particularly helpful in structuring analysis and strategy formulation.

SUMMARY

A business strategy must be congruent with the capabilities of a firm and the characteristics of its environment—both the market and nonmarket environments. Just as the environment has two components, a business strategy has both market and nonmarket components, and these components must be integrated. The nonmarket component is of greater importance when the opportunities of a firm are controlled by government, challenged by private politics, or involve moral concerns. Nonmarket strategies can be directed at competitive forces or at unlocking opportunities blocked by the nonmarket environment. Because strategies depend on the issues, interests, institutions, and information that characterize the nonmarket environment, they are more likely to be multidomestic than global. Nonmarket strategies are based on capabilities such as the knowledge and experience of managers in addressing nonmarket issues and the reputation of the firm for responsible actions. Nonmarket capabilities can be developed, and over the long run their development is part of a business strategy.

Positioning in the nonmarket environment provides a foundation for strategy and hence is a strategic choice of the firm. Positioning can attract opportunities and affect the set of issues the firm faces. Positioning takes place in legal, political, and public sentiment spaces. eBay's positioning in legal space has shielded it from certain liabilities and responsibilities. The brand-name pharmaceutical companies have established a strong position in political space, and BP had established a green position in the space of public sentiment. The benefits from positioning may not spill over from one space to another or even from one issue to another, as BP has learned. Positioning thus is often issue-specific.

Most companies focus on those nonmarket issues with a potentially significant impact on performance. Addressing nonmarket issues in an effective manner requires a framework that organizes analysis, reasoning, and strategy formulation. The framework illustrated in Figure 2-5 is composed of three stages: screening, analysis, and choice. The screening stage rules out those alternatives that are contrary to the law, company policy, or ethical consensus. The analysis stage focuses on the prediction of nonmarket actions and their likely consequences. The choice stage involves evaluating those consequences and any ethics claims and making choices based on those evaluations. The results of the choice stage are strategies for addressing the issue and policies that can be used to guide managers in the screening stage for future issues.

-- C A S E S --
Exclusive Resorts: Entrepreneurial Positioning and Nonmarket Defense

Brad Handler had just retired from eBay, where he had been the first lawyer and 35th employee at the company. In May 2002 he and his family joined his brother Brent and his family for a much deserved vacation at a luxury resort in Hawaii. The accommodations were fine but lacked many of the comforts of a home, such as a kitchen, space for young children, a room for a nanny, and accommodations for grandparents. While sitting on the beach, he realized there was a demand for luxury vacation residences that avoided the hassles of owning a second home and being tied to a single location. Brad and Brent decided to establish a luxury vacation residence venture. Brad's retirement lasted only a few months.

When he returned to California, Brad began researching the formats for such a venture. The first challenge was to position the new venture in both the market and nonmarket environments.

In the market environment, Brad and Brent identified a set of criteria for positioning the venture:

1. Serve the luxury end of the market.
2. Provide accommodations equivalent to a second home.
3. Provide the services and convenience of a fine hotel or resort.
4. Offer a choice of locations and accommodations.
5. Provide customers with liquidity of any deposits and refundable fees.
6. Provide assurance of availability of accommodations.
7. Separate the vacation aspect from the investment aspect.
8. Own rather than lease the residences.
9. Structure the revenue to cover the costs of the venture in a manner that reduced the risks to the principals.
10. Enter rapidly with a scalable format.

In the nonmarket environment the positioning criteria were to (1) avoid the onerous state regulation that accompanied certain forms of real estate ventures, (2) avoid the risk that promises to customers could be viewed as a security and hence subject to Securities and Exchange Commission (SEC) regulation, and (3) mitigate any nonmarket opposition to the venture.

The existing formats for vacation residence ventures were timeshares, fractionals, private vacation clubs, and destination clubs. Timeshares were the largest segment of the vacation residence market. Purchasers obtained either a deed or a right-to-use in a unit in a development,

so the vacation and investment aspects were inexorably linked. Some timeshares had earned a bad reputation because of high-pressure sales tactics, although practices had improved.

Private vacation clubs provided a variety of accommodations, including residences, at popular tourist destinations. These clubs were often operated by hotel chains such as Hilton, Hyatt, and Marriott and had been growing in popularity. Marriott Vacation Club International sold deeded units on a fractional basis in resorts and allowed owners to trade their weeks or exchange them for points redeemable at Club resorts. Other vacation clubs did not provide ownership but rather a right to use a room in the hotels owned or leased by the club. Vacation clubs were timeshares, but their marketing was softer.

A destination club provided both residences and travel and tour services, such as those offered by Abercrombie & Kent Destination Clubs. In 2000 Private Retreats offered a club that leased or owned residences in the $800,000 range in a variety of locations, and members could reserve the residences on a space available basis.

Positioning in the Nonmarket Environment

Positioning in the nonmarket environment was influenced by local, state, and federal law. Zoning was generally city or county law, and real estate law was state law, which meant that a venture with multiple locations could be subject to a myriad of regulations. No federal legislation pertained to timeshares and fractionals, but they were subject to regulation in most states.

The basic principle of timeshare law was that a promise made must be kept. This had a number of implications for the industry. First, a developer could not finance a development with a mortgage because, if the developer defaulted, the timeshare owners would be stuck with the mortgage obligation. Second, developers were not allowed to remove or substitute inventory. That is, they could not easily swap out owners from one timeshare development to a newer development. Third, most developers left once all the timeshares had been sold, leaving the timeshare owners responsible for the management of the facility under a homeowners association.

Under the regulatory system in California and other states, in addition to a fee interest in real estate, timeshare owners received a "right to use" that could take one of three forms: (1) a recurring basis, such as the 20th and 21st weeks of every year; (2) a fixed date, such as May 15 to May 29; or (3) a periodic right to use some portion of a year, such as one month a year. Brad reasoned that it should be possible to avoid regulation if members did not have any of the three forms of use.

The Federal Securities Act of 1933 required that, absent any available exemption, all securities be registered with the Securities and Exchange Commission (SEC) before they were offered to the public. The definition of *security* was broad and included an *investment contract,* which the Supreme Court ruled was a security if "a person invests his money in a common enterprise and is led to expect profits solely from the efforts of the promoter or a third party."[16]

Federal securities law had several implications for timeshares and the vacation residency industry. First, the buyers' investments in timeshares were not liquid. Second, timeshares substituted "exchanges" for liquidity, whereby one owner exchanged use of his or her time slot for use of another person's slot, possibly at a different location. Third, for the private vacation club and destination clubs, promotions that made promises based on the value of the real estate holdings could be viewed as securities and subjected to SEC and/or state registration requirements.

The Federal Trade Commission (FTC) provided scrutiny over the vacation residence industry because of the possibility of unfair or deceptive practices. In its "Timeshare Tips" the FTC stated, "Never consider the purchase of a timeshare as an investment. Timeshare resales usually are difficult."[17] The resale price of a timeshare was generally far less than the purchase price, since the purchase price covered the developer's sales and marketing expenses, which were roughly 50 percent of the sale price.

With respect to the third positioning criterion, whether rivals would take nonmarket action to restrict the new venture or attempt to put it under the same regulatory framework as timeshares would depend on how successful it was. If it were very successful, a challenge in the nonmarket environment was quite possible.

Positioning in the Market Environment

In the market environment, the principals, Brad and Brent Handler and Tom Fillipini, chose a country club model in which members belonged to the club but did not own any of the facilities. The three would own the club through a limited-liability company, and Brad would serve as chairman and CEO. They named the venture Exclusive Resorts and designed it for those seeking accommodations in luxury residences in attractive vacation locations that provided skiing, golf, beaches, natural beauty, and the style of major cities. The residences would have concierge and maid service as well as provide conveniences such as initial grocery shopping, trip planning, and reservations for activities and events. To accommodate members' demands, Exclusive Resorts

pledged to maintain a ratio of no more than 6 members per residence.

The membership fee was set at $375,000, of which 80 percent was refundable.[18] Annual dues ranged from $15,000 to $25,000 depending on whether the member selected 2 to 4 weeks of advanced reservations with total usage up to 60 days. Members would have access to the accommodations at any time, and the club guaranteed accommodations at any of its locations with notice of at least 90 days. If all the residences in a location were occupied, Exclusive Resorts pledged to rent an equivalent residence for the member. Exclusive Resorts planned to purchase multiple residences in the same location, both to accommodate members' demand and so that a concierge could be assigned to the residences. The first residences were in Beaver Creek, Colorado; Kohala Coast, Hawaii; New York, New York; and Los Cabos, Mexico.

After the initial residence purchases, Exclusive Resorts used the refundable portion of the membership deposit to purchase additional residences and used the annual dues to cover the maintenance of the residences. Exclusive Resorts also used mortgage financing but never more than 50 percent of the aggregate residence value.

Exclusive Resorts opened for memberships in the spring of 2003 and was an instant success. By mid-2004 it had over 750 members, 130 residences in 25 locations, 200 residences under contract or in the late stages of furnishings, and a substantial waiting list.[19] The average value of the residences was $2.5 million. Exclusive Resorts anticipated selling its residences on average after 7 years to replenish its inventory.

During its growth one of the biggest challenges was finding residences fast enough to accommodate those seeking membership. Exclusive Resorts concluded that it was necessary to develop some of its own properties and launched its first captive development in Hawaii.

As it expanded, Exclusive Resorts formed alliances and purchased other luxury residence companies. Alliances were formed with Virtuoso, a $3 billion luxury travel network; The Timbers, a developer and owner of resort club communities; and Marquis Jet Partnership, which made private jet service available for members. Exclusive Resorts also acquired two competitors, the Odyssey Club and Mirabella Estates.

To avoid being classified as a security, Brad and Brent structured the venture so that membership could not provide a profit. Paragraph 12 of the Club Membership Agreement stated that membership "is not an investment" and the member has no "interest in the Club's

---

[16]*SEC v. Howey Co.* U.S. Supreme Court, 328 U.S. 293 (1946).
[17]FTC, "Timeshare Tips," March 1997. Timeshares were traded on eBay.

[18]Refunds were governed by a three-in one-out rule under which a refund was provided once three new members had joined. Through mid-2004 fewer than 10 members had sought and received refunds. The membership could also terminate the club on a 75 percent vote, sell the properties, and distribute the proceeds, up to their 80 percent deposit, to the members.
[19]It received a membership inquiry from Steve Case, founder of AOL, who subsequently bought half the company.

income" and "will not share in any appreciation in the value of Club assets."

The paragraph also made it clear that a member had no "recurrent use or occupancy of a specific Club Property or Properties, or on an annual or other periodic schedule, or any specific time period of use. Rather, such rights were based on all Club Members' rights to occupy available Club Properties on a first-come, first-served basis, subject to the Club's reservation policies, including Club Members' use of non-Club Properties pursuant to the Availability Policy."

In recognition of possible regulatory risk, Paragraph 13 of the Club Membership Agreement stated, "Although the Club makes regular, prudent efforts to qualify its tax, regulatory and other legal obligations, government authorities could impose fees, taxes, charges, fines, penalties, cost or other liabilities on the Club related to (a) any new regulation applicable to the Club or the Club's failure to comply with any existing regulation, or (b) the Club's failure to pay any taxes associated with the sale of Club Memberships, Annual Dues, occupancy of Club Properties by Club Members, or any other aspect of the Club's business (collectively, '**Imposed Fees**')." If any Imposed Fees were incurred, Exclusive Resorts had the sole discretion to bill members or increase the annual dues.

Competition and Entry

In the marketplace Private Retreats and Abercrombie & Kent entered into a licensing arrangement and began selling memberships in Abercrombie & Kent Destination Clubs with two tiers. Private Retreats offered a luxury vacation residence club with residence values between $700,000 and $1.5 million. As a result of the success of Exclusive Resorts, Abercrombie & Kent offered another club, Distinctive Retreats, with average residence values of $2.5 million. These clubs were structured somewhat differently from Exclusive Retreats. First, members could use the residences for any length of time. Second, a Residence Daily Fee ranging from $75 to $250 per person was charged. Third, the membership fees were 100 percent refundable. Fourth, membership dues were in the $8,000 to $16,000 range. Abercrombie & Kent also offered access to its safaris, yachts, and tours.

The success of Exclusive Resorts spurred entry into the luxury vacation residence club industry. In addition to Abercrombie & Kent Destination Clubs, entrants included the Portofino Club with an 80 percent refundable $210,000 initial membership fee and annual dues of $15,000; Private Escapes with a fully refundable membership fee of $75,000, annual dues of $6,000, and a daily fee of $75; BelleHavens with residences with an average value of $1 million for a membership deposit of $200,000, annual fees from $8,000 to $18,000, and a refund of 90 percent of the membership deposit at the time of sale.

BelleHavens was unique in that the members actually owned the properties and hence could "sell" their memberships with sales governed by a two-in one-out rule.

Private Escapes introduced its Platinum Club with a pledge to share the appreciation of its real estate holdings: "Each year, the club will distribute 18% of the appreciation from its resort real estate holdings as dividends to you and the membership. No catch. When the properties appreciate, you get dividends. But if the market goes soft, you have no exposure. You may also choose to have your appreciation dividends issued as club credits, making them tax free and essentially doubling their value."[20]

Nonmarket Threats

As Exclusive Resorts' market success continued, nonmarket threats began to grow. Entry into the luxury vacation residence club business was surprisingly easy, and by mid-2004 a dozen or so clubs were being offered. These clubs were typically not as well capitalized as was Exclusive Resorts, and one concern was that some of them might fail and tarnish the image of the industry. This could scare away some prospective members and raise concerns among current members. Moreover, bankruptcies could lead to regulation. In addition, "equity" like club offerings could attract the SEC's attention. Bankruptcies or new regulatory activity had the potential to harm the timeshare industry as well.

Exclusive Resorts and the other luxury vacation residence clubs posed a threat to traditional timeshares and particularly to the luxury vacation clubs. Taking members away from the luxury vacation clubs could ripple through the timeshare industry. Similarly, failures by undercapitalized luxury residence or vacation clubs could raise concerns among consumers and weaken demand for fractionals and timeshares.

The American Resort Development Association (ARDA) represented the timeshare industry, including among its members timeshare developers and vacation club companies. ARDA members also included law firms, consulting firms, and others that provided services to the resort development industry. ARDA reported that in 2003 there were 5,425 timeshares worldwide with 1,590 in the United States. Sales of timeshares in the United States were $5.5 billion in 2002, and 3 million U.S. consumers owned timeshares with 92 percent using them on average nearly 2 weeks a year. The average size of a timeshare resort was 83 units.

Because timeshares were regulated by state laws, ARDA had developed considerable strength in states that regulated developments as well as those that regulated marketing to their residents. ARDA's objective was not to overturn state regulations but to obtain sensible re-regulation. ARDA had developed Model Timesharing

---

[20]www.private-escapes.com/platinum/dividends.html, August 16, 2004.

Act Guiding Principles that it advocated as a basis for state regulation.

ARDA expressed concerns about whether luxury vacation residence clubs were operating outside the law, since consumers did not have the protections of state timeshare law. In particular, club plans were not vetted by state regulators. ARDA was also concerned that the contractual arrangements were not transparent to consumers and that the promises made might not be kept. ARDA not only was concerned with risks to consumers but also feared that possible fraud or failures among the clubs could tarnish the entire resort development industry. ARDA was particularly concerned because entry into the luxury vacation residence club business was relatively easy. For example, Private Escapes' Platinum Club offering was made with only one residence, one yacht under contract, reciprocal privileges at six original Private Escapes properties, and 22 properties "coming soon."

ARDA wanted everyone in the resort development industry to play by the same rules even though their respective business models were different. ARDA sought to have the luxury vacation residence clubs registered in the states in which they held properties and in which they sold memberships.

ARDA asked four of its member law firms to construct a "model club" based on three luxury vacation residence clubs, including Exclusive Resorts. The law firms then assessed whether the model club would be required to register in each of seven states. The law firms concluded, consistent with ARDA's position, that registration was required in each state, including California, except where the law specifically allowed the club, as in Colorado.[21] Registration would subject the model club to the same requirements as timeshares. The law firms also examined the securities issue as well as whether club members were protected in the event of bankruptcy. ARDA sent the analysis to the Association of Real Estate Licenses Law Officials (ARELLO), the association of state real estate regulatory officials. Additionally, private lawyers from law firms within the industry contacted state regulators.

Several states wrote to Exclusive Resorts seeking additional information about its offering. The question was whether it might be required to register with the state under the laws and regulations that pertained to timeshares. If that were required, Exclusive Resorts would be subject to costly and burdensome regulations. In California the cost to register a timeshare development could run as high as $150,000. Moreover, a core component of the Exclusive Resorts model, that of inventory replacement via the sale of appreciated assets, would be prohibited. Several state attorneys general had contacted ARDA for its views on the luxury vacation residence club industry. ∎

SOURCE: This case was written by Professor David P. Baron based on interviews with Brad Handler and Howard C. Nusbaum of ARDA as well as information from public sources. Copyright © 2004 by the Board of Trustees of the Leland Stanford Junior University. All rights reserved. Reprinted with permission.

Preparation Questions

1. How well is Exclusive Resorts positioned in its market environment?
2. How well is it positioned in its nonmarket environment?
3. How serious are the nonmarket threats?
4. What should Exclusive Resorts do about the nonmarket threats?
5. Looking to the future, formulate an integrated strategy for Exclusive Resorts.

---

[21]Exclusive Resorts LLC was a Delaware company whose principal place of business was in Denver, Colorado.

Envirotest Systems Corporation (A)

The Opportunity

The Clean Air Act of 1990 called for an average 24 percent reduction in vehicle emissions by the end of the century and directed the Environmental Protection Agency (EPA) to issue revised regulations to expand and enhance state inspection and maintenance (I/M) programs. Not only would additional areas of the country be required to have an I/M program, but the programs currently in place in several states would have to be improved. Nearly all the existing programs were "decentralized" with testing and repairs conducted by service stations and repair shops. In many parts of the country these decentralized systems were believed to be ineffective in attaining clean air standards. Proponents of enhanced emissions testing argued that centralized testing using more sophisticated technology was required to achieve air quality standards. In a centralized system a motorist drove to a test-only facility where emissions were tested using a dynamometer, a treadmill-like machine that allowed emissions to be tested at various speeds rather than at idle, as in decentralized testing. Several centralized systems were in operation in 1990.

Seizing the Opportunity

In 1988 Chester Davenport and Slivy Edmonds established an investment fund to acquire companies that were expected to benefit from stricter government regulations. Davenport, a lawyer, had worked in several government positions, including serving as assistant secretary of transportation in the Carter administration. He also had practiced law and had successfully invested in several commercial real estate properties in Washington. His experience had brought him a wide set of contacts and considerable expertise in dealing with both government and the financial community. Edmonds was an experienced corporate finance specialist who brought financial expertise to the venture.

Recognizing the opportunity created by the Clean Air Act, in 1990 Davenport and Edmonds formed Envirotest Systems Corporation to acquire Hamilton Test Systems, Inc., from United Technologies Corporation for $51 million. Hamilton had been founded in 1974 in Arizona to operate the nation's first centralized, contractor-operated emissions testing facility. Envirotest provided test-only facilities and did no repairs. In 1990 it had four emissions testing contracts in effect. Although it was clear that the demand for emissions testing would increase substantially, there was uncertainty about how large an expansion the EPA would mandate and whether it would recommend the type of testing program Envirotest provided. Davenport was confident about the EPA's recommendations. As he explained, "It was my business to know these things."[22]

The success of Envirotest depended on the forthcoming EPA regulations, and in 1992 Davenport's expectations were realized. The EPA regulations required 182 metropolitan areas in 35 states to have either a basic or an enhanced I/M program. Fifty-three metropolitan areas with 15 million vehicles had no I/M program, and 15 states had either no program or a decentralized program. Envirotest estimated that a total of 59 million vehicles would be required to have an enhanced I/M program.

In addition to the I/M mandate, the EPA concluded that no decentralized program could be as effective as a centralized program. One of the EPA's concerns with decentralized systems was the inherent conflict of interest in a system in which the tester also made the repairs.

This concern was emphasized by proponents of centralized testing such as the Natural Resources Defense Council. A spokesperson said, "Under the old program, mechanics had an incentive to fail cars that should pass and a mechanic had an incentive to pass a car once he worked on it." The EPA concluded that a centralized program was superior to a decentralized program and decided that the pollution credits given for implementation of a decentralized program would be 50 percent less than for centralized systems.

The EPA estimated that centralized testing would cost less than decentralized testing and take less of a motorist's time. A test for nitrogen oxide, which was not included in many existing programs, would be added, causing more vehicles to fail. Under the EPA's regulations motorists could be required to pay up to $450 for repairs. Existing programs had caps ranging from $50 to $300.

The EPA required enhanced programs in 83 areas, and in those areas decentralized programs were not permitted unless the jurisdiction demonstrated that a decentralized program was as effective as a centralized program.[23] Under the Clean Air Act, implementation of the National Ambient Air Quality Standards was delegated to the states, and states could choose either a centralized or a decentralized program as well as the test procedures required. The EPA's regulations, however, placed the burden of proof on the states to demonstrate that a decentralized program could be as effective as a centralized program. The EPA, in effect, told the states that they would not be able to demonstrate equivalent effectiveness. If a state failed to adopt an acceptable program by November 1994, the EPA had the authority to ask the Department of Justice and the Department of Transportation to impose penalties on the state. Those penalties included withholding federal highway funds and reducing pollution offset credits that could be used for plant expansions in the state. For Pennsylvania, for example, nearly $1 billion of federal highway funds could be withheld.

Because of the EPA's rule making, in 1992 Envirotest acquired for $83.5 million virtually all of its largest competitor, Systems Control, Inc., renamed ETI, from a unit of Electronic Data Systems, a subsidiary of General Motors.[24] GM was forced to sell because of a conflict of interest between manufacturing and testing vehicles. The acquisition made Envirotest the nation's largest vehicle emissions testing company.

Market Strategy

Envirotest's market strategy focused on vehicle testing programs and direct service extensions. Envirotest designed, owned, and operated the test-only facilities and provided complete systems including public education about vehicle emissions testing. To avoid conflicts of interests, it made no repairs. This was a marketing advantage because one of the EPA's reasons for favoring centralized programs over decentralized programs was the inherent conflict of interest that arose when the same party did both testing and repairs.

---

[22]*Wall Street Journal*, March 4, 1994.

[23]An association of state air pollution–control officials met to review the EPA's regulations and generally concluded that states should switch to centralized testing.
[24]Envirotest sold the name Systems Control and its 50 percent interest in a joint venture in an I/M program in the state of Washington to the joint venture partner Sun Electric Corporation.

Envirotest had two types of customers: governments and motorists. Emissions testing contracts were let by states and municipalities through a competition typically involving the submission of bids in response to a request for proposals. Contracts with states extended for 7 years and provided for an exclusive emissions testing operator. Contracts could be terminated at will by a state, but damages could be imposed in that event.

Envirotest's other customer was the motorist, and Envirotest emphasized customer convenience and user-friendliness. Motorists were also constituents and voters, so states were particularly sensitive to the public reception of emissions testing. Contracts thus required centralized testing facilities to be located within specified distances of the bulk of the population—for example, within 5 miles of all the population in urban areas and within 10 miles of 80 percent of the population in rural areas. Contracts also provided for fines on the operator based on the length of time for completing the tests—for example, if 95 percent of the tests were not completed in 20 minutes or less.

Envirotest formed alliances as part of its bidding strategy. For its successful bid in Colorado, Envirotest formed an alliance with the leader in mechanics hotline services, experts in advanced troubleshooting and vehicle diagnostics, the developer of an onboard diagnostics technology, and a vehicle diagnostic database/expert system company.

Envirotest planned to invest $150 million to purchase land and construct testing facilities in Pennsylvania. In April 1993 it made an initial public offering raising $55 million in equity and $125 million in long-term debt. Envirotest also arranged a $130 million credit facility and project financing of up to $400 million from its investment bank. As important as having the funds available to build and operate several testing systems simultaneously was having the organizational capacity to manage multiple contracts. One benefit of acquiring ETI was obtaining experienced personnel.

A component of Envirotest's market strategy was to have leading-edge technologies, and hence it invested in research and development through its R&D facilities in Tucson. In addition to its centralized testing technologies, in 1993 Envirotest acquired Remote Sensing Technologies (RST) from Sun Electric Corporation, which had commercialized a remote sensing device.[25]

Envirotest engaged in a limited set of product extensions. It provided pre-emissions safety inspections, a quality assurance service, and a referee service. The referee service in Anchorage, Alaska, resolved disputes between motorists and repair shops. The quality assur-

ance program in California provided inspection of the state's 9,300 smog check stations. Its safety inspection services were operated both separately and within its emissions testing facilities.

Competitive Advantage and Capabilities

Envirotest had a competitive advantage because of its experience. Of the 16 centralized testing systems in the United States and British Columbia, Envirotest operated 10. Emissions testing had learning curve economies along two dimensions. The first was the usual development of technical sophistication and operational expertise. The other pertained to dealing with the public. An advantage of being the largest and most experienced company was that states could have a measure of confidence that Envirotest would effectively manage its interactions with the public.

Envirotest had many distinctive technical, operational, and organizational capabilities. It had unparalleled proprietary technologies that it had extended through several strategic alliances. It had two emissions testing technologies, one from Hamilton and the other from ETI, and had acquired a remote testing technology. It had extensive operating experience and a reputation for effective service. It also had the largest number of experienced professionals.

Nonmarket Strategy

One foundation of Envirotest's nonmarket strategy was its knowledge of governments in their three roles. Governments created demand (EPA), were customers (states and municipalities), and chose technology through the type of emissions testing system they selected (states and municipalities). Envirotest developed relationships with the EPA and was successful in being selected to develop the demonstration facility for the I/M 240 enhanced test required by the EPA for centralized testing facilities. This gave the company a marketing advantage that it could use as evidence that it was the most experienced contractor and had an unparalleled technology. Part of Envirotest's nonmarket strategy with respect to governments as customers was to encourage states to choose centralized testing rather than to attempt to demonstrate that an alternative system could perform as well.

A second foundation of its nonmarket strategy was sensitivity to the concerns of interest groups and the public. An important part of an emissions testing program was public education intended to build acceptance for the program. Envirotest participated in both the development and implementation of these programs. Envirotest also sought to manage effectively its interactions with "key participant groups," the most important of which were motorists and repair shops. Envirotest was willing to support exemptions for fleet operators, automobile dealers, and government agencies that wished to operate their own testing facilities.

---

[25]Remote sensing technologies involved portable roadside infrared monitors that examined vehicle emissions and photographed the license plates of vehicles. Vehicles emitting more than allowable levels were sent notices to go to a testing facility or repair shop.

The company also sought to develop effective relationships with interest groups at the state level. In Colorado, for example, it interacted with and attempted to be responsive to the concerns of the American Automobile Association, the American Lung Association, the Automobile Service Association, the Colorado Automobile Dealers Association, the Colorado Building and Construction Trades Council, and Coloradans for Clean Air.

As part of its constituency efforts, Envirotest lined up local suppliers and partners. For example, one of its partners was a Colorado firm that manufactured dynamometers. It also pointed to the number of people it would hire in a state and established a Minority/Women Business Enterprise program for minority and women contractors.

In bidding for state contracts, Envirotest used a three-stage contract award approach in which nonmarket strategies comprised the first of the three stages.[26] The first stage, called Pre-Bid Marketing, was founded on the premise that "participation in the legislative and regulatory authorization process for emissions testing programs [is] an important initial step in marketing its services. With the help of legislative consultants, the Company's marketing staff educates states and municipalities on the environmental and operational benefits associated with contractor-operated centralized programs, and attempts to build support for adoption of such a program among environmental and health organizations." Once legislation had been enacted, "interested parties (including the Company and its competitors) are often asked to assist the appropriate governmental authority in drafting the technical aspects of a bid request. This effort often includes reviewing bid criteria and recommending specified test programs."[27]

Competitive Advantage and Nonmarket Capabilities

Envirotest's three principal nonmarket capabilities were (1) its knowledge of and experience with government, (2) its sensitivity to the concerns of the public and interest groups, and (3) its reputation for dealing effectively with public concerns. Davenport not only had considerable experience and expertise, but he also had a set of relationships with influential members of the federal government and the public. As the company had grown and obtained additional emissions testing contracts, it had hired additional executives to manage its interactions with government.

Its sensitivity to public concerns led Envirotest to seek effective relationships with both organized interest groups, such as repair shops and automobile dealers, and unorganized interests such as motorists. Its educational and outreach programs constituted a capability that could be transferred to other states.

Its reputation for dealing effectively with interests and the public was an important capability, as government officials wanted to avoid a public outcry against emissions testing. A reputation for and experience with these matters provided a degree of assurance that served Envirotest well in contractor selection.

Market Threats

Envirotest faced a number of threats in its market environment. The centralized testing industry included four rivals: Sun-Systems Control, Gordon-Darby, Allen-MATRA, and Environmental Systems Products. Envirotest operated more testing programs than all the others combined and was the most formidable firm in the industry, but nevertheless it faced competition.

The threat of new entry came both from new firms that might enter the centralized testing business and from states that could choose to provide their own centralized testing facilities. With the pressure on government to become slimmer and the movement toward privatization and outsourcing, however, few states were likely to provide centralized testing themselves.

The threats from substitutes came at two levels. First, states had the authority to achieve air quality standards through a variety of means. For example, they could institute programs to scrap old cars, which accounted for a substantial proportion of the emissions in many states.[28] States could also implement remote testing programs directed at detecting vehicles with excessive emissions. Second, states could choose an alternative emissions testing approach—decentralized or remote testing—provided they demonstrated to the EPA that it would be as effective as centralized testing. Although Envirotest did not have a clear technological advantage in remote testing, it had pursued opportunities for remote testing programs. Remote testing had the advantage of identifying the worst polluting vehicles, including those whose emissions control systems had been tampered with, and requiring them to undergo repair and further testing, while not requiring testing of clean vehicles. California, for example, spent $250 million annually testing clean vehicles and $117 million annually repairing dirty ones.[29] ■

---

[26]The second stage involved the preparation of proposals/bids, and the final stage involved program implementation.

[27]Envirotest Systems Corp. Form 10-K for the fiscal year ended September 30, 1993. Securities and Exchange Commission, Washington, DC, 1993, pp. 11–13.

[28]Pre-1982 vehicles accounted for 25 percent of the vehicles on the road.

[29]California Research Bureau, "Motor Vehicle Inspection and Maintenance in California," Sacramento, CA, August 24, 1993.

Preparation Questions

1. What forces gave rise to the opportunity for Davenport and Edmonds?
2. Assess the effectiveness of Envirotest's market strategy. Is the company likely to be able to take full advantage of the opportunities presented by the Clean Air Act?
3. How effectively integrated are its market and nonmarket strategies? Are its market and nonmarket competencies complementary?
4. How significant are the threats in its market environment? Is it capable of dealing with those threats?
5. Does it face threats from its nonmarket environment? If so, how should it deal with them?

Molecular Insight Pharmaceuticals: Integrated Strategy for a Development Stage Molecular Medicine Company

Introduction

In early 2006 David Barlow, CEO of Molecular Insight Pharmaceuticals, Inc. (MIP), a development stage biopharmaceutical company, faced a set of challenges in bringing its lead product to market and in progressing its second product into the clinical trial stage. MIP researched, developed, and commercialized molecular imaging pharmaceuticals and targeted radiotherapeutics to meaningfully improve patient diagnosis and care. An emerging company in the late research and development phase, MIP focused on applying its proprietary platform technologies to develop product candidates that targeted markets with significant unmet needs in the areas of cardiology, oncology, and neurology. Zemiva, the company's lead cardiology product candidate for the rapid diagnosis of cardiac ischemia, had completed Phase 2b clinical trials. Azedra was a preclinical stage oncology product designed to treat a rare form of cancer—neuroendocrine tumors. In addition to developing these two products, Barlow was preparing MIP for its initial public offering (IPO).

Molecular Insight Pharmaceuticals

The company was founded in 1997, and the name Molecular Insight Pharmaceuticals, Inc. was adopted in 2003. The company's strategic intent was:

> To become the leader in the development and commercialization of unique molecular imaging pharmaceuticals to enable improved visualization and management of disease and targeted radiotherapeutics for cancer with meaningful safety and efficacy benefits.

Products and Technologies

Molecular imaging combined radiopharmaceuticals with nuclear medicine scanning to enable the visualization of altered protein expression, which frequently characterized the earliest evidence of disease. For example, current imaging tests to diagnose acute chest pain patients were only reliable for up to two hours after related symptoms had subsided. In contrast, Molecular Insight's Zemiva, by focusing at the molecular level, could potentially provide a reliable diagnosis of these patients up to 30 hours after symptoms ceased without the need for a stress test.

Targeted radiotherapy for cancer involved the delivery of curative radiation doses to malignant cells without damaging normal tissues. The technology precisely identified a tumor's location based on the expression of molecules produced during the transformation of normal cells into cancerous ones. Molecular Insight's Azedra could be used for treating a rare form of neuroendocrine tumors in children and adults.

MIP also possessed a set of patented, innovative technologies that enabled products to target particular types of cells. The company's three platform technologies—Ultratrace™, SAAC™, and Nanotrace Discovery™—aided imaging compounds to target specific cells, for example, neuroendocrine tumor cells and heart cells with decreased fatty acid metabolism.

Management Team

David Barlow joined MIP as chairman in 2000, after leaving his position as president of Sepracor Pharmaceuticals, initially to engage in private investments. He expanded his commitment to the company by becoming the CEO in 2003. Barlow had over 25 years of experience in the biopharmaceutical industry, which he reentered after receiving his MBA from Stanford University. He had established a strong track record of building companies and successfully commercializing new products. He was also experienced in working with regulatory agencies and with Congress on policymaking in the biopharmaceutical arena.

John Babich, Ph.D., a cofounder of the company, served as president and chief scientific officer of MIP. His research focused on molecular imaging and targeted radionuclide therapy. Prior to joining the company he had been an assistant professor of radiology at Harvard Medical School and a radiopharmaceutical chemist at Massachusetts General Hospital.

Barlow and Babich built an experienced management and scientific team to develop and commercialize new products that would create significant value for patients and providers. John McCray, chief operating officer, had worked with Barlow for over 20 years at Sepracor, Pfizer, and Rhone Poulenc Rorer. Dr. Nicholas Borys, chief medical officer, had 15 years of experience in pharmaceuticals and health care, including working for two oncology companies. Bob Gallahue, chief financial officer, had 15 years of experience working in public and private biotechnology companies. Vice president of research John Barrett, Ph.D., had conducted research for 20 years in oncology and angiogenesis and directed tumor imaging and therapy. Joshua Hammermesh, vice president of commercial and business development, joined the company from Genzyme Corporation, where he had served as business director of cardiac cell therapy. Priscilla Harlan, vice president of corporate communications, had worked in the biotechnology and pharmaceuticals industry for over 20 years, including directing corporate communications for Sepracor. James Kronauge, Ph.D., vice president of process chemistry, was an active researcher in radiology and nuclear medicine, who joined the company from positions at Harvard Medical School and Brigham and Women's Hospital. James Wachholz, vice president of regulatory affairs and quality assurance, had 20 years of experience in regulatory affairs at biotechnology and pharmaceutical companies, including Accentia Biopharmaceuticals and Sepracor.

Zemiva

Product Overview

Zemiva was a promising product in the late Phase 2 stages of clinical development. The product was designed to rapidly diagnose cardiac ischemia, enabling doctors to triage emergency department chest pain patients with suspected acute coronary syndrome (symptoms suggestive of a heart attack or unstable angina). The compound functioned on the basis that the heart is essentially a pump fueled by energy sourced primarily from the metabolism of fatty acids within the body. Metabolizing fat requires that a significant oxygen supply be delivered to the heart via the blood, and a decrease in oxygen, such as through blockages in the arteries, results in the heart switching from metabolizing fat to metabolizing carbohydrates such as glucose. Glucose requires far less oxygen, but is also a less robust energy source. The interruption of blood flow, and therefore oxygen delivery to the heart, causes cardiac ischemia. Zemiva enables the rapid visualization of reduced fatty acid metabolism associated with cardiac ischemia, thus identifying areas of damaged heart tissue.

Leading imaging products on the market in 2006 identified defects in cardiac blood flow only during stress, or up to two hours after cardiac symptoms ceased. In contrast, imaging using Zemiva detected areas of decreased fatty acid metabolism without the need for a stress test through a 30-minute procedure that could be performed up to 30 hours after chest pain had ceased. By enabling rapid imaging of chest pain patients in emergency departments, which was rarely done due to inherent limitations of existing products, Zemiva shortened the time to critical intervention and reduced damage to heart tissue. Its superior imaging ability also reduced the risk of misdiagnosis. The potential market for Zemiva was large: Over 6 million individuals annually presented at hospital emergency rooms with suspected acute coronary syndrome—chest pains suggestive of a heart attack or unstable angina. These patients typically received a blood test, an ECG, and an examination, but results were equivocal for 3.5 million patients, thereby requiring a lengthy series of additional tests and often hospitalization. By enabling timely diagnosis, Zemiva also had the potential to reduce the number of costly and unnecessary hospital stays associated with inconclusive diagnoses.

Intellectual Property Protection

Zemiva (iodofiltic acid ^{123}I) was MIP's brand name for BMIPP (^{123}I-BMIPP), a fatty acid analog linked to a radioisotope (^{123}I) used for imaging alterations in cardiac cell metabolism. BMIPP had never been marketed in the United States, and the U.S. patent for BMIPP had expired in 2003. The same drug, manufactured and sold in Japan by Nihon Medi-Physics, had a well-established safety profile from clinical experience in over 400,000 patients.[30]

MIP developed an intellectual property protection strategy with short-term and long-term objectives. In the short term, the company sought market exclusivity for Zemiva. Zemiva would be a new product in the United States, and MIP planned to utilize a provision in the Hatch-Waxman Act of 1984. The provision was enacted to induce companies to develop products with fragile or nonexistent patent protection by granting five years of market exclusivity upon a new drug application (NDA) approval (for any product not yet approved, in whole or part, in the United States). As the vast majority of new compounds were already patent protected beyond this five-year period, the provision was rarely utilized. MIP applied for protection for Zemiva as a novel substance under Hatch-Waxman, which, if granted, would provide a five-year data exclusivity period during which no company (typically a generic drug company) could reference safety and efficacy data on the drug in pursuit of its own regulatory approval. Under provisions of the Act,

---

[30]The Japanese manufacturer, Nihon Medi-Physics, was 50 percent owned by General Electric. To market the drug in the United States, the Japanese manufacturer would have to undergo the same development and approval process as MIP.

Zemiva, if approved, would not only receive five years of data exclusivity, but the FDA could not begin the review process for a generic version of Zemiva until after the five-year period had ended. Because the approval process for a generic drug took as long as 30 months, drugs that received exclusivity under Hatch-Waxman had effectively seven years of exclusivity before they could face generic competition.

MIP intended to follow a parallel strategy for Zemiva in Europe. European countries had enacted legislation similar to that in the United States but provided longer periods of market exclusivity: 10 years in the United Kingdom, France, Germany, Italy, Belgium, and Switzerland; and 6 years in other European countries.

In the longer term, MIP's intellectual property strategy was, prior to the expiration of its market exclusivity period, to replace the current racemic version of Zemiva with improved, patent-protected versions in the United States and Europe. MIP pursued three patent categories: a stereoisomer of BMIPP (patent granted); a production process for improved ^{123}I radioisotope labeling (patent granted); and BMIPP labeled with an alternate radioisotope (patent granted with foreign patent applications pending).

As the company anticipated the opportunity to develop and market additional compounds with little or no patent protection, particularly radiotherapeutics for cancer, it sought an extension of the five-year market exclusivity provision of Hatch-Waxman. Such an initiative would require the support of other pharmaceutical companies, but it would be opposed by generic pharmaceutical companies that would perceive it as a threat. Any legislative attempt to alter intellectual property protection laws generated intense politics.

Manufacturing

MIP had contracted with MDS Nordion[31] for the production of Zemiva used in its Phase 2 and Phase 3 clinical trials. As Zemiva neared the final stages of FDA approval, MIP faced a decision: whether to develop its own manufacturing capability or to contract with MDS Nordion or another pharmaceutical company. MDS Nordion was the logical choice due to its experience in producing Zemiva for the clinical trials. The company had originally been selected for the clinical trial production because it was the sole producer of the radioisotope ^{123}I, an essential component of Zemiva. Even if MIP were to contract with another pharmaceutical company to produce Zemiva, it would be dependent on MDS Nordion for the radioisotope.

For the longer term, MIP had concerns about relying solely on Nordion to supply ^{123}I. First, MIP was potentially susceptible to price pressure from a monopoly supplier. Second, a production interruption at MDS

Nordion's facility in Vancouver, as might occur from a security threat or terrorist action, could potentially halt the production of Zemiva. MIP's best option in the long term was to secure additional suppliers of ^{123}I, preferably located in the United States.

Sales

As with manufacturing, MIP had several options. The company could develop its own specialty sales force or contract with another pharmaceutical company for marketing. Barlow had extensive experience in building successful specialty sales teams. MIP estimated that a sales force of fewer than 100 specialty representatives would be sufficient to cover the target market of the hospital settings, which was expected to drive the bulk of Zemiva's initial demand. The American Medical Association (AMA) and other medical societies, which could be important in the FDA approval process, could also stimulate demand for Zemiva.

Food and Drug Administration (FDA) Approval

Approval of drugs by the FDA required a formalized series of steps. After the requisite research and clinical testing phases for a new drug were completed, the company sponsor was required to submit an NDA to the FDA. A compilation of the research conducted during the preclinical and clinical development phases, along with details of the product's chemical formulation, production process, labeling, and intended use were included in the application. After reviewing the NDA, the FDA determined the drug's official labeling, including a detailed description of the drug and its composition, indications, contraindications, and side effects. On average the FDA required 18 months to review and approve an NDA submission. Upon approval the product would be authorized to be marketed in the United States. If the sponsor wanted approval for additional indications, it had to file a supplemental NDA (sNDA) with the FDA.

MIP anticipated that Zemiva would receive FDA approval in 2009.

Financing Product Development

To fund the costly research and development process and clinical trials required for FDA approval, MIP required a steady infusion of new capital. Raising funds for the young company was a recurring challenge. When Barlow joined MIP, he made his first of several investments in the company, including writing checks to meet the payroll.

From its inception through 2003, MIP had raised $18 million from private investors. These funds were augmented by $4 million received through 26 research grants from the National Institutes of Health. The company often collaborated with leading biomedical research institutions on these research projects, including the University of Maryland, McLean Hospital, and McMaster University.

---

[31]MDS Nordion was a subsidiary of MDS Inc., an international health and life sciences company based in Canada.

From its inception through 2003, the company declined venture capital financing proposals largely due to unacceptable terms. Instead, MIP elected to raise funds from several individual investors. In 2003 the company raised $7 million in a Series A round. In 2004 it completed a Series B financing for $7 million; key investors included a leading health care investment banker and Cerberus International, its first institutional investor. In April 2005, MIP raised $28.6 million in an oversubscribed Series C financing. Principal investors in the round included Siemens Venture Capital and Tudor Investments. In November 2005, MIP filed with the Securities and Exchange Commission for an IPO in the amount of $57.5 million to finance the company through clinical development and NDA submissions of Zemiva and Azedra.

Reimbursement would be key to the success of MIP's products in the marketplace and required substantial long-term planning. Both Barlow and McCray had extensive experience in obtaining reimbursement. Medicare, an insurance program for eligible individuals over the age of 65 and those with disabilities, reimbursed physician visits and hospital costs, including certain drugs. MIP needed to ensure that hospitals received coverage for imaging procedures using Zemiva as well as for the product itself. Reimbursement for specific procedures was determined by the Centers for Medicare and Medicaid Services (CMS), an agency in the Department of Health and Human Services.

The process to obtain a new procedure code was bureaucratic and lengthy. MIP had to apply for a Healthcare Common Procedural Coding System (HCPCS) Level II National Code so that hospitals could obtain coverage for the imaging procedure using Zemiva. CMS developed the HCPCS Level II coding system to provide a comprehensive and standardized system that classified similar products that were medical in nature into categories for the purpose of efficient claims processing. MIP had options among several codes under which the imaging procedure using Zemiva was eligible, as well as the option to seek a new code. To obtain a new code, MIP could seek an endorsement from the AMA, which could request a modification of an existing code or a new code.

Failure to achieve an appropriate code in a timely manner could result in slower acceptance of Zemiva by hospitals and thus lower than anticipated sales of the product. MIP's reimbursement strategy included seeking advice on the company's options and garnering support in the application process for reimbursement to cover Zemiva. The CMS Current Procedural Terminology (CPT) Radiology Panel and the Cardiology Panel were both important in the coding process, and MIP began a dialog with members of each panel for guidance on Zemiva's application. MIP could apply for reimbursement for Zemiva during or after Phase 3 clinical trials, and the company planned to send letters to the radiology and cardiology division of several medical societies, including the Society of Nuclear Cardiology, the Society of Nuclear Medicine, the American College of Radiology, and the Society of Chest Pain Centers to inform them about Zemiva's impending approval and thus the need for a timely procedure code.

In addition to the coding issues, MIP had to deal with the payment process. The best outcome for the company would be to obtain "pass through" status for Zemiva, which would allow hospital outpatient departments to bill Medicare for the price MIP set for the drug. CMS had recently become cautious about granting pass through, and if pass through were not granted, insurers could make payments through the Ambulatory Payment Classification (APC) system under its nuclear medicine procedure APC.

Third-party payers also established reimbursement rates, which often corresponded to Medicare reimbursement rates. If CMS covered the procedure with Zemiva, private payers would in all likelihood also cover the procedure with Zemiva.

Azedra (Ultratrace MIBG)

MIP's second lead product candidate, Azedra, was a preclinical stage, targeted radiotherapeutic for the treatment of rare neuroendocrine tumors in children and adults. Azedra was based on an existing compound ($[^{131}I]$-MIBG), which was already approved and used as first-line therapy in Europe. In the United States, the product was available only on a compassionate use basis and primarily supplied by the University of Michigan. Obtaining permission to use the drug was onerous, requiring that physicians submit special requests to the FDA for each patient.

MIP had leveraged its proprietary Ultratrace™ radiolabeling technology to develop an enhanced, ultrapure version of MIBG. Azedra had the potential to enhance antitumor activity through increased tumor uptake of radioactive material and to reduce the side effects associated with the first generation MIBG product. Preclinical research had demonstrated potent antitumor activity and provided strong initial proof of concept for MIP's Ultratrace™ targeting technology. MIP had filed an investigational new drug (IND) application with the FDA and was preparing for clinical research.

MIP had received a patent for Azedra (Ultratrace MIBG), but the compound $[^{131}I]$-MIBG was no longer under patent in the United States. Another company thus could develop a rival product based on the compound. MIP again faced an intellectual property protection problem. Because the potential market for the drug was small, Azedra qualified for orphan drug status. The Orphan Drug Act of 1983 created incentives for companies to develop drugs for rare diseases that affected fewer than 200,000 individuals in the United States and addressed a medical need where no other treatment was available or provided significant benefits over other therapies. The FDA was authorized to grant orphan drug designation, which essentially gave a company seven years of market protection from generic versions, a protection similar to that from a "method-of-use" patent. Orphan drug status also made the sponsor company eligible for a 50 percent tax credit for research and development, reduced filing fees, and protocol assistance. Orphan drug designation could be awarded to a drug that had been on the market in the United States for other diseases or was used in other countries.

MIP had consulted the FDA regarding Azedra's development objectives and potential for orphan drug and fast track designations. Under the fast track process, MIP would work with the FDA to leverage the first generation MIBG experience in Europe and the United States. MIP and the FDA then would create an appropriately accelerated development program to study, review, and approve this potentially important medical advance. To facilitate this process, MIP planned to contact advocacy groups for neuroendocrine patients of all ages to provide their insights and support for the product. The company viewed medically based relationships with patient advocacy groups as mutually beneficial partnerships, both pre- and postproduct launch.

SOURCE: This case was prepared by Aneesha Capur under the supervision of Professor David Baron. Copyright © 2006 by the Board of Trustees of the Leland Stanford Junior University. The Trustees of Leland Stanford University acknowledge that they hold the copyright for the Case Study only and any underlying intellectual property rights owned by or licensed to Molecular Insight Pharmaceuticals, Inc. remain owned by Molecular Insight Pharmaceuticals, Inc. All rights reserved. Reprinted with permission.

Preparation Questions

1. What approach should MIP take in its interactions with the FDA and CMS?
2. What should MIP do about manufacturing for Zemiva? Sales?
3. Will IPO investors be nervous about the absence of patent protection for Zemiva, or is MIP's intellectual property strategy sufficient to reassure them? What, if anything, should MIP do to strengthen its strategy?
4. Is MIP's intellectual property protection strategy for Azedra sufficient?
5. How should MIP price Azedra once it is approved? What should it do about patients who cannot afford the drug?
6. Should MIP work with advocacy groups to support its orphan drug application for Azedra and in the FDA approval process?
7. Evaluate MIP's overall business strategy and the integration of its market and nonmarket components.

CHAPTER

3

The News Media and Nonmarket Issues

INTRODUCTION

The news media plays an important role in society by providing information to the public about matters affecting people's lives and the society in which they live. The news media also plays an important role in identifying nonmarket issues and stimulating action that affects their progress. The news media finds business of interest, and with stories instantly transmitted worldwide by the broadcast media and the Internet, a firm's actions are in the eye of the media and under the scrutiny of interest groups, activists, and government. Phil Knight, chairman and CEO of Nike, stated in Nike's 1996 annual report, "Yet no sooner had the great year ended than we were hit by a series of blasts from the media about our practices overseas." As this comment suggests, many companies dread media coverage of their nonmarket issues and have had to develop a capability for interacting with the media.

The essential role the news media plays in a democracy is accompanied by a responsibility to provide information in an accurate and unbiased manner so that individuals can formulate their own conclusions about issues. News organizations, however, face incentives, including those provided by profits, and pressures from competition among news organizations. Similarly, journalists face incentives associated with career and professional advancement. These incentives and pressures complicate the fulfillment of that responsibility. The news media itself is a diverse collection of organizations, including television, radio, Internet services, blogs, newspapers, magazines, and journals, and each faces its own set of challenges.

This chapter considers the role of the news media in the development of nonmarket issues. To analyze that role, a theory of media coverage and treatment is presented. This theory provides a basis for anticipating the impact of the news media on the progress of issues through their life cycles. The news media as an institution is then considered, focusing on the business and professional incentives that motivate news organizations, their editors, and journalists. Lastly, approaches to interacting effectively with the news media are presented, including recourse in the event of a dispute.

THE ROLE OF THE NEWS MEDIA IN NONMARKET ISSUES

In Chapter 1 the news media was identified as one of the institutions in whose arena nonmarket issues are addressed. Indeed, Cater (1959) referred to the news media as the "fourth branch" of government, formalizing Thomas Carlyle's 1841 description of British statesman Edmund Burke's characterization of journalists as the "Fourth Estate."[1] Editors and journalists are the "officeholders" of the institution. In addition to

---

[1]Quoted in Sparrow (1999, p. 5).

serving as an arena in which nonmarket issues are addressed, the news media plays an important role in identifying nonmarket issues and placing issues on the agendas of firms. Media coverage can

- Alert the public, activists, interest groups, and government officeholders to nonmarket issues.
- Raise concerns about the policies and practices of firms.
- Provide information about the likely effects of alternative courses of action.
- Reduce the costs of collective nonmarket action.
- Enhance a nonmarket strategy by conveying information provided by an interest group.
- Represent certain interests and principles consistent with the news media's perception of its role in society.

Interest groups and activist organizations, as well as government officeholders, are prepared to act on a variety of issues, and media coverage can inform them and spur action. Media coverage can also make a message widely known among the public and thereby reduce the cost of collective action. An interest group such as a union or trial lawyers may seize the opportunity created by media coverage of an event to further their interests. Media coverage can also provide a natural opportunity for a politician to advance an issue, represent constituents affected by it, or claim credit for addressing it.[2]

Nonmarket entrepreneurs outside of public office have developed strategies for attracting media coverage to call attention to issues, influence the public, and stimulate private and public politics. As considered in Chapter 11, environmental groups use the annual release of the EPA's Toxic Substances Inventory to hold press conferences to name the nation's largest polluters and call for more stringent environmental standards. Similarly, Greenpeace is effective in using media coverage to advance the issues on its agenda, as illustrated by the Chapter 4 case, *Shell, Greenpeace, and Brent Spar.*

A striking example of the role the news media can play in an activist group's strategy was provided by the Natural Resources Defense Council's (NRDC) campaign against Alar, a chemical used to make apples ripen more uniformly and stay crisp when stored. In a policy study, "Intolerable Risk: Pesticides in Our Children's Food," the NRDC argued that Alar increased the risk of cancer in children and called for a ban on its use. To advance its position through the media, the NRDC hired Fenton Communications. After the media campaign, David Fenton described the strategy.[3]

> Our goal was to create so many repetitions of NRDC's message that average American consumers (not just the policy elite in Washington) could not avoid hearing it—from many different media outlets within a short period of time. The idea was for the "story" to achieve a life of its own, and continue for weeks and months to affect policy and consumer habits. Of course this had to be achieved with extremely limited resources. . . .
>
> It was agreed that one week after the study's release, [Meryl] Streep and other prominent citizens would announce the formation of NRDC's new project, Mothers and Others for Pesticide Limits. This group would direct citizen action at changing the pesticide laws, and help consumers lobby for pesticide-free produce at their grocery stores.
>
> The separation of these two events was important in ensuring that the media would have two stories, not one, about this project. Thereby, more repetition of NRDC's message was guaranteed.
>
> As the report was being finalized, Fenton Communications began contacting various media. An agreement was made with *60 Minutes* to "break" the story of the report in late February. Interviews were also arranged several months in advance with major women's magazines like *Family Circle, Women's Day,* and *Redbook* (to appear in mid-March). Appearance dates were set with

---

[2]See Cook (1989) and Graber (2000).
[3]*Wall Street Journal,* October 3, 1989.

the *Donahue Show,* ABC's *Home Show,* double appearances on NBC's *Today Show* and other programs. . . .

In addition, we arranged for Meryl Streep and Janet Hathaway of NRDC to grant 16 interviews by satellite with local TV major market anchors. . . .

In the ensuing weeks, the controversy kept building. Articles appeared in food sections of newspapers around the country. Columnists and cartoonists took up the story. *McNeil/Lehrer,* the *New York Times,* and *Washington Post* did follow-up stories; as did the three network evening programs and morning shows. Celebrities from the casts of *L.A. Law* and *thirtysomething* joined NRDC for a Los Angeles news conference.

This episode illustrates the responsiveness of the media to an issue such as pesticide use and the media's role in stimulating nonmarket action that can advance an issue through its life cycle. Media coverage made the NRDC's message widely known, leading to demands by the public to ban Alar. Not only did the NRDC orchestrate newsworthy events, but it also timed them to extend the media attention. This was despite little scientific basis for NRDC's claims.[4]

This example is not intended to suggest that it is easy to use the media in a nonmarket strategy. The news media guards the independence of its editorial judgments and is careful to avoid being used as part of a nonmarket strategy. However, when an issue is of interest to viewers and readers, the news media has incentives to cover it. That coverage can serve the interests of activists, interest groups, public officeholders, or businesses. The Alar episode serves as a reminder of the potential effect of media coverage on the progress of an issue. Addressing the issue then is considerably more difficult.

MESSAGES AND THEIR INTERPRETATION

Because of the importance of the news media, firms and their managers must anticipate which issues will attract media coverage and how the media will treat them. Figure 3-1 illustrates the role of the media in informing the public and facilitating nonmarket action. Issues and events are observed by the media, which then decides whether to cover them and how to treat those it covers. Coverage and treatment provide messages to which readers and viewers are exposed and on which interest groups, politicians, firms, and others condition their perceptions and actions. Those actions can themselves be newsworthy, attracting further coverage and giving the issue a life of its own.

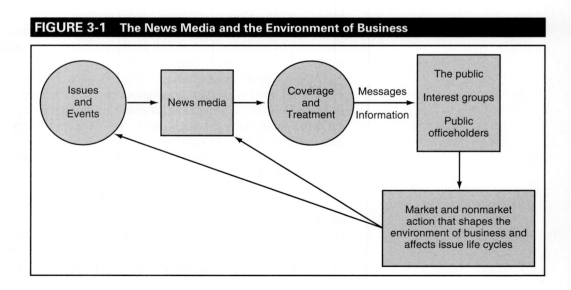

FIGURE 3-1 The News Media and the Environment of Business

---

[4]See the Chapter 3 case, *The Alar Episode,* in the fifth edition of this book.

The messages provided by the news media are interpreted in a variety of ways depending on individuals' prior information, beliefs, and preferences. Even though the interpretation of messages can vary, their impact can be systematic and hence important. In a series of laboratory experiments, Iyengar and Kinder (1987) investigated the agenda-setting role of the news media and the ways in which news stories affected viewers' attitudes toward issues and political leaders. Their research indicated that viewers attached greater importance to an issue after seeing news coverage of it. They also found that news coverage primes viewers by affecting "what springs to mind and what is forgotten or ignored."[5] These agenda-setting and priming effects are important to both the development of nonmarket issues and management's efforts to address them.

A THEORY OF NEWS MEDIA COVERAGE AND TREATMENT

To assess the role of the news media in nonmarket issues, a theory is needed for the stages of the process shown in Figure 3-1 in which the media observes issues and events and chooses whether to cover them and how to treat those it covers. The unit of analysis is the issue, and the theory is intended to explain and predict coverage and treatment. Treatment may take several forms:

- A straightforward presentation of facts and description of events
- An interpretation of the facts and events
- An exploration of their potential significance and ramifications
- Advocacy of a course of action

Advocacy is in principle, but not always in practice, to be restricted to the editorial page.

A variety of explanatory variables could be used in a theory of media coverage and treatment, but in the interest of parsimony only two are considered—the intrinsic audience interest in the issue and its societal significance as perceived by the news media. As indicated in the previous section, audience interest and societal significance may themselves be influenced by media coverage and treatment.

Intrinsic Audience Interest

The audience interest perspective begins with the observation that coverage and treatment decisions by news media are influenced by revenue and hence audience considerations. Subscription and advertising revenues are based on circulation and ratings, and the objective is to attract an audience by covering issues of interest to readers and viewers and treating those issues in a manner that will hold their attention. From this perspective, predicting which issues the media will cover requires determining which issues are of intrinsic interest to readers and viewers. Similarly, predicting the treatment an issue will receive requires determining what attracts and holds their attention. The principal predictions of the intrinsic audience interest perspective are that (1) coverage increases with audience interest, and (2) treatment will be chosen to appeal to and retain an audience.

Assessing intrinsic audience interest in issues such as international trade policy, product safety, environmental protection, and working conditions in overseas suppliers' factories generally lies in the realm of judgment rather than measurement. A product safety issue centering on a hazard to consumers attracts an instant audience, as in the case of lead in paint on children's toys, as considered in the Chapter 5 case, *Mattel: Crisis Management or Management Crisis*. In contrast, many international trade issues have limited audience interest due to their complexity and their indirect effects on people. Environmental issues matter to many people; so environmental stories have a natural audience. Moreover, the more proximate the consequences, the greater the audience interest.

---

[5]Iyengar and Kinder (1987, p. 114).

Societal Significance

The societal significance perspective views coverage and treatment as a reflection of the news media's perception of the significance of an issue to society. This perspective reflects the news media's role in serving democracy by providing information citizens need. Veteran journalist Edwin Newman (1984, p. 19) said, "We in the news business help to provide the people with the information they need to frame their attitudes and to make, or at any rate to authorize or ratify, the decisions on which the well-being of the nation rests." Louis H. Young (1978), former editor-in-chief of *BusinessWeek,* stated, "Reporters see themselves as guardians of the public's right to know." Applied to business issues, he described an incident involving a company's board of directors meeting and explained, "The magazine's position was—and is—that what the directors ate or drank was their business; but when they considered replacing the chief executive of a company it was the business of stockholders, both present and future."

A duty to provide information to the public places the news media in a watchdog role, and that role frequently is an adversarial one. Louis Banks, former managing editor of *Fortune,* noted, "The editorial mind-set is influenced by the periodic—and important—feats of investigative reporting or crisis coverage that bring out the natural adversarial aspects of the business-media relationship and reassure the media about their watchdog, top-dog role."[6]

The societal significance perspective emphasizes issues important to the social fabric and to tensions in that fabric. Two similar events will receive quite different coverage if one has a racial dimension and the other does not. Similarly, issues that have a human cause are more likely to be covered. Two similar health risks associated with food products will receive different coverage if one involves a man-made risk and the other a natural risk. The societal significance perspective also emphasizes forerunners of changes in the social fabric, particularly when moral concerns are raised. An issue such as the responsibility of U.S. companies for the working conditions in the factories of their overseas suppliers has societal significance, as Nike painfully learned.[7]

The societal significance perspective can be summarized as follows. The news media has a special role in a democracy and is assigned, or has assumed, the duty of serving the people's right to know about issues important to the fabric of society. In the United States this duty is recognized in the First Amendment, which protects the news media in its role of providing information to people. The greater the media's perception of an issue's societal significance, the more likely it is to be covered. Also, the greater the perceived societal significance, the more likely the treatment will be characterized by advocacy consistent with the media's vision of an informed democracy. Issues high on the societal significance dimension include health, safety, environmental protection, human rights, security, and social justice.

Combining the Perspectives

Combining these two perspectives provides a theory of news coverage and treatment as a function of intrinsic audience interest and the media's assessment of the societal significance of the issue. In this theory, treatment depends more on societal significance than on audience interest, whereas coverage depends more on audience interest.

Figure 3-2 illustrates the predictions of the theory, which are refined in the next section. The theory predicts that issues low on both the audience interest dimension and the societal significance dimension will receive little coverage. Most routine business news is in this category as are regulation and antitrust actions, and coverage usually is limited to the business press. Deregulation of the electric power or telecommunication industry has an important impact on economic efficiency, but economic deregulation has neither high audience interest nor high perceived societal significance. Further-

---

[6]*Fortune,* October 14, 1985, p. 207.
[7]See the Chapter 4 case, *Nike in Southeast Asia.*

FIGURE 3-2   Theory of Media Coverage and Treatment

more, economic deregulation is complex and thus difficult for the media to explain or for readers or viewers to understand. The treatment of such issues tends to be factual, objective, and balanced.

Issues that are high on the audience interest dimension but low on the societal significance dimension include the weather and natural disasters, sports, and entertainment. These issues receive considerable coverage and are generally treated in a factual and balanced manner.

Issues low on the audience interest dimension but high on the societal significance dimension include income distribution, foreign policy, and much of politics. Such issues are likely to receive only moderate coverage because of their limited audience interest. Their treatment, however, may involve a degree of position taking or advocacy. The working conditions in overseas factories are a distant issue for most readers and viewers, but when activists and unions framed it as a human rights issue, it received considerable coverage reflecting its high societal significance as perceived by the media. In its role as a protector of the public's right to know, the news media may advocate a course of action. Treatment of the issue, for example, frequently used the term "sweatshops."

Issues high on both the intrinsic audience interest and societal significance dimensions receive extensive coverage, and their treatment may involve both factual reporting and position taking and advocacy. These issues include health, safety, security, the environment, human rights, and both natural and man-made crises. A health risk, particularly the protection of society from such a risk, is high on both the audience interest and the societal significance dimensions. Consequently, the Alar issue received considerable coverage, and its treatment reflected the media's perceived duty to warn the public. The media covered the events organized by the NRDC because those events made the story more appealing to audiences. The coverage conveyed the NRDC's message, and by implication the media's treatment advocated that precautions be taken, including governmental action.

Coverage and treatment can differ between the print and broadcast media, between the *New York Times* and the *New York Post,* and Fox News and CBS News. Moreover, over time issues may change their location in the audience interest–societal significance space. Over the past three decades issues involving health risks and environmental protection have moved to the upper right in Figure 3-2. Similarly, the issue of the working conditions in overseas factories was propelled toward the upper right in the 1990s.

This theory of news media coverage and treatment is based on two sufficient conditions—societal significance and intrinsic audience interest. Other features of stories, such as visual effects, human interest, confrontation, and controversy, are also important. The theory is extended along these dimensions in the next section.

EXTENDING THE THEORY

Newsworthiness

The concept of newsworthiness extends the intrinsic audience interest and perceived societal significance dimensions. An issue is more newsworthy if it has a degree of immediacy or urgency. The massive television coverage of a natural disaster results in part because it is a breaking story. The risk to life and property makes it urgent. The burning of Amazon Basin rain forests has less urgency, but its link to global climate change makes it more immediate than it would otherwise be. A groundwater contamination issue has a greater degree of urgency if there is a threat to health.

An issue is more newsworthy if it has a human interest dimension with which the audience can identify, as in stories about victims of injustice, accidents, or natural disasters. A story is also more interesting if it is told by someone involved in the issue rather than by a correspondent. In an era of remote channel changers, television producers are reluctant to air a "talking head" segment with a correspondent telling a long and complex story. When the story is told by participants, however, the result is often more than just an eyewitness account, since the participants have an opportunity to make judgments about the issue or advocate action.

An issue often is more newsworthy if it involves a celebrity. The NRDC was correct in thinking that Meryl Streep would attract coverage for the Alar issue. Similarly, the news media may choose to cover an issue because it is entertaining, or it may add an entertainment dimension to the story. Particularly for television, an issue is more newsworthy if it has visual appeal.

A story is more newsworthy if it involves confrontation or controversy. An environmental issue is more newsworthy if it contains allegations that apple growers are creating hazards for an unsuspecting public. A story is more newsworthy if it links to an issue such as health with high intrinsic audience interest. In particular, linking Alar to the health of children not only provided a human interest dimension but also demonstrated that the news media was fulfilling its role by protecting the public's right to know. A common approach to developing confrontation and controversy in a story is to have each side tell its version of the issue. This provides balance, but it also highlights the controversy.

In contrast, stories about ideas are often difficult to write and present, particularly for a medium such as television. Stories about ideas provide limited opportunities for drama, human interest, or visual effects. The media thus may not give as much coverage to issues centering on ideas as they might merit in terms of their societal significance. To explain why the national news media was slow to cover the savings and loan crisis that cost the economy tens of billions of dollars, Ellen Hume wrote: "It was all too complicated and boring to interest many mainstream journalists. Regulatory changes—such as the accounting tricks and reduced capital requirements that helped paper over the first phase of the savings and loan crisis in the early 1980s—weren't big news. . . . When asked why TV hadn't covered the crisis much even after it made headlines in 1988, the president of NBC News, Michael Gartner, observed that the story didn't lend itself to images, and without such images, 'television can't do facts.'"[8] Hume added that as the issue developed, the victims (the depositors) did not complain because their deposits were federally insured. Controversy and conflict were absent. Media interest subsequently developed as the magnitude of the crisis became evident and as malfeasance was revealed.

The Cost of Coverage

News coverage is also a function of the costs of obtaining information and producing a story. Costs include assigning journalists to stories and beats, maintaining bureau offices, getting reporters to where the stories are breaking, and providing editorial and administrative support. Once journalists are assigned to a story and are on location, the marginal cost of coverage is reduced and the media is more likely to use stories from that source. As Edwin Newman (1984, p. 29) stated, "What is news on television often depends on where your reporters and cameramen are. If you keep people at the White House, you will be tempted to use stories from there, if only for economic reasons. . . . If you send reporters and camera crews on a trip with the secretary of state, you tend to use what they send back. If you staff a story day after day, you will have it on the air day after day."

Both the costs of obtaining information and budget pressures have forced most media organizations to rely increasingly on low-cost sources of information such as interest groups, government agencies, and businesses rather than developing the information firsthand. Firms and interest groups thus are frequently sources of the information the news media needs to present stories. These sources often strategically provide information, and journalists may end up relying on what their sources claim about facts rather than gathering those facts directly.[9] Brooks Jackson, a Cable News Network correspondent and former *Wall Street Journal* reporter, observed, "We usually depend on governmental institutions or groups like Common Cause or Ralph Nader or General Motors or somebody to make sense out of all this data for us."[10]

Balance and Fairness

Journalism standards and editorial controls require that a story be accurate and the treatment provide balance and fairness. Accuracy involves not only verifying facts but also ensuring that the story as presented portrays the situation correctly. Balance requires presenting both sides of an issue, which often involves providing an opportunity for the various sides to present their views on the issue. Fairness involves not only ensuring that those involved in an issue have an opportunity to present their views but that a person or subject is not presented or treated in an unjust manner. The latter is particularly relevant on those issues high on the societal significance dimension on which the media may take an advocacy position.

With the rise of cable and satellite television the number and variety of news programs has increased. These programs respond to consumer preferences and their nature has changed. The annual report "The State of the News Media" funded by the Pew Charitable Trusts concluded,

> A growing pattern has news outlets, programs, and journalists offering up solutions, crusades, certainty and the impression of putting all the blur of information in clear order for people. The tone may be just as extreme as before, but now the other side is not given equal play. In a sense, the debate in many venues is settled—at least for the host.[11]

---

[8]Ellen Hume, "Why the Press Blew the S&L Scandal," *New York Times,* May 24, 1990.
[9]Baron (2005) provides a theory of strategic provision of information by sources.
[10]Quoted in Ellen Hume, "Why the Press Blew the S&L Scandal," *New York Times,* May 24, 1990.
[11]www.stateofthemedia.org/2007.

THE NATURE OF THE NEWS MEDIA

News Organizations as Businesses

In the United States, news organizations are owned by for-profit companies, so profit is a primary objective. ABC is owned by Walt Disney, CBS by Viacom, NBC by General Electric, and Fox by the News Corporation. As profit-oriented firms, news media companies are interested in attracting readers and viewers, since subscription and advertising revenue depend on audience size. Reuven Frank (1991, p. 222), former president of NBC News, said "The product of commercial television is not programs. If one thinks of making goods to sell, the viewers are not the customers, those who buy the product. Advertisers buy the product, pay money for it. Programs are not what they buy, what they pay for is audience, people to heed their messages. The bigger the audience, the more they pay. . . ."

News organizations are in a highly competitive industry. They compete not only against other companies in the same medium but also across media. The traditional competition has been intensified with the rise of Internet news organizations that exploit synergies with broadcast news organizations. Competitive pressures have increased the importance of attracting an audience.[12] Competitive pressures also mean that there are strong incentives to be first with a breaking story, which can affect accuracy.

Young (1978, p. 2) offered a perspective on the implications:

As more organs of the media are owned by large corporations, whose prime interest is financial, the journalistic principles of a publication can be compromised by—or dissipated in—the business needs. The demand [is] for more circulation, more advertising, and more profit. To achieve these, the media will cater to populist—meaning antibusiness—fears and prejudices, entertain instead of enlighten, pander instead of lead. They reduce big issues to oversimplified personality battles, because both people and disputes make good reading and viewing.

This statement is surely too strong, but it indicates the tension between the incentives to attract an audience and the standards of the journalism profession.

The Profession

Media decisions are made by the people who choose careers in journalism. Journalists are younger, better educated, and more liberal than the American public. A survey by the American Society of Newspaper Editors (ASNE) found, "At the bigger papers, 61 percent of newsroom respondents described themselves as Democrats (or leaning toward Democrat) and only 10 percent as Republicans (or leaning toward Republican)."[13] In 1992, 89 percent of the Washington journalists surveyed voted for Bill Clinton and 7 percent for George H.W. Bush. Sixty-one percent of the journalists rated themselves as liberal or liberal to moderate and 9 percent as conservative or conservative to moderate.[14] Editors were more evenly balanced in their orientation and political preferences.

A widely shared perspective among journalists is that they are serving the public. Some journalists joined the profession in the wake of Robert Woodward and Carl Bernstein's triumph in the Watergate affair. Not only had journalists succeeded in uncovering illegal activity, but their work led to the resignation of a U.S. president. Journalists seek the "scoop that will echo around the world."

---

[12] The same type of competitive and performance pressures are present in government-owned media. Küng-Shankleman (2000) provides an analysis of the BBC and CNN as businesses in their market and nonmarket environments.

[13] ASNE, Chapter "Characteristics of the Respondents." www.asne.org.

[14] Povich (1996, p. 137).

Writing before Watergate, Epstein (1973, p. 219), who studied the operations of network television news programs, addressed journalists' views of their role and power.

> Privately almost all network correspondents expressed a strong belief in their ability to effect change in public policy through their work, if not as individuals, then certainly as a group. Some considered their self-perceived political powers "frightening" and "awesome," while others merely depicted them as a necessary part of the political process.

Journalism is governed by standards enforced by news media organizations and professional associations.[15] A journalist is trained to present the who, what, where, when, and why of a story. Journalistic judgments, however, can lead to quite different treatments of stories. As an example, the Institute of Medicine, a unit of the National Academies of Science, released a report on the health effects of indoor mold and moisture. On May 26, 2004, the headline in the *Wall Street Journal* read, "Indoor Mold Linked to Problems Such as Asthma and Coughing," the headline in the *San Jose Mercury News* read, "Report: Mold seen as irritant, but not as bad as feared," and the *New York Times* headline read, "Panel Finds Mold in Buildings Is No Threat to Most People."

Journalists seek professional attainment, recognition, and reward. A necessary condition for attainment is that a journalist's work be published or aired and have an impact. Journalists thus have strong incentives to present stories that will pass editorial scrutiny and be sufficiently newsworthy that editors will print or air them. Stories must also be read or viewed, so journalists seek to make their stories engaging. Making stories engaging, however, can result in inaccuracies, bias, and in some cases fabrication. The chapter case, *General Motors: Like a Rock? (A)*, considers such a situation.

Does the News Media Treat Issues Selectively?

The news media may not cover every issue under the same criteria. Most issues are treated under controls and editorial standards. On some issues, however, the media takes an advocacy approach, suspending the standards of fairness and balance. Epstein (1973, p. 233) wrote that

> controls tend to be disregarded when executives, producers and correspondents all share the same view and further perceive it to be a view accepted by virtually all thoughtful persons. News reports about such subjects as pollution, hunger, health care, racial discrimination, and poverty fall in this category. On such consensus issues, correspondents are expected by executives openly to advocate the eradication of the presumed evil and even put it in terms of a "crusade," as a CBS vice-president suggested with respect to the pollution issue. At times, however, what are assumed to be commonly held values turn out to be disputed ones in some parts of the country; and when executives are apprised of this (by affiliates and others), the usual "fairness" controls are applied to the subject.

There is certainly consensus on preferring less to more pollution, but often the real issue, as in the case of global climate change, is how much reduction in emissions is warranted by the cost and how that cost is to be distributed. On these dimensions, considerable disagreement exists.

In the wake of the firing of Jayson Blair for the fabrication of stories, the *New York Times* created the position of public editor devoted "to receiving, investigating, and answering outsiders' concerns about our coverage." Public editor Daniel Okrent described his conclusions about the coverage of social issues: "And if you think *The Times*

---

[15]The Poynter Institute provides information on journalistic ethics: www.poynter.org. Codes of ethics and responsibilities for journalists can be found at www.asne.org/ideas/codes.

plays it down the middle on any of [the social issues], you've been reading the paper with your eyes closed.... [It is] quite another thing to tell only the side of the story your co-religionists wish to hear. I don't think it's intentional when *The Times* does this. But negligence doesn't have to be intentional.... *Times* editors have failed to provide the three-dimensional perspective balanced journalism requires."[16] Okrent referred to *The Times'* coverage as "cheerleading," and his assessment is consistent with Epstein's observation about "consensus issues." The publisher of *The Times* described its consensus viewpoint as "urban."

Bias, Accuracy, and Fairness

The public widely views the media as biased. A survey by the ASNE (1999) revealed that 78 percent of the public believed that there was bias in news reporting.[17] There was little consensus, however, on the nature and direction of the perceived bias. The ASNE wrote, "The public appears to diagnose the root causes of media bias in two forms. First (and at best), bias is a lack of dispassion and impartiality that colors the decision of whether or not to publish a story, or the particular facts that are included in a news report and the tone of how those facts are expressed. Second (and at worst), they see bias as an intent to persuade."

Public confidence in the news media has declined for the past two decades as "The State of the News Media" found. The report stated, "since the early 1980s, the public has come to view the news media as less professional, less accurate, less caring, less moral, and more inclined to cover up rather than correct mistakes."[18]

Most nonmarket issues involving business are complex, and the ability to present that complexity and achieve accuracy, balance, and fairness differs considerably among media organizations. Some newspapers and magazines can present complex stories in a comprehensive manner and in enough detail to provide accuracy and balance. Television, however, may not be well suited to presenting complex stories, in part because of the brief time that can be allocated to a story. As Epstein (1980, p. 127) stated, "This enforced brevity leaves little room for presenting complex explanations or multifaceted arguments." As importantly, the need to retain viewer interest requires that a story be attractive and entertaining. The desire to develop human interest and controversy in a limited time slot can lead to sacrifices in balance and accuracy. Qualification and complexity, even when written into a story, may be edited out to provide time for other stories. Many complaints by business executives about television news coverage are due to the simplification needed to fit a story into a restricted time slot. Distortion in a story thus could result from simplification rather than bias.

Because journalists write for the audience and not for the protagonists in a story, the protagonists may view a story as not giving sufficient attention or credence to their side. The difference between the objective of providing information to the public and the subject's interest in a favorable portrayal can lead to a perception of bias.

The treatment of an issue, particularly when advocacy journalism is practiced and editorial controls are suspended, can put firms in a difficult position. News coverage of fires due to the use of space heaters may involve the victims telling of their plight and demanding that the manufacturer and the government take action. Given the framing of the issue, manufacturers may have considerable difficulty providing information about the safety features already incorporated, the possibility that the victims may have

---

[16]*New York Times,* July 25, 2004.
[17]Groseclose and Milyo (2005) found "a very significant liberal bias" in the news media. Eighteen of the 20 news outlets studied were found to be more liberal than the average U.S. voter and average member of Congress and "closer to the average Democrat in Congress than to the median member of the House of Representatives." Their methodology required no judgments about which media outlets were liberal or conservative or the degree of bias. They simply counted the number of citations a news publication made to each of 50 think tanks and computed a score by comparing those citations to citations of those think tanks in speeches by members of Congress. The positions of Congress members on a left–right scale were determined using a statistical procedure standard in political science based on rankings by interest groups. Baron (2006) provides a supply side theory of bias based on the career interests of journalists.
[18]www.stateofthemedia.org/2007.

misused the heaters, and the measures taken to reduce the likelihood of misuse. The fact that no space heater can be perfectly safe reduces the credibility of such explanations.[19]

Media coverage can also be alarmist, which can put firms in a difficult position. The media coverage in the Alar episode was alarmist, as was coverage of the outbreak of SARS in 2003. Health scares are frequently fanned by the media because "fear sells," but the media can also exercise restraint. Michael Fumento, writing in the *Washington Post,* commented on the media's restraint in the coverage of the first case of mad cow disease in the United States:[20]

> Part of the explanation for the paucity of panic, though probably only a minor one, may be that there's no cause for it—and even the media know this. . . .Watching the British over the last decade may also have helped us keep our heads level. . . . The United Kingdom's top BSE official said in 1996 that as many as half a million Britons would die from the bad beef, while an estimate in the *British Food Journal* a year earlier pegged potential deaths at as many as 10 million. . . . A 2001 study in *Science* magazine estimated the number [of cases] will probably top out at 200.

Sales at McDonald's and other restaurants in the United States were largely unaffected by the case.

Cost pressures on news organizations, journalists' incentives to have stories aired or published, deadlines and space constraints, and competitive pressures can result in inaccuracies in stories. Cost pressures, for example, led some news organizations to shift some fact-checking responsibilities to their reporters. This resulted in a number of serious violations of professional standards. News organizations responded by strengthening their internal controls. CNN, for example, established an internal watchdog office, the Journalistic Standards and Practices office. Cost and competitive pressures, however, work against stronger internal controls.

The Internet and Citizen Journalism

The sources of information about nonmarket issues and the firms affected by them have broadened substantially with the expansion of use of the Internet. The use of the Internet for news has increased with 70 percent of users reporting that they access news online, although the percent using online services daily is considerably lower at 27 percent, according to surveys by the Pew Research Center. The sources have also diversified with the advent of blogs and Web 2.0 sites. Usage varies with age, with young people relying more on the Internet for news than other sources. A survey of high school students by the Knight Foundation indicated that nearly a third of the respondents viewed blogs as news sources, although only 10 percent viewed blogs as trustworthy, compared to 45 percent for television news.

The rise of blogs and Web 2.0 formats allows citizens to be journalists, and although most focus on personal experiences, some use the Internet to comment on developments. With information and comments passed along on the Internet instantly, the media environment of firms has become more complex. Moreover, the public exposure of corporate actions has expanded. Activists also use blogs and Web 2.0 formats to disseminate information about companies. As indicated in Chapter 1, an activist with the Rainforest Action Network asked hostile questions of a Toyota executive at an auto show while filming with a video camera. The executive knocked the camera to the ground, and the film quickly appeared on YouTube.

Companies have also begun to use blogs and other online forums to disseminate information and communicate with stakeholders, journalists, and the public. These formats can be used to answer questions of stakeholders about the conduct of the company, counter critics, and supply additional information on issues beyond what the

---

[19]See the Chapter 12 case, *California Space Heaters, Inc.*
[20]*Washington Post,* January 18, 2004.

mainstream media report. Companies also use these forums to correct mistakes by the news media or to present another side to a story. Journalists increasingly use such information in the stories they write. These forums can also be used in times of crisis to communicate with consumers and others affected, as considered in Chapter 5.

BUSINESS INTERACTIONS WITH THE NEWS MEDIA

Business concerns with media coverage and treatment stem from several considerations. First, few companies like their activities to be publicly scrutinized. The media guards its independence and in particular does not serve as a public relations arm of firms. Second, the desire for balance and the incentive to develop controversy to make stories appealing often gives critics of the company an opportunity to deliver their message to the public. Third, some executives agree with Young that the media caters to antibusiness sentiments. Fourth, particularly in the case of television interviews, the control of the editing process gives the media the opportunity to select the parts of an interview that make the best story, and those may not be the parts business wants to have aired. Fifth, media treatment almost always results in oversimplification, precluding the presentation of a full account of a company's side of the story. Because of these concerns many firms have developed competencies for interacting with the media.

In interacting with the media, managers should be both cautious and realistic in their expectations. In a case against ABC's *Primetime Live,* Court of Appeals judge Richard Posner wrote, "Investigative journalists well known for ruthlessness promise to wear kid gloves. They break their promise, as any person of normal sophistication would expect. If this is 'fraud,' it is a kind against which potential victims can easily arm themselves by maintaining a minimum skepticism about journalistic goals and method."[21]

The Need for Information

Many business issues are newsworthy, and frequently only business has the information that can serve as the basis for a story. This provides firms with an opportunity to develop a relationship with news organizations in which they provide the information needed in exchange for stories that will be fair and balanced. As one prominent journalist commented, "We need access [to information] and sources can trade on access." Many firms sustain those relationships through their forthrightness and the credibility of the information they provide. Many firms have professionalized their interactions with the media by employing communications specialists and by giving their managers media training. Business interactions with the media are also broadening as more managers assume a role in interacting with the media.

Media Strategies

Media strategies guide interactions with the media and communication with stakeholders and the public. Evans (1987, pp. 84–87) identified six elements of an effective media strategy:

- The unusual is usual.
- Emphasize the consistency of business and the public interest.
- Remember your audience.
- Communicate through the press.
- The medium is the message.
- Establish credibility—not friendship.

A firm's interactions with the media should be tailored to the audience. In interacting with the media the firm is speaking not just with the journalist but, more importantly, with the audience. The information presented thus should be directed at the likely audience. In the case of an issue that will be covered only by the business press,

---

[21]*New York Times,* July 13, 1998.

the information should be tailored for a knowledgeable audience. If the audience is more general, the information should be accessible to the layperson.

For most nonmarket issues the interests of a firm are consistent with some aspect of the public interest or at least with the interests of stakeholders. Emphasizing the effects of the issue not on profits but on stakeholders can be effective, as can pointing out that the practice in question is consistent with the public interest. In interviews, managers thus should not only answer questions but also take the opportunity to make affirmative statements about the firm's position.

The development of relationships of confidence is easier with the business press than with the general media because of the business press's greater need for information and because it typically assigns journalists to regular beats. The journalist then has an incentive to develop expertise and a relationship with the firm, and the resulting stories may be more accurate and balanced. If a journalist demonstrates an understanding of the industry and the issues, the firm may choose to release its information first to him or her as a reward.

Developing relationships with journalists from the more general news media, particularly television, is often more difficult because fewer journalists are assigned to business beats. For those journalists, the incentive to develop expertise on the issues can be weak. A journalist assigned to an issue high on the social significance dimension—products with a health risk to children, for instance—may not have expertise on the issue. In such cases it is particularly important for a manager to communicate effectively with the journalist and not leave a media vacuum for others to fill.

Responses and Media Vacuums

On many issues—particularly those that may generate nonmarket action—business prefers to avoid media coverage. One tempting strategy is not to comment to the media in the hope that no story will appear. If it seems likely that the story will appear anyway, a "no comment" strategy can be risky. Especially on issues that are high on the societal significance dimension, the media may take an advocacy approach either directly or by airing the allegations of others. Leaving a vacuum that the firm's critics can fill with their side of the story can often be more damaging than having the firm tell its side of the story, even if that story is not compelling. Providing facts and demonstrating concern, even if the facts are not all favorable to the firm, can narrow the space in which critics can maneuver.

Just as allowing critics to fill a vacuum is generally not a good strategy, attacking critics is often not a good strategy, since it can create a second story that can prolong an issue. After a half-time employee of Électricité de France wrote a book criticizing French corporations for their rigid social norms and urging French workers to adopt "calculated loafing" and to "spread gangrene through the system from inside," her employer sent her a letter calling her before a disciplinary hearing. The letter was given to the news media, and coverage of the episode caused sales of the book to skyrocket.[22]

Many firms have concluded that there are some media representatives or programs with which it is better to not talk. Many will not talk with investigative journalism programs such as *60 Minutes* because of concerns about how they and their firm will be portrayed. They prefer a statement such as "The company refused to comment" to risking an interview from which the editors will extract a 15-second clip to be interspersed among interviews with the critics of the firm.

Media Interviews

Because of its importance in the development of nonmarket issues, managers frequently grant interviews to the media and are called on to speak to the public. Media training is customary in many firms, and a communications consulting industry has

---

[22]*New York Times,* August 14, 2004. Corinne Maier, *Bonjour Paresse,* Éditions Michalon, Paris, 2004.

FIGURE 3-3 Hewlett-Packard Company Media Guidelines

Hewlett-Packard Company's Twelve Guides for Conducting a Media Interview

• Assume everything you say is "on the record."
• Speak in plain English.
• State your main point or conclusion first.
• If you don't understand a question, say so.
• If presented with a "laundry list" of questions, identify the one question you are responding to before answering it.
• Don't hesitate to repeat an answer.
• Volunteer information to make your points and to give perspective.
• Use anecdotes and illustrations involving people.
• Have fun doing the interview, without being flippant, of course.
• Don't be afraid to admit mistakes.
• Don't expect the editor to clear the story with you before it is published.
• Never, never, never stretch the truth.

developed to support that training. Many firms provide guidelines for their managers in dealing with journalists. The Hewlett-Packard Company's guidelines are presented in Figure 3-3.

Perhaps the best advice for media interviews was given by the publisher of a major newspaper. He said that when dealing with the press, there were three cardinal rules. The first is "Tell the truth." The second is "Tell the truth." The third is "Always remember the first two." A pragmatic version of the publisher's cardinal rules was provided by a judge who said, "Always tell the truth—it's easier to remember." Answering truthfully is always a good policy, but simply responding to questions is not. Managers must be prepared to make affirmative points when responding to an interviewer's questions and seize opportunities to tell the company's side of the story.

When asked to appear for a television interview, some business executives ask to go on live so that their comments cannot be edited. Stations, however, typically will not agree to an unedited interview. The interviewee thus is often advised to answer questions in a manner that makes them difficult to edit. Sometimes a firm may ask the reporter to submit questions in advance, but that request is usually rejected. When agreeing to an interview, some firms find it prudent to audiotape or videotape the interview. Taping the interview provides a record of what transpired and can be useful if a dispute with the media arises. Taping may also caution journalists to be careful about what they write or broadcast. When agreeing to an interview, it is important to recognize that at times the media may already have the story in the can and may be seeking an interview to develop controversy. The chapter case, *Illinois Power Company (A),* presents such a situation.

Anticipating Issues

Many firms attempt to educate the media about important issues in their nonmarket environment. Some go further and attempt to communicate directly with the interest groups that are likely to be concerned with issues. To the extent that it can anticipate an issue, a firm is better positioned if it has laid the groundwork to deal effectively with the issue as it progresses through its life cycle.

When a nonmarket issue can be anticipated, the theory of the news media can be used to assess whether the issue is likely to be covered and, if so, the type of treatment it is likely to receive. For those stories that will be covered only by the business press, a firm can hope, and in many cases expect, that the journalist has a degree of expertise in the subject matter of the story. If, in addition, the issue is low on the societal significance dimension, the firm may need to do little more than provide the media with facts along with its side of the issue.

A broader set of news organizations is likely to be attracted to issues that are high on the societal significance dimension, making interactions with the media more complex. Such issues also may attract or be initiated by activist groups, as in the case of Alar. These groups can be expected to advance their side of the issue by providing information to the media. The Alar episode was more orchestrated than most, but the point is clear. Interest and activist groups can orchestrate events to advance their causes both in a planned manner and in response to an issue brought to their—and the public's—attention by the media.

When media coverage of an issue can be anticipated, the firm has the opportunity to prepare. Preparation includes gathering the relevant information about the issue and its context and assigning a spokesperson to interact with the media. Preparation also includes evaluating the messages likely to be conveyed by the media and its sources. As discussed in the context of Figure 3-1, the messages are a function not only of the coverage and treatment given to the issue but also of the information the audience already has. Individuals, interest groups, and politicians may evaluate a story in different ways. Some may consider the story in terms of their own self-interest, whereas others may look at it in terms of broader principles. These varied evaluations can result in market and nonmarket actions that affect the progress of the issue and cause change in the firm's environment. Firms and their managers thus must be sensitive to how those in the audience will evaluate the messages they receive.

Unanticipated Events

Because events such as environmental accidents can occur, firms should have a routine to follow in the event of a breaking story. For serious matters firms should have a crisis management plan as considered in Chapter 5. If the issue is one that need not be made public—embezzlement, for example—the first decision is whether to release the information to the news media or attempt to keep it confidential. The latter can be successful in many cases, but leaks occur more often than most managers expect.

If the incident is public, the first step is to gather as much information as possible as quickly as possible. There is little that can damage a firm more than having others uncover information that management itself does not have. An accurate record-keeping system that, for example, keeps track of the toxic wastes generated by a plant and where they are disposed can be essential. Having the facts readily accessible not only allows the firm to be in the position of being the best source of information for the media but also provides a basis on which management can develop a strategy for addressing the underlying issue. In implementing a strategy, it is also often wise for the firm to speak with a single voice. The spokesperson must have all the information on the issue so as not to be blindsided and to better anticipate the story's likely development.

RECOURSE IN DISPUTES WITH THE MEDIA

Private Recourse

The subjects of news coverage at times perceive stories to be incomplete, inaccurate, or unfair. Some take actions ranging from writing to the editor to correct inaccuracies to initiating legal action. Firms may also take economic measures against the media by, for example, withdrawing advertising in response to a story that management believes has misrepresented the facts. The Procter & Gamble example describes one such case. When neither economic measures nor legal action is warranted, companies can bring concerns about a story to the attention of the media. Some firms make a practice of notifying editors about their concerns, with the objectives of improving future stories and establishing a reputation for being ready to act.

The news media is governed by professional standards, and journalists and editors develop and maintain reputations for professionalism. Organizations such as the Society of Professional Journalists, Sigma Delta Chi, and the ASNE work to foster high professional standards and ethics in journalism. Media organizations discipline their

EXAMPLE

Procter & Gamble and Neighbor to Neighbor

Neighbor to Neighbor, an activist group located in San Francisco, opposed U.S. support for the government in El Salvador and called for the end of military aid to that country. The group claimed that coffee growers in El Salvador financed death squads with money obtained from exporting coffee to the United States. From the group's perspective, U.S. coffee companies that imported Salvadoran coffee beans were supporting the death squads.

Neighbor to Neighbor took its message to the American public by placing advertisements in the *New York Times,* the *New London Day* (Connecticut), and *The Progressive* magazine. The group also advocated a consumer boycott of U.S. coffee brands. The best-selling U.S. brand was Folgers, produced by the Procter & Gamble Company (P&G). To generate support for the boycott, the group produced a 30-second television commercial that it planned to air on several television stations. The commercial, narrated by Ed Asner, named only Folgers and showed an upside-down coffee cup dripping blood.[1] The inscription on the cup read "Seal of Salvadoran Coffee," and Asner said, "The murderous civil war in El Salvador has been supported by billions of American tax dollars and by the sale of Salvadoran coffee. . . . Boycott Folgers. What it brews is misery and death."[2]

Of the 30 television stations approached by Neighbor to Neighbor, all but two rejected the commercial. After reviewing it for taste and content, investigating its content, and obtaining legal advice on the possibility of libel suits, the CBS affiliate WHDH-TV in Boston broadcast the commercial twice in May 1990. Seymour L. Yamoff, president and general manager of WHDH-TV, stated, "The information on this particular commercial is correct. . . . We screen them for accuracy, libel, slander and 'Do they meet a standard of fairness?'" He also stated that the station had never broadcast such "issue advertisements" other than in election campaigns, and he could not recall any such advertisement being aired in Boston during the 20 years he had lived there.

P&G was shocked by the commercial. It purchased coffee from 30 countries, and less than 2 percent of its supply came from El Salvador. P&G was one of the largest television advertisers and provided advertising revenue of $1 million annually to WHDH-TV. That represented nearly 2 percent of the station's advertising revenue. The revenue from broadcasting the Neighbor to Neighbor commercial totaled less than $1,000.

P&G decided to withdraw its advertising from WHDH-TV and threatened to withdraw its advertising from any other station that broadcast the ad. WHDH-TV hired a *Washington Post* reporter, Scott Armstrong, to conduct an inquiry into the commercial. In the draft of his report, he concluded "that certain conclusions . . . were not substantiated."[3] As a result of the report, WHDH-TV adopted a new policy: "Any public-issue commercials submitted to the station in the future will be broadcast only after the truth of their claims has been determined."[4] "A Procter & Gamble spokesman said, 'We were satisfied that WHDH had on further review concluded that certain representations in the anti-Folgers ad were not substantiated and . . . it was an appropriate time to resume advertising on that station.'"[5] As a result of a peace accord between the government and rebels in El Salvador in March 1992, the boycott was called off.

[1]The print advertisements had mentioned other coffee brands in addition to Folgers.
[2]*Boston Globe,* December 12, 1990. A similar commercial calling for a boycott of Hills Brothers Coffee was aired on the West Coast where Hills Brothers had its largest market share.

[3]*Boston Globe,* December 12, 1990.
[4]*Boston Globe,* December 12, 1990.
[5]*Boston Globe,* December 12, 1990.

correspondents, editors, and managers who violate professional standards. Correspondents may be suspended, reassigned, or fired for violations. In the chapter case, *General Motors: Like a Rock? (A)*, NBC took disciplinary actions when it was revealed that its *Dateline* producers and correspondents had used a model rocket engine to ignite a fire during a test collision of a GM truck. NBC reassigned the correspondent and fired the producer of the *Dateline* segment. The senior producer and the executive producer of *Dateline* resigned, and Michael Gartner, president of NBC News, also resigned. NBC created the position of ombudsman to supplement its professional standards and to review segments produced for its news programs as well as programs such as *Dateline*.

Recourse to the Law: Defamation and Libel

Defamation is a branch of torts pertaining to false statements made to a third party that damage a person's reputation.[23] The category of "person" includes not only humans but legal entities such as corporations. Defamation takes the form of either libel or slander. Libel pertains to statements that are either written or broadcast, whereas slander pertains to statements that are spoken. A finding of slander requires a showing of actual damages, but a finding of libel generally does not require such a showing. Defamation cases are governed by state law and the common law. Defamation cases generally center on statements made in public, but in *Dun & Bradstreet v. Greenmoss Builders,* 472 U.S. 749 (1985), Greenmoss Builders was awarded $350,000 when Dun & Bradstreet issued an erroneous credit report. Thus, defamation more generally applies to a statement made to a third party.

A defendant in a defamation suit has several possible defenses, which fall into the categories of "truth" and "privilege." A defendant always has the defense that what was said, written, or broadcast was the truth. In some states truth constitutes an absolute defense, whereas in others it may be subject to limitations such as those arising from laws on privacy. For example, in some states it is illegal to disclose that someone has been convicted of a crime or has a disease.

The courts exercise judgment in assessing a truth defense. In 1990, 20 Washington State apple growers filed suit against CBS and the NRDC seeking $250 million in damages, alleging that the *60 Minutes* segment on Alar had led to a panic among consumers that cost the state's growers $150 million in sales. A federal district judge dismissed the suit because the plaintiffs had not shown that the broadcast was false. The judge stated, "Even if CBS's statements are false, they were about an issue that mattered, cannot be proven as false and therefore must be protected."[24] CBS had argued that its story was based on an EPA report, and the judge stated, "A news reporting service is not a scientific testing lab, and these services should be able to rely on a scientific Government report when they are relaying the report's contents."[25]

A degree of privilege is provided to the media by the First Amendment, which extends protection but does not provide an absolute defense. In *New York Times v. Sullivan,* 376 U.S. 254 (1964), the Supreme Court delineated a standard of proof required of plaintiffs in a defamation lawsuit.[26] The ruling requires plaintiffs who are "public figures" to show that the statement in question was made with actual malice—that is, either with knowledge that it was false or with "reckless disregard" for whether it was true.[27] Being careless or sloppy with the facts is not sufficient for a finding of libel. In a complex case, the court attempts to balance the rights of the plaintiff with the rights of the media as provided by the First Amendment. Although plaintiffs win some libel suits against the media, the media is generally successful in defending itself given the protection provided by the Constitution and Supreme Court rulings.

The rationale for the standard enunciated in *Sullivan* is that although persons retain rights to privacy, they lose a degree of privateness when they participate in "public" activities. The publicness of a plaintiff is not restricted to public officeholders but also pertains to private citizens who voluntarily appear in public. A corporate executive who makes public speeches or testifies in public hearings may be held to be a public figure in a defamation suit. Thus, a corporate plaintiff in a defamation suit may have to meet the standard of proof delineated in *Sullivan.*

---

[23]A tort is a civil wrong that damages a person or property.
[24]*Auvil v. CBS "60 Minutes,"* 836 F. Supp. 740 [E.D. Wash.].
[25]*New York Times,* September 15, 1993.
[26]This case arose when supporters of Martin Luther King placed an advertisement in the *New York Times* describing the activities of the Alabama police. The advertisement contained "several minor inaccuracies and exaggerations" (Schmidt, 1981), and an Alabama jury found that the supporters and the newspaper were guilty of defamation under state law. The Supreme Court viewed a standard requiring complete accuracy as conflicting with the First Amendment's protection of freedom of the press.
[27]If the plaintiff proves actual malice, the court presumes there is actual damage, relieving the plaintiff of the burden of proving damages.

To illustrate the application of this standard, in 1981 anchorman Walter Jacobson of CBS's Chicago television station WBBM stated in a commentary that Brown & Williamson Tobacco Corporation was trying to lure young people to its Viceroy cigarette by using a marketing strategy that related the cigarette to "pot, wine, beer, and sex." Jacobson based his commentary on a Federal Trade Commission (FTC) study that reported that a Brown & Williamson advertising agency had hired a consultant who had proposed such a strategy. The FTC study, however, did not indicate that Brown & Williamson had adopted the consultant's recommendations. Indeed, Jacobson's assistant had told him prior to the broadcast that the company had rejected the proposed strategy. In spite of having been so informed, Jacobson made his commentary. The jury concluded that Jacobson made a statement that he knew to be false and held for Brown & Williamson. The jury awarded $3 million in compensatory damages and $2 million in punitive damages against CBS and WBBM and $50,000 in punitive damages against Jacobson. A federal judge reduced the compensatory damages to $1, but the Court of Appeals reinstated $1 million in compensatory damages. The decision was appealed to the Supreme Court, which allowed the Court of Appeals decision to stand.[28]

A relatively untested aspect of the law pertains to information posted on the Internet. Such postings can be widely disseminated and could form the basis for a defamation lawsuit. Online service providers could also be the potential subject of a lawsuit if they played a role in maintaining a bulletin board or exercising editorial control over postings or access. The Communications Decency Act of 1996 provides a degree of protection to Internet service providers, and that law has protected eBay against defamation and other lawsuits, as indicated in Chapter 2. No case has yet reached the Supreme Court to clarify the application of the law, but the Court of Appeals ruled that AOL was not liable for postings on its Web site.

Libel laws differ considerably across countries. In the United Kingdom libel cases are easier for plaintiffs to win in part because defendants do not have the protection of *Sullivan*. In the 1980s McDonald's filed a libel suit against Greenpeace volunteers in the United Kingdom who had distributed leaflets criticizing the company's policies. In the longest trial in UK history the court ruled in favor of McDonald's and ordered the volunteers to pay £60,000. The court, however, soundly criticized McDonald's and its practices.[29] The episode, known as McLibel, attracted widespread public attention, support for the volunteers, and hostility toward McDonald's. In a complaint against the UK government for stifling their rights to criticize a company, the volunteers took their case to the European Court of Human Rights in Strasbourg, which in 2005 ruled in favor of the volunteers.

Political Recourse

The First Amendment provides protection to the news media, and *Sullivan* strengthens that protection in the case of public figures. Commercial speech, however, receives less protection. Although the apple industry failed to obtain relief in the courts, the Alar episode generated considerable sympathy for the industry. The American Feed Industry Association (AFIA), a trade association, seized the opportunity and hired a law firm specializing in food and drug issues to draft a model "food-disparagement bill" for introduction in state legislatures. The model bill would change state libel laws to provide a cause for action against a party that made "disparaging statements" or disseminated "false information" about the safety of a food product. Steve Kopperud, senior vice president of AFIA, said, "There has been long-standing frustration . . . that an activist organization, for the price of a full-page ad in

---

[28]Juries often award large judgments against the news media in libel cases, and judges frequently view the awards as excessive and reduce them.
[29]The volunteers appealed, but their appeal was rejected. A description of the case can be found at www.mcspotlight.org/case. A documentary film, *McLibel*, of the episode was produced and widely circulated.

USA Today, can say whatever it wishes to scare the public."[30] Thirteen states had enacted versions of the model bill, which have become known as "veggie-libel" laws. Critics of these laws argued that they placed the burden of proof on defendants to demonstrate conclusive scientific evidence, which they argued was a standard that would stifle free speech.

SUMMARY

The news media is a major source of information for those in the nonmarket environment. It alerts the public, activists, public officeholders, and interest groups to nonmarket issues and the activities of firms. Those interested in advancing an issue may attempt to use the media as a component of their nonmarket strategies. Although the media guards its independence, it may at times find components of those strategies to be newsworthy, as in the Alar episode.

Because the news media plays an important role in the development of nonmarket issues, managers must assess which issues the media is likely to cover and the treatment those issues are likely to receive. The theory of coverage and treatment predicts that the news media will cover issues with intrinsic audience interest or perceived societal significance. Stories are more likely to be newsworthy if they have broad audience interest, immediacy, human interest, controversy and conflict, and, for television, visual appeal. Societal significance pertains to the media's role as a protector of the public's right to know. In this role, the media may at times engage in advocacy by making judgments or supporting particular policies.

The media needs information for its stories, and on many issues business is the best and least-costly source of information. Firms thus have an opportunity to develop relationships with journalists who cover business issues on a regular basis. Managers may be called on to interact with the media, and to prepare for those interactions, they need to be fully informed about the issue in question as well as about the likely audience.

Business issues are often complex and may be difficult for television and the general media to cover. Although the media applies standards of accuracy, fairness, and balance to a story, it has incentives to make the story appealing to the audience and therefore may overemphasize conflict and controversy. It may also simplify a story to fit a time slot, a space limit, or a deadline. Many of the complaints about news coverage of business result from oversimplification.

The news media is both a business and a profession. Media companies are motivated by profit considerations, and journalists have career interests. Editorial controls govern conduct, and journalists are guided by professional standards. A tension, however, exists between those standards and corporate and individual incentives.

The subjects of media stories frequently believe that they were unfairly treated or that a story was inaccurate or biased. One means of recourse is a defamation lawsuit, but such lawsuits are typically costly and difficult to win. The standard under which a case is judged is important to its eventual outcome. For a public figure, the standard is articulated in *New York Times v. Sullivan.* This standard provides considerable protection for the media because a public figure must show actual malice and a "reckless disregard" for the truth.

Some critics have called for restraints on the news media. Despite its lapses and occasional abuses, the news media plays an essential role in a democracy, and the imperfections in the coverage and treatment of stories may be the cost borne for the benefits provided. As Thomas Jefferson wrote, "Were it left to me to decide whether we should have a government without newspapers or newspapers without a government, I should not hesitate to prefer the latter."[31]

---

[30]Marianne Lavelle, *National Law Journal,* May 5, 1997.
[31]Letter to E. Carrington, 1787.

-- C A S E S --

General Motors: Like a Rock? (A)

In 1992 the General Motors Corporation struggled through rocky management shake-ups and its third consecutive year of red ink. If any silver lining could be found in GM's financial cloud, it was its line of pickup trucks. Large pickups were one of GM's few profitable products from its ailing North American operations. Sales of Chevy and GMC full-size pickups exceeded half a million in 1991. Greater expectations for 1992 and 1993 coincided with a beefed-up marketing campaign centering on the theme "Like a Rock." However, as events unfolded, GM management found itself between a rock and a hard place.

In 1992 the Center for Auto Safety (CAS) petitioned NHTSA to recall some 5 million Chevrolet and GMC full-size pickup trucks. The CAS claimed that more than 300 people had died in side-impact accidents involving the trucks. Unlike most other pickups, GM class C/K pickups built during the years 1973 to 1987 were equipped with twin "side-saddle" gasoline tanks positioned outside the main frame rails. In 1987 GM made a design change in its trucks and brought the tanks inside the frame.

The CAS petition was not the first sign of a potential problem in GM's pickups. For years GM had managed to avoid the eye of the media by fighting on a case-by-case basis as many as 140 fuel tank–related lawsuits. Most were settled out of court with settlements occasionally exceeding $1 million. Throughout these legal proceedings, GM steadfastly defended the overall safety of its trucks. GM regularly pointed out that the NHTSA standard called for crashworthiness at 20 mph, and its pickups easily met that standard. In the 1970s GM regularly tested its trucks with side-impact crashes at 30 mph. In the mid-1980s it increased its internal standard to 50 mph. That fires sometimes broke out in the highest speed tests was not disputed but rather was viewed by GM as evidence that it was pushing its tests to the limit in an effort to make its trucks safer.

Data and interpretations concerning the relative safety of GM trucks were mixed. According to NHTSA, GM's side-saddle trucks were 2.4 times as likely as Ford's to be involved in deadly side-impact crashes. According to the Insurance Institute for Highway Safety—a research group supported by insurance companies—the GM trucks might be slightly more prone to fire than similar models built by Ford and Chrysler, but they could be far safer in certain kinds of accidents. This conclusion, according to GM, suggested a need for a broader and more appropriate criterion of safety—that of overall crashworthiness. At least one large database on accidents indicated that in terms of the overall probability of a fatal accident, GM trucks were marginally safer than their competitors.

In November 1992, NBC's *Dateline* aired a 15-minute segment entitled, "Waiting to Explode?" Its focus was the GM series C/K pickup trucks. In preparation for the segment, the NBC news crew hired three "safety consultants" to assist in conducting two crash tests of GM pickups on a rural Indiana road on October 24. Each test simulated a side-impact crash by using a tow truck to push a Chevy Citation along the road into a pickup. The pickup was parked on the road perpendicular to the oncoming car, which slammed into the pickup's passenger side. A minute-long videotape of the tests was aired, and correspondent Michele Gillen stated that the tests were "unscientific." In the first of the tests, Gillen stated that the car was moving at about 40 mph. The truck was jolted significantly, but no fire ensued. In the second test, a fire broke out at a speed stated to be 30 mph. In the broadcast one safety consultant described the fire as "a holocaust."

After the nationally televised broadcast that reached approximately 11 million viewers, GM officials examined the NBC test segment in slow motion. Suspicions arose. GM wrote to NBC almost immediately, stating that the show was unfair and requesting NBC's test data. NBC refused to comply. In a follow-up contact, GM asked NBC to allow it to inspect the pickups. On January 4 the producer of *Dateline* told GM the vehicles were "junked and therefore are no longer available for inspection."

In the meantime, 32-year-old Pete Pesterre, editor of the magazine *Popular Hot Rodding,* had been pursuing some suspicions of his own. He was intimately familiar with GM trucks. He had owned four of them and once was involved in a side-impact crash from which he emerged unscathed. After Pesterre wrote an editorial criticizing the *Dateline* segment, a reader from Indiana called Pesterre and informed him that he knew a Brownsburg, Indiana, firefighter who was at the scene of the NBC crash tests. When the Brownsburg Fire Department is on assignment, as it was the day NBC staged the crashes, its firefighters customarily videotape the action for subsequent use in training. GM contacted the fire chief, who provided a copy of the tape. Similarly, GM learned that an off-duty sheriff's deputy was on site and had also videotaped the tests. GM also acquired his tape.

To analyze the tapes (including NBC's), GM called on its Hughes Aircraft subsidiary to deploy digital-enhancement techniques for sophisticated frame-by-frame analysis. These investigations revealed that NBC had been less than precise about both the sequence and speeds of the two tests. The first test conducted was the second test aired. The GM/Hughes analysis suggested the actual speed was 39 mph instead of the 30 mph stated in the *Dateline* segment.[32] This test yielded the

---

[32] The 9 mph is important because energy is a function of the square of the velocity. To be precise, $e = .5MV^2$, where e is kinetic energy, M is mass, and V is velocity.

so-called holocaust. In the other test NBC claimed a speed of 40 mph, but GM/Hughes concluded the speed was 47 mph. No fire occurred in this test.

Another revelation came from the audio portion of the firefighter's tape. After the first test—which, although slower, did produce a fire—the firemen were noticeably unimpressed with the outcome. It was clear that the fire was confined to the grass, short lived, and not life endangering. One firefighter laughed, and one said, "So much for that theory."

Meanwhile, GM was able to locate and acquire the two wrecked Citations and the two wrecked pickups. The recovered pickups were sent to GM's plant in Indianapolis where workers discovered a model rocket engine in the bed of one truck. Inspections of the bottom of the truck uncovered flare marks and remnants of duct tape in two places where GM's video analysis had curiously shown both smoke and fire in frames prior to impact in the crash. Additional inspection of tapes and photographs fueled suspicions that a detonator or starter device had been wired to the rocket engine.

GM officials wanted to examine the trucks' fuel tanks but they had been stripped from the trucks. GM immediately went to court seeking a restraining order to bar one of the NBC consultants from disposing of the fuel tanks. Days later, through his attorney, GM learned that the consultant had given the tanks to a neighbor. Eventually GM obtained the tanks.

Having obtained the pickups and the tanks, GM identified and contacted the trucks' previous owners. From the owner of the truck that was struck and caught fire, GM learned that the gas cap was nonstandard. The owner had lost gas caps several times and in the last instance obtained one that did not fit correctly. GM also strongly suspected that the tank had been "topped off" with gasoline prior to the test. (Tanks are designed with 5 gallons of excess space to make topping off impossible with properly functioning fuel pumps.) GM sent the gas tank of the truck to an X-ray lab and a metallurgist to test whether, as NBC correspondent Gillen claimed, the tank was punctured and therefore was responsible for the fire. According to the experts, it was not punctured. GM had therefore amassed considerable data that supported a different theory about the crash results and the *Dateline* segment. The pieces of the puzzle were as follows:

- A possibly topped-off tank
- A faulty fuel cap in the truck involved in the fiery accident
- Rocket engines that flared prior to impact
- Footage indicating that the fire was confined primarily to grass and did not engulf the cab of the pickup
- Fuel tanks that, contrary to NBC claims, had not been punctured

Additionally, GM conducted background checks on NBC's "safety experts" and learned the following:

- The consultant referred to by NBC as "vice president of the Institute for Safety Analysis" had no engineering background but was a former stock-car driver with a BA in Asian studies.
- The second consultant worked as a "safety consultant" for trial lawyers and had worked as a consultant for ABC News in seven segments on auto safety. He majored in industrial design but did not complete college.
- The third was from the Institute for Injury Reduction, a nonprofit organization that tests products for plaintiffs' attorneys. He had no college degree but studied Japanese and had a diploma in Korean from the U.S. Government's Defense Language School.

On Monday, February 1, 1993, GM's executive vice president and general counsel, Harry Pearce, presented these findings to GM's board of directors. When asked how the directors responded, Pearce said, "They were shocked."

In January, GM had sent yet another letter to Robert Read, the *Dateline* producer, this time detailing GM's specific findings. Read responded without informing either NBC President Robert Wright or NBC News President Michael Gartner. In a subsequent letter to Read dated February 2, GM carbon-copied Wright and Gartner, finally bringing the case to the attention of top NBC officials. NBC management responded by having its top public relations advisers and NBC General Counsel Richard Cotton draft a letter from Gartner to GM. The letter asserted three separate times that the NBC story was entirely accurate. "NBC does not believe that any statements made . . . were either false or misleading . . . the *Dateline* report was and remains completely factual and accurate."[33]

On February 4, 1993, an Atlanta jury awarded $101 million in punitive damages and $4.2 million in compensatory damages to the parents of a 17-year-old boy killed in a fiery death in a GM C/K pickup. The parents had argued that the placement of the fuel tank outside the frame of the pickup made it vulnerable to puncturing during a collision. GM's defense in the trial had been that the boy had died instantly during the collision which, the GM attorney argued, occurred at such a high speed that the death could not be blamed on the truck's design.

On Friday, February 5—the morning after the verdict in the liability case and a few days before a scheduled press conference by the CAS—GM management had a weekend to consider some delicate strategic options. One major option was to file a defamation suit against NBC. Defamation was the communication (e.g., by journalists) to a third party (e.g., viewers) of an untrue statement of fact that injures the plaintiff (GM). A second major option was to go public with the

---

[33]*Wall Street Journal*, February 11, 1993.

information it had developed on the *Dateline* segment. With the liability verdict and its aftermath fresh in the news, GM would be taking a significant risk in drawing still more attention to its pickups. Said one Wall Street analyst, "A successful rebuttal won't make anybody go out and buy trucks. The publicity [of an aggressive defense by GM and an attack on GM's critics] can't do anything but harm GM."[34] This perspective reflected the rule of thumb that "any news is bad news" when it involves a major company, a less than perfectly safe product, and a high level of public sensitivity toward product safety. ■

SOURCE: This is an abridged version of a case written by Professor Keith Krehbiel. Royal Bryson provided valuable comments. Copyright © 1994 by the Board of Trustees of the Leland Stanford Junior University. All rights reserved. Reprinted with permission.

Preparation Questions

1. From GM's perspective, what are the nonmarket issues? What are their sources? Where are they in their life cycles?
2. Should GM fight the *Dateline* issue as a matter of principle? Why or why not?
3. What kind of media coverage should GM anticipate over the next week? Does GM have any control or influence over this situation?
4. Should GM file a defamation suit and/or go public with its findings about the *Dateline* segment?
5. In the position of Mr. Gartner at NBC, what would you have done upon receiving GM's letter and findings?

Illinois Power Company (A)

At 8:00 A.M. on November 26, 1979, the executives of Illinois Power Company, a medium-size utility headquartered in Decatur, Illinois, met to decide how to respond to a *60 Minutes* program that had been broadcast the night before.[35]

The *60 Minutes* segment had used Illinois Power's Clinton Nuclear Power Plant as an example of severe cost overruns and excessive delays, which the CBS report said were typical of nuclear power plant construction. In late 1979 public interest in the cost and safety of nuclear power was at a peak; the Three Mile Island nuclear accident had occurred in March 1979.

60 Minutes was among the most popular programs on television and frequently led the list of the most watched television shows. The program, which featured pugnacious reporters Mike Wallace, Dan Rather, Morley Safer, and Harry Reasoner, prided itself on being the advocate of the "average American." Each 1-hour program consisted of three 15- to 18-minute segments or stories. Usually, two of the three weekly stories focused on individual or bureaucratic malfeasance or misfeasance. The program's producers particularly liked to stage interviews during which one of the star reporters and a camera crew would burst unannounced into the office of the person to be interviewed.

The *60 Minutes* segment on Illinois Power featured interviews with three former Illinois Power employees, who claimed the cost overruns and production delays were due to mismanagement. The company believed that the three employees were using the charges as revenge for alleged mistreatment by the company. One employee had been fired; another resigned over wage increases he found unsatisfactory. The former employee who had suggested that *60 Minutes* do the story on Clinton had been denied permission to appear as an expert witness in state regulatory hearings after it was discovered he had falsified his academic credentials and work experience. Nevertheless, CBS featured him as Illinois Power's "sharpest critic."

More troubling to Illinois Power was that Harry Reasoner, who reported the story on the air, appeared to be misstating several key facts that had been discussed with him and explained at length. The story left the strong impression that Illinois Power was mismanaging the construction of the Clinton Nuclear Power Plant and expected its customers to pay higher rates to compensate for this mismanagement. Reasoner stated that the nuclear facility would come on line much later and at a much higher cost than Illinois Power was now predicting.

Illinois Power executives felt betrayed. They had welcomed the *60 Minutes* producer, reporter, and camera crews. Illinois Power had taken one precaution, however; it had filmed everything the *60 Minutes* cameras had filmed on Illinois Power property. Company executives believed they could show with these films that Harry Reasoner had deliberately misrepresented the facts in at least three instances.

Company executives were particularly concerned about the impact such a negative report would have on

---

[34]*Wall Street Journal*, February 8, 1993.
[35]A transcript of the *60 Minutes* segment is found in CBS News, *60 Minutes Verbatim*, Arno Press, New York, 1980, pp. 149–153.

the company's customers ("the residents of one-third of Illinois"), its shareholders, its employees, and its case for a 14 percent rate increase then before the Illinois utility regulatory commission. What could the company do now to counteract whatever damage had been done?

Among the alternatives suggested were to ignore the whole incident, sue CBS for damages (it would be necessary to show deliberate misrepresentation), request equal time under the Fairness Doctrine by petitioning the FCC, and seek a public judgment against CBS from the National News Council, a self-regulatory group of the media that published its deci-sions in the *Columbia Journalism Review*. Illinois Power's management wondered which would be the most effective in controlling the damage to the company, or whether the company ought to consider other alternatives. ■

SOURCE: This case was prepared by Kirk O. Hanson, Senior Lecturer in Business Administration, from publicly available sources as a basis for class discussion rather than to illustrate the effective or ineffective handling of an administrative situation. Copyright © 1981 by the Board of Trustees of the Leland Stanford Junior University. Reprinted by permission. All rights reserved.

Preparation Questions

1. Where is the *60 Minutes* story located in Figure 3-2? What makes it newsworthy?
2. If Illinois Power files a libel suit, under what standard is it likely to be tried? Is Illinois Power likely to win?
3. What should Illinois Power do about the impact of the story on its constituents and its nonmarket environment?

CHAPTER

4

Private Politics

INTRODUCTION

Many nonmarket issues are addressed in public institutions, as considered in Parts II and III of this book, which deal with lawmaking, regulation, and the legal system. The competition between firms and other interests over the resolution of these issues in the context of the institutions of government is called *public politics.* Other nonmarket issues are addressed largely outside, but often in the shadow of, public institutions. These issues are advanced by the strategies of individuals, firms, interest groups, activists, and NGOs and range from direct pressure, as in the case of consumer boycotts, to attempts to influence public sentiment. The competition between a firm and these other groups over the resolution of issues outside of government institutions is called *private politics.*

Private politics can be motivated by self-interest as well as by broader concerns. In some cases it arises because an individual becomes concerned about an issue, as in the instance in Chapter 1 of the person who telephoned Larry King and said that his wife had died from brain cancer caused by radiation from heavy use of a cellular telephone. More often, private politics originates from interest groups, as when U.S. labor unions act to demand higher wages and improved working conditions in the overseas factories supplying the apparel and footwear industries. Similarly, unions helped create and fund the organizations that led the campaign against Wal-Mart, as considered in the Part I integrative case, *Wal-Mart: Nonmarket Pressure and Reputation Risk (A).* Private politics is also initiated by activists, advocacy groups, and NGOs that serve the interests of others in addition to the interests of their members. The causes these individuals, interest groups, and NGOs pursue are important components of the nonmarket environment, and the issues on their agendas are frequently thrust onto the agendas of firms. Understanding their concerns, organization, and strategies is essential for formulating effective strategies to address the issues they advance and the pressures they generate.

Private politics affects the issues, interests, institutions, and information that comprise the nonmarket environment. First, those initiating private politics can identify issues about which management either is unaware or has not understood as important to others, as in the case of the possible health risks from cellular telephone radiation. Similarly, the actions of Greenpeace calling attention to Shell UK's plan to sink the oil storage platform, Brent Spar, in the North Atlantic generated intense private politics in Europe even though the plan had been approved by the UK government. Individuals and interest and activist groups thus play an important role in setting the nonmarket agendas of firms and in advancing issues through their life cycles. Oil companies now involve stakeholders as well as governments in developing disposal plans for oil platforms. Moreover, the issues these groups raise and the concerns they express may point in the direction of more effective and responsible management.

Second, these groups can affect the organization of interests by forming watchdog and advocacy groups and by mobilizing people to work for causes. These groups have been instrumental in advancing the causes of environmental protection, health and safety protection for consumers, and civil and human rights. These organizations are an increasingly important component of the nonmarket environment.

Third, the pressure these groups exert can affect the institutional configuration of the nonmarket environment. In public politics their actions have led to new laws, expanded regulatory authority, court orders, legislative oversight activities, and executive branch initiatives. These groups were the prime movers behind the creation of the Environmental Protection Agency and the Consumer Products Safety Commission, and organized labor worked for the creation of the Occupational Safety and Health Administration. In private politics activists have spurred the formation of private governance organizations such as the Fair Labor Association and the Forest Stewardship Council, which govern the private regulation of labor practices in overseas apparel and footwear factories and in timber harvesting and forest management, respectively. This private regulation has been growing as an alternative to government regulation.

Fourth, individuals, interest groups, and activists provide information that influences public and private politics. Rachel Carson's *Silent Spring* spurred the environmental movement by calling attention to the harmful effects of DDT. Activists at the Earth Island Institute spurred a public outcry and boycotts of tuna products when they produced a film showing dolphins drowning in nets used to catch tuna.[1] The news media plays a major role in disseminating this information, and an important component of private politics strategies is to attract media coverage, as illustrated by the campaign against the apple-ripening chemical Alar considered in Chapter 3.

Regardless of whether these groups are right in their causes, their actions can damage a firm, its reputation, and its constituents. Some products, rightly or wrongly, have been doomed by the actions of activists. Ralph Nader's attacks on the safety of the General Motors Corvair, for instance, contributed to the car's elimination. Activists have been vocal opponents of agricultural biotechnology, causing delays in new products and increased costs. The strength of activist groups varies across countries. The opposition to agricultural biotechnology has remained moderate in the United States as more products have been brought to market without the harmful effects claimed by their critics. Opposition to agricultural biotechnology, however, remains strong in much of Europe. Because of private politics, a major Swiss pharmaceutical company located biotechnology units just over the French border and connected those units by pipeline to its plant just inside Switzerland. In effect, the plant lies on both sides of the border with the biotechnology components located in France.

This chapter first considers the nature of private politics using activist campaigns as an example. The strategies used by interest and activist groups are then considered more generally, followed by a discussion of the organization of these groups. Strategies of firms for dealing with private politics challenges are then considered.

CAMPAIGNS

Activists organize corporate campaigns to advance the issues on their agendas, and a frequent component of a campaign is a boycott. Some boycotts are more symbolic than real, but many attract media and public attention. Boycotts against such companies as Starkist Tuna, General Electric, the Walt Disney Company, Nike, Shell, Citigroup, Boise Cascade, and Coca-Cola have attracted national and international attention. The Walt Disney Company was the subject of several boycotts. The National Hispanic Media Coalition organized a boycott because of Disney's record in hiring Hispanics. The Southern Baptist Convention organized a boycott to protest Disney's decision to extend employee benefits to gay and lesbian domestic partners. International labor groups called for boycotts of Disney toys because of the working conditions in the factories of its Asian suppliers. The Texas State Board of Education sold 1.2 million shares

---

[1]Putnam (1993) provides an analysis of the boycott of H. J. Heinz over the killing of dolphins in conjunction with tuna fishing.

in Disney to protest violence and sexually explicit movies produced by its Miramax Films subsidiary. The Immune Deficiency Foundation called for a boycott of Disney because of its movie *Bubble Boy,* and civil rights groups called for a boycott because of a racially offensive promotion on a radio station owned by Disney.

In the early 1990s General Electric came under attack for its operation of nuclear weapons facilities. A boycott and other pressures were directed at the company by the United Methodist Church, Physicians for Social Responsibility, and INFACT, an activist group that had led the campaign against Nestlé for its marketing of infant formula in developing countries. INFACT produced a documentary film, *Deadly Deception: General Electric, Nuclear Weapons and the Environment,* that won an Academy Award for best documentary in 1992. The award provided the filmmaker an opportunity to criticize General Electric in her acceptance speech, which was broadcast worldwide.

Corporate campaigns such as those against Disney and General Electric target the company directly, but activists are increasingly targeting the markets in which a company operates. Physicians for Social Responsibility claimed that its campaign against General Electric caused physicians to switch purchases of $43 million of medical equipment, such as magnetic resonance imaging machines, from General Electric to other suppliers. General Electric denied that the campaign had any effect, but in 1993 it sold its aerospace division, which included its nuclear weapons business.

The Rainforest Action Network (RAN) now focuses primarily on market campaigns. To stop timber harvesting in old growth forests, RAN first targeted retailers selling lumber and wood products, including Home Depot, Kinko's, and Lowe's, and then targeted home builders. Once it had affected the market for old growth products, it turned its attention to timber companies, beginning with Boise Cascade and moving to Weyerhaeuser.

Boycott targets may also be chosen because of opportunity. Greenpeace used the 2000 Olympics in Australia to launch a boycott against Coca-Cola, which was an official sponsor of the Olympics. The objective was to stop Coca-Cola from using hydrofluorocarbons (HFCs) as a refrigerant in its dispensing machines. Greenpeace Australia produced a downloadable poster under the caption "Enjoy Climate Change" depicting Coke's family of polar bears worriedly sitting on a melting ice cap. Greenpeace urged the public to download the posters and paste them on Coke machines. Activist and interest groups often use both private and public politics strategies, as the Pizza Hut example illustrates.

Do campaigns and boycotts have an effect on either the performance of firms or on their policies? Nearly all targets state that a boycott had no significant effect on their performance, yet some customers do stop purchasing the products of a boycott target. A boycott of Mitsubishi Electric organized by RAN led Circuit City to stop carrying Mitsubishi televisions. The loss of a large retailer could not have helped Mitsubishi sales. Some boycotts have been found to have significant effects. Chavis and Leslie (2008) found that the sale of French wines in the United States decreased significantly as a result of the informal boycott resulting from France's opposition to the invasion of Iraq in the aftermath of September 11. The question thus is better posed in terms of the magnitude of the effect on company performance.

Several studies have measured the stock price performance of companies that were the target of a boycott relative to the stock price performance of companies not subject to a boycott. The empirical evidence is largely inconclusive.[2] Moreover, the effects can depend on the nonmarket issue. Epstein and Schnietz (2002) studied the effect on the stock prices of firms identified as "abusive" by the antiglobalization demonstrations at the 1999 Seattle World Trade Organization meeting. Firms that were identified

---

[2]Davidson, Worrell, and El-Jelly (1995) found that the announcements of 40 boycotts between 1969 and 1991 resulted in a statistically significant decrease in the share price of the targets. Friedman (1985), Pruitt and Friedman (1986), and Pruitt, Wei, and White (1988) found evidence that boycotts significantly reduced the market values of target firms. Koku, Akhigbe, and Springer (1997), however, found that the market values of 54 target firms increased significantly. Teoh, Welch, and Wazzan (1999) found no significant effect of the boycott of South Africa on either U.S. firms or on shares traded on the Johannesburg Stock Exchange. Friedman (1999), Manheim (2001), and Vogel (1978) have studied individual boycotts in more detail.

EXAMPLE

Pizza Hut and Health Insurance Reform

In the summer of 1994 Congress was occupied with Clinton administration proposals to change the health care system. Interest group activity was intense. In July the Health Care Reform Project, an interest group formed by a coalition of organizations led by labor unions, released a report attacking Pizza Hut and McDonald's for providing less health care coverage for their employees in the United States than they provided in other countries.[1] The group sought mandatory employer-provided health insurance and universal coverage. To publicize its campaign, the group held a press conference and placed full-page advertisements in the *New York Times* and the *Washington Post.* The headline read "No Matter How You Slice It ... Pizza Hut Does Not Deliver the Same Health Benefits in America as It Does in Germany and Japan." The group also produced a commercial it planned to show on four New York and Washington television stations. Showing a young man delivering a pizza by bicycle, the commercial said that Pizza Hut provided health coverage for all its employees in Germany and Japan, "but for many workers in America, Pizza Hut pays no health insurance. Zero." Neither the advertisement nor the commercial mentioned McDonald's. The strategy of the interest groups was coordinated with one of its allies in Congress, Senator Edward Kennedy (D-MA), chairman of the Senate Labor Committee, who appeared at the press conference and asked, "What do they have against American workers?" He announced plans to hold committee hearings the next week on the issue and asked Pizza Hut and McDonald's to appear.

Under attack, Pizza Hut first addressed the immediate problem of the television commercial. Its Washington law firm wrote to the television stations pointing out its concerns with the commercial. The letter stated, "If you cause to be broadcast any statement to the effect that Pizza Hut does not offer health care coverage for its employees in the United States, the company will regard that false broadcast as having been made with knowledge of falsity or in reckless disregard of falsity."[2] This thinly veiled threat of a libel lawsuit caused the television stations not to broadcast the advertisement.

Pizza Hut then sought to explain more fully the underlying issue and defend its policies. It indicated that health care coverage was not provided for part-time, hourly employees for the first 6 months of employment, although employees could purchase a basic plan for $11 a month. After 6 months the company paid for a modest supplement to that insurance. Pizza Hut had 120,000 employees who worked 20 hours a week or less, and most of them had health care coverage through their families. Moreover, few part-time workers remained on the job for 6 months. Pizza Hut also explained that health care coverage was mandatory in Germany and Japan and was one of the reasons a pizza that sold for $11 in the United States sold for $19 in Germany and $25 in Japan. Pizza Hut claimed that the cost of a pizza would increase by 10 percent if the plan supported by the interest groups and Senator Kennedy were adopted.

Pizza Hut also had allies in Congress, and its home state senators, Robert Dole (R-KS) and Nancy Kassenbaum (R-KS), defended the company. Speaking on the floor of the Senate, Senator Dole said, "I don't know what company or industry will next be attacked by the White House, the Democratic National Committee or their allies, but from the arguments they use, I know they like their pizzas with a lot of baloney."[3]

Pizza Hut CEO Allan S. Huston appeared before Senator Kennedy's committee and defended the company's record and practices. Choosing to let Pizza Hut take all the heat, McDonald's declined to appear. Committee staffers placed a Big Mac, fries, and a soft drink on the table in front of the empty chair provided for McDonald's CEO. Senator Kennedy attacked the companies for "an unacceptable double standard."

Shortly afterwards, the Clinton administration's health care reform efforts collapsed in disarray, and the Health Care Reform Project closed its doors. Although Pizza Hut had incurred only minor harm, the issue of health care coverage for part-time workers was unlikely to go away. The issue had attracted considerable media attention because of the societal significance of health issues and the attention being given to health care reform. Moreover, organized labor and other interest and activist groups, as well as some members of Congress, would continue to raise the issue—perhaps with different tactics.

[1]Health Care Reform Project, "Do As We Say, Not As We Do," Washington, DC, July 1994.
[2]*New York Times,* July 16, 1994. See the section "Recourse to the Law" in Chapter 3 for the explanation for this language as a basis for a libel lawsuit.
[3]*New York Times,* July 24, 1994.

as environmentally abusive experienced a statistically and economically significant decrease in their share prices, whereas the share prices of firms identified as abusive of human rights were unaffected. Despite the varying evidence, most firms are concerned about the possibility of a boycott not only because of possible lost sales but also because the public attention, frequently under the scrutiny of the media, could harm their brands as well as their reputations and public images.

Many campaigns are designed to threaten a brand or the public face of a firm. RAN does not attempt to organize boycotts because it believes that it is too difficult to demonstrate to a target the effect of a boycott. Instead, in its campaigns RAN focuses on the public face and brand equity of its targets. The goal is to call attention to objectionable practices of the target, casting doubt on the public face the company has created through its public relations and advertising. RAN primarily targets consumer-facing companies with branded products so that consumers can take individual actions against the target. In the chapter case, *Anatomy of a Corporate Campaign: Rainforest Action Network and Citigroup (A)(B),* RAN conducted an aggressive campaign against Citigroup, focusing on its public face, and some consumers cut up their Citibank credit cards and some students pledged not to do business with Citigroup.

Which companies are most susceptible to boycotts or reputation damage? Figure 4-1 identifies characteristics of companies, their products, and their operating environment that make them susceptible. A consumer products company is susceptible because consumers can take action by switching to competing products. This is easiest when switching costs are low, as in the case of gasoline, tuna, or televisions. A company with a brand name is also susceptible because customers can punish it by not buying other products it sells. General Electric experienced this even outside its consumer product lines.

A company whose activities produce harmful externalities such as pollution or a health hazard could be subject to protests from those affected or from advocacy groups that support them. Operating in an interest group–rich environment, as in Europe or the United States, provides a ready set of groups that can initiate private politics. Also, multinational companies must be concerned about the effects of operations in one country that are of concern to interest groups and activists in other countries. Operations in developing countries may encounter fewer organized interest and activist groups, but groups in developed countries closely monitor activities in developing countries. Shell learned this from its decision not to intervene when the Nigerian government executed nine activists, including a Nobel Peace Prize nominee, who were protesting environmental degradation from oil fields operated by Shell. The organization of a company can also increase susceptibility. In a highly decentralized company such as Shell, a subsidiary in one country may not take into account or even be aware of the potential effects of its activities on private politics affecting subsidiaries in other countries.

The characteristics identified in Figure 4-1 can be used in the chapter cases *Shell, Greenpeace, and Brent Spar* and *Nike in Southeast Asia* to identify why the campaigns were successful.

FIGURE 4-1 Susceptibility to Private Politics

- Products
  - consumer products
  - products with low switching costs
  - a brand name that can be damaged
- Operating environment
  - activities that produce harmful externalities
  - operating in an interest group–rich environment
  - multinational/global operations—issues can spill over to other units and countries
  - operating in developing countries
- Organization
  - a decentralized organization, so that external effects, including intracompany, are not naturally considered

PRIVATE OR PUBLIC POLITICS?

The choice between public and private politics is strategic, and activists are increasingly choosing private politics. What can private politics accomplish that public politics cannot? One answer is that private politics can succeed where public politics would face interest group opposition or institutional gridlock.

During the 1970s and 1980s activists primarily focused on public politics, seeking legislation and regulation to compel firms to change their practices. In the 1990s many activist groups recognized that it was difficult to obtain change through government and turned to private politics by directly pressuring firms to change their practices. Commenting on the boycott campaign against ExxonMobil for its stance on climate change, Paul Gilding, former head of Greenpeace, said, "The smart activists are now saying, 'OK, you want to play markets—let's play.' [Lobbying government] takes forever and can easily be counter-lobbied by corporations. No, no, no. They start with consumers at the pump, get them to pressure the gas stations, get the station owners to pressure the companies and the companies to pressure governments. After all, consumers do have choices where they buy their gas, and there are differences now. Shell and BPAmoco (which is also the world's biggest solar company) both withdrew from the oil industry lobby that has been dismissing climate change."[3]

Michael Brune, executive director of RAN, said, "Companies were more responsive to public opinion than certain legislatures were. We felt we could create more democracy in the marketplace than in the government." Democracy in the marketplace means that citizen consumers express in markets their views on the performance of firms. If they object to logging in old growth forests, they can impose their will on the logging companies by refusing to buy old growth products. Moreover, they can refuse to buy from retailers, such as Home Depot, that purchased old growth products, and they could support demonstrations and protests against the retailers. This threat led Home Depot to pledge to change its practices.

Another example is fuel economy standards. When opposition to increased fuel economy standards mounted in Congress, in 2002 the Sierra Club turned to private politics. It began a 3-year campaign to pressure the big three auto manufacturers to increase the fuel economy of their light vehicles. As Carl Pope of the Sierra Club explained, "We're going now to the customers." A number of other activist groups also launched private politics campaigns against automakers and in particular against SUVs. Those groups included the Detroit Project, Earth on Empty, the Evangelical Environmental Network, and RAN.

In many cases activists integrate private and public politics campaigns. To address the issue of fuel economy, the Bluewater Network launched dual campaigns. In private politics it targeted Ford using advertisements, demonstrations, public criticism, and a consumer boycott. In commenting on Ford's planned introduction of its hybrid Escape SUV, executive director Russell Long said, "It's ridiculous for Bill Ford to portray his company as an environmental leader because of the hybrid Escape. Ford's new vehicles create more global warming pollution than any other major auto company."[4] Its public politics campaign focused on legislation in California that would require automakers to improve their fuel economy. Under federal law California is allowed, with approval by the Environmental Protection Agency (EPA), to set pollution standards more stringent than federal standards. The Bluewater Network drafted legislation calling for sharp reductions in pollutants and included carbon dioxide. The only way to appreciably reduce carbon dioxide emissions was to reduce the consumption of fossil fuels, and a major reduction could only be accomplished by reducing the fuel burned in automobiles and trucks. The legislation was enacted and signed into law by the governor, and as indicated in Chapter 1 was the subject of lawsuits by the auto industry. Elisa Lynch of the Bluewater Network said, "We wrote a bill that will stand up well in court." Although the law prevailed in the courts, the EPA denied the state's application for a waiver required to implement standards different from federal standards.

---

[3]*New York Times,* June 2, 2001.
[4]*Los Angeles Times,* no date. Ford had the lowest average mileage of the big three U.S. automobiles.

The Health Care Reform Project campaign against Pizza Hut and McDonald's involved private politics by the Project members and public politics led by its allies in Congress. Both components of the strategy were directed not at initiating or passing legislation but instead were intended to pressure the companies to provide more health care benefits to their part-time employees. A decade later a related campaign was launched against Wal-Mart as considered in the Part I integrative case, *Wal-Mart: Nonmarket Pressure and Reputation Risk (A)*.

In 2003 the AIDS Healthcare Foundation (AHF) launched a public and private politics campaign against GlaxoSmithKline (GSK) to force the company to make its AIDS drugs accessible to developing countries. AHF asked investors, including CalPERS, to pressure GSK to lower its drug prices for developing countries. It filed a lawsuit in the United States challenging GSK's patent on AZT, the first antiretroviral drug. It also filed a complaint in South Africa challenging GSK's pricing practices and a lawsuit in California alleging that GSK engaged in false advertising of its AIDS drugs. AHF lobbied the California state government to put pressure on GSK and its pricing policies. AHF organized protests and demonstrations against GSK in the United States and barred company personnel from its AIDS outpatient facilities in the United States.

ACTIVIST STRATEGIES

Activists choose nonmarket strategies just as firms do. They seek to pressure firms to change their practices, and although some have a large membership that could be mobilized for action against a target, most have limited resources and a small membership base. Activists thus face a collective action problem, and a campaign serves as a coordinating mechanism for those with concerns about the practices of firms. To elicit support from the public, citizens must learn about the issue of concern to the activist and about the firm's activities. The news media plays a central role by providing information about the issue, the firm's practices, and the target. Activists often take out advertisements in newspapers and magazines as part of their attempt to inform the public, but they also rely on "earned" media—that is, media coverage of the campaign itself. Information provision is intended to both harm the target and create a degree of common knowledge among members of the public to mitigate a free-rider problem through coordination; that is, eliciting participation by the public. The chapter case *Anatomy of a Corporate Campaign: Rainforest Action Network and Citigroup (A)(B)* illustrates RAN's approach to influencing a target.

The shared concerns of activists and elements of the public must be turned into action. This requires a strategy. The two basic strategies of activists are directly pressuring firms through private politics and working through public institutions using public politics. Direct pressure is applied by calling attention to the activities of a firm as in the Citigroup case. Activists often refer to this strategy as "naming and shaming." The activists identify a firm that has an objectionable activity and provide information to the public about the harm from that activity. In the case of Citigroup the activity was funding projects in developing countries that harmed or threatened ecosystems. Shaming involved showing photographs of environmental damage done by the projects financed.

The objective of shaming is to harm the target firm by damaging its brand, its reputation, or the morale of its employees. During the campaign on sweatshops Nike concluded that the criticisms of the company had made its advertising and marketing people more cautious and less creative. More often, shaming is believed to threaten a brand or reputation. The information provided is typically not verifiable by the public, but it can have credibility because of the "trust gap" discussed in Chapter 19. Surveys have shown that the public places considerably more trust in NGOs than in business firms, which makes both shaming more effective and an effective response by the firm more difficult. Moreover, what gives a firm strength in the marketplace can be a liability in the nonmarket environment. That is, a strong brand can mean that the potential damage from a campaign is greater.

The trust gap can create an asymmetry in the effectiveness of NGO and firm strategies. Because the public tends to trust NGOs more than firms, negative information provided by an NGO can have more impact on the development of an issue than can information provided by the target. Using the terminology of Chapter 3, one negative message by an NGO can offset several positive messages by a firm. Thus, not only can the reputation of a firm be harmed by an activist, but it can be difficult to repair the damage. That is, the trust gap can mean that the firm receives little credit for the good it does. As indicated in Chapter 1, environmental activists targeting Toyota because of its production of the Tundra and its opposition to higher fuel economy standards gave the company little credit for the Prius.

Shaming may involve attracting the media to the issue, communicating through community groups, or attempting to reach opinion leaders and public officeholders. The media may be attracted by events such as demonstrations, hanging banners on buildings, or press conferences at which studies are released or allegations made. Some activists have access to a network of organizations through which their concerns can be communicated. Others may enlist the aid of public officeholders, such as Senator Kennedy in the Pizza Hut example.

Pressure can be applied through centralized and decentralized activities. The campaign against Pizza Hut was centralized through labor unions. As an example of a decentralized strategy, the Emergency Planning and Community Right-to-Know Act requires the federal government to publish annually the Toxics Release Inventory, which lists for every plant in the country the emissions of over 300 possibly hazardous chemicals. Using data from the Inventory, the Natural Resources Defense Council holds an annual press conference and releases a study of the nation's biggest polluters. The Inventory and the media coverage alert local community groups to the emissions in their areas. Local groups, using private politics, then pressure firms in their areas to reduce their emissions. Partly as a result of these activities, several major companies, including DuPont and Dow Chemical, have reduced emissions below the levels required by EPA regulations.

The Internet has helped activists coordinate their actions and mount their campaigns on a broader and decentralized basis. Carol Browner, former head of the Environmental Protection Agency, said, "Environmental groups have become truly sophisticated in using the Web to move information to millions of people literally overnight, and to attack companies on a global scale."[5] The coordinated antiglobalization protests against international institutions that began in 1999 in Seattle against the World Trade Organization and continued against the International Monetary Fund, World Bank, and G-8 are ample evidence. The Internet has also become important in fundraising for NGOs, as the success of MoveOn had demonstrated. MoveOn wanted to raise $25,000 to take out an issue advertisement and sent out an appeal on the Internet. It received $400,000, launching the Internet as an important source of activist funding.

A first-mover advantage is often available to an activist. Moving first typically allows the activist both to attract the media with an event and frame the issue by raising concerns or making allegations about the target. Moving first can also provide an advantage if surprise leads the target to make tactical mistakes in responding to the activist's campaign. RAN begins its campaigns with a letter to the CEO of its target, often followed shortly thereafter by a demonstration, or a banner hang, or speaking at the target's annual meeting.

Activist groups also use their standing before courts, legislatures, and administrative organizations to petition, sue, and advocate action. Environmental legislation and certain health and safety legislation were written to give citizens the right to petition regulatory agencies for action and sue those agencies if they fail to act. In the Chapter 3 case, *General Motors: Like a Rock? (A)*, the Center for Auto Safety petitioned NHTSA to recall General Motors pickup trucks with side-mounted gas tanks. As illustrated in the Pizza Hut example, many activist groups have as allies legislators and

---

[5]*New York Times*, September 9, 2001.

officials in executive branch agencies who can influence the nonmarket agendas of firms. Access to public institutions is a lever activists often use to pressure firms to negotiate on issues. The public politics strategies used by activists are similar to those used by firms, as considered in Part II of this book.

Activists also use shareholder rights as a component of their strategies and campaigns. The most common tactic is to question the company at its annual meeting, and a more formal approach is to file a shareholder resolution with the Securities and Exchange Commission. Shareholder resolutions are filed on a variety of issues, including human and animal rights, diversity, community issues, the environment, and product-specific issues.[6] These resolutions are rarely successful but instead are intended as a component of a private politics strategy to put pressure on a firm and its reputation.

Many groups utilize litigation. A lawsuit may serve as a bargaining lever or may be used to force action by the target. The Natural Resources Defense Council initially followed an aggressive litigation strategy to spur enforcement of environmental regulations. As a means of obtaining lending commitments in their communities, community groups coordinated by ACORN routinely file lawsuits to block acquisitions by federally chartered banks.

Some activists and NGOs choose to work directly with firms and industries to improve practices. Two prominent such groups are Conservation International and Environmental Defense. Other groups, such as RAN and the Bluewater Network, prefer negative campaigns. RAN believes that praising a company that has good environmental policies has little effect in inducing other companies to adopt similar policies. Instead, negative campaigns can catch the attention of the public, the media, and the target.

These two approaches to achieving change can leave activist groups on opposite sides of an issue. Forest products are certified by independent third parties to have come from forests managed with certain social, environmental, and conservation practices. Competing certification systems have been established. The Forest Stewardship Council (FSC) was supported by RAN, Greenpeace, the Sierra Club, and other NGOs. The Sustainable Forestry Institute (SFI) was developed by the timber industry in cooperation with Conservation International and the Nature Conservancy. The groups backing the FSC criticized the SFI as letting the fox guard the henhouse.

Advocacy Science

A frequently used strategy of activists is to conduct a policy study or scientific investigation to call attention to an issue. Even when it involves only secondary sources, this practice of "advocacy science" can advance the activists' cause. As in the Alar case considered in Chapter 3, a study can attract the media, and hence the public, which adds a degree of credibility to the claims of the activists. It can also attract sympathetic legislators, who can provide support, introduce bills, and hold hearings at which activists can testify. Advocacy science is most effective if it can be coordinated with other actions to prolong attention to the issue and provide a series of newsworthy events.

Activists may also seize the release of studies by others to advance their causes, as illustrated by the fish farm activism example.

Target Selection

An important component of a private politics campaign is the selection of a target. Activists typically seek to change practices in an industry, but targeting an individual firm rather than an industry is preferred because the threat of harm is concentrated. Targeting is largely driven by strategic calculations, and activists frequently do not target a company directly but instead target its value chain, that is, its suppliers or customers. Target selection strategies vary widely. Activists sometimes target "worst offenders." For example, environmental activists concluded that ExxonMobil was the most obstinate opponent of measures to address global climate change. As a result,

---

[6]See Rehbein, Waddock, and Graves (2004) for a study of shareholder resolutions and the objectives of the groups filing the resolutions.

EXAMPLE

Fish Farm Activism

In 2004 a study published in the journal *Science* reported higher levels of polychlorinated biphenyls (PCBs) and dioxin in salmon raised in fish farms than in salmon caught in the wild.[1] The concentrations exceeded Environmental Protection Agency (EPA) standards. David Carpenter, of the University of Albany, one of the authors of the study, said, "We're not telling people not to eat fish. . . . We're telling them to eat less farmed salmon."[2] Wild salmon cost $15 a pound compared to $5 a pound for farmed salmon.

The Environmental Working Group and Center for Environmental Health (CEH) filed a notice with the State of California of their intent to file a lawsuit against fish farms, producers, and retailers for failing to notify consumers of the PCBs and dioxin. Michael Green, executive director of CEH, said, "We believe it's the responsibility of these companies to ensure the fish they sell is not contaminated with toxic chemicals. Our goal is to challenge them to change their practices so their fish is safe to eat."[3]

The tolerance level for PCBs set by the Food and Drug Administration was 2000 parts per billion, which was 50 times greater than the level in fish farm salmon. Also, "'The study tested salmon raw, with the skin on. Removing the skin and grilling it removes a significant amount of PCBs, dioxins and other pollutants stored in fish fat,' the FDA said."[4] "We do think the levels [in farmed salmon] should be lowered," said Terry Troxell, an FDA division director and toxicologist. "However, we don't believe there is a public health concern with the levels seen here. . . . Our message for consumers is not to alter their consumption of wild or farmed salmon."[5] The guidelines used in the research study were set by the EPA for recreationally caught fish, and the FDA standards were for commercially caught fish. The EPA stood by its guidelines.

Salmon are an important source of omega-3 fatty acids, which reduce the risk of heart disease. Salmon are also low in mercury. Martha Daviglus of the Northwestern University Medical School observed, "The benefits (of salmon) in my opinion are way over the risks of having cancer."[6] A Purdue University food toxicologist, Charles Santere, criticized the study for ignoring the benefits of salmon: "I would calculate 6,000 people getting cancer over their lifetime, that's an approximation, versus potentially saving the lives of 100,000 individuals every year."[7] He added, "In my view, the study says we should be eating more farmed salmon."[8] Eric Rimm of the Harvard School of Public Health commented, "To alarm people away from fish because of some potential, at this point undocumented, risk of long-term cancer—that does worry me."[9]

---

[1] The study was financed by the Pew Charitable Trust.
[2] *Associated Press,* January 8, 2004.
[3] *Vancouver Sun,* January 23, 2004.
[4] *Associated Press,* January 8, 2004.

[5] *Oakland Tribune,* January 10, 2004.
[6] *Philadelphia Inquirer,* January 21, 2004.
[7] *Los Angeles Times,* January 9, 2004.
[8] *The Times (London),* January 9, 2004.
[9] Associated Press, January 8, 2004.

European activists led a boycott of Esso products. In contrast, hoping that they would be responsive, activists sometimes target firms, such as BP and Starbucks, that have positioned themselves as socially responsible and environmentally friendly. Argenti (2004, pp. 110–111) explained the decision by the activist organization Global Exchange to target Starbucks to sell fair trade coffee: "Truly socially responsible companies are actually more likely to be attacked by activist NGOs than those that are not. . . . Our interviews with Global Exchange suggested that Starbucks was a better target for the fair trade issue because of its emphasis on social responsibility, as opposed to a larger company without a socially responsible bent." Starbucks had revealed itself as a soft target. King and Soule (2007) studied the firms targeted in social and union protests and concluded "that protestors tend to target large, weakly performing firms. Firms that have been targeted by protestors in the past are more likely to be protested against in the future."

Sometimes activists target the most well-known company or largest company in an industry. In the campaign against the prevailing labor practices in overseas apparel and footwear plants, activists targeted Nike. RAN chooses targets with a strong retail presence, brand identity, and a public face that could be damaged by a campaign. RAN chose Citigroup not only because of these characteristics but also because it was the industry leader and the worst offender from its perspective. Because it was the industry leader, success with Citigroup could ripple throughout the industry.

Several empirical studies have attempted to identify the characteristics of firms that make them more likely to be targeted. Using data on environmental campaigns Lenox and Eesley (2008) found that large firms, firms with greater toxic emissions, and firms that are more advertising intensive are more likely to be targeted. They also found that campaigns against larger firms and firms with higher emissions are more aggressive, and the target was more likely to concede to the activist demands the higher the emissions.[7] Rehbein, Waddock, and Graves (2004) found the firms with worse environment performance and product-related concerns had a higher probability of being targeted with a shareholder resolution. Hendry (2006) conducted interviews with five environmental NGOs and concluded that larger firms and firms closer to the consumer are more likely to be targeted, as are firms with a greater environmental impact. These studies are consistent with the factors identified in Figure 4-1.

In its global climate change campaign RAN chose as its target Ford rather than General Motors, even though GM had shown greater opposition to higher fuel economy standards. RAN's rationale was that (1) Ford had the lowest fleet fuel economy of the U.S. automakers. (2) Ford had a primary brand in the United States, whereas GM sold vehicles under a larger number of domestic brands (Chevrolet, Buick, Oldsmobile, Pontiac, Cadillac, GMC, Hummer, Saturn, and Saab). Thus, Ford's brand equity was a clearer target. (3) CEO and Chairman Bill Ford had been a supporter of the environmental movement and was thought to be sympathetic to environmental causes. A campaign would provide an opportunity to go further by embracing higher fuel economy. (4) Ford had broken its promise and announced that it would be unable to meet its fuel economy goal for SUVs. (5) Ford had been targeted by other environmental activist groups, including the Bluewater Network and the Sierra Club, and RAN's campaign would add to the pressure.

The Coastal Alliance for Aquaculture Reform of Vancouver, British Columbia sought reductions in ocean pollution from salmon farms that used floating nets in the ocean and decided to target a retailer that sold farmed salmon rather than the local salmon farmers themselves. The Alliance chose Safeway because it was one of the few grocery chains that operated in both Canada and the United States and because of its proclaimed policy of being a good corporate citizen. The group decided to take out a large advertisement in the *New York Times,* since 85 percent of the farmed salmon produced in British Columbia were sold in the United States and that is where most of Safeway's customers were. The ad featured dead seals, sea lice, and salmon feces under the heading "Ingredients for extinction," playing on Safeway's "Ingredients for life" advertising campaign.[8]

Activists also target individuals in both their personal and professional roles. Attention typically focuses on those perceived as influential and possibly influenceable. RAN directed attention to Citigroup CEO Sandy Weill by putting his picture in advertisements and on posters, and schoolchildren sent him valentines asking him to stop Citigroup's financing of environmentally destructive projects. Pro-choice demonstrators participating in the National Organization of Women's nationwide boycott picketed Domino's Pizza outlets, claiming that the chain opposed abortion rights. Although Domino's Pizza had no policy on abortion, its owner, Thomas S. Monaghan, had made a personal contribution of $50,000 to the Committee to End Tax-Funded Abortions.

A Generic Strategy of Activists

Although some campaign activities may be coercive, particularly when an individual is the target, the above examples show that potential targets must anticipate the actions of activist groups and be prepared to deal with the issues they place on the firm's

---

[7]For a broader set of campaigns Eesley and Lenox (2008) report results consistent with their study of environmental campaigns.
[8]*Globe and Mail,* June 23, 2007.

FIGURE 4-2 Activists' Generic Strategy

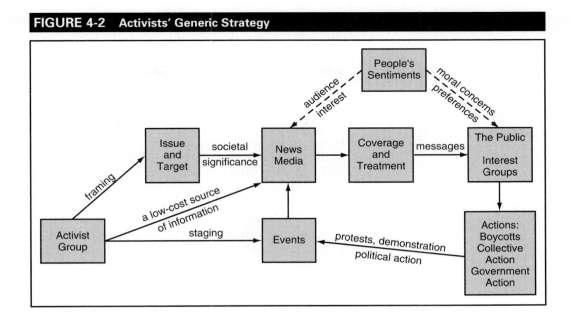

agenda.[9] Figure 4-2 characterizes a generic strategy used by many activist groups in advancing the issues on their agendas. This characterization draws on the role of the news media in informing the public about issues, as considered in Chapter 3. The activist group first identifies an issue such as health insurance or fuel economy and selects a target such as Pizza Hut or Ford. The activist group may have a first-mover advantage and frame the issue by identifying its societal significance and the company's role in the issue. The audience interest in an issue is determined by people's sentiments, and those sentiments may be based on moral concerns, as in the case of workers without health care insurance. To attract the news media, the activists may orchestrate events. The activists also seek to become a low-cost source of information for the journalists. For example, Greenpeace has photographers and camera crews that broadcast its actions worldwide. When media coverage is difficult to attract, some activist groups take out advertisements in newspapers.

People's responses to this strategy depend on their sentiments and concerns about the issue. The hope of the activists is that individuals and interest groups will take action in the form of protests, boycotts, and collective action, which may attract further news media coverage. In addition, government officials may be attracted to the issue. Greenpeace's actions in the chapter case, *Shell, Greenpeace, and Brent Spar,* attracted the support of motorists, labor unions, and government officials. The basic strategy of the activists thus is to frame the issue to attract the interest of the public and the news media and induce people and government officeholders to take actions that give the issue a life of its own.

ACTIVIST ORGANIZATIONS

Activists and Their Organizations

Activism can be a means of furthering interests, as when a labor union leads a boycott of a company whose workers it seeks to organize, as in the Part I integrative case on Wal-Mart. Or, a union may pressure companies regarding wages in their suppliers' factories in Asia with the objective of reducing the competitiveness of imports that threaten union jobs in the United States. For some, activism provides training for political office or for advancement in the network of interest groups participating in

---

[9]Baron and Diermeier (2007) provide a formal theory of activist campaigns and firms' nonmarket strategies.

public policy processes. For others, an activist group provides a forum to express personal visions. Most activists, however, are motivated by concerns about specific issues. Some are concerned about an environmental or health issue or about the well-being of workers in factories in developing countries. Some are concerned about human and civil rights. Some advocate specific policies such as higher fuel economy, whereas others see activism as a means of advancing a broader social agenda to reform corporate conduct.

The nonmarket environment is populated by thousands of interest and activist groups, although some of them have only brief life spans. Because these groups shape the nonmarket environment of business and the agendas of firms, managers must be aware of their capabilities, networks, and agendas. A number of activist groups were founded in association with Ralph Nader. These include the nucleus organizations: Center for Study of Responsive Law, U.S. Public Interest Research Group, Corporate Accountability Research Group, and Essential Information.[10]

Another set of activist organizations was spawned by David Brower, former executive director of the Sierra Club, who founded the Earth Island Institute (EII). Organizations founded through EII include the International Rivers Network and RAN. Activist organizations frequently form coalitions to advance particular issues. Antiglobalization activists have a broad network coordinated over the Internet and are capable of demonstrating wherever international economics organizations convene. The Ruckus Society provides training camps for participants in demonstrations and campaigns, and RAN contracts with Ruckus to supplement its own training camps. For demonstrations, protests, and other actions, RAN relies on four national networks of student organizations: Free The Planet, the Student Environmental Action Coalition, Students Transforming and Resisting Corporations, and the Sierra Student Coalition.

Activist organizations such as these are important elements of the nonmarket environment. These groups are often staffed by dedicated people pursuing a cause they view as just or at least opportune. They are also an important source of information for citizens, politicians, and the media.

Greenpeace

Greenpeace International has 2.8 million members from over 100 countries, offices in 40 countries, and a worldwide income of €177 million in 2006. Greenpeace began in 1971 with a high-profile effort to stop nuclear testing in the Aleutian Islands, and its most widely known incident occurred in 1985 when French commandos sank the Greenpeace ship *Rainbow Warrior* in New Zealand, where it was attempting to block French nuclear testing. That incident caused membership in the United States to climb to 1.2 million in 1991. Because of Greenpeace's opposition to the Persian Gulf War and the successes of the environmental movement, such as the ban on hunting whales, U.S. membership declined to 400,000 in 1997. Nevertheless, Greenpeace remains one of the most formidable environmental activist organizations, particularly in Europe.

Greenpeace has eight campaigns: climate change, toxic chemicals, nuclear power, oceans, genetic engineering, ancient forests, peace and disarmament, and sustainable trade. Internally, Greenpeace has two competing factions. The rubber suits argue for continued emphasis on high-profile, dramatic actions to call attention to issues. The technocrats argue for participation in policy processes and the search for alternative solutions to environmental problems. For example, Greenpeace supported development of a new, environmentally safe cooling system for refrigerators, which it argued should be adopted as an alternative to current HFC-based refrigerators. Its boycott of Coca-Cola in conjunction with the 2000 Olympics led to an announcement by the company, along with McDonald's and Unilever, that it would eliminate the use of HFCs in refrigeration by the 2004 Athens Olympics. The chapter case, *Shell, Greenpeace, and Brent Spar*, focuses on another of Greenpeace's high-profile actions.

---

[10]Griffin (1987) presents Nader's approach of forming public interest groups on college campuses.

RAN is a tax-exempt organization, and contributions are tax deductible for the donor.[11] The Sierra Club is also tax-exempt, but contributions are not tax deductible because the Club engages in political activities, such as lobbying and endorsing candidates. In 2001 the Sierra Club spent $370,000 on outside lobbyists, and in addition 9 other internal lobbyists and 11 staff lobbied. The Sierra Club Political Committee was a "hard money" PAC, and the Sierra Club Educational Fund raised soft money contributions.[12]

INTERACTING WITH ACTIVIST ORGANIZATIONS

Assessment

Because the nonmarket environment is populated by interest and activist groups, firms must develop approaches to dealing with these groups. Figure 4-3 highlights several basic steps successful firms have taken. First, a firm must assess its position and any possible private politics challenges to that position. This assessment begins by answering the question of what is demanded of the firm by the activists and, more importantly, by the public. A firm like McDonald's has a major public presence, making it the subject of a wide set of demands, as identified in the Chapter 1 case, *The Nonmarket Environment of McDonald's*. The demands made on an investment banking firm or consulting firm are much more limited.

The next step is to assess vulnerability to a private politics campaign. This involves assessing not only the firm's own vulnerability but also the vulnerability of those in its value chain. The determinants of vulnerability are identified in Figure 4-1 and are the same as those used by activists in selecting their targets.

It is also important to assess the extent of public support for the activists' agendas. This depends on the issue as well as the public. Agricultural biotechnology meets stronger opposition in Europe than the United States, and in the United States milk from cows treated with BST has stronger opposition than bioengineered soybeans. A number of firms have established forums with activist groups for exchanging information and viewpoints on issues. Firms generally prefer to interact with more moderate groups and avoid those that emphasize confrontation. Some interactions can lead to cooperative efforts to resolve problems, as in the McDonald's and Environmental Defense episode discussed later in the chapter. On some issues, however, firms fight the activists when they are confident that they are both right and can win the fight. In some cases, such as that of Nike and Disney, firms have underestimated the resolve of activists.

If a firm is potentially vulnerable, the next step is to consider whether it is possible to forestall a possible campaign through self-regulation, by working with constructive NGOs, or by making public commitments to new policies. Interacting with an outside group can provide benefits, particularly when the group has expertise. When it considered establishing oil operations in Iran, Shell met with Amnesty International to discuss how it might handle human rights matters in the country. On some issues firms

---

FIGURE 4-3   Addressing the Activist Environment

- Identify the relevant interest groups and activist organizations in your market and nonmarket environments.
- Understand their agenda, preferences, and capabilities.
- Understand the broader public support for their agenda.
- Consult with them on important issues; a number of companies have established regular forums for exchanging information and views.
- Cooperate when that is beneficial.
- Fight when you are right and can win—but be careful.

---

[11]The organization and overall strategy of RAN is considered in the case *Strategic Activism: The Rainforest Action Network*, Case No. P-44, Graduate School of Business, Stanford University.
[12]"Political Finance, The Newsletter," September 2002.

may view an NGO as part of the solution. This has become common on environmental issues in particular, as considered in Chapter 11. When partnering with an NGO, firms frequently prefer science-based NGOs with reputations for working with companies. Environmental Defense, Conservation International, and the World Wildlife Fund are frequent partners of companies. In some cases the formation of new organizations may be warranted. Staples joined with NatureServe, Conservation International, and the Nature Conservancy to form the Forest and Biodiversity Conservation Alliance. Major global banks worked with Conservation International to develop the Equator Principles for governing the financing of development projects.

When a firm is challenged by an activist group or NGO, the specific issues of concern must be evaluated. The frameworks developed in the previous chapters may be used to assess the challenge. Management should assess where the issue is in its life cycle and how rapidly it is progressing. Often the issues generated by activists and interest groups are early in their life cycles, and thus firms have an opportunity to affect their progress. The next step involves identifying other potentially interested parties and assessing how likely they are to become active on the issue. As indicated in Figure 4-2, activists may attempt to bring the issue to the attention of the public and government officials through media strategies. The theory of the news media presented in Chapter 3 can be used to assess how the media is likely to cover and treat the issue. Assessing the effectiveness of alternative strategies is often difficult when the issue is the subject of media and public attention, and that attention may advance an issue quickly along its life cycle. In the case of a boycott, the firm must assess whether customers and the public are likely to be aware of the issue and sympathetic to the position of the activists. Sympathy, however, does not necessarily translate into action, so the likelihood that individuals will actually respond must be assessed.

Many firms choose to meet with activist groups to show their concern, explain the steps being taken to address the issue, or indicate the complexities involved in addressing it. Meetings can also help the firm understand the motivations of the activists and how likely they are to persist in their efforts. When targeted by RAN, Citigroup quickly initiated discussions. Developing understanding and trust was difficult, however, because Citigroup found that it was not on the same wavelength as RAN. Citigroup eventually hired as a facilitator a former member of Greenpeace who subsequently had earned an MBA. In its meetings with RAN, Weyerhaeuser also used the services of a facilitator.

Strategy and Negotiations

Determining the most effective strategy requires understanding the nature and strength of the activists, the concerns that motivate them, the likelihood of media coverage, the likely support for the issue among consumers and the public, how much damage the activist could cause, how central the issue is to their agenda, and whether they are led by professionals or amateurs. Professionals are more difficult to co-opt, but they may be more practical as well. With limited resources, activists and interest groups must determine which issues to address, and they may abandon an issue that appears to be unwinnable or requires too much of their available resources.

When confronted with private nonmarket action, a natural reaction is to be defensive. A better response is to evaluate the claims and demands made by the activists and determine whether they have merit. In some cases a firm may conclude that the activist's position is correct. RAN targeted Kinko's as part of its Old Growth Campaign, and within a few weeks received a letter from Kinko's stating that RAN's demands were consistent with Kinko's environmental policies. In disbelief, RAN called Kinko's to argue for its demands. Kinko's was surprised, since its letter stated that it agreed with RAN—Kinko's would stop sourcing supplies from old growth forests.

McDonald's faced a major solid-waste disposal problem, and when invited by Environmental Defense (ED) to discuss the problem, it accepted. The result was a voluntary working arrangement with ED to develop an action plan that included waste reduction, recycling, and substitute packaging. The arrangement provided McDonald's with fresh ideas for addressing its waste disposal problem. This cooperative project is considered in more detail in Chapter 11, which also considers a cooperative project between Federal Express and Environmental Defense.

If the interactions with an activist group reach the point of bargaining over the resolution of the issue, a firm must assess the benefits and costs of alternative resolutions. It is also important to determine how an agreement will be monitored and how misunderstandings that might subsequently develop will be resolved. A firm also must assess whether its competitors will follow suit or whether the playing field will become uneven. Many firms prefer that the playing field be level, with their competitors adopting the same policies for dealing with the issue.

An important component of a strategy for addressing a private politics campaign is to shore up the support of a firm's employees, some of whom may be sympathetic with the demands made by the activists. During the Old Growth Campaign, a Home Depot employee gave RAN the intercom code used in all its stores. RAN's staff and others went into stores, entered the intercom code, and recorded messages such as "Lumber from old growth forests is on sale on Aisle 3," or "Tropical lauan from the habitat of the orangutan and Sumatran tiger on sale on Aisle 4." The intercom system provided an opportunity to review a message before it was broadcast. Activists thus could be gone with their shopping carts before the message was broadcast or could be in the next aisle recording another message, making it difficult for Home Depot personnel to find them. This was repeated by dozens of activists in stores across the United States.

In the Old Growth Campaign Weyerhaeuser was targeted by RAN after Boise Cascade had agreed to stop harvesting old growth timber. After an initial demonstration in Seattle and speaking at Weyerhaeuser's annual meeting, RAN paused its campaign as it prepared for a series of actions against the company later in the year. During the pause Weyerhaeuser published in its employee newsletter a lengthy interview with the executive responsible for sustainable forestry and for meeting with RAN. She explained the company's position and also warned of the actions that might be taken against the company. The objective was to protect employee morale by explaining the extensive steps the company was already taking to protect forests and manage them in an environmentally sound manner.

Negotiations with activists can be voluntary, as in the case of McDonald's decision to join with ED to address solid-waste problems. In many cases, however, the objectives of the activists and the interests of the firm are in conflict. In such cases, negotiations between the activists and the firm may be required to resolve the issue. Often negotiations take place in the shadow of threats. Examples of negotiations are the OnBank example and the chapter case on RAN and Citigroup. RAN and Citigroup discussed the issue for over 2 years with neither making any concessions.

In the OnBank example the activists had a one-shot opportunity—the required approval by the Federal Reserve Bank—to extract concessions from the bank. This made it relatively easy for the bank to "buy off" the activists, and because the bank had a strong incentive to resolve the issue and complete the merger, an agreement could be reached. RAN and Citigroup did not have a one-shot opportunity, and the discussions and negotiations were lengthy.

In cases where the stakes are high and monitoring of the firm's actions is difficult, the parties may require more than a simple agreement. To resolve issues of working conditions in factories in Southeast Asia, activists and footwear and apparel companies formed a private regulatory organization, the Fair Labor Association (FLA), to monitor working conditions in suppliers' factories. The FLA is considered in more detail in Chapter 23, but in brief it is a private governance organization established to maintain the agreement between the companies and the activists. The FLA has no enforcement powers, but it has informational powers stemming from its authority to inspect the working conditions in overseas factories and release its findings to the public.

To monitor its agreement with Home Depot, RAN used local volunteers. With some training it is possible to distinguish lumber from old growth trees from lumber from younger trees. Volunteers then walked through Home Depot aisles visually checking the lumber and reporting to RAN on their findings. RAN's only enforcement mechanism, however, was the threat to relaunch its campaigns against the company.

EXAMPLE

Negotiating with Activists: OnBank[1]

In response to charges that some financial institutions limited lending in inner-city neighborhoods, Congress enacted the Community Reinvestment Act (CRA). The CRA required federally chartered banks to lend in the communities in which their depositors lived. The Home Mortgage Disclosure Act (HMDA) required banks to report their mortgage lending by census tract. When two banks announced a merger, activist groups frequently seized the opportunity to challenge the merger. The groups asserted that the merging banks had not complied with the CRA, and they backed that assertion with data on mortgage lending by census tract filed in compliance with the HMDA.[2]

OnBank announced it would acquire another local bank, Merchants National Bank & Trust. When an inner-city resident's application to refinance his mortgage was rejected by OnBank, he turned to a community organization. The organization examined OnBank's lending record and found that it had seldom made loans in the community, had no branches in the inner city, and refused to participate in the city's Syracuse Housing Partnership. Merchants, however, had four branches in the inner city, participated in the Housing Partnership, and made significantly more loans in the inner city. Community organizations feared that the acquisition might result in Merchants operating as OnBank did. The community organizations began a letter-writing campaign to state and fed-

eral regulators calling attention to OnBank's lending record. OnBank countered with data showing that its record compared favorably with other banks in the state of New York. OnBank received endorsements from local organizations such as the United Way and the Urban League.

The community organizations gave OnBank a list of 26 concerns and proposed that they and the bank meet. The two sides met to discuss the issues, but the bank was unwilling to conclude an agreement. Meanwhile, OnBank was negotiating with state regulators, and when the state approved the acquisition, the community groups protested and attracted considerable media coverage. The acquisition still required approval by the Federal Reserve Bank, and the protests led to a second meeting at which regulators were present as observers. Little progress was made until the bank agreed to participate in a number of smaller working groups to address specific issues. The smaller groups made rapid progress, and with a threat of direct action against the bank and federal approval still pending, the bank and the community organizations reached an agreement to increase lending in the inner city.[3] The threat of direct action against the bank, the required regulatory approval, and the reporting of lending data by census tract provided the opportunity to pressure OnBank and obtain lending commitments.

---

[1]This example is based on an article in the *Wall Street Journal*, September 22, 1992.
[2]In response to complaints by banks the CRA was relaxed in 2005 for banks with assets under $1 billion.

[3]This process is repeated throughout the nation. Community organizations have formed an organization, the Association of Community Organizations for Reform Now (ACORN), that helps local organizations intervene in the bank merger approval process.

Challenging the Activists

The demands made in a campaign often are unreasonable or too costly to meet, and firms resist or fight back. Some firms decide that they will agree to disagree with the activist and bear whatever pressure the activist can muster. A target of a campaign may also fight back. This may involve filing a lawsuit against the activist organization. BP, for example, filed a lawsuit against Greenpeace as a result of its boarding a drilling rig under tow to an exploration location. A lawsuit, however, carries the risk of creating a second media story.

When targeted by RAN, Boise Cascade wrote to all of RAN's donors and wrote to the Internal Revenue Service challenging its tax status. This only generated sympathy for RAN and its cause, and Boise Cascade subsequently conceded to RAN's demands. Many firms, when opposing an activist campaign, choose not to attack the activist group but instead provide information about the issues in question in the hope of weakening public support for the campaign. A target may invest in reputation management by providing positive information about its record and making sure that employees are on board. Targets may also develop an alternative organization. The timber industry established the Sustainable Forest Initiative (SFI) to implement forest management standards that were more practical and less costly than those of the activist-backed Forest Stewardship Council (FSC).[13] One concern about the FSC has been that it cannot credibly commit not to ratchet up its sustainability standards nor can firms that accept its standards have a voice in the decision, since they are neither members nor are they represented.

In some cases, a firm may change the boundaries of the organization. Boise Cascade eventually agreed to RAN's demands, but doing so was not costly because it was in the process of selling its entire timber operations to a private equity firm and becoming a consumer products company. A number of cosmetics and pharmaceutical companies stopped animal testing of their products because of protests and violence by PETA and other animal rights organizations. Some of those companies farmed out their testing to independent companies, such as Huntingdon Life Sciences, which has become the subject of an intense and at times violent campaign by activists opposed to animal testing. SHAC (Stop Huntingdon Animal Cruelty) has also targeted pharmaceutical companies that use Huntingdon. SHAC picketed the homes of Chiron executives, including sending a hearse to the house of a Chiron executive to pick up her very-alive body. Environmental extremists also bombed Chiron's facilities. In 2004 the FBI arrested seven people for violence against Huntingdon and Chiron.

The opponents of activists have also sought to shed light on activists and their practices. Taking a page from the activists' book, opponents have begun to provide information on those who fund groups such as RAN.[14] For example, the Capital Research Center published a report on the Tides Foundation, which receives contributions from donors and foundations and distributes the funds to activist groups and projects. The report listed donors and recipients of the funds.

Activists and NGOs have been criticized for being both "unelected" and unaccountable. They do not stand for election to allow the public to express its evaluation of their performance. They do not have to abide by governance requirements, such as Sarbanes-Oxley, considered in Chapter 19, that apply to firms. Some opponents of activists seek to apply Sarbanes-Oxley to NGOs and nonprofits. Independently of Sarbanes-Oxley many corporations issue public reports on their social activities, and those reports increasingly discuss shortcomings as well as accomplishments. For example, in 2004 the Gap released its first corporate social responsibility report, which revealed shortcomings in the practices of some of its overseas suppliers. NGOs typically do not report on their shortcomings.

Activists and NGOs could be accountable to the public, government, their members, and financial supporters. SustainAbility, Ltd., a London consulting firm, published a report (2002), "The 21st Century NGO: In the Market for Change," asking for greater public accountability.[15]

SUMMARY

Private politics takes place outside the arenas of government institutions and typically is intended to cause a firm to change its practices. Private politics is often led by activist organizations and other NGOs that attempt to advance issues on their agendas through direct pressure and offers of collaboration. Activists play an important role in the nonmarket environment because they can (1) alert management to issues of concern to the public, (2) affect the organization of interests, (3) lead to changes in institutions, and (4) provide information to the public and government officials.

Private politics strategies are frequently integrated with public politics strategies. A private politics strategy may be composed of target selection, actions to attract the media, and efforts to develop public support. These strategies may involve advocacy

[13]See Sasser, Prakash, Cashore, and Auld (2006) for an analysis of why U.S. timber firms participate in the SFI rather than the FSC.
[14]See www.activistcash.com.
[15]*New York Times,* January 3, 2004.

science, policy studies, and media strategies to bring issues to the attention of a broader public. Activist organizations frequently interact with each other, and some form networks. Activist organizations employ a variety of strategies to advance the issues on their agendas, and frequently those strategies are organized as a campaign. The objective is to shine the spotlight of public attention on a firm with the hope that attention will cause it to change its practices. This is often complemented using public politics as a lever to encourage negotiations on the issue. An alternative private politics strategy is decentralized and centers on mobilizing local groups to take action, as in the case of a boycott. The framework presented in Figure 4-2 summarizes the strategy of many activist organizations.

In dealing with activist organizations, firms take a number of approaches. Some ignore the issues and the activists in the hope that their interest will wane or that they will fail to generate broader support. Many negotiate directly with the activists, as in the OnBank case. Others collaborate with the activists to find a solution to the identified problems, as in the case of McDonald's and ED. When a firm believes that its practices are appropriate or that the activist group is weak, it may oppose the activists. Most firms, however, prefer to negotiate rather than become engaged in a protracted confrontation that could attract the attention of the media, the public, and government officials.

------------------------------------- C A S E S -------------------------------------
Shell, Greenpeace, and Brent Spar

The North Sea was a mature petroleum province where several facilities had already been abandoned or were approaching the ends of their useful lives. There were about 400 offshore petroleum platforms in the North Sea, about half of which were in the United Kingdom sector. The removal of platforms was governed by a variety of international regulatory principles. According to the guidelines of the International Maritime Organization, any installation in shallow waters had to be completely removed and dismantled on land. A substantial portion (about 50 in UK waters) of the current installations, however, were in deeper water, and if approved, could be disposed of at sea. According to the British interpretation of international conventions and guidelines as well as UK legislation, operators had to submit their preferred disposal option, the Best Practical Environmental Option (BPEO), for government approval. Each such case for disposal then was individually considered on its merits. If the platforms were disposed of at sea, any remains had to be left at least 55 meters below the surface. Proposals had to be well documented and include a review of the options considered. The costs of abandonment were to be borne by the field licensee. Part of the cost (50 to 70 percent) was tax deductible.

Royal Dutch/Shell

The Royal Dutch/Shell Group of Companies was a multinational holding of service and operating companies engaged in various branches of the oil, natural gas, chemicals, coal, and related businesses throughout the greater part of the world.[16] The parent companies, Royal Dutch Petroleum Company (domiciled in The Netherlands) and "Shell" Transport and Trading Company, plc (domiciled in the United Kingdom), did not themselves engage in operational activities. There were about 295,000 shareholders of Royal Dutch and some 300,000 of Shell Transport. Royal Dutch and Shell Transport owned the shares in the Group Holding Companies, Shell Petroleum NV (The Netherlands), Shell Petroleum Company Limited (United Kingdom), and Shell Petroleum Inc. (USA). These Group Holding Companies held all Group interests in the operating companies, such as Shell UK and Shell Germany (Deutsche Shell AG). The management of each operating company, although bound by common standards, was fairly independent in its decision making and was responsible for the performance and long-term viability of its own operations. It could, however, draw on the experience and expertise of other operating companies.

By most international standards Royal Dutch/Shell was one of the most successful companies in the world. It was the largest corporation in Europe and the third largest in the world. In recent years Royal Dutch/Shell was Europe's most profitable company. Since 1992, however, it had been in the process of restructuring. One reason was that its return on capital lagged behind its main competitor, Exxon. According to C.A.J. Herkstroeter, president of the Group, the process of restructuring, although encouraging, was not yet satisfactory in terms of return on capital employed. Group companies had about 106,000 employees in 1994 (down from 117,000 in 1993). Its net income in 1994 was £4,070 million (up 36 percent from 1993), its return on capital was 10.4 percent (up from 7.9 percent from 1993), and its debt-to-capital ratio was 16.7 percent (down from 17.8 percent in 1993).

The Issue—Disposal of Large Offshore Petroleum Facilities

The Brent Spar was a cylindrical buoy, 463 feet high and weighing about 14,500 tons. Between 1976 and 1991 it was used as an oil storage facility and tanker loading buoy for the Brent field (which along with Brent Spar was 50 percent owned by Esso AG, a unit of Exxon Corporation). In 1991 a review concluded that the necessary refurbishing of the facility was economically unjustifiable. Brent Spar was thus decommissioned in September 1991. Shell UK, one of the operating companies of the Royal Dutch/Shell Group, considered several disposal options. These options were evaluated according to engineering complexity, risk to health and safety of workforce, environmental impact, cost, and acceptability to the British authorities and other officially designated parties. The latter included government bodies such as the Scottish National Heritage and the Joint Nature Conservancy Committee, as well as "legitimate users of the sea" (as specified in the 1987 Petroleum Act), mainly fishermen's associations and British Telecom International.[17]

Two options survived the initial screening process: horizontal onshore dismantling and deepwater disposal. The former consisted of the rotation of the buoy to the horizontal, transport to shore, and onshore dismantling. The latter involved towing the structure to a deepwater disposal site in the Northeast Atlantic and sinking the platform. The study commissioned by Shell UK concluded that deepwater disposal dominated on the grounds of engineering complexity, risk to health and safety of the workforce, and cost (about £11 million versus £46 million). Both alternatives were acceptable to the other parties consulted.

---

[16]Royal Dutch Petroleum Company, Annual Report, 1994.

[17]Rudall Blanchard Associates Ltd. (for Shell UK Exploration and Production), Brent Spar Abandonment BPEO, December 1994.

With respect to possible environmental impacts, the study concluded that both options were equally balanced. Whereas the environmental impact was expected to be minimal for both options, horizontal dismantling (due to its considerably higher engineering complexity) would involve an increased potential for mishaps that, if one were to occur in shallow inshore water, could have a significant impact on other users of the sea. In addition, a research team at the University of Aberdeen recommended deep-sea disposal. Consequently, Shell UK proposed deepwater disposal as its BPEO to the British Department of Energy, the relevant regulatory agency. In mid-February 1995 the British Energy minister, Tim Eggart, announced that Shell's BPEO was accepted. The European governments were informed about the decision and were given 3 months to protest the decision. Although some of the European governments, including Germany, were generally critical of deep-sea disposal, no government officially protested, and so Shell UK scheduled the towing of Brent Spar to the disposal site in the North Atlantic for mid-June.

Greenpeace

Founded in 1971, Greenpeace had grown to be the world's largest environmental group. It had about 3.1 million contributors worldwide and a budget of about $140 million. Offices were located in 30 countries with a full-time staff of about 1,200. In addition, Greenpeace owned four ships, a helicopter, and modern communications equipment. It could also draw on a wide network of thousands of volunteers. In 1994 Greenpeace was forced to cut its budget by about 10 percent and dismiss more than 90 staff members because of a drop in contributions mainly due to Greenpeace USA's opposition to the Persian Gulf War. The Greenpeace offices were fairly independent but coordinated their decisions through Greenpeace International, located in Amsterdam. Greenpeace strongholds were in Germany, the Netherlands, and the United States.[18]

One of the largest and most active Greenpeace sections was in Germany. Greenpeace e.V. (Germany) had about 120 full-time staff members, a budget of roughly $50 million, and could rely on over 500,000 enlisted volunteers.[19] Its German headquarters and the North Sea logistic centers were located in Hamburg. Greenpeace enjoyed high acceptance and popularity among the German public and had frequently captured center stage through spectacular actions, which was reflected in donations that reached a record in 1994. Greenpeace Germany alone contributed over 40 percent of the total budget of Greenpeace International. Recently, Greenpeace Germany had also been active in developing alternative solutions to environmental problems.

One of Greenpeace's principal strategies was to attract the public's attention through high-profile, confrontational actions, which were covered by Greenpeace photographers and film crews. "We try to keep it simple," said Steve D'Esposito, an American who was executive director of Greenpeace International. "One, we raise environmental awareness. Two, we want to push the world toward solutions, using the most egregious examples. The whole point is to confront; we try to get in the way. Confrontation is critical to get coverage in the press or to reach the public some other way."[20]

The Brent Spar Protests

After being informed about Shell UK's plans concerning Brent Spar in summer 1994, Greenpeace commissioned a policy study to consider the arguments for deep-sea disposal. The study concluded that total removal and not deep-sea disposal should be adopted as the BPEO, especially from the viewpoint of the environment.[21] By March, Greenpeace had devised a plan to board the Brent Spar. To win public support through television coverage, Greenpeace acquired satellite communications and video equipment.

On April 30, 1995, 14 Greenpeace activists from the United Kingdom, the Netherlands, and Germany landed on the Brent Spar by boat. They were joined by a group of nine journalists who with Greenpeace filmed the incident and broadcast it by satellite. After a 3-week occupation, the group was expelled by Shell. Although the UK media gave little coverage to the Greenpeace campaign, German television extensively broadcast footage of soaked activists. Harald Zindler, head of the section Campaigns of Greenpeace Germany, who organized the Brent Spar landing, recalled, "We were very happy when Shell decided to clear the platform. It portrayed Shell as an unresponsive and inconsiderate big business."[22] In response to the media coverage, expressions of outrage and protest in Germany and the Netherlands grew. Members of all German political parties and the German minister of the environment, Angelika Merkel, condemned Shell's decision to dump the rig in the deep sea. On May 22, the worker representatives on Shell Germany's supervisory board expressed "concern and outrage" at Shell's decision to "turn the sea into a trash pit."[23]

Under pressure, executives of Shell Germany met with Jochen Lorfelder of Greenpeace, who argued that 85 percent of German motorists would participate in a boycott. He told Shell that "in the four weeks it would take to tow the Brent Spar to its dumping site, Greenpeace would make life a nightmare for Shell." The chairman of Shell Germany explained that Shell UK's studies

[18]*Frankfurter Allgemeine Zeitung,* June 12, 1995.
[19]Interview with Harald Zindler, Greenpeace Germany, August 11, 1995.

[20]*New York Times,* July 8, 1995.
[21]Simon Reddy (for Greenpeace International), "No Grounds for Dumping," April 1995.
[22]Interview, August 11, 1995.
[23]*Wall Street Journal,* July 7, 1995.

indicated that deep-sea disposal was the best alternative for the environment. Lorfelder answered, "But Joe Six-Pack won't understand your technical details. All he knows is that if he dumps his can in a lake, he gets fined. So he can't understand how Shell can do this."[24]

On June 7 Greenpeace activists again landed on the Brent Spar but were soon expelled. The next day the Fourth International North Sea Conference began in Esbjerg, Denmark. One of the main topics was the disposal of petroleum facilities. Germany introduced a proposal that would rule out any disposal at sea. Norway, France, and the United Kingdom, however, blocked the proposal.[25] In the meantime, calls for an informal boycott of Shell by German motorists were mounting. Proponents included members of all German political parties, unions, motorists' associations, the Protestant Church, and the former chief justice of the German Constitutional Court, Ernst Benda.

In its media campaign, Greenpeace successfully appealed to the German enthusiasm for recycling. In their homes many Germans separated garbage into bags for metal, glass, paper, chemicals, plastic, and organic waste. Harald Zindler pointed out the appeal of Greenpeace's strategy to the general public: "The average citizen thinks: 'Here I am dutifully recycling my garbage, and there comes big business and simply dumps its trash into the ocean.'" Greenpeace always tried to keep its message simple and connect it to the public's everyday experiences and values.

Despite the mounting protests and another attempt by Greenpeace to board the rig, Shell began towing the Brent Spar to its dumping site on June 11 as scheduled. During the following week the boycott of German Shell gas stations was in full swing. Sales were off 20 to 30 percent[26] and in some areas up to 40 percent.[27] The mayor of Leipzig banned city vehicles from using Shell gasoline. Boycotts also spread to the Netherlands and Denmark. During the G7-summit at Halifax, Canada, German Chancellor Helmut Kohl criticized Shell and the British government for persisting with the proposed deep-sea dumping. Two days later a firebomb exploded at a Shell gas station in Hamburg.

Shell had used high-powered water cannons to keep a Greenpeace helicopter from approaching the Brent Spar, but on June 16, two Greenpeace activists again succeeded in landing on the rig by arriving before the water cannons had been turned on. They managed to stay on Brent Spar while the rig was being towed to its chosen disposal site. On June 19, the German economics minister, Guenther Rexrodt, announced that his ministry, too, would join the boycott. During this period the German public received inconsistent messages from Shell. Al-

though Shell Germany suggested that the project could be halted, Shell UK refused to stop the towing. Meanwhile in the United Kingdom, Prime Minister John Major was repeatedly attacked in Parliament but refused to reconsider the government's decision to approve Shell's proposal.

Shell's Climb Down

After a meeting of the Royal Dutch/Shell Group's managing directors in The Hague on June 20, Christopher Fay, chairman of Shell UK, announced that Shell would abandon its plans to sink the Brent Spar. Fay stressed that he still believed that deep-sea disposal offered the best environmental option but admitted that Shell UK had reached an "untenable position" because of its failure to convince other governments around the North Sea.[28] Shell UK would now attempt to dismantle the platform on land and sought approval from Norwegian authorities to anchor the Brent Spar temporarily in a fjord on the Norwegian coast.

The decision was received with joy by environmentalists and with an angry response by the British government. John Jennings, chairman of Shell Transport, apologized in a letter to the British Prime Minister. A variety of public relations experts criticized Shell's handling of the protests and its decision to abandon its original plans. Mike Beard, former president of the Institute of Public Relations, commented, "They failed to communicate the benefits of the course they believed to be right; they lost what they believed to be their case; and now they're having to defend something they don't consider to be defensible."[29]

In response, Dick Parker, production director of Shell Expro, defended the company's decision not to involve environmental interest groups like Greenpeace: "Greenpeace does not have formal consultative status under the guidelines set out for an offshore installation proposal. Other bodies who represent a wide range of interests or who are accountable to their members are part of the process, and we consulted them."[30] Following the decision to halt the project, Shell started an advertising campaign admitting mistakes and promising change.

Aftermath

In the June 29 issue of *Nature,* two British geologists at the University of London argued that the environmental effects of Shell UK's decision to dump the Brent Spar in the deep sea would "probably be minimal." Indeed, the metals of the Brent Spar might even be beneficial to the deep-sea environment. Disposing of the Brent Spar on land could pose greater risks to the environment.[31]

[24]*Wall Street Journal,* July 7, 1995.
[25]Accepted proposals of this conference were nonbinding.
[26]*Wall Street Journal,* July 7, 1995.
[27]*Wirtschaftswoche,* June 22, 1995.

[28]*Financial Times,* June 21, 1995.
[29]*Financial Times,* June 23, 1995.
[30]Shell UK (Sarah James, ed.), "Brent Spar," July 1995.
[31]E. G. Nisbet and C. M. R. Fowler. "Is Metal Disposal Toxic to Deep Oceans?" *Nature* 375:715, June 29, 1995.

Robert Sangeorge of the Switzerland-based Worldwide Fund for Nature said, "Deep-sea disposal seemed the least harmful option." He called the Brent Spar episode "a circus and sideshow that distracted from the big environmental issues affecting the world."[32] In response, however, a spokesperson for Shell UK reiterated that the company would stick to its decision to abandon deep-sea disposal.

The Brent Spar remained anchored in Erfjord, Norway. After an independent Norwegian inspection agency, Det Norske Veritas, had surveyed the contents of the Brent Spar, some doubts arose about Greenpeace's estimates of the oil sludge remaining on Brent Spar. Shell had previously estimated that the Spar contained about 100 tons of sludge. Greenpeace had estimated 5,000 tons. On September 5, Greenpeace UK's executive director, Lord Peter Melchett, admitted that the estimates were inaccurate and apologized to Christopher Fay. Shell UK welcomed the apology and announced its intention to include Greenpeace among those to be consulted in its review of options and the development of a new BPEO.[33] ■

SOURCE: This case was prepared by Daniel Diermeier from public sources, including materials supplied by the Shell Petroleum Co. Ltd. (London, UK) and Greenpeace e.V. (Hamburg, Germany), as well as an interview with Harald Zindler, head of the section Campaigns (Bereichsleiter Aktionen) of Greenpeace Germany. Copyright © 1995 by Daniel Diermeier. All rights reserved. Reprinted with permission.

Preparation Questions

1. From Shell UK's perspective, what was the issue in this case, and where was it in its issue life cycle?
2. In which institutional arenas was this issue addressed? Which interests were active on this issue?
3. Evaluate Shell UK's decision process in choosing a BPEO. Could it have effectively communicated its rationale for deep-sea disposal to the public? Was Shell UK right in abandoning its initial plan? How should Shell have managed the Brent Spar disposal? From the perspective of a major multinational corporation such as Royal Dutch/Shell, what strategy should be adopted to participate in, influence, and prepare for the development of this or similar issues? In what way, if any, might the organization structure of Shell have contributed to the Brent Spar debacle? Should the management of issues such as the disposal of the Brent Spar be centralized?
4. How did Greenpeace view this issue? What were its objectives and strategy? Why was it able to win the public opinion war? Could Greenpeace use the estimated costs of deep-sea and on-land disposal to its advantage? Why was Shell unable to explain its position and reasoning to the public?
5. Why did the German government not protest Shell's plan before the boycott? Why did the German government oppose deep-sea dumping? Why did the British government approve Shell's BPEO?
6. What should Shell UK do now about the Brent Spar?

[32]*Wall Street Journal,* July 7, 1995.

[33]*Financial Times,* September 5–9, 1995.

Nike in Southeast Asia

Phil Knight, chairman of the board and CEO, opened Nike's 1996 annual report with an account of the record revenues of $6.5 billion. One paragraph later, though, he added: "Yet no sooner had the great year ended than we were hit by a series of blasts from the media about our practices overseas." Nike had been widely criticized by labor and human rights groups over the working conditions and wages at its suppliers' factories in Asia. The media followed developments closely as revelations of sweatshops in the United States added to the public interest in Nike. *Doonesbury* likened Nike factories to Dickensian sweatshops.

Sourcing shoes from low-wage countries in Asia had been one of the foundations of the company's strategy. Nike had never owned a factory in Asia; instead the company contracted production from independent companies. Shoes and apparel thus were manufactured in independently owned and operated factories, and Nike took ownership of the product only when it left the factory. The factories were mostly owned by Korean and Taiwanese companies with whom Nike maintained long-term relationships.

In 1997 Nike bought the bulk of its shoes from China, Vietnam, and Indonesia. As the company's visibility increased, so did the scrutiny of its practices. Nike had to deal with allegations of subcontractors running sweatshops marked by poor working conditions, worker abuse, and below-subsistence wages. Shoes that sold for up to $140 were manufactured by workers earning about $2 a day in such countries as Vietnam and Indonesia.

Nike had contracts with a dozen factories in Indonesia in 1997, employing around 120,000 people. Both Nike's South Korean and Taiwanese manufacturing partners had come to Indonesia to take advantage of the low labor costs. In Nike audits, several incidents involving Korean and Taiwanese plant managers had been reported. The workers considered some managers too strict, or even abusive, shouting at or striking workers, or issuing punishments considered excessive for bad work or tardiness. In one case, a worker had to run laps around the factory because the shoes she assembled had defects.[34] Nike insisted that managers who were found to be abusive be transferred or removed. Employees and union activists from the Union of Needletrade, Industrial and Textile Employees (UNITE) in the United States confirmed that Nike's audits had been effective; at the Nikomas plant, for example, a security guard who hit a worker had been quickly fired by the owners.[35]

Underpayment of wages had led to several cases of unrest at Nike's Indonesian contract factories. In April 1997 workers at PT HASI staged a mass strike and protest. They demanded to be paid the new basic minimum monthly wage of 172,500 rupiah ($71.37), excluding allowances, that went into effect on April 1. A representative of the workers said that the company had included their "attendance" allowance in their basic wage, which meant that their minimum wage had actually stayed at last year's levels. The *Jakarta Post* quoted the personnel manager of the company as saying that because of its financial situation, it had been given permission by the manpower ministry to delay paying the 1997 minimum wage.

About 10,000 of the 13,000 workers at the factory marched 6 miles to the district parliament to demand the increase. Later in the week they burned cars and ransacked the factory's offices. The company then agreed to pay the minimum wage without including allowances for attendance, overtime, transport, holiday pay, and meals.[36] Nike claimed that its contract factories paid more than what most laborers would earn in other jobs. "We turn away more prospective employees than we could hire," Knight commented. "It sounds like a low wage and it is. But it's a wage that's greater than they used to make."[37]

In Vietnam, Nike's footwear plants had been under attack by both workers and media since 1996 when a 29-year-old Korean forewoman at the Sam Yang factory lined up 15 female Vietnamese workers and beat them around the face with an unfinished shoe because she was angered by the quality of their work. Workers staged an immediate strike, and the forewoman was fired the same day. Later, she was found guilty in a Vietnam court of "humiliating" workers.[38] In another incident a Taiwanese manager from the Pao Chen factory forced 56 slow workers to run laps until a dozen fainted. The manager was sentenced to 6 months in prison for physically abusing workers.[39]

The monthly minimum wage at foreign-owned factories in Vietnam was $45 in 1997, compared with about $20 per month at state-owned factories. The Nike contract factories were believed to pay the minimum wage, but some had been accused of paying the workers less than this in the first 3 months of employment, which was illegal.

When it came to average per-capita income, cost of living, and the value of workers' benefits, statements from Nike and claims from human rights groups such as the Vietnam Labor Watch (VLW) differed. Although Nike said that the annual per-capita income in areas where Nike factories were located was $200, VLW claimed it was $925. A *San Jose Mercury News* investigation found the average to be $446 in the areas where 14 of the 15 factories were located. According to Nike, most workers saved enough of their salary to send money home to their families. VLW interviewed 35 workers, and none said they could save money. The *Mercury News* found that 12 of 24 workers could save money. Nike claimed that workers received free health care, whereas the VLW said workers' health insurance was deducted from their paychecks. The *Mercury News* found that employers, by law, deducted and contributed 1 percent of employees' salaries to government medical insurance.[40]

Nike had its first "Code of Conduct" for its contract factories in 1992, after the initial criticism of its labor practices in Asia. In a Memorandum of Understanding signed by all Nike contractors, the contractors were required to comply with all local government regulations, including those on occupational health and safety. Nike banned the use of forced labor, and required environmental responsibility, nondiscrimination, and equal opportunity practices. The rights of association and collective bargaining were to be guaranteed. Nike's production managers, who were stationed at the factories, monitored working conditions on a daily basis. Enforcement was not a problem according to Nike; many factories produced exclusively for Nike, which gave the company tremendous leverage. Beginning in 1994 Nike hired the Indonesian office of the international accounting firm Ernst & Young to monitor the plants for worker pay, safety conditions, and attitudes toward the job. The auditors were to pull workers off the assembly line at random and ask them questions that the workers would answer anonymously. In September 1997 Nike severed contracts with four factories in Indonesia that did not pay workers the minimum wage. This was the first time Nike had fired contractors for noncompliance with its code of conduct.

[34]"Sweatshops Haunt U.S. Consumers," *BusinessWeek,* July 29, 1996.
[35]"Sweatshops Haunt U.S. Consumers," *BusinessWeek,* July 29, 1996.
[36]"Workers Win Pay Raise at Nike Plant in Indonesia," *Reuters Asia-Pacific Business Report,* April 23, 1997.
[37]"Protests as Nike CEO Addresses Stanford Students." *San Francisco Examiner,* April 30, 1997.
[38]"Culture Shock: Korean Employers Irk Vietnamese Workers," *Far Eastern Economic Review,* August 22, 1996.

[39]"Nike Aide in Vietnam Convicted," *Wall Street Journal,* June 1997.
[40]"Nike's Fancy Footwork in Vietnam," *San Jose Mercury News,* June 25, 1997.

In 1996 Nike established a Labor Practices Department to monitor subcontracted manufacturing facilities and upgrade conditions for factory workers around the world. The creation of the department was "a further step in Nike's ongoing commitment to have products made only in the best facilities with the best working conditions in the sports and fitness industry." Specific emphasis would be on Indonesia, China, and Vietnam.[41]

Nike had long promised independent monitoring of its factories, and in February 1997 it hired Andrew Young, civil rights activist and former U.S. ambassador to the United Nations and mayor of Atlanta, to review its labor practices. The appointment received a mixed reception; Nike and Young emphasized his independence, but critics claimed he was hired to promote the company's image.

Young's report was released in June 1997 and called conditions in Nike's overseas factories comparable with those in U.S. factories. The report stated, "The factories that we visited which produce Nike goods were clean, organized, adequately ventilated and well lit . . . . I found no evidence or pattern of widespread or systematic abuse or mistreatment of workers in the twelve factories." The Young report did not specifically address the wage issue, which Young considered too complex and beyond the capacity of his firm. Phil Knight said, "We will take action to improve in areas where he suggests we need to improve. For although his overall assessment is that we are doing a good job, good is not the standard Nike seeks in anything we do."[42] When the Young report was released, Nike took out full-page advertisements in major papers summarizing the key recommendations from the report.

The report was immediately criticized by human rights and labor groups. Thuyen Nguyen, director of VLW, noted that Young spent only 10 days visiting factories in China, Vietnam, and Indonesia; his tours were conducted by management, and he talked to workers through Nike interpreters. "Workers are not about to complain in front of the boss, especially in authoritarian countries where workers labeled troublemakers can be fired and jailed," wrote Nguyen.[43] Medea Benson, director of the human rights group Global Exchange, said, "I think it was an extremely shallow report. I was just amazed that he even admitted that he spent three hours in factories using Nike interpreters and then could come and say he did not find systematic abuse."[44]

In a letter to Phil Knight, a coalition of women's groups including the National Organization of Women, the Ms. Foundation for Women, the Black Women's Agenda, and the Coalition of Labor Union Women wrote, "While the women who wear Nike shoes in the United States are encouraged to perform their best, the Indonesian, Vietnamese, and Chinese women making the shoes often suffer from inadequate wages, corporal punishment, forced overtime, and/or sexual harassment."[45] Fifty-three members of Congress wrote to Phil Knight accusing Nike of "ruthlessly exploiting" workers. Knight invited the Congress members to visit the factories.

The criticism and actions against Nike also occurred at the local level. Protesters distributed leaflets at a Nike-sponsored event at Stanford University where Phil Knight had received his MBA.

Five months after Andrew Young's report, the heat was turned up further when an audit by Ernst & Young, initially intended for Nike's internal use, was leaked to the media. The report revealed unsafe conditions at the Tae Kwang Vina Industrial Ltd. Factory in Vietnam, including chemical levels 6 to 177 times that allowed by Vietnamese regulations. The audit also stated that dust in the mixing room was 11 times the standard and that a high percent of the employees had respiratory problems. Major problems detailed in the report were the unprotected use of dangerous materials, poor air quality, and overtime-law violations. Over 75 percent of the workers in the factory were said to suffer from respiratory problems. Nike said that the shortcomings in the audit had been addressed.

The publicity surrounding labor practices was worrisome to Nike management. In some regions around the world, surveys showed that the bad publicity had affected consumers' perceptions of Nike. Consumers were used to considering Nike a leader in its field, but here the company was stumbling. Bob Wood, vice president of U.S. marketing, stated, "It's obviously not good. It's something that we're really concerned about, but we haven't noticed any literal decline in demand or sell-through of our products because of it."

Knight admitted that Nike had been ill prepared for the media offensive. "Our communications staff is woefully inadequate to deal with this problem right now," he explained. "Our Washington, DC, office essentially is one guy, and he's always dealt essentially with the [international] trade, with the quota issues." In 1997 Nike's public relations department had a staff of approximately 10 people. According to Knight, "They should probably have fifty people in there, but they have to be the right people, and organized right." Martha Benson, a Nike spokesperson in Asia, explained, "We are about sports, not Manufacturing 101."[46]

Phil Knight could not have been more sure that Nike was a force for positive change in Asia. "Whether

[41]"Nike Establishes Labor Practices Department," Canada NewsWire, October 3, 1996.
[42]*New York Times,* June 25, 1997.
[43]"Report on Nike Work Force Glossed over Issues," Thuyen Nguyen. Letter, *New York Times,* June 30, 1997.
[44]*New York Times,* June 25, 1997.
[45]*New York Times,* October 20, 1997.
[46]*Wall Street Journal,* September 26, 1997.

you like Nike or don't like Nike, good corporations are the ones that lead these countries out of poverty," he said in an interview. "When we started in Japan, factory labor there was making $4 a day, which is basically what is being paid in Indonesia and being so strongly criticized today. Nobody today is saying, 'The poor old Japanese.' We watched it happen all over again in Taiwan and Korea, and now it's going on in Southeast Asia." ■

SOURCE: This is an abridged and edited version of a case prepared by Ann-Kristin de Verdier under the supervision of Professor David Brady. Copyright © 1998 by the Board of Trustees of the Leland Stanford Junior University. All rights reserved. Reprinted with permission.

Preparation Questions

1. How serious are the criticisms of the practices in the factories of Nike's suppliers in Indonesia and Vietnam? Are Nike's sales likely to be hurt by the criticisms and the actions of activists?

2. How effectively has Nike addressed the sequence of episodes? Was hiring Andrew Young wise?

3. What, if anything, should Nike do about the wages paid in its suppliers' factories in Asia? Is Phil Knight right in saying that companies like Nike can "lead countries out of poverty"?

4. How should Nike deal with the inevitable continued scrutiny its practices will receive?

Anatomy of a Corporate Campaign: Rainforest Action Network and Citigroup (A)

Citigroup, the world's largest project finance bank, provided financing for extractive projects such as mining, logging, and oil exploration. Some of these projects took place in developing countries and in rain forests and other endangered ecosystems. In 2000 the Rainforest Action Network (RAN) launched its Global Finance Campaign with Citigroup as the target. The goal was to convince Citigroup, and eventually all lenders, to stop financing destructive activities in endangered ecosystems.

Project finance referred to the financing of long-term industrial (e.g., pulp and paper mills), public service, and infrastructure (e.g., telecommunications) projects. The cash flows generated by a project were used to repay the debt financing.[47]

Creditors did not have recourse to the project companies (contractors) for failure to repay the debt—only to a project's specific assets, rights, and interests, which served as collateral for the funding. Most project finance deals were highly leveraged with project companies providing 20 to 40 percent of the required funds as equity. Typically, a lead bank arranged a project's financing and then opened the deal to participation by other banks and investors. The project finance market peaked in 2000, when $379 billion was funded globally.

Extractive Projects and Rain Forests

Environmental NGOs (nongovernmental organizations) had historically targeted logging and mining companies

directly. In the late 1990s, however, some environmental activist organizations, such as RAN, began to focus on the commercial banks financing extractive industries. The objective was to cut off funding for projects that led to the destruction of rain forests in developing countries. Through project finance, revolving credit facilities, or general corporate loans, many banks funded the extraction of timber, wood pulp, wood chip, and oil, in addition to open-pit mining for ores and land clearing for cattle farming, all of which contributed to the destruction of rain forests.

Tropical rain forests received between 4 and 8 meters of rain a year. Rain forests covered only 2 percent of the Earth's surface, yet they housed about half of the world's 5 to 10 million plant and animal species. According to the National Academy of Sciences, a 4-square-mile area of rain forest typically housed 1,500 species of flowering plants, 750 of trees, 125 of mammals, 400 of birds, 100 of reptiles, 60 of amphibians, and 150 of butterflies. Drugs for cancer treatment, heart problems, arthritis, and birth control came (in some cases exclusively) from rain forest plants. Rain forests also held years and years of carbon buildup in their vegetation. When this vegetation was burned or cut and left to decay, the carbon was released as CO_2. CO_2 released in this manner was the second largest factor contributing to the greenhouse effect.

The primary rain forests in India, Bangladesh, Sri Lanka, and Haiti had been destroyed. By 1985, 55 and 45 percent, respectively, of the Philippines' and Thailand's rain forests had been destroyed. According to the National Academy of Sciences, over 50 million acres of rain forest were destroyed a year.

---

[47]Michelle Chan-Fishel, "Project Finance Trends: Key players, regions, and sectors," Friends of the Earth–US, September 22, 2003.

The Rainforest Action Network

RAN was founded in 1985 with the mission of protecting tropical rain forests and the human rights of people living in them. RAN used tools such as citizen protests, media, nonviolent civil disobedience, and publications to bring awareness to the issues and pressure governments, corporations, and lending institutions. RAN had about two dozen employees, all in the United States, organized in three departments: operations, development (fundraising), and campaigns. RAN had a full-time media specialist who interacted with the news media and participated in campaign planning. Within the campaigns department, RAN typically had a campaign manager for each campaign and used an organizing staff of about five to support whichever campaign was active at the time.

In the mid-1990s RAN changed its focus from public policy to the private sector with the objective of changing the practices of companies with environmentally destructive practices. RAN executive director Michael Brune said, "Companies were more responsive to public opinion than certain legislatures were. We felt we could create more democracy in the marketplace than in the government."

RAN's Global Finance Campaign

Selecting a Target

In late 1999 RAN was concluding a successful 2-year campaign (led by Brune) targeting Home Depot, which had agreed to end by 2003 the sale of wood from endangered forests. For the Global Finance Campaign, RAN planned to use a model similar to the one used for Home Depot—target a large, brand-oriented, U.S.-based multinational company that had a strong retail presence, was a leader in its industry, and had a key role in facilitating the destruction of old growth forests and supporting extractive industries. Because RAN was a small organization with the goal of shifting the practices of entire sectors, not just individual companies, it relied on the ripple effect of targeting a market leader.

One company stood out as the best target—Citigroup, the world's largest bank. Citigroup was the leading global, emerging market project finance bank and the leading developing country project finance bank. Citigroup also had a key role in a number of specific projects that alarmed RAN, such as the Camisea pipeline in Peru (Citigroup was the financial advisor on the project but did not directly fund it) and the Chad-Cameroon pipeline under construction by ExxonMobil, Chevron, and a consortium of central African oil companies.[48] In researching Citigroup's involvement, RAN relied on data from Dealogic's ProjectWare, a database of project finance deals.

In 2000 Citigroup had net income of $13.5 billion on revenues of $111.8 billion and had customers in over 100 countries and territories. Citigroup's activities included global consumer banking, global corporate and investment banking, global investment management and private banking, and investment activities. Citigroup's global consumer group offered banking, lending, investment services, and credit cards to customers in over 50 countries and territories. The global consumer group reported core net income of $5.3 billion on $30.4 billion of revenues in 2000.[49]

Citigroup had a public image and a brand to protect (in particular, its large consumer banking operation and credit card business), which made it an attractive target. Ilyse Hogue, RAN's campaign manager for the Global Finance Campaign, said:

> Citigroup had poured $100 million into its brand image, most recently on its "Live Richly" marketing campaign, which was predicated on the notion that "there is more to life than money." We saw a company that was investing a lot in making the public believe that they operated in line with common social values. Part of Citi's vulnerability was the juxtaposition of what it articulated to the public with what we saw on the ground from Citi's finance activities.

RAN began the campaign expecting it to last up to 5 years but hoping to win in 3 years. RAN dedicated three staff members, including Hogue, full time to the Global Finance Campaign.

RAN had such limited resources and Citigroup was such a large target that many people thought RAN could not win the campaign. RAN believed, however, that Citigroup's vulnerability was its sensitivity to public opinion, so exploiting that vulnerability by publicizing Citigroup's environmental practices became the heart of RAN's strategy.

RAN's Strategy during the First Two Years of the Campaign[50]

In developing its strategy, RAN drew heavily on past campaigns and consulted with allies that had interacted with Citigroup and were interested in helping. RAN dubbed Citibank the "World's Most Destructive Bank" and on April 13, 2000 wrote to Citigroup CEO Sandy Weill, asking the company to recognize its role in, and take action to address, the destruction of the world's old growth forests and the acceleration of climate change. As with most of RAN's campaigns, this introductory letter presented the issues and a set of demands. Five days later a group of RAN campaigners addressed the board

---

[48]For years RAN had developed relationships with allies (e.g., other NGOs, indigenous federations, and others) on the front lines of the affected areas. These allies kept RAN apprised of project developments and enabled it to track the projects and their financing.

[49]Citigroup Inc. 2000 Annual Report.
[50]www.ran.org.

of directors and Sandy Weill at Citigroup's annual meeting, voicing their concerns in front of a room of shareholders. On April 19, Citigroup agreed to meet with RAN to discuss its connection with the fossil fuel and forest industries. Citigroup, however, took no action to address the issues.

After Citigroup's annual meeting, RAN organized a 3-day strategic brainstorming session, attended by about 20 ally organizations, to generate ideas, increase awareness, and spur interest in the campaign. Some of RAN's strategies included shareholder resolutions, high-profile media attention, paid advertisements, Days of Action with student networks, disruptions of Citibank branches, and other nonviolent civil disobedience (e.g., banner hangs). Hogue believed the media was one of the best arrows in RAN's quiver when going after a target's brand image.

In September 2000 RAN launched the campaign on college campuses, encouraging a boycott of Citigroup credit cards and job recruitment. Many of RAN's actions were designed to call the public's attention to the campaign objectives and attract media coverage, which was essential to informing the public. In October, RAN organized a Day of Action that included demonstrations in which participants cut up their Citibank credit cards and closed their Citibank accounts. In December, carolers gathered at Citigroup's headquarters and sang "Oil Wells" to the tune of "Jingle Bells." The campaign also targeted Sandy Weill. For Valentine's Day 2001, Weill received hundreds of valentines, asking him to show the Earth some love and stop funding rain forest destruction. April 2001 saw the second Day of Action, with 80 actions in 12 countries on five continents. The actions included hanging banners, marches, and leaving symbolic piles of wood chips and oil at Citibank branches. Also in April, 500 schoolchildren sent drawings to Weill asking him to stop funding rain forest destruction. In October, an oil pipeline under construction in an Ecuadorian cloud forest reserve was obstructed by dozens of indigenous women and children. Students across the United States gathered at local Citibank branches, bringing pledges from 12,000 students who refused to do business with the "#1 funder of global warming." In February 2002 students at 60 U.S. colleges participated in a National Student Week of Action, which included demonstrations as well as telephone calls and letters delivered to Citigroup.[51]

Much of RAN's media attention was "earned"— media coverage that RAN did not pay for, such as press coverage of Days of Action or articles written about the Global Finance Campaign. In addition, RAN paid for a number of advertisements in various newspapers and magazines criticizing Citigroup and challenging it to take leadership in protecting the environment.

Enlisting students was important to the success of the campaign, and RAN found that students at many universities were eager to participate. To mobilize student groups, RAN campaigners traveled to campuses to spur interest in the campaign. In addition, RAN hired organizers from Green Corps, an organization that trained young environmental activists to become future leaders. Green Corps had historically been politically aggressive but had not promoted the use of civil disobedience. Green Corps organizers were hired on a short-term basis and saturated campuses—educating students, organizing Days of Action, and establishing groups (or relationships with existing student groups) with which RAN could coordinate.

Students at Columbia University, through SEEJ (Students for Environmental and Economic Justice), played a significant role in the campaign over time. Citigroup had a substantial presence at Columbia—it had an affinity agreement with Columbia, and Citigroup's logo appeared on student identification cards. Nearly 4,000 Columbia students opened accounts with Citibank each year.[52]

RAN's ability to gain the support of young people, such as college students, was critical in getting Citigroup's attention. Many students refused Citibank credit cards as a result of the campaign and wrote letters to Citigroup to that effect. Hogue said, "Cards issued to college students are kind of a gateway drug, in Citigroup's mind. If Citigroup breeds brand loyalty by issuing credit cards to young people, then Citigroup has their business for college loans, mortgages, their kids' college, and retirement."

During the first 2 years of the campaign, RAN met frequently with Citigroup to discuss the issues—the difficulty was getting any real response or action from Citigroup. RAN was clearly frustrated by the lack of progress.

Response from Citigroup

Citigroup had assigned its vice president of community relations to interact with RAN, although she initially delegated day-to-day communications with RAN to others. Community relations typically dealt with issues like community reinvestment and partnering with Habitat for Humanity. As the campaign wore on, the vice president, who had a long tenure at Citigroup and was highly respected, began to develop expertise on project-finance and environmental issues.

After 2 years of campaign activity and regular meetings with RAN, Citigroup had to decide what to do about the RAN campaign. ∎

SOURCE: This is an abridged version of a case written by Research Associate Erin Yurday, Cornell MBA 1998, under the supervision of Professor David P. Baron. This case would not have been possible without the help of Mike Brune and Ilyse Hogue of Rainforest Action Network. Copyright © 2004 by the Board of Trustees of the Leland Stanford Junior University. All rights reserved. Reprinted with permission.

---

[51]During campaign activities, no activists were injured or served jail time. However, there were many arrests—of RAN staff, students, concerned citizens, and volunteers. Arrests sometimes led to fines or community service, but most charges were dropped.

---

[52]"SEEJ Members Influence Citigroup Corporate Agenda," *Columbia Daily Spectator*, February 3, 2004.

Preparation Questions

1. Identify the issues, interests, institutions, and information characterizing this nonmarket situation.

2. Was it strategically wise for RAN to launch a campaign on project finance? Can RAN realistically expect to affect project finance, which is provided by banks around the world?

3. Was Citigroup a good or bad target for RAN? Why not focus on the project contractors themselves?

4. Is Citigroup vulnerable to such a campaign? What harm can RAN impose on Citigroup, and how serious is that harm?

5. What should RAN do next in its campaign? Should it abandon the campaign? Should it accept a symbolic agreement with Citigroup and turn its attention elsewhere?

6. What action, if any, should Citigroup take in light of the RAN campaign?

Anatomy of a Corporate Campaign: Rainforest Action Network and Citigroup (B)

The Rainforest Action Network (RAN) launched its campaign against Citigroup in April 2000 with the objective of forcing Citigroup to recognize and take responsibility for its role in rain forest destruction through its financing. After two challenging years, RAN believed that the campaign was gaining momentum, but RAN was still meeting with Citigroup personnel who had little real authority. Ilyse Hogue, campaign manager for the Global Finance Campaign, said, "We were convinced that no one inside Citigroup with any decision-making ability was paying attention to us." RAN was at a low point in the campaign. Outside developments then suddenly put the spotlight on corporate governance and Citigroup. RAN took advantage of the opportunity and stepped up the pressure beginning in the summer of 2002.

Enron

In July 2002, following Enron's bankruptcy, billions of dollars of deals that Citigroup had structured for Enron came into question. Some of these deals made the funds flowing into Enron look like energy trades instead of loans. The funds were off balance sheet, hiding part of Enron's debt burden from ratings agencies, investors, and creditors. Some of the transactions also made Enron's core energy trading activities look as if they were generating more cash than they actually were.[53]

Jack Grubman

Coinciding with the Enron news was more bad news for Citigroup. Criticism of Jack Grubman, the star telecom analyst of Citigroup's Salomon Smith Barney, had been growing for some time—complaints focused on biased research resulting from his dual roles as investment banker and analyst. One example was Grubman's upgrade of AT&T from "neutral" to "buy" in 1999. At the time of the upgrade, AT&T was preparing a multibillion-dollar stock offering, and Salomon was seeking a lead role in the underwriting. Reports suggested that Weill, an AT&T board member, nudged Grubman to reassess AT&T. New York State Attorney General Eliot Spitzer and the National Association of Securities Dealers began investigating.[54]

Much of the Enron and Grubman related news was reported on July 22 and 23, 2002. On the 22nd, Citigroup's stock closed at $32.04, down 11 percent from the previous day's close. On the 23rd, Citigroup's stock fell another 16 percent, closing at $27.

Stepping up the Pressure in the Global Finance Campaign[55]

RAN had considered Citigroup a good target because of its pride in its brand name and its sensitivity to public opinion. Now that Citigroup had been implicated in the Enron and Grubman scandals, RAN stepped up the pressure.

A national Day of Action was planned for November 6, 2002, with 40 different actions, including a demonstration at Citigroup's headquarters by New York University students. On November 13, a full-page advertisement appeared in the *New York Times* with the headline, "Did you know that someone is using your Citigroup credit card without your authorization?" Later that month, activists blockaded all the Citibank branches in San Francisco's financial district using U-locks, kryptonite chains, and concrete-filled barrels. Activists in New York, Washington D.C., and Miami

---

[53]See the Chapter 19 case, *The Collapse of Enron.*

[54]Charles Gasparino, "The Stock-Research Pact: How Settlement Train Kept on Track," *Wall Street Journal*, December 23, 2002; Charles Gasparino, "Spitzer Staff Gathers Salomon E-Mails Criticizing Grubman," *Wall Street Journal*, July 16, 2002.
[55]www.ran.org.

locked themselves to the doors of Citibank branches, shutting them down. In December, over 2,500 letters and pictures from children across the United States were delivered to Weill, asking him to stop funding global warming and forest destruction. In January 2003, RAN launched a "Hometown Showdown," a two-month campaign in New York City, which included visiting Citibank branches, plastering posters around the city, and organizing student groups. The campaign got personal in January 2003 when activists visited Greenwich, Connecticut, where Weill lived, and plastered grocery stores with "Wanted" posters. The protesters delivered campaign information to Weill's neighbors and son. In February, at a Citigroup-sponsored parade in Hartford, Connecticut in which Citigroup employees carried red umbrellas with the slogan "On the Move," protestors appeared, holding a banner that read, "Citi: On the Move in the Wrong Direction. #1 in Rainforest Destruction."

In March, former Treasury Secretary Robert Rubin, a Citigroup executive and board member, was speaking at the Columbia Business School when students disrupted him. Other students hung a banner reading, "Rubin and Citigroup: Partners in Environmental Crime." According to an article in the *Columbia Daily Spectator*, at the lecture, a student asked Rubin, "How can you justify funding the pipeline in Ecuador?" Rubin replied that the pipeline was not a Citigroup project. The student asked again, "Is it not true that you're funding the pipeline?" Moments later, Rubin replied, "Yes, we are funding it."[56]

Also in March 2003, Weill arrived at Cornell University, his alma mater, to a festive rally and a banner reading, "Sandy Weill, Class of '55, Make Us Proud: Stop Funding Destruction." RAN president and founder Randy Hayes was invited to speak on these issues by a Cornell student group the night before Weill's speech. Hayes then accompanied the students into the speech and offered to debate Weill on the issues. In April a television commercial aired in New York City featuring Susan Sarandon, Ed Asner, Daryl Hannah, and Ali McGraw cutting up their Citigroup credit cards and showing graphic footage of the environmental damage from projects financed by Citigroup. RAN claimed that 20,000 Citigroup credit cards were cut up as a result of the campaign.

Next Step

By the spring of 2003, RAN believed that Citigroup was vulnerable from the Enron and Grubman scandals and the stepped-up campaign. Citigroup had kept RAN at a distance for three years by holding regular meetings but never progressing from discussions to negotiations. Citigroup knew that RAN was planning protests at Citigroup's upcoming April 15, 2003 annual meeting, marking the three-year anniversary of RAN's initial contact with Citigroup. ■

SOURCE: This case was written by Research Associate Erin Yurday, Cornell MBA 1998, under the supervision of Professor David P. Baron. This case would not have been possible without the help of Mike Brune and Ilyse Hogue of the Rainforest Action Network. Copyright © 2004 by the Board of Trustees of the Leland Stanford Junior University. All rights reserved. Reprinted with permission.

Preparation Questions

1. What damage, if any, is the RAN campaign doing to Citigroup?
2. Is RAN acting responsibly in campaigning against project financing? In its campaign tactics?
3. How vulnerable is Citigroup as a result of the Enron and Grubman scandals?
4. What should Citigroup anticipate next? What, if anything, should it do? Should it begin serious negotiations with RAN?
5. If Citigroup were to agree to negotiate, which agreements should RAN be prepared to accept and which to reject? What enforcement mechanism for the agreement should RAN seek?

---

[56]"SEEJ Members Influence Citigroup Corporate Agenda," *Columbia Daily Spectator*, February 3, 2004.

C H A P T E R
5
Crisis Management

INTRODUCTION

Crises happen even to firms that take measures to avoid them. Acts of nature and random events occur. Most crises involving businesses, however, have a degree of human involvement and at least the possibility that the firm was responsible for the crisis occurring. Human involvement could be on the part of the firm as in the case of the *Exxon Valdez* oil spill, a villain outside the firm as in the case of Tylenol laced with cyanide, or innocent persons in the case of patients experiencing side effects of a prescription drug. Crises require immediate attention and can have lasting effects on brands and the reputations of companies. Crises can also alter the operating practices of firms and industries. Medicines have tamper-resistant packaging, new oil tankers have double hulls, warnings on many prescription drugs are stronger, disclosure of pharmaceutical clinical trial results is broader, and postmarketing testing is conducted on some drugs.

Many firms, even those that have not experienced a crisis, have taken measures to reduce the likelihood of a crisis, formulated management preparedness plans, and developed crisis response plans. Wal-Mart had studied weather forecasts and projected the likely path of Hurricane Katrina and had delivered to its stores and distribution centers in the Gulf Coast states supplies that would be needed by people in the event of a disaster. When the hurricane struck, Wal-Mart was ready with portable generators, bottled water, and other needed items. In many cases, however, a crisis is difficult to forecast, but nevertheless firms can prepare for the types of crises that might develop and be prepared to respond.

This chapter addresses crisis management and its components: avoidance, preparedness, root cause analysis, response, and resolution. The focus is on crises that directly affect a firm's stakeholders and the broader public. The conceptual frameworks developed in the previous chapters provide the foundation for crisis management, and approaches specific to crisis management are introduced, particularly those associated with crisis response and communication.

THE NATURE AND CAUSES OF CRISES

A crisis may be defined as a situation in which harm to people or property either has occurred or is imminent. A crisis typically is unexpected, can escalate quickly, and can damage a firm's operating performance, its reputation, and the credibility of management. A crisis often requires a response or action under time pressure, so management must act with a sense of urgency. A crisis can attract the media and the attention of public and private politics actors. Moreover, the public may sympathize with those who were harmed, particularly if they were unsuspecting or unsophisticated. Many crises develop quickly, as in the case of Tylenol poisoning, but some fester for extended periods. The protests against Nike for alleged sweatshop conditions in the factories of its overseas suppliers continued for several years. (See the Chapter 4 case *Nike in Southeast Asia.*)

Tylenol   In 1982, seven people died from swallowing Tylenol capsules injected with cyanide. The crisis was identified when the Chicago medical examiner and fire department found that victims had in common the use of Tylenol. To prevent any further loss of life, Johnson & Johnson issued a nationwide recall of 31 million Tylenol capsules at a cost of $100 million. CEO James Burke personally appeared on television to explain the recall and answered questions at a news conference. The company's strong and rapid response and the evidence that the tampering had taken place in retail stores and not in the manufacturing process relieved Johnson & Johnson of responsibility.[1] Sales of Tylenol recovered quickly once the product was reintroduced. The company continues to be acclaimed for its quick action in an uncertain situation in which lives were at risk.

Exxon Valdez   The 1989 grounding of the *Exxon Valdez* and the accompanying spill of 11 million gallons of crude oil created an environmental crisis, and Exxon's response escalated the crisis.[2] Exxon responded by moving a team from Houston to Valdez, Alaska in 20 hours and was prepared to spray a chemical dispersant on the oil as called for in its oil spill procedures. For two days the Coast Guard prevented Exxon from doing so to run tests on the dispersant, and then a delay of an additional two days resulted because of bad weather that grounded aircraft. A report by Exxon revealed that the captain of the tanker was sleeping at the time of the grounding. Reports circulated that the captain, who had been assigned to the *Exxon Valdez* after completing alcohol rehabilitation, was drunk. Exxon was viewed by many people as directly responsible and in the eyes of many people as negligent. As considered below, the company's communication to the public provoked more criticism, and the damage to the company's reputation continues today.

Société Génerale   Although the specifics and timing are difficult to predict, some crises have a positive probability of developing. Rogue traders have caused billions of dollars of losses to financial markets firms, and firms engaged in financial services and commodities and currency trading have developed procedures and systems to control trading risks. Société Génerale, a leading financial services group in the euro zone, was proud of its control system, yet in 2008 a 31-year-old securities trader in France was revealed to have evaded the controls over three years, taking €50.4 billion in positions in European stocks. Unwinding the positions resulted in a loss of €4.9 billion, and forced the bank to quickly sell €5.5 billion in new shares to remain viable.

BP   An explosion at BP's Texas City, Texas refinery in 2005 killed 15 workers and injured another 170 people. The company had been warned of safety problems, and cost-cutting due to budget pressures may have led the company to delay dealing with the problems. The accident resulted in the company pleading guilty to criminal charges, paying fines, and facing liability lawsuits. The accident severely damaged BP's reputation—the company prided itself on its environmental and social responsibility programs—and dissipated public trust in the company.

THE PATTERN OF CRISIS DEVELOPMENT

Crises often have a pattern that can be conceptualized using the life cycle framework introduced in Chapter 1. Adapted for crisis management, the stages are identification, escalation, intervention, and resolution. The Chapter 4 case *Shell, Greenpeace, and Brent Spar* provides an opportunity to identify the stages of development of a crisis

---

[1]The Tylenol bottles were found to have been purchased in a small number of stores, and the batch numbers of the bottles quickly led police to conclude that the tampering had occurred in stores. The killer has never been identified.

[2]The oil spill was the largest in the United States but was exceeded by 21 other spills in other countries. The largest spill was 100 million gallons by the *Amoco Cadiz* off the Atlantic coast of France.

resulting from Shell's plans to sink an obsolete oil platform in the North Sea. The chapter case *Buffalo Savings Bank (A)* provides an opportunity to anticipate the possible development of a crisis associated with the forced refinancing of home mortgages.

The first stage in the life cycle of a crisis is *identification*. A crisis may result from a single event or from a series of developments over time. The subprime mortgage crisis of 2008 was the result of risky home mortgages issued over a period of several years that resulted in widespread defaults when the economy slowed. Similarly, the crisis centering on health risks from Merck's drug Vioxx resulted from accumulating evidence of risks to heart patients. A crisis can also result from a single event such as an accident, as in the case of Exxon officials who received a call from the captain of the *Exxon Valdez* that the ship had "fetched up hard aground" and was "leaking some oil." Some crises are revealed directly to the public whereas others are identified from inside the company. The Tylenol crisis was identified by a medical examiner and the fire department whose investigations identified the link between two deaths that were then traced to Tylenol capsules. The crisis at Société Génerale was identified internally and became public when the company notified law enforcement officials and regulators of its findings.

Some crises have unusual causes and come as a considerable surprise, as the Perrier example indicates.

Perrier and Benzene

Perrier mineral water, produced by Source Perrier S.A. of France, is a mixture of natural spring water and a gas obtained from wells near the source at Vergeze.[3] The gas from the well is basically carbon dioxide but contains a number of other elements including benzene and hydrogen sulfide. Benzene is a suspected carcinogen, and hydrogen sulfide is the gas that smells like rotten eggs. To remove the benzene and the hydrogen sulfide, Source Perrier used carbon filters and relied on the smell of hydrogen sulfide to know when to change the filter. Trouble developed when Perrier switched to gas from a new well that contained a lower concentration of hydrogen sulfide. Workers thus did not change the filters as often as needed to remove the benzene, and traces of benzene were left in the bottled mineral water. Routine tests in the United States disclosed benzene, and although the amounts were believed not to constitute a health hazard, the public was concerned and the media covered the issue extensively. Perrier initially dismissed the benzene reports, but after the disclosure, distributors in Japan, the Netherlands, and Denmark recalled the water. Perrier decided to issue a worldwide recall.

The second stage is *escalation*. Some crises explode as a result of media coverage, government actions, or company actions. In some cases such as that of the *Exxon Valdez* the crisis is exacerbated by the actions of the company, and in other cases the company's response quickly resolves the issue as in the case of the Tylenol poisonings. Other crises develop more slowly as in the case of side effects of drugs that are revealed through reports from hospital emergency rooms.

An important factor influencing the development of the public phase of a crisis is media coverage. Often media coverage begins before the firm can act, and hence the firm is forced into a reactive mode. Particularly in a reactive situation, communication with stakeholders, the public, and government through the media can be crucial to dealing with the crisis. A crisis and the accompanying media coverage can also lead to action by activists and NGOs as well as by government regulators. Congress is often interested in crises and can respond with legislation, as the chapter case *Mattel: Crisis Management or Management Crisis* indicates. Media coverage in a crisis can put a firm's reputation and brand at risk.

The effect of the media on the development and severity of a crisis can be assessed using the frameworks presented in Chapter 3. Greater media coverage can be expected when the issue at the core of the crisis is viewed as important to society and when the potential audience is large. Environmental degradation is an important societal issue and is of interest to a broad segment of society. Moreover, environmental issues often

---

[3]Perrier's label did not specify that its product was a mixture of water and carbon dioxide.

have a visual aspect that is attractive to media coverage. Although no deaths or human injuries resulted from the *Exxon Valdez* spill, media broadcasts showing dead birds, otters, and fish covered with oil shaped the public's assessment of the incident and made Exxon's task more difficult. The media can also adopt an advocacy mode, which can be to the detriment of the firm in the crisis. In some cases the media can also uncover information that can be helpful to the firm and calm a crisis.

Chapter 3 focuses primarily on institutionalized media, but with the Internet anyone can assume the role of the media. Disgruntled consumers, activists, and employees can post messages on blogs and videos on YouTube and other sites. These postings can identify or accelerate a crisis. The Internet also provides an opportunity for firms to communicate with stakeholders as well as its critics. A number of firms and their executives maintain blogs to communicate with the media and the public.

Intervention involves actions by the company or government to deal with the crisis. These actions include communication with stakeholders, the public, and government as well as substantive measures to resolve the crisis and lessen the likelihood that a similar crisis will occur in the future.

Some crises are more innocent but nevertheless serious, as the "PepsiCo and the Syringe Episode" boxed example indicates. Even when a crisis is due to fraud, an intentional hoax, or a simple mistake, it is essential for the company to intervene by communicating with the public and cooperating with law enforcement, regulatory, and public health officials. Particularly in a situation in which a company is certain that the claims are false, it is best to turn to law enforcement and regulatory authorities. In the Wendy's example, the news media also played an important role.

In some cases a potential crisis can be dissipated and die a natural death. Reports surfaced that McDonald's put worms in its hamburgers. Repeated denials by the company helped calm anxieties among customers, but founder Ray Kroc put the issue to rest by stating, "We couldn't afford to grind worms into our meat. Hamburger costs a dollar and a half a pound, and night crawlers six dollars."[4] Other absurd crises can fester. Periodically, Procter & Gamble is subjected to rumors that its moon and stars logo is a sign of devil worship. Despite their absurdity the rumors have persisted over several decades. In other cases the crisis can have more substantial consequences, even if it is a hoax or fraud, as illustrated in the Wendy's example.

Wendy's

In 2005 the media extensively covered the story of a woman who found a human finger in her chili at a Wendy's restaurant in San Jose, California. Wendy's explained that it was impossible for the finger to have been in its chili because of the process by which it was prepared and packaged. Moreover, any restaurant employee who had lost a finger would have reported it to the company and sought medical treatment. Nevertheless, sales at Wendy's restaurants dropped as a result of the incident and the media coverage.

The police and the local news media began to investigate the incident, and the investigations revealed that the woman had a history of questionable actions that had led to her arrest on several occasions. She also had filed lawsuits evidently intended to shake down companies, including a fast-food company. The police arrested her and her boyfriend for attempting to shake down Wendy's. The police found that the finger had been taken by her boyfriend from the site of an accident where he worked, and she had put the finger in her chili. Both the woman and her boyfriend were charged with fraud, convicted by a jury, and sentenced to prison.

Resolution involves turning the crisis into a manageable nonmarket issue. This may be accomplished by eliminating any further potential for harm, assuring the public and the media that the crisis has passed, or compensating those harmed. Source Perrier subsequently changed its procedures to regularly test the gas for chemical contaminants and reported that no benzene has been detected since the change. Resolution can also involve moving the crisis into the institutions of government. After the recall, the

---

[4]*Time*, 1992.

Tylenol crisis resided in the hands of law enforcement officials and the Food and Drug Administration.

The aftermath can persist long after the crisis has ended. A crisis involving a rogue trader leads to more costly and stringent internal controls in banks. Reputation damage can also persist, as in the case of Exxon. More stringent regulation can result as in the case of testing toys for lead. Frequently, when the crisis involves harm to people or damage to property, lawsuits follow. Trial lawyers represent victims and file lawsuits on their behalf. The lawyers typically receive one-third of any settlement or judgment and thus have strong incentives to pursue cases.

Even those crises in which a company had no responsibility can have a lingering effect on a company and its reputation. More people recall that a customer found part of a human finger in her chili at a Wendy's restaurant than recall that the woman planted the finger there in an attempt to extort a settlement from the company.

EXAMPLE

PepsiCo and the Syringe Episode[1]

On June 9, 1993 Earl and Mary Triplett of Tacoma, Washington, returned from a vacation and decided to have a late-night snack. Earl poured part of a Diet Pepsi into a glass for Mary, and he drank the rest of the contents with a straw. When he went to bed, he put the Diet Pepsi can in the sink. The next morning the Tripletts were surprised to find a syringe and needle in the can. Neither had been injured, but they quickly alerted authorities, and the local media reported the incident. After a second report the next day in the Seattle area, the Federal Drug Administration (FDA) warned Diet Pepsi drinkers in four western states served by the Alpac Corporation, the regional bottler for PepsiCo, to empty the contents of cans into a glass before drinking it.

The two incidents led to national news reports of possible product tampering and were quickly followed by a rash of other reports of incidents. Approximately 50 incidents of objects found in soft drink cans were reported in 23 states, mostly Pepsi products. No injuries were reported.

PepsiCo faced the issue of whether to recall products already on store shelves, cease production, or take other action. The company was confident that it was virtually impossible for a syringe or other object to get into a can. Craig A. Weatherup, president of PepsiCola North America, said, "It is 99.99 percent assured that nothing is happening in the facilities themselves, in the plants. It's literally, physically impossible."[2] When cans enter a bottling plant, they are covered by sheets, bound with straps, and checked for damage and quality. When they are ready for the bottling process, the straps are removed, and the cans are checked to see that they are empty. When the cans are ready to enter the bottling process, the sheets are removed and the cans are turned upside down and rinsed inside with water. The cans are then turned upright and filled by machines at a speed of 650 to 2,000 cans a minute. The filled cans proceed immediately to a seamer and are capped. The product is then inspected and packaged. A can is upright and open for less than one second.

PepsiCo inspected all its canning lines and examined its plant records searching for evidence of problems. It also investigated the origins of the cans reported in the incidents. Weatherup said, "These cans were produced at very different plants, some six months ago, some six weeks ago, some six days ago. And therefore there's no correlation between the complaints, when these cans were produced or where they were produced."[3] PepsiCo officials were confident that no tampering had taken place and that the syringes had gotten into the cans after they had been opened. PepsiCo concluded that a product recall was not warranted.

The FDA investigated the claims of objects found in Pepsi products in Washington and found no relation between the two incidents and that neither drink was contaminated. Roger Lowell, a district FDA director, said that the acidity of the soft drink would likely kill any bacteria or virus. FDA Commissioner David E. Kessler stated, "It is simply not logical to conclude that a nationwide tampering had occurred." The FDA's investigation could find no pattern in the reports. They were spread around the country and involved a variety of types of containers produced by different bottlers, in some cases months apart. The FDA had sophisticated forensic techniques, and

---

[2]*New York Times,* June 19, 1993.

[3]*New York Times,* June 19, 1993.

(Continued)

investigators were unable to confirm even one case of tampering. On June 14 the FDA decided not to issue a recall of Pepsi products.

When FDA Commissioner Kessler telephoned Weatherup on the evening of June 14, both knew that the claims of tampering were false. PepsiCo still had to deal with the public concerns. The company staffed telephone banks to answer consumer concerns and reassured its bottlers and distributors. The company also decided to produce a video of the canning process and sent it up by satellite on June 15. Bottlers and distributors were also concerned, and PepsiCo sent them information by fax twice a day. Some bottlers took steps of their own. The Buffalo Rock Company, a Pepsi bottler in Birmingham, Alabama, opened its plant to TV news crews.

Even though the claims appeared to be either hoaxes or hysteria, PepsiCo still faced a communications challenge. The company had to decide who would present the company's views to the public, and Weatherup was chosen because of his knowledge of the bottling process. On the evening of June 15, Weatherup and Kessler appeared on *Nightline* to defend the decision not to recall Pepsi products. Kessler knew that an arrest of a Pennsylvania man was imminent, and his assurance that there was no public danger helped calm public concerns. He also observed that in 1984 a single case of alleged tampering with Girl Scout Cookies resulted in 487 reports, none of which was ever verified. Weatherup then made appearances on *The MacNeil/Lehrer NewsHour,* the *Larry King Show,* and all three network news shows and morning news programs. He also made himself available for interviews by satellite. He urged consumers "to rely on their common sense and good judgment" and stated that no one had been injured and no contaminated drinks had been found. He assured the public that a syringe could not possibly have found its way into a can.

PepsiCo also faced the problem of reassuring retailers that pulling its products from their shelves was unwarranted. After Synthia Smith of San Jose, California, reported finding a syringe in a can of caffeine-free Pepsi, Safeway pulled Pepsi products from the store where she had bought it. The next day the store replaced the product with a batch from a different bottler. Debra Lambert, a spokeswoman for Safeway, said that there had been no appreciable decrease in Pepsi sales. She said, "Business was brisk after the product was replaced. People seem to be seeing it as a hoax." San Jose police searched Smith's home and found another syringe similar to the one she had reported finding in a Pepsi can. Her husband was a diabetic, and a recommended means of disposing of a syringe used for an insulin injection was to place it in an empty can.

An Aurora, Colorado, woman claimed to have found a syringe in a Pepsi can she opened at the supermarket checkout counter. A supermarket surveillance camera showed her taking an object out of her purse and placing it in the can she had just purchased and opened. She then showed it to the checkout person who saw a syringe in the can and reported it to the store manager. On June 17 PepsiCo released videotape it had prepared in which Weatherup narrated the events in the supermarket surveillance tape of the woman. Weatherup said his purpose was to "tell you what really happened."

The FBI arrested several people who had reported finding objects in Pepsi cans, local police arrested several others, and several others recanted their claims. Some of those arrested apparently had hoped to extort a cash settlement from PepsiCo. Product tampering hoaxes are not uncommon. In February 1993 the FBI had arrested Douglas John Knight after he deposited a $350,000 check extorted under FBI surveillance after he threatened to tamper with Pepsi products. In March 1993 Bobby Jo Johnson of Oklahoma City was convicted on charges of tampering with a Pepsi can.[4]

After the FBI had made over twenty arrests and the tampering claims had stopped, PepsiCo ran full-page advertisements in a dozen national newspapers, and bottlers ran advertisements in 300 to 400 local papers explaining the hoax and thanking customers for staying with its products. Weatherup stated: "We'd like to thank the millions of Americans who have stood behind us. We're eager to put this incident behind us. Consumer safety and product integrity are of utmost importance to us. We know that the American people, in their good sense and extraordinary fairness, will continue to support us as we go forward. It's time to get on with business."[5]

---

[4]Federal law against filing false tampering charges provides for a maximum penalty of five years in prison and a fine of $250,000.
[5]Pepsi news release, Somers, N.J., June 18, 1993.

COMPONENTS OF A CRISIS MANAGEMENT PROGRAM

Crisis management has five components: avoidance, preparedness, response, root cause analysis, and resolution. The timing of these components and the pattern of crisis development are depicted in Figure 5-1. The Brent Spar episode in Chapter 4 is a good example of a company without a crisis management plan to deal with the private politics that erupted over its plan for disposal of an obsolete oil rig.

FIGURE 5-1   Crisis Management and the Crisis Life Cycle

Avoidance

The most important component of a crisis management program is avoidance, and the next most important component is preparedness. The best approach to crisis management is to reduce the likelihood of a crisis developing, and an important precursor to doing so is an assessment of the exposure of the company in its nonmarket environment.

One aspect of an avoidance strategy is auditing. One type of audit focuses on risks and their causes. This is also the first step in developing measures for reducing risks that can damage the performance of the firm. Audit findings must be acted upon. In 2005 prior to the refinery explosion a BP health and safety business plan had warned that the refinery would "likely kill someone in the next 12–18 months."[5] The risk assessment should also include an assessment of the risk of litigation and regulatory actions.

Another type of audit focuses on reputation risk. This audit assesses the potential impacts of a crisis on the stakeholders of the firm and its reputation with them, the public, and government. Reputations are difficult to evaluate in terms of both their importance and the extent to which they can be damaged by a crisis and a company's response to it. A reputation for responsible management can be important in the marketplace, in relations with business partners, and with respect to groups and institutions in the nonmarket environment. Activists, NGOs, regulators, and legislators give additional scrutiny to firms with bad reputations.

Reputations are harder to build than they are to dissipate. Johnson & Johnson had developed a strong reputation not only for its handling of the Tylenol crisis but also for tangible concern for its stakeholders. That reputation mitigated the adverse publicity when it sued the American Red Cross for trademark infringement. The Red Cross had begun to license the red cross symbol to companies to use on products that competed with those of Johnson & Johnson, but a nineteenth-century agreement with Johnson & Johnson prohibited the Red Cross from using the symbol on commercial products.

Reputations are built by actions, through products, and by policies to which a firm adheres. Reputations are strengthened and maintained by conduct that accepts responsibility for actions and that benefits stakeholders and respects the public trust. Reputations are also strengthened by openness, forthright conduct, and transparency.

Many firms appear to overestimate the strength of their reputation and the protection it provides. Many people are skeptical of firms and their motives and have a low level of trust in business. This can make a reputation fragile and easily damaged.

---

[5]*Wall Street Journal*, March 14, 2008.

A crisis, accident, or scandal can severely strain a reputation, and failure to respond in a responsible manner can result in damage that is difficult to repair. Moreover, years of reputation building can be dissipated quickly. BP's reputation as an environmentally and socially responsible company was severely damaged by events over a two-year period. In addition to the refinery explosion, leaks in a pipeline in Alaska spilled oil in Prudhoe Bay and on the tundra, and price fixing in the propane market called into question its credibility, as well as the quality of its management.

A firm may be thought of as having a reputation or trust account that reflects the aggregate effect of its past actions and conduct. The balance in the trust account is increased by how effectively it operates its business and manages its interactions with stakeholders, the public, and government. The balance is decreased by crises, illegal acts, and public criticism of its conduct. Negative events can be more powerful than positive events. The public seems to remember negative events more than positive events, and hence one negative event can wipe out trust built by several positive events. This asymmetry is important to recognize and makes effective crisis management imperative.

The importance of reputation and trust, however, may not be as great as some commentators claim. As indicated in Chapter 1, Citigroup has been involved in a large number of scandals and illegal actions that resulted in fines and large settlements. In addition, it structured securities to keep risks off its books, as in the case of portfolios of subprime mortgages. When mortgage defaults and foreclosures mounted, the subprime mortgage market began to collapse along with the value of its portfolios. Citigroup was at best inaccurate and at worst misrepresented the magnitude of its potential losses, resulting in the firing of its CEO. Nevertheless, there is little evidence that the scandals and crises have impaired the company's ability to hire talented people or caused business partners to shun it.

Crisis Preparedness

An essential part of preparedness is organization. Firms susceptible to a crisis need a crisis management team that can be mobilized quickly and can substantively address the root cause of a crisis. Exxon was prepared for one dimension of an oil spill crisis—it had a cleanup plan. It was unprepared, however, for the public component of a crisis—that is, expressing remorse, assuming responsibility for the incident, interacting with the local residents, and dealing with the media and government.

In most cases a company wants one spokesperson who can speak for the company with a single, consistent voice. The spokesperson must be continuously informed about the facts of the situation as well as new developments. Two considerations are important in selecting the spokesperson. First, the person should be effective in communicating with the public and in interacting with the media. Second, the person should be knowledgeable about the central factors involved in the crisis. PepsiCo chose a person knowledgeable about the bottling process, which was at the center of the crisis.

The other aspect of organization is policies that help team members as well as others to act in response to developments. Johnson & Johnson operates under a long-established mission statement, "Our Credo," presented in Chapter 22, that emphasizes the primacy of serving its stakeholders. Exxon's cleanup procedures involved the quick application of a dispersant to reduce the environmental damage from a spill.

In addition to organization, firms may identify and earmark resources that can be mobilized if a crisis occurs. This can involve physical resources such as those to contain an oil spill or deal with a fire or explosion. It also can involve the identification of outside contractors that can provide assistance or experts whose advice can be quickly obtained.

An important part of preparedness is organizational learning. Some firms encounter crises frequently enough that they have an opportunity to refine and develop their approach to crisis management and improve their preparedness. In the Wal-Mart and Hurricane Katrina example that follows the company had experienced enough hurricanes that it had developed statistical data on the items people bought in anticipation of a hurricane and after it had struck. McDonald's had experienced crises resulting from mad cow disease in the United Kingdom and other European countries and had learned from those experiences. When the first case of mad cow disease was reported in the United States, it was prepared to act. It assured the public that its beef was safe and described the measures it took to avoid animals that might have the disease. Sales were unaffected.

Insurance against the cost of a crisis can also be purchased. Insurance is offered for natural disasters, industrial accidents such as fires, and liability for product injuries. More innovative insurance is also offered. XL Insurance offers food-and-drink product contamination insurance, which also covers product recalls. Insurance coverage is available for oil and chemical spills, political risks, and foreign direct investments. Insurance, however, only compensates for direct harm done to the insured and does not help manage in a crisis situation.

Preparedness: Wal-Mart and Hurricane Katrina

With over 3,300 stores in the United States Wal-Mart was experienced in dealing with crises of many types, including hurricanes. Analysis of its sales data revealed that prior to a hurricane people stocked up on items ranging from bottled water to generators, and after a hurricane had struck they bought chain saws and cleaning supplies. Wal-Mart operated an Emergency Operations Center in its headquarters and had begun tracking a storm in the Caribbean when it was upgraded to tropical depression status, some six days before it struck the Gulf Coast as Hurricane Katrina. Using forecasts of the National Weather Service and private meteorologists, the company projected the path of the storm. Wal-Mart initially sent supplies to its stores in Florida where the storm was projected to hit. To keep its stores operating, Wal-Mart used its truck fleet to deliver back-up generators, fuel, and dry ice. When the storm crossed the tip of Florida without causing much damage, Wal-Mart turned its attention to the Gulf Coast. With the aid of its meteorologists it projected landfall just east of New Orleans and immediately began sending generators and supplies to its distribution centers in the Gulf region.[6] Wal-Mart also sent a "loss-prevention" team to protect its stores from looting.

As the devastation from the hurricane and flooding became evident, Wal-Mart delivered $3 million of supplies to residents and relief and rescue personnel and donated $17 million in cash to relief organizations. Stores gave away clothing, food, and pharmaceuticals to desperate local residents, and truck drivers remained in the area hauling relief supplies to where they were needed. The company set up mini Wal-Marts in the backs of trucks, in tents, and remaining buildings to distribute free items such as food, water, clothing, and other essentials. Some Wal-Mart stores were used as shelters and headquarters for police and the National Guard. The mayor of Kenner, Louisiana, said, "The only lifeline in Kenner was the Wal-Mart stores. We didn't have looting on a mass scale because Wal-Mart showed up with food and water so our people could survive. The Red Cross and FEMA need to take a master class in logistics and mobilization from Wal-Mart."[7] When the hurricane hit, 126 Wal-Mart stores were forced to close because of lost power, storm damage, or flooding, but within two weeks all but 13 stores were operating and 97 percent of their employees were back at work or had been offered jobs elsewhere in Wal-Mart stores.

Root Cause Analysis

The first step in developing an effective response is to analyze the crisis. This is straightforward for many companies. Wal-Mart was accustomed to dealing with the impacts of hurricanes, having dealt with four in the year before Hurricane Katrina. When it is not straightforward, the four I's identified in Chapter 1 provide the starting point. This requires identifying the issues involved in the crisis. In the Tylenol crisis the issues were the likely tampering but more importantly the possibility of further harm to consumers. Information was incomplete, since the company had no idea how many capsules had been laced with cyanide. Nor did the company know whether capsules were

---

[6]Some other companies such as Home Depot also used their distribution systems to provide relief items.
[7]*Fortune*, October 3, 2005.

poisoned outside the Chicago area. The relevant institutions were the FDA and the court of public sentiment that would assess the company's handling of the crisis. The interests were primarily the consumers who were potentially at risk, in addition to Johnson & Johnson's shareholders and employees.

A second step is root cause analysis, which has the objective of identifying the causes of the crisis. This provides the basis for resolution of the present crisis, avoidance of future crises, and preparedness for crises that do result. In the Société Génerale case the root cause was flaws in the supervision and control system used to monitor trades. The bank quickly fixed the flaws, and it also continued to search for accomplices. The root cause in the BP crisis was cost-cutting that had led to unsafe working conditions, and the root cause in the *Exxon Valdez* crisis was a failure by the tanker crew and captain to follow procedures. In the Pepsi crisis it was clear to the company and the FDA that the incidents were hoaxes or fraud.

The root cause in the Tylenol crisis was product tampering, and as that became clear and the product recall progressed, Johnson & Johnson was absolved from responsibility. Nevertheless, product tampering remained a concern, and companies improved their packaging to make tampering more difficult and easier for consumers to detect if it had occurred. Similarly, rogue traders may be difficult to identify ex ante as a series of trading scandals had revealed. The root causes are multiple, but incentive compensation systems and inadequate controls and monitoring are important causes. One root cause of the subprime mortgage crisis was the incentives for mortgage brokers and lenders to issue mortgages to unqualified borrowers to collect fees up front. Another cause was the opportunity for firms to package mortgages and sell portfolios to investors who were either unable to assess their riskiness or relied on the reputation of the sellers.

In the early 1990s Denny's restaurants were revealed to have discriminated against African-American customers, resulting in lawsuits and widespread media attention.[8] The company identified the root cause as insensitivity to discrimination and a lack of training of employees. The company implemented an extensive training program and created opportunities for minorities to advance within the company. Several years later Denny's was ranked as the best company for minorities to work.

Response

Response includes actions to resolve the crisis, deal with the root cause, and communicate with stakeholders, the public, and government. The appropriate action depends on the root cause and the specifics of the situation. In the Tylenol crisis the principal concern was whether other bottles with cyanide-laced capsules could be on retailers' shelves or in consumers' medicine cabinets. With the guidance of "Our Credo" it was clear that Johnson & Johnson had to recall Tylenol, but whether the risks were confined to the Chicago area was unclear. The only way to be sure of eliminating further harm was to issue a nationwide recall.

In the Pepsi crisis the root cause was not product tampering, and neither people nor property were at risk of harm. No recall was needed, but PepsiCo still had to decide whether a recall was needed to reassure consumers. Consumers seemed little concerned, since no deaths or injuries had been reported. PepsiCo's challenge then was to communicate effectively with its customers and to work with government to end the crisis.

Effective and Ineffective Communication

Communication and rectification are the two principal components of crisis response. Since crises often develop quickly, information is often incomplete and speculation and rumors can fly. Even when information is complete or the crisis self-evident, it is important to communicate effectively with those affected by the crisis as well as the public more broadly. A large industry of communications specialists is available to provide advice on effective communication, and firms have developed their own capabilities. As considered in Chapter 3, many firms provide media relations training for their executives.

---

[8]See the Chapter 22 case, *Denny's and Customer Service.*

Communication with stakeholders can be crucial. PepsiCo faxed information twice a day to its bottlers and distributors to keep them abreast of the developments. Companies also need to communicate with employees who may be concerned about the role of their employer in the crisis. When Denny's identified the root cause of the discrimination, it began training its employees and also produced a television advertisement in which its servers and restaurant managers pledged to provide good service to all customers.

Companies also have to communicate to the public, and this communication often takes place through the news media. Interacting with journalists is considered in Chapter 3, and communication with journalists in a crisis is guided by the same principles. The difference is the time pressure resulting from the crisis and the possibility that the firm may not know the origins or causes of the crisis. Johnson & Johnson's first hint of a possible crisis came from an inquiry by a reporter covering the medical examiner's suspicions about the poisonings.[9]

In some crises the government can play an important role in communicating with the public, but the firm often has better information than the government, making cooperation with government essential. PepsiCo worked with the FDA to assure the public that no product tampering had occurred. Choosing a spokesperson knowledgeable about the root cause of the crisis can be important, particularly when the cause and nature of the crisis are complex. As mentioned above, PepsiCo chose as its spokesperson an executive who was knowledgeable about the bottling process.

The messages conveyed can be crucial to resolving the crises and protecting the reputation of the company. Communication specialists advocate messages that are truthful, sincere, and express concern for those affected. If people have been harmed, messages should express concern and sympathy for the victims, and, if appropriate, pledge aid to the victims. Because stakeholders and the public may be suspicious of the company as a result of the crisis, messages should be transparent and reassuring. For example, a message could be that the company is taking all possible steps to ensure that further harm does not result and that the problem does not reoccur. Credibility of the company and spokesperson are important, particularly when the company has a trust deficit. Some people assume the worst when a crisis erupts, and some people are suspicious of communication by businesses because of the incentives to protect the profits of the firm rather than to attend to those harmed by the crisis. For some people perception becomes reality.

In addition to communicating with stakeholders and the public, a firm in crisis must also communicate with government agencies. Johnson & Johnson worked with local governments and the FDA. Some crises result in new legislation or regulatory rule making, and companies need to anticipate these developments. Mattel lobbied Congress for new legislation mandating testing for lead in paint on toys. Communication may also be addressed to financial analysts, business partners, suppliers, dealers, and others in the firm's value chain.

The effectiveness of messages can be enhanced if they are corroborated by messages from independent sources. In some cases the media can play this role, and in others the government assumes this role. The FDA corroborated PepsiCo's message that the syringe could not have been put in the can during the bottling process. Similarly, police and medical examiner reports revealed that the poison in Tylenol capsules had been injected after the bottles were on retailers' shelves.

Systematic evidence on the effectiveness of crisis communication is difficult to come by, and some researchers have turned to laboratory experiments. Uhlmann, Newman, Brescoll, Galinsky, and Diermeier (2008) conducted an experiment in which 126 corporate executives evaluated three responses to a hypothetical crisis involving finding lead in paint on a toy. One response emphasized engagement and a pledge to investigate the incident and take appropriate action. A second response was defensive, challenging the independent investigation that had been conducted and stating that the

---

[9]Fink (2002).

company's safety procedures were effective. The third response was "No comment." The respondents were asked to evaluate the company, and the engagement message yielded a significantly more favorable evaluation than the other two, which had comparable evaluations. This study suggests that the message itself can affect the public's evaluation of the company and perhaps its reputation and brand.

Exxon

Exxon's communication with the public was ineffective at best. Immediately after the oil spill, an Exxon official accepted responsibility for the cleanup. Exxon also took out advertisements in 100 newspapers and magazines for "An Open Letter to the Public" from chairman Lawrence Rawl stating, "I want to tell you how sorry I am that this accident took place. We at Exxon are especially sympathetic to the residents of Valdez and the people of the state of Alaska." Rawl also appeared on television giving the same message. Later, in a statement to the press, the company said,

> The *Exxon Valdez* spill was an accident, a bad one. But accidents can happen to anyone. If Exxon's rules and regulations governing conduct aboard ship had been followed, the accident would not have occurred. If Exxon had been permitted to follow the cleanup plan immediately, the effects of the spill would not have been as extensive.[10]

Several messages conveyed in these statements drew criticism. First, the statements characterized the episode as an accident, but many observers viewed Exxon as having caused the oil spill. Second, Exxon seemed to blame the captain and crew, and the spill was clearly their fault, but Exxon was responsible for their conduct. Third, taking responsibility for the cleanup was not enough. Extensive media coverage showed not only the oil in the bay and on shore, but the public also saw repeated images of otters and sea birds covered in oil, some of which were dead and others in jeopardy. No cleanup could restore the lost wildlife and the damage to their habitat. Moreover, skeptics worried about whether the natural environment could ever recover from the spill. Fourth, the livelihood of fishers and other businesses in Prince William Sound were jeopardized. Fifth, although Exxon had been delayed by the Coast Guard from beginning its cleanup, placing blame on the government appeared to be an attempt to shift responsibility. Nor was it clear to the public that if Exxon had been able to implement its cleanup procedures immediately, the damage would have been significantly mitigated.[11] Sixth, although Exxon expressed sympathy for the residents of Valdez, it did little to aid them in the days after the spill. Within a year of the oil spill, however, Exxon had voluntarily compensated the people affected by the spill, but that was not sufficient to overcome the adverse effects of the media coverage and its earlier communication with the public. Residents subsequently filed a lawsuit for compensation for private harm.

What Might Exxon Have Done?

Exxon was in a difficult position and appears to have been more concerned with potential liability, and possible punitive damages, for the oil spill than with its reputation. Whether the risk to the company's reputation was more serious than the liability risk is not clear, but Exxon likely could have reduced its reputation risk, and perhaps avoided being labeled a pariah by many people, if had responded differently. Given the seriousness of the situation and the intense media and public attention, how effective any communication could have been remains speculative.

Exxon repeatedly referred to the oil spill as an accident, but it was not an accident caused by nature but by humans. The company accepted responsibility for the cleanup but it did not apologize. Apologizing and acknowledging its responsibility for the spill, as well as for the cleanup, likely would have helped the company communicate more effectively. Exxon also could have expressed remorse for its role rather than expressing

---

[10]*New York Times,* May 3, 1989. Quoted in Tyler (1997).
[11]Exxon had initially said that if it had been allowed to use the dispersant 50 percent of the oil could have been contained. Exxon later said that the containment would have been 35 percent. *Anchorage Daily News,* March 24, 1989.

sympathy. It also could have acknowledged the harm to animal life and to the livelihoods of local residents who depended on the Sound. Tangible actions, such as establishing a private fund for dealing with wildlife habitats and for compensating fishers who depended on the Sound, might have spoken larger than words. Moreover, top management could have gone to the scene to represent the company, talk with residents, and assure the public and government officials about the cleanup. Exxon was undoubtedly correct not to discuss whether the ship's captain had been drinking, since that was a factual matter to be addressed in court.

Concerns about Liability

In formulating a strategy for addressing a crisis, a firm must consider both its exposure to liability and its response to stakeholders and the public. Advice from legal counsel is essential, but managers should not underestimate the cost of reputation damage and harm to a brand that can result from an inadequate response.

Did Exxon's public statements, expressions of concern, and cleanup actions reduce its potential liability? The prior question is whether the harm from a liability judgment would exceed the harm from the additional reputation damage to the company if it had changed its approach to communicating with the public. Hindsight indicates that Exxon's reputation remains tainted by the *Exxon Valdez* episode, exposing the company to greater public and private politics pressure. Reputation damage is difficult to value, however. [12] Resolution of the litigation occurred 19 years after the oil spill.

It is not at all clear that the verdicts would have been different if Exxon had apologized and accepted responsibility for the episode and the conduct of the captain and crew. Trials involve discovery that results in the revelation of information, and witnesses can describe events. The failure to apologize or to admit responsibility thus may have had little effect on the outcome of litigation. Firms, however, rarely admit negligence, since that can provide the basis for punitive damages, as considered in Chapter 12. If the captain of the *Exxon Valdez* was drunk and asleep when the ship went aground, he and Exxon could have been found negligent. The Supreme Court has begun to cap the ratio of punitive damages to compensatory damages, but nevertheless those damages can be large.

The litigation record is now complete, and Exxon's assessment of the litigation risk at the time might have been different from what hindsight reveals. A jury acquitted the captain of criminal charges. Exxon faced five criminal charges, pleaded guilty to three lesser charges, and paid a $25 million fine. In addition to $2.1 billion in cleanup costs, Exxon paid $900 million in compensatory damages and several hundred million dollars to local fishers, for a total cost of $3.4 billion. A jury also awarded Alaskan residents $5 billion in punitive damages, but an appeals court ruled that the award was excessive and cut the award to $2.5 billion. Exxon appealed to the Supreme Court, and in 2008 the Court reduced the award to $507 million.

Resolution

The Tylenol crisis was resolved when no further deaths resulted and law enforcement authorities concluded that the tampering had been the work of a person who had opened the packages, removed and opened the bottles, injected cyanide, put the bottles back in the packages, and resealed them. Once that became clear, Johnson & Johnson reintroduced Tylenol with new packaging, and sales quickly recovered to pre-tampering levels. One lesson from this episode is that the problem should be fixed before the firm begins to resume its normal marketing activities.

As the *Exxon Valdez* episode indicates, some crises, and their effects, can persist. The reputation damage to Exxon continues, and for many people the company remains a symbol of irresponsibility. Many crises are difficult to resolve because of continued attention from the media, politicians, and trial lawyers. BP attempted to resolve one aspect of its refinery explosion crisis by negotiating a settlement with the

---

[12]Exxon had profits of $40.6 billion in 2007—the largest ever of any U.S. company.

Department of Justice. BP pleaded guilty to a felony violation of the Clean Air Act and paid a fine of $50 million. In 2008 the settlement was questioned by Representative John Dingell (D-MI) who asked whether BP "executives have culpability, and should have been held to account?"

The PepsiCo example illustrates effective management in a crisis situation. Even though the company knew that reports of objects found in its cans were false at best and fraud at worst, it had to reassure consumers and the public of the safety of its products. The company knew that the FDA had responsibility for food safety and would be investigating the reports. This was a boon to PepsiCo, since the FDA would likely corroborate its statements that it was impossible for these objects to get into a can. To demonstrate this PepsiCo uploaded film of its bottling process showing the speed of the operation and showing that a can was upright and uncapped for less than one second. As mentioned, one of its bottlers opened its plant to TV crews so that they could film the can filling process. PepsiCo also kept its bottlers informed of developments and the steps it was taking to deal with the crisis. Copycats continued to report objects in Pepsi cans, but the reports of arrests for filing false reports ended the copycatting.

A Hardball Response

In 2007 the government of Thailand issued compulsory licenses for the production of drugs used in the treatment of cancer, heart conditions, and AIDS. The licenses allowed generic drug makers in India and elsewhere to produce drugs whose patents had not expired. Abbott Laboratories held the patent on one of the drugs, which was an important second-line treatment for AIDS. (See the Chapter 18 case, *Compulsory Licensing, Thailand, and Abbott Laboratories*.)

Abbott chose a hardball response. The company announced that it was withdrawing all its applications for registering new drugs in Thailand, including an important new version of its AIDS drug that required no refrigeration. Abbott's decision was widely criticized by AIDS activists and public health officials. The criticism damaged not only Abbott's reputation but also that of the pharmaceutical industry more broadly. Few if any pharmaceutical companies would have responded as Abbott did. Whether the response improved Abbott's bargaining power with the government of Thailand or other governments that might issue compulsory licenses remains unclear.

Because of Abbott's actions the French AIDS activist group Act Up–Paris launched a cyber attack in which between 500 and 1,000 activists in 12 countries participated in an International Day of Action to overload Abbott's Web site during a 4-hour period, halting online sales. In response, Abbott filed a lawsuit in a French criminal court alleging that the group had violated two articles of French criminal law. Abbott was widely criticized by AIDS activists and NGOs, adding to the reputation damage.[13]

SUMMARY

Crises happen. They are typically unexpected, often escalate quickly, and frequently are characterized by incomplete information about their cause and likely development. Even though their occurrence may be difficult to anticipate and their development hard to predict, firms can improve their crisis management through planning and preparation.

Crises have patterns that progress through stages. Some crises are identified within a firm, but many are identified outside the firm by consumers, business partners, or government. Crises can escalate quickly, particularly when the news media covers the developments. How a crisis develops depends on the intervention of not only the firm but often government as well. In cases involving safety and health, natural disasters, or environmental damage, government agencies have expertise and can be an important source of information and action. Government can typically mobilize resources and deploy them to where they are needed. Firms and government agencies often work

---

[13]Abbott subsequently dropped the lawsuit.

together in resolving a crisis. Crises pass, but their effects can continue in the form of changes in management practices, new government regulations, or increased public scrutiny of the performance of firms.

Crisis management is intended to anticipate the possibility of a crisis and be prepared to respond effectively if one develops. The most important component of crisis management is avoidance; that is, reducing the probability that a crisis will occur. This can involve audits of risks and reputation to assess exposure and changes in management practices to reduce the likelihood of a crisis. Preparedness involves organization as well as identifying resources to be mobilized in the event that a crisis occurs. When a crisis occurs, a firm must respond appropriately and communicate with those involved as well as with the public and government. A response requires identifying the root cause of the crisis so that its effects can be contained and future crises avoided. A response also requires action to provide relief to those affected and steps to ensure that more are not affected. Effective communication can involve acceptance of responsibility, an apology to those affected, expression of concern for those affected, and assurance that the problem is being addressed and will not reoccur. Government agencies can play an important role in communicating with the public, identifying the source of the crisis, and helping address its effects. Once a crisis has been resolved, a firm must reassess its crisis avoidance measures and its preparedness.

The chapter case *Mattel: Crisis Management or Management Crisis* presents a case in which lead was found in the paint on Mattel toys. The case proceeds in chronological stages that allow the formulation of responses and strategies as the crisis unfolds. The chapter case *Merck and Vioxx* is similarly organized and focuses on what the company should do about a blockbuster drug as information about possible side effects becomes available. Crises are also present in the following cases: *Shell, Greenpeace, and the Brent Spar* (Chapter 4), *Obesity and McLawsuits* (Chapter 12), *DoubleClick and Internet Privacy* (Chapter 13), *Pfizer and Celebrex* (Chapter 20), and *Denny's and Customer Service* (Chapter 22). The Chapter 23 case *Siemens: Anatomy of Bribery* concerns a series of developments centering on questionable payments to obtain business.

------------------------------------- C A S E S -------------------------------------

Buffalo Savings Bank (A)

In September 1981 the Buffalo Savings Bank, a mutual savings bank located in Buffalo, New York, faced a dilemma. Although it was the largest mortgage lender in the area with $2.95 billion in assets and over 40,000 mortgages outstanding, the bank had a $10.3 million net operating loss during the first 6 months of the year. Gains from the sale of securities and other investments had resulted in a small profit, however.

The operating loss incurred by the bank was typical of the losses being incurred by other thrift institutions as a result of the high cost of short-term funds and the low yield on their long-term loan portfolios. In addition, the nation was in a recession. One opportunity for reducing the bank's operating losses was to call 900 "renegotiable rate mortgages," which because of the state usury law had been made at an 8.5 percent interest rate in 1975 and 1976 even though lenders in other states were receiving 10.5 to 11 percent on the mortgages they were extending.[14] To justify issuing mortgages at below-market rates, the bank had made the mortgages callable in 5 years to protect itself in the event of further increases in interest rates.[15] As bank president Ross Kenzie stated, "Most of our competitors were out of the market at the time. At least we made money available at the time.[16]

Kenzie had been a high-ranking officer of Merrill Lynch, but in 1979 after being passed over for promotion, he left to head the Buffalo Savings Bank. At Merrill Lynch, he had developed a reputation as a hard-nosed executive who had the unfortunate task of firing managers whose performance in the rapidly changing financial services industry was unsatisfactory. Kenzie joined Buffalo Savings Bank with the objective of generating growth by diversifying into real estate and mortgage banking and through the acquisition of other thrifts. A principal limit on his growth plans was the depletion of capital by the continuing losses on outstanding loans. As with other thrifts, Buffalo Savings Bank was being hurt by the imbalance between record high interest rates, which made funds expensive, and the low yield on its long-term loan portfolio.

Although the 900 renegotiable rate mortgages were callable after five years, the monthly payment on the mortgages had been calculated on the customary 25- or 30-year basis. Borrowers had been informed of the call provision, and one of the borrowers, Joseph Leto of Tonowanda, remembered noticing the clause when he closed his mortgage.[17] Richard K. Schueckler, vice president in charge of loan servicing, recalled, however, that the bank had also indicated to the borrowers that it had never before called in a mortgage instrument.

One alternative the bank was considering was to offer the 900 borrowers the option of refinancing their mortgages at an interest rate of 14 percent, even though the going rates on new mortgages were 17 to 18.5 percent. Refinancing the mortgages at 14 percent would yield the bank an additional $1 million annually in interest income. The bank, however, was concerned about the impact of the refinancing on the borrowers. For a $30,000 mortgage, the monthly payment with a 30-year term and an 8.5 percent interest rate was approximately $230. At 14 percent, the monthly payment would be $355, whereas the payment at an 18 percent rate would be $452. Although refinancing the mortgages at 14 percent would impose a significant additional cost on the borrowers, they would still be receiving a substantial benefit relative to the current market rate of interest.

Bank managers who favored calling the mortgages argued that the renegotiable rate mortgages were a form of risk-sharing between the bank and the borrowers and that the borrowers had been informed of this provision. Furthermore, they argued that the borrowers had received a benefit of 2 to 2.5 percent during the past 5 years compared with the market rate at the time the mortgages were extended. In exchange, the borrowers bore some risk that market rates 5 years in the future would exceed 8.5 percent. The fact that the bank was considering offering to renegotiate the mortgages at 3 to 5 percent below current market rates was viewed as a considerable concession.

Opponents of calling the mortgages argued that not only would the borrowers suffer from the higher monthly payments, but the bank might find its reputation impaired by calling the mortgages during a period of extremely high interest rates. After all, the bank's motto was "You can believe in Buffalo." ∎

---

[14]State usury laws on home mortgages were prohibited by the federal Monetary Control Act enacted in March 1980.

[15]In the early 1980s adjustable rate mortgages were not used, and renegotiable rate mortgages were also very uncommon. The renegotiable rate mortgages differed from adjustable rate mortgages because the mortgages were callable at the discretion of the bank and the interest rate if the mortgages were renegotiated was unspecified.

[16]Owner financing of home sales had begun by 1981, and loan contracts often specified balloon payments after a period of 3 to 5 years. Those payments would not start coming due until 1984.

---

[17]New York law required home buyers to be represented by an attorney, who in all likelihood would have reviewed the clause with the client.

Preparation Questions

1. What gave rise to this issue?
2. Apply the framework in Figure 5-1 to the issue of whether to call and refinance the mortgages.
3. What is likely to happen if the bank calls the 900 mortgages?
4. What specifically should the bank do about the 900 mortgages?

Mattel: Crisis Management or Management Crisis

Introduction

In late 2006 and early 2007 a number of imports from China were found to pose health risks. In the most serious case the deaths of 200 people in Haiti and Panama were linked to syrup from China containing the chemical diethylene glycol used in antifreeze. British Airways withdrew Chinese toothpaste from its in-flight pouches for the same reason. Large quantities of imported dog food were found to contain the chemical melamine, resulting in death and injury to as many as 4,000 pets. An investigation by the Chinese government found that two suppliers had intentionally used melamine to save money and increase the protein content. The U.S. Food and Drug Administration (FDA) banned the importation of certain seafoods from China because of contamination. Representative Bart Stupak (D-MI) commented, "While I am pleased that the FDA realizes the danger these Asian and Chinese seafood imports pose to the American people, I am concerned that it requires congressional prodding of the FDA to take the steps necessary to keep American consumers safe."[18] No serious injuries or fatalities were reported in the United States.

Safety and health concerns were not limited to food. In November 2006 the retailer Target recalled 200,000 Kool Toyz action figures because of lead contamination and sharp edges. On June 13, 2007 RC2 Corporation recalled 1.5 million of its Thomas & Friends toy trains because of high lead levels in the paint. RC2 quickly fired both the company producing the trains and the paint vendor but did not disclose their names. Some 8,000 toy factories in China employed 3 million people, producing most of the world's toys. Approximately 80 percent of the toys sold in the United States were made in China.

China was at first defensive. It banned two shipments of food from the United States and even released a statement that an FDA regulation allowed the toxic chemical diethylene glycol in toothpaste. The FDA stated that its regulation allowed as an additive polyethylene glycol, not diethylene glycol. China subsequently announced that it was strengthening its food safety regulations and ordered 180 food plants to close. It also said inspectors had uncovered 23,000 violations of food safety regulations. The *China Daily* reported finding industrial chemicals in foods ranging from candy to seafood to pickles and biscuits. In July a high-ranking official of China's Food and Drug Administration was sentenced to death for corruption and approving counterfeit drugs.

With safety concerns about imports from China on the minds of readers, on July 26, 2007 the *New York Times* carried a feature article on the precautions Mattel, the world's largest toymaker, took to ensure the safety of its toys. In contrast to other toymakers Mattel owned the factories in China where its most popular toys, such as Barbie dolls and Hot Wheels cars, were made. Those factories accounted for half the company's dollar volume with the rest coming from toys manufactured under contract, often by suppliers with long-term relationships with the company. Mattel also operated a testing laboratory in Shenzhen, China where employees tested products for safety, including possible misuse of the toys. Jim Walter, a Mattel vice president, said, "We are not perfect; we have holes. But we're doing more than anyone else." Professor S. Prakash Sethi of the City University of New York, who regularly conducted inspections of Mattel suppliers' factories, said, "Mattel is the gold standard."[19]

Mattel had strict requirements for its contract suppliers, which were subject to inspections by independent auditors. Products were tested at the factory and supplies were tested at the door. The *New York Times* article stated, "Elisha Chan, the director of product integrity and corporate responsibility, is charged with guarding against dangerous defects like lead-based paint. Suppliers are closely monitored, he says, and sending in fake or tainted supplies is a ticket to losing the contract with Mattel. And some vendors have, says Mr. Chan." The article also stated, "Many Western companies operating in China do not test their raw materials, even though suppliers are known for substituting cheaper materials to pad their profits." Dane Chamorro with the consultancy Control Risks commented, "This is very common. The samples you get are always fantastic; but once they rope

---

you in they can cut back. And a lot of Chinese companies will do anything to cut costs."[20] Lead paint, for example, reportedly cost from 30 to 60 percent less than paint without lead.

Other commentators placed the blame on the Western companies that pressured their suppliers to keep costs down and meet tight deadlines. Dara O'Rourke, a professor at the University of California, Berkeley, stated, "There is a lot of scapegoating China, but I would argue that this was caused by a system that is designed to push down costs and speed up delivery."[21]

On July 30, after the RC2 and Target recalls, the Sierra Club wrote to 10 companies that it would file a lawsuit against them if within 60 days they did not file a report with the Environmental Protection Agency (EPA) on their lead-tainted products. The letter claimed that the companies were required to report to the EPA under the Toxic Substances Control Act. A Target spokesperson stated, "We have no indication that Target has violated any EPA laws relating to this matter."[22] The action by the Sierra Club was part of a broader campaign by activists, NGOs, and public health officials against products containing lead, which in large enough quantities can cause brain damage, organ failure, and death.

Mattel, Inc.

In 2000 Mattel had a loss of $431 million on sales of $4.566 billion. To turn the company around, Mattel hired CEO Robert A. Eckert from Kraft Foods. Eckert sold off a number of product lines to focus on toys, and by 2006 the company had net income of $593 million on sales of $5.650 billion. Its principal brands in addition to Barbie and Hot Wheels were American Girl and Fisher-Price. Mattel made *Fortune* magazine's 100 best companies to work for in 2008, ranking 70th.

In the 1980s Mattel began to build factories in China, and by 2007 it owned 12 factories there, which it used to produce its most popular toys.[23] During Eckert's tenure Mattel consolidated its remaining production among a smaller set of suppliers in China, but it continued to rely on 30 to 40 suppliers with whom it had long-term relationships. Those suppliers had, however, over time used subcontractors which were not under Mattel's supervision. Since 1996 suppliers' factories had been subject to a code governing working conditions, and factories were subject to inspection by an independent organization.

Mattel claimed not to squeeze its suppliers and had a policy of paying extra for materials that were safe, including lead-free paint. Thomas A. Debrowski, head of worldwide operations, said, "We insist that they continue

to use certified paint from certified vendors, and we pay for that, and we're perfectly willing to pay for that."[24] Mattel had 200 employees in China responsible for training and supervising suppliers, but those employees were not stationed permanently at the factories of the suppliers.

The Crisis

The first hint of a crisis came from France. The French retailer Auchan had hired Intertek, a large testing company, to test the toys it stocks. On June 6 Intertek found high levels of lead in the paint on some Mattel toys. Mattel intercepted the shipment to France and did not report the problem immediately because the items were not being sold in the United States.

The incident led Mattel to undertake an internal investigation, which found lead in the paint of a number of its toys. Mattel traced the products back to the Lee Der Industrial Company with headquarters in Hong Kong and factories on the mainland, including the city of Foshan. Lee Der was founded in 1993 by Xie Yuguang and Zhang Shuhong, who managed the factory in Foshan. Zhang was respected by employees, and the company treated its employees fairly, paying overtime and paying on time. Zhang was known to provide workers with iced tea and fruit on hot summer days as well as for lending money out of his own pocket to employees who needed an apartment or other assistance.[25]

Further investigation revealed that a Mattel-certified paint supplier, Dongxing New Energy Company, had run out of yellow pigment and arranged on the Internet to buy 330 pounds of powder from a local company, Dongguan Zhongxin Toner Powder Factory, that was not certified by Mattel. Dongguan Zhongxin had provided fake documentation on the powder certifying its quality. Neither the powder nor the paint was tested, although Lee Der had testing equipment at its factory in Foshan.

Mattel had to determine whether to announce a voluntary product recall or to have the Consumer Product Safety Commission (CPSC) decide whether to recall the toys. The CPSC would have to investigate, and it was understaffed and was required to satisfy procedural requirements before it could order a recall of the products. A voluntary recall by Mattel would be faster and could be coordinated with the CPSC, which was required to monitor the progress of any nationwide recall. If Mattel decided on a voluntary recall, it had to decide whether to recall only those items known to be contaminated or to issue a broader recall in case other batches of products also were contaminated. Mattel also had to decide whether to make public the source of the problem and name the contractors involved and whether to fire them. It also would have to notify retailers to stop selling the

[20]*New York Times*, July 26, 2007.
[21]*New York Times*, September 21, 2007.
[22]*Wall Street Journal*, July 30, 2007.
[23]Mattel closed its last factory in the United States in 2002. Approximately 65 percent of its toys were manufactured in China, with some production in Indonesia and Mexico.
[24]*New York Times*, August 29, 2007.
[25]*Los Angeles Times*, August 24, 2007.

product and communicate with consumers for the return of contaminated products already purchased.

Mattel also had to assess whether its current policies and procedures were sufficient to ensure safety. In addition to procedures such as factory audits and inspections, technology could be used to mitigate certain risks. For example, in addition to conducting tests at its testing laboratories, it could deploy testing equipment to individual factories, as it had done in its factory in Tijuana, Mexico. A handheld device for detecting heavy metals had recently been developed and could provide a first-level screening. Mattel also had to anticipate how the product safety issue might evolve in the next few months.

What should Mattel do?

The Decision and Aftermath

Mattel decided to voluntarily recall the toys but delayed the recall until it could put up a Web site with information for retailers and consumers about how to return the products, according to David Allmark, general manager of Fisher-Price. On August 2 Mattel issued a voluntary fast-track recall in cooperation with the CPSC. The recall covered 83 toys with 1.5 million units worldwide, of which 967,000 were in the United States, two-thirds of which had not yet reached retailers' shelves. The recall was broader than needed, but the company sought to err on the side of caution. Mattel also announced that it was reviewing its procedures for ensuring product safety. Eckert said, "We apologize to everyone affected by this recall, especially those who bought the toys in question. We realize that parents trust us with what is most precious to them—their children. And we also recognize that trust is earned. Our goal is to correct this problem, improve our systems, and maintain the trust of families that have allowed us to be part of their lives by acting responsibly and quickly to address their concerns."[26] In a video posted on Mattel's Web site Eckert said, "I can't change what has happened in the past, but I can change how we work in the future." Eckert mentioned that he had four children. Videos mocking the company quickly appeared on YouTube, including one involving a character called "Tickle Me Lead-Mo."[27]

In its announcement of the recall Mattel explained the source of the problem, naming Lee Der and its supplier. Lee Der suspended production at the factory in Foshan, but on August 6 Zhang received a new order from Mattel which would allow the factory to resume production. He called the production manager and told him to tell the workers to report for work. On August 7 he learned that Mattel had disclosed the name of his company as having produced the recalled toys. Two days later China's Administration of Quality Supervision and Inspection and Quarantine banned Lee Der from exporting. The next day Zhang closed the factory and told

the production manager to start selling the equipment. Zhang then hanged himself in the factory.

"'After the recall was announced, the company flew a delegation to China to meet with manufacturers,' said a Mattel spokesperson last week. Factory owners were asked to gather in a room where Jim Walter, Mattel's senior vice president of worldwide quality assurance, reiterated basic safety standards. The attendees were required to sign a new safety contract. 'They needed to reaffirm what they had agreed to in previous years,' said the spokesperson."[28] Walter explained, "The message was very clear. If you cannot do these things, please let us know. No problem, but you won't be doing business with us."[29]

The Crisis: Phase II

During a conference call with Mattel supervisors in Hong Kong on the safety issue, one of the supervisors received a call from the testing laboratory in Shenzhen reporting that lead had been found in the paint of a toy car known as "Sarge," based on a character in Disney's movie *Cars*. The cars were made by Hong Kong–based Early Light Industrial Company, which had supplied Mattel for 20 years and was owned by Francis Choi, one of Asia's wealthiest persons. Early Light had outsourced the painting to another company, Hong Li Da, which unknown to Early Light purchased paint from an unauthorized supplier. The lead paint problem was detected by Early Light, and Choi said, "We informed Mattel immediately."

What should Mattel do?

The Decision and Aftermath

On August 14 Mattel issued another voluntary fast-track recall of 436,000 Sarge die-cast vehicles. Mattel credited detection of the problem to its reemphasis to suppliers of its standards, along with expanded testing. Mattel announced the lead paint had come from Hong Li Da and that Early Light Industrial was not responsible for the problem.

At the same time Mattel voluntarily recalled 18.2 million toys worldwide with small, powerful magnets that could come loose. This supplemented a November 2006 recall. The company stated that it had "implemented enhanced magnet retention systems in its toys across all brands."[30] Mattel made it clear that the problem was due to its own design error and not to problems with its suppliers. The day before the recall Mattel had begun an advertising campaign designed to assure consumers of its commitment to product safety.

Jim Walter also announced strengthened procedures the company was implementing. The procedures had three components. First, every batch of paint was required

[26]Mattel, Inc. press release, August 2, 2007.
[27]*Wall Street Journal*, August 15, 2007.
[28]*Wall Street Journal*, August 14, 2007.
[29]*New York Times*, August 15, 2007.
[30]Mattel, Inc. press release, August 14, 2007.

to be tested. Second, production controls were strengthened and unannounced factory inspections were increased. Third, every production run of finished toys was tested. Mattel also announced that it had met with all its suppliers to make certain that they fully understood the new procedures. It began to use the hand-held device for initial screening for heavy metals.

Some parents had purchased lead detection kits to test their children's toys. The CPSC reported in August that the kits were unreliable, producing both false positives and false negatives.

On September 4 Mattel voluntarily recalled worldwide 850,000 units of 11 products made in China because of "impermissible levels of lead." The products were in the Barbie and Fisher-Price brands. Mattel said that the recall was the result of "the company's ongoing investigation of its toys manufactured in China. . . ."[31] On October 25 Mattel recalled 55,550 units of one product sold in Canada, Ireland, the United Kingdom, and the United States because of "impermissible levels of lead." Mattel identified the supplier in China and the subcontractor. Mattel was cooperating with the CPSC.

Some small U.S. companies that produced their toys in the United States seized the opportunity to promote their use of lead-free paint. Whittle Shortline Railroad proclaimed its products as "100 percent kid-safe," and owner Mike Whitworth said, "We are little bitty, but we are taking some leaps and bounds here. Actually, we have seen about a 40 percent jump since late June."[32]

One remaining issue was what to do with the recalled product. Most consumers never returned recalled products, although RC2 reported that 60 percent of its Thomas & Friends toy trains had been returned. Rachel Weintraub, director of product safety at the Consumer Federation of America, described the issue, "The first step is the product is recalled. The second step is the manufacturer gets some of the product back. And the third step is: What happens next?"[33] Recalled toys could legally be sold in other countries if the recall was voluntary. The EPA required testing of recalled products and a disposal plan for recalled products containing lead. Concentrations above 5 ppm required special disposal procedures. Otherwise, the products could be disposed of in landfills.

The Scope of the Crisis

The recalls by Mattel and other companies put pressure on the Chinese government and its export-driven industries. The government was sensitive to criticism, particularly as it was racing to complete preparations for the 2008 Olympic Games. Moreover, Mattel's product recalls had resulted in thousands of Chinese workers losing their jobs. China Labor Watch, a worker rights organization based in New York, seized the opportunity and released a report alleging brutal conditions and illegal practices in toy factories in China.[34]

The State Council of China released a report in August stating that 85 percent of its food exports passed quality inspections, up from 78 percent a year earlier. The State Council also announced that it had established a cabinet-level committee headed by Vice Prime Minister Wu Yi to improve the quality and safety of products made in China.

Mattel was concerned about its relationship with the Chinese government. After the waters had calmed somewhat, Mattel sent Debrowski to China to apologize. Debrowski said that Mattel's recalls over lead paint were "overly inclusive" and that the larger recall involving magnets was due to a design error by Mattel and not to Chinese manufacturers. Debrowski's apology caused an uproar in the United States where Mattel was accused of kowtowing to China and the suppliers on which it relied. Senator Charles Schumer (D-NY) said, "It's like a bank robber apologizing to his accomplice instead of to the person who was robbed. They're playing politics in China rather than doing the right thing."[35] A Mattel spokesperson explained that Debrowski had apologized to the Chinese people as customers, as Mattel had apologized in other countries.

The crisis quickly moved into government arenas. Hearings were held in the United States, and the European Union took up the issue led by the consumer affairs commissioner Maglena Kuneva and members of the European Parliament. Dwight Justice of the International Trade Union Confederation said, "Companies are not afraid of being punished if they don't apply standards in factories in China." Critics called for mandatory testing of products, but Anne Starkie-Alves, head of the Toy Industries of Europe association, warned about the volume of imports and said of current practices, "I think there are very good systems in place."[36] Peter Mandelson, commissioner for international trade, warned about inaction, "If the EU doesn't take defensive measures when they are justified, we will risk encouraging a backlash against China's trade growth. Given the mood in Europe, the burden of proof is shifting to China to demonstrate that it is trading fairly and that its goods are safe."[37]

In Senate hearings Mattel CEO Eckert apologized to Congress and pledged that the company was changing its practices to prevent safety problems. He announced that the company was now testing each batch of products for lead and requiring all its suppliers to buy only

[31]Mattel, Inc. press release, September 4, 2007.
[32]*New York Times,* August 15, 2007.
[33]*New York Times,* December 22, 2007.

[34]"Investigations on Toy Suppliers in China: Workers are still suffering," August 2007. www.chinalaborwatch.org.
[35]*New York Times,* September 21, 2007.
[36]*New York Times,* September 15, 2007.
[37]*New York Times,* September 18, 2007.

from authorized vendors. Mattel, along with other U.S. toy manufacturers, called for mandatory testing by independent laboratories. Toys 'R' Us complained that information provision about recalls needed to be improved, so that retailers would not unknowingly continue to sell recalled products. Senators called for stronger measures including possible criminal prosecution for selling dangerous products.

Hearings were also held in the House, which in December approved a bill that would reduce the allowable lead content in consumer products, strengthen the CPSC, and improve the tracking of recalled products. Safety activists said the bill did not go far enough and sought a stronger bill reported by committee in the Senate. The Senate bill would increase the maximum fine that could be imposed from $1.8 million to $100 million and allow state prosecutors to enforce the federal law, but the Senate delayed acting on the bill.

Management Crisis?

In November 2007 *Consumer Reports* discovered lead in Mattel's Fisher-Price blood-pressure cuff in its toy medical kit and alerted the attorney general of Illinois, which had standards more stringent than federal standards. Illinois regulators tested the product and found that the lead content of the plastic cuff was 4,500 to 5,900 parts per million. Although there was no federal standard for lead in plastic, the lead content was roughly 8 times the federal standard for lead in paint. Mattel also had tested the product and found "higher than anticipated" lead levels. A Mattel spokesperson stated that the product met both U.S. federal and European Union safety standards for lead in plastic. In August Toys 'R' Us had recalled vinyl baby bibs and offered refunds to consumers because some of the bibs had lead in the plastic. The lead concentrations in the

bibs were revealed by testing at independent laboratories sponsored by the *New York Times* and a California environmental group. The lead concentrations did not exceed federal standards, but they exceeded Toys 'R' Us' own standards, resulting in the recall. The company said the bibs posed no health risk unless they were so worn that pieces could break off and be swallowed by a child. Toys 'R' Us spokesperson Julie Vallese said, "Parents shouldn't be alarmed."[38]

In December Mattel recalled the toy medical kit but only in Illinois and notified retailers that it was accepting the return of the toys. Mattel did not make a public statement about the return. Consumers could also return the toys, and Mattel gave instructions on the Internet. It was not clear that there was any risk from the lead, since sucking on the plastic was unlikely to release the lead, according to scientists.

As a result of Mattel's limited recall, in December Representative Elijah Cummings (D-MD) wrote to Mattel asking it to stop using lead in its products. In January Mattel responded by reporting that 70 percent of the products had been returned. This response did little to calm the critics. On January 29, 2008, 56 members of Congress wrote to Mattel expressing concern for the lack of action by the company. The letter stated, "We challenge you to live up to your words and set a standard for the entire industry by completely eliminating the use of lead in all the children's products manufactured by Mattel."

What should Mattel do? ■

SOURCE: This case was prepared from public sources by Professor David P. Baron. Copyright © 2008 by the Board of Trustees of the Leland Stanford Junior University. All rights reserved. Reprinted with permission.

---

[38]*New York Times*, August 18, 2007.

Merck and Vioxx

On September 30, 2004, Merck voluntarily withdrew its $2.5 billion blockbuster drug Vioxx (rofecoxib) because new clinical research showed a significantly higher probability of cardiovascular events, such as heart attacks, for patients who took the drug for over 18 months. Merck's market capitalization fell by 27 percent on the day of the announcement and subsequently fell another 13 percent. The withdrawal met with instant praise for the quick decision, but soon the praise turned to questions as information became available about whether the company should have recalled the drug years earlier.

Merck defended itself in a series of full-page advertisements in major newspapers. In three full-page ads on November 21, 2004, Merck defended its actions, restated its commitments to patients, and attempted to assure in-

vestors about its financial strength and its future. The first ad stated:

> **We extensively studied** VIOXX before seeking regulatory approval to market it.
> **We promptly disclosed** the clinical data about VIOXX.
> When questions arose, **we took additional steps, including conducting further prospective, controlled studies** to gain more clinical information about the medicine.
> When information from these additional prospective, controlled trials became available, **we acted promptly** and made the decision to voluntarily withdraw VIOXX.

Vioxx, along with Pfizer's Celebrex and Bextra, were Cox-2 inhibitors used to treat patients with chronic pain. Traditional painkillers, such as aspirin and ibuprofen, blocked the Cox-1 and Cox-2 enzymes that cause pain. Blocking Cox-1 enzymes had the benefit of reducing cardiovascular risks, such as blood clots and heart attacks, but it could contribute to intestinal and stomach problems including stomach bleeding and ulcers. Cox-2 inhibitors did not block Cox-1 enzymes, so relative to traditional painkillers they provide benefits to patients at risk from intestinal and stomach bleeding. Vioxx had sales of $2.5 billion in 2003, Celebrex had sales of $1.9 billion, and Bextra, a newer version of Celebrex, had sales of $687 million.

The Initial Marketing Decision for Vioxx

Early Merck memoranda suggested that the company recognized that sales would be limited if Vioxx were restricted to patients with stomach or intestinal bleeding. If the drug were marketed as a general-purpose painkiller for arthritis and other persistent ailments, sales could be much higher. If Merck were to market Vioxx as a general-purpose painkiller, it would use direct-to-consumer (DTC) advertising.

In designing clinical trials for Vioxx in the mid-1990s Merck recognized that to show its effectiveness trial subjects could not take aspirin. Consequently, the trials could show increased blood clots and cardiovascular events. A Merck scientist proposed that patients with a high risk of cardiovascular problems be kept out of the clinical trials. Information on the final design of the clinical trials was not available.[39]

The Food and Drug Administration (FDA) approved Vioxx for sale in 1999. The Phase III clinical trials required by the FDA for approval found "there was not an increased risk of cardiovascular events with VIOXX compared with placebo or VIOXX compared with other non-naproxen non-steroidal anti-inflammatory drugs (NSAIDS)."[40] ∎

Preparation Questions

1. Should Merck seek to market Vioxx as a general-purpose painkiller with heavy DTC advertising or limit its marketing to those patients with gastrointestinal problems?
2. Should Merck conduct additional clinical trials to evaluate the risks of blood clots and cardiovascular events?

[39]*Wall Street Journal,* November 1, 2004.
[40]Merck, "Merck Announces Voluntary Worldwide Withdrawal of VIOXX®," www.vioxx.com/rofecoxib/vioxx/consumer/index.jsp. Naproxen is marketed over-the-counter as Aleve.

The Success of Vioxx

Merck aggressively promoted Vioxx as a general-purpose pain reliever for arthritis and other conditions. In 2000 it spent $161 million on DTC advertising for Vioxx. Continued heavy advertising and traditional marketing to doctors resulted in 2003 sales of $2.5 billion worldwide.

The VIGOR Clinical Trials

In early 1999 Merck began a clinical study called VIGOR to demonstrate the effectiveness of Vioxx for patients with gastrointestinal problems. The control was naproxen, and participants were prohibited from taking aspirin. Patients with heart problems were not included in the trials. The results were released in March 2000 and showed that patients receiving Vioxx had fewer gastrointestinal problems than those receiving naproxen.[41] The results also showed that of the 4,047 people taking Vioxx, 101 had cardiovascular adverse events, such as blood clotting, whereas 46 of the 4,029 taking naproxen had such events. Because earlier studies had shown no greater cardiovascular problems with Vioxx than with a placebo, Merck suspected that the difference in cardiovascular adverse events was due to the beneficial effects of naproxen rather than to problems with Vioxx.[42] Merck and the FDA began discussions about what information from the VIGOR trial would be included in the new label for Vioxx. ∎

Preparation Questions

1. In light of the results of the VIGOR trials, should Merck issue a warning to doctors and patients?
2. Should Merck reduce its DTC advertising of Vioxx?
3. Should Merck conduct new clinical trials designed to identify any cardiovascular adverse effects of Vioxx?
4. What information should Merck support for inclusion on the new Vioxx label?

[41]The results of the study were published in the *New England Journal of Medicine* in November 2000.
[42]Ted Mayer, an attorney representing Merck, later explained, "The known antiplatelet properties of naproxen strongly suggested that a property of naproxen was responsible for the differential rates in the Vigor trial." *Wall Street Journal,* November 1, 2004.

The APPROVe Study

In August 2001 researchers at the Cleveland Clinic published an article in the *Journal of the American Medical Association* raising concerns about Vioxx's cardiovascular risks. In 2002 a researcher at the Catalan Institute of Pharmacology in Barcelona criticized Merck's handling of Vioxx. The same criticism had been published in the British medical journal *The Lancet*.

The FDA was also concerned about the results of the VIGOR trial and particularly a Merck press release entitled "Merck Confirms Favorable Cardiovascular Safety Profile for Vioxx." In a September 17, 2001, letter to Merck the FDA called the press release "simply incomprehensible" and said that Merck had engaged "in a promotional campaign for Vioxx that minimizes the potentially serious cardiovascular findings that were observed. . . ." The letter also stated that "patients on Vioxx were observed to have a four- to five-fold increase" in heart attacks.[43] The new label for Vioxx mentioned both the gastrointestinal and cardiovascular results of the VIGOR trial.

As a result of the VIGOR trial, Merck researchers began discussing the possible risks associated with Vioxx and the other Cox-2 inhibitors. In May 2000 Merck considered conducting a cardiovascular study on Vioxx but decided not to do so. Earlier in 2000 Merck had begun enrolling patients for a 156-week study named APPROVe to demonstrate the effect of Vioxx on "the recurrence of neoplastic polyps of the large bowel" in patients with colorectal adenoma. In the study Merck used a placebo as the control and decided to monitor patients carefully for cardiovascular events. Merck established an external safety review board for the study. The board reviewed the interim results periodically. In May 2003 the panel noted a 20 percent higher risk of heart attack and stroke and by February 2004 the risk was 80 percent higher. Two of the five board members had consulting arrangements with Merck.[44]

An article published in *Circulation* in May 2004 found that Vioxx was "associated with an elevated relative risk" compared to Celebrex and to no pain reliever. Vioxx was also criticized at a medical conference in August by an FDA researcher.

In September 2004 the cardiovascular results in the APPROVe study showed 15 heart attacks or strokes per 1,000 patients with Vioxx compared to 7.5 with the placebo. Merck decided to withdraw Vioxx from the market. Merck reported, "In this study, there was an increased relative risk for confirmed cardiovascular (CV) events, such as heart attack and stroke, beginning after 18 months of treatment in the patients taking VIOXX compared to those taking placebo. The results for the first 18 months of the APPROVe study did not show any increased risk of confirmed CV events on VIOXX, and in this respect are similar to the results of two placebo-controlled studies described in the current US labeling for VIOXX."[45]

Preparation Questions

1. In light of the criticism of Vioxx and the letter from the FDA, should Merck have withdrawn Vioxx or issued warnings to doctors and patients prior to learning the results of the APPROVe study?

2. Should Merck have conducted a specific cardiovascular study?

[43]*Wall Street Journal*, October 5, 2004.

[44]*Wall Street Journal*, February 7, 2005.
[45]Merck, "Merck Announces Voluntary Worldwide Withdrawal of VIOXX," September 30, 2004.

The *Lancet* Article

In November 2004 researchers published a "meta-analysis" that combined the data from all the published studies on Vioxx.[46] Combining the data resulted in a larger sample size and narrower confidence intervals, which enabled the authors to conclude that the cardiovascular risk was higher with Vioxx. Merck criticized the statistical approach because the studies combined were not comparable, since some studies compared Vioxx with a placebo and non-naproxen NSAIDs, the VIGOR study used naproxen as the control, and the APPROVe study used a placebo. Merck stated that the meta-analysis showed nothing that had not already been published by Merck and that the increased cardiovascular risks were only due to the VIGOR study comparing Vioxx with naproxen. In its response to the article in *The Lancet*, Merck stated that "it was vigilant in monitoring and disclosing the cardiovascular safety of VIOXX and that the company absolutely disagrees with any implication to the contrary." Merck provided a detailed response to the article. ■

Preparation Question

1. What more, if anything, should Merck do in response to the article in *The Lancet*?

[46]Juni et al., *The Lancet*, November 5, 2004.

Congressional Hearings

The Senate Finance Committee held hearings in November on whether the FDA was doing enough to ensure post-approval safety of drugs. The FDA's Dr. David Graham stated, "I would argue that the FDA as currently configured is incapable of protecting America against another Vioxx." He testified that five drugs, Accutane, Meridia, Crestor, Bextra, and Serevent, should be reexamined to determine if they should be withdrawn. Earlier in the year Graham had examined the health records of 1.4 million Kaiser Permanente patients, including 40,405 who took Celebrex and 26,748 who took Vioxx. He found that the risk of heart attacks and sudden cardiac death was three times higher in patients that took high doses of Vioxx. He estimated that Vioxx was responsible for an additional 27,785 deaths from 1999 through 2003. His analysis was posted on the FDA Web site.

Another FDA official, Dr. Sandra Kweder, head of the Office of New Drugs, disagreed with Graham. Dr. Steven Galson, the FDA's director of drug evaluation and research, later said that Graham's numbers "constitute junk science" and were "irresponsible."[47] ■

Preparation Question

1. Should Merck provide testimony on the adequacy of the FDA's post-approval safety monitoring? How should it respond to Dr. Graham's study?

[47]*New York Times,* November 19, 2004.

------------------------------------- P A R T I -------------------------------------

Integrative Case
Wal-Mart: Nonmarket Pressure and Reputation Risk (A)

"It's time for Wal-Mart to understand that their company practices run counter to the very values that make this country great—fairness, opportunity, and equality."

Senator Edward Kennedy

"Some well-meaning critics believe that Wal-Mart stores today, because of our size, should, in fact, play the role that is believed that General Motors played after World War II. And that is to establish this post–World War middle class that the country is proud of. . . . The facts are that retail does not perform that role in this economy."

H. Lee Scott, CEO Wal-Mart

Introduction

By 2005 the company founded by Sam Walton operated over 5,482 stores in 16 countries and employed 1.3 million associates in the United States, making it the second largest employer after the federal government. For fiscal 2005 net income was $11.2 billion on sales of $312.4 billion, compared to $10.3 billion and $288 billion, respectively, in fiscal 2004. An estimated 100 million customers shopped at Wal-Mart stores. Wal-Mart's stock price, however, had languished over the past several years. Wal-Mart had an inward focus emphasizing its two key constituencies—its customers and its associates. Sam Walton had believed that dealing with the public was a waste of time and saw little need to be concerned with a broader constituency.

When Wal-Mart became the largest U.S. company in sales in 2002, it began to attract increased attention. Its expansion into the grocery business, however, was a precipitating event. Wal-Mart entered the grocery business in 1988, and its presence grew with the expansion of its supercenters. By 2002 it had become the largest grocery chain and was larger than Safeway and Albertson's combined. In 2003–4 in Southern California Safeway, Albertsons, and Kroger supermarkets locked out their union employees, demanding that they make wage and benefit concessions so that the supermarkets could be more competitive with Wal-Mart. After four months the union conceded, agreeing to lower wages and benefits for new workers. The unions were threatened and decided to attack Wal-Mart directly. They redirected their efforts from attempting to organize Wal-Mart employees to private and public politics and formed activist organizations to attack the company and its reputation.

Wal-Mart was criticized for providing low wages and inadequate health care benefits, driving small merchants out of business, damaging the culture in small towns, harming the environment, and violating workers' rights.

A series of incidents attracted attention, and a number of lawsuits were filed against the company alleging violations of labor laws, discrimination, and poor working conditions in overseas factories supplying the company. Wal-Mart also became a focus of the media. It had been the subject of 950 articles a week in 2001, but by 2004 it was the subject of 2,165 articles a week. Many of those articles were critical of the company's practices and repeated the allegations of the company's critics.

As the nonmarket pressure on Wal-Mart intensified, some observers linked the pressure to its stock price. Wal-Mart's stock price had fallen by 27 percent since 2000 when H. Lee Scott became CEO. Lisa Featherstone, writing on Salon.com, argued that Wal-Mart's low stock price was due "to what they call 'headline risk,' which is Wall Street-speak for bad press. That lagging stock price may become a critical pressure point for activists pressuring Wal-Mart to change its ways."[48] By its silence Wal-Mart had left a vacuum that its critics were more than happy to fill.

CEO Scott commented, "Over the years, we have thought that we could sit in Bentonville, take care of customers, take care of associates, and the world would leave us alone. It just doesn't work that way anymore."[49] Members of the board of directors asked for a reputational audit of the company. Wal-Mart concluded that a focus solely on customers and associates was no longer viable and that a nonmarket strategy was needed to address the criticism it faced and change its deteriorating reputation. That strategy required engagement with its environment as well as addressing the private and public politics the company faced.

Central to any nonmarket strategy was reducing the threat to its reputation by countering the nonmarket opposition it faced and by better positioning the company in its broader environment. A nonmarket strategy also had to be synergistic with the company's market strategy. For example, Wal-Mart wanted to attract higher-income customers who would purchase bigger-ticket items.[50] Higher-income customers were thought to be more sensitive to the issues raised by the company's critics.

Market Strategy

Wal-Mart's market strategy was based on low prices backed by efficiency. Growth was a key component of its

---

[48]*Wall Street Journal*, August 16, 2005.
[49]*Wall Street Journal*, July 26, 2005.
[50]Target Stores had achieved higher per store growth than Wal-Mart in part by appealing to higher income shoppers.

business strategy, and initially the company had focused on small towns and the suburbs of large cities. As those markets became saturated, Wal-Mart sought other ways to grow sales and profits. It revised its market strategy and entered new geographic markets and expanded the offerings in its existing stores. The principal available markets were in urban areas in the United States and in other countries. Wal-Mart announced that it would add between 555 and 600 stores globally in 2006, including 270 to 280 supercenters compared to 266 opened in 2005. CEO Scott said, "We could be three or four times bigger in the U.S."[51] Wal-Mart, however, had experienced local opposition to store openings in Chicago, Los Angeles, and New York City.

The second component of Wal-Mart's growth strategy was expanding its offerings. The company had entered the automotive service market, sold pharmaceuticals, and sold jewelry. It began selling groceries for two reasons. One was a cost advantage relative to supermarkets. The other was to attract higher-income customers who would also shop for higher margin electronic and other products. Wal-Mart also sought to offer banking and other financial services in its stores, but it had been blocked in several attempts. Its latest attempt was a pending application to form an industrial bank in Utah. On a trial basis the company began to provide health care through in-store clinics.

A central pillar of Wal-Mart's business model was to avoid unionization, and it had successfully defeated numerous attempts to organize its workers.[52] When employees at a store began to solicit signatures to request a union certification vote, the company would send a team of labor experts to the store to organize opposition to the drive. Management held mandatory associates' meetings to provide anti-union information. One message was that rather than pay union dues to hire someone to speak for them, associates could speak directly to management to address any problems. The company provided "I can speak for myself" buttons to employees.

Another pillar of its market strategy was its workforce. Despite the criticisms of Wal-Mart for low wages and inadequate benefits, people were eager to work for the company. One reason was the opportunity for advancement, provided in part by the growth in the number of its stores. CEO Scott said, "At Wal-Mart you can, without a high school degree, start as a cart pusher in the parking lot and end up being a regional vice-president."[53] Wal-Mart stated that "Nationally, more than 9,000 hourly associates were promoted into management jobs last year, and two-thirds of our store management started their careers with Wal-Mart in hourly positions."[54]

Eleven thousand people applied for the 400 jobs at a new store in Oakland, California that opened in 2005. The average wage paid in the Bay Area was $10.82 an hour. Melvin Brown, 52, who had applied for a job, said, "I think this is a good place to work. It seems like everybody gets along well with everybody."[55] "Lisa Jackson, 34, a Wal-Mart employee for nine years, working as a cashier, truck unloader, and overnight stock clerk, is now a manager of the electronics department at the new Oakland store. 'I love my job,' Jackson said. 'I like the people, and I love what I do.'"[56] Wendall Chin, coalition director for the Alameda County Central Labor Council said, "Wal-Mart is one of the largest employers in the world—they have to be a model for the society they are promoting. If they don't provide a decent lifestyle, it's scary. . . . It's not just about jobs. It's (having) a good job that you can raise a family on."[57]

Private Politics

Opposition to its geographic expansion in the United States developed quickly, led by local NIMBY groups, unions, and organizations aligned with unions. Some of its product line extensions also met with opposition from interest groups potentially threatened by the extensions. Wal-Mart also came under fire for a number of its operating practices. For example, it contracted with custodial firms to clean its stores, and some of those firms employed illegal aliens. In 2003 Immigration and Naturalization Service agents raided 60 Wal-Mart stores and arrested 245 illegal aliens working for 12 contractors. Wal-Mart's contracts with the custodial firms prohibited them from employing illegal workers, but critics claimed that Wal-Mart knew that illegal workers were used. Wal-Mart settled a government lawsuit for $11 million and agreed to establish stricter controls to ensure that contractors hired legally eligible workers.[58] The company denied that it knew that illegal workers were used.

In addition to criticism for specific issues such as contractors employing illegal workers, Wal-Mart faced a well-organized and well-financed set of campaigns. The campaigning organizations were backed by the unions that had tried and failed to organize Wal-Mart workers and that were threatened by its product extensions, particularly the sale of groceries. In 2005 the Service Employees International Union (SEIU) provided funding to establish Wal-Mart Watch to campaign against the company. The SEIU pledged $1 million to finance the campaign and supported a staff of 36 in Washington, D.C. The Union of Food and Commercial Workers (UFCW) had failed to organize Wal-Mart employees and suspended its organizing efforts.

---

[51]*Wall Street Journal*, October 26, 2005.
[52]Other large retailers such as Home Depot and Target were also nonunion.
[53]*Business Week*, October 3, 2005.
[54]*San Jose Mercury News*, September, 2004.

[55]*San Francisco Chronicle*, August 17, 2005.
[56]*San Francisco Chronicle*, August 17, 2005.
[57]*San Francisco Chronicle*, August 17, 2005.
[58]The 12 contractors pleaded guilty to criminal charges and paid $4 million in penalties.

It established an Internet-based organization, WakeUp WalMart.com, and supported a staff of six in Washington, D.C. The organization carried the campaign to the Internet, and over 160,000 people signed up to participate in the campaign.

The campaigns were headed by Democrat operatives who had worked on presidential campaigns. WakeUp Wal-Mart was led by Paul Blank, former political director for Howard Dean's presidential campaign, and Chris Kofinis, who worked on the campaign to draft Wesley Clark. The media team for Wal-Mart Watch was led by Jim Jordan, former director of the John Kerry campaign, and Tracy Sefl, a former Democratic National Committee aide who was responsible for press reports about President Bush.[59] MoveOn.org, which financed political campaigns, led the public and governmental aspects of the campaign.

A documentary film, *Wal-Mart: The High Cost of Low Price*, by Robert Greenwald, extended the campaign to theaters. Wal-Mart viewed the film as inaccurate and misleading and produced a short film pointing out the factual errors. Wal-Mart promoted a favorable film, *Why Wal-Mart Works & Why That Makes Some People Crazy,* by Ron Galloway. A press release said, "The riveting documentary explores why Wal-Mart is one of the greatest success stories in business history, how it improves the lives of individual working Americans and their communities, and the social pathology behind the escalating attacks on the company by special interest groups."[60] Wal-Mart challenged Mr. Greenwald to show both films side-by-side.[61]

One criticism of Wal-Mart was that it harmed the culture of small towns by driving small merchants out of business through its low prices. Commentators noted that other companies such as Home Depot, Lowe's, and Zales also drove small merchants out of business but did not face the same criticisms. Another criticism focused on the health care benefits available to its part-time and full-time employees. Unions and their allies also complained that Wal-Mart's low wages depressed the wages of workers in other companies. Ironically, the greatest beneficiaries of Wal-Mart's business strategy were low-income consumers who benefited from its low prices.

In December 2004 six unions announced an unusual campaign against Wal-Mart. The $25 million campaign was not directed at organizing workers but at publicizing its claim that Wal-Mart was depressing wages and benefits. The unions argued that now that Wal-Mart was the largest U.S. company it had an obligation to be a model for other companies, as General Motors had been

decades earlier.[62] Greg Denier of the UFCW said, "This isn't a campaign, this is a movement. There's no precedent for this. It's a movement to confront the reality of Wal-Martization. No other company has ever had the global economic impact that Wal-Mart has."[63] A Wal-Mart spokeswoman responded, "You need to ask one question: Is it fair to ask American consumers to pay higher prices to subsidize a relatively small pocket of individuals just because they are making the most noise."[64]

In April 2005, 50 groups, including unions, environmental groups, and community organizations joined together to work through the Center for Community and Corporate Ethics with the objective of forcing Wal-Mart to change its practices. The Center was formed with $1 million from the SEIU. Andy Grossman, executive director of the coalition and former executive director of the Democratic Senatorial Campaign, said, "We're focusing on Wal-Mart because of the huge impact it has on each of the different parts of American life it touches. They do provide goods at the lowest price, but that sometimes comes at a high cost to society."[65] Carl Pope, executive director of the Sierra Club, said, "We recognize that we are much more likely to win the battle against a giant like Wal-Mart if we act on multiple fronts. You don't want to challenge Wal-Mart just on health care or just on the environment or just on sex discrimination. You want to pressure them on all three. This is an assault on a business model. We're not trying to shut Wal-Mart down."[66]

In solidarity with the lead unions, on August 10, 2005 members of the National Education Association and the National Federation of Teachers picketed Wal-Mart stores and held rallies at schools in 34 cities in 24 states to protest Wal-Mart practices. The "Send Wal-Mart Back to School" campaign was supported on WakeUpWalMart.com and was initiated by the UFCW.[67] The teachers urged parents not to buy their children's school supplies at Wal-Mart. Although the members of the teachers unions repeated the usual allegations about low wages and benefits, their true motivation may have been closer to home. Wal-Mart had long had a commitment to education, providing $45 million in scholarships and grants to teachers, but it also supported policies that were anathema to the teachers unions.[68] One protesting

[59]*The New York Times,* November 1, 2005.
[60]Business Wire, November 17, 2005.
[61]*New York Times,* November 1, 2005.

[62]After World War II General Motors and the United Auto Workers reached collective bargaining agreements that promised gains in real income to workers regardless of the state of the economy or the company's profitability. The real income of workers rose sharply, and the agreements became the pattern for the automobile industry. Nelson Lichtenstein, "Wal-Mart's Bargain with America," *San Jose Mercury News,* September 12, 2004.
[63]*New York Times,* December 11, 2004.
[64]*New York Times,* December 11, 2004.
[65]*New York Times,* April 3, 2005.
[66]*New York Times,* April 3, 2005.
[67]*San Jose Mercury News,* August 11, 2005.
[68]See www.walmartfacts.com. Wal-Mart made over $170 million in charitable donations in 2004. Most of the donations were made to local community organizations chosen by local store employees.

teacher complained that the Walton Family Foundation had contributed to school-voucher campaigns and supported tax credits for families sending their children to private schools. Don Dawson, a math teacher, said, "We don't solve problems in public education by taking money away. We can't afford to go backwards."[69]

The UFCW and the SEIU also joined with the community activist group ACORN to form the Wal-Mart Workers Association to work for better conditions for Wal-Mart employees. Wade Rathke of ACORN explained, "We are building something that's never been seen; it's neither fish nor fowl. We're focusing on Wal-Mart because it is the largest employer in the area—and in the whole nation—and is setting standards that affect communities and employment relations across the nation."[70] The association intended to engage Wal-Mart on issues relating to working conditions. For example, some employees complained that Wal-Mart reduced the number of hours they could work. Wal-Mart explained that it used an algorithm to determine how large a staff was needed at various times in the month.

The UFCW in conjunction with WakeUpWalMart .com sponsored full-page advertisements on November 14, 2005 under the heading "Wal-Mart vs. America." The ad stated: "You Decide":

Wal-Mart's America vs. Our America

600,000 workers without company health care vs. Affordable health care
2 million women suing for discrimination vs. Equal pay for equal work
Repeated child labor law violations vs. Protecting children
Poverty-level wages vs. Living wages
Corporate special interest lobbyists vs. The American people

WakeUpWalMart commissioned Zogby International to conduct a national survey of people's attitudes toward Wal-Mart. The poll revealed that "56 percent of Americans agreed with the statement 'Wal-Mart was bad for America. It may provide low prices, but those prices come with a high moral and economic cost.' In contrast, only 39 percent of American adults agreed with the opposing statement, 'I believe Wal-Mart is good for America. It provides low prices and saves consumers money every day.'"[71]

WakeUpWalMart carried the campaign to a higher level. The group recruited 65 ministers to sign a letter to CEO Scott. The letter stated, "Jesus would not embrace Wal-Mart's values of greed and profits at any cost, particularly when children suffer as a result of those misguided values."[72] In a break of solidarity Tracy Sefl of

Wal-Mart Watch replied, "What would Jesus do, indeed. I think he would say the ad was a mistake. We heard from numerous supporters who were offended."[73] Wal-Mart spokesperson Sarah Clark commented, "To us, these are both campaigns directed by union leadership intended to criticize a company trying to help working families. There are well-meaning critics out there. These two organizations don't fall into that category."[74]

Public Politics

The unions and other critics of Wal-Mart saw little hope for action by the federal government, but the states provided some hope. In a move intended to put pressure on the governor, the California state legislature passed a bill requiring an "economic impact" statement for any new store with at least 130,000 square feet, 20,000 types of items, and more than 10 percent of sales from nontaxable goods. The only type of store that would meet those conditions was a Wal-Mart supercenter that sold groceries. The bill had been backed by the California Labor Federation. The governor vetoed the bill, and the state legislature was unable to override the veto.

One opportunity for Wal-Mart's critics lay in pressures on state budgets from the rising cost of Medicaid, the federally-mandated, but state-funded, health care program for low-income individuals. The pressures had increased because of rising health care costs and federal welfare reform. "The expansion of Medicaid to cover the working poor has fundamentally broadened the nation's safety net and changed the lives of low-wage workers in the USA. It also has put enormous strain on federal and state finances and made taxpayers the health insurance provider for millions of workers at Wal-Mart, McDonald's and other low-wage employers. . . . 'People who left welfare went into jobs paying $5.15 to $7.15 an hour,' says Michael Paxton, the county's [Washington County, Ohio] welfare director. 'Medicaid and food stamps and child care assistance make it possible for people to work at low wages.' . . . Many workers choose Medicaid over insurance offered by their employers because it is less expensive. Wal-Mart workers pay $273 a month for the company's family medical coverage and get fewer benefits than Medicaid."[75]

In April 2005 Wal-Mart Watch ran a full-page ad alleging that Wal-Mart wages forced thousands of its employees to use food stamps and Medicaid for health care. In the internal memo leaked to the media, a Wal-Mart vice-president wrote that 5 percent of its associates were on Medicaid compared to 4 percent nationally and that 46 percent of the children of Wal-Mart's associates were uninsured or on Medicaid.

Regardless of Wal-Mart's impact on state Medicaid expenditures, many states had incurred large increases in their health care expenditures, putting pressure on state

[69]*San Jose Mercury News,* August 11, 2005.
[70]*New York Times,* September 3, 2005.
[71]WakeUpWalMart press release, December 1, 2005.
[72]*Wall Street Journal,* January 11, 2006.

[73]*Wall Street Journal,* January 11, 2006.
[74]*Wall Street Journal,* January 11, 2006.
[75]*USA Today,* August 2, 2005.

budgets. Unions recognized this burden and devised a strategy to appeal to state governments. The AFL-CIO developed a model bill to be introduced in state legislatures, and their efforts were directed at over 30 states. The Maryland General Assembly passed the bill, popularly known as the Wal-Mart bill, which required all employers in the state with 10,000 or more employees to spend at least 8 percent of their sales on medical benefits for their employees or pay the difference into the state's health insurance program. Only four companies had 10,000 employees, and Wal-Mart was the only one to which the law would apply. The Republican governor vetoed the bill, but the heavily Democrat state legislature overrode the veto.[76] The governor had said that the law would chill business activity in the state. Wal-Mart had announced that it would build a distribution center on the Maryland Eastern shore employing up to 1,000 workers, and legislators from the region feared that the company would switch the distribution center to another state. Referring to the unions, a Wal-Mart lobbyist said, "They have a power we can't match, and we worked this bill very hard."[77] Bills had been introduced in 12 states.

The override in Maryland spurred new efforts in states such as California. Wal-Mart had 70,000 employees in California, and another 68 companies had 10,000 or more employees. The state legislature earlier had passed a bill requiring the disclosure of the names of all companies with 25 or more employees receiving public health care, as under Medicare. The governor vetoed the bill, and it was not overridden.

Issues

Wal-Mart faced a number of additional issues, some of which arose from its product extensions and some from its operating practices.

Groceries

By 2005 Wal-Mart had 1,866 supercenters selling groceries. Supermarkets bore the brunt of Wal-Mart's expansion. Albertson put itself up for sale, and Winn-Dixie announced plans to cut 22,000 jobs, or 28 percent of its workforce.

In response to the unions and their allies, Wal-Mart quoted a columnist for the *Sacramento Bee*, who studied the conflict with the UFCW and wrote, "So for the sake of 250,000 grocery store clerks and baggers and their employers, the other 35 million people in this state are asked to agree to pay billions of dollars more than they ought to for the necessities of life and to deprive themselves of choices that could make their lives better. You don't have to be a Wal-Mart shopper to see that this is not a bargain that makes sense."[78]

Banking

At the beginning of 2005 Wal-Mart announced that it would issue a Wal-Mart Discovery credit card in cooperation with GE Consumer Finance. The credit card would have no fee and give 1 percent cash back. Wal-Mart also had bank branches of its partners in 1,000 of its stores, and it had begun a venture with SunTrust that would place co-branded money centers in stores. Wal-Mart was on the road to realizing its objective of offering financial services to its customers.

In 2005 Wal-Mart filed an application with the Federal Deposit Insurance Corporation (FDIC) for permission in Utah to open an industrial bank, also known as an industrial loan corporation, to process the credit and debit card transactions from its stores. Federal law prohibited a nonfinancial institution from engaging in banking, but an industrial bank was not classified as a bank under federal law. An industrial bank was state-chartered and regulated and was supervised by the FDIC. Wal-Mart's objective was to process its 140 million transactions a month at lower cost. Other companies, including American Express, Daimler-Chrysler, General Electric, Merrill Lynch, Toyota, and Target Corporation operated industrial banks in Utah, and Berkshire Hathaway had applied to establish one. General Electric and Target used their banks to issue commercial credit cards.

In 1999 Wal-Mart had attempted to enter the banking business by buying a savings and loan bank in Oklahoma. In response Congress enacted a provision prohibiting commercial companies from buying thrifts, and the planned acquisition was called off.[79] Wal-Mart was also thwarted in its attempt to form a partnership with a bank in Toronto to open branches in 100 of its stores. It also attempted to acquire an industrial bank in California, but under pressure from interest groups the state legislature passed a law prohibiting commercial companies from owning a bank.

The FDIC extended its comment period on Wal-Mart's Utah application to two months, since in contrast to the maximum of six comments received on a typical application more than 1,100 comments were received on the Wal-Mart application. In response to the application, a coalition formed to oppose Wal-Mart. The coalition included the Independent Community Bankers of America, the National Grocers Association, National Association of Convenience Stores, and the UFCW. Local banks feared that Wal-Mart would open branch banks in its stores. Wal-Mart Watch also filed a petition with 11,000 signatures opposing the application.[80] WakeUpWalMart launched an Internet-based campaign against the application. The FDIC announced it would hold a public hearing on the application.

---

[76]Overriding a veto in Maryland required a 60 percent vote of each chamber of the legislature.
[77]*New York Times*, January 13, 2006.
[78]*New York Review of Books*, April 7, 2005. The columnist reported that he was not a Wal-Mart shopper.

[79]The provision was included in the Gramm-Leach-Bliley Act.
[80]*New York Times*, October 15, 2005.

In-Store Health Care

Wal-Mart had provided pharmacy departments in its stores for years, and a natural extension was to provide health care. Federal law prohibits "self-referrals" which prohibits pharmacies from operating clinics, so Wal-Mart partnered with InterFit Health and other providers to open clinics in its stores in several states. CVS, Target, Rite-Aid, Brooks Eckerd Pharmacy, and Costco also planned to open clinics in their stores. The clinics provided basic diagnostic services and medical care by nurse practitioners. The clinics were drop-in, and prices were low. The clinics were also open long hours corresponding to pharmacy hours.

Unionization

Employees at two Wal-Mart stores in Canada had voted for a union, but the union members had failed to negotiate a contract with Wal-Mart and later voted to decertify the union. Employees also voted for a union at a store in Quebec. That store had been operating at a loss, and Wal-Mart decided to close it. The UFCW–Canada filed a complaint with the Quebec labor relations board. The board found against Wal-Mart, concluding that the closing of the store was not "real, genuine and definitive," since Wal-Mart could reopen the store because it had a long-term lease on the building and had not found another tenant for it.[81]

Unions had repeatedly tried to organize workers at Wal-Mart stores in the United States. Every attempt had failed. In 2004 butchers at a store in Texas voted 7–3 for a union, and Wal-Mart responded by switching to prepackaged beef, eliminating the position of butcher. In 2005 the National Labor Relations Board ruled that employees of Wal-Mart Tire and Lube Express in Loveland, Texas could hold a union election. The campaign for an election was led by one employee, supported by the UFCW, who was able to obtain signatures of a majority of the employees to request an election. The employees, however, voted 17–1 against the union. The union alleged that the employees were intimidated and appealed the election result. A National Labor Relations Board examiner found in favor of Wal-Mart and recommended that the election be certified. Debbie Moore, a former union member who now worked for Wal-Mart and along with her co-workers had voted 19–0 against a union in another election, explained her vote, "Right now, in this day and era, I don't think I need a union to pay for anybody to protect me."[82]

Store Openings

Wal-Mart's strategy of opening stores in urban areas met with protests in Chicago, Los Angeles, and New York. The opposition was led by unions and their allies and in some cases by local NIMBY groups. In Chicago one store application was rejected and another approved. Voters in one Los Angeles suburb rejected a change in zoning laws that would have allowed the construction of a Wal-Mart supercenter, and the company abandoned plans to open a store in Queens.

Alderwoman Emma Mitts, who represented a West Side ward in Chicago, explained her support for the opening of a Wal-Mart store in her ward: "For a lot of people, this will be their first job of any kind. This is where they'll learn that in the world of work, you have to show up on time, you have to look good, you have to be helpful and courteous. Our young people are going to learn how to stock shelves, how to answer customers' questions, how to make change. Don't underestimate what it will mean to our community to have a place where young people can learn skills like these."[83]

Environment

In 2001 Wal-Mart reached a settlement with the Environmental Protection Agency and the Department of Justice for violations of the Clean Water Act in 17 locations. Wal-Mart agreed to implement a $4.5 million environmental management plan and pay a $1 million civil fine.[84] In 2004 Wal-Mart paid a $3.1 million civil fine for storm water violations at 24 construction sites.

The Coalition of Tri-Lakes Committees in Colorado opposed the opening of Wal-Mart stores. It argued that although MTBE was no longer used in Colorado, "fuel from other states such as California that still allow use of MTBE could be brought here by visitors to the state. MTBE from gasoline that leaks from vehicles on the Wal-Mart parking lot could be washed off by storm water and could contaminate the surrounding environment and groundwater."[85]

Wal-Mart was also criticized for the footprint of its stores and parking lots, which reduced green spaces and wetlands and contributed to urban sprawl. The company was also criticized for generating disposal problems from in-store restaurants and for the solid waste disposal problem generated by the packaging of the products it sold. The company also generated substantial greenhouse gases, particularly from its huge truck fleet.

Health Care Benefits

Critics claimed that Wal-Mart failed to provide company health care benefits for 900,000 of its workers. Wal-Mart reported that 48 percent of its employees were covered by its health insurance plans, compared to the national average of 67 percent and 46 percent in retailing.[86] Wal-Mart provided no retiree medical benefits.

---

[81]*New York Times,* September 20, 2005. The board did not examine Wal-Mart's explanation that the store was closed because it was losing money.
[82]*Wall Street Journal,* August 15, 2005.

[83]*New York Times,* July 6, 2004.
[84]EPA News Release, June 7, 2001.
[85]www.coalitiontlc.org/wal-mart.htm.
[86]Henry J. Kaiser Family Foundation. *Wall Street Journal,* December 3-4, 2005.

In response to its critics, in 2005 Wal-Mart offered a low-cost health insurance plan with monthly premiums 40 percent lower than its other plans. The new plan had a $1,000 deductible after three visits to a doctor and three generic prescriptions. The premiums were $23 a month for a single worker, $37 for one parent and children, and $65 a month for two parents and children. In its first year the plan attracted 53,000 current and new employees, including 31,000 who switched from other Wal-Mart plans.[87] The company also offered a health insurance plan for $11 a month designed for employees with low health care needs. Unions continued to criticize Wal-Mart for not providing an affordable health care plan for employees with higher health care needs.

In October 2005 an incendiary internal Wal-Mart memorandum to the board of directors was leaked to the media. The memo primarily focused on reducing health care costs. Wal-Mart's benefits costs had increased from $2.8 billion to $4.2 billion three years later. Its associates were also aging more rapidly than the population. M. Susan Chambers, vice president for benefits, called for hiring healthier employees as a means of reducing costs.[88] To discourage unhealthy associates and job applicants, she suggested designing "all jobs to include some physical activity (e.g., all cashiers do some cart-gathering)."[89] She also suggested offering educational benefits in an attempt to attract younger, and presumably healthier, employees. She defended her memo stating, "This is not about cutting. This is about redirecting savings to another part of their benefit plans."[90]

Wages

Wal-Mart maintained that its wages and benefits were high relative to retailing in general and to comparable firms. Critics claimed that Wal-Mart, because of its size, should provide wages and benefits high enough to support a family with a single wage-earner. "If Wal-Mart spent $3.50 an hour more for wages and benefits of its full-time employees, that would cost the company $6.5 billion a year. At less than 3 percent of its sales in the United States, critics say, Wal-Mart could absorb these costs by slightly raising its prices or accepting somewhat lower profits."[91]

Wal-Mart's Susan Chambers wrote that "the cost of an associate with seven years of tenure is almost 55 percent more than the cost of an associate with one year of tenure, yet there is no difference in his or her productivity. Moreover, because we pay an associate more in salary and benefits as his or her tenure increases, we are pricing that associate out of the labor market, increasing the likelihood that he or she will stay with Wal-Mart."[92]

In response to a critical book review in the *New York Review of Books*, Wal-Mart took out a two-page ad "to set the record straight." The company reacted to a critique "so riddled with mistakes and blinded by ideology that it offered a fundamentally erroneous view of the way we do business and the contributions we make to thousands of communities."[93] In response to the criticism that Wal-Mart wages were too low to support a family, the company pointed out that only 7 percent of its associates were single wage earners supporting a family and that its average wage was nearly twice the minimum wage. The ad pointed out that "74 percent of its hourly associates were full-time compared to 20–40 percent at comparable retailers, which meant that Wal-Mart provides considerably more health care benefits than do comparable retailers, who typically do not provide benefits for part-time workers. In contrast, Wal-Mart offers health care benefits to part-time as well as full-time associates."

The Labor Research Association (LRA) used Costco as an example of a successful retailer that paid higher wages than Wal-Mart.[94] The LRA claimed that Costco paid $16 an hour, compared to $12 a hour at Sam's Club, and that 82 percent of Costco's employees were covered by its health plans. Many Costco employees were represented by unions, and their wage and benefits agreements served as the reference point for the rest of Costco's employees.

Employment Practices

Wal-Mart had experienced a number of challenges to its employment practices. In 2005 Wal-Mart paid $135,540 to settle Department of Labor charges that workers under the age of 18 had operated dangerous equipment such as chain saws and cardboard balers. The settlement had an unusual provision criticized by congressional allies of unions. The Department of Labor agreed to a six-month agreement that gave Wal-Mart 15 days notice before it investigated any "wage and hour" complaint and allowed it to avoid fines if it brought its stores into compliance within 10 days of being notified of a violation. A Department of Labor inspector general criticized the 15 days notice provision because it violated its own handbook. Earlier Wal-Mart had been fined by the state of Maine for violation of child labor laws. An internal audit by Wal-Mart revealed numerous instances in which minors worked too late at night or during school hours.

---

[87]*Wall Street Journal,* December 3-4, 2005.
[88]WellPoint, a large health care insurer, reported that 7 percent of its customers accounted for 63 percent of its medical costs (*Wall Street Journal,* October 27, 2005).
[89]"Supplemental Benefits Documentation," Board of Directors Retreat FY06, Wal-Mart Stores, Inc.
[90]"Supplemental Benefits Documentation," Board of Directors Retreat FY06, Wal-Mart Stores, Inc.
[91]*New York Times,* May 4, 2005,

[92]"Supplemental Benefits Documentation," Board of Directors Retreat FY06, Wal-Mart Stores, Inc.
[93]*New York Review of Books,* April 7, 2005.
[94]The LRA "provides research and educational services for trade unions." LRA Online, "The Costco Challenge: An Alternative to Wal-Martization." July 5, 2005.

Wal-Mart also was sued by three former employees who alleged that the company had shaved time off their payroll records when they failed to punch in after a meal break or failed to punch out at the end of a shift. The lawsuit was spurred by a newspaper article mentioning the practice. Plaintiffs' attorneys sought class-action status for the lawsuit.

A group of employees in California filed a lawsuit, which was granted class-action status, alleging that they had been denied compensation for lunch breaks not taken as required by California law. The law required a 30-minute, unpaid lunch and dinner break. Wal-Mart claimed that the employees had failed to file for the pay on a timely basis. A jury awarded the workers $57 million in compensatory damages and $115 million in punitive damages. Wal-Mart said that hourly employees "did take substantially all of their meal periods" and planned to appeal the decision. Scott Brink, a Los Angeles attorney who represents employers in labor issues, said, "California has the most stringent and Byzantine wage and hour laws in the country. Wal-Mart has found itself caught, apparently, on some of these very technical wage and hour laws that are peculiar to California."[95] Wal-Mart revised its practices and now "sends alerts to cashiers when it is time for their meal breaks."[96] A lawsuit in Pennsylvania on the same issue was granted class-action status in 2006.

Discrimination

In 2001 six women employees filed a lawsuit against Wal-Mart alleging that they were paid less than men with comparable qualifications and were not promoted at the same rate as men. Witnesses for the plaintiffs provided evidence that women were paid between 5 and 15 percent less than men, and a federal judge in San Francisco granted class-action status to the lawsuit to cover 1.6 million current and former workers. Wal-Mart denied the allegations and appealed the decision to grant class-action status. Wal-Mart's lead attorney stated, "The judge has precluded Wal-Mart from arguing that certain individuals should not be part of the class, that there were reasons they might have received less pay or were passed over for promotion."[97] The U.S. Ninth Circuit Court of Appeals agreed to hear Wal-Mart's appeal.

Activists also regularly introduced shareholder resolutions at Wal-Mart's annual meeting on issues ranging from executive compensation to environmental reporting. One resolution sponsored by the National Council of Women's Organizations called on the company to have more than 2 women on its 14-person board. The company urged shareholders to vote against the resolutions, and they did so by votes of at least 80 percent.

Wal-Mart began using a "mapping" process on its Web site to suggest other DVDs of "similar interest" to buyers of DVDs. A blogger noticed that buyers of DVDs such as *Charlie and the Chocolate Factory* and *Planet of the Apes* were referred to movies with African American themes such as *Martin Luther King: I Have a Dream/ Assassination of MLK.* The movies were also linked to *Home Alone* and *The Powerpuff Girls.* Within two minutes the story was up on Crooks and Liars and hundreds of comments followed. Wal-Mart responded quickly by changing the process and apologizing, stating that the process had malfunctioned.

Wal-Mart did not extend health care benefits to domestic partners unless required by state law. It, however, updated its ethics code to prohibit discrimination against "immediate family members" including domestic partners in certain states that had changed their laws on domestic partnerships and civil unions.

In another incident, Wal-Mart was sued by a disabled man, whose disability resulted from cerebral palsy as a child. The man had applied for a position in the pharmacy department and was hired but reassigned to a job that required collecting garbage and shopping carts from the parking lot.[98] A federal jury awarded the man $7.5 million for discrimination. Wal-Mart planned to appeal the award.

Working Conditions in Suppliers' Overseas Factories

In 2005 the International Labor Rights Fund filed a lawsuit in California state court alleging sweatshop conditions in the factories of Wal-Mart contractors in five countries. The lawsuit claimed that Wal-Mart's code of conduct represented a legal obligation to the workers in its suppliers' factories. Wal-Mart responded that it employed 200 inspectors who made 12,000 monitoring visits in 2004. If violations of its policies were found, the contractors were required to correct the problems or were discontinued. In 2004 1,200 factories were suspended for at least 90 days for violations, and 108 were permanently banned. Wal-Mart said that the Labor Rights Fund had "a history of presenting opinions as fact" and had ties to the UFCW.[99] Four of the workers represented in the lawsuit were California supermarket workers who claimed they suffered lower wages and benefits because of low prices made possible by violations of Wal-Mart's code.

Critics demanded that Wal-Mart agree to unannounced and independent inspections rather then use its own inspectors. Apparel and footwear companies that participated in the Fair Labor Association (FLA) were subject to inspections by independent organizations certified by the FLA.

---

[95]*San Francisco Chronicle,* December 23, 2005.
[96]*San Francisco Chronicle,* December 23, 2005.
[97]*Los Angeles Times,* August 6, 2005.
[98]*New York Times,* February 24, 2005.
[99]*New York Times,* September 16, 2005.

Hurricane Katrina

In the aftermath of hurricane Katrina that devastated New Orleans and the Gulf Coast, city, state, and federal agencies failed to provide essential relief. In contrast Wal-Mart had anticipated the threat and was prepared. When Katrina was upgraded to storm category, Wal-Mart began to plan for an emergency. It stocked its stores with supplies people would need if the storm struck, and it established staging areas that were stocked with items such as generators and bottled water.[100] After the hurricane struck, Wal-Mart donated $17 million for the relief effort, provided $3 million of supplies to relief workers and displaced citizens, and made vacant buildings available for relief agencies.

Newspapers published a photograph of a line of Wal-Mart trucks loaded with relief supplies for New Orleans being blocked by FEMA officials.[101] On "Meet the Press" the president of Jefferson Parish, outside New Orleans, said that if "the American government would have responded like Wal-Mart has responded, we wouldn't be in this crisis."[102] *Fortune* published a four-page article on the relief provided by local store managers and the company under the headline "The Only Lifeline Was the Wal-Mart."[103] ■

Preparation Questions

1. Identify the primary issues facing Wal-Mart. Should Wal-Mart have been able to anticipate the issues it now faces?

2. Which interests are opposed to Wal-Mart and what are their costs of organizing for nonmarket action? Which interests are aligned with Wal-Mart and what are their costs of organizing for nonmarket action?

3. In which institutional arenas will the issues be resolved? What role will government institutions play?

4. How effective has Wal-Mart's strategy been in addressing the pressures on the company? How will the likely resolutions of these issues affect Wal-Mart's ability to execute its market strategy?

5. Should Wal-Mart stop its opposition to the unionization of its associates?

6. Should Wal-Mart agree to independent inspections of its suppliers' factories?

7. Should Wal-Mart select its employees based on their expected health care costs? Should it include physical work in every job?

8. What should Wal-Mart do about the environmental pressures it faces? Should it undertake environmental initiatives?

9. What should Wal-Mart do in the aftermath of the Wal-Mart bill in Maryland? Should it switch its distribution center to another state? What should it do about similar bills in other states?

10. Should Wal-Mart make concessions to improve the chances for approval of its industrial bank application in Utah? For example, should it pledge not to open branch banks?

11. As the largest private-sector employer in the United States, should Wal-Mart be a model or should it straightforwardly serve its principal constituents—its associates and customers?

[100]*Wall Street Journal*, September 12, 2005.

[101]*New York Times*, September 14, 2005.
[102]*San Jose Mercury News*, September 7, 2005.
[103]*Fortune*, October 3, 2005.

C H A P T E R

6

Nonmarket Analysis for Business

INTRODUCTION

This chapter presents frameworks for analyzing political and nonmarket action on issues characterized by opposing interests. The frameworks provide the foundation for strategy formulation and implementation in Chapters 7 and 8, respectively. Although the focus is on public politics—the competition among interests in the arenas of government institutions—the approach also applies to private politics as considered in Chapter 4. The approach is presented in the context of U.S. institutions, but, as indicated in Part IV of the book, it is also applicable to settings outside the United States. The approach is illustrated using a case involving Boeing and tax benefits on foreign leasing.

The perspective here is that the nonmarket actions taken by pluralistic interests in the context of government institutions determine the outcomes of nonmarket issues involving private politics. The study of individual interests and the manner in which they are transformed into nonmarket action thus is one foundation for the analysis of nonmarket issues. In public politics nonmarket action is transformed into outcomes through government institutions—legislatures, administrative agencies, regulatory agencies, courts, and international accords. The characteristics of these institutions are the other foundation of nonmarket analysis. Because these institutions structure the nonmarket actions of individuals, firms, and interest groups, the approach presented here is referred to as *structured pluralism*.

Structured pluralism is illustrated in Figure 6-1 in the context of the issues, interests, institutions, and information that characterize the nonmarket environment. The nonmarket issue is the unit of analysis. The actions of the pluralistic private interests

FIGURE 6-1 Structured Pluralism

affected by the issue compete in the arenas of government institutions. Those institutions have structures and procedures under which their officeholders consider alternatives for resolving the issue. The officeholders have preferences derived from their policy interests and, through the constituency connection, the interests of their constituents. Information comes from two sources. First, research and public policy analysis provide technical information about the likely consequences of alternative policies. Second, interests provide politically relevant information to institutional officeholders. The outcome of this process is a public policy to address the issue.

A FRAMEWORK FOR THE ANALYSIS OF NONMARKET ACTION IN PUBLIC POLITICS

Interests and Interest Groups

The term *interests* has a dual use in nonmarket analysis and strategy formulation. One refers to those individuals, firms, and organizations with a stake in an issue. The other refers to the magnitudes of their stakes. Interests in the first usage are the actors (as in interest groups), and interests in the second usage are the stakes of the actors, which provide incentives for nonmarket action.

The framework begins with an assessment of the incentives. Stakes may be distributive or moral. Most issues have *distributive consequences,* as measured by benefits and costs, surpluses and rents, or profits and losses. In the example analyzed in Chapter 7, convenience stores, sporting goods manufacturers, and the charcoal and barbecue industries identified the effects of an extension of daylight saving time on their sales and profits. Issues may also involve *moral concerns*. In the chapter case, *Scrubbers and Environmental Politics,* the motivation of some environmentalists was moral rather than distributive. The moral determinants of nonmarket action are often more difficult to assess than the distributive consequences, but on some issues they are as important.

Incentives, whether distributive or moral in origin, can cause an individual, firm, union, nonprofit organization, NGO, or activist group to become active on an issue. They may act on their own, but they may also organize, coordinate, and mobilize for collective action. Interest groups form among individuals and organizations with aligned interests. A necessary condition for formation of an interest group is that the benefits from collective action exceed the costs of organization. Interest groups may organize around a single issue, such as an extension of daylight saving time. High-tech companies, public accounting firms, and other firms formed an ad hoc coalition to coordinate their actions to obtain uniform national standards for securities fraud lawsuits. Interest groups may also be organized by a political entrepreneur who mobilizes the common interests of dispersed individuals, by a trade association that represents firms in an industry, or by a labor union that represents workers. Although interest groups form because of an alignment of interests, they are sustained by the fruits of their efforts. Once uniform national standards for securities fraud lawsuits had been enacted, the coalition disbanded.

Interest groups can also have aligned interests that lead them to act in parallel rather than jointly. The Daylight Saving Time Coalition and the RP Foundation Fighting Blindness both worked to extend daylight saving time, although the former represented business interests and the latter represented individuals afflicted with night blindness. Aligned interests also allow specialization. Environmental interest groups engage in a wide range of nonmarket activities, and many focus on particular issues or strategies. The Sierra Club has a broad agenda, the Wilderness Society focuses on open lands, and Greenpeace uses confrontation to draw attention to environmental issues.

In some cases an interest group may be successful in having the government establish an agency through which its interests can be served. The Small Business Administration, the Department of Agriculture, and the Export-Import Bank are examples of such agencies. Environmental interest groups, however, repeatedly have sought without success a cabinet department for environmental protection. Members of Congress interact directly with interest groups and have established means of responding to their interests—the agriculture and small business committees of both chambers are examples.

Constitutions and laws grant rights to individuals and organizations to pursue their interests and to protect those interests from the actions of others. U.S. trade law gives firms, labor unions, and communities rights to seek relief from imports. Similarly, wilderness groups exercise their rights before the courts to block the commercial development of public lands. Whatever their motivation, interest groups have become skillful in putting pressure on elected and administrative officeholders through direct action, their standing before the courts and regulatory agencies, and their rights to participate in governmental processes. The chapter case, *Tobacco Politics,* provides an opportunity to assess the interests involved in the tobacco issue.

The Amount of Nonmarket Action

From the perspective of structured pluralism, a principal driver of public policies is the nonmarket action taken by interests. That nonmarket action includes activities such as lobbying, grassroots and other forms of constituent activity, research and testimony, electoral support, and public advocacy. The extent of these activities is a function of their costs and benefits, and the optimal amount of nonmarket action maximizes the excess of benefits over costs for the interest.

To assess the nonmarket actions of interests, the supply-and-demand framework from economics can be used. The demand side pertains to the benefits associated with nonmarket action on an issue, and the supply side pertains to the cost of taking, or supplying, nonmarket action. An increase in the benefits results in more nonmarket action, and an increase in the costs results in less nonmarket action. One component of the nonmarket strategy of a firm is thus to work to increase the benefits for the interests on its side of an issue and decrease the benefits of the interests on the other side of the issue. Another component is to reduce the cost of nonmarket action for the interests on its side of the issue through, for example, the formation of an association or coalition.

The demand for nonmarket action can be characterized in terms of three factors. One is the aggregate benefits to the interests on a side of an issue. The second is the per capita benefits for an individual interest, such as a taxpayer, firm, or union. The third factor is alternative means, referred to as substitutes, for achieving the benefits by, for example, turning to a different institutional arena.

The cost of nonmarket action has three components. The first includes the costs of organizing for collective action. The second includes the direct costs of undertaking nonmarket action, including the cost of lobbying, maintaining a Washington office, and preparing testimony, as considered in Chapter 8. The third component is the effectiveness of nonmarket action, which depends, for example, on the size of the interest group and its coverage of legislative districts. The following sections consider the demand and supply of nonmarket action in more detail.

The Demand for Nonmarket Action

The demand for nonmarket action is derived from the distributive consequences of an alternative, such as a bill before Congress. For firms, those consequences are reflected in sales, profits, and market value. Employee interests are measured in terms of jobs and wages. For consumers, the distributive consequences are measured in terms of the prices, qualities, and availability of goods and services.

The demand for nonmarket action depends on the *aggregate benefits* for an interest. In the Boeing example the aggregate benefits to taxpayers from eliminating the tax breaks on foreign leasing exceeded the aggregate benefits to Boeing from preserving the tax breaks. In the daylight saving time example, the benefits to firms stemmed from the increase in demand for their products, and those benefits were greater the longer the extension. In the chapter case, *Scrubbers and Environmental Politics,* eastern coal interests would benefit from mandating scrubbers because the demand curve for high-sulfur eastern coal would be shifted outwards. Conversely, consumers of the electricity generated from eastern coal would be worse off because the combination of eastern coal and scrubbers was more costly than burning low-sulfur western coal.

Aggregate benefits are important indicators of the demand for nonmarket action. In many cases, however, the *per capita benefits* are a better measure of the incentive to take nonmarket action, since individual interests compare their potential benefits to the cost of participation. If the benefits are substantial and concentrated, the per capita benefits can be high, and those who benefit will have an incentive to act. The per capita benefits for Boeing as a company were $200 million a year from preserving the tax breaks on foreign leasing. The members of the Daylight Saving Time Coalition each anticipated substantial benefits from an increase in the demand for their products.

If the aggregate benefits are widely distributed, however, the per capita benefits can be small, providing little incentive for nonmarket action. Although the aggregate benefits to taxpayers from eliminating tax breaks on foreign leasing were larger than the benefits to Boeing, the per capita benefits for an individual taxpayer were very small. Individual taxpayers generally take little nonmarket action because their per capita benefits are typically exceeded by their costs of taking action. In some cases nonmarket action can occur even when benefits are not large on a per capita basis. Proposition 13, a public referendum in California that reduced property taxes, resulted from political entrepreneurship that allowed individuals to lower their property taxes by simply casting a vote.

Substitutes

On some issues the benefits from nonmarket action can be obtained through other means, referred to as *substitutes*. The benefits from nonmarket action are lower when there are other means of generating them, and the closer these substitutes come to replicating the benefits, the smaller are the incentives to act. Substitutes may be available in the market environment or in the nonmarket environment. On an issue such as unitary taxation—the taxation of corporate profits on a worldwide basis by a state—a foreign electronics firm considering where to locate a new U.S. subsidiary has an incentive to support the repeal of California's unitary taxation law. That firm, however, has available the market substitute of locating its subsidiary in Oregon, which repealed its unitary taxation law. The alternative of avoiding unitary taxation by locating in Oregon reduces the benefits from, and hence lowers the firm's incentives for, taking nonmarket action to change the California law.[1]

An example of a public substitute is pursuing an objective in a different institutional arena. In the chapter case, *Tobacco Politics,* farmers had a substitute to opposing the tobacco settlement. They could seek government subsidies to compensate them for reducing their acreage in tobacco and transitioning to other crops. In the case of Internet wine sales the wineries sought state legislation to allow direct interstate sales of wine to consumers. A substitute in the six states that allowed intrastate but not interstate direct sales was to file lawsuits seeking equal treatment for interstate direct sales. If a lawsuit were successful, the demand for new legislation in that state would be reduced.

The Costs and Effectiveness of Nonmarket Action

The amount of nonmarket action also depends on cost, or supply, considerations. One cost is associated with identifying, contacting, motivating, and organizing those with aligned interests. If the number of affected individuals or groups is small, the *costs of organizing* are likely to be low. When the number is large, those costs can be high. Taxpayers are costly to organize because they are numerous and widely dispersed, whereas pharmaceutical companies are relatively easy to organize. The costs of organization can be reduced by associations and standing organizations. Labor unions, the Sierra Club, and business groups such as the National Federation of Independent Business reduce the cost of organizing for nonmarket action.

The cost of organizing is greater the more serious is the *free-rider problem,* considered in Appendix A. If the number of potential members of a group is small, the

---

[1]Under pressure from a number of countries, California revised its unitary taxation law. In 1994 the Supreme Court upheld the law allowing the taxation of profits on a unitary basis.

importance of one additional participant can be significant enough to justify each member's participation. Furthermore, as indicated in Appendix A, when groups are small, punishment and exclusion are easier to apply to those who free ride. If the group is large, a potential participant may conclude that joining in collective action will have little effect on the outcome and hence may decide to free ride. Interest groups attempt to reduce the free-rider problem by bundling together nonmarket action and services for their members. Many industry associations collect market data that they make available only to their members. The Sierra Club publishes a magazine and also arranges trips for its members. The free-rider problem also can be mitigated when interests expect to address a series of nonmarket issues, since they then have longer-run incentives.

Another component of the cost of organizing is mobilizing interest group members to deliver collective nonmarket action. Members may be mobilized on an ad hoc basis to address a particular issue. They may also be represented by a formal organization that can monitor issues and act when the interests of the group can be served. In addition to this readiness function, formal organizations monitor the progress of issues through their life cycles. Trade and professional associations, unions, the National Federation of Independent Business, and environmental groups provide these functions.

Effectiveness

Effectiveness refers to the impact of a given level of nonmarket action on the outcome of an issue. Effectiveness depends on several factors, including the number of members of an interest group and their geographic distribution. Those members are also constituents of legislators. For a firm, potentially relevant constituents are its stakeholders—shareholders, employees, suppliers, distributors, and in some cases customers.

Numbers   There are few automobile manufacturers, but they have many employees, extensive dealer organizations, many suppliers, and millions of customers. The Sierra Club has 1.3 million members and supporters, and the National Federation of Independent Business has over 600,000 member firms. The greater the *number* of members of an interest group, the greater is its potential effectiveness, but the costs of organizing and mobilizing those members can be high. In addition, members may have an incentive to free ride.

Coverage   Particularly for issues addressed in legislative arenas, the effectiveness of nonmarket action depends on the geographic location of interest group members. Nonmarket strategies based on the constituency connection between voters and their representatives are more effective the greater the number of political jurisdictions covered by the group. Although small businesses do not have the resources of large businesses, they are politically effective because they are numerous and located in every political jurisdiction. Automobile assembly plants are concentrated in a relatively small number of congressional districts, but the *coverage* of the auto companies' dealer and supplier networks is extensive. General Motors CEO Rick Wagoner attended the national auto dealers convention in 2008 to deliver a message and generate coverage of state political jurisdictions. The issue of concern to Wagoner was the possibility that states would enact their own regulations on greenhouse gases emissions to force large increases in automobile and truck fuel economy. Wagoner's message was, "We need to work together to educate policymakers at the state and local levels on the importance of tough but national standards." Wagoner explained why dealers were important in implementing General Motor's strategy at the state level, "Dealers are very effective in the political process because we don't have a plant in every state. We have dealers in every state."[2] The greater the coverage by the members of an interest group, the more effective is its nonmarket action.

Resources   A nonmarket strategy must be financed, and the greater the *resources* available to an interest group, the greater the set of activities that can be funded.

---

[2]*San Jose Mercury News,* February 10, 2008.

Financial resources fund research, lobbying, legal services, grassroots campaigns, and the group's administrative staff. The greater a group's stake in an issue, the greater are the resources that potentially can be contributed to a nonmarket strategy. Pharmaceutical companies have ample resources, and when the stakes are high, as in the case of reimportation of drugs or Medicare coverage of prescription drugs, substantial resources are allocated to nonmarket action. The members of the Sierra Club also have ample resources, but their willingness to contribute to the Club's nonmarket campaigns is more limited.

Supply Side Summary Supply side considerations imply that the costs of organizing interests are higher when the costs of identifying and mobilizing those with common interests are higher. These costs are also higher when the free-rider problem is more prevalent and fewer means are available to mitigate it. Nonmarket action is more effective when the group has more members, their resources are greater, and it has more extensive coverage of legislative districts. A strategy that reduces the costs of collective action or increases effectiveness will increase the impact of the group's nonmarket action.

The effectiveness of nonmarket action also depends on the actions others take on an issue. A grassroots political campaign in which members of an interest group contact their congressional representatives can be quite effective. If, however, an interest group on the other side of the issue responds by mounting its own grassroots campaign, the effectiveness of the first campaign will be reduced. Consequently, the assessment of the benefits from nonmarket action must take into account the likely actions of opposing interest groups. In many cases there are synergies between the actions of groups with aligned interests, even when those actions are independent. In the daylight saving time case, the independence of the actions of the coalition of businesses and the RP Foundation Fighting Blindness increased the effectiveness of the other's nonmarket action.

The Distributive Politics Spreadsheet

The analysis of the demand and supply sides can be summarized in a spreadsheet as presented in Figure 6-3 for the Boeing case. The distributive politics spreadsheet pertains to a specific alternative, such as a bill to revoke the tax benefits on foreign leasing, or equivalently to a particular change from the status quo. The spreadsheet is organized in terms of the interests that would benefit from the adoption of the alternative, and hence support it, and the interest groups that would be harmed by the alternative, and hence oppose it. The top panel of the spreadsheet pertains to the supporting interests and the bottom panel to the opposing interests. The spreadsheet is intended to summarize rather than substitute for the analysis of the benefits and costs of nonmarket action.

The demand side information summarized in the spreadsheet for each interest includes the available substitutes, the aggregate benefits, and the per capita benefits for individual members of the interest group. The supply side information includes the number of members, their coverage of political jurisdictions, their resources, and their costs of organizing for nonmarket action, including the effects of the free-rider problem.

The information summarized in the spreadsheet provides the basis for predicting the nonmarket action likely to be generated by the interests. This prediction then is used in conjunction with institutional characteristics to assess the likely outcome of the issue and to formulate strategies to influence the outcome. The Boeing example illustrates the link between the analysis summarized by the spreadsheet and strategy formulation.

Institutions are not included in the spreadsheet because they are viewed as arenas in which the nonmarket actions of interests are deployed, as indicated in the next section. The institutional officeholders who decide the fate of the nonmarket alternative are also not included in the spreadsheet, since they are regarded as part of the institution.

THE NATURE OF POLITICAL COMPETITION

When interests are opposed, their nonmarket actions may be viewed as competing in an institutional arena. The actions of these interests, coupled with the characteristics of the institution and its officeholders, determine the outcome of the competition. The outcome may be a win for one side and a loss for the other. The ratification of the North American Free Trade Agreement (NAFTA) was a win for business and consumers and a loss for organized labor. In other cases, the outcome may be a compromise influenced by all the competing interests. In the daylight saving time example in Chapter 7, the outcome was in the center of the distribution of preferences of members of Congress, whose preferences reflected the interests of their constituents.

Building on the work of Lowi (1964), Wilson (1980) categorized the nature of political competition on an issue as a function of the concentration or dispersion of the benefits and costs from an alternative.[3] Although this categorization focuses on the nature of the politics and not on the outcome, it is useful for distinguishing among types of competition and provides a context for formulating strategies as considered in Chapter 7.

The Wilson-Lowi matrix presented in Figure 6-2 pertains to the benefits and harm from a nonmarket alternative, such as the enactment of a bill, relative to the status quo. The columns of the matrix correspond to those interests that would benefit from the alternative relative to the status quo. The rows of the matrix correspond to interests that would be harmed by the alternative relative to the status quo. The benefits or harm are said to be *concentrated* if the per capita effects are high. If the per capita effects are low, they are said to be to be *widely distributed*. Eliminating the tax breaks for foreign leasing would concentrate harm on Boeing and a few other exporters. The increased tax revenue was widely distributed among taxpayers. On some issues the benefits (or harm) may be widely distributed across interests, yet some benefits (or harm) may be concentrated for some specific interests. Interests with concentrated effects have a stronger incentive to take nonmarket action, whereas interests with widely distributed effects have weaker incentives.

If both the benefits and the harm are concentrated, both supporters and opponents have incentives to act. If, in addition, their costs of nonmarket action are low,

FIGURE 6-2   Nature of Political Competition: Wilson-Lowi Matrix

Qualifications: 1. Magnitudes of costs and benefits
2. Costs of organizing and effectiveness of nonmarket action

---

[3]Heckathorn and Maser (1990) provide a reformulation of Lowi's typology from a transactions cost perspective.

interest groups will be active on both sides of the issue. The resulting competition, according to the Wilson-Lowi matrix, takes the form of *interest group* politics. The outcome is then largely determined by the amounts and effectiveness of the nonmarket action generated by the interests on each side of the issue. Legislation that pits business against labor is typically characterized by interest group politics. International trade policy, which often finds business opposed by labor unions and environmentalists, is also characterized by interest group politics.

When the consequences from an alternative are widely distributed, the incentives to take nonmarket action are weak. When this is the case for both the interests who would benefit and those who would be harmed by the alternative, the political competition is said to be *majoritarian*. The outcome then is determined by the preferences of a majority. The politics of Social Security are majoritarian because each individual benefits from Social Security but is also taxed to support it, albeit by different amounts. The politics of the extension of daylight saving time were at one level majoritarian, since everyone was affected.

When the benefits from an alternative are concentrated and the harm is widely distributed, the interests that benefit have stronger incentives to take nonmarket action than do those who incur the harm. The competition then takes the form of *client* politics with the beneficiaries working to become the clients of the institutional officeholders—that is, to have the officeholders serve their interests. In client politics, the beneficiaries face little risk of opposition from the other side. Firms seeking a subsidy for ethanol used in motor fuels are engaged in client politics. The extension of daylight saving time had a component of client politics because some benefits were concentrated on businesses and the harm was widely distributed among individuals on the western edges of time zones.

When the benefits are widely distributed and the harm is concentrated, those bearing the harm have a stronger incentive to take nonmarket action than do the beneficiaries. Wilson refers to this situation as *entrepreneurial* politics, since if the alternative is to be adopted over the status quo, an entrepreneur is needed to mobilize or represent those with widely distributed benefits. A member of Congress, an activist, or a business leader can be a nonmarket entrepreneur. The elimination of tax breaks in the Boeing example involved entrepreneurial politics, since the benefits were to taxpayers and the harm was borne by exporters.

In terms of the concentration and distribution of benefits and harm, entrepreneurial politics is the opposite side of the coin from client politics. On which side of the coin the political competition is located depends on the alternative in question relative to the status quo. In entrepreneurial politics, benefits from the alternative are widely distributed, whereas the harm from the alternative is concentrated. This favors the status quo, and for the alternative to be adopted a political entrepreneur is needed to mobilize the interests with widely distributed benefits. In client politics the benefits to the interest groups supporting the alternative are concentrated, and the harm to those supporting the status quo is widely distributed, so other things being equal, the alternative is favored over the status quo.

One strategy of interests is to attempt to change the nature of the politics of an issue. The politics of the extension of daylight saving time was basically majoritarian because everyone would be affected by an extension. Although a majority of people likely preferred the extension, their benefits were widely distributed. Some benefits, however, were concentrated, and those beneficiaries worked to change the politics from majoritarian to client through collective action. The Daylight Saving Time Coalition, representing business, and the RP Foundation Fighting Blindness, representing those suffering from night blindness, reduced the costs of nonmarket action for the beneficiaries. Those opposing the extension were unable to organize effectively and unable to prevail against the better organized supporters of an extension.

The Internet wine sales example illustrates the application of the Wilson-Lowi matrix, and the chapter case *Repeal of the Luxury Tax* provides an opportunity to combine the assessment of the nature of the political competition and the analysis of which interests will be active on the issue.

Internet Wine Sales[1]

The Twenty-first Amendment to the Constitution ended prohibition and also gave the states the right to regulate the sale of alcohol. All but three states adopted a three-tier system in which producers (tier one) sold to distributors (tier two) who sold to retailers (tier three) and then to the consumer. This system made interstate direct sales of alcoholic beverages illegal.

Over the past decades the number of wineries increased 500 percent to 2,700, most of which were family-owned "cottage businesses" shipping fewer than 25,000 cases a year. During the same period the number of distributors (wholesalers) decreased from 5,000 to 400.

The development of the Internet made possible an online market in wine with the potential to broaden the availability of wines, benefiting both consumers and wineries. Online retailers quickly appeared. Direct sales from wineries to consumers, however, would bypass distributors, costing them significant business. The distributors sought a ban on direct sales, and the wineries sought specific permission for direct sales. By 2003, 26 states allowed direct sales, and 24 states banned direct sales, including five states in which a direct sale was a felony.[2] In Virginia rival bills backed by the two sides were introduced in the state legislature. This example considers the demand and supply of nonmarket action and the political competition in Virginia.

The principal interests were consumers, wineries, retailers, and distributors.[3] Consumers had a large aggregate stake, but their per capita stakes were small. Moreover, they were costly to organize, particularly in light of the free-rider problem. Consumers could not be expected to be active on this issue, although their interests could be represented by the wineries or by political entrepreneurs in the state government. The wineries were organized primarily through the Wine Institute from California and Wine America. The 50 largest wineries accounted for 95 percent of the wine sales in the United States, and their wines generally had broad distribution. The smaller wineries had limited access to interstate markets, so their interests in direct sales were strong. Their per capita stake was high, and they were already organized, so their costs of nonmarket action were low. The effectiveness of their action, however, was limited because most of the wineries were out of state. Fortunately for the wine industry, Virginia also had wineries, providing some direct coverage of state legislative districts. The out-of-state wineries, however, had a degree of political effectiveness because they could represent the interests of Virginia consumers. Five wine industry associations and centers formed Free the Grapes to represent the interests of consumers and the wineries. Retailers of wine would be harmed by Internet wine sales, and their interests were aligned on this issue with those of the distributors. The distributors were represented by the Wine and Spirit Wholesalers of America, and Southern Wine and Spirits played the lead role. The distributors had large stakes and were well organized, and their costs of acting were low.

In terms of the Wilson-Lowi matrix, consider first the bill to specifically allow direct sales. The harm would be borne by the distributors, and that harm was concentrated. Consequently, the nature of the politics was either interest group or entrepreneurial. The principal beneficiaries of direct sales would be consumers, and if they were the only interest benefiting, the politics would be entrepreneurial. The wineries could be viewed as representing the interests of consumers in entrepreneurial politics, but they had their own interests and were the ones to take nonmarket action. The politics thus were primarily interest group with some elements of entrepreneurial politics. Consider next the alternative of a ban on direct sales. The benefits from a ban would accrue to the distributors, so the politics were either client or interest group. Again, if only consumer interests were present, the politics would be client, but the presence of the organized wineries made it interest group politics, again with some elements of client politics.

The nature of the politics does not predict the outcome, which requires a more fine-grained analysis of the demand, supply, and effectiveness of nonmarket action. The Boeing example provides such an analysis. In Virginia consumers and the wineries won. Direct sales by out-of-state wineries were allowed with a permit, but they were required to remit taxes and ship their wines by a common carrier registered with the state.

---

[1]This example is based on Wiseman and Ellig (2004).
[2]The legal strategies pertaining to direct shipments are considered in Chapter 12.
[3]In Virginia retail sales of liquor but not wine were through state Alcohol Beverage Control stores.

Institutions and Institutional Officeholders

Although the Wilson-Lowi matrix identifies some of the important characteristics of the politics of a nonmarket issue, it does not provide a complete theory of the outcome. For example, although the free-rider problem and the coverage of political jurisdictions as well as the effectiveness of nonmarket strategies can affect the nature and the intensity of the politics and hence the outcome, outcomes also depend on the institutions that deal with the issue. This chapter and Chapters 7 and 8 consider issues addressed in legislative institutions and particularly the U.S. Congress. Appendix B provides information on Congress and the legislative process. The characteristics of Congress, such as the committee structure and the legislative process, can be important. The position taken by a cabinet agency or the president can also be important.

Since an institution provides an arena in which interests deploy their nonmarket strategies, the preferences of those who hold offices in the institution can affect the outcome. Officeholders may support an interest group or work to advance their own policy agendas. They may attempt to influence other officeholders or trade their vote on an issue of lesser importance for the vote of another officeholder on a more important issue. Legislators, however, are constrained by both their duty to represent their constituents and their desire to be reelected. The constituency connection thus constrains their behavior. One means of determining how legislators are likely to vote on a political alternative is to examine the interests of their constituents and how those interests would be affected by the alternative in question. The implications of this constituency connection for strategy formulation are developed further in Chapters 7 and 8.

MORAL DETERMINANTS OF COLLECTIVE ACTION

On some issues, moral concerns motivate individuals and groups to take nonmarket action. Moral concerns are the subject of Part V of this book, and only a brief discussion of these concepts is presented here. Assessing how individuals with various moral concerns view a nonmarket alternative can be difficult. The equally difficult task is determining how many people have a particular moral concern and how likely they are to act in the arenas of government institutions or through private politics.

Because moral concerns can differ among individuals, nonmarket competition can take place on moral dimensions, as in the cases of abortion and genetically modified foods. Just as one would not expect all physicians to perform abortions, neither would one expect all people of goodwill to agree on issues regarding genetically modified foods, working conditions in the factories of foreign suppliers, or drug testing of employees. The difficulty in predicting when moral concerns will lead to nonmarket action arises not only from the differences among individuals but also because the conviction with which those concerns are held can differ.

Despite these difficulties, managers must attempt to understand the moral motivations of individuals and interest groups and the strategies they are likely to employ. A church group concerned about a corporation's marketing activities in developing countries may use a private politics strategy that is quite different from exporters seeking a higher lending authorization from the Export-Import Bank. The exporters may use low-profile strategies such as lobbying and coalition building. The church group may initiate shareholder resolutions, pressure institutional investors, and demonstrate to attract the attention of the news media and government officeholders. In the Part III integrative case, *Credit Card Regulation,* some consumers felt they were deceived by credit card companies and were subjected to unfair charges. Their complaints had both distributive and moral motivations, and members of Congress sought to represent their interests and concerns.

BOEING IN A PICKLE

Since 1962 the investment tax credit had provided incentives for capital investment through credits deducted from a firm's tax liability. By the 1980s, however, a number of companies were incurring operating losses and had no tax liability to which the credits could be applied. With the nation in a recession Congress passed the Economic Recovery Tax Act (ERTA) of 1981 to stimulate economic activity. ERTA allowed companies with losses to purchase capital equipment and "sell" the investment tax credit to a profitable company that could use the credit to reduce its taxes. Thus, a steel company with operating losses could obtain a new rolling mill by having a lessor take title to the mill and then lease it back to the steel company. The lessor would receive the investment tax credit plus the tax benefits from accelerated depreciation, and the lease payments by the steel company would be lowered by the amount of those benefits.[4] ERTA thus restored the incentives for capital investment of those companies with operating losses.

Prior to ERTA many foreign sales were made under lease arrangements designed to capture the investment tax credit. A U.S. lessor would purchase capital equipment from a U.S. manufacturer, take the investment tax credit and the tax benefits from accelerated depreciation, and lease the equipment to a foreign customer. The tax benefits were then shared among the three participants in the transaction. Commercial aircraft had frequently been sold through these leasing arrangements. Investment tax credits were available for aircraft purchased by a U.S. lessor and leased to a foreign airline if the aircraft were used substantially in regular service to the United States. The "substantially" condition involved a modest number of landings on U.S. territory in a year.

Foreign leasing inadvertently became an issue because of the way ERTA was written. Its language allowed tax-exempt entities to make the same type of lease arrangements a steel company or a foreign airline could make. In addition, ERTA allowed the sale and leaseback of assets already owned by a firm or a tax-exempt entity. Tax-exempts thus could sell an existing asset to a lessor, who would take the investment tax credit and the accelerated depreciation benefits and lease the asset back to the tax-exempt at a price reflecting the tax benefits.

The number of tax-exempt entities that could benefit from such leasing was enormous. Every municipality, museum, school district, university, library, nonprofit corporation, and government entity could use it. The pace of leasing by tax-exempts began to accelerate in 1983, and the federal government became alarmed about the potential loss of tax revenues, particularly because of the record federal budget deficit and the sluggish economy. In addition, several leasing plans attracted media attention. Bennington College announced plans to sell its campus to alumni and then lease it back, with the alumni passing back to the college the tax benefits allowed by ERTA. The Navy planned to lease 13 cargo ships instead of purchasing them, with the "purchaser" of the ships taking the investment tax credit and the depreciation benefits and passing back to the Navy a portion of the tax benefits in the form of a price reduction. Transactions such as the Navy's and sale-and-leaseback transactions such as that planned by Bennington College were clearly contrary to the intent of ERTA.

The House Ways and Means Committee had drafted ERTA, and members of that committee had a vested interest in its original intent. Representative J. J. (Jake) Pickle (D-TX), a ranking member of the committee, was determined to eliminate the abuses of ERTA. His idea was that those who were exempt from taxes should not receive tax benefits. This was expressed as, "People who don't pay taxes should not get tax breaks."[5] This slogan was quickly interpreted to include foreign lessees, since foreign firms do not pay U.S. taxes. U.S. exporters that had used leasing for foreign sales suddenly faced the risk of losing the tax benefits on which they had relied.

In May 1983 Representative Pickle introduced a bill, H.R. 3110, that would deny the investment tax credit and accelerated depreciation benefits to tax-exempts and to foreigners who leased assets from U.S. lessors.[6] Hearings were held 2 weeks later, and H.R. 3110 was passed by the Ways and Means Committee on July 27. Floor action in

---

[4]The economic efficiency rationale for this provision of ERTA was that it would equalize marginal tax rates across firms and thus lessen distortions in the pattern of capital investment. The political pressure from industries unable to use the investment tax credits was undoubtedly the impetus for the provision, however.
[5]*Fortune,* September 19, 1983, p. 52.
[6]Straight-line depreciation would be allowed on foreign leasing.

the House was scheduled for the end of October. Senators Robert Dole (R-KS) and Howard Metzenbaum (D-OH) introduced a similar bill in the Senate.

At the then-current volume of leasing, the Department of Treasury estimated that the bill would increase tax receipts by $1.65 billion per year, with foreign leasing accounting for $570 million. Approximately $300 million of the $570 million was attributable to Boeing, which used leasing for nearly half its foreign sales of 747s.[7] The other exporters affected included oil drilling rig manufacturers, producers of containers for ocean shipping, and other aircraft manufacturers.

In 1983 the 747's only competitors were the DC-10 and the Airbus A300. The A300's range did not allow it to make transoceanic flights, so many observers believed that the 747 had little foreign competition for flights to the United States. The DC-10 had a smaller capacity than the 747 but a similar range. McDonnell-Douglas was rumored to be phasing out the DC-10 because of lagging sales.

Boeing maintained that it was locked in a fierce competitive struggle with the highly subsidized Airbus, a consortium of four European companies supported by their home governments. According to Boeing, foreign airlines used their wide-bodied aircraft on many routes that involved a trade-off between long legs and short hops. For some foreign airlines, the A300 was a substitute for the 747, according to Boeing. An airline that operated routes in Asia as well as a route to the United States could fly 747s on the U.S. route and A300s on the Asian route, with a series of hops if necessary. Alternatively, it could use 747s on the Asian routes and fly each aircraft on the U.S. route sufficiently often to qualify for the leasing tax benefits. Boeing thus argued that elimination of the tax benefits on foreign leasing would result in a loss of U.S. exports. Critics of foreign leasing, however, maintained that Boeing would not lose sales because it faced no competition. Furthermore, if sales would be lost, then U.S. taxpayers must be subsidizing foreigners. Representative Pickle wanted such subsidization stopped.

One means by which Airbus was subsidized was through government export financing at below-market interest rates. To compound Boeing's problem, the U.S. Export-Import Bank (Eximbank) had recently stopped providing subsidized export financing for 747s. This decision reflected the Eximbank's limited lending authorization and its conclusion, strongly criticized by Boeing, that the 747 faced no effective competition.[8]

In addition to Pickle's bill, hearings were scheduled before the Senate Finance Committee, chaired by Senator Dole, for the end of September. Neither senator from the state of Washington was a member of the Finance Committee, and Republican Slade Gorton was in his first term in the Senate. Longtime Senator Henry Jackson had died in August 1983 and had been replaced by the former Republican governor Daniel Evans, who was in the process of campaigning to retain his seat in the November special election.

Boeing's problem was how to deal with the challenge posed by Representative Pickle's bill.

ANALYSIS OF BOEING IN A PICKLE

The Nonmarket Issue

The issue of eliminating the tax benefits on leasing by tax-exempt and foreign entities arose suddenly as a result of the rapid increase in leasing by tax-exempts. The potential loss of tax revenue for the federal government was large, and the issue advanced quickly to the legislative stage of its life cycle. Although the politics of the issue were basically distributive, the sale-and-leaseback deals on existing assets by tax-exempts

---

[7]In 1983 the 747 was the only Boeing aircraft still in production that was certified for transoceanic flights. The 767 was not yet certified because of a Federal Aviation Administration's (FAA) administrative rule that permitted transoceanic crossings by twin-engine aircraft only if they remained no more than 60 minutes flying time from an acceptable airport. Approval was later granted, allowing the 767 to make transoceanic flights.
[8]The Eximbank had limited lending authority, requiring it to support those sales where its financing would have the greatest incremental effect on exports. See Baron (1983) for an analysis of Eximbank financing.

constituted abuse of ERTA's intent because those deals neither created jobs nor stimulated economic growth. The tax abuse coupled with the record federal budget deficit meant that the issue was likely to advance quickly through the rest of its life cycle. The dilemma for Boeing was that its leasing was threatened by the actions of the tax-exempts.

The following analysis illustrates the approach presented in this chapter.[9] The analysis is intended to develop an understanding of the politics of the issue and the relative strengths of the interests involved. This provides a basis for making judgments about the likely outcomes and therefore about strategy.

Distributive Consequences

The demand for nonmarket action depends on the value of the associated tax benefits. The investment tax credit ranged up to 10 percent and represented a cash inflow for the entity holding title to the asset. The value of the accelerated depreciation was the present value of the difference in the tax liability between accelerated and straight-line depreciation. On a sale of a $100 million 747, the tax benefits threatened by Pickle's bill were approximately $20 million, composed of a $10 million investment tax credit and approximately $10 million due to accelerated depreciation. At a sales rate of ten 747s a year, Boeing's tax benefits at stake were approximately $200 million.[10]

Although the magnitude of the tax benefits from foreign leasing is straightforward to estimate, the distribution of those benefits is more complex. A foreign leasing transaction involves three parties: the aircraft manufacturer, the foreign lessee, and the U.S. lessor. The share of the tax benefits captured by each party depends on the competitiveness of the aircraft and leasing markets. The leasing industry includes large banks, some insurance companies, and several leasing companies. Because of the number of potential lessors, competition would be expected to leave them with competitive profits. The bulk of the benefits thus should accrue to the aircraft manufacturer and the foreign airline.[11]

The distribution of the tax benefits between the manufacturer and the airline depends on whether other aircraft are close substitutes for the 747 for the route configuration of the airline. Indeed, each airline can be considered individually, since sales result from negotiations between the airline and aircraft manufacturers. For an airline for which there is no substitute for the 747, Boeing is in the position of a monopolist and captures the tax benefits. For example, consider a foreign airline that is willing to pay no more than $100 million for a 747. With foreign leasing Boeing can make the following arrangement. It can sell the 747 to a lessor for $125 million, with the lessor taking the 20 percent tax benefits of $25 million and leasing the aircraft to the foreign airline for $100 million. If the Pickle bill were enacted, Boeing would reduce its price to $100 million, retain the sale, and no jobs would be lost. Boeing would, however, have lost $25 million as a result of the Pickle bill.

If there were some degree of competition from the A300, the tax benefits from leasing would be shared between the foreign airline and Boeing. If the A300 were a close substitute, the foreign airline might capture all the benefits. In that case, the elimination of the tax benefits would result in the loss of sales and jobs. U.S. taxpayers in that case would be subsidizing the foreign airlines. In other cases Boeing and the airline would each capture a share of the tax benefits.

The Eximbank apparently concluded that the 747 faced little competition and that Boeing captured the bulk of the tax benefits from its financing. Representative Pickle and his staff came to the same conclusion. Even if there were a degree of competition, Representative Pickle and the other supporters of the bill had an attractive issue. If there was competition and foreign airlines captured a portion of the benefits, then U.S.

---

[9]This is not a description of Boeing's analysis.

[10]The difference between this figure and the Treasury estimate of $300 million is that the Treasury was reporting the tax collections reflecting the accelerated depreciation during the first years after the sale. The $200 million is a present value that takes into account the lower depreciation in later years.

[11]If the lessors captured a substantial share of the tax benefits, Boeing could establish its own financing subsidiary as McDonnell-Douglas had done. That would permit Boeing to realize the depreciation tax benefits but not the investment tax credit.

taxpayers were subsidizing foreign airlines that competed with U.S. airlines. If there was little competition and Boeing captured the benefits, U.S. taxpayers were subsidizing a large, profitable company. Boeing was in a pickle.

Boeing maintained that foreign leasing allowed it to make sales that otherwise would be lost to Airbus and that Pickle's bill would cost jobs at both Boeing and its suppliers. In its testimony before the Senate Finance Committee, Boeing could expect to be asked why it could not lower its price to avoid losing sales if the tax benefits were eliminated. Boeing could also expect to be asked if the tax benefits on foreign leasing subsidized the foreign airlines that competed with U.S. international airlines.

To assess the impact of the Pickle bill, Boeing must determine if there are any public or private substitutes for the leasing. One obvious private substitute is to lower its price, which is possible, since Boeing is far down the learning curve on an aircraft that it had been producing for nearly 20 years. The other possible private substitute is to arrange for foreign lessors to make the lease arrangements, taking advantage of their own domestic tax laws. Other countries, however, did not have investment tax credits, so even if foreign lessors financed Boeing's exports, the tax benefits would be much lower. The Eximbank was unlikely to reverse its withdrawal of financing for 747s, so that public substitute was not a realistic alternative. The U.S. government was even less likely to subsidize a profitable company.

This analysis suggests that Boeing is likely to be capturing most, or at least a substantial share, of the tax benefits. If the tax benefits were lost through Pickle's initiative, except for some airlines for which the A300 was a close substitute, Boeing would retain the bulk of its sales by reducing its prices. Boeing thus stood to lose profits but probably few aircraft sales as a consequence of the Pickle bill—at least that was the conclusion reached by Representative Pickle, the Ways and Means Committee, and the Eximbank.

Boeing's Nonmarket Agenda and Objectives

Boeing had several issues on its nonmarket issue agenda, including Eximbank policy, U.S. pressure on Airbus and its parent countries, antitrust concerns in the U.S. aircraft industry, the high value of the dollar, the Reagan administration's increased defense spending from which it expected to benefit, and the media and public attention being given to defense contractors. The foreign leasing issue had little direct relationship to these other issues, but the action the company took could affect its ability to deal with the other issues.

Choosing an objective is a central component of a nonmarket strategy, and Boeing could pursue the following objectives:

1. Defeat of the Pickle bill
2. An exemption for job-creating leases consistent with the intent of ERTA
3. An exemption for job-creating export leases consistent with the intent of ERTA
4. An exemption for its own leases
5. Grandfathering of current orders
6. A phaseout of the tax benefits on foreign leasing

The best outcome for Boeing would be the defeat of Pickle's bill, but there is considerable support for the bill, and it is likely to pass in some form.[12] Objective 2 is consistent with the original intent of ERTA, but a substantial tax loss would remain because tax-exempts would still be able to use leasing for new projects although not for sale-and-leaseback deals. This objective is unlikely to be achievable. Objective 4 singles out Boeing without any particular justification, and so it, too, is unlikely. Therefore, Boeing's primary objective should be 3, with 5 and 6 as contingent objectives in the event that an exemption for job-creating export leases cannot be obtained. This objective means that the interests of other exporters are aligned with Boeing's interests, whereas the interests of tax-exempts are opposed.

---

[12]One indication of this was that the Senate bill was introduced by Senators Dole and Metzenbaum, who were from different parties and had quite different positions on many issues. Their support signaled that this was not a partisan issue.

The Nature of the Politics

The principal beneficiaries of the Pickle bill are taxpayers and those who would benefit from lower interest rates if the federal budget deficit were reduced.[13] These benefits are widely distributed and small on a per capita basis. The harm resulting from Pickle's bill is concentrated among tax-exempts, exporters of capital goods that use lease financing, and lessors. In the framework of the Wilson-Lowi matrix, the politics of Pickle's bill are entrepreneurial, and Pickle is the entrepreneur. This issue is attractive to a politician because it involves good government—the elimination of a tax abuse—and the entrepreneur can claim credit for it. Boeing's objective, however, is not to defeat the Pickle bill, which was expected to pass, but instead is to obtain an exemption for job-creating export leases. The relevant alternative thus is the exemption, and using the Wilson-Lowi matrix again, Boeing, the other exporters, and lessors are clients with concentrated benefits from an exemption with widely distributed costs for taxpayers.

Interests and the Demand for Nonmarket Action

Boeing accounts for over half the tax benefits associated with foreign leasing, so the other exporters have smaller stakes in the issue than Boeing has. Employees, suppliers, shareholders, and local communities that depend on the exporters would also benefit from an exemption to the extent that sales would be lost. The lessors are likely to earn competitive profits on foreign leasing but still have an incentive to take action on the issue.[14] Since a relatively small number of firms is affected, general business associations such as the Chamber of Commerce and the National Association of Manufacturers are unlikely to be active on the issue.

The tax-exempts have a strong demand for nonmarket action in opposition to the Pickle bill. They also oppose an exemption for export leases because if the exemption fails, Boeing would then join them in opposing the Pickle bill. Although the impact on any one tax-exempt is small compared with the impact on Boeing, in the aggregate their demand is great. Many tax-exempts are already squeezed by federal budget reductions and the recession. Furthermore, they have few, if any, substitutes for replacing the tax benefits. Collectively, their demand is very high.

The interests of taxpayers are opposed to those of Boeing and the tax-exempts. The benefits to taxpayers from the Pickle bill correspond to the additional tax receipts, which would contribute to a lower federal budget deficit and hence lower interest rates and increased economic activity.

The Supply Side

The affected exporters not only are few in number but also are geographically concentrated. Boeing's affected employment, if it lost sales, would be in Seattle. Oil drilling rig exporters are concentrated on the Gulf Coast, and container manufacturers are few in number. The exporters thus have poor coverage of congressional districts, even though they have considerable resources. Boeing has a supplier network whose coverage is extensive, and it could attempt to organize its suppliers for nonmarket action. Boeing, however, may not want to mobilize its suppliers in a grassroots campaign because the overt use of political pressure by a defense contractor could attract media attention and result in a backlash.

The tax-exempts are numerous, their coverage of congressional districts is virtually complete, and many of their leaders and supporters have access to members of Congress. Although they have few resources, they have the ability to deliver considerable nonmarket pressure. To assess their strategy, it is useful to distinguish between those tax-exempts that already have a leasing deal in hand or in the planning stages and those that do not. The recipients of the benefits of leasing in the latter group are as yet

---

[13]U.S. airlines that competed with foreign airlines would also benefit to the extent that the foreign airlines captured some of the tax benefits.
[14]No lessor testified in the House hearings on the Pickle bill, although one association of lessors involved primarily in domestic leasing sent a letter that was entered into the hearing record.

unidentified, so it is difficult to mobilize them for nonmarket action. The former group, however, has identifiable benefits and a strong incentive to organize and act.[15] Their benefits, however, can be protected by simply grandfathering existing deals. Grandfathering would allow Pickle and Dole to avoid constituency pressure on them and their colleagues while preventing further drains on the Treasury.

Taxpayers are numerous, have complete coverage of congressional districts, and have large resources. They are costly to organize, however, and given their low per capita benefits, cannot be expected to be active on this issue. Their interests are represented by a political entrepreneur, Representative Pickle.

Boeing's ability to generate effective nonmarket action on this issue is limited. It could attempt to mobilize its shareholders, but most are unlikely to contact their representatives on an issue such as this. Furthermore, a letter from Boeing stressing the urgency of this issue could cause some of them to sell their shares. Boeing employees have a demand for nonmarket action if sales would be lost, and their costs of organizing are low. Their coverage of congressional districts, however, is limited to the Seattle area. Consequently, their nonmarket action is likely to have only a limited effect, although their unions could represent them. Similarly, the communities potentially affected by the bill are geographically concentrated. Boeing could obtain coverage of congressional districts by mobilizing its suppliers. Their demand for nonmarket action varies considerably as a function of their volume of 747 subcontracts, but in all likelihood enough suppliers could be mobilized to supply a moderate amount of nonmarket pressure. As a defense contractor, however, Boeing is cautious about taking high-profile actions.

The Distributive Politics Spreadsheet

Figure 6-3 presents a distributive politics spreadsheet summarizing this analysis. The conclusion from this analysis is that the supporters of an exemption for job-creating export leases are unlikely to be able to generate a great amount of nonmarket action. Attention should thus be directed to the contingent objectives of grandfathering and a phaseout of the tax benefits.

Institutions and Institutional Officeholders

Although Congress is the institutional arena in which this issue was contested, the executive branch was also interested in the budget consequences. A White House working group had begun meeting to develop measures to curb the leasing by tax-exempts.

Boeing might have been able to enlist the support of executive branch agencies concerned with exports. The Department of Commerce and the U.S. Trade Representative were potential supporters. The Department of the Treasury had stated that the additional tax receipts from eliminating the tax benefits on export leasing were not as important as the exports potentially at risk, but the Treasury could not be expected to work on Boeing's behalf.

Boeing's best hope was to have an exemption for job-creating export leases incorporated into the Senate Finance Committee's bill. Success in the Finance Committee would likely mean success on the Senate floor. If the committee did not provide an exemption, the chances of having an exemption amendment adopted on the Senate floor were not good, given the limited coverage of Boeing and the other exporters. Obtaining an exemption through a floor amendment in the House would be difficult because it would be necessary to obtain from the Rules Committee an open rule or a modified rule to allow the amendment. Ways and Means bills sometimes receive a closed rule that prohibits amendments, and Representative Pickle would certainly seek one. There was little hope of successfully introducing an amendment in the House.

---

[15]Some of the groups testifying were the National Housing Rehabilitation Association; American Federation of State, County, and Municipal Employees; YMCA; National Conference of Black Mayors; Municipal Finance Officers Association; Bennington College; and the Preservation Alliance of Louisville and Jefferson County.

FIGURE 6-3 Distributive Politics Spreadsheet

Alternative being analyzed: Exemption for job-creating exports

Supporting Interests

	Demand Side — Benefits from Supporting an Exemption			Supply Side — Ability to Generate Nonmarket Action	Effectiveness			Prediction
Interests	**Substitutes**	**Aggregate**	**Per Capita**	**Numbers**	**Coverage**	**Resources**	**Cost of Organizing**	**Amount of Nonmarket Action**
Boeing Company	lower price	large	large	small	little	large	small	moderate
• shareholders	sell shares	large	small	large	extensive	large	very high	little
• employees	few	large	substantial	large	little	limited	very low	little
• suppliers	other business	substantial	moderate	substantial	extensive	moderate	high	moderate
Communities								
• Boeing	few	substantial	considerable	small	little	small	low	little
• suppliers	few	moderate	moderate	considerable	extensive	small	high	limited
Oil rig mfgrs.	lower price	moderate	small	few	little	moderate	low	little
Container mfgrs.	lower price	moderate	small	few	little	moderate	low	little
Lessors	other loans	moderate	moderate	small	little	large	low	little

Opposing Interests

	Demand Side — Benefits from Opposing an Exemption			Supply Side — Ability to Generate Nonmarket Action	Effectiveness			Prediction
Interests	**Substitutes**	**Aggregate**	**Per Capita**	**Numbers**	**Coverage**	**Resources**	**Cost of Organizing**	**Amount of Nonmarket Action**
Taxpayers	none	large	very small	huge	complete	huge	very high	little
Tax-exempts	none	substantial	substantial	large	extensive	small	low	large

The likelihood that the Pickle bill would pass in the House meant that if Boeing were successful in obtaining an exemption in the Senate, it would have to preserve that exemption in a conference committee. The contingent objective of grandfathering current orders might be a reasonable compromise to achieve in conference. Pickle would be among the House conferees.

The key institutional actor was Senator Dole. Although Boeing had a major facility in Wichita, much of the work there in 1983 was on defense contracts. The Senator had won with nearly two-thirds of the vote in the last election and was electorally safe. His current policy interest was in reducing the federal deficit, and his personal objectives were to become Senate majority leader and position himself for a possible run for the presidency. To achieve the first objective, he had to avoid offending his Senate colleagues, who were under pressure from their constituents to preserve leasing deals for tax-exempts in their states. Dole could easily accommodate them and still be fiscally responsible simply by grandfathering their deals. The bill then would have clear sailing through the Senate.

The final opportunity for Boeing then would be the president. It was unlikely that he would veto this bill, which promoted fiscal responsibility, since he had been berating Congress for its unwillingness to cut spending. If a veto were likely, Congress had ways to protect the bill. One was to consolidate the Pickle bill with other pending tax legislation the president wanted passed. That could insulate the leasing provisions from a veto.

Nonmarket Strategy Formulation

For a nonmarket strategy to be successful on an issue characterized by client politics, the client must demonstrate to enough members of Congress that either their constituents would benefit from an exemption or their own policy interests would be served. Given the belief that the 747 faced little competition, it would be difficult to demonstrate either that many jobs would be preserved by an exemption or that the trade deficit would be significantly affected. Indeed, the pressure on Congress came from the tax-exempts, and members were busy working to protect their constituents' deals. A client can attempt to build a coalition, but in this case there were only a few potential coalition members (the other exporters and the lessors), and their coverage of congressional districts was very limited.

Boeing's best strategy was to provide information through lobbying arguing that export leases created jobs in a manner consistent with the objectives of ERTA. In doing so it could distinguish between its lease transactions and sale-and-leaseback transactions that did not create jobs. Boeing could also emphasize its importance in lowering the U.S. trade deficit. The trade deficit, however, was of much less concern to members of Congress than the budget deficit. Boeing also could challenge as inflated the Treasury estimate of the increase in tax revenues from eliminating the tax benefits on foreign leases.

Members of Congress were uncertain about Boeing's claims about the effects on sales and jobs, so Boeing could enlist the aid of some of its customers, such as Singapore Airlines, to attest to the impact of this legislation on their orders. In the upcoming hearings, senators, however, were likely to ask if Boeing could not lower its price to retain sales. This would reduce Boeing's profits, but few in Congress were concerned about lower profits for a quite profitable company.

Boeing could remind the members of the Finance Committee that it faced unfair competition from a highly subsidized Airbus and that eliminating the tax benefits on foreign leasing would place it at a further disadvantage. This argument, however, had not stopped the Eximbank from ending its financing of 747s. Moreover, Congress preferred to try to stop unfair competition than to subsidize U.S. firms. Furthermore, all U.S. exporters were complaining about losing sales because of the high value of the dollar.

In pursuing its objectives, Boeing could enlist the aid of the congressional delegation from the state of Washington. The House delegation was small, however, and the senators had little seniority. Senator Evans was spending much of his energy campaigning for election in November, and Senator Gorton was in his first term. Neither was on the Senate Finance Committee. Boeing thus had relatively weak representation in Congress, and few other members were likely to view Boeing as their client.

Because of the other issues on its nonmarket issue agenda and because of the sensitivity of overt political activity by a defense contractor, Boeing generally prefers to maintain a low profile. Using suppliers for a grassroots campaign would have too high a profile for this issue.[16] A grassroots program involving employees would also be high profile and would likely have been insufficient to attain Boeing's primary objective given the limited coverage of congressional districts.

Boeing's best nonmarket actions were lobbying and coalition building. Lobbying the Senate Finance Committee was essential. Boeing would be able to address the complexity of the issue in its discussions with key committee members and their staffs. It also could discuss its contingent objectives and the importance of protecting orders already in hand. In its lobbying, Boeing should stress the effects of lost sales on its suppliers and on its own operations and employees. The cost of lobbying was low compared with the potential consequences, and Boeing should use its executives in the lobbying.

Boeing could form a coalition with other firms that used leasing to finance exports, or it could coordinate its nonmarket activities with them. McDonnell-Douglas, oil drilling rig manufacturers, container manufacturers, engine manufacturers, and a few other exporters had incentives to act, although the aggregate effect on them was smaller than on Boeing. These companies were relatively few in number and had relatively poor coverage of congressional districts. The same was true of lessors, so there was a mismatch between their demand for nonmarket action and their ability to supply nonmarket pressure.

Boeing should, of course, modify its market strategy by developing alternative means of financing foreign sales.

The Outcome

The Pickle bill had strong support from members of Congress who wanted to stop the tax abuse and the drain on tax revenues. As is clear from the previous analysis, exporters were unable to generate sufficient nonmarket pressure to stop the Pickle bill. The bill was incorporated in the Deficit Reduction Act of 1984. The final provisions eliminated the tax benefits for both tax-exempts and foreign leases, but the current projects of many of the tax-exempts were grandfathered. Straight-line depreciation was allowed for foreign leases, but the depreciation period had to extend for the life of the asset or 125 percent of the lease term. The other tax benefits were phased out over several years. Grandfathering was provided for wide-body aircraft, containers, and drilling rigs. The provision for Boeing read: "The amendments in this section shall not apply with respect to any wide body, 4-engine commercial passenger aircraft used by a foreign person or entity if (i) on or before November 1, 1983 the foreign person or entity entered into a written binding contract to acquire such aircraft, and (ii) such aircraft is placed into service before January 1, 1986." Boeing thus achieved its contingent objectives.[17]

SUMMARY

The analysis of nonmarket and political action has two foundations—interests and institutions. Interests can arise from distributive consequences and moral concerns. Distributive consequences can be assessed in terms of the benefits and costs from an alternative. The moral determinants of nonmarket action are based on considerations of well-being, rights, and social justice.

Interests give rise to a demand for nonmarket action, and that demand depends on the private and public substitutes available. The incentive to act depends on the per capita benefits, and if the aggregate benefits are high but the per capita benefits are low, incentives for nonmarket action can be weak.

---

[16]Boeing undoubtedly wanted to avoid media attention because the political entrepreneur had the better side of this issue. A large, profitable company seeking to preserve tax benefits—or subsidies, as its critics called them—had the potential for unfavorable media treatment, which could hurt a defense contractor.
[17]The case *Leasebacks by Tax-Exempt Entities* in the fifth edition of this book considers the second chapter in the foreign leasing saga.

The costs of nonmarket action are of three types. The first is the cost of organizing interests and joining together for collective action. The second is the direct cost of implementing a nonmarket strategy. The third is associated with the effectiveness of a given amount of nonmarket action. If the number of affected interests is small, the costs of organization are likely to be small. The larger the number of affected interests, the more likely they are to encounter the free-rider problem. The effectiveness of nonmarket action depends on the number of people affected, their resources, and their coverage of legislative districts. The paradox of collective action is that while effectiveness increases with the number of interests affected and with their coverage of legislative districts, dispersed groups often have low per capita benefits and high costs of organization, resulting in little nonmarket action.

The analysis of the benefits and costs of taking nonmarket action can be summarized in the distributive politics spreadsheet. The chapter case, *Scrubbers and Environmental Politics,* provides an opportunity to apply nonmarket analysis and the distributive politics spreadsheet to a legislative issue.

The nature of political competition depends on the relative concentration and dispersion of the benefits and harm from enactment of a nonmarket alternative. The categories of client, interest group, entrepreneurial, and majoritarian politics characterize the nature of the political competition, but the outcome depends on additional factors, including the characteristics of the institutions in whose arenas the competition takes place.

The Boeing case indicates the complexity of even a relatively straightforward issue. It also illustrates the difference between the demand for nonmarket action and its supply. Taxpayers have low per capita benefits relative to their costs of taking nonmarket action and thus had to be represented by a political entrepreneur. The tax-exempts had benefits that exceed their costs, so they were active. Boeing and other exporters had a high demand for nonmarket action and low costs of organizing, but their effectiveness was limited by a lack of coverage of congressional districts. As a defense contractor, Boeing preferred a low-profile strategy to avoid compromising its effectiveness on other issues. Boeing's best political strategy was to lobby using the message that sales and jobs would be lost. The best that Boeing was able to achieve, however, was a phaseout of the benefits and the grandfathering of orders in hand.

-------------------------------- A P P E N D I X   A --------------------------------

Nonmarket Action and the Free-Rider Problem

The Benefits and Costs of Nonmarket Action

Pluralist theories predict that common interests, such as those that result from a potential increase in industry profits, lead to nonmarket action consistent with those interests. These demand-side theories draw implications about nonmarket activity directly from the interests of individuals and firms, as measured by surpluses and rents. Olson (1965), however, argued that such theories ignore the costs of taking nonmarket and collective action. Those costs are an important determinant of the effectiveness of those with common interests.[18] The higher those costs, the lower is the nonmarket action taken and therefore the less effective are those with common interests.

Taxpayers have a common interest in lower taxes, and consumers have a common interest in lower prices. With some exceptions neither taxpayers nor consumers have been particularly effective in public politics, in part because their costs of organizing for collective action are high relative to the per capita benefits they would receive as a result of that action.[19] The (per-capita) benefits for an individual consumer from eliminating sugar import quotas are outweighed by the costs of taking nonmarket action. Large groups thus may have a high demand for political action, but their costs of acting can also be high. Common or aligned interests therefore do not translate directly into nonmarket success but instead are mediated by the costs of nonmarket action.

The Free-Rider Problem and Collective Action

The costs of nonmarket action can be reduced through *collective action*. On many nonmarket issues, a firm's interests are aligned with those of other firms, labor, or suppliers. With an alignment of interests, collective action is possible. Outcomes of nonmarket issues, however, often have the property of a public good in the sense that they pertain to everyone, regardless of whether they contributed to realizing the outcome. For example, preventing a shift in demand due to restrictions on credit card charges benefits all firms in the credit card industry regardless of whether they contributed to preventing the shift. When the benefits from nonmarket action accrue to those who do not contribute, a *free-rider problem* may be present.[20]

Consider an industry composed of n small firms. Suppose that nonmarket action by any one firm costs that firm c and yields benefits b for each of the n firms in the industry, for a total benefit of nb. For example, participation by an individual firm increases the likelihood that taxes will not be increased, which is a public good for the firms in the industry. Whenever $nb > c$, the firms in the industry are better off if an individual firm participates in the collective action. Consequently, it is collectively rational for all firms to contribute to the nonmarket action when $nb > c$. If all n firms contributed, the total benefits would be n^2b.

What is collectively rational, however, may not be individually rational. An individual firm has an incentive to contribute to the collective action only if the cost c it incurs is less than the benefits it receives from its own participation, and those benefits are only b. Consequently, if $c > b$, an individual firm has no incentive to participate even though its participation produces collective benefits nb to the industry that exceed its costs c.[21] The firm then prefers to free ride on the efforts of the other firms, since doing so saves it the cost c and it loses only the benefits b from its own contribution. The incentive to free ride is thus $c-b > 0$. Each firm has an incentive to free ride, and the possibility of collective action is in doubt. The free-rider problem thus is present when $b < c < nb$.[22] The characteristic of such dilemmas is that what is collectively rational is not individually rational.

The larger the number of potential participants, the more serious is the free-rider problem. Large groups such as consumers and taxpayers often have difficulty overcoming this problem. The Consumer Federation of America, for example, has no individual members, but instead its members are other organizations. Large groups thus must develop other means to induce participation. Some groups form associations to reduce the cost of nonmarket action. Some groups encourage participation by providing selective benefits that can be denied to those who do not participate. The largest organized

[18]See Moe (1980) and Hardin (1982).
[19]This does not mean that the interests of consumers and taxpayers are not reflected in political outcomes. Their interests can be represented by a government officeholder, who can claim credit for having done so, or by an NGO such as the Consumer Federation of America or the National Taxpayers Union.

[20]See Shepsle and Boncheck (1997) for an introduction to collective action.
[21]If $c > b$, each individual firm benefits sufficiently from its own participation to act on its own, so there is no collective action problem. For example, many private equity and venture capital firms had a strong incentive to avoid a tax increase in the Chapter 7 case *Carried Interest Taxation*.
[22]The free-rider problem is a special case of a prisoners' dilemma. In a prisoners' dilemma each player has a dominant strategy, and if each plays that strategy the outcome is worse for both than is the outcome if both participated.

interest group in the United States is AARP (American Association of Retired Persons), which has a membership of over 30 million. AARP is politically active on a variety of issues of concern to its members, and it attracts members in part by providing selective benefits to them. AARP, for example, offers its members discount prices on pharmaceuticals and supplemental health insurance, as well as discounts on travel and accommodations.

Labor unions also face a free-rider problem in obtaining contributions from members to undertake nonmarket activities. The unions have solved this collective action problem by obtaining legislation that requires mandatory dues from everyone in a collective bargaining unit, and those dues can be used for nonmarket action as well as supporting candidates in federal and state elections.[23]

One possibility for resolving the free-rider problem and other social dilemmas is cooperation in which the parties take into account not only the consequences for themselves but for the other parties as well. Cooperation in this sense is mutual altruism. In the context of the free-rider problem, each firm would participate at a cost c and receive nb in benefits—provided that all others participated. If a firm agrees to participate, however, it has an incentive to defect from the cooperative agreement. This would save the firm c and its benefits would be reduced by only b, which is less than c. The temptation is thus not to participate and free-ride on the participation of others. Indeed, if a firm harbors some doubt

about whether others will participate, not participating becomes even more compelling. Such doubts can lead to no participation.

This reasoning suggests that free-rider problems are difficult to resolve, yet many are resolved. Resolution often occurs because the free-rider problem is repeated rather than encountered only once. In that case, players have a stake in the future, and the set of strategies that players can employ is much broader. A player can, for example, reward or punish another player for the choice made in the previous round, and the expectation of punishment for failure to participate can induce participation. In employing these strategies, the players do not take into account the interests of the other party in their reasoning about how to play, so altruism is not involved. This resolution of the free-rider problem is thus noncooperative rather than cooperative.

Behavior generated by repeated play can be supported by the creation of an institution to punish deviations from the mutually beneficial actions. The World Trade Organization was created to lower trade barriers for the mutual benefit of its members and has a dispute resolution and punishment mechanism to deal with violations of the trading rules.[24] Similarly, firms that repeatedly take nonmarket action on issues on which their interests are aligned may be able to solve the free-rider problem by forming an association that acts on the behalf of its members on a series of issues and can monitor and punish free riding.

---

[23]Union members can file a statement each year to take back the portion of their dues that would otherwise go to electoral support.

[24]The World Trade Organization is considered in Chapter 18.

---------------------------------- A P P E N D I X   B ----------------------------------

The Organization of Congress

The Congress is bicameral. The House of Representatives is composed of 435 voting members serving 2-year terms and elected from districts with approximately the same population.[25] The 10 largest states account for half the members, whereas Alaska, Delaware, Montana, North Dakota, South Dakota, Vermont, and Wyoming have only one representative each. House districts are reapportioned after each census, and as a result of the 2000 census, the West and the South gained seats at the expense of the Northeast and the Midwest. The Speaker is the presiding officer of the House and is selected by the majority party and elected by the entire House.

Each of the 50 states has two senators, serving staggered 6-year terms. States with a small population thus have relatively more weight in the Senate, and states with large populations have relatively more weight in the House. The vice president presides over the Senate and has a vote in case of a tie.

The Constitution specifies neither how the chambers are to be organized nor how they are to conduct their business. Over time, they have developed their own formal and informal organizational structures and procedures. The formal organization is found in the committee structure and the legislative process. The informal organization is found in the party organization within the chambers. Each party elects a leader, whips, a secretary of the party conference, and heads of policy and steering committees. The primary responsibility of the whips is to generate party discipline on those issues on which the party has taken a position. Although parties and the party organization of Congress are important, members have considerable latitude in their voting, and party discipline is not the rule.

The Legislative Process

During the 109th Congress (2005–2006), 6,432 bills were introduced in the House and 4,102 in the Senate, yet only a few hundred were enacted.[26] Most bills are written by members of Congress, and bills originating in the executive branch (the Presidency) are introduced by a member of the president's party. Many bills are introduced with little expectation that they will even be considered, and some are introduced to appeal to interest groups or particular constituents. When submitting a bill a member will often seek cosponsors, but cosponsorship does not commit a member to support the bill if it comes to the floor for a vote. The number of cosponsors also does not necessarily translate into votes because interest group activity

often intensifies with the submission of a bill and can result in some members changing their positions.

Figure 6-4 illustrates the legislative process.[27] When a bill is introduced, it is referred to a committee. The committee can then consider the bill or, in the case of most bills, take no action on it. A bill is usually considered first by a subcommittee, which, by a majority vote, sends it to the full committee. A subcommittee cannot, however, effectively block a bill that a committee majority wishes to consider because the committee can consider the bill directly. Much of the substantive legislative work in Congress is done in committees, including amending and rewriting ("marking up") bills.

When a bill receives a majority vote in committee, it is ready to be scheduled for consideration on the floor of the chamber. In the House the bill goes to the Rules Committee, which assigns an amendment rule that governs floor consideration. The Rules Committee may assign a restrictive rule, which specifies or restricts the amendments that can be offered, or an open rule, which places no restrictions on the amendments that may be offered on the floor. Amendments on the floor, however, are governed by a standing rule of the House that prohibits nongermane amendments.[28] Special orders are used to schedule legislation and limit the time allocated to floor debate. Little true debate actually takes place, and many speeches on the floor are made to appeal to constituents.

The legislative process in the Senate is similar to that in the House except that all bills are technically considered on the floor under an open rule. In practice, however, the Senate operates under unanimous consent agreements (UCAs) specifying which amendments are to be considered on the floor. These agreements are negotiated under the auspices of the Senate leadership. An objection to a UCA by any senator prevents it from taking effect.

Senate rules allow members to speak on the floor for an unlimited time, and senators opposed to a bill can speak continuously (a filibuster), thus preventing a vote on a bill. Cloture can be invoked by a vote of 60 senators, preventing any member from speaking for more than an hour and precluding nongermane amendments. The minority party in the Senate frequently uses a filibuster to extract concessions from the majority or at times to kill a bill. A filibuster thus makes it more difficult to change the status quo.[29]

Before a bill can be enacted, it must be passed by both chambers in identical language. The bills passed by

---

[25]Representatives from the District of Columbia, American Samoa, Guam, Puerto Rico, and the Virgin Islands are members of the House but do not have a vote.
[26]See Ornstein, Mann, and Malbin (2008) for longitudinal data. Any legislation pending at the end of a Congress dies.

[27]Oleszek (2004) provides detailed information on the legislative process and on congressional procedures.
[28]On a majority vote, the House may waive any of its rules.
[29]See Krehbiel (1996) and Brady and Volden (1998) for theories of gridlock and Krehbiel (1998, 1999) for a theory in which filibusters and vetoes play an important role.

FIGURE 6-4 How a Bill Becomes a Law

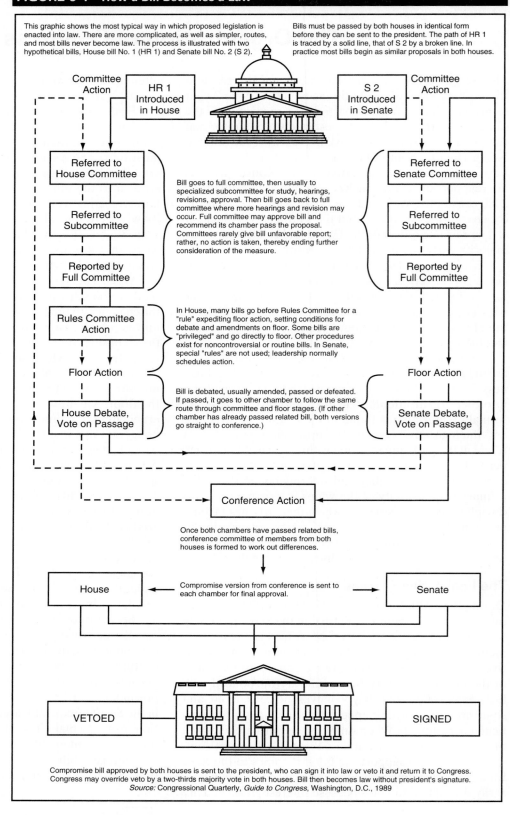

This graphic shows the most typical way in which proposed legislation is enacted into law. There are more complicated, as well as simpler, routes, and most bills never become law. The process is illustrated with two hypothetical bills, House bill No. 1 (HR 1) and Senate bill No. 2 (S 2).

Bills must be passed by both houses in identical form before they can be sent to the president. The path of HR 1 is traced by a solid line, that of S 2 by a broken line. In practice most bills begin as similar proposals in both houses.

Committee Action
HR 1 Introduced in House
S 2 Introduced in Senate
Committee Action

Referred to House Committee

Bill goes to full committee, then usually to specialized subcommittee for study, hearings, revisions, approval. Then bill goes back to full committee where more hearings and revision may occur. Full committee may approve bill and recommend its chamber pass the proposal. Committees rarely give bill unfavorable report; rather, no action is taken, thereby ending further consideration of the measure.

Referred to Senate Committee

Referred to Subcommittee

Referred to Subcommittee

Reported by Full Committee

Reported by Full Committee

Rules Committee Action

In House, many bills go before Rules Committee for a "rule" expediting floor action, setting conditions for debate and amendments on floor. Some bills are "privileged" and go directly to floor. Other procedures exist for noncontroversial or routine bills. In Senate, special "rules" are not used; leadership normally schedules action.

Floor Action

Floor Action

House Debate, Vote on Passage

Bill is debated, usually amended, passed or defeated. If passed, it goes to other chamber to follow the same route through committee and floor stages. (If other chamber has already passed related bill, both versions go straight to conference.)

Senate Debate, Vote on Passage

Conference Action

Once both chambers have passed related bills, conference committee of members from both houses is formed to work out differences.

House

Compromise version from conference is sent to each chamber for final approval.

Senate

VETOED

SIGNED

Compromise bill approved by both houses is sent to the president, who can sign it into law or veto it and return it to Congress. Congress may override veto by a two-thirds majority vote in both houses. Bill then becomes law without president's signature.
Source: Congressional Quarterly, *Guide to Congress*, Washington, D.C., 1989

each chamber seldom have the same language or substantive provisions and must be reconciled before they are sent to the president. Conference committees composed of representatives of each chamber and selected by the majority party leadership are usually used to reconcile major legislation.[30] Members of both parties from the committee that reported the bill plus the authors of principal amendments are typically appointed to the conference committee. Conference committees are important because the conferees have to bargain when the bills passed by the two chambers differ substantially. Thus, conference committees are often the focus of political activity. As an indication of the importance attached to conference committees, over 100 members of the House served as conferees on the 1990 amendments to the Clean Air Act. If the conferees from the two chambers agree on common language, the bill is returned to the floor of each chamber for a final passage vote. If approved by both chambers, it is sent to the president for signature or veto.

A bill passed by Congress becomes law when the president signs it or when Congress overrides a presidential veto on a vote of two-thirds of the members of each chamber. When a bill is passed while Congress is still in session, the president must act on the bill within 10 days or it automatically becomes law. If Congress is no longer in session, the president can choose not to act on the bill, and then it dies.[31] The authority to veto legislation gives the president considerable power.

Because legislation can be stopped at a number of points in the legislative process, it is more difficult to enact than to stop legislation. To be enacted, a bill must clear a number of hurdles. Committees represent an important hurdle, which gives power to the committees and their chairs. A majority of the members of the parent body can circumvent any hurdle that a chairperson or committee might erect, however.

Committees

Most of the work of Congress is done in committees, and each chamber chooses its own committee structure. The standing committees of the 110th Congress are listed in Figure 6-5. The House has 20 and the Senate

---

FIGURE 6-5   Standing Committees of the 110th Congress

House of Representatives	Senate
Agriculture	Aging (Special)
Appropriations	Agriculture, Nutrition and Forestry
Armed Services	Appropriations
Budget	Armed Services
Education and the Workforce	Banking, Housing and Urban Affairs
Energy and Commerce	Budget
Financial Services	Commerce, Science and Transportation
Government Reform	Energy and Natural Resources
Homeland Security	Environment and Public Works
House Administration	Ethics (Select)
International Relations	Finance
Intelligence (Select)	Foreign Relations
Judiciary	Governmental Affairs
Resources	Health, Education, Labor and Pensions
Rules	Indian Affairs
Science	Intelligence (Select)
Small Business	Judiciary
Standards of Official Conduct	Rules and Administration
Transportation and Infrastructure	Small Business and Entrepreneurship
Veterans' Affairs	Veterans' Affairs
Ways and Means	

---

[30]Instead of convening a conference, Congress often uses the procedure of amendments between the chambers to reconcile differences between bills. As in the daylight saving time example presented in Chapter 7, one chamber can simply adopt the language of the other's bill. A bill may go through several iterations of amendments between the chambers before common language is reached. This means that achieving reconciliation typically involves implicit bargaining.

[31]This is called a pocket veto.

has 17 standing committees, each of which has several subcommittees. Each chamber may also have select and special committees, and there are five joint committees.

Committees have policy jurisdictions, but those jurisdictions can overlap when issues cut across formal boundaries. In the House, for example, an environmental protection issue such as regulation of an agricultural pesticide could be under the jurisdiction of the Agriculture Committee as well as committees with environmental jurisdictions. Committees thus often battle over jurisdictions and hence over influence on legislation.

Government expenditures are governed by a complex process requiring both an authorization and an appropriation. The House Agriculture Committee or the Armed Services Committee may authorize expenditures for an agricultural subsidy program or a new weapons system, but the funds for those programs are provided by the Appropriations Committee. The process is designed to have the authorization committee act first, with the Appropriations Committee then providing funding no greater than the amount authorized. In recent Congresses authorization committees have begun to require program funding at particular levels. Beginning in the 1990s, the budget process has involved complex bargaining between the president and Congress over both the budget and the funding of individual programs.

Authorization committees have the responsibility for enacting legislation and reauthorizing programs with fixed expiration dates. In addition to their legislative roles, authorization committees have oversight responsibilities. Committees attempt to influence the policies of regulatory and administrative agencies by holding hearings and threatening legislative or budgetary action.

Committee membership is proportional to a party's representation in the chamber, and party conferences assign their members to committees. Newly elected legislators give a ranking of their committee preferences, and the party conferences do their best to assign members to the committees they have requested. Members of the House generally serve on two standing committees, and some also serve on select or joint committees. In the Senate, each member serves on several committees. Members accumulate committee-specific seniority, and the members of each committee are ranked by seniority within their party. Seniority is usually not transferable if the member changes committees. Because committee and subcommittee chairs are generally selected according to seniority and because chairpersons have strategic positions, members do not frequently change committees. Remaining with the same committee also gives members an incentive and an opportunity to develop expertise in its policy jurisdictions.

The chairs of committees and subcommittees are members of and are selected by the majority party. When the Democrats captured majorities in both the House and Senate in 2007, all chairs changed from Republicans to Democrats.

Approximately half of the House majority party and virtually all the Senate majority party are chairs of a committee or subcommittee. Committee chairs are selected by a party conference, and incumbents generally retain their chairs. Occasionally, however, a chair is replaced. When they became the majority party in the House in 1995, the Republicans passed over several more senior members in selecting committee chairs. In 2005 the Republicans replaced the chair of the Veterans Affairs Committee, and they passed over a more senior member in choosing the chair of the Appropriations Committee. Committee chairs traditionally have chosen the chairs of their subcommittees. In addition to their role as the first stage of legislative activity, subcommittees have the opportunity to hold hearings to direct public attention to issues and provide interest groups with a forum to advance their interests.

Committee and Personal Staffs

Members of Congress each have a personal staff that includes a chief, a press secretary, legislative assistants, and administrative assistants. The staff keeps the member informed about legislation, hearings, and other developments and also serves as an important link between members and their constituents and interest groups. A substantial portion of staff time is devoted to providing constituents with services such as assisting with lost Social Security checks, assisting with immigration problems, and interacting with government agencies. The staff also responds to constituents' letters on issues, often acknowledging the receipt of the letter, expressing concern for the issue, and stating that attention is being given to it. From 1960 to 1980 legislators' personal staffs expanded considerably; but since 1980 staff size has been relatively stable.

Committee staffs have shown a similar pattern. The committee staff is directed by the chair of the committee and, at quiet times, may serve as an adjunct to his or her personal staff. The committee staff is important in drafting legislation, marking up bills, and interacting with interest groups. For firms, trade associations, and other interest groups, the staff represents an important point of access to the legislative process and to information about the committee's activities. The majority party is allocated a substantially larger number of committee staff positions than the minority party. In 1995 the Republicans reduced the committee staff in the House by about one-third.

Legislators and Their Constituents

Whatever are their personal policy objectives, legislators must be reelected to have a continuing opportunity to achieve those objectives. Legislators thus vote on bills based on two considerations: their reelection incentives and their policy preferences.[32] Elected representatives thus are

---

[32]See Fiorina (1989) and Mayhew (1974) for analyses of congressional behavior.

responsive to the preferences of their constituents not only because they have a duty to represent them but also because they want to be reelected. To enhance the reelection of incumbents, many states have gerrymandered their congressional (and state legislature) electoral districts so that few are competitive. For example, in the 2004 elections in California not a single congressional seat, state Assembly seat, or state Senate seat changed party.

An electoral constituency includes voters, campaign volunteers, and providers of campaign resources. The reelection motive gives legislators an incentive to be attentive to the interests of those likely to vote. It also gives them an incentive to develop a personal constituency by providing services to constituents. Mayhew (1974) refers to this as the *constituency connection*. The reelection motive also may provide an opportunity for interest groups with electorally important resources to influence the behavior of legislators.

Mayhew characterized members of Congress as exhibiting two types of behavior: *credit claiming* and *blame avoidance*. Credit claiming is the practice of claiming credit for legislative or oversight activity that is in the interest of constituents. Because it is difficult for most constituents to know the actual effectiveness, or in some cases even the position, of a legislator, credit claiming may go beyond actual accomplishments. Interest groups, however, monitor legislators and often have a good idea of their effectiveness.

Blame avoidance involves distancing oneself from unpopular events, policies, or positions that might provide an opportunity for an electoral challenger. To avoid blame for the savings and loan crisis mentioned in Chapter 3, several members who had served on the important congressional banking committees chose to leave those committees.

Parties

Political parties are important in legislative politics, yet legislators have a considerable degree of independence from party positions and party leaders. In Congress, parties attempt to maintain discipline in voting in committees and on the floor. On issues important to their constituents, however, members often depart from the party position. One measure of the degree of party-line voting is the percentage of roll-call votes in which a majority of one party voted contrary to a majority of the other party. In 2002 only 45 percent of the roll-call votes in the Senate and 43 percent of those in the House had this partisan characteristic.

Parties in the United States are relatively weak compared to parties in many other countries, particularly those countries with a parliamentary system of government. One reason is that in the United States nominations for elected office are controlled locally rather than by a national party. In addition, issues important to voters are often local rather than national, which allows members to develop local, personal constituencies to improve their reelection prospects. This personal vote is developed through district work, directing federal funds to the district, and constituent service. Parties are also relatively weak in the United States because most campaign contributions are made directly to candidates rather than to parties, which gives members a further degree of independence.

The Presidency and the Executive Branch

The president has a range of powers—some granted by the Constitution, some delegated by Congress, and some derived from public support.[33] The Constitution assigns to the president the right to veto legislation as well as certain powers in foreign affairs. Congress has delegated to the president the authority to negotiate treaties and trade agreements. The president also has authority in certain administrative areas, as granted by legislation. President Reagan had a substantial impact on regulatory rule making through his executive authority. In 1981 he issued an important executive order requiring a cost-benefit analysis of new regulations proposed by executive branch agencies. When President Clinton took office, he modified the order, requiring a review of costs and benefits only for major regulatory rule making. President Bush strengthened the role of the office that reviews regulations.

The president also appoints, with the consent of a majority of the Senate, the heads of cabinet departments, the members of regulatory and other commissions, and the top levels of executive branch agencies. The executive branch thus is responsive to the policy objectives of the president. The executive branch agencies and cabinet departments have influence not only on the administration of laws but also on policy formation through their expertise and their ability to develop policy proposals.

The president submits an annual budget to Congress. Although Congress may make any changes it chooses, the president, through pressure, bargaining power, and the veto, has considerable influence over the final product. The budget process is typically characterized by intense bargaining between the Office of Management and Budget and the congressional leadership.

In reasoning about political behavior, it is important to recognize that the absence of certain behavior does not mean that it is not important. For example, presidents cast relatively few vetoes, even when the president and Congress are from different parties. The infrequency of vetoes does not, however, mean that the veto is unimportant. The threat of a veto causes Congress not

---

[33]The president can be removed from office only through impeachment by the House and a trial in the Senate. Andrew Johnson and Bill Clinton have been impeached, but neither was convicted.

to pass some legislation that it would otherwise pass and causes it to modify legislation that it does pass so as to avoid a veto.

One of the most important powers of the president is the responsibility, with the consent of a majority of the Senate, to appoint members of the federal judiciary. In addition to deciding individual cases, the judiciary inter-prets the Constitution and federal statutes. The precedents established by court decisions have lasting effects. Through their appointments, the Reagan and (George H.W.) Bush administrations changed the Supreme Court from one with a liberal and judicial activist orientation to one with a more conservative orientation reflecting judicial restraint.

--- C A S E S ---
Tobacco Politics

The tobacco industry has long been an economic jugger-naut. By one estimate, as of 1998 tobacco accounted for 500,000 jobs and generated up to $170 billion in revenue annually in the United States—an amount approximately equal to the gross domestic product of Columbia.[34] Tobacco was grown in 20 states and was one of the most successful cash crops. Renewed efforts to regulate tobacco were fueled by new reports on the effects of secondhand smoke, such as one claiming that smoking accounted for as many as 400,000 deaths annually.

The federal government's efforts to control tobacco and cigarette advertising can be traced to 1954, when Representative John Dingell (D-MI) proposed a bill banning interstate advertising of tobacco products and alcoholic beverages. Although Representative Dingell's proposal did not succeed, in 1970 President Nixon signed a bill banning cigarette advertising on radio and television. In the 1980s several additional measures were passed that restricted smoking, including a ban on smoking on domestic airline flights. The 1990s saw further action taken against the tobacco industry, with legislation enacted to limit tobacco advertising and ban smoking in federal buildings.

Throughout this period, antismoking advocates portrayed the tobacco industry as an all-powerful, evil empire that held lawmakers in its hip pocket. Antismoking advertisements in the late 1990s claimed that tobacco companies consciously targeted teenagers in their advertising campaigns in the hope of recruiting and addicting the nation's youth. The threat to the tobacco industry and its beneficiaries increased significantly in November 1997, when S.1415, the National Tobacco Policy and Youth Smoking Reduction Act, was introduced by Senator John McCain (R-AZ).

Provisions of the Act

S.1415 was an outgrowth of an agreement reached on June 20, 1997, known as the Tobacco Resolution. The agreement between the major tobacco companies, state attorneys general, and class action lawyers provided the tobacco industry with protection from future punitive damages lawsuits and set caps on damage payments in exchange for a substantial per-pack tax increase and lump-sum damages payments.[35] Overall, the bill would

constitute a significant increase in the regulatory role of the federal government with respect to the tobacco industry. As proponents of the bill portrayed it, the bill required tobacco companies to pay $506 billion over 25 years to cover health care expenses related to smoking. The mechanism for funding this transfer was a $1.10 excise tax on the price of each pack of cigarettes. The bill also provided block grants to states to deal with medical costs stemming from tobacco use. In return for the tax increase, the liability of tobacco companies would be capped at $6.5 billion per year.

In addition to the monetary and legal provisions, the bill also restricted tobacco advertising and promotion. Tobacco companies would be prohibited from advertising on billboards, in public arenas, and on the Internet. In an attempt to reduce underage smoking, human or cartoon characters such as R. J. Reynolds's "Joe Camel" were to be banned from advertising campaigns. Companies also would not be allowed to sell items of clothing bearing their brand name, provide gifts to customers, sponsor public events, or pay for product placements in television programs or movies. Advertisements could no longer use phrases such as "low tar" or "light" that would imply that a given cigarette brand was less dangerous than another brand.

Other provisions would affect the regulation and distribution of tobacco. The Food and Drug Administration (FDA) would have the power to regulate nicotine like a drug, including, with the consent of Congress, the power to ban it altogether. Retail stores would have to apply for licenses to sell tobacco, and tobacco companies would have to disclose all corporate documents about their product, which would then be placed in a national depository for public use.

Interests

In addition to the tobacco companies, other interests would be affected. Trial lawyers for plaintiffs in individual and class action lawsuits would receive a financial windfall. To avoid the public fallout and demands for accountability associated with the payment of extremely large fees, the bill created a payment mechanism whereby three "arbitrators" representing lawyers and tobacco companies would determine the actual payment figures. In addition, tobacco companies agreed to provide the class action lawyers, who were instrumental in the agreement, an annuity of up to $500 million a year.[36]

---

[34]The $170 billion estimate is from Alan Greenblat, "Growing Ranks of Cigarette Tax Critics Invigorate Big Tobacco's Lobbying Effort," *Congressional Quarterly Weekly Report*, May 16, 1998, p. 1306. Bulow and Klemperer (1998), however, report that retail sales of cigarettes were only $50 billion, which suggests that the $170 billion figure includes multiplier effects.
[35]Bulow and Klemperer (1998) provide an excellent overview of the provisions of the resolution.

[36]Bulow and Klemperer (1998).

State attorneys general who had filed state lawsuits wanted S.1415 to pass for two reasons. The first was to recover damages associated with smoking that could be used to cover state Medicaid expenses. The second and more subtle reason was the expectation of political gains from public sentiment for helping to pass what was being promoted as a major blow against the tobacco industry.

Foremost among the bill's supporters were dozens of antismoking groups, including the Coalition on Smoking OR Health, Americans for Nonsmokers' Rights, Action on Smoking and Health (ASH), Airspace, The BADvertising Institute, Smoke*Screen, the National Center for Tobacco-Free Kids, Effective National Action to Control Tobacco (ENACT), the American Heart Association, and the American Lung Association.

Wholesalers would be hurt by the per-pack excise tax provision because of the way the tax was to be collected. Wholesalers would have to extend credit to many retailers, and the book value of wholesalers' inventory would be higher, resulting in higher insurance costs and "shrinkage" (theft). In estimating the damage at $367 million over 5 years, the American Wholesalers Marketers Association's spokeswoman, Jacqueline Cohen, explained, "Your shrinkage will grow."[37]

Cigarette-only stores would benefit under the proposed legislation because they would be exempt from point-of-sale promotional restrictions that would affect other retailers. Some of these stores were "adult bookstores."

Convenience stores would be hurt by the excise tax and the registration requirements. Convenience store cigarette sales accounted for approximately 40 percent of U.S. cigarette sales, and cigarettes alone comprised 20 percent of the average convenience store's total business.[38] A 1997 Department of Agriculture study confirmed the suspicion that many of these stores would likely not survive price and distribution reforms such as those included in S.1415.

The National Association of Convenience Stores, an international trade association, represented almost 3,300 convenience store operators, petroleum marketers, and suppliers, with 63,000 convenience stores around the world. In 1996 the convenience store industry posted $151.9 billion in sales.[39]

Grocery chains would also be hurt, since tobacco companies currently paid $2 billion annually in slotting fees to obtain prime placement for their products. Grocery retailers were organized in a number of associations, including the Food Marketing Institute (FMI)—a trade organization of over 100 grocers, including Giant-Eagle, Dominick's, Piggly-Wiggly, Safeway, and Tom

Thumb. The FMI's annual trade show hosted over 35,000 representatives from the supermarket industry. Additionally, the National Grocers Association had a membership of 2,060 and a budget of $5 million. It had food retailer members in 50 states and also included 60 wholesale food distributors.

The advertising industry would also be affected. By one account, tobacco advertisements and promotions totaled $5 billion, and the provisions of S.1415 chipped away at virtually every advertising approach used by firms.[40] Although print advertisements only generated $20 million in revenue, the prohibition on billboard advertising would eliminate $290 million in revenue. Point-of-purchase displays would also be prohibited and would reduce retailer revenues from slotting fees. The American Association of Advertising Agencies, with membership of 6 percent of the 13,000 U.S. agencies, accounted for 75 percent of advertising revenue in the United States.[41]

Tobacco farmers naturally opposed S.1415, but a 1997 Department of Agriculture study found that the preponderance of jobs attributed to tobacco were in the retail and wholesale trade—not in farming per se. Furthermore, the bill as drafted was sensitive to farmers' concerns, providing transition payments for them. Meanwhile, the foreign market for cigarettes continued to grow.

Concert promoters would be rocked by the expected loss of underwriting, which was dependent on prominent displays of advertisements. Likewise, organizers of golf tournaments would be driven to find alternative sources of underwriting revenue, while the net proceeds for tennis promoters would decline.

Not even universities escaped the reach of tobacco politics. By one estimate as many as 70 percent of university portfolios included tobacco stock, and some portfolio managers began to contemplate alternative investment strategies due to heightened public antitobacco sentiment and/or reduced profitability of tobacco firms. Harvard and Johns Hopkins had already divested, and Yale's board of trustees considered selling $16.9 million of tobacco stock from its $6 billion portfolio. ■

SOURCE: This case was prepared for class use by Professor Keith Krehbiel and Alan Wiseman using publicly available information. Copyright © 1998 by the Board of Trustees of the Leland Stanford Junior University. All rights reserved. Reprinted with permission.

---

[37]Greenblat (1998).
[38]Greenblat (1998).
[39]www.cstorecentral.com/public/nacs/rf05.htm.

[40]Greenblat (1998). Data provided by Bulow and Klemperer (1998); Table 10, however, suggests that all tobacco marketing expenses are treated as advertising expenses in the $5 billion figure. Most marketing expenses are promotional allowances such as price cuts for distributors and coupon and retail value-added promotions, neither of which would be prohibited by the bill.
[41]Some legal scholars believed the advertising provisions in S.1415 would be subject to court challenges on grounds of violating the First Amendment.

Preparation Questions

1. For each of the following groups, assess the likelihood that it will engage in nonmarket action on S.1415, and identify the specific cost and/or benefit characteristics underlying your assessment: smokers, tobacco companies, tobacco farmers, trial lawyers, antismoking groups, cigarette-only stores, grocery stores, convenience stores, advertising agencies, concert and event promoters, and universities.

2. Using the Wilson-Lowi matrix, what kind of politics best characterizes the activity surrounding McCain's bill?

3. Assess the prospects for coalition formation.

4. What outcome do you predict for the bill and why?

Scrubbers and Environmental Politics

In 1972 the Environmental Protection Agency (EPA) promulgated a "new source performance standard" (NSPS) for new coal-fired power plants, capping sulfur dioxide emissions at 1.2 pounds per million Btus (MBtus) of energy produced. As part of the stationary source emissions control section of the Clean Air Act Amendments of 1977, Congress had the task of implementing the NSPS for new power plants. The issue before Congress was not whether the NSPS would be attained but whether to specify how it would be achieved. More specifically, the issue was whether to require power companies to use a particular technology—a scrubber—to remove sulfur from their emissions.

Coal was produced both in the eastern and the western parts of the United States, but the technologies of extraction and the qualities of the coal differed greatly. Most of the coal in the East (West Virginia, Kentucky, Illinois, Indiana, Pennsylvania) was found in deep seams, requiring shaft mining. Shaft mining was labor intensive, and the coal miners were organized by the United Mine Workers (UMW). The wages earned by UMW members were high, and employee benefits were generous. Much of the coal mined in the East had a high sulfur content of up to 12 pounds per MBtus with an average of approximately 4 pounds. Sulfur dioxide emissions were a principal contributor to acid rain.

In Montana and Wyoming, coal lay just below the surface, and the extraction technology was strip mining, which was capital rather than labor intensive. Western coal was clean, with a sulfur content of approximately 1 pound per MBtus. Miners in the West generally were not unionized, and their wages and benefits were lower than those of the eastern UMW miners. The UMW had tried unsuccessfully to organize the western miners.

The EPA had concluded that scrubbers could remove approximately 90 percent of the sulfur oxides, although this determination was based on engineering data rather than actual applications. A scrubber was a large and very costly system that sprayed a water and limestone mixture inside a smokestack, causing a chemical reaction that removed sulfur from the smoke. Sludge was produced by the

reaction and collected at the base of the scrubber, leaving a substantial waste disposal problem. A scrubber could require 400 tons of limestone and thousands of gallons of water a day to remove 200 tons of sulfur dioxide. When they worked, scrubbers were effective in sulfur removal but their initial reliability had been low, in part because of the corrosion caused by the chemical reaction and in part because the apparatus could become clogged by the sludge.[42] Scrubbers were thus often shut down while the power plant continued to operate. Not only were they quite expensive to build, they were also costly to operate.

The EPA concluded that the most efficient means— the lowest cost to society—of meeting emissions standards in the Midwest and certain parts of the East would be for new power plants to burn low-sulfur western coal. This would allow emissions standards to be met without having to build and use scrubbers. (Despite the difference in transportation costs, it was less expensive to use western coal in eastern power plants than to use eastern coal and scrubbers.) If scrubbers were mandated, however, it would be less expensive for power plants in the East to burn high-sulfur eastern coal than low-sulfur western coal, since scrubbers would have to be used with either type of coal. Some experts warned, however, that unless significant advances were made in scrubber reliability, emissions in the East would actually be higher with mandated scrubbing and the burning of eastern coal than if scrubbers were not required and western coal were burned.

Environmental groups, which were particularly strong in the West, expressed little concern about the possibility of worsened air quality in the East if scrubbers were mandated and power companies used high-sulfur eastern coal. The western environmentalists were primarily interested in preventing air-quality degradation in the West, and they preferred lower emissions in the West than allowed by the 1.2 pounds per MBtus NSPS. The NSPS for the West could be achieved without using scrubbers, but the environmentalists preferred that

---

[42]By the mid-1980s scrubber technology had improved significantly.

scrubbers be mandated to reduce emissions below the NSPS. The environmentalists recognized that this would increase the cost of electricity in the West, but they preferred cleaner air. ■

Preparation Questions

1. From a social efficiency perspective, should Congress mandate scrubbers?
2. Which interests are affected by this issue? Which are likely to take nonmarket action?
3. Prepare a distributive politics spreadsheet and assess which interests will be active on this issue.
4. Are there any opportunities for coalition formation that would allow coalition members to achieve their primary objectives?
5. What do you predict Congress will do and why?

Repeal of the Luxury Tax

In 1990 Congress, with the acquiescence of the Bush administration, enacted legislation imposing a 10 percent federal luxury tax on the sale of furs and jewelry costing more than $10,000, automobiles costing more than $30,000, boats costing more than $100,000, and aircraft costing more than $250,000 (except for aircraft used at least 80 percent for business). Effective in 1991 the tax was applied to the difference between the price and the tax base, so the tax on a $1,000,000 yacht was $90,000. The luxury tax was a component of the Deficit Reduction Act of 1990 and was viewed not as a significant source of additional revenue but as a symbol that the rich should bear a larger share of the tax burden. The tax yielded $251 million in 1991 and $146 million in the first half of 1992 with the vast majority coming from the sale of automobiles.

As the economy slowed, sales of boats costing at least $100,000 began to decrease, falling from 16,000 in 1987 to 9,100 in 1990. In 1992 after the luxury tax was imposed, only 4,200 boats were sold. Sales of boats 35 feet or longer fell from 1,300 in 1989 to 400 in 1991, with sales revenue falling from $2.5 billion to $800 million. Employment in the industry decreased from 600,000 to 400,000 in 1993. Hatteras Yachts of New Bern, North Carolina, experienced a 50 percent decrease in sales and was forced to lay off 1,000 of its 1,800 employees. Viking Yacht of New Gretna, New Jersey, was forced to cut its workforce to 65 people. Yacht manufacturers from Minnesota, Wisconsin, Maine, Connecticut, and Florida experienced similar declines. As one potential customer who decided to stick with his current yacht rather than purchase a new one said, "I don't care how much you spend for a boat, $190,000 in taxes is ludicrous."[43] Some purchasers of yachts registered their boats in the Bahamas and the Cayman Islands to avoid the luxury and state sales taxes. The National Marine Manufacturers Association and its members blamed the collapse of the market on the luxury tax.

The light aircraft industry was also hard hit, as were the other industries subject to the tax. Jaguar auto sales fell by 55 percent, and the company decided to rebate the luxury tax of over $3,000 to customers.

The luxury tax had been enacted by inserting it in a large tax bill during conference committee deliberations, and opponents had little opportunity to oppose it. Once in place and its effects were realized, opposition mounted. "The purpose [of the tax] was to tax the rich and their toys," said Republican Senator John H. Chafee of Rhode Island, a big boat-building state. "What it really did was hurt the toymakers."[44] Senator Robert Dole (R-KS) of Kansas, where light aircraft manufacturers were located, said, "A lot of middle-class people are losing their jobs."[45]

Opponents of the tax pressured Congress and the Bush administration, and Senator Dole introduced a bill to repeal the tax. The repeal bill was included in a more comprehensive bill, but Congress was unable to reach agreement on the package. Opponents saw another opportunity in the spring of 1993 as President Clinton pushed for a deficit reduction package that would include increases in personal and corporate income taxes in addition to an energy tax. ■

Preparation Questions

1. Use supply-and-demand analysis to identify the incidence of the luxury tax for producers and consumers. Summarize your analysis in a distributive politics spreadsheet.
2. Are the consumers or producers of luxury goods more likely to be politically active on this issue? Why?
3. Are the interests of U.S. automobile manufacturers aligned with those of yacht builders?
4. What is the nature of the politics of this issue?
5. Are the opponents of the luxury tax likely to be successful?

---

[43]*BusinessWeek,* August 3, 1993.
[44]*BusinessWeek,* August 3, 1993.
[45]*Wall Street Journal,* June 12, 1991.

CHAPTER

7

Nonmarket Strategies for Government Arenas

INTRODUCTION

For many firms and industries the rules of the game are established by legislation. For 65 years the Glass-Steagall Act imposed walls between the banking, insurance, and securities industries, and after decades of effort by industry members the Act was repealed in 1999 by the Gramm-Leach-Bliley Act. The Telecommunications Act of 1996 opened telecommunications markets but left some barriers to entry in certain segments of the market. Congress regularly passes legislation imposing a moratorium on any new taxes on the Internet.

This chapter addresses the nonmarket strategies used by business and other interests to participate effectively and responsibly in nonmarket issues addressed in legislative arenas. The First Amendment to the Constitution grants to persons, including firms, the right to free speech and the right to petition government. Business and other interests thus have the right to participate in government processes, and that participation requires effective strategies. The chapter considers the strategy process, presents generic nonmarket strategies, and provides examples. The integration with market strategies is addressed through the chapter cases. The context is U.S. institutions, but the approach is also applicable to other countries, as indicated in Part IV of the book.

Strategy formulation in the nonmarket environment differs in a number of ways from its counterpart in the market environment. First, nonmarket issues attract a broader set of participants than those involved in markets. Second, important components of nonmarket strategies are implemented in public view, which requires sensitivity to the concerns of that broader set of participants. Third, the logic of collective and individual nonmarket action is different from the logic of market action. Fourth, in the nonmarket environment issues are not resolved by voluntary agreements as in markets but in most cases by government institutions with the power to set the rules of the game. In their strategy formulation and implementation, firms and other interests must ensure that their strategies are not only effective but also responsible. In the framework for the analysis of nonmarket issues presented in Figure 2-5, nonmarket strategies must be evaluated for responsibility in both the screening and the choice stages.

This chapter first considers the issue of responsible nonmarket action and the legal basis for business participation in government policy processes. Then, a perspective on understanding the outcomes of nonmarket issues is presented to provide a foundation for strategy formulation. The process of nonmarket strategy formulation is developed with a focus on strategic assets. Three basic strategies are then presented and illustrated with examples. A representation strategy is based on the constituency connection between voters and their representatives and involves directing constituent pressure to government officeholders. A majority building strategy involves building a majority to support or oppose legislation and focuses on pivotal legislators. Informational strategies focus on the strategic provision of technical and political information to officeholders. These generic strategies are then related to the nature of nonmarket competition as considered in Chapter 6. Implementation of nonmarket strategies is the subject of Chapter 8.

RESPONSIBLE NONMARKET ACTION

In the long run, a firm has influence on nonmarket issues to the extent that its interests are aligned with those of people. In the short run, however, firms and such other interests as labor unions and activists can have greater influence. An important issue thus is the appropriateness of interests attempting to influence public decisions. In addressing this issue, an analogy to markets is useful. In market competition, a firm that faces little competition has market power that enables it to restrict output and raise its price. Society has two responses to such a situation. First, it may rely on market forces. A high price can attract entrants to the industry and provides incentives to develop substitute products that can reduce the market power of the incumbent firm. Second, society may use its powers to control the exercise of market power through, for example, antitrust or regulation, considered in Chapters 9 and 10, respectively.

In nonmarket competition, society also has two responses to the exercise of nonmarket power. First, it can rely on countervailing influences from opposing interests to mitigate that power. The pluralism of competing interests can be effective in limiting power, but participation can be asymmetric because of the free-rider problem and other costs of organizing and taking nonmarket action. In some cases, advocacy groups can represent the interests of those with high costs, and watchdog groups can alert the public and government officeholders, thereby limiting the exercise of nonmarket power. Second, society can control the exercise of nonmarket power or require disclosure of nonmarket actions. For example, corporations are prohibited from making contributions to federal election campaigns, and contributions by a political action committee (PAC) are strictly limited and must be publicly reported. In addition, actions such as hiring a lobbyist and holding ex parte meetings with regulators require public disclosure. These responses to the exercise of nonmarket power, however, leave a substantial gray area in which firms must exercise judgment, and at times restraint, to ensure that nonmarket strategies are responsible and do not exceed the limits of public acceptability. The Chapter 8 case, *Responsible Lobbying?*, addresses these concerns.

Criticisms of Business Nonmarket Action

Business Objectives and the Public Interest

One criticism of nonmarket action by business is that it can be contrary to the public interest. What is in the public interest, however, is often the subject of fundamental disagreement. For example, the antidumping laws that impose duties on imported goods sold at lower prices than in the exporting country are viewed by economists as harmful to consumers and the economy. Yet, antidumping laws have been in place for over 80 years in the United States and have been adopted by most countries. Firms, labor unions, interest groups, and governments use the antidumping laws against foreign imports, even though that may be contrary to some conceptions of the public interest.

From a pluralist perspective, the public interest is identified by the interests of individuals and groups in the context of political institutions. The public interest thus can be advanced by business participation, since the interests of firms are ultimately the interests of those who have a stake in their performance, including shareholders, employees, retirees, customers, suppliers, and the communities in which they operate.

Firms have the right to participate in political processes irrespective of the particular interests they represent. In *First National Bank of Boston v. Bellotti*, 435 U.S. 765 (1978), the Supreme Court held that the First Amendment protects the right of corporations to make expenditures and participate in the political competition on a state ballot proposition. The Bank of Boston had challenged a Massachusetts law prohibiting a corporation from making expenditures to influence the vote on public referenda that did not "materially" affect the corporation. The Supreme Court held that the Bank of Boston's right under the First Amendment derived less from its right to speak than from the public's right to hear what others have to say. The court stated that freedom of speech "embraces at least the liberty to discuss publicly and truthfully all matters of public concern without previous restraint or fear of subsequent punishment. . . ." In addition, the court ruled that a state could not single out a set of entities, such as corporations, because of the interests they represent. The court stated that the prohibition in the Massachusetts law was "an impermissible legislative prohibition of speech based on the identity of the interests that spokesmen may represent in public debate over controversial issues. . . ."

Two years later, the Supreme Court overturned a ruling by the Public Service Commission of New York that had prohibited Consolidated Edison from including messages about public issues in its billing envelopes.[1] The court held that the prohibition was an impermissible restriction on speech. In *Pacific Gas & Electric Co. v. Public Utilities Commission of California,* 475 U.S. 1 (1986), the Supreme Court ruled that a company cannot be compelled to include messages from other groups in its billing envelopes. The California Public Utilities Commission (PUC) had ordered Pacific Gas & Electric to include an insert from a consumer group with its bills. The Supreme Court held that a corporation cannot be forced to associate with ideas to which it objects any more than can an individual. The majority opinion stated that the PUC order "discriminates on the basis of the viewpoints of the selected speakers and also impermissibly requires appellant to associate with speech with which appellant may disagree . . . that kind of forced response is antithetical to the free discussion that the First Amendment seeks to foster."

The rights accorded corporations by the First Amendment can also override certain restrictions imposed by legislatures. In *Eastern Railroad Conference v. Noerr Motor Freight,* 365 U.S. 127 (1961), the Supreme Court ruled that collective nonmarket action, such as joint lobbying to influence government, does not violate antitrust laws against collusion because the First Amendment grants the right to petition government. Firms thus have the right to form and participate in coalitions and associations to conduct nonmarket activity.[2]

Unwarranted Power

In *Austin v. Michigan Chamber of Commerce,* 494 U.S. 652 (1990), the Supreme Court upheld a Michigan law that prohibited corporations from making independent expenditures on behalf of a candidate.[3] Justice Thurgood Marshall, writing for the majority, referred to "the corrosive and distorting effects of immense aggregations of wealth that are accumulated with the help of the corporate form." In his dissent, Justice Antonin Scalia wrote, "The fact that corporations amass large treasuries is not sufficient justification for the suppression of political speech unless one thinks it would be lawful to prohibit men and women whose net worth is above a certain figure from endorsing political candidates." These opinions reflect disagreement about whether a corporation has the same freedom of speech as a person and whether its resources pose a threat to democratic processes.

The criticism that business has unwarranted power also arises because some interests may not participate due to their high costs of acting. Other interests thus are necessarily "overrepresented." Corporate participation in political activities, however, can give voice to people whose interests might otherwise be unrepresented. Just as unions represent their members, corporations can give voice to their stakeholders.[4] Firms represent the interests of their shareholders and pensioners when they act to increase shareholder

---

[1] *Consolidated Edison Company v. Public Service Commission of New York,* 199 S. Ct. 2326 (1980).

[2] The protection of the First Amendment does not extend to "sham" organizations. See also *Mine Workers v. Pennington,* 381 U.S. 637 (1965), and *California Motor Transport Co. v. Trucking Unlimited,* 404 U.S. 508 (1972). The Noerr-Pennington doctrine may not apply to nongovernmental legislative bodies such as standard-setting bodies; see *Allied Tube & Conduit Corp. v. Indian Head,* 486 U.S. 492 (1988).

[3] An independent expenditure is made directly, for example, by taking out an advertisement supporting a candidate rather than through a candidate's campaign organization.

[4] See Hirschman (1970) for an analysis of the voice issue.

value. Similarly, firms often represent the interests of employees and suppliers on issues affecting sales, which determine employment and purchases from suppliers. In the chapter case, *Wal-Mart and Its Urban Expansion Strategy,* the company's interests were aligned with those of the prospective employees who would be hired if its stores were approved by the Chicago city council. Firms may also represent the interests of customers. In the Part II integrative case, *Fuel Economy Standards 2007,* the automakers represented the interests of SUV and truck buyers whose options could be restricted by a major increase in fuel economy standards.

Often, the nonmarket power of business is controlled because it is naturally divided. Business differs from many single-interest groups because business interests are often fragmented, leaving firms on opposite sides of issues. U.S. automobile manufacturers and auto dealers were on the opposite sides of the enactment of lemon laws. American exporters interested in opening foreign markets to domestic goods oppose protectionist measures because they are concerned about retaliation by other countries. Generic and brand-name pharmaceutical companies are on opposite sides of many issues, including patent enforcement and market exclusivity. In the telecommunications industry local service companies and long-distance companies are on opposite sides of many issues such as network access, as considered in the Chapter 10 case, *The FCC and Broadband Regulation.* Because business interests on many issues are fragmented, so is business power.

Business nonmarket power is also checked by the power of other interest groups. There are many well-funded environmental groups, and they have been effective in advancing their agendas through both public and private politics. Activist groups also serve as a check on business power. The news media plays an important role in monitoring the nonmarket activities of business and other interest groups.

Business interests can also be aligned with activist groups. Shaffer and Ostas (2001) studied the enactment of state automobile lemon laws. Prior to the enactment of the laws, car buyers could seek recourse in the case of a lemon by filing a lawsuit under warranty law. The defendant in a lawsuit was generally the auto dealer that sold the car, since the automobile manufacturer was shielded by a privity rule that limited a consumer's ability to sue down the supply chain to the producer. Lemon laws were pushed by consumer and activist groups, yet the enactment of these laws was due more to the support by automobile dealers. The lemon laws in most states shifted responsibility from auto dealers to auto manufacturers, and the 25,000 dealerships located in every congressional district worked hard for the laws. On this issue auto dealers' interests were aligned with those of consumer and activist groups.

The abstract ability to exercise power is also not the same as its actual use. Business PACs could make their campaign contributions on a partisan basis, but instead they contribute to both Democrats and Republicans. In contrast, labor PACs contribute almost exclusively to Democrats. Business may also exercise self-restraint on the use of its power. In the example presented in Chapter 6, because of its broader nonmarket agenda, Boeing did not mobilize its supplier network to oppose restrictions on the tax treatment of leasing to foreign customers. Similarly, an increasing number of companies do not have PACs.

The Possibility of Manipulation

A third criticism of business nonmarket activity goes beyond interests and power and focuses on manipulation. Manipulation can take two basic forms. One involves misrepresentation or activities that play on ignorance, fear, or biases. As considered in Chapter 8, providing false or misleading information rarely is beneficial in the long run. An example is the tobacco company CEOs swearing in a congressional hearing that they believed that cigarette smoking was not addictive. Under the Racketeer Influenced and Corrupt Organizations Act, the Department of Justice filed a fraud case in 2004 seeking $280 billion in damages from five tobacco companies for "a half-century campaign of deception, half-truths and flat-out lies." Enron consistently misrepresented information about its financial condition and the propriety of its financing deals, as considered in the Chapter 19 case, *The Collapse of Enron.* In the framework for nonmarket analysis presented in Chapter 2, nonmarket strategies with these characteristics are to be rejected in the screening stage.

The second form involves exploiting institutional features. For example, a company may exploit a gray area or a loophole in the law that it knows will be closed by the government. In the Chapter 20 case, *Tax Shelters,* KPMG was accused of marketing abusive tax shelters. Similarly, Long-Term Capital, a darling of the financial services industry until its collapse in the 1990s, was found by a federal court to have engaged in tax-beneficial deals that were without economic substance. In the Chapter 10 case, *Enron Power Marketing and the California Market,* the company exploited flaws in the design of the California electricity market and was accused of price manipulation.

As another example, to induce pharmaceutical companies to bring generic drugs to market quickly when a patent on a drug expired, Congress passed a law granting a 6-month exclusivity period to the first company to bring a generic drug to market. Pharmaceutical companies with drugs whose patents were about to expire responded with "authorized generics" in which the companies contracted with generic drug makers to bring authorized copies of the patented drugs to market, thereby effectively eliminating the incentives of other generic drug companies. In the context of the framework in Chapter 2, strategies that exploit institutional features are to be evaluated in the screening stage to determine whether they are responsible.

The distinction between participation in and manipulation of public processes can be a fine one. In 1984 Johnson & Johnson, the maker of Tylenol, the best-selling nonprescription pain reliever, faced a new competitive challenge when the Food and Drug Administration (FDA) allowed the nonprescription sale of the drug ibuprofen, an antiarthritis drug previously available only by prescription. Upjohn estimated that within 2 years ibuprofen would garner 10 to 15 percent of the $1.3 billion pain-reliever market. Bristol-Myers planned to market Upjohn's ibuprofen under the brand name Nuprin, and American Home Products planned to market its version under the brand name Advil.

To counter this competitive challenge, Johnson & Johnson filed a lawsuit against the FDA challenging the sufficiency of the warnings on ibuprofen labels as well as the procedures under which it had approved the nonprescription sale. The suit alleged that the FDA had authority over the advertising only of prescription drugs, not over-the-counter drugs. Johnson & Johnson claimed injury by the alleged improper approval, stating that it would have a "direct and immediate impact" on Tylenol sales. Bristol-Myers responded, calling the suit "an arrogant and unconscionable effort by Johnson & Johnson to keep an important new drug off the nonprescription pain-relief market."[5]

By 1989 the tables had turned as American Home Products, which makes Anacin as well as Advil, asked the FDA to require drugs containing acetaminophen to include in their labels a warning about possible kidney damage from extended use.[6] The objective was to handicap the market leader, Tylenol, which has acetaminophen as its principal ingredient. The tables turned further in 1994 as American Home Products filed suit against Syntex and its marketing partner Procter & Gamble, charging that their FDA-approved advertising for their recently approved pain reliever Aleve involved "unwarranted and unsubstantiated claims." Were the Johnson & Johnson and American Home Products actions responsible uses of the companies' standing before the FDA and the courts, or did they involve manipulative use of institutional procedures? The Chapter 12 case, *Patent Games: Plavix,* considers another set of strategies used by pharmaceutical companies.

NONMARKET STRATEGY FORMULATION

Managers and Nonmarket Strategies

Because of the importance of nonmarket issues for the performance of firms, responsibility for formulating nonmarket strategies ultimately rests with management. From the lower levels of a firm, nonmarket issues often are seen as regrettable complications

---

[5]The suit failed, and ibuprofen was marketed on a nonprescription basis beginning in 1985.
[6]The basis for the submission was a May 1989 study by the National Institute of Environmental Health Sciences that suggested that daily use of drugs containing acetaminophen for over a year could cause kidney damage. This possibility was confirmed in a study reported in 1994 in the *New England Journal of Medicine.*

FIGURE 7-1 Approach to Nonmarket Strategy Formulation

that reduce autonomy and create headaches. The higher managers are in an organization, however, the more likely they are to appreciate that the progress of these issues can be affected by the firm's participation. They are also more likely to be involved in the formulation and implementation of nonmarket strategies.

Most managers address nonmarket issues on an episodic rather than a continual basis. They thus need parsimonious frameworks for formulating effective and responsible strategies. Much of the task of strategy formulation involves bringing together the approach to nonmarket analysis presented in Chapter 6, institutional knowledge, and the analysis of the nonmarket environment developed in Part I of this book. The following sections present this approach and provide examples.

As indicated in Figure 7-1, the nonmarket strategy of a firm competes in institutional arenas against the strategies of other interests. The outcome of this competition often involves the delegation of administrative responsibility to an agency or a regulatory commission. Nonmarket strategies thus focus both on the initial institutional arena in which an issue is addressed and on the subsequent delegation to administrative or regulatory agencies. The foundation for those strategies is nonmarket analysis.

Nonmarket Analysis

Nonmarket analysis forms the basis for effective strategies. Building on Part I and Chapter 6, nonmarket analysis includes the following components.

- Assessing the characteristics of the issue and where it is in its life cycle
- Identifying the interests affected by the issue
- Assessing motivations and incentives
- Analyzing the likely demand for and supply of nonmarket action
- Assessing the nature of the politics of the issue
- Identifying the institutional arenas in which the issue will be addressed
- Assessing institutional characteristics
- Identifying the relevant institutional officeholders and their constituent and policy interests

If the issue is primarily distributive, the Wilson-Lowi matrix (Figure 6-2) provides a first step in assessing the nature of the competition. To predict the likely outcome, the demand for and costs of generating nonmarket action must be assessed to determine which interests are likely to participate and their effectiveness. The distributive politics spreadsheet (Figure 6-3) provides a format for summarizing this analysis. If the issue has moral dimensions, the likelihood of morally motivated nonmarket action must be assessed.

Objectives

The specification of objectives is an essential component of a nonmarket strategy not only because objectives focus attention but also because they affect which interests will be aligned with and against a firm. In the example in Chapter 6, the objective of seeking an exemption for export leasing put Boeing on the opposite side of the issue from the tax-exempt organizations. Contingent objectives must also be specified and pursued in case the primary objectives cannot be achieved. The primary objective may be the defeat of a legislative proposal, but if the proposal is likely to pass in some form, a more realistic objective is to seek wording that lessens its impact, provides alternative means of compliance, or allows time to adjust. Boeing's secondary objectives were to grandfather orders in hand and obtain a gradual elimination of the tax benefits. The choice of objectives is a central feature of the chapter case, *Carried Interest Taxation.* In the Part II integrative case, *Fuel Economy Standards 2007,* the domestic auto industry abandoned its primary objective of preventing higher fuel economy standards and adopted its contingent objective of obtaining flexibility in meeting the standards and measures to protect U.S. jobs.

Selection of Institutional Arenas

In which institutional arenas nonmarket issues are addressed is typically determined by the forces that put the issues on the firm's agenda. Boeing had no alternative but to address the foreign leasing issue in Congress. In some cases, however, a firm has the opportunity to choose the institutional arena. A firm injured by unfair foreign competition can file a petition for relief under a number of sections of U.S. trade law. As considered in Chapter 18, the section selected determines the process and the institutions that will govern it. The processes differ—some are administrative, whereas others encourage negotiations with the other countries involved. In the Chapter 18 case, *Cemex and Antidumping,* Cemex, the Mexican company that has become the world's third largest cement producer, sought to overturn an antidumping order in the institutional arenas of the International Trade Commission, the International Trade Administration, the U.S. Court of International Trade, the General Agreement on Tariffs and Trade, the North American Free Trade Agreement, and finally Congress. Similarly, high-tech companies addressed the issue of frivolous securities fraud lawsuits first in the courts, then in Congress, then in a state referendum, and finally back in Congress.

Firms may also pursue an objective at either the federal or the state level. In the Chapter 8 case, *Internet Taxation,* opponents of Internet taxes worked at the state level to stop new taxes and worked at the federal level to impose a moratorium on all new taxes. Firms seeking protection from hostile takeovers had little success in Congress or with the Securities and Exchange Commission, so they turned their attention to the states. Pennsylvania enacted a law that made it more difficult to acquire firms incorporated there. Business has had only limited success at the federal level in its attempts to reform the liability system, but it has had success at the state level. Firms can also select institutional arenas at the local level. When Home Depot was stymied by the Mountain View, California, city council in its attempt to open a home improvement center, it circulated a petition for a ballot initiative that would enact the zoning change needed to allow it to build its store.

Nonmarket Strategy Choice

Strategies are the link between objectives and the specific actions taken to achieve them. When there is competition among interests, as in the case of interest group politics, the effectiveness of a strategy depends on the strategies of others active on the issue. Strategy formulation thus is not a linear process but instead involves adjustments that take into account the strategies of other interests as well as the progress of the issue through its life cycle. One aspect of the strategy challenge therefore is to anticipate the strategies of other participants. The chapter case, *Carried Interest Taxation,* considers such a situation.

One basic principle underlying strategy formulation in interest group politics is that the weight of nonmarket action for and against an alternative affects the outcome.

Therefore, a strategy should increase the benefits to those with aligned interests and reduce their costs of taking nonmarket action. For example, a firm may reduce the costs of participation for its employees, suppliers, and customers. Conversely, a strategy could reduce the opposing side's incentives to take nonmarket action. Identifying substitutes, for example, can reduce the incentives to oppose the objective sought. As discussed in the Appendix, the Daylight Saving Time Coalition effectively eliminated opposition by the National Association of Broadcasters by including in the legislation a provision asking the Federal Communications Commission to authorize AM radio stations to begin broadcasting before sunrise. In the Boeing example, opposition from tax-exempt organizations was reduced by grandfathering those deals already under way. In the chapter case, *Wal-Mart and Its Urban Expansion Strategy,* Wal-Mart sought a way to reduce the opposition by unions.

The nonmarket strategies available to firms are the same as those available to other interest groups, but their appropriateness and effectiveness can differ. Activists often rely on high-profile campaigns to attract the attention of the media and the public. Such strategies are seldom effective for business and, if undertaken, may embroil the firm in a highly visible controversy that constrains its ability to act on other issues. The set of effective nonmarket strategies for firms thus is often smaller than the set of strategies used by other interests.

Unilateral and Coalition Strategies

A firm may have a choice between forming a coalition or acting unilaterally to address an issue. If the issue could increase industry demand, the firms in the industry are in a similar situation. Moreover, the success (or failure) of the nonmarket strategy would produce a public good (or bad) for the industry members. Such issues are best addressed at the industry level through an ad hoc coalition or an industry association. Even if the firms in an industry address an issue collectively, an individual firm may choose to supplement the industry strategy. In the Part II integrative case, *Fuel Economy Standards 2007,* the automobile industry primarily worked through the Alliance of Automobile Manufacturers, but individual companies also took actions on their own to strengthen the industry effort as well as serving their own interests.

An industry strategy potentially suffers from two problems: the incentive to free ride and the heterogeneity of interests. In the Chapter 2 case, *Exclusive Resorts: Entrepreneurial Positioning and Nonmarket Defense,* Exclusive Resorts was the clear market leader in the luxury residence club market and sought to form an industry association to counter the nonmarket strategy of the timeshare industry. The smaller firms, however, chose to free ride, so Exclusive Resorts was forced to act alone.

On many issues the interests of firms in an industry differ. The greater the heterogeneity of their interests, the more difficult it is to form a coalition. In addition, firms may have different views about the best strategy. As the AIDS pandemic grew, the pharmaceutical industry came under nonmarket pressure to increase the availability of AIDS drugs to developing countries that lacked the means to pay for them. An industry response was precluded by the fact that only a few companies had AIDS drugs. Those companies sought to address the issue jointly, but Pfizer objected to the preferential pricing approach of the other companies. Pfizer broke ranks and provided its drug at no cost.

Nonmarket Assets

Firms and interest groups build their strategies on nonmarket assets. Access to institutional officeholders is an important asset to be developed and maintained. Access to members of Congress is a necessary condition for effective lobbying. That access can be based on the constituency connection, campaign contributions, or a reputation for providing reliable information. Some firms obtain access by hiring former government officials or retaining well-connected advisors and consultants. Some firms attempt to develop personal relationships between their managers and government officeholders.

The reputation of the firm and its top management is also an important asset. The success of Intel has been due both to its leading-edge technology and respect for its leaders. Reputation also depends on how responsible are the nonmarket actions of the firm and its managers. Actions that are deceptive, manipulative, or represent an abuse of power can quickly damage a reputation and depreciate its value. Government officeholders as well as interest and activist groups can have long memories.

The costs of collective action are a significant obstacle to nonmarket action, so any means of lowering those costs represents an important asset. A trade association reduces the costs of collective action, particularly for industries with many firms and for issues on which it is important to present a common rather than a fragmented position. The U.S. timber industry responded to the sustainability movement by developing within its industry association its own sustainability standards.

When seeking legislation, it is often effective for the firms in the industry to adopt a common position. When an industry seeks to defeat legislation, a fragmented position may be more effective by revealing to officeholders a wider set of contentious dimensions and adverse consequences of the legislation.

The Rent Chain

An important nonmarket asset is the alignment of the firm's interests with those of constituents of government officeholders. The value of this asset depends on the number of people affected, their resources, and their coverage of political jurisdictions. A large employment base or an extensive supply or distribution network is a potentially important asset. Its value increases as its coverage of political jurisdictions broadens, since greater coverage provides a broader base for lobbying and grassroots activities. Automobile dealers represent an important political asset of the automobile industry because they are numerous, have substantial resources, and provide extensive coverage of congressional districts. This asset, however, can be a liability when interests are not aligned, as in the case of the enactment of lemon laws.

Porter (1985) introduced the concept of a value chain that identifies the stages of a firm's operations in which value is created for its owners. Nonmarket strategies are also directed at creating value, and the *rent chain* is the analogous concept.[7] The underlying principle of the rent chain is that the greater the rents affected by a nonmarket issue, the greater are the incentives to take nonmarket action to protect or increase those rents. The rent chain represents a basis for influence in the nonmarket environment, particularly in the context of distributive politics.

A rent is a surplus. In the long run the rent of a firm equals its profit, but in the short run a rent can differ from profit because of sunk costs. Rents are also earned by the factors of production. Employees earn a rent if their wages and benefits are higher than what they could earn in alternative employment. When jobs are threatened by a nonmarket alternative, employees have an incentive to act to protect their rents. Labor unions are thus one of the strongest supporters of protectionist measures when the jobs of their members are threatened by imports. The United Steel Workers and steel producers joined to seek quotas on imports, as considered in Chapter 18. Rents can also be earned by distributors, retailers, and customers, which can motivate them to take nonmarket action. Rents are thus a fundamental source of incentives for nonmarket action.

A firm's rent chain includes those stakeholders that benefit from their interactions with the firm. When a nonmarket alternative, for example, increases the demand for a firm's products, the rents of the firm increase, and employees and suppliers benefit in addition to shareholders. Interests are then aligned along the rent chain, and hence there is the potential for collective action. Because rents are earned by the factors of production—in supply chains, in the channels of distribution, and by customers—the rent chain is larger than the value chain. The relationship between the rent chain and the value chain is illustrated in Figure 7-2. To the extent that jobs, supply contracts, alliance relationships, and communities are affected, the firm has an additional basis for appealing to government officeholders. Grassroots strategies are based on the rent chain, and lobbying also draws strength from information about the effects of alternatives on the rents of constituents.

The rent chain provides two types of strategic advantage. First, it can provide enfranchisement, giving the firm the right, or opportunity, to participate in public

---

[7]This concept is developed in more detail in Baron (1995a).

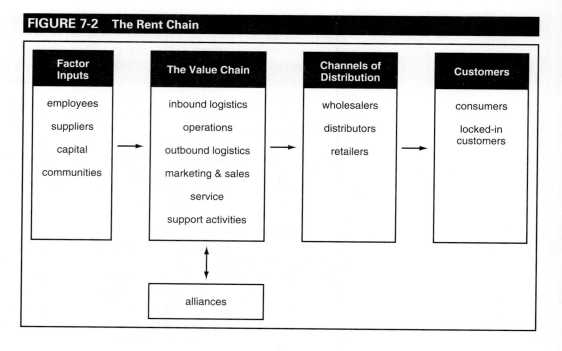

FIGURE 7-2 The Rent Chain

processes. Many U.S. pharmaceutical firms believed it was important to locate facilities in Japan to be able to participate effectively in the regulatory and consultative processes that set drug prices. In a country where market opportunities are controlled by government regulation and where administrative directives are pervasive, locating a portion of the rent chain in that country can be important for obtaining access to legislators and regulators. Second, a rent chain can provide the basis for generating nonmarket action through the constituency connection. Toshiba's strategy considered later in the chapter included such a component.

The rent chain can also be mobilized on issues outside governmental institutions. In 1992 Wal-Mart was the subject of a critical story on NBC's *Dateline,* alleging that some of the company's Asian suppliers used child labor. The story also raised concerns about whether Wal-Mart's Buy America program for creating jobs by sourcing products in the United States was being compromised. In response to the allegations, several of Wal-Mart's suppliers, including large companies such as General Electric Lighting and smaller companies such as Brinkman Corporation and Cheyenne Lamps, took out advertisements in newspapers with headlines, "We Support Wal-Mart's Buy America Program."

Implementation

Implementation of nonmarket strategies pertains to the selection of specific actions and the assignment of tasks to organizational units and individual managers. This can involve designating managers to lobby in Washington, undertaking a grassroots strategy, hiring a Washington law firm to provide technical advice on a legislative issue, or forming an ad hoc coalition. The specifics of strategy implementation are considered in Chapter 8.

Strategies are implemented over time, so contingent strategies should be developed. This is particularly important because the nonmarket competition on an issue may move from one institutional arena to another. Alternatively, in the context of Figure 7-1, a firm that fails to achieve its objective in a legislature may continue its nonmarket activity before the administrative agency to which responsibility has been delegated. If unsuccessful at that stage, the firm may take the issue to an administrative or judicial arena. In the Part II integrative case *Fuel Economy Standards 2007,* the automobile industry stopped opposing higher fuel economy standards in Congress and focused on the rule making by the National Highway Traffic Safety Administration to implement the standards. In the Chapter 12 case, *Obesity and McLawsuits,* McDonald's and the fast-food industry took actions in the judicial arena, Congress, and state legislatures.

UNDERSTANDING OUTCOMES

In formulating a nonmarket strategy to be implemented in an institutional arena, it is helpful to have a theory about how the institutional decision will be made. The Boeing example in Chapter 6 provides a theory of outcomes based on the strength and effectiveness of interests. The Boeing example involved a complex set of alternatives based on whether jobs were created. Some issues have a simpler set of alternatives that can be arrayed on one dimension. For example, the alternatives may be the budget for a government program, the stringency of an environmental standard, or the patent duration for pharmaceuticals. The alternatives in the example considered in the Appendix were the number of weeks of daylight saving time. If (1) the alternatives are one-dimensional, (2) the legislative process is open so that all alternatives can be considered, and (3) voters have a most-preferred alternative, or ideal point, and prefer alternatives closer to rather than farther from that ideal point, then the outcome is the median of the ideal points. The median ideal point will receive at least a majority of votes against any alternative to either its left or its right. That is, including the median, there is a majority of voters on one side or the other that will defeat any other alternative. The logic of this theorem is developed further in the daylight saving time example.

The *median voter theorem* is powerful because it is only necessary to know voters' ideal points and not their entire preference ordering over alternatives. Moreover, if the median ideal point is known, it is not necessary to know the exact location of the other ideal points. Although the median voter theorem does not extend to alternatives with more than one dimension, related results suggest that outcomes are likely to be close to the intersection of the medians on each dimension.

The median voter theorem is an important tool for analyzing legislative outcomes in an open process: that is, a process in which any alternative can be proposed. If the issue under consideration is one-dimensional and the ideal points of the members of a legislature can be estimated, the outcome can be predicted. Moreover, strategies can focus on pivotal legislators who could change the median and hence the outcome.

Legislators' ideal points are not directly observable, but information on them can be inferred from their voting records. Interest groups analyze roll-call votes on issues on their agendas and provide scores for each member of Congress. The League of Conservation Voters provides ratings based on how members of Congress voted on environmental issues. Similarly, Americans for Democratic Action (ADA: a very liberal group), the Chamber of Commerce (COC) (a more conservative group), and the American Federation of State, County and Municipal Employees (AFSCME), a union with 1.3 million members, provide ratings based on issues important to them.[8] These ratings are used by analysts as an indicator of the relative location of the ideal points of members of Congress on various policy dimensions. Following are the 2006 ratings for the current Senate minority leader Mitch McConnell (R-KY), Speaker of the House Nancy Pelosi (D-CA), Senate majority leader Harry Reid (D-NV), and House minority leader John Boehner (R-OH).[9]

	Americans for Democratic Action	Chamber of Commerce	League of Conservation Voters	AFSCME
Mitch McConnell (R-KY)	5	100	0	0
Nancy Pelosi (D-CA)	95	40	100	100
Harry Reid (D-NV)	90	50	57	100
John Boehner (R-OH)	5	100	0	0

---

[8]For each member of Congress, the *Almanac of American Politics 2008* (Barone and Cohen, 2007) presents ratings by the following organizations: League of Conservation Voters, Americans for Democratic Action, Chamber of Commerce, AFSCME, Information Technology Industry Council, National Taxpayers Union, Club for Growth, Family Research Council, American Civil Liberties Union, and American Conservative Union. Each group selects a different set of issues on which to score members, so the ratings are not necessarily comparable. Similarly, the issues differ from year to year, so intertemporal comparisons are problematic.
[9]The ratings for the two chambers are not directly comparable because the two chambers do not always have roll-call votes on the same issues.

These ratings indicate that both McConnell and Boehner are conservative (low ADA scores) and responsive to business concerns (high COC scores), Reid and Pelosi are liberals (high ADA scores) and responsive to union interests (high AFSCME scores), and McConnell and Boehner are not responsive to environmental issues, whereas Reid and Pelosi are.

GENERIC NONMARKET STRATEGIES

Three generic nonmarket strategies are *representation, majority building,* and *information provision.* These strategies are not mutually exclusive but instead can be used together when there are synergies. Representation strategies are based on the consequences of alternatives for constituents of government officeholders. The Toshiba example and the Chapter 6 case, *Repeal of the Luxury Tax,* involve representation strategies. These strategies may involve the mobilization of a rent chain and may include a grassroots campaign, coalition building, and public advocacy, as considered in Chapter 8.

Majority building strategies focus on developing the needed votes in a legislature to enact or defeat a bill. A majority building strategy can build on a representation strategy, as when the rent chain is mobilized in districts of pivotal legislators. The chapter case, *Federal Express and Labor Organization,* involves majority building strategies.

Informational strategies focus on providing information to government officeholders. Informational strategies can be coupled with representation and majority-building strategies, as when a firm lobbies to provide information in conjunction with a grassroots strategy involving the mobilization of its rent chain. Informational strategies are important in the chapter case, *Carried Interest Taxation.*

Representation Strategies

A representation strategy is based on the connection between elected officeholders and their constituents. Because members of Congress are interested in reelection, they are interested in serving their constituents. A firm's stakeholders are constituents, so a firm has an opportunity to build support for its objectives by representing stakeholders' interests. It may go further by mobilizing them for nonmarket action. Automakers represent the buyers of SUVs and light trucks when they seek flexibility in meeting higher fuel economy standards. Pharmaceutical companies represent the interests of patients who benefit from their drugs when they work with patient advocacy groups to obtain fast track approval of new drugs.

When its attempts to overturn U.S. antidumping duties were unsuccessful, Cemex established a production base in the United States. In 1996 it acquired a cement plant in Texas and built ready-mix plants in the Southwest. This gave the company a rent chain and constituent base on which it could deploy a representation strategy to obtain relief from the duties. Its U.S. operations were geographically concentrated, however, limiting its coverage of congressional districts. To overcome its coverage deficit, Cemex formed an alliance with the 180,000 member National Association of Home Builders (NAHB). Their legislative objective was an amendment to U.S. trade law to allow the Department of Commerce to temporarily suspend antidumping duties in times of shortage of a good.[10] The coalition deployed a representation strategy, but it was countered by a representation strategy of the U.S. cement producers, and the status quo prevailed. In response, Cemex then acquired

---

[10]The European Union has such a provision in its international trade laws, and suspensions are allowed under GATT.

EXAMPLE

Toshiba and Trade Sanctions

The U.S. Department of Defense observed that Soviet Union submarines were operating more quietly than in the past, making tracking more difficult. A Pentagon investigation revealed that Soviet propeller technology had improved substantially, possibly due to the sale of highly sophisticated milling equipment to the Soviet Union by the Toshiba Machine Company of Japan. Any such sale would be in violation of the regulations of the Coordinating Committee for Multilateral Export Controls (CoCom), an international agreement that prohibited the export to communist countries of technology that could improve their military capability.

When a U.S. newspaper reported the Pentagon investigation in March 1987, the Japanese Ministry of International Trade and Industry (MITI) shrugged off the report. U.S. pressure, however, eventually led MITI to investigate. MITI found that the Toshiba Machine Company had twice sold milling machines to the Soviet Union in violation of both CoCom regulations and Japanese law. This machinery could have enabled the Soviets to improve their propeller technology. Toshiba Machine Company was 50.1 percent owned by the Toshiba Corporation (referred to as Toshiba hereafter), which reportedly was unaware of

the illegal sales. The MITI investigation also revealed that Toshiba Machine had falsified export documents to qualify for export licenses and that the trading company Wako Koeki had illegally arranged for computer software for the milling machines to be supplied by Kongsberg Vaapenfabrik, a government-owned Norwegian defense contractor.

The uproar in the United States was immediate. Several consumer boycotts of Toshiba products were reported, and members of Congress smashed Toshiba products on the lawn of the Capitol. A $1 billion sale of Toshiba laptop computers to the U.S. Department of Defense came under fire. Some U.S. companies canceled purchase agreements with Toshiba, and others were noticeably nervous about dealing with it.

Political entrepreneurs were eager to represent constituents angry over the sale of the milling machines. In mid-June the House passed a nonbinding resolution calling on the Department of State to seek compensation from Japan for damages. Bills barring Toshiba sales to the Defense Department and banning all Toshiba imports to the United States for a period of 2 to 5 years were speeding through Congress. Legislatively imposed sanctions seemed a certainty.

the largest independent U.S. cement company, expanding both its value chain and its rent chain.

The formulation and implementation of a representation strategy are considered in the Toshiba example.

Strategy Formulation

Toshiba's problem was characteristic of client politics. Because sanctions seemed inevitable, the relevant status quo was that sanctions would be imposed, and Toshiba's objective was to limit them. On the other side of the issue, the costs from opposing a reduction in the sanctions were widely distributed rather than concentrated on identifiable interest groups. Pressure for sanctions came from the public and from members of Congress, who wanted to prevent further illegal sales to the Soviet Union and claim credit for doing so.

To limit the sanctions, Toshiba adopted a multifaceted strategy that addressed the threat of sanctions and the concerns the incident had caused.[11] The facets included putting its house in order and directly addressing the political issue in the United States. In Japan, Toshiba's strategy had two components. The first was to ensure that no further illegal sales were made by any of its subsidiaries or affiliated companies.

---

[11]The account presented here is based on public sources and does not necessarily reflect the reasoning of Toshiba executives. Instead, the presentation is intended to analyze Toshiba's strategy and its implementation.

The second was to work with the government to ensure that other Japanese companies would also comply with CoCom regulations.

In the United States reaction to the sales did not distinguish between the Toshiba Machine Company and the Toshiba Corporation. Toshiba Machine had U.S. sales of $100 million. Toshiba, with U.S. sales of $2.6 billion, was a much more visible target. One component of Toshiba's strategy was to direct attention to the Toshiba Machine Company. This involved providing information about the relative independence of Toshiba Machine and the fact that Toshiba had been unaware of the sales. A second component of its strategy was to protect Toshiba Machine's business in the United States. The fact that Toshiba Machine had production plants and hence stakeholders in the United States allowed Toshiba to argue that sanctions would hurt constituents. A third component of its strategy was to attempt to place time limits on any sanctions and allow exceptions for certain exports such as spare parts and specialized products, particularly those used for defense purposes. Furthermore, Toshiba sought to grandfather sales agreements already signed. A final component of Toshiba's U.S. strategy was to focus attention on the future rather than on the past. Toshiba emphasized the measures it was taking to ensure that such violations would not happen again.

Strategy Implementation

To implement its strategy, Toshiba took a number of steps in Japan and the United States. Both Toshiba and the Japanese government acted to put their own houses in order. In an act of contrition, the chairman as well as the president of Toshiba resigned their positions. Toshiba increased by 80 its staff responsible for verifying compliance with export regulations. MITI announced that it would increase its surveillance of exports, strengthen penalties for violations, and contribute more to the support of CoCom's secretariat in Paris. MITI also offered to provide the U.S. Department of Defense with the same milling machines that had been sold to the Soviet Union so that it could develop improved submarine detection devices. The Japanese government hurriedly prepared strengthened laws on CoCom compliance.

Toshiba's strategy in the United States was implemented on a broad scale, reportedly at a cost of $30 million. It took out full-page advertisements apologizing for its actions and pledged not to make any further illegal sales. In other quarters Toshiba attempted to assure its critics that it was taking steps to prevent further violations.

Toshiba mounted a major lobbying campaign. To obtain access to Congress and the executive branch, it hired several former government officials, including the former chairman of the House Budget Committee, a well-known Republican lawyer who had served in the Nixon administration, a lobbyist who had served in the Nixon White House, and a former deputy U.S. trade representative.

Toshiba used its rent chain in a grassroots strategy by bringing to Washington the managers of many of its U.S. operations. It also flew a number of its suppliers and customers to Washington to impress on Congress the harm to U.S. interests that harsh sanctions would cause. Toshiba's employment of 4,200 people in the United States provided a link between possible sanctions and constituents' jobs. For example, Toshiba had a microwave oven plant in Tennessee and was able to enlist the governor to write to each member of the state's congressional delegation warning that retaliatory measures directed at Toshiba could have a direct impact on over 600 employees in the state. Even potential employment provided a basis for generating political action. The governor of Indiana, who had been working to attract a Toshiba facility to his state, asked the Indiana congressional delegation to oppose sanctions.

Toshiba had little difficulty enlisting the support of its customers, many of whom relied on its products. The Electronic Industries Association argued that over 4,000 jobs held by employees of Toshiba's customers were threatened by the sanctions. Some 40 companies, including Apple and Honeywell—importers of Toshiba printers and semiconductors, respectively—opposed the proposed sanctions. Toshiba suppliers also rallied to its defense. Toshiba was able to enlist other allies as well. In a letter to the House Armed Services committee chairman, an assistant secretary of defense wrote that Japan was "succeeding in punishing the guilty, establishing stronger controls, and funding antisubmarine warfare programs which will help the United States and Japanese navies."[12]

The Outcome

The sanctions eventually imposed against Toshiba were considerably less severe than initially expected, and Toshiba's nonmarket strategy was given considerable credit for the outcome. The sanctions included a ban on imports by Toshiba Machine and Kongsberg for 3 years and a ban on any sales to the U.S. government for the same period. The parent company in Japan was also banned from sales to the U.S. government for the same period. However, exceptions were provided for products necessary for national security, spare parts, servicing and maintenance, and for those items already under contract.

Majority-Building Strategies

Vote Recruiting

A majority is required to enact legislation, or in the case of a presidential veto, two-thirds of the members of both the House and the Senate are required to overturn the veto. Conversely, to defeat legislation a blocking majority of votes is required or, in conjunction with a veto, one-third of the members of the House or Senate is required. Strategies directed at legislatures focus on building a majority for or against an alternative.[13] The chapter case, *Wal-Mart and Its Urban Expansion Strategy,* concerns building a majority in the Chicago city council for permission to open two stores.

A key component of a majority-building strategy is *vote recruitment.* Votes are recruited by interest groups and by public officeholders. For example, the majority and minority leaders in the House and Senate recruit votes on some issues by providing favors to legislators. Similarly, the president frequently recruits votes by providing favors to members of Congress. President Clinton used this approach to recruit votes of congressional Democrats for the North American Free Trade Agreement.

Votes may be recruited by interest groups through a variety of means. One is in conjunction with a representation strategy based on the constituency connection. Votes can also be recruited through vote trading. A legislator who has strong preferences on issue A and does not care about issue B may be willing to trade her vote on B for a vote on A of another legislator who has strong preferences on B. Consequently, an interest group with allies in the legislature may be able to enlist them in vote trading and recruiting.

Votes are also recruited by providing politically valuable support for a legislator. This could involve pledges of electoral support or endorsements by constituent groups such as those in a firm's rent chain. Other means include assisting in voter mobilization and supplying volunteers as practiced by labor unions, providing endorsements and advertisements as used by the Sierra Club and other environmental interest groups, and campaign contributions. There is little evidence that campaign contributions influence congressional voting, and the caps on contributions are very low. Campaign contributions are thus better thought of as developing access to members of Congress for the purpose of lobbying, as considered in Chapter 8. Support also includes opportunities for legislators to claim credit for serving the interests of their constituents.

---

[12]*The New York Times,* March 14, 1988.
[13]Baron (1999) introduces the concepts of majority building and vote recruitment strategies for client and interest group politics.

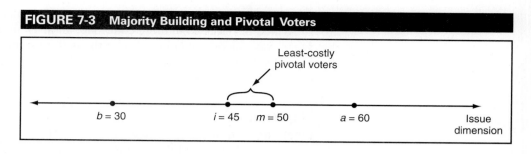

FIGURE 7-3   Majority Building and Pivotal Voters

Pivotal Voters

A vote recruitment strategy focuses on *pivotal voters*—those most likely to switch the outcome between victory and defeat.[14] To identify the pivotal voters in a vote recruitment strategy, consider an issue for which the alternatives can be arrayed on a line. Consider a 101-member legislature that operates under simple (50 percent) majority rule and is considering two alternatives, $a = 60$ and $b = 30$, as depicted in Figure 7-3. Also suppose that the preferences of each legislator are represented by the distance of an alternative from her ideal point—the outcome she most prefers.[15] To simplify the exposition, assume that legislators' ideal points are uniformly distributed along the line in Figure 7-3 with the legislator the farthest to the left having ideal point 0 and the legislator farthest to the right having ideal point 100. The median legislator is denoted by m and has an ideal point at 50. Since alternative a is closer to m than is alternative b, the median legislator prefers a.

Consider client politics in which an interest group prefers b to a. The first step in a vote recruitment strategy is to identify the pivotal voters. The pivotal voter is indifferent between a and b and is the one with an ideal point at 45, which is the midpoint between a and b, as illustrated in Figure 7-3. In the absence of a vote recruitment strategy by the interest group, alternative a would be enacted on a vote of 56 to 45, assuming that the indifferent voter (45) votes with the majority. Consequently, for alternative b to win, the interest group and those in the legislature who prefer b to a must recruit six votes. That is, the 45 legislators with ideal points to the left of 45 will vote for b regardless of whether the interest group recruits them; they are natural allies of the interest group on this issue, and consequently, only six additional votes are needed to form a majority for b.[16] Any six legislators who would vote for a are pivotal, but the interest group prefers to recruit those votes that are least costly. The least-costly votes are of those legislators who only mildly prefer a to b. These are the legislators with ideal points between (and including) 45 and 50. The focus of a vote recruitment strategy is thus on these six legislators.

There is no reason to recruit legislators with ideal points from 51 through 100. First, their votes are not needed to pass b. Second, recruiting their votes would be more costly because they prefer a to b more strongly than the legislators with ideal points between 45 and 50. Using the same logic, recruiting the vote of legislator $m = 50$ is more costly than recruiting the vote of legislator 45, because m prefers a to b more strongly than does legislator 45. Consequently, greater support or a more valuable vote trade must be provided to m than to legislator 45.

Multiple Pivots

The U.S. legislative process is more complicated than the example just considered because it has multiple pivots. First, it is a bicameral system, which requires that both the House and Senate pass a bill in identical language before it can become law. To enact legislation, it may be necessary to recruit pivotal voters in both chambers. To defeat

---

[14]A formal theory of vote recruitment in client politics is presented in Snyder (1991).
[15]The preferences of legislators can be assessed based on the characteristics of their constituents and their past voting record using the interest groups ratings discussed earlier in the chapter.
[16]If the interest group and its allies in the legislature are uncertain about the preferences of legislators, they may want to recruit more than six votes as insurance.

legislation, however, it is only necessary to build a majority in one of the two chambers, so other things equal it is easier to defeat than to enact legislation. Second, senators can filibuster a bill, and cloture—stopping the filibuster and proceeding to a vote— requires a vote of 60 senators. Third, the president can veto a bill, and overriding the veto requires two-thirds of both the House and Senate.[17] Institutions in other countries also have multiple pivots. In Japan, a two-thirds vote in the lower house of the Diet can enact legislation without approval by the upper house. The Council of Ministers of the European Union operates with qualified majority rule, which requires 255 of the 345 votes to approve legislation. The Chapter 15 case, *The European Union Carbon Tax,* involves a pivot at the qualified majority and the chapter case, *Federal Express and Labor Organization,* involves a pivot at the majority needed to overcome a filibuster.

Competition and Majority Building

The vote recruitment strategy considered in the context of Figure 7-3 involves only one interest group and thus corresponds to client politics, where opposing interests have weak incentives to take nonmarket action. This strategy is also used in interest group politics in which the opposing interest group has already implemented its strategy and the interest group supporting *b* has the last move. For example, in the chapter case, *Federal Express and Labor Organization,* organized labor deployed its strategy by enlisting its allies in the Senate to undertake a filibuster against a bill sought by Federal Express. Given that organized labor had already deployed its strategy, Federal Express was in the situation depicted in Figure 7-3.

When two interest groups are actively competing, majority building becomes more complicated. Suppose that interest group G_a supports the status quo *a* and group G_b supports alternative *b*. Because G_b seeks to overturn the status quo, it naturally moves first. If it attempts to build a majority by recruiting votes, the opposing interest group can recruit a majority among any of the legislators to preserve the status quo. For example, if in Figure 7-3 G_b were to recruit the votes of legislators 45 through 50, group G_a could counter either by attempting to recruit those same legislators or by attempting to recruit voters to the left of 45 who only mildly prefer *b* to *a*. Consequently, group G_b must employ a *majority protection* strategy that may require recruiting more than the minimal number of pivotal voters. That is, group G_b may have to recruit a supermajority of voters and provide them with sufficient support to protect each majority against the strategy of the opposing interest group.[18]

Agenda Setting

If the legislative process is open so that legislators can easily offer amendments, and if there is no vote recruitment, the winning alternative is typically centrally located among the preferences of legislators, as in the daylight saving time example in the Appendix. That is, in an open process the median voter theorem provides the basic prediction of the outcome. If interests can recruit pivotal voters, the outcome can be moved, as considered in the context of Figure 7-3.

If the legislative process is relatively closed and a committee's bill, for example, is protected from amendments by a closed rule, strategic agenda setting is possible. In the European Union the Commission is the principal agenda setter, and under some legislative procedures amendments by the European Parliament are difficult to make. The committee in the first example and the Commission in the second are agenda setters. Nonmarket strategies are often directed at agenda setters.

Agenda-setting strategies focus first on recruiting the agenda setter and then on building support for the alternative on the agenda. Consider Figure 7-3, and suppose that the status quo is *a*. Also, initially assume that there are no interest groups attempting to recruit votes. If the agenda setter has an ideal point at 30, it can place the alternative *c* = 41 on the agenda and a majority will vote for it against the status quo *a*. To see

---

[17]Krehbiel (1998) (1999) provides a theory of legislation that considers these pivots.
[18]Groseclose (1996) and Groseclose and Snyder (1996) present theories of competitive vote recruitment.

this, note that the pivotal voter $m = 50$ just prefers $c = 41$ to $a = 60$. Consequently, an interest group on the left with an agenda-setter ally with ideal point 30 can obtain $c = 41$ without having to recruit any votes.[19]

The ability of an agenda setter to use the status quo to its advantage is mitigated to the extent that there is vote recruitment competition between interest groups. A strategy that involves agenda setting is thus more likely to be effective in client politics. An agenda setter's power is also limited by the ability of others to offer amendments or counterproposals. When amendments are freely allowed, the median voter theorem is applicable, and in the absence of vote recruitment the outcome is likely to be centrally located.

Informational Strategies

Information is a politically valuable resource. Information enables officeholders to better serve their constituents and pursue their policy interests. Interest groups thus employ informational strategies in an attempt to influence outcomes. Informational strategies are based on the superior information an interest group has about, for example, the consequences of alternatives for constituents. Thus, a necessary condition for an informational strategy to be effective is that the interest group is better informed about some aspect of the issue than are government officeholders. Informational strategies typically involve providing information favorable to the firm or interest group. That is, firms advocate "their side of the issue" as in a court where lawyers advocate the side of their clients. Officeholders understand this and take the advocacy into account in updating their beliefs. Even though it may be provided strategically, the information can be beneficial to the officeholder.

The strategic provision of information is a, if not the, principal component of lobbying, testimony in legislative or regulatory proceedings, and public advocacy. To implement an informational strategy through lobbying, an interest group may invest in obtaining access to legislators or administrative officials. Influence thus often has two stages. The first involves obtaining access, and the second involves the strategic provision of information. In public processes such as those of many regulatory agencies, interests have due process rights to participate in the process and provide information. In legislative institutions, however, access to a pivotal legislator is not guaranteed and may have to be developed. A firm's rent chain can provide access through the constituency connection.

Lobbying involves the strategic provision of two types of information—*technical* and *political*. Technical information pertains to the likely consequences of alternatives. Political information pertains to the effects of alternatives on the constituents of officeholders. Political information is often provided in conjunction with representation and majority building strategies. Both technical and political information may be provided strategically—advocating the outcome sought by the interest. This may involve the strategic advocacy of a position, the choice of methodologies that generate data and conclusions favorable to an interest, or the emphasis on favorable, and deemphasis on unfavorable, information. Some informational strategies are counteractive—that is, they are undertaken to counter the information provided by an opposing interest.

Information must be credible to have an effect. Credibility can be established in several ways. First, the information may be verifiable in the sense that the officeholder or her staff can check its validity. Second, if it is not verifiable, information can be credible if the group's interest is aligned with the interests of the officeholder. That is, the

---

[19]Viewing the alternative placed on the agenda as a function of the status quo, note that a more extreme status quo allows the agenda setter to obtain an outcome closer to his or her ideal point. For example, if the status quo were 70, the agenda setter could place the alternative $c = 31$ on the agenda and it would pass. If the status quo were 80, however, the agenda setter would put the alternative $c = 30$ on the agenda, since that is its ideal point.

officeholder can rely on the information the interest group provides because she knows that the interest group would not provide the information unless it wanted her to act on it. A member of Congress whose constituents have strong environmental preferences may rely on the information provided by the Sierra Club. Third, if an interest group and the officeholder have divergent preferences, the information provided can be credible if it is confirmed by information provided by a nonaligned or opposing interest. This information need not be identical to provide confirmation. Fourth, an interest may commission a study by an organization that has a degree of independence. Studies are frequently used to bolster advocacy. Credibility is considered in more detail in Chapter 8.

A concern about informational strategies is whether an interest is legally or morally obligated to provide information that it prefers not to disclose. Unless there is specific legislation or regulation compelling the provision of information, a firm is generally not legally obligated to provide such information. It would be illegal, however, for a pharmaceutical company to withhold data on the safety of an approved drug, and it would be immoral, and probably illegal, to make false claims about a product's performance. It is both allowed and commonplace, however, for interests to advocate their side of an issue or to provide estimates based on methodologies likely to provide answers favorable to their side. A common example is a trial in which the plaintiff and the defendant provide expert witnesses who reach different conclusions regarding an issue. In executive and legislative institutions, the same type of advocacy takes place. Some pharmaceutical companies, however, have been accused of withholding negative clinical test results that failed to demonstrate that a drug was an effective treatment for a health condition. This issue is the subject of the Chapter 5 case, *Merck and Vioxx*.

Public Officeholders as Targets of Nonmarket Strategies

In public politics, nonmarket strategies are ultimately directed at government officeholders, who as in a legislature are often in a collective decision setting. These officeholders have duties to their institution and to their constituents. The constituency connection provides a basis for developing allies among officeholders. Allies are legislators who see the firm's interests as consistent with their own. Some allies may support bills that benefit the firm, whereas others may simply be willing to listen to the firm's position on an issue.

The interests of officeholders may also depend on career concerns. Those career concerns include reelection, running for higher office, advancement in a bureaucracy, and employment after government service. Because of career concerns, most officeholders are risk averse and wary of taking actions that risk their advancement or jeopardize their electoral prospects.

When officeholders seek to avoid risk, the status quo is often favored. An interest group seeking to preserve the status quo can thus adopt a strategy emphasizing the uncertainty inherent in the issue. This may involve counteractive lobbying that calls into question the information provided by the proponents of a change from the status quo. Another strategy that is often effective is raising new dimensions of the issue. Toshiba, for example, emphasized the importance of its products to U.S. defense contractors. In the chapter case, *Carried Interest Taxation,* private equity and venture capital firms emphasized the uncertain effect on economic growth of taxation of their stakes in ventures. Through its informational lobbying Boeing attempted to emphasize the uncertainty about the consequences of failing to renew China's MFN status, as indicated in the example.

Conversely, an interest that seeks to change the status quo should focus on reducing uncertainty about the consequences of the change. In the Chapter 6 case, *Repeal of the Luxury Tax,* yacht builders provided specific information about the loss of jobs caused by the luxury tax. Such information must be credible, and its corroboration by other interests contributed to the repeal.

China and Most Favored Nation Status

Prior to China's admission into the World Trade Organization (WTO), the United States had annually extended most favored nation (MFN) status to China. Congress had refused to grant permanent MFN status because of human rights concerns, disclosures that China had supplied missiles and chemical weapons technology to Iran, and revelation that it had attempted to gain influence in the United States through illegal campaign contributions. In 1997 the extension was in trouble in Congress.

Boeing, the largest U.S. exporter, was involved in intense market competition with Airbus, based in France and three other countries, for a $4 billion sale to China. China was expected to purchase an estimated $140 billion of aircraft over the next 20 years. In early April at the United Nations human rights conference in Geneva, the United States voted for a resolution to condemn China, whereas France voted against the resolution, causing it to fail. With President Chirac of France scheduled to visit China in May, Boeing faced a considerable challenge to obtain the sale.

Larry S. Dickenson, vice president of international sales for Boeing, noted the advantage France had obtained through its vote on the human rights motion: "When President Chirac arrives in Beijing in a few weeks, I am sure he will be rewarded for that stance."[1] When President Chirac arrived in China, the government announced that it would purchase 30 Airbus aircraft valued at $1.5 billion. China's Premier Li Peng explained the decision to buy from Airbus: "They do not attach political strings to cooperation with China."[2]

Boeing and other U.S. firms, such as the Ford Motor Company, used informational and representation strategies in support of both MFN and China's admission into the WTO. Representative Todd Tiahrt (R-KS), who had worked for Boeing for 14 years, said he talked with Boeing lobbyists "once a week, sometimes daily. They never fail to bring [MFN] up."[3] After President Chirac's visit, the president of Boeing's commercial aircraft business, Ronald Woodard, said, "The Chinese just bought 30 Airbus planes to reward Europe for not punishing human rights. The Europeans love the fight over MFN."[4]

The information provided by Boeing and other companies pertained to the effects on the companies, their stakeholders, and the constituents of members of Congress, as well as to broader consequences. Dickenson identified the long-term seriousness of the matter:

"If we lose the opportunity to get China into a rule-based organization like the WTO now, it will take us another five years to get back to the spot we're in today."[5] He added, "I told [Congress] about Airbus, Chirac's visit, what was likely to happen. I told them the realities: that every time there's a blip in U.S.-China relations, it helps our foreign competitors."[6]

Analysis

In this case, Boeing could provide information on (1) the likelihood that sales would be lost, (2) the profits that would be affected if sales were lost, (3) the effects on its, and its suppliers', stakeholders, (4) future sales that might be jeopardized, and (5) the effects on the competitive positions of Airbus and Boeing. Some of this information was soft in the sense that an officeholder was unable to verify its accuracy and completeness. In particular, the information in (1), (4), and (5) was to varying degrees soft and difficult to evaluate. Other information, such as that in (3), was hard in the sense that the officeholder could understand the data by inspection; for example, Boeing could identify the aircraft it was offering to China, the current subcontractors, and the possible lost sales. Because Boeing had superior information, it had an opportunity to advocate its position strategically. This could involve emphasizing favorable information and remaining silent about unfavorable information. It could also involve emphasizing worst-case scenarios, such as the maximum number of jobs that could be lost, or utilizing data that presented its side of the issue in a favorable manner. Boeing, however, had a lengthy nonmarket agenda and interacted regularly with Congress and the executive branch. It thus had an incentive to build and maintain a reputation for providing reliable information.

Informational strategies can be integrated with broader nonmarket strategies including those of other interests. The major companies with business at risk in China divided lobbying responsibilities. Boeing lobbied representatives from Alabama, Kansas, and Washington, and General Motors lobbied representatives from Georgia, Michigan, and Texas. The companies also backed grassroots organizations that supported continuation of MFN status. Boeing backed the Kansas Alliance for U.S.-China Trade, which had grown to include 120 member companies that did business with China. Similarly, in California 350 companies participated in the Coalition for U.S.-China Trade. MFN was granted.

---

[1] *New York Times,* April 29, 1997.
[2] *Business Week,* June 16, 1997.
[3] *Business Week,* June 16, 1997.
[4] *Business Week,* June 16, 1997.

[5] *New York Times,* April 29, 1997.
[6] *Wall Street Journal,* June 24, 1997.

INSTITUTIONS, INTERESTS, AND STRATEGY CHOICE

Institutions and Responsiveness

The choice among the three generic nonmarket strategies depends on the interests involved with the issue and the institutions in whose arenas the issue will be addressed. The significance of institutional arenas for strategy is illustrated in Figure 7-4. Institutions can be arrayed in terms of their political responsiveness to constituent interests. Institutions that are highly responsive to constituent interests are legislatures and the presidency, or more generally institutions whose officeholders are directly elected. In contrast, the courts are not very politically responsive but instead make their decisions based on the Constitution, statutes, and case law precedents. Regulatory and administrative agencies are somewhere in between, depending on their policy domain and mandate. The figure provides more detail on the responsiveness of the institutions.

In politically responsive institutions success depends more on the ability of interests to supply nonmarket action, and in less politically responsive institutions success depends more on the provision of technical information. For judicial institutions informational strategies, and particularly strategies that provide technical information and legal argument, are most effective. In legislative arenas representation strategies are more important, since they can be based on the constituency connection. Informational strategies that provide political information about the impact of a bill on constituents, for example, are often used in conjunction with representation strategies in politically responsive institutions.

The choice of a nonmarket strategy for issues addressed in regulatory or administrative agencies depends on their political responsiveness. An agency with a narrow mandate such as the International Trade Commission (ITC; see Chapter 18) is less politically responsive than is an agency with a broad mandate such as the Environmental Protection Agency (EPA). Representation strategies tend to be more effective in the EPA than in the ITC. Similarly, the Department of Justice and Federal Trade Commission are closer to the courts than are the Department of Commerce and United States Trade Representative.

Interests: Client and Interest Group Politics

The choice among nonmarket strategies is related to the nature of the politics of an issue, as characterized in the Wilson-Lowi matrix presented in Chapter 6. In client politics the benefits are concentrated on the clients, whereas harm is widely distributed. Because the opposition is not active in client politics, the client interest group usually adopts a low-profile strategy outside the view of the public. Lobbying and information provision are typically the centerpieces of such a strategy. The information is often political—about the constituents who would benefit from the alternative sought by the client or about how that alternative would serve the policy interests of the officeholder.

FIGURE 7-4   Institutions and Responsiveness

	Institutions	
Courts	*Regulatory Administrative*	*Congress Presidency*
less	*degree of political responsiveness*	*more*
To what are the institutions responsive?		
Constitution	statutes and mandate	constituents
due process	due process	interest groups
statutes	interests with standing	policy agenda
the record	court review	(administration)
precedents	congressional and	congressional
ideology	executive pressure	committee agendas

In a legislative arena the strategy frequently focuses on both majority building and agenda setting with a particular focus on committees. In conjunction with a majority building strategy, a firm may use a high-profile strategy of organizing and mobilizing its stakeholders and those of other interests into a coalition that can take coordinated action and improve the coverage of legislative districts. The Daylight Saving Time Coalition's strategy of adding candy manufacturers by including Halloween is an example.

The danger in a behind-the-scenes nonmarket strategy in client politics is that watchdog groups and opponents in the legislature will shine light on the activities of the client. The label often given to client relationships is "special-interest" politics, and many members of Congress seek to avoid such politics. Clients thus often wrap their objectives and messages in the rhetoric of the public interest.

Interest group politics usually involves more visible strategies. A high-profile strategy could include public advocacy and grassroots activities. Firms engaged in interest group politics also use lobbying and coalition building. The formation of the Daylight Saving Time Coalition was important in achieving an extension that had for many years been stalled in Congress. Informal alignments of interests can also be important, as in the case of the Coalition and the RP Foundation Fighting Blindness.

If a coalition seeks new legislation, its chances of success are enhanced if its allies are able to restrict the opportunities of others to amend the proposal in ways that could split the coalition. This can at times be accomplished by incorporating the desired legislation in a larger bill to give it a degree of protection. Representative Pickle incorporated his bill ending the tax benefits for tax-exempts and foreign leasing into a larger tax bill. In the chapter case, *Federal Express and Labor Organization,* the company and its allies were successful in having a provision inserted in the bill in conference committee, after which no amendments were allowed.

Competition between interest groups gives more importance to pivotal legislators, often increasing the cost of vote recruitment in majority building strategies. Providing substitutes for opposing interests can be effective in reducing their incentives and conserving the resources of the interest group and its allies. The Daylight Saving Time Coalition supported pre-sunrise authorization for radio stations to eliminate their opposition. The cost of a vote recruitment strategy can also be reduced by proposing compromises. In the foreign leasing example in Chapter 6 Boeing was able to attain its secondary objective of preserving its orders already in hand and having the tax benefits phased out over several years.

When a firm is on the side of dispersed benefits in entrepreneurial or majoritarian politics, a number of strategies are available. One is to identify pockets of interests that can be organized and mobilized. The basic politics of the extension of daylight saving time was majoritarian, but there were pockets of interests—convenience stores, recreation and sports products firms, candy makers, and nursery firms—that could be organized. This transformed the politics from majoritarian to client politics. A second strategy is to identify other aligned interests, as in the case of the Daylight Saving Time Coalition and the RP Foundation Fighting Blindness. A third strategy is to seek a nonmarket entrepreneur who can either organize those with dispersed benefits or represent them from within the government institution. To the extent that an entrepreneur is able to mobilize dispersed interests, the potential of collective action can be realized. Particularly when interests are not well informed about an issue, a nonmarket entrepreneur can alert those interests and provide information on the possible consequences of the issue. Pharmaceutical companies use this approach in mobilizing patient advocacy groups that benefit from particular drug therapies.

SUMMARY

Nonmarket action by firms as well as other interests must meet standards of responsibility. Firms have the constitutional right to speak on issues and to petition government, and those actions should be forthright and transparent. The nonmarket power of firms is often controlled by the differences in their interests. In addition, the power of business is often limited by the actions of groups such as organized labor, NGOs, and activists. Firms must avoid the temptation to manipulate public processes and should exercise restraint in the gray area between manipulation and the acceptable exercise of their rights.

The formulation of nonmarket strategies is the responsibility of managers, and the strategy process has as components:

- Nonmarket analysis (Chapter 6)
- Specification of primary and contingent objectives
- Selection of institutional arenas
- Strategy formulation
- Development and utilization of nonmarket assets, including the rent chain
- Implementation (Chapter 8)

The principal nonmarket strategies used by firms are representation, majority building, and information provision. Representation strategies are based on the link between the firm's rent chain and an officeholder's constituents. Majority-building strategies involve building a majority in support of or in opposition to a legislative alternative. These strategies focus on pivotal legislators and agenda setters. Informational strategies involve the strategic provision of technical and political information as in advocacy and are often used in conjunction with representation and majority-building strategies.

The choice among strategies depends on institutions and interests. Institutions can be arrayed in terms of their political responsiveness. Representation strategies are used for politically responsive institutions such as Congress and the presidency. Strategies involving the provision of technical information are associated with less politically responsive institutions including the courts and some regulatory and administrative agencies. Strategies involving the provision of political information are often used in conjunction with representation strategies. In legislatures majority-building strategies are often supported by representation and informational strategies.

The nature of the politics also affects the strategy choice. In client politics firms face no direct opposition, and firms typically prefer low-profile strategies implemented through lobbying. In interest group politics firms may be forced to adopt a higher profile strategy to counter the opposition. In client politics majority-building strategies are relatively straightforward to formulate, but in interest group politics a firm may need not only to build a majority but also to protect that majority from the majority-building strategies of those on the other side of the issue.

-------------------------------- **A P P E N D I X** --------------------------------

The Politics of the Extension
of Daylight Saving Time

Since the Uniform Time Act was enacted in 1966, daylight saving time had begun on the last Sunday in April and lasted 6 months until the last Sunday in October.[20] Bills to extend daylight saving time were introduced in Congress beginning in 1976, and the battle for an extension lasted for 10 years, concluding in 1986 with a 3-week extension to the first Sunday in April. The forces that led to the extension are representative of those present on many nonmarket issues affecting business.

Two contrasting approaches can be taken to explain the extension. The public interest perspective predicts that the alternative that best serves the public will be adopted. In this case, the public interest would select the extension that yielded the greatest differences between aggregate benefits and costs. This perspective was first advanced in 1784 when Benjamin Franklin argued to the French that they could save 96 million candles per year from an extra hour of daylight.[21] During World Wars I and II the United States adopted daylight saving time, and in World War II it lasted for 3½ years. During the oil crisis of 1973–1974, the United States extended daylight saving time as a means of saving energy. The waning of the oil crisis and protests from parents who objected to their children having to walk to school in the early morning darkness led to the elimination of the extension. Subsequently, the Department of Transportation (DOT) estimated that the extension during the oil crisis saved 6 million barrels of oil and traffic decreased 2 to 3 percent. The extension of daylight saving time in 1986 occurred at a time when energy savings were not considered important. A variety of business interests would benefit from an extension including recreation and retail businesses. In addition the RP Foundation Fighting Blindness representing people affected with night blindness was an important participant in the nonmarket competition.

The second approach focuses on the nonmarket competition resulting from the actions of those whose interests are affected by the length of daylight saving time. For most nonmarket issues it is better to view nonmarket action as arising from the interests of individuals, firms, and groups than to view nonmarket outcomes as the result of the pursuit of the public interest. This does not mean that public policy analysis has no effect on the outcome of political activity. Often it does. Even in those cases, however, public policy analysis should not be viewed as the determinant of the outcome of the nonmarket activity. Instead, public policy analysis is better viewed as providing information about the consequences of alternatives for the various interests affected.

In the case of the extension of daylight saving time, Congress was the relevant institution and lobbying was the principal action of the proponents and opponents of an extension. To predict the outcome of the nonmarket competition, the first step is to use the framework presented in this chapter to understand the effectiveness of the interests. The second step is to understand how the institution resolves the competing interests and their actions. In this case, the median votes theorem provides the understanding. The third step is to identify the design of effective nonmarket strategies for firms and other interests given the characteristics of the relevant institutions and their decision-making processes and procedures.

The Legislative History of the Extension

In 1976 the Senate passed a bill extending daylight saving time to 8 months and 1 week, but the House did not act. In 1981 the House passed a bill providing for a shorter extension, but the Senate did not act. In 1983 the House rejected an extension. Finally, in 1985 the light at the end of the tunnel began to appear. Representative Edward J. Markey (D-MA), chairman of the Subcommittee on Energy Conservation, introduced a bill that would extend daylight saving time to the third Sunday in March and the first Sunday in November. The Subcommittee approved the bill by voice vote. The Energy and Commerce Committee, however, approved an amendment by Howard C. Nielson (R-UT) that moved the starting date back 2 weeks to the first Sunday in April. Approving the amended bill by voice vote, the committee sent it to the full House, which approved it by a 240 to 157 vote in October 1985.

In July 1985 Senator Slade Gorton (R-WA) introduced a bill extending daylight saving time, but opposition by senators from rural and Midwestern states led by Senators Wendell Ford (D-KY) and J. James Exon (D-NE) blocked the bill in the Commerce Committee. With the committee gates closed, Senator Gorton introduced his extension bill as a rider to an authorization bill for fire prevention and control programs. The amendment provided the same starting date as the House bill, but to recruit additional votes Gorton removed the 1-week extension in the fall. By a 36 to 58 vote the

---

[20] States retained the right not to adopt daylight saving time. The dates had been chosen because the weather was generally similar at the beginning and end of the period.

[21] *Fortune,* November 12, 1984, p. 147.

Senate defeated a motion to table the amendment and then by voice vote adopted the amendment and the bill. The House and Senate thus had both passed extensions of daylight saving time, but the measures were not identical. Rather than convene a conference to reconcile the bills, the House chose to enact the Senate bill. An authorization bill for fire prevention and control had been working its way through the House, and on June 24, 1986, the House, by unanimous consent, agreed to drop the 1-week extension in November and adopted the Senate bill.

The Politics of Daylight Saving Time

The politics of daylight saving time can be understood as a competition between those interests favoring and those opposed to an extension. Congress was the institutional arena for that competition. Senator Ford characterized the differences in interests as "any Kentucky mother who has sent a first-grader out to catch a bus on a dark, misty April morning takes a dim view about . . . electricity that might be saved on the East and West coasts and the number of afternoon tennis games that might be played here in Washington."[22]

The effects of an extension were broadly distributed, and at the beginning of the nonmarket competition in 1976, interests were poorly organized and their strategies only loosely coordinated. The status quo prevailed. The benefits to a number of groups, including recreation and business interests, were substantial, however, so interest groups had an incentive to form.

An extension of daylight saving time would affect a wide array of economic activity. As James Benfield, a lobbyist who served as executive director of the Daylight Saving Time Coalition, explained, "Here's a way to increase economic activity by doing nothing more than changing the time on your wrist. . . . We are simply fine-tuning our use of time to adjust for daily life patterns and to translate those patterns into dollars for business."[23] An extension would shift the demand curve outward for a variety of goods. The Barbecue Industry Association estimated that an extension would increase the sales of briquettes by $56 million and starter fluid by $15 million. The Kingsford Company was an active supporter of the extension. Bob Lederer of the American Association of Nurserymen stated, "When daylight saving time comes, people think spring and they start buying plants. And if daylight saving comes earlier, people will buy a lot more plants."[24] The Sporting Goods Manufacturers Association estimated that golfers would spend $7 million more on clubs and balls and would play 4 million more rounds of golf a year. Expenditures for tennis balls and rackets could increase by $7 million per year. Hardee's estimated that an extension would increase

sales by an average of $800 per week per store. The Southland Corporation estimated that daylight saving time could increase sales at its 7-Eleven stores by $30 million annually. Pamela Sederholm, a spokesperson for 7-Eleven, said, "Women shop in daylight hours at a 7-Eleven. They go to supermarkets when it's dark."

Benfield conceived the idea of including Halloween in the extension to bring the candy industry into the coalition.[25] Candy makers were interested in an additional hour of daylight on Halloween because some parents would allow their children to extend their trick-or-treating. Those candy companies were represented by the Chocolate Manufacturers Association, the National Candy Brokers Association, and the National Confectioners Association. Representative Markey said, "This small step could make trick-or-treating for young children a much safer experience."[26] The deletion of the fall extension by Senator Gorton was a substantial blow to the candy interests—as well as to children.

Firms measured the impact of an extension in terms of their sales and profits. Increased sales also mean that customers benefit. Similarly, increased sales mean an increase in employment. The difference between the incentives of a firm (or its shareholders) and the incentives of customers and employees is both in the magnitude of their benefits and the cost of taking nonmarket action. Firms have relatively low costs of taking nonmarket action and thus may act when those with higher costs would not act. Customers and future employees typically are widely dispersed and costly to organize, so they would not be expected to be active on the daylight saving time issue. Their interests, however, were represented by the firms that benefited from an extension. Thus, an important consequence of the participation of firms in nonmarket activity is that they often represent the interests of those who might otherwise not be represented due to high costs and low per-capita benefits. Firms regularly inform members of Congress of the jobs that would be created and other benefits that would accrue to their constituents.

An important factor in political competition is the alignment of interests among dissimilar groups. An interest group with a strong incentive to support the extension of daylight saving time was the RP Foundation Fighting Blindness, which had 400,000 members who suffered from retinitis pigmentosa and other eye diseases that caused night blindness. Although their interests were not directly economic, as were those of 7-Eleven and Kingsford, they had an incentive to support an extension just as business had. The fact that individuals with night blindness were disadvantaged could, however, be more compelling to some members of Congress than the economic interests of firms, customers, and employees.

---

[22]*Congressional Quarterly Weekly Report,* May 24, 1986, p. 1177.
[23]*Fortune,* November 12, 1984, p. 150.
[24]*Fortune,* November 12, 1984, pp. 150–151.

[25]He was successful in expanding the coalition from 4 members in 1983 to 16 in 1985.
[26]*Congressional Quarterly Weekly Report,* May 4, 1985, p. 839.

On most issues, there are opposing interests, and one nonmarket strategy is to provide substitutes to reduce the adverse consequences to those opposed to the issue. The National Association of Broadcasters, for example, opposed the extension. Although most of the 2,450 AM radio stations licensed to operate only in the daytime had a PSA (presunrise authorization) that allowed them to begin broadcasting with reduced power at 6:00 A.M., nearly 450 did not have a PSA.[27] For many of these stations the most profitable advertising time was the morning commute hours, and profits would be reduced by an extension that would add an hour of broadcast time in the evening and eliminate an hour in the morning. This opposition was relatively easy to accommodate because adjustments in authorizations for AM radio stations were virtually costless to the supporters of the extension. As Benfield argued, the Federal Communications Commission (FCC) could extend the broadcast time in the morning. The amendment offered by Senator Gorton contained a provision allowing the FCC to make appropriate adjustments in broadcast authorizations.

In other instances there may be no means of satisfying opponents. Some Christian fundamentalists opposed the extension because they viewed it as contrary to God's will. Some Orthodox Jews opposed the extension because their morning prayers cannot begin earlier than 45 minutes before sunrise, and the length of the prayers might make them late for work. A number of other groups also opposed the extension.[28] Some parents opposed it because their children would have to go to school in the dark. This was more of a problem on the western edges of time zones.[29] Some farmers objected to the extension, and their interests were represented by a number of members of Congress. Representative Thomas A. Daschle (D-SD) said, "The time shift would hurt farmers, particularly the estimated 30 percent who hold second jobs and who would have less daylight to perform morning chores." Even more important, he said, was the safety threat to "children who would wait in the dark for school buses as early as 6:30 A.M."[30] These interests were represented by organizations such as the PTA and the American Farm Bureau.

The Role of Information

One feature of political competition is the provision of information about the consequences of political alternatives. The DOT and the National Safety Council reported that the extension of daylight saving time would not significantly increase the risk to school children. Opponents of the extension attacked DOT's accident data

from the 1974–1975 extension and argued that it was insufficient to warrant any conclusion. In 1986 the DOT countered when Secretary Elizabeth H. Dole wrote to Senate majority leader Robert Dole (R-KS) stating that DOT studies concluded that an extension "would reduce traffic deaths nationwide by a minimum of 22, injuries by a minimum of 1,525, and societal costs from auto accidents by a minimum of $28 million [annually] . . . with possible savings being as much as twice as large."[31]

The impact of such facts is difficult to determine, but whatever their significance, politics is not primarily a competition among facts. Politics is better viewed as a competition of interests, and information is important to the extent that it helps identify the relationship between political alternatives and their consequences for those interests. Through the efforts of the Daylight Saving Time Coalition, many legislators learned of the benefits to businesses and their constituents. Complaints from farmers, parents, and others provided information that led Representative Daschle and Senators Exon and Ford to oppose an extension.

An Analytical Characterization of the Politics of Daylight Saving Time

The next step in the analysis is to move from interests to outcomes. In the case of daylight saving time, the median voter theorem provides that step. The alternatives before Congress can be summarized by the length of daylight saving time, as measured by the number of weeks constrained by beginning and ending on a Sunday. The principal alternatives are displayed in Figure 7-5. The status quo q is farthest to the left, and Representative Markey's bill, denoted by m, is farthest to the right.

Because of the constituency connection, members of Congress were concerned about the interests of their constituents. Particularly in states and districts at western edges of a time zone, pressure from farmers and parents of school-age children outweighed the pressure from the supporters of the extension. Senators Ford and Exon, then, can be thought of as preferring a length of daylight saving time at, or perhaps to the left of, the status quo. This is illustrated in Figure 7-5 by a preference function with a peak at their most preferred length, their ideal point, and declining the farther an alternative is from that point.[32] The preferences of Representative Markey, whose district was on the eastern edge of a time zone, are also illustrated in Figure 7-5. Indeed, each member of Congress can be thought of as having preferences of a similar form.

---

[27]*Congressional Quarterly Weekly Report,* May 24, 1986, p. 1177.
[28]Some opposition defied logic. Representative Thomas F. Hartnett (D-SC) asked "how big the mushrooms are going to be with that extra hour of daylight in the evening" (*Fortune,* November 12, 1984, p. 150).
[29]DOT estimated that dawn would be, on average, at 6:48 A.M. but would occur at 7:00 A.M. on the western edges of time zones.
[30]*Congressional Quarterly Weekly Report,* May 4, 1985, p. 839.

---

[31]*Congressional Quarterly Weekly Report,* May 24, 1986, p. 1177. Sood and Ghosh (2007) estimated that the extension of daylight saving time significantly reduced crashes for vehicle occupants and crashes involving pedestrians.
[32]Daschle's district was also at the western edge of a time zone, whereas Gorton's state was at the eastern edge.

FIGURE 7-5 Median Voter Theorem and Daylight Saving Time

If the House had only two alternatives, *q* and *m,* representatives would simply vote for their preferred alternative. The alternatives were not restricted, however, because the legislative process was open and any number of weeks of daylight saving time could be proposed. Legislators could thus introduce alternatives they preferred to either *q* or *m*. For example, an alternative to the right of *q* and to the left of the median would be preferred to *q* by all those representatives with ideal points to the right of the median plus some of those to the left. It thus would defeat *q* on a majority vote. Indeed, the only alternative that could not be defeated in this manner by some other alternative is the median of the ideal points of the legislators. That is, any other alternative would receive fewer than half the votes against the median. Hence, the median is the majority-rule winner. In the House, Representative Nielson's amendment *n* to the Markey bill was closer to the median and was preferred by a majority to both *q* and *m*.

In the Senate Commerce Committee Senators Ford and Exon were successful in preserving the status quo

against Senator Gorton's bill *g*. Senator Gorton, however, was able to attach his bill as a rider to an authorization bill. A majority of the Senate preferred *g* to *q,* as reflected by the 36 to 58 vote defeating the motion to table *g*. The fact that Senator Gorton's proposal provided a week less of daylight saving time than the Nielson amendment may indicate that Gorton believed that *n* was farther from the median of the ideal points in the Senate.

The House and the Senate had thus passed extensions that were preferred to the status quo, but before an extension could become law, the two chambers had to reconcile the two bills. Bargaining between the chambers resulted in the House agreeing to *g,* which was enacted.[33]

---

[33]In 2005 Congress again extended daylight saving time effective in 2007. Daylight saving time now begins the second Sunday of March and ends the first Sunday of November. The public policy explanation for the extension was energy savings, but as *ABC News,* July 26, 2005, headlined, "Are Golf, Shopping Behind Daylight Saving Time?"

------------------------------------ C A S E S ------------------------------------
Federal Express and Labor Organization

Historically, labor relations for the Federal Express Corporation had been governed by the Railway Labor Act (RLA), which required that unions attempting to organize the employees of a company must do so nationally. Federal Express had operated as an "express company" under the RLA. Organized labor, however, claimed that a bill enacted in 1995 subjected Federal Express to labor organization under a different law, the National Labor Relations Act (NLRA), which allowed unions to organize workers locally. Avoiding unionization was a key element of Federal Express's market strategy. Of its 110,000 domestic employees, only its 3,000 pilots were unionized.[34] Because local organization was usually easier for a union than national organization, Federal Express wanted Congress to pass new legislation that would clearly place its labor practices under the RLA.

Federal Express's nonmarket objective was to have a Senate ally attach a relatively small amendment (a "rider") to a much larger bill (a "vehicle"). The legislative vehicle in this instance was the annual authorization bill for the Federal Aviation Administration, which was regarded as a "must-pass" measure. The substantive aim of the rider was to remove the jurisdictional ambiguity associated with the status quo by clearly making Federal Express's labor relations subject to the RLA.[35] Although minor in comparison with the larger bill, the amendment would have attracted attention and opposition if offered outright on the Senate or House floors, so Federal Express deferred to the judgment of one of its Senate allies who successfully negotiated for insertion of the amendment in the conference committee. When the bill and rider came back to the Senate for a vote on final passage, however, senators aligned with organized labor decided to mount a fight. They sought to block the vote on final passage of the conference report (and hence the bill) unless and until the rider were dropped. They began a filibuster.

To stop the filibuster (i.e., to invoke cloture) and thereby move to certain passage of the bill and the rider, Federal Express and its supporters in the Senate had to build a majority of at least 60 votes. Suppose that supporters were willing to trade votes or other support of varying value to recruit the needed votes to stop the filibuster. Let the status quo q denote the current ambiguous labor jurisdiction, and let the conference committee bill b denote unambiguous RLA jurisdiction. Along with the filibuster pivot f (the 41st ideal point) in the Senate, these points are identified in Figure 7-6.

Assume that each senator has a symmetric utility function, so that his or her preference for q or b is determined by the relative distances from his or her ideal point to q and b. For convenience, assume also that the shapes of senators' utility functions are symmetric and that their ideal points are uniformly distributed (equally spaced) over the line as shown. The median senator's ideal point is shown as m, and Federal Express's allies have ideal points on the right side of the spectrum. Finally, assume that if the support provided or votes traded are sufficiently valuable, a senator will vote for b. Remember, however, that Federal Express supporters do not want to trade more votes or provide more support than is necessary. ■

Source: This case was prepared by Professors David P. Baron and Keith Krehbiel for the purpose of illustrating theories of vote recruitment. Although it is based on an actual legislative history, it is not intended to suggest that Federal Express dealt with this nonmarket issue in this manner. Copyright © 1997 by the Board of Trustees of the Leland Stanford Junior University. All rights reserved. Reprinted with permission.

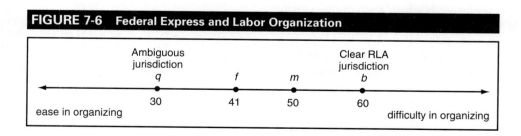

FIGURE 7-6 Federal Express and Labor Organization

Ambiguous jurisdiction
Clear RLA jurisdiction
q f m b
30   41   50   60
ease in organizing   difficulty in organizing

---

[34]"This Mr. Smith Gets His Way in Washington," *New York Times,* October 10, 1996.

[35]Public laws cannot mention private companies explicitly. Therefore, the language that accomplished this task was necessarily opaque. The provision simply inserted the term "express company" into the Railway Labor Act of 1926. The term had been stricken—some claimed accidentally—from the law in 1995 when Congress eliminated the Interstate Commerce Commission, which had regulated surface transportation.

Preparation Questions

1. Which senators will not receive support or vote trades and why not?
2. Which senators will receive support or vote trades and why?
3. Which senator will receive the most valuable support or vote trades and why?

4. Does it make a difference if an opposing group (say, the AFL-CIO) were simultaneously working to offset the efforts of Federal Express and its legislative allies by implementing its own vote recruitment strategy?

Carried Interest Taxation

Introduction

Congress threatened to increase from 15 percent to 35 percent the tax rate on the income of partners in private equity firms, venture capital firms, and some real estate and oil and gas partnerships. Partners in these firms received a share, typically 20 percent but as high as 30 or 40 percent for some elite firms, of the gain on investments above a predetermined high water mark, with the remainder going to the limited partners and outside investors. The 20 percent economic interest in the venture typically was greater than the partners' investment of their own capital, so the economic interest did not represent a return on capital. Their economic interest was referred to as carried interest or "sweat equity" as some in the industry referred to it. Carried interest was currently treated as a long-term gain and taxed at the long-term capital gains rate of 15 percent. Legislation passed by the House of Representatives would treat carried interest as ordinary income, which was taxed at a 35 percent rate.

Victor Fleischer, a law professor at the University of Illinois-Chicago, testified in a congressional hearing, "This quirk in the tax law is what allows some of the richest workers in the country to pay tax on their labor at a low rate."[36] On his blog Harvard University economics professor Greg Mankiw quoted economist and columnist Paul Krugman who had asked, "why does Henry Kravis pay a lower rate on his management fees than I pay on my book royalties?" Mankiw answered, "In both cases, a person (investment manager, author) is putting in effort today for a risky return at some point in the future. The tax treatment should be the same in the two cases."[37]

Douglas Lowenstein, president of the Private Equity Council, argued, "The proposal would undo decades of established partnership tax law and create a new standard that reserves capital gains rates only for those with the wherewithal to invest equity into an enterprise. Congress should not raise private equity taxes by 130 percent and create the risk that some of the benefits of this economic activity could be discouraged. Partners 'who

invest their time and effort to add value to an asset they own' are rightfully paying the lower capital gains rate on the resulting investment profits."[38]

Background

Some critics of the current tax treatment, including unions, were opposed to private equity firms because jobs were frequently eliminated when acquired firms were restructured. Other critics cited the extremely high incomes of private equity firm partners. Stephen A. Schwarzman, a co-founder of the Blackstone Group, earned $684 million in 2006 and held a $3 million birthday party that included entertainment by Martin Short and Patti LaBelle. Blackstone went public in June 2007 with a market capitalization of $33 billion, and Schwarzman's share was valued at $7.5 billion. The bill to increase the tax on carried interest was introduced in the House the day after Blackstone went public.

Senator Gordon Smith (R-OR) chided his colleagues, "It seems to me we were brought to this hearing because of the extravagant lifestyle of one person."[39] The legislative threat, however, was not due to extravagance but to an unrelated issue. The threat was due to a flaw in the personal income tax law and a "pay as you go" pledge by congressional Democrats. The flaw was the adjusted minimum tax (AMT) which threatened an additional tax burden on 23 million taxpayers. In 1968 the AMT had been enacted to make certain that wealthy individuals could not avoid personal income taxes. The flaw was that the income at which the AMT took effect was not adjusted for inflation. If Congress did not act, the AMT exemption income would fall from $62,550 in 2006 to $45,000 in 2007 for taxpayers filing joint returns with the average increase in taxes estimated at $2,000 per taxpayer. Most members of Congress viewed the AMT as unneeded and a political hazard and wanted it eliminated.

In 1990 Congress adopted a "pay as you go" rule in a bipartisan effort to reduce the budget deficit. Congress began to waive the rule in the late 1990s and in 2002 the

---

[36]*International Herald Tribune,* September 22, 2007.
[37]http://gregmankiw.blogspot.com, July 19, 2007.

[38]*Daily Deal/The Deal,* October 26, 2007.
[39]*Los Angeles Times,* September 19, 2007.

Republican-controlled Congress allowed the provision to expire.[40] When the Democrats won majorities in both chambers in 2006, they resurrected the pay as you go provision to demonstrate their fiscal responsibility in light of what they claimed was uncontrolled spending by the Republican Congress.[41] The rule required that any tax revenue lost from the reduction or elimination of the AMT be made up by increases in revenue from other taxes.

Legislation

Charles Rangel (D-NY), the new chairman of the House Ways and Means Committee, introduced major tax reform legislation in the form of the Tax Reduction and Reform Act of 2007. The $796 billion (over 10 years) bill provided for the permanent repeal of the AMT and a reduction in the corporate profits tax rate from 35 percent to 30.5 percent.[42] To make up the lost revenue, the bill would tax carried interest at 35 percent and impose a 4 percent surtax on individual incomes above $150,000 and $200,000 for couples filing a joint return.[43] The bill would also eliminate a special tax rate for manufacturers, disallow for tax purposes the use of the LIFO accounting method for inventories, and disallow certain deductions associated with untaxed foreign profits.

Democrats called the bill the "mother of all tax revisions," and Republicans labeled it the "mother of all tax hikes," since the pay as you go rule required that the lost tax revenue be made up by tax increases. The business community generally applauded the provisions eliminating the AMT and reducing the corporate tax rate, but opposed the tax increases.

The Bush administration opposed any increase in taxes. Secretary of the Treasury Hank Paulson argued that a tax increase would "hurt the ability of our businesses and workers to compete in a global economy. The proposed new surtax on individual income would burden millions of small businesses, and undermine job creation."[44] Representative Jim McCrery (R-LA), ranking minority member of the Ways and Means Committee, said that Rangel was exploiting the AMT to "lock Congress into a system where we are guaranteed to raise taxes by $3.5 trillion over 10 years. That will hurt our nation's competitiveness and cost us American jobs."[45]

The Carried Interest Provision

The higher tax on carried interest would raise $25.7 billion over 10 years. The director of the Congressional Budget Office, Peter R. Orszag, testified: "Most economists would view at least part, and perhaps all, of the carried interest as performance-based compensation for management services . . . rather than a return on financial capital invested by that partner." Alan Auerbach, a University of California–Berkeley economics professor, estimated that the proposed tax increase on carried interest would likely not decrease the assets of pension plans by more than 2 basis points a year nor raise the cost of partnerships by more than 20 basis points a year. He stated, "If half of the tax increase were shifted to investors, this tax burden would imply a reduction of at most around 2 basis points in the annual return of these pension funds' assets, and quite possibly less."[46]

The private equity industry had anticipated the threat to the tax treatment of carried interest and had begun hiring experts and lobbyists. Private equity firms spent $5.5 million on hired lobbyists in the first six months of 2007. Blackstone paid Ogilvy Government Relations $3.74 million during the first half of 2007.[47] Over 20 lobbying firms were working for the industry, and the industry hired former members of Congress and Clinton administration officials to lobby against the tax increase. Peter G. Peterson of Blackstone and David M. Rubenstein of the Carlyle Group had personally lobbied members of Congress. Lisa McGreevy, chief lobbyist for the Managed Funds Association, said, "I have already done more than 250 meetings on the Hill and have the swollen feet to prove it."[48]

Money managers also contributed to congressional campaigns with hedge funds contributing $4.4 million with 77 percent going to Democrats. Venture capital firms contributed $6.3 million with a majority going to Democrats, according to *Congressional Quarterly*.[49] Some staffers for members of Congress warned that the intense lobbying by the private equity industry was creating enemies on the Hill. According to the *Financial Times,* the Private Equity Council and the Managed Funds Association "tend to blame each other for black eyes to the industry's reputation."[50]

Bruce Rosenblum, managing director of the Carlyle Group and chairman of the Private Equity Council composed of Blackstone, Carlyle, and nine other firms, testified that "Another possible consequence is that U.S. firms will become less competitive with foreign PE firms,

[40]*Wall Street Journal,* November 9, 2007.
[41]Waiving the rule required a majority in the Senate and in the House both a majority and approval by the Democrat leadership (*Wall Street Journal,* November 9, 2007).
[42]Rangel argued that the U.S. corporate income tax was too high and hurt U.S. competitiveness.
[43]The surtax on high-income filers was estimated to increase tax revenues by $634 billion over 10 years.
[44]*Financial Times,* October 26, 2007.
[45]*Daily Deal/The Deal,* October 26, 2007.

[46]*Pensions and Investments,* September 17, 2007.
[47]Blackstone was also fighting a bill that would ban the listing on stock exchanges of partnerships that pay no corporate income tax (*Financial Times,* November 1, 2007). Another provision would tax such firms at the corporate tax rate of 35 percent.
[48]*Financial Times,* November 1, 2007.
[49]*New York Times,* November 2, 2007.
[50]*Financial Times,* November 1, 2007.

and even foreign governments with huge investment war chests. As governments the world over are striving to make their tax systems more competitive to attract foreign capital and challenge U.S. dominance, this Congress is considering a proposal that would go in the opposite direction."[51]

The U.S. Chamber of Commerce echoed this position. The Chamber stated that the tax increase on carried interest would affect 15.5 million Americans in 2.5 million partnerships.[52] Russell Read, chief investment officer of CalPERS, which had a $17.5 billion stake in private equity, said referring to a tax increase, "My personal expectation is that this will be a factor. How large it will be is really difficult to know."[53] CalPERS took no position on the issue of the taxation of carried interest nor did the National Conference on Public Employee Retirement Systems (NCPERS). NCPERS had initially opposed the tax increase on carried interest but withdrew its opposition because "a majority of our members do not share that opinion."

Others were also active. The Real Estate Roundtable wrote to members of Congress and testified in hearings. Adam Ifshin, president of DLC Management, a real estate development firm, testified before the House Ways and Means Committee, stating in written testimony, "The bill presents a barrier to entry for those who bring the ideas, the know-how, and the effort to those with money to invest. Development and redevelopment in many communities would suffer, no question about it."[54]

In September 2007 the Access to Capital Coalition was formed by a group of minority and women money managers with the financial backing of the Private Equity Council. Willie E. Woods, Jr., stated, "The present carried interest policy has been essential to attracting top talented minorities and women to the industry as independent firms and fund managers. Its elimination, consequently, would have the unfortunate effect of impeding this great progress."[55]

The business opposition to the tax increase on carried interest was not unanimous. Leo Hindrey, Jr., managing partner of InterMedia Partners LP, a private equity firm, stated in testimony before the House Ways and Means Committee, "A tax loophole the size of a Mack truck is right now generating unwarranted and unfair windfalls to a privileged group of money managers, and, to no one's surprise, these individuals are driving right through this $12 billion-a-year hole. Congress, starting with this committee, needs to tax money management income— what we call carried interest—as what it is, which is plain

old ordinary income."[56] William D. Stanhill, founding partner of Trailhead Investors in Denver, stated in testimony, "I don't think it's fair for . . . teachers and firefighters to subsidize special tax breaks for me and other venture capitalists. Or for private equity and hedge fund managers."[57] He also stated that a higher tax rate would not affect venture capital, "We get ample compensation, financial and psychic, for the work we do and the risks we take."[58]

Warren Buffett supported a tax increase. Referring to when he ran an investment partnership, he said, "I was managing money for other people . . . believe me, it's an occupation. I believe you should tax people on carried interest."[59] Earlier in June he had told a gathering of 400 venture capitalists and money managers gathered to raise funds for Senator Hillary Clinton (D-NY), "The 400 of us [here] pay a lower part of our income in taxes than our receptionists do—or do our cleaning ladies, for that matter. If you're the luckiest 1 percent of humanity, you owe it to the rest of humanity to think about the other 99 percent."[60]

In October the Service Employees International Union staged a protest against the Carlyle Group with a street theater depicting executives such as David Rubenstein as "Fat Cat Tycoons." For Halloween the union repeated the performance, including a protester dressed as "Sugar Daddy David Rubinstein" who handed out candy to mock lobbyists.[61]

Professor Fleischer commented, "The Private Equity Council has done a great job using sound bites to shape the debate. It started out as a debate about the tax rates that wealthy fund managers pay. Now it's about whether tax reform would hurt pensioners, minorities, and destroy capitalism as we know it."[62]

In September venture capitalists gathered for lunch in Palo Alto, California, and Mark Heesen of the National Venture Capital Association (NVCA) warned the group that "We are in a true battle." The NVCA sought to distance itself from the money management firms. Emily Mendell of the NVCA stated, "We are making distinctions between the long-term nature of venture capital investment versus the shorter-term economics that the other funds employ. We have a unique argument— we don't do arbitrage, we don't do financial engineering, we make assets from nothing. We build companies." Ted Schlein, a partner at Kleiner Perkins Caufield & Byers and chairman of NVCA, said, "If Congress is serious about promoting a competitiveness and innovation agenda and supporting new energy technologies, then it

[51]*Pensions and Investments,* September 17, 2007.
[52]*Los Angeles Times,* September 7, 2007.
[53]*Los Angeles Times,* September 7, 2007.
[54]Ifshin had testified on behalf of the Real Estate Roundtable and the International Council of Shopping Centers, many of which are organized as partnerships. *Washington Post,* September 7, 2007.
[55]*Washington Post,* September 7, 2007.

[56]*Pensions and Investments,* September 17, 2007.
[57]*Pensions and Investments,* September 17, 2007.
[58]*International Herald Tribune,* September 22, 2007.
[59]*Financial Times,* November 15, 2007.
[60]*Financial Times,* November 15, 2007.
[61]*Mergers and Acquisitions Journal,* December 1, 2007.
[62]*New York Times,* October 3, 2007.

should be extremely thoughtful before it passes legislation which will discourage investments in the startups and small businesses that are key players in these arenas." Jonathan Silver, a venture capitalist with Core Financial Partners, stated in testimony before the House Ways and Means Committee, "Early-stage companies would be harder to form and fund, reducing the overall number of venture-backed companies and hurting the lifeblood of our entrepreneurial ecosystem."[63]

Legislative Developments

The Senate was considering a bill to increase the tax on carried interest only for private equity firms that went public. Blackstone wrote to Senator John Kerry (D-MA) that the bill under consideration by the Senate Finance Committee would increase the Group's taxes by $525 million a year and partners' taxes by $175 million and would reduce its market capitalization by $10.5 billion. Senator Kerry had compared "private equity executives with other entrepreneurs who risk their own capital and therefore merit special tax treatment."[64] Senator Charles Schumer (D-NY) planned to introduce a bill that would increase taxes on all partnerships in addition to those generating carried interest.

On an 88–5 vote the Senate passed its own tax bill, which eliminated the ATM for 19 million taxpayers, reducing their taxes by $51 billion. The Senate, however, opposed any tax increase and waived the pay as you go rule. Senate Majority Leader Harry Reid (D-NV) had decided not to push the tax on carried interest because Republicans had threatened a filibuster and Democrats would be unable to invoke cloture and bring the bill to a vote. Senator Barack Obama (D-IL) issued a statement

in response: "If there ever was a doubt that Washington lobbyists don't actually represent real Americans, it's the fact that they stopped leaders of both parties from requiring elite investment firms to pay their fair share of taxes, even as middle-class families struggle to pay theirs."[65]

Rangel's tax reform bill became bogged down because of its complexity, and needing to deal with the AMT issue so that the Internal Revenue Service could prepare the 2007 tax forms and tax refunds would not be delayed, Rangel introduced a bill to provide a one-year fix. The $76 billion bill would freeze the AMT for one year, extend some popular tax credits for families, and increase the tax on carried interest.[66] On November 1 on a 22–13 vote the Ways and Means Committee passed the bill, and the full House approved it within a week on a 216–193 vote. After the committee vote Lowenstein of the Private Equity Council said, "We are disappointed with the committee's actions today, and we will continue to oppose legislation to change the tax treatment of carried interest. We remain hopeful that in the end this legislation will not be enacted into law."[67]

With time fleeting, the House and Senate conferred and agreed to the House freeze on the AMT but dropped the tax increase on carried interest, sending the bill to President Bush for his signature.

Lisa McGreevy of the Managed Funds Association commented, "This issue is definitely still on the table and will stay there until major tax reform is passed."[68] ■

Preparation Questions

1. Evaluate the strategy used by the private equity industry to deal with the threatened increase in taxes on carried interest.

2. Should the venture capital industry join with the private equity industry, or should it separate from the private equity industry? That is, is it better for the venture capital industry to join with the private equity industry in a broad coalition to defeat higher taxes on carried interest, or should the venture capital industry pursue, either as a primary or a contingent objective, an objective such as taxing as ordinary income carried interest associated with

   money management and private equity but not taxing carried interest on venture capital investments associated with creating jobs?

3. Now that Rangel's legislative effort failed, will the carried interest issue go away?

4. If the tax on carried interest were increased, what would be the effect on the private equity and venture capital markets? How should firms in those industries adjust their market strategies?

5. Formulate a strategy for the venture capital industry to deal with the carried interest taxation issue.

---

[63]*International Herald Tribune,* September 22, 2007.
[64]*Financial Times,* August 25, 2007.

[65]*Mergers and Acquisitions Journal,* December 1, 2007.
[66]The freeze was designed to keep the number of taxpayers subject to the AMT at the same level as in 2006. The income level was set at $66,250 for joint filers and $44,350 for single filers. The tax credits were detailed in *Accounting Today,* December 17, 2007.
[67]*Los Angeles Times,* September 2, 2007.
[68]*Financial Times,* November 1, 2007.

Wal-Mart and Its Urban Expansion Strategy

Wal-Mart was the world's largest corporation with sales of $256 billion, a $9 billion profit, and 1.3 million associates, as it called its employees. Wal-Mart was the most admired company in *Fortune*'s annual survey. In addition to its traditional merchandise Wal-Mart had expanded to sell pharmaceuticals and groceries. In the United States its strategy had been to locate in small towns and suburban areas. Only 38 of its 3,000 stores were located in cities with populations of at least 1,000,000. With attractive sites in its traditional areas becoming scarce, Wal-Mart embarked on an urban expansion strategy. The company had 53 Wal-Mart and Sam's Club stores in the Chicago metropolitan area, but none in the city itself. In 2004 Wal-Mart sought approval to build two stores in Chicago.[69] The stores would employ 600 workers.

Wal-Mart's market strategy emphasized low prices, low costs, helpful sales people, an efficient distribution system, bargaining power over suppliers, and low wages compensated for by opportunities to advance as the company opened new stores. Although the company paid low wages, those wages were comparable to those paid by its competitors such as Target and K-Mart. Wal-Mart provided health insurance to its employees after 1,000 hours of employment. Wal-Mart also employed many elderly workers who were eligible for Social Security and Medicare.

Wal-Mart had experienced a host of labor incidents that generated criticism. In late 2003 Immigration and Customs Enforcement agents raided several Wal-Mart stores, taking into custody 200 undocumented workers employed by custodial service companies that cleaned the stores. It was also revealed that some Wal-Mart employees had been forced to punch out and continue working, and some minors had worked too many hours. Wal-Mart was also criticized for refusing to sell some magazines and CDs and concealing parts of the covers of some magazines. The media reported that in high crime areas Wal-Mart had a policy of locking night shift employees in the building to prevent "shrinkage" from theft. In many cases there was no one with a key to unlock the doors in the case of an emergency, and employees had to call a store manager to have the doors unlocked. Employees could use the emergency exits, but Wal-Mart had made it clear they were not to do so except in a true emergency such as a fire. Some employees said that they had been told that they would be fired if they used the emergency exits. Wal-Mart was also named in the largest-ever class-action lawsuit on behalf of 1.6 million women alleging job discrimination in promotions.

Activists and union leaders criticized Wal-Mart for its low wages and because its low prices put pressure on other companies, including small retailers. Wal-Mart became a political symbol as Democratic presidential primary candidates Howard Dean and Richard Gephardt criticized the company for its health benefits. Wal-Mart had become a symbol of low pay and was accused of driving down wages across the country.

Wal-Mart had a history of opposing unionization, and its employees had rejected unions on a number of occasions. John Bisio, a Wal-Mart spokesperson, explained that the reason "our associates haven't wanted third-party representation is because they have faith in the company, and it provides them with tremendous opportunity."[70]

In Southern California supermarkets faced increased competition from Wal-Mart superstores that sold groceries. To remain competitive, the supermarkets sought to require their employees to bear a share of their health care insurance costs. The United Food and Commercial Workers (UFCW) struck Kroger, Albertsons, and Safeway for 5 months before agreeing to have employees share in the insurance costs.

Earlier in the year Wal-Mart had sought to open a 60-acre shopping center in Inglewood, California, but local opposition led the city government to reject the changes in zoning rules needed for the project to go ahead. Wal-Mart then campaigned to put the matter before the voters, but in a public referendum voters rejected it by a 60–40 vote.

The Chicago Stores

Wal-Mart planned to open stores on the sites of a closed Ryerson Tull steel facility on the south side and a recently closed Helene Curtis plant on the west side. Both communities were poor and largely African American.

The opposition to Wal-Mart in Chicago was led by the Chicago Workers' Rights Board, which represented a coalition of labor, religious, and civic groups. At a rally an economist from the University of Illinois at Chicago predicted that Wal-Mart's entry would cost more jobs than it would create. He said, "As a rule, Wal-Mart squeezes more sales out of each man hour, so they can generate the same dollars out of fewer workers. So, you'll have a net loss."[71] The unions focused on the specific threat. "The Chicago Federation of Labor has made three demands of the retailing behemoth it called 'Public Enemy No. 1': that Wal-Mart agree not to sell groceries at any of its Chicago stores to avoid driving down the wages of its supermarket competitors, that the company remain neutral in any union-organizing campaign, and that it pays its Chicago employees a 'living wage.'"[72]

---

[69] Wal-Mart stated that it had no current plans to sell groceries in the proposed new stores.

[70] *New York Times,* May 6, 2004.
[71] *Columbia Chronicle* via U-Wire, May 17, 2004.
[72] *Chicago Sun-Times,* May 26, 2004.

Elizabeth Drea of the UFCW said, "Wal-Mart has a well-documented history of violating workers' rights and devastating communities with its predatory practices."[73] She added, "Wal-Mart usually comes in and pays the minimum wage, which forces all other workers' wages downward. That means there's a long-term impact many people may not be willing to explore."[74]

The NGO Good Jobs First produced a study reporting that Wal-Mart had received over $1 billion in state and local tax subsidies during its decades-long expansion. The study was financed in part by the UFCW.[75] A Wal-Mart spokeswoman responded that in the past decade "Wal-Mart has collected $54 billion in sales taxes, paid $4 billion in local property taxes, and paid $192 million in income and unemployment taxes to local governments. 'It looks like offering tax incentives to Wal-Mart is a jackpot investment in local government,' she said."[76]

Mark Brown, writing in the *Chicago Sun-Times,* said, "Of course, if Chicagoans prefer to keep their tax dollars closer to home, they can shop at Target or Lowe's or Home Depot or any of numerous other discount retail stores operated with nonunion workers, all of which have opened new locations in the city in recent years without a peep from organized labor that I can recall. . . . Labor's main concern seems to be in protecting its workers in the grocery business, because some Wal-Mart stores operate full-service groceries, although the company says that's not part of its initial plan here."[77]

Alderwoman Emma Mitts, who represented the West Side ward in which a store would be located, explained her support for the stores, "For a lot of people, this will be their first job of any kind. This is where they'll learn that in the world of work, you have to show up on time, you have to look good, you have to be helpful and courteous. Our young people are going to learn how to stock shelves, how to answer customers' questions, how to make change. Don't underestimate what it will mean to our community to have a place where young people can learn skills like these."[78] She estimated that the unemployment rate in her ward was 60 percent. In response to the criticisms of Wal-Mart, Mitts said, "We want to take the worst retailer in the world, the worst, as they say, and make it the best. But you know something? To make them the best, you've got to have them inside."[79]

Wal-Mart's average compensation for its associates in the Chicago area was $10.77, which it argued was not low relative to small retailers or large retailers, including Home Depot and Target. "A February 2004 report from

U.S. Representative George Miller (D-CA), a senior member on the House Committee on Education and the Workforce, says that the average Wal-Mart employee nationally earns $8.23 an hour, below the average supermarket employee's wage of $10.35 an hour."[80] Bisio said, "As far as having an impact on the overall economy, if you talk to the Chambers of Commerce in any town where we're present, they'll tell you that we not only create jobs, but we also help attract revenues for ourselves and neighboring retailers, which generates taxes that pay for law enforcement jobs and roads and everything else."[81]

Alderman Howard Brookins, Jr., in whose South Side ward the Ryerson Tull facility was located, said, "I don't understand any opposition. Target and Home Depot aren't unionized and they're in the city."[82] Brookins added, "When [Wal-Mart] said they were interested in coming, there was interest from other businesses. Restaurants such as Red Lobster and Applebee's, that weren't interested in coming into the inner city before, signed onto the project."[83]

After Wal-Mart opened a store in Los Angeles, local merchants did not experience the disaster critics had predicted. "'The traffic is definitely there. We're seeing more folks,' says Harold Liecha, a cashier at Hot Looks, a nearby clothier. . . . But the larger picture is that many [shops] that were there before the big discounter arrived are still there. There are new jobs now where there were none. And a moribund mall is regaining vitality. In short, Wal-Mart came in—and nothing bad happened."[84]

Wal-Mart had worked to build support for the stores in both the communities and Chicago more broadly. Approval of each store required 26 votes from the 50-member city council, and the council usually deferred to the wishes of the relevant alderman. This, however, was not business as usual, and despite support from Mayor Richard Daley, the city council postponed a vote on the stores.

Mr. Bisio observed, "In Chicago, you have to be willing to step out of your so-called comfort zone and what you're used to doing. We recognize that there are experiences there that are different from other places. Organized labor is very strong there. We know we're going to be subject to great scrutiny, and we really want to adhere or conform to the spirit of how things are done in Chicago."[85] ■

Source: This case was prepared from public sources by Professor David P. Baron. Copyright © 2004 by David P. Baron. All rights reserved. Reprinted with permission.

---

[73]*USA Today,* May 26, 2004.
[74]*Columbia Chronicle via U-Wire,* May 17, 2004.
[75]Good Jobs First also lobbied for a living wage.
[76]*New York Times,* May 24, 2004.
[77]*Chicago Sun-Times,* May 6, 2004.
[78]*New York Times,* July 6, 2004.
[79]*New York Times,* May 6, 2004.

[80] *Columbia Chronicle via U-Wire,* May 17, 2004.
[81]*New York Times,* May 6, 2004.
[82]*Crain's Chicago Business,* April 5, 2004.
[83]*Columbia Chronicle* via U-Wire, May 17, 2004.
[84]*BusinessWeek,* May 10, 2004.
[85] *New York Times,* July 6, 2004.

Preparation Questions

1. Should Wal-Mart give up on entering Chicago?
2. If not, should it agree to the demands of the Chicago Federation of Labor?
3. What should it do to build a majority in the city council?
4. Formulate an integrated strategy for Wal-Mart's urban expansion.

CHAPTER

8

Implementing Nonmarket Strategies in Government Arenas

INTRODUCTION

Nonmarket strategies must be implemented effectively, and conversely, the effectiveness with which strategies can be implemented affects the choice among them. For example, implementing an informational strategy as considered in the previous chapter requires access to government officeholders, the development of politically relevant information, lobbying, and perhaps public advocacy. If access cannot be obtained or politically relevant data cannot be developed, an informational strategy is unlikely to be effective. Strategy formulation and implementation thus are necessarily intertwined. This chapter considers the following implementation activities: (1) lobbying, (2) electoral support, (3) grassroots and constituency campaigns, (4) coalition building, (5) testimony, (6) public advocacy, and (7) judicial actions. As the following PacifiCare example indicates, companies use a portfolio of activities in implementing their nonmarket strategies.

Nonmarket issues often receive media and public attention, and that attention can shape and accelerate nonmarket activity. An important decision in any nonmarket strategy is whether a firm's actions should be high or low profile. A low-profile strategy emphasizes behind-the-scenes actions such as lobbying and is intended to reduce the chances of a reaction from opposing interest groups or public officeholders. Most companies prefer low-profile strategies. A high-profile strategy involves more visible activities, including grassroots campaigns, public advocacy, and broad-scale lobbying. Whether a nonmarket strategy is implemented in a high- or low-profile manner depends on the nature of nonmarket competition, as considered in Chapters 6 and 7. In opposing higher fuel economy standards, the auto industry initially used a high-profile strategy to raise concerns among the public about safety, cost, and choice and a low-profile strategy in building a coalition of firms and unions that would be harmed by higher standards. By 2007 the high-profile strategy was no longer viable, as considered in the Part II integrative case, *Fuel Economy Standards 2007*.

LOBBYING

Lobbying is a central component of most representation and informational strategies. Lobbying is the strategic communication of *politically relevant information* to government officeholders. That information may be provided to the president, a governor, executive branch officials, members of Congress or state legislatures, their staff, and committee staff. Lobbying also occurs at regulatory and administrative agencies, where it often takes place in ex parte meetings. Lobbying requires access, and access may be obtained through the constituency connection, campaign contributions, and personal relationships. In contrast to public advocacy and testimony before congressional committees, lobbying typically takes place behind the scenes.

EXAMPLE

PacifiCare's Nonmarket Portfolio

In the second half of the 1990s health maintenance organizations (HMOs) were under attack from patients, doctors, activists, and state and local governments. The health care industry had defeated President Clinton's attempt to restructure the industry, and although HMOs and other managed care providers had been responsible for holding down the cost of health care, complaints mounted from patients who wanted both unrestricted access to care and the lower cost associated with managed care.

Individual HMOs conducted a wide variety of nonmarket activities to avoid more extensive regulation and additional restrictions on their operations. PacifiCare Health Systems, with 1997 revenue of $9 billion and profits of $107 million, was the fifth largest HMO in the country. It provided managed care for group plans and Medicare beneficiaries in nine states plus Guam. As with other health care providers, PacifiCare faced a series of government initiatives to expand the scope of regulation.

To address these challenges, PacifiCare's leadership developed a nonmarket strategy with a broad portfolio of activities and an infrastructure to support it.[1] PacifiCare had a vice president for public affairs, a vice president for government affairs, and a senior vice president who had been the head of a state Democratic Party and an unsuccessful senatorial candidate. PacifiCare had no Washington office and relied on a trade association, the American Association of Health Plans, for some lobbying and monitoring work. PacifiCare contributed $900,000 to the association. PacifiCare was also active at the state level and hired a public relations firm to help introduce it to state policymakers.

PacifiCare's political action committee (PAC), which received contributions from about 250 of its executives, contributed approximately $100,000 to Republican and Democratic candidates in the 1997–1998 election cycle. PacifiCare also provided an equivalent amount of soft money to Democratic and Republican House and Senate reelection organizations and the Democratic Leadership Council. These contributions helped provide access to members of Congress for informational lobbying about issues on the company's agenda. It planned to spend $130,000 in 1998 to collect data and prepare research reports for use in its lobbying.[2] It also retained two lobbying firms headed by former Democrat staffers.

To address specific issues such as the Clinton administration's Patient Bill of Rights, PacifiCare participated in the 1,000-member Health Benefits Coalition, which successfully portrayed the administration's campaign as a costly intrusion by government. PacifiCare also used its rent chain by hiring a grassroots lobbying firm, which prepared lists by congressional district of satisfied PacifiCare patients who were willing to write or call members of Congress.

To repair the tarnished image of HMOs, PacifiCare joined with Cigna Corporation, WellPoint Health Networks, and other providers to form the Coalition for Affordable Quality Healthcare. The coalition initially planned to spend $6 million on an advertising campaign. A spokesperson said, "We are concerned we're getting a bad deal with the media and the only way around this anecdote-a-day is to try to appeal directly to the public to make them aware of the benefits of HMOs."[3] The campaign was in response to congressional hearings in which people claimed to have been denied care for serious illnesses.

Despite the low public opinion of HMOs, the industry was able to block the Clinton administration's efforts in 1998. Health care issues retained salient, however, and PacifiCare and other health care providers faced continuing challenges at the federal and state levels.

---

[1]This section is based on the article "Capital Clout: A Buyer's Guide," *Fortune*, October 26, 1998, by Jeffrey H. Birnbaum, and on other public sources.

[2]*Fortune*, October 26, 1998.
[3]*Dallas Morning News*, September 4, 1998.

Firms and other interests spend much more on lobbying than on any other implementation activity. According to data compiled by the Center for Responsive Politics, companies, unions, and other organizations spent $2.8 billion in 2007 on registered lobbying in Washington, DC.[1] In addition, these interests spent substantial amounts on lobbying not subject to reporting requirements.

---

[1]www.opensecrets.org/influence.

TABLE 8-1 Business Lobbying Expenditures	
	2007 (millions)
Health	$448
Pharmaceuticals/health products	228
Hospitals/nursing homes	92
Health professionals	71
Health services/HMOs	52
Misc. health	5
Finance, insurance, & real estate	418
Misc. business	359
Communications/electronics	334
Energy and natural resources	270
Transportation	230
Agribusiness	100
Construction	46
Total	$2,205

Source: Center for Responsive Politics, www.opensecrets.org/lobbyists.

Lobbying expenditures by sector are reported in Table 8-1, and not surprisingly, the largest expenditures are in sectors in which government policy and regulation are important. This is consistent with Figure 2-2, which relates the importance of nonmarket strategies to the control of opportunities by government versus markets. As discussed in a later section, the pattern of lobbying expenditures is quite different from the pattern of campaign contributions. The health industry spent $448 million on registered lobbying in 2007, whereas its campaign contributions were $99 million in the 2005–2006 election cycle. In contrast, lawyers and lobbyists spent only $30 million on lobbying, but made campaign contributions of $195 million. The lobbying expenditures by individual companies vary with their nonmarket agendas. In 1999 Schering-Plough spent $9.2 million on lobbying in its unsuccessful attempt to extend the patent on its allergy drug Claritin.[2]

Lobbying also takes place at state and local levels. Lobbying expenditures in California totaled $272 million in 2006, as reported by the Center for Public Integrity.

The Nature of Lobbying

Particularly in Congress, lobbying is important because of the large number of bills under consideration; for example, over 5,000 bills may be introduced in the House in a session. Members necessarily know little about many of the bills, so they have a demand for information. Conversely, in some cases members will check with lobbyists to determine whether the draft language of a bill is acceptable to them—that is, whether the interest group the lobbyist represents will support or at least not oppose it. This serves as a useful barometer of the political support or opposition a bill is likely to receive.

The scope of lobbying has broadened considerably over the past two decades. This broadening has had four components. First, managers have become more active participants in lobbying, just as they have become more deeply involved in formulating nonmarket strategies. Second, the professional lobbying industry has grown substantially as more interests participate in public policy processes. Third, the professional lobbying industry has become increasingly specialized with firms focusing on mobilizing constituents, grassroots lobbying, and research and technical services as well as the more traditional functions of monitoring government, providing access, and communicating

---

[2]See the chapter case, *Pharmaceutical Switching*.

information. Fourth, on majoritarian issues such as health care policy that affect large numbers of people, lobbying coordinated with communication directly to citizens through the mass media has become more common.

Lobbying is strategic in the sense of advocating one's position or countering the information provided by the other side. Analogous to a court trial, an interest advocates its side of an issue, and interests on the other side of the issue advocate their positions. Lobbying is also strategic in the sense that it is targeted to influential or pivotal officeholders and timed to the stages of the institutional process governing the issue. Lobbying does not involve threats or coercion and should not involve false information. Crying wolf and making false claims rarely is effective in the long run. Members of Congress and their staffs have heard such claims before and can have long memories.

Executives are often effective lobbyists because members of Congress and other government officials want to hear about a firm's concerns from the people in charge. A busy member of Congress will more often meet with a CEO or other high-ranking manager than with a representative of the firm's Washington office. High-level managers also have better knowledge of the firm's activities than do professional lobbyists and thus can be more specific. They also can make commitments that others cannot.

Technical and Political Information

Lobbying conveys two types of information: technical and political. Technical information consists of data and predictions about the consequences of alternative policies. In the Part II integrative case, *Fuel Economy Standards 2007,* the automobile companies urged reliance on sound science and engineering, emphasized the benefits of ethanol, and provided information on the effects on costs. In the chapter case, *Internet Taxation,* both supporters and opponents of Internet taxation provided technical information on the effects on the economy and the tax revenue lost by states.

Political information pertains to the impact of an alternative on the constituents or policy interests of an officeholder. In the *Fuel Economy Standards 2007* case the coalition formed by the automobile companies provided information on the higher prices auto buyers would have to pay and the need for flexibility in meeting the standards so as to preserve jobs. Since consumers and employees are constituents, that information had an impact. To support their lobbying, many firms develop data on their rent chains, including the number of employees and the supply contracts in each congressional district. This enables the firm to tell members of Congress how much business in their districts could be affected by a legislative proposal. The task of the lobbyist is to provide information that links the interests of the firm with those of legislators.

As an example of political information, consider the 1986 attempt to eliminate the tax credit for employing disadvantaged youths. The Treasury had estimated that eliminating the credit would increase tax collections by nearly $500 million a year, helping to reduce the federal budget deficit. One of the largest employers of youth, and thus one of the largest recipients of the tax credit, was the fast-food industry. The lobbying message of Pizza Hut was that the tax credit was an employment program that served constituents and was consistent with the policy objective of providing opportunities for disadvantaged youth. The members of the tax-writing committee understood that Pizza Hut would benefit from retention of the tax credit, but they also understood that Pizza Hut's interests were aligned with those of the disadvantaged. The tax credits were retained.[3]

When lobbying Congress, information should be provided at several levels, as illustrated in Figure 8-1. The CEO or other high-ranking managers may directly lobby a member of Congress with access facilitated by a professional lobbyist or government affairs professional. In addition to lobbying at the top, lobbying also takes place at the level of the member's personal staff and the staff of the relevant committees. The staff is the eyes and ears of the member, and providing information to a key staffer may be as effective as meeting with the member. Technical information and detailed policy studies are best presented to the staff rather than the member. Political information

---

[3]The credits came under attack again in 1993. See Chapter 22.

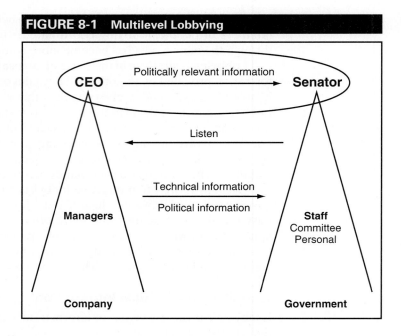

FIGURE 8-1 Multilevel Lobbying

can also be presented to the staff, which is generally quite knowledgeable and well equipped to evaluate such information.

The following are principles of effective lobbying:

- Know the institutional arenas in which the issue is addressed (e.g., Congress works through committees).
- Look for alignments of interests and explore opportunities to build coalitions.
- Time lobbying to the stages of the institutional decision-making process. (Lobby committee members, then pivotal floor members in advance of a floor vote.)
- Target key officeholders.
- Know the officeholder's interests and goals and frame messages accordingly.[4]
- Respect the officeholder and staff; in most cases they are intelligent and savvy.
- Educate but don't just talk. Listen to the officeholder and staff for information about their interests and concerns and for strategic advice about process, the preferences of other officeholders, and so on.
- Make straightforward presentations. Members of Congress are busy, understand politics well, and can see beyond window dressing. (Managers and professional lobbyists often leave a detailed written statement with members or their staff.)
- Explore compromises or concessions that might help resolve officeholders' concerns.
- Give credit to the officeholder.
- Establish access and maintain continuing relationships for the future (e.g., meet with committee staff even if there is no pending issue). Don't wait until there is a crisis.

Credibility and Relevance of Information

Information provided through lobbying must be both credible and relevant. Credibility requires an established reputation, self-evident data and analysis, or corroboration by others with different interests. A firm may have developed a reputation for providing

---

[4]Information on members of Congress and governors is provided in the *Almanac of American Politics 2008*, Barone and Cohen (2007).

technical information or for being a reliable predictor of the effects of legislative alternatives on the constituents of a government officeholder. Lobbying information that is backed by data and studies is generally more effective. Even if information is only soft and cannot be backed by conclusive data, lobbying can be effective when the interests of the firm and the government officeholder are aligned, as in the Pizza Hut example. Firms operating on the Internet used this alignment in conveying information about the possible effects of Internet taxes on growth, entrepreneurship, and employment. Information can also be credible if it can be corroborated by information provided by a party with opposing or nonaligned interests. The automakers' information about the relation between safety and vehicle size was corroborated by studies by the Insurance Institute for Highway Safety and by universities and was supported by a report by the National Academy of Sciences.

Politically relevant information is something that is not known to the government officeholders and their staffs; that is, "Tell me something I don't already know." Consider an issue that threatens the business of a firm. Officeholders understand that firms are interested in profits, and information about the effect on profits is unlikely to be helpful. For example, a regulatory issue that would lower the profits of all firms in an industry could still leave a level playing field. If a firm, however, can credibly demonstrate that constituents will be hurt, firms will fail, and jobs will be lost or new businesses not started, the message can be effective. The messages of the opponents of Internet taxation focused on this.

The provision of technical and political information through lobbying is consistent with the perspective of pluralism that public policies are determined by a competition of interests in the arenas of government institutions. Better information provided to officeholders then results in policies that in principle better serve the interests of citizens. This process can be subverted by the provision of false or manipulated information. As considered in Chapter 7, providing such information is irresponsible. Moreover, false or manipulated information is often exposed, which can damage a reputation and reduce the effectiveness of future nonmarket strategies. In addition, lobbying that is too aggressive can cause a backlash, as in the chapter case, *Responsible Lobbying?*

Access

Congressional decentralization in the early 1970s gave additional autonomy to subcommittees and thereby increased the number of influential positions substantially. Successful lobbying thus requires more than developing relationships with a few powerful committee chairpersons. A firm that interacts with Congress on a variety of issues must maintain access to several committees and their relevant subcommittees. Lobbying typically focuses on members who hold strategic positions, such as a committee or subcommittee chair, and members who may enlist the support of others. On many issues, lobbying executive branch agencies can also be important. The Department of the Treasury, for example, can have a significant effect on the outcome of a tax issue through its expertise in predicting the revenue effects of alternatives. The Department of Commerce is often a willing advocate of business interests. On a trade issue, lobbying may target the Office of the U.S. Trade Representative in addition to members of Congress. These agencies do not have direct constituents as does a member of Congress, so technical information is relatively more important than political information, although the latter is important to their political principals in Congress and the White House.

Members of Congress and executive branch officials have only limited time to meet with lobbyists and must allocate access. Those who have access possess an important asset. The key to continued access is the ability to provide politically valuable resources. Those resources include information about the effects of political alternatives on constituents, technical information pertaining to the likely consequences of alternatives, and information about the support that can be mustered for or against an alternative. Those resources also include electoral support, endorsements, and campaign contributions. Former officeholders are frequently useful to provide contacts, access, and expertise. Public Citizen reported that 43 percent of the members who left Congress from 1998 to 2005 became registered lobbyists.

Federal Express, which faces a continuing set of issues addressed in Congress, has developed access through a variety of means. As Doyle Cloud, vice president of regulatory and government affairs, explained, "We have issues constantly in Washington that affect our ability to deliver the services our customers demand as efficiently as possible."[5] In 2007 Federal Express spent $5.5 million on lobbying, including outside lobbying firms. Using outside firms is common, particularly for their contacts and established relationships with government officials. Federal Express also had on its board of directors Howard H. Baker, Jr., former Republican Senate majority leader, and George J. Mitchell, former Democratic Senate majority leader. Federal Express and its managers also were the second largest corporate campaign contributor in the 2005–2006 election cycle, contributing $1.5 million. Federal Express also made its four corporate jets available to members of Congress on a regular basis.[6]

Timing and Focus

Lobbying should be timed to the stages of the legislative process. Some interests begin early and work with members of Congress in drafting new legislation. At the subcommittee or committee stage, the appropriate focus is the committee members, particularly the chair and ranking minority member. When legislation is being drafted or marked-up, lobbying often focuses on the committee staff who do the drafting. Because majority rule governs the committee process, lobbying is also directed at those who are likely to be pivotal, as considered in Chapter 7. Larry Whitt, vice president of Pizza Hut, explained, "We focus on those on the fence."[7] Lobbying for support on the floor requires a broader effort and again focuses on pivotal members.

On an issue in conference committee, the focus is on the conferees. In the case of the tax credit for employing disadvantaged youth, the House bill provided a 2-year extension, whereas the Senate bill provided a 3-year extension. Having been successful in both chambers, Pizza Hut turned its attention to the conference committee. Peyton George, a lobbyist for Pizza Hut, stated, "I've figured out my list of who will be the conferees, and I'm trying to maintain contact with every one of [them]."[8]

Government Allies

The effectiveness of lobbying can be enhanced by developing allies in Congress. The Semiconductor Industry Association (SIA) encouraged the formation of the Congressional Support Group, a caucus composed of senators and representatives who worked to support the SIA's legislative agenda. Because many SIA members were headquartered in California, the California congressional delegation also represented its interests. Having allies in government can make a difference in the outcome of a nonmarket competition. Not all expressions of support by members of Congress, however, are credible. For example, in response to constituent or interest group pressure, members of Congress may introduce or cosponsor bills they know will not pass.

Executive branch officials may also act as allies if doing so will help them further their agency's policy objectives. The Department of Commerce may support a firm seeking to open a foreign market to U.S. goods and may take a position opposing a bill supported by organized labor.

Controls on Lobbying

The First Amendment to the Constitution establishes the right to petition government, so lobbying is a relatively unregulated activity. The principal law governing lobbying is the Lobbying Act of 1946. In *United States v. Harriss*, 347 U.S. 612 (1954) the Supreme

---

[5]*New York Times,* October 12, 1996.
[6]Although members are required to reimburse the company at the equivalent of first-class airfare, the corporate jets provide privacy and convenience to their passengers. In most cases, the flights take members of Congress to fundraising events. "Mr. Cloud said that during political seasons, Federal Express might fly a group of lawmakers about once a week." *New York Times,* October 12, 1996.
[7]*Peninsula Times Tribune,* February 23, 1986.
[8]*Wall Street Journal,* June 25, 1986.

Court interpreted the act as pertaining only to the direct lobbying of Congress by a hired lobbyist. Therefore, activities that involve a firm's own managers and Washington representatives are not considered lobbying under the law, although Washington representatives of firms may be required to register. The act also does not cover public relations and grassroots political activities or consultants and advisors.

Recent legislation has focused on disclosure. Lobbyists are required to register with the clerk of the House and the secretary of the Senate. They must file quarterly reports listing the issues and bills on which they are lobbying, the positions they support, how long the lobbying is likely to take, and details about how their efforts are funded.

In 1995 with unanimous votes by both the House and Senate, Congress passed the Lobbying Disclosure Act that requires lobbyists to report the fees they receive as well as their expenditures. The act also requires registration of those who lobby the executive branch and the staffs of Congress members. This provision was estimated to have increased the number of registered lobbyists by a factor of 3 to 10. In 2005 there were 34,785 registered lobbyists in Washington, according to the Center for Responsive Politics.

Laws as well as House and Senate rules prohibit gifts to members of Congress, including dinners and privately paid travel to conventions and events.[9] Laws prohibiting gifts also cover executive branch officials. In 1997 Tyson Foods pleaded guilty to providing the secretary of agriculture in the Clinton administration with $12,000 of illegal gratuities. Tyson paid a criminal fine of $4 million and costs of $2 million. The Robert Mondavi winery hosted a visit by the secretary that included wine and dinner. The $187 for the wine and $207 for the dinner for the secretary and his friend resulted in $150,000 in civil penalties for the winery, including paying for a public education program on bribery and gratuity laws.

The Ethics in Government Act of 1978 addressed the "revolving door" of officials who leave government service and then lobby their former employers.[10] The act restricts the contacts of former executive branch officials and regulators with their former agencies for a 2-year period and former members of Congress and congressional staff from lobbying Congress for 1 year after their terms in office end.[11] The law also prohibits officials who were involved in trade or other negotiations from lobbying their former offices for 1 year.

The interactions of business and other interest groups with regulatory agencies are limited by ex parte requirements. Public notice of meetings with regulatory officials is required unless all interested parties are present.

ELECTORAL SUPPORT

Electoral support focuses on providing electorally important resources to candidates. Unions and some interest groups endorse candidates, provide volunteer workers, staff get-out-the-vote campaigns, align with political parties, contribute to campaigns, and fund political advertising for and against candidates. Firms provide a much narrower set of electoral support, and as the PacifiCare example indicates, electoral strategies are only one component of companies' nonmarket portfolios. Moreover, business spends much more on lobbying than on electoral resources, and its contributions to charities dwarf both. Corporate contributions were approximately $300 million in the late 1990s, compared to lobbying expenditures of $3 billion and charitable contributions of $35 billion.[12] This section considers the myths and realities of corporate campaign contributions, the legal context for campaign contributions, the pattern of contributions, and the role of contributions in corporate nonmarket strategies.

---

[9]Senate rules allow gifts or meals up to $50 and up to $100 from any individual.
[10]Not all ex-government employees take jobs in business. Joan Claybrook, former head of the NHTSA, headed Public Citizen, and David Pittle, a former commissioner of the Consumer Products Safety Commission, became the technical director of Consumers Union.
[11]The prohibition extends to 2 years in areas for which they had primary responsibility.
[12]Milyo, Primo, and Grosclose (2000).

Myths and Realities of Campaign Financing

A popular impression about campaign financing is that huge amounts of money are involved, contributions buy favor from officeholders, and corporations provide the bulk of the funding. These are largely myths. Ansolabehere, de Figueirdo, and Snyder (2003) studied campaign finance and were left with quite different conclusions. Despite the popular impression, campaign expenditures by all candidates for federal office have not grown relative to the size of the economy, although expenditures in real terms have increased. For the 2005–2006 election cycle, campaign spending in federal elections was approximately $3 billion. Expressed as a percent of GDP, expenditures decreased during the 20th century until the campaign financing reforms in the mid-1970s and have been essentially constant since then.[13] The bulk of the contributions are made by individuals. In the 1999–2000 election cycle 21 million individuals contributed $2.4 billion, whereas PACs contributed $600 million. Moreover, the number of PACs declined 12 percent since 1988, and only 60 percent of the Fortune 500 firms had a PAC.

For the presidency, the Bush campaign spent $339 million and Democrats spent $465 million, including primaries in 2004. Republicans spent $579 million and Democrats $512 million on Congressional races. PAC contributions represented 34 percent, 14 percent, and 0.4 percent of contributions to House, Senate, and presidential races, respectively. Individuals contributed $1.34 billion, and PACs contributed $302 million. Fifty-six percent of the PAC contributions were to Republicans and 43 percent to Democrats.[14]

Empirical studies show little effect of campaign contributions on congressional voting, and despite examples suggesting the contrary, contributions seem to have little effect on policy. Moreover, if contributions did buy favor from elected officials, business would be expected to contribute up to the campaign limits. Average PAC contributions to campaigns, however, were $1,700 compared to a limit of $10,000 for primary and general election campaigns. Moreover, few corporate PACs contributed the maximum. Ansolabehere, de Figueirdo, and Snyder asked the rhetorical question, "Why is there so little money in politics?" Their conclusion is that there is not more money in campaigns because money has little direct effect on policy.

A second question then is why companies contribute at all. The conclusion of Ansolabehere, de Figueirdo, and Snyder was that contributions are a form of consumption or entertainment for the executives of the contributing companies. As indicated by the decline in the number of PACs, fewer companies are finding the entertainment worth the cost. Most companies that do make campaign contributions make them to gain access to members of Congress for lobbying.

Election Financing Laws

Federal election financing is regulated by the Federal Election Commission (FEC) under the Federal Election Campaign Act (FECA), as amended in 1974. Corporations are prohibited by the Tillman Act of 1907 from making contributions to the federal election campaigns of candidates. Contributions by unions were prohibited in 1943. State campaign contribution laws can vary substantially from federal law. In California, corporations may make direct contributions to state election campaigns.[15]

At the federal level, corporations, labor unions, trade and professional associations, and groups of individuals may form multicandidate PACs for the purpose of soliciting contributions and distributing them to candidates or expending them independently in election campaigns.[16] A major turning point for PAC activity was a 1976 FEC ruling that employees as well as shareholders could contribute to corporate PACs.

---

[13]Spending for the 2000 presidential election increased, however.

[14]The data were through December 14, 2004.

[15]For information on state contribution limits, see www.ncal.org/programs/legismgt.about.ContriLimits.htm.

[16]The FEC designates six categories of PACs: corporate, labor, nonconnected, trade/membership/health, cooperative, and corporation without stock. The organization and operation of PACs are discussed by Handler and Mulkern (1982).

Most contributions to corporate PACs are now made by employees, primarily management, and contributions must be voluntary.[17]

Unions collect funds for political contributions through dues, but members cannot be forced to contribute to the union's political activities. The Supreme Court has held that individuals may not be compelled to support political positions they oppose. Applied to unions, this means that members and covered nonmembers can be forced to pay only that fraction of the dues used for collective bargaining purposes.[18]

Campaign financing law distinguishes between expenditures in electoral campaigns and contributions to those campaigns. In *Buckley v. Valeo*, 424 U.S. 1 (1976), the Supreme Court ruled that any limit on campaign expenditures threatens the freedoms of speech and association and thus violates the First Amendment. This decision also overturned state laws limiting campaign spending.[19] As a result of this decision, candidates are not restricted in their personal expenditures. In 2000 Jon Corzine (D-NJ) spent $60.2 million of his own funds to win a Senate seat by 3 percent of the vote. Hillary Clinton (D-NY) raised $40.8 million to finance her 2006 New York Senate race.

Although expenditures are not limited, limits on contributions to candidates' campaigns have been upheld by the Supreme Court. The court reasoned that such limits represent less of an abridgment of First Amendment rights than limits on expenditures.[20] Contributions to a candidate's campaign are called *hard money* contributions and are strictly limited, as indicated in Table 8-2.

Violations of campaign contribution regulations can lead to substantial penalties. A prominent lobbyist was convicted of making illegal campaign contributions to the same secretary of agriculture mentioned previously and was fined $150,000 and ordered to write an essay on the election laws. The essay was distributed to the members of the American League of Lobbyists.[21]

In 2002 Congress enacted the Bipartisan Campaign Reform Act (McCain-Feingold) to restrict fundraising and spending by political party committees outside federal limits and to restrict issue ads mentioning candidates. The FEC, however, did not ban "527" groups, although it did fine Swift Boat Veterans for Truth, the League of Conservation Voters, and MoveOn.org for failing to register as "political committees" that would be subject to contribution limits.

The Pattern of Campaign Contributions

Campaign contributions are an important aspect of electoral politics, if not of nonmarket strategies of business. PAC contributions constitute, however, a relatively small

TABLE 8-2	Hard Money Contribution Limits (2007–2008)				
Contributor	To Candidate Committee (per election)	To National Party (per year)	To State and Local Parties	To PAC or Other Political Committee	Aggregate Total
Individual	$2,300*	$28,500*	$10,000	$5,000	$108,200*
PAC	$5,000	$15,000	$10,000	$5,000	None

Note: *Amounts are adjusted for inflation in odd years.

---

[17]See Sabato (1984) for a study of PACs. See www.opensecrets.org and www.fec.gov for data on campaign contributions.
[18]In 1998 the Supreme Court held that federal labor law permitted dues collected from nonunion workers in the private sector to be used only for collective bargaining purposes. In 1986 it had made a similar ruling for public employees. In 1991 the Court extended this principle in ruling that public employee union members cannot be forced to support lobbying and other political activities.
[19]In 1998 the Supreme Court declined to review this decision.
[20]Independent expenditures on campaigns were held to be immune to restrictions in *FEC v. National Conservative Political Action Committee*, 470 U.S. 480 (1985), but in *FEC v. Massachusetts Citizens for Life*, 479 U.S. 238 (1986) the Supreme Court stated that restrictions on expenditures by for-profit corporations would be upheld.
[21]*New York Times*, September 29, 1998.

percent of campaign financing. Corporations accounted for 35 percent of total PAC contributions in the 1997–1998 election cycle.[22]

PAC contributions are primarily made to incumbents, and because a substantial majority of incumbents were Democrats until 1995, a majority of PAC contributions had gone to Democrats. When the Republicans became the majority party in both the House and Senate in 1995, PAC contributions shifted to the Republicans. When the Democrats won majorities in the House and Senate in 2006, contributions shifted again. Corporate PACs contribute slightly more to Republicans than to Democrats. Labor PACs contribute almost exclusively to Democrats.[23] The largest PACs contributing to candidate campaigns are mainly not corporate but are formed by realtors, beer wholesalers, homebuilders, trial lawyers, unions, and auto dealers

Many PACs have higher direct expenditures on issues and candidates than contributions to candidate campaigns. In the 2005–2006 congressional election cycle the PACs with the greatest total expenditures were EMILY'S List, MoveOn.org, Service Employees International Union, American Federation of Teachers, and the American Federation of State, County, and Municipal Employees. The objective of many of the largest spenders is to affect election outcomes rather than to seek access.

Purposes of Campaign Contributions

Campaign contributions are made for three basic purposes. The first is to affect the outcomes of elections, the second is to obtain access to present or future officeholders, and the third is to obtain services. Most contributions by individuals are made for the first purpose, as are the contributions by labor unions. Business, however, takes a more pragmatic approach and tends to make contributions to those most likely to win, largely for the purpose of facilitating access for lobbying. The fact that a high percentage of contributions are made to incumbents reflects this. As former Senator Rudy Boschwitz (R-MN) commented, "All they're [corporate PACs] doing is buying a bunch of access and playing the damn thing like a horse race. They don't do it philosophically. They do it on who's going to win."[24] The role of campaign contributions in providing access was explained in a deposition by former Senator Alan Cranston (D-CA) in the "Keating five" ethics inquiry: "The only thing I will grant is that the person who makes a contribution has a better chance to get access than someone who does not. All senators know you may get ten, twenty, thirty, fifty phone calls a day, people trying to reach you, and you cannot answer all those phone calls. So you answer those from those whose names you recognize and who you think you have some obligation to at least hear out."[25]

An access theory of campaign contributions predicts that the more valuable the services the candidate can provide, the more an interest group will be willing to contribute. This suggests that access to those members of Congress who hold strategic positions should be more valuable than access to those members who do not. In particular, it implies that senior members, and particularly the chairs of committees and subcommittees, should receive more contributions than other members.[26] The data support this prediction. Similarly, members of the committees that deal with legislation affecting an industry may receive contributions from the firms in those industries. In addition, this theory predicts that the bulk of contributions are made to incumbents. In the 1999–2000 election cycle incumbents received 87 percent of PAC contributions. In part this reflected the incumbency advantage, and in part it reinforced that advantage.

Studies by Hall and Wayman (1990) and Wu (1994) indicate that another purpose of campaign contributions is to develop allies and encourage them to work for

---

[22]Milyo, Primo, and Groseclose (2000).
[23]Organized labor also provides substantial in-kind support in addition to campaign contributions. Unions provide volunteer workers who staff phone banks, ring doorbells, deliver campaign materials, and help register voters.
[24]*New York Times,* September 26, 1988.
[25]*New York Times,* November 30, 1990.
[26]See Kroszner and Stratmann (1998) for a study of financial services PACs and their contributions to committees.

legislation that both the member and the contributor support. Thus, campaign contributions could affect legislative outcomes by mobilizing congressional efforts on behalf of legislation rather than by directly affecting the votes of the recipients.

Many firms would like not to make political contributions but believe that they are caught in a prisoners' dilemma. That is, if no other interest group were to make contributions, an interest group that made a contribution could be important to the candidate and might see benefits flow from its contribution. Conversely, if many firms and interest groups contribute, a noncontributor might be at a disadvantage, possibly suffering a loss of access. Contributing, then, is a dominant strategy, resulting in a situation in which interest groups contribute, with their contributions then yielding little or no benefits. All could be better off not contributing.

GRASSROOTS AND CONSTITUENCY CAMPAIGNS

Grassroots campaigns are based on the connection between constituents and their elected representatives. Grassroots campaigns are often a component of a broader representation strategy and are often tactical in nature. Labor unions, community interest groups, environmental groups, the National Rifle Association, and many other interest groups engage in grassroots nonmarket activity intended to demonstrate the breadth and intensity of their members' interests on issues.[27] Beginning in the 1980s, firms and industries adopted this strategy and applied it effectively to issues on their nonmarket agendas. The grassroots campaign by Toshiba (Chapter 7) was effective because it revealed the potential costs to employees, suppliers, and customers. Grassroots campaigns have become sufficiently pervasive that a grassroots lobbying industry has developed to organize the campaigns. The industry includes firms that, for example, translate data by postal zip codes into congressional districts. This allows shareholder, retiree, supplier, and customer lists to be organized by district to target members of Congress. In the PacifiCare example, the company organized patients by congressional district. Grassroots activity has also become increasingly specialized. Some political consulting firms now provide "grass-tops" services: They recruit prominent citizens to lobby their representatives or senators on issues.

Mobilization

Members of interest groups and stakeholders of firms must be mobilized for effective grassroots action. Mobilization involves providing information to stakeholders on the significance of an issue and helping to reduce their costs of participation. Letter-writing campaigns are the least expensive grassroots activity. They are also difficult to implement because constituents often are unwilling to spend the time to write a letter or send a telegram. Volume can be generated through the use of preprinted letters, postcards, or e-mail, but recipients know that postcards generally do not reflect the same intensity of preferences as handwritten letters. Although handwritten letters have a greater impact than postcards, there is a trade-off with volume. Some congressional offices sort and count mail by issue and distinguish between letters and postcards. Others, however, just weigh the postcards. In a survey of congressional staff Lord (2000) found that letter writing and telephone calls had the greatest effect and petitions and mass-mailing responses the least effect.

A more effective means of demonstrating grassroots preferences is to have constituents go to Washington or a state capital to lobby. Labor unions developed this tactic by organizing "bus-ins" in which busloads of union members converged on Washington to lobby and engage in other political activities. "Fly-ins" are the modern counterpart of bus-ins. For example, overseas U.S. firms participate in the American Chamber of Commerce (ACC). The Asian chapters meet annually to discuss a variety of governmental and nonmarket issues pertaining to international trade policy, government relations, and U.S. policy pertaining to foreign operations. Members of the ACC

---

[27]See Fowler and Shaiko (1987) for an analysis of the grassroots activities of environmental organizations.

chapters then fly to Washington to conduct a "knock-around" in which they knock on as many doors as possible to explain their positions on issues.

Grassroots activities may be directed at government officeholders, as in the case of a fly-in, or they may be directed at constituents. The former are components of informational strategies and are a form of lobbying. The latter are components of representation strategies and are intended to develop public support for an alternative. As the PacifiCare example indicates, the health care industry has used this strategy effectively. Constituent-based grassroots strategies are frequently accompanied by mass advertising, Internet, or e-mail campaigns to inform the public and officeholders and to recruit participants, often by giving a toll-free number they can call for more information. The Internet has become an important force in generating grassroots actions such as letter writing and e-mailing members of Congress. The activist organization MoveOn.org sent out an e-mail appeal for $25,000 to pay for an advertisement, and it received $400,000 in response. The Internet now is an important vehicle for raising funds for both public and private politics.

Business Grassroots Campaigns

A business grassroots strategy involves corporate stakeholders as identified by the rent chain. These stakeholders can include employees, shareholders, retirees whose pensions depend on company performance, franchisees, suppliers, and in some cases customers. Not all constituencies are equally easy to organize and mobilize, however.[28] Shareholders and pensioners may be mobilized to some extent, but alerting them to a potentially serious issue may cause them to sell their shares.

To the extent that their interests on an issue are aligned with those of the firm, employees may be relatively easy to include in a grassroots program. Mobilizing employees can generate criticism, however. In the last days of the Clinton administration's attempt to restructure the U.S. health care system, IBM asked its employees to oppose bills mandating employer-provided health insurance. Some employees complained about the request, and IBM was publicly criticized for changing its practice of not involving employees in political issues.

More recently, however, companies have begun to embrace grassroots strategies involving employees. Companies such as International Paper and Sun Microsystems make information on policy issues and voting records of members of Congress available to their employees on company Web sites. International Paper then encourages employees to write their representatives on policy issues and may recommend a candidate to employees requesting such information.[29] Cigna urged its employees to write members of Congress on tort reform legislation in 2004.

Some firms also take positions on ballot initiatives and referenda. Silicon Valley firms urged their employees to vote no on Proposition 211 that would make it easier for plaintiffs to win securities fraud lawsuits. In the same election a number of companies, including Atlantic Richfield, Hewlett-Packard, Pacific Gas & Electric, and Southern California Edison, publicly opposed Proposition 209, which would ban affirmative action in public contracts, education, and employment.

Suppliers and customers are frequently mobilized when their rents are affected. The grassroots campaign organized by Toshiba to weaken sanctions resulting from its illegal sales to the Soviet Union relied heavily on its U.S. production base, its suppliers, and its customers. Toshiba's U.S. production provided a link between possible sanctions and jobs at its suppliers. Similarly, Toshiba had little difficulty enlisting the support of its customers, many of whom depended on its products.

The Effectiveness of Grassroots Programs

The effectiveness of a grassroots program depends on the supply-side factors considered in Chapter 6 as well as on the credibility of the program itself. The larger the number

---

[28]See Keim (1985) and Baysinger, Keim, and Zeithaml (1985) for an analysis of corporate grassroots programs.
[29]*Wall Street Journal,* September 3, 2004.

of participants in a grassroots program and the more extensive their coverage of political jurisdictions, the more effective it is likely to be. These factors determine the amount of pressure that can be transmitted through the constituency connection. This pressure, however, must be credible. The following two examples, both of which involved attempts to defeat legislation, illustrate the credibility dimension of a grassroots campaign.

Legislation was introduced in Congress to require financial institutions to withhold taxes on the interest and dividend income of savers and trust fund beneficiaries. Supporters of the proposal included Treasury officials and members of Congress concerned with the federal budget deficit. In addition to the considerable administrative expense to financial institutions, the legislation would reduce the short-term cash flow to savers and beneficiaries, who would receive lower quarterly payments as taxes were withheld. The financial institutions were in a position to mobilize a dispersed constituency of savers to oppose the bill. Their grassroots campaign generated over 22 million letters and postcards, and the interest-withholding issue died.

In 1987 the Pharmaceutical Manufacturers Association (PMA) campaigned against the adoption of a catastrophic illness program for the elderly. Pharmaceutical companies were concerned that federal budget pressures would lead to the substitution of generic for brand-name drugs and perhaps to price controls, or reimbursement limits, on drugs. The PMA hired a political consulting firm to conduct a $3 million grassroots campaign opposing the program. Even though the campaign generated over 100,000 contacts between constituents and members of Congress, it was largely ineffective. Congress members knew that their constituents did not understand the program under consideration. Moreover, it may have worsened relations with members of Congress. As Senator Lloyd Bentsen (D-TX) said, "I know the difference between grassroots and Astroturf."

In his survey of congressional staff Lord (2000) found that corporate constituency activity was relatively more effective in influencing how members of Congress voted on legislation, and professional and executive lobbying were relatively more important in influencing the content of legislation. The effect of constituency actions was greater in the House than the Senate presumably because members of the House face elections every 2 years. Among the corporate constituents, employee contacts with staff and members had the largest effect.

COALITION BUILDING

Coalition building is an important component of many nonmarket strategies. Coalitions are the principal means of forging a majority from a collection of minorities. Business coalitions are of three types: peak organizations, trade associations, and ad hoc coalitions. Peak associations emphasize issues that affect more than one industry, trade associations represent a single industry, and ad hoc coalitions tend to be issue specific. Trade associations and individual firms also participate on issues addressed by peak organizations and trade associations, respectively.

Many of the most effective coalitions are ad hoc and issue specific, as in the case of the Daylight Saving Time Coalition. Some are not formal coalitions but instead are alignments of interests, as in the case of the Daylight Saving Time Coalition and the RP Foundation Fighting Blindness considered in Chapter 6.[30] At times, two interest groups may find themselves working on the same side of one issue and opposite sides of another. Automobile manufacturers, dealers, and the United Auto Workers (UAW) opposed increases in fuel economy standards, but the automakers and the UAW were on opposite sides of the North American Free Trade Agreement, and automakers and dealers were on opposite sides of the lemon law discussed in Chapter 7.

Peak Associations

Peak, or umbrella, organizations include firms from a number of industries and thus represent a range of interests. In the United States these organizations include the U.S.

---

[30]See Salisbury (1992) for an analysis of interest group alignments.

Chamber of Commerce, the National Association of Manufacturers, the Business Roundtable, the American Business Conference, the National Federation of Independent Business, and the National Small Business Association, among others. These organizations support issues such as liability reform, tax reductions, trade liberalization, and regulatory reform. The heterogeneity of the interests of their members and their desire to maintain a reasonable internal consensus, however, limits the scope of the issues on which they act. Consequently, individual firms do not rely solely on peak organizations to represent their interests but instead participate in trade associations and often take independent nonmarket action.[31]

As an example of an umbrella organization, the Chamber of Commerce is the oldest general business organization in the United States and has a budget of over $70 million. The Chamber focuses on tax, labor, trade, and regulatory issues. An important source of strength for the chamber is its 3,000 state and local chambers, which give it complete coverage of congressional districts. To generate political pressure, it organized over 2,700 Congressional Action committees, composed of local businesspeople who have personal contacts with members of Congress. The chamber also had a public interest lobby, the Grassroots Action Information Network, that conducted grassroots campaigns. The Chamber's National Chamber Alliance for Politics provided electoral support to candidates.

The National Federation of Independent Business (NFIB) focuses on the concerns of small business. The influence of small business should not be underestimated. Although individual small businesses may have limited resources, collectively their resources are large. The NFIB, for example, has 600,000 members and offices in Washington and every state capital, which gives it comprehensive coverage of political jurisdictions. It has been effective in lobbying and mobilizing small firms by reducing their cost of participation in collective action. The NFIB worked effectively for President Bush's tax cut plan. About 85 percent of NFIB members pay their business taxes through their individual tax returns, and the tax plan allowed the immediate expensing of an additional $75,000 of equipment. Small business has also been effective in obtaining exemptions from certain regulations. Its effectiveness is strengthened by the access provided by the small business committees in the House and Senate.

Trade Associations

Trade associations serve a variety of market and nonmarket functions.[32] Market functions include the collection of market and industry statistics, the development of technical standards, and in some cases research. Nonmarket functions center on reducing the cost of collective action, particularly by reducing the costs of information acquisition. Trade associations also monitor legislative activity, regulatory rule-making activities, and administrative actions. In the Chapter 2 case, *Exclusive Resorts: Entrepreneurial Positioning and Nonmarket Defense,* the American Resort Development Association worked at the state level for constructive re-regulation of the timeshare and vacation club industry. Trade associations also reduce the cost of lobbying, grassroots programs, and other political strategies.

The Pharmaceutical Research and Manufacturers Association (PhRMA), with a 2004 budget of $150 million, allocated $72.7 million for lobbying Congress, $4.9 million for lobbying the FDA, and $48.7 million for advocacy aimed at state governments. Funds were also allocated to fight a union-led campaign for lower drug prices in Ohio, support policy research, hire economists to discuss pharmaceutical issues, oppose the Canadian discount drug system, fund public advocacy, and foster ties with minority congressional caucuses and medical organizations.[33] Small firms are more likely than large firms to rely on trade associations.

---

[31]Peak organizations are more important in a number of countries other than in the United States. The *Keidanren* in Japan and the peak organizations in Germany and other European countries are quite influential.
[32]See Lynn and McKeown (1988) for an analysis of trade associations.
[33]*New York Times,* June 1, 2003.

Ad Hoc Coalitions

Ad hoc coalitions are interests that join together on specific nonmarket issues. High-tech companies, public accounting firms, underwriters, and others that had been subjected to frivolous securities fraud lawsuits formed the Uniform Standards Coalition to work for federal legislation requiring security fraud lawsuits to be filed in federal rather than state courts. The Coalition was successful, and after legislation was enacted in 1999, the Coalition disbanded.

Although firms in the same industry are often aligned on issues, they may be opposed on some nonmarket issues. In 1992 British Airways announced it would invest $750 million in USAir, forming a global alliance. Robert L. Crandall, chairman of American Airlines, criticized the investment on the grounds that the arrangement provided the United Kingdom increased access to the U.S. market, while U.S. airlines remained restricted in their access to the U.K. market. Crandall was subsequently joined by the CEOs of United Airlines, Delta Air Lines, and Federal Express. USAir countered their lobbying with a grassroots letter-writing campaign by its employees, but the relentless lobbying by the four airlines caused British Airways to cancel the investment and alliance.[34]

The alignment of interests on some issues can be broad. The clean air legislation pending in Congress during the 1980s led to the formation of the Clean Air Working Group, which included 2,000 businesses and trade associations. Aligned with the group were labor unions representing auto, construction, and other workers. This allowed the opponents of stringent legislation to speak from a relatively unified position on the 1990 amendments to the Clean Air Act.

Coalitions and Consensus

The alignment of interests not only affects who participates in a coalition but also the bargaining within a coalition. When interests are closely aligned, as in the case of the Uniform Standards Coalition, bargaining is relatively easy because disagreements are likely to be small. On an issue where interests are poorly aligned, the bargaining can be more complex and lengthy.

On some issues, disagreements among members of a coalition may be irreconcilable. In 1999 eBay and eight other Internet service providers, including Amazon.com, America Online, DoubleClick, and Yahoo!, formed NetCoalition.com. The coalition's mission was to serve as "the collective public policy voice of the world's leading Internet companies. . . ." Within a few months, however, the collective voice split over the issue of database protection.[35] eBay backed legislation to protect its databases, and other members backed rival legislation that, according to eBay, would provide little if any protection. eBay withdrew from the coalition.

Jet ski or personal watercraft (PWC) manufacturers faced a host of nonmarket issues related to safety, pollution, noise, and disruption of fishing, canoeing, and other water sports. One strategy used by the PWC manufacturers was to argue that any new regulations on jet skis should also apply to boats. The purpose was to force boat manufacturers to oppose the new regulations. PWC manufacturers and boat producers belonged to the National Marine Manufacturers Association (NMMA), which worked against the proposed regulations. Genmar, the world's largest independent boat manufacturer, however, objected to being aligned with the PWC manufacturers and quit the NMMA in protest.[36]

Trade associations can be effective on those nonmarket issues that have similar impacts on their members. In those cases a trade association can effectively speak with one voice before congressional committees, regulatory agencies, and executive branch agencies. As the jet ski example indicates, however, on matters that affect members quite differently, consensus may not be possible. The pharmaceutical politics example illustrates this even in the case of an industry with relatively homogeneous interests.

---

[34]The following year British Airways invested $340 million in USAir, but by 1996 the alliance had disintegrated.
[35]See the Chapter 13 case, *eBay and Database Protection.*
[36]The Genmar chairman stated, "I am convinced the PWC industry will ultimately force new regulations and restrictions on the boating industry that will cause irreparable damage to us all due to their product's potential dangers and the abuse of our lakes and rivers." Genmar press release, November 19, 1997.

EXAMPLE

Pharmaceutical Politics

The Food and Drug Administration (FDA) required extensive laboratory and clinical testing that could take from 5 to 10 years or more, and many millions of dollars, before a new drug was approved for sale. Because a drug is patented before testing begins, a new drug might have only a few years of patent protection before generic drug manufacturers could introduce a chemically identical drug. The companies retained some protection because generic drugs also had to be tested, which could take up to 5 years to complete even though their active ingredients were chemically identical to the already approved drugs. Furthermore, a federal appeals court had ruled that testing by a generic drug manufacturer could not begin until the patent on the original drug had expired.

The Generic Pharmaceutical Industry Association (GPIA) sought legislation requiring the FDA to establish simplified approval procedures for generic drugs, requiring proof only that a generic drug was biochemically identical to an already approved drug. Legislation to expedite the approval of generic drugs was introduced in both the House and the Senate, and it received considerable support. Changes in the generic drug approval process would have a major impact on the brand-name drug companies because patents on over 150 drugs with annual sales of $4 billion either had recently expired or were about to expire.

The Pharmaceutical Manufacturers Association (PMA), representing the makers of brand-name patented drugs, opposed the legislation, arguing that the revisions in FDA testing requirements would reduce their incentives to develop new drugs. This, it was argued, would result in fewer drugs being discovered, which in turn would reduce the quality of health care.

The PMA sought outright defeat of the legislation. Once it became apparent that this objective could not be realized, it reached a compromise in negotiations among the GPIA and the chairpersons of the cognizant congressional committees. The compromise would extend patent protection for certain brand-name drugs and speed the approval process for generic drugs.

Consensus on the compromise could not be sustained within the PMA, however. Eleven companies were furious with the compromise and succeeded in having the head of the PMA and its chief lobbyist fired. The CEOs of the companies, including American Home Products, Hoffman-LaRoche, and Merck, then lobbied intensely over the next few weeks to strike from the compromise bill the provision that would speed the approval of generic drugs.[1] Their efforts failed, however, and they were only able to obtain a provision pertaining to exclusive-marketing rights for nonpatented drugs.

---

[1]*Dun's Business Month,* January 1986, p. 36.

TESTIMONY

Companies testify before regulatory agencies, congressional committees, administrative agencies, and courts. In a regulatory setting, *testimony* is important not only because the information presented can affect regulatory decisions, but also because it creates a record that may serve as a basis for judicial review. Many regulatory rulings are challenged in the courts, and the courts will at times consider both substantive and procedural challenges to a ruling. Testimony thus not only must stand up to cross-examination during the hearing, but it should also provide a basis for a possible court action.

Congressional hearings serve a variety of purposes ranging from issue identification to information provision. A hearing provides an opportunity to present a position that may be backed by a policy study conducted by a firm, association, or coalition. Testimony of firms and interest groups, however, is often preceded by lobbying, so for many members of Congress hearings provide little new information.

Hearings are not always held to obtain information. Some are held to generate publicity and mobilize support for a particular position. For example, trial lawyers and consumer groups have opposed liability reform, and one of their tactics is to bring accident victims to congressional hearings to testify against limits on liability awards. Hearings can also be managed to promote the side of the issue supported by the committee chair. Testimony on the chair's side of an issue may be scheduled in the morning so that television stations will be able to prepare the story and edit the tape in time for the evening news. Testimony on the other side may be scheduled late in the afternoon, when it is too late for the evening news. By the next day, that testimony is often too old for television. Hearings thus can provide a stage on which a committee chair can play out a story to advance a policy interest or cater to constituents.

Stephen Breyer (1982, pp. 317–340), now a Supreme Court justice, gave a detailed description of the 1974 oversight hearings on regulation of the airline industry. Breyer, who then served on the committee staff, characterized the hearings as "drama" to be orchestrated. In preparation for hearings, the committee staff prepared a script that included an opening statement for the chair and a set of questions to ask each witness. Because the chair already knew much of what the witness would say, the chair was able to direct the dialogue. Breyer also discussed the tactics used by members of Congress in their questioning of witnesses. One tactic was to ask a zinger—a question whose only possible answer would support the Congress member's own position. As an example, in the foreign leasing example in Chapter 6, Representative Pickle asked the general manager of Boeing, "Are we not subsidizing the competition of our own foreign carriers? [international airlines]"[37]

PUBLIC ADVOCACY

On some issues, particularly those characterized by majoritarian politics, firms use *public advocacy* to communicate directly with the public. The health care industry demonstrated the effectiveness of mass communication with its "Harry and Louise" advertisements, raising alarms about the Clinton administration's plans to restructure the health care industry. The ads turned the public against the administration's plan, contributing to its collapse. As indicated in the PacifiCare example, the industry continued with this approach in its criticism of the Clinton administration's patients' bill of rights.

During the political activity on the Clinton administration's health care restructuring proposal, pharmaceutical firms concerned about possible price controls and mandated rebates adopted a nonmarket strategy that included a communication component. The industry's basic strategy was to emphasize the discovery of new drugs and the incentives needed for research and development. The industry association added "Research" to its name and undertook lobbying and public advocacy with the message that the discovery of new drugs would be jeopardized by price controls.

Several major pharmaceutical companies also formed a coalition, Rx Partners, that conducted media tours in 65 cities and hosted a series of breakfasts for members of Congress. Individual firms also took action. Several companies conducted public education campaigns similar to those of Rx Partners. Bristol Myers held 350 meetings with community groups and lobbied extensively in Congress. Several companies conducted advertising campaigns that emphasized the discovery of new drugs. They also stressed the beneficial therapeutic value of existing drugs, which, invariably, some member of Congress or a relative had used. As the threat of price controls dissipated, the industry turned to advertisements containing personal testimony on the benefits of pharmaceuticals.

How a message is framed can be important when communicating with the public and government officeholders. An example is provided by the plan developed by AT&T and the Federal Communications Commission (FCC) to lower long-distance telephone rates toward the cost of service. The reduction was to be accomplished by introducing usage-independent access charges to be paid monthly by residential and business customers for long-distance service. The FCC and AT&T chose the term "access charge" because the monthly charge would cover the costs of the connection, or access, to the interstate telephone network. The reaction to the plan shocked the FCC and AT&T. Customers, consumer groups, and politicians complained about having to pay for access they might not use. The uproar nearly resulted in legislation barring the plan. As the FCC scaled back the plan, it renamed the charges "end-user charges." The new term implied "use" and did not serve as a lightning rod. The damage had already been done, however.

---

[37]Hearing, Committee on Ways and Means, House of Representatives, Washington, DC, June 8, 1983, p. 212.

JUDICIAL ACTIONS

Judicial actions pertain not only to those cases in which a firm finds itself the defendant but also to those in which it initiates legal action as a component of a nonmarket strategy. Judicial actions are taken in state and federal courts, which are governed by statutory and common law. Judicial actions are also taken in quasi-judicial arenas, such as those of regulatory and administrative agencies, which are governed by administrative law. Judicial strategies are used to enforce rights, obtain damages for breach of contract, and address unfair competitive practices under the antitrust laws. Many firms aggressively protect their intellectual property by filing patent and copyright infringement lawsuits.[38]

Rambus, Inc., a chip designer, has used litigation as a means of forcing companies to pay it royalties on its patents. It has filed numerous lawsuits in the United States and other countries against companies it claimed had used its patented designs in memory chips. In 2008 it won a court case that allowed it to obtain $133.4 million from Hynix Semiconductors and to pursue lawsuits against Nanya Technology, Micron Technology, and other chip manufacturers, which could result in royalty income between $700 million and $10 billion. Rambus' share price increased 39 percent after the verdict.

Lawsuits are also used to deter competitors from taking certain actions and to caution the media or regulatory or administrative agencies. Firms frequently file lawsuits against regulatory agencies, alleging an inadequate basis in the record for their rule making. General Motors filed suit against the Department of Transportation because of its preliminary decision to recall GM pickup trucks with side-mounted gas tanks.[39] The secretary of transportation backed down and did not order a recall. On the other side, environmental and activist groups often file lawsuits against agencies for not adequately enforcing the laws.

A judicial strategy can also be used to open markets. The coalition working for the direct to consumers sale of wine via the Internet used litigation to overturn protectionism by states. Florida, Michigan, New York, North Carolina, Texas, and Virginia allowed intrastate direct sales by wineries within their states but prohibited interstate direct sales. The coalition filed lawsuits to overturn the ban, but the Court of Appeals upheld the ban.[40] The Supreme Court agreed to hear an appeal by the coalition, and in *Heald v. Engler* (2005) the Supreme Court overturned the Court of Appeals and ruled that the Constitution does not allow the discriminatory treatment of intrastate and interstate direct shipment of wine.

Judicial action, particularly in the courts, can be costly. The Department of Justice's antitrust suit against AT&T took 8 years before it was settled out of court with the breakup of the Bell system. It is estimated to have cost AT&T $360 million and the government $15 million.[41] In arenas governed by administrative law, cases, such as petitions to the International Trade Commission for relief from injury by imports, often proceed more expeditiously and at lower cost because of legislatively imposed time limits. Although lawsuits can be extremely costly, awards can also be high. As a fledgling company, MCI successfully sued AT&T on antitrust grounds, and its award was used to finance its expansion. MCI also filed a number of other lawsuits against both AT&T and the FCC seeking the opportunity to provide expanded telecommunications services. The lawsuits helped open the telecommunications market to competition.

In 1998 PepsiCo filed an antitrust lawsuit against the Coca-Cola Company alleging that it used exclusionary practices and abused its dominant position in the fountain-dispensed segment of the soft drink market. Most restaurant chains had avoided carrying Pepsi because PepsiCo owned their competitors: Pizza Hut, Taco Bell, and Kentucky Fried Chicken. In 1997, however, PepsiCo spun off its restaurants and began to aggressively pursue the fountain business, which accounted for 27 percent of soft drink sales.

---

[38]See Chapter 12.
[39]See the Chapter 3 case, *General Motors: Like a Rock? (A).*
[40]See Wiseman and Ellig (2004).
[41]Shipper and Jennings (1984, p. 115).

The lawsuit alleged that Coca-Cola's exclusive contracts with independent distributors hindered PepsiCo's efforts to win the accounts of restaurant chains, since those distributors would not distribute to restaurants that would like to carry Pepsi. Coca-Cola said that the lawsuit "smacks of desperation."[42]

Regulatory and administrative law channels may be used for a variety of purposes, including to protect rights, handicap a competitor, or gain a direct advantage. When the FDA attempted to streamline its rules for approving generic drugs, the brand-name pharmaceutical companies filed lawsuits challenging its authority to do so. Thwarted in this administrative channel, the generic drug companies took their cause to Congress, as the "Pharmaceutical Politics" example indicates.

ORGANIZING FOR NONMARKET EFFECTIVENESS

Firms that expect to be involved in issues addressed in government arenas must anticipate rather than simply react to developments. Consequently, they need to organize and be prepared for action. It is essential to monitor issues, and for many firms this means full-time representation in Washington and in the capitals of key states. For other firms, associations can be a cost-effective means of providing intelligence, although this may not be sufficient if the firm's interests differ from those the association represents. Most large firms also have a government affairs department that provides expertise and monitors the development of issues. A department may include lawyers, communications experts, former government officials, lobbyists, and analysts.[43]

Washington offices serve as the eyes and ears of firms. They provide information on developing issues and are a locus of expertise about issues, institutions, and officeholders. Because nonmarket issues are often episodic in nature, many firms on occasion engage the services of political consulting firms, Washington law firms, or public relations firms. Similarly, lobbyists may be hired for a specific issue. The size of a firm's permanent staff thus is determined relative to the cost and effectiveness of outside alternatives.

Because lobbying is the centerpiece of most firms' interactions with government, most employ lobbyists who are either political professionals or experienced managers responsible for presenting the firm's concerns to government officials. Their responsibilities typically include maintaining relationships with members of Congress, executive branch officials, and government agencies. Access is a necessary condition for lobbying, so many firms make a practice of maintaining contact with those members of Congress in whose districts they have their operations and with the committees that regularly deal with issues on their nonmarket agendas. Firms also provide training for their managers who are involved in nonmarket issues. That training often emphasizes sensitivity to the possible public reaction to the firm's activities and the development of personal skills for participating effectively in government arenas.

DEVELOPING NONMARKET CAPABILITIES

Companies develop capabilities in implementing nonmarket strategies. Google's most important nonmarket capability is the credibility it had earned from its success in Internet technology and applications. The public and governments listened when Google spoke not because of its power but because of its success. More was required, however, to deal with the myriad of issues it faced and those that would arise in the future. In 2005 it opened an office in Washington with one employee, a lawyer responsible for intellectual property issues. Alan Davidson of Google commented, "Washington and its policy debates are important. We can't ignore them."[44] As Google's nonmarket agenda

---

[42]The lawsuit was dismissed in 2000.

[43]A detailed description of the organization of a Washington office in the heyday of the politics of the oil industry is provided in the case "Gulf Oil Corporation: Public Affairs and the Washington Office" in Fox (1982, pp. 287–306).

[44]*Washington Post*, June 20, 2007. See the Chapter 1 case, *The Nonmarket Environment of Google*, and the Chapter 15 case, *Google in China*.

grew, its executives began to make Washington a regular stop on their trips. Its executives testified before Congress on expanding the number of highly educated workers allowed to immigrate to the United States and on the future of videos on the Internet. Google also was dealing with the human rights and censorship issue, intellectual property, and telecommunication regulation regarding possible Internet capacity policy.

As the number of nonmarket issues it faced grew, it decided to develop its nonmarket capability and to do it by building on its technology expertise. It increased its staff in Washington and began interacting with members of the government. Adam Kovacevich of its Washington office explained, "We're trying to approach government in a 'Googley' way—some things we're doing are traditional and some aren't."[45] One approach was to show members of Congress and their staffers how they could use Google applications in their constituency activities and election campaigns. Jamie Brown, a Google lobbyist, explained, "The vast majority of my time is spent educating people about the company and its economic footprint." One of her principal activities was to conduct "Google 101" seminars to educate congressional staffers about the company. Robert Boofstin of Google said, "We're more and more under the microscope. It would be disingenuous to say we weren't trying to have influence with decision makers and people who try to influence them."[46]

In July 2007 YouTube and CNN hosted a debate among Democratic presidential candidates. Google took the opportunity to demonstrate its products to the candidates' campaign staffs. Google argued that its ads were a cost-effective way to reach voters. Google also created a space called "You Choose" on YouTube where presidential candidates could post videos.

In 2006 Google established NetPAC, a political action committee, and explained, "We started this NetPAC in order to be able to support officeholders and candidates who share our vision of promoting and preserving the Internet as a free and open platform for information, communication and innovation. Google has thrived thanks to the opportunities of the free market so we believe it is important to look at policymakers as they make decisions that impact our users and business."[47]

Google sought to emphasize policy over politics and opened its Public Policy Blog to advocate its policy positions.[48] "We're seeking to do public policy advocacy in a Googley way. We want our users to be part of the effort," explained Andrew McLaughlin. Google, however, had not attempted to enlist its users on its behalf for any of the issues on its agenda.

SUMMARY

Firms and interest groups have broad nonmarket portfolios. Lobbying is essential in addressing issues in legislative, regulatory, and administrative arenas. Lobbying involves demonstrating to officeholders that the interests of their constituents or their own policy interests are aligned with those of the firm and its stakeholders. Providing politically relevant information to officeholders is at the heart of effective lobbying. That information may be technical or political, relating to the constituents or policy interests of officeholders. Lobbying often focuses on committees and their staffs. Testimony in hearings is related to lobbying and can be coordinated with it. Access to policymakers is necessary for lobbying. It can be attained through the constituency connection, personal relationships, former government officials, and in some cases campaign contributions. Lobbying remains a relatively unregulated activity.

Corporate electoral support primarily involves campaign contributions, since firms rarely endorse candidates. These contributions are typically made to obtain access to members of Congress and otherwise seldom play a major role in the nonmarket strategies of most firms.

[45]*San Jose Mercury News,* June 2, 2007.
[46]*Wall Street Journal,* July 20, 2007.
[47]*The Guardian,* October 24, 2006.
[48]http://googlepublicpolicy.blogspot.com.

Grassroots campaigns are based on the rent chain and are designed to influence legislators through the constituency connection. Firms and interest groups often organize and mobilize their constituents for grassroots activities, including letter-writing and visiting Washington for personal lobbying. The effectiveness of those activities depends on their credibility as well as on their scale. Grassroots campaigns are often coordinated with public advocacy. Public advocacy is used to inform both the public and those involved in policymaking processes.

Coalition building is an important component of many nonmarket strategies. Firms participate in peak organizations, trade associations, and ad hoc coalitions. Peak organizations address general business issues rather than industry-specific matters. Trade associations are important, particularly for issues that pertain to a specific industry. Ad hoc coalitions address specific issues and often bring together interests that may not be aligned on other issues. When members of a coalition have heterogeneous interests, the maintenance of the coalition requires effort, and its activities are determined through internal bargaining. Large firms often supplement coalition activities with their own individual nonmarket strategies.

Judicial strategies are implemented both in the courts and in regulatory arenas governed by administrative law. These strategies can be effective but can also be expensive.

Most large firms are organized to address nonmarket issues in government institutions. That organization may involve a Washington office, professional lobbyists, a government affairs department, associations and coalitions, and management training. This organization supports but does not substitute for management involvement in nonmarket strategy formulation and implementation.

The chapter cases *Pharmaceutical Switching* and *Internet Taxation,* and the Part II integrative case, *Fuel Economy Standards 2007,* involve issues that require a nonmarket strategy and an implementation plan.

-------------------------------------- C A S E S --------------------------------------
Responsible Lobbying?

Our goal is about cervical cancer prevention, and we want to reach as many females as possible with Gardasil. We're concerned that our role in supporting school requirements is a distraction from that goal, and as such have suspended our lobbying efforts.

Dr. Richard M. Haupt, Merck, February 20, 2007

Caution: Too much lobbying may result in an overdose of suspicion. Push too hard and you may experience political acid reflux.

Ellen Goodman, *Boston Globe,* March 1, 2007

Introduction

In 1965 a German doctor, Harald zur Hausen, received a postdoctoral fellowship at the University of Pennsylvania where he first conjectured that cervical cancer was caused by a virus.[49] Subsequently, the human papilloma virus (HPV) was identified as the cause of cervical cancer. HPV was transmitted only through sexual activity, often had no visible symptoms, and was generally eliminated by the body's immune system. Nevertheless, the Food and Drug Administration (FDA) estimated that worldwide there were 470,000 new cases of cervical cancer a year and 233,000 deaths a year. In the United States there were 9,710 new cases and 3,700 deaths a year. Treatment for cervical cancer cost the Medicare system $1.7 billion a year, and private insurance paid more. Karen Lustgarten of Planned Parenthood said, "Cancer prevention is preferable to cancer treatment at any age."[50]

Approximately 80 percent of all cervical cancers were caused by HPV types 16, 18, 31, and 45.[51] In 2006 Merck received FDA approval for the first vaccine, Gardasil, for HPV. Gardasil protected against types 16 and 18, which accounted for 70 percent of cervical cancers and 90 percent of genital warts. Gardasil was highly effective for women who had not been infected and less effective for women who had HPV.

Merck priced the vaccine at $360 for the three injections and was also working on programs for the use of Gardasil in developing countries at much lower prices. Analyst Steve Brozak of W.B.B. Securities projected sales of Gardasil at $1 billion a year and billions more if states mandated vaccination.[52] Sales in 2006 were $235 million.

Prior to FDA approval, Merck began to develop a market for Gardasil. It launched an intensive campaign to get states to make vaccination of girls entering middle school mandatory. The campaign generated a backlash against mandatory vaccination, and Merck suspended its campaign. Merck had to reflect on its failure and decide what to do next.

In 2005 Merck had sales of $22 billion and profits of $4.6 billion. The company, however, was fighting on a case-by-case basis hundreds of thousands of lawsuits on its painkiller drug Vioxx, which the company had withdrawn from the market in 2004. The company had established a reserve of $970 million for Vioxx litigation expenses. Merck's biggest drug, Zocor, had lost patent protection in 2006, and another of its major drugs, Fosamax, would lose patent protection in 2008.

Gardasil and Approvals

The technology used in Gardasil was developed in 1993 by CSL Limited of Australia, which discovered how to make tiny shells that would lead the body's immune system to attack HPV. The National Cancer Institute and Medimmune, Inc. began working to develop a vaccine, and Medimmune later licensed its technology to GlaxoSmithKline.

Dr. Kathrin Jansen of Merck also began working on a vaccine in 1993, and Merck licensed the technology from CSL in 1995. Jansen conceived of using a yeast to make the shells. Merck had a large library of yeast that had been developed for research on a hepatitis-B vaccine, and Jansen and Merck yeast experts succeeded in developing ways to grow large quantities of the shells. This research provided the foundation for Gardasil.[53]

Gardasil was approved on June 8, 2006 for protection against HPV types 16 and 18 for cervical cancer and against HPV 6, 11, 16, and 18 for precancerous lesions and genital warts for women 9 to 26 years. Gardasil was also approved for use in a number of other countries including Mexico, Australia, Canada, Brazil, and elsewhere. The European Agency for the Evaluation of Medicinal Products approved the vaccine in October 2006 for the 25 member nations of the European Union.

The Centers for Disease Control (CDC) Advisory Committee on Immunization Practices recommended that women between 9 and 26 years of age be vaccinated against HPV and that vaccinations be given at ages 11 and 12 before girls became sexually active.[54] Vaccination was intended not only to protect the person vaccinated but also to reduce the likelihood of transmission of HPV.

---

[49]He received the 2008 Nobel Prize in Medicine for his discovery.
[50]*Palm Beach Post,* February 20, 2007.
[51]Over 100 types of HPV had been identified.
[52]Associated Press, January 30, 2007.

[53]The National Cancer Institute and Medimmune used host cells from butterfly caterpillars, but scaling to large quantities proved difficult.
[54]A booster shot might be required 5 to 10 years after the vaccination. Merck was monitoring women who had been vaccinated.

Gardasil was endorsed by the American Academy of Pediatrics, which stopped short of recommending mandatory vaccinations.[55]

HPV was primarily transmitted through sexual activity. A CDC survey of physicians revealed that 46 percent would vaccinate 10–12-year-olds and 89 percent would vaccinate 16–18-year-olds. Some 11 percent believed that vaccination might increase sexual behavior.[56] A survey of pediatricians published in the *Journal of Adolescent Health,* however, reported that "half the pediatricians expect parents to resist vaccinating their child against any sexually transmitted infection. About 42 percent expect parents to fret that immunization may lead to riskier sexual behaviors, and fully 70 percent said they expect safety concerns about the HPV vaccine to weigh on parents' decision to immunize children."[57]

The CDC Advisory Committee also voted to add Gardasil to the federal program that pays for vaccines for low-income children up to 18 years of age. This vote was important because private insurers would then cover the vaccination. WellPoint, Incorporated, one of the largest private health insurers, announced that it would provide coverage.

Gardasil was effective in stopping cervical cancer among those who did not have HPV, but its effectiveness in the 9 to 26 age group would be lower because many of the women already had HPV. A study of "female students at Rutgers University in New Jersey found that 26 percent were already infected with HPV when they arrived as freshmen. The rate was 60 percent after three years of college."[58]

Merck had tested Gardasil on boys aged 9 to 15 for prevention of genital warts and head and neck cancer, and additional tests were underway. Merck had not yet sought FDA approval for Gardasil for males. Initial testing had shown that it was likely to be effective for the prevention of genital warts. Although Gardasil had only been approved for females, doctors could prescribe the drug for males. Insurance plans, however, were not required to cover prescriptions for males, since the drug had not been approved for them.

GlaxoSmithKline (GSK) was close behind Merck in developing an HPV vaccine. A 2004 article published in the medical journal *Lancet* reported successful tests of its vaccine Cervarix. By 2006 GSK had tested its vaccine on 16,000 women worldwide and had Phase III clinical trials under way on 35,000 women in 25 countries. The company had submitted a marketing application with the European Agency for the Evaluation of Medicinal Products in March 2006 and planned to submit an application to the FDA for marketing approval in the spring of 2007. One Phase III study showed that Cervarix was 100 percent effective for women 9 to 55 years of age. GSK estimated that the market for HPV vaccines could reach $7.5 billion within a few years.

The CDC issued a publication, "Human Papillomavirus: HPV Information for Clinicians," for health care professionals. In the publication the CDC wrote, "Although this vaccine offers a promising new approach to the prevention of HPV and associated conditions, this vaccine will not replace other prevention strategies, such as cervical cancer screening. . . . Vaccine providers should notify vaccinated females that they will need regular cervical cancer screening as the vaccine will not provide protection against all types of HPV that cause cervical cancer." Pap tests introduced in the 1950s had reduced the death rate from cervical cancer by 70 percent, and a new DNA-based test for HPV had recently been approved by the FDA.[59]

Market Development

While conducting Phase III trials, Merck began wrestling with the issues surrounding the marketing of its vaccine. The issues centered on public acceptance, mandating the vaccine, and obtaining reimbursement from the government and private insurers. Merck also knew that Medimmune and GlaxoSmithKline, among others, were working on a vaccine.

In anticipation of the approval of Gardasil Merck began developing the market. In 2005 it provided financial support for a public education campaign, *Make the Connection,* established in 2005 by the Cancer Research and Prevention Foundation and Step Up Women's Network.[60] The campaign featured the Internet site www.maketheconnection.org and included a series of educational events in 15 cities beginning in September 2005. The campaign also included television "public service announcements" similar to the direct-to-consumer advertisements used by pharmaceutical companies. The announcements featured Kimberly Elise and Elizabeth Röhm, who discussed cervical cancer and urged the viewers to contact their doctors. The campaign asked women to make a commitment to talk to their doctors about cervical cancer. For each commitment Merck pledged to contribute 1 dollar, up to a maximum of $100,000, to the Cancer Research and Prevention Foundation for cervical cancer programs.

Merck lobbied extensively at the state level in support of mandatory vaccination and conducted a television advertising campaign for Gardasil. "It aired TV ads featuring young girls skipping rope while reciting the slogan,

[55]*Wall Street Journal,* April 16, 2007.
[56]*Wall Street Journal,* May 17, 2006.
[57]*Wall Street Journal,* November 30, 2005.
[58]*Wall Street Journal,* November 21, 2002.

[59]The Pap test was developed by Cornell University pathologist George Papanicolaou. Precancerous lesions identified by a Pap test were typically surgically removed.
[60]The Cancer Research and Prevention Foundation, founded in 1985, provided grants for cancer prevention, education, and prevention programs. Step Up Women's Network, founded in 1998, focused on strengthening community resources for women and girls.

'I want to be one less' woman to battle the disease." The ads stated that Gardasil "'may help protect you' from HPV strains 'that may cause 70% of cervical cancer.'"[61]

Merck also worked with Women in Government to promote vaccination in line with the CDC Advisory Committee's recommendation. Women in Government was formed in 1988 for elected women in state governments and focused on public policy issues, particularly those affecting women. One of those issues was preventing cervical cancer. In 2004 it launched its "Challenge to Eliminate Cervical Cancer Campaign." President Susan Crosby said, "Cervical cancer can be our first victory in the war on cancer. By ensuring that women are educated about this disease and the virus that causes it, and that they have access to preventive technologies, regardless of socioeconomic status, we can ensure that no more women die of this preventable disease."[62]

Women in Government released a study, "Partnering for Progress 2007: The 'State' of Cervical Cancer Prevention in America," that evaluated the states on their performance on cervical cancer incidence and mortality. The study concluded that the states that performed best were those that provided reimbursement for HPV testing. Women in Government also concluded that vaccinations were an essential part of the campaign to eliminate cervical cancer. Crosby said, "To truly achieve this goal, we must make FDA-approved HPV vaccines available to all age-appropriate girls and women. That is what our recommendations, including the middle school entry requirement, are designed to do."[63] More specifically, the organization's policy recommendation regarding "School Entrance Requirements" was, "States should require cervical cancer/HPV vaccination for girls to enter middle school, in conjunction with other adolescent vaccines required at this time, and should allow parents to opt out in accordance with states' existing exemption allowances (e.g., medical, religious and/or philosophical)."[64]

Women in Government held an "HPV & Cervical Cancer Summit" in Washington, D.C., and conducted activities in all the states. The organization held dinners and meetings on HPV and cervical cancer in a number of major cities in the United States. "In early January [2007], Women in Government held a conference for some 60 state legislators in Marco Island, Fla., paying for their airfare and hotel rooms. One of the speakers was Christine Baze, a pop singer and cervical-cancer survivor. As she performed songs on the piano, Ms. Baze told the story of her battle with the disease and said she wished a vaccine had been available to her. Ms. Baze says Women in Government paid her a $2,500 fee and covered her travel and lodging. She says she didn't receive any money from Merck for the appearance, but the company has paid her $7,500 to speak at three other events."[65]

Women in Government received contributions from Merck, GlaxoSmithKline, and Digene, which had developed the first FDA-approved test to detect HPV DNA.[66] Merck's Deborah Alfano sat on Women in Government's business council in 2006. The organization posted model legislation on its Web site.

According to the National Conference of State Legislatures, bills to mandate, fund, or educate the public about HPV and cervical cancer had been introduced in 34 state legislatures.[67] Many of the bills were introduced by members of Women in Government, and many of the bills requiring mandatory vaccinations included an opt out provision for religious or moral reasons.

Merck used a combination of traditional lobbying and a public information and advocacy approach relying on television advertisements. It increased its budget for lobbying in states like Texas.

Merck was not the only company to work with health advocacy groups to raise awareness of HPV and cervical cancer and its treatment. The Partnership to End Cervical Cancer, a 20-member coalition of medical, public health, and NGOs plus GlaxoSmithKline and Digene Corporation, stated, "Comprehensive vaccination programs work—as we've seen with the significant reduction or elimination of smallpox worldwide and measles in the Western Hemisphere. Today, the Partnership is making the commitment to play a leadership role in the campaign to end as much of cervical cancer as can be prevented with these vaccines and screening in this country."[68] GSK provided financial and administrative support for the partnership.

Digene had worked to educate women and governments about the importance of testing and began a direct-to-consumer advertising television campaign in 2006 to educate women about the importance of testing for HPV. It expanded the campaign to more cities in 2007. Digene also provided support to the Academy for Educational Development and the Coalition of Labor Union Women for their five-year campaign to reduce cervical cancer.

State Actions

Health care programs, and particularly mandated vaccinations, were the responsibility of the states. In some states health departments were responsible for public health programs such as vaccination programs. The New Hampshire Health Department decided to provide the vaccine to girls under 18 at no cost, and the governor of

---

[61]*Wall Street Journal,* April 16, 2007.
[62]Women in Government, press release, September 21, 2006.
[63]PR Newswire, September 12, 2006.
[64]Women in Government, September 12, 2006.

[65]*Wall Street Journal,* April 16, 2007. Baze spoke at the 2006 HPV & Cervical Cancer Summit.
[66]At least 25 of the 81 sponsors were pharmaceutical companies. www.womeningovernment.org/home/support_ sponsors.asp.
[67]www.ncsl.org/programs.health/HPVvaccine.htm.
[68]PR Newswire, September 13, 2006.

South Dakota announced a similar program. In most states legislation was required to provide the funds for such programs or to require mandatory vaccination.

A bill introduced in the Florida legislature would require vaccination of girls of age 11 or 12 before they could enroll in a public or private school. Parents were allowed to opt out their children after having received information on cervical cancer. Virginia was moving more rapidly than other states, and the legislature had passed a mandatory vaccination bill. The governor was reviewing the opt out provision before deciding whether to sign the bill.

In Texas Governor Rick Perry issued an executive order requiring that girls entering the sixth grade as of 2008 be vaccinated against HPV.[69] For those not covered by insurance he also ordered that the vaccine would be free for girls aged 9 to 18 and covered by Medicaid for women from ages 19 to 21. Krista Moody, a spokesperson for the governor, explained, "The governor believes we should protect as many young women as possible—rich and poor, insured and uninsured—while maintaining parents' rights to opt their daughters out of receiving the vaccine."[70]

Critics

As the public and organized private groups became aware of Merck's efforts to promote and secure a first-mover advantage for Gardasil, and particularly mandatory vaccination, criticism grew. The criticism focused not only on Merck's efforts but also on the wisdom of mandatory vaccination and whether a state should wait until more evidence of side effects had accumulated.

Critics in Texas claimed that Governor Perry's action was the result of cronyism. Dawn Richardson, president of Parents Requesting Open Vaccine Education, said, "He's circumventing the will of the people. There are bills filed. There's no emergency except in the boardroom of Merck, where this is failing to gain the support they had expected."[71]

Merck had contributed $6,000 to Perry's election campaign. Perry's former chief of staff, Mike Toomey, was a lobbyist, one of whose clients was Merck, and Representative Dianne Delisi, the state director of Women in Government, was the mother-in-law of Perry's current chief of staff. Delisi had met in September with the governor's budget director for an "HPV Vaccine for Children Briefing," according to her calendar. She had also met with Toomey three times, and two other Perry staffers had met with a Merck lobbyist.[72] The wife of Perry's former chief of staff was a nurse who had pro-

moted health and spoken at a Women in Government conference on cervical cancer.[73] Cathie Adams of the Texas Eagle Forum commented, "We have too many coincidences. I think that the voters of Texas would find that very hard to swallow."[74]

Public criticism of Governor Perry's order grew, and the Texas legislature held a hearing on the order and began considering rescinding it. The state House of Representatives voted 118 to 23 to rescind the governor's order, but the Senate took a different approach by passing a bill that prevented the state from mandating vaccinations before 2011. The House approved the bill on a 132 to 2 vote.[75]

A bill to mandate vaccination began hearings in California in March 2007 and was met with skepticism. Opponents of the bill said the California children would be "guinea pigs" and that parents rather than the state should make the decision about vaccinations for a virus that was transmitted by sexual activity.

Criticism of the vaccine had begun with some conservative Christian groups claiming it would encourage premarital sex. Stephen Cable, president of Vermont Renewal, echoed a theme of a number of conservative organizations, "To think that an 11-year old would be forced to take this vaccine, based on the assumption they'll be sexually active, it's more than annoying. . . . There are a lot of parents who haven't heard about this (legislation). When they do, the hair will be standing up on the back of their necks."[76] "In recent weeks, opposition to state mandates has grown among parents who want the freedom to make such a medical decision on their own, and who are worried about exposing their children to the unforeseen side effects of a new vaccine. Physicians and consumer advocates have also questioned the need to immunize young girls against a disease that is no longer very prevalent in the U.S. and doesn't develop until much later in life."[77] A spokesperson for the Center for Medical Consumers stated, "Parents should be concerned that the only company that makes this vaccine is pushing behind the scenes for mandatory laws."[78]

Mandating the vaccine also drew fire from family values groups. The Minnesota Family Council said a mandate "undermines abstinence and excuses premarital sex. It's not dealing with a contagious disease that someone can get in public. It's specifically resulting from a particular behavior."[79]

State senator Janet Greenip of Maryland opposed legislation mandating the vaccine stating, "The vaccine is

---

[69]Texas had not mandated two other vaccines approved in recent years for meningitis and whooping cough.
[70]*New York Times,* March 14, 2007.
[71]Associated Press, February 3, 2007. The citizens group had worked for opt out provisions for other vaccines.
[72]Associated Press, February 22, 2007.

[73]*New York Times,* February 17, 2007.
[74]Associated Press, February 22, 2007.
[75]*New York Times,* April 26, 2007.
[76]Associated Press, February 22, 2007.
[77]*Wall Street Journal,* February 21, 2007.
[78]*Wall Street Journal,* February 7, 2007.
[79]*Pioneer Press,* February 22, 2007.

very important, but I'm reluctant to make it mandatory. If it is good, people will do it."[80] Dr. Mark Myers, executive director of the National Network for Immunization Information, however, cautioned, "A lot of us are concerned that if you allow people to opt out of one vaccine, they will opt out of other vaccines that are due at the same time."[81]

One concern raised was whether Gardasil had been sufficiently tested in very young girls. Of those tested only 1,184 were preteen girls. The National Vaccine Information Center, an organization formed by parents concerned about the harm from vaccines, reported that through the end of 2006, 385 adverse events had been reported associated with the use of Gardasil. The CDC stated that the adverse events were not a cause for concern. When the FDA approved Gardasil, it ordered Merck to track a number of 11- and 12-year-olds in a postmarketing study scheduled to be completed in 2009. The FDA action requiring a postmarketing study was common.

The Health Information National Trends Survey (HINTS) conducted by the National Cancer Institute collected data from 3,000 women between the ages of 18 and 75. Only 40 percent had heard of HPV and fewer than half were aware of the connection to cervical cancer. A study of 645 adults by the Annenberg National Communication Survey found that 56 percent had heard of HPV and 42 percent had heard about a vaccine. The respondents were asked to read three statements about the vaccine and asked if they would get vaccinated. When the statement stated that the vaccine protected against cervical cancer, 63 percent of the women indicated that they were "very likely" or "somewhat likely" to get vaccinated, compared to 43 percent when the statement said it protected against cervical cancer and a sexually transmitted infection.[82]

Critics contended that Merck's lobbying campaign was intended to obtain mandatory vaccination before GlaxoSmithKline's vaccine for HPV was approved. Vera Hassner Sharav, a critic of pharmaceutical companies, called the HPV vaccine campaign the "Help Pay for Vioxx" losses campaign.[83]

Cathie Adams, president of the Texas Eagle Forum, commented on the relationship between Women in Government and Merck, "What it does is benefit the pharmaceutical companies, and I don't want the pharmaceutical companies taking precedent over the authorities of parents." Referring to Merck's lobbying campaign, she said, "It's corrupt as far as I'm concerned."[84]

In February two women legislators in Minnesota removed their names from sponsorship of a school-mandated vaccine. The Minnesota Medical Association called for the appointment of a scientific advisory board to study whether the vaccine should be mandated. Minnesota already required vaccination for hepatitis B, which is sexually transmitted.

Debbie Halvorson, the majority leader of the Illinois Senate, said she would continue to work for a mandatory vaccination. She said, "If the people out there are thinking that Merck is doing all this, and pushing our buttons, they need to just step away. The fact that I'm doing what I'm doing has nothing to do with Merck." Halvorson had had a hysterectomy as a result of human papilloma virus.[85]

Closing

Margaret McGlynn, Merck president for vaccines, responded to critics of its lobbying campaign by stating, "Each and every day that a female delays getting the vaccine there is a chance she is exposed to human papillomavirus."[86] Merck spokesperson Janet Skidmore said, "What we support are approaches that achieve high immunization rates. We're talking about cervical cancer here, the second-leading cancer among women."[87] Patti Stinchfield, an immunization expert in Minnesota and a member of the CDC's vaccine advisory committee, commented, "It's hard to argue against a vaccine that prevents cervical cancer in your sisters and aunts and mothers. That's where the argument goes if you want to argue against this vaccine."

In response to the criticism, Merck's Dr. Haupt commented on the views of medical organizations and public health officials, "They believe the timing for the school requirements is not right. Our goal is to prevent cervical cancer. Our goal is to reach as many females as possible. Right now, school requirements and Merck's involvement in that are being viewed as a distraction to that goal."[88] Merck suspended its lobbying but indicated that it would continue its educational efforts directed at health officials and legislators.

Dr. Joseph A. Bocchini, chairman of an American Academy of Pediatrics committee on infectious diseases, said, "If the public had enough experience with the vaccine and had enough knowledge about HPV, the question about whether to get the vaccine or give it to their daughters wouldn't be an issue."[89] Dr. Bocchini praised the decision by Merck to stop its lobbying campaign for school-mandated vaccinations. He said that the focus should be on educating parents.[90]

In April an article in the *Wall Street Journal* questioned the efficacy of mandatory vaccination, suggesting

[80]Associated Press, January 19, 2007.
[81]*New York Times*, February 17, 2007.
[82]*Cancer Vaccine Week*, December 4, 2006.
[83]*New York Times*, February 17, 2007.
[84]Associated Press, January 30, 2007.

[85]*New York Times*, February 21, 2007.
[86]*New York Times*, February 17, 2007.
[87]Associated Press, January 30, 2007.
[88]*New York Times*, February 21, 2007.
[89]*New York Times*, February 17, 2007.
[90]*Wall Street Journal*, February 21, 2007.

that it would be better to rely on Pap screening. In May researchers published an article in the *New England Journal of Medicine* analyzing 12,167 women three years after vaccination. Whereas Gardasil was 98 percent effective for women who had never been infected by HPV, it was only 44 percent effective when women who had previously been infected were included. Gardasil was only 17 percent effective in preventing precancerous lesions.[91] ∎

Preparation Questions

1. What was Merck's motivation for its market development strategy?
2. Were the components of its market development strategies responsible?
3. Should Merck have been able to anticipate the opposition that developed to its strategy?
4. Should it have suspended its lobbying for mandatory vaccinations? In which circumstances and under what conditions should it resume its lobbying?
5. Design a marketing program for the use of Gardasil for males.

---

[91] *Wall Street Journal,* May 10, 2007.

Internet Taxation

On May 10, 2000, the House of Representatives passed H.R. 3709, the "Internet Non-Discrimination Act," by a resounding majority of 352–75. The bill provided a 5-year extension of an existing moratorium on new Internet taxes that was due to expire in 2001.[92] The bill had been embraced by a diverse coalition of consumer groups, Internet users, and high-tech companies that argued that the imposition of taxes on electronic commerce would slow both the development of the Internet and the growth in the U.S. economy.

In the Senate intense lobbying by a diverse set of interests caused Senator John McCain (R-AZ), chairman of the Commerce Committee, to cancel a hearing on a bill to make the tax moratorium permanent. When questioned about the cancellation, McCain said the topic of Internet taxes was "incredibly complex [and had] not been nearly fleshed out enough."[93] At the same time the legislation stalled in the Senate, the solidarity of the high-tech community on the Internet taxation issue began to slip. In a June hearing before the Joint Economic Committee, Intel Chairman Andy Grove argued for applying sales taxes to transactions on the Web, saying that he felt there was no "justification" for the online tax advantage. At the same hearing, Hewlett-Packard CEO Carly Fiorina warned that "to apply the current system of taxation to the online world would be disastrous." She, however, criticized those opposed to any Internet taxes, saying that such a stance was "unrealistic."[94] A new report by the General Accounting Office (GAO) estimated that state and local governments stood to lose anywhere between $300 million and $3.8 billion in sales tax revenue in 2000.[95]

Precedents and Mail-Order Sales

The controversy surrounding Internet taxation resulted from court decisions that exempted from taxes mail-order sales to out-of-state residents. In two landmark court cases, *National Bellas Hess v. Department of Revenue of the State of Illinois* (386 U.S. 753, 1967) and *Quill v. North Dakota* (504 U.S. 298, 1992), the U.S. Supreme Court concluded that requiring mail-order merchants to calculate, collect, and remit the appropriate tax to the appropriate authorities would constitute an undue burden because of the approximately 35,000 state and local tax rates in effect. The Court decided that merchants were only required to collect sales taxes from customers that resided in a state where the merchant had a "nexus." A nexus, loosely defined, was a physical presence, such as a warehouse or retail outlet.

The Supreme Court decisions effectively absolved merchants of their responsibility for tax collection on out-of-state sales, but responsibility for the remittance of

---

[92] The existing moratorium prohibited the imposition of "multiple and discriminatory" taxes on electronic commerce. These taxes included those that subjected buyers and sellers to taxation in multiple states and localities, as well as taxes on goods specifically sold over the Internet by companies that did not have brick-and-mortar counterparts in the state. Discriminatory taxes included taxes imposed on Internet sales but not on catalog sales. The moratorium also prohibited the federal government from imposing taxes on Internet access or electronic commerce generally.
[93] *Wall Street Journal,* June 22, 2000.

[94] *Atlanta Journal and Constitution,* June 8, 2000.
[95] *Report to Congressional Requesters,* "Sales Taxes: Electronic Commerce Growth Presents Challenges; Revenue Losses Are Uncertain," United States General Accounting Office, June 2000.

the tax remained for consumers. Most states required the remittance of "use" taxes for goods bought from out-of-state vendors. The rate of these use taxes was usually identical to the state sales tax rates for goods sold within the state. It was the responsibility of individual consumers to report to their state government how much tax they owed and pay accordingly. Use taxes provided governments with a legal basis to collect revenue on out-of-state purchases, but such collection rarely occurred. Compliance was very low, as most consumers were unaware that they were required to pay the use tax. Few states attempted to collect from individual consumers.[96] Although the inability to collect use taxes on catalog sales had not led to new tax legislation, the rise of the Internet significantly changed perceptions about the scale of purchases potentially free from state and local taxes. As more transactions migrated to the Web, state and local governments feared a substantial erosion of their tax bases.[97]

Fears of dwindling revenues were accompanied by the concerns of offline Main Street merchants who felt that the tax advantage of online stores gave them a significant advantage. These issues led to the introduction of bills in several state legislatures, all of which were aimed at providing some form of tax collection on online sales, at least from their own residents. Online merchants, however, argued that they had to bear delivery costs, which, as with catalog sales, offset the tax exclusion. The online merchants also argued that they did not use state resources other than for delivery and hence should not be required to fund state services.

While state and local governments were clamoring for action, the federal government was effectively putting on the brakes. The Internet Tax Freedom Act (ITFA), introduced in Congress by Representative Christopher Cox (R-CA) and Senator Ron Wyden (D-OR), was passed as part of the Omnibus Appropriations Act of 1998. Placing a 3-year moratorium on new Internet taxes, the ITFA also created the Advisory Commission on Electronic Commerce to study issues related to the taxation of the Internet and to recommend to Congress by April 2000 an appropriate tax policy.

The Advisory Commission consisted of 19 members, eight from industry and consumer groups, eight from state and local government, and three from the Clinton administration. Early in its deliberations the Commission separated into three camps. One camp, in-cluding executives such as C. Michael Armstrong of AT&T and Theodore Waitt of Gateway, was in favor of taxing electronic commerce, provided that an equitable collection mechanism could be devised. A second group included representatives of state and local governments and was prepared to support any tax regime that would allow recovery of revenues lost to electronic commerce. A third group, represented by Governor James Gilmore (R-VA) and Grover Norquist of the Americans for Tax Reform, opposed any taxes on online commerce.[98]

The Commission considered a variety of alternatives ranging from no taxes to a flat tax on all electronic transactions. One alternative considered would keep the current tax system intact but would require credit card companies to act as trusted third parties in collecting use taxes from consumers and remitting them to the relevant governments.[99] While the Commission was studying the tax options, new measures were being introduced in Congress to address the Internet tax question. Wyden and Cox introduced new legislation asking the World Trade Organization to consider a permanent global moratorium on Internet taxes. Senator McCain introduced legislation to make the ITFA tax moratorium permanent. On the other side of the aisle Senator Ernest Hollings (D-SC) introduced legislation mandating a uniform 5 percent tax on all remote sales, including Internet and mail-order transactions.

As the April deadline approached, the Advisory Commission was unable to reach a consensus for "official" recommendations, which required the agreement of 13 members. An agreement could not be achieved because the members representing the Clinton administration and state and local governments abstained on necessary votes, arguing that the Commission had been subverted by industry interests and was not operating with the consensus of the relevant stakeholders.[100] Congressional leaders urged the Advisory Commission to make unofficial policy recommendations nonetheless. Among the unofficial recommendations was an additional 5-year extension on the existing tax moratorium, which was quickly incorporated into the pending Internet Non-Discrimination Act.

Interests and their Stakes

Online consumers were, not surprisingly, opposed to the Internet taxes. According to one poll, 57 percent of Internet users took tax rates into account when making purchasing decisions.[101] Similarly, 75 percent of online consumers reported that they would be less likely to purchase goods online if they were required to remit taxes for their purchases. Furthermore, large-sample

---

[96]States that took measures to collect use taxes met with little success. Several states, such as New Jersey, had a separate line for use taxes on residents' income tax forms. In 1997 less than 1 percent of New Jersey residents reported use taxes. (Robert J. Cline and Thomas S. Neubig, 1999, "Masters of Complexity and Bearers of Great Burden: The Sales Tax System and Compliance Costs for Multistate Retailers," Technical Report, Ernst and Young Economics Consulting and Quantitative Analysis.)

[97]All states except Alaska, Delaware, Montana, New Hampshire, and Oregon had a sales tax.

[98]*New York Times*, September 13, 2000.
[99]*Washington Post*, October 4, 1999.
[100]*Washington Post*, March 22, 2000.
[101]*Atlanta Journal and Constitution*, July 2, 2000.

statistical studies indicated that taxing online sales could reduce online purchases by as much as 30 percent.[102]

Many members of the high-tech community opposed online taxes, arguing that instituting taxes on the Web would chill the growth of the Internet in at least two ways. First, if taxes were imposed, consumers might choose not to shop online, constricting the Web's expansion. The demand for many companies' products and services was directly proportional to how many people were using the Web. Second, executives argued that the high costs associated with collecting and remitting use taxes under the current system would lead to the death of many online firms. The possibility of chilling the Internet's expansion and the high compliance costs led most high-tech companies to support an extended moratorium. They argued that given time more consumers would experiment with, and gain confidence in, online commerce, and during the moratorium some solution might be developed to handle the burdensome compliance costs. Recent research had supported this infant industry argument for an extension of the tax moratorium.[103] Many high-tech leaders viewed the Internet as an essential component of the infrastructure of both business and society, and its public goods characteristics warranted as extensive an expansion of the Internet as possible.

Among the groups that voiced opposition to "discriminatory" taxes (i.e., taxes that targeted online products but had no catalog or telephone-order counterparts) was the Information Technology Association of America (ITAA), which represented over 26,000 companies, including Compaq, IBM, MCI-Worldcom, and Microsoft. The American Electronics Association represented over 3,000 companies in the high-tech and electronics industry and also opposed new Internet taxes.

To counter the advocates of online taxes, companies formed several ad hoc coalitions. The Global Business Dialogue on Electronic Commerce was a consortium of several major companies, including Disney, Hewlett-Packard, and IBM, and was co-chaired by America Online CEO Steven Case and Time-Warner CEO Gerald M. Levin.

Another ad hoc coalition, the Internet Tax Fairness Coalition (ITFC), was formed by 11 companies and associations. ITFC was "committed to ensuring that any taxation imposed on electronic commerce not thwart the development of the Internet marketplace."[104] Mark Nebergall of the ITFC also stressed fairness: "In order to achieve a true 'level playing field,' remote merchants must enjoy the simplicity and predictability of sales tax collection and remittance enjoyed by brick-and-mortar stores. Otherwise, the burden on remote sellers amounts to a competitive advantage for merchants deciding to stay out of electronic commerce." The ITFC also argued that virtually all sectors of the U.S. economy, including state and municipal governments and Main Street businesses, had benefited from the growth of the Internet. Furthermore, there was currently no efficient technology to collect taxes under the present tax system. The ITFC argued that any hasty decision on Internet taxation could hinder the country's economic growth.

Opposing the tax moratorium were conventional brick-and-mortar businesses that viewed the tax advantage to online retailers as unfair competition and injurious to their business. The National Retail Federation (NRF) represented retailers ranging from small independent shops to major department stores. Representing shopping centers was the International Council of Shopping Centers, which had 38,000 members. An ad hoc coalition was formed specifically to address the Internet tax question. The E-Fairness Coalition, composed of several interest groups and major retail firms, including the International Council of Shopping Centers, the American Booksellers Association, Tandy/Radio Shack, and Wal-Mart, claimed to represent over 350,000 retail outlets. It consistently argued for a "level playing field" where "customers [were] treated fairly regardless of where they [chose] to shop."[105]

State and local governments strongly favored some form of Internet sales taxation. Arguing that online commerce would lower their tax revenues by as much as $20 billion a year by 2002, state governors had begun pressuring their representatives in Washington. The governors were represented by the National Governors Association (NGA), a national lobbying organization representing the interests of the 50 states. A counterpart to the NGA was the National Council of State Legislatures (NCSL), which represented state legislatures.

City and county governments had voiced their opposition to any tax-moratorium extension.[106] City governments were organized primarily through the U.S. Conference of Mayors, which represented approximately 1,100 cities with populations of at least 30,000. Eighteen thousand smaller cities and towns were represented by the National League of Cities. In legislative matters the National Association of Counties represented over 1,800 counties, covering almost 75 percent of the U.S. population.

The June report by the GAO added to the concerns of state and local governments. The GAO estimated that they would lose sales tax revenue up to $3.8 billion in 2000 and up to $12.4 billion in 2003. A University of

[102]Austan Goolsbee, 2000, "In a World Without Borders: The Impact of Taxes on Internet Commerce," *Quarterly Journal of Economics,* 115(2): 561–76. Goolsbee also argued that the implementation of online current use taxes would lead approximately 20 to 25 percent of the current consumer base not to shop online.

[103]Goolsbee, ibid. For a discussion of other research on these topics, see Wiseman (2000).

[104]The members were America Online, Charles Schwab, Cisco Systems, First Data Corporation, and Microsoft, as well as the American Electronics Association, Information Technology Association, Investment Company Institute, Securities Industry Association, and Software and Information Industry Association.

[105]www.e-fairness.org.

[106]*Chicago Sun Times,* July 24, 2000.

Tennessee study estimated the sales tax loss at $20.1 billion in 2003. The GAO also estimated that the losses in 2003 would be $20.4 billion if the taxes not collected on mail-order catalog and telephone sales were included.

Congressional Activity

Any legislation on Internet taxation implicitly dealt with interstate commerce and hence was referred to the cognizant committee in each chamber of Congress. Under the Rules of the House, the Judiciary Committee, chaired by Henry Hyde (R-IL), had jurisdiction over all legislation dealing with "interstate compacts generally," which included Internet taxation. The Standing Rules of the Senate assigned matters dealing with interstate commerce to the Commerce, Science and Transportation Committee, chaired by Senator McCain. During his bid for the Republican presidential nomination McCain had come out in favor of a permanent moratorium on all Internet sales taxes.

Congress faced other vexing taxation issues created by technological change. State and local governments imposed taxes of between $4 and $7 billion on telephone usage, but with the growth of cellular telephone usage the state and local governments faced the question of which tax rates applied to cell phones. In July 2000 Congress resolved the issue by enacting legislation specifying that the applicable taxes were those for the address to which the bill was sent. Exceptions were made for corporations that provided cellular telephones to their employees, allowing the company to designate the area code in which the phone was registered as the location for taxation. Lisa Cowell, executive director of the E-Fairness Coalition, commented, "A lot of politicians have stopped hiding behind this bogeyman of 'it can't be done' because no one knows where the customer is."[107]

While the Internet Non-Discrimination Act had sailed through the House without serious complications, the procedural differences between the House and the Senate raised possible problems for the moratorium extension. Any senator could filibuster the bill, which if cloture were not invoked, would likely kill the bill, since the Senate had important pending legislation remaining. One senator, in particular, had voiced opposition to an extended moratorium and had proposed an alternative scheme to remedy the problem of multiple and conflicting tax jurisdictions. Senator Byron Dorgan (D-ND) proposed that online sellers be required to collect and remit use taxes at point of sale, and states could join a "compact" to collect and distribute tax revenues. To join the compact, states would have to adopt uniform definitions of taxable products and have a flat use-tax rate for the entire state. As of June 2000, several states had announced their participation in this "streamlined sales tax project," an NGA initiative to create uniformity in

tax laws so as to facilitate online collection. Working with the NGA, the NCSL organized a tax project to simplify state sales taxes. Wal-Mart was one of five retailers that volunteered to test a pilot technology to distinguish among the myriad of state and local tax laws. If successful, the program would be a major step toward making taxation of online sales practical.

State Activity: California

Legislative activity at the state level complicated the movement toward a uniform federal solution for the tax issue. In August 2000 the California state legislature passed legislation requiring Internet merchants with brick-and-mortar stores in California to collect sales taxes on purchases made online by California residents. If enacted, Barnesandnoble.com and Borders.com would have to collect taxes on purchases made by California consumers, since they had retail outlets in California even though their Internet businesses were housed outside California.[108] Barnesandnoble.com and Borders.com claimed that their online companies were separate from their brick-and-mortar companies and hence were not affected by the nexus principle. Borders.com, however, directed customers to a Borders store if they wanted to return a book. Although proponents of the bill hailed it as a "fair and square measure," other parties, such as the American Electronics Association, argued that California was trying to "shoehorn e-commerce business into an old tax system that doesn't make any sense."[109] As the legislation arrived on Governor Gray Davis's desk, observers wondered what its enactment might mean for the future of electronic commerce and state tax autonomy.

International Activity

International developments were also complicating U.S. attempts to resolve the Internet taxation issue. The 1999 Human Development Report of the United Nations made a formal recommendation to impose a $0.01 "bit tax" for every 100 e-mails sent between users. The tax would raise an estimated $70 billion a year for underdeveloped countries. Both the Clinton administration and Congress urged the WTO to impose bans on the bit tax and similar Internet-specific taxes. Embracing the sentiments of the Clinton administration, at its Seattle meeting in December 1999 the WTO decided to extend for 2 years an existing moratorium on Internet taxes, effectively striking down the bit tax proposal.

Other international organizations were also weighing in on the tax question. In October 1998 the 29-nation Organization for Economic Cooperation and Development (OECD) proposed the Ottawa Taxation Framework

---

[107]*New York Times,* July 19, 2000.

[108]Amazon.com did not have a nexus in California and thus did not collect taxes from California residents. It collected state sales taxes in its home state of Washington.
[109]*San Francisco Chronicle,* August 31, 2000.

Conditions. In the hope of developing a uniform taxation scheme for online commerce, the Ottawa Conditions envisioned a tax plan that was economically neutral, efficient, simple, fair, and flexible.[110] The conferees agreed that any taxation scheme should levy taxes on goods based on where they were consumed rather than where they were produced. The flexible nature of Internet commerce, however, raised difficult questions about how to determine where, precisely, goods purchased online were consumed.[111] The OECD established several industry and government working groups to examine these issues in more detail. The United States and the European Union (EU) used the OECD as a forum for their negotiations on Internet taxation.

Most member states of the European Union imposed a value-added tax (VAT) on electronically delivered goods and services supplied by EU companies to EU residents. In June 2000 the EU Commission proposed extending the VAT to non-EU companies, despite the existing WTO moratorium. Specifically, the proposal required any firm selling more than €100,000 worth of electronic goods into the European Union to be registered with one of the 15 member states' tax authorities and charge that state's rate. The VAT rates of the EU member states varied from 15 percent in Luxembourg to 25 percent in Denmark and Sweden. The VAT accounted for approximately 40 percent of the tax revenue of the EU member states and financed the entire EU budget.[112]

The Commission was heavily criticized by the United States for acting unilaterally despite continued negotiations within the OECD. Stuart Eizenstat, Undersecretary of the Treasury Department, argued that the proposal "if implemented, could well hinder the development of [the] global medium of [electronic] commerce." Similarly, Andy Grove came out against the VAT, calling it "e-protectionism."[113] Implementation issues also arose as to how such taxes would be collected, as well as whether the necessary unanimous endorsement of all member states of the European Union could be expected. Mark Bohannon of the U.S.-based Software and Information Industry Association called the Commission report "fatally flawed" because it was impossible to determine where a customer in cyberspace resided.[114]

Companies

A variety of companies would be directly affected by an Internet tax, and others would be indirectly affected. A tax would have a major impact on Amazon.com, the largest online retailer. A sale to a customer in California saved the customer the sales tax of approximately 8 percent, and a sale to a Texas customer saved 8.5 percent.[115] The tax savings helped compensate for delivery costs, which were paid by the customer. Despite not facing sales taxes, Amazon.com lost $207 million before special equity arrangements on sales of $578 million in the quarter ending June 20, 2000.

Amazon.com had worked behind the scenes to oppose any Internet taxes. Its perspective was revealed in its commentary on the California bill to impose taxes on sales by those online companies that claimed that their Internet companies were separate from their brick-and-mortar stores. "Paul Misener, vice president for global public policy at Amazon.com, said he does not see any need to tax Internet sales in general since so many state and local governments are running surpluses right now. 'We really have to see the problem first,' he said. 'This is almost a solution in search of a problem.' Misener added that if online sales are taxed, it should be at a lower rate than off-line transactions because sales made over the Internet 'use fewer state and local resources.' Amazon opposes the... bill because it does not recognize this principle, even though the bill would affect one of the company's biggest competitors: Barnesandnoble.com."[116]

Cisco Systems, the leading supplier of servers for the Internet, supported the Internet Non-Discrimination Act because state governments were running surpluses and "the often-confusing tax rules of 7,500 separate jurisdictions could severely impede development of this rapidly expanding medium for global trade, investment, and communication. State and local governments should use an extended moratorium period to simplify their existing, complex tax structures."[117]

Cisco worked on the Internet taxation issue primarily through the Internet Tax Fairness Coalition and the American Electronics Association. Katrina Doerfler of Cisco, testifying on behalf of the American Electronics Association, articulated five principles for any legislation on Internet taxation. "One, impose no greater tax burden on electronic commerce than other traditional means of commerce. Two, support simplicity in administration. Three, retain and clarify nexus standards. Four, avoid new access taxes on the Internet. And, five, consider tax issues in a global context."[118] ■

SOURCE: This case was written by Alan Wiseman under the supervision of Professor David P. Baron. Copyright © 2000 by the Board of Trustees of the Leland Stanford Junior University. All rights reserved. Reprinted with permission.

---

[110]OECD Committee on Fiscal Affairs, "Implementing the Ottawa Taxation Framework Conditions," June.

[111]*Financial Times*, "Plan for Taxing Internet Commerce Outlined," October 9, 2000.

[112]In contrast, sales taxes accounted for approximately 25 percent of the tax revenue of U.S. states and none of the federal government's tax revenue. The VAT systems in Europe were less complicated than the sales tax systems across the U.S. states.

[113]*BusinessWeek*, June 26, 2000.

[114]*New York Times*, September 30, 2000.

[115]Customers in the state of Washington were required to pay the sales tax.

[116]*San Jose Mercury News*, September 12, 2000.

[117]www.cisco.com/warp/public.

[118]Hearings, House Committee on the Judiciary, Subcommittee on Commercial and Administrative Law, June 29, 2000.

Preparation Questions

1. How would the market strategy of Amazon.com be affected by the application of state and local sales taxes to online sales?
2. How would the market strategy of Cisco Systems be affected by the application of state and local sales taxes to online sales?
3. How much influence are the various interests identified in the case likely to have on the issue of Internet taxation?
4. Are there any interests not identified in the case that are likely to be active on this issue? Will they be able to overcome the free-rider problem?
5. What is likely to be the outcome of the Internet Non-Discrimination Act?

Pharmaceutical Switching

If the FDA agrees to these switches, the changes discussed today will be the tip of the iceberg. It is likely that many products will be proposed for such changes of status on a very frequent basis by those who have a strong self-interest in the change.[119]

Bert Spilker, Pharmaceutical Research and Manufacturers Association

U.S. spending on prescription pharmaceuticals increased by 19 percent to $131.9 billion in 2000, the fifth consecutive year of increases above 13 percent. One factor contributing to the increased spending was direct-to-consumer advertising of prescription drugs, which was allowed under relaxed Food and Drug Administration (FDA) guidelines in 1997. Pharmaceutical companies responded aggressively to the opportunity. In 1999 Schering-Plough spent $137.4 million on advertising for Claritin, an antihistamine used to treat allergies.[120] Sales of Claritin reached $2.5 billion in the United States in 2000.

Prescription pharmaceuticals were covered by insurance programs, whereas over-the-counter (OTC) drugs were not. The increased spending on prescription drugs imposed a substantial burden on insurance companies. In an unprecedented action on July 22, 1998, Robert C. Seidman, vice president and chief pharmacy officer of Blue Cross of California, a unit of WellPoint Health Networks, Inc., filed a Citizen Petition with the FDA seeking an exemption for three second-generation antihistamines, Allegra (fexofenadine), Claritin (loratadine), and Zyrtec (cetirizine), used to treat allergic rhinitis. The exemption would in effect switch the drugs from prescription to OTC status. The petition noted that over 100 antihistamines were already sold over the counter, and those first-generation drugs were more

"dangerous" than the second-generation nonsedating drugs. The petition stated that prescription status "deprives a majority of patients ready access to quality pharmaceutical care" and places an undue burden on patients. The petition also noted, "Patients are seeking greater ownership of their health care and often prefer to self-medicate when feasible."

A switch would not only put the second-generation antihistamines under considerable price pressure but would also disrupt the product planning of their manufacturers. Moreover, a switch initiated by an insurance company could lead to future petitions for switches of other prescription drugs.

On May 11, 2001, an FDA advisory committee composed of doctors and researchers voted overwhelmingly that the three second-generation antihistamines could safely be marketed over the counter. Although the vote was not binding, the FDA usually acted in accord with the judgments of its advisory committees. The pharmaceutical companies strongly objected to the committee's vote and faced the challenge of developing a strategy for dealing with the threat.

The Petition

Claritin (loratadine) was first marketed in Belgium and Canada in 1988, and in 1989 Canada switched it to the OTC market. In 2001 loratadine was sold on a prescription-only basis in approximately 80 countries, and in 17 countries it was sold "behind the counter," requiring the supervision of a pharmacist. In four countries, Canada, Australia, New Zealand, and the Philippines, it was sold over the counter.[121] Allegra was produced by Aventis Pharmaceutical, and Zyrtec was produced by UCB SA and marketed in the United States by Pfizer. In 2000 U.S. sales of the three drugs were nearly $4.5 billion with Claritin accounting for $2.5 billion, Allegra $1.1 billion, and Zyrtec $800 million.

---

[119]*San Jose Mercury News,* May 12, 2001.
[120]In 1999 AstraZeneca and Pfizer each spent $79.5 million on Prilosec and Viagra respectively. In the first half of 2000 Merck spent $94.6 million on Vioxx.

[121]Schering-Plough, "Briefing Book," April 12, 2001, p. 7.

Making the three nonsedating antihistamines available on a prescription-only basis was part of the conservative approach used by the FDA. Two other nonsedating antihistamines, terfenadine (Seldane) and astemizole, had been approved on a prescription-only basis and after a few years of marketing were withdrawn from the U.S. market because of a serious safety concern associated with cardiac arrhythmias.

The petition by Blue Cross was unprecedented. The only other switch petitions had been filed by pharmaceutical companies seeking approval to move their drugs to the OTC market. A number of widely used OTC drugs, including Actifed, Bactine, Dimetapp, Pepcid, Sominex, and Tagamet, had been switched by their makers to the OTC market. In 1982 the FDA had initiated a switch of metaproterenol, but criticism by physicians led it to return the drug to prescription status.

In January 1999 the FDA indicated that it needed more time to evaluate the petition. In June 2000 it held a hearing to review the process of switching a drug from prescription to OTC status. The FDA also established an OTC Switch Review Team in the Center for Drug Evaluation and Research (CDER) and scheduled the May 11 meeting. The staff noted that Canadian regulators had studied the postmarketing experience with Claritin and had taken no significant regulatory action since it was first sold on the OTC market. A review of the safety and scientific evidence by the FDA staff concluded that the second-generation antihistamines had "certain safety advantages" as well as cognition advantages relative to first-generation antihistamines, many of which were marketed as OTC sleep aids. The Federal Aviation Administration allowed pilots to fly while taking Claritin and Allegra but not first-generation antihistamines.

The FDA had earlier ruled in a separate docket that antihistamines as a class could be sold on the OTC market and that consumers could diagnose allergies and treat them without consulting a doctor. Paradoxically, the sedating antihistamines were available over the counter, whereas the nonsedating antihistamines were available only by prescription. Referring to the Claritin advertisements that proclaimed that the drug was safe like "a sugar pill," Blue Cross's Seidman said, "If they are marketing these like candy, then they should be sold like candy."

The joint advisory committee composed of the Pulmonary-Allergy Drug Advisory Committee and the Nonprescription Drugs (OTC) Advisory Committee met on May 11 to review evidence on whether the three antihistamines could be used safely by consumers without the intervention of a doctor. The Food, Drug and Cosmetics Act stated that drugs were to be sold on a prescription-only status only if a "learned intermediary" was required for proper use. The question to be answered for each of the three drugs by the joint committee was, Does loratadine (fexofenadine, cetirizine) have a safety profile acceptable for OTC marketing; that is,

can it be used safely without a learned intermediary? The Durham-Humphrey Amendment to the Food, Drug and Cosmetic Act added, "A drug is expected to be made available without a prescription if, by following the labeling, consumers can use it safely and effectively without professional guidance." The FDA had implemented that requirement by asking three questions: Can the condition be adequately self-diagnosed? Can the condition be successfully self-treated? Is the self-treatment product safe and effective for consumer use under conditions of actual use?

After reviewing safety data and hearing presentations from WellPoint, Aventis, and Schering-Plough, the committee voted 19–4 in the cases of Claritin and Zyrtec and 18–5 in the case of Allegra that a learned intermediary was not required for safe and proper use. If the FDA followed the advice of the joint committee, the implications would be profound. " 'This is a new paradigm,' said John Jenkins, director of the FDA's office of drug evaluation."[122]

Opposition to a Switch

In its presentation at the May 11 meeting Schering-Plough made three broad points: "1. Prescription status may be necessary to protect and optimize public health. 2. The safety profiles of the second-generation antihistamines in an OTC setting are not fully known. 3. Allergies are frequently chronic, complex diseases with serious co-morbidities."[123] The principal co-morbidities were asthma, sinusitis, and otitis media. The principal concern cited by Schering-Plough was that allergies occurred with more serious conditions such as asthma. The company stated that 78 percent of asthma patients have nasal symptoms, and 38 percent of allergic rhinitis patients have asthma. This resulted in 3 million Claritin prescriptions being co-prescribed with asthma medications.

Schering-Plough argued that OTC sales of Claritin would lead consumers not to visit their doctors when they had allergy symptoms, leaving many of the co-morbid conditions such as asthma undiagnosed and untreated. Dr. Robert J. Spiegel, chief medical officer for Schering-Plough, noted that asthma cases had increased by 75 percent from 1980 to 1994, and deaths increased from 11.5 to 18.0 per million people.[124] Schering-Plough concluded that the FDA should make a decision on the switch only after a "robust assessment," which would require evidence on the following:[125]

- Ability to accurately self-diagnose the condition
- Assessment of risk of initial misdiagnosis

---

[122]*San Jose Mercury News,* May 12, 2001.
[123]Robert J. Spiegel, Schering-Plough, Presentation to FDA Advisory Committee, May 11, 2001.
[124]Robert J. Spiegel, Schering-Plough, Presentation to FDA Advisory Committee, May 11, 2001.
[125]Schering-Plough, "Briefing Book," April 12, 2001, p. 9.

- Assessment of label comprehension under conditions of use
- Assessment of risk of disease exacerbation or common co-morbid conditions due to subsequent misdiagnosis
- Assessment of risk of incorrect dosing (voluntary and/or inadvertent)
- Assessment of potential outcomes of OTC use

In a filing in conjunction with the May 11 hearing, the American Academy of Otolaryngology—Head and Neck Surgery wrote, "We believe that it is critical for patients with severe allergy problems to see a physician . . . There is great public health risk in inappropriate and/or over utilization of these potent second generation drugs owing to inaccurate self-diagnosis and potential over-medication. In addition, we believe that pharmacists provide important patient education on adverse interactions of drugs."[126] Dr. Hari Sachs, a member of the Nonprescription Drugs Advisory Committee, said, "The bottom line for all of us is the asthma question, which is a big red flag. As a pediatrician, I am always surprised at the kids who come into my office wheezing—and their parents think it's a cold or an allergy."[127]

Similarly, the American Academy of Allergy, Asthma and Immunology wrote that "OTC availability will eliminate the physician from the care process of patients taking antihistamines. . . . Allergies are not necessarily a self-diagnosable condition."[128] The Academy also stated that "the cost of these drugs will likely make them unavailable to those patients who received them through insurance covered formularies."[129] That is, the OTC price of the drugs would be higher than the current insurance copayment. During the Advisory Committee meeting, "Andrea Apter, a panel member and associate professor at the Hospital of the University of Pennsylvania, expressed concern about access to the drugs for the low- and moderate-income clients who now rely on insurance coverage." "'That situation applies to everything we review' for over-the-counter switches, said Charles Ganley, director of the FDA's division of over-the-counter drugs. If that were the criteria, 'nothing will ever get taken to over the counter.'"[130]

In its presentation to the advisory committee, Aventis argued that the FDA should follow the practice used in past switches, which included a comprehensive New Drug Application (NDA) supplement that presented new safety data based on post-approval clinical trials or post-marketing data. Aventis pointed to the same issues raised by Schering-Plough, arguing that OTC status would make the patient responsible for diagnosis, selection of the medication, and dosage. At the May 11 meeting

Dr. Francóis Nader of Aventis Pharmaceutical argued that Allegra was undergoing ongoing clinical development, postapproval and effectiveness trials, and extensive safety monitoring.[131] Nader reminded the committee of the experience with Seldane and argued that once a drug was sold over the counter the collection of post-marketing data became more difficult. Dr. Nader added, "The patients would be playing a costly trial-and-error game with their health, their quality of life and their money."[132] During the meeting, however, advisory committee member Alastair Wood of the School of Medicine of Vanderbilt University asked the drug companies, "Can you give me an example of a specific safety concern you are pursuing?"[133]

As Ira A. Loss, an analyst for Washington Analysis, said, "The drug companies are against it. And the doctors don't like the idea that the number of office visits might fall. It's hard to find an honest broker in the whole deal."[134]

Reactions to the Committee Vote

Robert Seidman of WellPoint celebrated the committee's vote, stating, "Patients can readily self-diagnose and patients can safely use these drugs. This goes to a societal need—it's in society's best interest for these safe and effective drugs to be made available without a prescription."[135] WellPoint also argued that if the costs of pharmaceuticals were not controlled, insurance companies could withdraw their coverage for pharmaceuticals. Seidman explained, "One of the reasons we filed the petition was to protect consumers from out-of-control drug costs. I'm afraid if we do nothing we'll get to the point where there will be no prescription drug benefits at all."[136] Uwe Reinhardt, a health economist at Princeton University, said, "My message to the American people is: 'Get used to it.' Every year for the next decade you will see your benefit package cut."[137]

Larry Sasich of Public Citizen, a public-interest activist group, said, "It's purely self-serving on the part of (WellPoint) to shift cost from their bottom line to the pockets of consumers."[138] Public Citizen had long campaigned against high pharmaceutical prices, yet it did not support the switch to the OTC market where the price would be substantially lower. Several consumer groups, including Families USA, the National Consumers League, and American Association of Retired Persons (AARP), had not taken a position on the issue. Ronald

---

[126]Letter from G. Richard Holt to CDER, April 20, 2001.
[127]*Los Angeles Times,* May 12, 2001.
[128]Letter from Emil J. Bardana, Jr., to FDA, April 19, 2001.
[129]Letter from Emil J. Bardana, Jr., to FDA, April 19, 2001.
[130]*San Jose Mercury News,* May 12, 2001.

[131]Francóis Nader, "Non-Sedating Antihistamines Rx-to-OTC Switch," May 11, 2001.
[132]Francóis Nader, "Non-Sedating Antihistamines Rx-to-OTC Switch," May 11, 2001.
[133]*San Jose Mercury News,* May 12, 2001.
[134]*New York Times,* May 12, 2001.
[135]*Los Angeles Times,* May 12, 2001.
[136]*Sacramento Bee,* May 11, 2001.
[137]*Washington Post,* May 10, 2001.
[138]*Wall Street Journal,* May 11, 2001.

Pollack of Families USA said that although most consumers would benefit from a switch, it "could result in making drugs less available to a very vulnerable part of the population [low-income consumers with prescription-drug coverage]. . . ."[139]

After the vote Dr. Spiegel of Schering-Plough stated, "We don't believe this would be in patients' best interest. We're concerned that the insurance company is trivializing the importance of the patient–physician relationship."[140] He explained, "The second-generation antihistamines tend to be used for long-duration use," and he cited company data indicating an average duration of use of over 60 days.[141]

Commenting on the positions of the drug companies, Stephen W. Schondelmeyer, an economist at the University of Minnesota, asked, "Is the industry saying that American consumers are not as wise in using medicine as consumers in Canada or Mexico or England?"[142]

Dr. Robert Brook, professor of medicine at UCLA and director of the Rand Corporation's health practice program, stated, "This [committee vote] is consistent with the movement we're seeing in medicine, which is to give consumers more control over their lives. I suspect that, as we get more sophisticated with drugs and their safety margins, we're going to see more of this."[143]

The patient-advocacy group Allergy and Asthma Network/Mothers of Asthmatics (AAN/MA) spoke in favor of prescription-only status. President Nancy Sander said, "The average consumer does not possess the knowledge and skills necessary to safely self-diagnose and treat allergy symptoms without medical guidance. At best, their efforts are experimental. Stand in the cold and cough section of the grocery store and you'll witness confused consumers seeking medical advice from stocking clerks as to which medications they should take home to try. . . . The health insurers say nonsedating antihistamines are safe. And I agree. But only when used as prescribed by a physician."[144]

Blue Cross of California, WellPoint Health Networks Inc.

WellPoint Health Networks was a leading managed care company serving 9.7 million medical members and over 40 million specialty members. WellPoint Pharmacy Management was the nation's leading health-plan-owned pharmacy benefit management company serving 27.8 million people.[145] WellPoint was formed in 1992 to operate Blue Cross of California's managed care business. WellPoint subsequently acquired the group life and

health businesses of Massachusetts Mutual Life Insurance and John Hancock Mutual Life Insurance companies. WellPoint also acquired Rush Prudential Health Plans of Illinois and Blue Cross and Blue Shield of Georgia.[146] Total revenue for 2000 was $9.2 billion, and net income was $342.3 million, a 21 percent increase over the previous year. For 3 consecutive years WellPoint had been voted the most-admired health care company in *Fortune* magazine's annual survey. "Our success in attracting customers is a result of our focus on offering products that deliver choice and flexibility," said Leonard D. Schaeffer, WellPoint's chairman and chief executive officer.[147]

Blue Cross of California estimated that it would save $45 million annually if the three drugs were switched to the OTC market. In addition, the company would not have to pay for physician visits for patients who chose to self-diagnose.

Schering-Plough Corporation

Schering-Plough was a research-based, worldwide pharmaceutical company with four major therapeutic areas: allergy/respiratory, anti-infective/anticancer, dermatology, and cardiovascular. Its products were sold in 125 world markets. In 2000 the company had net income of $2.4 billion on sales of $9.8 billion and total assets of $10.8 billion. Spending on research and development was 13.6 percent of sales in 2000, and its gross margin was 80.6 percent. Sales for the first quarter of 2001 were down 3 percent from the year-earlier quarter, and net income was down 10 percent. The company's leading product was Claritin (and Claritin D), and Claritin sales were up 8 percent over the year-earlier quarter. Over 85 percent of the $3 billion Claritin revenue came from the United States. The company's OTC products included Dr. Scholl's foot care products, Lotrimin, Tinactin, Chlor-Trimetron, Coricidin, Di-Gel, St. Joseph's aspirin, Solarcaine, and Coppertone sun care products.

Schering-Plough's Market Strategy

Claritin received FDA approval in 1993 as a prescription drug and as such was promoted primarily through doctors. In 1997 the FDA revised its regulations, making possible direct-to-consumer (DTC) advertising of prescription drugs in the broadcast media. Schering-Plough and other pharmaceutical companies then began to directly advertise to consumers on television, radio, and through other media. The advertisements gave a toll-free number to call for information, referred to magazine advertisements where warnings were required, and instructed viewers to "ask your doctor." The marketing strategy was to induce consumers to ask their doctors for the drug by brand name. This strategy proved to be quite

[139]*Wall Street Journal,* May 11, 2001.
[140]*New York Times,* May 11, 2001.
[141]*The Pink Sheet,* May 21, 2001.
[142]*New York Times,* May 12, 2001.
[143]*Los Angeles Times,* May 12, 2001.
[144]Letter to FDA Advisory Committee, May 11, 2001, www.aanma.org.
[145]www.wellpoint.com.

[146]Blue Cross is a national trade association.
[147]www.wellpoint.com.

successful. Schering-Plough reportedly spent $322 million on advertisements for Claritin in 1998 and 1999, and U.S. sales reached $2.5 billion.[148] A 2001 survey by *Prevention Magazine* found that 72 percent of the respondents recalled an advertisement for Claritin.

The Pharmaceutical Research and Manufacturers of America explained the rationale and success of DTC advertising.[149]

Advertising allows the pharmaceutical companies to educate consumers directly about possible treatment options. A study released by *Prevention Magazine* found consumers give high marks to pharmaceutical advertising because it "allows people to be more involved with their health." Further, the study found DTC advertising "is an extremely effective means of promoting both the public health and prescription medicines" and concluded that "the benefits of DTC [direct-to-consumer] advertising could go far beyond simply selling pharmaceutical medicines: These advertisements play a very real role in enhancing the public health." More importantly, the survey found that DTC advertising prompted an estimated 21.2 million Americans to talk to their doctors about a medical condition or illness they had never discussed with their physicians before. In other words, millions of people who had previously suffered in silence were encouraged to seek help.

An Ohio State University study of 246 North Carolina patients taking Allegra, Claritin, or Zyrtec revealed that 65 percent did not have allergies. The study, however, was funded by a company that was marketing a blood test for allergies. Dr. Steven D. Shaefer of the New York Eye and Ear Infirmary said, "It's hard to separate those people who have sinusitis from those who have allergic disease."[150]

The U.S. Senate took an interest in DTC advertising. The Consumer Affairs Subcommittee of the Commerce Committee scheduled hearings for May 22 but decided to postpone them.

A second component of the market strategy for Claritin was to set a high price. Drug prices in the United States were considerably higher than in most other countries. The price of Claritin averaged $2.13 a tablet in the United States, whereas in Canada the price was $0.70 before taxes. WellPoint estimated that Claritin might sell in the OTC market for $15 for a month's supply compared to $60 to $80 as a prescription drug. Part of the increase in U.S. spending on pharmaceuticals was due to high prices, and some critics of the industry pointed to DTC advertising, which allowed pharmaceutical companies to establish market power and obtain higher prices.

A third component of the market strategy was driven by the length of the patent. Because of the unusually long review process for Claritin, Schering-Plough had succeeded in having the patent extended to December 2002. The company subsequently mounted a formidable campaign to extend the patent beyond its 2002 expiration date. "To press its case in Washington, the company has paid millions of dollars in political contributions and assembled a high-powered, strange-bedfellows team of lobbyists (including former senators Howard Baker and Dennis DeConcini, the Gore-confidant Peter Knight, and Linda Daschle, wife of the Senate minority leader Tom Daschle); it has also encouraged repeated attempts by Congressional supporters to insert language favorable to Schering into legislation at the last instant."[151]

Once the patent expired, a generic version of loratadine produced by Geneva Pharmaceuticals, a unit of Novartis, could be marketed with a 180-day period of exclusivity.[152] After that period other generics could enter once FDA approval had been granted. Teva Pharmaceuticals had received tentative FDA approval for its generic version of loratadine. Six other companies had also filed to sell generic versions of loratadine, including two that planned to sell on the OTC market.[153]

Schering-Plough had two basic alternatives for dealing with the generics. It could leave Claritin as a prescription-only drug using DTC marketing and its brand name to maintain a price premium over the generics. Second, it could voluntarily move Claritin to the OTC market, which would take the generics with it, since FDA regulations prohibited selling the same drug on both the prescription and OTC markets. The company had employed this strategy in 1991 with Gyne-Lotrimin, used in the treatment of vaginal yeast infections.

To replace Claritin, Schering-Plough had developed a third-generation antihistamine, Clarinex (desloratadine), and filed an NDA in October 1999.[154] Clarinex would be sold as a prescription drug and heavily advertised, as was Claritin. Schering-Plough's strategy was to try to migrate prescription demand from Claritin to Clarinex, but to do so in a manner that would leave Claritin in a strong position when switched to the OTC market. Schering-Plough recognized that migrating prescriptive demand to Clarinex would be easier if Claritin were still on a prescription-only basis.

In January 2001 Clarinex was approved for sale in the European Union, and the FDA issued an "approvable" letter for the drug indicating that there were no outstanding clinical or scientific issues.[155] The FDA,

---

[148]Stephen S. Hall, "Prescription for Profit," *New York Times Magazine,* March 11, 2001.
[149]www.phrma.org.
[150]*Wall Street Journal,* May 18, 2001.

[151]Stephen S. Hall, "Prescription for Profit," *New York Times Magazine,* March 11, 2001.
[152]Schering-Plough had sued Geneva Pharmaceuticals alleging patent infringement.
[153]Stephen S. Hall, "Prescription for Profit," *New York Times Magazine,* March 11, 2001.
[154]Desloratadine was developed for Schering-Plough by Sepracor, Inc. Separately, Sepracor had developed a new antihistamine with the brand name Zoltara, and it hoped for FDA approval in 2001.
[155]Desloratadine was marketed in Europe under the brand names Aerius and Neoclarityn.

however, withheld approval because of quality control problems in Schering-Plough's New Jersey and Puerto Rico manufacturing facilities. The company temporarily shut down its production facilities and embarked on an extensive Good Manufacturing Practices program. CEO Richard Jay Kogan stated, "I am taking full responsibility for resolving these matters in a timely manner and securing FDA confidence in the quality and reliability of our manufacturing systems and controls."

The Clarinex strategy would be put at risk by an FDA decision to switch Claritin to the OTC market, since Schering-Plough would not have an opportunity to migrate demand to Clarinex. Moreover, if Claritin were given OTC status, the FDA might at some point do the same with Clarinex. Bert Spilker of the Pharmaceutical Research and Manufacturers Association said a switch "would chill many areas of research and development . . ."

Schering-Plough's Nonmarket Strategy

Schering-Plough had advertised Claritin as safer than the nonprescription antihistamines and having side effects like "taking a sugar pill," so it could not argue that Claritin was not safe when sold over the counter. The company instead took the position that more postmarketing studies should be conducted. With regard to the switching process the FDA Review Team had concluded, "The switch of a prescription drug to OTC marketing requires a review of the post-marketing safety data and a determination that a consumer can adequately use the product in an OTC setting." Schering-Plough used this statement to argue that insufficient data on postmarketing safety were available. "'It took about 10 years to realize the cardiac toxicity of the once-popular antihistamine Seldane,' said Chandler May, a researcher funded by the drug companies. 'The science needs five or 10 years to say if Claritin is safe at this level or Allegra is safe at that level.'"[156]

Schering-Plough argued that it was better positioned to monitor consumer use and safety data. Spiegel said, "What we don't know is as you move away from [prescription status], how might the benefit decrease and the risk increase."[157]

One alternative for Schering-Plough was to fight the FDA on a step-by-step basis as the FDA decision-making process progressed. One possible focus was on the OTC label for the drug. Some members of the advisory committee argued that the labels should include warnings about use by the elderly and young children. In its presentation to the advisory committee WellPoint had anticipated this and provided a draft label with the following warnings:

> If you are pregnant or nursing a baby seek the advice of a health care professional before using this

product. KEEP THIS AND ALL OTHER DRUGS OUT OF THE REACH OF CHILDREN. In case of accidental overdose, seek professional assistance or contact a Poison Control Center immediately.

Schering-Plough could also file a lawsuit to challenge an FDA-mandated switch. William O'Donnell of Schering-Plough said, "We think this (move) raises many legal and policy issues. Any switch would be considered an unprecedented departure from past agency policy and would implicate the sponsor's statutory and constitutional rights."

Another alternative was to attempt to enlist congressional and White House support for prescription-only status. One natural opportunity was the appointment of a new commissioner for the FDA.

Aventis and UCB/Pfizer

Aventis and Pfizer were both much larger companies than Schering-Plough, and Allegra and Zyrtec respectively accounted for a much smaller percent of their sales. In 2000 Aventis had sales of €22.3 billion and net income of €1.1 billion.[158] In the first quarter of 2001 sales were €5.865 billion, and net income was €317 million. Allegra sales reached €384 million in the first quarter, and U.S. sales accounted for one-third of the sales of Aventis Pharma. Allegra and Zyrtec had longer remaining patent lives than Claritin.

Pfizer had sales of $29.6 billion and net income of $3.7 billion, which was down 25 percent from the previous year because of merger expenses. In the first quarter of 2001 Pfizer earned $1.9 billion. UCB had sales of €2.204 billion, and net income of €269 million. Zyrtec was one of the two principal drugs of UCB's Pharma Group.

Pfizer declined to participate in the May 11 panel meeting and immediately after the vote presented the FDA with a 49-page legal brief stating grounds on which it was prepared to sue the FDA. The brief argued that a switch would infringe Pfizer's proprietary information, since a public hearing was required and the FDA would be forced to disclose proprietary information that would deprive it of property. Lisa Kennedy of Aventis Pharmaceuticals also said the company would file suit. She said, "Decisions about the product should be made in agreement with us and health care professionals."[159] "If the agency goes forward, we would definitely challenge it."[160]

The FDA Decision

For its final decision the FDA had to follow administrative procedures established in the Food, Drug and

[156]*Washington Post*, May 10, 2001.
[157]*Wall Street Journal*, May 11, 2001.
[158]Aventis was formed in December 1999 by the merger of Hoechst AG and Rhone-Poulenc SA.
[159]*Saint-Louis Post Dispatch*, May 11, 2001.
[160]*New York Times*, May 16, 2001.

Cosmetics Act and the Administrative Practices Act. The procedures could include a public hearing, notice of proposed decisions in the *Federal Register,* and a comment period. Any decision by the FDA could be appealed to the federal courts, but preventing a decision from taking effect would require a preliminary injunction by a federal judge.

Whether the FDA had the authority to force the drugs to be sold over the counter was unclear. David A. Kessler, former commissioner of the FDA and dean of the Yale University School of Medicine, said, "It appears the FDA has the authority." Ira Loss observed, "The statute does not prevent them from doing this, but it doesn't say they can either."[161] David F. Weeda, a former FDA attorney who now represented pharmaceutical companies, said, "It's a legal question that has not been answered in court. In my gut, I think that it is going to be a close case."[162]

The Bush administration had yet to appoint a commissioner for the FDA, and the switching issue was certain to be raised in the Senate confirmation hearing on the appointee. ■

Preparation Questions

1. Assess the significance of an FDA-mandated switch on Schering-Plough, Aventis, UCB, and Pfizer.
2. How would a possible switch affect Schering-Plough's market strategy and product planning process?
3. What are the implications of a possible switch for the pharmaceutical and health care insurance industries?
4. Formulate an integrated market and nonmarket strategy for Schering-Plough.
5. Formulate an integrated market and nonmarket strategy for WellPoint.

---

[161] *New York Times,* May 16, 2001.
[162] *New York Times,* May 11, 2001.

-- P A R T   I I --

Integrative Case
Fuel Economy Standards 2007

Introduction

After more than 20 years of stable fuel economy standards, in 2007 the stars aligned and Congress was poised to enact a 40 percent increase. The automobile industry had initially opposed any major increase, but with an increase seeming inevitable, it had turned its attention to the details of the pending legislation. As often was the case, the devil was in the details, and individual firms had differing interests. They sought both to lessen the burden of higher standards and obtain a competitive advantage—or at least to preserve opportunities to deploy their distinctive competencies. The Senate had passed a fuel economy bill, and the House was considering fuel economy standards as part of a broader energy bill.

History of Fuel Economy Standards

The 1973–4 Arab oil embargo resulted in oil shortages and high prices for gasoline and heating oil in the United States. Congress responded by enacting a Corporate Average Fuel Economy (CAFE) system that required an increase in automobile fuel economy from 14.2 miles per gallon in 1974 to 27.5 mpg in 1984. Subsequently, the Department of Transportation set standards for light trucks, which at the time were primarily used for work. At a substantial cost the automobile industry was able to meet the 27.5 mpg standard. The CAFE system was not only costly, but it also had differential effects on individual manufacturers. The standards advantaged automakers that already had higher fuel economy vehicles and disadvantaged the Big Three U.S. automakers, Chrysler, Ford, and General Motors, which lost substantial market share primarily to Asian automakers. The lost market share also meant that auto workers, and particularly members of the United Auto Workers (UAW), lost jobs.

Only Congress could increase the CAFE standard for automobiles, and efforts were made to increase the standard, particularly in 1990 and 2002. In 1990 Congress considered a bill to increase fuel economy standards by 40 percent by 2001 based on automakers' actual 1988 fuel economy. Despite the invasion of Kuwait by Iraq during the congressional debate, the bill failed to pass because of several factors. First, both organized and unorganized interests opposed the proposed increase. The automakers were unanimous in opposing the major increase proposed, and the UAW joined the industry in an attempt to save members' jobs. Suppliers and the communities in which jobs were threatened also opposed the legislation. In addition, oil prices, which had been predicted to increase, instead had fallen substantially in real terms.

Consumers were not concerned with fuel economy, and their focus turned to light trucks and SUVs, which were classified as light trucks. Automakers were able to rally opposition by consumers using the themes that higher CAFE standards would increase costs, decrease consumer choice by eliminating large, more powerful vehicles, and reduce safety by forcing automakers to produce smaller, less safe vehicles. The final factor was the staunch efforts of Congress members such as John Dingell (D-MI), chairman of the House Commerce Committee, and Senator Carl Levin (D-MI), who used their positions to organize congressional opposition to the bill.

The 2002 attempt to increase CAFE standards resulted from concerns about global climate change, and although the evidence was strong that climate change was real, skeptics remained. Moreover, many citizens were unconvinced that they should bear higher costs to deal with the threat of climate change, and President George W. Bush opposed any increase. Despite the heightened security concerns as a result of the September 11, 2001 terrorist attack, the same alignment of interests and the supporters of the auto industry in Congress were sufficient to defeat the proposed legislation.

Despite unchanged CAFE standards, automakers had through technological advances improved the fuel efficiency of their vehicles by 60 percent since 1984, but that gain was not translated into improved fuel economy. Instead, automakers responded to consumer demand by using the gain in efficiency to increase the size, weight, and horsepower of vehicles, resulting in little change in fuel economy. In the mid-1980s Honda's Civic CRX was 12 feet in length with a weight of 1,700 pounds, whereas a 2007 Civic was 3 feet longer and 900 pounds heavier. The Honda Fit was larger than the 1980s CRX.[163]

By 2007 several changes in the market and nonmarket environments had occurred. First, the evidence on climate change was much more conclusive, and many Americans believed that costly measures were warranted. As David Doniger of the Natural Resources Defense Council (NRDC) observed, "People get it now. They didn't pay much attention to global warming five years ago."[164] Second, certain interests such as the Big Three automakers and the UAW were considerably weaker than in the past. Membership in the UAW had fallen from 750,000 in 1995 to 550,000 in 2006 and was half the membership of 20 years earlier. Third, the price of

---

[163]*Wall Street Journal,* May 31, 2007.
[164]*New York Times,* April 7, 2007.

gasoline had risen to over $3.00 a gallon, and few expected it to fall significantly. Fourth, the conflicts in Afghanistan and Iraq heightened security concerns, and the risk of dependence on the foreign supply of oil was more salient.[165] Fifth, in the 2006 elections Democrats had won a majority in both the House and the Senate and pledged to increase fuel economy standards. Sixth, in his 2007 State of the Union Address President Bush asked for a major increase in fuel economy standards to be implemented in a cap-and-trade system with the National Highway Traffic Safety Administration (NHTSA), an agency in the Department of Transportation responsible for developing attribute-specific standards for vehicle classes. Seventh, the state of California had taken the initiative to regulate fuel economy indirectly. In 2002 the California legislature had enacted legislation establishing stringent standards for greenhouse gas emissions, and those standards would require major increases in fuel economy. The auto industry had filed a lawsuit to block the California standards.

The 2007 Legislative Effort

Energy legislation and higher fuel economy standards were high on the agenda of the Democratic leadership in Congress, and the leadership pushed a 35 mpg standard for 2020 for the combined car and light truck fleet. In January 2007 the House passed H.R. 6, the Renewable Fuels, Consumer Protection, and Energy Efficiency Act of 2007. The bill, however, did not address vehicle fuel economy standards because of disagreements between the Democratic leadership and Representative Dingell, chairman of the House Energy and Commerce Committee.

Senator Debbie Stabenow (D-MI) explained her support for the automobile industry, "I am very proud to represent people who work hard every day in this industry, and the auto industry is the linchpin of Michigan's economy, making up 22 percent of our state's workforce. The Big Three employ nearly 400,000 Americans in 176 major facilities in 34 states. I think it is not an exaggeration to say that the automobile industry created the middle class of this country. As we move forward together, we need to achieve our goals and also allow them to continue to be strong and an important part of our middle income wage base."[166]

In February NHTSA presented a draft of the Bush administration proposal for reducing gasoline consumption by 20 percent over the next 10 years. This would be attained by increasing the use of alternative fuels and increasing fuel economy standards by approximately 4 percent a year through 2017. Fuel economy standards would be based on the size, or footprint, e.g., the wheelbase, of the vehicle class. Daniel Becker of the Sierra Club welcomed the Bush initiative. Dave McCurdy, president of the Alliance of Automobile Manufacturers, said, "Automakers support reforming and raising car fuel-economy standards, consistent with the need to preserve jobs and consumer choice. Determining the right level for the future will require sound science and engineering, in an open process that involves everyone."[167] The reference to jobs was for the sake of the UAW. Representative Fred Upton (R-MI) said the cost of meeting the higher standards would be $2,000 per vehicle.

Auto Industry Strategy

The industry argued that the sharply higher standards would force automakers to produce small cars and limit the choices available to consumers. Automakers emphasized the themes of safety and choice. The Alliance of Automobile Manufacturers ran radio advertisements stating, "Why can't they let me make the choice? I'm all for better fuel economy, but for me safety is my top concern."[168] In print ads the industry claimed that the standards under consideration in Congress would force consumers to buy smaller vehicles. One ad said the Senate proposal would "take your pickup truck away."

In April 2007 automakers began to change their strategy. Instead of opposing higher fuel economy standards, they decided to work from the inside to influence what appeared to be an inevitable increase. Derrick M. Kuzak, group vice president of Ford, commented, "We very much want to work with Congress. We recognize that CO_2 is an issue and we want to be part of the solution, but it has to be technology-based, and affordable."[169] Doniger of the NRDC observed, "They're coming to the table so they can avoid being on the menu."[170] Automakers turned their attention to the details of achieving a fleet-wide standard. Michael Stanton, president of the Association of International Automobile Manufacturers, said, "We're all trying to position ourselves."[171]

In early June the CEOs of Daimler-Chrysler, Ford, and General Motors lobbied members of Congress on the energy and fuel economy bills under consideration. After the Senate Energy and Commerce Committee approved a fuel economy bill, the Alliance of Automobile Manufacturers knew that sharply higher fuel economy standards were inevitable. In a broad coalition with the UAW, suppliers, and dealers, in conjunction with other groups including the National Association of Manufacturers, it

---

[165]Since 1990 domestic oil production had declined from 7.4 million barrels a day to 5.2 million, and imports had increased from 5.9 to 10.1 million barrels a day (*New York Times,* January 22, 2007). Cars and light trucks accounted for 20 percent of U.S. CO_2 emissions.
[166]Debbie Stabenow, Testimony, Committee on Energy and Natural Resources, U.S. Senate, January 30, 2007, p. 3.

[167]*Wall Street Journal,* May 15, 2007. The members of the Alliance were BMW, Daimler-Chrysler, Ford, General Motors, Mazda, Mitsubishi, Porsche, Toyota, and Volkswagen.
[168]*New York Times,* June 20, 2007.
[169]*New York Times,* April 7, 2007.
[170]*New York Times,* April 7, 2007.
[171]*Wall Street Journal,* April 9, 2007.

changed the tone of its messages. One ad stated, "We don't have all the answers to questions about fuel economy standards. No one does. But we are committed to helping find them."

Robert Lutz, vice chairman of General Motors, warned, "Meeting these accelerated and very, very steep standards would consume the quasi-totality of our investment in engineering resources." He added, "Anybody who thinks that the auto industry will invent some sort of device that will eliminate or absorb CO_2 is dreaming."[172] Lutz estimated that the cost of an average vehicle would increase by $5,000 to $6,000.[173] Goldman Sachs estimated that a fuel economy standard of 35 mpg would reduce Ford's bottom line by $750 million a year.[174]

Consumers were also concerned about new fuel economy standards. Barry McCahill, president of the SUV Owners of America, said, "They're saying this will save a lot at the pump—but people aren't being told that all these technological improvements will have a pretty significant price tag. If we get smaller vehicles with less towing capacity, well, for a lot of people that's going to be a deal-breaker."[175] Light trucks had made a recovery in spite of high gas prices and accounted for 55 percent of sales in October 2007, compared to 2 percent for hybrids.

The Big Three wanted an attribute system in which vehicles with larger wheelbases would have lower standards than vehicles with smaller wheelbases, as included in the Senate bill and the Bush administration proposal. The automakers also wanted the flexibility of using credits earned by exceeding the standard for one attribute class to cover a deficiency in another attribute class. This would allow automakers that exceeded the fuel economy for small vehicles to overcome a shortfall for their large vehicles. This would support the current strategy of selling small vehicles for low prices while selling large vehicles for high prices.

Automakers also sought the opportunity to buy and sell credits. Analogous to a cap-and-trade system used in the regulation of environmental externalities, an automaker that exceeded the fuel economy standards could sell credits to an automaker that was below the standard. This would benefit specialty manufacturers as well as allowing additional flexibility to manufacturers producing both high and low mileage vehicles.

Since attribute-based standards would have to be set by an administrative agency, one issue was which agency would be given the responsibility for the standards. One alternative would be NHTSA, which was expected to be more sympathetic to the auto industry. Another alternative was the EPA, which was expected to be less sympathetic. Moreover, if NHTSA were given

sole responsibility over tailpipe emissions, states such as California, which required an EPA waiver, could be blocked from setting their own standards.

John German of the American Honda Motor Company anticipated the implementation of higher fuel economy standards. He testified, "What we have said is that the standard should be set by an expert agency like NHTSA. They are the one who can evaluate the trade-offs between—the rate of technology development is very unpredictable. . . . But the issues are so complicated that it really takes an expert agency like NHTSA to sort them out."[176]

An issue that divided the auto industry was the basis for how standards would be set. CAFE standards were the same (e.g., 27.5 mpg) for all automakers, and an alternative was to require each manufacturer to achieve the same percentage increase, as in the failed 1990 legislation. The percentage approach would disadvantage high mileage automakers such as Honda and Toyota, and favor low mileage automakers such as Ford and General Motors. Michael Stanton of the Association of International Automobile Manufacturers said his members were "adamantly opposed to anything that treats us differently than other manufacturers."[177]

Most environmental groups had sought a single fuel economy standard for cars and light trucks, and the bills backed by the Democratic leadership included a single standard. Automakers preferred separate standards, which would allow a lower standard for trucks, enabling manufacturers to emphasize their strengths in the light truck market.

The auto industry sought to preserve the flex-fuel credit that gave a 50 percent fuel economy bonus for vehicles capable of running on alternative fuels such as ethanol. Environmental groups advocated the elimination of the bonus, since few of the vehicles ever used ethanol as a fuel.

Automakers had avoided CAFE standards on some SUVs and trucks by making them heavy enough to qualify as medium trucks, which were not subject to fuel economy standards. Environmentalists sought to include medium and heavy trucks in any standards system, but these trucks were used for work and hence came in a wide variety of types. The bills under consideration in Congress would cover medium and heavy trucks, and the industry sought to have NHTSA set standards based on feasibility considerations, including cost and technology.

Industry members emphasized the need for tax incentives to bring down the cost of new technologies. The auto makers sought tax credits and loan guarantees for the cost of retooling and the development of new technologies. Senator Stabenow and the UAW lobbied for a provision in the House bill to provide loan guarantees.

[172] *Wall Street Journal,* April 9, 2007.
[173] National Post's Financial Post & FP Investing, December 11, 2007.
[174] National Post's Financial Post & FP Investing, December 11, 2007.
[175] *Christian Science Monitor,* December 5, 2007.

[176] John German, Testimony, Committee on Energy and Natural Resources, U.S. Senate, January 30, 2007, p. 49.
[177] *Wall Street Journal,* April 9, 2007.

Automakers also sought other tax incentives. One existing incentive was a consumer tax rebate for the purchase of qualifying hybrid vehicles. The rebate had been increased to a maximum of $2,000, but it declined when the number of vehicles sold in a year reached 60,000. The 60,000 limit was supported by the UAW because most of the qualifying vehicles were produced by companies such as Honda and Toyota, whose workers are not represented by the UAW. Toyota was working to eliminate the limit in any new legislation.[178]

Individual companies also had special concerns. In 2004 Nissan had successfully obtained an exemption from NHTSA that waived for the 2006–2010 model years the two-fleet rule that required automakers to meet standards on both their domestic and imported fleets. If the exemption had not been granted, Nissan said it would have to move production from its plants in Tennessee and Mississippi to its plant in Mexico. Nissan came out in support of higher fuel economy standards in what commentators said was an attempt to preserve its special exemption. The bill under consideration in the Senate would extend the exemption for three years.

Under the current regulatory system NHTSA could make exceptions for "low-volume producers" with global annual production of no more than 10,000 vehicles. The Senate bill defined a low-volume producer as one with less than 0.4 percent of the U.S. market (approximately 60,000 units). This would benefit Porsche, which had sales of 34,227 in 2006.[179] Porsche was actively working to preserve the provision, lobbying both Congress and the White House Office of Management and Budget.[180] Barbara Nocera of Mazda North American Operations, however, warned that the 0.4 percent level would make it easier for automakers from China and India to make inroads in the U.S. market.[181]

Higher fuel economy standards would provide a relative advantage to automakers with existing technologies yielding higher mileage. For example, diesel engines were 20–30 percent more fuel efficient than conventional internal combustion engines and accounted for nearly half the new car sales in Europe. German automakers announced plans to sell diesel vehicles in the United States.

Honda also announced production plans for new generation diesel automobiles and trucks that met the strict U.S. emissions standards for particulates and NO_x. John German of Honda explained, however, why the impact of diesel vehicles would not be as great in the United States as in Europe. He said, "Diesel fuel in Europe is cheaper than gasoline is in Europe; differential

taxation.... [and] the emissions standards in Europe are less stringent ..."[182]

FedEx Systems had joined with Environmental Defense for a project to demonstrate the feasibility of using hybrid electric versions of its pickup and delivery trucks. The trucks met FedEx's performance standards and increased fuel economy by 40 percent while decreasing particulate and greenhouse gases emissions, but the cost of the truck was almost twice as much as its standard truck.

Congressional Action

The Senate Commerce, Science and Transportation Committee adopted the attribute-based approach to fuel economy standards as well as the provisions for transferring and trading credits and most of the other provisions providing flexibility sought by the auto industry. The bill established an average fuel economy standard of 35 MPG by 2020 for all cars and light trucks manufactured for sale in the United States, and after 2020 the standard would increase by 4 percent a year through 2030. The Senate bill would also eliminate the credits for vehicles that could run on alternative fuels.

Senator Levin of Michigan said, "We will be continuing to oppose it. This is not over by any stretch."[183] The UAW opposed the bill because it would lead automakers to move small car production offshore and did not specify requirements for flex-fuel vehicles.[184] John W. Snow, chairman of Cerebus Capital Management, which was in the process of purchasing 80.1 percent of Chrysler, pledged that his firm would oppose the demanding standards in the Senate bill. He supported a modest increase in standards, "not a set of standards that are so one-sided that they can't be met and which have the risk of sinking the U.S. auto industry."[185]

The fuel economy bill was incorporated in the energy bill H.R. 6 reported by the Energy and Natural Resources Committee. The Energy Committee also considered a provision that would have established a Renewable Portfolio Standard (RPS) requiring electric utilities to generate 15 percent of their electricity from wind, solar, or biomass energy by 2020. Ben Lieberman of the Heritage Foundation commented, "The only reason renewable electricity needs to be mandated in the first place is that these alternatives are far too expensive to compete otherwise."[186] Senator Pete V. Domenici (R-NM) offered an amendment that would have allowed utilities to meet the goal through nuclear power, but Democrats defeated it. Domenici responded with the threat of a filibuster, and the RPS was abandoned. The

[178]*Wall Street Journal,* April 9, 2007.
[179]*Automotive New Europe,* December 10, 2007.
[180]The CAFE system included fines for not meeting the mileage standards, and companies such as BMW, Mercedes-Benz, and Porsche regularly paid the fines. In 2006 Porsche paid $3.6 million in fines.
[181]*Automotive News,* November 26, 2007.

[182]John German, Testimony, Committee on Energy and Natural Resources, U.S. Senate, January 30, 2007, p. 53.
[183]*New York Times,* June 22, 2007.
[184]*Wall Street Journal,* June 22, 2007.
[185]*New York Times,* July 12, 2007.
[186]*International Herald Tribune,* December 10, 2007.

Senate leadership also refused to consider a provision eliminating $32 billion in tax breaks for the oil industry because Republicans were certain to mount a filibuster against the provision and there were not enough votes for cloture.

The two Democrat senators from Michigan had recruited colleagues to support amendments to relax the standards. Bargaining within the Senate resulted in two concessions to the Michigan senators. First, the 4 percent annual increase after 2020 was eliminated in favor of requiring "maximal feasible increases" in standards taking into account technology and economic impact. Second, the credit for vehicles that run on alternative fuels was continued but phased out gradually through 2020. The Senate then passed the energy bill H.R. 6 incorporating the compromise fuel economy standards.

The auto industry and its supporters had worked to obtain provisions in the Senate bill to make it easier to achieve the standard, and they sought to preserve them while avoiding any changes by the House that would make the fuel economy system more stringent. In any bargaining with the House over a bill for final passage, the Michigan senators could again try to weaken the standards.

In the House Chairman Dingell and Rick Boucher (R-VA) introduced a bill that would set fuel economy standards of 36 mpg for cars by 2021 and 30 mpg for light trucks by 2024. The bill also contained an "anti-backsliding" provision that would prevent an automaker from decreasing its fleet average fuel economy. This provision would aid the UAW by disadvantaging already high

mileage automakers. The bill also contained a provision that would block states from setting standards more stringent than federal standards. House Speaker Nancy Pelosi (D-CA) reacted angrily to the bill and urged the House to reject it.

The Democratic leadership in the House included in the energy bill two controversial measures, one of which would increase taxes on oil companies by $32 billion by eliminating tax breaks for exploration and development, and the other which would require electric utilities to generate 15 percent of their power from wind, solar, or biomass energy. Opposition had mounted to the requirement, particularly in the South, where wind power was not a feasible alternative.

The House also had to adopt fuel economy standards to be included in the energy bill, and Speaker Pelosi and Chairman Dingell began bargaining over the details of the bill. Dingell agreed to the 35 mpg standard but sought to ease the burden on the industry.

Whatever bill Congress passed would leave a number of features of the current fuel economy standard system in place and potentially subject to rulemaking by the agency assigned responsibility for implementation. One feature was a set of fines for not meeting fuel economy standards. Another was whether automakers would be required to meet standards for both their domestic and imported fleets. ■

SOURCE: This case was prepared from public sources by Professor David P. Baron. Copyright © 2008 by the Board of Trustees of the Leland Stanford Junior University. All rights reserved. Reprinted with permission.

Preparation Questions

1. What objectives—primary and contingent—should the Big Three pursue? Can they stop the 35 mpg standard?
2. What specifically should the automakers seek to preserve from the Senate bill?
3. Formulate a nonmarket strategy for the Big Three to influence Congress and the subsequent implementation of any legislation that might be passed. What should Toyota do?
4. How should the market and nonmarket strategies of the auto companies be integrated?

C H A P T E R

Antitrust: Economics, Law, and Politics

People of the same trade seldom meet together, even for merriment and diversion, but the conversation ends in a conspiracy against the public or in some contrivance to raise prices.

—ADAM SMITH, 1776

INTRODUCTION

Antitrust policy is an amalgam of social policy, economics, law, and administrative practice.[1] Antitrust policy had its origins in the populist movement of the 1870s when a number of states enacted statutes to regulate economic activity and control the exercise of economic power. At the federal level, this movement led to the Interstate Commerce Act of 1887, which provided for federal regulation of interstate commerce, and the Sherman Act of 1890, the first federal antitrust statute. These acts resulted from political pressure by farmers and others concerned about railroad cartels, the railroads' pricing practices, and the distribution of power between farmers and railroads. The laws thus represent both social and economic policy.

As social policy, the antitrust laws express concern about concentrations of economic power and the potential for abuse inherent in that concentration. This parallels the concern about the concentration of political power and the preference for its dispersion in the electorate and among the institutions of government. Just as the Constitution controls political power through checks and balances among the branches of government and through popular elections, antitrust policy has focused on controlling economic power.

Antitrust policy also reflects economic policy. The basic objective is to protect competition and by doing so to benefit consumers. Antitrust thus is concerned with the structure of markets, the conduct of market participants, and the resulting performance of those markets. Protecting competition does not mean protecting competitors; vigorous competition can result in firms being driven from the market. Moreover, practices that may appear to be anticompetitive must be evaluated in terms of their effects on consumers. Antitrust economics has both a theoretical and an empirical component. Theory has been an indispensable guide for reasoning about the relationships among structure, conduct, and performance. Empirical research has provided evidence about those relationships.

Antitrust law includes statutes and the court decisions interpreting those statutes. The principal federal statutes are the Sherman Act, the Clayton Act of 1914, and the Federal Trade Commission Act of 1914. These acts are broadly worded, employing such terms as *monopolize, restraint of trade,* and *unfair practices.* This has required the courts to interpret the acts in the context of the specifics of individual cases.[2] Antitrust law is thus both statutory and interpretive. It is also the subject of politics as interest groups, politicians, and public policy specialists attempt to influence the law.

---

[1]The antitrust policies of Japan and the European Union are considered in Chapters 14 and 15, respectively.
[2]See Carp and Stidham (2001) for information on the U.S. federal courts.

Although there have been few major changes in the antitrust statutes in recent years, antitrust has not been static. Change comes from its administration and enforcement. At the federal level, public enforcement is provided by the Antitrust Division of the Department of Justice (DOJ) and the Federal Trade Commission (FTC). During the 1980s the DOJ and the FTC made significant changes in antitrust policy through their merger guidelines, which revised the policies governing federal enforcement. Similarly, enforcement policies on vertical restraints of trade changed considerably. During the 1990s the pace of antitrust enforcement increased substantially. The antitrust laws, however, are enforced less by government than by private litigants—often by one firm filing a lawsuit against another. Over 90 percent of the lawsuits filed under the federal antitrust laws are brought by private litigants. Consequently, decisions made by courts on cases brought by private litigants cause antitrust law to evolve, even when there is no legislative or government enforcement activity.

Much of the recent evolution of antitrust law, and of antitrust policy more broadly, has resulted from changing economic and legal thought about markets, business strategies, and performance. This thought has a coherence and perspective not necessarily found in the historical record of court decisions, and it has shaped a number of recent decisions. Three approaches, or schools of thought, to reasoning about antitrust are considered in this chapter.

The traditional or structure-conduct-performance school focuses on the structure of industries and on conduct that may foreclose opportunities or diminish competition. In the 1970s new understandings of the functioning of markets and the nature of competition were developed by the Chicago school of economics; these understandings had a major impact on antitrust enforcement and court decisions.[3] More recently, industrial organization economists have challenged some conclusions of the Chicago school by considering more closely the implications of informational asymmetries, repeated play, and strategic interactions among market participants. This perspective has qualified a number of the conclusions of the Chicago school.

These understandings of the purpose of antitrust policy and its appropriate application are particularly important in the United States because of the adversarial nature of judicial proceedings. Both plaintiffs and defendants have incentives to make the best cases they can and to use whatever new understandings support their sides. Consequently, new theories and empirical evidence quickly find their way into court proceedings. Hearing these arguments, judges make decisions that can be influenced by how compelling the theories are, in addition to the facts of the case, empirical evidence, and legal precedents. Antitrust law thus is shaped by economic thought.

Antitrust policy has broad implications for management. Firms must conform to the law, but in many cases and for many practices, there is a considerable gray area in which the requirements of the law are unclear or untested. Similarly, because antitrust law evolves, a practice that once was allowable under the law may no longer be allowable. Practices that were once illegal may now be legal. Legal counsel is thus essential when issues or practices may have antitrust implications. Managers, however, must have an understanding of antitrust law, enforcement practices, and antitrust thought, since they must recognize when a policy or practice may raise antitrust concerns.

The purpose of this chapter is to provide an introduction to antitrust law and thought, the forces that have shaped antitrust policy in recent years, and the forces that may shape its future development. The next section introduces the principal antitrust laws and discusses their enforcement, both by the government and private litigants. The following section considers the two rules under which antitrust lawsuits are tried: a rule of reason and a per se rule. The three schools of antitrust thought are then introduced and applied to vertical arrangements, predatory pricing, collusion and price-fixing, and mergers. The antitrust guidelines used by the DOJ and FTC to review mergers are then considered. The effects of antitrust decisions on market opening are discussed, and the politics of antitrust are considered.

---

[3]Much of the theory was developed by economists and legal scholars at the University of Chicago.

ANTITRUST LAW

The Antitrust Statutes

The principal antitrust statutes, excerpts from which are presented in Figure 9-1, have remained largely intact for over 90 years. Section 1 of the Sherman Act pertains to unreasonable *restraints of trade* with a focus on joint conduct. Section 2 focuses on unilateral conduct and proscribes attempts to monopolize or to maintain a *monopoly*. The Sherman Act thus pertains to the reality of monopoly and restraints of trade and to the process of obtaining or maintaining a monopoly.

The Clayton Act goes further by addressing potentially anticompetitive actions. The Clayton Act contains terms such as "may be" and "tend to," which address monopolization and restraints in their incipiency. The Federal Trade Commission Act goes beyond the other two acts by prohibiting unfair methods of competition and *unfair or deceptive acts*. The broad language employed leaves considerable room for interpretation and thus a substantial role for the courts.[4]

The Sherman Act does not provide for private lawsuits, but Section 4 of the Clayton Act states "that any person who shall be injured in his business or property by reason of anything forbidden in the antitrust laws may sue therefore in any district court of the United States. . . ." This allows private parties to bring lawsuits for practices that are illegal under either the Sherman Act or the Clayton Act. Section 4 also provides for treble damages. Section 7 of the Clayton Act prohibits mergers that may substantially lessen competition or create a monopoly.

FIGURE 9-1   Excerpts from the Antitrust Statutes

Sherman Act

Section 1.   Every contract, combination in the form of trust or otherwise, or conspiracy, in restraint of trade or commerce among the several States, or with foreign nations, is hereby declared to be illegal. ...Every person who shall make any contract or engage in any combination or conspiracy hereby declared to be illegal shall be deemed guilty of a felony. . . .

Section 2.   Every person who shall monopolize, or attempt to monopolize, or combine or conspire with any other person or persons, to monopolize any part of the trade or commerce among the several States, or with foreign nations, shall be deemed guilty of a felony. . . .

Clayton Act

Section 2.   (a) That it shall be unlawful for any person engaged in commerce . . . to discriminate in the price between different purchasers . . . where the effect of such discrimination may be substantially to lessen competition or tend to create a monopoly in any line of commerce, or to injure, destroy or prevent competition . . . nothing herein contained shall prevent differentials which make only due allowance for differences in the cost of manufacture, sale, or delivery. . . .

Section 3.   That it shall be illegal for any person [to enter an arrangement] . . . on the condition . . . that the lessee or purchaser thereof shall not use or deal in the goods . . . of a competitor or competitors, where the effect . . . may be to substantially lessen the competition or tend to create a monopoly in any line of commerce.

Section 7.   That no corporation engaged in commerce shall acquire, directly or indirectly, the whole or any part of the stock or other share capital . . . where in any line of commerce in any section of the country, the effect of such acquisition may be substantially to lessen competition, or tend to create a monopoly.*

Federal Trade Commission Act

Section 5.   (a)(1) Unfair methods of competition in commerce, and unfair or deceptive acts or practices in commerce, are hereby declared unlawful.**

*As amended by the Celler-Kefauver Act of 1950.
**As amended by the Wheeler-Lea Act of 1938.

---

[4]See Areeda and Kaplow (1997), Areeda and Hovenkamp (2004), and Gavil, Kovacic, and Baker (2008) for comprehensive treatments of antitrust law and Spulber (1989) and Viscusi, Vernon, and Harrington (2005) for the economics of antitrust.

The Robinson-Patman Act of 1934 strengthened Section 2 of the Clayton Act's prohibition of price discrimination. The Robinson-Patman Act was intended to protect small businesses and merchants from their larger competitors, which were able to obtain lower prices on their supplies. Small grocers, for example, sought protection from supermarkets, which used their greater buying power to obtain lower prices. Critics of the Robinson-Patman Act claim that it causes firms to be wary of price competition, resulting in higher prices for consumers. Proponents, however, contend that it is necessary to prevent small firms from being driven out of business, which would increase concentration and lessen competition.

Practices that come under the antitrust laws are classified as horizontal or vertical. A *horizontal* practice is one that involves activities in the same industry. A merger, for example, is horizontal if the two firms operate in the same industry. Horizontal arrangements include monopolization, predatory pricing, price fixing, bid rigging, the allocation

---

FIGURE 9-2   Arrangements and Practices Subject to Antitrust Scrunity

Horizontal

Horizontal merger—A merger is horizontal if it involves two firms in the same industry. A horizontal merger comes under Section 7 of the Clayton Act and under Section 2 of the Sherman Act, if it would create a monopoly.

Horizontal price fixing (collusion)—Horizontal price fixing includes explicit or implicit agreements to control prices in an industry or with respect to a product. Horizontal price fixing comes under Section 1 of the Sherman Act.

Monopoly—Concerted efforts to monopolize come under the purview of Section 1 of the Sherman Act, and the unilateral attempt to monopolize comes under Section 2 of the Sherman Act.

Price discrimination—Price discrimination involves charging customers different prices that are not justified by cost differences of serving those customers. Price discrimination comes under Section 2 of the Clayton Act, as amended by the Robinson-Patman Act.

Vertical

Boycotts and refusals to deal—A manufacturer refuses to sell to a distributor or a retailer. If two or more parties agree to refuse to deal with another party, it is a boycott. These practices are considered under Section 1 of the Sherman Act.

Exclusive dealing—A manufacturer grants another firm an exclusive right to distribute or market a particular product. Exclusive dealing comes under Section 3 of the Clayton Act.

Exclusive territory—A manufacturer grants an exclusive territory to a seller, and no other seller is permitted to sell in the territory. Exclusive territories come under Section 1 of the Sherman Act.

Resale price maintenance—A manufacturer requires a retailer to sell only at a price at least as high as a price it specifies. Such cases come under Section 1 of the Sherman Act.

Tying—Tying is the practice of bundling one product with another. For example, Mercedes-Benz requires its dealers to carry only Mercedes-Benz parts. * Tying arrangements come under Section 3 of the Clayton Act and Section 1 of the Sherman Act.

Vertical integration—Vertical integration involves the joining together, in terms of a merger or venture, of firms at various stages of a production process or channel or distribution. A vertical merger comes under Section 7 of the Clayton Act. ** A vertical contract that forecloses or restrains competition comes under Section 3 of the Clayton Act.

Conglomerate

Conglomerate merger—A conglomerate merger involves two firms that do not operate in the same industries either as competitors or as part of a channel of distribution or supply. Conglomerate mergers come under Section 7 of the Clayton Act. The concern in the case of a conglomerate merger is the elimination of a potential competitor.***

*The DOJ dropped its antitrust suit against Mercedes-Benz because it concluded that a tying arrangement could only be anti-competitive if it is based on horizontal market power.

**See *Brown Shoe Co. v. U.S.*, 294 (1962), in which the Supreme Court invalidated the merger between Brown Shoe and the G. R. Kinney retail chain.

***See *Federal Trade Commission v. Procter & Gamble Co.*, 368 U.S. 568 (1967).

EXAMPLE

Monopoly

In basic economic theory a monopoly is present when a firm has a dominant position in a market and can restrict its output to increase the price consumers pay. In some markets, however, a monopoly may be the inevitable result of competition. For example, if there are benefits from standardization, competition can drive the market to concentrate on a single standard. If that standard is proprietary, as in the case of Microsoft's Windows operating system, a monopoly results. A monopoly achieved as a result of market forces combined with a superior product is not illegal, since consumers can benefit from the competition to become the standard and from the development of a superior product.

Monopoly is the subject of Section 2 of the Sherman Act. In *United States v. Aluminum Co. of America,* 148 F2d 416 (2d Cir 1945), Judge Learned Hand formulated a two-step procedure for deciding monopolization cases under Section 2.[1] The first step is to determine if the defendant has a monopoly. The second step is to determine if the monopoly was willfully acquired or unreasonably maintained or if it was the result of "superior skill, foresight and industry."

[T]he offense of monopoly . . . has two elements: (1) the possession of monopoly power in the relevant market and (2) the willful acquisition or maintenance of that power as distinguished from growth or development as a consequence of a superior product, business acumen, or historical accident.

Having a monopoly thus is not illegal, as in the case of a firm that becomes a monopoly through a superior product with which others are unable to compete. Willful monopolization or maintenance of a monopoly through anticompetitive practices is illegal.

For example, the online person-to-person auction market tipped to eBay, which has over 80 percent of the market. Similarly, Microsoft has over 90 percent of the personal computer operating system market. Having such monopolies is not illegal if they were achieved through superior performance and characteristics of the market, such as the characteristics of information technologies considered in Chapter 13. Maintaining a monopoly using anticompetitive practices is illegal, as is using a monopoly position in one market to attempt to monopolize another related market. In the chapter case, *The Microsoft Antitrust Case,* the Department of Justice alleged that Microsoft used anticompetitive practices to maintain its monopoly in the PC operating system market and used that monopoly to attempt to monopolize the Internet browser market.[2]

[1]Early cases broke up the oil [*Standard Oil Co. v. United States,* 221 U.S. 1 (1911)] and tobacco [*United States v. American Tobacco Co.,* 221 U.S. 106 (1911)] monopolies.

[2]Monopolization cases are rarely filed. The most recent case prior to the Microsoft case was against IBM for monopolization of the computer industry. That case was filed on the last day of the Johnson administration in 1969 and dropped by the Reagan administration.

of customers, and group boycotts. The concern with horizontal arrangements is that they may increase market power, leading to lessened competition and higher prices.

Vertical practices are those involving firms in a supply arrangement or a channel of distribution. Vertical practices include the allocation of territories by a manufacturer among distributors or retailers, refusals to deal, exclusive dealing arrangements, resale price maintenance, reciprocal arrangements, and tying. Vertical practices also include the merger of a manufacturer and a supplier or distributor. Figure 9-2 provides brief definitions of the principal practices of concern under the antitrust laws.

Exemptions

A number of exemptions from the antitrust laws are provided. The Norris-LaGuardia Act of 1932 strengthened the statutory exemption the Clayton Act provided to unions. The economic activities of labor unions taken in their own interest, such as strikes, are protected. Exemptions are also provided for agricultural cooperatives and for certain activities of industries, such as insurance, that are regulated by government.[5] Exemptions for joint export trading activities are also provided under the Webb-Pomerene

[5]The exemption for the insurance industry is provided in the McCarron-Ferguson Act, and the exemption for agricultural cooperatives is provided by the Capper-Volstad Act of 1922.

Act of 1918 and the Export Trading Company Act of 1982. A partial antitrust exemption was established for joint research and development ventures and for certain insurance pools. Exemptions can also be provided by specific legislation, as in the Soft Drink Interbrand Competition Act considered later in the chapter.

The 1.2 million–member National Association of Realtors excluded online real estate brokers from obtaining the listings on its multiple listing services. The Realtors had no exemption, and the Department of Justice filed a lawsuit alleging that excluding online brokers restricted competition. In 2008 the DOJ and the National Association of Realtors reached a consent agreement providing equal access to online brokers.

Baseball never had a statutory exemption from the antitrust laws but was protected by a 1922 Supreme Court decision, which had been upheld in subsequent decisions because the courts believed that it was the role of Congress, not the court, to change the antitrust status of baseball.[6] In 1998 Congress modified the antitrust exemption by no longer exempting labor agreements, but a partial exemption continues.

ENFORCEMENT OF THE ANTITRUST LAWS

Government Enforcement

Both the DOJ and the FTC have the authority to enforce the Sherman and Clayton Acts, but only the FTC can enforce the Federal Trade Commission Act.[7] Their dual enforcement responsibilities led the DOJ and the FTC to reach an interagency liaison agreement in 1948. As a result of the agreement, cases are allocated primarily by industry and secondarily by the nature of the complaint.[8] For example, the DOJ has enforcement responsibility for computer software and the FTC for semiconductors, so the DOJ filed the antitrust lawsuits against Microsoft and in 2008 the FTC began a formal investigation of Intel. Most enforcement activities are civil rather than criminal, and only the DOJ can bring criminal charges under the antitrust laws. Bringing criminal charges requires a grand jury indictment, and the standards of proof are higher than in a civil case.

In criminal cases the available penalties are fines and imprisonment. In civil cases injunctive relief can be granted, contracts dissolved, and business units ordered divested. Fines cannot be imposed in civil cases except to compensate the government for actual damages when it is a purchaser of goods and services. The courts not only decide cases but also approve consent decrees, such as that which split AT&T into seven regional operating companies and a residual AT&T. The DOJ can enforce the antitrust laws only through lawsuits filed in federal courts, but the FTC has authority to issue orders directly. The FTC can also seek injunctions in federal court, for example, to block a proposed merger, as in the chapter case *The Staples–Office Depot Merger?*[9]

The FTC is an independent commission with five commissioners appointed, subject to Senate confirmation, by the president to 7-year terms. It can initiate its own investigations of practices it believes may violate the antitrust laws. As a consequence of an investigation, the FTC may negotiate a consent decree with a firm. If a firm refuses to agree to a consent decree, the FTC can continue the case through an administrative law procedure. A hearing is held before an administrative law judge, who issues an opinion and recommendation for action. The case is then decided by a majority vote of the commission. As penalties, the FTC can issue cease and desist orders that have the effect of injunctions against the activity in question. If a firm violates an order, the FTC

---

[6]See *Federal Baseball Club of Baltimore v. National League of Professional Baseball Clubs,* 259 U.S. 200 (1991), *Toolson v. New York Yankees, Inc.,* 346 U.S. 356 (1953), and *Flood v. Kuhn,* 407 U.S. 258 (1972).
[7]Technically the FTC has no authority to enforce the Sherman Act, but in practice, it does. The courts have held that practices violating the Sherman Act constitute "unfair" methods of competition under Section 5 of the Federal Trade Commission Act.
[8]See Shugart (1990, p. 947).
[9]See Clarkson and Muris (1981) for an analysis of FTC policy and enforcement. See Weaver (1977) for a study of FTC enforcement policy and Elzinga and Briet (1976) for a study of antitrust policies.

can impose fines. Both the orders issued by the FTC and the court decisions in cases brought by the DOJ can be appealed to the U.S. Court of Appeals.

A consent decree is an agreement reached by the litigants under the sanction of a court. It does not involve a judicial determination and hence does not signify a violation of the law. A consent decree generally involves restrictions on the actions of the defendant. It binds only the consenting parties and does not set a precedent for other cases. A consent decree may remain in effect indefinitely and requires the agreement of the plaintiff, the defendant, and the court to lift or modify it. In 1997 a federal court lifted, effective in 2001, a 1956 consent decree that had restricted IBM's sales and service practices on its mainframe and mid-range computers. The judge concluded that IBM's market power "has substantially diminished."

The Hart-Scott-Rodino Antitrust Improvements Act of 1976 amended Section 7 of the Clayton Act to enhance the enforcement of the antitrust laws pertaining to monopolization and restraint of trade through mergers.[10] Hart-Scott-Rodino requires pre-merger notification to the DOJ and the FTC of plans to merge.[11] In 2000, 4,926 mergers were reported to the DOJ and FTC under Hart-Scott-Rodino. The DOJ and FTC decide which agency will review a merger based on "expertise and experience." A merger cannot be completed for 30 days, and during this period the agencies can require the firms to submit information about the market effects of their merger. For example, the firms may be required to submit information about their market shares in the market segments in which they both participate. In 2001 the Hearst Corporation agreed to pay a $4 million fine for failure to produce key documents as required by Hart-Scott-Rodino. If the DOJ or FTC decides that there are grounds to challenge the merger, it seeks a preliminary injunction. In most cases, this convinces the firms to abandon their plans to merge. The chapter case, *The Staples–Office Depot Merger?*, concerns an FTC action to obtain a preliminary injunction against a merger.

The 1974 Antitrust Procedures and Penalties Act classified as felonies violations such as price fixing and increased the allowable fines. Fines against corporations can be as high as $10 million per count in criminal cases. Individuals, including managers of corporations, can be fined up to $350,000 and can be imprisoned for up to 3 years. Since 1990 the federal government has been able to collect treble damages. Federal sentencing guidelines enacted in 1991 allow fines to be based on the amount of business affected, in addition to other factors. In 1999 Roche Holdings, BASF, and Rhone-Poulenc (now Aventis) pleaded guilty to criminal price fixing in vitamins, and Roche paid $500 million in fines and BASF $225 million. Rhone-Poulenc paid no fine in exchange for cooperating with the government. The chapter case, *Price Fixing in the Airways,* considers a recent case.

The Robinson-Patman Act prohibits price discrimination not justified by cost differences in serving customers. In addition to a cost difference defense, a firm can defend itself by arguing that the price discrimination was necessary to meet competition. The Clayton Act assigns the burden of proof in a price discrimination case to the plaintiff to show that there has been discrimination. Given a prima facie case, the defendant has the burden to show that the discrimination was justified by, for example, cost differences.[12] During the past 25 years the DOJ and the FTC have effectively stopped enforcing the Robinson-Patman Act because of their view that it stifles competition. Private antitrust lawsuits continue to be filed.

The DOJ and the FTC have also stopped enforcing the prohibition against resale price maintenance, although private enforcement continues. Resale price maintenance pertains to restrictions imposed by manufacturers on the prices that can be charged by retailers. In the 1930s small retailers sought protection from price competition by having manufacturers establish minimum resale prices. States passed "fair trade laws" that

---

[10]See Federal Trade Commission (1990).
[11]Notification is required if the acquirer will have a 15 percent stake or a $15 million investment in the acquired firm and the acquirer has either sales or assets of $100 million or the acquired firm has assets of at least $10 million. If the acquired firm is a manufacturer, the asset figure is replaced by sales of $10 million.
[12]A prima facie case is one that needs no further demonstration.

required retailers to sell at the prices specified by contracts signed with manufacturers. The Miller-Tydings Act of 1937 allowed states to exempt price maintenance agreements from coverage under Section 1 of the Sherman Act as long as there was competition from other brands. The McGuire Act extended this to nonsigners of resale price contracts. In 1975 Congress repealed the Miller-Tydings and the McGuire Acts and withdrew the states' authority for fair trade laws.

The explanation for the lack of government enforcement of the resale price maintenance and price discrimination provisions of the antitrust laws is found in the changing schools of antitrust thought considered later in the chapter. To indicate the type of case to which the DOJ and the FTC object, Cuisinart was found to have violated the antitrust laws by requiring sellers of its food processors to maintain a minimum retail price. Cuisinart held a dominant share of the market for food processors at the time the lawsuit was filed, but its share was largely due to its having developed the original product. Cuisinart had no fundamental horizontal market power, since entry into the food processor market was easy. Furthermore, the high minimum price established by Cuisinart stimulated entry, which quickly eroded its market share. Prices fell substantially when entry occurred. The resale price agreement, if it had continued, would likely have had little effect on the market for food processors. To clarify its policy, in 1985 the Antitrust Division of the DOJ issued revised guidelines indicating that it would not investigate vertical accords when a firm has less than a 10 percent market share. A market share above 10 percent could lead to an investigation.

In spite of the lack of enforcement against certain vertical arrangements, federal enforcement of the antitrust laws is active. During the 1990s the pace of federal antitrust enforcement accelerated considerably. In part this was due to the increase in merger activity, but vigorous enforcement of price fixing and other antitrust violations also occurred. In 1998 three former Archers-Daniel-Midland executives, including the son of the chairman of the board, were sentenced to 2 to 3 years in prison for price-fixing of lysine and citric acid. An FBI videotape of a price-fixing meeting is available from the DOJ.[13]

In 1998 the DOJ filed an antitrust case against Visa and MasterCard alleging that their prohibitions preventing banks from issuing other credit cards such as Discover and American Express was exclusionary. The district court found against Visa and MasterCard and ordered them to allow banks to issue other cards. The companies appealed, but the Court of Appeals upheld the lower court decision. The companies then appealed to the Supreme Court, which rejected the appeal, opening a $1.3 trillion market to American Express and Morgan Stanley's Discover card. Private lawsuits were filed after the decision.

Although the federal antitrust agencies are usually successful in obtaining at least a consent decree in the cases they bring, companies do win cases. In 1994 in a case brought by the DOJ alleging that General Electric had engaged in price fixing for industrial diamonds, the judge ruled that the DOJ had presented insufficient evidence and dismissed the case without requiring the company to present a defense.

Private Enforcement

Even though the federal government has decided not to file price discrimination and resale price maintenance lawsuits, private lawsuits are filed. Most antitrust cases are the result of private lawsuits.[14] The number of private antitrust suits increased beginning in the early 1960s and peaked at over 1,600 in 1977, declining to 570 in 1997. The decline was a function of a number of factors, including Supreme Court decisions that made it more difficult for some plaintiffs to prevail in cases involving vertical restraints and predatory pricing. Firms also instituted compliance programs that contributed to the decrease.

---

[13]The videotape is available from the U.S. Department of Justice, Antitrust Division, Freedom of Information Act Unit, 325 Seventh Street, NW, Suite 200, Washington, D.C., 20530.
[14]Viscusi, Vernon, and Harrington (2000, p. 68) report that approximately 90 percent of antitrust lawsuits filed in U.S. courts during the 1970s and 1980s were private. See also White (1988).

Most antitrust lawsuits are brought under the Sherman Act, and cases pertaining to vertical arrangements represent a somewhat higher percent of the total than those pertaining to horizontal practices. Of the total cases in their study, Salop and White (1988) found that 36.5 percent were filed by competitors and 27.3 percent by dealers. Of the cases filed before 1980, 71 percent were settled out of court and 11 percent were dismissed. Of the 12 percent of the cases that continued, plaintiffs prevailed in approximately 30 percent. Only 5.4 percent of the cases went to trial. AMD, the second largest producer of microprocessors, has filed complaints and lawsuits resulting in four antitrust cases against Intel, the largest producer of microprocessors.

The treble damages provision of the Clayton Act provides strong incentives for a private party to file an antitrust lawsuit. If a suit is filed against a firm by the DOJ, private parties often follow with private lawsuits. For example, the DOJ action against British Airways in the *Price Fixing in the Airways* chapter case was followed by a private class action lawsuit. A court decision for the government is interpreted by the courts as providing a prima facie case against the defendant, greatly increasing the likelihood that private cases will be decided in favor of the plaintiff. In the vitamin price-fixing case, private class action lawsuits were filed against seven drug companies. The companies settled the lawsuits for $1.1 billion. The companies also reached a $340 million settlement with state attorneys general, bringing the total fines in the United States to $2.2 billion.

In 1996 Wal-Mart and other retailers filed an antitrust lawsuit against Visa and MasterCard, which had imposed an "honor-all-cards" policy on merchants, requiring them to accept debit cards if they accepted Visa and MasterCard credit cards. The merchants alleged that this was illegal tying under Section 1 of the Sherman Act and also that Visa and MasterCard were attempting to monopolize the debit card market in violation of Section 2 of the Sherman Act. As the case was going to trial in 2003 a settlement was reached in which Visa paid $2 billion and MasterCard $1 billion to the merchants and agreed to revise their policies and reduce their charges for debit cards.[15]

Treble damages are understandably controversial. Their proponents argue that they provide an important incentive for private enforcement. Critics contend that treble damages provide an incentive to challenge the practices of competitors, thereby making firms reluctant to compete on a number of dimensions, including price.

Private suits can have significance beyond their impact on the parties involved. When a private antitrust case is tried and appealed, higher court decisions can establish a precedent that is then followed by courts in similar cases. Many of the important interpretations of the antitrust statutes and the precedents followed by the courts have come from private lawsuits.

Per Se Violations and the Rule of Reason

The courts have held that there are some sufficiently egregious acts that on the face of it violate the antitrust laws. These acts are said to be *per se* illegal, and the only defense allowed is that the defendant did not commit the act. The Supreme Court established this rule in *Northern Pacific Railroad Co. v. U.S.*, 356 U.S. 1 (1958), stating, "There are certain agreements or practices which because of their pernicious effect on competition and lack of any redeeming virtue are conclusively presumed to be unreasonable and therefore illegal without elaborate inquiry as to the precise harm they have caused or the business excuse for their use."

In contrast, other cases are considered by the courts under a *rule of reason*.[16] Under this rule, a restraint of trade, for example, is illegal if it is unreasonable. Per se violations are presumed to be unreasonable. The rule of reason was needed because much of the language of the antitrust laws is too sweeping and a literal interpretation

---

[15]The lawyers for the plaintiffs asked for fees of $600 million, but the judge reduced the amount to $220 million.

[16]The rule of reason was first articulated by the Supreme Court in *Standard Oil Co. of New Jersey v. United States*, 221 U.S. 1 (1911), which broke up the Standard Oil Trust. A judicial rule is a standard of interpretation for a law that is ambiguous in the absence of that interpretation.

would be harmful to competition and efficiency. Section 1 of the Sherman Act, for example, might be interpreted as prohibiting supply contracts because they restrain the opportunities for others. Similarly, combinations such as partnerships might otherwise be held to be in violation of the Sherman Act. The DOJ case against Visa and Master-Card for exclusionary practices was tried under a rule of reason.

A defendant has two defenses under a rule of reason. The first is the same as under a per se rule—the defendant did not commit the act in question. The second is that, although the defendant committed the act, it was not unreasonable to do so. The burden of proof is on the plaintiff to show that it is unreasonable. In evaluating whether an act is unreasonable, courts look to its purpose and effect. In the case of vertical arrangements, the stimulation of interbrand competition is a purpose the courts recognize. In evaluating the effect of an act, the courts examine whether it restrains or promotes competition and whether it is the least restrictive means of achieving the purpose. A court may hold for the plaintiff if either the purpose or the effect is unreasonable.

The courts do not decide which rule is applicable on a case-by-case basis but instead hold that certain practices are per se illegal and others are not. Presently, price-fixing, output restraints, and the allocation of customers among competitors are per se violations of the antitrust laws. Some practices that in the past were considered per se offenses are now considered under the rule of reason. For example, in 1997 the Supreme Court ruled that maximum price resale maintenance, where a manufacturer sets a maximum price that retailers may charge, is not per se illegal and is to be considered under a rule of reason.[17] In 2007 the Supreme Court extended this to minimum resale price maintenance on the grounds that it could stimulate interbrand competition.

A variety of arrangements and practices have come under the scrutiny of the antitrust laws, as indicated in Figure 9-2. A treatment of each of these requires more space than is available, so the following sections focus instead on antitrust thought and on the application of that thought in the areas of vertical restraints, predatory pricing, collusion, and mergers.

ANTITRUST THOUGHT

Antitrust policy, enforcement practices, and court decisions are influenced by the prevailing schools of thought about the purposes of antitrust policy and the likely consequences of specific practices. The *structural* or *structure-conduct-performance school* of thought prevailed into the 1970s, when it was confronted with the understandings of the *Chicago school.* The Chicago, or law and economics, school viewed the objectives and principles of antitrust policy differently, particularly with regard to vertical arrangements. It has had considerable influence on legal education, the courts, and the enforcement activities of the DOJ and FTC beginning with the Reagan administration. In addition, the courts have adopted many understandings of the Chicago school, and several Chicago school scholars have been appointed to the federal judiciary.

In the 1990s antitrust practice and policy were influenced by the work of industrial organization (IO) economists, who focused on new considerations such as network externalities and compatibility and on theories of oligopoly that take into account the strategic interactions among market participants in imperfectly competitive markets. This *new IO* approach challenges some of the understandings of both the structural and the Chicago schools. The new IO approach is a collection of theories rather than a unified perspective from which broad conclusions can be drawn. Furthermore, courts have only cautiously embraced its theories, in part because of the complexity and subtle reasoning involved. Nevertheless, it represents an important force in antitrust thought.

These three approaches agree on many points but differ on others. Figure 9-3 contrasts the approaches.

---

[17]*State Oil Company v. Khan,* 522 U.S. 3; 118 S.Ct. 27 S.

FIGURE 9-3   Structural, Chicago School, and New IO Perspectives

Dimension	Structural	Chicago School	New IO
• Purpose of antitrust policy	Social and political as well as economic objectives.	Economic objectives—efficiency with a focus on prices.	Economic objectives; static and dynamic efficiency.
• View of markets	Markets are fragile and prone to failure.	Markets are resilient; market imperfections can be addressed through incentives.	Most markets are resilient, but some have imperfections such as network externalities; strategic behavior can limit efficiency.
• What is needed	Government to protect society from economic power.	Competition is the best protector of consumers and economic efficiency.	Competition is the best protector of consumers, but government intervention can be required.
• Perspective on consumers	Need to protect consumers from others and from themselves; e.g., unfair practices.	Consumers are responsible for their own decisions and will protect themselves.	Consumers can protect themselves when they have choices.
• Requirements for markets to function efficiently	Protect competitors to prevent monopoly; avoid foreclosing opportunities for competitors.	Conditions for perfect competition are sufficient but not necessary.	Both innovation and competition are required for efficiency; dynamic efficiency is important.
• Relationship between the number of competitors and market performance	More competitors means more competition.	Competition can be effective with only a few competitors.	Competition can be effective with a small number of competitors.
• Entry	High barriers to entry reduce efficiency; potential entry may not limit the power of incumbent firms.	Few barriers to entry; barriers are due to the efficiency of incumbent firms; potential entry limits the economic power of incumbents.	Barriers to entry can be present; e.g., from the economies of standardization.
• Sources of economic power	Market power derives from horizontal power and from vertical arrangements.	Market power can only arise from horizontal power.	Market power derives from horizontal factors but can be extended through vertical arrangements and strategic behavior.
• Collusion	Increases profits, so firms can be expected to collude.	Is difficult for firms to enforce and thus is unlikely.	Is possible with repeated encounters.
• Where is collusion most likely	In concentrated markets.	In industries with government regulation or protection.	In industries with repeated encounters and easy monitoring, as well as in regulated and protected industries.
• Interpretation of the relationship between concentration and profits	Positive correlation indicates that more concentration reduces market efficiency and increases profits.	Positive correlation is more likely due to lower costs of larger firms.	Positive correlation can be due to lower costs, market power, or strategic opportunities.
• Relevant market for antitrust scrutiny should be	Defined narrowly so that pockets of concentration can be detected and addressed.	Defined broadly to include substitutes and imports.	Defined broadly to include substitutes and imports.
• Conclusion about antitrust	Proscribe many practices as per se offenses.	Judge business practices in terms of their effects on efficiency and prices; use the rule of reason.	Judge business practices in terms of impact on present and future competition; use rule of reason except for egregious practices such as price fixing.
• Values underlying the perspective	Efficiency and fairness; government protection.	Economic efficiency; individual choice and responsibility.	Economic efficiency; individual and collective responsibility.

The Structural Approach

From the perspective of social and economic policy, government intervention in markets is intended to improve economic performance and further the social objective of limiting economic power. From this perspective, concentrations of economic power should be checked, just as political power is checked. Because economic power can result in the unfair treatment of competitors and consumers, government has a responsibility to protect citizens and society from the presence, and the abuse, of economic power. Antitrust policy and regulation are the principal public instruments for checking that power.

The structural approach views the performance of markets as determined by the conduct of market participants, which is largely determined by the structure of the market, such as the number of competitors and barriers to entry. This approach takes as its starting point the economic theories of monopoly and perfect competition. Perfect competition serves as the standard for evaluating an industry, and monopoly is its antithesis. Monopolistic pricing can be characterized by the generalized Lerner index, given by

$$\frac{p - mc}{p} = \frac{1}{n\varepsilon}$$

where p is price, mc is marginal cost, n is the number of firms in the industry, and ε is the price elasticity of demand.[18] The left side of the index is the percentage markup on price; for a monopoly ($n = 1$), the markup equals one divided by the elasticity of demand. As the number of firms increases, the markup decreases and price approaches marginal cost, which is the case of perfect competition. Market power is thus the ability to command a price above marginal cost and that power is greater the smaller the number of firms in an industry, other things equal. In the chapter case, *The Staples–Office Depot Merger?*, the FTC and the court concluded that prices were higher in markets with only one office supply superstore than in markets with two or three superstores.

The structural approach thus views economic power as a function of the number of firms in the industry or, correspondingly, their market shares. The smaller the number of firms, the more likely they are to restrict output to raise prices and worsen the performance of a market. The focus of antitrust policy thus should be on the structure of the industry, and industries with substantial *concentration*—a substantial market share held by a small number of firms—should be regarded with suspicion. The structural approach finds support for this conclusion in empirical studies that show a positive correlation between industry concentration and profitability, as predicted by the Lerner index.

Improving performance in the market requires dealing with industry structure as well as the conduct of market participants. Remedies for antitrust violations should include breaking up monopolies, ordering the divestiture of business units, requiring tight standards for mergers, and requiring the licensing of technologies. Because a larger number of firms correlates with more competition and lower prices, the more firms in the industry the better. To ensure that there are enough firms for vigorous competition, it may be desirable to protect firms from their rivals, particularly from predatory behavior or from unfair advantages such as not being able to purchase inputs at low prices (as reflected in the Robinson-Patman Act).

The Lerner index implies that market power arises from horizontal considerations. Market power can also result from vertical arrangements in channels of distribution, as when a manufacturer requires a distributor or retailer to maintain a minimum price, carry only the manufacturer's replacement parts, or sell only within a specified territory. From the perspective of the structural approach, it is important to avoid foreclosing opportunities for competitors, since competition would then be less vigorous. Vertical arrangements thus should be viewed with suspicion because they can foreclose opportunities for competitors and increase economic power.

The economic power of the incumbent firms in an industry can be checked by entry into the industry. The structural approach, however, is concerned about possible *barriers to entry*. Barriers to entry are said to include such factors as technological advantages, advertising and brand names, and capital requirements. Because of barriers to entry and economic concentration, the structural approach often views markets as fragile. Government thus has a role in helping markets function more efficiently.

When there are barriers to entry and economic power is concentrated in a relatively small number of firms, incumbent firms may have an opportunity to collude. The structural approach views collusion as more likely the more concentrated the industry.

---

[18]This relation is derived from a Cournot model of oligopoly.

Collusion can take the form of price fixing among firms in an industry or in a channel of distribution. Empirical research finding a positive correlation between concentration and profitability could reflect such collusion. This provides another rationale for focusing on concentrated markets.

Because economic power harms consumers through higher prices, the structural approach holds that markets should be viewed narrowly to identify market segments in which economic concentration is present. Similarly, it is important to keep market opportunities open. Consequently, restraints of trade and market foreclosures should be limited to those that are absolutely necessary, and antitrust should proscribe practices that foreclose opportunities or restrain competition. Many of those practices should be per se illegal.

In summary, the structure-conduct-performance paradigm views performance as following from conduct, which follows from the structure of markets. Antitrust policy thus should be concerned about concentration, barriers to entry, possible collusion, and exclusionary practices. Antitrust enforcers should closely scrutinize market structure for economic concentration, market foreclosures, and restraints of trade. Antitrust remedies should include structural as well as conduct remedies.

The Chicago School

The Chicago school views the objective of antitrust policy as economic efficiency, which may be understood in its simplest form as the maximization of producers' plus consumers' surplus. Since economic efficiency depends on the level of prices, the focus is on the prices consumers pay. Thus, a price equal to marginal cost is efficient, whether it results from a perfectly competitive market or a monopolistic industry in which price is held down by the threat of entry. The focus of the Chicago school is on performance—the prices in markets—rather than on the structure of markets.[19] The Chicago school recognizes the potential for horizontal market power and its abuse but believes that competition, not government, is the best protector of consumers and the best promoter of economic efficiency.

Perfect competition is the ideal, but the conditions for perfect competition—many firms, a homogeneous product, technologies available to all firms, and complete information—are viewed as sufficient but not necessary for economic efficiency. Competition can be efficient even with few firms in an industry since, given the opportunity, firms will compete vigorously.

The Chicago school is skeptical about the nature and scope of barriers to entry. Claimed barriers such as advertising, brand-name advantages, and capital requirements are unlikely to be true barriers. Capital markets are viewed as efficient, so investors will provide capital for ventures that have prospects for at least a market rate of return. Barriers to entry are likely to be due to the cost advantages of incumbent firms, and the inability of a potential entrant to raise capital could be due to efficiency advantages of incumbent firms. Thus entry may be limited not by structural barriers but by economic efficiency. Indeed, incumbent firms are those that have already survived competition.

The positive correlation between industry concentration and profitability that the structural approach views as reflecting the exercise of economic power could, according to the Chicago school, result from the greater efficiency of those firms that have survived the competitive process. Furthermore, larger firms may have lower costs because of economies of scale. Their markups thus could be higher but their prices lower than if the firms in the industry were smaller. That is, if as firms become larger their costs decrease and competition is present to force prices down, consumers benefit. The firms could also benefit because of their lower costs and greater market shares. Consequently, both markups and profits could increase with concentration, yet higher concentration could result in lower prices for consumers.

The Chicago school also views collusion among firms as unsustainable because of the difficulties in monitoring and enforcing collusive agreements. Colluding firms have

---

[19]See Posner (1976) for an analysis of antitrust policy from the Chicago school perspective.

a strong incentive to cheat on an agreement by, for example, making secret discounts to customers to increase sales. A collusive agreement may have the structure of a prisoners' dilemma in which each firm finds it in its interest to cheat on the agreement. Unless there is a clear mechanism for monitoring the agreement, collusion is unlikely to be sustainable.

From the Chicago school's perspective, collusion is most likely to be sustainable when there is government protection or regulation. Government regulation that precluded entry into the airline and trucking industries was viewed as having resulted in implicit collusion, with much of the rents captured by labor rather than by firms. Consistent with this perspective, during the Reagan administration the DOJ pressed its antitrust case against AT&T because it believed that regulation was inhibiting competition and technological progress. The DOJ, however, dropped its antitrust case against IBM because whatever market power IBM might have had was being dissipated by the rapid technological change in the computer industry.

Because barriers to entry are low and collusion is difficult to sustain, competition—both existing and potential—can be expected. Because it is the performance of the market that is important, the rule of reason should be used by courts in judging practices under the antitrust laws. Correspondingly, few practices should be per se illegal. In particular, vertical restraints are harmful only if the firm has horizontal market power, which should be assessed for its consequences for prices.

In assessing horizontal power the relevant market should be defined broadly. Both present and potential competition should be considered because either can hold prices down. The relevant market also includes not only the product in question but also close substitutes for that product. The definition of the relevant market should also include imported as well as domestic products. In the case of capital goods, the relevant market should include the market for used goods. In the case of a commodity such as aluminum, it should include the scrap and recycling markets as well as aluminum produced directly from bauxite. As an example of this perspective, Eastman Kodak has a 70 percent share of the U.S. color film market, 60 percent of the color paper market, and 70 percent of the wholesale photofinishing market. Its market dominance and practices had twice resulted in antitrust consent decrees. In 1994, however, the courts lifted both consent decrees. The courts concluded that Kodak did not have substantial market power because it had only a 36 percent market share worldwide. The courts concluded that if Kodak were to exercise market power by restricting output to obtain high prices, imported film would quickly rush into the U.S. market, forcing prices down.

In summary, the Chicago school views the objective of antitrust policy as economic efficiency and views competition as the best means of achieving efficiency. Perfect competition is not the only means of achieving efficiency, however, as competition among a few firms can be sufficient to drive prices down to marginal costs. Barriers to entry are viewed with skepticism and collusion is viewed as difficult to sustain, so market forces should correct most attempts to restrain trade. Furthermore, the relationship between profitability and concentration may be due to costs that decrease with the size of firms rather than to the exploitation of market power. Because the objective is economic efficiency, the focus of antitrust policy should be on performance, and the market in which that performance is assessed should be viewed broadly.

The Chicago school does not conclude that conduct such as vertical arrangements should be legal. Instead, it concludes that vertical arrangements could be pro-competitive rather than anticompetitive. Hence, they should not be per se illegal but rather should be considered under a rule of reason. This allows firms to adopt those practices that stimulate competition and enhance efficiency but also allows successful prosecution of practices that harm efficiency.

The New IO Approach

The new IO approach to antitrust is derived from the economics of modern industrial organization. This approach rejects the static equilibrium approach taken by the Chicago school and focuses on the opportunities for strategic behavior not initially considered by the Chicago school.[20] For example, even when firms act in a noncooperative manner, implicit collusion could result from repeated interactions among market participants and could be sustained by expectations that cheating would be met by punishment by other market participants. Similarly, interactions over time may allow firms to develop a reputation for a particular mode of behavior, such as price cutting in response to entry into a market that can deter potential entrants.

The possibilities for such strategic behavior are greater when there is incomplete information about factors important to the strategy choices of a firm. A potential entrant may have incomplete information about the costs of incumbent firms and thus may be reluctant to commit the capital required for entry, since it could turn out that the incumbent firms actually had costs lower than anticipated. Furthermore, incumbent firms may be able to deter entry by signaling that they have low costs even when they have high costs.

The new IO approach is also concerned with the potential for anticompetitive behavior in markets characterized by network externalities and where compatibility and standardization are required. For example, the benefits from standardizing software development on a small number of platforms, such as Microsoft's Windows operating system, can result in the development of market power for the suppliers of the platforms. Similarly, network effects are important in businesses ranging from Internet commerce to credit cards to commercial real estate. In addition to supply-side economies of larger networks, there may also be demand-side increasing returns, as considered in Chapter 13. This generates incentives to compete to develop the largest network, and the winner then has an "essential facility" and hence market power. Moreover, the owner of an essential facility may be able to use it to thwart innovation or block alternative technologies that provide the potential for competition. The threat to Microsoft's dominance of the desktop operating systems market from the Internet and the Java programming language was alleged by the DOJ to have led to anticompetitive practices.

As summarized in Figure 9-3, the new IO perspective on antitrust focuses on the objectives of static and dynamic efficiency; thus, it is concerned not only about the performance of markets at a point in time but also about innovation and incentives to develop new products and processes. Most markets are viewed as resilient, although some markets have imperfections such as those due to network externalities. Therefore, although competition and ensuring choice among products are the best protectors of consumers, government intervention may be warranted to ensure that standardization on a particular technology does not lead to market abuse and that incentives and opportunities for innovation are not thwarted. Most markets can be efficient even if there is only a small number of competitors, provided that barriers to entry are low, but otherwise markets may require scrutiny. For example, switching costs and the efficiencies from standardization can make it virtually impossible for a firm with a new technology to enter a market dominated by an incumbent. Easy entry thus cannot be assured.

The new IO perspective agrees with the Chicago school that market power derives from horizontal considerations but holds that it can be extended through vertical arrangements. For example, the DOJ alleged that Microsoft attempted to extend its market power to the Internet by bundling its Internet browser with its operating system and giving its browser away for free.

The new IO perspective acknowledges that competition with only a few firms can be efficient in a one-time encounter, but it also recognizes that repeated encounters provide an opportunity for implicit collusion. Collusion is more likely the better is the monitoring of the actions of firms. The price fixing cartels in vitamins, lysine, and citric acid are evidence of the ability of firms to collude. The positive empirical relationship between concentration and profits thus could be due to lower costs or to collusion and market power. In examining the likelihood that market power will impair static and dynamic efficiency, the new IO perspective views the relevant market as broadly defined.

---

[20]See Holt and Scheffman (1989) for a discussion of this approach and its implications for antitrust.

With respect to antitrust enforcement and policy, the new IO perspective concludes that business practices should be evaluated in terms of their effects on static and dynamic efficiency under the rule of reason except in egregious situations such as price fixing. Individuals can protect themselves when choice is available in the market, but government intervention can be warranted when choice and innovation are stifled through exclusive practices and the exercise of market power.

The new IO approach concludes that there are situations in which firms can employ anticompetitive strategies, as in the case of products that exhibit network externalities or have compatibility and standardization characteristics, as well as when implicit collusion can be supported by repeated encounters. The new IO approach has not at this point presented a comprehensive theory of antitrust economics, however. Instead, the approach is a collection of theories about behavior under particular structural and informational conditions.

EXAMPLES OF THE DIFFERENCES IN ANTITRUST THOUGHT

Vertical Arrangements

The principal area in which the structural and Chicago schools differed was in regard to vertical arrangements. These arrangements take a variety of forms, but most involve restrictions imposed by a manufacturer on the sale or distribution of its products. Because most of these arrangements involve the foreclosure of a market opportunity or a restraint of trade, a number of vertical practices had been held by the courts to be per se illegal. Economic understandings developed by the Chicago school, along with a Supreme Court required to interpret laws containing imprecise and general language, changed the law on vertical arrangements. Many of the vertical arrangements that had been per se illegal during the 1970s are now considered under a rule of reason. Furthermore, the courts have upheld the use of many of the previously illegal vertical arrangements. These changes have occurred in the absence of new legislation.

Vertical price restrictions had been per se illegal since the Supreme Court decision in *Dr. Miles Medical Co. v. John D. Park & Sons,* 220 U.S. 373 (1911). Nonprice vertical restrictions were not per se illegal, however, until the decision in *U.S. v. Arnold Schwinn & Co.,* 388 U.S. 365 (1967). In *Schwinn,* the Supreme Court decided that vertical nonprice restrictions on the resale of goods, such as territorial restrictions, restrictions on customers served, refusals to deal, and exclusive dealerships, were per se illegal.

The Chicago school found little logic in the court's reasoning, since from its perspective a vertical arrangement could be harmful to competition only if there were horizontal market power. That is, vertical arrangements do not create market power but can extend market power, for example, from a dominant market position. Indeed, vertical arrangements generally are viewed as tolerable unless there is horizontal market power. When that power is present, vertical arrangements should be judged under a rule of reason.

In reasoning about vertical arrangements, the Chicago school distinguished between *interbrand* and *intrabrand* competition. Intrabrand competition refers to competition between sellers of the same brand, as in the case of two Toyota dealers competing against each other. Those dealers also compete against the sellers of other makes of automobiles—interbrand competition. If interbrand competition is vigorous so that a manufacturer does not have horizontal market power, restrictions on intrabrand competition will have little impact on the efficiency of the market.

Moreover, vertical arrangements that restrict intrabrand competition can make interbrand competition more efficient by, for example, strengthening dealer networks. Competition among stronger networks holds down prices, and stronger dealer networks can reduce costs and better serve consumers on the nonprice dimensions of sales. Restrictions on intrabrand competition can also reduce transactions costs in a firm's channels of distribution, as Williamson (1975) has emphasized.

In addition, the Chicago school argued that competition does not take place only on price. Many products require the provision of information to enable consumers to use the product effectively. Also, many products must be supported with service, both at the time of purchase and later. To provide information and customer service, manufacturers establish dealer networks. The networks, however, are often plagued by the free-rider problem. Customers can visit a dealer to obtain information and then buy from a discount store that offers neither information nor service. Customers then are free riding on the information provided by the licensed dealers. This weakens the dealer network, resulting in less information being provided to consumers. Consumers then may make less-informed decisions, reducing economic efficiency. Indeed, one reason dealers charge a higher price than discount stores is that they must have a margin adequate to cover the costs of a well-trained sales staff and a service facility.

In *Continental TV v. GTE Sylvania,* 433 U.S. 36 (1977), the Supreme Court, influenced by this reasoning, changed the precedent established in *Schwinn.* The court held that nonprice vertical restraints should be considered under a rule of reason. GTE Sylvania, a producer of television sets, had experienced declining sales. By the beginning of the 1960s it had only 1 to 2 percent of the U.S. market. Sylvania distributed its television sets through both company-owned and independent distributors, which supplied retailers. In an attempt to increase its sales, Sylvania changed its method of distribution by eliminating its distributors and selling directly to franchised retailers. Sylvania also required its retailers to sell only from a specified location. This provision allowed Sylvania to control the number of retail outlets in an area. The objective of the changes was to attract a smaller but stronger group of retailers that would have the incentive to promote Sylvania TV sets. The franchised dealers could sell other brands and were not restricted in the prices they could charge.

The change proved successful. Dealers promoted Sylvania sets, increasing its market share to 5 percent by 1965. In 1965 Sylvania decided to authorize a new retailer in San Francisco. Continental TV, a Sylvania dealer there, protested and asked permission to sell Sylvania TVs in Sacramento. Sylvania refused, and Continental decided to sell them there anyway. Sylvania then refused to sell to Continental. Continental sued, and the federal district court, following *Schwinn,* held in its favor. The Court of Appeals reversed the decision and ordered a retrial on the grounds that it did not believe that *Schwinn* was applicable in this case. Continental appealed, and the Supreme Court took the case as an opportunity to reconsider whether vertical arrangements such as the one in question should be per se illegal.

The Supreme Court concluded that "Per se rules of illegality are appropriate only when they relate to conduct that is manifestly anticompetitive." As indicated in *Northern Pacific,* such conduct must have a "pernicious effect on competition" and have no "redeeming virtue." In considering whether this was true of the practice in *Sylvania,* the court found that "The market impact of vertical restrictions is complex because of their potential for a simultaneous reduction in intrabrand competition and stimulation of interbrand competition. . . ." The court then held that a vertical restriction could not be said a priori to have a pernicious effect on competition or to have no redeeming virtue. Hence, nonprice vertical arrangements were not per se illegal. The court pointed to the possible redeeming virtues, stating:

> New manufacturers and manufacturers entering new markets can use the restrictions in order to induce competent and aggressive retailers to make the kind of investment of capital and labor that is often required in the distribution of products unknown to the consumer. Established manufacturers can use them to induce retailers to engage in promotional activities or to provide service and repair facilities necessary to the efficient marketing of their products. Service and repair are vital for many products, such as automobiles and major household appliances. The availability and quality of such services affect a manufacturer's good will and the competitiveness of his product. Because of market imperfections such as the so-called "free rider" effect, these services might not be provided by retailers in a purely competitive situation. . . .

The Supreme Court affirmed the decision of the Court of Appeals and thus changed the per se rule of illegality for vertical practices to a rule of reason, reversing what had served as law for the previous 10 years. Since *Sylvania,* most nonprice vertical restrictions have been considered under a rule of reason. The new IO perspective generally agrees with this result, as does the structural perspective.

The Supreme Court followed the *Sylvania* decision with two decisions extending the applicability of the rule of reason in nonprice vertical arrangements. In *Monsanto Co. v. Spray-Rite Service Co.,* 465 U.S. 752 (1984), the court held that terminating a price-cutting dealer after complaints from several other dealers was not a per se violation. In *Business Electronics Corp. v. Sharp Electronics Corp.,* 485 U.S. 717 (1988), the court held that terminating a dealer relationship because another dealer had complained about its price cutting was not a per se violation unless there had been an agreement between the manufacturer and the complaining retailer. The rationale for these decisions was again that the practices could have the redeeming virtue of strengthening the dealer networks and stimulating interbrand competition and thus should be tried under a rule of reason.

Predatory Pricing and Entry Deterrence

The traditional perspective on predatory pricing is that a firm can drive a competitor out of a market by cutting prices below the competitor's costs. A firm with deep pockets can bear the short-term losses from the price cutting, and once the weaker rival is forced from the market, it can set higher prices to recoup its losses. The standard used to determine if a firm is engaging in predatory pricing is whether price is below marginal cost. Marginal cost is not easy for a court to measure, however, so a standard such as average variable cost is often used as the proxy.[21]

The Chicago school's criticism of this view of predatory pricing focused on its aftermath. Suppose a firm were to engage in predatory pricing and successfully drove a competitor out of the market. Could it then set a higher price than prior to the predation? The answer depends on whether there are barriers to entry in the industry. If there are not, and the Chicago school is skeptical about the presence of barriers to entry, then raising the price will simply attract new entrants. This will force the price down, and the predation will have been for naught. Recognizing this, a firm will not engage in predatory pricing in the first place.

If there were high barriers to entry, a firm could exercise market power. The principal barrier to entry recognized by the Chicago school is due to the sunk costs of incumbent firms. Even those sunk costs, however, are not a long-run deterrent to entry because once an entrant has entered the market, its costs are also sunk, and the incumbent firm no longer has a reason to price below long-run costs. The entrant will anticipate this and not be deterred from entering. Also, if an incumbent firm has sunk costs, a competitor already in the market is also likely to have sunk costs. Prices thus would have to be cut below short-run marginal costs to drive out that competitor.[22]

Even if predatory pricing were possible, it may not be desirable to drive a smaller competitor from the market. An industry leader would have to incur losses on a larger volume of sales. Predation in this case might not be in the interest of an industry leader, even if there were barriers to entry.

The conclusion of the Chicago school is that predation is unlikely to be successful, so it will not be attempted. The price cutting observed in markets is instead likely to be the result of competition rather than of predation. Applying antitrust law to alleged predation thus would discourage firms from competing on price, resulting in higher prices.

Research from the new IO perspective, however, casts some doubt on these conclusions. One theory of potential entry is based on the recognition that a potential entrant may not know if an incumbent firm has a cost advantage. Because of this incomplete information about the incumbent's costs, the incumbent may be able to

---

[21]See Areeda and Turner (1975).

[22]This argument would not hold if an incumbent had a cost advantage over a competitor or a potential entrant. The incumbent then could set a price just low enough that the potential entrant would stay out of the market. In this case, the threat of potential entry limits the incumbent firm's ability to increase its price but does not necessarily force the price down to the cost of the most efficient producer.

signal that it has low costs, even though its costs are actually high. The incumbent can do this by setting a price equal to the average of what a low-cost and a high-cost incumbent firm would choose. This pricing strategy can deter some entry that would be desirable from the perspective of economic efficiency.[23]

Another theory developed from the new IO perspective indicates that an incumbent firm may have an incentive to engage in predatory pricing in several geographic or product markets so as to develop a reputation as a "tough" competitor, thus discouraging entry by new firms.[24] The development of such a reputation hinges on potential entrants' incomplete information about, for example, the costs of the incumbent firm. A reputation for toughness, then, may deter entry into a market even if no real barriers to entry are present. In the supermarket industry Safeway developed a reputation as a tough competitor, which, according to some economists, has deterred entry.

Whatever the appropriate economic theory of predatory behavior, antitrust scrutiny of price cutting poses a serious concern. In practice it is difficult to distinguish between vigorous price competition and predatory pricing. Even in a competitive industry, prices can rise and fall in response to shifts in demand, and when entry occurs, prices will adjust as other firms change their outputs or exit the industry. Applying antitrust law in situations in which prices are being cut could stifle price competition. For example, new entrants may set low prices to build market share and utilize their capacity efficiently. Precluding an incumbent firm from responding to those prices would restrain competition and possibly prevent output from being produced at the lowest possible industry cost.

As an example, in 1992 American Airlines revamped its pricing by grouping fares into four classes, and it then cut full-fare prices substantially. Continental and Northwest filed an antitrust suit under the Sherman Act charging that American was trying to drive them out of the market with predatory prices and then use its increased market power to raise prices. The plaintiffs asked for damages of $1 billion, which would be trebled in the event of a guilty verdict. Robert Crandall, CEO of American, said that Continental and Northwest were "hoping to accomplish in the courtroom what they couldn't accomplish in the marketplace." A jury acquitted American.

As another example, in the chapter case, *The Microsoft Antitrust Case,* the court did not conclude that Microsoft's decision to give away its Internet Explorer (IE) browser for free was anticompetitive, even though that decision was a major blow to its rival Netscape. Its Navigator browser was selling at $15 to $20 a copy to licensees, and Netscape was forced to set its price to zero. Pricing IE at zero, which is its marginal cost, is economically efficient. The court concluded that a price of zero benefited consumers, and the competition to win in the browser market stimulated substantial improvements in browser quality, also benefiting consumers. Pricing at zero in this case was not predatory.

Collusion and Price-Fixing

All schools of thought agree that collusion and horizontal price fixing are anticompetitive, and the DOJ has vigorously prosecuted price fixing and obtained large fines, criminal convictions, and prison sentences for those found guilty. The schools, however, disagree about how likely it is that collusive arrangements can be sustained.

The structural perspective on collusion and price fixing is that firms will collude when possible, so tight antitrust supervision is necessary. The Chicago school, however, points to historical evidence indicating that cartels broke down as a result of cheating by their own members. Furthermore, the larger the number of firms required to collude, the more difficult it is to prevent cheating and defection. For collusion to be sustained, the colluders must have a means of detecting cheating, as in the case of bidding on government contracts when the bids are publicly reported. In the chapter case, *Price Fixing in the Airways,* cheating was easier to detect because trans-Atlantic airfares were publicly posted.

---

[23]See Milgrom and Roberts (1982) for a development of this theory.
[24]See Kreps and Wilson (1982) for a development of this theory.

The new IO approach, however, reaches the conclusion that collusion and price-fixing are easier to sustain than suggested by the Chicago school. Moreover, the number of convictions provides evidence that price fixing is not uncommon. Because firms in the same industry will be in competition over time, firms have a broad set of strategies that could sustain implicit collusion.[25] A firm that believes that another firm is cheating on an implicit agreement to maintain high prices can punish that firm by lowering its own price. If the second firm is confident that the first firm indeed has an incentive to punish any perceived cheating, the second firm will have no incentive to cheat in the first place. The threat of punishment in repeated encounters thus can, in principle, enforce high prices even when there is neither an explicit agreement nor communication among the firms. Price-cutting thus could be a means of punishing deviations from implicit collusion rather than an indication of either vigorous competition or predation.

In the chapter case, *Price Fixing in the Airways,* British Airways and Virgin Atlantic fixed fuel surcharges on passenger flights, and airlines carrying cargo across the Pacific also fixed prices. The number of airlines involved was small, so coordination was not difficult. The price fixing continued for two years and was revealed as a result of a leniency program of the Office of Fair Trade in the United Kingdom. The program provides leniency for a company that reports price fixing to the authorities. Virgin Atlantic and Lufthansa reported the price fixing on Atlantic and Pacific cargo fares respectively. The airlines said that the price fixing had occurred at lower levels in the company, and when brought to the attention of higher-level management, the leniency program provided incentives to report the price fixing to authorities.[26]

Mergers and Merger Guidelines

Mergers can create horizontal market power or restrain competition in supply or distribution channels. The passage of the Celler-Kefauver Act in 1950 decreased the number of mergers, but when the Reagan administration took office in 1981, it signaled that it did not view mergers with the same hostility as had prior administrations. Indeed, mergers were viewed as potentially beneficial to efficiency and competition. Mergers can yield cost efficiencies and synergies that benefit consumers. Mergers can also remove ineffective management and eliminate inefficient cross-subsidization of one line of business by another.

To provide guidance to firms about when it was likely to initiate an antitrust investigation, the DOJ issued revised merger guidelines in 1982.[27] The FTC issued similar guidelines, and in 1992 the agencies jointly issued updated guidelines.[28] The guidelines reflect both structural and Chicago school perspectives by identifying where market power may be present and whether it can be exercised. The guidelines also reflect the new IO perspective with respect to the dynamics of competition. In contrast to the structural perspective, the guidelines do not assume that market power automatically will be exercised. Market power is viewed as a horizontal concept, and nonhorizontal mergers, either vertical or conglomerate, that do not affect market concentration are not necessarily a threat to competition. Nonhorizontal mergers are a concern only to the extent that they have horizontal consequences, such as eliminating a potential entrant.

The merger guidelines identify collusion as the means to the exercise of market power. The exercise of market power requires a restriction of output to increase prices and profits. Since the smaller a firm's market share the more it has to restrict output to achieve a given price increase, unless a firm has a dominant market position, collusion must be the means to the exercise of market power. In accord with the Chicago school's perspective, the greater the number of firms that would have to collude to restrict output, the more likely collusion is to break down. Collusion is easier the more

---

[25]Green and Porter (1984) present and empirically test this theory.
[26]The European Union also has a leniency program under which the first firm receives 100 percent leniency, the second 50 percent, and the third 30 percent.
[27]Ordover and Willig (1983) provide an evaluation of the DOJ merger guidelines.
[28]Department of Justice and Federal Trade Commission, Horizontal Merger Guidelines, Washington, DC, April 2, 1992.

homogeneous the product, since then there is only one dimension of competition that must be monitored under an explicit or implicit collusive arrangement. Collusion is more difficult when products are differentiated and substitutes are available in the relevant markets and is easier when repeated encounters provide an opportunity to punish cheating on the collusive arrangement.

In its definition of the relevant market, the DOJ and FTC focus on "economically meaningful" markets. These are defined in terms of products and geographic areas in which a firm could restrict output and thereby increase price above prevailing levels. To do so, a firm would have to have horizontal market power. Assessing market power involves consideration of substitute products, since an attempt to raise prices may cause consumers to switch to a substitute. It also takes into account imports and the resale market for durable goods.

To assess the potential for achieving price increases in the case of horizontal mergers, the DOJ and FTC use the Herfindahl-Hirschman Index (HHI) to measure concentration in an industry. The HHI is defined as the sum of the squares of the market shares of firms, or

$$HHI = \sum_{i=1}^{n} s_i^2$$

where n is the number of firms in the industry and s_i is the market share of the ith firm expressed as a percent. The HHI is zero for a perfectly competitive industry and is 10,000 for a monopoly. If two firms with 10 percent market shares merge, the HHI increases by 200. For an industry with 10 firms with equal market shares, the HHI is 1,000, and for an industry with two firms with 30 percent shares and eight firms with 5 percent shares, the HHI is 2,000.

The merger guidelines state that the agencies will not challenge a merger in which the postmerger HHI is below 1,000. They are unlikely to challenge a merger in which the postmerger HHI is between 1,000 and 1,800 (six equal-sized firms) unless the merger would increase the HHI by more than 100. In the case of an industry with an HHI above 1,800, they are unlikely to investigate if the merger increases the HHI by less than 50, and are likely to investigate if the HHI increases by at least 100. The agencies, however, will take into account other factors that affect market power or its exercise.

In 2004 the FTC reported on its merger enforcement actions in industries other than grocery, oil, chemicals, and pharmaceuticals. Table 9-1, adapted from Gavil, Kovacic, and Baker (2004), reports the enforcement data, where "Closed" means that no action was taken by the FTC and "Enforced" means that some antitrust action was taken. The data indicate that concentration, and particularly the increase in concentration, plays a central role in enforcement decisions.

The use of the HHI requires identification of the relevant market for determining shares. One approach is to identify the scope of substitutes for the product. Another approach is to use data to identify which products compete with which others. This approach was used by the FTC in the chapter case *The Staples–Office Depot Merger?*[29] Using product price data, the court defined the relevant market as office supply superstores, and since there were only three superstores, the HHI was high. Moreover, the HHI would increase substantially if two superstores merged.

TABLE 9-1 Horizontal Merger Enforcement 1996–2003		
	Increase in HHI 0–299	*Increase in HHI 300 or more*
Postmerger HHI 0–2,399	Enforced: 0 Closed: 6	Enforced: 3 Closed: 16
Postmerger HHI 2,400 or more	Enforced: 2 Closed: 7	Enforced: 183 Closed: 45

[29]See also Baker (1997) and Dalkir and Warren-Boulton (1999) for analyses of the "Staples–Office Depot" case.

A merger, however, can result in greater efficiency, and in 1997 the FTC issued a revision to the merger guidelines. The FTC identified the potential efficiencies from a merger and stated that the efficiencies considered should be net of the efficiencies that would have been realized in the absence of a merger. The FTC also stated that any efficiency claims must be verifiable and substantiated. It also stated that efficiencies would likely carry little weight if the merger were to create a monopoly or near-monopoly. The efficiency considerations played an important role in the *Staples–Office Depot* case.

In addition to the structural factors involving market concentration, the antitrust agencies take into account technological change and the rate of innovation in an industry. In an industry that experiences rapid technological change, a large market share of merging companies may be of little concern because market share can be won or lost relatively quickly. Similar reasoning led to dropping the government's antitrust suit against IBM.

In 2007 Whole Foods Market, the largest marketer of natural and organic groceries, sought to acquire the second largest firm, Wild Oats Markets, for $565 million. The FTC investigated the proposed merger and concluded that it would reduce competition and increase prices of premium natural and organic food. The FTC sought a preliminary injunction in federal courts to prevent the firms from merging. The companies argued that there was no distinctive market for natural and organic groceries and that the relevant market was broad, since Safeway, Wal-Mart, and others also sold those groceries. The judge agreed with the companies that the relevant market was larger than the premium grocers, and denied the request for a preliminary injunction. The FTC filed an appeal of the judge's decision, and the court of appeals reversed the lower court decision. The definition of the relevant market is the crucial issue in *The Staples-Office Depot Merger?* case.[30]

The antitrust enforcement agencies frequently negotiate with merging companies under the "fix-it-first" approach in which areas of antitrust concern are fixed prior to a merger being consummated. For example, in 2004, after initially opposing it, the FTC approved the merger of Nestlé and Dreyer's Grand Ice Cream after potentially anticompetitive features had been fixed. Dreyer's sold three of its brands, and Nestlé sold its U.S. distribution assets. Similarly, in 1996 the FTC required Ciba-Geigy and Sandoz to sell part of their gene-therapy technology as a condition for their merger to form Novartis.

In 2000 AOL and Time Warner announced a merger that the FTC delayed because of concerns about anticompetitive effects. After nearly a year of negotiations to fix the concerns, the companies and the FTC agreed to a consent order that allowed the merger to be completed. AOL Time Warner agreed to make Earthlink's ISP service available to subscribers on Time Warner's cable system before AOL could offer its broadband ISP service. AOL Time Warner also agreed not to discriminate against independent ISPs and not to price discriminate on DSL service and competing services unless there were cost differences.

Mergers often come under the jurisdictions of other countries. The European Union approved the AOL Time Warner merger with the stipulation that Bertelsmann AG withdraw from a joint venture in Europe in which AOL's CompuServe and Vivendi SA participated. In 2001 the United States also approved a merger between General Electric and Honeywell after the companies agreed to some minor fixes. The European Union, however, rejected the merger, causing the companies to abandon their merger plans. This decision is considered in more detail in Chapter 15.

COMPLIANCE

Compliance with the antitrust laws involves both procedures and policy. Firms provide training and guidance to employees who may encounter situations in which antitrust concerns are present. For example, in its "Standards of Business Conduct," Hewlett-Packard provides guidance on trade practices (vertical arrangements), price discrimination, unfair practices, and competitor relations (horizontal practices). Cisco Systems

---

[30]In 2008 Staples reached an agreement to acquire Corporate Express, NV for $4.8 billion.

requires employees to watch an antitrust primer on its Web site. Companies with dominant market positions restrain their competitive practices and language. Cisco and Intel do not use the term *leveraging*, as in "leveraging from a dominant position."

A firm may find itself in a situation in which a contemplated practice falls in an area in which the antitrust laws and the court decisions interpreting them are unclear or changing. In addition to seeking the advice of counsel, the firm should examine whether the purpose of its practice is anticompetitive. In *Sylvania* the court held that the policy of territorial restrictions served the purpose of stimulating interbrand competition. In such a case a firm should use a practice that is the least restrictive in achieving the desired purpose. On retrial the court acquitted GTE-Sylvania because it concluded that the practice of terminating a dealer that violated its policy was the least restrictive means of achieving the intended purpose of strengthening its dealer network. Hewlett-Packard's policy on terminating relationships is cautious despite the decisions in *Sylvania, Monsanto,* and *Sharp:* "Terminating relationships with customers can lead to litigation. It is therefore important that the decision to terminate be made carefully and for valid business reasons. HP's Legal Department should be consulted before terminating any such relationship without the customer's consent. Possible termination of one customer's contract should not be discussed with another customer."[31]

THE POLITICS OF ANTITRUST

Antitrust policy has important distributive as well as efficiency consequences for firms and consumers, so it is the subject of nonmarket action.[32] In the 1970s the FTC adopted an aggressive posture and initiated several new investigations, some of which were directed at such politically influential industries as insurance and funeral homes. The resulting political pressure on Congress led it to pass the Federal Trade Commission Improvements Act of 1980, which reined in the FTC.[33] The framework for nonmarket analysis presented in Part II of this book provides the basis for analyzing the politics of antitrust policy.

Most proposed changes in the antitrust laws fail because of the intensity of the ensuing politics and the complexity of the issues. In 1986 the Reagan administration proposed amending Section 7 of the Clayton Act (which deals with mergers) by replacing "may be" and "tend to" with "significant probability." It also proposed relaxing merger standards for firms that had been injured by foreign competition. Because of a concern that private antitrust lawsuits were being used to stifle competition, the administration proposed eliminating treble damages except for price-fixing violations. The FTC and the Reagan administration also proposed that the FTC authority over unfair advertising be eliminated, because the term "unfair" was too vague to be enforced. None of these initiatives was successful.

Democrats in Congress have also sought revisions in the antitrust laws, attempting to counter DOJ and FTC decisions to stop bringing suits for certain vertical restraints. They also attempted to revise the standards established by the Supreme Court in *Monsanto* and *Sharp* involving nonprice vertical arrangements. In 1991, for example, the Senate passed a bill that would make it easier to win cases against retail price maintenance practices. Both activist groups and discounters who had been cut off by manufacturers backed the bill, arguing that consumers were injured by the nonprice arrangements. They were opposed by manufacturers and specialty retailers, who viewed vertical arrangements as promoting interbrand competition. The bill failed.

The politics of antitrust also manifests itself in legislative action seeking exemptions or providing for affirmative defenses in antitrust lawsuits. For decades the soft drink industry had been organized around exclusive territories for its distributors. Soft drink manufacturers produced syrup, which was sold to bottlers that were allowed to distribute the soft drink only in a specified geographic area. In 1971 the FTC issued complaints against seven national-brand soft drink syrup manufacturers, including

---

[31]Hewlett-Packard Company, "Standards of Business Conduct," Palo Alto, CA, 1989.
[32]See Shugart (1990) for a perspective on antitrust and interest group politics.
[33]See Weingast and Moran (1983), Moe (1985), and Wilson (1989, Chap. 13) for differing perspectives on the relationship between the FTC and Congress.

Coca-Cola, PepsiCo, Seven-Up, and Canada Dry. The complaints charged that exclusive territorial distributorships were illegal vertical restraints of trade. With the strong support of the National Soft Drink Association, in 1972 a bill was introduced in the Senate to permit exclusive territorial arrangements for soft drink manufacturers.

The FTC complaint was resolved in 1978 when the FTC ruled that the exclusive distributorships were anticompetitive. The decision was appealed and was still before the courts when Congress finally acted. After 10 years of effort, the soft drink manufacturers and their bottlers succeeded in 1980 in obtaining an effective antitrust exemption. The Soft Drink Interbrand Competition Act provided protection from antitrust lawsuits if soft drinks were in "substantial and effective competition." Despite opposition by the DOJ, the bill passed the Senate on an 86 to 6 vote, passed the House on a voice vote, and was signed by President Carter.[34]

SUMMARY

The principal antitrust laws are the Sherman Act, the Clayton Act, and the Federal Trade Commission Act. The Sherman Act pertains to monopolization and restraints of trade. The Clayton Act addresses monopolization and restraints of trade in their incipiency and provides the basis for government authority over mergers. The act also restricts price discrimination. The Federal Trade Commission Act prohibits unfair competition and unfair and deceptive acts.

Both the DOJ and the FTC have enforcement responsibilities for the Sherman and Clayton Acts, but only the FTC can enforce the FTC Act. Considerable enforcement of the antitrust laws occurs through private lawsuits, most of which are filed by one firm against another. Private lawsuits are encouraged by the prospect of treble damages.

Antitrust enforcement and court decisions are influenced by schools of thought about the role of antitrust policy and the likelihood of adverse economic consequences from business practices. The structural approach is based on the structure-conduct-performance paradigm and focuses on the structure of industries and on practices that may foreclose opportunities for competitors. The Chicago school focuses on economic efficiency and consumer prices and views markets as both resilient and the consumer's best protection. Both the structural approach and the Chicago school view horizontal market power as a concern but differ about how likely collusion is and how substantial are barriers to entry. The Chicago school concludes that most practices should be considered under a rule of reason, whereas the structural approach supports a broader application of the per se standard. The new industrial organization perspective emphasizes the strategic interactions among competitors that can result from repeated interactions and incomplete information. These strategic interactions have the potential to sustain implicit collusion and limit entry into industries. This perspective also focuses on factors such as network externalities and standardization that can provide the basis for anticompetitive practices.

These schools of thought have influenced the thinking of government antitrust officials and judges. In the case of vertical arrangements and resale price maintenance, the courts reversed earlier decisions in holding that those practices are no longer per se illegal but are to be considered under a rule of reason. Certain arrangements that enhance interbrand competition but harm intrabrand competition have been held by the courts to be legal under the antitrust laws.

The DOJ and FTC have applied revised guidelines to the surveillance of mergers. The guidelines are based both on industry structure and on the likelihood that market power can be exercised. The government has used a fix-it-first approach to reduce the anticompetitive effects of mergers that otherwise would produce efficiencies.

Antitrust policy has important distributive consequences and so is the subject of considerable political activity. The complexity of the issues, however, makes significant legislative changes in the antitrust laws difficult to achieve.

---

[34]The case *The Malt Beverage Interbrand Competition Act* in Baron (1996) considers the beer industry's unsuccessful attempt to obtain similar protection.

------------------------------------- C A S E S -------------------------------------
Price Fixing in the Airways

Crude oil prices increased rapidly in the 2004–2006 period and the increase in fuel costs placed a burden on airlines. Airlines began to add "fuel surcharges" to air fares, adding a new instrument of price competition. British Airways (BA) contacted Virgin Atlantic Airways and began discussing the situation in 2004, and the discussions resulted in increases in the surcharge from £5 to £60 on return trans-Atlantic flights over the next two years. Virgin's legal department subsequently notified the United Kingdom's Office of Fair Trading (OFT) that the two firms had colluded to fix the fuel charges. Virgin was taking advantage of a "leniency policy" included in the Competition Act of 1998, which provides immunity to firms that reveal illegal competitive action. The objective of the policy was to provide an incentive to disclose wrongdoing. In response to Virgin's disclosure BA admitted guilt and established a £350 million reserve for fines. Two BA executives resigned as a result of the price-fixing. The European Union was also conducting an investigation of the price fixing and could levy substantial fines.

BA cooperated fully with the OFT, and stated that its policy was "to conduct its business in full compliance with all . . . the laws." As a result of its investigation in 2007 the OFT fined BA £121.5 million, the largest civil penalty it had ever imposed.[35] Simon Williams, director of cartel operations for the OFT, said, "Had BA not made admissions and cooperated from the outset, they would have been fined many millions of pounds more . . . tens of millions of pounds."[36] Philip Collins, the head of the OFT, said the fine would "send an important message . . . about our intention to enforce the law.[37] Ryanair CEO Michael O'Leary commented, "The fuel surcharges levied by British Airways and Virgin Atlantic are just their latest price-fixing scam. The flag-carriers have been price fixing for years. . . ."[38] Ryanair had not added fuel surcharges.

A few hours after the OFT announced the fine, in a case filed by the United States Department of Justice (DOJ), a court imposed a $300 million fine on British Airways, the second largest fine ever imposed in a DOJ case. The fine also covered a separate case in which BA and Korean Air Lines admitted to fixing prices and surcharges on air cargo flights.[39] Korean Air

Lines was also fined $300 million, and Qantas paid $61 million. The price fixing conspiracy was exposed by Lufthansa AG, and Lufthansa and Virgin were notified that restitution would be required for customers even though the companies were conditionally accepted into the DOJ "corporate leniency" program. William W. Mercer of the DOJ said, "When British Airways, Korean Air and their co-conspirators got together and agreed to raise prices for passenger and air-cargo fares, American consumers and businesses ended up picking up the tab for their illegal conduct."[40] Craig Kelly, a lighting manufacturer in Sydney, complained, "We just missed out on contracts of upwards of a million dollars because of price. It could very well have been the cartel margin that Qantas was ripping us off that was enough to push us over the edge and lose the contract.[41]

In addition to the fines by the antitrust authorities the airlines faced the likelihood of class action cases in the United States on behalf of customers who were overcharged because of the price fixing. Michael Hausfeld, a U.S. attorney, said he would be filing a representative action lawsuit in the UK to give consumers "the opportunity to recover that which was robbed from them."[42] BA CEO Willie Walsh said, "I want to reassure our passengers that they were not overcharged. Fuel charges are a legitimate way of recovering costs."[43] Walsh also stated, "The activities that went on were in breach of the law and fines were established in accord with the guidelines. They could have been as high as $850 million but we cooperated fully with the investigation, which was the right thing to do."[44] Walsh blamed the price fixing on "a very limited number of individuals within British Airways."[45]

In 2008 British Airways and Virgin Atlantic Airways reached a $200 million settlement in a class action lawsuit filed in federal court in the United States alleging price fixing on fuel surcharges. The plaintiff's law firm also had filed a separate class action lawsuit alleging price fixing on trans-Pacific routes. ∎

---

[35]The maximum fine allowable under European Union law was 10 percent of sales.
[36]Reuters, August 1, 2007.
[37]The Economist, August 4, 2007.
[38]Daily Mail, August 4, 2007.
[39]The investigation involved authorities in the United States, the United Kingdom, South Korea, and elsewhere. The fine was composed of $200 million for cargo flights and $100 million for passenger flights.

[40]Wall Street Journal, August 2, 2007.
[41]Daily Telegraph (Australia), January 17, 2008.
[42]Guardian, August 18, 2007. In the United Kingdom a "representation action" under the OFT law is the counterpart of a class action lawsuit.
[43]Wall Street Journal, August 2, 2007.
[44]Sunday Telegraph, August 3, 2007.
[45]USA Today, August 2, 2007.

Preparation Questions

1. What were the incentives that led the airlines to fix prices?
2. Show how a leniency program can put price fixers in a prisoners' dilemma.
3. What procedures should be put into place to ensure that employees do not engage in price fixing?
4. How hard is it to conceal price fixing?

The Staples–Office Depot Merger?

On September 4, 1996, Staples, the fast-growing No. 2 office supply retailer, agreed to buy Office Depot, the industry leader, in a transaction valued at $3.36 billion. Staples and Office Depot were among the pioneers that a decade earlier developed the successful concept of office supply superstores. By pursuing aggressive marketing strategies, charging low prices, and leveraging their buying power and efficient mass supply channels to cut costs, the companies created a profitable, rapidly growing industry. Staples had the second largest superstore chain in the United States with approximately 550 stores in 28 states, $3 billion annual revenues, and net income of $74 million. With more than 500 stores in 38 states, Office Depot had the largest sales, approximately $5.3 billion, and net income of $132 million. The only other office supply superstore chain was OfficeMax.

The companies identified significant cost reductions as the main reason for the merger. Thomas Stemberg, chairman and CEO of Staples, said, for example, that the two companies bought envelopes from three separate vendors. "We'd entertain proposals from all three," he said, "and we'd say, you can have all of the business or none of it."[46] Stemberg also commented on the combined entity's ability to pass through the savings to customers: "Both Staples and Office Depot were founded a decade ago to bring savings to purchasers of office products. The combined company, with over $10 billion in revenues, will be able to offer even greater value to our customers through increasing operating efficiency and purchasing scale."[47]

The companies, as well as commentators, anticipated from the outset that the transaction would raise antitrust concerns: "The merged organization—with 1,100 stores in 96 percent of the country's largest metropolitan areas—will reduce the number of distributors for manufacturers, giving them less bargaining power. The deal is also likely to draw close scrutiny from the U.S. antitrust regulators."[48] David Fuente, chairman and CEO of Office Depot, stressed both that the companies did not compete with each other in many geographical areas and that the market was much larger than the merged companies. Fuente said, "The reality today is that there's very little overlap in our store base and geographical locations, and two or three years from now that might not be the case if both companies continue to grow at the pace that we were predicting."[49] Fuente also stated, "Our new company operates in an office products industry which is very large, highly fragmented and growing rapidly. As a result of this strategic combination, we will be better positioned to participate fully in the enormous growth opportunities that exist in our industry."[50] Juris Pagrabs, vice president of investor relations of Office-Max, the third largest office supply superstore chain, offered a positive view on the announced merger: "We think the merger is quite good for the industry. It's better to have two players instead of three."[51]

The Federal Trade Commission (FTC) did not share this view. The FTC contended that the overall expected effect of the proposed merger on customers would be negative, since it expected the merger to reduce competition significantly in many markets. Underlying this contention was a claim that the expected pass-through to customers of the efficiencies created by the merger would not be large enough to offset the effect of the reduction in competition. The issue thus revolved around the assessment of the expected economic consequences of the planned merger. To assess these effects, verbal pronouncements such as "reduction in competition," "respective market," and "efficiencies that pass through to customers" had to be reduced to quantifiable measures.

The Antitrust Review

Following the procedure required by Hart-Scott-Rodino, Staples and Office Depot filed a Premerger Notification and Report Form with the FTC and the Department of Justice on October 2, 1996. This was followed by a 7-month investigation by the FTC, in which additional information was requested from the companies, hundreds of boxes of documents were examined, depositions of 18 officers and employees of both Staples and Office Depot were taken, and (ex parte) discovery of third-party information was made. The FTC voted 4 to 1 to challenge the merger.

[46]*Wall Street Journal,* September 5, 1996.
[47]*Business Wire,* September 4, 1996.
[48]*Wall Street Journal,* September 5, 1996.

[49]*Wall Street Journal,* September 5, 1996.
[50]*Business Wire,* September 4, 1996.
[51]*Wall Street Journal,* September 5, 1996.

In an attempt to satisfy the FTC's objections, Staples and Office Depot negotiated a consent decree with the FTC staff that would allow the merger if the companies would sell 63 stores to OfficeMax for $109 million to reduce the concentration in those local markets. The FTC, however, in a shock to the companies, rejected the negotiated consent decree by a vote of 3 to 2, and in a revision of its merger guidelines it expressed skepticism about projected cost efficiencies from mergers that cannot "be verified by reasonable means." The FTC then filed a motion with the District Court of the District of Columbia on April 9, 1997, seeking a preliminary injunction to block the merger. The matter thus was for the court to decide.

The Court's Review

In deciding whether to issue a preliminary injunction, the court required the FTC to show (1) that its challenge was likely to succeed on the merits after complete consideration of the facts, and (2) that in "balancing the equities" it was of greater harm to let the transaction proceed and later try to reverse it than to enjoin it until the review process reached its final conclusion. Since the preliminary proceedings raised the key issues that would be raised in the complete review process, the hearing on the preliminary injunction would in effect resolve the entire case. The findings of fact by the court would determine whether those conditions were satisfied.[52]

Likelihood of Success on the Merits

The Geographic Market

There was no dispute that the appropriate geographic market was 42 metropolitan areas in which Staples and Office Depot competed with each other prior to the merger agreement, as well as several areas in which they planned to begin competing in the near future.

The Product Market

The court defined the product market for antitrust purposes as "the sale of consumable office supplies through office superstores," thereby accepting the FTC's claim that although the products Staples and Office Depot sold had perfect functional substitutes sold at other stores such as Wal-Mart, the market should be viewed as office superstores only. The court based its conclusion on pricing data.

The FTC compared Staples' prices in geographic markets in which Staples was the only office superstore (termed one-firm markets) with markets in which it competed with Office Depot or OfficeMax (two-firm markets), or both (three-firm markets). Prices in one-firm markets were, on average, 13 percent higher than in three-firm markets.[53] Prices were compared at one point in time (January 1997), and they were based on a sample representing 90 percent of Staples's sales. Additional, less comprehensive data showed that average prices were well over 5 percent higher in one-firm markets than in two-firm markets. Based on the merger guidelines, price differences of 5 percent or more were viewed by the court as indirect evidence that office supply superstores were a distinct product market for antitrust purposes. The FTC presented similar evidence regarding Office Depot's prices based on a sample of 500 items (also from January 1997). Prices in Office Depot–only markets were on average well over 5 percent higher than they were in three-firm markets. Additional data showed that on average Office Depot's prices were highest in its one-firm markets and lowest in its three-firm markets.

The FTC also had to determine if the office superstores represented a largely independent market or were part of a much broader office supply market of which the companies had only a 5.5 percent market share. To do this, the FTC considered the cross-elasticity of demand between products in the superstore market and their functional substitutes in the broader markets. (The cross-elasticity of demand is the percentage change in the demand for one product divided by the percentage change in the price of another product.)

Retail and discount chains other than office superstores carried consumable office supplies (functional substitutes), and the court identified the set of other sellers such as Wal-Mart, Kmart, and Target; wholesale clubs such as BJ's and Price Costco; computer and electronic stores such as Computer City and Best Buy; independent retail office supply stores; mail-order firms; and contract stationers. The court concluded that "these competitors, albeit in different combinations and concentrations, are present in every one of [the superstores' markets]." Despite this fact, Staples and Office Depot were able to charge higher prices in their one-firm markets than they did in their two- and three-firm markets. The court found a lower price sensitivity to the existence of other superstore competitors. For example, Staples maintained a "warehouse-club-only" price zone, which was a zone where it competed with a warehouse club but not with other superstores. The data the FTC presented showed average variation in prices of only 1 to 2 percent between warehouse-club-only zones and one-firm markets; that is, the cross-elasticity of demand was low, suggesting that the stores were not competing in the same market. These findings led the court to conclude that the office superstore market was distinguishable from other markets for consumable office supplies and should thus be considered the relevant market for antitrust purposes.

---

[52]These findings were based on the public version of the decision. The court examined specific price data submitted by the parties in classified documents. The public version of these documents, as well as the decision, withheld all these data.

[53]These price data had been submitted by the companies.

Perceptions and Behavior of Market Participants

The court also based its definition of the product market on several additional considerations. First, in all of their internal documents and communications, both Staples and Office Depot viewed the relevant competitive market as comprised of office superstores only. For example, when determining whether to enter a new metropolitan area, both companies repeatedly referred to markets without office superstores as "noncompetitive," regardless of the existence of other sellers of office supplies. Staples used the phrase "office superstore industry" in strategic planning documents. In a monthly report entitled "Competitor Store Opening/Closing Report," which it circulated to its Executive Committee, Office Depot reported all competitor store closings and openings, but the only competitors referred to were Staples and OfficeMax.

Also, both companies price checked the other superstores much more frequently and extensively than they price checked other retail outlets. Executives of nonsuperstore competitors, who were summoned to testify by the FTC, were aware of the distinct nature of the superstore market. The court concluded that Staples and Office Depot considered the other superstores as their primary competition.

Cost Differentials

Staples and Office Depot offered two cost explanations for the average price differentials between one-, two-, and three-firm markets. The first explanation was that there were differences in wages and rents across localities. These differences, however, were not correlated with the price differences across localities, so the court rejected this explanation.

The second explanation was related to differences in advertising and marketing costs. Indeed, these costs were higher, on average, in one-firm markets than in two- and three-firm markets. Yet, the court found that the differences in costs were too small to account for the significant price differentials shown by the FTC. The court rejected the second explanation as well.

Distinctive Features

The court also distinguished between the superstores and other distribution channels in terms of appearance, physical size, format, variety of items offered, and the type and character of targeted and served customers. The court concluded that "office supply superstores look far different from other sellers of office supplies. ... No one entering a Wal-Mart would mistake it for an office superstore."

The Probable Effect on Competition

Concentration

Once the relevant product market had been defined, the concentration analysis was straightforward. The court examined the concentration within each identified geographic market. The HHIs in many of the geographic markets were at "problematic levels" even before the merger. The least concentrated market had an HHI of 3,597, and the most concentrated had 6,944. In contrast, if the merger were completed, the least concentrated market would have an HHI of 5,003, and many areas would have an HHI of 10,000 (i.e., monopoly). The merger guidelines stated that unless mitigated by other factors, an increase in the HHI in excess of 50 in a postmerger, highly concentrated market raised significant competitive concerns. The average increase in the HHI caused by the Staples–Office Depot merger would have been 2,715 points. The court also examined concentration statistics. The merged Staples–Office Depot was expected to hold a dominant market share in 42 geographic markets across the country. In 15 markets the combined market share would be 100 percent.

The court's definition of the relevant product market had, in effect, determined the concentration issue. If the product market had been defined more broadly as, for example, "consumable office supplies" or "office supplies," the concentration figures would have been much lower. The product market definition had a similar effect on the consideration of entry.

Entry

The court assessed the existence and significance of barriers to entry with respect to the relevant market. Staples and Office Depot claimed that the rapid growth in overall office supply sales had encouraged, and would continue to encourage, expansion and entry. They pointed to the fact that all office superstore entrants had entered within the last 11 years. They also offered testimony regarding the general ability of mass merchandisers of various types to change store configurations and shift shelf space to accommodate new demands. Yet, the FTC showed that new superstore entrants did not survive as selfsustaining businesses. The number of office superstore chains dropped from 23 to 3 over the few years preceding 1997. All but Staples, Office Depot, and OfficeMax had either closed or been acquired. The failed office superstore entrants included large, well-known retailers such as Kmart, Montgomery Ward, Ames, and Zayles.

The court determined that a "new office superstore would need to open a large number of stores nationally to achieve the purchasing and distribution economies of scale enjoyed by the three existing firms." The court thus found that it would be extremely unlikely that a new office superstore would enter the market and thereby lessen the anticompetitive effects of the proposed merger.

The court also concluded that even in one-firm markets no retailer had successfully expanded its consumable office supplies to the extent that it constrained superstore pricing increases to less than 5 percent. Entry into the relevant market was therefore rejected as a factor likely to offset the merger's expected anticompetitive effects.

Efficiencies

Staples and Office Depot submitted an Efficiencies Analysis that predicted that the combined business would achieve savings of between $4.9 and $6.5 billion over the first 5 years. The companies also claimed that additional dynamic efficiencies would result because the superstores' suppliers would become more efficient as a result of the increase in their sales to the combined business. Staples and Office Depot argued that two-thirds of the cost savings would be passed along to consumers.

The court, however, found these figures to be inflated and unreliable and preferred the evidence and expert testimony the FTC provided. First, the court noted that the estimates provided by the companies exceeded by almost 500 percent the figures that were presented to the two boards of directors in September 1996, when they approved the transaction, and which had been disclosed to the companies' shareholders and the SEC in the Joint Proxy Statement/Prospectus of January 1997. Second, the companies estimated only the overall savings that the merger was expected to yield and did not deduct the savings both companies would generate as standalone entities if the merger did not materialize. Third, large parts of the argued savings were unverifiable—the companies' experts could not provide figures and explicit methods of calculation to justify the projections.

The court also found the companies' projected pass-through of savings to customers in the form of lower prices to be unrealistic. The court did not find a convincing argument for the combined business to increase significantly its pass-through rate to two-thirds from the historical pass-through rate of 15 to 17 percent established by the evidence.[54]

Pricing Practices

The court used the historical pass-through rate as an indication of the likely future rate. In a similar manner, as an indication of the likely future behavior and practices of the combined entity, the court used the historical pricing practices of the two companies, which had been established in identifying the relevant product market.

This further supported the likely anticompetitive effects of the merger: "The evidence of the defendants' own current pricing practices, for example, shows that an office superstore chain facing no competition from other superstores has the ability to profitably raise prices for consumable office supplies above competitive levels. ... Since prices are significantly lower in markets where Staples and Office Depot compete, eliminating this competition with one another would free the parties to charge higher prices in those markets, especially those in which the combined entity would be the sole office superstore." The court concluded that the FTC had shown that its case was likely to succeed on its merits. The court then considered the equities.

Balance of Equities

The court concluded that "'Unscrambling the eggs after the fact is not a realistic option in this case." The combined company's postmerger plans included consolidation of warehouse and supply facilities, closing 40 to 70 superstores, changing the name of Office Depot stores to Staples, renegotiating contracts with manufacturers and suppliers, and consolidating management, which was likely to lead to layoffs of many Office Depot key personnel.

The court then considered the possible private equities. Staples and Office Depot argued that the principal private equity at stake was the loss to Office Depot shareholders, who would likely lose a substantial portion of their investments if the merger were enjoined. While acknowledging this possible harm to Office Depot shareholders "at least in the short term," the court concluded that such private equity alone did not justify a denial of preliminary injunction where the public equity clearly supported it.

The court issued the preliminary injunction requested by the FTC. Shortly thereafter, Staples and Office Depot terminated their merger agreement. ■

SOURCE: This case was written by Professor David P. Baron and Chen Lichtenstein based on public sources. Copyright © 1998 by the Board of Trustees of the Leland Stanford Junior University. All rights reserved. Reproduced with permission.

Preparation Questions

1. What was the key finding by the court that effectively decided the case for a preliminary injunction?
2. Was the court's analysis of the pricing data appropriate for determining the likely effects of the merger?
3. Could Staples and Office Depot be reasonably expected to pass two-thirds of any cost efficiencies through to consumers?
4. Since Staples and Office Depot and their attorneys understood the antitrust laws and the facts the court would examine, why did they believe that the FTC and the courts would not block the merger?
5. As a commissioner of the FTC, how would you have voted on the consent decree negotiated by your staff?

---

[54]One of the FTC's expert witnesses presented uncontroverted evidence that Staples had historically passed through 15 to 17 percent of firm-specific cost savings in the form of lower prices to consumers.

The Microsoft Antitrust Case

At a 1995 meeting with Intel, Microsoft's chairman and CEO Bill Gates said, according to an Intel executive, "This antitrust thing will blow over. We haven't changed our business practices at all."

On May 18, 1998, the U.S. Department of Justice (DOJ) together with 19 state attorneys general filed an antitrust action against Microsoft Corporation under Sections 1 and 2 of the Sherman Act (the Act). The DOJ complaint was filed to restrain anticompetitive conduct by Microsoft, the world's largest supplier of computer software for personal computers (PCs), and to remedy the effects of its alleged past unlawful conduct.

The DOJ specifically alleged four violations of the Act:

1. *Microsoft engaged in "unlawful exclusive dealing and other exclusionary agreements"* (Section 1 of the Act). The DOJ contended that Microsoft's agreements requiring other companies not to license, distribute, or promote non-Microsoft products, or to do so only on terms that materially disadvantage such products, and its agreements with PC manufacturers restricting modification or customization of the PC boot-up sequence and screens "unreasonably restrict competition." The DOJ claimed that "the purpose and effect of these agreements are to restrain trade and competition in the Internet browser and PC operating system markets."

2. *Microsoft engaged in "unlawful tying"* (Section 1 of the Act). The DOJ viewed the Windows operating systems and Microsoft's Internet Explorer browser as separate products—they were sold in different markets, their functions were different, there was separate demand for them, and they were treated by Microsoft and other industry participants as separate products. The DOJ claimed that it was socially "efficient for Microsoft not to tie them and/or to permit [PC manufacturers] to distribute Windows 95 and Windows 98 without Microsoft's Internet browser software." The DOJ argued that "Microsoft had tied and plans again to tie its Internet browser to its separate Windows operating system, which has monopoly power." The "purpose and the effect of this tying are to prevent customers from choosing among Internet browsers on their merits and to foreclose competing browsers from an important channel of distribution."

3. *Microsoft illegally maintained its monopoly of the PC operating systems market* (Section 2 of the Act). The DOJ contended that Microsoft

"possesses monopoly power in the market for PC operating systems" and claimed that Microsoft had maintained that power through anticompetitive conduct.

4. *Microsoft attempted to monopolize the Internet* (Section 2 of the Act). The DOJ claimed that Microsoft had targeted Internet browsers because they had the potential to facilitate the development of products to compete with its Windows operating system and thereby "erode Microsoft's Windows operating system monopoly." Microsoft allegedly engaged in a "course of conduct, including tying and unreasonably exclusionary agreements," for the purpose of obtaining a "monopoly in the Internet browser market."

The 1995 Consent Decree

The DOJ also sought to show that Microsoft remained dismissive of a long-running antitrust investigation, even after Microsoft had signed a consent decree with the DOJ in 1995. The DOJ had filed an action against Microsoft under Section 2 of the Sherman Act for "unlawfully maintaining its monopoly in the market for PC operating systems." The complaint alleged, among other things, that Microsoft had engaged in anticompetitive agreements and marketing practices directed at PC manufacturers, and the consent decree restricted those practices.

In 1997 the DOJ filed a complaint against Microsoft alleging that it had violated the consent decree. In response, Judge Thomas Penfield Jackson, in whose court the 1998 antitrust case was also tried, issued a preliminary injunction requiring Microsoft to offer Windows independently of Internet Explorer. In July 1998 a federal Court of Appeals overturned Judge Jackson's order, stating that the courts should not be "second guessing the claimed benefits of a particular product design." This ruling gave Microsoft an argument to use in the 1998 case. It could argue that consumers benefited from the integration of Internet Explorer and the Windows operating system.

Microsoft's Position

Microsoft maintained that because of the nature of the industry it did not have a monopoly in the PC operating systems market nor could it become a monopoly in the Internet browser market, despite its market shares in these markets. According to Microsoft the rapid change in technology and in the business environment did not allow a single company to establish and maintain a monopoly. Microsoft also argued that antitrust law definitions, such as a monopoly identified by market share, did not apply to the software market as they did to traditional markets. Since it could not be categorized as a monopoly, Microsoft contended that its business conduct, even if as depicted by the DOJ, did not amount to unlawful conduct. Microsoft also rejected many of the DOJ's factual claims regarding its actual conduct and intent. For example, Microsoft argued that Windows and Internet Explorer were integrated to provide consumers with a superior product.

Microsoft also argued that its competitors employed strategies similar to its own. Moreover, the fact that firms with little market power used the same competitive strategies suggested that there were efficiencies associated with those practices. Although competitive strategies identical to those of a dominant firm were likely to be harmless when used by firms with little or no market power, when used by a firm with substantial market power, the efficiency benefits of those strategies could be outweighed by their anticompetitive effects.

The Trial

An industry's economics are key in any antitrust case and in particular in the Microsoft case. The DOJ proved at least some of its alleged "course of conduct" factual claims with credible clarity, so the court's decision focused on fundamental economic issues rather than on factual controversies. The trial consisted of two phases. The first was a decision by Judge Jackson on the facts of the case and the specific allegations made by the DOJ. If Judge Jackson found for the DOJ, the second phase would focus on remedies for the illegalities.

The DOJ's Case

The DOJ's complaint was based on a set of factual claims, which together were intended to establish Microsoft's "unlawful course of conduct." The first determination by the court was the relevant market. The judge ruled that Intel-based desktop operating systems constituted the relevant market.

The DOJ sought to demonstrate the following:

- Microsoft possessed monopoly power in the market for PC operating systems (OS). Its Windows operating system was used on over 80 percent of all Intel-based PCs, the dominant type of PC in the United States. More than 90 percent of all new Intel-based PCs were shipped with a pre-installed version of Windows. PC manufacturers had no commercially reasonable alternative to Microsoft's operating systems for their PCs.
- Barriers to entry in the market for PC operating systems were high. One of the most important barriers stemmed from network effects and was due to the number of software applications that must run on an operating system

to make it attractive to end users. End users wanted a large number of applications, and because Windows was the dominant operating system, most applications were written to run on Windows. It would be prohibitively expensive to create an alternative operating system to run the programs that ran on Windows.

- Consequently, the most significant potential threat to Microsoft's operating system monopoly was not from existing or new operating systems but from new software products that could support, or themselves become, "platforms" to which applications could be written and which could be used on multiple operating systems. The specific threat to Windows was from Internet browsers and the Java programming language.

The Threat of Internet Browsers and Java

The DOJ cited Microsoft CEO Bill Gates as saying in May 1995 that the Internet posed a serious potential threat to Microsoft's Windows operating system. Mr. Gates warned his executives:

A new competitor "born" on the Internet is Netscape. Their browser is dominant, with a 70 percent usage share, allowing them to determine which network extensions will catch on. They are pursing a multi-platform strategy where they move the key API [applications programming interface] into the client [the browser] to commoditize the underlying operating system.

The DOJ asserted that Internet browsers posed a competitive threat to Microsoft's operating system monopoly in two basic ways.

- If application programs could easily be written to run on multiple operating systems, competition in the market for operating systems could be revitalized. The combination of browser technology and the Java programming language developed by Sun Microsystems for writing software that would run on any operating system threatened one of the key barriers to entry protecting Microsoft's operating system monopoly. Browsers represented the most significant vehicle for the distribution of Java technology to end users. Microsoft recognized that the widespread use of browsers could increase the distribution and use of Java and hence threaten Microsoft's operating system monopoly.
- A browser was itself a "platform" to which many applications were being written. Instead of writing software to run on Windows, software developers could write to the browser platform. Since the browser would run on any

operating system, software applications would be decoupled from the operating system. PC companies thus could use other operating systems on their computers.

The DOJ presented documents and e-mail messages indicating that Microsoft regarded Java as a key threat. A Microsoft document said that it was a "strategic objective" for Microsoft to "kill cross-platform Java" by expanding the "polluted Java market"—Microsoft's altered version of Java. A senior Microsoft executive identified Java as "our major threat" in an e-mail and added that Netscape's Internet browser was Java's "major distribution vehicle."

Microsoft's Alleged Response to the Threat

Microsoft embarked on an extensive campaign to market and distribute its own browser, Internet Explorer (IE). Microsoft executives had described this campaign as a "jihad" to win the "browser war." The DOJ acknowledged that continued competition on the merits between Navigator and Internet Explorer would result in greater innovation and the development of better products at lower prices. The DOJ alleged, however, that Microsoft was unwilling to compete on the merits. The DOJ cited Microsoft's Christian Wildfeuer writing in February 1997 that Microsoft concluded that it would "be very hard to increase browser share on the merits of IE 4 alone. It will be more important to leverage the OS asset to make people use IE instead of Navigator."

The DOJ alleged that Microsoft engaged in anticompetitive conduct to halt this threat.

- One measure was to develop a polluted version of Java that would run on the Windows OS but not on other operating systems. This could force a recoupling of software applications to Windows.
- A second step was to bundle IE with Windows and provide it free. To bundle IE with Windows, Microsoft removed IE from the Add/Delete menu so that neither PC manufacturers nor users could delete it.
- The DOJ argued that providing IE at no additional cost to PC manufacturers that preloaded Windows or to users who purchased Windows constituted predatory pricing. The alleged intent was to drive Netscape, which charged $10 to $15 to PC manufacturers who preloaded it, out of the market. Netscape was forced to provide Navigator for free, eliminating much of its revenue.
- The DOJ also alleged that giving away IE for free represented illegal leveraging from its operating system monopoly in an attempt to monopolize the browser market.

- The DOJ alleged that Microsoft provided discounts to PC manufacturers that agreed not to preload Navigator. Microsoft was said to "take $7.50 off the unit price of Windows if PC makers agree to carry a 'Windows' logo on their machines and submit to certification by Microsoft's labs."[55] Microsoft maintained that price discounts to PC makers were not favoritism to reward them for not carrying rival products but instead were volume discounts.
- Microsoft's contracts with PC manufacturers were alleged to be exclusionary. While not prohibiting PC manufacturers from preloading Navigator, the contracts were written to discourage the use of rival products. Contracts restricted the ability of PC manufacturers to modify the start-up sequence and desktop. Microsoft also allegedly required PC manufacturers to favor its products and threatened to terminate their license to use Windows if they failed to do so. The DOJ produced documents from Compaq and depositions of its executives indicating that Compaq might have taken the Netscape Navigator icon off its desktops and chosen Internet Explorer because of fear of retaliation by Microsoft. Microsoft pointed to depositions by Compaq executives stating that Microsoft had never objected to the Navigator icon appearing on the desktop. Microsoft had objected when Compaq planned to delete the Internet Explorer icon.
- Microsoft was alleged to have illegally tied IE to Windows by not giving original equipment manufacturers (OEMs) and consumers the opportunity to purchase one without the other. Tying occurs when a firm conditions the purchase (or license) of one product on the purchase (or license) of another product. Procompetitive reasons for tying include cost savings and quality control (it could be easier to identify the source of quality problems with a tied sale than if the products were sold separately). Tying could, however, be an anticompetitive leveraging practice if it foreclosed competition in network markets.
- Microsoft allegedly withheld APIs from software developers that threatened its products.
- Microsoft built incompatibility into its products. For example, when Microsoft's Real Media player was installed, RealNetwork's media player would not work.[56]

---

[55] *Wall Street Journal*, March 1, 1999.
[56] Microsoft was able to eliminate the source of the incompatibility.

Microsoft's Defense

Microsoft challenged the government's witnesses and sought to support its fundamental line of argument. Microsoft argued that it did not have monopoly power, any apparent monopoly power could quickly be dissipated in a dynamic industry, its behavior and practices were not abusive and were similar to standard practices in the industry, and consumers were not harmed but instead benefited from its practices. As the defendant Microsoft did not have to prove its arguments but instead needed only to raise substantial doubt about the DOJ's allegations.

Microsoft witnesses argued that the relevant market was not operating systems but was much broader and included the Internet and handheld computers, for neither of which Microsoft had a dominant position. Microsoft argued, for example, that it was not a monopolist, since it faced competition from Sun's Java programming language and Internet browsers.

Microsoft argued that if it had monopoly power in operating systems, it would have charged a much higher price for Windows. A government witness countered that all that the price charged for Windows indicated was "that Microsoft is not maximizing its short-run profits."

Many economists viewed pricing IE at zero as economically efficient, since the marginal cost of producing an additional copy of IE was essentially zero. Moreover, consumers benefited from competition in browsers, since improvements in browser quality resulted from the competition. A government witness, however, testified that it would be difficult to determine the exact standard for concluding that a price for Internet Explorer was predatory, but the fact was that Microsoft charged a "zero price" and had spent $100 million a year since 1995 developing IE.

Microsoft executives denied allegations of coercive behavior and argued that consumers benefited from its innovations. Paul Maritz, senior group vice president, testified, "Ironically, the very thing that makes Windows valuable to computer manufacturers, software publishers and customers ... is now under attack in this lawsuit. The popularity of Windows, owing entirely to Microsoft's efforts to innovate, evangelize and license the software cheaply to promote wide distribution, is derided as monopoly."

Much of Microsoft's defense was directed at countering the testimony of government witnesses. A considerable portion of that testimony centered on recollections of and notes taken at private meetings between Microsoft and companies such as Apple, Intel, and Netscape. Microsoft witnesses provided different interpretations of what had transpired at the meetings than had the government's witnesses. Paul Maritz, for example, testified that Microsoft opposed Intel's development of software because that software was second-rate and that Microsoft had withheld software support for Intel's MMX microprocessor because of overzealous intellectual property claims by Intel. Maritz also denied that he had ever told an Intel executive that Microsoft would "cut off Netscape's air supply." He also said that Microsoft's reluctance to continue producing software for Apple's Macintosh was due to concerns that Apple might fold.

Microsoft also denied that it had harmed Netscape through exclusive arrangements with and financial incentives to PC makers and Internet service providers. A Microsoft attorney stated, "Whatever those arrangements were, whatever measure of exclusivity they created for a period of time, Netscape was able to gain a substantial number of new users. There was no foreclosure of consumer choice."[57]

A Microsoft executive testified that it had not attempted to undermine Java. The DOJ, however, produced a memo from Bill Gates stating that he was "hardcore about NOT supporting" Java. When the executive tried to explain what Gates meant, the judge abruptly cut him off, stating that it was abundantly clear what Gates meant.

Microsoft's direct testimony was attacked effectively by DOJ lead attorney David Boies. The *Wall Street Journal* wrote, "Microsoft's defense is in disarray and its executives and economist have been battered so badly on the witness stand that the judge has questioned key elements of the Redmond, Wash., software giant's case."[58] The *New York Times* referred to the trial as "a humbling courtroom experience" for Microsoft.[59] *Fortune* said, "We're seeing Microsoft's defense go down in flames."[60] Microsoft countered that the DOJ's attacks amounted to showmanship and that the case would be decided on the facts and the law.

One major faux pas for Microsoft occurred in Senior Vice President James Allchin's testimony. Allchin showed a videotape produced by Microsoft that purported to show "performance degradations" in the Windows 98 operating system when Internet Explorer was removed from the system. The videotape had been produced to challenge the testimony of a government witness that Internet Explorer could be removed from the Windows operating system without any significant performance degradation. The government consultants who reviewed the videotape noticed that the title bar displayed the words "Internet Explorer" even though the Microsoft narrator said it had been removed. Allchin maintained that the computer shown was the one from which its browser had been removed. Two days later Microsoft admitted that the videotape was prepared in a studio and showed a number of different computers to

---

[57]*New York Times,* February 28, 1999.
[58]*Wall Street Journal,* February 18, 1999.
[59]*New York Times,* February 28, 1999.
[60]*Fortune,* March 1, 1999.

simulate its claims about performance degradation. Microsoft then prepared a new videotape that observers said showed that the system without Internet Explorer performed well, although applications requiring a browser, of course, did not work.

Developments Outside the Courtroom

Two developments occurred during the trial that lent support to Microsoft's argument that the market was constantly changing and monopoly power was a transient phenomenon at most. In November 1998 AOL announced that it would acquire Netscape for $4.2 billion and form an alliance with Sun Microsystems. Microsoft asserted that the deal fundamentally changed the industry's landscape and that it therefore was sufficient grounds for the DOJ to drop the lawsuit. DOJ witnesses such as William Harris, chairman and CEO of Intuit Corporation, stated that they did not view the new alliance as an industry shift that would diminish Microsoft's dominance.

Microsoft also asserted that Linux, a free UNIX operating system, posed a potential threat to Windows because several of Microsoft's chief competitors were writing software to run on it. On March 1, 1999, Oracle, Intel, Dell, and Hewlett-Packard all announced substantial investments in Linux, and IBM announced greater offerings of computers using Linux. Although Linux had several million devotees around the world, it held an insignificant share of the operating system market. A DOJ expert witness firmly rejected the proposition that it threatened Windows: "Whatever role Linux may have, it is not expected to constrain the monopoly power of Microsoft. . . . If you truly believe this product is going to constrain Microsoft's market share, then run, don't walk, to your broker and sell Microsoft stock short."

Remedies

If the court found against Microsoft, the next issue would be which remedies to impose. Many companies in the industry, including rivals of Microsoft, were fearful that the cure imposed could be worse than the disease. The principal fear was that some form of government supervision or oversight of the industry would be imposed that would impede innovation and technological change.

Possible remedies were generally classified as behavioral or structural. Behavioral remedies sought to eliminate the abusive conduct and exclusionary practices without altering Microsoft's control of the Windows operating system. Structural remedies focused on eliminating Microsoft's Windows operating system monopoly either by breaking up the company or by replicating the source of its power through the creation of clones. Behavioral remedies were favored by those who worried that breaking up Microsoft's monopoly could lead to multiple industry standards that would impede

the development of software applications. Many commentators and industry members, however, were skeptical that behavioral remedies would be sufficient to curb Microsoft's alleged monopoly power and abusive conduct. Opposition to behavioral remedies resulted not only from skepticism about their effectiveness but also because such remedies would require supervision or regulatory oversight of the industry. Most industry members and economists feared any supervision or oversight of a dynamic industry with rapid product development and obsolescence.

Most behavioral remedies under discussion focused on breaking Microsoft's hold on PC manufacturers that resulted from its licensing agreements for Windows. A number of PC manufacturers had sought more flexible licensing agreements, and under antitrust scrutiny Microsoft had recently granted some leeway.

Behavioral remedies could include stopping Microsoft from using exclusive contracts prohibiting PC manufacturers from offering other Internet browsers. Another behavioral remedy would be to require Microsoft to publish its "most-favored customer" prices and make those prices available to all OEMs. This would reduce the likelihood that Microsoft could punish an OEM by not offering it a discount available to other OEMs. More generally the court could impose a pricing "transparency" policy under which Microsoft would set fixed prices for its products. A third behavioral remedy would require Microsoft to publish the APIs, or software hooks, required to write software for the Windows operating system. This would address the alleged strategy of releasing APIs in stages or selectively to favored software developers.

In February 1999 the 1,400 member Information Industry Association (IIA), of which Microsoft was a member, presented a report to the DOJ urging it to "seriously consider" structural remedies.[61] The structural remedy preferred by the IIA was to break Microsoft into three standalone companies. One would have the Windows operating system, including the CE and NT systems. Another would have Microsoft's software business, and the third would have its Internet and electronic commerce businesses.

An alternative structural remedy was to break Microsoft into three to five clones, referred to as "Baby Bills," each of which would have Microsoft's source codes for Windows and its other products. A related proposal was to auction the Windows code and brand name to several companies. These remedies would introduce competition and break the alleged monopoly power of Microsoft. The IIA report, however, concluded that this type of remedy could be harmful if it led to multiple technical standards.

---

[61]The initial draft reportedly recommended structural remedies, but lobbying by Microsoft led to the wording "seriously consider."

The Trial Court: Conclusions of Law and Findings of Fact

On April 3, 2000, Judge Jackson ruled that Microsoft had violated the Sherman Act. Microsoft's conduct was found to have violated the Sherman Act not because of the practices themselves, many of which were standard in the industry, but because they were used by a monopolist to maintain its monopoly. As conclusions of law, he found that the relevant market was "Intel-based PC operating systems" and that Microsoft had a monopoly. The judge concluded that Microsoft's conduct had a "significant exclusionary impact." He also concluded that "middleware [Navigator and Java] threatened to demolish Microsoft's coveted monopoly power" and that Microsoft engaged in a "deliberate assault upon entrepreneurial efforts. . . ." He cited Microsoft's efforts in the OEM channel to stifle innovation, including tactics such as requiring the installation of IE and bundling proprietary software. The former constituted illegal tying of one product with a monopoly product, which he concluded was in effect a per se violation of the Sherman Act. The latter constituted "exclusionary behavior in the IAP [Internet access provider] channel," which also constituted a violation of Section 1 of the Sherman Act.

The judge also concluded that Microsoft's behavior was as a whole "predacious" and cited providing IE for free and offering promotional inducements to bundle it with other offerings. In addition, he concluded that Microsoft used its control of technical information (APIs) to induce Internet service vendors to distribute the so-called "polluted" version of Java. Judge Jackson also found that although Microsoft had used exclusionary contracts, such as inducing Compaq not to distribute Navigator, those contracts "did not ultimately deprive Netscape of the ability to have access to every PC worldwide to offer an opportunity to install Navigator." These exclusive contracts thus were not themselves sufficient to constitute a violation of Section 1.

Judge Jackson's Remedies

At the conclusion of the trial Judge Jackson urged the DOJ and Microsoft to reach a settlement of the case. In a highly unusual move he appointed a distinguished U.S. Court of Appeals judge, Richard Posner, to convene the parties and seek a settlement. Efforts to reach a settlement failed.

On June 7, 2000, Judge Jackson ordered both structural and behavioral remedies in response to his findings that Microsoft had violated the Sherman Act. The remedies largely followed those recommended by the DOJ and the 19 state attorneys general. Jackson's decision was notable in that it took an arguably hostile tone toward the company. He stated that Microsoft was "unwilling to accept the notion that it broke the law" and that it had "proved untrustworthy in the past."

The structural remedy involved breaking Microsoft into two separate companies. One, referred to as "ops," would have Microsoft's operating systems business, including Windows 2000, Windows ME, and Windows CE. The other, referred to as "apps," would have all other lines of business, including software applications (e.g., Microsoft Office, Exchange, IE) and Internet services (e.g., MSN, Hotmail, Expedia, CarPoint). Microsoft was ordered to submit to the court a plan for creating the two companies. The breakup would be complete at the management level with a "firewall" between the two companies.

In addition to the structural remedy, Judge Jackson's ruling included a set of behavioral remedies intended to restore viable competition in the operating system and applications markets. The behavioral remedies were to last for 10 years and pertained to Microsoft's conduct with respect to customers and rivals. In response to allegations that Microsoft had illegally tied IE to the Windows operating system, Judge Jackson ruled that Microsoft must allow OEMs to remove any applications from the operating system. OEMs could modify the start-up sequence and desktop, including removing Microsoft icons, and would be given 30 days' notice before Microsoft could terminate a Windows license. Microsoft would have to license operating systems products under uniform conditions with the exceptions of volume discounts. Microsoft would be prohibited from interfering with any non-Microsoft middleware, discriminating against a hardware or software company for using non-Microsoft products, favoring Microsoft over non-Microsoft products, or linking licenses to the use of Microsoft products. Microsoft would also be required to continue to offer the previous version of its Windows OS when it introduced a new version. This was intended to limit Microsoft's ability to force migration.

To ensure the "interoperability" of software and hardware, Judge Jackson ordered Microsoft to allow hardware, software, and computer makers access to technical information and developers to view the "relevant necessary portions" of code. This included all APIs and portions of the OS code. The APIs and code would be available only in a "secure facility."

The Court of Appeals Decision

Microsoft appealed the decision and in its appeal attacked the conduct of Judge Jackson for statements made outside of the courtroom. Microsoft asked that he be removed from the case. On June 28, 2001, the U.S. Court of Appeals issued a unanimous decision affirming some of the trial court's conclusions, vacating some of its orders, and remanding some to a different district court for resolution.

In its most important ruling the Court of Appeals vacated the order breaking Microsoft into two separate companies. In doing so the Court observed that divestiture had traditionally been reserved for firms that had grown through acquisition and merger, but the Court left the door open for a divestiture order. The District Court was ordered to reconsider the appropriateness of divestiture and whether there was a sufficient relationship between the maintenance of monopoly and the illegal conduct to warrant the full structural remedy of divestiture. The Court of Appeals also ordered the district court to hold full evidentiary hearings on appropriate remedies.

The Court of Appeals concurred with Judge Jackson's conclusion about monopoly power: "We uphold the District Court's finding of monopoly power in its entirety." This conclusion was important not only for the present case, but also because in private antitrust cases the plaintiffs would not have the burden of proving that Microsoft had monopoly power.

The Court of Appeals concurred that Microsoft's conduct violated the Sherman Act. First, its license restrictions on OEMs were found to be anticompetitive. Second, the exclusion of IE from the Add/Remove program of Windows so that a user could not remove IE was found to be a violation of Section 2. The Court stated, "Microsoft failed to meet its burden of showing that its conduct serves a purpose other than protecting its operating system monopoly." The Court also held that Microsoft developed a polluted version of Java that would run only on Windows, and this "conduct is exclusionary, in violation of Sec. 2 of the Sherman Act."

The Court of Appeals reversed without remand Judge Jackson's conclusion that Microsoft attempted to monopolize the browser market. The Court stated that the Department of Justice had not properly defined the relevant market nor established that there were barriers to entry.

Judge Jackson had concluded that the tying or bundling of IE with Windows was in effect a per se violation of Section 1 of the Sherman Act. The Court of Appeals, however, concluded that per se analysis was inappropriate and remanded the issue to the District Court to be considered under a rule of reason.

The Court of Appeals also strongly criticized the conduct of Judge Jackson and disqualified him from the case. The court found "no evidence of actual bias" but concluded that "the trial judge engaged in impermissible ex parte contacts by holding secret interviews with members of the media and made numerous offensive comments about Microsoft officials in public statements outside the courtroom, giving rise to an appearance of partiality." Consequently, the court vacated the remedies ordered by Judge Jackson and on remand assigned the case to a different trial judge to be assigned by random draw. The new judge would determine the remedies.

The headline of the front page article of the *Wall Street Journal* on the day after the Court of Appeals decision was "With Its Old Playbook, Microsoft Is Muscling into New Web Markets: Using Aggressive Bundling, It Roils High-Tech World with Windows Overhaul."

The Settlement and Next Stage

Claiming victory, the DOJ did not appeal the decision. Microsoft, however, appealed the decision and Judge Jackson's findings of fact, but the Supreme Court refused to consider the appeal. Faced with a complex and potentially lengthy case dealing both with tying and remedies, District Court Judge Colleen Kollar-Kotelly appointed a mediator to attempt to settle the case. In November the DOJ and Microsoft reached a settlement. The state attorneys general engaged in brief negotiations with Microsoft, obtaining some potentially important changes in the settlement. In a highly unusual development, however, nine state attorneys general refused to accept the settlement. Thomas F. Reilly, attorney general of Massachusetts, said, "There is no question in my mind that Microsoft will use this agreement to crush the competition, and they will have the imprimatur of the U.S. government to do it."[62] Kelly Jo MacArthur, general counsel for RealNetworks, said, "This is a reward, not a remedy. This agreement allows a declared illegal monopolist to determine, at its sole discretion, what goes into the monopoly operating system in the future."[63] She was referring to Microsoft integrating its Media Player into Windows XP, in effect giving it away for free just as IE had been integrated into Windows without charge. Scott McNealy, CEO of Sun Microsystems, asked, "Does anyone think this settlement is going to change Microsoft's behavior? These guys are unfettered."[64] Michael Morris, senior vice president and general counsel of Sun Microsystems, said, "I think everybody who isn't a Microsoft vassal understands, and has been saying, this is the most bizarre, pointless, ridiculous antitrust settlement that anyone could have possibly imagined. It doesn't even pass the red face test."[65] In a more dispassionate statement professor David Yoffie and research associate Mary Kwak, co-authors of *Judo Strategy*, referred to the settlement as "a spectacular victory for Microsoft."

Microsoft chairman Bill Gates said the case had "a profound impact on me personally and on our company" and "we will focus more on how our activities affect other companies." He added, "While the settlement goes farther than we might have wanted, we believe that settling this case now is the right thing to do to help the industry, and the economy, to move forward."[66] CEO Steve Ballmer observed that during the lawsuit "our industry didn't rise to support us the way we might have supposed as an industry leader."[67] Bill Gates said that Microsoft was "committed to becoming a better industry leader."

[62] *New York Times,* November 6, 2001.
[63] *Wall Street Journal,* November 5, 2001.
[64] *New York Times,* November 5, 2001.
[65] *San Jose Mercury News,* November 3, 2001.
[66] *New York Times,* November 3, 2001.
[67] *Wall Street Journal,* November 5, 2001.

U.S. assistant attorney general Charles A. James, who headed the antitrust division of the DOJ and negotiated the settlement, said, "The settlement will promote innovation, give consumers choice and provide computer manufacturers and the industry with more certainty as they go forward in marketing their products. This consent decree will remedy the problems that were caused by Microsoft's unlawful conduct, prevent the recurrence of those problems and restore competition in the software industry."[68] Observers speculated that Mr. James was eager to settle the case to remove uncertainty from the economy in the wake of the September 11 terrorist attacks.

The terms of the settlement were as follows:

- Microsoft can integrate any product into Windows.
- PC makers can hide any Microsoft feature, and Microsoft cannot restrict or retaliate against any PC maker that installs non-Microsoft software.
- Microsoft must license Windows on the same terms to all PC makers and must publish its prices on a Web site.
- Microsoft must share certain technical information for middleware, both for desktop systems and server software for the Internet, with software developers. Microsoft retains all intellectual property rights but must license that property to allow PC makers and software developers to exercise their rights under the agreement. Microsoft cannot retaliate against any software developer.
- Microsoft must appoint an internal compliance officer to ensure that its executives and board members understand the terms of the settlement.
- A three-person technical committee, with one member appointed by Microsoft, one by the DOJ, and one by agreement of both parties, was established to determine which parts of the software code need to be released to competitors, to monitor compliance, and to hear complaints. The committee has no enforcement authority but can inform Microsoft and the courts of serious complaints, possibly leading to a court enforcement hearing.
- The consent decree extended for 5 years, and if Microsoft willfully and systematically violated the terms, it would extend for an additional 2 years.

Judge Kollar-Kotelly set two tracks for the case. On the first track, under the Tunney Act a 90-day review period began in which the judge must decide if the settlement is in the public interest. The public and the parties in the case could make comments. In this track the DOJ and Microsoft would be on the same side in defending the settlement. On the second track to resolve the case pursued by the nine remaining states, the judge scheduled hearings on remedies to begin March 11, 2002.

In 2002 both Sun Microsystems and Netscape/AOL filed private antitrust lawsuits against Microsoft. ∎

SOURCE: This case was written by Professor David P. Baron and Chen Lichtenstein from publicly available information from the following sources: court filings made by the U.S. Department of Justice and by the Microsoft Corporation, transcripts of testimonies and related materials posted on the Department of Justice and Microsoft Corporation's Web sites, and court reports. Copyright © 1998 by the Board of Trustees of the Leland Stanford Junior University; revised 2001. All rights reserved. Reproduced with permission.

Preparation Questions

1. Should the DOJ have brought an antitrust case against Microsoft?
2. Does the evidence indicate that Microsoft violated the Sherman Act?
3. Did Microsoft's conduct benefit consumers?
4. Were Judge Jackson's remedies appropriate? Should a structural remedy be used?
5. Were the terms of the settlement appropriate? Sufficient?
6. What, if anything, should be done with Microsoft's operating system monopoly and its dominance in other software applications?

---

[68]*New York Times,* November 5, 2001.

10

Regulation: Law, Economics, and Politics

INTRODUCTION

Markets and property rights are the centerpieces of the free enterprise system. Markets allow people to exchange goods and services, and property rights allow them to gain from trade. Markets also provide information by establishing prices that reflect the cost of society's resources used to produce goods and services. Under some conditions, however, markets may not function efficiently, inhibiting gains from trade. When there are market imperfections, government intervention in markets could improve their efficiency. This intervention can be the responsibility of the judiciary, as in the case of antitrust law enforced through the courts, or it can be the responsibility of regulatory agencies responsible for particular markets or imperfections. Regulation is government intervention in economic activity using commands, controls, and incentives. Both regulation and judicial enforcement are based on legislatively enacted statutes. This means that regulation can be used for purposes other than making markets more efficient. Regulation is thus a political as well as an economic instrument.

Regulation takes place through a public process that is open and allows participation by interested parties. In contrast to antitrust, regulation is not implemented through judicial institutions but instead by independent commissions and agencies of the executive branch. The courts, however, have played an important role in interpreting regulatory statutes, assessing their constitutionality, and ensuring that regulatory decisions satisfy due process requirements.

Regulatory decisions and rule-making proceedings are extremely important to many firms, industries, and interest groups. Kerwin (1994, p. 194) reported a survey of 180 interest groups that found that two-thirds of the groups saw participation in regulatory rule making as at least as important as lobbying Congress.

Regulation includes a broad set of interventions:

- Controlling prices (electric power, local telephone service)
- Setting price floors (crops, minimum wages)
- Ensuring equal opportunity (banning discrimination in employment)
- Regularizing employment practices (overtime)
- Specifying qualifications (occupational licensure)
- Providing for solvency (financial institutions, insurance, pension plans)
- Controlling the number of market participants (broadcast licenses, taxi medallions)
- Limiting ownership (media, airlines)
- Requiring premarketing approval (toxic chemicals, pharmaceuticals)
- Ensuring product safety (pharmaceuticals, toys, food)
- Mandating product characteristics and technology (automobile safety standards)
- Establishing service territories (local telephone service)

- Establishing performance standards (automobile emissions standards)
- Controlling toxic emissions and other pollutants (sulfur dioxide emissions trading)
- Specifying industry boundaries (insurance, banking, and stock brokerage boundaries)
- Allocating public resources (spectrum allocations)
- Establishing technical standards (telecommunications interconnections)
- Controlling unfair international trade practices (antidumping)
- Mandating disclosure and restricting terms (credit cards)
- Providing information (labeling)
- Rationing common pool resources (fisheries)

As this list indicates, regulation is a broad subject and often specific to particular industries, products, and conditions. The focus of this chapter is the nature of regulation. Two principal perspectives are considered—one based on the correction of market imperfections and the other based on the political economy of regulation. The institutional focus is on regulation administered by government agencies and commissions with applications to telecommunications and electric power. Environmental regulation is considered in Chapter 11, and the regulation of international trade is considered in Chapter 18.

The next section identifies periods of regulatory activity in the United States, and the following section considers the constitutional basis for regulation. Regulatory agencies and the regulatory process are then discussed. The nonmarket environment of regulatory agencies is considered with an emphasis on external influences on agencies. The economic rationale for correcting market imperfections is presented, including natural monopoly, externalities, public goods, asymmetric information, and moral hazard. The broader political economy of regulation is then considered along with the distributive objectives of regulation. The chapter concludes with an analysis of deregulation in the telecommunications and electric power industries.

PERIODS OF REGULATORY CHANGE

The United States has experienced four major periods of regulatory change. The first occurred during the populist era of the late 1800s as a result of nonmarket action by interest groups. Farmers succeeded in establishing regulatory bodies at the state level to control the market power of grain elevators and railroads. This was extended to the federal level with the passage of the Interstate Commerce Act in 1887, which established the Interstate Commerce Commission (ICC) with the authority to regulate railroad rates. In the same tradition, legislation was enacted early in the 20th century to shore up regulatory and antitrust powers that had been narrowly construed by the courts.[1]

The second period was the progressive era and the New Deal. Regulation was extended to labor markets and industries, including electric power, food, pharmaceuticals, trucking, air transport, securities, and communications. Much of this regulation was industry specific and focused on pricing, entry, and conditions of service.

The third period, which began in the 1960s and accelerated in the 1970s, brought social regulation. In contrast to the earlier regulation that focused on the economic regulation of industries, social regulation addressed externalities and hazards. Regulation was extended to consumer products, the environment, and the workplace. The new social regulation differed substantially from the regulation of earlier periods. The new regulation cut across industries by focusing on issues such as safety, health, and the environment. This changed the nature of the politics of regulation. In the past, the politics had been dominated by industry interests, as when the railroads used ICC regulation to limit competition from the emerging interstate trucking industry. The new social regulation brought to the politics of regulation a new set of interest groups, including safety and health activists and environmentalists.

---

[1]See McCraw (1981) for the history of regulation. The Sherman Antitrust Act was enacted in the same era.

The fourth period brought economic deregulation to several industries, including electric power, natural gas transmission, telecommunications, air transport, and surface transportation. Public policy analysts, regulators, and executive branch officials recognized that regulation, which had been intended to keep prices down, seemed instead to lead to higher costs and higher prices. Beginning in the 1970s several regulatory systems were dismantled, and market forces were substituted to improve economic efficiency. In some industries, such as electric power and telecommunications, economic regulation is steadily being replaced by market competition. The deregulation movement also led to the substitution of market-like mechanisms, such as auctions and the trading of pollution permits, for regulatory control and allocation procedures. On January 1, 1996, the first regulatory agency, the Interstate Commerce Commission, closed its doors.

The past four decades have witnessed two quite different regulatory movements. The social regulation that began during the 1960s has expanded at the same time as deregulation has occurred in a number of industries. Although new regulatory agencies have not been created in recent years, the authority of some existing social regulatory agencies such as the Environmental Protection Agency has been expanded. Economic regulation has moved in the other direction as markets and competition have been substituted for government controls. These two movements have come together as market-like mechanisms have been substituted for some social regulation, as in the case of the trading of sulfur dioxide allowances considered in Chapter 11.

THE CONSTITUTIONAL BASIS FOR REGULATION

Government regulation can be traced to the 1100s when the English monarchy began to contract with private parties for the provision of services. The monarchy granted rights-of-way to stage lines and in return retained the authority to regulate services and prices. Private property committed to a public use thus became subject to government controls. This contractual relationship between the state and a firm provided the basis for the evolution of regulatory authority through the common law.[2]

The U.S. Constitution provides the authority for regulation but also limits its application. Section 8 of Article I of the Constitution gives Congress the power "To regulate Commerce . . . among the several States. . . ." The Fifth Amendment to the Constitution limits this power by stating, "No person shall be deprived of life, liberty, or property, without due process of law; nor shall private property be taken for public use without just compensation." The Fourteenth Amendment extends the due process protection to actions taken by the states.

Many of the legal principles of regulation in the United States have come from court decisions that draw on the common law. The common law doctrine that private property committed to a public use could be regulated was extended to property that was "affected with a public interest." In *Munn v. Illinois,* 94 U.S. 113 (1877), the Supreme Court upheld an Illinois statute regulating the prices charged by grain elevators, which in the state constitution had been declared "public warehouses." The court cited the English common law principle that when "affected with a public interest, [private property] ceases to be *juris privati* only. . . . Property does become clothed with a public interest when used in a manner to make it of public consequence, and affect the community at large. When, therefore, one devotes his property to a use in which the public has an interest, he, in effect, grants to the public an interest in that use, and must submit to be controlled by the public for the common good. . . ." In this sweeping statement, the court established the government's right to regulate private property. However, the court went on to warn: "We know that this is a power which may be abused; but there is no argument against its existence. For protection against abuses by the legislatures the people must resort to the polls, not to the courts." In upholding minimum price regulation of milk sold in grocery stores, the Supreme Court ruled in *Nebbia v. New York,* 291 U.S. 502 (1934) that the same principle applied to

---

[2]The common law is considered in Chapter 12.

enterprises not affected with a public interest. The government's authority to regulate is thus extremely broad.

The Fifth and Fourteenth amendments, however, place limits on regulation.[3] In *Smith v. Ames,* 169 U.S. 466 (1898), the Supreme Court held that "What a company is entitled to ask is a fair return upon the value of that which it employs for the public convenience."[4] This established the right of public utilities to obtain a fair return on their capital and led to cost-of-service regulation. The due process provisions of the Constitution are also important factors in structuring regulatory processes, as considered later in the chapter.

REGULATORY COMMISSIONS AND AGENCIES

The principal federal regulatory agencies are listed in Figure 10-1. Regulatory agencies are of two basic forms—independent commissions and executive branch agencies. Independent commissions include the Federal Communications Commission, Federal Trade Commission, Federal Reserve System, International Trade Commission, Federal Energy Regulatory Commission, Securities and Exchange Commission, National Labor Relations Board, Consumer Products Safety Commission, and Nuclear Regulatory Commission. The Federal Communications Commission, for example, has five commissioners appointed by the president and confirmed by the Senate. They serve 7-year terms, and no more than three commissioners may be from the same political party. Most commissions make decisions through majority-rule voting and formal rule-making procedures.

Agencies typically have a single administrator appointed by the president or a cabinet secretary. Most executive branch regulatory agencies are located in a cabinet department, as in the case of the Federal Aviation Administration, National Highway Traffic Safety Administration, Occupational Health and Safety Administration, and

FIGURE 10-1 Principal Federal Regulatory Agencies and Commissions

Federal Reserve System (1913)

Federal Trade Commission (1914)

International Trade Commission (1916) (formerly the Tariff Commission)—considered in Chapter 18

Federal Energy Regulatory Commission (1930) (formerly the Federal Power Commission)

Food and Drug Administration (1931) [HHS]

Securities and Exchange Commission (1934)

Federal Communications Commission (1934)

National Labor Relations Board (1935)

Federal Aviation Administration (1948) [DOT]

Federal Maritime Commission [1961]

Equal Employment Opportunity Commission (1965)—considered in Chapter 20

Environmental Protection Agency (1970)—considered in Chapter 11

National Highway Traffic Safety Administration (1970) [DOT]

Consumer Product Safety Commission (1972)

Occupational Safety and Health Administration (1973) [DOL]

Nuclear Regulatory Commission (1975) (formerly the Atomic Energy Commission)

Note: The cabinet departments in which agencies are located are shown in brackets.
Source: Congressional Quarterly, *Federal Regulatory Directory,* 7th ed., Washington DC, 1994.

---

[3]The "takings" clause in the Fifth Amendment has been the subject of political and legal activity intended to require public compensation for the loss of value due to regulations such as zoning and environmental protection.
[4]See also *Federal Power Commission et al. v. Hope Natural Gas Co.,* 320 U.S. 591 (1944).

Food and Drug Administration. The Environmental Protection Agency is an independent executive branch agency not housed in a cabinet department.[5]

Most states also have regulatory commissions and agencies. Considerable economic activity such as local telephone and electricity service is regulated by the states and not the federal government. Most states also have regulatory agencies to deal with environmental, occupational safety, and health issues. As indicated in Chapter 11, federal law delegates the implementation of certain federal regulations to the states. States, for example, are responsible for developing implementation plans for achieving clean air standards.

DELEGATION, RULE MAKING, DUE PROCESS, AND DISCRETION

Article I, Section 1 of the Constitution grants Congress the sole power to enact laws. It does not authorize Congress to delegate policymaking to agencies. Yet regulatory agencies promulgate rules, establish policies, and resolve disputes. Prior to 1935 courts held that the delegatee was simply making a determination in the implementation of a law enacted by Congress. In 1935 the Supreme Court overturned as unconstitutional two delegation provisions of the National Industrial Recovery Act. Subsequently, the courts have not overturned a congressional delegation.[6] Instead, the courts have sought to ensure that the exercise of any delegated authority is consistent with the constitutional protections of the Fifth and Fourteenth Amendments and the common law doctrine of consistency.

Congress also was concerned about the exercise of agency powers and enacted the Administrative Procedure Act (APA) of 1946 to provide for public notice and comment prior to agency action. Agencies also adopt their own rule-making procedures in a manner consistent with the APA. Under the APA, agencies can use either a formal or an informal rule-making process.[7] The informal model of rule making requires publishing in the *Federal Register* a Notice of Proposed Rule Making (NPRM) and a request for the submission of comments. The agency may also hold a public hearing on the proposed rule. The agency next reviews the comments received, revises the rule, and publishes it in the *Federal Register* with an effective date at least 30 days in the future. Under the formal model, the agency employs a quasi-judicial process involving hearings conducted by an administrative law judge, the presentation of evidence, and the cross-examination of witnesses. A formal record of the proceedings is kept and may be reviewed by the courts. Appearances may be made and testimony given by any interested party. The authorizing statutes of some agencies also prescribe public hearings for certain types of actions. Under this model, the agencies are restricted by ex parte rules against having contacts with interested parties outside the proceedings.[8]

The APA grants parties the right to sue for judicial review of an agency action. One basis for that review is the failure to follow the procedures required for an action. This is review under the framework of *procedural due process*. The APA [Section 706(2)(A)] requires that agency actions not be "arbitrary, capricious, an abuse of discretion, or otherwise not in accordance with law." Because of the right to judicial review, agencies are careful to follow procedures and base their decisions on the record. Nevertheless, in 2003 the Court of Appeals overturned as "arbitrary and capricious" an NHTSA rule allowing automakers to choose one of two tire-pressure monitoring systems when the record showed that one system was clearly superior in the court's view. NHTSA announced a new NPRM, and the process began again.

An important procedural due process decision pertained to the bases for changing a regulatory rule. NHTSA began rule-making proceedings on air bags in 1967. In 1977, the first year of the Carter administration, it promulgated a rule requiring new

---

[5]For a description of the regulatory agencies, see Congressional Quarterly (1994).
[6]See Mashaw and Merrill (1985, pp. 2–5).
[7]See Kerwin (2003), and Breyer (1982, pp. 378–381). Magat, Krupnick, and Harrington (1986) and Owen and Braeutigam (1978) consider the administrative processes of regulation.
[8]See Mashaw and Merrill (1985, pp. 470–476).

automobiles to be equipped with a passive restraint system—either an air bag or automatic seat belts. The Reagan administration opposed the rule, and the new administrator of NHTSA revoked it in October 1981. The revocation was based not on new information but rather on a reevaluation of the previous record. The administrator concluded that because auto manufacturers planned to use seat belt systems that were easily detachable, the benefits from the rule would not justify the costs. The insurance industry, one of the principal interest groups that had worked for the passive restraint rule, filed a lawsuit challenging the revocation, and the case reached the Supreme Court.[9] The court ruled that the revocation was arbitrary and capricious because NHTSA had failed to develop new evidence to justify a change in the rule.[10]

The courts also review regulatory actions for *substantive due process*. The basic concern under substantive due process is whether an action exceeds the scope of the mandate of the regulatory agency.[11] Regulatory decisions thus are required to bear a relationship to a proper public purpose. In *Nebbia,* the Supreme Court stated:

> So far as the requirement of due process is concerned, and in the absence of other constitutional restriction, a state is free to adopt whatever economic policy may reasonably be deemed to promote public welfare, and to enforce that policy by legislation adapted to its purpose.... If the laws passed are seen to have a reasonable relation to a proper legislative purpose, and are neither arbitrary nor discriminatory, the requirements of due process are satisfied.... With the wisdom of the policy adopted, with the adequacy or practicality of the law enacted to forward it, the courts are both incompetent and unauthorized to deal.

The courts have traditionally been reluctant to substitute their judgments for those of a legislature.[12] The Court of Appeals overturned telecommunications regulations "for failure to give fair weight to Congress's directive that the Commission unbundle only those elements that would impair the viability of entry . . .," leading to the chapter case, *The FCC and Broadband Regulation.* The Court of Appeals also overturned an FCC rule prohibiting ownership of a local television station by a cable company and expressed skepticism about the FCC's national television ownership rule, leading to the chapter case, *The FCC Media Ownership Rules.*

Rule making is the most important activity of most regulatory agencies. Agencies must follow the procedures specified in the APA and procedures specified in their authorizing statutes. Interested parties participate in both formal and informal rule-making procedures, but they also attempt to influence agency actions outside those procedures. Contacts with firms and other interests are generally required to be disclosed in advance through ex parte notification requirements, which contributes to the relative openness of regulatory processes. Lobbying and other forms of information provision are the principal approaches to influencing agency decisions in addition to participation in formal rule-making procedures.

THE NONMARKET ENVIRONMENT OF REGULATORY AGENCIES

Regulatory agencies operate in a complex environment, and even "independent" regulatory commissions are subject to a variety of influences, as illustrated in Figure 10-2. Commissioners and administrators of regulatory agencies are appointed by the president, and most require Senate confirmation. The appointment of regulators can have an important impact on regulatory policy and practice, as the discussion of the deregulation of the

---

[9]*Motor Vehicles Manufacturers Assn. v. State Farm Insurance Co.,* 463 U.S. 29 (1983).
[10]For the majority, Justice Byron R. White wrote, "We have frequently reiterated that an agency must cogently explain why it has exercised its discretion in a given manner, and we affirm this principle again today." See Mashaw and Merrill (1985, pp. 343–354).
[11]See Mashaw and Merrill (1985, pp. 318–385).
[12]See Edley (1990) for a treatment of administrative law and judicial review.

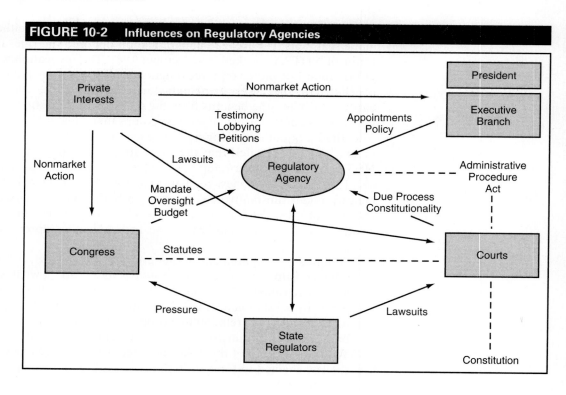

FIGURE 10-2 Influences on Regulatory Agencies

airline industry in Chapter 1 indicates. When President Carter sought to deregulate the surface transportation industries, he needed a majority of pro-deregulation commissioners on the ICC. When his appointment of the chairman gave the pro-deregulation side a four-to-three majority, with four seats vacant, he chose not to fill the vacancies. The ICC then began to deregulate. The executive branch can also influence regulatory commissions through the policy expertise of cabinet agencies. The president thus has a number of instruments to influence regulatory agencies, particularly those in the executive branch.

The president also exercises considerable influence through the ability to direct the review of regulations. President Carter issued an executive order requiring analysis of all new regulations and established the Regulatory Analysis Review Group to review those analyses. Shortly after taking office, President Reagan issued Executive Order 12291, which required that "regulatory action shall not be undertaken unless the potential benefits to society from the regulation outweigh the potential costs to society." The order required regulatory agencies to prepare a Regulatory Impact Analysis for any proposed rule.[13] The Office of Management and Budget (OMB) reviewed the agencies' analyses and could request changes. The order was an important tool in the Reagan and George H. W. Bush administrations' efforts to limit regulation. When he took office, President Clinton modified President Reagan's order by restricting the reviews by OMB's Office of Information and Regulatory Affairs (OIRA) to "significant" regulations and by requiring that OMB take into account "qualitative" as well as quantitative measures of costs and benefits. OMB estimated that the benefits from the regulations reviewed by OMB ranged from $96 billion to $484 billion and the costs ranged from $40 billion to $46 billion.[14] The influence of the president on specific rules is indicated by the example.

Congress exercises considerable influence over regulatory agencies through its budgetary and oversight authorities. Congressional influence also comes from its ability to revise and block changes in statutes. The Reagan administration attempted to

---

[13]See Weidenbaum (2004, p. 171).
[14]OMB, Report to Congress on the Costs and Benefits of Federal Regulations, March 12, 2007.

Regulatory Rule Making in the Bush Administration

The George W. Bush administration set out to make regulation less burdensome and to apply better data and science to the analysis of regulatory rules. The Data Quality Act required regulatory agencies to set standards for the quality of their scientific studies, including the quality not only of the data but also of the analysis of the data. OIRA played the lead role in the evaluation of proposed new rules and modification of existing rules.

As examples of the changes, the Bush administration relaxed costly requirements for hospital emergency rooms that had led a number of hospitals to close their emergency rooms. At the urging of the U.S. Conference of Mayors, the EPA revised brownfields regulations to allow the sale of contaminated sites to private parties that would assume clean-up responsibilities. In response to a surge in lawsuits pertaining to eligibility for overtime pay, the administration put into place new rules under the Fair Labor Standards Act that required mandatory overtime for an addi-

tional 1.3 million workers but allowed employers to decide whether employees earning between $23,660 and $100,000 were administrators and hence not eligible for overtime. Unions claimed that this threatened the overtime pay of 6 million workers. Under the Clean Air Act the EPA proposed a system of tradable mercury permits to achieve reductions in mercury pollution.[1] New rules issued under the Endangered Species Act counted hatchery-raised salmon as well as wild salmon in determining whether a species was endangered. Following complaints by the governors of western states, the administration revised rules issued in the final days of the Clinton administration prohibiting logging and other activities in "roadless areas" of national forests. Under the new rules governors of states could ask the Forest Service for permission to authorize logging.

---

[1]Tradable permit systems are considered in Chapter 11.

deregulate in the area of social regulation, but the congressional oversight committees with responsibilities over the regulatory agencies joined with interest groups to oppose those efforts. For example, the Reagan administration sought to eliminate the Consumer Products Safety Commission (CPSC), but Congress refused.

Congress has power over regulatory agencies because it writes their legislative mandates and reauthorizes those agencies whose statutes require it. The CPSC requires reauthorization every 3 years, yet from 1981 to 1990, threatened by a possible presidential veto, Congress could not agree on reauthorization legislation. The difficulty in reauthorization resulted in part because, in contrast to the statutes establishing economic regulation that use broad terms such as "the public interest," the statutes establishing social regulation often have very detailed language. For example, the reauthorization bill passed in 1990 required the CPSC to establish safety standards for automatic garage door openers.[15] Congress also can include provisions in budget appropriations bills that prevent regulatory agencies from spending any funds on particular programs or regulatory initiatives. For example, in the 1990s Congress prohibited the Department of Energy from spending on any new rule making on energy efficiency standards.

Congress and its committees also provide oversight of regulatory agencies and can pressure regulators through oversight hearings in which regulators can be called to task for their actions. Members of Congress also frequently call or write regulatory agencies asking for explanations of agency actions. The agencies always answer.

Federal regulatory agencies can also be influenced by state regulatory agencies. The National Association of [state] Regulatory Utility Commissions strongly criticized Congress for imposing a moratorium on new energy efficiency standards. State regulatory commissions also make their interests known to their state's congressional delegation and may file lawsuits against federal regulatory agencies.

Private interests affect regulatory agencies directly through their participation in hearings and other regulatory proceedings and indirectly through pressure on

---

[15]*Congressional Quarterly Weekly Report,* October 27, 1990.

Congress and the executive branch. The statutes for some regulatory agencies give citizens rights to petition for action. In the Chapter 8 case, *Pharmaceutical Switching,* a citizen's petition was filed asking the FDA to switch Claritin to the over-the-counter market. Private interests also lobby regulatory agencies, although ex parte contracts with regulators must be disclosed in advance. Private interests also often take their cases to the courts. Activists file lawsuits to force regulators to enforce what the activists see as the agency's mandate. Firms frequently appeal regulatory decisions. Fox Television successfully appealed an FCC order blocking the acquisition of local television stations. The chapter case, *The FCC Media Ownership Rules,* considers the FCC review of those rules.

The courts have a considerable influence on regulation, reviewing regulatory actions for constitutionality and for consistency with statutes. In both the "Broadband" and "Media Ownership Rules" chapter cases the FCC decisions were appealed to the courts. As considered in Chapter 11, many of the rules promulgated by the EPA are appealed.

EXPLANATIONS FOR REGULATION

Two theories have been offered to explain where regulation is and is not imposed. The first is the theory of market imperfections, which predicts that regulation will be instituted to correct market imperfections. The second theory is political and predicts that interest groups seek regulation to serve their interests. The regulation of the prices charged by grain elevators that gave rise to *Munn v. Illinois* allowed farmers, rather than grain elevators, to capture the profits from the sale of their crops. The same interests were important in the passage of the Interstate Commerce Act and the Sherman Antitrust Act. The market imperfections perspective is grounded in economic theory, and the next section examines five types of market imperfections: natural monopoly, externalities, public goods, asymmetric information, and moral hazard.[16] The following section then considers political explanations for regulation.

MARKET IMPERFECTIONS

Natural Monopoly

A monopoly is natural if one firm can produce a given set of goods at lower cost than can any larger number of firms. A *natural monopoly* results when costs are decreasing in the scale of output or in the scope of the set of goods a firm produces. The classical theory of natural monopoly predicts that a monopolist will restrict its output, raising its price above marginal cost. The restriction of output causes economic inefficiency because some consumers who are willing to pay the cost of the resources required to satisfy their demand are prevented from doing so by the restricted output. This inefficiency is referred to as a *deadweight loss* (DWL), since an opportunity to achieve economic gains is forgone.

The case of a monopoly is illustrated in Figure 10-3, which presents a demand curve (D) and the monopolist's average cost (AC) and marginal cost (MC) curves. The marginal and average cost curves are decreasing because of economies of scale. A monopolist exercises its market power by restricting its output to the point q_2 at which marginal revenue (not shown) equals marginal cost, resulting in a price p_2 that is above average and marginal costs. The profit of the firm is the difference between the price p_2 and average cost multiplied by the quantity q_2; that is, profit is the area FAHG. *Consumer surplus* is the area under the demand curve above the price p_2. A deadweight loss results because there are consumers who are willing to purchase the product at a price above the marginal cost of producing it. These units are the difference between q_0 and q_2, and the deadweight loss is the shaded area ABC.

---

[16]See Breyer (1982, Ch. 1), Spulber (1989), and Viscusi, Vernon, and Harrington (2005) for discussions of the nature of market imperfections.

FIGURE 10-3 Monopoly and Deadweight Loss

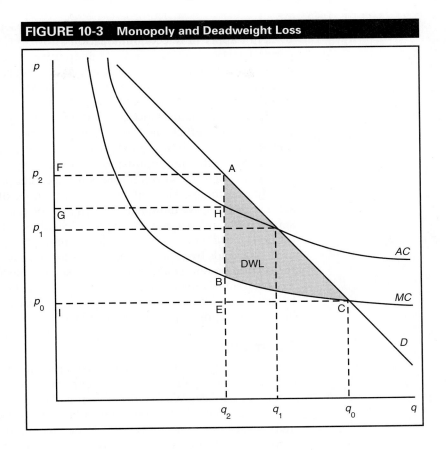

In the case of a natural monopoly, economic theory recommends that government set price equal to marginal cost, or p_0, so that all consumers who are willing to pay the incremental cost of the resources expended to satisfy their demand will purchase the good. Lowering the price to p_0 has two effects. The first is the elimination of the deadweight loss because output expands from q_2 to q_0. The second is a pure transfer from the firm to consumers consisting of the profit FAHG and the area GHEI, which represents a gain in consumer surplus and a loss of profit from lowering the price from p_2 to p_0.

In the presence of decreasing costs, however, pricing at marginal cost does not provide sufficient revenue to cover the total cost of the firm. Total costs could be covered by a government subsidy financed by taxes. This alternative is generally opposed, however, because taxes distort the activity on which they are levied and subsidies weaken the incentives of the monopolist to be responsive to consumer demands. Consequently, either regulated prices are set equal to average costs, denoted p_1 in Figure 10-3, or costs are covered through fixed charges, such as monthly charges. For example, under cost of service regulation consumers pay usage-independent monthly charges to cover the fixed costs of electric power plants, including a fair rate of return on capital.

Before concluding that regulation is warranted in the case of a natural monopoly, two questions must be answered. The first is whether there are any natural monopolies. If there are, the second is whether significant economic efficiency would be gained by regulation. With respect to the first question economies of scale and scope certainly exist over some sets of goods and services, but these economies may be exhausted at output levels that allow more than one supplier to be in the market. Empirical studies indicate, for example, that the large electric power plants in the United States have exhausted the achievable economies of scale. Moreover, advancements in gas turbine generators have resulted in highly efficient power generation at much smaller scales. A natural monopoly can also result if having more than one supplier would result in an uneconomical duplication of facilities. Local electricity distribution systems within cities may remain a monopoly to avoid duplicate sets of distribution wires. This rationale does not apply in telecommunications, however, since cable television and wireless communications systems provide alternatives to local wire connections. A monopoly could also result from network effects and standardization, as considered in Chapter 13 and as found in the Chapter 9 case, *The Microsoft Antitrust Case*, with respect to computer operating systems.

If there is a natural monopoly, it does not necessarily follow that there is substantial economic inefficiency. First, if entry into the industry is easy, the threat of potential competition may limit the extent to which an incumbent monopolist will restrict its output. Second, a monopolist may choose to use nonlinear pricing, involving fixed charges and a low unit price; that is, a price near p_0. This can both increase profits and benefit consumers. Third, if there are a number of possible suppliers of a monopoly service, competitive bidding for the right to be the monopolist can be used to lower the supply price and increase economic efficiency. Similarly, an alternative to the regulation of the electric power industry is for communities to own the local distribution system and solicit bids from power companies for the supply of electricity.[17] As considered in the section on deregulation, industries such as electric power and telecommunications had been subject to price regulation based on a natural monopoly rationale. Competition, however, continues to replace regulation in these industries, not only improving pricing but also inducing more efficient production.

Externalities

Externalities are of two types. A pecuniary externality is present when the actions of one economic agent affect other economic agents through changes in the prices of goods and services. When a firm builds a plant, its demand for labor drives up the wage rate in the local labor market, unless labor is perfectly elastically supplied. This pecuniary externality does not result in economic inefficiency because the wage rate in the labor market is determined by the forces of supply and demand. Thus, a pecuniary externality does not provide a rationale for regulation.

Pecuniary externalities do, however, affect rents and hence may motivate nonmarket action. The oil shocks of the 1970s increased prices dramatically, and politicians responded by enacting a complex regulatory system to lower the price of oil so as to reduce the rents of the owners of U.S. crude oil reserves. The price controls, however, both dampened the incentive to find new domestic crude oil and stimulated the demand for oil, resulting in increased oil imports. The resulting inefficiency was sufficiently costly that crude oil price regulation was eliminated by the early 1980s.[18] The increases in oil prices in 2007–2008 have not resulted in price controls or new regulation.

The second type of externality is nonpecuniary and occurs when an action of one economic agent directly affects the preferences or production opportunities of another economic agent. An individual who drives an automobile generates pollution that both is unhealthy and affects visibility. Similarly, one firm's waste disposal site may pollute another's water supply. These externalities result in a divergence of private costs from social costs. Economic inefficiency results unless agents take into account the full social costs of their activities. Externalities provide an efficiency rationale for regulation to align private and social costs, as considered in Chapter 11 on environmental protection. Energy-efficiency regulation of household appliances may be warranted because burning carbon-based fuels to generate electricity causes externalities in the form of pollution and the release of gases that contribute to global climate change. Energy-efficiency regulation is, however, only a second-best form of regulation, as considered in Chapter 11 in the context of incentive-based systems for environmental protection.

---

[17] See Joskow and Schmalensee (1983) and White (1997) for an assessment of the potential for competition in electric power.

[18] See Breyer (1982, pp. 164–171) and Kalt (1981) for analyses of the inefficiency resulting from crude oil price regulation.

Public Goods

A *public good* is one whose consumption by one person does not reduce its availability for others. When a person consumes a private good such as an apple, it is not available for consumption by others. When a person consumes a good such as national defense or a radio broadcast, however, the amount of the good available for consumption by others is not diminished. For a private good, economic efficiency requires that the marginal utility from consumption equals the price of the good, or, more correctly, that the marginal rate of substitution of one private good for another equals the ratio of their prices. Since a public good is available to all economic agents in a quantity undiminished by their consumption, economic efficiency requires that the sum of the marginal utilities of all individuals equals the price of the public good.[19] Many public goods are "local" in the sense that at some point adding more people diminishes the amount of the good available for others due to congestion, as in the case of a bridge at rush hour.

For some public goods, such as national defense, bridges, and roads, government provision is customary. Government provision, however, does not imply that a good has the characteristics of a public good. Many goods, such as public housing, food stamps, and soil-bank programs, are provided by government to redistribute income rather than because they are public goods. Also, public goods can be supplied by the private sector. Radio and television broadcasts are provided by private enterprises subject only to noneconomic regulation. Similarly, the government privatized its Landsat satellite system, which provides data and photographs of the earth's surface.

A fundamental problem with either private or public provision of public goods centers on the "revelation of preferences." If those who benefit from a public good are asked to pay for it based on how much they value it, people may understate their valuations and free ride on the payments of others. Because of the free-rider problem, public provision may be warranted. This, however, does not resolve the problem of determining the public's aggregate valuation of the good and thus whether it should be supplied in the first place. If individuals could be excluded from consuming the public good, the revelation and free-rider problems could be resolved—at least in principle. For example, preventing satellite dish owners from obtaining free television programming induces customers to pay for Direct TV and the Dish Network.

Asymmetric Information

A market imperfection can also result from *asymmetric information*. If people have different (private) information at the time they act, markets may not perform efficiently, even when there are advantageous trades that could be made. Akerlof (1970) considered the case of a used car market in which each seller knows the true value of the car she wants to sell, but the buyers know only the probability distribution of the values of the cars that might be offered for sale. For each used car there is a potential buyer who is willing to buy it, but a buyer cannot through casual inspection determine the true value of any particular used car offered for sale. All the buyer knows is that a car might be a lemon, might be high quality, or might be somewhere in between.

Because a potential buyer does not know the true value of any particular car, the maximum amount the buyer is willing to pay is the average of the values of those cars that will be offered for sale. Potential sellers with high-quality cars find that the amount buyers are willing to pay is less than the value of their cars. They thus will not offer their cars for sale. Buyers recognize this and understand that the only cars that will be offered for sale will be those of low quality. The average value of those low-quality cars is low, however, so buyers will be willing to pay only a low amount. The low amount buyers are willing to pay again means that the potential sellers of cars at the high end of the remaining range will not offer their cars for sale. Buyers will then be willing to pay even less for any car offered for sale. The market thus may collapse with no sales

---

[19]In this sense, an externality is also a public good (or bad), since the efficient provision of goods involving externalities requires that the sum of the marginal utilities and disutilities from its supply be equated to its marginal cost.

being made. This is clearly inefficient, because for every used car there is a buyer who is willing to buy it if its true value were known.

This phenomenon, known as *adverse selection,* also occurs when sellers have incomplete information about customers. Insurance, in principle, is to provide coverage for individuals with similar risk characteristics. When those characteristics cannot be readily observed, people with quite different risks can be placed in the same pool. High-risk individuals have an incentive to buy insurance, which can drive up the price of insurance and cause some low-risk individuals not to buy insurance. Insurance companies respond to this adverse selection by requiring a physical examination for life insurance and basing auto insurance rates on observables such as accident and traffic citation histories and the number of years of driving experience.

When market participants have incomplete information and acquiring information is costly, the mandated provision of information through regulation may be warranted. Regulation may not be warranted in all situations involving asymmetric information, however. Information has value, so there is a demand for it. In the used car example, a potential buyer may take the car to a mechanic for inspection. More generally, individuals may invest in information acquisition or hire agents who are more knowledgeable than they are. On the supply side, manufacturers can offer warranties to signal to consumers that their products are of high quality.[20] Some dealers, for example, offer warranties on their used or pre-owned cars.

Information, however, can remain undersupplied when it is in the self-interest of its possessor not to supply it. Manufacturers are understandably reluctant to release negative information about their products because doing so may reduce demand. The Chapter 5 case, *Merck and Vioxx,* concerns the issue of how much and when information should be released about clinical drug trials. Consequently, consumers may be inadequately informed about hazards. Similarly, an employee may be incompletely informed about possible health and safety hazards in the workplace. In such situations, regulation could be warranted. The liability system, considered in Chapter 12, however, is an alternative to regulation.

Moral Hazard

Moral hazard refers to inefficient actions induced by policy instruments that cause people not to bear the full consequences of their actions. In the case of medical care, fully insured individuals have an effectively unlimited demand for medical care, since they bear none of the cost of the care they receive. In addition, individuals may not have the proper incentive to take socially efficient preventive measures because they know that the cost of any illness or accident will be covered by insurance. For example, federally funded flood insurance encourages people to live in areas prone to flooding and can lead to socially inefficient location decisions.

Regulation is one response to moral hazard problems, but regulation can also cause moral hazard problems, making the regulation itself less effective. In a controversial article Peltzman (1975) argued that automobile safety regulation induced drivers to take more risks, thus reducing the effectiveness of mandatory safety standards. Peterson and Hoffer (1994) studied data on automobile personal injury and collision insurance claims from 1989 to 1991 and for each model compared data for those vehicles with an airbag to those with no airbag. Their data indicated that the number of accident claims was systematically higher for the identical automobile model with air bags than those without an airbag. The authors concluded that although these results were consistent with Peltzman's argument, they could be due to higher-risk drivers being more likely than lower-risk drivers to choose automobiles with airbags.

As an example of moral hazard, the 1986 Emergency Medical Treatment and Active Labor Act (EMTALA) requires all hospitals that both participate in Medicaid and have an emergency room to provide a medical screening evaluation to anyone who

---

[20]See Spence (1973) for the seminal work on signaling.

comes to their emergency room and to stabilize a patient's condition if there is a medical emergency. The rules implementing EMTALA also require that physicians be on call to treat a wide variety of conditions in emergency rooms. Patients were also granted the right to sue the hospital. Uninsured individuals who could not pay began using emergency rooms for their health care, imposing a heavy cost burden on hospitals. Moreover, doctors began to refuse to be on call because they could be exposed to fines or a lawsuit. The response of an increasing number of hospitals, particularly those in low-income areas, was to close their emergency rooms. In 2003 and 2004 six hospitals in the Los Angeles area closed their emergency rooms to avoid the costs of EMTALA. The regulation had induced behavior that reduced rather than expanded the availability of emergency care.

Moral hazard can also occur within a firm. To increase the incentives for individuals to report corporate wrongdoing, federal laws allow a whistle-blower to receive 10 to 30 percent of any judgment won in court. In response to such laws, companies have instituted internal disclosure and ethics systems to reduce the likelihood of wrongdoing and encourage the reporting of suspected wrongdoing at an early stage. Moral hazard results because the reward provided by the federal law encourages employees to avoid the companies' internal control systems, wait for sufficient evidence to accumulate, and then go directly to the public authorities. This makes the internal systems less effective in stopping wrongdoing.

In industries in which cost-of-service pricing and rate-of-return regulation are used, cost increases are passed on to consumers. The incentive for the firm to hold down costs is thus weakened. This is a form of moral hazard because the firm does not bear the full consequences of the higher costs that result from its own decisions.

The principal means of dealing with this market imperfection is to structure incentives so that the moral hazard is taken into account in decision making. In the case of medical insurance, copayments can be required and reimbursement limits imposed. Moral hazard can also be addressed by monitoring the behavior of individuals to increase the likelihood that they take proper care. Imposing fines for not wearing a seat belt is an example of monitoring. Moral hazard is also reduced by breaking the link between cost increases and the prices charged for services, as in price cap regulation used in some states for telecommunications.

Markets can also resolve some potential moral hazard problems. A common problem in markets is the incentive for sellers to shirk on the quality of the goods or services they sell. For example, if quality can be observed only through use, a seller may have an incentive to shirk. If, however, consumers can sully the reputation of the firm by informing other consumers that the firm shirked on quality, shirking can be reduced or eliminated. Consumers can follow the strategy of purchasing from the firm as long as its reputation for producing high-quality products is unsullied and not purchasing from it if its reputation is ever sullied. If the potential gain from future sales is sufficiently great, the firm will have no incentive to shirk on quality.[21]

Government Imperfections

Market imperfections in many cases warrant government regulation. In some cases, however, regulation may be a cure that is worse than the disease. Wolf (1979, p. 138) argues that government intervention to deal with a market imperfection or failure may itself be subject to a "nonmarket failure."[22] He argues that the market failure "rationale provides only a necessary, not a sufficient, justification for public policy interventions. Sufficiency requires that specifically identified market failures be compared with potential nonmarket failure associated with the implementation of public policies. . . ."

Market imperfections are thus only a necessary condition for regulation to improve economic efficiency. Regulation is not perfect, and even well-intentioned regulation can

---

[21]See Kreps (1990) for an exposition of this theory.
[22]See also Wolf (1988).

in some instances worsen the performance of markets. In addition, regulation is not always intended to correct market imperfections but instead can be the result of political forces that serve objectives other than economic efficiency. The next section considers the political economy of regulation.

THE POLITICAL ECONOMY OF REGULATION

Capture and Rent-Seeking Theories

One theory of economic regulation is that it is initially imposed to address a market imperfection, but through interaction with the firms they regulate, regulators begin to see the firms' problems as their own. Regulation then evolves over time to serve the interests of regulated firms in addition to, or instead of, the goal of economic efficiency.[23] This *capture* theory predicts that regulation initially will be found where there are market imperfections and over time will evolve to serve the interests of the regulated industry.

Observing that much of the economic regulation of industries increased costs and generated rents, Chicago school economists provided a different explanation for where regulation would be found. Their focus was not on market imperfections but on the ability of interest groups to obtain regulation through political pressure. From this perspective, regulation is demanded by interest groups and supplied through the political process.[24] Regulation thus was not established to address market imperfections and then captured but instead was established to benefit politically effective interests. Once established, regulation continued to serve those interests. From this *rent-seeking* perspective, the railroads in the 19th century sought regulation to support their cartel agreements, which were plagued by defections and cheating. Similarly, regulation in the airline and trucking industries was sought in part to serve the interests of incumbent firms by limiting entry and passing on cost increases through higher regulated prices. This perspective and the supporting empirical evidence provided the impetus for the deregulation of a number of industries.

Regulation is also supplied in response to the demands of interest groups other than business. This is clearest in the context of social regulation where, for example, environmental groups successfully overcame agricultural interests in obtaining the regulation of pesticides and where organized labor succeeded in obtaining workplace safety and health regulation. During the early 1990s consumer complaints about basic cable television prices led Congress to establish price regulation over the veto of President Bush.

Firms also seek federal regulations to avoid individual states imposing different regulations. Appliance manufacturers sought uniform energy-efficiency standards across the states to avoid having to produce different models for different states. Some Internet service and content providers supported federal Internet privacy standards to preclude the enactment of disparate state standards. Companies also seek regulation to level the playing field by requiring competitors to meet the same standards they meet. When McDonald's decided to implement a no-smoking policy in its company-owned restaurants, it sought uniform federal regulation to impose a no-smoking policy on all restaurants. The large toy companies such as Mattel and Hasbro sought mandatory testing for lead in paint on children's toys, so that other companies would not free ride on the safety reputation built by their own testing.

Fairness

Regulation is also used to accomplish fairness goals. This can involve policies such as lifeline rates for telephone service for low-income people and the provision of aid such as food stamps. Fairness can also be sought in cases in which consumers do not or cannot easily take precautions. During the economic slowdown in 2008 the prac-

---

[23]See Bernstein (1955) and Quirk (1981).
[24]See Stigler (1971), Posner (1974), and Peltzman (1976).

tices of financial services companies became a center for attention. Some consumers found themselves burdened by high interest payments on their borrowing on credit cards.[25] In some cases consumers had poorly understood the terms under which the cards were issued, and in other cases those terms were silent about certain practices. For example, for some consumers who had credit card balances at two different interest rates, such as an introductory rate and a standard rate, interest paid was applied to the balance with the lower interest rate. In other cases, when a cardholder exceeded a prespecified limit and a penalty rate was applied, that rate was applied to all balances and not just to future borrowing. Moreover, consumers complained that not all the terms of the credit card use were disclosed by the issuers and that some disclosures were difficult to understand. Consumers complained to members of Congress and to regulators, and their advocates such as the Consumer Federation of America campaigned for restrictions on card issuers. Regulators had the authority to restrict or ban many of the practices that generated complaints, but fearing that the regulators would not go far enough, members of Congress introduced legislation to restrict the practices. These issues are considered in more detail in the Part III integrative case, *Credit Card Regulation.*

Other Public Purposes: Media Ownership Rules

Regulation can also be used for other public purposes. For example, the Federal Communications Commission (FCC) has traditionally been fearful of concentrations of ownership in the news media that might stifle the full reporting of news or restrict the diversity of views expressed. To support diversity objectives and avoid concentrations of ownership, the FCC had promulgated media ownership rules that restricted the number and type of media outlets that could be owned by the same company. Over time the structure of the media industry changed as a result of the growth of television and the decline of newspapers and the advent of the Internet as a source of news. These changes required that the media rules should be reexamined. This generated intense nonmarket action with some companies seeking to preserve the status quo and others seeking changes that would benefit themselves. The chapter case, *The FCC Media Ownership Rules,* addresses the nonmarket activities and the regulatory process centering on one set of revisions.

In 2008 FCC chairman Kevin Martin again sought to promulgate new media rules to accomplish two objectives. One was to strengthen newspapers whose circulation and advertising revenue had been declining. The other was to limit the power of the largest cable company, Comcast Communications. Martin voted with the other two Republican members of the FCC to relax the newspaper-broadcast cross-ownership rule that applied to the 20 largest media markets. The new rule would allow a company to own both a newspaper and either a television station or radio station if there were at least eight other independent sources of news. If the company was a television station, it could not be one of the four largest in the market. This relaxation benefited newspapers, but the newspapers complained that the revision was so minor that it would have no effect on developments in the markets.

Martin joined with the two Democrat members of the FCC to limit further acquisitions of cable companies by large cable providers, the largest of which was Comcast with nearly 30 percent of the market. By a 3–2 vote the FCC issued a rule that prohibits any company from owning cable systems serving more than 30 percent of the market nationally. This rule making followed a number of other actions that restricted the practices of cable systems and accelerated the provision of video services by telephone companies.

The two rules were criticized from all sides. A group of 25 senators led by Byron Dorgan (D-ND) notified Chairman Martin that they would lead a legislative effort to revoke any media rules the FCC promulgated.

---

[25]This occurred at the same time as the subprime loan crisis that caused many borrowers to lose their homes.

Preemption

A major regulation issue is whether a decision by a federal regulatory agency preempts lawsuits in state courts. The Food and Drug Administration (FDA) has the responsibility for approving drugs and medical devices, and the companies making these products claimed that FDA approval precluded lawsuits in state courts that sought damages for injuries due to the products. The companies argued that approval of the products by an expert agency meant that the government had judged that the products were safe, although not without some risks, to be marketed and that additional enforcement of safety through the courts was inappropriate. That is, the FDA had already taken into account in its decision the benefits and costs associated with the product, and the courts should not make decisions pertaining to only one side of that assessment.

Preemption has attracted considerable nonmarket action as firms have sought to obtain explicit language in new legislation to provide preemption, and other interest groups such as trial lawyers and consumer groups have opposed such language. The courts have also addressed the issue in response to cases brought before them, and in a major decision in 2007 the Supreme Court ruled that FDA approval of a medical device shielded the manufacturer from class action lawsuits by people claiming injury from the product. The Supreme Court was also considering a related case pertaining to pharmaceuticals. The court decisions on preemption are considered in more detail in Chapter 12.

A NONMARKET THEORY OF REGULATION

Although the capture and rent-seeking theories are insightful, they give insufficient attention to market imperfections, as is most apparent in the regulation of externalities such as pollution. These theories also give insufficient attention to the role of institutions in structuring the competition among interest groups, and they lack an account of the organization, strategies, and effectiveness of those interest groups. As indicated in Figure 10-2, regulation takes place in a complex institutional and political environment, and the mandates and procedures of those institutions, as well as the policy objectives of the executive branch, can be important. In the case of the regulation of basic cable television prices, members of Congress saw the issue as sufficiently popular with constituents that it was worthwhile for them to enact the Cable Television Act of 1992 and claim credit for it. Price regulation was eliminated during the Clinton administration. By 2008 members of Congress were again calling for restrictions on rate increases for cable television.

Regulation and regulatory change can be more fully understood through the frameworks presented in Parts I and II of this book combined with the characteristics of the regulatory environment, as illustrated in Figure 10-2, and the analysis of market imperfections. This *political economy* theory views regulation as shaped by market imperfections, institutions and their officeholders, and the nonmarket action of private interests. The impact of nonmarket action on regulatory agencies is direct, as well as indirect through Congress and the executive branch. In addition, regulation has procedural requirements imposed by both legislation and due process rights. The economic efficiency objective of addressing market imperfections also influences the policymaking process, particularly if that objective is embraced by the presidential administration. The civil service personnel of the agencies and the nature of bureaucracy also play a role.[26]

Interest group politics represents a strong force for change in some cases and for preservation of the status quo in others.[27] Regulatory change in the telecommunications and electric power industries considered later in the chapter illustrates the importance of institutions as well as of interests. The example of ATV regulation illustrates that firms can simultaneously seek to obtain certain regulations and avoid others.

---

[26]See Wilson (1989).
[27]See Noll and Owen (1983), Wilson (1980), and Francis (1993) for studies of the politics of regulation.

EXAMPLE

The Political Economy of Regulation: ATVs

The Consumer Products Safety Commission (CPSC) maintains an information system in which accidents that require hospital emergency room treatment are reported to the CPSC. In 2005, 137,000 people went to the hospital as a result of accidents involving ATVs, and 40,400 children under the age of 16 required treatment in hospital emergency rooms. The commission staff estimated that 90 percent of the children injured were riding adult-size vehicles. The commission had identified 467 people who had died from accidents involving ATVs, and the staff believed that when all the data were in, the number would reach 700.

Sales of ATVs had fallen from 912,000 in 2004 to 856,000 in 2006. Moreover, imports from China had increased substantially, putting pressure on the established manufacturers such as Yamaha, Kawasaki, and Polaris. The established manufacturers both supported and opposed regulation of their industry and products. They sought a commission rule that would remove restrictions on the power and size of youth ATVs. The commission had not acted, perhaps because it faced another problem with youth ATVs. Whereas the established manufacturers were required to comply with safety regulations, the products of "new entrant" manufacturers were not required to meet those regulations. The CPSC issued a public statement "that children are at risk of injury or death due to multiple safety defects" from the Kazuma Meerkat 50, a youth ATV imported from China. The commission stated that the ATV had no front wheel brakes, no parking brake, and could be started in gear.[1] The CPSC had not ordered a recall because it lacked a quorum: The Senate had refused to confirm the nominee, who then withdrew from consideration.

The Specialty Vehicle Institute of America (SVIA), which represented the established manufacturers, sought regulation of all ATVs, including those in the "new entrant" category. The SVIA lobbied Congress to enact legislation making regulation uniform across all manufacturers.

The SVIA also faced regulation of another type. Carolyn Anderson, co-founder of Concerned Families for ATV Safety, had lost her 14-year old son to an ATV accident and sought a rule by the CPSC banning children under 16 from using ATVs. She said, "Kids under 16 don't have the judgment, they don't have the physical strength a lot of time. They're short on common sense."[2] The American Academy of Pediatrics agreed. Dr. Gary Smith, chair of the Committee on Injury, Violence and Poison Prevention of the Academy, said, "The Academy feels strongly that children aren't developmentally ready until about the age of 16 to operate a complex machine such as an ATV. It has to do with maturity, with judgment, with coordination, with strength."[3]

The SVIA already participated in a voluntary agreement with the CPSC in which retailers were not supposed to sell to people who might let children operate the vehicles. The SVIA opposed going farther. Tim Buche, president of the SVIA, said, "A lot of parents want their kids to ride ATVs. ATVs are loads of fun every day for millions of Americans when used safely and responsibly."[4]

---

[1]*Wall Street Journal,* June 6, 2007.

[2]Associated Press, June 3, 2007.
[3]Associated Press, June 3, 2007.
[4]Associated Press, June 3, 2007.

Regulation is also shaped by the efficiency consequences of policy alternatives and the policy responses to those consequences. The impetus for deregulation in the transportation industries came from information provided by public policy analysts, the staff of regulatory commissions, and policymakers in the executive branch.[28] Regulatory policy is thus a product of both interest group actions and institutions and their officeholders.[29]

To illustrate the perspective, consider the case of social regulation and small business. One distinctive feature of much of the social regulation enacted over the past 35 years is the regularity of special provisions for small businesses. Many regulations provide small businesses with exemptions, streamlined reporting procedures, reduced compliance burdens, smaller penalties, or less stringent standards. Brock and Evans

---

[28]See Derthick and Quirk (1985) for a study of the influence of policy analysts on regulatory policy.
[29]Harris and Milkis (1989) provide an analysis of regulatory change at the FTC and EPA.

(1986, Table 4.2) listed 29 federal regulatory programs that provide "tiers" of regulation based on the size of firms. For example, the Family Leave Act of 1993 exempts firms with fewer than 50 employees. Furthermore, the Regulatory Flexibility Act of 1980 encourages regulators not to burden small businesses unduly.

Small business receives these exemptions in part because the compliance costs, and particularly their administrative components, are disproportionately burdensome for small business. Exemptions, however, are also due to the effective political organization of small businesses. As indicated in Chapter 8, small businesses are numerous, have complete coverage of legislative districts, and in the aggregate have substantial resources. Small business is also well organized for nonmarket purposes, with the National Federation of Independent Business and the National Small Business Association having considerable influence in Washington and in state capitols.

Redistribution and Cross-Subsidization

In addition to addressing market imperfections, regulation can be used to redistribute income. Rent control in the housing market is an example, and cable television price regulation is another. In telecommunications the distribution of rents between local and long-distance providers depends importantly on the "access charge" paid for access to the local loops of incumbent telephone companies. These rents have generated nonmarket action at the state level. De Figueiredo and Edwards (2007) showed that the access charges set by state public utilities commissions depended significantly on the campaign contributions made to state legislators by the incumbent companies seeking high access charges and by the entrants to the local telecommunications market seeking low access charges.

Regulation can also be used to redistribute income through cross-subsidization of one customer class by another. Because of distributive concerns, state regulatory agencies have instituted lifeline rates for low-income consumers. In California, at the end of 2001 the number of low-income individuals receiving lifeline rates for basic telephone services reached 3.7 million. Lifeline rates require cross-subsidization by other customers, which in California took the form of a 4 percent surcharge on basic telephone service.

Cross-subsidization occurs when one group of customers pays more and another group pays less than the cost of providing their service. Inefficiency results on both sides of the cross-subsidization. When a price is below costs, some consumers receive service even though the cost of satisfying their demand is greater than their willingness to pay for it. When a price is above costs, some consumers who are willing to pay the cost of the resources required to produce their service are denied the opportunity to do so.

Cross-subsidization is a common feature of the economic regulation of industries. Long-distance and business telephone services have been used to cross-subsidize basic residential service. When airline fares and routes were regulated, long-distance flights cross-subsidized shorter flights, and high-density airline routes cross-subsidized low-density routes. Cross-subsidization is unsustainable when entry into the industry is possible, since customers who are paying more than the cost of their service have an incentive to seek alternative suppliers. Much of the deregulation movement in the United States has been the result of forces created by cross-subsidization. The entry of MCI into the long-distance telecommunications market occurred because AT&T's long-distance rates were used to cross-subsidize other services. MCI offered services at prices that did not include the cross-subsidization, and customers switched to it. Similarly, as the airline industry was being deregulated, entry occurred first on high-density, long-distance routes.

COST-OF-SERVICE REGULATION

Regulation in a number of industries has centered on cost-of-service pricing. In industries such as airlines and trucking, entry was controlled and industry-wide prices were set with cost increases passed on to consumers in the form of higher prices. This allowed inefficiencies to creep into the industries. Because industry-wide wage increases affected all firms similarly and the increased costs could be passed through to consumers, firms had weak incentives to resist wage demands. This moral hazard feature of cost-of-service regulation allowed organized labor, such as the Teamsters, to capture substantially higher wages than would otherwise have been possible.[30] When deregulation occurred in those industries and entry was permitted, wage rates and union membership began to fall. Similarly, in the airline industry pilots and machinists captured high wages, and with deregulation the growth of nonunion carriers threatened unionized airlines and their union members.

In the electric power, natural gas transmission, and telecommunications industries prices were set on a firm-by-firm basis to yield the revenue required to cover the firm's actual costs plus an allowed return on equity capital. Price changes occurred only with regulatory approval, and the approval process was similar to formal adjudication. Data and analyses were presented by the firm in support of the price changes, comments were requested from interested parties, hearings were held, witnesses testified and were cross-examined, and the commission issued an order specifying the prices. Much of the contention in this process centered on the rate of return the firm was allowed. In some cases, the emphasis on rate of return caused regulation to focus more on the profits earned by firms than on production efficiency or efficient pricing.

Cost-of-service regulation of telecommunications service focused on the rate of return in part because neither the regulators nor the firms had reliable data on the costs of providing individual services. The cost structure of telecommunications involves large common costs of facilities, such as network and switching equipment, used for a variety of services. In addition, network externalities complicate the determination of costs. Moreover, the firms' accounting and information systems were not designed to identify costs of individual services, making it virtually impossible to base prices for individual services on their actual costs.

This cost-of-service regulatory system has been blamed for inducing high costs and slowing the introduction of new technology in telecommunications. Firms were said to invest in excess capacity and higher-quality equipment than needed because that increased their asset base. Since profits were determined by applying the allowed rate of return to the asset base, higher profits resulted. This also caused other inefficiencies. AT&T was said to have inhibited the rate at which new technology was introduced because it did not want to write off existing assets and lose the return allowed on those assets. These inefficiencies coupled with cross-subsidization led to deregulation.

DEREGULATION

Telecommunications

Over the past 50 years, interstate telecommunications regulation has evolved from strict cost-of-service regulation of a monopoly (AT&T and the Bell system) to reliance on competition with only limited supervision by regulators. Intrastate telecommunications services were also tightly regulated by state public utility commissions, and competition is emerging at the state level. Regulation of interstate long-distance service traditionally focused on who was permitted to provide service and what prices could be charged for those services. After World War II a series of technological advances changed the cost structure of the industry with microwave transmission technology reducing costs dramatically. In the 1950s state police departments and oil and gas pipeline companies received permission to build microwave systems tailored to their specific needs and dedicated to their own use.[31] Entry into the industry had begun.

Technological progress continued, and for several decades both real and nominal prices for telecommunications services decreased. Despite the lower prices, the price structure in telecommunications resulted in considerable economic inefficiency. Because of the early public policy objective of achieving universal service, basic residential service was cross-subsidized by business and long-distance services. This

---

[30]See Rose (1987).
[31]Pipeline companies already had rights of way and thus could readily construct microwave systems.

cross-subsidization continued as a result of nonmarket pressure from consumers and from politicians who sought to represent their interests. Technological change in the form of microwave and satellite systems and electronic switching equipment, however, made it possible for large business customers to bypass the Bell network by establishing their own private telecommunications systems. Bypass was sufficiently attractive that the system of cross-subsidization was in jeopardy.

Entry of new service providers had been blocked by the FCC, but as a result of court decisions overturning several FCC decisions, competitors such as MCI and Sprint were allowed to enter increasingly broad segments of the interstate telecommunications market. The breakup of the Bell system further complicated the practice of cost-of-service and rate-of-return regulation.[32] The FCC faced the problem of restructuring the rates for long-distance and local service in light of bypass, entry, and competitive pressures.

Telecommunications deregulation thus was spurred by technological change and cross-subsidization, which provided opportunities for new entrants to offer selected services at prices substantially below regulated prices. Technological change essentially eliminated any remaining vestiges of natural monopoly in the industry. For example, local connections could be provided by cable television connections and wireless communications systems in addition to copper wire. Deregulation proceeded most rapidly at the federal level with more modest steps taken by states.

State regulation had also been rampant with cross-subsidization, with intrastate long-distance service subsidizing local service and business service subsidizing residential service. State deregulation has focused less on cross-subsidization and instead on incentive regulation intended to provide firms with flexibility to operate more efficiently and to pass on some of the efficiency to customers. Kridel, Sappington, and Weisman (1996) reviewed the empirical literature on state deregulation and concluded that the evidence on the effects of the regulatory initiatives was mixed; that is, it is "premature to conclude that incentive regulation has been an overwhelming success." They noted, "There is no evidence that incentive regulation has led to streamlined regulatory proceedings."

At the federal level Congress had attempted for 20 years to amend the Communications Act of 1934, which had remained largely as originally written despite dramatic technological change. Finally, a compromise among the three principal sets of companies—long-distance carriers, regional Bell operating companies, and cable television providers—was reached in the Telecommunications Act of 1996. This complex act sought to open both local service and long-distance markets to competition, provided that the entrant's market was open to competition.

The Telecommunications Act of 1996 was a milestone in the transformation of virtually all segments of the telecommunications market from tight regulation to competition. The Act and continued technological change resulted in restructuring of the industry. Through mergers and acquisitions AT&T and the seven regional Bell operating companies plus GTE have consolidated, leaving four companies: AT&T, Verizon, Bell South, and Qwest.

Entry occurred in fits and starts in the local and interstate telecommunications and cable television markets. In 2001 SBC, now AT&T, won approval to offer long-distance service to Texas residents, marking the next step in competition in the interstate long-distance market. Verizon subsequently entered the interstate long-distance market, becoming one of the largest providers.

The Telecommunications Act required the incumbent local-exchange carriers (ILECs) to lease elements of their networks to other companies entering their markets. The entrants, referred to as competitive local exchange carriers (CLECs), sought low prices for the network elements, and the state regulators provided discounted prices to spur entry and drive down prices for consumers. Some 300 CLECs entered, but many failed when the technology bubble burst in 2001 and 2002. The FCC was responsible for determining which network elements should be provided to the

[32]See Temin (1987) for a history of the Bell system and its change. See Fisher, McGowan, and Greenwood (1983) for an analysis of the breakup.

CLECs, but the courts overturned the FCC's decisions because they went beyond the courts' interpretation of Congress's directive to provide "only those network elements that would impair the viability of entry. . . ." The FCC's decisions affected not only voice communications but also the provision of broadband. The chapter case, *The FCC and Broadband Regulation,* concerns the FCC's attempt to determine which network elements were necessary to avoid impairing entry.

Electric Power

The electric power industry represents approximately 3 percent of GDP and is nearly the size of the telecommunications and airline industries combined. Electricity prices vary greatly across the states with average 1999 retail prices of 11.75 and 9.3 cents per kilowatt hour in New Hampshire and California, respectively, at the high end, and 4.0 and 4.2 cents per kilowatt hour in Idaho and Kentucky, respectively. The price differences are in large part due to historical factors including the high costs of nuclear power plants still in the rate base. Technological change in electric power has also had an important effect as improvements in gas turbine generators have lowered costs and greatly reduced the minimum efficient scale in the industry. Moreover, legislation required electric utilities to purchase electricity, often at high prices, from qualified facilities such as cogeneration plants and renewable energy sources.[33] In addition, line losses from electricity transmission have been reduced.

These technological changes have made it both feasible and economical to transmit electricity to distant customers. For example, the lower cost of power in adjacent states provided incentives for California's customers to import electricity. In 1992 Congress passed the Energy Policy Act, which required a transmission company to "wheel" electricity from a producer in one state through its lines to a customer in a third state. This, in effect, made wholesale electricity a competitive market. Brokers and trading companies such as Dynegy and Enron made a market in electricity, where industrial customers bought electricity on the spot market in 15-minute blocks. The potential for competition led a majority of states to deregulate their electric power markets.[34] The actions taken by the states varied considerably, and only the most extensive deregulation effort, that in California, is considered here.[35]

Electricity prices in California were nearly double the prices in neighboring states. This had two effects. First, the price gap plus nonmarket forces, including stringent environmental regulation and NIMBY protests, led to no additions of electric power generation capacity during the 1990s. This also meant that California power plants were older and required more maintenance. Second, industrial customers in the state sought access to the cheaper power available just across the border. If power were imported and the market opened to competition, however, the California utilities would have stranded investments—investments in generating plants that were no longer economical to operate. This stranded investment was estimated at $28 billion.[36] Opening the market would cause the California electricity producers to default on their bond obligations. Default could undermine the credit rating of the state government, forcing it to pay higher interest rates on its bonds, since the investments in generating plants had been made with the approval of state regulators.

The state government and the electric utilities essentially struck a bargain in which the stranded investments were addressed and the market opened to competition. Any California customer was free to purchase electricity from any supplier. An industrial customer or a municipality with its own local distribution system thus could purchase electricity from the lowest bidder in a deregulated retail market. The wholesale market was also opened, and California began to import electricity from neighboring states. California utilities were not permitted to sign long-term supply contracts, so they bought power on the spot market. Consumers received an immediate 10 percent reduction in their

---

[33]The high-price contracts with qualifying facilities began expiring at the end of the 1990s.
[34]Wilson (2001) analyzed in detail the market for electricity and the management of that market.
[35]White (1997) analyzed the political economy of electric power deregulation across the states.
[36]Moody's Investor's Service estimated the stranded investment of U.S. electricity producers at $135 billion.

electricity rates, and those rates were frozen for 4 years to provide income to electricity producers to cover a portion of their stranded investments. Also, government agencies issued $7.4 billion in bonds, the proceeds from which were used to pay off a portion of the stranded investments. Taking the $7.4 billion off the electricity companies' books allowed the 10 percent price reduction. Consumers, however, were billed for the debt service on the state bonds and thus received little benefit during the 4-year price freeze.

Strong economic growth in California during the 1990s and the failure to build new generating capacity reduced the peak-load reserve capacity in the state to almost zero. During the summer of 2000 a drought in the Northwest reduced the supply of hydroelectric power and reduced electricity exports to California. California utilities were forced to increase their purchases of electricity on the wholesale market, and the wholesale price skyrocketed. California utilities could not increase prices to their customers and were obliged to meet demand, so they purchased electricity on credit. When the utilities were unable to pay for the electricity, some qualifying facilities, some of which had not been paid for 6 months, refused to generate electricity. Power shortages developed in Northern California leading to occasional rolling blackouts. Pacific Gas & Electric, the utility in Northern California, declared bankruptcy. Southern California Edison also ran out of credit and sought relief from the state government.

In January 2001 the California governor, using executive authority, signed secret $43 billion long-term electric power contracts, many at very high prices. Prices to retail customers were increased only slightly, so the demand for electricity did not drop. The crisis ended in May 2001 as a result of several factors. First, substantial retail price increases were finally adopted, which reduced demand. The higher prices, however, would pay only for future purchases of electricity. Second, cool weather throughout the summer reduced peak demand by approximately 10 percent. Third, the Federal Energy Regulatory Commission instituted a price monitoring system for the western United States and a price mitigation plan for California. Within 2 months wholesale prices in the West had fallen by 80 percent.

The power crisis was over, but the California deregulation effort had been crippled. Moreover, the state of California was stuck with long-term power supply contracts at high prices and volumes that at times forced it to resell power at substantial losses. To pay for the power, the state was forced to issue bonds for past electricity purchases that ultimately would be paid by California residents. California voters recalled the governor in 2003.

The failure of the California power market was due to several factors. First, risks, such as the drought in the Northwest, were larger than had been contemplated. Second, nonmarket pressures had prevented construction of new power plants in California. Third, the prohibition against utilities signing long-term contracts forced them to pay spot prices on the wholesale market. Fourth, the fixed retail prices meant that consumers did not curtail their demand when the wholesale price of electricity skyrocketed. Fifth, the refusal of the California Public Utility Commission to raise retail prices caused the utilities to bear all the risk, and they quickly became insolvent. The rules governing the electricity market were revised, and the market began to operate more efficiently.

Part of the volatility of wholesale prices was due to the trading strategies of companies such as Enron that exploited flaws in the design of the California electricity market. The chapter case, *Enron Power Marketing, Inc. and the California Market,* concerns these trading strategies.

Auctions

The FCC has innovated by substituting auctions for its comparative license award system for allocating the radio spectrum. The FCC had traditionally allocated broadcast licenses, for free, by evaluating applications using a set of noneconomic standards.[37] With the development of cellular telephones, the FCC had to allocate portions of the radio spectrum for that service, and it initially turned to the same system it used to allocate broadcast licenses.

---

[37]See Breyer (1982, pp. 71–95) for a description and critique of this system.

It became clear, however, that the traditional allocation system was cumbersome and inefficient and, with a major segment of the radio spectrum to be allocated in 1995 for personal communications services, the FCC needed a better mechanism. For decades economists had urged the use of auctions to allocate scarce public resources such as the radio spectrum. Auctions award resources to the highest bidders—the ones with the highest-valued uses for the resource. In a competitive market the highest-valued uses are determined by how effectively the bidders can compete to serve customers. Auctions thus yield economically efficient outcomes; that is, resources (the spectrum) are allocated to their highest-valued use. Moreover, auctions capture for the government and the public the rents that previously went as gifts to the selected applicants. The 1995 auction for spectrum licenses suitable for personal communications systems attracted 70 bidders and raised $7 billion for the federal Treasury—$7 billion that under the previous system would have been a windfall gain to those receiving the licenses.

The FCC continued to use auctions to allocate the radio spectrum. A 1996 auction restricted to small bidders for a 30-MHz block of the broadcast spectrum generated $10.2 billion in proceeds. The 2008 spectrum auction discussed in Chapter 2 generated $19.6 billion. Cramton (1997) provided a detailed analysis of the first four FCC auctions and concluded that they were well designed and effective in both allocating the spectrum efficiently and in extracting the rents from bidders and to the public treasury.[38] Other countries began to use auctions to allocate licenses. In Europe spectrum auctions brought in over $100 billion, but overbidding weakened many of the successful bidders.

SUMMARY

Government regulation has a long history in the United States, beginning in the populist era, expanding during the New Deal, and taking new directions during the period of social regulation. Although considerable deregulation has occurred, particularly at the federal level, there is still considerable economic regulation in many industries.

The government's right to regulate is unquestioned and broad but limited by due process and the constitutional protections against the taking of property without compensation. Regulation is conducted by commissions and agencies located at both the federal and the state levels. To implement their guiding statutes, regulatory agencies issue rules through formal and informal procedures.

Regulatory commissions and agencies are embedded in a complex institutional environment. They are influenced by the executive branch, Congress, private interests, and the courts. The president has considerable influence through both the appointment process and the policies advocated by executive branch agencies. Agencies have a considerable range of discretion, which allows the president to influence regulation. In addition to writing the authorizing statutes for a regulatory agency, Congress controls the agency's budget and has oversight responsibility. Private interests affect regulatory agencies directly through testimony and lobbying and through their influence with Congress and the executive branch. The nature and scope of regulation are also shaped by the courts, which review statutes, policies, and individual rules in response to lawsuits filed by private parties.

Regulation is provided in response to both market imperfections and nonmarket forces. Market imperfections include natural monopoly, externalities, public goods, asymmetric information, and moral hazard. One role of regulation is to correct these market imperfections, but regulation itself is imperfect and could be worse than the imperfection it is intended to correct. In some cases regulation is intended to protect incumbent firms and in other cases to redistribute income or provide fairness. The political economy perspective on the locus and form of regulation emphasizes the role of private interests in shaping regulation. Institutions and the regulatory agencies themselves have an important impact, and regulators at the federal level have actively worked for deregulation in the airline, electric power, natural gas transmission, surface transportation, and telecommunications industries.

---

[38]See the special issue of the *Journal of Economics & Management Strategy*, Vol. 6, Fall 1997, for additional analysis of auctions for spectrum allocations.

--- C A S E S ---
The FCC and Broadband Regulation

Broadband deployment is the central communications policy objective in America today.

—Michael Powell, FCC Chairman

Broadband should be a national imperative for this country in the 21st century, just like putting a man on the moon was an imperative in the last century. To stay competitive, educate the workforce and increase productivity, the United States must have ubiquitous broadband.

—John Chambers, President and CEO of Cisco Systems

Introduction

The Telecommunications Act of 1996 provided a structure for the deregulation of the telecommunications industry from long distance to local service. The Act allowed the remaining regional Bell operating companies, referred to as incumbent local exchange carriers (ILECs), to provide interstate long-distance service once their local service areas were open to competition from other carriers, including AT&T, MCI, and Sprint, as well as from resellers. Verizon was the first ILEC to offer long-distance service, and within 2 years it had become the third largest provider. The Act delegated authority to the Federal Communications Commission (FCC) to spur local competition by requiring the ILECs to provide access to their network by providing unbundled network elements (UNEs) to competing carriers. Some 300 companies, referred to as competitive local exchange carriers (CLECs), began to offer telecommunications services, including broadband. Some built their own fiber optics networks but most leased UNEs from the ILECs and rebundled them to provide UNE-Platforms (UNE-Ps) for their services. UNE-Ps were used by the CLECs for both voice and DSL broadband service. Although voice was by far the bigger revenue source, broadband was crucial to many business opportunities.

The CLECs included not only newly formed companies such as DSL providers NorthPoint and Rhythms NetConnections but also AT&T, MCI, and Sprint. The CLECs were able to compete against the ILECs because they leased the UNEs at theoretically calculated costs referred to as TELRIC prices. In addition, some state regulatory commissions ordered discounts of up to 50 percent from those prices. The ILECs referred to this as false competition and argued that the UNE discount eliminated their incentives to invest in new facilities. Under current regulations any upgraded DSL equipment and technology would have to be made available to CLECs at the prices set by state regulatory commissions.

During the late 1990s the telecommunications industry embarked on an aggressive build out of fiber optics capacity based on what turned out to be major overestimates of demand. The telecommunications meltdown left many of the CLECs bankrupt and the ILECs in precarious financial conditions.

Internet broadband service was provided by ILECs and CLECs through the DSL technology and by cable companies using cable television lines. Cable modem service was available nearly 2 years before DSL service was offered, and cable had captured two-thirds of the broadband market. The ILECs claimed that the false competition dampened their incentives to the point that they had little reason to expand their DSL capacity. Moreover, in March 2002 the FCC declared that cable modem service was an information service, so cable companies were not required to share their facilities or provide open access for competing carriers and ISPs.

President Bush appointed Michael Powell as chairman of the FCC, and Republicans became a majority on the Commission. In 2002 the FCC began its Triennial Review of the UNE requirement for both voice and broadband services. The FCC was required to make its decision by February 20, 2003.

The Federal Communications Commission

The five FCC commissioners were three Republicans—Kathleen Abernathy, Kevin Martin, and Michael Powell—and two Democrats—Jonathan Adelstein and Michael Copps. The FCC made decisions using majority rule.

Chairman Powell advocated quick deregulation of voice and broadband services and argued that deregulation should not be "a reward for competition" but instead should be an instrument to spur competition. In particular, he wanted to stimulate new investments in digital technology.

In contrast, Commissioner Copps, a liberal Democrat and former aide to Senator Fritz Hollings (D-SC), opposed rapid deregulation and supported a major, continuing role for state public utility commissions (PUCs) in telecommunications regulation. Copps had informally organized the opponents of deregulation in the telecommunications industry.

Commissioner Martin had a position between those of Powell and Copps. Martin had been a senior White House adviser to President Bush. He favored a longer transition to deregulation so that orderly competition could be developed. In a speech on December 12, 2002, Martin stated, "ILECs should receive the benefits of making investments in new infrastructure deployment, but competitors should maintain the ability to receive access to end-user customers at the service capacity levels that they currently receive."[39] He believed in states' rights and advocated devolving regulatory responsibility to state regulatory commissions where possible.

Commissioner Abernathy had served as a staff member in the FCC and as legal advisor to former FCC chairman James Quello. In the private sector she had practiced law and served as vice president of AirTouch Communications, U.S. West, and BroadBand Office Communications.

Commissioner Adelstein had been a Senate committee staff member and aide to Senator Tom Daschle (D-SD). He joined the Commission in December 2002.

The FCC UNE Triennial Review

In 1996 the FCC had ordered the unbundling of seven network elements. In response to a U.S. Supreme Court decision, in 1999 the FCC reconsidered the unbundling decision and required that six elements be unbundled:[40]

1. Loops, including loops used to provide high-capacity and advanced telecommunications services
2. Network interface devices
3. Local circuit switching (except for large customers in major urban markets)
4. Dedicated and shared transport
5. Signaling and call-related databases
6. Operations support systems

The DC Circuit Court of Appeals overturned the 1999 FCC decision and ordered that the UNE Triennial Review be more "fine-grained" and "identify more precisely how incumbent local-exchange carriers must provide competitors access to their ubiquitous networks."[41] On December 12, 2001, the FCC issued a Notice of Proposed Rule Making (NPRM) with the principal objective of determining how to apply the statutory standards, as well as whether and how the Commission should take into account other goals of the Act, such as encouraging broadband deployment, investment in facilities, and technological innovation. The NPRM requested comments on whether new facilities should be exempt from the unbundling requirement and whether certain facilities, such as fiber-optic cable, with advanced telecommunications capabilities should be exempted.[42]

Broadband Technology

The principal technologies for residential broadband service were DSL (digital subscriber line) and cable modems. DSL operated at higher frequencies than voice service and came in a variety of flavors. Asymmetric DSL, for example, had a maximum download speed of 1.5 to 8 megabits per second but a maximum upload speed of only 640 kilobits. DSL service was limited because users had to be within three miles of a provider's central switching office. In addition, DSL was costly due to the costs of order taking, installation, and support and maintenance services. DSL service could be provided at substantially higher speeds if fiber ran close to a residence and the copper wire pair to the residence was short. DSL also required dedicated switches in the central office and hence was costly to provide, as was fiber to the curb of residences that were not in high-density locations.

Cable generally operated at a higher speed than DSL and had the capacity to provide the very high-speed service needed for advanced applications.[43] The actual speed at which cable modems operated, however, could be lower because of congestion resulting from many customers using the Internet at the same time. Congestion could be relieved by laying additional fiber-optic cable to a node and increasing switching capacity at the cable system head end, but providing that capacity was costly.

Catch 22: The Broadband/Content Dilemma

Cisco Systems pointed to the existing benefits of broadband, including entertainment, e-learning, national security, teleworking, and telehealth.[44] But the next killer application was over the horizon, and without it many consumers were reluctant to subscribe to broadband service. Without substantial penetration of broadband, many content providers were hesitant to commit the major investments to provide new, innovative services. And, without new, innovative content many consumers were unwilling to pay $40 to $50 or more a month for broadband service. Moreover, the technology to provide some applications was limited by the current speed of DSL and cable modems, which content providers believed prevented them from reaching their capabilities.

"Everyone understands that getting some serious movement in broadband is critical to restoring growth in our industry," said Cisco lobbyist Jeff Campbell. "Right now, the tech sector is in a vicious cycle. Content-rich applications aren't being developed because few people have the high-speed connections needed to use them. Yet, consumers aren't signing up for broadband because of the lack of new applications."[45]

---

[39]Telco Business Report, December 16, 2002.
[40]The Supreme Court had required the FCC to reexamine the "necessary" and "impair" standards of the Act. *AT&T Corp. v. Iowa Utilities Board,* 525 U.S. 366 (1999).
[41]FCC, Notice of Proposed Rulemaking, FCC 01-361. *Verizon Inc. v. FCC,* 122 S.Ct. 1646 (2002).
[42]FCC, Notice of Proposed Rulemaking, FCC 01-361, paragraph 24.

[43]Cable systems used coaxial cable to the customer premises in conjunction with fiber optic trunks.
[44]Cisco's Broadband Primer (www.cisco.com/gov) identified the bandwidth required for various services. For example, movies on demand required from 1 to 7 megabits per second.
[45]*San Jose Mercury News,* November 3, 2002.

Perspectives on Voice and Broadband Regulation and the Triennial Review

ILECs

Commenting on the Telecommunications Act of 1996 and the unbundling requirement, Verizon CEO Ivan G. Seidenberg said, "The deal was we would make our network open to competitors on a nondiscriminatory basis. Nobody ever said we'd give it away at below market prices." The ILECs not only complained about the UNE discounts but also accused the CLECs of cream skimming by entering the most attractive markets and serving the most profitable customers. The ILECs sought to limit the role of state commissions in regulating broadband.

The FCC had set Total Element Long Run Incremental Cost (TELRIC) pricing rules for UNEs, but state PUCs were responsible for specific pricing orders. The ILECs complained that TELRIC understated the cost of capital by failing adequately to take risk into account. In addition, some state commissions had ordered price discounts to stimulate competition from the CLECs to force consumer rates down. "In Massachusetts, the straight 'resale' discount is 29 percent, or 25 percent if competitors use Verizon for operator and directory-assistance services. But competitors can exploit UNE-P to get a 46 percent discount, according to Michael Glover, the Verizon senior vice president and deputy general counsel. On high-end residential and business lines, Glover said, the discount can be as much as 70 percent off Verizon's retail cost."[46]

SBC claimed that UNE discounts forced it to provide 4 million lines below cost, which it said was a major reason it had to lay off 11,000 employees in 2002. The discounts on voice services eroded profits, reducing the funds available to invest in digital and other voice capacity, and the discounts on UNEs for broadband service dampened incentives to invest in DSL capacity. SBC's senior vice president for the FCC explained, "The wholesale business is important to us—we'd rather have competitors use our lines. We are willing to offer our network to competitors as long as the prices are compensatory."

One objective of the ILECs was to eliminate the UNE requirement on new fiber optics facilities and UNE capacity. "For the old wire, old rules should apply. For any new fiber that's laid, the new rules should apply," said Business Software Alliance president Robert Holleyman.[47]

CLECs

CLECs served approximately 11 percent of the switched telephone lines. Some 11.9 million lines were provided by CLECs that used none of their own facilities, and an additional 4 million were provided by CLECs that used a combination of owned facilities and UNEs. All CLECs used the "last mile"—the ILEC copper wire twisted-pair connection to a customer premise. Some CLECs provided their own switching, whereas others leased switching capacity from the ILECs. Some CLECs argued that their use of UNEs was a temporary step leading to their own facilities build out. Developing their own facilities would free them from their dependence on the ILECs, but all CLECs sought to preserve access to the last mile. The CLECs were represented by the Competitive Telecommunications Association (CompTel) and the Association for Local Telecommunications Services (ALTS).

The number of CLECs had fallen from 300 to approximately 70, according to ALTS. A number of CLECs, such as NorthPoint Communications and Winstar Communications, had attempted to build their own fiber-optics networks but had gone out of business.[48] Covad Communications had emerged from Chapter 11 bankruptcy and was a major DSL provider. Covad relied on line sharing, access to the unused high-frequency band on the copper pair to the customer premises, for its services.

In response to the ILECs' attempts to convince the FCC to eliminate the current UNE discounts, MCI Mass Markets president Wayne Huyard wrote to the 50 state utility commissions asserting that the ILEC efforts were "characterized by threats, distortion and political manipulation. . . . It's classic monopolistic maneuvering. Pressure regulators to change the rules, eliminate the competition, and re-monopolize the market."[49]

A number of smaller CLECs formed PACE (Promoting Active Competition Everywhere) to support access to UNE-P. CEOs of the participating companies set out for Washington in January 2003 to carry their message to the FCC and the Bush administration.

CLECs, CompTel, and PACE urged the FCC to maintain a major role for state regulatory commissions in promoting local competition based on UNEs. The group wrote, "In the *Triennial Review,* the Commission must . . . conduct a refined and fact-specific analysis of factors previously identified by the Commission. Most, if not all, of these factors are highly fact-specific and may vary from geographic region to geographic region, and accordingly, state commissions are, no doubt, best situated to conduct these analyses."[50]

Cable Companies

The largest multiservice operator (MSO) was Comcast, which acquired AT&T Broadband in November 2002. Comcast had 21.6 million subscribers, followed by Time Warner Cable with 10.9 million subscribers and Charter Communications, Cox Communications, and Adelphia Communications with approximately 6 million each. The

[46]*Boston Globe,* October 14, 2002.
[47]*San Jose Mercury News,* November 3, 2002.
[48]Some commentators believed these companies were victims of unfair squeeze tactics by the ILECs.
[49]*Rocky Mountain News,* October 18, 2002.
[50]Ex parte letter, www.comptel.org/press/oct24_2002.html.

25 largest MSOs served over 63 million cable television subscribers. In addition to cable television the MSOs provided broadband cable modem service to over 9 million subscribers. Compared to cable television service, broadband did not require paying for content, as with television programming. Brian Roberts, CEO of Comcast, explained that subscribers were "sending Comcast about $45 a month without significant programming costs."[51] The cable industry was represented by the National Cable Television Association (NCTA).

Because of the FCC ruling that cable access to the Internet was an information service, cable broadband services were not subject to the UNE requirements. The ILECs complained that this gave the cable companies an unfair competitive advantage and diminished their incentives to expand their broadband facilities. The cable companies countered by arguing that over half the new customers dropped their second telephone line when they subscribed to broadband service, which explained why ILECs had been slow to deploy DSL.

Equipment Suppliers and High-Tech Companies

High-tech equipment suppliers wanted rapid expansion of broadband service and competition between DSL and cable modem broadband. In November, CEOs of companies in the High Tech Broadband Coalition (HTBC) held a press conference prior to calling on FCC commissioners and National Telecommunications and Information Administration (NTIA) officials.[52] The CEOs argued that the UNE requirement discouraged the ILECs from expanding their broadband networks and that renewed capital expenditures for broadband deployment were essential for generating the demand for the next generation of Internet services. Cisco Systems commissioned a broadband study, "Customers at the Gate: Mounting Demand for Broadband-enabled Services," based on a survey of U.S. households. The report concluded that even the most conservative estimates put the demand for Internet-delivered services for the home at $25 billion a year.

Equipment suppliers had been hurt by the slump in the telecommunications industry. Catena Networks CEO Jim Hjartarson pointed to the dramatic drop in equipment demand. He said that Catena had laid off 55 percent of its employees and that "North America's technical prowess is being jeopardized."[53] Michael Norris, CEO of NextLevel Communications, which had laid off 70 percent of its staff, said, "We're losing a great resource. I don't come to Washington often but the issues here are incredibly important."

Consumer and Activist Groups

The American Civil Liberties Union, the Center for Digital Democracy, and the Consumer Federation of America argued that the threat of only a few monopoly Internet service providers meant that the FCC should require cable and telecommunications companies to allow other Internet service providers, such as EarthLink and United Online, onto their systems. Companies including Amazon.com and Microsoft were concerned about the control of content availability. Content providers were concerned that the cable companies would increase their share of the broadband market and become monopoly gatekeepers to the Internet and a bottleneck to the provision of content and variety. The consumer groups and the concerned companies advocated "open access" to cable systems.

In November representatives of the Media Access Project, ABC Disney, and other content providers met with commissioner Abernathy seeking a "nondiscrimination" rule that would allow broadband users to connect to any Web site of their choosing. "[Y]our electric company doesn't care if you use their service to hook up a hair dryer or a sex toy. Your Internet service should not be able to control where you go, either," said Andrew Schwartzman, head of the Media Access Project.[54]

The Media Access Project and the Alliance for Community Media joined with companies including Microsoft, eBay, Apple, RadioShack, Disney, and Yahoo! to form the Coalition of Broadband Users and Innovators. The coalition urged the FCC to "ensure that transmission network operators do not encumber relationships between their customers and destinations on the network." The coalition was concerned that broadband network operators would impose restrictions that would inhibit "innovative content, services, and devices on the broadband network."[55]

State regulators were also concerned about possible FCC actions. The National Association of Regulatory Utility Commissioners (NARUC) weighed in by meeting with FCC commissioner Martin to urge him to stop major changes in the regulatory system and preserve their role in setting discounts for competitive carriers.

The Competitive Landscape in Broadband

High-speed Internet connections by cable or DSL were estimated to be available to approximately 70 percent of U.S. households, but only 17 percent had subscribed. According to Morgan Stanley, cable served 11.7 million households and telecommunications companies served 6.4 million. Broadband subscriptions were projected by InStat/MDR to increase by 38 percent in 2003, 23 percent in 2004, and less than 20 percent in 2005.

[51]*Wall Street Journal*, January 8, 2003.
[52]The HTBC was formed in April 2002 by six trade associations: the Business Software Alliance, Consumer Electronics Association (CEA), Information Technology Industry Council, National Association of Manufacturers, Semiconductor Industry Association, and Telecommunications Industry Association (TIA).
[53]Washington Telecom Newsletter, November 14, 2002.

[54]Cable World, November 25, 2002.
[55]Coalition of Broadband Users and Innovators, press release, November 18, 2002.

The competitive situation in telecommunications was that CLECs leased UNEs at discount rates and resold those lines to customers in competition with the ILECs. Herschel Abbott of BellSouth referred to it as "false competition." Chairman Powell also viewed the current system as not providing real competition. Real competition required rival networks, he argued. CLECs, however, could not be expected to build their own networks quickly, since the estimate for the capital required for each telephone line was $2,000, or $360 billion for the nation. Fiber optic cable to the curb or home would be costly.

The "false competition" had several effects. First, the ability to obtain lines at discounted rates enabled AT&T and WorldCom to enter the local service voice telecommunications market and garner an 11 percent share. For those companies local service was viewed as more prof-itable than long-distance service. Second, prices for local service had been pushed down, benefiting consumers and pleasing state regulators. Moreover, some state regulators had increased the UNE discounts to encourage competition. Third, consumers were being offered a greater variety of plans.

The elimination of UNE discounts could have a dramatic effect on the industry. As AT&T vice president Len Cali said, "Without the wholesale rates, this is an unsustainable business."[56] Doug Allen, writing in *Network Magazine*, argued that without the discounts the interexchange carriers (AT&T, Sprint, MCI) were "business-wise, toast" and that most CLECs that resold services were "dead."[57] ■

Preparation Questions

1. Are there any market imperfections in broadband that require correction through regulation?
2. What are the likely consequences in the voice and broadband marketplaces of reducing the set of network elements that must be unbundled?
3. What are the likely consequences of requiring "just and reasonable" rates for UNEs?
4. As an equipment manufacturer such as Cisco Systems, what would you urge the FCC to do with regard to UNEs and broadband?
5. What are the principal dimensions of disagreement among the interests?
6. What theory could be used to predict the likely FCC decision on UNEs and broadband?
7. What strategies should the ILECs, CLECs, and cable companies use to advance their perspectives before the FCC?

[56]*Wall Street Journal,* January 6, 2003.
[57]*Network Magazine,* November 1, 2002.

Enron Power Marketing, Inc., and the California Market

Using names such as Death Star, Get Shorty, Fat Boy, and Ricochet, Enron Power Marketing (EPM) deployed an array of electricity trading strategies to take advantage of imperfections in the design of the market for power in California. In a December 2000 memorandum an outside lawyer and an EPM lawyer reminded the company that the California market rules prohibited "gaming" the trading system and warned that penalties could include "fines and suspension" and actions by "the appropriate regulatory or antitrust enforcement agency."[58] In late April 2002 that memorandum and a later memorandum by lawyers engaged by Enron were discovered.[59] The Enron board of directors waived at-torney-client privileges and confidentiality rights and turned the memos over to the Federal Energy Regulatory Commission (FERC).[60] An Enron attorney said that it was "the responsible and honest thing" to do. FERC chairman Patrick Wood decided to make the memoranda public, stating, "We have to try to get to the bottom of this and tell the truth. If the capital markets perceive that regulators and customers and elected officials and everybody else are getting comfortable with understanding what went on in California, then you can restore confidence."[61]

Deregulation in the electricity market required establishing a market in which buyers and sellers could trade electricity on a continuous basis.[62] Markets for a nonstorable good such as electricity must be designed

[58]Memorandum from Christian Yoder of EPM and Stephen Hall, Stoel Rivers LLP, December 8, 2000.
[59]Memorandum from Gary Fergus (Brobeck, Phleger & Harrison, LLP) and Jean Frizzell (Gibbs & Bruns LLP), no date. The two memoranda were available at www.ferc.gov. The lawyers engaged by Enron reviewed the December memorandum and met with traders to discuss the strategies described. They concluded that some of the information in the December memorandum was incorrect. Both memoranda stated that other traders used some of the same strategies.

[60]In 2002 EPM and its trading technology were sold to UBS Warburg, a unit of UBS AG of Switzerland. Six hundred thirty-five employees moved from Enron to UBS.
[61]*New York Times,* May 12, 2002.
[62]The development of the wholesale electricity market was spurred by the Energy Policy Act of 1992.

and regularized to allow supply and demand to be equilibrated almost minute by minute. One of the largest markets was established in California, where large customers were allowed to purchase electricity from any supplier. The efficiency of such markets can be improved by traders who act as middlemen between electricity producers and customers. EPM, Dynegy, El Paso, Reliant Resources, Duke Power, American Electric Power, Williams, and a number of other companies traded power. In 2000 EPM had an estimated 13.0 percent of the U.S. wholesale electricity market, and the next largest share was 8.9 percent.[63] Enron was believed to have had a significantly larger share of the California market.

No new electricity generation capacity had been built in California during the 1990s, and strong economic growth caused the state to import electricity from other states and Canada, particularly during peak periods. With reserve capacity in California below the minimum needed to ensure that demand could be met, the system was at risk. When a drought in the northwest reduced the power generated by hydroelectric facilities, the California market faced shortages and much higher wholesale prices. Despite the increases in wholesale power prices, the regulated retail prices remained fixed.[64]

The state's energy system and the market for electricity were coordinated by the Independent Service Organization (ISO), which operated the state's power grid. The power grid had a limited capacity, since no new transmission capacity had been built in many years. Moreover, the system had bottlenecks that limited the amount of power that could be moved between the north and south of the state.

The ISO was responsible for ensuring that California's power needs would be met. The ISO attempted to forecast demand and supply and balance the system both in real time and in advance. A trader that contracted to supply large retail customers such as manufacturing plants submitted a daily "schedule" of deliveries for the day-ahead market, and the ISO checked whether there was both a buyer and a seller for each megawatt before scheduling its transmission across the state's power lines.

EPM's "inc-ing" strategy involved overscheduling power deliveries to Enron Energy Services, Enron's retail unit, which contracted with large retail customers. The overscheduling led the ISO to anticipate higher demand and to plan to buy power the next day. Often those purchases were from Enron at high prices. An EPM trader referred to this as the "oldest trick in the books." Enron was in effect speculating based on its forecasts of demand, scheduled power generation, and the ISO's

predicted behavior, which was influenced by EPM's scheduling. According to the second memorandum, this strategy offset the practice of independently owned utilities that regularly underestimated their load (demand for their power). In addition to trading on its own account, EPM served as "scheduling coordinator" for other companies. Two power suppliers allegedly involved in the generation side of this practice were Puget Sound Electric and Powerex, a unit of BC Hydro of Canada. Both companies denied having violated either ISO or FERC rules. EPM's strategy was believed to be legal and, according to an ISO official, consistent with the ISO rules at the time. California politicians charged that the companies using this strategy reaped billions of dollars of profits from the California market.

The Get Shorty strategy took advantage of the ISO's policy of maintaining reserve capacity to handle unexpected surges in demand. The ISO referred to this reserve generating capacity as "ancillary services," and power generators were paid to maintain idle capacity that could be switched on at short notice. EPM used a strategy of shorting the ancillary services and then covering them the next morning at a lower price. This speculation was not always successful, since on at least one occasion the ISO asked EPM to deliver ancillary services it had shorted but failed to cover. The December memorandum stated, "This strategy might be characterized as 'paper trading' because the seller does not actually have the services to sell. . . . As a consequence, in order to short the ancillary services, it is necessary to submit false information that purports to identify the source of the ancillary services."

In the Death Star strategy, EPM profited by relieving congestion in the power grid for deliveries between the north and south of the state. The ISO relieved congestion by paying power suppliers to reduce their deliveries on the congested part of the grid and sell their power elsewhere. EPM would overschedule power to be delivered, knowing that the ISO would not be able to determine whether there were actual users for the power. Since the power grid appeared to be overloaded, the ISO would pay power suppliers, including EPM, to relieve congestion by selling their power elsewhere, such as out of the state.

In its "load shift" strategy EPM overscheduled supply into a congested area and underscheduled power into an uncongested area. EPM then would "reduce" deliveries into the congested area, receiving congestion relief payments, and "increase" deliveries in the uncongested area. In this practice EPM did not have to actually contract for the power, and even if it had contracted for the power, it could sell the power at a loss and still profit. The December memorandum stated, "Because the congestion [relief] charges have been as high as $750 per megawatt-hour, it can often be profitable to sell power at a loss simply to be able to collect the congestion payment."

EPM also took advantage of a price cap imposed by California regulators to prevent price spikes due to shortages. The normal price for electricity was $30 to $40

[63]"Report on EnronOnline," FERC, May 16, 2002.
[64]Pacific Gas & Electric (PG&E) went bankrupt by buying power at wholesale prices with its customers paying at the fixed retail rate. When it filed for bankruptcy, PG&E was estimated to owe Enron $500 million.

a megawatt-hour, but price spikes of as high a $1,200 occurred in 2000 and in the spring of 2001 as the ISO desperately sought to obtain power. The price cap of $250, however, covered only California. During a price spike EPM could buy power at $250 in California, export it from the state, and sell it at a higher price. EPM referred to this as arbitrage. The December memorandum stated that this "appears not to present any problems, other than a public relations risk arising from the fact that such exports may have contributed to California's declaration of a Stage 2 Emergency yesterday."

Ricochet trades, or "megawatt laundering," involved completing the arbitrage opportunity by reselling the exported electricity back to the ISO, which was unconstrained in the price it could pay for imported power. In a Ricochet trade EPM would buy power at the $250 price cap during a price spike and sell the power to a party outside the state. That party would charge a small fee, and resell the power to EPM. EPM then would sell the power to the ISO at prices as high as $1,200. Ricochet trading involved other parties often without their knowledge of the nature of the trade. Portland General Electric (PGE), a unit of Enron, Inc., reported that it had participated in a trade in which EPM sold power to a third party, which sold it to PGE, which then sold it to EPM. In June 2001 FERC imposed a price cap of $250 throughout the Western states, ending this arbitrage opportunity.

The December memorandum indicated that some of EPM's trading practices were "potentially criminal," and EPM reportedly halted the practices in December 2000. During the first several months of 2001 electricity prices in California continued to increase and shortages

resulted in rolling blackouts and wholesale price spikes. To alleviate the energy crisis, or because he panicked as his critics contended, Governor Gray Davis committed $43 billion of state funds to buy power under long-term contracts at prices substantially above normal market prices. The energy crisis in California abated during the summer 2001 due to below normal temperatures, lower natural gas prices, and new generating capacity coming on line. The governor subsequently sought to renegotiate the contracts and obtain refunds from energy traders.

After the revelation of the two memoranda Senator Diane Feinstein (D-CA) wrote to U.S. Attorney General John Ashcroft asking for a criminal investigation of Enron's trading practices. She wrote that the memos from the Enron lawyers "indicate that Enron was not only manipulating prices in the West, but also engaged in a number of calculated strategies . . . to either receive payment for energy not delivered or increase price. In my book, this is outright fraud."[65]

R. Martin Chavez, CEO of Kiodex, an energy risk management company, said, "Energy trading is a football game; it ain't bridge. If you want a nice game because electricity is an important public good, then set up a nice game."[66] Recalling his days as head of energy risk management at Goldman Sachs, he said, "The whole reason for the existence of traders is to make as much money as possible, consistent with what's legal. I lived through this: If you didn't manipulate the market and manipulation was accessible to you, that's when you were yelled at."[67] ■

Preparation Questions

1. Was EPM doing anything wrong in its trading strategies? Was this not just taking advantage of opportunities available in the market?
2. What were the flaws in the California market design?
3. Were EPM's strategies different from the types of strategies used on Wall Street?
4. How should Enron have conducted its trading business?

---

[65]*Wall Street Journal,* May 8, 2002.
[66]*New York Times,* May 12, 2002.
[67]*New York Times,* May 8, 2002.

The FCC Media Ownership Rules

Media ownership had been regulated for decades, but in a little-noticed section of the Telecommunications Act of 1996 Congress required the Federal Communications Commission (FCC) to review the justifications for its regulations every 2 years. In addition, the D.C. Court of Appeals had remanded several FCC decisions requiring better justifications for its rulings and orders.[68] In the

Fox decision the court stated, "Section 202(h) carries with it a presumption in favor of repealing or modifying the ownership rules. . . . [T]he Commission may retain a rule only if it reasonably determines that the rule is 'necessary in the public interest.'" The FCC emphasized "diversity, location, and competition," and its restrictions on media ownership were justified by concerns that viewpoints could be restricted by dominant companies and that a diversity of views should be encouraged.

As required by the Telecommunications Act, the FCC issued a Notice of Proposed Rule Making (NPRM)

---

[68]*Sinclair Broadcasting Group, Inc. v. FCC,* 284 F.3d 148, 168–69 (D.C. Cir. 2002) and *Fox Television Stations, Inc. v. FCC,* 280 F.3d 1027, 1048 (D.C. Cir. 2002).

in 2001 on two broadcast ownership rules—the Broadcast-Newspaper Cross-Ownership Rule and the Local Radio Ownership Rule. In September 2002 the Commission issued a NPRM for the biennial review required by the Telecommunications Act. The review included the Television-Radio Cross-Ownership Rule, the Dual Network Rule, the Local Television Multiple Ownership Rule, and the National Television Ownership Rule. The focus of this case is the National Television Ownership Rule and the Local Television Multiple Ownership Rule.

The FCC

The five FCC commissioners were three Republicans—Kathleen Abernathy, Kevin Martin, and Michael Powell—and two Democrats—Jonathan Adelstein and Michael Copps. The FCC made its decisions using majority rule.

FCC chairman Powell expressed three objectives for the Commission's review of the media ownership rules. The first was to promote "diversity, localism, and competition" in the broadcast media and to do so in a manner that would withstand court scrutiny. Diversity referred to the number of "voices" available to the public. Localism referred to the local ownership of media organizations, which was valued because it promoted local programming. Competition was the preferred means of promoting progress in the media. The second was to recognize "the explosion of new media outlets for news information and entertainment." The third was to formulate rules that would allow ownership changes "while ensuring that no company can monopolize the medium."[69] The FCC scheduled a vote on revised media ownership rules for June 2, 2003. Three weeks before the scheduled vote, Powell circulated a draft set of rules.

Powell contended that free broadcast television was in jeopardy from cable and satellite TV. He and Commissioner Martin argued that the economics of the news business had changed and that the traditional concern with providing a diverse set of views was of less concern now due to the rise of cable and satellite systems and the Internet. Martin was viewed as the strongest supporter of media ownership deregulation among the commissioners.

Commissioners Copps and Adelstein argued that there was little evidence that mergers led to better or expanded news programming. As a result of the Telecommunications Act the FCC had relaxed rules on radio ownership, and Copps argued that the number of station owners had decreased by 34 percent as a result of the change and the number of minority owners had decreased by 14 percent. Michael Bracy of the Future of Music Coalition said, "Radio clearly is the coal mine canary" and claimed that radio listeners had declined to the lowest level in the past 27 years.[70] Adelstein

commented, "Radio is a very sick canary in the coal mine, and we're about to infect television with the same disease." Copps pointed to Clear Channel Communication, which owned 1,200 radio stations, and criticized it for its homogenized programming.[71] Andrew Levin of Clear Channel responded, "Deregulation revived local radio."

The Media Ownership Rules

The National Television Ownership Rule prohibited a company from owning television stations that reached more than 35 percent of the national audience.[72] However, as a result of acquisitions that the FCC was unable to block because of court decisions, both CBS, a unit of Viacom, and Fox, a unit of the News Corporation, owned stations reaching 39 percent of the households. The FCC reported that of the 1,340 commercial stations Viacom owned 39, Fox 37, NBC 29, and ABC 10. Powell had initially questioned whether any cap was required, given the growth in cable systems and the Internet as sources of news. The networks sought a much higher cap and expected to benefit by attracting more advertising and having greater power in buying programming. Jay Ireland, president of the NBC television stations, said, "To leave these rules in place would subject television broadcasters to unfair and burdensome constraints that prevent them from competing against other forms of media."[73]

Local affiliates strongly opposed relaxation of the regulation, fearing that greater size would increase the power of the networks. Independent programmers also opposed relaxation of the rule. They had been hurt by changes in 1996 that allowed the networks to produce their own programming, and relaxation of the 35 percent rule would give the networks greater control over programming. Affiliated stations not owned by the networks also opposed relaxation so as to preserve their independence.

Powell's draft would raise the cap to 45 percent and retain the UHF viewer rule, which for the purposes of the National Television Ownership Rule counted two viewers of UHF stations as one viewer. The UHF "discount" allowed media companies to reach more than 35 percent of the national audience. Powell argued that the UHF discount had spurred the growth of new networks, such as UPN (owned by Viacom), Paxson Communications (32 percent owned by NBC), WB (owned by AOL Time Warner), and Fox.

Since almost all UHF viewers received their signal by cable, there was little reason to continue the discount, according to Commissioner Copps. Gene Kimmelman of the Consumers Union referred to the UHF discount as "total hypocrisy" and said, "If the theory

---

[69]*New York Times,* June 3, 2003.
[70]*New York Times,* May 28, 2003.

[71]The United States had approximately 10,800 commercial radio stations.
[72]The 35 percent limit was based on potential rather than actual viewers; i.e., on the number of people who could watch a channel.
[73]*Seattle Times,* February 28, 2003.

behind changing the rules is that the FCC needs to keep up with market conditions, to preserve a significant discount for UHF stations is simply a fraud on the regulatory process." Andrew Schwartzman, head of the Media Action Project, said that the UHF discount "eviscerates the cap."[74]

The Local Television Multiple Ownership Rule pertained to the ownership of television stations in local markets and was based on the "eight-voices test." Before a company could own two stations in a local market, eight separate voices (television stations) were required. The networks would benefit from relaxation of the eight-voices rule, as would media companies such as the Tribune Company, Gannett, Belo, E.W. Scripps, and Sinclair Broadcasting.[75] The FCC's eight-voices test effectively precluded a duopoly in small markets, but television stations in small markets argued that they could provide better news coverage if they were allowed to merge. Moreover, consolidation would ease the burden of providing digital broadcast capability for HDTV as the FCC required by 2007. A digital antenna capable of transmitting HDTV signals cost between $3 and $5 million. Powell's draft would allow a company to own two stations in a market with at least five stations and three in a market with at least 18 stations, provided that only one was among the four largest. In markets with 11 or more stations, the FCC would consider on a case-by-case basis the merger of two of the top four stations.

Perspectives and Preferences

The disagreement between the Republican and the Democrat commissioners resulted from a difference in perspectives. The Democrats focused on the fear of greater media concentration and the corresponding reduction in the diversity of views available to the public. The Republicans focused on the increase in the number of media outlets over the past 50 years, the emergence of cable and the Internet as sources of news and entertainment, and the lack of evidence that mergers and the growth of media conglomerates had resulted in any harm to the public. Commenting on the predominance of the networks in prime time, Abernathy said, "Four companies air the programming that is chosen by approximately 75 percent of viewers during prime time. To me, the critical fact is that these providers control no more than 25 percent of the broadcast and cable channels in the average home, even apart from the Internet and other pipelines. Given these other viewing options, I can only presume that this means that Americans are watching these providers because they prefer their content, not because they lack alternatives."[76]

Commissioner Martin commented,

I recall having extremely limited choices on our family television set when I was growing up. There was no cable. There was no satellite. Even with our roof antenna, we received just five channels—the three major networks, one independent, and one public television station. . . .

While my parents still live in the same house, they now have access to seven broadcast networks, hundreds of digital cable channels (including a local cable news channel), many more radio stations, and thousands of sites on the Internet. Indeed, people today have access to more information from more diverse sources than at any time in our history.

Commissioner Abernathy chided the Democrats for focusing on "fear and speculation about hypothetical media monopolies." She argued that with "the breakneck pace of technological development, and the ever-increasing number of pipelines into consumers' homes, it is simply not possible to monopolize the flow of information in today's world. Indeed, the fall of Communism in the 1980s and of military dictatorships in the 1990s shows that diverse viewpoints cannot be suppressed even by authoritarian governments, much less by private media companies."[77]

To build public opposition to changes in the media ownership rules, commissioners Copps and Adelstein held hearings around the country to provide a forum where critics could voice their opposition.[78] Copps argued that diversity had not increased despite the increase in the number of media sources. He claimed that 90 percent of the leading cable channels were owned by the companies that owned the major networks and the cable systems. A Nielsen survey revealed that 80 percent of Americans obtained their news from television or newspapers and only 6 percent from the Internet. Moreover, the 20 most-visited Internet news sites were owned by 16 large media companies, and the top five sites had more visits than the next 15.

The organized opponents of possible changes in the media ownership rules included the National Organization of Women (NOW), Leadership Conference on Civil Rights, Writers Guild of America, United States Conference of Catholic Bishops, Parent Teachers Association, and National Rifle Association (NRA). The critics warned of media monopolies that could control the information the public received. Wade Henderson of the Leadership Conference said, "Diversity of voices, not merely the variety of programming, is what matters."[79]

---

[74] *New York Times,* May 13, 2003.
[75] *New York Times,* May 11, 2003.
[76] Separate Statement of Commissioner Kathleen Q. Abernathy, June 2, 2003.

[77] Separate Statement of Commissioner Kathleen Q. Abernathy, June 2, 2003.
[78] They held over a dozen hearings but had to fund the hearings from their own office budgets because the FCC provided funding for only one hearing outside Washington.
[79] *New York Times,* May 28, 2003.

NOW organized a protest outside the FCC building demanding that it "halt further media consolidation and act to preserve the openness and diversity of the Internet." The FCC hearings attracted 750,000 communications, by far the largest number ever received by the FCC.

The NRA opposed revisions in the ownership rules for quite different reasons. It opposed allowing the large media companies to become larger, since those companies were opposed to the right to bear arms. The NRA message to its 4 million members was that the "gun-hating media giants like AOL Time Warner, Viacom/CBS and Disney/ABC . . . could literally silence your NRA and prevent us from communicating with your fellow Americans by refusing to sells us television, radio or newspaper advertising at any price."[80] Nearly half the 750,000 communications were generated by the NRA.[81]

The opposition on the left was led by advocacy and activist groups. MoveOn.org, Common Cause, and the Free Press financed television and newspaper advertisements criticizing any relaxation of the rules. Some of the ads showed the face of Rupert Murdock, head of the News Corporation, with the caption "This Man Wants to Control the News in America. The FCC Wants to Help Him."

The opposition to relaxation of the ownership rules was informally coordinated by four people. Gene Kimmelman of the Consumers Union focused on building support in Congress for legislation to preserve the 35 percent cap. Andrew Schwartzman of the Media Access Project focused on lobbying the FCC. Mark Cooper, research director of the Consumer Federation of America, provided economic analysis on the extent of diversity in media markets. Jeff Chester of the Center for Digital Democracy focused on providing information to the news media.

In a joint press release by the Consumers Union and the Consumer Federation of America, Cooper stated, "Encouraging further concentration by relaxing the current rules on media ownership, . . . would reduce the prospects of competition in local markets, diminish the provision of local news and information and limit the diversity of local perspectives." Kimmelman said, "Merging the dominant local newspaper with a major local TV station is dangerous to our democracy because it combines the key watchdogs who keep an eye on each other, and point out each other's abuses in the market or in their reporting."[82]

The Center for Digital Democracy joined with the Writers Guild of America and independent producers to protest the impending FCC decision. Award-winning writers and producers urged Senators John McCain (R-AZ) and Fritz Hollings (D-SC), chair and ranking minority member, respectively, of the Commerce Committee, to stop the FCC from relaxing the media ownership rules. Norman Lear wrote, "We built these companies in the seventies and eighties under the watchful eye of an FCC that was committed to keeping the playing field even, protecting against the vertical integration of the major broadcasting networks that would, if they had been allowed, have forced independent companies such as ours to take a minority interest in the very shows we had created, giving majority ownership to the network in order to get on the air."[83]

The supporters of relaxation of the media ownership rules were generally well-organized industry groups with aligned preferences. In the case of the National Media Ownership Rule, however, the networks were pitted against their local affiliate stations. On the other rules the media companies were aligned, well organized, and represented by high-powered lobbying firms. The broadcast companies reportedly had 70 meetings with FCC officials, whereas public interest groups had only five meetings.[84]

Congressional Action

As details of Powell's draft were revealed, members of Congress swung into action. Bills were introduced in both the House and Senate. Senators Hollings and Ted Stevens (R-AK) introduced a bill to preserve the 35 percent cap. Senator Byron Dorgan (D-ND) commented, "There has been galloping concentration in virtually every area of the media industry. It's hard to argue that we need more."[85] Senator McCain had agreed to hold hearings on the bill despite his view that "the FCC was set up to be an independent agency and should be so." Senator Hollings threatened to attach a rider to an appropriations bill to prohibit the FCC from spending funds to implement its decision. The House was believed to be more sympathetic to the FCC's perspective than was the Senate. Representative David R. Obey (D-WI) announced his intention to attach a provision to an appropriations bill to preserve the 35 percent cap. The Bush administration supported the relaxation of the media ownership rules, and the president threatened to veto any measure overturning the FCC decision. Whatever rules the FCC chose were certain to be challenged in the courts.

The proponents of the bills in Congress along with the two Democrat commissioners called for a postponement of the FCC vote so that further consideration could be given to the alternatives. Powell responded, "This isn't like wine. It doesn't get better with age." He refused to postpone the vote. ■

---

[80]Some media organizations refused NRA ads.
[81]Many of the other communications were from an online petition circulated by MoveOn.org.
[82]Joint press release, May 12, 2003.

[83]Center for Digital Democracy, May 12, 2003.
[84]The number of meetings was identified in a study by the Center for Public Integrity (*Wall Street Journal,* June 2, 2003).
[85]*Wall Street Journal,* May 14, 2003.

Preparation Questions

1. To what extent does Powell's draft respond to the changes in the media industries?
2. How closely aligned are the preferences of the commissioners?
3. What theories could be used to predict which majority will prevail in the FCC?
4. As the CEO of a major television network, what strategy would you adopt to advance relaxation of the ownership rules? As the owner of an affiliated local television station, what strategy would you adopt to oppose relaxation of the media ownership rules?
5. What is the FCC likely to decide? Why?
6. What is likely to happen in Congress? Why?

11

Environmental Management and Sustainability

INTRODUCTION

The public, government, and business recognize the importance of environmental protection and sustainability. Those benefits include improved human health, a more vibrant natural environment, the preservation of ecosystems, and a more sustainable relationship with the natural environment. Achieving these benefits is also expensive. Compliance with existing environmental regulation costs each person in the United States nearly $900 a year in 2004—or a total of $250 billion annually, representing 2.1 percent of GDP. Any new programs to meet other environmental goals, such as addressing global climate change, would add to that cost. The cost of environmental protection and sustainability require not only that the environment be protected and sustainability be achieved but that they be accomplished as efficiently as possible. Although there is widespread agreement about general goals, there remains considerable disagreement about how much protection is appropriate and about the distribution of the burden of that protection. These disagreements generate the politics of environmental protection and sustainability.

This chapter focuses on public and private managerial policies for environmental protection and sustainability. The following section considers the global climate change challenge, and the next section introduces a framework for reasoning about externalities that provides the foundation for cap-and-trade systems. The experiences with the U.S. sulfur dioxide cap-and-trade system and the European Union cap-and-trade system for carbon dioxide are then reviewed. Environmental regulation is then considered with a focus on the policies of the Environmental Protection Agency (EPA). The politics of environmental protection are then addressed. The management of environmental and regulatory issues from a firm's perspective is then considered. Examples include BP's internal emissions trading system, Intel's participation in the EPA's XL program, environmental innovation at Home Depot, Wal-Mart's aggressive environmental programs, an experiment by FedEx, the Responsible Care program in the chemical industry, and McDonald's and Dow Chemicals' cooperative programs with environmental groups.

THE ENVIRONMENT AND SUSTAINABILITY

Goals and Actions

Environmental protection and sustainability are widely accepted goals, although disagreement remains about how costly attaining these goals would be. Environmental protection goals pertain to ecosystems, climate change, pollution, habitats, and more, and sustainability pertains to energy, forests, and the environment more generally. The principal instruments for attaining these goals come from government, but private initiatives can also play a role, as can the policies of firms and the practices of individuals. Twenty-six companies including General Electric, General Motors, and DuPont joined with six environmental groups including Environmental Defense and the Natural Resources Defense Council to form the U.S. Climate Action Partnership. The partnership has urged the adoption of strong government action to reduce greenhouse gases emissions. Venture capital firms have begun investing in energy startups and companies developing technologies to reduce carbon emissions, including negative carbon technologies. Companies such as Wal-Mart have implemented aggressive corporate environmental programs. Some of these programs are responses to public and private politics pressure, but many are adopted voluntarily in the absence of direct pressure. Individuals have taken simple measures such as replacing incandescent light bulbs with compact fluorescent bulbs as well as more extensive measures such as installing solar panels and bicycling to work.

Responsibility for environmental protection and sustainability has broadened. Financial institutions, for example, are now held responsible not only for their own carbon footprint but also for the consequences of their lending. JPMorgan Chase, Bank of America, Citigroup, and Goldman Sachs have environmental and sustainability policies. As a consequence of pressure from activist groups and its leadership in establishing the Equator Principles, Citigroup has a greenhouse gases reporting system for the project finance it provides. The bank also has a Sustainable Development Investment Program to fund private equity investments in renewable energy and other environmental improvement prospects.

Global Climate Change

The scientific evidence on global climate change identifies humans as a major contributor to global warming through the release of greenhouse gases. The increase in greenhouse gases emissions is due to a variety of factors, the two most important of which are population growth and economic growth. The U.S. Census Bureau estimates that the world population increased from 3 billion in 1959 to 6 billion in 1999 and projects a population of 9 billion by 2042. Africa and Asia account for approximately three-quarters of the world population and are projected to account for nearly 90 percent of the growth over the next 30 to 40 years. Economic growth has increased more rapidly than population, resulting in an increase in per capita income of 119 percent from 1959 to 1999.

The energy intensity of economic activity has decreased steadily in much of the world by approximately 1.5 percent a year. Denmark has perhaps the lowest energy intensity with a slightly more than 5 Btu/\$1,000 of GDP in 2005. The energy intensity in China had declined from 13 Btu/000 in 1990 to 7 Btu/000 in 2000, but with the recent economic boom energy intensity increased to 8 Btu/000 in 2005, which is the world average. For the United States the Btus/000 have decreased from 12 in 1990 to slightly more than 9 in 2005. Although energy intensity has decreased steadily in the United States because of population and economic growth, the total emissions of CO_2 have increased by 17.5 percent between 1990 and 2006 and by 38.6 percent since 1974.

Policy

The United States may adopt a cap-and-trade system for reducing carbon emissions. A bill under consideration in 2008 was the Lieberman-Warner Climate Security Act, which would cover 87 percent of U.S. greenhouse gasses emissions and would impose caps to reduce emissions by 7 percent by 2012 (compared to 2006 levels), 39 percent by 2030, and 72 percent by 2050. The act would also cap the Kyoto mechanism measures (offsets) at 15 percent of the reductions in each year. Incentives would also be provided for carbon capture and storage and biogenic carbon sequestration. Energy efficiency standards would be increased for appliances and buildings.[1] The Energy Information Administration of the Department of Energy estimated that the price of

---

[1] These measures were in addition to those in the Energy Independence and Security Act of 2007, which increased automobile fuel economy standards and restricted the use of incandescent lights.

electricity would increase from 5 to 27 percent by 2020 and 11 to 64 percent by 2030. Real GDP would decrease slightly, and the greatest economic impact of the act would be on the manufacturing sector.

Goals such as those in the Lieberman-Warner bill could be achieved using a variety of instruments. One is to increase energy productivity. In two major studies McKinsey & Co. evaluated the opportunities to reduce energy use and found that half of the projected increase in worldwide energy demand could be avoided by investments that had an internal rate of return of at least 10 percent.[2] The capital expenditures required would be $170 billion a year for 13 years, of which half would be in the industrial sector, one quarter in the residential sector, and the remainder in the commercial and transportation sectors. The greatest opportunity is in the residential sector through better insulation, the use of fluorescent lighting, and more efficient hot water heaters.

If such attractive investment opportunities are available, why are these investments not being made automatically? One explanation is that there are market failures and transactions costs that impede the investments. Individuals may be poorly informed about the opportunities or may be credit constrained, preventing them from retrofitting their homes to reduce energy use. In addition, the transactions costs, including hassle, of making improvements may seem larger to home owners than the modest savings that can be achieved. Because of uncertainty about whether consumers will actually buy a more energy-efficient appliance, manufacturers may be reluctant to produce enough of the appliances to realize the potential economies of scale. One response to these market failures and transactions costs are government subsidies and incentives for reducing energy use. Another is a moral commitment to bear a cost of providing a public good that will benefit others.

Tradeoffs

Even if there are attractive investment opportunities, they are unlikely to be sufficient to deal with global climate change. Tradeoffs thus must be made. Most measures to mitigate the harm from externalities require tradeoffs. Tradeoffs are involved in decisions by consumers as well as policies of governments. For example, the use of compact fluorescent bulbs in place of incandescent bulbs causes a mercury pollution problem, since the fluorescent bulbs contain about 4 mg of mercury, a toxic substance. At the government level, Congress has mandated increased production of ethanol as a substitute for oil. Corn has been the principal crop used for ethanol production, and the demand for corn has increased, leading farmers to increase their production at the expense of other crops.[3] The demand for ethanol has resulted in higher prices for corn, palm, and other crops, and combined with droughts in some parts of the world and increasing demand for food, crop and food prices escalated rapidly in 2008, putting a substantial burden on many developing countries as well as households. The Food and Agriculture Organization of the United Nations and the Organization for Economic Cooperation and Development issued a report stating, "The energy, security, environmental, and economic benefits of biofuels production based on agricultural commodity feed stocks are at best modest, and sometimes even negative."

These concerns have refocused biofuel enthusiasts on second-generation feed stocks made from nonfood crops such as reeds, jatropha, and wild grasses. Scientists warned, however, that these nonfood crops were often invasive and posed environmental risks. Plans for a giant reed plantation in Florida have been opposed by some environmental groups, and jatropha, which is grown in eastern Africa, has been banned in Australia. The International Union for Conservation of Nature warned, "Don't let invasive biofuel crops attack your country."

The U.S. Green Building Council provides standards and certification for sustainable buildings and provides LEED certification for new construction and retrofitting.

---

[2]McKinsey & Co., "The Case for Investing in Energy Productivity," February 2008; "Curbing Global Energy Demand Growth: The Energy Productivity Opportunity," May 2007. The estimates were based on a price of $70 for a barrel of crude oil.

[3]In contrast, Brazil uses the stalks from sugar cane to produce ethanol and has become nearly self-sufficient.

Certificate levels are Certified, Silver, Gold, and Platinum, representing successively higher levels of sustainability—and costs. San Francisco has adopted stringent building standards requiring the use of clean energy and sustainable building materials. A study by the city's Office of Economic Analysis (OEA) concluded the greenhouse gas emissions would be reduced over time but at a cost of $30 million to $700 million a year through 2027. The OEA indicated that a carbon tax would have an immediate effect on emissions and would distort economic activity less. The tax, however, would increase utility rates by 16.5 percent.

The chapter case, *Emerging Nanotechnology Regulation: Samsung's SilverCare Washing Machine*, involves the balancing of lower energy consumption in washing clothes and possible harm as a result of water pollution.

SOCIALLY EFFICIENT CONTROL OF EXTERNALITIES

Social efficiency is attained when aggregate well-being is maximal. Aggregate well-being takes into account the harm from an externality and the social costs of reducing that harm. Just as it is not socially efficient to prevent all accidents, it is not socially efficient to prevent all pollution or return carbon concentrations in the atmosphere to pre–industrial revolution levels. Instead, that pollution which is not too costly to prevent should be prevented. The control of externalities, however, has often taken the form of *command-and-control* regulation in which regulators order engineering controls, such as scrubbers for electric power plants, or require the best available technology for pollution abatement. This approach deals with the source of the harm, but it takes into account neither the benefits of the avoided harm nor the cost of abatement. Command-and-control is a blunt instrument that imposes uniform controls and standards on dissimilar sources of pollution, resulting in excessive abatement costs. In contrast, social efficiency requires that the polluter and those affected by the pollution externality take into account both the harm and the costs of abatement. For each source of pollution, social efficiency requires that costs and benefits be considered and that reductions in pollution be attained at the least cost. The lower the cost of reducing pollution, the larger are the reductions that can be made.

Incentive approaches take into account the benefits and costs of attaining environmental objectives and achieve those objectives by aligning the social and private costs of pollution and its abatement. These approaches attain social efficiency by requiring polluters to internalize the social costs of their pollution externalities. These approaches also decentralize pollution-control decisions because the generators of pollution rather than regulators have the responsibility for evaluating alternative abatement strategies and technologies. Rather than dictating how environmental goals should be achieved, incentive approaches impose a cost on pollution-causing activities, leaving it to individual polluters to decide how best to respond. Incentives then drive these decisions toward the least-cost means of attaining environmental objectives. The incentives to reduce costs also provide incentives to redesign production processes to reduce pollutants, eliminate harmful components of products, develop better pollution control technologies, and develop alternative production technologies.

The principles underlying incentive approaches to achieving social efficiency in the presence of externalities are provided by the Coase theorem. It addresses the private attainment of social efficiency and the conditions for its attainment.

The Coase Theorem

The *Coase theorem* pertains to market imperfections, including externalities and public goods. It focuses on the standard of social efficiency and provides a conceptual foundation for both regulation and the liability system considered in Chapter 12. The theorem does not address other standards, such as distributive objectives and social justice, that could be used in evaluating alternative social arrangements and public policies. The Coase theorem has gained influence in the economics of externalities and public goods and in the law through applications to issues such as breach of contracts, nuisance law, and torts.[4] Coase's (1960) original exposition focused on externalities.

Coase observed that an externality is reciprocal in the sense that at least two parties are required. In the case of noise pollution, there would be no externality without the polluter or in the absence of anyone to hear the noise. In the case of a toxic risk from an oil refinery, an externality exists because of both the refinery and the presence of homes and businesses near it. When an externality is recognized to be reciprocal, it is clear that there is more than one means of achieving social efficiency. Coase's analysis began with an entitlement protected by a *property rule*. A property rule prohibits other parties from infringing the entitlement without the consent of the party holding it. Homeowners are protected by a property rule that prohibits other persons from taking their home without consent or forcing them to sell it at a price they deem inadequate.

As an example of Coase's analysis, suppose firm A discharges pollutants into a river whose water is used as an input to a production process by a downstream firm B. In principle, the two firms can voluntarily reach an agreement to internalize the externality regardless of which firm has the entitlement. That is, social efficiency can be achieved whether A has the entitlement to pollute or B has the entitlement to be free from pollution. If A has the entitlement to pollute, B has an incentive to bargain with A to reduce the pollution. B would be willing to pay A to the point at which the marginal harm done to B's production equals the marginal cost of reducing pollution at A. This minimizes the total cost of abatement and harm from pollution, resulting in social efficiency.

If B has the entitlement not to have its production harmed by the pollution, A has an incentive to bargain with B to allow A to discharge some amount of pollution into the river. A is willing to pay B up to A's marginal cost of abatement. B would require a payment equal to the marginal harm it would incur from the pollution, so in an agreement the marginal cost of abatement would equal the marginal harm. The assignment of the entitlement to B thus also results in the socially efficient level of pollution. The Coase theorem example illustrates this logic in more detail and extends the analysis to include abatement alternatives.

The Coase theorem states that, in the absence of transactions costs that would impede the bargaining over these private agreements, the socially efficient outcome can be realized if the entitlement is assigned to either party. The role of government thus is to assign entitlements to the parties and allow them to reach private agreements that internalize the externality. Although social efficiency is attained with either assignment of the entitlement, the assignment affects the distribution of the social costs of the externality and its control. The Coase theorem example illustrates this in more detail.

Since it is reciprocal, one approach to dealing with an externality is to remove one side of the reciprocal relationship between polluter and those harmed by the pollution. Many plants have closed because of the costs they would have to bear to reduce their pollution. Conversely, to reduce the harm to local residents, the American Electric Power Company bought for $20 million the town of Chesire, Ohio, where one of its coal-fired power plants was located. The amount paid was three times the value of the homes, and the residents quickly accepted the offer.[5] Similarly, Exxon paid $4 million to purchase 110 homes and businesses to create a safety zone around its Baton Rouge, Louisiana, refinery. From the perspective of the Coase theorem, the entitlements in these two cases were held by the homeowners and were protected by a property rule. The firms bargained to purchase those entitlements, thereby bearing the cost of reducing the risk of harm.

Although social efficiency can be achieved with any assignment of entitlements, the distributive consequences can differ substantially. Environmental politics often arises from the existing assignment of entitlements and its implications for the distribution of the benefits and costs of environmental protection. As an example, residents of the Old Diamond neighborhood of Norco, Louisiana, conducted a 12-year private and public politics campaign against Shell. The neighborhood was located between a Shell chemical

---

[4]See Polinsky (2003) for an exposition of the role of the Coase theorem in the law.
[5]*New York Times Magazine,* February 8, 2004.

plant and an oil refinery owned by a Shell joint venture. The plants met EPA emissions standards, and Shell had reduced its emissions. The residents, however, wanted further reductions or a higher price for their homes. The entitlement rested with Shell, but the pressure of the campaign finally forced Shell to buy the residents' homes.

EXAMPLE

The Coase Theorem

To illustrate the concept of social efficiency, suppose company A produces apple cider up river from a brewery B. Company A can produce 0, 100, or 200 gallons of apple cider, and its corresponding profit is 0, 40, and 70. The company's plant also pollutes the river in proportion to production, and the pollution causes harm to the brewery's product of 0, 20, and 60, respectively. These data are summarized in Table 11-1. Social well-being or social value is the aggregate of the profit of company A and the harm to company B. As indicated in the table, the social value is maximized at a production level of 100, which yields profit of 40 and harm of 20 for a social value of 20.

Identifying the social optimum is one thing; attaining it is another matter. Company A has an incentive to maximize its profit by producing 200 gallons, which yields a profit of 70. The harm, however, of 60 results in a social value of 10. One means of achieving social efficiency is through bargaining between A and B.

For bargaining to take place, entitlements must be clearly assigned and their protection specified. Suppose that B has the entitlement not to be harmed by pollution, and the entitlement is protected by a property rule. B thus will not allow A to produce at all unless it is compensated for the harm it incurs. A is willing to pay up to 40 to be able to produce 100 units, and B requires compensation of at least 20 for the harm. Suppose that as a result of their bargaining they split the difference, with A paying 30 to B to be allowed to produce 100 units accompanied by the pollution. Next, consider whether A wants to induce B to allow A to increase its production from 100 to 200. If it does, its profit increases by 30, but B requires at least 40 more to compensate for the additional

harm. A thus is not willing to pay enough to induce B to bear the additional harm. Consequently, the bargaining between A and B results in the socially optimal output of 100 and a social value of 20. Through bargaining, the two parties have *internalized the externality.*

Coase considered such situations and asked whether social efficiency would be obtained regardless of how the entitlement was assigned. That is, suppose that A is assigned the entitlement to produce, and pollute, as much as it chooses and the entitlement is protected by a property rule. A would then want to produce 200 units. B, however, would incur harm of 60, so it is willing to offer A up to 40 if A will reduce its production from 200 to 100. Since A loses only 30 in profit from cutting back its production to 100, the two parties can strike a bargain (at 35 if they split the difference). It is straightforward to verify that B will not be willing to compensate A enough to induce it to cut its production to zero. The socially efficient outcome has again been obtained. The Coase theorem states that social efficiency can be achieved regardless of which party has the entitlement.

Although social efficiency is achieved with either assignment of entitlements, the distributive consequences of the assignments are quite different. If the entitlement is assigned to B, A has profit of 10 (= 40 – 30) and B has 10 (= 30 – 20). If the entitlement is assigned to A, A has a profit of 75 (= 40 + 35) and B has –55 (= –20 – 35). (Note that B's profit is not included here.) These distributive consequences are the source of politics as people seek to have the entitlement assigned to them.

The Coase theorem is more general than indicated by the analysis of a property rule. A property rule is distinguished from a *liability rule.* A liability rule does not prohibit a party from interfering with another party, but if harm is done, compensation must be paid to the injured party. In the example, suppose that the entitlement is assigned to B and is protected by a liability rule. Then A will produce 100 units and compensate B for the actual harm of 20. A will not increase its production to 200 because its

(Continued)

TABLE 11-1	Production, Harm, and Social Value			
A			***B***	***Social***
Production	***Emissions***	***Profit***	***Harm***	***Value***
0	0	0	0	0
100	10	40	−20	20
200	20	70	−60	10

profit would increase by only 30, but additional compensation of 40 would be required. Similarly, A would not reduce its output to 0. Social efficiency is again achieved. The same is true if the entitlement is assigned to A and protected by a liability rule. In this case, B would enjoin A from producing 200 and would be required to compensate A for the loss of profits of 30. B is willing to do so since it avoids harm of 40, so A will produce 100, again achieving social efficiency.

As in the case of a property rule the distributive consequences of the assignment of the entitlement protected by a liability rule differ. When the entitlement is assigned to B and protected by a liability rule, A has 20 and B has 0. When the entitlement is assigned to A, A has 70 and B has −50.

This analysis can be extended to include an abatement alternative. Suppose that, as indicated in Table 11-2, A and B each have an abatement alternative. Each can reduce the pollution by 50 or 100 percent at different costs. A can reduce the pollution by 50 and 100 percent at costs of 15 and 30 respectively, and the corresponding costs for B are 20 and 40 re-

spectively. The socially efficient outcome is then for A to produce 200 and to pay 30 to reduce pollution by 100 percent. The social value is 40. This outcome is achieved regardless of to whom the entitlement is assigned and whether it is protected by a property or a liability rule. For example, if the entitlement is assigned to B and protected by a liability rule, A will produce 200 and, rather than compensate B by 60 for the harm, will install the 100 percent abatement technology at a cost of 30. A's profit is then 40, and B incurs no harm.

TABLE 11-2	Abatement and Social Value			
Reduction in Emissions, %	**Cost of Abatement**		**Social Value***	
	A	**B**	**A Abates**	**B Abates**
0	0	0	10	10
50	15	20	25	20
100	30	40	40	30

*Based on production of 200.

Transactions Costs and the Limits of the Coase Theorem

The Coase theorem implies that when bargaining between the parties to an externality is possible, social efficiency can be achieved. Consequently, from the Coasean perspective social efficiency is a problem only when there are impediments to bargaining. These impediments are referred to as *transactions costs* because they are associated with the process of arriving at a transaction or agreement. When the parties involved are identifiable and their number is small, transactions costs are likely to be low and private agreements can be reached, as in the case of the power plant in Ohio and the oil refineries and chemical plant in Louisiana. When the parties are difficult to identify or are large in number, however, transactions costs can be prohibitively high, preventing private arrangements.

Consider air pollution from automobile emissions. Millions of automobiles generate pollution, and many more people are affected by that pollution. The costs would be exorbitant if all these individuals attempted to reach agreements about measures to reduce emissions or the amount of driving allowed. Because of the very high transactions costs associated with private bargaining, automobile emissions are controlled through government regulation.

In the case of an externality such as automobile emissions with high transactions costs of bargaining, either a command-and-control approach specifying particular controls can be used or performance standards can be set. Performance standards are preferred because they allow firms to choose the most cost-effective means of achieving those standards based on their superior information about the costs of alternatives. This approach is decentralized with localized information being used to achieve abatement at the lowest cost.

A market is the logical extension of a decentralized system in which entitlements are assigned and can be traded. Markets, or incentive-based systems, have become an effective means of achieving environmental goals at the least cost to society. These systems are considered next.

CAP-AND-TRADE SYSTEMS

Cap-and-trade systems, or *tradable permits systems,* cap the total allowed emissions of a particular pollutant such as sulfur dioxide or carbon dioxide, issue permits (entitlements) for that amount, and allow the permits to be traded.[6] Cap-and-trade systems are used for sulfur dioxide emissions and nitrogen dioxides, and several systems are in operation regionally, as in Southern California. A tradable permits system has been adopted to reduce greenhouse gases emissions in conjunction with the Kyoto Protocol on global climate change. Although the United States did not ratify the Kyoto Protocol, a voluntary compliance system has been established and permits are traded on the Chicago Climate Exchange. The European Union has implemented a cap-and-trade system for carbon dioxide, and the United States is considering implementing a similar system. BP established an internal tradable permits market for greenhouse gases.

The Coase theorem applies to this type of system. That is, given the amount of pollution permitted, the permits can be allocated to polluters for no charge, can be allocated to the public, or can be auctioned to the highest bidder. With any of these allocations, social efficiency can be achieved provided the permits can be traded. The allocation of the permits, however, affects the distribution of the burden of the emissions reduction and hence motivates politics. The politics of a tradable permits system are considered in the scrubbers example later in the chapter.

The control of an externality in a market-based system has three components. The first is providing incentives for abatement by internalizing the cost of the harm done by the pollutants. The second is allowing parties to respond to those incentives by choosing the most efficient means of abatement. These means include reducing output, installing pollution-control equipment, redesigning products and production processes to reduce the pollutants generated, and reducing the harm from emissions, as when oil refineries create safety zones around their facilities. The third component involves reflecting in the prices of goods and services, the costs of abatement and the social costs of the harm from the remaining pollution. This allows consumers to take into account the full social cost of the goods they consume. These three components operate simultaneously. An equilibrium results when (1) all advantageous trades have been made, (2) emitters have taken the abatement measures they prefer given the market price of permits, and (3) the quantities of products consumers purchase result in total emissions equal to the number of permits issued.

A cap-and-trade system is equivalent to a system in which an emissions tax is imposed on each unit of pollution emitted, provided the tax is set so as to reduce the pollution to the level of the cap. A tradable permits system is said to be superior to an emissions tax because the amount of abatement is known in advance with a permits system, whereas with an emissions tax the amount is known only after firms have responded to the tax.

An emissions tax is favored by some economists because it is transparent and easy to implement compared to having to develop a market. The Congressional Budget Office in 2008 concluded that a tax could achieve environmental objectives "at a fraction of the cost" of a cap-and-trade system. Moreover, an emissions tax may be less vulnerable to pressure from industry and labor, as suggested by the European Union's experience with its cap-and-trade system in which too many permits were issued and emissions actually increased. Industry opposes emissions taxes because companies would have to pay the tax, and prefers a cap-and-trade system in which they are given the permits for free.

Emissions taxes or fees are used in Scandinavia for CO_2 emissions, and in Southern California for organic gases, nitrogen oxides, carbon monoxide, sulfur oxides, and particulate matter. Maine uses an emissions fee that increases from $3.28 per ton for emissions up to 1,000 tons to $15.85 per ton for emissions over 4,000 tons. Fees or taxes are used for landfills, grazing on public lands, and hazardous waste disposal. The Chapter 15 case, *The European Union Carbon Tax,* considers such a system.

---

[6]The Chapter 20 case, *Environmental Justice and Pollution Credits Trading Systems,* provides another example of a tradable permits system.

A cap-and-trade system has an advantage in that it allows people with different preferences to express them in the market for permits. If people have a preference for lower levels of pollution, they can purchase permits and retire them, thereby reducing emissions. Some people have purchased permits and given them as gifts. The Cleaner and Greener Green Energy program facilitates the donation of permits. The Nature Conservancy purchases land and holds it as open spaces.

Cap-and-trade systems and emissions tax approaches to environmental protection also provide incentives for dynamic efficiency. Firms have incentives to invest in research and development to find more efficient means of reducing or avoiding their emissions. If they can do so, they can sell their permits. Similarly, the pollution-control technology industry has an incentive to develop new abatement technologies because firms have a continuing demand for emissions reduction rather than a demand that arises only when more stringent engineering controls are mandated, as in a command-and-control system.

Despite their efficiency advantages, objections arise because under incentive approaches some firms will reduce emissions considerably whereas others will reduce them less. Some people who view pollution as a social wrong rather than as an external cost of production believe that all firms should be forced to reduce their emissions by the same amount so that, for example, neighboring residents all receive the same reduction in pollution. The chapter case, *Environmental Justice and Pollution Credits Trading Systems,* addresses this issue and the politics it generated.

Cap-And-Trade Systems to Address Acid Rain

The bulk of the sulfur dioxide emissions that cause acid rain come from coal-fired electric power plants in six states: Indiana, Illinois, West Virginia, Pennsylvania, Ohio, and New York. New power plants are subject to New Source Performance Standards (NSPS), but existing power plants had not been subject to emission limits. These six states, and others as well, had lower electricity prices because their plants did not have to meet stringent controls. Adding a scrubber to remove the sulfur dioxide, for example, could increase the cost of electricity by 15 percent. Since the damage from acid rain occurred primarily in the northeastern states and Canada, addressing the issue involved benefits for one region and costs to another. Bargaining thus focused on both efficiency and the distributive consequences of policy alternatives. The political competition over acid rain went on for a decade, culminating with the Clean Air Act Amendments of 1990, which provided for an 87 million pounds, or 45 percent, reduction in sulfur dioxide emissions from the 1980 level and a 2 million pounds reduction in nitrogen oxide emissions.

The amendments addressed efficiency through a tradable permits, or cap-and-trade, system and the distributive consequences through a number of special provisions. Called "allowances" rather than permits, the system reduced the cost of abatement by allowing electric power companies to use the most efficient means of achieving emissions standards. They could choose low-sulfur coal, coal washing to remove sulfur before burning, new technologies such as fluidized bed combustion, or a scrubber. More importantly, the system permitted firms to trade allowances in a market, providing incentives for the efficient distribution of abatement across firms.

In the initial phase of the program, the EPA administrator annually allocated allowances to 110 coal-fired power plants in 21 states in the Midwest, South, and East according to formulas specified in the legislation.[7] The EPA administrator conducts an annual auction of allowances from a reserve formed by taking a percentage of the allowances allocated to the plants.[8] Unused allowances could be carried forward to the next year and transferred or sold to other companies.

The value of the sulfur dioxide allowances issued in 2004 was estimated at $3.6 billion, and the spot price in 2004 had skyrocketed from $200 per allowance to $650 per

---

[7]See Joskow and Schmalensee (1998) for a study of the political economy of the allocation of allowances.
[8]The proceeds are distributed back to the plants from which the allowances were originally obtained.

allowance. Spot prices in the EPA auction reached $883 in 2006 and declined to $380 in 2008 as a result of reductions in emissions by power plants. The economic harm from a ton of sulfur dioxide emissions is estimated to be $4,000.[9] A total of 22.4 million allowances were traded in 2006.[10] The tradable allowances system has been estimated to cost 50 percent, or $2.5 billion per year, less than a uniform command-and-control approach.[11] A 2005 study concluded that by 2010 the acid rain program would yield benefits of $122 billion at an annual cost of $3 billion for a benefit-cost ratio of 40 to 1. With a tradable permits system, emissions must be monitored to ensure that they do not exceed the permits held by the firm. The sulfur dioxide cap-and-trade system uses continuous monitoring by sources and is verified by the EPA and posted on the Internet for public inspection.[12] If a source emits more sulfur dioxide than the allowances it has, a fine of $2,900 per ton of excess emissions is imposed (in 2003).

Power companies were also allowed to transfer allowances among their own plants. New power plants completed after enactment of the amendments were not allocated any allowances and had to purchase them from existing plants. New power plants were already subject to the NSPS of 1.2 pounds of SO_2 per MBtu, so their emissions were substantially below the emissions levels of existing plants. In 2000 the emissions cap under the Clean Air Act Amendments was extended to cover all power-generating units above 25 megawatts and all new units. By 2006 sulfur dioxide emissions were below the cap of 9.5 million tons.

The distributive consequences of the tradable allowances system depend in large part on how the allowances are allocated. Since regulated electricity prices are cost-of-service based, the full costs of both allowances and abatement are borne by the customers of the electric power plants. If the allowances were initially allocated to the EPA and auctioned, the power companies and their customers would bear the costs of abatement plus the payments for the allowances. Taxpayers across the nation would be the beneficiaries. If the allowances were initially allocated to the power companies, taxpayers would receive nothing, and the power companies and their customers would bear only the costs of abatement. As the Coase theorem indicates, the efficiency consequences of assigning the allowances to the EPA or the power companies are identical, so the choice between the two methods is a distributive matter. Assigning the allowances to the power companies would produce concentrated benefits in the 21 states and particularly in the six states that emit the most sulfur dioxide. The loss to taxpayers would be widely distributed. Client politics prevailed, and the allowances were allocated for free to the power companies, resulting in lower costs for the power plants and their customers.

The EPA also established an emissions trading system for nitrogen oxide similar to the one for sulfur dioxide. The program reduces by 28 percent the emissions in 22 states and the District of Columbia and covers coal-fired and oil-fired power plants and industrial boilers. Nitrogen oxide is a major component of smog and can flow to downwind states. In 2006 nitrogen oxide emissions were less than half the 1990 levels.

GLOBAL CLIMATE CHANGE AND EMISSIONS TRADING SYSTEMS

In 1998 the Clinton administration signed the Kyoto Protocol on global climate change, which called for country-specific reductions in carbon dioxide emissions by 2010. The U.S. target was a 7 percent reduction from 1990 levels. The protocol had strong opposition in the Senate, which in 1997 adopted a resolution opposing the protocol unless developing countries, particularly China and India, made firm commitments to reduce their emissions. President Clinton chose not to submit the protocol to the Senate for ratification. The Clinton administration argued that the Kyoto agreement would have little

---

[9]The value of the nitrogen dioxide allowances was estimated at $1.4 billion.
[10]Cantor Environmental Brokerage reports market prices for allowances (www.emissionstrading.com).
[11]Joskow, Schmalensee, and Bailey (1998); Schmalensee et al. (1998); and Stavins (1998) evaluated the market for SO_2 allowances and concluded that by 1994 it was functioning relatively efficiently.
[12]www.epa.gov/airmarkets.

effect on costs, but the Department of Energy predicted that gasoline prices would increase by nearly 40 percent and electricity prices between 20 and 86 percent in real terms by 2010. President Bush announced that the United States would not ratify the Kyoto Protocol. Australia also rejected the Kyoto Protocol. Russia approved the protocol in late 2004, enabling it to go into effect.

The signatories to the Kyoto Protocol agreed to use an emissions permits trading system to reduce the cost of achieving their commitments. Countries can earn credits, referred to as Kyoto measures, toward their Kyoto goals by investing in emissions reduction programs in developing countries. The European Union took the lead on multination emission trading with the European Trading System (ETS) commencing in 2005. The ETS is a cap-and-trade system that covers 12,000 facilities in 15 EU member states. The EU goal is an 8 percent reduction by 2012 from a 1990 base.

The United States and Carbon Emissions

The United States under the Bush administration adopted a voluntary approach to greenhouse gases reductions with a 2012 goal of an 18 percent reduction in emission per unit of GDP. Greenhouse gases are traded on the Chicago Climate Exchange under a voluntary cap-and-trade system. Twenty-five U.S. power companies formed the Power Tree Carbon Company to plant trees, and American Electric Power reported that it had planted 22 million trees, sequestering 9.1 million tons of CO_2, at a cost of $12 million.[13] Excelon reported eliminating 24.8 million tons of CO_2 by upgrading its nuclear power plants to increase their capacity. Power and coal companies with funding from the federal government formed the FutureGen Project to develop a coal-fired electricity and hydrogen plant with 100 percent CO_2 sequestration. Escalation of estimated construction costs, however, led the government to withdraw its funding, leaving the project in doubt. States in the northwest and in the northeast began work on regional trading systems for greenhouse gases. Although voluntary approaches had some effect, mandatory approaches were required to achieve overall reductions in carbon emissions.

Emissions Trading in the European Union

The Kyoto Protocol called for the use of a cap-and-trade mechanism to achieve reductions in greenhouse gases emissions. To meet a portion of its Kyoto goal of a reduction of 8 percent by 2012 from 1990 levels, the European Union (EU) introduced a cap-and-trade mechanism. The European Trading Scheme (ETS) began in 2005, and the individual members of the EU issued the permits to the companies in their countries. Pressure from the companies and unions that feared the loss of jobs as a result of pursuing the Kyoto goals resulted in the issue of more permits than the emissions companies had made in the previous year. The market value of the permits was around €20 per tonne of CO_2, but when the EU released a report that there was an extra supply of credits, the market collapsed with the price reaching €1. Not facing any cost of emissions, the firms increased their emissions. For example, Point Carbon, a carbon market research and consulting firm in Oslo, Norway, reported that the firms in the EU increased their carbon emissions by 1.1 percent in 2007. Emissions had also increased in the previous two years by about 1 percent.[14] The EU announced that it would reduce permits allocated for 2008–2012 by 6.3 percent below projected levels, and the price of a permit rose to the €15–25 range.

The European Environment Agency (EEA) reported that through 2005 the EU-15 (the members of the EU prior to 2004) had reduced their emissions by 2 percent, but the reduction had come in the early 1990s. In its 2007 report the EEA lamented that more progress had not been made but, based on the pledges of the member states, concluded that the member states would meet the Kyoto target "if Member States implement existing and additional measures fully and quickly, and make use of carbon sinks

---

[13]*Electric Utility Week,* March 29, 2004.
[14]The U.S. Energy Information Administration reported that carbon emissions in the United States increased by 0.6 percent in 2005, decreased by 1.3 percent in 2006, and increased by 1.6 percent in 2007.

and Kyoto mechanisms."[15] The EEA also reported that the programs already in place would by 2010 reduce emissions to 4 percent below 1990 levels. In addition, the other policies under consideration were anticipated to reduce emissions by 3.9 percent, and the EU-15 planned to use carbon sinks to reduce emissions by another 0.8 percent and Kyoto mechanisms by 2.5 percent. Ten of the EU-15 planned to use Kyoto mechanisms.

Kyoto mechanisms referred to credits bought by countries to help finance projects in developing countries that would reduce greenhouse gases. Qualifying projects had to be such that they would not be undertaken absent the funds provided by the sale of the credits. Projects were qualified by the United Nations under its Clean Development Mechanism (CDM) program, and approval was given by the CDM board. In its first year the board approved almost all the proposed projects, but concerns began to mount that some of the projects would have been funded independently of the credits. In addition some of the projects were found not to have generated the reductions projected. The board then applied additional scrutiny to the proposed projects and began to reject a higher percentage. In 2007 the board rejected 9 percent of the proposals and approved 57 percent with the rest delayed.[16] The average time to approval increased from 3 months to 8 months.

Emissions Trading Within BP plc (British Petroleum)

Emissions trading can occur not only among firms and nations, but also within firms. To address the global climate change issue, in 1998 BP plc committed by 2010 to reduce its emissions of greenhouse gases (GHGs) by 10 percent from 1990 levels.[17] BP's greenhouse gases policy was guided by a target for the earth of 500 to 550 parts per million (ppm) of GHGs compared to the present level of 370 ppm and 280 ppm before the industrial revolution.

To achieve its goal, BP worked with Environmental Defense to develop an internal GHGs trading system for the company. Each BP business unit was given an annual cap that it had to meet either through reduction projects or by purchasing allowances (permits) on the internal company market. No additional allowances are given for growth, although the baseline was adjusted in the case of an acquisition. A central broker within the company administered the market. In the first year of the market 2.7 million tons of allowances were traded, and an average price was $7.60 per ton. Trading operated as it does in the basic theory of tradable permits systems. A chemicals unit that installed a new furnace that improved combustion freed allowances that it could sell to a business unit whose cost of CO_2 reduction was greater than the price of an allowance.

BP's internal trading system was instrumental in enabling the company to achieve its 2010 goal in 2001. Having achieved its goal, BP ended its emissions trading system and set a new goal of no increase in GHG emissions through 2012. BP also participated in the UK emissions trading scheme and the sulfur dioxide and nitrogen oxides trading systems in the United States.

REGULATION AS OPPORTUNITY

The ETS provided for trading of credits and in 2007 the trade volume reached €40 billion. Most of the trade occurred between companies and financial institutions, and 90 percent of the remaining trades were made on the European Climate Exchange operated by Climate Exchange plc. In 2008 the market capitalization of the company was $1.3 billion.[18] The volume of trade attracted traders, and financial institutions set up trading desks. Some financial services firms such as Credit Suisse began to package carbon credit projects and repackage them into risk tranches.[19] Interest in trading was spurred

---

[15]European Environment Agency, "Greenhouse gas emission trends and projections in Europe," November 27, 2007.
[16]*Wall Street Journal,* April 12-13, 2008.
[17]BP's response to the global climate change issue is considered in more detail in Chapter 22.
[18]*Wall Street Journal,* March 13, 2008.
[19]*Fortune,* April 28, 2008.

as well by the anticipation that the United States would in the near future adopt a cap-and-trade system for carbon emissions.

In addition to opportunities in trading, firms were formed to serve as intermediaries between the purchasers of carbon credits and those with projects in developing countries for reducing emissions. Those projects required approval by the UN CDM board, and the firms assisted those with projects in the developing countries in preparing the proposals.

One such firm was EcoSecurities Ltd., which arranged projects in a number of countries and by early 2008 had 171 million tons of carbon credits available through 2012. EcoSecurities went public in 2005, and its share price skyrocketed. When the CDM board tightened its project approval procedures, EcoSecurities was forced to write off a substantial part of the portfolio and its share price fell by 70 percent.[20]

To identify and implement energy conservation measures, firms hire energy services companies (ESCOs) such as units of large companies including Trane, Siemens, and Johnson Controls as well as start-ups such as Ameresco. For example, these firms evaluate the opportunities for energy use reductions in a factory or office building and install retrofits. Many organizations such as governments, schools, hospitals, and universities are capital constrained, and ESCOs offer turnkey services in which they pay for retrofits, in return for which they receive the energy cost savings under a long-term performance contract extending up to 15 years. The projects of ESCOs are financed by specialized financial services companies such as Hannon Armstrong and increasingly by banks. The Clinton Climate Initiative is a cooperative project of ESCOs, banks, and 45 cities across the world to achieve $5 billion in energy efficiency investments in municipal and other buildings.

The chapter case, *Regulation as Opportunity: Cummins, Inc.,* considers another opportunity created by environmental regulation.

GOVERNMENT POLICY: THE EPA

The EPA, an independent agency located in the executive branch, is headed by an administrator appointed by the president and confirmed by the Senate.[21] The EPA was created by an executive order of President Nixon in 1970 to bring together in a single agency a number of environmental regulation programs then housed in different federal agencies. Congress quickly passed several measures expanding the new agency's responsibilities. The EPA is now responsible for administering the major acts listed in Figure 11-1. As was characteristic of the new social regulation, the acts were written in the fear that they would not be enforced because the agencies would be captured by industry. The acts thus are often highly detailed and frequently include timetables intended to force the agency to act.[22] Many of these measures established specific goals for environmental protection without reference to costs. The goals in some cases were unrealistic and served more as symbols than as commitments.[23] The Federal Water Pollution Control Act of 1972, for example, established the goal of eliminating all discharges of pollutants into navigable waters by 1985.

Federal environmental regulation is a major undertaking. The EPA had a budget of $7.2 billion in 2008 and over 17,000 employees. The EPA has responsibility for air and water quality, drinking water safety, waste treatment and disposal, toxic substances, and pesticides. The Department of the Interior has responsibilities for some conservation programs, and the Department of Agriculture has responsibilities for some pesticide control programs.

A number of the statutes assign to the states the responsibility for formulating implementation plans for attaining federal environmental standards. Under the Clean Air Act, states are responsible for developing State Implementation Plans to meet air

---

[20]*Wall Street Journal,* April 14, 2008.
[21]See *Congressional Quarterly* (1994) for a description of the EPA and its powers.
[22]Vogel (1986) provides a comparison of U.S. and UK environmental policy.
[23]See Kneese and Schultze (1975) for an early critique of environmental legislation.

FIGURE 11-1 Principal Environmental Acts

Federal Insecticide, Fungicide and Rodenticide Act of 1947 (amended in 1972, 1988)

Clean Air Act of 1963 (amended in 1970, 1977, 1990)

Solid Waste Disposal Act of 1965

Air Quality Act of 1967

National Environmental Policy Act of 1969

Water Quality Improvement Act of 1970

Federal Environmental Pesticide Control Act of 1972

Federal Water Pollution Control Act (Clean Water Act) of 1972 (amended in 1987)

Marine Protection, Research and Sanctuaries Act of 1972

Noise Control Act of 1972

Endangered Species Act of 1973

Safe Drinking Water Act of 1974 (amended in 1997)

Toxic Substances Control Act of 1976 (amended in 1988)

Resource Conservation and Recovery Act of 1976

Clean Water Act of 1977

Comprehensive Environmental Response, Compensation, and Liability Act of 1980 (amended in 1986) [Superfund]

Emergency Planning and Community Right-to-Know Act (1986)

Water Quality Act of 1987

Ocean Pollution Dumping Act of 1990

Pollution Prevention Act of 1990

Oil Pollution Act of 1990

Reclamation Projects Act of 1992

Food Quality Protection Act of 1996

quality standards. This gives the states a considerable role in environmental protection. States have their own environmental laws and regulatory agencies as well, and some enforcement is delegated to those agencies.

Enforcement

The EPA enforcement process requires the filing of a notice of a complaint and a hearing before an administrative law judge (ALJ). The ALJ's decision can be appealed to the agency's administrator and to the courts. Under some statutes the EPA has the authority to forward cases to the Department of Justice, which can file a civil proceeding in federal district court. Typically, however, the EPA seeks voluntary compliance. Some environmental laws also allow lawsuits by private citizens against polluters who violate regulations.

The federal government can seek both civil and criminal convictions of polluters, both of firms and individual managers. In 1997 the EPA referred for prosecution 278 criminal cases and 425 civil cases with total fines of $264.4 million. In the wake of the Alaskan oil spill by the *Exxon Valdez,* felony and misdemeanor criminal charges were brought against Exxon and the captain of the tanker. The captain was acquitted of three of the four charges, including the felony charges, and convicted on one charge of misdemeanor negligence. In 1991 Exxon agreed to a settlement with the federal and Alaska governments in which it pleaded guilty to three misdemeanor charges and agreed to pay $1.15 billion in civil and criminal fines and restitution, of which $287 million was for actual damages. In addition, Exxon spent over $2 billion on the cleanup. In 1994 a federal court jury found that Exxon had acted in a negligent and reckless manner and ordered it to pay $5 billion in punitive damages to Alaskans. After a series of appeals, punitive damages were reduced to $507 million, which equaled the compensatory damages.[24]

---

[24]See Chapter 12.

Standards Setting and Engineering Controls

EPA regulation has largely been command and control, in which uniform rules or standards are ordered and then enforced. This type of regulation is often a blunt instrument, imposing uniform rules in dissimilar circumstances. Under this approach the EPA, for example, sets emissions limits for each pollution source, where a source may be as specific as an individual piece of equipment in a chemical plant. Uniform stationary-source pollution standards that ignore differences in abatement costs and achievable benefits across emissions sources have created both economic inefficiency and administrative nightmares. This experience contributed to the decision to use a cap-and-trade system.

The EPA sets emissions standards and air quality standards. In 2008 the agency set stringent standards for soot emissions by trains and ship diesel emissions. The agency also tightened the standard for ozone from 84 parts per billion to 75 parts per billion. The soot regulations drew praise and the ozone regulations drew criticism from environmental groups.

In addition to establishing overall standards, such as for ambient air quality, the EPA specifies engineering controls to reduce emissions. The engineering controls, in order of increasing stringency, are the "best practicable technology," "best conventional technology," "best available technology," and "maximum achievable control technology." The use of engineering controls has been criticized on efficiency grounds, but its advocates believe it is necessary to force polluters to comply. The Chapter 6 case, *Scrubbers and Environmental Politics,* illustrates the politics of mandated controls.

The command-and-control approach is a blunt instrument and often imposes high administrative costs on firms and limits their flexibility in responding quickly to market changes and product developments. For example, an Intel semiconductor plant may have 35 to 40 chemical process changes a year, and each change can require EPA approval. For a company like Intel that introduces a new generation of microprocessors every year or two, the delay caused by the required process approvals can be more costly than the administrative and compliance costs. To deal with such problems Intel and the EPA reached an agreement on simplifying the permit and compliance process in the context of the EPA's Project XL. The example on page 352 describes the Intel project.

Incentive Approaches

In addition to imposing engineering controls and establishing standards, the EPA has increasingly used incentive approaches.[25] One approach used in local air quality regulation under the Clean Air Act is the "bubble" program. Under the command-and-control approach, engineering controls are specified for each individual processing unit in an oil refinery, chemical plant, or steel mill. Under the bubble policy, the EPA sets permitted emissions levels for the entire plant—imagine a bubble around the plant—and allows the producer to achieve those levels in the most efficient manner. The plant, for example, may achieve the required reduction on a single processing unit or through controls on several units.

Another program to improve the efficiency of air quality regulation in nonattainment areas—those that do not meet federal air quality standards—uses *credits* and *offsets.* For example, under the Clean Air Act Amendments of 1990, the EPA allocates credits to states for implementing enhanced auto emissions testing and maintenance programs.[26] Under the offset program, to construct a new plant in a nonattainment area a firm must reduce pollutants elsewhere in the area by the amount to be released by the new plant. The firm can reduce emissions at another of its facilities or may purchase credits from another firm. In 1995 the California Institute of Technology and the Pacific Stock Exchange created an electronic market for trading credits in four Southern California counties. The Regional Clean Air Incentives Market (RECLAIM) hosts

---

[25]Ellerman, Joskow, and Harrison (2003) provide an introduction to incentive approaches in the United States. Fiorino (2006) discusses and evaluates environmental program innovations at the EPA.
[26]See the Chapter 2 case, *Envirotest Systems Corporation (A),* for the management and politics of an auto emissions testing program.

EXAMPLE

Intel and the Project XL

The objective of the EPA's Project XL is to "provide a forum for companies to test new technologies and alternative regulatory approaches that eventually might be used by more companies to boost efficiency and achieve better environmental protection." In 1996 Intel and the EPA reached an agreement on the first XL project at its Chandler, Arizona, semiconductor plant.[1] The plant was subject to regulations under four principal statutes administered by five different EPA offices:

- Clean Air Act administered by the Office of Air Quality Planning and Standards
- Clean Water Act administered by the Office of Wastewater Management and the Office of Wetlands, Oceans, and Watersheds
- Resource Conservation and Recovery Act administered by the Office of Solid Waste
- Pollution Prevention Act administered by the Office of Prevention, Pesticides, and Toxic Substances

In addition, the Intel plant was subject to regulation by the Arizona Department of Environmental Quality, the Maricopa County Bureau of Air Pollution Control, and the city of Chandler.

The Intel project had two principal features: (1) elimination of case-by-case process change reviews by the EPA, provided that Intel emissions remained below a capped amount, and (2) preapproval of major plant expansions, provided that emissions remain below a cap for the entire site. Environmental groups initially criticized the agreement. The National Resources Defense Council (NRDC) said, "We are disappointed with the environmental performance required by this agreement."[2] Local environmental and labor groups also criticized the agreement, charging that it "allows Intel to expose its employees and the communities of Chandler and Phoenix to increased toxic chemical hazards."[3] Intel has remained well below the emissions caps.

According to the EPA, "Intel also has avoided millions of dollars in production delays by eliminating 30 to 50 new source permit reviews a year. The company has found the emissions caps so successful that it will invest $2 billion to build a new wafer fabrication facility (Fab 22) at the site. Under the existing cap, Intel can proceed with expansion without first going through regulatory review." The Project XL was one of the factors that led Intel to build its Fab 22 at the Chandler site.

The project also included an informational component. The project allowed Intel to use a consolidated reporting system for all the regulatory statutes, with the exception of the Toxic Release Inventory. Intel invited local stakeholders to participate in designing environmental reports, and those reports were made available on Intel's Web site. Intel also participated in an emergency preparedness program with the city of Chandler.

[1]EPA, "Project XL Progress Report: Intel Corporation," 100-R-00-031, January 2001.

[2]*New York Times*, November 20, 1996.
[3]*New York Times*, November 20, 1996.

---

trades of credits in sulfur dioxide and nitrogen oxides. Trading has been active, and a state review concluded that the program was efficient and effective.[27]

The EPA does not have the authority to tax pollution, but Congress has taken an interest in pollution taxes. In 1989 a federal law imposed a tax on chlorofluorocarbons (CFCs) as a means of reducing the use of the ozone-depleting chemicals while production was being phased out. To address the global climate change issue, some firms, members of Congress, and environmentalists have urged the use of a broadscale carbon tax on fuels. In 1993 the Clinton administration attempted to have a closely related Btu tax enacted by Congress, but the political pressure from those who would bear the distributive consequences of the tax caused the plan to fail. The Chapter 15 case, *The European Union Carbon Tax*, concerns a similar measure.

Superfund

The EPA administers the Superfund for the cleanup of existing toxic waste disposal sites. Estimates placed the number of sites requiring Superfund cleanups as high

---

[27]Each trade is listed at www.aqmd.gas/reclaim/reclaim/html.

as 20,000, and cost estimates were as high as $600 billion. Under the Superfund program the EPA attempts to identify the source of the dumping and force it to clean the site. If the EPA does the cleanup, it can go to court to recover the costs. In 2007 the EPA secured nearly $1 billion from private parties. As of 2004 the EPA had completed work on 61 percent of the over 1,500 sites on the National Priorities List. The Superfund program has been criticized both for moving too slowly and for spending funds where there was little hope of a successful cleanup. In recent years the pace of cleanup of toxic waste sites has increased. Of the $30 billion spent by business and government on the Superfund program, however, a third is estimated to have gone to lawyers in litigation over who is liable for the cleanup costs. Another criticism of the program is that it requires the same cleanup level of all sites, regardless of their future use or the costs of cleanup.

In addition to the litigation costs the Superfund has been criticized for its "retrospective liability" feature that requires companies to pay for the cleanup of wastes that had been disposed of legally. The Clinton administration responded to this criticism by proposing to exempt small firms. The criticisms and disagreements over the Superfund caused its congressional reauthorization to be mired in politics for most of the 1990s, and the taxes imposed on firms to fund the program expired in 1995. The Superfund is now financed by the federal budget and by fees imposed on identified polluters. Approximately 70 percent of the cleanup costs are paid by the party held responsible for the pollution with the rest paid by the government.

State Policy Initiatives

Electric utilities have incentives to build new capacity to meet projected demand, and to reduce the incentives to build new capacity, regulators in California have begun a program in which utilities are rewarded for their energy savings. The California Public Utilities Commission (CPUC) establishes energy-savings goals for each utility, and for any savings beyond the target, it retains 12 percent, which is higher that the rate of return allowed by the CPUC on new investments. If the savings are within 85–100 percent of the target, the utility receives 9 percent; within 65–85 percent there is no return; and below 65 percent a penalty is imposed. The state estimates that the total bonuses and penalties could be in the $324 million to $450 million a year, and the CPUC has estimated spending $2 billion over 3 years on conservation programs. One program is to subsidize compact fluorescent light bulbs. Consumers pay for these programs in their utility bills, including an approximate $8 per pack of two light bulbs. California regulators expect that the program will eliminate half the new capacity that otherwise would be built, although lighting savings are primarily at night and capacity is determined by daytime peak demand.

Pacific Gas & Electric has introduced its ClimateSmart program that allows households to offset their carbon footprints. Customers participating in the program calculate their carbon footprint based on their PG&E bills, identify other measures they are taking to reduce energy use, and agree to pay extra on their bill to fund new greenhouse gas reduction projects, such as planting trees in California. The cost for an average household would be approximately $5 a month.

THE POLITICAL ECONOMY OF ENVIRONMENTAL PROTECTION

The Nature of Environmental Politics

Environmental issues are of concern to most people, and hence to interest groups and the news media, and often advance rapidly in their life cycles. Since most of the costs of environmental protection are borne by private parties, government budget considerations have imposed few limits on the advance of environmental issues.[28] The costs of environmental protection are borne by firms, their employees, and consumers, and those costs generate opposition to more stringent regulation. Similarly, the benefits of environmental protection are both widespread and concentrated on those with strong

---

[28]Some regulation does have budget effects. For example, municipalities are one of the largest water polluters, and the federal government provides subsidies to municipalities for the construction of waste treatment plants.

concerns about particular issues such as health impairment from pollution, air quality at the Grand Canyon, wetlands, logging in national forests, or cattle grazing on Bureau of Land Management lands. Environmental issues thus are the subject of intense public politics.[29] Environmental issues are also the subject of private politics led by environmental and activist groups, as considered in Chapter 4 and in the Chapter 4 case, *Anatomy of a Corporate Campaign: Rainforest Action Network and Citigroup (A)(B)*.

Environmental issues are complex, in part because of scientific uncertainty about the consequences of pollution, incomplete information about the costs and benefits of environmental protection, and disagreements about alternative approaches, such as emissions taxes and cap-and-trade systems, to protection. Environmental issues are also complex because of differing perspectives about the protection of entitlements. From the social efficiency perspective, the entitlement to be free from the hazards of pollution should be protected by a liability rule because the transactions costs associated with a property rule would be prohibitive. Yet many individuals treat the environment and their health as if they were protected by a property rule. They seek to prohibit activities that may pose a risk to their health or to the environment. In one instance, Congress responded to these sentiments by enacting the Delaney amendment, which prohibited the use of any food additive found to be a carcinogen in laboratory animals. Environmental politics—including the NIMBY movement—thus is motivated both by distributive consequences and normative perspectives about the protection of the environment and health.

Judicial Politics

The politics of environmental protection often moves into judicial arenas. The NRDC sued the EPA, seeking enforcement of the Delaney amendment for pesticides used in the production of foods. As a practical means of dealing with potential risks, the EPA had followed a practice of allowing pesticide use if the risk to human health was "negligible." The courts held for the NRDC, requiring the EPA to enforce the Delaney amendment. This decision required the banning of dozens of widely used pesticides. The court decision added to the pressure for congressional action to repeal the Delaney amendment, which occurred in 1996.

Environmental groups have succeeded in inserting citizen provisions in environmental statutes. Under the citizen provision of the Clean Water Act the environmental group Water Keeper Alliance sued Smithfield Foods, the nation's largest hog producer, alleging that runoff from its hog farm in North Carolina polluted the state's rivers. Such lawsuits are not uncommon, but this one was potentially important because it was financed by the trial lawyers who had successfully filed class action lawsuits against the tobacco companies. Such litigation can also be backed by interests seeking to preserve their rents. Some populist farm groups backed the lawsuit because the efficiency of Southfield's operations threatened many family-owned hog farms.

Advocacy Science

Much remains unknown about environmental hazards and their control, and this scientific uncertainty is a source of contention in environmental politics. For example, the EPA estimated that 8 million homes were contaminated by dangerous levels of radon, a naturally occurring radioactive gas formed as radium decays in the ground. The EPA projected that the exposure to radon over a lifetime could cause 20,000 lung cancer deaths a year. The EPA issued an Indoor Radon Health Advisory that said, "Radon causes thousands of deaths each year." Other scientists placed the number of households with radon concentrations at the EPA's action level as low as 100,000. In one study, the lung cancer rate of people exposed to radon was found to be no different from that of people who were not exposed.[30] The EPA then issued voluntary guidelines for new homes and an information pamphlet for homeowners.

---

[29]See Greve and Smith (1992), Rosenbaum (2007), and Vaughn (2007) for treatments of environmental politics.
[30]*New York Times*, January 8, 1991.

The scientific uncertainty about the harm to the environment caused by pollution and about the risks to people's health, as in the case of radon, provides an opportunity to use advocacy science—proclaiming dangers to health and the environment—as a component of a private politics strategy. The Alar episode considered in Chapter 3 provides an example of the effectiveness of such a strategy. Because the media sees health and environmental risks as having societal significance and considerable audience interest, environmental issues quickly find their way to the public's attention and are frequently contested in full view of the public. These issues often arise from data provided in epidemiological studies. Feinstein (1988) characterized the pattern: "The episodes have now developed a familiar pattern. A report appears in a prominent medical journal; the conclusions receive wide publicity by newspapers, television, and other media; and another common entity of daily life becomes indicted as a menace to health—possibly causing strokes, heart attacks, birth defects, cancer. . . . The reported evidence is almost always a statistical analysis of epidemiological data, and the scientific tactics that produced the evidence are almost always difficult to understand and evaluate." He criticized the studies because "the research methods seldom have the precautions, calibrations, and relative simplicity that are taken for granted in other branches of science."

Another source of contention in environmental politics results from laboratory studies. Studies of health risks are often conducted on laboratory animals, which are exposed to pollutants at concentrations higher than human beings would ever encounter.[31] The laboratory results then must be extrapolated to the size and weight of people. Whether such results bear a reasonable relationship to the health risks to human beings can be a matter of disagreement.

Distributive Politics

In addition to concerns about hazards, environmental politics is motivated by the distributive consequences of environmental policy, the costs of environmental protection, and the benefits from the reduction in pollution and hazards. Much of the battle over the Clean Air Act Amendments requiring reduction of sulfur dioxide emissions from power plants was between "clean" and "dirty" states. The clean states wanted credit for their accomplishments and wanted to avoid having to pay the dirty states' cleanup costs. The dirty states were primarily in the Midwest, and many of them also mined high-sulfur coal. Their representatives in Congress sought both to hold down electricity prices and preserve jobs for coal miners. The dirty states also sought cost sharing through federal tax subsidies for scrubbers and sought compensation for jobs lost. Similar concerns arose when the cap-and-trade system for sulfur dioxide emissions was designed. Environmental groups sought lower emissions, and power companies sought to have the allowances given to them for free rather than have them auctioned.

At the federal level, attention had focused primarily on major sources of pollution, often exempting small business. The 1990 amendments to the Clean Air Act, however, addressed emissions not only by automobiles and electric power plants but also by dry cleaners, furniture manufacturers, and printers. In spite of their claims of hardship, these firms were required to install costly pollution-control systems. Joe Gerard, vice president of the American Furniture Manufacturers, stated, "What's unnerving for our industry is that the law would affect the application of [wood] finishing materials, and that's what gives us our competitive edge over imports." Linda Greed of the NRDC responded: "Everything that comes down the pike, we're told it'll put them out of business. . . . When they come up with the data to show it costs too much, they usually do get some relief. But when it's just arm waving, they don't. We hear it too often to be credible."[32]

The benefits from environmental protection accrue to people quite broadly, as in the case of the air quality improvements. The basic structure of environmental politics thus is entrepreneurial. The broad public sensitivity to environmental and health issues has meant that there are many political entrepreneurs seeking to represent the dispersed

---

[31]This is often because of the short life span of some laboratory animals and the desire to reduce the cost of experiments and speed completion of the research.
[32]*Wall Street Journal*, November 13, 1990.

beneficiaries. Particularly when the costs of environmental protection are paid through prices rather than taxes, the government has often been responsive to environmental political entrepreneurship. The growth and sophistication of environmental interest groups and the strong incentives of those who would bear the cost of reducing emission mean that the politics of environmental policy have an important element of interest group politics.

To illustrate the politics of environmental protection and sustainability, consider the U.S. effort to regulate carbon emissions. The Bush administration opposed mandatory reductions, but the new administration supports a mandatory cap-and-trade system. Consider the Lieberman-Warner bill. Majoritarian politics arises because everyone would benefit from emissions reductions and the associated costs would be borne by virtually everyone. Since the benefits in all likelihood outweigh the costs, support is present for the bill. The distributive consequences of the bill, however, are not uniformly distributed. The manufacturing sector will bear most of the cost, and the cost will be passed on in terms of higher prices. The electric power industry will bear the cost, and the impact on those companies will depend on how credits are allocated. If the credits are allocated based on the kilowatts of electricity emitted, companies such as Calpine that burn natural gas and companies that have a high proportion of nuclear generation could have higher profits by selling their permits. Companies, and their customers, that rely on coal generation would bear the bulk of the cost. If, however, permits were to be allocated on the basis of a baseline of carbon emissions, the impact on companies relying on coal generation would be substantially reduced. Although the power companies may not overtly oppose a cap-and-trade system, the politics will have a strong flavor of interest group competition. Moreover, companies are likely to seek subsidies or tax credits to offset costs and invest in the development of new technologies.

Interest group politics will also be present on another dimension. One argument against a major reduction as called for in Lieberman-Warner is that other countries may not adopt similar measures, placing U.S. firms at a competitive disadvantage. The same argument has been made within the European Union as it considers its carbon emissions policy beyond 2012. The Kyoto Protocol expires in 2012, providing another opportunity to enlist all nations including China, India, and the United States in a carbon emissions reduction agreement.

As another example of the political economy of environmental protection and sustainability, the alternative energy industry, including wind, solar, geothermal, biomass, marine, and hydrokinetic, has been supported by a 30 percent investment tax credit. The credit was set to expire at the end of 2008 and was in jeopardy because of a disagreement between the House, which had adopted a pay-as-you-go rule requiring that other taxes be increased to cover any extension of the credit, and the Senate, which did not require an offset. This is a case of client politics because the benefits from the tax credit accrue to alternative energy producers and the costs are widely distributed among taxpayers. The American Wind Energy Association argued that 116,000 jobs and $19 billion in investments were in jeopardy because of failure to extend the credits. In an election year Congress was likely to find a way to extend the credits.

Private and Public Politics

There are many environmental NGOs active in public politics at the federal, state, and local levels. Environmental groups testify regularly in legislative and regulatory hearings, and some demonstrate to attract media coverage to their side of the issue. Environmental groups are also active in private politics, as considered in Chapter 4 and in the Chapter 4 cases, *Shell, Greenpeace, and Brent Spar* and *Anatomy of a Corporate Campaign: Rainforest Action Network and Citigroup (A)(B)*. Some environmental groups have been active participants in the antiglobalization protests against the World Trade Organization and other international economic organizations such as the World Bank and the International Monetary Fund. Environmental groups also monitor the activities of government officials. The League of Conservation Voters annually rates members of Congress based on their votes on a set of environmental bills. The Sierra Club and some other environmental groups endorse candidates in federal and state elections. The example on the Equator Principles illustrates the role of environmental groups and private politics at the global level.

EXAMPLE

The Equator Principles

Project finance provided the funding for dams, pipelines, telecommunications systems, transportation systems, mines, power plants, and other infrastructure projects. The financing was typically secured by the anticipated revenue from the project. Many of these projects were in developing countries, and environmentalists complained that some of the projects caused environmental damage and disrupted the lives of indigenous peoples. For example, the Three Gorges dam in China displaced many thousands of people and resulted in considerable environmental damage in addition to the power it provided for the country. In 1996 the Export-Import Bank (Eximbank) of the United States refused to provide financing for the dam because of concerns about potential environmental damage. Within the Organization for Economic Cooperation and Development (OECD), the Eximbank began to promote better environmental standards, but as chairman James Harmon observed, "To my amazement, opposition to our proposal was not only intense, but came from virtually every OECD member."[1]

The campaign for higher standards was subsequently led by NGOs. Environmental groups advocated stronger guidelines for projects and targeted individual lenders as well as the construction companies. WestLB of Germany had been targeted because of a pipeline project in Ecuador. The Rainforest Action Network (RAN) targeted Citigroup because of its major role in project financing. RAN blamed Citigroup for contributing to "rainforest destruction, climate change and the disruption of the lives of indigenous peoples." RAN's tactics included hanging a large banner across Citigroup's headquarters "accusing it of 'banking on' global warming and deforestation." RAN also urged college students not to accept Citigroup credit cards and for those with cards to cut them and mail the pieces to the bank. In addition to targeting by individual environmental activist groups, a group of 100 advocacy groups signed the Collevecchio Declaration calling for financial institutions to adopt more responsible lending practices.[2]

Under pressure from the NGOs four banks, ABN Amro, Barclays, Citigroup, and WestLB, began discussions under the auspices of the International Finance Corporation (IFC), the private-sector financing unit of the World Bank.[3] The IFC hosted negotiations involving the four banks and environmental groups, and

the result was the Equator Principles, a set of voluntary principles for project financing. In addition to the initial four banks, Credit Lyonnais, Credit Suisse, HVB Group, Rabobank, Royal Bank of Scotland, and Westpac joined in the initial signing of the Principles. By late 2008, 60 banks had subscribed to the principles. In 2007, 71 percent of the $74.6 billion of project finance debt in emerging market economics was subject to the Equator Principles.

The Equator Principles applied to all projects of $50 million or more and categorized projects as A, B, or C (high, medium, and low) for their environmental or social impact. For A and B projects an environmental assessment was required, and the loan contracts from subscribing banks included a covenant stipulating that the borrower must comply with the environmental assessment. If a borrower did not fulfill its commitments, the bank could declare the loan in default. The principles are available at www.equator-principles.com.

Citigroup proclaimed, "We are extremely proud to be part of this voluntary, private-sector initiative and we are confident that we will see more and more banks active in project finance adopt these principles in the coming months." Peter Woicke of the IFC said, "The adoption of these principles by the private sector marks a profound victory for sustainable development....some of the banks came under pressure from NGOs. They also realized without the best graduates they cannot compete, and the best people want to work for companies which pay attention to environmental and social issues."[4]

Fred Krupp of Environmental Defense praised the actions of the banks: "This is a major step forward in trying to achieve environmental standards for the global economy."[5] He added, "It is remarkable to have a private bank committing to this even ahead of supposedly green governmental institutions like the European public export credit agencies."[6]

Those sentiments were not widely shared within the environmental activist community. Ilyse Hogue of RAN said, "We're glad to see banks responding to pressure that's been brought on them. But I think that you'll find broad consensus around the NGO (nongovernmental organization) community that the Equator Principles don't go far enough. The loopholes are wide enough for bulldozers to move through."[7] Michelle Chan-Fishel of Friends of the Earth commented, "We

---

[1]*Financial Times,* April 9, 2003.
[2]*Wall Street Journal,* June 4, 2003.
[3]The IFC had 175 member countries and authorized capital of $2.45 billion. The IFC provided loans and equity capital for projects to improve the lives of people in developing countries.

---

[4]*Financial Times,* June 4, 2003.
[5]*Financial Times,* April 7, 2003.
[6]*Financial Times,* April 9, 2003.

(*Continued*)

(*Continued*)

are pleased that banks are responding to public pressure and are trying to address the environmental and social impact of their transactions. But one of the key weaknesses of most corporate-led voluntary initiatives is the lack of accountability in implementation mechanisms. This may be the fatal flaw of the Equator Principles."[8] The participating banks met with the NGOs, including Environmental Defense, Friends of the Earth, and RAN, to discuss progress and implementation of the Equator Principles. The environmental groups were generally satisfied with Citigroup's implementation.

[7]*Wall Street Journal,* June 4, 2003.

[8]*Financial Times,* June 4, 2003.

Company policies can also generate public and private politics. Tesco, the largest retailer in the United Kingdom, announced a carbon label program to inform customers of the carbon emissions associated with the products they buy. The program covers all products it sells ranging from food to appliances. The program requires suppliers to determine the carbon associated with their products, which is a complicated matter since a product could be produced in several plants and countries. In the first phase of implementing its carbon label program, Tesco placed an airline sticker on products shipped by airfreight. The stickers generated protests from companies and governments of developing countries that complained that their fresh food products were being discriminated against. Abraham Barns, an agricultural attaché in Kenya's embassy in the UK, said, "The moment consumers looked at this sticker, they would stigmatize those products."[33]

The Bush administration applied a more consistent and refined cost-benefit analysis on new regulations issued by agencies including the EPA. One controversial aspect of the cost-benefit analysis was the use of life-expectancy analysis, which estimates benefits based not on the number of deaths prevented by a regulation but the number of years that life expectancy would be increased. This meant that the benefits from preventing a death of an elderly person were lower than from preventing a death of a younger person. This approach was used in medical research and had been used for years by the Food and Drug Administration. When environmentalists learned in a footnote in a report that the EPA used it as a secondary method in estimating benefits, they labeled it a "senior citizen death discount" and ran an advertisement showing an elderly person with a price tag hanging from her glasses. On the tag was written "37% off." Fearing that the method would lead to less stringent regulation, environmentalists and health care advocates created a firestorm of criticism that led the EPA to end use of the method.[34]

NIMBY and Private Politics

In 1989 William Ruckelshaus, former EPA administrator and then CEO of Browning-Ferris industries, a worldwide waste disposal company, wrote of the coming solid waste disposal crisis, "More than a third of the nation's landfills will be full within the next decade. New York will exhaust its capacity in 9 years, Los Angeles in 6, and Philadelphia is out of capacity now and must engage in continuous negotiations to dispose of its 800,000 tons per year. Why? Nobody wants garbage put down anywhere near where he lives, the 'not-in-my-backyard' syndrome—the dreaded NIMBY."[35] The NIMBY movement focuses on local environmental concerns, particularly as they involve possible risks to person or property. The movement is often directed toward refuse disposal sites, toxic waste sites, chemical and oil plants, and other facilities that may emit toxins. Hamilton (1993) studied the location decisions and expansion plans of hazardous waste disposal and incineration facilities and found that companies take into account the anticipated opposition by local groups in making their site decisions for capacity expansion.

The NIMBY movement has been energized by information provided by the federal government's Toxics Release Inventory (TRI), which provides detailed information on the

[33]*BusinessWeek,* March 17, 2008.
[34]The life-expectancy approach is considered in more detail in Chapter 20.
[35]*Wall Street Journal,* September 5, 1989.

emissions by 22,000 plants of over 300 chemicals believed to have health consequences.[36] The TRI is a result of the "right-to-know" amendment to a 1985 Superfund reauthorization bill. The amendment was passed by the House on a 212 to 211 vote.[37] The TRI has become the focus of considerable nonmarket activity with some industries seeking to have chemicals they emit dropped from the TRI and industries such as agriculture, forestry, and mining working to preserve their exemptions. Environmentalists have sought to eliminate exemptions and expand the list of chemicals. The release of the TRI has become a strategic event for environmentalists. The NRDC uses the data in the TRI to release the names of the largest emitters of those chemicals listed by the EPA as "probable human carcinogens."

In addition to allowing national organizations to take action, the TRI facilitates private politics in the form of local NIMBY action. The data in the TRI are provided for each plant, so emissions can be identified for individual communities. This allows local citizens to take nonmarket action against the plants. As an example, in 1989 the NRDC released an analysis of the TRI data listing Shendahl of Northfield, Minnesota, as the 45th largest emitter of the 11 chemicals analyzed by the NRDC. Shendahl had been legally emitting 400 tons a year of methylene chloride, a chemical whose emission was unregulated at both the federal and state level. The firm had no visible chemical emissions and had routinely been issued a permit for the discharges.[38]

When residents of Northfield learned of the emissions, their reaction was immediate. Within a week of the revelation, Shendahl announced that it would reduce emissions by 90 percent by 1993 and eliminate them entirely by 2000, switching to flammable solvents. Residents and activists formed Clean Air Northfield to continue the pressure. The activists charged that the company had withheld information on its emissions from the public, knowing in 1985 that the EPA had listed methylene chloride as a probable carcinogen. One activist group sought closure of the plant, but employees, arguing that the plant was the largest employer in town, sought an orderly reduction in emissions to save their jobs. The Amalgamated Clothing and Textile Workers Union, which represented the employees, was concerned that reducing emissions by the planned 90 percent might cause a hazardous accumulation of methylene chloride inside the plant, threatening employees. The union sought and won contract rights to monitor the emissions reduction program. The activists and the union also took action at the state level, persuading the state to include in Shendahl's emissions permit a required 93 percent reduction by 1995. Clean Air Northfield then lobbied the state government for the elimination of all methylene chloride emissions.

Empirical studies by Hamilton (1995) and Konar and Cohen (1997) found that the market value of companies included in the TRI fell upon release of the TRI, and those with the greatest decreases subsequently had the largest reduction in their toxic releases. Maxwell, Lyon, and Hackett (2000) studied voluntary reductions in TRI releases and concluded that reductions were larger the higher the local membership in the Sierra Club and the NRDC. Since the toxic chemicals released were within the levels permitted by environmental regulations, the identified effects were likely due to local environmental pressures and private politics that caused firms to reduce their emissions.

MANAGEMENT OF ENVIRONMENTAL PROTECTION ISSUES

The management of environmental issues involves both external and internal activities. Externally, firms and their managers must address a set of issues that arise in their market and nonmarket environments. These issues may be addressed in government institutional arenas such as Congress, state legislatures, courts, and regulatory agencies; or outside those institutions, as with NIMBY activities and direct interactions with environmentalists.

Environmental issues have become so important, pervasive, and costly that high-level attention must be given to them. Some firms have established committees of their boards of directors to assume oversight responsibility for environmental matters. Some CEOs

---

[36]Firms are required to notify the federal, state, and local governments of any emission of the chemicals.
[37]See Hamilton (1997) for a study of the voting on the amendment.
[38]This account is based on an article in the *New York Times*, January 2, 1991.

have personally declared a commitment to environmental protection. When DuPont Chairman Edgar S. Woolard, Jr., assumed the role of the company's chief environmentalist, the level of awareness rose. DuPont's vice president for safety, health, and environmental affairs commented on the difference: "I used to have to do a real selling job to line up people....Then suddenly it wasn't just me trying to get the organization to do things, it was Ed. Now they call all the time."[39] Some firms established corporate environmental groups and audit units. IBM created the position of vice president for environmental health and safety in its corporate office and gave that office responsibility for ensuring compliance with environmental regulations and company policies. Home Depot has been aggressive in its environmental policies, particularly in its wood procurement, as considered in the example.

To implement its new environmental lending policy for project finance, Citigroup placed the group responsible for its Environmental and Social Risk Management policy in a position in which it interacted directly with senior lenders. Ilyse Hogue of RAN commented, "Having only five full-time staff dedicated to what the majority of the world is concerned with still falls short. But they have made smart choices by not locating [Environmental and Social Risk Management] staff in a marginalized environmental affairs office, instead placing them in positions of power with real access to senior decision-makers. That has really been key."[40]

A commitment from top management may be necessary for successful management of environmental matters, but it is not sufficient, since compliance takes place at the level of the individual facility. Sensitivity to environmental issues and compliance responsibility must be distributed throughout the firm. Furthermore, ideas for waste reduction and pollution control often are generated at the plant level. The Carrier Corporation, for example, was able to eliminate through engineering redesign its degreasing operation in the manufacture of air conditioners.

Wal-Mart was the subject of an unrelenting private politics campaign as considered in the Part I integrative case, *Wal-Mart: Nonmarket Pressure and Reputation Risk (A)*. Wal-Mart began to work with Conservation International and the Natural Resources Defense Council on environmental initiatives.[41] The company evaluated the packaging of products it sold and found that reducing packaging also reduced shipping costs. Wal-Mart also opened an Environmental Demonstration Store and planned to open another. The store used solar panels, wind turbines, burned the used oil from oil changes, and burned fat used to fry chickens.[42] It also had a computerized heating and cooling system and used low-mercury fluorescent lamps and electronic ballasts.

In 2005 Wal-Mart announced a $35 million, 10-year Acres for America program to offset the nearly 140,000 acres that its current stores occupied plus its planned expansion over the next 10 years. The company formed a partnership with the Fish and Wildlife Foundation for the purchase of the acreage. The land would be available for hunting, fishing, and other outdoor activities and for sustainable logging.

In October 2005, Wal-Mart announced a major environmental initiative focused on reducing energy use. The initiative included improving the efficiency of energy use in its supercenters and other stores. It also pledged to improve the fuel efficiency of its huge truck fleet by 25 percent over three years and by 100 percent over 10 years. The company announced that it would invest $500 million annually to reduce its emissions of greenhouse gases by 20 percent over seven years. Wal-Mart also pledged to use its power to encourage its suppliers to be more energy efficient and to reduce their packaging. The initiative drew praise from Environmental Defense and the Sierra Club. A spokesperson for WakeUpWal-Mart.com, however, said, "It is a diversionary tactic. Wal-Mart understands that they have a growing public relations disaster on their hands."[43]

---

[39]*New York Times*, March 3, 1991.
[40]www.equator-principles.com/inc/printversion.php
[41]This material is from the Chapter 19 case, *Wal-Mart: Nonmarket Pressure and Reputation Risk (B): A New Nonmarket Strategy*. For more detained information on Wal-Mart's sustainability strategy, see the case *Wal-Mart's Sustainability Strategy*, OIT-71, Graduate School of Business, Stanford University.
[42]"Lee Scott on Why Wal-Mart Is Playing Nicer," *BusinessWeek*, October 3, 2005.
[43]Michael Barbaro and Felicity Barringer, "Wal-Mart To Seek Savings In Energy," *New York Times*, October 25, 2005.

Many companies attempt to instill the attitude that environmental matters are the responsibility of all employees. Many have established Environment, Health, and Safety (EHS) programs with explicit goals and public reporting on the progress made on those goals. BP reports publicly on its EHS performance, which is independently reviewed as part of its sustainability reporting.

Managers must interact with a host of regulatory officials, ranging from those who grant permits and inspect facilities to those who write implementation regulations. Managers should deal with regulators on the basis of trust and mutual respect but must also be prepared to suggest new means for achieving environmental goals and to oppose rules that may be overly burdensome. Managers should recognize that just as they face competing pressures for profits and environmental goals, regulators face competing pressures from environmental groups, oversight by political principles in Congress, and monitoring by those who bear the cost of regulation. Recognizing the pressures regulators face can be important in developing workable relationships.

Many firms have extended their internal environmental management programs to include external advice and consultations with local communities. Dow Chemical formed a Corporate Environmental Advisory Council to advise the company on its environmental stewardship policies and programs. Dow also encouraged its plant managers to form community advisory councils to address local issues and assure the community that its activities met environmental standards. Dow's emphasis was on pollution prevention through the four Rs: reduce, reuse, recycle, and recover. Source reduction was the preferred method followed by recycling and recovery.[44] The example illustrates the importance of source reduction in pollution. King and Lennox (2002) found that source reduction reduces total production and pollution control costs as argued by Porter and van der Linde (1995).

---

[44]See Popoff (1992).

EXAMPLE

Dow Chemical and Local Environmentalists

In 1996 Dow Chemical, in conjunction with the NRDC, invited five local activists to join in a project at its Midland, Michigan, plant complex to make environmental improvements that would also save the company money.[1] Despite concerns about the possible release of proprietary information, Dow agreed to reduce toxic chemicals by 35 percent and to reduce emissions into the air and water by the same amount. These reductions were beyond any required by government regulations and were to be achieved only through pollution prevention approaches. More strikingly, Dow allowed the environmentalists to choose which toxic chemicals to be included, and it accepted without challenge the 26 selected.

Dow and the environmentalists agreed to use an outside environmental engineering expert to provide recommendations for how to achieve the reductions. Often the reductions were for small changes in processes or equipment settings that reduced the pro-

duction and release of the toxic chemicals. Many of these changes had been overlooked by Dow engineers, whose focus had been on satisfying regulations rather than going beyond those requirements. Dow reported that it spent $3.1 million on process changes yielding cost savings of $5.4 million a year. A major part of the savings occurred in its waste treatment facilities, which no longer had to treat certain toxics. Moreover, the company exceeded the targeted 35 percent reductions.[2]

The project also had less tangible benefits. Samuel Smolnik, vice president for global EHS, commented on a practical benefit of the project, "When you reduce waste and emissions, a community is a lot more willing to issue permits for other operations down the road."[3]

The NRDC offered to cooperate with other companies and expressed disappointment that it had no takers. Part of the explanation may be due to its other stances, such as its criticism of Intel's Project XL program with the EPA, discussed earlier in the chapter.

---

[1]This example is based on an article in *New York Times,* July 18, 1999.

[2]The final project report is available from the NRDC.
[3]*New York Times,* September 9, 2001.

With increasing frequency companies are joining with environmental groups to discuss issues and solve particular environmental problems. As indicated in Chapter 4, most companies prefer moderate, science-based groups such as Conservation International and Environmental Defense. Environmental Defense (ED) has embraced the objective of efficiency in pollution control and advocates the use of incentive approaches to achieve that end. This earned ED a role in the development of the provisions of the Clean Air Act Amendments of 1990 and in the design of the emissions permits trading system for the Kyoto Protocol. As indicated previously, ED also joined with BP to develop an internal tradable permits system for CO_2 emissions. ED has also developed a working relationship with McDonald's, resulting in over 20 joint projects. Their first project, a waste reduction program, is discussed in the example.

EXAMPLE

McDonald's and Waste Reduction

McDonald's is the largest restaurant system in the world and also one of the world's largest generators of solid waste. For a number of years McDonald's had been reducing its use of packaging materials. The packaging weight for a Big Mac, fries, and a shake had been reduced from 46 grams in the early 1970s to 25 grams by the 1990s. McDonald's had also conducted a number of waste reduction experiments, including a test program in 800 restaurants to recycle polystyrene containers. Environmental groups, however, pressured the company to make further reductions in its solid waste.[1] The Citizens' Clearinghouse for Hazardous Waste worked for 3 years, pressuring McDonald's to replace its polystyrene clamshell sandwich container. McDonald's replaced it with paper in 1990.

In the same year McDonald's decided to work with ED on the solid waste reduction issue. ED had a staff of over 110, including scientists, engineers, economists, and attorneys. It also had both a moderate stance on environmental protection and considerable experience in dealing with solid waste issues. The relationship began when Ed Rensi, president of McDonald's U.S.A., accepted ED president Fred Krupp's invitation to discuss the waste issue. After a number of joint staff meetings, McDonald's and ED established a joint task force project to study options for reducing solid wastes. The task force studied McDonald's operations and its 39 regional distribution centers and visited suppliers and disposal and recycling facilities. Each ED member also worked for a day in a McDonald's restaurant to gain an appreciation for its operations.

In 1991 the task force released its final report, identifying 40 steps that could reduce McDonald's solid wastes by 80 percent.[2] An important part of the task force study was a detailed investigation of McDonald's solid waste generation. The study revealed, for example, that 79 percent by weight of on-premise waste was generated behind the counter. "'The results of the task force far exceed all of our expectations and original goals,' said Keith Magnuson, McDonald's director of operations development and a task force member. 'We started out to study waste reduction options. Instead, we developed a comprehensive waste reduction plan that is already being implemented.' . . . 'The task force has set forth a long-term vision bolstered by concrete actions to be taken in the short term,' said Dr. Richard Denison, a senior scientist with ED and a task force member."[3]

The task force study also resulted in changes in McDonald's decision-making criteria. In its purchasing decisions on disposable packaging, McDonald's had considered three factors: availability, functionality, and cost. As a result of the task force study, it added a fourth: waste reduction.

In addition to the specific measures, the task force emphasized instilling a commitment to waste reduction throughout the McDonald's system. Three-quarters of McDonald's 8,500 U.S. restaurants were owned by independent franchisees. In addition, McDonald's had over 100 packaging suppliers. McDonald's had a tradition of standardization and strict enforcement of policies, so institutionalizing the waste reduction commitment was not difficult. Overall compliance assurance rested with the Environmental Affairs Department, but the commitment was lodged in all areas of its operations, including with suppliers and franchisees. McDonald's senior environmental officer reported directly to the board of directors on progress in implementing the task force recommendations.

---

[1]See the Chapter 1 case, *The Nonmarket Environment of McDonald's.*
[2]The McDonald's Corporation–Environmental Defense Fund Waste Reduction Task Force report is available at www.environmentaldefense.org.

[3]McDonald's Corporation press release, April 16, 1991. In contrast to these statements, the original agreement between McDonald's and ED sought options rather than an action plan and contained language allowing for separate opinions to be issued and for either side to withdraw from the project.

Environmental Activism at Home Depot

Home Depot was founded in 1978 and became the world's largest home improvement specialty retailer with 1,707 stores in all 50 states. Its sales reached $64.8 billion in 2003 and earnings were $4.3 billion. Home Depot was the world's second largest retailer and had 300,000 associates. It had frequently been ranked as one of the nation's most-admired companies.

After Earth Day in 1990 Home Depot established its Environmental Principles and initially focused on recycling and offering some green products. In 1992 the company faced its first challenge from environmental groups. The Rainforest Action Network (RAN) challenged the company to eliminate its use of old growth tropical timber. Home Depot phased out its line of teak furniture and pledged to buy wood from sustainable sources. Environmental activists, including RAN, again targeted Home Depot and other companies in 1997 to stop their use of old growth redwood, and Home Depot and the other companies did so. RAN then launched its old growth market campaign in 1998, again targeting Home Depot. RAN hung a banner on Home Depot's headquarters and held protests at hundreds of stores.[1] Concerned about the public criticism of its timber sourcing, Home Depot agreed to stop buying old growth products. It also agreed to give preference to Forest Stewardship Council (FSC) certified wood.[2]

Home Depot's environmental practices were recharged when in 2000 Ron Jarvis was appointed as merchandising vice president with authority to terminate timber supply contracts. When Jarvis learned that an Indonesian supplier was using slash-and-burn harvesting, he cancelled the contract. Subsequently, Home Depot reduced by 90 percent its sourcing from Indonesia, where illegal logging was commonplace. The remaining purchases were from sources with sustainable practices. Rewarding those sources for their practices, however, did not cause other loggers in Indonesia to change their practices.[3] Jarvis also cancelled all purchases from Gabon when suppliers refused to change their practices.

When it was targeted by the activists, Home Depot realized that it had no means of identifying the sources of the wood products it sold nor how much wood it purchased from those sources. It began a major tracking effort that bore fruit in 2002. Home Depot now knows the source of every wood product

it sells. In 1999 it issued its first Wood Purchasing Policy, and in 2002 it issued its current Policy. Ninety-four percent of its wood products now comes from North American timber, where forestland has increased by 1.5 percent during the past decade.[4] Home Depot pledged to purchase wood only from "forests managed in a responsible way and to eliminate wood purchases from endangered regions of the world. . . ."

Home Depot went beyond its own practices and began corporate environmental activism. Along with Lowe's and other companies, it joined with environmentalists to convince the Canadian government to stop logging in the Great Bear Rainforest in British Columbia. Home Depot joined with The Nature Conservancy and a British agency to put bar codes on timber from Borneo. Home Depot had reduced its purchases of Indonesian lauan by 70 percent and worked with The Nature Conservancy, Tropical Forest Foundation, Tropical Forest Trust, and the World Wildlife Fund to improve practices in Indonesia. RAN executive director Michael Brune, however, criticized any purchasing from Indonesia: "This is not a time to establish small toeholds of good production."[5] RAN wanted all purchases from Indonesia halted.

Home Depot recognized only FSC certification, but the supply was too small to satisfy its demand, let alone other retailers and home builders. Home Depot decided to increase the supply. It worked with Tembec, a large Canadian lumber producer, to increase FSC certified lumber. Tembec agreed to obtain FSC certification for all its lumber by 2005, compared with 25 percent in 2003.[6]

After a call from the environmental activist group Forest Ethics claiming that tree farms were wiping out the natural forests in Chile, where Home Depot purchased 10 percent of the country's timber production, Jarvis called the heads of the two timber suppliers in Chile that had been targeted by a boycott by U.S. and Chilean activists. The timber executives disputed the activists' claim, stating that in the past they had cleared less than a million acres of forests and had discontinued the practice. The companies now planted their tree farms on agricultural and ranch land. Jarvis invited the activists and the Chilean timber producers to Home Depot's headquarters in Atlanta to discuss the matter. The next meeting was in Chile, where the timber companies gave the activists a tour of their farms.

[1]See the case *Strategic Activism: The Rainforest Action Network*, Case No. P-44, Graduate School of Business, Stanford University.
[2]FSC was backed by environmental groups including RAN and Greenpeace.
[3]*Wall Street Journal*, August 6, 2004.

[4]www.homedepot.com.
[5]*BusinessWeek*, November 24, 2003.
[6]Canada News Wire, December 3, 2003.

(Continued)

(*Continued*)

Jarvis said, "I basically told both sides, 'If you want to win on this, you have to give.'"[7] The timber companies agreed not to buy recently cleared land for their tree farms and made some changes in their practices. The activists agreed to call off the boycott and praised the companies. Randy Hayes, president of RAN, observed, "If you've got Home Depot carrying your water, you're going to get a lot farther than as just an environmental group."[8] The environmentalists stopped targeting Home Depot.

Ron Jarvis commented, "I think that maybe this is a template we can use in other countries."[9]

Source: This case was prepared from public sources by Professor David P. Baron. Copyright © 2004 by David P. Baron. All rights reserved. Reprinted with permission.

[7]*Wall Street Journal,* August 6, 2004.

[8]*Wall Street Journal,* August 6, 2004.
[9]*Wall Street Journal,* August 6, 2004.

Not all cooperative arrangements between environmental NGOs and companies produce positive results. Federal Express and Environmental Defense joined in a project to explore the feasibility of a hybrid-electric truck that would be more environmentally friendly than its standard pickup and delivery trucks. William Logue, executive vice-president of FedEx, reported on the experience with the 93 trucks in its Opti-Fleet E700 fleet. Compared to its standard trucks, the hybrids were "shown to increase fuel economy by 40 percent while decreasing particulate emissions by 90 percent and greenhouse gases by more than 25 percent." He also said, "The Opti-Fleet E700 costs almost twice as much as a standard pickup and delivery truck and, while we embarked on this program with a rallying call for others in the transportation sector to get on board, very few companies have committed to the technology, and the main reason is cost."[45]

VOLUNTARY COLLECTIVE ENVIRONMENTAL PROGRAMS

A number of voluntary self-regulation programs have been established. These programs are relatively new, and their effectiveness has only begun to be evaluated. The International Organization for Standards has established ISO 14001, a worldwide voluntary environmental program for improved environmental management systems. In contrast to government regulation, ISO 14001 does not establish environmental standards or specify pollution-control practices. Instead, it emphasizes managerial processes to improve environmental performance. Over 36,000 companies have obtained ISO 14001 certification, with over 1,500 in the United States. Delmas (2000, 2001) studied the participation of firms in ISO 14001. Potoski and Prakash (2005) studied participation of U.S. facilities in ISO 14001 and concluded that, although it is costly, participation provided reputational benefits for participants. They, however, were not able to determine how effective it was in achieving improved environmental performance beyond that required by government and induced by private politics.

The Responsible Care program is a worldwide EHS voluntary regulation program operated by the chemical industry. Initiated in Canada in 1985, Responsible Care was established in the United States in 1989 following the accident at the Bhopal chemical facility that killed thousands. Responsible Care programs are now conducted by chemical industry associations in 47 countries that account for over 90 percent of chemicals production. Responsible Care focuses on improved practices for human and environmental protection. In addition to the direct benefits from improved practices, the program provides reputational benefits to the industry. Participation is voluntary, and many chemical companies do not participate. Among the participants, companies with public faces and brand names are overrepresented, suggesting that the reputational benefits are important to those firms.

King and Lennox (2002) evaluated the Responsible Care program in the United States and found that companies with poor performance were disproportionately represented in the program. They also found that participants did not improve their per-

[45]William J. Logue, "Testimony." Committee on Energy and Natural Resources, U.S. Senate, January 30, 2007.

formance at a faster rate than companies not participating in the program. The former is consistent with the hypothesis that companies with the worst performance have the most to gain from an improvement in the collective reputation of the industry, and the latter is consistent with the hypothesis that some participants shirk on their commitments to improve performance. Responsible Care subsequently strengthened their standards and provided for voluntary inspections of facilities.

A number of programs such as Responsible Care have been called "greenwash" by environmental groups. The allegations are that the programs sound good to the public, but they fail to live up to their promises. That is, performance does not match the proclamations of the programs. The same criticisms have been levied against some of the voluntary programs run by the EPA and other government agencies. For example, Lyon and Kim (2007) found that participation in the Department of Energy's voluntary greenhouse gas registry had no effect on the carbon emissions per unit of electricity generated by electric utilities.

SUMMARY

Environmental protection and sustainability have broad support among the public, government, and the business community. Environmental protection is costly, however, and the more efficient the approach taken to reduce pollution, the greater reduction can be attained for any given expenditure. Conversely, for a given level of pollution reduction, the approach used to achieve that reduction affects the costs that society must bear. The social efficiency approach to environmental protection seeks to minimize the sum of the harm from pollution and the cost of reducing that harm.

An emissions tax system imposes a charge on pollutants emitted, which increases the costs of emissions and provides incentives to reduce them. A cap-and-trade system caps emissions, issues permits equal to the emissions cap, and allows the permits to be traded. A polluter with relatively low costs of reducing emissions has an incentive to reduce emissions by more than its permits require and sell the unused permits to another firm that has higher costs of reducing emissions. Both systems provide incentives to achieve social efficiency. The EPA has also used other incentive approaches in its bubble, offset, and credits programs, but the most successful system in operation is the transferable permits program for controlling sulfur dioxide emissions that cause acid rain. The transferable permits system has substantially reduced pollution control costs, benefiting companies and their customers and also benefiting the environment. Cap-and-trade is also used in implementing the Kyoto Protocol, and the European Emissions Trading System has been in operation for several years but with only limited success.

Environmental policies such as a cap-and-trade system are the product of a political competition in which distributive consequences and efficiency considerations weigh large. The Clean Air Act Amendments of 1990 involved bargaining on several specific measures affecting those distributive consequences. On the acid rain provisions, bargaining occurred on both the stringency of the cap and the distribution of the permits. The same incentives for nonmarket action are present in the effort in the United States to establish a cap-and-trade system for carbon emissions.

Environmental issues spark a wide range of private politics in addition to public politics at the federal and state levels. At the local level, environmental groups have been increasingly active in addressing environmental issues. The NIMBY movement and private politics have grown in importance. NGOs have been successful in pressuring firms to strengthen their environmental and sustainability programs.

Environmental protection and compliance are important components of management responsibility. Firms and their managers must address a variety of nonmarket issues that involve local communities, environmental groups, legislators, and regulators. A number of firms and environmental groups have developed relationships that allow them to address issues in a nonconfrontational manner. Some firms have worked directly with environmentalists, as in the case of the McDonald's–Environmental Defense project on reducing the company's solid wastes. Firms have developed a variety of innovative voluntary programs that go beyond the requirements of regulation.

--------------------------------------- C A S E S ---------------------------------------
Regulation as Opportunity: Cummins Inc.

Introduction

Motor vehicles were a major source of pollution and the greenhouse gas CO_2. Emissions standards for automobiles had been sufficiently tightened that new automobiles were quite clean. Diesel-powered vehicles, however, remained a major source of pollution, particularly nitrogen oxide (NOx) and fine particulates. Heavy trucks and off-road vehicles in the United States were diesel-powered, and a number of companies produced diesel truck engines. Truck manufacturers and diesel manufacturers had opposed more stringent regulations. After a long and contentious political contest between the oil industry and the automobile industry, Congress passed new standards that required gas stations by October 15, 2006 to begin selling ultra low sulfur diesel (ULSD) fuel with a sulfur content of 15 ppm compared to 500 ppm in the current diesel fuel.[46] In addition new emissions standards were imposed effective on January 1, 2007 with tighter standards being phased in through 2010.[47] At that time diesel engines would be as clean as gasoline engines.

The impending diesel emission standards had created a boom in the sale of heavy trucks, as trucking and construction companies sought to avoid having to buy trucks equipped with the new emissions control systems. The new standards were said to increase the cost of a $100,000 truck by $7000–$10,000. As a result of the boom analysts predicted that the industry would slump badly in 2007, and several manufacturers had begun to lay off workers. Caterpillar, a major producer of diesel engines and nonroad vehicles, revised downward its earnings forecast, and its share price promptly fell 15 percent.

Nearly half the automobiles sold in Europe were diesels, compared to less than 1 percent in the United States.[48] Diesels had several advantages. First, in most countries in Europe, diesel fuel was less costly than gasoline largely because of lower taxes. Second, diesels delivered about 30 percent better fuel economy than gasoline-powered vehicles. Third, diesel engines generated higher torque than gasoline engines, yielding greater power and better performance.[49] In addition, the greater fuel economy of diesels would reduce CO_2 emissions as they replaced gasoline vehicles.

Diesel vehicles were somewhat more expensive than gasoline vehicles.[50] In the United States the prices of diesel fuel and gasoline were approximately the same, but the explanations for the low sales of diesel-powered passenger vehicles were (1) the bad reputation developed in the 1970s when diesel automobiles were unreliable and dirty and (2) the stringent emissions standards in California and four other states. The performance problems had been eliminated in the new generation diesel vehicles, but the reputation lingered with many consumers.

Not surprisingly, European automobile makers had an advantage in the market for light vehicles. In 2006 the only diesel automobiles sold in the United States were made by Volkswagen and Daimler-Chrysler. Volkswagen planned to withdraw its current diesel models from the U.S. market and replace them in 2007 with new versions meeting the 2007 standards.

One limit on the sale of diesel light vehicles was the stricter emissions standards in California and 4 other states. Some vehicles, such as the Jeep Grand Cherokee to be introduced in 2007, would be sold only in the other 45 states. The engine would be produced in Berlin by Mercedes-Benz. Mercedes planned to introduce three new diesel models to be sold in the 45 states. The Daimler-Chrysler vehicles used the Bluetec emissions-cleansing technology, which involved injecting urea into the fuel stream to reduce NOx emissions.

Cummins Inc.

Cummins Inc. had 2005 sales of $9.9 billion and net income of $550 million. Its products were sold through 550 distribution centers and 5,000 dealers. In 2005 Cummins Emissions Solutions had revenue of $500 million. Cummins' financial performance had, however, caused concerns over the years. Mike Osega, publisher of *Diesel Progress* magazine, said, "Cummins is the Mark Twain of the engine business. Their demise has been predicted by everyone in the last 20 years. But they keep getting better."[51]

Cummins saw an opportunity created by the more stringent regulations. A company that could develop a new generation of engines that was both energy

---

[46]By 2010 all diesel fuel had to meet the 15 ppm standard.
[47]The diesel fuel for nonroad vehicles was required to meet the 15 ppm standard by 2010.
[48]Ultra clean diesel fuel with 10 ppm was available in Europe. As of September 2009 new diesel automobiles and vans in new lines would be required to be equipped with a particle filter and for existing lines as of January 2011.
[49]In 2006 an Audi diesel race car won the Le Mans 24-Hour race with an average speed of 134 miles per hour.

[50]The price premium for diesel vehicles was approximately one-third that for hybrid vehicles, and diesels were said to be more efficient than hybrids for highway driving. Diesel engines were also much less complex than the systems in hybrids.
[51]*New York Times,* November 10, 2006.

efficient and met the emissions standards could have a competitive advantage in an expanding market for diesel vehicles, particularly in light trucks. The natural advantages of diesel power were projected to develop a market in pickup trucks and SUVs. Cummins had been focusing on engines for heavy trucks and non-road vehicles.

Cummins' strategy had several components. One was to develop a new energy-efficient engine. Another was to prepare to enter the light vehicle market. A third component was to develop an effective emissions control system.

Cummins partnered with the Department of Energy with the assistance of Dodge Truck Engineering to develop a light truck clean diesel engine with a 50 percent fuel economy improvement compared to a 1997 gasoline-powered vehicle. The engine would also reduce emission of particulates and NOx.

The market for light trucks, including SUVs, pickups, and vans, was over 8 million units a year. Cummins partnered with Dodge to introduce a Dodge Ram Heavy Duty with turbo-diesel 6.7 liter engine, producing 350 horsepower at 3,000 RPM and 650 lb.-ft of torque. With the cleaner diesel fuel the truck could be sold in all 50 states, meeting the 2007 heavy-duty emissions standards. Cummins announced that it would invest $250 million to reopen a partly idled factory and hire 600 workers to produce light duty diesel engines for trucks below 8,500 pounds gross vehicle weight.

In addition to the 2007 standards a particular challenge to diesel engine manufacturers was to meet the EPA's more stringent 2008 standards for hydrocarbons, nitrogen oxide (NOx), and particulates. The NOx and particulates standards were substantial challenges for the diesel engine industry.

Emissions Controls

As part of its strategy Cummins established in 2002 the Cummins Emissions Solutions to develop improved emissions controls systems to allow diesels to meet the upcoming new emissions standards.[52] In addition to developing a more energy-efficient engine, Cummins developed and produced emissions control systems for diesels. Its Diesel Particulate Filter (DPF) was designed to reduce particulate matter in the exhaust by 90 percent. In conjunction with the DPF Cummins produced a diesel oxidation catalyst that allowed the DPF to regenerate its capacity. Christina M. Vujovich, vice president of marketing and environmental policy, said, "We didn't want to take on after-treatment just because it was sexy

to do. We only wanted to take it on because it provided additional value to customers."[53] John C. Wall, vice president and chief technology officer, commented, "You really like to have all that in your control, so that you're not at the mercy of someone else not turning up with their part of the costume." He added, "As we remind our engineers, the EPA has never bought a single engine from Cummins. This is really about how do you create customer value."[54]

The Launch

EPA Administrator Stephen L. Johnson chose the Cummins test facilities in its headquarters town Columbus, Indiana, to kick off the U.S. transition to the new ultra-low sulfur diesel fuel. Johnson proclaimed, "Over the last century, diesels have become our nation's economic workhorse—reliable, fuel efficient and long-lasting. Today, . . . America's economic workhorse is becoming America's environmental workhorse."[55]

Cummins Engine Business President Jim Kelly stated, "Achieving the new, lower emissions level would not have been possible without ULSD. This cleaner fuel allows Cummins and others to produce engines that are capable of meeting the new standards without sacrificing performance and reliability."[56]

Cummins was renowned for its commitment to corporate social responsibility, particularly its community involvement teams. Its mission was "making people's lives better by unleashing the power of Cummins." Legendary president and chairman J. Irwin Miller had articulated the company's version of corporate responsibility: "Our success as a corporation will be increasingly influenced by our ability to understand the environment within which we do business. Corporate responsibility involves far more than the development of new social programs. A social profile is an essential part of the selection of new plant sites, market penetration, and consideration of potential ventures. We have a responsibility to use our resources to respond to the needs of the society which gives us our charter. We can, in the long run, be a healthy company only in so far as we exist and serve within an economically and socially healthy society." In 2005 Cummins was named "Best Corporate Citizen" by *Business Ethics* magazine. Cummins was one of 42 companies named to Dow Jones' Sustainability World Index.[57] ■

---

[52]In 2006 Cummins entered into a private-public partnership with the California South Coast Air Quality Management District to demonstrate that advanced technology diesel engines could meet the EPA 2010 on-highway standards.

[53]*New York Times,* November 10, 2006.
[54]*New York Times,* November 10, 2006.
[55]Stephen L. Johnson, Statement, Columbus, Indiana, October 10, 2006.
[56]Jim Kelly, Statement, Columbus, Indiana, October 10, 2006.
[57]Twelve hundred companies applied to be included in the Index.

Preparation Questions

1. Which industries/companies benefited from the new regulations and which were hurt?
2. How attractive are the opportunities for Cummins created by the new environmental standards?
3. Is Cummins likely to gain a competitive advantage in the markets for diesel engines and emissions control systems? Why or why not?
4. Is it wise for Cummins to commit itself to a proprietary emissions control technology rather than selecting the best technology the market produces?
5. Did Cummins' commitment to corporate social responsibility contribute to its strategy for seizing the opportunity created by the more stringent emissions standards and the ultra low sulfur diesel fuel? Would engine manufacturers who were only interested in profits have adopted the same strategy as Cummins?

Emerging Nanotechnology Regulation: Samsung's SilverCare Washing Machine

Ancient Egyptians drank from silver cups for its health benefits and tossed silver coins into water barrels to clean them. More recently, nanosilver had been added to bandages to aid healing.

Samsung developed a line of eco-friendly washing machines that washed clothes at low rather than high temperatures. Samsung claimed a "92% energy savings over hot water sanitization." The tub was coated with silver, and during use "metallic silver atoms electrolytically stripped of an electron are injected during the wash and rinse cycles, allowing over 100 quadrillion silver ions—which act as a super cleaning solution—to penetrate deep into the fabric to sanitize clothing without the need for hot water or bleach. . . . Prominent scientists have shown that [washing in cold or warm water] commonly results in clean wet laundry with a significant microbial contamination. Samsung's SilverCare washer specifically targets the microbial contamination of the typical American washing methods." [58] "Samsung is committed to being first to market with advanced technologies that benefit and enhance people's lives, and the new washers with SilverCare technology are a perfect example," said Peter Weedfald, senior vice president.

The SilverCare technology was eco-friendly in two ways. First, washing in cold or warm, as opposed to hot, water reduced energy consumption. Second, bleach was not needed to reduce microbial health risks.

Milliken & Company, a manufacturer of fabric, yarn, and chemicals, put its silver-ion biocide and a stain treatment in all the carpets, fabrics, and upholstery it produced. Its silver-ion biocide was intended to reduce odors. [59]

Pure Bioscience of El Cajon, California produced a microbial product, Axenhol, which used as an active ingredient silver dihydrogen citrate. Pure Bioscience claimed that the product was "less toxic to humans and the environment than triclosan, the additive produced by Ciba that is widely used in products labeled 'antibacterial.'" [60]

Gillian Morris, industry manager of the Chemicals and Materials practice of Kline & Company, commented on the difference in attitudes about nanotechnology and the use of silver ion biocides: "The Japanese are quite sophisticated in terms of the technology and demand for protection and the method in which it is delivered to the final article. On the other hand, in Europe, there is growing concern about overexposure to antimicrobial substances. The fear is that sanitizing everything may reduce people's natural immunity to common germs and help antibiotic-resistant strains of bacteria to develop." [61] The European Union's Biocidal Products Directive governed such products.

The Woodrow Wilson International Center for Scholars maintained a list of products that used nanotechnology and had identified a list of 350 as of late 2006. [62] The most widely used nanoparticle was nanosilver.

Emerging Regulation

Nanotechnology had the promise of providing benefits to consumers, producers, and the environment; for example, in cleaning toxic waste spills and sites. Environmentalists, however, warned of the risks to health and the environment. [63] Dr. Jennifer Sass of the Natural Resources

[58]Samsung Electronics America, Press Release, March 23, 2006. "[T]his process removed or killed 99.9% of odor-causing bacteria."
[59]Associate Press Financial Wire, October 20, 2006.

[60]Knight-Ridder/Tribune Business News, April 28, 2006.
[61]Kline & Company, Press Release, August 22, 2006.
[62]www.nanotechproject.org/comumerproducts.
[63]The National Science and Technology Council, "Environmental, Health, and Safety Research Needs for Engineered Nanoscale Materials," Washington, DC, 2006.

Defense Council (NRDC) warned, "Nanoparticles behave unpredictably and could harm human beings, wildlife and the environment."[64] Sass criticized the Environmental Protection Agency: "In the face of such a significant jump in the number of everyday products containing untested and unlabeled nanoparticles, the Environmental Protection Agency is moving much too slowly to ensure that they are safe."

The National Association of Clean Water Agencies (NACWA) wrote to the EPA on February 14, 2006 asking that the silver in washing machines be regulated because silver is highly toxic to marine life, even in small amounts. The NACWA represented wastewater treatment agencies that were required to meet strict toxicity requirements of the Clean Water Act for their discharges. The letter stated, "To allow unrestricted use of a product that intentionally releases silver into the environment would be an irresponsible neglect of the principles of environmental sustainability that should strongly influence such decisions."[65]

In response to the NACWA the EPA announced that it would regulate the silver ions released in a Samsung SilverWash machine as a pesticide under the Federal Insecticide, Fungicide and Rodenticide Act (FIFRA). The EPA's jurisdiction under FIFRA apparently resulted from Samsung's claims about the microbial properties of its SilverCare technology. The EPA filed a notice in the Federal Register.

This was not a decision to regulate nanotechnology per se, since Samsung had not filed a pesticide registration application. The EPA stated, "Recent press articles have referred to the Samsung washing machine as a product of nanotechnology. However, since we have not yet received an application for registration from Samsung, the agency has not yet come to any conclusions about whether a washing machine that releases silver ions or any other similar product involves nanomaterial." The EPA potentially could regulate nanomaterials under the Toxic Substances Control Act (TSCA).[66]

In response to the decision the NRDC wrote to the EPA stating, "We are confident that once EPA has specifically examined nanosilver pursuant to the appropriate FIFRA risk assessment provisions, EPA will recognize the significant harm that this substance inflicts on the environment (particularly aquatic organisms) and will be compelled either to prohibit or significantly restrict its use."

Jim Jones, director of the Office of Pesticide Programs of the EPA, said of the EPA's planned regulation, "We will be able to evaluate them and ensure that these products are not going to do damage to the aquatic environment." The EPA could require manufacturers to provide scientific evidence that their products did not produce environmental risks. Jones, however, made it clear that the regulation would apply only to those products advertised as germ-killing. He explained, "Unless you're making a claim to kill a pest, you're not a pesticide."[67] Mae Wu, an attorney with the NRDC, noted, "It sounds like a major legal loophole and is probably something that will have to be dealt with in the courts."[68]

The NRDC wrote to Jones praising the agency for its action, arguing that nanosilver was a pesticide and asking for stronger action.[69] The NRDC called attention to the products marketed by the Sharper Image and Samsung's SilverCare™ Technology. The NRDC stated, "Animal studies suggest that nanoparticles can cause inflammation, damage brain cells and cause pre-cancerous lesions."

Earlier, Tri-TAC, an advisory group for the California Association of Sanitation Agencies, the California Water Environment Association, and the League of California Cities, had written to Jones and the California Department of Pesticide Regulation asking for regulation of Samsung's "SilverWash" washing machine.[70]

Although regulation under FIFRA was a concern to the nanotechnology industry, a greater threat was that TSCA could be used to ban products thought to pose an "unreasonable risk." A product containing nanomaterials could be classified as a new chemical, requiring the maker to register it, in which case the burden was on the government to show that the material was hazardous. The government, however, could require the maker to provide the data needed to conduct a risk assessment. In addition, the Food and Drug Administration was preparing regulations of medical and cosmetic products containing nanomaterials.[71] In addition to existing regulatory authority, Congress could establish new requirements such as labeling of products with nanomaterials or requiring premarketing approval. In 2005 the House of Representatives Science Committee had held hearings on nanotechnology, but no legislation advanced to the floor.

The city of Berkeley, California drafted an ordinance to regulate nanomaterials because of their potential hazards. Nabil Al-Hadithy, the city's hazardous materials manager, explained, "There has been a great number of attempts to regulate them, and they've all amounted to nothing because of the fear of upsetting industry, which leaves workers and the community at some unknown risk. It's the unknown that's a concern to us."[72]

---

[64]NRDC Press Release, November 27, 2006.
[65]Inside Washington Publishers, December 1, 2006.
[66]Silver ions likely would be classified as nanomaterials, which are defined by the National Nanotechnology Initiative as "of roughly 1 to 100 nanometers" in size. The silver ions of concern to the environmentalists were from 20 to 30 nanometers in size.

[67]*Washington Post,* November 24, 2006.
[68]*Washington Post,* November 24, 2006.
[69]NRDC letter to Jim Jones, November 22, 2006.
[70]Tri-TAC letter to Jim Jones, January 27, 2006. Tri-TAC letter to Dr. Tobi Jones, California Department of Pesticide Regulation, January 27, 2006.
[71]The American Bar Association prepared a series of white papers on the potential for the regulation of nanotechnology-based products under existing acts. http://abanet.org/environ.
[72]*San Francisco Chronicle,* November 24, 2006.

Samsung and the Sharper Image

Samsung, which was selling its washing machines in Asia, had to decide what to do in light of the EPA's pending regulation.

The Sharper Image, an upscale specialty retailer, sold a variety of consumer products including slippers and socks containing silver ions. The products were said to be "anti-germ, anti-mold, and anti-fungus." In the aftermath of the EPA decision to regulate nanosilver the Sharper Image quietly dropped its statements about the benefits of anti-microbial particles in its products. ■

Preparation Questions

1. As the Sharper Image would you take any further steps beyond dropping the claims about the antimicrobial particles?
2. What should Samsung do with its SilverCare technology and its washing machine? Should it conduct scientific tests to establish that the technology does not pose environmental risks?
3. The NanoBusiness Alliance represented companies that made or used nanomaterials. Its mission was to serve as "a collective voice for the emerging small tech industry and develop a range of initiatives to support and strengthen the nanotechnology community. . . ." Develop a nonmarket strategy for the industry to address possible regulation of nanomaterials.

Environmental Justice and Pollution Credits Trading Systems

As executive vice president for West Coast operations of Westco Oil Company, Jeremy Bentley was proud of the environmental accomplishments of his company in California. Emissions at the company's Long Beach refinery had been reduced, and oil spills at its marine terminal in El Segundo had been reduced dramatically.

Jeremy was aware of the Environmental Protection Agency's environmental justice campaign and supported its concern about the siting of facilities, such as hazardous waste disposal sites, in areas in which minorities and the poor were overrepresented. He was shocked, however, when Westco was confronted by the environmental justice movement. Not only were the arguments made by the activists novel, but they struck at the heart of the evolving system of air pollution control being implemented in the Los Angeles area and elsewhere in the United States. That system emphasized attaining environmental goals using the least costly means of abatement. Attaining the goals at least cost to society required greater reductions in emissions at facilities with low costs of abatement and smaller reductions at facilities with high costs of abatement.

To implement this system the South Coast Air Quality Management District (AQMD) had established a pollution credits trading program that allowed abaters to earn credits for emissions reductions and sell those credits to emitters of pollution that had high costs of abatement. The trading of credits reduced the aggregate costs of attaining environmental goals, and the AQMD had supported the development of markets in credits. Under one program approved by the AQMD, automobile scrap yards bought old, high-pollution automobiles for $600 to

$700 and received a credit that they could sell either to the AQMD, a company such as Westco, or an environmental group. If a company purchased a credit, it would not have to reduce its emissions by as much as it would otherwise have to reduce them. Under Jeremy's leadership Westco had participated in the AQMD program and purchased credits that it used at its marine terminal. Jeremy had also purchased credits through other programs and used those credits at its Long Beach refinery.

Environmental justice and pollution credits trading systems collided in July 1997 in Southern California as environmental groups and advocates for low-income groups, led by the interest group Communities for a Better Environment, filed lawsuits seeking to force the EPA to rescind the authority granted to the AQMD and the California Air Resources Board to operate a pollution credits trading system. One focus of the lawsuits was the pollution credits trading system and the purchase and scrapping of old, high-pollution automobiles. One lawsuit filed by Communities for a Better Environment against five oil companies including Westco alleged that residents in San Pedro and El Segundo had been exposed to harmful hydrocarbon emissions because the companies violated the federal Clean Air Act by failing to reduce emissions at their marine terminals. Instead, the companies had earned pollution credits by purchasing and scrapping 7,400 old cars as allowed under the AQMD program. Westco had been one of the leading purchasers of the credits.

Unocal, which had initiated the program to purchase and scrap high-pollution cars, operated a subsidiary, Eco-Scrap, that purchased old cars for companies that wanted to earn pollution credits. Spokesman Barry Lane said, "We still believe that the emission control program is of great value, it makes good sense."[73]

In another lawsuit, the Center on Race, Poverty and the Environment and the National Association for the Advancement of Colored People joined Communities for a Better Environment in alleging that the pollution credits trading system violated the civil rights of minorities by subjecting communities in which they were disproportionately represented to high levels of health-threatening pollutants. The lawsuit cited Title VI of the Civil Rights Act of 1964, which prohibits discrimination, such as against minorities and women, in programs and activities receiving federal funds.

In conjunction with the filing of the lawsuits, the activist and advocacy groups held a press conference at which local residents told of the harmful effects of the pollutants. Fifth-grader Laurie Johnson, who was on medical leave from Wilmington Park Elementary School, reported that she and other children at the school had health problems attributable to the emissions. She said, "It's time for our corporate neighbors to be responsible and give us a hand."[74] Sixty-nine-year-old Lily Camarillo, who lived near a Texaco refinery, said, "I've raised several kids there, lost three others and you wouldn't believe the problems we've had. Headaches, sick stomachs; my daughter has leukemia."[75]

Richard Drury, attorney for Communities for a Better Environment, turned the pollution credits trading system principle on its head by arguing that it exposed residents to the equivalent of "thousands of cars idling at each marine terminal." He also said, "It's a good thing to get old cars off the road; they cause a lot of pollution. But you don't trade the health of workers and the residents who live near those facilities in exchange for that."[76] Later on CNN he said, "If you have enough money, you can buy enough pollution credits and pump out as much pollution as you want to. That's going to create toxic hot spots."[77]

AQMD spokesman Tom Eichorn stated, "These people think they're being affected by air pollution problems . . . our job is to respond to their complaints." But he added that the agency did not believe that emissions were higher than before the pollution credits trading system was instituted.[78] Barry Wallerstein of the AQMD said, "The preliminary analysis by our legal department indicates that we're in full compliance with federal law."[79] "James Lents, the AQMD's outgoing executive officer, said he believes that the agency is not violating civil rights because toxic hot spots around industries are

reduced under a separate rule, which prohibits fumes that pose a risk exceeding 100 cases of cancer among every million people exposed. However, that standard is less stringent than environmentalists and some health officials have wanted. AQMD board members, skeptical of the cancer danger posed by the [hydrocarbon] fumes, set the scaled-back standard in 1994."[80]

Faced with moral accusations, lawsuits, and community pressure, Jeremy had to decide what to do. First he wanted to evaluate the moral claims being made by the activists and residents. Then, he would have to assess whether their claims, if morally supported, warranted a change in Westco's environmental protection programs. Jeremy also wondered whether he should meet with the residents or the activists to see if there was common ground from which they could work to resolve the issues.

Environmental Justice

The environmental justice movement began with concerns raised by activists that the poor and minorities were disproportionately affected by pollution. Since housing prices were naturally lower near industrial areas, low-income individuals tended to disproportionately locate in those areas. Concern for their well-being centered not only on issues of poverty and opportunity but also on the effects of pollution on their health. In 1992 the EPA issued a report raising the environmental justice issue. When President Clinton appointed Carol Browner, an environmentalist who had worked for Vice President Al Gore, to head the EPA, she initiated an environmental justice program. In 1994 President Clinton issued an executive order directing federal agencies to ensure that public health and environmental programs were nondiscriminatory and provided environmental justice. The president referred to Title VI of the Civil Rights Act in his order.

Many environmental interest groups and activists opposed the use of pollution credits trading systems. Some were suspicious of using incentive systems to control a social bad such as pollution. Some preferred uniform command-and-control regulations that forced a direct abatement requirement on all pollution sources and hence would result in a similar reduction in pollution in every locale rather than different levels of abatement across locales, depending on where the pollution credits were used. More fundamentally, however, most of the activists preferred lower emissions than allowed by legislation and EPA regulations.

As some commentators observed, with the mainstream environmental groups "under the thumb of Vice President Al Gore, their political patron," the cause of environmental justice has been led by some of the smaller and newer environmental interest groups.[81] In

---

[73]*Los Angeles Times,* July 23, 1997.
[74]Copley News Service, July 23, 1997.
[75]Copley News Service, July 23, 1997.
[76]*All Things Considered,* National Public Radio, July 24, 1997.
[77]*CNN Today,* August 1, 1997.
[78]Copley News Service, July 23, 1997.
[79]*CNN Today,* August 1, 1997.

[80]*Los Angeles Times,* July 23, 1997.
[81]*In These Times,* July 28, 1997.

the 1990s those groups emphasized the twin themes of health, particularly for those at risk, and of environmental justice. These groups argued that pollution control policies should take into account the special interests of low-income people who disproportionately live and work in areas of high pollution. President Clinton and Vice President Gore embraced both the concept of environmental justice and the use of pollution credits trading systems.

In 1997 the U.S. Court of Appeals gave individuals the right to challenge state environmental permits on the grounds of a disparate effect on low-income and minority groups. The Supreme Court, however, chose to review the decision.

As the EPA began its implementation planning, the environmental justice movement met with increasing opposition as business groups and members of Congress became concerned about the objectives of the movement and the consequences of such a policy. The U.S. Chamber of Commerce and the National Black Chamber of Commerce led a campaign to revoke the EPA's environmental justice program.[82] "We fully support the U.S. Chamber's efforts to repeal the EPA's misguided policy," Black Chamber president Harry Alford said. "This represents the beginning of a close working relationship between the U.S. Chamber and our organization to support black businesses around the country."[83] "It's an economics problem; it isn't race," Alford said. "If you're going to dump trash, you're going to dump it on land that's cheap. We feel the EPA is exploiting the Civil Rights Act and exploiting the black communities in an attempt to gather a vocal constituency in its ever-growing fight against big business."[84]

Alford was particularly concerned that the policy would drive jobs away from the areas in which minorities live. He pointed to the case of a permit sought by Shintech, a Japanese-owned company, to build a $700 million polyvinyl chloride plant in Louisiana's St. James Parish. Local activists had protested the plant, even though it would bring badly needed jobs to the parish.

Alford and others also argued that the EPA's environmental justice program would hinder attempts by cities to attract businesses to so-called "brownfields," some half million abandoned industrial sites, most of which were located in inner city areas. The U.S. Conference of Mayors spoke out against the EPA's environmental justice program, urging the EPA to develop a new policy that would encourage rather than hinder brownfield developments.

Congress also took an interest in the EPA program. The House Appropriations Committee inserted language in the EPA's fiscal 1999 appropriation barring it from taking any new civil rights actions under the program. The House Commerce Committee launched an investigation of the EPA's environmental justice program.

In a challenge to President Clinton, Carlos Porras, director of Communities for a Better Environment for Southern California, said, "[Environmental justice] is a defining issue for the president's administration. This has national significance and we're very interested to see where the Clinton administration draws the line."[85]

Pollution Credits Trading Systems

For decades economists and business leaders had advocated the use of pollution credits trading systems to achieve environmental objectives at the least cost to society. Pollution credits trading systems had been implemented in the Midwest and Northeast for sulfur dioxide and nitrogen oxides, and several systems were in place in Southern California to control a number of pollutants. Many other states were considering using similar systems, and with the recent promulgation of costly new federal regulations regarding microscopic airborne particulates, additional states and regions were expected to consider these systems.

To illustrate the difference between pollution credits trading systems and the traditional command-and-control approach, consider an environmental objective of reducing emissions of hydrocarbons by 50 percent in the oil industry in the Los Angeles basin. Under a command-and-control system all pollution sources would be required to reduce their emissions by 50 percent. In a pollution credits trading system the 50 percent reduction would be achieved by requiring a source to hold a permit for each pound of hydrocarbons emitted. Permits would be issued equal to 50 percent of the prereduction emissions. For example, one permit could be issued for each pound of hydrocarbon emissions allowed with the permits allocated among the emitters according to some baseline such as their prereduction emissions. Then, an emitter with low costs of abatement that reduced its emissions below the number of permits it was allocated could sell its excess permits, or credits, to an emitter with high costs of abatement, which would reduce its emissions by less than 50 percent. Thus, low-cost abaters would reduce their emissions by more than high-cost abaters, allowing the environmental objective to be achieved at the lowest total cost. In characterizing pollution credits trading systems, David Roe, a senior attorney for Environmental Defense, said, "What this allows for the first time is that companies that have the technical ability to go beyond the law in reducing their emissions have a reason to do it."[86]

[82]The National Black Chamber of Commerce had 180 chapters representing 62,000 black-owned businesses.
[83]*Washington Times*, July 20, 1998.
[84]*National Journal*, July 11, 1998.

[85]*Los Angeles Times*, July 23, 1997.
[86]*Wall Street Journal*, July 24, 1997.

As an example, consider a region with three pollution sources a, b, and c in locations A, B, and C, respectively. Suppose the sources each have been emitting 200 pounds of hydrocarbons and that the new environmental objective is to cut emissions by 50 percent to 300 pounds in total. Also assume that each source is allocated 100 permits. Suppose that the costs of abatement for each source are as given in Table 11-3.

TABLE 11-3

Pounds Abated	Costs of Abatement by Source ($)		
	a	b	c
100	10	15	20
200	20	30	35

For example, if source a were to abate 100 pounds, its cost would be $10, and if it were to abate 200 pounds, the cost would be $20. The corresponding costs for source c are $20 and $35, respectively. If under a command-and-control system each source were to reduce its emissions by 100 pounds, the total cost of the 300 pounds of abatement would be $10 + 15 + 20 = \$45$.

The environmental objective of a 300-pound reduction can, however, be attained for $35 if a reduced its emissions by 200 pounds (at a cost of $20) and b reduced its emissions by 100 pounds (at a cost of $15). Source a would then have zero emissions, b would have emissions of 100, and c would have emissions of 200.

For this outcome to be realized, source c must purchase 100 credits. By purchasing the 100 credits, c would avoid the abatement cost of $20 that it would incur if it were to abate 100 pounds. By reducing its emissions by 200 rather than 100 pounds, a incurs a cost of only $10. Since c is willing to pay up to $20 for 100 credits and a requires only $10 of compensation to reduce its emissions from 100 to 0 pounds, the two sources can reach an agreement. Thus, source a reduces its emissions by 200 pounds, source b reduces its emissions by 100 pounds, and source c purchases 100 credits from a rather than reducing its emissions. The equilibrium price for a credit is $15, since if a were to attempt to sell credits for more than $15, b would offer to sell credits for slightly less. Then the competition between a and b would drive the price down to $15. Similarly, if the price were less than $15, b would offer to buy credits from a. Then b and c would compete for the credits, driving the price up to $15. The distribution of the cost of achieving the environmental objective with a price of $15 is then $5, $15, and $15, respectively, for sources a, b, and c.

In designing a pollution credits trading system, an important factor is the geographic region the system covers. The basic principle is that the region include those affected by the emissions, as in the Los Angeles basin. Then the focus is on the aggregate reduction in emissions in that region rather than in specific locations. In the example, a reduction of 200 pounds was achieved by source a and 100 pounds at b. This result can also be stated in terms of the remaining emissions, which are 0, 100, and 200 pounds in locations A, B, and C, respectively. ∎

Preparation Questions

1. Evaluate a pollution credits trading system from the perspective of a system that maximizes the aggregate utility of all.
2. Compare command-and-control and pollution credits trading approaches in terms of economic efficiency.
3. Evaluate the claims of the activist and advocacy groups based on conceptions of justice. Is the AQMD's "separate rule" for hot spots an appropriate response to justice concerns?
4. Do oil companies have a duty to reduce their emissions at their marine terminals and refineries rather than purchasing credits, even though doing so would reduce the efficiency of the pollution credits trading system?
5. What should Jeremy Bentley do and why? Should he voluntarily stop purchasing credits? Should he meet with the residents and activists?

CHAPTER
12

Law and Markets

INTRODUCTION

Markets are the cornerstone of a free enterprise system. For markets to function efficiently individuals must be confident that the terms of their exchanges will be fulfilled. An exchange may be supported by a contract that establishes mutual expectations about terms such as the quality and quantity of an item, delivery, and payment. An exchange may also carry with it some residual obligations not explicitly included in the contract. For example, a party may be responsible for harm to the other party or to third parties caused by the item exchanged. That harm could involve environmental damage, personal injury during use, or adverse health consequences. An exchange may also involve other risks for the parties. For example, does a party actually have a property right to the item to be exchanged? Can the attributes of the item be easily appropriated by a third party without payment? Does the contract cover the possible events that could affect its execution? What if there is an extenuating circumstance, such as an act of nature or human intervention, that leads one party to breach the contract? Is compensation due? What if there is an accident or injury associated with the item exchanged? These uncertainties can impair the functioning of markets and the realization of the gains from trade. The law plays a principal role in reducing such uncertainties and in supporting exchange in markets.

Law is established by constitutions, statutes enacted by legislatures, and decisions made by judges. Statutory law, for example, specifies the length of a patent and the statute of limitations on filing lawsuits. The common law, or judge-made law, is a body of law that has evolved through cases brought before the courts by private parties. The decisions made by judges serve as precedents for future cases, and the set of precedents establishes a body of law. Judges also interpret statutes, and their interpretations become part of the law. This chapter addresses aspects of the law that support the functioning of markets and private agreements. The subjects considered are property (with a focus on intellectual property), contracts, and torts (with an emphasis on products liability).

Despite its importance the law is not the principal means of reducing uncertainty and improving reliance in exchanges. The alternative to public order provided by the law is private order based on private assurances among trading partners. Private means of assurance include trust, honesty, reputations for fulfilling promises, and bargaining to resolve disputes. Anyone who has purchased a mail-order item relies more on the reputation of L.L. Bean or Lands' End than on law. Similarly, buyers on eBay pay in advance for items, relying on the descriptions and pictures of items offered and on the reputations of sellers established through feedback from other buyers. Disputes are also resolved between a company and a customer through return and refund policies. On eBay the parties to a dispute can use an online dispute resolution mechanism, and if that does not work, an online mediator can be engaged for a modest fee.[1]

---

[1] See the Chapter 13 case, *eBay: Private Ordering for an Online Community*.

In some instances the law plays even less of a role in resolving disputes. A private ordering could be established through face-to-face and repeated interactions that allow norms to develop and be sustained. Ellickson (1991) studied the norms of ranchers and homeowners in Shasta County, California, and found that they settled disputes based on norms largely without reliance on the law and often in a manner contrary to the law. The ranchers and homeowners were able to rely on norms and punishments, primarily through gossip, because they had repeated interactions and were proximate. Repetition and proximity allowed norms to be respected.

Private orderings, however, function in the shadow of the law, which provides a final recourse for disputes. The homeowners at times resorted to lawsuits when the norms failed to resolve recurring problems. Similarly, cases of suspected fraud on eBay are turned over to law enforcement authorities. In areas where the stakes are high, the law remains the principal basis for supporting expectations about future performance. The cost of developing a new drug is over $1 billion, and a pharmaceutical company wants assurance that other companies will not simply copy its discovery. Patent law and its enforcement provide the assurance, and the decisions of judges have refined the law of patents to address new issues that arise.

This chapter first considers the common law and contrasts it with civil law. The concept of property is then introduced, and the establishment of incentives to develop property are analyzed. The focus is on intellectual property and its protection through patents and copyrights. Contracts are then considered along with principles governing their enforceability and breach. Torts and the liability system are considered next with a focus on establishing incentives to guide the actions of buyers and sellers to reduce accidents associated with a product. Products liability is considered both because of its importance and because it illustrates the evolution of the common law. The chapter cases deal with product safety, possible liability for a health problem, and patent protection.

THE COMMON LAW

One perspective on the law is that it is imposed from above by a legislature or, in earlier times, by a ruler. In issuing decrees even a ruler may look for guidance to how the people have organized their activities. For example, people privately developed practices for the control and management of land, and in England the king often looked to those practices as the basis for the king's law.[2] That law then evolved both as the practices of people evolved and through the precedents set by the king's court and subsequently by public courts. The resulting body of law is referred to as the *common law*. It is used in the United Kingdom, the United States, and most of the other former English colonies. Common law countries typically have an adversarial system of litigation in which each party advocates its side of the dispute and judges and juries render decisions based on the evidence, the arguments provided, and precedents.[3]

The role of the common law is to help people accomplish what they want to accomplish. The advantage of the common law is that it can adjust to changing circumstances without having to wait for new statutes established by legislation. The common law evolves through lawsuits filed by people in response to the problems they need addressed. As considered in a later section, the evolution from a law of warranty to the law of products liability occurred as a result of the changing nature of products.

In contrast, on the European continent, in Latin America, and elsewhere, *civil law* is used rather than common law. Civil law was developed by the Romans and served as the basis for the Napoleonic Code written after the French revolution by legal scholars commissioned by Napoleon. The Napoleonic code spread through the European continent and to the colonies of those countries. Civil law is also used in Louisiana and Puerto Rico in the United States, Quebec in Canada, and Scotland in the United Kingdom. Japan has a civil law system developed from German civil law. Civil law is written

---

[2]See Cooter and Ulen (1997, Ch. 3).
[3]See Carp and Stidham (2001) for information on the courts.

in codes based on legal principles, and judges decide cases based on those codes and the principles expressed in them. Civil law thus does not evolve in as flexible a manner as does the common law. Civil law countries typically do not use an adversarial system, and in many cases a judge is as much a fact finder as an adjudicator. Civil law countries also generally do not use juries as widely as in the United States, where the Constitution grants persons the right to a jury trial in both criminal and civil cases.

The origins of commercial law are similar to those of common law. The origins were in the medieval Merchants Law and in institutions such as the law merchant that developed to facilitate long-distance trade. Trade centered around fairs, such as the Champagne fair, to which merchants would travel great distances to arrange the exchange of goods. The trades often involved future delivery, with merchants agreeing to deliver goods of a particular quality in the future. The traders themselves were often from different regions and relied on their reputations for fulfilling promises. Disputes naturally arose even when merchants sought to fulfill their promises. The law merchant was an office established by merchants to resolve disputes. Moreover, over time merchants developed understandings about how particular uncertainties were to be handled. These understandings formed the basis for the development and evolution of commercial law.

In the United States the common law governs a number of important domains, including property, contracts, torts, products liability, and some aspects of labor contracting. The decisions of judges and the precedents established have been codified in a number of areas. On some matters statutes have been enacted to address specific issues in the domain of the common law.

PROPERTY

Property is a set of rights to control a tangible or intangible thing. In the terminology of the Coase theorem introduced in Chapter 11, a property rule protects an entitlement by allowing the holder to use the entitlement, transfer it to another person, or prevent unwanted infringement of that entitlement. That is, a property right is the right to do whatever one chooses with the entitlement. Some property is well defined, whereas others are more difficult to define. Real property in the form of land, buildings, and physical assets is well defined. Ideas, inventions, and expressions are more difficult to define. The former are easier to protect than the latter, and their protections may differ. Real property is generally protected indefinitely, whereas intellectual property is generally protected for a limited time.

The economic efficiency rationale for property is twofold. First, property rules facilitate bargaining, allowing economic transactions to be made and gains from trade to be realized. Second, property rules provide incentives to create assets, as in the case of intellectual property.

Bargaining

Property allows persons to reach mutually beneficial agreements. To illustrate this, consider a manufacturer that wants to buy components from two suppliers and assemble them to produce a final product. Component a is supplied by firm A, and component b is supplied by a number of firms in a competitive market. The manufacturer can produce its final product by buying a and b and assembling them at a cost of $100. Because of complementarities in its technology, supplier A could assemble the two components at a cost of $80 and supply the assembled components to the manufacturer. The manufacturer and supplier A thus have an incentive of $20 to reach an agreement under which firm A assembles the two components. Because the manufacturer and firm A have property rights they can bargain with confidence to reach an agreement. How the gain of $20 is divided by the manufacturer and firm A depends on their bargaining power as determined by their reservation values, but any division is efficient. The courts are not concerned with how the gain is divided, provided that the manufacturer and firm A have bargained over the division.

Incentives and Appropriability

The second efficiency role of property is to provide incentives to create assets. The incentives are clear in the case of physical assets such as a house. The incentive to build a house arises from a property rule that allows the holder to exclude others from the use of the house, with enforcement provided by public authorities. In the case of intellectual property, exclusion can be considerably more difficult. A music recording company that releases a recording can have thousands of copies distributed instantaneously over the Internet. Similarly, a pharmaceutical company can develop a new drug, but once developed it is easy to copy. The same is true for any invention whose technology can be copied at low cost. Many intellectual creations have low costs of replication, making exclusion difficult. It thus can be hard for the creator to appropriate the returns from the creation. When those returns are not appropriable, the incentives to create are weakened. Since innovation and discovery are engines of economic growth, means are needed to strengthen those incentives. The law of property is intended to provide for appropriability by the creator.

Some means of establishing appropriability are private.[4] Firms may keep their intellectual assets proprietary. Microsoft keeps its Windows XP and Vista codes proprietary. The formula for Coca-Cola is kept secret. Similarly, some production technologies are kept within the company. The private protection of intellectual assets is often incomplete or expensive, however. Recording companies may be able to encrypt their products, but codes can be cracked.

INTELLECTUAL PROPERTY

The characteristics of intellectual assets and the difficulty in excluding others from their use implies that those assets can be undersupplied in markets. To address this undersupply, protection is publicly provided. Article I of the Constitution states, "Congress shall have the Power . . . to promote the Progress of Science and useful Arts, by securing for limited times to . . . Inventors the exclusive Right to their respective writing and Discoveries." The issues for Congress and the courts are then what can be protected, what type of protection should be provided, and the duration of that protection.

The basic tradeoff in the protection of intellectual property is between the benefits to society from the use of ideas and inventions and the incentives for their creation. Consider the issue of the duration of a patent. A patent grants a monopoly on use of the invention, and the longer the duration, the greater are the returns that may be appropriated, and hence the greater are the incentives to invent. The longer the duration of the monopoly, however, the lower are the benefits to society, since the holder of the patent restricts use so as to appropriate the monopoly returns. This is illustrated in Figure 12-1.

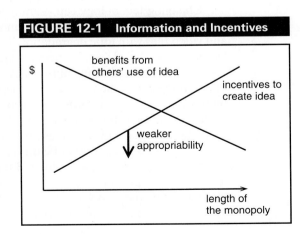

FIGURE 12-1 Information and Incentives

---

[4]Some incentives to develop information can be provided by the opportunity to take financial positions in the information. For example, some private equity investment firms appropriate returns from their investment in information by acquiring stakes in companies.

FIGURE 12-2 Appropriability of Returns

The optimal duration of a patent maximizes the sum of the benefits to society and to the inventor. The same principle applies to the breadth of protection for an invention or idea.

The appropriability of the returns from a discovery thus depends on two principal factors. The first is how easy it is for others to replicate the discovery. The second is the strength of the public protection for the discovery. Figure 12-2 is adapted from Teece (2000, p. 19) and relates these factors to appropriability. The cost of replicating a CD is very low, whereas the cost of replicating an oil refining process may be high. The protection given to pharmaceutical patents in the United States is generally tight, whereas the protection in India was loose because Indian patent law granted a patent if the method of production of a product was original or different. Hence, one company's patented drug could be produced in India by another company that used a different manufacturing process. Returns to pharmaceuticals in India were weakly appropriable, whereas in the United States they are more strongly appropriable. In 2005 India changed its patent law to allow patents on products and discoveries, including drugs. The change was required by the World Trade Organization, but it was also supported by Indian pharmaceutical companies that sought to develop their own proprietary drugs and needed assurance of appropriability.

Changing technology can dramatically alter the costs of replication of intellectual creations. The Internet and MP3 technology made it possible to exchange digital music and video files with little degradation in quality. Napster seized the opportunity provided by the technological developments to launch a peer-to-peer file sharing service. This lowered the costs of replicating music to close to zero, reducing the appropriability of returns to recording companies, music publishers, and film studios. Appropriability also depends on intellectual property protection accorded to recordings and films and whether peer-to-peer services infringe copyrights. Moreover, enforcing intellectual property rights is costly because legal proceedings are expensive and it is difficult to identify the persons copying files. As illustrated in Figure 12-3, the high cost of enforcement means that protection is loose rather than tight, and technological change reduced the cost of replication. The appropriability of returns in the music and film industries was weakened, and the remaining question was how far it would go. The example reviews the issues and the next round of the intellectual property dispute involving digital piracy.

Intellectual Property Protection

The principal forms of protection for intellectual assets are *patents, copyright, trade secrets,* and *trademarks.*

FIGURE 12-3 Appropriability of Returns and Peer-to-Peer Systems

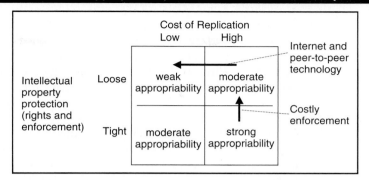

Intellectual Property Enforcement and Digital Piracy

Napster began with software written by 19-year-old Shawn Fanning that allowed people to exchange digital music files on the Internet. A user downloaded Napster's software and registered with the service, receiving a user name and a password. Users could upload and download MP3 files with ease. Napster operated central servers to maintain a "hotlist" of where to find requested music and routed users to the locations. Napster was so successful that the number of registered users reached 62 million.

Venture capitalists were reluctant to invest in Napster, however, for two reasons. One was the concern about how it would generate revenue. The other was whether its service was legal. Music publishers and record companies quickly filed a copyright infringement lawsuit charging that Napster facilitated digital piracy. The courts concluded that Napster had contributorily and vicariously infringed copyrights.[1] The court issued an injunction against Napster and required it to put in place software to block 100 percent of the copyrighted material before it could reopen. Napster appealed, and the Court of Appeals rejected its appeal [*A&M Music, Inc. v. Napster, Inc.,* 2001 WL 115033 (9th Cir., February 12, 2001)].[2]

Napster closed, and the user bases skyrocketed at Morpheus, KaZaA, and Grokster. In addition, Gnutella networks allowed peer-to-peer exchanges of music files. In contrast to Napster, these peer-to-peer services had no central computers but instead coordinated file sharing from the computers of users. These free services threatened the appropriability of returns of the recording companies, music publishers, and film companies.

The entertainment companies developed a three-pronged nonmarket strategy to increase the appropriability of returns. First, they filed lawsuits against several thousand individuals using peer-to-peer systems. Second, they filed copyright infringement lawsuits against the services providing the peer-to-peer services. Third, they sought federal legislation to strengthen appropriability.

For the second prong, the legal issues were similar to those in the Napster case, but the peer-to-peer systems had attempted to position themselves in a manner that gave them a stronger defense. These systems described their software as a general technology for sharing any kind of file. Although their systems could be used for sharing files that violated copyright, their software had other noninfringing uses. The rationale for this positioning derived from *Sony Corp. of America v. Universal City Studios,* 464 U.S. 417 (1984), in which Sony successfully defended its VCR, which could be used to violate copyright by sharing or reproducing television programs and movies. The court concluded that a VCR had substantial noninfringing uses, such as time-shifting programs, that did not violate copyrights. The court ruled in favor of Sony. In 2003 the Court of Appeals concluded that Grokster and StreamCast, which made Morpheus, had not violated copyrights because they did not operate central computers and had no means to prevent piracy. The entertainment industry appealed, and the Supreme Court ruled unanimously that the companies

---

[1]In 2000 a federal court ruled that the Digital Millennium Copyright Act did not protect Napster.

[2]For an analysis of the decision, see Matthew Antonelli, C. Raj Kumar, Bernadette McCann-Ezring, Chad Peterman, and Jeffrey Steck, "Unanimous Ninth Circuit Substantially Affirms Lower Court Injunction against Napster," *Intellectual Property & Technology Law Journal,* May 2001.

(*Continued*)

(Continued)

could be sued.[3] Grokster paid $50 million and closed the service, whereas StreamCast contested the issue on remand and was found guilty. As a result of the court decisions, LimeWire, which was not a party to the litigation, stopped distributing its file sharing program.

In response to the entertainment industry's efforts to restrict file sharing on open networks such as KaZaA, new ventures were formed to facilitate sharing among a designated group of people. Grouper Networks provided software that allowed groups up to 30 to share movies, music, and photos. For example, a family could form a group to share home videos. The company was positioned to lessen the risk of copyright infringement. For example, instead of exchanging music files, the software allowed a group member to stream music from another member's computer. Movies, however, were shared by exchanging files. The new venture had some of the virtues identified in the *Sony* decision, but the Internet enforcement director of the Motion Picture Association

of America said, "We do think it's a problem. It's something we're watching."

The third prong of the rights holders' nonmarket strategy focused on the Induce Act under consideration in Congress. The bill would make companies that create peer-to-peer software liable for copyright infringement. The bill was backed by the entertainment industry and opposed by Silicon Valley firms that feared that the bill would impede the development of new technology. The Consumer Electronics Association sought to narrow the scope of the bill, and the U.S. Copyright Office sought to widen the scope. A quick resolution of the issues was unlikely.

As fate would have it, in 2004 Shawn Fanning launched a new venture, Snocap Inc., that would allow copyright holders to set a price and terms of use on copyrighted files that could be exchanged on peer-to-peer systems. This time the venture was supported by recording companies such as Vivendi's Universal Music Group, and the first peer-to-peer system to participate with the venture was Mashboxx, which was headed by the former president of Grokster. Mashboxx, however, had difficulty getting launched because of a lack of funding. Mashboxx also threatened to sue LimeWire for patent infringement.

In 2008 Sweden joined the mix by arresting four people with Pirate Bay for facilitating copyright infringement.

---

[3]*Metro-Goldwyn-Mayer Studios v. Grokster Ltd.* 545 U.S. 913 (2005). The plaintiffs included the Motion Picture Association, the Recording Industry Association, and 27,000 music publishers and songwriters. The state attorneys general of 40 states, individual recording artists, and other organizations, including professional sports leagues, joined the plaintiffs in friend-of-the-court briefs.

Patents

A patent may be granted for an invention of "any new and useful process, machine, manufacture, or composition of matter, or any new and useful improvement thereof." A patent establishes a property right that allows the holder to exclude others from using the invention; that is, a patent grants a monopoly to the inventor. Patents are also granted for designs and for plants. As a result of a 1981 Supreme Court decision, computer software may be patented, but software patents are not easily obtained. Patents are also granted for designs and for plants as well as for business methods such as eBay's "buy-it-now" feature. The principal type of patent is a utility patent, which has a duration of 20 years beginning with the filing of the patent application with the Patent and Trademark Office. The number of patent applications filed in 2006 was 443,652, nearly double the number from 10 years earlier, and 183,187 were granted. Patents are enforced by the courts, which may enjoin others from infringing the patent or may order compensatory damages.[5] Beginning in 2005 the Supreme Court in a series of cases has made it more difficult for a patent holder to enforce its patent against infringement, including ordering royalties rather than imposing an injunction for infringement. In 2008 the Court ruled that a patent holder could not require royalties from downstream users of a product produced under a license from the patent holder.

In addition to the duration of a patent, the breadth of the patent is important. Breadth pertains to issues such as whether a patent for a discovery also covers closely related applications and improvements thereon. Inventors seek as broad a patent as

---

[5]Treble damages can be awarded but seldom are, unless there is intentional and continuing infringement. See Bouchoux (2001).

> ## EXAMPLE
>
> ### Mickey Mouse Politics and Law
>
> The copyrights on the early Mickey Mouse cartoons (e.g., *Steamboat Willy*) were due to expire in 2003, and Pluto, Goofy, and Donald Duck would lose their protection in 2009. Disney and other entertainment and media companies saw this as an opportunity to extend the duration of copyright. The European Union had issued a directive in 1993 to set the copyright duration at 70 years, and the U.S. interests, arguing for harmonization, sought a 20-year extension to 70 years. The issue was characterized by relatively quiet client politics, and in 1998 Congress provided the extension by passing the Sonny Bono Copyright Term Extension Act.
>
> The opponents of the extension soon challenged the Act in the courts. The opponents included individuals and companies that relied on public access to materials. They made two arguments. First, they argued that the extension violated Article I of the Constitution by essentially giving nearly unlimited rights to creations. Second, they argued that the law stifled free speech in violation of the First Amendment. The district court, the Court of Appeals, and in 2003 the Supreme Court upheld the Act. In the majority opinion Justice Ruth Bader Ginsburg wrote that Congress had acted within its authority as granted by the Constitution and that copyright was intended to "promote the creation and publication of free expression." With respect to the wisdom and the public policy effects of the extension, Ginsburg wrote "that it is generally for Congress, not the courts, to decide how best to pursue the copyright clause's objectives. . . ."

possible, whereas competitors and potential users of the invention want a narrow patent. The appropriate breadth of patents is a source of contention both within the courts and among legal scholars.

Patents are the driving force in the pharmaceutical industry, providing strong incentives for research, development, and testing of new chemical entities. A patent on a new drug and approval for marketing by the Food and Drug Administration gives the innovating company a monopoly on the sale of the drug. Reflecting this monopoly, the company appropriates returns by charging a high price. When a patent expires, generic versions of the drug can be marketed. This typically drives the price down significantly and widens the use of the drug. This increases the benefits to society of the drug. Not only do pharmaceutical companies have strong incentives to innovate, but they also have strong incentives to enforce their patent rights and to obtain extensions of their patents through congressional and other actions. The Chapter 1 case, *The Nonmarket Environment of the Pharmaceutical Industry,* and the chapter case, *Patent Games: Plavix,* address these issues. The latter case considers the lengths a company may go to protect a patent.

Licensing makes an invention available to others and hence increases the benefits to society from the invention. Licensing also allows the discoverer to appropriate returns. Licensing is attractive when there are complementary goods whose value is enhanced by the intellectual asset.[6] A biotechnology company that develops a gene may license it to another company that can use it to develop a noncompeting pharmaceutical. Similarly, to appropriate returns an engineering company may license a refining technology to oil companies rather than go into the oil refining business. In some cases an intellectual asset may be given to the producers of complementary products. Microsoft provided its application programming interfaces (APIs) to software developers because the more software written for Windows, the greater the demand for its operating system and other proprietary software.

Copyright

Works of original expression may receive a copyright allowing the recipient to restrict use, reproduction, and distribution of the work. A copyright can be claimed even without a filing with the government. The first copyright law in 1790 established a maximum duration of 28 years. Since then Congress has extended the duration 11 times. The most

---

[6]See Teece (2000, Ch. 8) for strategic considerations in licensing.

recent extension in 1998 was stimulated by the imminent expiration of the copyright on early Mickey Mouse cartoons, as considered in the example. The duration of a copyright is now the life of the author plus 70 years, or in the case of a disguised authorship it is the minimum of 75 years or 100 years after creation. The breadth of a copyright pertains to which uses are allowed without authorization by the author. The fair use doctrine allows limited unauthorized use for research, scholarship, and literary criticism.

An important issue in information technology and information services industries is whether the "look and feel" of software or a Web site can be protected by copyright. This is an unsettled matter. In an important case Apple Computer filed a copyright lawsuit against Microsoft arguing that the user interface of its Windows operating system copied the look and feel of Apple's system. The court held in favor of Microsoft.

The issue of what may be copyrighted has required both legislation and court interpretation. Consider the issue of whether compilations of facts can be protected by copyright. A 1991 Supreme Court decision (*Feist Publications, Inc. v. Rural Telephone Service Co.,* 499 U.S., 340) held that "facts," even if collected through "sweat and effort," remained in the public domain. Earlier court decisions had held that databases were protected by copyright under the "sweat of the brow" doctrine. This doctrine prevailed despite 1976 amendments to the Copyright Act that required a degree of creativity or originality for compilations of data to be protected. In *Feist* the court affirmed the originality and creativity requirement and stated that "all facts—scientific, historical, biographical and news of the day . . . are part of the public domain available to every person." For example, the telephone white pages cannot be copyrighted because they are simply an alphabetical list of names and numbers, whereas the Yellow Pages can be copyrighted because the information is arranged by category, which has a degree of originality. eBay had been concerned about whether auction aggregators could copy its database of online auctions and provide listings to their users, as considered in the Chapter 13 case, *eBay and Database Protection.*

Trademarks and Trade Secrets

A trademark provides social and private value. The social value results from reducing search costs for consumers by allowing branding of products. Branding can also support a reputation for quality, uniformity, or service. The word Coke is a trademark, as are eBay and Intel. Trademarks can be registered at the federal or state levels and if maintained can be perpetual. Remedies for infringement can take the form of injunctions and compensatory damages. The requirement for a trademark is distinctiveness. Generic terms such as "online auction" cannot be protected by a trademark, but the name eBay can be protected. As mentioned in Chapter 2, a new entrant into the online auction market used a front page that closely resembled eBay's homepage. The most defensible trademarks are those that are "arbitrary and fanciful," and an eBay attorney explained, "eBay is a completely coined name. It means nothing."[7] eBay filed a successful trademark infringement lawsuit against the entrant.

As an example of a trademark dispute Johnson & Johnson, the health care company that makes Tylenol, Band-Aids, and Johnson's Baby products along with pharmaceuticals, sued the American Red Cross for infringing its red cross trademark. Johnson & Johnson had begun using the red cross symbol in 1887 before the American Red Cross was established. In 1895 the two parties entered into an agreement under which the American Red Cross acknowledged Johnson & Johnson's "trademark for chemical, surgical and pharmaceutical goods of every description."[8] Johnson & Johnson did not oppose the occasional sale of products by the American Red Cross as a fund-making device and itself was a supporter, having contributed $5 million over the past 3 years. In 2004, however, the American Red Cross began licensing the red cross symbol to companies for use on a variety of products that competed with Johnson & Johnson products, such as first-aid kits. The company filed the lawsuit after the failure of several

---

[7]*San Jose Mercury News,* July 31, 2001.
[8]*New York Times,* August 9, 2009.

months of negotiations, about which a company spokesperson said, "We deeply regret that it has become necessary to file this complaint. The company has the highest regard for the American Red Cross and its mission." The organization's president characterized the company's action as "obscene" and said it was done "simply so that J & J can make more money."[9] A judge ruled in favor of the American Red Cross.

A trade secret is almost anything that is unique and of value or potential value to a company. This includes process information, operating methods, programs, and business plans. To receive protection the information must be adequately protected by the company on a continual basis. Trade secret protection can be perpetual, and the secrets do not have to be registered. Remedies for violations of trade secrets include injunctions and compensatory damages. Trade secret law has been used to prohibit employees who move from one company to another to take along information from their former employer. Google protects its search engine as a trade secret rather than through patents, since patents require the disclosure of information.

CONTRACTS

Contracts are governed both by the common law and by statutes pertaining to particular types of contracts and transactions. This section focuses on the principles of contract law derived from the common law, which developed over time to resolve economic problems associated with noncontemporaneous trades. People benefit from the exchange of goods and services, and because of their knowledge of the specific circumstances, people know best how to realize the gains from trade. The objective of the law is to support people in what they want to do by addressing impediments to those trades. In this sense the common law looks to what people do and want to do to arrange and complete exchanges. Contracts are one means by which people arrange mutually advantageous trades.[10]

In a contract both parties seek assurances. A mortgage lender wants assurance that the borrower will repay the loan with interest. To make it costly for the borrower to fail to repay the loan, the house is pledged as collateral. The borrower wants to induce the lender to provide funds by pledging the house as collateral, and without a contract no lender would extend funds with a repayment period that extends over 25 to 30 years. Contracts make the mortgage lending market possible. Contracts thus are mutually advantageous to the participating parties.

Contracts are also entered into to induce *reliance*. Reliance refers to a change in behavior by a party. For example, an electric power plant wants a steady source of coal, and rather than develop a mine itself, it prefers to have a coal company with the required expertise develop the mine. Opening a mine requires major expenditures that the coal company is unwilling to make without assurances that the coal will have a buyer. To induce the coal company to make the reliance expenditures, the power company must provide assurances to the coal company. The power company may agree to build a generating plant at the mine mouth and to purchase at market prices specific quantities of coal for an extended period such as 50 years. With such an assurance, the coal company is willing to make the reliance expenditures. In the event of default on the contract by the power company, the reliance expenditures provide a basis for damages.

A contract is an agreement over which parties are to have bargained. The contract then is mutually advantageous, making each party better off than it would be in its absence. As in the case of mortgage lending, some markets would not exist if it were not for contracts. Contracts cover promises to take particular actions in the future, such as making mortgage payments, and the promises are credible because the failure to follow through on them is costly. For example, a lender may foreclose on the house provided as collateral.

---

[9]*New York Times,* August 9, 2007.
[10]Other means include contemporaneous exchange (at the grocery store), relational contracts built on long-term relationships (as in supply chains), and reputation (as in online auctions).

Contracts, however, are seldom complete in the sense of providing for all the possible contingencies that could arise. The transactions costs associated with completely specifying the responsibilities of the parties in every conceivable circumstance are typically too high, so contracts have a degree of incompleteness. When one of those contingencies arises, the courts may be called on to resolve the ambiguity or resulting conflict. The Genentech and City of Hope example illustrates this in the case in which a long-term licensing contract contained sections that appeared to have conflicting implications.

Contracts can be either written or oral and generally involve an offer, acceptance, and consideration. Consideration is what a promisee gives to a promisor to induce the latter to make the promise, and mutual consideration is usually given. In the purchase of an automobile, the seller gives the automobile as consideration to the buyer to elicit a promise to pay for the car. To induce the seller to provide the car, the buyer gives the seller a down payment and a promise to pay as well as recourse to the car in the event of breach of the contract. In the case of financing the purchase of a house, the buyer provides as consideration a lien or deed of trust on the house to induce the lender to provide the funds. The lender provides the funds to induce the borrower to agree to the lien or deed of trust.

EXAMPLE

Genentech and City of Hope

In 1976 as a fledgling company, Genentech entered into a contract with the City of Hope Medical Center (COH) under which two COH researchers agreed to splice a human gene into bacteria to synthesize the DNA for human insulin.[1] In 1978 the scientists were successful, resulting in the first genetically engineered pharmaceutical and the birth of the biotechnology industry. The contract provided that all research findings and resulting patents were the property of Genentech, and Genentech obtained 127 patents related to the COH research. Upon the discovery Genentech licensed the DNA patent for human insulin to Eli Lilly & Co. Under the license Lilly agreed to pay a 6 percent royalty to Genentech and a 2 percent royalty to COH. COH had received $285 million in royalties from human insulin and also from the human growth hormone.

In the mid-1990s COH began inquiring into Genentech's licensing of the DNA patents to pharmaceutical companies other than Lilly. Genentech had licensed the patents to 22 companies, and COH filed a breach of contract lawsuit, claiming that Genentech owed it $445 million in additional royalties. COH also claimed that Genentech intentionally concealed the licensing, which opened the possibility of punitive damages. COH based its lawsuit on a paragraph of the

16-page contract that stated, "Should Genentech license any third party under any patent acquired by it hereunder, then Genentech shall secure from that party and pay to City of Hope the same royalty City of Hope would have received had Genentech itself carried out the licensed activity."

Genentech rejected COH's claim and argued that the governing section of the contract was the section that stated, "Genentech shall pay to City of Hope a royalty of 2 percent of the net sales of all polypeptides (proteins) sold by it or its affiliates, provided only that manufacture of the polypeptide employs DNA synthesized by City of Hope under this agreement."[2] Genentech stated that the term "provided only" meant that royalties were due only on products that used the DNA developed by the COH scientists. Genentech not only argued that it had not violated the contract but that the case was actually about patent law and hence should be tried in federal, not state, court.

The case was tried in state court in 2001 and the jury split 7 in favor of Genentech and 5 in favor of COH. Since nine votes were required to decide the case, the judge was forced to declare a mistrial. The case was retried and the jury voted 9 to 3 that Genentech had breached the contract and 10 to 2 that it had done so with fraud or malice. The jury awarded COH $300 million in compensatory damages and $200 million in punitive damages.

---

[1]COH is a world-renowned nonprofit cancer research center that in addition to giving birth to the first genetically engineered pharmaceutical also pioneered bone marrow transplants and opened a facility to produce experimental drugs for untreatable diseases.

[2]*San Francisco Chronicle,* September 10, 2001.

Enforceability

The central issues in contracts are which contracts are enforceable, when can they be breached, and what damages are due in the event of a breach. A contract may be voided if an individual, such as a minor, does not have the authority to enter into it. Similarly, a contract to sell one's vote in an election is voidable because the right to vote is inalienable; that is, it is not transferable. A contract is generally not enforceable if it is illegal or unconscionable and is voidable under certain conditions such as fraud or a mistake. These conditions may be augmented by statute. In California individuals have 3 days during which they can cancel certain contracts. Unconscionability may be either procedural or substantive. The former pertains to contracts entered into under duress or unfair circumstances such as when one party has no bargaining power. The latter pertains to contracts that, for example, may obligate a person to pay a penalty that has no relation to the value of the item purchased.

Duress and unconscionability are ex ante concepts in the sense that the conditions are present when the parties agree to the contract. Circumstances may develop after signing a contract that make it unenforceable. One such circumstance is impossibility, where a party is unable to fulfill a contractual promise. For example, an act of nature such as a fire may destroy a company's plant, making it impossible to fulfill a supply contract. The responsibility in such a case should be assigned to the party that is able to cope with the situation at the least cost. For example, if the buyer can obtain the contracted supplies from another producer, the factory owner may have no remaining obligation. If the buyer had made reliance expenditures, however, for a unique product produced by the destroyed plant, the factory owner may be responsible for damages. In the case in which reliance expenditures are made by the buyer, the factory can take out insurance against the risk of both the fire and the inability to fulfill the contract.

Another situation that can make a contract unenforceable is frustration of purpose. If an event occurs that causes the purpose of the contract to disappear, the courts have held that the contract is unenforceable, since there is no point to its fulfillment. As with impossibility, damages may be awarded. From the perspective of economic efficiency, responsibility for the risk that the purpose of the contract could vanish should be assigned to the party that can best avoid the risk or, if that is not possible, deal with it ex post at the least cost. This principle of the least-cost avoider is considered in more detail in the following section on torts.

Breach

Contracts and their enforcement provide credible commitments about the actions of parties. These contracts, however, cannot be complete, so circumstances can arise under which one or both parties prefer not to fulfill its commitment. In such circumstances the parties could mutually agree, perhaps with the payment of compensation, to terminate a contract. A party may also unilaterally *breach* a contract. Breaches are allowed because under some circumstances it is economically efficient not to fulfill the conditions of the contract. For example, if a change in the market makes a necessary input to the production process prohibitively expensive, it may be better to breach a purchase contract and allow the buyer to contract for a product made with different inputs.

If the circumstances can be anticipated under which it may be economically inefficient to fulfill the commitments, the contract can be written to specify the obligation each party has to the other in those circumstances. There may be disagreement, however, about whether the circumstances are as claimed by the breaching party. One purpose of contracts is to reduce transactions costs associated with circumstances that develop during fulfillment of the agreement. When contract terms do not specify the obligations of the parties, the contracting parties can anticipate the consequences of a broken promise by referring to the rules used by courts for ordering remedies.

Remedies

Courts use two basic types of remedies in the event of breach: damages and specific performance. Damages can be conpensatory for the harm caused or punitive, as in the

Genentech and City of Hope example. Compensation for foreseeable damages depends on the baseline used by the courts.[11] One baseline is to leave the plaintiff as well off as she expected to be if the contract terms had been fulfilled. These *expectations damages* can differ from the amount required to allow the plaintiff to contract with someone else for the provision of the product or service. For example, in the case of an antique a promisee may have expected to pay a certain amount for the item, but finding another identical item may be considerably more expensive because of search costs, transportation costs, and special handling. In such a case the court could order *consequential damages* based on the opportunity cost of the next best alternative. Another rule for awarding damages is to put the promisee in the same position she had been in prior to signing the contract. This rule corresponds to *reliance damages,* since it compensates the promisee only for reliance expenditures made as a result of the contract. In some cases the courts may simply require the defendant to return the item provided by the promisee. For example, an auto dealer may repossess an automobile when a purchaser defaults on payments.

Court awards of damages take place ex post, and anticipation of those awards provides ex ante incentives to fulfill promises, while leaving the flexibility to breach contracts when it is efficient to do so. The parties to a contract may also write into the contract contingencies in the event of breach. This *liquidated damages* approach is ex ante and is based on the principle that more complete contracts can be more efficient. Liquidated damages are limited to compensation for harm and are not intended as penalties for particular actions.

In cases in which it is difficult to determine the actual damages incurred as a consequence of a breach, the courts may provide relief in the form of *specific performance.* This generally involves an order directing the promisor to take the action called for in the contract. The court could, for example, order the antiques dealer to deliver the item to the buyer.

Many contracts contain mandatory arbitration clauses that require disputes to be resolved outside the courts. The purpose of these clauses, which have been used for credit card and brokerage accounts for years, are intended to avoid the legal and administrative costs associated with a court case. Arbitration clauses are being used more broadly by a wider set of industries. Arbitration itself can be costly, so some companies have turned to jury waivers. In signing a contract such as a residential lease or an automobile loan agreement, an individual may waive the right to trial by jury. The purpose of the waiver is to avoid what some companies view as unreasonable awards by juries. In some states, including California, such waivers have been held to be in violation of the state constitution.

TORTS

Torts are civil wrongs—wrongs done by one person to another.[12] The law of torts is common law that evolves through decisions made by judges in cases brought by private plaintiffs. The common law of torts evolves as innovative cases are brought before the courts. Obesity has become a health concern, and trial lawyers have brought lawsuits against restaurants for their alleged contribution to obesity and the associated health risks. The chapter case, *Obesity and McLawsuits,* concerns the litigation against McDonald's. Tort claims also are laid to rest. In 2002 the claims of 1,900 plaintiffs who said their health was damaged by radiation from the 1979 Three Mile Island nuclear plant accident were finally resolved when the Court of Appeals upheld the district court's summary dismissal of the claims. The court concluded that not enough radiation leaked to cause adverse health effects. The plaintiffs decided not to appeal the decision to the Supreme Court.

---

[11]In *Hadley v. Baxendale, Restatement (Second) of Contracts,* § 351(1) 1979, the court held that the defendant was not responsible for damages in circumstances that could not be reasonably foreseen. This decision is consistent with the notion that the common law provides incentives for actions to increase economic efficiency, and if something cannot be foreseen, no action can be based on it. Hence, there is no efficiency rationale for awarding damages.

[12]See Franklin and Rabin (1996) and Cooter and Ulen (2007) for treatments of the law of torts.

The law of torts is applied in situations in which, because of transactions cost, for example, people are unable to bargain over the compensation that will be due in the event of a wrong such as an injury. Accidents that involve damage to real property or injury to a person are one subject of torts. The purpose of the tort system is to provide incentives to people and firms to take care to avoid harm. A study by Towers Perrin Tillinghast estimated that the cost of the tort system in the United States was $246 billion in 2003, or $845 per person. In 1950 the cost per person was $12 (not adjusted for inflation).[13]

The basic elements of a tort case are an injury, an action that caused the injury, and the breach of a duty owed to the injured party. In the case of an automobile accident, the injury may have been caused by a brake failure, and if the brake failure was due to a faulty design or a failure of a part, the injured party may be able to recover damages from the automaker. If, however, the injured party was at fault as a result of negligence, the court may find for the defendant and not award damages. For example, if the owner of an older car had a safety inspection that revealed that the brake pads and rotors needed replacement and brake fluid was leaking but the owner did not have repairs made, the court could find that the owner had acted negligently. This could relieve the automaker of liability or reduce the damages awarded.

Some tort lawsuits that involve similar wrongs may be consolidated by the courts into a class action lawsuit. Class action lawsuits increased substantially in numbers during the 1970s and 1980s but in recent years have declined as a result of legislation and court decisions. Particularly in securities litigation the number of class action cases has plummeted since the peak in 1998.[14]

To identify the role of the law of torts in markets, the issue of product safety is used. The next section introduces the product safety problem and the concept of social efficiency. The following sections introduce the role of the liability system in achieving social efficiency, the development of the law of products liability, and the performance of the products liability system.

THE PRODUCT SAFETY PROBLEM AND SOCIAL EFFICIENCY

Safety is a primary concern for responsible management and occupies a prominent place on the nonmarket agendas of most firms. No firm wants injuries in its workplaces or associated with one of its products, yet preventing all injuries could be prohibitively costly if not impossible. The issue thus is the extent of care to take in reducing the number and severity of injuries. The principal and most comprehensive source of institutional guidance on safety is the law of torts. Lawsuits filed by injured persons bring both a specific case and broader issues of responsibility into the institutional arena of the courts. The law of products liability has developed from these cases, and the awards courts make and the costs of litigation and liability insurance provide firms with incentives to take care in manufacturing and in the incorporation of safety features, instructions, and warnings.[15]

The product safety problem can be conceptualized as shown in Figure 12-4. The producer makes a number of ex ante decisions including product conception, research and development, design, manufacturing, and marketing. Once the product is put on the market, it becomes the property of the consumer. Ex post some consumers may be injured or incur property damage through their use of the product. From the perspective of social efficiency, decisions by both the producer and consumers should take into

---

[13]Towers Perrin Tillinghast, "U.S. Tort Costs: 2004 Update," 2004.

[14]The leading law firm, Milberg Weiss, in filing class action securities lawsuits made illegal kickbacks to plaintiffs in 225 lawsuits extending over several decades. The law firm's most feared securities class action attorney, William Lorach, was fired and sentenced to 2 years in prison for his participation, and Melvin Weiss, co-founder of the firm, pleaded guilty to criminal conspiracy charges and was sentenced to 30 months in prison. The law firm, renamed Milberg, paid a $75 million criminal fine.

[15]The law of torts served as the principal source of institutional guidance on a broad range of safety issues until the 1970s, when the wave of social regulation led to the creation of regulatory agencies, such as the National Highway Traffic Safety Administration (NHTSA), the Consumer Product Safety Commission (CPSC), and the Occupational Safety and Health Administration (OSHA), to address particular safety issues. These agencies focused on specific hazards and mandated controls and safety standards.

FIGURE 12-4 The Product Safety Problem

account the social cost of possible injuries to persons and property as well as the costs of preventing those injuries.

Both producers and consumers take into account the social costs of the care they take to reduce injuries. The producer can make design changes, improve manufacturing quality, add safety features, and provide instructions and warnings. The consumer can develop skill in using the product and take precautions against accidents. In the case of a chain saw the producer can add safety features such as a safety tip, provide warnings about the hazard of kickback, and provide instructions on proper use, including a videotape. The consumer can purchase goggles, a hard hat, and steel-tipped boots. The costs of these measures constitute the cost of care by the producer and the consumer. The cost of care also includes any loss of benefits, for example, from the product because of safety features or additional costs from use. In the case of a chain saw a safety tip reduces the cutting length of the blade and increases the weight of the saw, contributing to fatigue of the user. Similarly, using a chain saw safely can lengthen the time required to complete a job.

Social efficiency requires balancing the costs of injuries and the costs of care. This perspective is illustrated in Figure 12-5, which graphs costs as a function of injuries prevented. The social cost of injuries decreases as more injuries are prevented. If all injuries were prevented, however, the cost of care—the cost of injury avoidance—would be very high. In the case of a chain saw, this would require not producing the product. Total social costs are the sum of the costs of care and the costs of injuries, as illustrated in the figure. The socially efficient number of injuries prevented, or equivalently the optimal amount of care, minimizes total social costs and is determined by a tradeoff between the cost of injuries and the cost of preventing them.[16] As shown in the figure, society tolerates some injuries because preventing them is too costly. That is, society prevents those injuries that are not too costly to prevent. Society allows chain saws to be produced and used despite many thousands of injuries annually.

The cost of care curve in Figure 12-5 reflects the most efficient, or least cost, combination of care taken by producers and consumers. Thus, for any given level of injuries prevented, the socially efficient allocation of care between the producer and consumers is that which minimizes the total costs of care. This is referred to as the principle of the *least-cost avoider;* that is, efficiency requires care by the producer or the consumer or both, depending on which has the lower cost of preventing injuries.

---

[16]The socially efficient number of injuries prevented is identified by the point at which the marginal social cost of injuries equals the marginal cost of care.

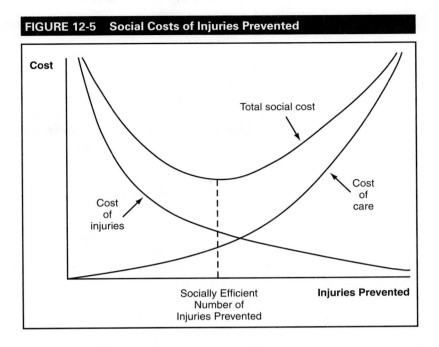

FIGURE 12-5 Social Costs of Injuries Prevented

Cost

Total social cost

Cost of care

Cost of injuries

Socially Efficient Number of Injuries Prevented

Injuries Prevented

The social costs of injuries and the cost of care taken by producers are reflected in the prices consumers pay for products. The higher price required to cover these costs reduces the demand for a product and thus the injuries resulting from it. Consumers will not purchase a product whose price and the associated cost of taking care during use exceed the benefits anticipated from its use. Those who value the product more highly than those costs will purchase it. Over 1.5 million chain saws are sold each year.

As illustrated in the lower part of Figure 12-4, the institution of liability is intended to assign the ex post social costs of injuries to producers and consumers so that each takes the efficient level of care. The prices of products demanded and supplied then fully reflect those costs. This then results in the socially efficient number of injuries prevented, as illustrated in Figure 12-5.

In the United States and in other countries, the institution of liability is the principal institution that guides producers and consumers in product safety decisions. Liability operates through the courts, which assign the social costs of injuries to consumers and producers through the damages assessed in cases brought by injured consumers. These assignments of costs are intended to induce consumers and producers to take the socially efficient level of care. By aligning private and social costs, the liability system not only provides incentives for the socially efficient level of care, but also allows decentralized decision making on the part of producers and consumers rather than relying on government regulation through command and control.

The actual institution of liability, however, differs from this ideal. Distributive considerations influence courts, which can focus on compensating the injured as well as on aligning private and social costs. These distributive consequences also motivate nonmarket action to alter liability standards. Products liability law and measures to reform it are considered in more detail after the distinction between liability and property rules is developed.

ENTITLEMENTS, LIABILITY, AND SOCIAL EFFICIENCY

Entitlements and Their Protection

Starting from the perspective of the Coase theorem, Calabresi and Melamed (1972) defined an entitlement, or right, as the ability of an individual to control a particular resource or to take an action, with the state protecting that control or action from infringement. The type of the protection given to entitlements is important. Calabresi and Melamed distinguished between two types of rules for protecting entitlements—property rules and liability rules.[17]

A *property rule* prohibits other parties from infringing the entitlement without the consent of the party holding it. Homeowners are protected by a property rule that prohibits a person from either taking their home without consent or forcing them to sell it at a price they deem inadequate.

A *liability rule* protects an entitlement in quite a different manner. When an entitlement is protected by a liability rule, a person may infringe the entitlement but must compensate its holder for the objectively assessed harm resulting from that infringement. Although a home is protected by a property rule against infringement by a person, it is protected only by a liability rule against infringement by the state. Eminent domain is a liability rule that permits the state to take a home for a public purpose and requires the state to compensate the owner for its objectively assessed value. Even if owners would prefer to hold out for greater compensation, as would be their right under a property rule, eminent domain does not allow them to do so. An injury in an accident associated with a product is governed by a liability rule.

The remarkable feature of the Coase theorem is that in the absence of transactions costs social efficiency is achieved when entitlements are protected with either a property rule or a liability rule.[18] An entitlement protected by a property rule allows parties to a possible accident to bargain over the allocation of care to reduce the likelihood of an accident. This bargaining was illustrated in the section of this chapter on property. To illustrate the role of a liability rule in protecting an entitlement, consider the case of chain saws and the risk of kickbacks; for example, the chain saw bucks sharply back toward the user as a result of hitting a knot in a tree, the chain binding in the cut, or from boring with the tip. If the entitlement to compensation for an accident is assigned to the chain saw user and is protected by a liability rule, the manufacturer will add a safety feature, such as a safety tip to prevent boring, if the cost of the feature is less than the expected cost of the additional harm from not adding the feature. If the cost is greater, the feature will not be added. This is consistent with social efficiency, which requires that the accidents to be avoided are those that are not too costly to avoid. The chapter case, *California Space Heaters, Inc.,* provides an opportunity to consider such decisions.

As another example of the role of a liability rule in inducing social efficiency, consider the case of a swimming pool in a person's backyard. An externality is present because of the swimming pool and the presence of neighbors. Because the greatest likelihood of injury centers on neighborhood children, they will be the focus here. If the swimming pool owner posts a clear and obvious warning not to trespass, anyone who trespasses and is injured in the pool is in some sense "at fault." From the perspective of fault, the swimming pool owner should be protected so that people neither trespass nor use the pool without the owner's consent. The costs of avoiding harm then would be assigned to the neighborhood children and their parents. Parents then would take care in supervising their children when they are outside and take measures such as building a fence around their own yards to prevent their children from going to the pool. Is this assignment likely to result in social efficiency; that is, is it likely to result in actions that minimize the sum of the costs of harm and the costs of the care by the pool owner and the neighbors? No, it would be more efficient for the pool owner to build a fence around the pool than for all the neighbors to build fences to keep their children away from the pool. This suggests that the swimming pool owner should be assigned the costs of injuries—that is, be liable for injuries associated with the pool. That assignment then creates incentives to build a fence around the pool.

Protecting certain entitlements with a liability rule is believed to involve fewer transactions costs than protecting them with a property rule. For example, it would be

---

[17]Calabresi and Melamed also consider inalienability rules. When an entitlement is protected by an inalienability rule, an individual is not allowed to give up or transfer the entitlement, even voluntarily. An individual's entitlement to vote in a public election is governed by an inalienability rule, since a person is not permitted to transfer that entitlement to another person.
[18]This feature is also considered in Chapter 11 in the context of the control of externalities.

prohibitively expensive to negotiate agreements between each motorist and every other motorist and all pedestrians regarding compensation for injuries. Consequently, accidental injuries are governed by liability rules rather than by property rules. The next section addresses the issue of transactions costs and their implications for the use of property and liability rules.

The Assignment of Social Costs and the Choice Between Liability and Regulation

The Coase theorem pertains to situations in which entitlements can be clearly assigned and private agreements can be reached without substantial transactions costs. When entitlements are not well defined or there are substantial transactions costs, the assignment of responsibility for the social costs of injuries is a task for government.

Calabresi and Melamed provide five principles for the assignment of costs and the choice between the institutions of liability and regulation.

1. The assignment of entitlements should favor knowledgeable choices between social benefits (e.g., preventing injuries) and the social costs of obtaining them.
2. When it is unclear whether the social benefits exceed the social costs, "the cost should be put on the party that is best located to make such a cost-benefit analysis."
3. When there are alternative means of achieving social benefits (or of avoiding social costs), the costs of achieving them (or avoiding social costs from accidents) should be assigned to the party that can do so at the lowest cost.
4. When it is not clear who that party is, "the costs should be put on the party or activity which can with the lowest transactions costs act in the market to correct an error in entitlements by inducing the party who can avoid social costs most cheaply to do so."
5. Given principles 1 through 4, protect the assignment with a liability rule or government regulation, depending on which is more likely to lead to social efficiency.

Breyer (1982) gives examples of the application of the *Calabresi and Melamed principles* to safety and pollution:

> When it is uncertain whether a benefit (such as a lawnmower with a certain risk) is worth the potential costs (such as the harm of related accidents), one should construct liability rules such that the costs (of the harm) are placed on the party best able to weigh the costs against the benefits. This principle is likely to place costs upon the party best able to avoid them, or, where this is unknown, on the party best able to induce others to act more safely. This principle seems to argue for making the lawnmower manufacturer strictly liable if he is best able to weigh the benefits, risks, and avoidance costs involved. Similarly, in the case of pollution, the rule would place liability on the factory owner, for he is in the best position to determine whether it is more efficient to curtail pollution or to compensate the victims of his noisome emissions.

In the case of lawnmower safety, the fifth principle pertains to the choice among government regulation, voluntary standards, and reliance on the liability system.

Principles 3 and 4 call for placing social costs on those who can most efficiently reduce them or induce others to take care to reduce them. In many cases, this means that the producer should be liable, as in the case of a cell phone with a risk of fire or explosion from a lithium-ion battery. In other cases, the producer and the consumer should each bear some portion of the social costs of injuries, so as to induce each to take the efficient level of care.[19]

---

[19]These principles also provide the basis for the choice among remedies for breach of contract, as discussed earlier in the chapter.

In the case of a chain saw, the producer is better placed than is the consumer to determine whether, for example, the social benefits of a safety feature exceed its costs. If accidents can be reduced either by a safety feature or by care taken by the consumer, the producer is likely better placed to determine which can do so at lower cost. For example, the producer is better placed to determine if a safety tip is more effective in reducing the risk from kickback than are warnings to the consumer not to bore with the tip. If the hazard is from a branch falling on a chain saw user, the consumer is best placed to reduce the risk by, for example, wearing a hard hat. The producer then may be liable only if it failed to inform consumers about the hazard. If it were not clear whether a safety feature would reduce the hazard at lower cost than a precaution taken by the consumer, the costs should be put on the party best able to correct an error in the assignment of the cost. Surely the producer is better placed to induce the consumer to change his behavior through warnings and instructions than is the consumer able to induce the firm to change its product. In the case of a chain saw, liability rather than regulation is used to govern the provision of safety, although the industry has adopted some voluntary standards to lessen the risk that a producer would free ride on the safety reputation generated by other producers.

PRODUCTS LIABILITY

The Development of Products Liability Law

Products liability is a branch of the common law of torts. Products liability cases that are litigated—particularly those that reach a state or the U.S. Supreme Court—establish legal precedents under which future cases are decided. Those precedents also provide the basis for plaintiffs' and defendants' expectations about likely court decisions in their own cases and so provide the basis for settlements.

The issues brought before the courts change over time, and the common law evolves to address those changes. Technological progress has changed the nature of many consumer products, particularly as electronics replaced mechanical functions. It is now often more difficult to determine a product's likely hazards through casual inspection. In this situation the Calabresi and Melamed principles suggest shifting the cost of injury prevention toward the producer because the producer is likely to have a lower cost of preventing injuries through design and manufacture than the consumer has in inspecting the products and taking precautions. The producer is also better placed to take actions in the market, such as providing warnings and instructions that can induce consumers to take care. Court decisions have followed a similar logic, resulting in evolving legal standards on which courts decide cases.[20]

The common law of products liability has evolved considerably since the 1950s, with legal standards originating in the law of contracts evolving into a standard of *strict liability* under which a producer may be held fully responsible even if it was not at fault and could not have prevented the injury. Some activists and legal scholars have advocated going further to a system of absolute, or total, liability. Under such a system a producer would be held liable for any injury associated with a product. Such a system would be equivalent to a producer attaching to each product it sells an insurance policy with no deductible or copayment.

This section provides an introduction to the principal changes in and central principles of products liability. One reason for the complexity is that products liability is largely state law, and not all states have adopted the same legal standards. Nearly all states have adopted the standard of strict liability, but some allow certain defenses that others do not allow. For example, a number of states now allow state-of-the-art design defenses, which have made liability less strict. Firms thus have the challenge of dealing

---

[20]Some legal scholars, such as Posner (1981), argue that social efficiency is the cornerstone of legal justice and that court decisions will in the long run produce a common law that supports efficiency. Rubin (1983) and Priest (1977) have argued that the natural incentives for parties to bring lawsuits when social efficiency gains can be realized will lead to new legal precedents that promote social efficiency.

with dissimilar laws across the states. This has led some business groups and some lawyers to advocate a uniform federal code for products liability.

The law pertaining to product safety developed from the laws of contracts and *warranties,* which focus on economic well-being. The law of warranties is codified in the Uniform Commercial Code, which has been adopted for commercial transactions by all the states. In addition, the Magnuson-Moss Warranty Act of 1975 regulates the content and clarity of written warranties. Warranties include those expressly made by the producer and those implied by, for example, the fact that the product was put on the market for sale. *Express* warranties are made in writing by the producer and, as part of the sales agreement, represent obligations binding on the producer. If the manufacturer states that a chain saw will cut at a particular speed and it does not, the consumer may sue for damages under the law of warranty.

Implied warranties are not made by producers but are held by the courts to be associated with a product put on the market. Products are held to have an implied *warranty of merchantability.* A chain saw is supposed to cut wood—if it does not, the consumer may sue. However, a chain saw is not supposed to cut cement blocks or metal pipe. A product also has an implied warranty for fitness for a particular purpose. A food or drink carries an implied warranty of *fitness for human consumption.*

The legal foundations provided by the law of contracts and warranties were transformed through two steps into the current law of products liability. The first step was a movement away from the rules of contract law by expanding the concept of who has standing to sue whom. In addition, certain principles of tort law were applied to injuries associated with products. The second was the replacement of the standard of negligence by strict liability. A negligence standard is still used in many parts of tort law, but the standard of strict liability is used in most jurisdictions in cases of products liability.

At the turn of the 20th century, state laws generally required *privity of contract* in which a party incurring a loss of property associated with the use of a product could sue only the party from whom the product had been purchased. A producer who sold a product through a retailer could not be sued by a consumer because the consumer had privity of contract only with the retailer. This standard changed when the State Appeals Court of New York in *MacPherson v. Buick Motor Company,* NY Court of Appeals, 111 N.E. 1050 (1916), held that an injured consumer could sue the manufacturer when the manufacturer had been negligent in failing to detect a defect in a product. The court stated, "If the nature of a thing is such that it is reasonably certain to place life and limb in danger when negligently made, it is then a thing of danger. . . . If he is negligent, where danger is foreseen, a liability will follow." This decision not only eliminated the privity requirement but also led to injuries associated with products being treated as torts. This began the development of products liability.

The limits of privity of contract were further eroded by a court decision that extended the implied warranty of merchantability to cover an automobile driver, in this case the spouse of the purchaser, who was not in privity with the seller.[21] These two cases extended the reach of tort law to users other than the purchaser and back through the channel of distribution to the manufacturer. In most jurisdictions, a consumer is now able to sue the producer as well as virtually all those in the channel of distribution through which the product passed. In addition, other people, including injured bystanders, can sue for damages.

The *MacPherson* decision applied to cases in which negligence was shown. *Negligence* is defined as "the omission to do something which a reasonable man, guided by those ordinary considerations which ordinarily regulate human affairs, would do, or the doing of something which a reasonable and prudent man would not do."[22] The second phase of the evolution of products liability was the abandonment of the negligence standard and its replacement by the standard of strict liability in tort. Under a negligence standard, the burden of proof was on the plaintiff to show that the

---

[21]*Henningsen v. Bloomfield Motors,* 32 N.J. 358, 161 A.2d 69 (1960).
[22]*Black's Law Dictionary* (Black, 1983, p. 538).

producer was at fault. Fault was determined by whether the producer had taken *due care* in the manufacture of the product and whether adequate warnings had been given. Cases often focused on showing that the product had a defect that caused an injury that would not have occurred had the manufacturer exercised due care.

Under strict liability the concept of fault is irrelevant and negligence is not required.[23] The courts do not inquire into who was at fault but instead are concerned only with whether the product in question was associated with the injury.[24] The courts also may not allow a due care defense, so a producer may be held liable even if everything possible had been done to prevent the defect that caused the injury.

The transformation to strict liability was the result of a set of cases decided in state courts. In *Escola v. Coca-Cola Bottling Co.,* 24 Cal. 2d 453, 150 P.2d 436 (1944), a case involving a person injured by an exploding Coca-Cola bottle, California Supreme Court Judge Traynor stated in a dissenting opinion: "I believe the manufacturer's negligence should no longer be singled out as the basis of a plaintiff's right to recover in cases like the present one. In my opinion it should now be recognized that a manufacturer incurs an absolute liability when an article that he has placed on the market, knowing that it is to be used without inspection, proves to have a defect that causes injury to human beings." Judge Traynor provided two rationales for his conclusion: one based on ex ante social efficiency and one based on which party can best bear the distributive consequences of the injuries. "Even if there is no negligence, however, public policy demands that responsibility be fixed wherever it will most effectively reduce the hazards to life and health inherent in defective products that reach the market. It is evident that the manufacturer can anticipate some hazards and guard against the recurrence of others, as the public cannot. Those who suffer injury from defective products are unprepared to meet its consequences. The cost of an injury and the loss of time or health may be an overwhelming misfortune to the person injured and a needless one, for the risk of injury can be insured by the manufacturer and distributed among the public as a cost of doing business."

Judge Traynor's call for a system of absolute liability has not prevailed, but his opinion influenced later court decisions that established the somewhat narrower standard of strict liability. In *Greenman v. Yuba Power Products,* 59 Cal. 2d 57 (1963), a person injured by a piece of wood when using a shop tool was awarded damages under the principle that "a manufacturer is strictly liable in tort when an article he places on the market, knowing that it is to be used without inspection for defects, proves to have a defect that causes injury to a human being." The explanation given for strict liability was "to insure that the costs of injuries resulting from defective products are borne by the manufacturers that put such products on the market rather than by the injured persons who are powerless to protect themselves." The definition of strict liability given in the *Restatement (Second) of Torts (1965)* is presented in Figure 12-6.[25]

FIGURE 12-6 Strict Liability Section 402A of the *Second Restatement of Torts* (1965)

(1) One who sells any product in a defective condition unreasonably dangerous to the user or consumer or to his property is subject to liability for physical harm thereby caused to ultimate user or consumer, or to his property, if (a) the seller is engaged in the business of selling such a product, and (b) it is expected to and does reach the user or consumer without substantial change in the condition in which it was sold.

(2) The rule in Subsection (1) applies though (a) the seller has exercised all possible care in the preparation and sale of his product, and (b) the user or consumer has not bought the product from or entered into any contractual relation with the seller.

---

[23]Negligence, for example, due to careless manufacturing may expose a company to punitive damages.
[24]Even proof of direct causation need not be given, as indicated by the DES decision considered later in the chapter.
[25]A restatement is a collection of the rules established through court decisions, prepared by the American Law Institute, an association of legal scholars. A restatement is intended to reflect the case law in a majority of the states. A restatement is not itself the law but instead provides guidance to plaintiffs, defendants, and the court in reasoning about particular cases.

The courts have adopted a broad interpretation of what constitutes a defect in a product. Defects include those that come from manufacturing, as, for example, a defective Coca-Cola bottle. It is often difficult to prove whether a product had a manufacturing defect, so many courts assume that if a person was injured by a product, the product was defective. Defects can also result from the design of the product. If a shop tool were designed in such a manner that a piece of wood could fly out of it during use, the product may be said to have a defect. Defects also can be associated with the instructions provided with a product or with the warnings given. Producers thus have a *duty to warn*. A defect in a warning is complicated because it involves both the warning given by the producer and the consumer's understanding of it. Many firms tailor their warnings to the lowest common denominator, and some use pictographs because some consumers cannot read. The adequacy of warnings and instructions is evaluated by the courts.

Design defects include both those that are knowable and in some cases those that are unknowable—for example, because of the limitations of science at the time the product was manufactured. Manville was held liable for some asbestos-related injuries because of a failure to warn even though the court concluded that the danger was unknown to science at the time and thus the company could not have warned against it.[26] A defense that a firm used *state-of-the-art design* may not prevail when a standard of strict liability is applicable.[27] Producers have thus been held liable for injuries from "defects" that were neither knowable nor preventable.

Warnings about the product's proper and intended use may not protect producers from liability. Proper and intended use is an imprecise concept. Is the proper and intended use of a screwdriver only to turn screws, or does it include opening paint cans and serving as a chisel? Because a product such as a screwdriver can be anticipated to be used for a variety of purposes, courts have assigned to producers the duty to *anticipate misuse*. A manufacturer of a pickup truck, for example, was held liable for an injury caused by a rollover when a user attached a camper that exceeded the truck's stated carrying capacity. In recent years companies have substantially increased their warnings. After an award to a woman scalded when she spilled a cup of its coffee, McDonald's added the warning on its cup, "Caution: Contents Hot." A manufacturer of a Batman costume warned, "Parents: Please exercise caution . . . cape does not enable user to fly."

Since the *Restatement (Second),* products liability has become both more important and increasingly controversial as courts have addressed a variety of difficult issues. In 1998 the American Law Institute issued the *Restatement (Third) of Torts: Products Liability* to reflect changes in the law as developed in the states. The *Restatement (Third)* is itself controversial; for example, it does not reflect the law in California and Oregon, and the Supreme Court in Connecticut has rejected the restatement as it pertains to design defects. How influential it will eventually be is unclear.

The *Restatement (Third)* distinguishes between manufacturing defects, design defects, and inadequate instructions and warnings defects. Strict liability applies only to manufacturing defects and applies "even though all possible care was exercised." A design is defective if a "reasonable alternative design" is available to reduce or avoid a foreseeable risk. The burden is assigned to the plaintiff to show that there is a reasonable alternative design. This assignment represents a departure from the law in many states and makes establishing liability considerably more difficult for the plaintiff. The *Restatement (Third)* also requires that an improved design be used rather than a warning to reduce or avoid a foreseeable risk. It also states that a manufacturer has a duty to warn if a risk is identified after the sale.

Allowable Defenses Under Strict Liability

Some defenses are allowed under strict liability, but they vary among the states. In all of these defenses, the burden of proof is on the defendant. The only absolute defense is

---

[26]*Beshada v. Johns-Manville Prods. Corp.,* 90 N.J. 191, 447 A.2d 539 (1982).
[27]Some states allow state-of-the-art defenses.

that the product was not associated with the injury or was not the *proximate cause* of the injury. The concept of proximate cause was broadened considerably in the DES case to that of probabilistic causation. A woman whose mother had taken the drug DES during her pregnancy developed cancer over 20 years later.[28] The woman did not know which of several manufacturers had produced the DES her mother had taken, but the court held for her and apportioned damages among the producers according to their market share.[29] Third-generation DES lawsuits have been filed as granddaughters of women who had taken DES sought compensation.

The other defenses are not absolute. One is based on the *assumption of risk* by the consumer. If a consumer voluntarily and knowingly assumes a risk, a producer may be protected. Such assumptions are routine for surgery and certain medications, but they may provide little protection if the patient did not understand the risk. The burden of proof is on the defendant to prove that the assumption was both voluntary and understood. A producer may also have a defense if the consumer accepted a known and avoidable danger.

As indicated in the statement of strict liability in Figure 12-6, a producer may have a defense if a product had been altered by someone other than the producer in a manner that caused injury to the plaintiff. A *correction of a defect* may also provide a degree of protection in some instances.

In some jurisdictions a defense of *contributory negligence* on the part of the plaintiff is allowed. The burden of proof is on the defendant to show that the plaintiff was negligent in the use of the product; if proven, the defendant may avoid damages or have the damages reduced by the plaintiff's share of responsibility.[30] Producers are generally held responsible for anticipating misuse, however.

A producer may be able to use *disclaimers* to limit liability, but the courts have held some disclaimers to be invalid. The Magnuson-Moss Act prohibits producers from disclaiming express warranties and any implied warranties that go with it. Disclaiming is a concept from contract law and as such is intended to be a factor over which the parties bargain. Otherwise the courts may hold that it is invalid. One type of disclaimer that is upheld by courts is that associated with an assumption of risk in which a consumer voluntarily and knowledgeably agrees to bear the risk. Courts, however, typically examine closely whether the consumer actually understood the disclaimer. Disclaimers that limit the remedies available to parties, such as the right to sue, may not be upheld.

In most jurisdictions, products liability cases are covered by a *statute of limitations,* which is often 4 years. For capital equipment, a *statute of repose* serves the same function as a statute of limitations, but the time allowed is much longer. Compliance with government safety standards can in some cases be used as a defense, although such standards may be viewed by the courts as providing only the minimum level of safety.

Preemption

Some federal legislation preempts states from adding requirements beyond those stated in the law. This preemption could be explicit or implicit in the law. A 1976 law dealing with the FDA pre-market approval of medical devices contained a preemption clause that prohibited states from imposing "any requirement . . . different from, or in addition to" the federal law. In 2008 in an 8-1 decision, *Medhome v. Riegel* (No.66-179), the Supreme Court held that this explicit preemption precluded the imposition of damages by state courts in a liability lawsuit pertaining to a large class of medical devices.[31] The case pertained to injuries due to the risks from a medical device that the FDA had already taken into account in its pre-market approval of the devices. An

---

[28]The FDA banned DES in 1971 as a result of an abnormal cancer rate in the daughters of women who had used the drug.
[29]*Sindell v. Abbott Laboratories,* 26 Cal. 3d 588, 607 P.2d 924 (1980). In 1989 the Supreme Court let stand a New York court verdict holding DES manufacturers liable.
[30]See Cooter and Ulen (1988, pp. 354–360) for an analysis of the efficiency consequences of a contributory negligence defense. Negligence is not the same as misuse but is better understood as gross misuse.
[31]Cases alleging manufacturing defects would be unaffected by the decision.

award of damages was judged to be precluded by the statute. Justice Antonin Scalia provided an efficiency argument in the majority opinion that what state courts do is consider the danger of the device but not its benefits. He wrote, "The patients who reaped those benefits are not represented in court."

In contrast to the explicit preemption in the medical devices statutes, pharmaceutical companies claimed that a similar preemption was implicit in the pre-market approval for drugs. In 2008 the first case to reach the Supreme Court resulted in a 4–4 tie with Chief Justice John Roberts not participating. The tie allowed the Court of Appeals decision allowing a liability lawsuit involving a diabetes drug to go to trial. In its 2008–2009 session the Supreme Court agreed to hear a broader case centering on whether the FDA's approval of labels preempts lawsuits alleging a failure to disclose information or adequately warn.

If the Supreme Court upholds preemption, the victims of injuries due to disclosed risks that had been weighed by the FDA would not be able to receive compensation through the tort system. Compensation instead would be provided by insurance or by funds provided by states or federal governments.

Damages

The principal form of damages awarded in liability cases is *compensatory*—compensation for the loss incurred. The determination of compensation is straightforward in the case of property that has a readily established value. In other cases measurement is more difficult. It is possible to determine the cost of medical care for an injury, but measuring pain and suffering or the loss of a limb or a life is more difficult. Juries do make such decisions, however. Moreover, trial lawyers have available detailed data on the damages awarded in personal injury lawsuits. For example, Jury Verdict Research (2001) annually publishes its *Personal Injury Valuation Handbook,* which provides data on awards in a variety of categories such as vehicular liabilities and products liability with breakdowns by type of injury. In 1999 the median jury award in products liability cases was $1.8 million compared to $500,000 six years earlier. Awards ranged from $11,000 to $285 million. Part of the explanation for the higher awards is that trial lawyers have shied away from cases they expect will yield only modest awards. Jury Verdict Research conducts statistical analysis of cases and awards and provides probabilities of a plaintiff victory and predictions of awards for particular types of cases. For example, the median jury awards for burns and leg fractures were $891,000 and $500,000, respectively. Most cases do not reach trial, and out-of-court settlements are substantially lower than awards in litigated cases, perhaps because stronger cases are more likely to be litigated than weaker cases.

In cases in which both the producer and the consumer are responsible for the injury, some courts assess *comparative damages.* If the consumer is found to be 30 percent at fault for an accident and the producer 70 percent at fault, the producer is assessed damages equal to 70 percent of the consumer's loss. *The Restatement (Third) of Torts: Products Liability* requires comparative damages. Comparative liability is used in all but six states and the District of Columbia.

Defendants often complain about the magnitude of some awards. The awards may reflect the sympathy jurors feel for accident victims and the deep pockets they see in firms. The awards in many of these cases are reduced by the trial judges or on appeal. Most cases are settled out of court with the settlement amounts not made public. The largest settlement was in 1998 when a class action suit against Dow Corning involving silicone breast implants was settled for $3.2 billion.

The number of personal injury lawsuits of all types has declined in recent years, although class action lawsuits and "mass torts," such as those involving tobacco and asbestos, increased until the mid 2000s. The overall decline in the number of cases in California, for example, has been attributed to several factors, including declines in accident rates, trial attorneys pursuing fewer but larger award cases, the use of alternative dispute resolution mechanisms such as arbitration, court decisions making certain types of cases more difficult to win, and tort reform. The size of awards and settlements has continued to increase. Settlements, awards, and court costs in asbestos cases have totaled nearly $54 billion, and projections are that the total will be over $200 billion. Eighty-five corporations have gone bankrupt as a result of the litigation.[32]

In most jurisdictions *punitive* damages can be assessed. The legal standard for imposing punitive damages is higher than that for compensatory damages and generally requires a finding of negligence and fault. This allows defendants to use defenses, such as state-of-the-art design, that may not be allowable under strict liability. Jury Verdict Research reported that in 1995 and 1996 punitive damages were awarded in 12 percent and 6 percent, respectively, of the products liability cases litigated. The median awards were $1.25 million and $2.5 million, respectively. In 1999 punitive damage awards increased substantially. The magnitude of some of the punitive damages awards has attracted considerable attention. In a case in which a Pinto's gas tank caught fire and caused injury, a jury awarded $3.5 million in compensatory damages and $125 million in punitive damages. The judge reduced the punitive damages to $3.5 million.[33] In 1994 the Georgia Court of Appeals struck down the award of $105 million in punitive damages mentioned in the Chapter 3 case, *General Motors: Like a Rock? (A)*, involving an accidental death in a GM pickup truck with gas tanks mounted outside the frame walls.

The Politics of Products Liability

The costs and consequences of liability cases, and the proportion of awards that go to trial lawyers, provide strong incentives to take liability issues into the legislative arena. Liability costs not only affect safety decisions, but they also affect the prices of products and in some cases whether products are produced. In part because of soaring liability costs, production in the small aircraft industry fell from 17,811 aircraft in 1978 to 964 in 1993. Cessna Aircraft stopped producing single-engine, piston-powered aircraft in 1986 because of liability costs. The plight of the industry led to enactment of the General Aviation Revitalization Act, which prevents lawsuits against manufacturers for accidents associated with aircraft more than 18 years old. When the law went into effect in 1994, Cessna announced that it would resume producing single-engine, piston-powered aircraft.

Producers of medical implants such as heart valves have been subject to numerous liability lawsuits. Fearing that they would be included as defendants, the suppliers of biomaterials began to stop supplying implant makers. The amount of biomaterials used in an implant is small and represented little loss of revenue to the suppliers. Implant makers and patient advocacy groups feared that a shortage would develop and worked for federal legislation shielding suppliers from liability. The Biomaterials Access Assurance Act was enacted in 1998.

Business has worked for over two decades for federal products liability legislation.[34] With Republican majorities in both houses of Congress as a result of the 1994 elections, business hopes for reform were buoyed. The American Tort Reform Association—which includes 300 nonprofit organizations, professional societies, trade associations, and businesses—has actively worked for tort reform. The 60,000-member Association of Trial Lawyers and its consumer advocate allies, such as Public Citizen, renewed their opposition to reforms and geared for another battle.[35]

The foci of the federal efforts were (1) caps on punitive damages for small companies, (2) limits on the liability of wholesalers and retailers in products liability lawsuits unless they altered a product, (3) heightened standards for punitive damages by requiring evidence of "conscious, flagrant disregard" for safety, (4) restrictions on damage awards if the plaintiff misused a product or was under the influence of alcohol or drugs, and (5) a cap on noneconomic (pain and suffering) damages. Federal tort reform, however, succumbed to filibusters in the Senate and a presidential veto during the Clinton administration. In 2004 the House passed bills to cap pain and suffering awards

---

[32]See White (2004).
[33]See Cooter and Ulen (1988, pp. 403–407) for an analysis of Pinto cases.
[34]See Cohen (1990) for a review of the early legislative efforts.
[35]The trial lawyers renamed their association the American Association for Justice.

at $250,000 and penalize lawyers who file frivolous lawsuits and engage in venue shopping. The Senate, however, did not act on the measures. A filibuster in the Senate by Democrats stopped a bipartisan compromise to move class action lawsuits from state to federal courts.

After the 2004 elections President Bush pledged to try again on tort reform. At an economic conference attended by the president, selected economists, and business executives, Home Depot CEO Robert Nardelli described the concerns of business: "What you have today is business on one side, and you've got the trial lawyers on the other side. . . . You've got deep pockets colliding with shallow principles." Todd Smith, president of the Association of Trial Lawyers of America, responded, referring to the president and his tort reform objectives, "He [unashamedly] advocates legislation that would protect insurance-industry profits and prohibit any punishment for the makers of dangerous drugs like Vioxx, while penalizing your mother for being abused in a nursing home or your daughter for having her baby killed by medical malpractice."[36] In 2005 the Bush administration prevailed and Congress passed a law requiring most class action lawsuits to be tried in federal rather than state courts. The law was intended to stop venue shopping, where plaintiffs attempt to have cases tried in jurisdictions friendly to plaintiffs.

Tort reform at the state level has been more successful than federal efforts. Many states have acted to cap and otherwise limit damage awards. In addition to the limits imposed by recent Supreme Court decisions, 36 states have adopted some limits on punitive damages. In addition, many states have capped awards in medical malpractice cases in an attempt to slow the increases in the cost of insurance for doctors. Several states have also abolished or otherwise restricted joint and several liability. The American Tort Reform Association (www.atra.org) tracks changes in tort law in each state. One proposal for reform is to have punitive damage awards paid to the government rather than the plaintiffs. This would preserve the deterrence effects of punitive damages without providing additional incentives for trial lawyers to file lawsuits.

In a study of the effects of changes in state liability laws over the 1970 to 1990 period, Campbell, Kessler, and Shepherd (1998) found that states that had decreased their levels of liability awards experienced statistically significant higher gains in productivity of approximately 1 to 2 percent.[37] Other studies have indicated that high levels of awards in liability cases reduce innovations.[38] As indicated in the next section, businesses shied away from Mississippi because of its litigation record.

IMPERFECTIONS IN THE LIABILITY SYSTEM

The products liability system has been criticized on equity, distributive, and efficiency grounds.[39] The equity arguments often express a belief that cases should be decided on the basis of fault and negligence. In particular, firms consider it inequitable to be assessed damages when there was nothing they could have done to prevent the injury. Objections have been made to the inability to use state-of-the-art design as a defense in cases governed by strict liability. In the absence of a statute of repose for capital equipment, this means that an injured party may be able to sue successfully for an injury caused by a product manufactured many years earlier when technological capabilities were more limited. The *Restatement (Third) of Torts* addresses this issue.

The distributive objection is that the awards in many cases are too large and seem to provide a prize, as in a lottery, rather than providing compensation for actual losses. The deep pockets of producers are seen by some jurors as a means of helping those who were unfortunate enough to have been injured. Criticism has centered on damages awarded for pain and suffering, which some argue are often unreasonable and

[36]*San Jose Mercury News,* December 16, 2004.
[37]Kimmel (2008) reached a similar conclusion, finding that an additional tort reform increased productivity by 1 percent.
[38]See Viscusi and Moore (1993) and Huber and Litan (1991).
[39]See Viscusi (1991) for an analysis of products liability and recommendations for reform.

unguided by legal standards. Whether awards are too large is unclear, however, and limits on awards remain the subject of considerable disagreement.

Most products liability cases are filed in state courts, and trial lawyers shop for the state venue most likely to favor their cases. The state of Mississippi earned a national reputation for large jury awards to plaintiffs, and many trial lawyers attempted to have their cases tried there.[40] Venue shopping focuses on Mississippi's 22nd Judicial Circuit, which the American Tort Reform Association designated a "Judicial Hellhole."[41] The governor of Mississippi pushed for state tort reform, citing not only the bad reputation the state had earned but also the business opportunities the state had lost. In explaining why Toyota had decided not to build a plant in the state, the company stated that "the litigation climate in Mississippi is unfavorable. . . ." Similarly, the CEO of Caterpillar explained why the company was not expanding operations in the state: "Unfortunately, Mississippi's current lawsuit environment makes us very reluctant to consider expanding our activities in the state."[42] Mississippi took the first steps toward reform by eliminating joint and several liability, reducing the liability of retailers, and capping awards for noneconomic damages at $1 million except for medical liability, which was capped at $500,000.

As the Coase theorem indicates, the distributive consequences of a legal standard can be independent of their efficiency consequences. However, liability awards can force firms into bankruptcy or dissuade them from producing certain desirable products. Because a number of pharmaceutical companies had stopped producing certain vaccines as a result of liability costs, Congress passed the Childhood Vaccine Act of 1986, which established a no-fault compensation system and capped pain and suffering awards. Similarly, there might be no nuclear power plants in the United States were it not for the Price-Anderson Act, which limits liability in the case of an accident.

Some critics argue that the development of drugs to treat conditions associated with pregnancy has been chilled by lawsuits such as those involving Bendectin, a drug used to treat morning sickness. Congenital abnormalities occur naturally in about 3 percent of newborns, and pharmaceutical companies can face lawsuits if a mother used one of their products. As the silicone breast implants example indicates, liability cases can result in large settlements even when there is little scientific evidence linking a product to a disease.

In addition to concerns about the standards on which cases are decided and awards based, the liability system is costly to operate. Court costs and legal expenses for defendants are high, and under the contingent fee system, attorneys for plaintiffs typically receive one-third of any award or settlement. Of the $54 billion cost of asbestos litigation, approximately $34 billion has gone to lawyers (White, 2004). Investigating the facts in a case can also be expensive. Products liability cases are frequently consolidated into class action lawsuits, which generally reduces the costs of litigation. The high cost of taking a case to trial encourages settlements, but it can also encourage frivolous lawsuits that seek to extract a settlement from defendants who prefer to avoid the legal fees and court costs.

A particular concern of business is *joint and several liability*. In a case in which several parties have a role in an injury, such as a manufacturer and a distributor or a manufacturer and a government, all may be held liable. A motorist who hits a pothole, loses control of the car, hits a telephone pole, and is injured may sue both the city government and the telephone company under the principle that the harm to the victim is indivisible.[43] In such a case, the damages awarded are allocated among the defendants in proportion to their responsibility for the injury. But if one of the defendants is unable to pay its share of the damages, the defendant with "deeper pockets" can be required

---

[40]In a dispute over legal fees in a case involving Hurricane Katrina, Mississippi lawyer Richard F. Scruggs, who had received millions of dollars in fees in asbestos and cigarette litigation, pleaded guilty in 2008 for conspiring to bribe a federal judge in Mississippi and was sentenced to 5 years in prison.
[41]Madison County, Illinois has also been called a judicial hellhole.
[42]*Associated Press State & Local Wire,* April 28, 2004.
[43]See Cooter and Ulen (2004, pp. 362–64, 429–431).

EXAMPLE

Silicone Breast Implants

In the 1970s and 1980s, 600,000 women received silicone breast implants in the United States. In 1982 a woman claimed that she became seriously ill when her breast implants leaked into her body. She sued and received an award of over $1 million. The Dow Corning Company subsequently was sued by 170,000 women, filing bankruptcy in 1995 as a result of a proposed settlement that collapsed shortly thereafter. Three other manufacturers settled the claims against them later in 1995. In 1998 Dow Corning reached an agreement with the plaintiffs in which it agreed to pay $3.2 billion over 15 years.

The litigation was coordinated by trial lawyers and was well orchestrated. The trial lawyers hired Fenton Communications to conduct a public relations campaign to highlight the claims of serious illness resulting from the implants.[1] The settlements reached were in spite of consistent scientific evidence that there was no link between the leaks and serious illness. The American College of Rheumatology stated that the scientific evidence was "compelling" that there was no link between implants and systemic disease. The Council on Scientific Affairs of the American Medical Association stated, "To date, there is no conclusive or compelling evidence that relates silicon breast implants to human auto-immune disease." The American Academy of Neurology stated that "existing research shows no link between silicon breast implants and neurological disease." Dr. Marcia Angell, executive editor of the *New England Journal of Medicine* and author of a book on breast implants, said that 15 scientifically valid epidemiological studies had been conducted and none showed any higher rate of illnesses among women with breast implants than women without them. She referred to the systemic diseases reported by women as "coincidental." Dr. David Kessler, who in 1992 as head of the Food and

Drug Administration banned the sale of silicone-gel implants and later became dean of the Yale University School of Medicine, said, "There's no evidence that they cause systemic disease."[2]

Citing a Supreme Court decision calling on judges to act as "gatekeepers" to rule out unscientific testimony and speculation in favor of "pertinent evidence based on scientifically valid principles," a federal district court judge hearing implant cases barred plaintiffs' expert witnesses from testifying that the implants can cause systemic diseases.[3] A special panel of independent experts appointed by the judge studied the issue for 2 years and in December 1998 issued its report concluding that there was no evidence that implants induce systemic diseases. The plaintiffs vowed to continue to press their cases.

The evidence continued to accumulate. A 1999 Institute of Medicine study found no increase in risk of cancer, autoimmune diseases, or neurological problems. A National Cancer Institute (NCI) study published in 2001 concluded there was no increased risk of cancer. Louise Brinton, an NCI researcher said, "[The study] helps lay to rest much of the concern."[4] Dr. Stuart Bondurant, chair of the Institute of Medicine committee, said, "We could find no evidence to support a causal relationship between the breast implants and any systemic disease. As far as I know there has been no information since the report was written that would naturally change that conclusion."[5]

In 2000 the FDA approved for marketing saline-filled breast implants produced by two companies, and in 2006 it approved two silicone-gel breast implants produced by the same two companies.

---

[1]Fenton Communications was the firm that orchestrated the nonmarket campaign against the apple-ripening chemical Alar discussed in Chapter 3.

[2]*New York Times*, July 11, 1998. The European Union never banned the implants, but in 2001 it required that recipients be at least 18 years of age.
[3]Some women suffered some scarring and hardening of tissue from leaks.
[4]*Milwaukee Journal Sentinel*, April 27, 2001.
[5]*New York Times*, October 11, 2003.

---

to pay the entire award. This standard focuses on compensating the injured party rather than providing appropriate incentives for care.

Another criticism is that punitive damages awards are governed neither by statute nor clear constitutional guidelines. Instead, juries have been largely free to assess punitive damages as they see fit. The imposition of punitive damages without standards to guide their award has been a source of concern to both firms and jurists. In a concurring opinion, Supreme Court Justices Sandra Day O'Connor and Antonin Scalia, discussing punitive damages, wrote, "The impact of these windfall recoveries is unpredictable and potentially substantial . . . this grant of wholly standardless discretion to determine the severity of punishment appears inconsistent with due process."[44]

Although there are no explicit constitutional limits on punitive damages, in 1996 the Supreme Court threw out as constitutionally excessive a decision against BMW of North America in a case in which a jury awarded $4,000 in compensatory damages and $4 million in punitive damages because the paint on a new car had been retouched.[45] In an important decision in 2003 the Supreme Court overturned a punitive damages award that exceeded the compensatory damages award by a ratio of 145 to 1.[46] The court stated that the award was an "irrational and arbitrary deprivation of the property of the defendant." The court also stated that an award with a double-digit ratio was unlikely to be constitutional and that when compensatory damages are substantial an award "at or near the amount of compensatory damages" would likely be justified. The decision quickly had effects as the Court of Appeals ruled that punitive damages of $5 billion against ExxonMobil for the *Exxon Valdez* oil spill were excessive and reduced the award to $2.5 billion. Exxon appealed the decision, arguing that the $3.4 billion it had already paid for compensation, criminal fines, and clean-up was sufficient punishment. In 2008 the Supreme Court reduced the award to $507 million, which was the amount of compensatory damages.

From the perspective of producers, damage awards are difficult to predict, complicating the estimation of the ex post consequences of their ex ante decisions. The insurance system allows firms to insure against that risk, but the insurance system itself is imperfect and costly to operate. Also, many firms are unable to purchase liability insurance. In response, Congress passed the Risk Retention Act of 1981, which allows firms in the same industry to form their own insurance pool.

The standard of strict liability is said by some to assign too much of the cost of injuries to firms and too little to consumers, distorting the incentives for care. This can cause firms to take more care and consumers to take less care than is efficient. The *Restatement (Third) of Torts* reflects this concern by allowing defenses in design defect cases. Efficiency is improved by allowing a defense of contributory negligence and assigning damages on a comparative basis. In an imperfect world, however, the Calabresi and Melamed principles indicate that liability should be assigned to that party who is best placed to evaluate costs and benefits and to induce the other party to take appropriate care. Producers are generally better placed than consumers for these purposes, so efficiency may be served by assigning liability to producers rather than to consumers.[47]

Tort law evolves as cases with new issues are brought before the courts. This means that tort innovation is ongoing. As an example, shortly after Mattel's second toy recall, a lawsuit was filed in Los Angeles on behalf of a California family claiming that Mattel was negligent and should establish a fund to pay for medical monitoring of children who might have been harmed by the toys. The lawsuit filed by attorney Jeffrey Killino of Philadelphia sought class action status. The lawsuit was based on the medical monitoring theory that a fund could be ordered by the courts even though there was no evidence of actual injury. A 1993 California Supreme Court decision had supported a fund for monitoring if there was "a reasonably certain consequence" of exposure to a toxic substance.[48] In 1997 the U.S. Supreme Court rejected the establishment of such a fund, but the decision did not apply to state courts. Justice Stephen Breyer cautioned against medical-monitoring funds because they could harm plaintiffs "who depend on a tort system that can distinguish between reliable and serious claims on the one hand, and unreliable and relatively trivial claims on the other."[49]

---

[44]*Bankers Life & Casualty v. Crenshaw,* 486 U.S. 71 (1988). Quoted in Mahoney and Littlejohn (1989).
[45]*BMW of North America v. Gore,* U.S. Supreme Court, 116 S.Ct. 1589 (1996).
[46]*State Farm Mutual Automobile Insurance Co. v. Campbell,* No. 01-1284, 2003 WL 1791206 (2003).
[47]See Epstein (1980) for an argument supporting strict liability.
[48]*Wall Street Journal,* August 20, 2007.
[49]*Wall Street Journal,* August 20, 2007.

SUMMARY

The law is an important institution for improving the efficiency of markets and private agreements. The United States has three basic types of laws. The first are those enacted by Congress, state legislatures, and local government bodies. The second includes rule making and decisions of administrative agencies, frequently involving an administrative law judge, as considered in Chapter 10. The third is the common law, which is law developed from the rulings of judges on cases brought by plaintiffs. Common law consists of the precedents established by those decisions and forms the basis for important branches of the law including the law of property, torts, and contracts. The common law evolves as courts address new issues brought before them by plaintiffs.

The fundamental efficiency perspective on the law is provided by the Coase theorem, which identifies two basic principles. The first is that when transactions costs are low, efficiency can be attained by assigning the entitlement to either party to a transaction, agreement, or hazard. The second is that efficiency can be attained with either a property rule or a liability rule. When transactions costs are high, as in the case of accidents, a liability rule is more efficient. In some cases regulation may be used, particularly if there is a market imperfection.

In the case of real property a property rule is natural, since the parties can reasonably be expected to bargain to an efficient outcome. In the case of an idea or invention, an intellectual property rule is required to allow the creator to appropriate returns from the creation. Appropriability is stronger the tighter is intellectual property protection and the higher the cost of replicating the creation. Intellectual property is protected by patents, copyright, trademarks, and trade secrets.

The law of contracts allows parties to make credible commitments to future actions. This can provide the needed assurances for noncontemporaneous trades and for reliance expenditures. Contracts may be unenforceable if they are made under duress, violate statutes, or are unconscionable. Breach of a contract can be efficient, and courts award damages for both efficient and inefficient breach and may order specific performance such as fulfillment of the contract. Damages may be awarded based on expectations, reliance, or opportunity costs, and the parties to a contract may stipulate liquidated damages. Contracts may be judged unenforceable ex post or damages may be reduced because of impossibility or a frustration of purpose.

Torts are civil wrongs, and strict liability in torts applies to manufacturing defects and in most states to many other types of defects. Under strict liability a producer may be held liable even if it has exercised all possible care. The social efficiency role of products liability is to provide incentives to producers and consumers to take appropriate care to avoid those injuries that are not too costly to avoid. The assignment of the entitlement to consumers is generally supported by the Calabresi and Melamed principles. In practice, courts have also assigned the entitlement to consumers to compensate them for the losses they incur. Under strict liability that compensation can be independent of fault. The defenses allowed under strict liability vary among the states and include the absence of proximate cause, the assumption of risk, product alteration, and contributory negligence.

Products liability law continues to evolve as courts consider cases involving new issues. This has led to a broadening of the definition of products liability and at the same time a narrowing of the grounds for lawsuits as reflected in the *Restatement (Third) of Torts*. The Supreme Court has also limited punitive damages. Tort reform has occurred in many states, and to a limited extent at the federal level. Business has sought federal legislation to limit liability awards and expand the allowable defenses, but the political competition over this legislation has been intense.

-- C A S E S --

California Space Heaters, Inc.

California Space Heaters had developed a line of unvented, convection kerosene space heaters using a new technology and was making preparations to sell them. For a modest purchase price the heaters could heat a room economically, without requiring a central heating system. A particular advantage of the heaters was that they allowed the consumer to focus the heat where and when it was needed. Because of high energy prices in the early 1980s, the demand for the heaters was expected to be brisk. Demand was anticipated to be particularly strong among low-income consumers and homeowners who had electric heating systems, especially in the East where electricity prices were very high. The heaters would also inevitably be used by people whose electricity had been cut off.

Although the heaters were very economical, there were safety hazards associated with their use, ranging from the risk of fire to adverse health effects from their emissions. The hazards were functions of the heater's design, its maintenance, and the conditions of use, including the fuel used. The company could incorporate a variety of safety features in the heaters, but safer heaters had a significantly higher cost and somewhat lower efficiency, requiring more fuel for the "effective warmth" produced.

In terms of hazards, a heater could cause a fire if it were placed too near curtains or furniture. The heaters could be designed so that the temperature could be as low as 320 degrees or as high as 500 degrees. The higher the temperature, the more efficient the heating but the greater the fire hazard, and the greater the risk that small children and others could be burned by touching the heater. The temperature in the heater depended in part on the wick adjustment, which could be controlled manually or by a thermostat. Fires could also occur from "flare up." Should that happen, closing the shutoff valve would extinguish the flame.

Ignition also posed a fire hazard. Electric spark ignition of the wick was safer than match ignition. Fires were a risk each time the fuel tank was refilled, particularly if the unit was already hot. This risk could be reduced by incorporating a removable fuel tank that could be filled outside the house. A siphon could also be incorporated into the tank to lessen the risk of spills when using a funnel. Because kerosene expands when warmed, the tank should never be completely filled; instead, some air space should be maintained to allow for expansion. Kerosene itself was difficult to burn without a wick, but if spilled, a carpet or curtains could act as a wick. The units with electric spark ignition—a battery-operated ignition device—could be equipped with an automatic cutoff system that instantly stopped combustion if the

heater were tipped over or jarred. These units could also be equipped with a power-loss shutoff system that stopped combustion if the batteries lost power.

In addition to the risk of fire, toxic emissions from the heaters posed a potential hazard because the heaters were not vented to the outside as were central heating systems and fireplaces. Inhaling noxious fumes could be harmful, particularly if substandard kerosene were burned or combustion were incomplete. Kerosene came in two grades: 1K, which had a low sulfur content and was appropriate for the heaters, and 2K, which had a higher sulfur content and was inappropriate. Grade 2K kerosene was used in diesel automobiles and trucks and was available at many gasoline stations, whereas 1K kerosene usually had to be purchased at a hardware or specialty store. Since the two grades of kerosene could not be distinguished without conducting a chemical test, consumers could not easily verify which grade they had purchased and had to rely on the supplier. Gasoline should never be used in the heater, nor should fuel oil, which has a significantly higher sulfur content than kerosene.

Proper ignition involved raising the wick, igniting it, and lowering it until the flame burned cleanly. Some consumers might attempt to regulate the heat by adjusting the height of the wick. If the wick were set too low, combustion was less complete and emissions were increased. A wick stop could be incorporated into the heater to prevent the wick from being lowered too far. Because the heater rested on the floor, it could be difficult to adjust the wick properly, requiring the consumer to bend low to see the flame.

The hazard from improper combustion and the burning of the wrong kerosene centered on carbon monoxide and nitrogen dioxide emissions, which posed particular problems for asthmatics, children, the elderly, and pregnant women. EPA standards for outside air were 9 parts per million (ppm) for carbon monoxide and 0.05 ppm for nitrogen dioxide.[50] U.S. Navy standards for submarines were 15 and 0.5 ppm respectively, and NASA's standards for the space shuttle were 25 and 0.5 ppm. The company's studies indicated that its heaters would not meet the EPA standards but would meet the Navy and NASA standards by a comfortable margin. The EPA had not issued standards for indoor air nor was it expected to do so within the next few years.

The risk associated with emissions could be reduced by using a kerosene additive that improved clean burning. The wick should be replaced each year, since

---

[50]The EPA standard was set to protect individuals with angina while they exercised.

the cleanliness of the burn depended on wick quality. Even if combustion were complete and the proper grade of kerosene were used, however, injury or asphyxiation could occur if the room were inadequately ventilated and the heater consumed too much of the oxygen in the room. A window should be left open to prevent oxygen depletion.

Kerosene heaters using old technologies had been banned by several states and municipalities, but most state legislatures had decided to allow the new-technology heaters because of the savings in fuel costs they provided. No federal safety standards for kerosene heaters had been promulgated, but such standards could be forthcoming if injuries resulted from the heaters. The cognizant regulatory agency was the Consumer Products Safety Commission (CPSC), but the CPSC had been immobilized recently and was unlikely to mandate standards, at least for several years.

The design alternatives available to California Space Heaters centered on the safety features that could be incorporated into the heaters. Table 12-1 lists the potential hazards and the design steps, beyond the least expensive model, the company could take to respond to the hazards. Each safety feature was expected to be effective in reducing the specific hazard. The production process for the heaters involved standard technologies and methods, so the chance of a manufacturing defect was slight.

Consumers could also take care to reduce the likelihood of accidents and injury, such as making sure the room was properly ventilated. They could purchase the proper grade of kerosene and could use the "clean burn" additive that sold for $3.99 per 12-ounce bottle. The heater should be cleaned and the wick changed at least at the beginning of each heating season. The consumer should, of course, purchase the appropriate wick.

The least expensive model of kerosene space heater with match ignition could be manufactured for $44, and the standard markup was 100 percent for a discount store and slightly higher in an appliance store. With proper use, the least expensive model was safe. The demand for the low-end heaters was expected to be strong and price elastic. At a price of $88 sales could reach 2 million units per year. The safest and most expensive model the company could make would include all the safety features listed in Table 12-1. It could be manufactured for $189. The demand for the safest heater was expected to be limited. The venture capitalist backing the company commented, only partly in jest, that at a price of $378 the only sales would be to the wealthy for use in their ski cabins.

To indicate the savings attainable from use of the heaters, a marketing analyst compared the cost of heating a house to 68 degrees with heating it to 55 degrees and using a kerosene space heater to bring the living room up to 68 degrees. The estimated savings was $470 a year for a house in New England that used fuel oil; if the house had electric heat, the savings would be $685 per year. Smaller savings could be attained with a portable electric heater, which cost less than a kerosene heater.

The heaters could be marketed through various channels of distribution, ranging from discount stores to appliance stores to heating and air-conditioning shops. Appliance stores might be interested in carrying a full line of heaters, but discount stores were expected to be interested in only the least expensive model. Heating and air-conditioning stores were not expected to stock the heaters but would order them for customers. Their customers were likely to be interested in the more expensive models. The channels of distribution differed significantly in their ability to provide consumers with information on safety features and proper use.

TABLE 12-1   Heater Hazards and Remedies

Potential Hazard	Design Remedy	Cost
temperature adjustment	thermostat	$ 7.50
overheating due to flare-up	automatic temperature shutoff	22.00
tank overflow	tank level gauge	3.00
tip-over fire	automatic cutoff	8.00
contact fire	low burn temperature	*
spill during filling	siphon filling system	12.00
ignition fire	electric spark ignition	19.50
	large tank	12.00
fire during refilling	removable tank**	6.00
noxious emissions		
substandard kerosene	none	
incomplete combustion	(a) wick stop	6.50
	(b) electric wick adjustment	32.00
oxygen depletion	none	—

* Estimated loss in efficiency of $40 per year.
** Only effective if tank is removed and taken outside.

The company consulted a lawyer who indicated that products liability lawsuits were probable should there be injuries or adverse health consequences associated with the use of the heaters. Strict liability in tort would in all likelihood be the applicable liability standard, so the company could be held liable even if an injury were due to foreseeable misuse by a consumer. The costs to the company included the cost of liability insurance, legal and court costs, and the management time required by the cases. These costs could be reduced by adding more safety features to the model. The lawyer had investigated the cost of insurance and roughly estimated that insurance costs plus legal fees might be as much as $55 per unit for the lowest priced model and $10 per unit for the safest model given the estimated sales. The lawyer also estimated that the purchasers of the lowest-cost heaters were less likely to file lawsuits in the event of an injury because they were less familiar with the legal process.

The likelihood of an injury associated with a heater was difficult to estimate, but the company's engineers gave a ballpark estimate of one in a million of a manufacturing defect resulting in a death or a permanent disability from a fire. They estimated that the likelihood of a fire death from misuse was approximately five in one hundred thousand with the least expensive model over the life of the heater and four in a million with the most expensive model. The lawyer asked the engineers for estimates associated with each safety feature, but so far they had provided only two estimates. They estimated that adding electric spark ignition to the least expensive model would reduce the probability of a death by 50 percent, whereas electric wick adjustment would reduce the probability of a death by less than 2.5 percent. ■

Preparation Questions

1. How should California Space Heaters reason about its responsibility for the safety of its heaters and their use?
2. What safety features should be incorporated into the heaters? Should electric spark ignition be incorporated? Electric wick adjustment? What criteria should be used for those decisions?
3. What other actions should be taken in the design or marketing of the heaters?
4. How should prices be set; that is, on what cost basis?

Patent Games: Plavix

In 2001 Apotex, a Canadian manufacturer of generic drugs, filed an application with the U.S. Food and Drug Administration (FDA) to market clopidogrel bisulfate as a generic version of the world's second–best-selling drug, Plavix, an anticlotting drug. Sanofi-Aventis, the French pharmaceutical giant, held a composition of matter patent on Plavix, but Apotex claimed that the 1989 Sanofi patent was invalid because the ingredient clopidogrel bisulfate could be inferred from an earlier 1985 patent that had expired. Sanofi-Aventis argued that the later patent was valid and would not expire until 2012.[51] In 2002 Sanofi-Aventis filed a patent infringement lawsuit in federal court, claiming that the patent provided it with exclusive rights to produce and market Plavix. Plavix was marketed in the United States by Bristol-Myers Squibb, and U.S. sales were $3.5 billion in 2005 with worldwide sales of over $6 billion. Plavix was the best-selling of Bristol-Myers Squibb's drugs and was crucial to the success of the company.

Apotex was a privately held generics producer located in Toronto, Canada, and its CEO, Richard Sherman, was known as an aggressive risk taker. Sherman said, "They say I stalk my prey. I say I don't ever shy away from a fight."[52] He added, "The system is being screwed up by greedy people who see this big pot to be split, and they have no interest in consumers, who get screwed by paying more than they should for medications they need." He referred to the payments that drug makers made to keep generic drugs off the market as "poison pills." Sherman had a net worth of $3.7 billion, according to *Forbes* magazine.

The FDA approved Apotex's version of Plavix in January 2006. The approval allowed Apotex to market the drug at its own risk. That is, if it marketed the drug and lost the patent infringement case, it could be liable for damages. Apotex had invested millions of dollars to construct production facilities and began to produce clopidogrel bisulfate in late 2005.

Bristol-Myers Squibb and Sanofi-Aventis learned that Apotex had built an inventory of clopidogrel bisulfate, and with a trial on the merits of the patent infringement lawsuit scheduled for June 2006, they initiated settlement negotiations with Apotex. On March 21 the three companies reached an agreement granting Apotex the right to market its generic drug in September 2011, eight months before the patent on Plavix would expire.

---

[51]*Wall Street Journal*, September 2, 2006.

[52]*Ottawa Citizen*, August 19, 2006.

The agreement gave Apotex a six-month period before the companies could offer their own generic. Bristol-Myers Squibb and Sanofi-Aventis also agreed to pay Apotex at least $40 million if the agreement were approved and a $60 million break-up fee if the agreement were rejected on antitrust grounds. In a required disclosure, Sanofi-Aventis and Bristol-Myers Squibb stated that there was a significant risk that the agreement would not receive antitrust approval. The trial on the patent infringement lawsuit was postponed pending approval of the agreement.

Bristol-Myers Squibb was operating under a 2003 consent decree with the Federal Trade Commission (FTC) and state attorneys general pertaining to attempts to delay the entry of generic versions of two of its drugs—Taxol and BuSpar. Under the consent decree the FTC and the state attorneys general had to approve any Bristol-Myers Squibb arrangements that could be anticompetitive. The agreement with Apotex was submitted to the regulators for review. The FTC had expressed opposition to agreements that restricted the introduction of generic drugs. On May 5 the state attorneys general told the three companies that they would not approve the agreement, and the FTC also was said to be opposed. The FTC was reportedly concerned about the break-up fee and the six-month period before Bristol-Myers Squibb and Sanofi-Aventis could begin marketing their own generic drug.

After the agreement was rejected, Bristol-Myers Squibb CEO Peter R. Dolan sent executive vice president Dr. Andrew G. Bodnar to Toronto to negotiate a modified agreement that would satisfy the regulators. The modified agreement was submitted on May 26 to the FTC and state attorneys general. It did not include the six-month period and allowed Apotex to license and manufacture a generic version of Plavix in June 2011.

Apotex said that in addition to the modified agreement submitted to the FTC and the state attorneys general, Bodnar had made two oral agreements with Sherman that had been in the original agreement but were not in the modified agreement. One was that Bristol-Myers Squibb and Sanofi-Aventis would not market its own generic version of Plavix until Apotex's generic had been on the market for six months. The other was that Bristol-Myers Squibb and Sanofi-Aventis would pay Apotex the $60 million break-up if the modified agreement were rejected by the government.

One provision retained in the modified agreement was that Bristol-Myers Squibb and Sanofi-Aventis could not file for an injunction to stop generic sales of clopidogrel until five days after a sales launch. The modified agreement also limited damages to 50 percent of Apotex's sales of the generic if it launched the drug and the modified agreement were rejected and Apotex lost the patent infringement case.[53] These provisions were to

remain valid even if the agreement were rejected by the government.

Robert S. Silver, an attorney for Apotex, demanded payment of the $60 million break-up fee after regulators rejected the initial agreement. On May 27 one day after the modified agreement had been concluded, Dr. Bodnar sent an e-mail message to Sherman stating, "You explicitly assured me that you would not initiate such action at this point and would wait until matters had resolved themselves. Unless Silver immediately withdraws his demand, I will consider myself not bound by any restriction as to this issue to which I am bound by agreement with you."[54]

On July 26 Federal Bureau of Investigation agents raided Bristol-Myers Squibb's headquarters, including the office of CEO Dolan, as the Antitrust Division of the U.S. Department of Justice began a criminal investigation of the agreement. The investigation was initiated at the request of the FTC. Bristol-Myers Squibb commented that it "believes that all of its conduct relating to the proposed Plavix settlement has been entirely appropriate and coordinated throughout with senior outside counsel."

The state attorneys general indicated that they would not accept the modified agreement, and the FTC indicated that it was not satisfied with the modifications. This rejection and the provisions of the agreement that remained valid gave Apotex an opportunity to market clopidogrel with only limited risk.

Apotex launched its generic drug on August 8. Sherman said, "There should be no mistaking that our decision to launch a generic version of this blockbuster product at risk is a testament to our commitment to patients, consumers, and taxpayers." The drug had an expiration date of nearly two years, so drug distributors could buy large quantities and sell it out of inventory. Apotex had talked with the major drug distributors prior to launching its sales, and they had expressed eagerness to purchase the drug, since they had mandates to obtain drugs at the lowest possible cost. Medco Health Solutions and other pharmacy benefits companies purchased the generic, and Rite Aid said it would have the generic on its shelves in a day. Apotex charged $124 for a 30-day supply, compared to a price of $148 for Plavix. Bristol-Myers Squibb was reported to be offering rebates. Verispan LLC, which provided information on prescription sales, reported that Apotex's generic drug had 60.2 percent of total prescriptions written and 74 percent of new prescriptions for the week ending August 18.[55]

Surprised by Apotex's flooding the market, Sanofi-Aventis responded by filing a lawsuit in federal court seeking an injunction to halt the sales. Prior to the first

[53]*Wall Street Journal,* September 2, 2006.

[54]*New York Times,* August 18, 2006.
[55]AFX.COM, September 1, 2006.

hearing on the lawsuit, Apotex's lawyers advised Sherman to disclose the oral agreements, and on August 17, 2006 Apotex filed a statement in federal court revealing the oral agreements. Bristol-Myers Squibb said that the side agreements had been suggested by Sherman and that they had refused. Bristol-Myers Squibb held that there were no oral agreements.

After Apotex began shipping its generic, Sherman said in an interview, "I thought the FTC would turn [the modified agreement] down, but I didn't let on that I did. But they seemed blind to it."[56] He also commented, "They couldn't see that maybe certain things were going to end them up in prison."[57] Sherman's belief that the modified agreement would be rejected was supported by a July 7 letter to three U.S. senators in which Sherman wrote, "I must comment on the well-publicized perception that Apotex has entered into an anticompetitive settlement with Sanofi/Bristol-Myers Squibb concerning clopidogrel (Plavix). That perception is incorrect. Apotex has negotiated only to remove barriers to immediate launch. To achieve that objective, we entered into a somewhat bizarre arrangement that will enable immediate launch, if and when the FTC refuses to approve a settlement."[58]

At the hearing on the lawsuit seeking an injunction, attorneys for Bristol-Myers Squibb claimed that failure to issue an injunction would "kill future clinical efforts." Federal judge Sidney Stein granted a preliminary injunc-

tion, halting sales on August 31. Judge Stein wrote that Sanofi-Aventis "clearly established a likelihood of success on the merits." The judge, however, refused to order Apotex to recall the product it had already shipped, and Bristol-Myers Squibb was required to post a $400 million bond to compensate Apotex if it won the lawsuit. Apotex had asked for a $4 billion bond and said that the amount of the bond was "grossly inadequate." Apotex filed with the U.S. Court of Appeals for an emergency stay of the injunction,[59] and the U.S. Court of Appeals rejected the appeal, ending Apotex's foray. Analysts estimated that Apotex had shipped several hundred million dollars worth of clopidogrel.

In 2005 Bristol-Myers Squibb and the U.S. Attorney in New Jersey had reached a deferred-prosecution agreement in a case involving charges of conspiracy to commit securities fraud relating to an accounting scandal. Under the agreement Bristol-Myers Squibb agreed to exemplary conduct for two years and supervision by an independent federal monitor, retired judge Frederick B. Lacey, appointed by the court. The U.S. attorney asked Lacey to examine the Apotex affair, and Lacey conducted a review. In September 2006 Lacey told the Bristol-Myers Squibb board of directors that CEO Dolan should be fired. The board promptly did so. Bristol-Myers Squibb's share price had fallen 60 percent since Dolan was appointed CEO in 2001. ■

Preparation Questions

1. Why did Bristol-Myers Squibb and Sanofi-Aventis seek a settlement rather than let the patent infringement case go to trial?
2. Should Bristol-Myers Squibb and Sanofi-Aventis have attempted to pay Apotex to prevent it from launching a generic version of Plavix?

3. Was Sherman's strategy that of a shrewd business executive? Did Sherman act ethically in his strategy?
4. Should the FTC and the state attorneys general have rejected the agreements?
5. Did Bristol-Myers Squibb likely violate the deferred prosecution agreement?

---

[56]*Wall Street Journal,* September 2, 2006.
[57]*New York Times,* August 15, 2006.
[58]*New York Times,* August 15, 2006.

[59]The judge stated that the claims of an oral side agreement were not affecting his decision "as of now."

Obesity and McLawsuits

In 2001 New York trial lawyer Samuel Hirsch filed a liability lawsuit against McDonald's alleging that his 5-feet 10-inch, 272-pound client had become obese from eating at McDonald's and other fast-food restaurants. The man had continued to eat at fast-food restaurants despite two heart attacks. After dropping that lawsuit, Hirsch represented two obese teenagers who claimed to have eaten at McDonald's regularly for several years and to have developed obesity-related illnesses.

Hirsch was advised by professor John Banzhaf of the George Washington University Law School, whose students had earlier filed a lawsuit against McDonald's for claiming that its french fries were fried in vegetable oil when they were also par-fried in beef fat at the potato processing plant.[60] The case was settled in 2002

---

[60]The Daily Buzz, www.foodservice.com, March 12, 2004.

for $12.5 million. Banzhaf "teaches unique world-famous courses—'Legal Activism' [Law 637], which has been dubbed 'suing for credit' and 'Sue the Bastards'—where his law students, which the press dubbed 'Banzhaf's Bandits,' learn to become public interest lawyers by bringing their own legal actions. . . . He and his students are widely known for bringing hundreds of innovative public interest legal actions. . . ."[61]

After their success in litigation against tobacco companies, trial lawyers sought a new mass tort, and obesity was their next campaign. Banzhaf said, "A fast-food company like McDonald's may not be responsible for the entire obesity epidemic, but let's say they're 5 percent responsible. Five percent of $117 billion is still an enormous amount of money."[62] The Public Health Advocacy Institute of Boston held a seminar at Northeastern University on "Legal Approaches to the Obesity Epidemic." Brian Murphy, an attendee and a recent graduate of the Rutgers Law School, said, "It's a very important and pressing issue, and its outcome will be with us for years to come. I'm hoping to be able to build a career out of this."[63]

Lisa A. Rickard, president of the U.S. Chamber Institute for Legal Reform, stated, "Lawyers hungry for more money should resist the temptation to take a bite out of the fast-food industry. Overweight Americans will not find the solution to obesity in the courtroom but in making wise choices to eat smaller portions and healthier foods wherever they go."[64] Brendan Flanagan of the National Restaurant Association commented that "people who are filing these suits are trying to legislate via the court system."[65]

Obesity

Interest in the obesity issue intensified after a government study revealed that Americans had become heavier and that obesity had become a serious health problem. A study released in February 2004 by the Centers for Disease Control and Prevention (CDC) stated that in 2000, 400,000 deaths were caused by obesity-released illnesses compared to 435,000 deaths caused by tobacco.[66] The Surgeon General estimated that health care costs resulting from obesity were $117 billion annually, and the Department of Health and Human Services began an advertising campaign promoting personal responsibility and urging more exercise and less eating. The U.S. government and the World Health Organization urged food manufacturers and restaurants to offer healthier foods.

The body mass index (BMI), defined as a person's weight in kilograms divided by height in meters squared, was used to measure obesity. A BMI in the 19 to 25 range was considered healthy, 26 to 30 was overweight, and over 31 was obese. The BMI had increased by 0.9 from 1971–75 to 1988–94, and the proportion of people considered obese increased from 15 to 31 percent from 1980 to 2000.[67] Sixty-four percent of American adults were overweight or obese. The average weight of an adult male had increased from 168 pounds in the early 1960s to 180 pounds at the beginning of the 21st century. The average weight for an adult female increased from 143 to 155.

Substantial increases in weight occurred throughout the 20th century with the BMI for people in their 40s increasing by 4 units.[68] This increase was accompanied by only a modest increase in calorie intake. During the last century, however, technological change reduced the strenuousness of work both in the home and in the marketplace. Another long-term factor was a substantial decline in the relative price of food as a result of technological progress in agriculture. Lakdawalla and Philipson estimated that in the post-WWII period approximately 40 percent of the increase in BMI was due to the expansion in the supply of food, and 60 percent was due to demand-side factors such as a decrease in physical activity.[69]

From 1977–78 to 1994–96 the average intake of calories increased from 1826 to 2002. Surveys based on food diaries indicated that the increase did not come from meals but instead from snacks between meals. Cutler, Glaeser, and Shapiro concluded, "Fast food has certainly increased, from about 60 calories per day to over 200 calories per day. But this increase is largely at formal meals, where it has been offset by reduced home consumption."[70] They concluded that "the evidence also rules out the view that fattening meals at fast-food restaurants have made America obese." Their explanation for the increase in obesity was that technological change had led Americans to switch from home-prepared food to mass-produced food. For example, the total potato consumption in the United States increased by 30 percent from 1977 to 1995 as a result of improved technologies for producing potato chips and french fries. The lower cost of mass-produced food also led to greater consumption.

---

[61]http:banzhaf.net.
[62]*Time,* August 3, 2003.
[63]*Time,* August 3, 2003.
[64]Press release, U.S. Chamber of Commerce, July 2, 2003.
[65]Associated Press Online, March 10, 2004.
[66]Obesity is associated with greater risk of developing type 2 diabetes, chronic lower back pain and joint disorientation, cardiovascular diseases, certain cancers, respiratory problems, and depression.

[67]Cutler, Glaeser, and Shapiro concluded that demographic changes did not explain the increase in obesity. David M. Cutler, Edward L. Glaeser, and Jesse M. Shapiro, "Why Have Americans Become More Obese?" Working paper, National Bureau of Economic Research, n.d.
[68]Dora Costa and R. Steckel, "Long-Term Trends in Health, Welfare, and Economic Growth in the United States." NBER Historical Working Paper No. 76. National Bureau of Economic Research, Cambridge, MA, 1995.
[69]Darius Lakdawalla and Tomas Philipson, "The Growth of Obesity and Technological Change: A Theoretical and Empirical Examination." Working Paper 8946, National Bureau of Economic Research, Cambridge, MA, May 2002.
[70]Cutler, Glaeser, and Shapiro, op. cit.

In a report prepared for the U.S. Chamber of Commerce, Todd Buchholz argued that the increase in obesity was caused by a variety of factors, including the lower real price of food, changes in the nature of work, and the failure to exercise more as the calorie intake increased.[71] Buchholz reported that in 1961 consumers spent 17 percent of their income on food and in 2001 spent 10 percent. He also cited U.S. Department of Agriculture (USDA) data indicating that the ratio of the prices of restaurant meals to supermarket prices had declined from 1.82 in 1986 to 1.73 in 2001. Moreover, a smaller percent of people were employed in jobs requiring physical work than in the past. Buchholz also argued that fast food meals derived fewer of their calories from fat than "a typical home meal from 1977–78."

Buchholz argued that the greatest increase in BMI from 1971–75 to 1988–94 was accounted for by college-educated people rather than those who had a high school education or less. On average Americans were consuming 200 more calories a day and not compensating for it with exercise. The USDA's "Continuing Survey of Food Intakes by Individuals" indicated that Americans were not eating larger meals but instead were eating more between meals.

McDonald's Market Response to the Obesity Issue

For nearly 20 years McDonald's had provided nutrition information in each of its restaurants, but it did not provide information for individual menu items. After the government reports on obesity, McDonald's announced that it was discontinuing its supersize meals to simplify its menus. It also introduced the "Go Active" meal with a salad, water, a pedometer, and an activity log; an all-white-meat chicken McNugget; and other healthier items. McDonald's, the International Olympic Committee, and the American College of Sports Medicine opened a Web site, www.goactive.com. McDonald's also introduced an educational campaign, Real Life Choices, about how to track diets and put menu items into three categories: Watching Calories, Watching Fat, and Watching Carbohydrates.[72] McDonald's also provided nutritional information on its Web site. Chuck Horton of Virginia commented, "If I want to eat healthy, I'll eat at home. I come to McDonald's for one reason: the fries. . . . I think this healthy eating thing has gone too far."[73]

Obesity Lawsuits

In dismissing the case brought by Hirsch on behalf of the two teenagers, U.S. District Court Judge Robert W. Sweet wrote "that the dangers of over-consumption of . . .

high-in-fat foods, such as butter, are well-known. Thus any liability based on over-consumption is doomed if the consequences of such over-consumption are common knowledge. . . . Thus, in order to state a claim, the Complaint must allege either that the attributes of McDonald's products are so extraordinarily unhealthy that they are outside the reasonable contemplation of the consuming public or that the products are so extraordinarily unhealthy as to be dangerous in their intended use. The Complaint—which merely alleges that the foods contain high levels of cholesterol, fat, salt and sugar, and that the foods are therefore unhealthy—fails to reach this bar."[74] He also wrote that under New York law, "The standard for whether an act or practice is misleading is objective, requiring a showing that a reasonable consumer would have been misled by the defendant's conduct."[75]

Judge Sweet, however, left the door open for a lawsuit based on showing that fast food was addictive or that it was deceptive because it contained more harmful content than consumers anticipated. He wrote that "Chicken McNuggets, rather than being merely chicken fried in a pan, are a McFrankenstein creation of various elements not utilized by the home cook." Judge Sweet also stated that this lawsuit could "spawn thousands of similar 'McLawsuits' against restaurants."

Strategy Alternatives

To deal with the McLawsuits, McDonald's and other restaurants could continue to defend themselves in court on a case-by-case basis. Cases could be brought in both state and federal courts, and the incentive for trial lawyers was to attempt to qualify for a class action lawsuit.

Some state courts were believed to be friendlier than federal courts to plaintiffs. Mississippi in particular had been a favorite venue for trial lawyers, who would shop in the state for plaintiffs whom they could represent. A study by Harris Interactive for the U.S. Chamber of Commerce and the U.S. Chamber Institute for Legal Reform concluded that Mississippi had the worst, most unfair liability system among the 50 states.[76] The new governor of Mississippi had campaigned on the theme that the state had earned a reputation as hostile to business, which discouraged companies from locating in the state. The governor sought legislation to limit and cap tort awards. Many states had placed caps on medical malpractice awards, and in tort cases states had imposed limits on punitive awards. A number of states also adopted liability standards based on comparative liability and had narrowed and limited joint and several liability.

---

[71]Todd G. Buchholz, "Burger, Fries and Lawyers: The Beef Behind Obesity Lawsuits," U.S. Chamber of Commerce and the U.S. Chamber Institute for Legal Reform, July 2, 2003.
[72]PRNewswire, January 6, 2004.
[73]Associated Press Online, April 16, 2004.

[74]*Pelman v. McDonald's Corporation,* 2003 U.S. Dist. Lexis 707, 13.
[75]*Second Opinion in Pelman v. McDonald's,* September 3, 2003.
[76]Harris Interactive, Inc. "State Liability Ranking Study." U.S. Chamber of Commerce and the U.S. Chamber Institute for Legal Reform. March 8, 2004.

McDonald's could also seek legislation to shield restaurants and food processors from liability. Legislation could be pursued in federal or state legislatures. The House of Representatives, whose members faced reelection every 2 years, were often responsive to issues that appeared to be popular with voters. The House quickly passed the Personal Responsibility in Food Consumption Act, dubbed the cheeseburger bill, on a 276–139 vote. The bill provided protection from obesity and weight-based lawsuits unless the weight gain had been due to the violation of a state or federal law. Author of the bill Ric Keller (R-FL) said, "We need to get back to the old-fashioned principles of common sense and personal responsibility and get away from this new culture where everybody plays the victim and blames other people for their problems."[77] James Sensenbrenner (R-WI) was more direct, stating that "fat people should 'look in the mirror' and that parents need to monitor children's eating habits to make sure that 'little Johnny' doesn't become 'big Johnny.'"[78] House Speaker Dennis Hastert (R-IL) commented, "We as Americans need to realize that suing your way to better health is not the answer. Trial lawyers need to stop encouraging consumers to blame others for the consequences of their actions just so they can profit from frivolous lawsuits against restaurants."[79] The White House added, "Food manufacturers and sellers should not be held liable for injury because of a person's consumption of legal, unadulterated food and a person's weight gain or obesity."[80] During floor debate on the bill representatives cited a Gallup poll indicating that 89 percent of those surveyed "oppose the idea of holding fast-food companies legally responsible for the diet-related health problems of fast-food junkies." The bill had also been introduced in the Senate, but the Senate was often less willing to go along with such measures than was the House.

Commenting on the cheeseburger bill, Representative James McGovern (D-MA) said, "It protects an industry that doesn't need to be protected at this particular point and we're dealing with a problem that doesn't exist. The problem that does exist is that we have an obesity problem in this country."[81] Neil Barnard, president of the Physicians Committee for Responsible Medicine, commented, "[The bill] is an unsavory attempt to protect corporate profits at the expense of American health. The bill strips the public of its right to seek any redress against food manufacturers for their contribution to the obesity crisis, and the related epidemics of heart disease and diabetes. Given that we are just now beginning to discover the industry's involvement, granting them sweeping immunity is, at best,

dangerously short-sighted."[82] Ben Cohen of the Center for Science in the Public Interest (CSPI) argued, "If Congress really believed in personal responsibility, it would help them make responsible choices by passing legislation that would require fast-food chains to post signs showing the calorie count for each item on their menu."[83]

The restaurant industry backed the Commonsense Consumption Act, the state version of the cheeseburger bill, which would shield restaurants and food processors from liability. As of mid-2004 the cheeseburger bill had been introduced in 23 state legislatures, and 12 had enacted it.

The public attention to the obesity issue led to the introduction of the Menu Education and Labeling Act (MEAL) in the House and the Senate in November 2003.[84] The so-called McMenu bills applied to chains with 20 or more locations operating under one trade name. The Senate bill required disclosure "in a statement adjacent to the name of the food on any menu listing the food for sale, or by any other means approved by the Secretary [of Health and Human Services], the number of calories, grams of saturated fat plus trans fat, and milligrams of sodium contained in a serving of the food, offered for sale, in a clear and conspicuous manner" and "information, specified by the Secretary by regulation, designed to enable the public to understand, in the context of a total daily diet, the significance of the nutrition information that is provided."

In April 2004 Ruby Tuesday, Inc. began providing nutritional information on its menus for every item served. The nutrition analysis cost the 750-restaurant chain $650 per menu item, and whenever the chain changed a portion size for an item, it would have to determine the nutritional information and reprint the menus. Moreover, the company found that customers' ordering was unaffected by the information. After 4 months the company stopped providing nutritional information on its menus and substituted cards at every table with the information. For years McDonald's had provided nutritional information on a placard in each restaurant, and in 2004 began to provide that information on tray liners.[85]

The fast-food industry also faced the possibility that state attorneys general would use the same strategy they used against the tobacco industry by filing lawsuits seeking reimbursement for Medicare costs of obese people.

Later in the year the CDC concluded that its estimate of the number of deaths from obesity contained errors and stated that it would substantially revise downward its estimate. Other researchers were also concerned about the CDC's estimates and criticized the

---

[77]The Daily Buzz, www.foodservice.com, March 11, 2004.
[78]The Daily Buzz, www.foodservice.com, March 11, 2004.
[79]Associated Press Online, March 10, 2004.
[80]Associated Press Online, March 10, 2004.
[81]Associated Press Online, March 10, 2004.

[82]The Daily Buzz, www.foodservice.com, March 9, 2004.
[83]The Daily Buzz, www.foodservice.com, March 11, 2004.
[84]The CSPI supported the MEAL bill.
[85]Wall Street Journal, August 31, 2004.

assumptions on which the estimates were prepared, suggesting that the actual number of deaths was far lower. For example, the death rates used by the CDC were based on people who became obese early in their life, whereas many people became obese later in life. Their death rates from obesity were believed to be considerably lower. ■

SOURCE: This case was written by Professor David P. Baron based on public sources. Copyright © 2004 by David P. Baron. All rights reserved. Reprinted with permission.

Preparation Questions

1. Given the *Restatement (Second) of Torts*, assess the likelihood of a plaintiff prevailing against McDonald's on an obesity lawsuit.
2. How would the doctrine of comparative liability address the obesity issue?
3. Is McDonald's likely to prevail in the courts?
4. Should McDonald's portray the lawsuits as being led by trial lawyers eager for large fees?
5. What market and nonmarket strategies should McDonald's use to address the obesity issue?
6. Should McDonald's fund research on a possible obesity–fast-food link, such as addiction? If so, should it pledge in advance to release the results of the research regardless of the results? Should it instead require the researchers to sign a nondisclosure agreement so that it could keep the results secret in the event that they supported a possible link?
7. Will the cheeseburger bill be broadly adopted? How active should McDonald's be in supporting the bills?
8. In which institutional arenas is McDonald's most likely to be successful?

C H A P T E R

13

Information Industries and Nonmarket Issues

INTRODUCTION

Information has become an important product, and the information industries have been a major source of growth in the past two decades. The Internet is a powerful information network that has had major economic and social impacts. The Internet allows communication of information among remote users, serves as a platform for online markets, and provides opportunity to individuals and businesses. Despite the bursting of the dot-com bubble, the potential for commercial activity facilitated by the Internet remains enormous. What has proven to be difficult is capturing value from that potential. One fundamental problem stems from the public goods nature of information. Information is costly to produce, but once it has been produced it is cheap to reproduce and transmit.

Associated with the promise and reality of the Internet are nonmarket issues that pose challenges for business, government, and individuals. The Internet is a network, and associated with networks are economics quite different from that in markets for physical goods. A number of lines of business, both online and offline, are characterized by network externalities, and complementary goods make compatibility and standardization important. This can mean that a market tips, leaving one firm with the bulk of the market; that is, the market is winner-take-all or at least winner-take-most. The market for desktop computer operating systems tipped to Microsoft, and the online auction market tipped to eBay. Winner-take-most markets pose a set of nonmarket issues including antitrust concerns, as addressed in *The Microsoft Antitrust Case* in Chapter 9.

As considered in Chapter 12 the Internet allows the sharing of files, which has hurt the recording, music publishing, and movie industries and threatens fee-based services. This has raised intellectual property issues for both online and offline companies. More fundamentally, the public goods nature of information raises the issue of the appropriability of the returns from the investment in developing information.

Substantial commercial activity has migrated to the Internet. Some of it consists of online versions of offline mail-order and catalog sales and brick-and-mortar retailers, but much represents new business activity such as the online offerings of Amazon.com and other companies. Some of the online revenue is taken from brick-and-mortar merchants, creating nonmarket opposition to online business. In particular, most online transactions escape the sales taxes that would be paid on offline transactions. The tax revenue lost to state and local governments has resulted in efforts to tax online transactions, as considered in the Chapter 8 case *Internet Taxation*.

Online transactions require providing personal information to the seller, and that information could be made available for a variety of uses. Moreover, browsing on the Internet is tracked via cookies deposited on a user's personal computer and by spyware and adware. In some cases anonymous browsing data can be matched with personal information, as when users identify themselves by participating in a sweepstakes, a drawing, or an online poll. Online searches are monitored, as is some e-mail, advertisements are attached to them, and data on searches is retained by Google, Microsoft, and Yahoo for extended periods. Online privacy concerns have been raised about the use of both personal and anonymous information. These concerns can reduce commercial activity on the Internet, and the information industries have attempted to deal with these concerns through self-regulation in lieu of government regulation.

Hosting online auctions has proven to be a profitable business model, giving eBay a market capitalization of $39 billion. eBay has developed a huge online community of traders in the United States and many other countries, and that community is eBay's principal business asset. The community is composed of remote and largely anonymous individuals, and payments are made by buyers before they have an opportunity to physically inspect the items. These features would normally impede trade, but instead trade flourishes on eBay as well as on other online auction sites. This results from the potential gains from trade and the development of trust among members of the eBay community and between community members and eBay as a company. The development and nurturing of a community are fundamental components of the success of Yahoo!, Amazon.com, and other online business, yet what allows these dispersed and anonymous communities to function effectively?

This chapter is concerned with nonmarket issues arising from the Internet and information industries, and the cases in this chapter and in several other chapters provide more detailed settings for these issues. The economics of the Internet and winner-take-most markets is considered in the next section, and the following section introduces the online privacy issue and the concept of self-regulation. The public policy issue of whether transactions on the Internet should be taxed is then considered. The chapter concludes by considering the provision of order for an online community such as eBay's. The chapter cases address the protection of online privacy, online communities, and database protection. Other cases about information industries include the following:

- *The Nonmarket Environment of Google* (Chapter 1)
- *Internet Taxation* (Chapter 8)
- *The Microsoft Antitrust Case* (Chapter 9)
- *The European Union Data Protection Directive* (Chapter 15)
- *Google in China* (Chapter 16)
- *Sophis Networks and Encryption Export Controls (A)* (Chapter 18)
- *Social Entrepreneurship: Kiva* (Chapter 17)

THE ECONOMICS OF ONLINE MARKETS

In describing Microsoft's business strategy, CEO Bill Gates said, "We look for opportunities with network externalities—where there are advantages to the vast majority of consumers to share a common standard. We look for businesses where we can garner large market shares, not just 30% to 35%."[1] Gates was referring to properties of Microsoft's software products that yield increasing returns for users. This and additional features of the economics of software were central to the Chapter 9 case, *The Microsoft Antitrust Case*. Some of these features are also present in the chapter case, *eBay: Private Ordering for an Online Community*.

A product such as an apple or an automobile is said to have rivalry in consumption in the sense that if one person consumes or uses it, others cannot. One person's consumption thus precludes another person's consumption. One person's use of Microsoft's Windows, however, does not preclude another person from using it, since the cost of producing another copy is essentially zero. Although it is extremely costly to develop, it is cheap to reproduce once developed.

---

[1]"Microsoft, 1995," HBS Case 9-795-147, Tarun Khanna and David Yoffie, Harvard Business School.

Software such as Windows often has another important property.[2] When an additional person uses Windows, the first user is actually better off because, for example, the two users can swap files. A third person using Windows provides even more benefits because that person can swap files with each of the first two people. The number of ways that two people can swap files is two, since one person can give a file to the other and the other can give a file to the first person. With three people there are six ways—or links—that files can be shared. With four people the number is 12. When there are n users the general formula for the number N of possible links is $N = n(n - 1)$. For example, if $n = 4$, there are 12 possible combinations.[3] The value of Windows to any person increases when there are others who use it, and the more users, the more valuable is the product to all users. That is, the average number ($N/n = n - 1$) of links is increasing in n.

The property that the value of a product to each user increases the more people who use it is what Gates meant by *network externalities*. The term *network* applies to the underlying economics of a product, not to the hardware or software associated with the product. Network effects, or network externalities, are present when an individual's demand for a product is positively related to use by other individuals.[4] Network externalities yield increasing returns on the demand side of the market. Network effects are also present in more traditional industries, such as transportation, but the development of industries such as computers, telecommunications, software, and online markets has been driven by these effects.

Many products such as software have another important property. Their value to a consumer is greater if there are *complementary products*. Windows is more valuable to a consumer if there is a word processor or e-mail program that works with it. Complementary products thus also create increasing returns on the demand side, since the greater the number of complementary products, the greater is the value of Windows. Both network externalities and complementary products can yield *demand-side increasing returns*.

Complementary products require *compatibility* so that they may operate together in a seamless manner. Compatibility is facilitated by *standardization*. A common standard allows developers of software and other complementary products to write to a single platform. Although multiple standards could exist in industries with network effects and demand-side increasing returns, consumers have incentives to use products compatible with those used by others. A common standard allows all the products to work together.

A standard can be *open* or *proprietary*. The advantage of an open standard is that software developers are more willing to write for an open standard because they face less risk of developing a product that cannot be used elsewhere. Linux is an open source system based on the UNIX operating system, and the number of users preferring it as an alternative to Windows has grown. The advantage of a proprietary standard is that it is easier to appropriate returns. Windows has become the standard to which software developers write, and Microsoft maintains it as a proprietary standard. Microsoft, however, makes its APIs (application programming interfaces) available to software writers to encourage the development of complementary products.

In 2000 eBay adopted a strategy to attract complementary products. It announced that it would make public its APIs written in XML so that Web sites could link to its online auction site. For example, sports Web sites could provide a link to eBay auctions for sports memorabilia, and Topps could provide access to eBay baseball card auctions from its site. Releasing its APIs also allowed independent software developers to write programs that benefited its community. More importantly, eBay hoped that its architecture would become the (open) standard and serve as an operating

---

[2]See Saloner, Shepard, and Podolny (2001, Ch. 12) for a discussion of the economics of industries with demand-side increasing returns. Shapiro and Varian (1999) provide a comprehensive analysis of the market for information and the network economy. Saloner and Spence (2002) examine electronic commerce and provide a set of cases on e-commerce companies.

[3]This is known as Metcalfe's law.

[4]See Besanko, Dranove, Shanley, and Schaefer (2006) for an introduction to network effects. See also Shapiro and Varian (1999) for a treatment of competitive strategy in information and network industries.

system or platform for electronic commerce. eBay planned to charge a licensing fee for its architecture as a means of appropriating returns.

Although it is more efficient to write software applications for one rather than multiple operating systems and although network effects are strongest with a single standard, this does not imply that the winning standard must be owned or controlled by a single firm. For example, technologies that become standards can be licensed by their owner. Even when standards are proprietary, competition to become the standard can be intense, and competition among multiple standards can persist when network effects are sufficiently limited, or offsetting factors sufficiently strong, to permit multiple networks to survive in the marketplace. AOL's and Yahoo!'s networks and Microsoft's MSN have survived, and Google quickly developed a network.

The presence of demand-side increasing returns means that the company wants as large a *user base* as possible, and as soon as possible, since the product then is more valuable to all. Moreover, the greater the user base, the greater is the incentive for software developers to write to Windows. Microsoft could, for example, set a low price for Windows so as to gain rapid adoption and hence expansion of its user base. It could even be desirable for Microsoft to develop a browser and give it away for free to increase the number of users of Windows. And, since the cost of producing another copy of Internet Explorer (IE) is zero and a browser increases the demand for PCs and hence Windows, a negative price for the IE could be justified.

The threat to a user base is that users may switch to another competing product. If there are costs of switching, however, the user base may be *locked in*. For example, when databases are written for Windows, it can be costly to switch them to a Linux or Apple format. Similarly, if employees are trained on Windows and its complementary products, it can be costly to retrain them for Linux or Apple. Thus Windows is protected from competing operating systems by high switching costs. Even if another operating system were better, it would be difficult to take users away once Windows established its user base. Linux and Apple, however, have the advantage of not being tied to a dominant firm.

These factors interact and may result in *positive feedback*. Software developers prefer to write to an operating system used by many people, and conversely the greater the number of popular software applications written for it, the greater the demand for the operating system. A larger installed base thus attracts software developers. The greater the availability of compatible software, the greater is the value to consumers, and network externalities further increase the value to consumers. New consumers thus choose the operating system, further increasing the user base, and the cycle of incentives continues.

This positive feedback may cause the market to *tip* in favor of one product. The classic example is the competition between alternative formats for videotape recorders. Sony introduced its Betamax format, and Matsushita introduced its VHS format. Content producers had a strong incentive to put their movies on a single format to reduce production and distribution costs. Similarly, videotape rental stores had an incentive to stock only one format, since that would allow them to hold less inventory. Consumers had an incentive to coordinate on the format for which more content was produced. They also benefited from demand-side increasing returns when more content providers and retailers chose a single format. In such a situation the market can tip in favor of one of the products. Videotape rental stores and content producers wanted to standardize on the format that would ultimately have the larger market share. As soon as they suspected that one format would win, they concentrated on that format. The VHS format appeared to be winning in the marketplace, and content producers, retailers, and consumers all focused on VHS. The market tipped. Betamax was then shut out and disappeared from the market, even though it might have been the better technology. In 2008 the market for HD recorders was on the verge of tipping to Blu-Ray rather than HD DVD.

The possibility of tipping means there is a strong *first-mover advantage*. The first mover has the opportunity to build an *installed base* of users before competition appears and may be able to attract complementary products and generate demand-side increasing returns. The first mover often has the best chance of having the market tip in its favor. For example, the online auction market in the United States tipped to eBay, which was the first online auction service. In Japan, however, Yahoo! Auctions was the first mover, and the market tipped to it.

A tipped market means that a single winner takes most of the market. Moreover, once a market has tipped, it may be difficult to unseat the incumbent. One possible means of doing so is to leverage from the installed base of users for a complementary product. For example, RealNetworks was the first mover in audio and video streaming on the Internet, and the market tipped in its favor. Microsoft attempted to change that by introducing its MediaPlayer, but the market remained tipped in favor of RealNetworks. Microsoft's next attempt to unseat RealNetworks was to integrate MediaPlayer with its Windows XP operating system, in effect giving away MediaPlayer for free. Microsoft thus was leveraging from its Windows operating system monopoly in an attempt to dominate another market. eBay entered the Japanese market late, and its hope of unseating Yahoo! Auctions was to leverage off its dominant market position in the United States and other countries where it was by far the largest online auction service. Its efforts were unsuccessful, and eBay withdrew from Japan.

In some markets, tipping may be irreversible due to lock-in or to a product becoming a de facto standard. A new operating system such as open source Linux, for example, has a considerable challenge in attempting to unseat Windows. Linux has a large number of ardent users, and some large users are concerned about being dependent on a monopolist Microsoft. Moreover, a number of foreign governments have been concerned that Windows has a secret "back door" that could allow the U.S. government access to their computer systems. Microsoft responded by offering discounts to governments and by establishing a Government Security Program. Participating governments are given access to much of the Windows source code and the code for its Office suite. The Chapter 18 case, *Sophis Networks and Encryption Export Controls (A),* is concerned with security.

The economics of information markets has important implications for competitive strategy, and it also raises a host of nonmarket issues. Many of those issues revolve around antitrust concerns. For example, the practices used to compete for a user base could ultimately be anticompetitive. A firm could, for example, use predatory pricing, although when the marginal cost of production is zero it is not clear that giving away a product is predatory, particularly if the product is complementary to a proprietary product. Once a market has tipped, the winner has strong incentives to fend off new technologies that may threaten its dominant position. Microsoft belatedly recognized that the Internet and the Java programming language threatened its Windows monopoly by allowing software to be written for any operating system. Microsoft then engaged in a set of anticompetitive practices to stop the distribution of Java. This included producing the so-called polluted version of Java that would run only on Windows. *The Microsoft Antitrust Case* in Chapter 9 considers these issues in more detail.

INTERNET PRIVACY

Privacy, both online and offline, is like motherhood and apple pie. When asked in surveys if they want privacy, respondents invariably answer yes. When asked to list the issues they are concerned about, however, privacy is seldom mentioned by respondents. A survey of 150,000 Web sites by WebSideStory in 2001 found that fewer than 1 percent of Internet users blocked cookies when visiting a Web site. Zero-Knowledge Systems, whose software package Freedom allowed individuals to block cookies and protect personal information, found little demand for its product and shut down its Freedom Network because of a lack of revenue. In a survey of online purchasers, 43 percent responded that they would sell their personal data for a $100 gift certificate.

Many online customers, however, remain concerned about how their personal information might be used. Some of these individuals are reluctant to purchase online or to conduct Internet activities that require personal information. Yet catalog and mail-order companies thrive, and few people are reluctant to use a credit card at a brick-and-mortar establishment. Moreover, a 2003 survey showed that 60 percent of adults believed that the posting of a privacy policy by a Web site meant that the site was not gathering or sharing personal or other information. Many sites share that information with business partners and others, as their privacy policies state.

In the United States Internet privacy has largely been governed by self-regulation by Internet companies, as companies have formulated privacy policies and established independent organizations to certify those policies. Moreover, government has been reluctant to regulate a rapidly evolving industry and technology. Perhaps the importance of Internet privacy and broader privacy issues is indicated by the growing number of companies that have established the position of chief privacy officer. Some 40 percent of the *Fortune* 500 companies have a chief privacy officer. This section introduces the Internet privacy issue and the self-regulation efforts of companies and identifies a number of current issues. The chapter case, *DoubleClick and Internet Privacy,* concerns a company that planned to merge anonymous data on Internet browsing with personal information obtained online and offline.

Technologies other than the Internet also raise privacy issues. The Global Positioning System (GPS) can pinpoint the location of an object quite accurately. This can be invaluable when a motorist seeks directions, but it also has the potential to provide the information to others. Similarly, antitheft tracking systems and telematics on rental cars provide location and tracking information and can detect if a renter has been speeding. Cellular telephone use allows locations to be identified, and telephone caller ID provides information that could be used for a variety of purposes. The development of radio frequency tags and their use in products raise a myriad of privacy concerns. The rapid development of information technologies will continue to generate a host of new privacy concerns.

Privacy issues associated with the Internet range from the use of personal information provided to electronic commerce sites by customers to the use of Web bugs that record who visits personal Web pages. DoubleClick used the banner ads it placed on a Web site to deposit a cookie, a text file with a unique ID number, on a user's computer. The cookie allowed DoubleClick to identify when that computer visited a Web site in its network. DoubleClick collected click-stream data and used that information to develop profiles of the visitors to a Web site, target advertisements on Web sites, and personalize advertisements to the ID numbers.

Spyware and adware are the second generation of monitoring technology. Adware programs are deposited on a user's computer, and in contrast to DoubleClick, which tracked visits to Internet sites that participated in its network, these programs can track each click a user makes when browsing anywhere on the Internet. Using these data the programs provide pop-up advertisements with messages tailored to the user's browsing. The program Gator provided by Claria Corporation was downloaded along with free Internet programs and recorded browsing activity that, like DoubleClick's system, was associated only with an ID number of the program deposited on the user's computer. The pop-up ads were popular with advertisers because the ads could appear on any Web site. Some companies objected to ads for others appearing on their Web sites, and Hertz and Dow Jones filed lawsuits charging that the ads violated copyright and trademark laws. Gator was deposited on over 30 million computers.[5]

Whereas Gator is downloaded with a user's consent, spyware is a secret program that goes beyond adware and collects personal information such as passwords and credit card information. Privacy watchdog organizations along with many users have complained about the programs, and several companies have developed software to remove adware and spyware from computers. Privacy on the Internet involves a technology race, and adware and spyware companies have responded by better hiding their programs. CoolWebSearch adware can change its name and location on a user's computer several times a day, making it difficult to find and eliminate.[6]

---

[5]Claris sold gator.com to hostgator.com in 2008.
[6]*New York Times,* September 19, 2004.

Businesses are necessarily customer oriented and focus on the value or benefits they provide to customers, clients, and Internet users. Focusing on benefits, however, can cause one to overlook rights. Privacy advocates focus on rights rather than benefits. Those rights need not be established by government but instead can be established by moral principles. Some privacy advocates argue that an individual's privacy is protected by a property rule, using the terminology of Chapter 12. This would mean that an individual's privacy cannot be infringed without that person's consent.

Why a person has a privacy right and the nature of any such right are moral questions. Conceptions of moral rights are developed in Chapter 21, and only some basic concepts are introduced here. Minimal conditions for establishing rights require that individuals be able to make knowledgeable choices for themselves regarding privacy. In the case of the Internet a basic principle is the *right to know,* and this right imposes duties on companies using the Internet. A right to know could pertain to what data would be collected, how it would be used, whether it would be shared, how long it would be stored, and how secure it would be. A second basic principle is *choice;* that is, choice of whether to have data collected. This could be based on either an opt-out or opt-in policy. A third basic principle is to be *free from arbitrary treatment.* For example, an individual could have the right to inspect the data collected and to correct any incorrect information. The chapter case, *DoubleClick and Internet Privacy,* and the Chapter 15 case, *The European Data Protection Directive,* provide opportunities to apply these principles. The "Gmail and Privacy" example illustrates initial concerns raised about Google's free e-mail service.

EXAMPLE

Google: Gmail and Privacy

Consumers really need to look this gift horse in the mouth because it has rotten teeth and bad breath.

—Beth Givens, Privacy Rights Clearinghouse[1]

That's why I'm a little baffled by this. We take people's trust in us very seriously. If we were to violate that trust, that would hurt our business seriously.

—Larry Page, President–Products, Google[2]

We are not going over to the dark side. Consumers can expect us to treat their e-mail as private and with a great deal of respect. I don't think we are doing anything unreasonable.

—Wayne Rosing, Vice President, Google[3]

On April Fool's Day 2004 Google launched a beta version of a free e-mail service—Gmail—with one gigabyte of memory provided for each user. In exchange a user agreed to allow Google to search its e-mail messages for keywords and receive targeted advertisements displayed with the message. Google requested volunteers, and hundreds of thousands of Internet users applied for the service. The response

---

[1]CBSNEWS.com, April 7, 2004.
[2]*San Jose Mercury News,* April 2, 2004.
[3]*Financial News,* April 7, 2004.

from privacy advocates was quite different. Privacy groups strongly criticized Google and Gmail and warned consumers of the dangers associated with the service. Politicians joined in the criticism with a California state legislator introducing a bill to stop the service. Google was dismayed by the response to its offering, since Gmail was accompanied by a strong privacy policy.

The one gigabyte of memory provided was up to 500 times greater than that of the free e-mail services offered by Yahoo! and Microsoft's Hotmail. Gmail also allowed the user to organize messages in a variety of convenient ways. Google provided a Gmail Privacy Policy, which included the statement, "By using Gmail, you agree to the collection and use of your personal information as described in this policy."

The only personal information required from a Gmail user was a first and a last name. Gmail did not use cookies to identify a user but instead identified the user's location by the service hub where the user logged on. The Gmail system searched incoming e-mail messages for keywords selected by advertisers, and when found, a text advertising message appeared along with the message. Ads were placed via Google's widely used AdSense.

Advertisers received information on Gmail users when they clicked on an advertisement.

(Continued)

(Continued)

Google's Gmail Privacy Policy stated, "Advertisers receive a record of the total number of impressions and clicks for each ad. They do not receive any personal information about the person who viewed the ad. If you click on an ad, Google will send a referring URL to the advertiser's site identifying that you are visiting from Gmail. Google does not send personally identifiable information to advertisers with the referring URL. Once you are on the advertiser's site, however, the advertiser may collect personal information about you. Google does not control or take responsibility for the privacy policies of other sites."[4] Cofounder Sergey Brin commented, "We wouldn't store anything related to what ads show up in your e-mail messages. That is one of the misconceptions."[5]

The Privacy Concerns

The privacy concerns stemmed from the user's understanding of Gmail, the possibility that Gmail information could be combined with tracking data from other Google searches, possible access to the data from outside Google, and more general considerations about privacy in society. As the privacy policy stated, when a user closed his or her Gmail account, the data could be retained for an indefinite period. Google used cookies with its search engine to provide convenience to users. The cookies allowed Google to keep track of the Web pages visited by its users.

California state senator Liz Figueroa introduced a bill to block the service. She stated, "I cannot urge you strongly enough to abandon this misbegotten idea. I believe you are embarking on a disaster of enormous proportions, for yourself, and for all your customers. The proposal is little different from asking people to let the phone company listen in on their calls and butt in at any time to say, 'This call is brought to you by. . . .'"[6] She called Gmail a Faustian bargain.

Twenty-eight privacy organizations, including the Consumer Federation of America, the Electronic Privacy Information Center (EPIC), and Privacy International, wrote to Google urging that Gmail be suspended. The organizations wrote that Gmail "sets potentially dangerous precedents and establishes reduced expectations of privacy in e-mail communications. These precedents may be adopted by other companies and governments and may persist long after Google is gone."

Google responded that the searches of e-mail messages would be done solely by computers with no human involvement. Pam Dixon of the World Privacy Forum countered, "The fact that it's machines is irrelevant. Machines are much more efficient than humans and far more able to be privacy invasive than humans because they can read so much more. We're concerned that users of Gmail, who must give Google their names to sign up, may have their names correlated with the search terms they type in when searching. This can be done through cookies and IP addresses."[7] Wayne Rosing responded, "We do not keep that data in correlated form, it's separated in various ways and we have policies inside the company that do not allow that kind of correlation to happen. We consider any program or programming that correlates user data with user identity to be a violation of trust and we do not do that."[8] Google was cautious in its response, since it knew that it could be forced under subpoena to supply both Gmail and search data. Rosing pointed out that antispam and antivirus filters also searched e-mail messages.

Simon Davies of Privacy International filed complaints with 17 countries in Europe as well as in Canada and Australia. Davies stated, "We will be filing simultaneous complaints with the data privacy regulations of every other European nation on April 22 should we not receive a satisfactory response from the ICO [UK's information commission]. Germany, for example, has much stricter policies regarding privacy and they would not blink at taking severe action. Sweden, as well, has shown a willingness to address similar issues."[9] Davies suggested that the privacy policy could violate Article 7(a) of the European Union's Data Protection Directive, which requires that a consumer give informed and unambiguous consent to the use of personal information. Davies said, "The service is fundamentally unlawful, under EU law, under the Data Protection Act. EU law is explicit on this point. There's a sanctity in communications that must be protected."[10] Davies warned, "If millions of people have their communication history kept on Google computers, then that storehouse becomes a very valuable source of information for a range of unintended consequences."[11] Michael Allison of the Internet Crimes Group in New Jersey said, "Google could create a potential monster—people with wicked ways could use it for everything from extortion to harassment."[12]

---

[4]www.google.com/gmail/help/help/privacy.html.
[5]*Washington Post*, May 13, 2004.
[6]A Web user checked Figueroa's Web site and reported that not only did it collect personal information but it did not have a privacy policy (*Washington Internet Daily*, April 15, 2004).

[7]ClickZ News, www.clickz.com, April 2, 2004.
[8]ClickZ News, www.clickz.com, April 2, 2004.
[9]IDG News Service, www.infoworld.com, April 15, 2004.
[10]Marketplace Morning Report, April 20, 2004.
[11]www.cbsnews.com, April 7, 2004.
[12]*Daily Telegraph*, April 14, 2004.

(Continued)

A spokesperson for the UK's ICO stated, "As long as Google makes it clear that it is monitoring e-mail usage and passing that information on for marketing purposes, there shouldn't be a problem. But I want to make it clear that Google has not even launched the service yet, and has agreed to work with us to make sure that its notification process is very clear."[13]

A Google spokesperson said, "We are confident that Gmail is fully compliant with data protection laws worldwide. Google actively solicits user feedback on our privacy policies. If they can be made clearer or otherwise improved, we want to hear about it. We look forward to a detailed dialogue with data protection authorities across Europe to ensure their concerns are heard and resolved."[14]

Chris Hoofnagle of EPIC said, "Individuals would be throwing away the protections of their communications for a few dollars. We don't see this as any different than letting a company listen in on your phone conversations and letting the Postal Service open your mail."[15] He also said, "It's an interference into an area where people have enjoyed a great deal of privacy. It's like a telemarketer listening in to your phone call and then trying to sell you something."[16]

Harrison Rainie, director of the Pew Institute and American Life Project, commented, "You tell people the trade-off you're making is you're letting yourself be followed significantly in exchange for some convenience. Most people say, that's fine."[17] Matthew Berk, an Internet analyst, said, "At the end of the day, consumer behavior will defer to convenience. When it comes to privacy concerns the bark is always far worse than the bite."[18] In 1999 Scott McNealy, CEO of Sun Microsystems, had said, "You have zero privacy anyway. Get over it."[19]

---

[13]www.infoworld.com, n.d.
[14]IDG News Service, www.infoworld.com, April 15, 2004.

[15]www.cbsnews.com, April 7, 2004.
[16]*San Jose Mercury News,* April 2, 2004.
[17]*Wall Street Journal,* April 6, 2004.
[18]*Wall Street Journal,* April 6, 2004.
[19]*Wall Street Journal,* April 6, 2004.

Privacy has been the subject of considerable legislation, although none has established specific Internet privacy rights. The Privacy Act of 1974 restricted information gathered for one government purpose to be used for another purpose or shared with another government agency. For example, the Internal Revenue Service was prohibited from sharing income tax information with other agencies. In 1988 Congress enacted the Video Privacy Protection Act that prohibited videotape rental companies and service providers from disclosing information about rentals or requests by individuals. The 1994 Driver's License Privacy Protection Act prohibited states from selling driver's license information. The Fair Credit Reporting Act regulated the disclosure of credit application data and credit histories. The Electronic Communications Privacy Act prohibited unauthorized access to e-mail, and other statutes prohibited unauthorized wiretaps. In 1998 Congress passed the Children's Online Privacy Protection Act, which prohibits collecting information from children under the age of 13 unless authorized by their parents. In 1999 Congress passed the Financial Services Modernization Act, which limited disclosure of nonpublic personal information to nonaffiliated third parties unless disclosure and opt-out requirements were met.

Although there has been no federal legislation establishing basic Internet privacy rights, a variety of bills have been introduced in Congress. Business has generally opposed these measures as unneeded and potentially harmful to the development of the Internet. A number of companies, however, would support federal legislation if it were needed to block states from enacting a set of dissimilar Internet privacy laws. As an example of possible federal legislation, the McCain-Kerry bill introduced after the DoubleClick episode would have required clear, conspicuous, and easily understood notice and full disclosure of how personal information would be used. Internet users would be given an easy opt-out of any data collection. The bill also would have granted a safe harbor to companies that complied with a seal program such as TRUSTe. Enforcement would have been by the Federal Trade Commission (FTC), which could act if a company violated its privacy policy. The bill would also have required state attorneys general to file privacy lawsuits in federal rather than state courts. The bill was never enacted.

Individual states have been hesitant to enact laws, however, because industry self-regulation has worked reasonably well and because of concerns that they may be branded as hostile to the information industries. Some states have acted to limit spyware and adware, and some such as Minnesota and Nevada require ISPs to keep customer information confidential. California and Utah require disclosure of the information a firm shares with others, and California, Nebraska, and Pennsylvania require the posting of privacy policies on Web sites and prohibit false, misleading, or deceptive statements.[7]

The principal reason government has not enacted legislation to require privacy protection is self-regulation by companies. Companies argued that self-regulation was working and that improvements in technology were providing more ways for Internet users to choose the level of protection they preferred. Self-regulation generally has the following components:

- Policies and practices of companies
- Certification by independent, nongovernmental organizations; for example, the seal programs of TRUSTe and others
- Compliance through self-assessment, including in some cases public release of the assessment, and organizational arrangements such as having a chief privacy officer
- Complaint resolution
- Backstopping by the FTC authority over unfair and deceptive practices (e.g., stating a privacy policy and then violating it)
- Education and outreach regarding privacy protection alternatives
- Providing technology alternatives
- Monitoring of company practices by activist and watchdog groups
- Personal protection by individuals (e.g., setting a browser to reject cookies)

Self-regulation has so far been relatively successful in forestalling government action, although incidents, such as those involving DoubleClick, and certain programs, such as adware and spyware, provide motivation for government action. In 2004 the FTC took the first public action against spyware by filing a lawsuit against the owner of two spyware companies charging "unfair or deceptive acts or practices in or affecting commerce."

As an example of a privacy policy consider the case of eBay.[8] To participate in an auction, either as a buyer or seller, a person had to become a member of eBay. The member agreed to abide by the eBay User Agreement and related policies and to provide personal information, such as name, address, e-mail address, and credit card information. A Privacy Policy posted on the eBay Web site governed the use of the information. The policy was a long, legal statement, but embodied the following core privacy values:

- We do not sell or rent your information to third parties.
- We do not give your personally identifiable information to advertisers.
- We let you select how you may be contacted by us when you join our community.
- We use safe, secure encryption technology to protect your personally identifiable information.
- We have no tolerance for spam (unsolicited, commercial e-mail).[9]

To ensure that the privacy policy could be understood by those who were not lawyers, the company developed a simple chart. For each piece of personal information collected during the member's registration, such as name or e-mail address, the chart described how the information could be used by each of five classes of organizations: advertisers, internal service providers, external service providers, eBay community representatives, and in response to legal requests. The information might be provided

- Not at all
- Only in aggregate form with no personal identification
- With the member's agreement

---

[7]www.ncsl.org/programs/lis/privacy/eprivacylaws.htm.
[8]This material is from the case "eBay: Private Ordering for an Online Community," P-37, Graduate School of Business, Stanford University, August 2001.
[9]pages.eBay.com/help/privacycentral1.html.

- To fulfill an eBay service requirement
- If the member was involved in a transaction
- In response to a subpoena

Even companies with policies and security systems can have problems, however. Victoria's Secret reached a settlement with the New York state attorney general agreeing to pay a fine and improve its security. A customer discovered that the company left a hole in its security system that gave access to customer accounts.

An important source of contention centers on the type of choice given to Internet users. Most companies prefer opt-out, where a user must affirmatively choose not to have data collected or browsing tracked. Privacy advocates argue that opt-out places too great a burden on individuals and that most will not bother to read the notice explaining the data collection and hence will not exercise choice. Privacy activists support opt-in, where an Internet company would not be allowed to collect or share data without the individual affirmatively agreeing to have the data collected and used. The difference in participation rates is believed to be very large between these two alternatives. The prevalent practice in the United States is opt-out, whereas in the European Union opt-in is required for personally identifiable information (PII).

The European Union (EU) has taken a different approach to Internet privacy. It enacted a directive (law) providing strong privacy protection for PII. In addition, companies are not allowed to transfer PII outside the European Union unless the recipient country provides "adequate" protection. A credit card company may want to transfer PII to its headquarters in the United States for billing and other purposes. Since self-regulation is the basic policy of the United States, the issue is whether U.S. policy satisfies the EU requirement of adequate protection. This issue is considered in more detail in Chapter 15 and in the case, *The European Union Data Protection Directive*, in that chapter. To update its electronic company telephone directory, General Motors was required to obtain permission from employees in the European Union to include their office telephone numbers, which were viewed as personal information by the European Union. Sending the numbers outside the European Union could be a criminal offense in some EU countries. GM had 200 of its affiliates sign contracts stating that they would not misuse the telephone numbers.

Confidence in the Internet is a public good, but the provision of that public good is subject to a free-rider problem. Some Internet companies infringe on the privacy of users who anticipated that the information they provided would remain private. To address this problem independently of government, a group of companies formed an independent governance organization, TRUSTe, to establish privacy standards, monitor compliance, and grant a seal to Web sites that met its standards. TRUSTe has evolved into a private government in which Web sites voluntarily participate. TRUSTe legislates standards such as opt-out requirements for the transfer of personal information, regulates participating Web sites by requiring TRUSTe approval for any changes in consumer privacy notices, and enforces standards by reviewing privacy policies of participants and submitting unique user information to a site and monitoring where that information turns up. TRUSTe also has established a judiciary. It provides a dispute resolution program for Internet users, makes decisions on individual complaints, and has an appeals panel for users and participating Internet sites. TRUSTe was selected by the Department of Commerce to provide a seal for compliance with the Safe Harbor Provisions for ensuring privacy of PII transmitted from the European Union to the United States. TRUSTe also recognizes firms for their privacy policies.[10]

THE INTERNET AND TAX POLICY

In 1998 Congress passed the Internet Tax Freedom Act, which imposed a 3-year tax moratorium prohibiting states from enacting any new tax on Internet access and any tax that singled out the Internet. Nine states had already enacted Internet access

---

[10]The recipients of the Most Trusted Companies for 2007 were Hewlett-Packard, Intuit, and AOL.

taxes, but the big issue was a tax on sales transacted on the Internet. No state had enacted such a tax. The moratorium did not ban the collection of the sales tax on Internet transactions, but if such collection were required, it would have to apply as well to mail-order and telephone sales. Amazon.com, based in the state of Washington, for example, collected the state sales tax from Washington residents but not from customers in other states.

Customers are obliged to pay the sales tax, but because of a Supreme Court decision, states are prohibited from ordering out-of-state mail-order companies to collect the taxes unless they have a physical location (nexus) in the state. The "singled-out" language of the moratorium had been supported by electronic commerce companies that sought as allies the mail-order and telephone sales companies. Internet sales represented less than 2 percent of U.S. retail sales, whereas catalog and telephone sales represented 3.4 percent. New York became the first state to require online retailers to collect the sales tax on sales to residents of the state. Both Amazon and Overstock.com filed lawsuits claiming that the New York law was unconstitutional.

The potential growth of electronic commerce was the concern. The General Accounting Office estimated that states would lose $12.5 billion in uncollected sales taxes in 2003. The Center for Business and Research at the University of Tennessee, however, in 2004 estimated that the tax loss on Internet sales would be between $20 billion and $35 billion and could reach $54 billion by 2011. States were concerned about their ability to provide public services if that much tax revenue were lost.

In addition to the lost tax revenue by states, brick-and-mortar retailers lost sales. They viewed Internet retailers as having an unfair advantage because they did not collect taxes, and that advantage loomed larger each year. The retailers were also concerned about the advantage of mail-order and telephone sales companies. Those concerned about the tax advantage included not only the major retail chains such as Wal-Mart but also the small, Main Street retailers.

Online retailers argued that they did not utilize state services and that collecting taxes due would be prohibitively costly. In the United States not only do states, counties, and municipalities impose taxes, but so do school, library, and mosquito abatement districts. The United States has approximately 7,600 state and local tax jurisdictions, and electronic commerce companies argued that it would be too costly to have to determine and collect the taxes due in each of those jurisdictions. Electronic commerce companies were also concerned about having to undergo multiple tax audits. In response, 30 states launched a tax simplification project with the objective of dramatically reducing the number of different tax rates and jurisdictions. The challenge was substantial, since, for example, clothing was not taxed in 13 states and in six of the other states a handkerchief was not considered clothing. The tax simplification project resulted in the Streamlined Sales and Use Tax Agreement, and Senator Mike Engi (R-WY) introduced a bill in 2007 that would allow states joining the agreement to require remote sellers to collect sales and use taxes on their sales. Fifteen states have changed their tax codes to comply with the requirements of the Agreement.

Many online retailers believed that they could be forced into bankruptcy if they had to collect taxes on their sales. Avoiding sales taxes was an important factor in their survival. The Direct Marketing Association's chairman said, "It literally will put a lot of small and medium-sized businesses out of business."[11]

Some public policy analysts argued that the Internet was a public good and part of a nation's infrastructure. They favored the current moratorium on Internet taxation because it would lead to greater use of the Internet and hence more investment in infrastructure capacity. The infrastructure included not only the Internet and the servers on which Web sites operated but also connections to the Internet. Bill Gates had called for more rapid deployment of DSL lines as a part of infrastructure investment. The telecommunications and cable companies that provided access generally supported the moratorium, as did equipment manufacturers.

---

[11] *San Jose Mercury News,* May 12, 2001.

The moratorium on taxes on Internet transactions was temporary, and Congress was the institutional arena in which the issue was considered. Three basic alternatives were available. The first was to let the moratorium expire, allowing the states to take their own actions. The second was to extend the moratorium while the states attempted to simplify their tax structures. The third was to make the moratorium permanent. The Chapter 8 case, *Internet Taxation,* addresses these issues in more detail.

ONLINE COMMUNITIES

The business model of some Internet companies centers on developing a community of users who interact with each other as well as with the company. The interactions may center on trades, as in the case of online auctions, or the sharing of information as in the case of Facebook, MySpace, Ning, and Twitter. This section focuses not on social networks but on commercial networks that involve transactions and have some of the characteristics of online markets.

The purpose of developing a community is to allow members to benefit from interactions that may have demand-side increasing returns due to network externalities. For example, eBay has the largest community of online buyers, and this means that sellers are attracted to its site. The fact that more sellers list their items on eBay than on any other online auction site means that buyers prefer to look for items on eBay first. The incentives for buyers and sellers are reinforcing and generate positive feedback. Moreover, users may become locked into eBay. A seller might have an interest in switching to Yahoo! Auctions, which had been free, but unless buyers also switched, the seller would face a thin market. Buyers would not switch because the other sellers remained on eBay, and the sellers remained there because the buyers were there. Buyers and sellers who traded in a particular class of items could collectively switch to another online auction site, but they would incur high costs, since coordinating their switching would be extremely difficult.[12] Collective switching was attempted once and failed. These collective switching costs meant that it was difficult for groups of traders to be taken away from the eBay community.[13] The eBay community reached 114 million registered members in 2004.

To illustrate the role of community, it is useful to consider the traders and their interactions. eBay's online community was composed of anonymous and remote individuals who were unlikely to have repeat dealings. Trade was impersonal with, for example, a seller knowing only the eBay user name of bidders until the winner of the auction provided a shipping address. Buyers did not have an opportunity to inspect the goods on which they bid, and the winning bidder paid for the item prior to shipment. Moreover, since public enforcement was costly, trades were neither supported by explicit contracts nor in most cases by public enforcement of implicit contracts. Unlike an offline auction house eBay never saw the items offered for sale nor certified their authenticity or quality or the accuracy of the descriptions provided by the sellers. Furthermore, eBay did not act as an agent of the seller or the buyer, certify the creditworthiness of buyers, nor play a role in settling the transaction.[14] Despite the inherent opportunities for abuse in such a setting, the unenforceability of implicit contracts among traders, and eBay's very limited role, trade flourished with approximately 2.5 billion auction items offered in 2008. At any given time the number of listings was approximately 115 million.

On its Web site eBay explained, "The key to eBay's success is trust. Trust between the buyers and sellers who make up the eBay community. And trust between the user and eBay, the company." Trust among the members of the eBay community was supported

---

[12]See Saloner, Shepard, and Podolny (2001, p. 313).
[13]This section is based on Baron (2003b).
[14]eBay thus differed from other venues such as the New York Stock Exchange, where in its early years members (brokers) acted as agents of investors, provided information about creditworthiness, used their information about prices, and helped enforce contracts through a "miniature legal system" (Banner, 1998).

by a multilateral online *reputation mechanism* based on feedback provided voluntarily by the transacting members. The reputation mechanism not only provided information to traders but also established a target for punishment, since members could simply not trade with a member with a bad reputation. The reputation mechanism was supplemented by rules designed by eBay to govern who could be a member, which items members could trade, and how they were to conduct themselves on its Web site. The mechanism was also supported by programs, such as eBay-provided insurance against fraud, designed to reduce the cost of trust.

The multilateral online reputation mechanism, the rules, and eBay's programs provided a *private ordering* for eBay's community. This was in contrast to offline markets. Offline markets were supported by the public order—that is, laws and their enforcement. This public order was supplemented by the reputation of the seller and by the use of contemporaneous transactions. For noncontemporaneous offline trades, order was supported by reputation and enforceable contracts.

eBay's private ordering existed in the shadow of the public order. Public order in the form of policing for activities such as fraud or the breach of implicit contracts was costly for a community of dispersed individuals whose only interaction was through a Web site. Because fraud was a threat to its community, eBay established an enforcement group to investigate allegations, spot shill bidding, and monitor its site. When illegal activity was spotted, eBay put the victims in contact with law enforcement officials and cooperated in their investigations. The public order also led eBay to position itself to avoid regulations and liabilities such as those associated with the sale of items that infringed copyrights, as considered in Chapters 2 and 12. The public order also affected the scope of its activities as well as the relations between the company and its members.

Early in its existence eBay established its Feedback Forum where members could provide feedback on other members, enabling them to establish an online reputation. The private ordering that developed was supported by the basic honesty of people and by a set of norms that continued to guide eBay. The company hoped they would guide its members as well:

> eBay is a community where we encourage **open and honest communication** between all of our members. We believe in the following five basic values.
> We believe people are basically good.
> We believe everyone has something to contribute.
> We believe that an honest, open environment can bring out the best in people.
> We recognize and respect everyone as a unique individual.
> We encourage you to treat others the way that you want to be treated.[15]

The establishment and updating of an online reputation required information and communication. Those with the best information were the traders themselves, since they knew whether the quality of the good was as described in the auction listing, payment had been timely, and the good was delivered as promised. Most members would transact with many different members rather than have repeat dealings with the same person, so bilateral reputation formation was insufficient to establish trust. A seller's reputation, however, was based on the experiences of all those who traded with her and could generate trust. A multilateral reputation mechanism also provided for uncoordinated, multilateral punishment of a seller who violated the trust of other traders. Punishment was administered by not bidding on items offered by a seller with a bad reputation or bidding less for those items or, in the case of sellers, by refusing to sell to a buyer with a bad reputation. eBay could also administer punishment by suspending or banning a user or by providing information to public law enforcement authorities in the case of fraud. This multilateral reputation mechanism generated incentives similar to those in a long-term relationship between a buyer and a seller. eBay did not participate in the reputation and information systems other than to establish rules such as whether feedback could be retracted.

---
[15]Emphasis in the original.

One potential problem with a reputation mechanism is that a reputation can be exploited. For example, a member who had developed a good reputation could begin to harvest short-term benefits by taking advantage of his trading partners, who were relying on that reputation. This would result in negative feedback weakening the member's reputation somewhat, but a prior high rating would decrease slowly. To deal with these problems, eBay summarized in a convenient table the number of positives, neutrals, and negatives for the past week, month, and 6 months. This allowed a potential trader to check whether the other member's behavior had changed.

A private ordering can be supplemented through design to increase its efficacy. Over time eBay developed a set of rules for its community to reduce the cost of trust and provided a set of services to reduce the risks of trading. In some cases, the rules were a response to incidents that identified weaknesses in the private ordering. For example, as the community grew and became more anonymous, eBay required members who were not otherwise identifiable to provide credit card information to establish their identity.

The chapter case, *eBay: Private Ordering for an Online Community,* considers these aspects of community in more detail.

SUMMARY

The economics of some information markets are quite different from the economics of the markets for consumption goods. Network externalities or complementary products can generate demand-side increasing returns. The increasing returns provide incentives to develop an installed base of users as quickly as possible, so the first mover has an advantage. A firm also has an incentive to build a user base by charging low initial prices. If the firm can lock in the user base because of high switching costs, for example, positive feedback can result and the market may tip. In such cases, the winner takes most of the market. This raises a number of antitrust concerns not about being a monopoly but about the practices used to obtain and maintain the monopoly.

Privacy on the Internet is of concern to users and to legislators and regulators. Privacy pertains to both personal information such as that provided to complete a purchase and anonymous data such as browsing or search information. The FTC has authority to take enforcement actions against Web sites that have privacy policies but then violate them. Other than that authority, privacy on the Internet is largely a matter of self-regulation by Web sites and self-protection by users. Self-regulation has a variety of components, the most controversial of which is opt-out versus opt-in. Most electronic commerce companies use opt-out, which critics argue places too great a burden on Internet users. Opt-in, however, would greatly reduce the data available to Internet companies.

The collection and remittance of sales taxes on Internet transactions is not required unless the seller has a physical nexus in the state. States and brick-and-mortar retailers have pressed for requiring collection of the taxes. The loss of tax revenue and sales provided incentives for political action, but opposition was strong from the electronic commerce companies and from mail-order and telephone sales companies that feared that they might be subject to the same requirements. The opponents of Internet taxation argued that with 7,600 tax jurisdictions collection and remittance of the taxes would be prohibitively costly. Some states have begun to simplify their tax codes. Congress has passed moratoriums against Internet-only taxes, but a permanent resolution of the issue has remained elusive.

A number of Internet companies develop online communities. These communities can benefit from demand-side increasing returns, but they are composed of remote and anonymous individuals. In the case of online auctions, anonymity provides members with opportunities to take advantage of other members. Web sites thus must provide order for their communities. That order can be private in the sense that it does not rely on the law, or public. Trust is the centerpiece of eBay's online community, and reputation is the basis for trust. Reputations on eBay are based on feedback from trading partners and are the foundation for the private ordering of its community. eBay supplements the reputation mechanism with a set of policies and rules intended to support trust by reducing the likelihood of opportunistic behavior.

--- C A S E S ---
DoubleClick and Internet Privacy

It is clear from these discussions that I made a mistake by planning to merge names with anonymous user activity across Web sites in the absence of government and industry privacy standards.

—Kevin O'Conner, CEO of DoubleClick

Introduction

DoubleClick, the industry leader in Internet advertising services, saw its $1.7 billion strategic investment in Abacus Direct dissolve in the face of a privacy firestorm over the merger of the Abacus data on offline purchasing with information gleaned from the browsing of Internet users. DoubleClick tracked Web activity on its DoubleClick Network of 1,500 Web sites and placed banner advertisements on 11,000 sites. The information it collected was identified only by an ID number assigned to a cookie deposited on the user's computer by the banner advertisements. DoubleClick's DART software technology processed the anonymous information to generate user profiles for tailoring advertisements for Web sites. Abacus Direct was the leader in collecting information from catalog purchases and using that data to target advertising and catalog configurations to consumers. Abacus had 5-year buying profiles on 88 million households, including name, address, demographic information, estimated income, and purchases.

DoubleClick recognized that the value of targeted online advertising would be substantially increased if information from consumers' online browsing activities could be linked with their offline purchase activities. Rates for targeted advertising based on anonymous profiling were 50 to 100 percent higher than for untargeted bulk advertising, and rates for targeted ads based on the merged databases would be even higher.

DoubleClick's plans were interrupted in February 2000 when *USA Today* disclosed its plan to merge its anonymous online data with Abacus Direct's database. A firestorm erupted, and DoubleClick quickly suspended its plan to merge the databases. It then faced the problems of developing a strategy for regaining public confidence and for the collection and use of information going forward.

DoubleClick

Kevin O'Conner founded DoubleClick in 1996 to serve advertisers on the Internet. By early 2000 DoubleClick had 1,800 employees, 7,000 customers, offices in 30 countries, and a market capitalization of $10 billion. Its revenue for the first quarter of 2000 was $110 million, an increase of 179 percent over the year-earlier quarter. Its gross profit was $53 million, but heavy marketing expenses resulted in a loss of $18 million. Forrester Research projected that online advertising would increase from $3.3 billion in 1999 to $33 billion in 2004.

Shortly after founding DoubleClick, O'Conner stated in an interview that the company would not collect and keep information that identified a person. He said that linking data to names and addresses "would be voluntary on the user's part, and used in strict confidence. We are not going to trick people or match information from other sources."[16] In accord with this policy DoubleClick allowed Internet users to opt out of its data collection system. Its opt-out policy was available on its own Web site at the end of a lengthy legal notice and a description of cookies.

To target advertisements to Internet users' interests, DoubleClick tracked their click-stream data. The technology for tracking click-stream data began with cookies. A cookie is a small text file deposited on a user's hard drive that contains an ID number associated with the computer but not the user. Cookies were a major convenience to many users. They enabled a portal such as Yahoo! to remember a user's password and immediately bring up personalized pages and information. They also allowed advertising and other content to be targeted by ID number. When a user visited a Web site that had deposited a cookie on the user's hard drive, the visit and ID number were recorded. DoubleClick collected the visit information through its network of Web sites, which included popular sites such as AltaVista and Travelocity. Since the ID number was associated with a computer and DoubleClick had no information on who owned or used the computer, the information remained anonymous. Abacus Online, however, was different.

DoubleClick's Abacus Online Strategy

DoubleClick's market strategy was to integrate the two databases to offer advertising better tailored to Internet users' actual purchasing behavior as well as their browsing. To implement its strategy DoubleClick formed Abacus Online. Participating Web sites identified users by name but were required to post a notice explaining the information to be collected and giving users the opportunity to opt out. Participating users could also choose whether to receive targeted advertisements. DoubleClick was actively recruiting companies and Web sites to join Abacus Online. AltaVista and Travelocity had not yet decided whether to join.

Sites participating in Abacus Online would not only allow click-stream data to be collected, but they also

---

[16] *Forbes,* November 4, 1996.

would collect personal information when individuals identified themselves to the site—for example, when they made a purchase, completed a survey, or signed up for a drawing. With that personal information the ID number assigned to the cookie could be associated with the user. The click-stream data then could be combined with Abacus Direct's database of offline information. DoubleClick operated one such site, Netdeals.com, where users could sign up for drawings for prizes, giving their name, age, and street and e-mail addresses. Users who agreed to receive "valuable offers" were added to its database.

DoubleClick explained its objective: "This is about getting the right ad to the right person at the right time. It's important for users to understand that the only time DoubleClick will actually have personally identifiable information attached to a browser is when the user has volunteered [it] and been given notice and choice."[17] DoubleClick had no intention of selling or disclosing information on individuals' Internet use to any third party. The information would only be used internally to enhance the value of its services to advertisers. DoubleClick also pledged that it would not collect data on medical, financial, or sexual transactions or browsing or on children's browsing.

DoubleClick argued that the information would benefit consumers because advertisements would be tailored to their interests and purchasing behavior. Just as consumers using Amazon.com received messages about books that might be of interest based on their past purchases, DoubleClick would provide advertisements of interest to users of a Web site based on the purchasing and browsing behavior of those who visited the site. Similarly, just as a consumer could design a personalized page on a portal such as Yahoo!, DoubleClick would provide personalized information for the consumer. Because advertisements were provided on virtually all Web sites, a consumer would benefit from receiving advertisements of interest rather than blanket ads.

Kevin O'Conner said, "There are some people on the Internet who want to go back to the old days when there was no advertising and it was government controlled. We believe that [the Internet] is a tremendous thing and that it should be free. That means it is going to be funded by advertising."[18] O'Conner pointed to recent polls indicating that 70 percent of Internet users understood that the Internet was free because of advertising and that two-thirds liked the personalization of information.[19] Broadcast television and radio were also funded by advertisements, and magazines and newspapers were largely funded by ads.

Dana Serman of Lazard Freres predicted, "Over time, people will realize it's not Big Brother who's going to show up at your door in a black ski mask and take your kids away or dig deep into your medical history. This is a situation where you are essentially dropped in a bucket with 40 million people who look and feel a lot like you do to the advertising community."[20]

Internet Privacy

The U.S. Constitution does not have an explicit privacy provision other than the Fourth Amendment's restrictions on searches and seizures by government. A number of court decisions, however, established certain privacy rights supported by constitutional interpretation.[21] A right to privacy was also established in a number of state constitutions, including that of California. Although there was no legislation specifying Internet privacy rights, other legislation reflected the sensitivity of privacy issues.

The Federal Trade Commission (FTC) had jurisdiction over unfair and deceptive practices, and in 1999 the FTC reached a decision not to regulate Internet privacy. One commissioner, however, dissented and advocated immediate action on privacy. The FTC established an Advisory Committee on Online Access and Security.

Self-Regulation and the Activist Landscape

The e-commerce industry had taken steps to provide better security and privacy and to stop theft and fraud on the Internet. Two industry groups, the Online Privacy Alliance and the Electronic Commerce and Consumer Protection Group, advocated continued self-regulation by Internet companies.[22] A number of Internet companies had established TRUSTe to certify the privacy policies of Web sites, and other organizations also provided certification.[23] This self-regulation and the complexities of the privacy issue had led the U.S. government to go slowly in establishing explicit consumer privacy rights for the Internet. Not everyone, however, was satisfied with self-regulation. Marc Rotenberg of the Electronic Privacy Information Center (EPIC) said, "Self-regulation is inviting a race to the bottom."

When it acquired Abacus Direct in 1999, DoubleClick was criticized by privacy activists who feared

---

[17]*USA Today,* February 2, 2000.
[18]*Guardian,* February 25, 2000.
[19]*Wall Street Journal,* March 7, 2000.
[20]*Washington Post,* February 18, 2000.
[21]See *Griswold v. Connecticut,* 383 U.S. 479 (1965).
[22]The Online Privacy Alliance had 85 corporate and association members. The members of the Electronic Commerce and Consumer Protection Group were AOL, AT&T, Dell, IBM, Microsoft, Network Solutions, Time Warner, and Visa U.S.A.
[23]TRUSTe was established in 1996 based on the principles that users have a right to informed consent and that "no single privacy principle is adequate for all situations." TRUSTe granted a site a "trademark" if it met the tests of (1) adoption and implementation of a privacy policy, (2) notice and disclosure, (3) choice and consent, and (4) data security and quality and access (to personal information). By mid-2000 approximately 2000 Web sites had received TRUSTe approval.

that it would integrate the information it collected on-line with the personalized information in Abacus Direct's database. Some activists drew analogies to George Orwell's *1984*, and Jason Catlett, head of JunkBusters, a for-profit consulting company, said, "Abacus is now becoming part of a company that will be despised by anyone who values privacy."[24] In response to the criticism, DoubleClick and nine other Internet advertising and on-line profiling companies formed the Network Advertising Initiative to develop privacy protection guidelines.

JunkBusters and EPIC had earlier created a storm when they revealed that Intel planned to put a serial number on its Pentium III processor, allowing identification of the computer on which it was installed. EPIC threatened a boycott, and Intel quickly backed down and abandoned its plan. A number of other companies had also had privacy incidents and were forced to change their policies. Lexis-Nexis was forced to abandon its plans to provide personal information to other companies. Similarly, in 1997 America Online (AOL) planned to release its subscribers list to telephone marketers despite an earlier pledge not to do so.[25] Referring to Marc Rotenberg of EPIC, Steve Case, chairman of AOL, said, "The guy can create a privacy uproar at the click of a mouse."[26]

Privacy activists were also suspicious of companies' stated privacy policies. First, policies could be changed at any time. For example, in August 1999 Amazon.com changed its policy and introduced "purchase circles" that used personal data and purchase data to identify publicly the best-selling products by geography, employer, university, or organization. Second, companies could violate their policies and escape detection. In November 1999 RealNetworks was revealed to be collecting information on users' Internet activity without disclosure and in violation of its own privacy policy.[27] The company apologized and stopped the practice.

A basic objection to the collection of click-stream data was that it was invisible to users. Activists argued that average consumers did not know their activity was being tracked let alone how the information was being used. Another objection was that the identifiers of consumers were persistent and the user did not have a relationship with the company doing the tracking, as when a consumer made a purchase using a credit card.

Some activists opposed the transformation of the Internet from an anonymous environment to one in which individuals were identified and their Internet use monitored. As one commentator put it, "You can escape your surroundings through the Internet, but your actions can easily catch up with you."[28]

The Reaction to Abacus Online

Shortly after Abacus Online was revealed, the Center for Democracy and Technology (CDT) launched a consumer education campaign to alert Internet users.[29] CDT provided an Operation Opt-out Web site allowing consumers to opt out of DoubleClick's system and urging them to write letters to DoubleClick protesting its policies. Several thousand letters were also sent to Web sites that participated in the DoubleClick Network.

Jason Catlett of JunkBusters described Abacus Online as, "Thousands of sites are ratting on you, so as soon as one gives you away, you're exposed on all of them. For four years, [DoubleClick] has said [the services] don't identify you personally, and now they're admitting they are going to identify you."[30] He added, "If you don't like Yahoo!'s privacy policy, you don't have to use its site. But it's very difficult for consumers to avoid DoubleClick because most don't know when it is collecting information."[31] Richard Smith, a privacy advocate, added, "Computers are like elephants: they never forget. And they are watching us all the time."[32] Other critics likened DoubleClick to the computer HAL in the movie *2001* and referred to the company as "Doublecross." Jonathon Shapiro, senior vice president of DoubleClick, said, "We are good actors. We've been leaders in protecting consumer privacy for the past four years, and we think our commitment to providing notice and choice to consumers puts us ahead of the curve."[33]

DoubleClick pointed out that since its founding 50,000 people had opted out of its tracking. Tom Maddox, editor of *Privacyplace*, argued, "People don't know they have to opt out."[34] David Banisar of Privacy International said, "This is not permission. That is fraudulent on its face."[35] Barry Steinhardt of the American Civil Liberties Union said, "The onus should be on the data collector to get your affirmative consent, in a knowing way. You shouldn't have to bargain for your privacy."[36]

Privacy advocates argued that consumers should have access to the data collected so that they could

[24]*Forbes*, November 24, 1999.
[25]Peter P. Swire and Robert E. Litan, *None of Your Business.* 1998, Brookings Institution: Washington, DC, p. 10. AOL continued to sell its subscribers list but notified its subscribers of the practice.
[26]*Business Week*, May 15, 2000.
[27]Its free RealJukebox allowed users to convert music to a digital format and play it on a personal computer. People downloading the software were required to give their e-mail address and zip code and were assigned a Globally Unique Identifier. The software transmitted daily information to RealNetworks on songs downloaded by users. RealNetworks was TRUSTe approved.

[28]Esther Dyson, *Los Angeles Times*, March 20, 2000.
[29]Members of CDT included America Online, AT&T, Business Software Alliance, Disney WorldWide, Ford Foundation, Markle Foundation, Microsoft, the Newspaper Association of America, the Open Society Institute, and Time Warner.
[30]*USA Today*, January 26, 2000.
[31]*U.S. News & World Report*, March 6, 2000.
[32]*Financial Times*, January 29, 2000.
[33]*Los Angeles Times*, February 3, 2000.
[34]*San Francisco Chronicle*, January 27, 2000.
[35]*USA Today*, January 26, 2000.
[36]*Financial Times*, January 29, 2000.

correct errors and decide whether to continue allowing the data to be collected. They also argued for an opt-in policy under which consumers would have to give their express permission before any information could be collected on them. In June 2000 the Supreme Court let stand a Court of Appeals decision voiding part of a statute that had required local telephone companies to obtain opt-in permission before using billing records to sell new services to customers. US West had filed the lawsuit so that it could use an opt-out policy instead.

Personal Assurance of Internet Privacy

Most people seemed willing to give personal information and credit card numbers to catalog companies such as L.L. Bean and Lands' End. Information on credit card transactions was routinely collected, and financial services companies had for many years used data that passed through their systems to target consumers. Moreover, the growth of the Internet and electronic commerce had been very rapid under the self-regulation approach without explicit Internet privacy rights. A Forrester Research poll of 10,000 Internet users revealed that two-thirds were willing to provide personal information, but 90 percent wanted control over how that information was used.

Users had a growing array of direct means of assuring privacy, including both those taken by ISPs and those taken individually. ISPs had privacy policies and published those policies on their Web sites. A growing number had their policies and practices certified by independent companies and organizations, such as TRUSTe, BBBOnline, and SecureAssure. SecureAssure affixed a seal to a Web site that pledged not to sell personal information about a user to a third party without express permission.[37] In contrast, sites with BBBOnline and TRUSTe approval could sell data.

Another means of avoiding online profiling was to block cookies from being deposited on a computer. Cookies could be blocked by simply configuring Internet Explorer (IE) or Netscape Navigator to reject them. On IE go to Tools, Internet Options, Security, and choose high. On Navigator go to Edit, Preferences, Advanced, and select the option.

Economic theory predicted that if there were a demand for Internet privacy the marketplace would supply the means of achieving it. Webroot.com's Windows Washer allowed a user to cleanse certain areas of Windows of cookies. Some companies, including TopClick International, Anonymizer.com, and Zero-Knowledge, provided anonymous surfing of the Internet using technologies that masked a user's identity. Zero-Knowledge's Freedom program gave users digital pseudonyms and routed their surfing through a variety of servers to cloak their activity. Anonymizer acted as an intermediary and

encrypted a user's inquiries. Hundreds of re-mailers removed revealing information from e-mail messages. Earth Proxy provided free downloadable software intended to inhibit tracking software.

Purchasing items on the Internet, however, required a billing record, which gave sellers information on purchasers. Infomediaries such as PrivaSeek offered subscribers downloadable software that allowed them to decide what information was made available when they purchased online. In May 2000 at a weekend privacy retreat organized by the U.S. Chamber of Commerce, Microsoft and a number of other companies displayed technologies to protect consumers. One technology demonstrated by DataTreasury Corporation allowed transactions to be made within its secure system.

In 1998 the World Wide Web Consortium, backed by a group of companies including America Online, AT&T, IBM, and Microsoft, formed P3P, the Platform for Privacy Preferences Protection, along with the Massachusetts Institute of Technology and universities in France and Japan. P3P was unveiled in June 2000, and Microsoft announced that it would incorporate it in its next version of Windows. Both Microsoft and America Online said they would offer it as a plug-in to their browsers. P3P software allowed Internet users to specify the personal data they wanted to divulge to a Web site, and P3P technology notified them when a site requested additional information. The participants in P3P were reported to have been unable to agree on more than a notification procedure. Marc Rotenberg of EPIC referred to P3P as "pretty poor privacy," criticizing it for being an opt-out rather than an opt-in procedure and requiring too much initiative by Internet users. He said, "It is not a technology to protect personal privacy. It's a means to enable the disclosure of personal information."[38] Dr. Horst Joepen, CEO of Webwasher.com, a German software privacy company affiliated with Siemens, characterized P3P as "too little, too late."

Government Action

As a result of the privacy concerns raised about Abacus Online, the Center for Democracy and Technology filed a complaint with the FTC, which began an inquiry into DoubleClick's data collection and advertising practices. CDT, the Privacy Rights Clearinghouse, Consumer Action, the Gay and Lesbian Alliance Against Defamation, and the American Civil Liberties Union subsequently filed a "Statement of Additional Facts and Grounds for Relief" with the FTC.

In addition to the FTC inquiry the New York State attorney general initiated an informal inquiry. The attorney general of Michigan referred to DoubleClick's plan as "a secret wiretap" and announced that she would file suit against the practice. "The average consumer has no

---

[37]The fee charged by SecureAssure ranged from $200 to $2,500 a year.

[38]*New York Times,* June 22, 2000.

idea that they are being spied upon," she said, and the lack of warning constituted "a deceitful practice under our consumer-protection act."[39] She said that DoubleClick's policy was like putting a "bar code" on a consumer's back. A California woman filed a lawsuit alleging that DoubleClick violated her state constitutional right to privacy.

Legislation on Internet privacy had been introduced in Congress by Senators Burns and Wyden, Senator Leahy offered another bill, and Representative Markey introduced another. A number of members of Congress supported a federal Internet privacy agency. The Clinton administration was also concerned about online privacy but favored self-regulation. The administration backed the P3P technology and installed it on the White House Internet site.

In May 2000 the FTC reversed its position and voted 3 to 2 to ask Congress for new legislation granting it rule-making authority to regulate privacy on the Internet. The FTC sought required notice of privacy policies, including telling Internet users how the data would be used and allowing them to inspect and correct their information. Companies would also be required to implement security measures to prevent unauthorized disclosure. In a statement FTC chairman Robert Pitofsky said, "This is not a report that comes to the conclusion that self-regulation has failed. On the contrary, self-regulation has made considerable progress. But in certain respects it looks as if self-regulation would be more successful if there was some backup legislation."[40] In his dissent commissioner Orson Swindle called the FTC request "breathtakingly broad."

The FTC's survey of Internet sites revealed that only 41 percent posted a privacy policy that told users how data was used and only 20 percent of the major Internet sites had adequate privacy policies. Commissioner Swindle said the survey was "embarrassingly flawed." The Direct Marketing Institute countered with a survey showing that 93 percent of major Internet sites had privacy policies and most of them told users how their data would be used.

Industry generally supported self-regulation and opposed government regulation, but some companies feared that states would enact their own Internet privacy laws. Internet privacy legislation had been introduced in 17 states. A number of companies believed that some federal regulation was an acceptable price if it would preempt state regulation. Tod Cohen of eBay said, "We would work with the FTC, Congress and the administration to develop a national standard." Robert Levitan, CEO of Flooz.com, commented, "I would like to think that industry could self-regulate, but I think we all have accepted the fact that there will be some regulation. We're not jumping up and down complaining about regulation. We're just saying, let's do it wisely."[41] Andy Grove, Chairman of Intel, stated, "I would prefer to recognize this trend and get ahead of the possibility that . . . states are going to take matters in their own hands."[42]

Doubleclick's Challenge

In putting Abacus Online on hold, Kevin Ryan, president of DoubleClick, said, "I think we could have done a better job of communicating. Because we are the largest and most successful Internet company in our space, we certainly attract more attacks than other people."[43] He observed, "There are always going to be controversies when people start using new technologies. When credit cards were introduced, people wouldn't use them because they were worried that the credit card companies would be tracking them. And when people first started using the Internet, they wouldn't buy anything because they were worried about credit card fraud. But they got over it."[44] ■

SOURCE: This case was prepared from public sources by Professor David P. Baron. Copyright © 2000 by David P. Baron. All rights reserved. Reproduced with permission.

Preparation Questions

1. How important is the privacy issue to Internet users? Is Kevin Ryan correct in his belief that users will get over their concern about privacy?

2. Why was there uproar over DoubleClick's strategy when there was little concern about Abacus Direct's offline data collection?

3. Should DoubleClick have anticipated the reaction to Abacus Online and the merger of the databases?

4. Is anonymous click-stream tracking and profiling objectionable? Is sending targeted advertising messages to a computer using cookie ID numbers objectionable?

5. How can DoubleClick restore consumer and public confidence in its business? Should it institute an opt-in policy?

6. What type of Internet privacy rights should individuals have? Is self-regulation adequate to protect those rights? Is legislation needed? Is consumer ignorance of privacy protection issues and alternatives a sufficient rationale for government regulation of Internet privacy?

7. What should DoubleClick do about the FTC inquiry and request for new legislation?

---

[39]*Washington Post,* February 17, 2000.
[40]*New York Times,* May 22, 2000.
[41]*New York Times,* May 22, 2000.
[42]*National Journal,* June 17, 2000, p. 1924.
[43]*Washington Post,* February 18, 2000.
[44]*U.S. News & World Report,* March 6, 2000.

eBay and Database Protection

I don't want to sound flip, but when people tell me, "The Internet's like the Wild West," I like to remind them we used to hang cattle rustlers in the Wild West.[45]

—Edward Miller

The popularity of online auctions pioneered by eBay led not only to rival Internet auction sites for items ranging from antiques to automobiles and from real estate to time with celebrities, but it also spawned a group of "auction aggregators." Companies such as Bidder's Edge, AuctionRover.com, and ultimatebid.com searched Internet auction sites, extracted data, and provided it to their users. Bidder's Edge, for example, provided information on auctions in a variety of categories corresponding to those on eBay's front page. A person searching for a Roman coin on Bidder's Edge received information on coins available on eBay, Yahoo!, and Amazon.com. This provided comparative information and convenience to users, but it was based on information extracted from eBay's site. One of eBay's most important strategic assets was its database and the information it gained from conducting auctions. This information was invaluable for the design of auctions and for identifying service enhancements and other business opportunities, including partnering with other service providers. The aggregators threatened the value of that asset.

eBay and Online Auctions

Pierre Omidyar founded eBay in September 1995 with the business concept of providing an Internet site, Auction Web, where person-to-person trading could take place. Buyers and sellers flocked to the site, and Auction-Web became eBay in September 1997. eBay recruited Meg Whitman, who had been a general manager of Hasbro and president and CEO of FTD, to serve as president and CEO, and Pierre Omidyar continued as chairman. eBay's growth was spectacular. By mid-2000 eBay had over 15.8 million registered users who traded items in more than 4,320 categories. On any day approximately 4.3 million auctions were active on eBay's site, with 500,000 new items listed every day. Nearly 1.8 million visits were made to its site on an average day, and the average visit was 20 minutes.

An online auction involved listing an item for sale with a closing date and time. The seller provided a description of the item, and most provided pictures. The seller could specify a minimum opening bid, a bid increment, and a reserve price that was not disclosed to bidders, although bidders were told whether the reserve had been met. A bid consisted of an initial bid and a maximum bid, which authorized eBay to increase the bid to the maximum if forced by another bidder. Often, there was a flurry of bidding just before the closing. Transactions between the seller and the high bidder were executed without eBay's involvement. Sellers and buyers were identified by their account names, and they earned reputations through feedback from their trading partners. The feedback was summarized and available to buyers and sellers.

eBay's principal asset was its ability to aggregate buyers and sellers on its Web site, for which it charged small fees for listings and sales. eBay strove for a high level of user satisfaction, and its reputation helped maintain its leadership among the online auction sites that had followed in its footsteps. eBay also sought to ensure the privacy of its users. Its privacy policy was TRUSTe-approved, and eBay was a founding member of the Online Privacy Association.

eBay's revenue in 1999 was $224.7 million, and its net income was $11 million. The first half of 2000 saw a doubling of revenue from the previous year and net income increased by nearly 400 percent to $17.9 million. In 2000 its market capitalization reached $30 billion, reflecting its leading position in the online auction market and its seemingly unlimited potential. In spring 2000, however, its market capitalization fell to $16 billion with the market decline in high-tech stocks.

eBay's rivals ranged from small niche Web sites to Yahoo! and Amazon.com. eBay, however, was estimated to host nearly 90 percent of the online auctions in the United States and to have 85 percent of the market. eBay had expanded into international markets and was a leading online auction site in Canada, Germany, Australia, and the United Kingdom. It planned to expand into France and Italy. In February 2000 eBay entered the Japanese market, where Yahoo! Japan Auctions was the leader.

Auction Aggregators and Database Protection

Bidder's Edge and two dozen other auction aggregators, or "auction portals" as some preferred to be called, searched across auction sites to provide listings and price information for their users. The opportunity for auction aggregators was provided by a 1991 U.S. Supreme Court decision (*Feist Publications, Inc. v. Rural Telephone Service Co.*, 499 U.S., 340) in which the Court held that "facts," even if collected through "sweat and effort," remained in the public domain. In *Feist* the court stated that "all facts—scientific, historical, biographical and news of the day . . . are part of the public domain available to every person." This ruling gave auction aggregators a legal defense for extracting "facts" from eBay and other online auction sites.

---

[45]*Wall Street Journal*, April 10, 2000.

The first auction aggregator appeared in the spring of 1999, and in September eBay declared that the listings on its Internet site were its "property" and prohibited auction aggregators from searching its site. Bidder's Edge stopped its searches and took out a full page ad in the *New York Times* protesting eBay's move. Undaunted, other auction aggregators resumed listing eBay items on their sites, and seeing itself at a competitive disadvantage, Bidder's Edge did also.

eBay attempted to work with the auction aggregators and offered a license for free and a small bounty for each user directed to eBay's site. Five aggregators took licenses, allowing them to query in real time eBay's system as a user would. The license, however, prohibited copying data. eBay entered into negotiations with Bidder's Edge on a license, but little progress was made. As Kevin Pursglove of eBay explained, "This is a clear-cut example of one business trying to get a free ride off eBay's success. What we've been trying to do is reach out to these third parties and establish some appropriate business guidelines." AuctionRover, for example, had agreed to eBay's conditions and had a separate eBay tab on its Web site. Scot Wingo, CEO of AuctionRover, said, "We've taken a more pro-eBay approach. Our competitors have taken a more, if you pardon the vernacular, 'screw eBay!' approach."[46]

Bidder's Edge obtained data from nearly 100 online person-to-person and merchant auction sites, providing users with an overview of available items, comparison information, and tracking services of items available for auction. Items available on eBay, however, accounted for 69 percent of Bidder's Edge's database. Instead of querying eBay's system to fulfill a user's search request, Bidder's Edge used a robotic program that daily copied approximately 80,000 pages, which were stored on Bidder's Edge's computers and updated recursively. A query by a visitor to the Bidder's Edge Web site was then answered by searching its rather than eBay's database. Since Bidder's Edge searched recursively, the information it provided to its users was necessarily stale and could be inaccurate. Bidder's Edge accounted for between 1.1 and 1.53 percent of the queries received by eBay and imposed a heavy load on eBay's computers. More importantly, eBay believed that those using Bidder's Edge and other auction aggregators' sites were not receiving the full value of its Web site and the eBay community.

eBay used a Robot Exclusion Standard and a robots.txt file that notified those searching its site that robotic searches were prohibited. Compliance was voluntary, and search sites such as Yahoo! and Google respected the Standard. Bidder's Edge, however, did not. eBay also had a security unit that detected any unusual number of queries from an IP number and blocked those suspected of violating its policies. Bidder's Edge used proxy servers to avoid eBay's IP blocks.

In addition to eBay there were other Internet service providers that sought to protect their databases. Reed Elsevier PLC and Thomson Corporation provided a comprehensive database of court cases and decisions. Reed Elsevier's Lexis unit was locked in a legal battle with Jurisline.com, whose founders had leased Lexis's 160 CD-ROMs for $2,365, copied them, and provided the data free on its Internet site. Jurisline contended that the data were developed from court records, which were public information and hence could not be copyrighted.

Other Internet service providers were concerned about database protection and access but had quite different interests. Virtually all companies that searched across Internet sites to bring information to users wanted to maintain access to information on Web sites. These companies included America Online, Yahoo!, and other portals and search engines. In addition, shopping bots feared that they would be shut out of the information they used to provide price and other comparisons for consumers.

Intellectual Property Law and Databases

Intellectual property law provided protection for information through patents, trademarks, copyrights, and trade secrets. The Coalition Against Database Piracy (CADP), however, argued that existing intellectual property laws provided little protection for databases. According to the CADP, "copyright law only protects a database to the extent that it is creative in the selection, arrangement or coordination of the facts it contains. Copyright law does not shield the database's factual content from thievery. Very few databases meet this 'creativity' requirement because all the things that make a database valuable and user-friendly—its comprehensiveness and its logical order (whether alphabetical in print products or random in electronic products)—are deemed to involve no 'creative' selection, arrangement or coordination."[47]

CADP also argued that the U.S. Anti-Hacking Statute as well as state contract and misappropriation laws provided inadequate protection. Moreover, state laws could vary considerably. The Anti-Hacking Statute has "never been held to apply to a published database at all—no matter what its format. Nor would the statute apply in a situation where a database producer—like eBay—makes information available over the Web without a password or firewall protecting it." State contract law applied only to signed agreements. Moreover, "[m]isappropriation is an ill-defined state law doctrine and it does not provide database creators with uniform, nationwide protection."[48]

---

[46]*MSNBC,* November 2, 1999.

[47]CADP Web site, www.gooddata.org.
[48]CADP Web site, www.gooddata.org.

Strategy Alternatives

One alternative available to eBay was to attempt to establish through the courts intellectual property rights to the data on its auctions. If successful this would allow it to block the auction aggregators. The *Feist* decision, however, placed a heavy burden on eBay to demonstrate creativity. Another possibility was to use the Computer Fraud and Abuse Act to claim that the aggregators were committing fraud. If eBay decided to take legal action, it could direct its action against Bidder's Edge or it could name additional auction aggregators as defendants.

eBay could also seek a preliminary and ultimately a permanent injunction against Bidder's Edge and other auction aggregators. To obtain a preliminary injunction, eBay would have to demonstrate probable success in a trial and convincingly show that the absence of an injunction would cause irreparable injury. Although eBay believed it would prevail, it recognized that pursuing a court resolution could be both costly and time consuming. Moreover, decisions could be appealed, and in the rapidly changing field of Internet law, legal innovation could thwart what appeared to be the current law. In addition, since eBay was by far the largest online auction site, legal action might attract the attention of federal or state antitrust authorities and possibly raise issues of unfair business practices, the exercise of market power, or the use of the courts to stifle competition.

For several years companies, including Reed Elsevier and other publishers, had backed the Collections of Information Antipiracy Act to protect their databases. In 1998 the bill had passed the House of Representatives but the Senate had not acted. Another alternative for eBay was actively to support the bill when it was reintroduced.

The World Intellectual Property Organization (WIPO) also sought stronger protection of intellectual property in light of the *Feist* decision.[49] A treaty negotiated under the auspices of WIPO provided additional protection for creative works and limited protection for online information that could be protected by copyright. Each signatory was to enact legislation to bring its laws into accord with the treaty, and the United States did so in the Digital Millennium Copyright Act of 1998. The Act established liability for online copyright infringement and protected ISPs from liability from material posted on their services, but it did not overturn *Feist*.

eBay could also attempt to use technology to thwart attempts to extract information from its database. A technology fix in the form of a firewall, however, could make its site less convenient for consumers. It could also lead to a technology race as aggregators developed software to overcome the barriers erected by eBay.

eBay and Public Policy

As with many high-tech companies, eBay had begun to address public issues. In the past 2 years it had established a Washington office and hired professionals to represent it. It had also established a PAC, the eBay Committee for Responsible Internet Commerce, which had contributed to members of Congress. eBay executives began to make Washington one of their regular stops on the East Coast.

In July 1999 eBay and eight other Internet service providers, Amazon.com, America Online, DoubleClick, Excite@Home, Inktomi, Lycos, theglobe.com, and Yahoo!, formed NetCoalition.com. The coalition's mission statement read, "As the collective public policy voice of the world's leading Internet companies, NetCoalition.com is committed to building user confidence in the Internet through responsible market-driven policies; preserving the open and competitive environment that has allowed the Internet to flourish; and ensuring the continued vitality of the Internet through active dialogue with policymakers." Meg Whitman explained, "We want to be active participants in the dialogue that is addressing the critical issues facing the burgeoning Internet industry. As a group we can be a valuable resource and a powerful educational tool for policymakers and the public."

Within a few months, however, the "collective voice" split over the issue of database protection. eBay backed legislation to protect its databases, and other members backed rival legislation that, according to eBay, would provide little if any protection.

Legislation

The Collections of Information Antipiracy Act was reintroduced in February 1999 as H.R. 354 by Representative Howard Coble (R-NC), chair of the Subcommittee on Courts and Intellectual Property of the Judiciary Committee. Seventy-five other House members cosponsored the bill. The bill had been redrafted to address concerns with earlier versions, and the Judiciary Committee reported it in October 1999. The bill would provide substantial protection to those who collected information, including those that did so on the Internet. Facts were not protected by the bill and remained in the public domain, but the effect of the bill would be to overturn *Feist*. The bill had not yet been introduced in the Senate, since Senator Orrin Hatch (R-UT), Chairman of the Judiciary Committee, had decided to wait until the House acted before taking up the issue.

The Judiciary Committee expressed the basic principle underlying H.R. 354.

> Developing, compiling, distributing and maintaining commercially significant collections requires substantial investments of time, personnel, and effort and money. Information companies, small and large, must dedicate massive resources to gathering and verifying

---

[49]WIPO is one of 16 specialized agencies of the United Nations system of organizations.

factual material, presenting it in a user-friendly way, and keeping it current and useful to customers. . . . But several recent legal and technological developments threaten to derail this progress by eroding the incentives for continued investment needed to maintain and build upon the U.S. lead in world markets for electronic information resources.[50]

H.R. 354 allowed an injured party to bring a civil action in U.S. court for actual damages as well as for any profits earned by the defendant and attributable to the action in question. An award for actual damages could be trebled by the court. Any person who violated the Act "for purposes of direct or indirect commercial advantage or financial gain" could be subject to a fine not to exceed $250,000 and imprisonment of not more than 5 years or both.

Interests benefiting from the status quo countered with a rival bill, H.R. 1858, the Consumer and Investor Access to Information Act of 1999, introduced in May under the sponsorship of Representative Tom Bliley (R-VA), chairman of the Commerce Committee. The bill was referred to the Commerce Committee and reported in October.

H.R. 1858 focused on the value of information to consumers and the benefits to Internet users from being able to obtain comparisons of information from different databases. The bill would proscribe "the sale or distribution to the public of any database that: (1) is a duplicate of another database collected and organized by another person or entity; and (2) is sold or distributed in commerce in competition with that other database."[51] Enforcement responsibility would be assigned to the Federal Trade Commission. The bill also prohibited the misappropriation of real-time securities market information but restricted the ability of market information providers to control that information. This would protect the access of online brokers to financial market information. Yahoo!, America Online, research librarians, telecommunications companies, the U.S. Chamber of Commerce, Consumers Union, CharlesSchwab, and Bloomberg L.P. backed H.R. 1858.

eBay viewed H.R. 1858 as worse than the current state of the law. Joining eBay in supporting H.R. 354 were Reed Elsevier, Thomson, the American Medical Association, the New York Stock Exchange, and the National Association of Realtors (NAR).

Interests

The e-Commerce Coalition, with nearly 300 members, was formed to support database protection and H.R. 354

in particular. eBay was a principal member of the Coalition, which argued that H.R. 354 "would strike a balance between protecting the huge investments of e-Commerce database developers and maintainers and recognizing the need for continued open access to information. Thus, it is aimed at the misappropriation of collections of information, not at uses that do not affect marketability or competitiveness. Its goals are to stimulate the creation of even more collections of information and to encourage more competition among those collections."[52]

Online auction companies, Internet service providers, and publishers were not the only ones concerned about their databases. One of the largest and most valuable databases was the Multiple Listing Service of real estate properties. Dennis R. Cronk, president of NAR, stated, "The piracy of online data poses a threat to everyone who is using the Internet to gain real estate information."[53] The NAR was capable of generating considerable grassroots support for, or opposition to, pending legislation.

Companies providing print databases also sought protection. Fifteen companies and associations formed the CADP to work in support of H.R. 354 and against H.R. 1858. The CADP argued that H.R. 354 was pro-Internet and pro-consumer, and it established an Internet site gooddata.org to provide information on the issue. The CADP argued that "H.R. 1858 only bars thefts that result in duplicative databases (i.e., those substantially similar to the original database). This allowed 'free riders' to avoid liability by the simple contrivance of cutting and pasting the stolen data so that the 'new database' is not a 'duplicate' of the original—a simple task today for anyone with a computer."[54]

In February 2000 the CADP released a public opinion poll in support of H.R. 354. Gail Littlejohn of Reed Elsevier stated, "This data confirms what we have known all along—the American people share the view that database piracy is a serious problem and that there is an urgent need to enact antipiracy legislation this Congress. . . . Consumer access to accurate information is being compromised when anyone can copy and steal a privately owned database with no fear of penalty. Without protection, databases are in jeopardy, and consumers will lose access to trusted information."[55] Harvard law professor William Fisher, however, said, "There are huge advantages to enabling people when navigating the Internet to have as much information as possible."[56]

The opponents of H.R. 354 argued that it would give too much protection to databases, effectively creating data monopolies. Brokerage companies, for example, were concerned about their ability to obtain and provide their

---

[50]House Report 106–349, September 1999.
[51]The Act provided certain exclusions for certain news and sports activities, law enforcement activities, scientific and educational activities, government databases, databases related to Internet communications, computer programs, subscriber lists, certain legal materials, and certain securities market data.

[52]www.theecommercecoalition.org.
[53]The NAR had 750,000 members.
[54]www.gooddata.org.
[55]Coalition Against Database Piracy, February 3, 2000.
[56]*Fortune,* June 26, 2000, p. 200.

customers with real-time stock quotes. Bloomberg feared that it would be prevented from providing stock price analysis: "The bill would mean they would have absolute ownership right over something as basic as stock quotes." A spokesperson for the Chamber of Commerce said, "Factual data is the nuts and bolts of the information age. If you try to control its use, you're going to stifle commerce."[57]

NetCoalition.com also waded into the battle. "As Congress considers the database issue, it must balance the objective of preventing database piracy with the equally important objective of preserving legitimate access to information, that does not conflict with the principles [in *Feist*]. Accordingly, additional database protection should be narrowly crafted to address specific, defined problems. NetCoalition.com believes that H.R. 1858 meets this test and, against the background of the many existing forms of protection, achieves the necessary balance between protection and access."[58] In February, 2000, NetCoalition.com wrote to every member of the House urging them to support H.R. 1858 and to oppose H.R. 354.

Matthew Rightmire, director of business development of Yahoo!, argued, "H.R. 1858 has a critical provision which protects Yahoo! and other search engines against liability for linking to or listing categories of data. Absent such a provision, Yahoo! and others could be liable simply for acting like a card catalogue for facts and information available on the Internet."[59] He added, "Yahoo! is somewhat uniquely positioned to comment on this issue. We have spent and continue to spend a great deal of effort developing our own databases. At the same time, we aggregate and disseminate large amounts of information. In our view, legislating on the availability of information is not unlike two porcupines making love: it must be done very carefully. And, in both cases, there are significant unintended consequences which must be avoided."

Database Protection in the European Union

The European Union (EU) adopted a Directive on the Legal Protection of Databases, effective January 1998.[60] For EU citizens and firms the Directive established copyright protection for "the intellectual creation involved in the selection and arrangement of materials" and established a 15-year *sui generis* (specific to the investment) right for an investment "in the offering, verification or presentation of the contents of a data base." This *sui generis* right effectively established the sweat of the brow doctrine for databases developed within the EU.

Henry Horbaczewski, testifying on behalf of the CADP, stated, "CADP does not advocate adopting a database protection law that mirrors the EU Directive but ignores traditionally accepted U.S. concepts of protecting intellectual property. Nonetheless, the United States database industry cannot endorse enactment of a law [H.R. 1858] whose deficiencies in regard to domestic protection also increase the discrepancies between U.S. and EU law." He also stated, "Without comparable U.S. legislation, U.S. databases will not be protected from piracy in Europe, thereby placing the U.S. database industry at a significant competitive disadvantage in the huge EU market. Each day that passes without fair, balanced and comparable U.S. legislation gives the EU database-producing industry another leg up on its U.S. competitors."[61]

The Challenge

Its database and the community it had developed were important strategic assets for eBay, and its challenge was to protect those assets while allowing information to flow freely on the Internet. James Carney, CEO of Bidder's Edge, however, argued, "We're no different from any other search engine. Yahoo! and Lycos garner lots of information every day from sites without exclusive permission. If eBay is right and the courts agree, that would rip the guts out of the Web itself."[62]

Edward Miller, representing the NAR, recognized the reluctance of most members of Congress to regulate the Internet. He said, however, "I don't want to sound flip, but when people tell me, 'The Internet's like the Wild West,' I like to remind them we used to hang cattle rustlers in the Wild West."[63] ■

SOURCE: This case was written by Professor David P. Baron based on public sources and interviews with eBay personnel. Copyright © 2001 by David P. Baron. All rights reserved. Reprinted with permission.

Preparation Questions

1. How important to eBay is the protection of its database from auction aggregators and other search engines? In what ways do the auction aggregators harm eBay?

2. What strategy should eBay adopt to protect its intellectual property?

3. Should eBay take legal action against Bidder's Edge? If so, on what grounds should it file?

---

[57]*New York Times,* June 6, 2000.
[58]NetCoalition.com.
[59]Testimony on H.R. 1858, House Commerce Committee, June 15, 1999.
[60]Parliament and Council Directive 96/9/EC.

[61]Testimony before the House Commerce Subcommittee on Telecommunications, Trade, and Consumer Protection, July 15, 1999 on H.R. 1858, the Consumer and Investor Access to Information Act of 1999.
[62]*Mass High Tech,* November 8–14, 1999.
[63]*Wall Street Journal,* April 10, 2000.

4. Should eBay use technology to attempt to thwart the aggregators?

5. What are the possible consequences for the Internet and electronic commerce of H.R. 354 and H.R. 1858?

6. Would enactment of H.R. 354 establish monopoly rights to information and limit the availability of information to Internet users?

7. What specifically should eBay do to move H.R. 354 through the House? Should it attempt to mobilize the eBay community in support of H.R. 354?

eBay: Private Ordering for an Online Community

By providing a safe trading place on the Internet, the eBay community has flourished. Not only does eBay provide an efficient medium for people to buy or sell items directly from or to a large number of people, it's a forum where buyers and sellers develop reputations and, in some cases, it can change people's lives.

—eBay Web site[64]

By the end of 2000 eBay hosted the world's largest online trading community of 22 million buyers and sellers. When it started in 1995, the eBay community consisted of a small group of people trading Pez dispensers. It grew dramatically in the next few years, and millions of items in thousands of categories were offered for sale at any given moment. eBay was used by people selling a few items from their attics and as a primary distribution method for personal businesses. Buyers included collectors and hobbyists, carpenters buying tools, and people searching for homes or automobiles.

This community of buyers and sellers was the core of eBay's business. Many were passionate, avid defenders of the community. eBay worked to nurture, develop, and grow its community. It sought to make the experience of buying and selling on its site both pleasant and safe. Since community members remained anonymous, trust among traders was essential. The principal instrument of trust was the reputation members developed based on feedback from their trading partners. As its community grew in size and diversity, eBay established rules of conduct to supplement the reputation mechanism. The reputation mechanism and the rules of conduct provided order for eBay's community. As the community grew, that private ordering was both extended and broadened.

In addition, new issues arose on a regular basis, and old ones had to be revisited. By late 2000, some of these issues included

- Whether contact information to facilitate communication between members should be made available while protecting the community from spam and privacy violations
- Members conducting their transactions outside the eBay marketplace

- The sale of controversial items such as those associated with hate crimes
- The sale of banned and regulated items

Background

In 1995 Pierre Omidyar founded eBay, Inc., which operated an Internet site AuctionWeb for person-to-person trading, inspired by his girlfriend's desire to find other collectors with whom to trade Pez dispensers. The initial participants were people with similar hobbies, but the number of buyers and sellers grew by word of mouth, and soon many different items were being traded. The growth continued and became difficult to manage, and Omidyar tried to slow it by charging fees. The growth continued unabated, however, and AuctionWeb was inundated with small checks. The person-to-person Internet auction industry had begun.

In the fall of 1997 Omidyar eliminated the Auction-Web brand and the site began operating under the name of eBay. In May 1998 Meg Whitman joined the company as president and CEO, after serving as general manager of Hasbro and president and CEO of FTD. Omidyar continued as chairman. In 2000 more than 256 million items were listed for sale on eBay, in a wide range of categories, including antiques, collectibles, computer hardware, musical instruments, camera equipment, fine art, coins, stamps, cars, and real estate. By the end of 2000 eBay had local sites in 60 cities in the United States and country-specific sites in Austria, Australia, Canada, France, Germany, Ireland, Italy, Japan, Korea, New Zealand, Switzerland, and the United Kingdom.

In 2000 the company had $431 million in revenue, almost double the previous year, and $59 million in net income, an increase of more than three times over 1999. Market capitalization was over $8 billion at the end of 2000. In July 2000 eBay acquired Half.com, an online marketplace for sales at fixed prices. This provided an online outlet for sellers of discounted mass-market items, as well as a way for companies to sell overstocked or used merchandise.

eBay operated as an online venue for buyers and sellers. Sellers listed items and provided descriptions, often including photographs. An auction was then conducted in which potential buyers could bid on the item until a fixed time. The seller specified the conditions of the auction (such as the minimum opening bid, bid incre-

---

[64]pages.eBay.com/community/abouteBay/community/profiles.html.

ments, and the reserve price, if any), as well as the time the auction would close. Potential buyers could place an initial bid and a maximum bid and authorize eBay to increase the bid to the maximum if forced by another bidder. Bidding was often active as the auction neared its closing time, sometimes driven by automated "sniping" programs that some buyers used to get their bid in just before the auction closed. After the auction ended, the sales transaction was completed between the seller and high bidder without eBay's involvement. eBay charged a small fee for listing an item for sale plus a fee based on the final sales price.

In creating an online marketplace, eBay operated much like a newspaper classified section. It facilitated person-to-person transactions but did not take possession of the items being sold. It had no information about an item beyond the description provided by the seller, did not certify the items sold, did not handle the exchange, and assumed no liability for the sale. It exercised control over buying and selling only in restricting which items could be listed on its site (for instance, illegal items could not be listed) and on the configuration of the auctions. Even then eBay could not control listings before they were placed, only whether a listing could remain on the site.

Traditional auction houses differed from eBay in many ways. Some auction houses served as the agent of the seller and were responsible for obtaining the best price for the items sold. They also served the buyer by authenticating the items. eBay performed neither of these roles. Some auction houses served as the bailee of the seller, took possession of the items, and provided a guarantee to either sell or return the items. eBay did not serve these functions either.

Community Development

The foundation of eBay's business was its community of buyers and sellers. The size, growth, happiness, and loyalty of the community was its principal competitive advantage. For the eBay community to flourish, members had to be secure and confident in their interactions with one another. The eBay community was analogous to a real-world society in which people interacted with each other under a set of shared rules and expectations. In small, isolated communities in which everyone knew each other and had a strong sense of shared values, little regulation was required. However, as the community grew, became more diverse, and individuals felt more anonymous, trust could become problematic.

Trust Among Members

eBay's fundamental challenge was to establish trust among remote and anonymous traders who might never interact again. Reputation served to establish trust. If a remote trader reneged on a sale or delivered an item different from its description, the other party could sully the reputation of the seller. Similarly, if a trader lived up to her promises, the trading partner could bolster her reputation. Such a reputation mechanism could engender trust but required an information system to report reputations to new trading partners and allow those reputations to be updated. Almost from its inception, eBay used a feedback system that involved the posting of comments on a trade and a scoring rule to aggregate the feedback.

Feedback

The most important vehicle for establishing trust was feedback, which allowed buyers and sellers to evaluate each other based on their experiences in eBay transactions. They could rate the transaction experience as positive, negative, or neutral and could also provide a written evaluation. Members obtained points when they received positive feedback and lost them when they received negative feedback. The feedback record, both the total points or score and the comments, established a community member's online reputation. The score and comments were automatically available to potential trading partners whenever an item was listed for sale or a bid was made. Reputation represented an asset for a trader and was jealously guarded, since negative feedback could ruin a seller's business. The feedback system also allowed sellers to determine if bidders had paid promptly in the past.

Initially, community members could provide feedback even if they had not been involved in a specific transaction. For instance, a member might provide comments on how a seller had handled a request for additional information about a listed item. This "nontransactional" feedback was listed but was not reflected in the seller's numerical score. While this kind of feedback provided information, it also made the system vulnerable to "feedback bombing," an unhappy person flooding the system with feedback messages. Eventually, nontransactional feedback was eliminated. By late 2000 the system allowed only the parties to a transaction to provide feedback about each other.

Another issue was feedback removal. This was important because of the potential for feedback extortion. If feedback could be retracted, a buyer could give negative feedback and make a demand on the seller in exchange for removing the feedback. The importance of a member's online reputation made such threats serious. eBay's rules thus allowed removal of feedback only in specific situations, such as when it had been sent to the wrong address or when it contained personal information that was prohibited by another eBay policy. In cases not covered by the written policy, feedback was removed only by court order.

Although unwarranted feedback could not be removed, members could respond to the feedback given them, and the response was listed along with the original comment. For instance, a buyer might provide feedback stating that the seller was late in delivering. The seller might reply that he was waiting for the buyer's check to clear and report how long it had taken from receipt of the check to the shipment of the item. Potential bidders could evaluate the situation for themselves before deciding if they wanted to bid on an item offered by that seller.

Rules of Operation

The eBay community was subject to the laws that governed society as a whole ("public law," which creates a "public order") as well as to rules that eBay developed to supplement the feedback mechanism creating "private order" for its community. The rules eBay developed were intended to further the interests of the community, and of eBay, within the overall constraints of public law. Those rules were based on a guiding principle—do what is good for the community and what is good for the enterprise. eBay's community was subject to the public laws regulating sales. Sales of illegal goods, such as controlled substances, were prohibited, as were sales of counterfeit goods or sales of items such as software or music in violation of copyright laws.

Public law also prohibited fraud, such as failure to deliver the purchased item, listing an item with a misleading description, and manipulating auctions (for example, "shill" bidding in which the seller engaged accomplices to place bids intended to drive the price higher, which is illegal in some jurisdictions). eBay worked with law enforcement officials to assist victimized members and help ensure that community members could deal with each other in an atmosphere of trust. eBay's view of fraud was realistic. It believed that it could stop the amateur, but stopping the determined professional would be very difficult. To combat fraud, the company employed two former federal law enforcement officers and in both San Jose and Salt Lake City maintained support staff dedicated to fraud and piracy issues.

In addition to protecting the community from illegal activity, eBay's rules supported trust among members. Those rules were stated in the User Agreement that each member agreed to when registering to join the eBay community. Violations of the agreement were punishable by warnings and temporary or permanent suspension from eBay. The agreement was supplemented by policies, such as a detailed privacy policy, and processes, such as the feedback mechanism. These rules, policies, and processes constituted the private ordering of eBay.

Tools for Assisting Safe Transactions

In addition to the feedback system for building reputations, community members could use a number of tools to make their transactions more secure or to resolve disputes. Some of these were developed by eBay, while others were provided by third parties that contracted with eBay.

Insurance

Most purchases on eBay were protected by a free insurance policy administered by Lloyd's of London as part of the standard eBay service. The policy protected against items that were purchased but not delivered or those that were of substantially less value than described (such as bidding on a gold item and receiving a copper one). The policy provided coverage up to $200, with a $25 deductible.

Escrow

To protect buyers and sellers in high-value transactions, eBay contracted with Tradenable, a third-party escrow service company. The service was available with the agreement of both buyer and seller and was generally used for purchases of over $500. When using the service, the buyer paid the purchase price to Tradenable, which notified the seller. The seller shipped the item to the buyer. When the buyer received and accepted the item, Tradenable paid the seller. The escrow service fees were paid as agreed between the buyer and seller.

Payment Methods

Transactions took place directly between the buyer and seller; eBay was not a party to any transaction. Payment for an item was made in a manner agreeable to both buyer and seller. This might be by credit card, check, or through an Internet payment system. eBay established one such system, called Billpoint, through which buyers could establish an account that would be used to pay sellers. Similar systems, such as PayPal, were provided by third-party companies and were available to eBay traders.[65]

Dispute Resolution

Disputes between buyers and sellers occasionally arose. eBay believed that a respected, independent third party could assist in resolving these disputes. The company contracted with SquareTrade to provide a free online dispute resolution service for eBay members. When a member filed a complaint, it notified the other party, and the two could use online negotiation tools within a secure portion of the SquareTrade Web site to resolve the disagreement. Most conflicts were resolved using this system. If a dispute were not resolved using the online system, for a $15 fee the parties could request a Square-Trade mediator, who would mediate the dispute online.

Sellers could obtain a SquareTrade Seal if they agreed to participate in dispute resolution in the event of a problem, committed to SquareTrade's standards for online selling, and had their identity verified. The SquareTrade Seal then was displayed when they listed items for sale, providing additional information to buyers in evaluating the seller's trustworthiness.

---

[65]eBay subsequently acquired PayPal.

Authentication

For many items, confirmation of authenticity of items was important. eBay did not authenticate, as it never saw the items offered on its site. However, it did refer sellers to experts who could provide authentication services. Referrals were made for authenticating art works, stamps, coins, sports memorabilia, Beanie Babies, comics, and trading cards. Some buyers also hired their own experts to authenticate items before purchasing.

Trust in eBay

Trust between community members and eBay was also important. Three primary issues—privacy, community support, and fraud prevention—were central to that trust.

Community Support

As eBay grew, it learned that many users felt that it was their community and objected strenuously to unilateral changes by eBay. In one early case, eBay changed the system by which feedback scores were graphically displayed. That system used stars shown after the member's user name. The eBay employee charged with revising the system changed the colors of the stars, implementing the change without consulting the community. Two weeks of flaming e-mails, angry phone calls, and upset chatboard postings ensued. Finally, the employee rescinded the changes and asked the community members what they wanted. For two weeks she received input, leading to extensive dialog with the users. eBay learned that its community was powerful and wanted to be consulted on issues affecting it.

In 1997 there were only 40 categories of items for sale, but the postings increased dramatically and additional categories were needed. eBay evaluated the items listed and developed new listing categories, again without consulting the community. The result was 4 weeks of angry e-mails and phone calls. Not only were users passionate about their community, but they were also much more knowledgeable about the items traded than eBay employees could ever hope to be. Categories that made sense to a generalist were viewed as inappropriate by those with detailed knowledge of the items and how people collected them. For instance, there were many types of buttons of interest to different groups of traders. Eventually, four categories were created for buttons, three in the collectibles part of the site and one in the hobbies and crafts section.

Voices

These experiences led eBay to solicit user input in decisions affecting the community—primarily the features and functionality of the site. eBay customer service representatives were open with users and were required by the company to respond to user e-mails as quickly as possible. Ideas for changes were discussed with users, and

their comments were considered when making changes. eBay was uncertain whether the users participating were a vocal minority or if they represented the majority opinion. However, they were passionate, and passionate people were evangelists, accessible to anyone interested in the company, including competitors and investors. It was important for them to be committed to eBay.

When eBay went public in an IPO in 1998, communications had to be more controlled. The company was subject to SEC disclosure regulations and to intense scrutiny by the press. To continue communications with its community and at the same time exercise control over disclosures, a mechanism was needed to interact with its community while keeping pending changes confidential.

The company decided to form a group called "Voices," consisting of 12 people from the eBay community. eBay defined the types of people it wanted for Voices—initially a broad spectrum of buyers and sellers—and the community suggested candidates. Those selected agreed to participate for 1 year, without compensation, and to sign a nondisclosure agreement. They were brought to eBay for 2 days of meetings with key eBay personnel. eBay discussed its plans with the group but spent significant time listening to the group. After returning home, the group continued to discuss issues with eBay by e-mail and telephone.

New Voices groups were started each quarter, and occasionally a Voices group would be constituted for a shorter period to focus on a particular issue, such as how to improve the way in which eBay dealt with a specific item category. More generally, Voices helped eBay make better decisions on issues affecting the community.

In some cases, decisions were made without Voices input, as in the case of a legal requirement. Sometimes even these were discussed with one or more Voices groups before implementation or a public announcement. This allowed eBay to better understand the likely reaction of the community, implement the change more effectively, address anticipated concerns in the announcement, and prepare responses (FAQs) to concerns raised by the announcement.

Enforcement and Fraud Prevention

Members remained concerned about the potential for fraud even though the fraud rate was very low.[66] eBay actively supported law enforcement efforts to identify and prosecute fraud. When a member contacted eBay regarding potential illegal activity, eBay identified the appropriate law enforcement official and in some cases assisted in the investigation. In some cases the scope of

---

[66]The fraud rate on eBay was low, at approximately one case per 40,000 listings, in part due to eBay's efforts to prevent fraud and the community's vigilant policing efforts. However, the large number of listings on its site required continual diligence in identifying and eliminating fraud.

illegal activity was not apparent based on an initial complaint. eBay frequently was able to identify additional victims and put them in contact with the appropriate law enforcement officials.

Two cases illustrate eBay's involvement in detecting and prosecuting fraud. In one case, a seller offered a wide variety of items for sale, including sunglasses, Rolex watches, diamonds, rare coins, and computer equipment. However, the items did not exist. Buyers made their payments and received no goods. The buyers had no way of knowing the true identity of the person who had defrauded them. When eBay received complaints, it had the information needed to identify the seller and connect the victims with the appropriate law enforcement officials. eBay also determined who had "won" auctions from the fraudulent seller, notified them of the suspected fraud, and gave them the contact information. Without eBay's involvement, law enforcement could not have determined the full extent of the fraud or identified all the victims.

In another case, an unusual coin, described as an "1879c Morgan Hill Silver Dollar," was offered for sale. A photograph was included in the listing, showing the coin encased in a plastic container with a serial number from a grading service (an independent firm that authenticates coins). The bidding was heavy, reaching well over $100,000. A community member, who was a coin expert, contacted eBay to express his concern about the coin's authenticity. The member had never heard of the coin and suggested that eBay investigate. eBay's lawyers contacted the grading service. The service had never heard of such a coin, and the serial number in the listing corresponded to a Lincoln penny. Apparently, the seller had digitally created the photograph in the listing and was attempting to defraud buyers. eBay contacted the Secret Service, which investigated and arrested the seller.

eBay also formed a group to detect fraud by screening for suspicious activity using a profile. When it found potentially fraudulent behavior, it investigated further, and if necessary contacted potential victims and law enforcement officials.

Issues Facing eBay and Its Community

Many issues faced eBay and its rapidly growing community at the end of 2000. Addressing them in a manner that sustained trust among community members and between the community and eBay was essential to an increasingly diverse and dispersed community of traders. Four issues illustrate the challenges: communication between members, off-site transactions, the sale of controversial items, and recalled and regulated items.

Communication Between Members

Originally, members had access to all other members' e-mail addresses and thus could communicate directly with each other. When an item was listed for sale, the seller's e-mail address and the addresses of each bidder were also displayed. This was done to facilitate communication in the belief that visibility would encourage good conduct. It was a natural consequence of eBay's philosophy that "people are generally good."

As the community grew and more people became aware of eBay, problems arose. One problem was that outsiders could collect members' e-mail addresses ("e-mail harvesting") and use them for their own purposes, such as sending unsolicited e-mail ("spam").

eBay's competitors could also collect e-mail addresses and solicit business. In 1997 OnSale, Inc. sent unsolicited e-mail to eBay members announcing its competitive auction service. OnSale had used software to gather e-mail addresses from eBay's site.[67] OnSale had registered as an eBay member and thus agreed to the eBay User Agreement. Violation of the agreement was sufficient for eBay to force a halt to this practice.

In 1999 using information it had taken from the eBay database, another competitor, ReverseAuction, sent e-mail messages to eBay users, stating incorrectly that their eBay user IDs would soon expire and suggesting that they join ReverseAuction. In this case, the Federal Trade Commission intervened, resulting in a consent decree that forced ReverseAuction to notify eBay users who had registered with its site, prohibiting it from making further misrepresentations, and imposing other sanctions.[68] eBay later sued ReverseAuction and obtained a monetary award.

In addition to e-mail harvesting and spamming, privacy was a concern, as members did not want their e-mail addresses broadly publicized. However, it was still important for members to be able to communicate regarding transactions. A potential buyer needed to be able to ask questions of the seller. Buyers and sellers also needed to communicate after the auction was completed to finalize the payment and shipping arrangements and deal with any post-sale issues.

Some companies requested e-mail addresses from eBay. A manufacturer of crystal collectibles, for instance, would benefit from a list of all people who bid on items it had made, as well as those who bid on competitors' products. Such requests identified a potential business opportunity for eBay. It could partner with companies that were interested in selling to a highly targeted audience. Members with specialized interests might also see such partnerships as beneficial. However, providing member contact information to other companies or organizations was not possible within eBay's existing privacy policy.

---

[67]"Internet Spam," EDGE: Work-Group Computing Report, EDGE Publishing, November 10, 1997.
[68]Daniel R. Valente, "Database Protection in the Next Century," *Information Today*, June 1, 2000. The consent decree, filed in federal court on January 6, 2000, can be found at www.ftc.gov/os 2000/01/reverseconsent.htm.

The ability of users to communicate with each other for legitimate purposes, while protecting privacy and preventing spam, continued to pose problems. The eBay legal staff and community relations personnel were constantly assessing the balance between protecting the company and community versus the benefits of open communication. Should they place new restrictions on the community? How should they handle requests by manufacturers to partner and provide targeted e-mail lists?

Off-Site Transactions

Sales outside the eBay marketplace were a concern to eBay as an enterprise, since it did not receive fees for off-site transactions. The company was also concerned that off-site transactions deprived the participants of eBay's services in case of problems. The number of these transactions was unknown, but eBay believed that it was significant.

In one type of off-site transaction, the seller, after the auction, would note the e-mail addresses of losing bidders and contact them directly, offering to sell them the same or a similar item without going though eBay. The initial auction thus served as an advertisement for off-site sales. In another type, a buyer and seller that had a successful transaction using eBay might conduct additional business off-site in the future. Off-site transactions also occurred when sellers included hyperlinks in their listings that directed potential bidders to their own Web sites, where they could make purchases without going through eBay.

Off-site transactions were a difficult issue for eBay and its community. On the one hand, if off-site transactions were successful, its members would be happy and likely to continue to use eBay for other transactions. On the other hand, eBay lost revenue from off-site transactions, and members lost the protections eBay offered, such as feedback, insurance, payment options, and dispute resolution services. Moreover, if the off-site transactions were bad experiences for buyers, trust between eBay and the community could be weakened. In some cases, the buyer might be confused, thinking that the eBay protections applied to a purchase that had not been made on the eBay site.

In one case, a member sold a Rolex watch on eBay. The seller then contacted the second-highest bidder and offered to sell another Rolex. The person agreed, sending several thousand dollars to the seller. When he received the watch, he found that it was a fake. The member sued eBay (unsuccessfully) even though it had been an off-site transaction not covered by the User Agreement.

eBay advised its members not to participate in off-site transactions because of the potential risks. The User Agreement and Listing Policy prohibited practices that circumvented eBay's fee structure, such as the sale of catalogs that offered items for sale outside the eBay venue.[69] eBay believed that off-site transactions still caused a serious loss of business and potentially placed members in jeopardy. Was this something they should give high priority? What could eBay do to prevent off-site transactions?

Controversial Items

Items that were legal to buy and sell but were offensive to members of the eBay community were a concern. Three obvious examples were Nazi memorabilia, material from hate groups such as the Ku Klux Klan, and items associated with heinous crimes, sometimes called "murderabilia." While such items could be objectionable, they were legal to sell in the United States. Also, prohibiting their sale would represent a form of editorial censorship.

eBay's basic policy was that as long as the sale of an item was legal, it could be sold on the site. Exceptions were items subject to a myriad of local laws and regulations that made sale on eBay impractical, such as alcohol, tobacco, and firearms.

Items Related to Hate Groups This issue was contentious but not clear-cut. On the one hand, Nazi-related items might be offered for sale by a World War II veteran who had obtained them during the war. Such items might be of interest to museums, academic institutions, or history enthusiasts. On the other hand, a neo-Nazi group might try to use eBay to sell its paraphernalia. The seller could also try to express his or her philosophy and include hyperlinks to the group's Web site. The eBay listing policy prohibited hate speech and required that the listing be limited to things relevant to the sale of the item. The potential for abuse, however, existed.

eBay did not want to become, or be perceived as, a platform for the expression of hate. Such a perception might damage the company's reputation and cause people to avoid the site. Moreover, eBay recognized that just the knowledge that hate-related items were listed would disturb some members, weakening its community.

eBay was expanding internationally, and some countries, such as France and Germany, prohibited the sale of Nazi-related items. These items were not allowed on the Web sites serving France and Germany, but eBay's reputation could be harmed in those countries if the items were sold in the United States.

Items Related to Crimes There were several classes of items associated with notorious criminals and crimes. For instance, items associated with the assassination of President Lincoln were likely to be of historical interest and probably not widely objectionable. However, items associated with a recent mass murderer were likely to be objectionable to large segments of the eBay community and extremely traumatic to the families of the victims. If

---

[69]pages.ebay.com/help/community/png-list.html.

objectionable items should be prohibited, could this be done in an objective, fair manner?

Recalled and Regulated Items

Problems with the sale of recalled items first surfaced in early 2000, when a community member complained about a listing for "Jarts." eBay investigated and learned that a "Jart" was a lawn dart that had been recalled by the Consumer Products Safety Commission. They further learned that there were several such listings on its site.

eBay realized that members might be cleaning out their attics, selling old toys and other items without knowing that the items had been recalled. This was possible in a variety of categories, such as baby toys, cribs,

and power tools. In addition, some people might be unwittingly selling items made from endangered species or trading items internationally that were prohibited by import/export regulations. How could the company address the innocent sale of recalled products and other items that were prohibited by law without inhibiting the sale of other similar items that were legal? ■

SOURCE: This is an abridged version of a case prepared by Research Associate David Hoyt under the supervision of Professor David P. Baron. The case is based on public information and interviews with eBay employees. However, certain information has been deleted or revised for teaching purposes. Thus, some information may be presented that is factually incorrect. The case was edited by Mary Petrusewicz. Copyright © 2001 by the Board of Trustees of the Leland Stanford Junior University. All rights reserved. Reprinted with permission.

Preparation Questions

1. How did eBay's position as a venue affect the development of its community policies?
2. What are the fundamental problems eBay addressed in building trust among its members and between its members and the company? Are its policies and practices appropriate for building trust?
3. How do eBay's policies regarding communication between members affect the community? How might they hurt eBay? What should eBay do to optimize communication between members without negative results?
4. How do off-site transactions affect eBay and its community? What should the company do to address the issue of off-site transactions?
5. How should eBay address the sale of items associated with hate groups and crimes? How does the company's statement of values affect this issue?
6. What should eBay do regarding the potential sale of recalled products and other problem items?

-------------------------------------- P A R T   I I I --------------------------------------
Integrative Case
Credit Card Regulation

Credit cards provide a variety of services for consumers. They provide convenience while shopping. They serve as ATM cards. Many Americans also use theirs for regular unsecured borrowing. The economic slowdown in 2007–2008 caused hardship to many people. Consumers were burdened by rising energy and food prices, many were burdened by the mortgages crisis, and some saw themselves as victims of abusive practices by credit card issuers. Cardholders complained about a variety of practices ranging from penalty fees, suddenly adjusted interest rates, billing practices, repayments applied to the lowest interest rate balances, and fees for cash advances. Consumer protection was a major focus of Democrats when they won majorities in both houses of Congress in 2006, and in an election year dealing with credit card practices could be politically popular.

Credit card practices were largely unregulated, but disclosure of terms of card agreements was governed by Regulation Z of the Federal Reserve System. The Fed was under pressure because of the mortgage crisis and from critics who expected it to do more to stop credit card abuse. The Fed had initiated a new rule to consider strengthening disclosure requirements, and along with the Comptroller of the Currency (OCC) and the Office of Thrift Supervision (OTS) it issued for comment new rules not only to improve disclosure but also to ban certain abusive practices. Congress was also concerned about credit card practices, and bills had been introduced in the House and Senate to ban a variety of practices. The bills under consideration in Congress involved more restrictive regulation than the Fed's draft rules.

The credit card issuers opposed both the Fed's draft rules and the bills under consideration in Congress. The major issuers, however, had individual and collective reputations to maintain and were wary that any abusive practice on their part could damage their reputation. They had to devise a strategy for addressing the regulation issues contained in the draft rules and the bills.

Credit Card Usage[70]

The first credit card was issued by the Diners Club in 1950, and the first widely available card was issued by Bank of America in the late 1950s. Charges to credit cards increased from $69 billion in 1980 to $1.8 trillion in 2005. Household debt had increased from $59 billion to $830 billion over the same period, and credit card borrowing accounted for much of the increase. Consumers held nearly 700 million credit cards.

Until about 1990 credit cards charged a single interest rate of approximately 20 percent and charged few fees. The cards were generally available only to people with good credit ratings. The credit card industry was transformed by legislation that required the disclosure of information about credit card terms and conditions. This provided a basis for issuers to compete more intensely by providing information to consumers. Beginning about 1990 issuers began using risk-based, or individualized, pricing, which resulted in multiple interest rates and a variety of penalty fees. This resulted in more efficient pricing, and average interest rates fell and the percentage of people with cards increased. According to the GAO, "the top six issuers indicate that, in 2005, about 80 percent of their active U.S. accounts were assessed interest rates of less than 20 percent—with more than half having rates of 15 percent or less."[71] For 2005 the average interest rate was 12.3 percent for the 28 popular cards examined by the GAO. The GAO concluded that competition and the innovations in credit card terms resulted in lower interest rates.

Most consumers were convenience users and never paid a penalty fee. Thirty-five percent of cardholders paid a late fee, and 13 percent paid a penalty fee for being over the credit limit. The average penalty fee for a late payment or exceeding the credit limit was $32. For the six largest issuers, which accounted for 61 percent of all credit cards, about 48 percent of their cardholders did not pay a finance charge for at least 10 months in 2005. The six largest issuers reported that 11 percent of their cardholders paid penalty interest rates and 35 percent had been assessed a late fee. They reported that unpaid interest and fees represented only about 10 percent of the balances of those people who had filed for bankruptcy.

The Credit Card Industry

Some 6,000 depository institutions issued credit cards in 2005, but the share issued by the six largest issuers had increased over time. The six largest credit card issuers in terms of balances outstanding were Citigroup ($139.6 billion), Chase Card Services ($135.4 billion), MBNA America ($101.9 billion), Bank of America ($58.6 billion), Capital One Financial Corp. ($48.6 billion), and Discover Financial Services ($48.4 billion).[72]

---

[70]This section is based on the report by the General Accounting Office, "Credit Cards: Increased Complexity in Rates and Fees Heightens Need for More Effective Disclosures to Consumers," GAO-06-929, September 2006. The GAO study included structured interviews with 112 consumers conducted by a consulting firm and surveys of the largest 6 issuers, which did not include issuers who were primarily engaged in subprime lending.

[71]GAO, op. cit., p. 5.
[72]MBNA was acquired by Bank of America in 2005.

Credit card issuers participated in a card association such as MasterCard and Visa, both of which had gone public in recent years. When a consumer used a credit card in a store, the association cleared the authorization request by the acquiring bank used by the merchant, and when the consumer paid the bill sent by the issuer, the association transferred the funds to the acquiring bank. The acquiring bank received an average fee of approximately $0.50 on a $100 purchase, and the association received approximately $2.00 with the merchant receiving $97.50.

Issuers typically used variable and multiple interest rates on most of their cards. Rates varied with the market rate of interest and were often reset monthly. Issuers also used multiple interest rates depending on the use of the card. Different interest rates were used for cash advances, balances transferred from another credit card, and balances resulting from purchases. Recently, some issuers had begun offering low introductory interest rates for a limited period.

One factor driving the growth of the credit card industry was the advance in credit risk measurement that allowed card issuers to put cardholders into risk classes to which differential pricing was applied. This risk-based pricing allowed lower rates and better terms to be offered to low-risk cardholders and higher rates with more limitations to high-risk cardholders. This reduced the cost of capital to issuers and attracted entrants to the industry. Competition then in principle drove rates down to competitive levels. This also meant that one group of cardholders did not cross-subsidize other groups. Risk-based pricing also meant that when a cardholder's risk changed, the interest rate on credit card borrowing should change. For the issuers this meant a change on the entire borrowing rather than just on new borrowing.

The decline in interest rates was due to entry into the industry in addition to more efficient pricing.[73] Beginning in the early 1990s new banks, referred to as monoline banks, that focused only on credit cards entered the market. These new banks attracted customers by offering lower interest rates. Monoline banks included MBNA America, Providian Financial, and Capital One.

The decline in interest rates was also due to new disclosure rules instituted in 1988 that required issuers to provide information on interest rates and some fees in a tabular format referred to as the Schumer box. This increased consumer awareness of costs and led many to switch from one card to another, which intensified competition.

At the same time that average interest rates were decreasing, fees were increasing. Over time more of the funds collected by issuers were represented by penalty fees and less by interest payments. Late fees were also tiered. Most issuers had a smaller late fee for balances below $100 or $250, a higher fee for balances up to $1,000, and a yet higher fee for balances of $1,000 or more. Fees for exceeding the card credit limit increased by 95 percent between 1995 and 2005, and increasingly these fees were being tiered. In recent years, however, some cards had dropped their over-the-limit fees. Issuers had also introduced fees for foreign transactions and fees associated with convenience checks. While these fees had increased, annual fees had been eliminated on many cards.

Issuers also increased the use of penalty fees for cardholders whose risk had increased. These fees were imposed for late payments and exceeding the card limit. The GAO estimated that the industry collected $15 billion annually in penalty fees and $17 billion a year in overdraft fees. These penalty fees were typically described in disclosure documents accompanying a credit card. Beginning in the 2000s some issuers began assessing a cardholder's risk based on the holder's actions with respect to other creditors, such as mortgage lenders. This practice was referred to as "universal default" and often resulted in the repricing of balances at default rates. The OCC became concerned and required national banks to disclose these practices. Many issuers then stopped using universal default. The six largest issuers no longer used universal default.

Credit card companies continued to regularly review the risk associated with their unsecured lending on credit cards, and if the cardholder's credit rating had worsened or payments on mortgages or other consumer loans were delinquent, they could increase the interest rate on both existing and new balances. This was analogous to the cardholder borrowing short-term in the unsecured loan market.

Issuers were not prohibited from repricing rates, but they were required under Reg Z to notify cardholders in writing at least 15 days before any changes took place. In addition, in some states consumers had the opportunity to opt out of the higher fees. Bank of America, for example, allowed cardholders to opt out of higher rates and pay off their balances. Few consumers exercised this right.

Banks repriced cardholders when they were delinquent because the risk of default was higher on those accounts. Bank of America reported that cardholders who accepted a higher interest rate when delinquent were 50 percent more likely to default than the average customer.[74]

Another practice of issuers that drew the ire of cardholders was the allocation of payment when a cardholder paid down a balance. For most of the popular cards repayments were credited to the lowest interest rate balances, and those balances had to be fully repaid before higher-interest rate balances could be paid down. This increased the interest received by the issuer and made it more difficult for cardholders to reduce the burden of their borrowings.

---

[73]The issuers' cost of funds also decreased.

[74]George Baer, Bank of America, Testimony before the Subcommittee on Financial Institutions and Consumer Credit, March 13, 2008.

Complaints

The GAO reported that consumers had a variety of complaints about credit card policies. One complaint was that during an authorization sale cardholders were not blocked from making purchases that would put them above the card limit and yet later an over-the-limit fee was imposed. A consumer group also complained that a payment that was one day late did not warrant a large increase in the interest rate, as was the practice with some cards.

A complaint also came from a consumer who incurred a late fee, which then put her over the card limit, resulting in another fee. Consumers also complained about "any time, any rate" provisions that allowed an issuer to increase interest rates for any reason and at any time. A practice that drew the ire of consumers and consumer groups was double cycle billing. Some issuers charged interest on the portion of a balance that was repaid during the allowed payment window.

Other complaints centered on the penalty interest rates, which were frequently over 20 percent. Interest rates imposed in the event of universal default could be even higher. There was no federal cap on interest rates, and a 1978 Supreme Court decision held that a national bank was subject to the interest rate regulations of the state in which it was chartered and not to the interest rate regulations in the states where it did business. Credit card issuers then located in states with no cap on interest rates or with very high caps, effectively eliminating any limits on the interest rates charged. Rates were thus held down by competition rather than regulation.

Disclosure in the Schumer box was required on interest rates, fees, and how finance charges were calculated. For example, default-repricing fees were disclosed in the Schumer box. Reg Z, however, did not require disclosure of fees not related to the opening of an account. Fees for reproducing billing statements or for replacing a lost or stolen credit card or for making a payment by telephone did not have to be disclosed. Issuers, however, reported that they informed cardholders of these fees at the time they requested the service.

The interviews conducted for the GAO study revealed that many consumers did not understand the terms and conditions of their credit cards. The usability consultant hired by the GAO used standard software that analyzed text based on quantitative measures such as the number of syllables in words and the length of sentences. Half the adults in the United States read at or below an eighth-grade level, whereas the disclosures were gradually written at a tenth- or twelfth-grade level. The consultant concluded that solicitation letters required an eleventh-grade education and cardholder agreements required a twelfth-grade reading comprehension. A consumer advocacy group conducted a similar analysis and reached the same conclusion. The consultant also concluded that the material in agreements on annual percentage rates, grace periods, balance computation, and payment allocation methods required a fifteenth-grade education, whereas the description of fees in solicitation letters required only a seventh-grade level. There were also complaints about the organization and formatting of the information in disclosures. The GAO (p. 6) concluded that "The disclosure materials that consumers found so difficult to use resulted from issuers' attempts to reduce regulatory and liability exposure by adhering to the formats and language prescribed by federal laws and regulations, which no longer suit the complex features and terms of many cards." In particular, the regulations did not encourage issuers to group related information together.

The interviews with consumers identified specific aspects that were not well understood, including default interest rates, other penalty rate increases, late payment fees, using a credit card to obtain cash, grace periods, and balance computation methods. Some consumer groups also complained about marketing credit cards on campuses and the deals made between universities and issuers.

Regulation

Regulation of the credit card industry rested with the Federal Reserve Board for the disclosure of information (Reg Z) under the 1968 Truth in Lending Act (TILA). The Federal Reserve also was responsible for the Truth in Savings Act under which it had issued Regulation DD. The OCC supervised national banks, the Federal Deposit Insurance Corporation (FDIC) oversaw state-chartered banks that were not members of the Federal Reserve System but had federally insured deposits, the OTS oversaw savings associations with federally insured deposits, and the National Credit Union Administration oversaw credit unions with federally insured deposits. The Federal Trade Commission Act delegated responsibility for unfair or deceptive practices to the Federal Reserve for banks, OTS for thrifts, and the National Credit Union Administration for credit unions.

The 2005 Bankruptcy Abuse Prevention and Consumer Protection Act directed the Federal Reserve to implement new disclosure requirements such as explaining the implications of making only the minimum payments on credit cards. The Federal Reserve issued an advanced notice of proposed rulemaking requesting public comment on Regulation Z. The OCC urged the Federal Reserve to conduct in-depth interviews with consumers and use usability testing.

The Fed issued a proposed revision to Reg Z, but concluded that improved disclosure was not sufficient to provide fairness to consumers and that action had to be taken to prevent deceptive and unfair practices. Chairman Ben S. Bernanke said the draft Fed rules "are intended to establish a new baseline for fairness in how credit card plans operate. He pointed to issuers that reserved the right to change interest rates at any time and on balances already outstanding and allocated payments "to minimize the benefits of [promotional rates] and maximize interest charges."[75]

Federal Reserve Governor Randall S. Kroszner, chair of the Board's Committee on Consumer and Community Affairs, described some of the credit card practices as "traps for the unwary." He announced the new proposed rules under the authority assigned by the FTC Act.[76]

- Creditors were required to give consumers at least 21 days to make payments before being considered late.
- Creditors were prohibited from allocating payments to pay off the lowest interest rate balances first.
- Creditors could no longer increase interest rates on existing balances at any time except in limited circumstances such as when rates were indexed to a market interest rate or the account was delinquent for 30 days.
- Creditors could no longer use the two-cycle balance computation method.
- Subprime credit card offers in which prior to receiving the card most of the credit line was used up by security deposits and account opening fees were restricted.
- Creditors were prohibited from imposing fees because a hold (e.g., checking into a hotel and not knowing the final charges) put a balance over the limit.
- Overdraft fees were prohibited unless a consumer had been given the opportunity to opt out.

Consumer groups were pleased with the Fed's proposed rules but wanted legislation as well. Gail Hillebrand of the Consumers Union in San Francisco said, "It's about time federal regulators offered consumers some relief from unfair bank practices." Travis Plunkett of the Consumer Federation of America (CFA), said, "This is a good first step, but Congress still needs to act. More needs to be done."[77] The CFA and Consumers Union were joined in their statement by Consumer Action, National Consumer Law Center, Demos, Service Employees International Union, and U.S. PIRG.

The Fed's proposed rules were greeted with a mix of skepticism and hostility by issuers. Steve Frieberg, CEO of Citigroup's global cards business, commented, "Clearly, we're looking for more flexibility [in the rules]."[78] Dennis Moroney of the Tower Group said, "The riskiest consumers will be hit the hardest."[79] In strong language, Edward L. Yingling, head of the American Bankers Association, said, "The Federal Reserve's proposal is an unprecedented regulatory intrusion into marketplace pricing and product offerings. We are deeply concerned that these rules will result in less competition, higher consumer prices, fewer consumer choices and reduced consumer access to credit cards. In short, everyday consumers will bear the real cost of these proposals."[80] Kenneth Clayton, general counsel of the American Bankers Association, was more cautious: "While the proposal might address certain issues, it might unintentionally create bigger problems for consumers."[81] Paul Weston, executive vice president of ICBA Bancard, a unit of the Independent Community Bankers of America, said the rules would lead some community banks to stop issuing credit cards.

The 75-day comment period for the Fed's proposed changes to the regulations began, after which the Fed would weigh the comments and then issue final rules.

Legislation

A bill, The Credit Cardholders' Bill of Rights: Providing New Protection for Consumers, was introduced in the House in February 2008 by Representative Carolyn B. Maloney (D-NY), chair of the Subcommittee on Financial Institutions and Consumer Credit. The bill had the backing of the Financial Services Committee chair Barney Frank (D-MA) and was supported by consumer advocacy groups. Senators Christopher Dodd (D-CN) and Carl Levin (D-MI) introduced a bill, The Credit Card Accountability, Responsibility and Disclosure Act, to restrict credit card practices.

In August 2007 Maloney had proposed "Gold Standard" Credit Card Principles to provide guidance to credit card issuers. The principles were:[82]

- Issuers should issue credit cards on terms that the individual can repay.
- Issuers should clearly explain account features, terms, and pricing at relevant times.
- Issuers should provide customers notice and choice with respect to changes in terms.
- Issuers should encourage responsible, successful credit use, especially among new credit entrants and customers with special needs.

Maloney said, "One of the things consumers are very disturbed about is when they have a contract on a card and the terms change."[83] She also commented, "What they are most concerned about is when they are given fees and fines for things they were unaware of. Credit card customers ought to be able to fully understand their accounts and control them."[84]

---

[75]Ben S. Bernanke, Statement, May 2, 2008.
[76]Randall S. Kroszner, Statement, May 2, 2008. The OCC and OTS announced identical rules.
[77]*Los Angles Times,* May 2, 2008.
[78]*BusinessWeek,* May 26, 2008.
[79]*BusinessWeek,* May 26, 2008.

[80]*New York Times,* May 3, 2008.
[81]*BusinessWeek,* May 26, 2008.
[82]Carolyn B. Maloney, August 3, 2007.
[83]*Wall Street Journal,* February 7, 2008.
[84]*Washington Post,* December 2, 2007.

Maloney also said that banks' reliance on fees makes it "abundantly clear that we do need new laws and rules to protect consumers, to protect the market.... Financial institutions have a right to make a profit, but they don't have a right to make an extra profit because they messed up elsewhere," referring to their losses on mortgage lending.[85]

Maloney's bill had the following provisions:

- Prohibit universal default.
- Restrict "any time, any reason" interest rate changes.
- Require 45 days advance notice of interest rate changes unless the increase was due to expiration of an introductory rate or a change in an index market interest rate. Allow cancellation of an account without a fee in response to an advance notice.
- Prohibit double-cycle billing.
- Require information to be provided about the amount required to pay off a balance.
- Prohibit an issuer from reporting any information to a credit bureau before a card has been used.
- Require that payments on cards with multiple balances be allocated equally among the balances.
- Allow opt-out of over-the-limit fees.
- Require the Federal Reserve System to collect information on certain terms and practices such as the use of multiple interest rates.
- Prohibit within the first year subprime or "fee-harvester" cards from imposing fees in excess of 25 percent of the credit limit.

Issuers' Positions

Kenneth Clayton, head of the Card Policy Council of the American Bankers Association, expressed concern about legislation pertaining to credit cards: "It impacts our ability to price our products, manage risk, and ultimately our ability to offer low-rate competitive products for consumers." Maloney responded, "What the bill fosters is fair competition and the values of a free market. It includes no price controls, no rate caps, no fee setting, and it doesn't dictate any business models to companies."[86]

Carter Franke, senior vice-president of JPMorgan Chase testified before Representative Maloney's subcommittee "on behalf of the 20,000 Chase Card Services employees." He reminded the subcommittee that in 2007 Chase had implemented its *Clear & Simple* program making it easier to manage accounts and giving cardholders more options. For example, customers could stop courtesy approval of over-the-limit fees, could choose their own payment date, and set up automatic payments.[87] Chase also had stopped using credit bureau information on customers. He also pointed to the anticipated strengthening of Reg Z by the Federal Reserve. He stated that Federal Reserve action was "preferable to the legislation currently under discussion and that Congress should let the Fed's process continue to determine its effectiveness." He also stated that restrictions on individualized pricing would turn back the clock on the progress that has brought "credit cards to many more people at much lower average prices." He explained the importance of adjusting interest rates based on default risk and reported that 30 percent of late payers eventually defaulted on their loans. He said, "Whenever a bank's ability to adjust pricing at the first sight of default indications is diminished, our experience tells us that expensive defaults will rise." Default imposed costs on other customers, and those who defaulted could cut themselves off from mainstream credit, requiring them "to turn to payday lenders and sub-prime credit sources where interest rates can be extraordinarily high."

John G. Finnerman, Jr., general counsel of Capital One, also argued that action by the Federal Reserve was preferable to legislation. He reminded the subcommittee that Capital One did not engage in "Universal Default" pricing or double-cycle billing and imposed late fees only if a customer was late twice by more than 3 days during a 12-month period. Moreover, Capital One automatically "unrepriced" if the customer had no late payments for 12 consecutive months. He said that Maloney's bill would unfairly penalize issuers like Capital One that did not have abusive practices. He also argued against mandating a formula for how payments are applied to different forms of borrowing. He warned that interest rates would increase. ∎

Preparation Questions

1. How serious are the complaints by cardholders and advocacy groups? Why are issuers using the practices that draw the complaints?
2. Most people do not use their cards for borrowing. How does this affect the politics of credit card regulation?
3. Is regulation or legislation the better way to address serious complaints?
4. Can a promise of self-regulation by the major issuers divert the Fed and Congress from imposing more stringent rules on credit card practices?
5. What strategy should a large issuer such as Chase or Capital One adopt? What should be its primary and contingent objectives?

---

[85]*USA Today*, February 7, 2008.
[86]*Wall Street Journal*, February 7, 2008.

[87]Citi Cards also stopped universal default and "any time, any reason" repricing.

C H A P T E R

14

The Political Economy of Japan

INTRODUCTION

The characteristics of market and nonmarket environments of business differ across countries. These characteristics are important for the formulation of both market and nonmarket strategies. Market strategies are typically adapted to the tastes of local consumers even in the case of a global brand such as McDonald's or Toyota. In a similar manner nonmarket strategies must be tailored to the issues, interests, institutions, and information in individual countries. This chapter presents an approach to nonmarket strategy based on these characteristics using as the context the nonmarket environment of Japan. The emphasis is on political economy—the interaction between government, the public, and interests—and on strategies for addressing nonmarket issues. Chapters 15 and 16 present similar analyses for the European Union and China, respectively, and Chapter 17 considers emerging markets.

Culturally, Japan is relatively homogeneous, which facilitates the structuring of political and social activity. Cultural homogeneity is a consequence of a variety of factors, including Japanese isolation prior to 1853, its resistance to immigration, the absence of fundamental religious differences, relatively small regional differences, and a uniform national education system. This relative homogeneity combines with culture to generate a system in which consultation and consensus are easier to achieve and sustain than they are in many Western nations. Nevertheless, interests are often in conflict, and the willingness to sacrifice for the sake of tradition or for the good of the nation has diminished. The pluralism of interests in Japan is sufficiently diverse that interests are increasingly difficult to bring into agreement, and change is continual if not rapid.

A conventional perspective on understanding political and social structures in a country is based on cultural and historical explanations. For effective management in the nonmarket environment and for addressing specific nonmarket issues, cultural and historical explanations operate at too aggregate a level. On specific issues, interests are the primary driving force, and they and their actions must be the focus of analysis. Moreover, interests are diverse and change more rapidly than do culture and history. Culture and history remain important, but their role is in providing structure and continuity to political and social relationships. The pluralism of interests implies that the framework of structured pluralism introduced in Chapter 6 is the starting point for understanding the environment of business in a country.[1] That framework—modified to fit Japan by including the influence of culture and history—provides a basis for understanding the nonmarket environment and how firms address nonmarket issues in the context of Japanese political and social institutions. This perspective is illustrated in Figure 14-1.

---

[1]Curtis (1975, pp. 60–61) provides an early discussion on the pluralism of interests in the business community in Japan. See also Muramatsu and Krauss (1987).

FIGURE 14-1 Structured Pluralism and Culture and History

Structured Pluralism

- Interests change more rapidly than culture and history
- Interests motivate the action that shapes business opportunities
- Institutions intermediate between interests and opportunities

The political economy of Japan is complex and requires a more complete treatment than can be given here. The focus thus is on a characterization of the nonmarket environment in terms of the four I's—issues, interests, institutions, and information—and the cultural underpinnings of the interactions between interests and government. The organization of business in Japan differs from that in the United States due to long-term relationships, many of which are supported by patterns of interlocking ownership among firms. Because of the importance of government in the national economy and the extensive regulation and administrative guidance of many industries, firms in Japan develop a set of relationships with public officeholders and the bureaucracy. Some of these relationships are formalized by a system of advisory committees and consultation processes. Others are developed and maintained through political contributions, the hiring of retired bureaucrats, and personal connections. Firms not only develop relationships but also develop the ability to monitor government activities to obtain the information needed to interact effectively with the political parties, the parliament, and the bureaucracy. These relationships provide the foundations for lobbying, electoral, and coalition-building strategies and for their integration with market strategies.

The chapter begins with a characterization of the nonmarket environment, with an emphasis on issues involving government. The institutional focus is on the parliament and the legislative process, the political parties, and the bureaucracy. The judicial system and the antimonopoly law are then considered. Cultural foundations are identified, and a framework for political exchange is presented to tie together these components. The organization of business is then considered with an emphasis on business–government interactions. Nonmarket strategies based on information, lobbying, and interactions with the bureaucracy are discussed. The chapter concludes with a consideration of corporate nonmarket styles. The chapter cases, *The Breakup of Nippon Telephone and Telegraph?, The Privatization of Japan Post,* and *Uniqlo: Success Breeds Nonmarket Challenges,* provide opportunities to consider strategy formulation in the context of the structural pluralism framework.

ISSUES

The principal systemic-level issues in the political economy of Japan have centered on deregulation of the economy, a massive financial crisis, a sluggish economy, a large government budget deficit, a large trade surplus, and political reform and stability. The

Japanese economic miracle ended at the beginning of the 1990s with the bursting of the real estate bubble that had driven prices to astronomical levels. Land prices in the business districts of six major cities fell by over 80 percent between 1990 and 1999. Growth was sluggish during the 1990s and worsened with a recession commencing in 2001. The Nikkei stock average reached a 16-year low, and unemployment reached a postwar high of 5.4 percent in 2001. Most of the large banks had huge nonperforming loans from earlier real estate lending and continued to carry the loans on their books. Since 2003 the economy has been growing, although at a rate far below the growth rates in the 1970s and 1980s.[2]

Government efforts to resuscitate the economy were having little success. The government lowered to zero the discount rate—the interest rate at which the Bank of Japan lends to banks—but the principal instrument used to attempt to stimulate the economy was fiscal policy. The government had increased public spending to the point at which the budget deficit reached 8 percent of GDP and public debt reached 130 percent of GDP. The economy not only was stagnant but deflation was occurring. Consumer and producer prices in 2001 were below 1995 price levels because cheap imports from East Asia poured into the country as consumers sought lower priced goods and firms sought to reduce their costs. The trade surplus with the United States was still large, but Japan was running a large and growing trade deficit with China. Corporate profits had plunged, and 15 major banks had approximately $145 billion of bad loans. Despite Japan's economic woes, personal income remained high and Japanese exports were strong.

The recent economic recovery has been important domestically, but it has contributed to a global problem. Japan's greenhouse gas emissions have been increasing. The country's 2012 target under the Kyoto protocol is to reduce its emissions 6 percent below 1990 emissions. As of March 2007 Japan's greenhouse gas emissions were 6.4 percent above 1990 levels.

Japan also faced serious demographic problems. Its population was aging; by 2020, 27.4 percent of the population would be 65 and older. Their retirement and health care costs would have to be borne by a shrinking workforce. Moreover, the birth rate was low, and if it did not increase, the population would decrease dramatically, according to one government forecast.

Japan also faced a set of specific issues including the further opening of domestic markets to international competition, the evolution of antitrust policy, and specific legislative and deregulation measures pertaining to particular industries. Managers in Japan faced the challenge of developing strategies to address the proposed deregulation measures in the context of a sluggish economy and pressure for more rapid economic reforms. In a 2008 study the OECD ranked Japan's energy sector last among wealthy countries in terms of openness and protection by regulators. Investor groups outside Japan began to pressure the government to lift restrictions.

As an example, the financial services industry in Japan was heavily regulated by the Ministry of Finance (MOF). The industry faced a set of issues arising from both within the industry and outside the country. Japan's foreign trade surplus and the difficulty foreign firms had in entering the Japanese market had generated continuing pressure for change. Under pressure from the United States and the European Union, the financial services markets were gradually being opened. Some liberalization of the insurance industry, for instance, had resulted from external pressure that led the government to allow entry into the auto and commercial fire insurance markets. In 1995 Japan and the United States reached an agreement that allowed a broader set of foreign firms to compete for the management of Japan's $1 trillion pension fund market—a market in which only trust banks and insurance companies had been allowed to operate. By 1999 other insurance markets were deregulated, and insurers were no longer required to use the rates set by the national rating agency.

---

[2]Ito (1992) provides information on the structure and performance of the Japanese economy.

The Ministry of Finance forced the banks to shed some of their nonperforming loans by writing off bad debts, which in 2 years decreased from $400 billion to $242 billion, and the major banks consolidated into four large banks. The government reduced the budget deficit and undertook a program of privatizing government-owned companies. The economy began to grow in 2003, and deflation stopped. Optimism returned.

A major issue facing the financial services industry was the government's huge postal savings system, which was the world's largest bank and largest life insurance company. The postal savings system offered high interest rates on deposits, providing what the banks viewed as unfair competition. The postal savings system had $12 trillion in deposits and insurance policies. Since the early 1990s deposits in the postal savings system had increased 73 percent, and deposits in banks had decreased 15 percent. The banking and insurance industries urged privatization of the postal savings system, and economists argued that it was distorting the capital markets by funneling funds into quasi-government companies that provided public projects to maintain voter support for the government. The chapter case, *The Privatization of Japan Post,* considers these issues in more detail.

INTERESTS

Interests in Japan are pluralistic, as they are in the United States. In the United States, however, coalitions are fluid and frequently issue-specific, and interactions with the government are often episodic. In Japan, interests are also varied, but coalitions in Japan are less fluid, and patterns of interaction with government are structured by formal and informal long-term relationships. If Japanese businesses disagree on a trade issue, they are more likely to seek consensus within industry and general business associations and then consensus with the government. They are less likely to contest the issue in public. Business, however, is not a unified interest group in its interactions with government. Interactions with government are conducted by peak organizations, such as the Keidanren (Federation of Economic Organizations), *keiretsu* (business groups), industry associations, and individual firms. Cross-shareholdings in *keiretsu* result in complex aggregations of interests that cannot be as issue-specific as they are in the United States.

The interactions among firms, the governing political parties, and the bureaucracy are complex and intermediated by a set of formal and informal arrangements. Advisory committees established by government ministries facilitate communication, policy formulation, and consensus building between the bureaucracy and interest groups. The career path links between the political parties and the bureaucracy facilitate interactions between them. Also, many high-ranking bureaucrats take positions in business or seek elected office after they retire, which facilitates the coordination of nonmarket activity.

Japan does not have an encompassing labor movement as do countries such as Sweden and Germany. In Japan, employees of large corporations are unionized, but the unions tend to represent workers at a single enterprise. These enterprise unions are linked in federations and associations, but union members in Japan identify with both their employer and their union. Enterprise unions are not required by law but evolved in the 1950s as a result of conflict between business and national unions, which had adopted a radical posture. Business defeated the national unions, and most workers organized into enterprise unions and focused on employment-specific matters, although some radical elements remained. The movement of jobs offshore and the decline in some unionized industries resulted in a decline in union membership with only 19.6 percent of the workforce belonging to a union.

Japan has activist and public interest groups, but in contrast to the United States they are fewer in number, less active, and less demonstrative. Dispersed groups, such as consumers and urban residents, are neither well organized nor broadly represented. Their direct influence in the nonmarket environment is thus limited, but political parties attempt to anticipate the interests of these "floating voters" to garner their electoral support.

INSTITUTIONS

The Japanese government was modeled after the British parliamentary system, but it has uniquely Japanese characteristics and an overlay of American-style institutions. The country has 47 prefectures, each headed by a governor, and each has its own government—as do cities and municipalities. The powers of the prefecture governments, however, are considerably less extensive than those of state governments in the United States.[3] The principal institutions of Japanese government are the Diet (Parliament), the electoral and party systems, and the bureaucracy. In addition to its parliamentary structure, Japan has a constitution that guarantees individual rights and a supreme court with the power to declare laws unconstitutional.

The Diet

The government is parliamentary, so the executive and the legislature are aligned. The Diet is composed of two houses with unequal powers.[4] The lower house, the House of Representatives, elects the prime minister and is the more powerful and the focus of most legislative activity. For example, it can enact legislation by a two-thirds vote even if the upper house disapproves it. The upper house, the House of Councillors, can block legislation unless overridden by a two-thirds vote in the lower house. The lower house can vote no confidence in the prime minister, which requires him to either resign or dissolve the lower house and call new elections. The Liberal Democratic Party (LDP) had been in continuous control of the lower house since 1955, but as a result of scandals and its failure to enact electoral reforms, it lost its majority in 1993. Several groups of dissident LDP members split from the party, resulting in party fragmentation and shifting government coalitions. The LDP, however, remained the largest party and returned to office shortly thereafter, leading coalition governments. In 2008 the LDP had a majority of the seats in the lower house and had lost its majority in the upper house.

The lower house has 480 members. Electoral reform enacted in 1994 replaced multimember districts by a system in which the majority of members are elected from single-member districts and the rest are elected under a proportional representation system. Elections are scheduled every 4 years, but under the parliamentary system the prime minister may call an early election. The upper house has 252 members who serve 6-year terms, with half elected every 3 years. One hundred "national constituency" members of the upper house are elected at large through a proportional representation system. The rest are elected by prefectures, each of which has at least two seats.

In a parliamentary system, a government—the prime minister and the cabinet—serves with the consent of the parliament—the support of a majority of the members of the lower house. A majority party can thus form a government, but in the absence of a majority party, a coalition is required. Even if it has a majority the LDP may form a coalition government as it has done with the New Komeito Party since 2005. In forming a coalition government, parties bargain over the allocation of ministries among the parties, the selection of the prime minister, and the principal policies the government will implement. The prime minister is elected by the lower house, but in practice the president of the LDP is prime minister. In 2008 Yasuo Kukuda was prime minister and president of the LDP.

The government is of the cabinet form, with the cabinet assuming collective responsibility for policy. The cabinet consists of the ministers who head the principal ministries plus the heads of a few other agencies. The prime minister does not have formal powers with regard to legislation, as the U.S. president has through the veto. The prime minister, however, has a number of crucial roles, including convener of the cabinet, spokesman for the government, and representative of the nation in international affairs. The prime minister consults with coalition parties and key interest groups and at times with opposition leaders before taking major initiatives. Decisions often await the

---

[3]See Reed (1986).
[4]See Baerwald (1974).

development of consensus. On some issues the prime minister must build majorities to support policy reforms, as in the chapter case, *The Privatization of Japan Post.*

The houses of the Diet have a committee structure. The lower house has standing committees, most of which corresponded to the principal ministries and agencies. In addition to dealing with the budget, the Budget Committee serves as a forum for questioning the cabinet about policies. Diet committees have relatively small staffs, and many staff members are provided by the ministries themselves. Since much of the major legislation is written in the ministries, the Diet committees have traditionally been weak compared with the bureaucracy. During the past decade, however, the Diet has exercised more power, and committees have begun to play a more significant role.

Political Parties and the Electoral System

The 1994 electoral reforms replaced multimember districts with a majority of single-member, plurality-winner districts with proportional representation used for the rest of the seats. A single-member district system typically leads to a two-party system, whereas proportional representation results in many parties.[5] Existing parties have splintered, new parties had formed and many dissolved, and coalitions had come and gone.[6] Some members had left the LDP to form new parties, and those parties formed the opposition. The opposition was led by the Democratic Party of Japan (DPJ), which had merged with the Liberal Party.

Electoral reform was spurred by scandals involving large contributions by businesses to the LDP and other political parties. One of the rationales for establishing single-member districts was to eliminate the competition for funds among members of the same party, which was prevalent in the previous system of multimember districts. The reforms included public financing of parties based on the number of votes received.

Contributions to parties and candidates in Japan have been important not only for electoral purposes but because members of the Diet seek to develop personal relationships with constituents. Among other things this involves holding parties, attending weddings and funerals at which gifts are typically given, and organizing excursions for constituents. To maintain constituency support, many Diet members have a *koenkai,* a local organization that serves to organize and mobilize support for the member. Because of restrictions on electoral campaigns, a *koenkai* is officially a cultural organization, and as Reischauer (1988, pp. 264–265) indicates, it conducts constituency activities on a year-round basis. Curtis (1999) argues that *koenkai* have become more important with the fragmentation of the political parties.

One function of a Diet member is to represent constituents' interests not only in the Diet but also before the bureaucracy. For example, Asao Mihara, an LDP member of the lower house from Fukuoka, "has to spend nearly all his time and most of the funds he can collect from supporters acting as a middleman between his constituents and the central government in Tokyo. This includes submitting petitions to bureaucrats on behalf of local businessmen and steering central government-funded public works projects in the general direction of Fukuoka."[7]

Members of the Diet also participate in groups, known as *zoku,* that intermediate between interest groups and the bureaucracy. *Zoku* are important to a ministry because they can represent the ministry's interests in the Diet and the LDP when there are interministerial disputes. In exchange for this support, the ministry may serve the interests that provide the political support for the *zoku* members. In addition to the *zoku,* Diet members have formed caucuses that support policies that cut across both factions and *zoku.* The principal function of the *zoku,* however, is to represent interest groups. The agriculture *zoku* succeeded in obtaining $60 billion over 6 years for relief for rice farmers who had been hurt by the opening of the Japanese market to imports.

---

[5]Duverger's (1954) law predicts that single-member, plurality-winner districts will result in two-party competition, since with three or more parties some votes will be wasted. A proportional representation system can sustain more parties.
[6]See Curtis (1999) for an analysis of the parties through the 1990s.
[7]*Far Eastern Economic Review,* March 9, 1989.

The construction *zoku* supports the construction industry before both the ministry for construction and the political parties.

Party Organization

Parties play an important role in governing in a parliamentary system. A majority party resolves a variety of matters internally, including proposed legislation before it goes to the legislature. Because the LDP has been the largest party in Japan, its structure and functioning are considered here.

Although it is conservative in its orientation, the LDP is neither strongly ideological nor homogeneous, nor does it have a well-defined legislative program. Instead, its program arises out of the work of the party, the Diet, and the bureaucracy. The LDP is a flexible collection of interests and politicians who have mutual incentives in governing.

The LDP is composed of factions. The factions are not ideological but form around leaders and provide a base from which the leader can seek top ministerial positions.[8] Because the size of the factions is important in intraparty bargaining and the subsequent distribution of rewards, LDP leaders attempt to increase the size of their factions by attracting junior Diet members. For a member of the Diet, a faction provides a vehicle for reaching higher office and a means of participating in legislative activity. LDP members have an incentive to join a faction because the success of the faction and its leader could be important to their personal advancement in the party and appointments to positions in the government.[9]

The LDP has developed an extensive internal decision-making process formalized in the Policy Affairs Research Committee (PARC).[10] PARC has sections, the policy jurisdictions of which correspond to the ministries and Diet committees. PARC takes positions on issues before the government. For example, the posts and communications section of PARC opposed the privatization of Japan Post.

The Legislative Process

The policy formation and legislative process is illustrated in Figure 14-2. The top portion of the figure represents the bureaucratic component of the legislative process, as considered in the following section. The lower portion represents the components of the process that take place within the governing party or coalition. In both portions, interest groups are consulted early in the development of policies. Interest group activity thus begins before the Diet considers legislation.

In the lower portion of the figure, PARC committees formulate policies and at times draft legislation, although most legislation is written by the bureaucracy. The draft legislation is reviewed by the government's executive committee, which includes representatives of all the parties in the governing coalition. Once the proposal is approved by the executive committee, it is forwarded to the appropriate ministry. Next, it goes to the cabinet for approval; if it is approved there, it is submitted to the Diet. Legislation drafted by a ministry passes through a similar process.

By the time a bill is introduced in the Diet, consensus has been developed within the policymaking apparatus of the governing coalition, support has been obtained from the bureaucracy, and the cabinet has given its approval. In addition, the government may have negotiated with the opposition parties on the legislative process for a bill.[11] Thus, most of the legislative work has been completed before the bill is introduced in the Diet. In many cases, Diet consideration involves going through the formalities—the outcome has been determined long before a vote is taken. Interest groups thus have a strong incentive to be involved early in this process and to develop relationships with the bureaucracy and the parties to obtain access to the policymaking process. Because Diet action comes at the end of the policymaking process, much of the interest group activity and nonmarket competition takes place out of the public view.

---

[8]In 2008 the LDP had five principal factions identified by the name of their leader: Machimura, Tsushima, Ibuki, Koga, and Tanigaki

[9]Prior to the public funding of elections, factions were used to raise campaign funds for their members.

[10]See Reischauer (1988, pp. 273–274) and Fukui (1970, pp. 83–89).

[11]See Curtis (1999, pp. 118–120).

FIGURE 14-2   Policy Formulation and Legislative Process

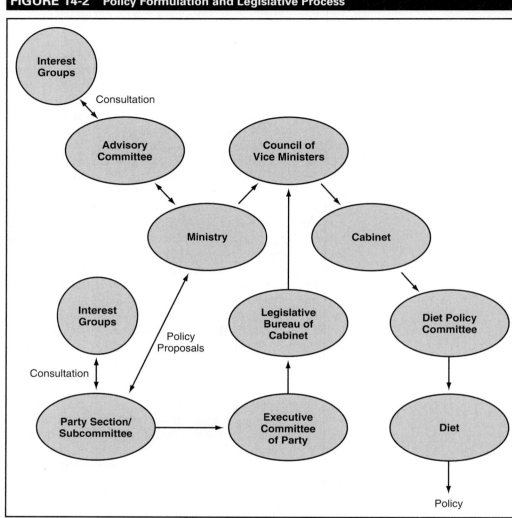

The Bureaucracy
Structure and Power

The bureaucracy in Japan has traditionally been viewed as the central force in government, and interactions with the bureaucracy have been essential to many businesses. Japanese culture confers respect on the bureaucracy, but its status has also been due to its expertise, dedication to the national interest, the innovativeness and leadership some ministries have demonstrated, and the economic prosperity Japan has enjoyed. The bureaucracy has also developed exchange relationships with interest groups that give it the political strength needed to develop and administer policies in its jurisdictions. In the 1990s, however, scandals and poor economic performance reduced public confidence in the bureaucracy.[12]

The ministries differ significantly in their functions and their importance. The Ministry of Economy, Trade and Industry (METI), has a planning and economic rationalization function and is the lead ministry in international trade negotiations. The posts and telecommunications ministry has a substantial regulatory role, and the construction

---

[12]As an example of a scandal that reduced the respect for the bureaucracy, to benefit certain pharmaceutical companies the Ministry of Health and Welfare delayed the introduction of heated blood products that reduce the risk of HIV infection. Hundreds of people unnecessarily contracted AIDS because of the delay. As another example, in 2001 the Ministry of Foreign Affairs revealed a kickback and entertainment slush fund system that led to the firing of two senior bureaucrats and the disciplining of 326 other civil servants.

ministry plays an important role in the expenditure of government funds. Japan does not have a system of separate regulatory commissions, so many ministries have regulatory as well as policy and administrative responsibilities.

A ministry is generally headed by a politician from one of the government parties. The ministry is administered by two vice ministers. The parliamentary, or political, vice minister is a member of the lower house of the Diet, who typically is rotated through the position. The day-to-day affairs of the ministry are supervised by the administrative vice minister, who is a career civil servant.

A ministry has influence as a function of several factors. The two most important are (1) its expertise in resolving problems and devising effective policies and (2) its authority to direct resources or control economic activity through guidance, regulation, and the allocation of government funds.[13] One source of power of the bureaucracy is its ability to act without having to enact new laws. The ministries have considerable discretion within their jurisdictions and often use informal administrative guidance to implement their policies.

Ministries such as METI have in some cases been effective in encouraging the development of certain industries, but the power of the ministries is found less in their industrial policies than in their regulatory, licensing, resource allocation, and supervisory functions. Many regulatory requirements are nontransparent, causing particular difficulty for foreign and other firms unfamiliar with the system. This requires firms subject to the requirements to maintain relationships with the bureaucrats to obtain needed information.

Ministries in Japan also have been powerful because of the absence of separate regulatory commissions. The MOF, for example, had formal authority over tax collection, the government budget, financial market regulation, tax policy, and the regulation of financial institutions. In the United States these are the responsibility of, respectively, the Internal Revenue Service, the Office of Management and Budget, the Securities and Exchange Commission, the Department of the Treasury, and for the regulation of financial institutions the Federal Reserve System, the Comptroller of the Currency, the FDIC, and the Office of Thrift Supervision. Although an independent agency, the Bank of Japan (the central bank) has been informally controlled by the MOF. The administrative vice ministers and senior bureaucrats at a number of agencies also come from the MOF.

In the mid-1990s the bureaucracy came under criticism from business, the public, and politicians who argued that it was impeding the deregulation needed to improve the efficiency of a number of sectors of the economy in which regulation served to protect firms and the status quo. Shoichiro Toyoda, chairman of Toyota, argued, "Japan must shift from an economy burdened by regulations and bureaucracy to one in which the private sector can operate unfettered. We must also downsize the public sector and create a small, efficient government."[14] Such criticism led to a restructuring of the ministries in 2001, as considered later in the chapter.

Career Bureaucrats

The bureaucracy attracts some of the best university graduates in Japan, which adds to its expertise and contributes to its influence. In 1997, 45,000 applicants from universities took the advanced civil service examination for 780 positions in the senior civil service. The ministries choose from among the successful candidates. The MOF chooses first, and the Ministry of Internal Affairs and Communication (MIC) and METI choose next. These new bureaucrats become members of the career *gumi*, or career team. At the Ministry of Finance approximately 800 of the 80,000 employees are career bureaucrats. Graduates of Tokyo University (Todai) dominate the highest ranks of the ministries; its graduates held the administrative vice minister post in 11 of the 12 ministries

---

[13]The expertise of the bureaucracy was accentuated because the prime minister, Diet members, and the Diet committees had very small staffs, requiring the politicians to rely on the ministries for information and expertise.

[14]*New York Times,* April 17, 1997.

in 1994. In 1994, 90.5 percent and 78 percent of new MOF and METI classes, respectively, were composed of Todai graduates.

The class that enters a ministry constitutes a cohort that moves up, and eventually out of, the ministry hierarchy together.[15] Throughout this process, no member of a cohort will be in a position of hierarchical superiority to another member of the same cohort.

Job rotation is an important part of the career path of a bureaucrat, and a shuffle of positions occurs every June. Job rotation develops the breadth and human capital needed for a consensual system in which conflicts are resolved through bargaining and accommodation. It also reduces the likelihood that a bureaucrat will become too closely allied with interest groups that could exert unwarranted influence and divert the ministry from its mission.

The links between ministries and business are facilitated by the *amakudari* ("descent from heaven") system.[16] After 30 years in a ministry, one member of the cohort will become a vice minister. During this period others will resign and "descend" to careers in universities, business, public enterprises, or a government-owned financial institution such as the Export-Import Bank. Others will run for political office; approximately one-third of the LDP Diet members in 1994 were former bureaucrats. Postretirement employment tends to be easiest for bureaucrats from ministries that have regulatory authority over industries, since those industries are most in need of the relationships and information channels the ex-bureaucrats can provide. One factor in the chapter case, *The Breakup of Nippon Telephone and Telegraph?*, was a ministry's concern for the placement of its career bureaucrats.[17]

Advisory Committees

The links between the bureaucracy and business are strengthened by over 200 ministerial advisory committees composed of bureaucrats, Diet members, representatives of relevant business and labor organizations, academics, and others. The explicit purpose of the advisory committees is to develop consensus on policies, regulations, or standards before they are proposed as legislation or implemented by the bureaucracy. The ministries also use advisory committees to persuade business and other interest groups to support—or at least not to oppose—the policy directives the ministry seeks to implement. The advisory committees also serve as communication channels that keep the bureaucracy informed about issues of concern to interest groups and keep the interest groups informed about the activities of the ministry.

Political Reform

The slumping economy and old-style politics provided an opportunity for economic and political reform. Reform was popular with the public and brought Prime Minister Koizumi into office. One reform objective was to rein in the soaring budget deficit. Japan had attempted to spend its way out of its economic slump, but critics argued that this strategy resulted only in high deficits and a soaring public debt. The new government pledged not to use government spending to stimulate the economy. One benefit of controlling the government budget deficit was to reduce pork barrel spending, which was one of the foundations for the "pipe" through which public expenditures flowed to the local level.

Criticism of the government, continuing scandals, a stagnant economy, and weakening electoral support led the LDP to reform the government. The reform, implemented in 2001, had three components: (1) increase the power of the cabinet relative to the bureaucracy, (2) restructure the bureaucracy, and (3) streamline the government.

---

[15]See Atsuyuki (1978) for a description of a bureaucrat's career. Bronte (1982, p. 137) describes the cohort process in some detail. See "Inside MOF; The Men from the Ministry," *Tokyo Business Today,* January 1995, for a description of the career path in the MOF.

[16]Amakudari bureaucrats are to wait 2 years before joining a firm that deals with their ministry, but they can obtain a waiver of the requirement from the National Personnel Authority (*Japan Economic Journal,* May 26, 1990).

[17]See Yayama (1998, pp. 109–111) for a discussion of NTT and the interests of bureaucrats.

FIGURE 14-3 Ministries

- Cabinet Office
- Internal Affairs and Communication
- Justice
- Foreign Affairs
- Finance
- Education, Culture, Sports, Science, and Technology
- Health, Labour, and Welfare
- Agriculture, Forestry, and Fisheries
- Economy, Trade, and Industry
- Land, Infrastructure, and Transport
- Environment

To increase the power of the prime minister and the cabinet, a ministerial-level Cabinet Office was established with a staff and administrative responsibilities. The Financial Services Agency (FSA) became part of the Cabinet Office and had regulatory, planning, and inspection responsibilities formerly held by the MOF. In 2004 the FSA ordered Citigroup to close its private banking operations in Japan after finding a series of violations of regulations.[18] The Cabinet Office formally has greater power than any of the ministries.

The bureaucracy was reformed by merging some of the ministries and establishing a new Ministry of the Environment. The ministries are listed in Figure 14-3. Their number was reduced from 12 to 10, and some of their implementation responsibilities were separated from their policymaking responsibilities. A set of Independent Administrative Institutions (IAIs) were established to assume implementation responsibilities. The IAIs are autonomous institutions associated with ministries and responsible for implementing policies. They are subject to external, independent ex post evaluation of their performance. The establishment of the IAIs was intended to reduce the influence of interests on the administration of policies and regulations.

The reform was also intended to streamline the national government and downsize the personnel by 25 percent. This involved the elimination and consolidation of bureaus and divisions within the ministries. For example, the Pearl Inspection Station was eliminated. The streamlining also involved delegating some responsibilities to local governments.

Part of the old-style politics centered on the public and quasi-public corporations, many of which had close connections with the LDP. Japan had 77 public corporations supported by government financing and another 86 quasi-public corporations. The Japan National Oil Corporation, for example, had losses totaling $3.5 billion at the time. The Japan Highway Public Corporation had been criticized for waste and pork barrel spending. Privatizing these companies would both improve economic efficiency and eliminate their use for political purposes. Many of these companies, however, had considerable support from within the LDP and the ministries. The government planned to privatize the public highway corporations, expressway corporations, and a bridge authority. In 2004 Japan began the privatization process for two companies, Impes, an oil and gas producer, and the Electric Power Development Company.

An important component of the government's economic reform program was to privatize the postal savings system. Its $2 trillion of deposits made it the largest savings system in the world, and it was also the world's largest life insurer. Japan Post was said to have an unfair competitive advantage over banks and insurance companies. It was also used to funnel funds to support political objectives. The postmasters, an important support group for the LDP, opposed privatization. The privatization of Japan Post posed a major challenge for the government, as indicated in the chapter case.

---

[18]Citigroup also closed another subsidiary in Japan as a result of compliance problems.

THE JUDICIAL SYSTEM AND THE ANTIMONOPOLY LAW

The Japanese judicial system is patterned after the civil code systems of continental Europe rather than the adversarial system found in the United Kingdom and the United States. Japan has no common law but has antitrust, labor, and securities laws patterned after those in the United States. A striking feature of the Japanese legal system has been the reliance on conciliation of disputes. The Japanese people traditionally place great value on harmony and the absence of confrontation and conflict. They seek to resolve disputes "within the family" without recourse to the courts, and hence there has been a low demand for the resolution of disputes in the courts. Van Wolferen (1989, p. 214) reported that Japan had one lawyer for every 9,294 citizens, compared with 1 for every 360 in the United States and 1 for every 1,486 in Germany.

Japan has an Anti-Monopoly Law (AML), which is enforced by the Fair Trade Commission (FTC). Enforcement is different from that in the United States for cultural reasons, say its proponents—or by intention, say its critics. Frequently, when the FTC concludes that a company has violated the AML, it issues a warning.[19] This administrative sanction is said to be a mark of shame that both causes the practice to end and serves as a deterrent to others. In 2003 the FTC ordered Intel to stop tying discounts on microprocessors to promises not to purchase microprocessors from rivals. Fines are also used and have been increased to bring them closer to those in the European Union and the United States. Criminal charges are rarely brought against executives found to have violated the AML.[20]

Critics contend that the FTC does more to sanction collusion than to deter it. On approval by the appropriate ministry and the FTC, cartels are legal in Japan for the purpose of rationalizing an industry. There are approximately 270 approved cartels, some of which were responses to voluntary restrictions on Japanese imports to the United States. Cartels were believed by many to insulate industries from certain market forces. As mentioned previously, automobile insurance companies had been required to charge prices established by a rating agency, which critics argued created a cartel.[21]

Some segments of the construction industry operated under an illegal system of bid rigging, price fixing, and market allocation known as *dango*. In the *dango* system, construction companies met in private to decide what bids to make and which company would win the contract.[22] In 1988 the FTC ruled that 140 construction companies had colluded on bids for work at the U.S. naval base at Yokosuka. The FTC issued a warning but imposed small fines totaling $2 million. The U.S. Department of Justice then hired a Japanese law firm to represent the United States, and within a year 99 construction companies agreed to pay $32.6 million to settle the bid-rigging claims. The settlement represented approximately 25 percent of the value of the contracts in question. Under pressure from within Japan and from the United States, the FTC issued new guidelines for the construction industry defining an additional set of illegal practices.

CULTURAL FOUNDATIONS

Japanese culture emphasizes harmony and the role of formal and informal hierarchical relationships, such as that between a superior and a subordinate. At the same time, Japanese business practices emphasize horizontal relationships, flexibility, and consensus. The cultural explanation for these practices lies in part in the importance of groups in Japanese society and the relationship between the individual and the group and between groups and society.

---

[19]See Upham (1987, Ch. 5) for a discussion of litigation and industrial policy.
[20]Private antitrust suits are allowed in Japan but are rarely filed because of limits on discovery, the absence of class actions, high filing costs, and the requirement that the FTC issue a finding of a probable violation before a case can proceed.
[21]See Lake (1998, p. 129).
[22]McMillan (1991) estimated that *dango* increased the price of public works contracts by 16 to 33 percent. In addition, *dango* represented a barrier to trade.

A cultural explanation for the societal value of harmony can be found in the religious tradition in which a person progresses toward a closer relationship with or deeper understanding of the "universe."[23] Work is also a path to a closer or deeper relationship with the universe, which has led to an ethic of diligence and a desire for harmony with other individuals and with groups in the work environment. Employment practices such as lifetime employment and a seniority system sustain this ethic.[24] A group, including a business group, thus is to be nourished and its members to act in harmony so that the group can progress, thereby allowing its members to progress. Groups balance a need to adapt to their environment, and hence for their members to act in a concerted manner, with a desire for individuals to express their individual intentions and interests. This may require leaders to modify their expectations toward their subordinates and may require subordinates to suppress their own interests. Doi (1988, pp. 22–23) argued that this consensus building through accommodation by both leaders and subordinates resolves the fundamental tension in groups. The desire to build consensus for government actions and the extensive consultation processes of the bureaucracy are consistent with this perspective.

Taka (1994) characterized the social environment in which individuals and groups are located in four concentric circles of "family, fellows, Japan, and the world." Appropriate behavior depends on the principal relationships in each circle. The notion that appropriate behavior differs among the circles, and the relationships in them, derives from early Confucianism, which held that although all persons are equal, a person is "to treat others in proportion to the intimacy of their relations."[25] A fundamental cultural value that characterizes these relationships is *on*, which refers to obligation and its fulfillment. *On* "is the indebtedness of subordinate to superior for the superior's benevolence in supplying resources to the subordinate."[26] In a fundamental sense, *on* can never be fully repaid and the remaining obligation serves to perpetuate the relationship.

The first circle centers on the *ie,* or family, which is viewed as a group that continues through time. In a business context the second, or "fellows," circle focuses on relationships with friends and colleagues. Viewing a company as analogous to a family, the principal relationship within the work environment is the hierarchical superior–subordinate relationship. This circle also includes the relationships among individual businesses and the ministries relevant to their industry. The fellows circle also includes the businesses in a *keiretsu,* which are expected to contribute to and draw assistance from other fellow members, but each is expected to have a positive balance of benefits over obligations remaining.

Taka characterizes the Japan circle as functioning under the principle of free competition. This is consistent with the notion of Confucian capitalism, the term given to the organization of the economy in terms of markets and groups, including *keiretsu,* supply networks, and long-term relationships among companies.[27] The bureaucracy in Japan may also be viewed from this perspective. In Japan a *samurai* was both a military and a civil officer—a bureaucrat. Morishima (1988, p. 38) states, "In Confucian political thought, those who play the most important roles in society are the bureaucrats."

In the Japan circle, businesses have mutual interests supported by reciprocal behavior, including that with government, that maintain harmony within the country through the accommodation and subordination of interests. This occurs among businesses and business groups in the context of a larger group—the business community— or the business community in relation to government. An economic phenomenon consistent with this value is the rescue of failing firms. When a firm is failing, a group or

---

[23]The Confucian support for this perspective is found in the concept of persons having within them a microcosm of the universe that is connected with the outer universe. The Buddhist underpinning of this perspective is the view that all human beings are the same.

[24]A seniority system also is consistent with the Confucian value of respect for elders.

[25]The five basic Confucian relationships are parent and child, husband and wife, older sibling and younger sibling, friend and friend, and superior and subordinate (ruler and subject). Confucianism is considered in more detail in Chapter 16.

[26]Hamilton and Sanders (1992, p. 24).

[27]Morishima (1988, pp. 36–38) addresses the Confucian bases for capitalism.

an industry rescues the firm. The rescuer is not always a Japanese firm—in 1994 creditors asked Ford Motor Company to assume managerial control of the failing Mazda, in which Ford had an ownership share. In 2005 three companies in the Mitsubishi *keiretsu* rescued Mitsubishi Motors, as they had in 2004.

The outer, or world, circle requires an outward orientation, but order is maintained among those who share the understandings of the inner three circles. Reciprocal relationships are less important in this circle, and business relies more on law to resolve conflicts.

TYING THE COMPONENTS TOGETHER: A FRAMEWORK OF POLITICAL EXCHANGE

The framework of political exchange brings together the institutions and processes of government and their interactions with interests. Interests have incentives for nonmarket action, and culture and institutions structure those actions, as indicated in Figure 14–1. The outcome of a nonmarket issue affecting business depends on the alignment and strategies of interests and the relevant institutions—the Diet, the governing parties, and the bureaucracy. Because of the powerful bureaucracy and the cultural values of harmony and consensus, political competition is not as freewheeling as in the United States. Much of the action takes place within the governing coalition or in behind-the-scenes consensus-building activities involving the government coalition, the bureaucracy, and interest groups. This nonmarket action is less visible than it is in the United States.

One path of influence for interests has been through parties and their leaders, but interests have often sought assistance from a broader set of officeholders. *Zoku* and caucuses give Diet members an opportunity to respond to the needs of interest groups. From the perspective of interest groups, *zoku* provide another access point to the government and are an important link between interest groups, the governing parties, and the Diet.

The bureaucracy plays a central role in the maintenance of interest group relationships, and to some extent ministries have been politicized. The most politicized ministries are those whose actions have a direct impact on industry, professional groups, and other organized interests through expenditure programs and regulation.

Political Exchange

The interactions between interest groups and the government can be viewed as political exchange in which interests provide political support and the government provides policies that benefit the interests. This takes place through a set of relationships, referred to as an *iron triangle,* formed by interest groups, political parties, and the bureaucracy. During the 1990s the importance of these iron triangles diminished somewhat, but they remain important for many businesses and interest groups. Okimoto (1989) classified these exchanges into four categories: (1) clientistic exchange, (2) reciprocal (pork barrel) exchange, (3) untied financial support, and (4) generalized voter support. Only reciprocal exchange is considered here.

Reciprocal Exchange

Reciprocal exchange, illustrated in Figure 14-4, involves government regulatory policies, licensing, and expenditures that benefit particular interest groups. In turn, those interest groups provide support for the governing parties. The parties and the interests recognize that future benefits depend on maintaining the system. Reciprocal exchange occurs in regulated industries such as electric power, telecommunications, and transportation. In these sectors the ministries, which are the regulators, again serve as intermediaries.[28] Expenditure programs primarily affect the construction, transportation, and defense industries. The businesses in these industries are generally not heavily involved in international trade and seek benefits from government programs. In the context of Figure 2-2, the regulation and expenditure programs of the ministries make nonmarket strategies essential.

---

[28]Aoki (1984) characterizes this as administrative pluralism in which the bureaucracy acts as a referee among competing pluralist interests.

FIGURE 14-4   Reciprocal Exchange

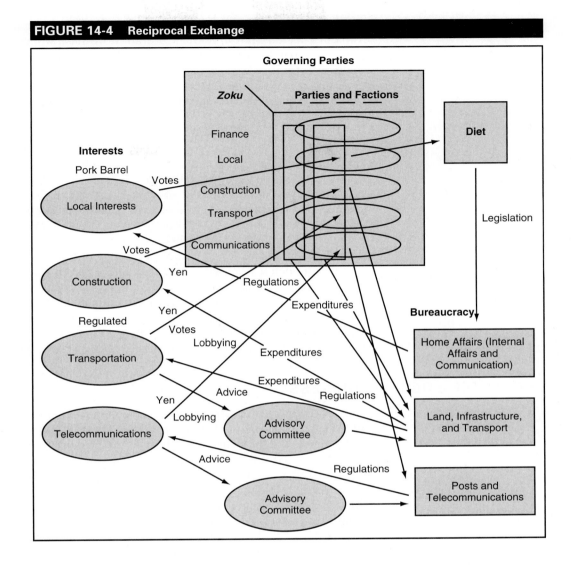

The governing coalition may be thought of as a matrix with Diet members belonging to a party, and also to a faction, as well as to a *zoku* or caucus. The points of access for an interest group, then, may be through a party, particularly those in the governing coalition, a *zoku,* or a caucus. The points of access to the bureaucracy include direct relationships and the advisory committee system.

The Ministry of Land, Infrastructure, and Transport is one of the most important participants in reciprocal exchange. Construction accounts for nearly 15 percent of GDP, and every project must be licensed by the ministry. In addition, as Yayama (1998, pp. 105–107) indicates, the Ministry benefits selected contractors through the "designated bidders" system in which only certain companies are allowed to bid on certain contracts. Because of the magnitude of the funds allocated by the ministry and its licensing function, construction companies have been strong supporters of the traditional system and are important participants in the *koenkai* of many LDP Diet members. The ministry provides the bureaucratic support for this exchange. The creation of IAIs may lessen this politicization and reduce the influence of the ministry.

The nature of political concessions to interest groups is illustrated by the case of small enterprises. Small enterprises have been one of the traditional support groups for the LDP, and in exchange the LDP provided a set of specific benefits, such as preferential tax treatment and favorable regulation, as a means of protecting them. To protect small retailers, the government restricted the growth of large stores, and this restriction was in part responsible for Japan's large retail and wholesale sector. To strengthen the reciprocal relationship among small merchants, the bureaucracy, and the LDP, the government enacted the Large-Scale Retail Store Law, which required any store that sought to expand beyond 1,500 square meters to obtain approval from the Small and Medium Enterprise Agency of MITI (now METI). When approval was sought, other stores in the neighborhood were consulted. Their protests often delayed an opening for years. In exchange for this regulatory protection, small merchants and wholesalers typically supported the LDP.

When some large stores began to build stores smaller than 1,500 square meters side by side, local retailers pressured municipal and prefecture governments seeking additional protection. Those governments began to enact regulations that placed additional restrictions on large stores. These regulations were "illegal" because they conflicted with the national law, and MITI sought to void them. The municipal and prefecture governments sought and received support from the Ministry of Home Affairs (MHA) (now MIC), which opposed MITI on this issue. The bureaucratic battle was arbitrated by the Cabinet, which eventually decided in favor of the MHA and the local merchants. Regulations were established requiring notice to the prefecture government of any plan to open a store with more than 500 square meters. These regulations, along with subsequent legislation, provided a role for local government in the protest process, strengthened the role of the local merchants, and allowed the merchants to appeal decisions to the ministries.[29] The Part IV integrative case, *Toys 'Я' Us and Globalization,* involves a retailer seeking to enter the Japanese market and facing this set of restrictions and the underlying reciprocal exchange relationship.

CHARACTERISTICS OF BUSINESS

Many of the most prominent Japanese companies are part of a network or group intended to provide mutual benefits to its members. In the United States, corporations tend to have wholly owned subsidiaries, and cross-shareholding of publicly traded companies is atypical. In Japan, business groups are supported by interlocking ownership, which serves both to facilitate coordination and insulate the group from outside forces. As Sonji Noguchi, a general manager at the Industrial Bank of Japan (IBJ), which had the largest shareholdings of any bank, explained: "When we issue stock, friendly companies hold it. When they issue stock, we hold it. . . . If I own 1,000 shares of IBJ, I don't feel I own the company. It's just an investment. It's the relationship."[30] The groups typically have no more than one firm in any industry, so cooperation rather than rivalry characterizes behavior within a group. Groups compete vigorously against each other, however. The companies in a group remain independent and serve their own interests first.

The interlocking networks, called *keiretsu*, are of three types: (1) the three groups, Mitsui, Mitsubishi, and Sumitomo, formed from the prewar, family-controlled *zaibatsu*, (2) groups formed around major banks, and (3) groups formed around major industrial companies. Members of the first two groups are referred to as horizontal *keiretsu*, whereas those in the third are called vertical *keiretsu*.[31] The firms in a *keiretsu* are independently managed, but each *keiretsu* has a "presidents' club" that meets regularly and focuses on group maintenance activities, the exchange of information, and, when necessary, the resolution of conflicts among members.

Vertical *keiretsu* are centered around a major manufacturing company such as Toyota or Matsushita Electric and involve supply and distribution networks. These groups may include wholly owned subsidiaries, partially owned subsidiaries, and independent suppliers. The form of the relationship varies with some subsidiaries supplying other companies in addition to their parent and the parent purchasing from competitors

---

[29]These regulations were subsequently largely eliminated.
[30]*New York Times*, June 27, 1989. The stagnant economy in the 1990s forced many *keiretsu* companies to raise funds by selling some of the shares they held, reducing the extent of cross-shareholdings.
[31]Gerlach (1992) provides an analysis of the *keiretsu* and other alliances in Japan and of the implications of these networks for corporate business strategy.

of a subsidiary. Toyota directly controlled 13 suppliers with ownership shares in 1990 ranging from 8.9 to 49 percent, and another 178 companies, organized into three societies, supply Toyota. Matsushita maintains a distribution network of 25,000 small "National shops" that account for much of its sales in Japan.

Maintenance of the network relationships in a vertical *keiretsu* involves implicit or relational contracting. As practiced in Japan, relational contracting is characterized not only by the absence of formal contracts but also by mutual adjustment led to changing circumstances. Within a *keiretsu,* long-term supply relationships are frequently augmented by a market allocation system in which suppliers receive fixed shares of the purchase orders of a company, but the quantity purchased varies with the level of demand. The relationship between NTT and a group of its suppliers had been so stable that the suppliers were referred to as the NTT "family." (See the chapter case, *The Breakup of Nippon Telephone and Telegraph?*.) Market allocation and long-term relationships made it difficult for new firms, both Japanese and foreign, to enter certain Japanese supply markets.

Implicit contracts also govern the employment relationship in most large firms. The compensation system in Japanese firms typically has three principal components: (1) an annual bonus, (2) pay graduated by seniority, and (3) a contingent retirement payment. Many Japanese employees receive a significant part of their income in the form of an annual bonus, which can be reduced along with hours worked when the firm has to improve its profits. Consistent with the cultural analogy to a family, most firms had based wages on seniority. These firms hired young employees directly from high schools and universities and offered them lifetime employment, so workers looked forward to a rising income stream.[32] These features of the compensation system provided strong incentives for employees to remain with the company, and they also aligned the interests of employees with those of the company.

Although lifetime employment and seniority systems continue to be used by many companies, pressure for improved efficiency and lower costs as well as the economic slump in Japan have generated change. Layoffs have occurred, and some companies have skirted the lifetime employment policies by hiring temporary workers. Compensation systems also have changed. As Osamu Sakuri, president of the Sumitomo Trust Bank, explained: "Under the lifetime employment system we could not offer appropriately high salaries to obtain top talent. Nor could we hire on a short-term basis."[33] Merit-based, rather than seniority-based, pay has become much more common, and companies such as Fujitsu put all employees on merit pay. In addition, companies such as Matsushita are giving employees more control over their retirement programs rather than providing all the funds at the time of retirement.

BUSINESS–GOVERNMENT INTERACTIONS

The Organization of Business for Nonmarket Action

Mutual gains, such as those from long-term relationships among businesses, also result from relationships with the government. Japanese firms cultivate relationships with politicians and bureaucrats that provide the foundation for participation and influence. When a Japanese firm faces a nonmarket issue that involves the government, it already has well-established relationships that provide it access. Firms participate in ministerial advisory committees and develop relationships with the relevant ministries and their career bureaucrats. They may employ *amakudari* bureaucrats or use them as advisors and counselors. Firms develop contacts with the relevant Diet committees and with the *zoku* and caucuses concerned with policy in their industries.

---

[32]Lifetime employment was available only to a small proportion of the workforce. Tachibanaki (1984) estimates that in the late 1970s approximately 9.7 percent of males and less than 2 percent of females had lifetime employment. He argued that this was quite similar to the United States, except that in the United States a much higher percent of young employees engaged in job shopping.
[33]Quoted in Mroczkowski and Hanaoka (1989, p. 50).

Firms also participate in industry associations and Keidanren committees. These relationships represent major assets to a firm, and considerable effort and resources are expended to maintain them.

These relationships do not guarantee success on nonmarket issues, but they can be important for effective participation in the Japanese system. The success of a nonmarket strategy in Japan depends on the strength of the interests and the nature of the exchange relationship between business and government. Opposition to entry into an industry, for example, is naturally weakest for those products that have no Japanese competitor. A company such as McDonald's was able to enter the Japanese market with relative ease because the fast-food market segment was unoccupied. The same was true for Blockbuster.

A firm seeking access to an industry in which the relationship between interest groups and the government is characterized by clientistic or reciprocal exchange may, however, find the opposition formidable. In industries such as agriculture, construction, and financial services, the U.S. government has played a major role in opening the markets. In other cases long-term arrangements through *keiretsu* limit the ability of foreign as well as new Japanese firms to break into some markets. For example, a principal impediment to increased sales by foreign semiconductor manufacturers was the long-standing supply relationships and market allocation policies of both *keiretsu* and independent firms.[34]

Nonmarket Strategies

Electoral Strategies

The principal nonmarket strategies used in Japan are electoral, coalition building, relationship building, and lobbying. Electoral strategies had been a central component of the nonmarket strategies of most large firms, and political contributions had been a part of those strategies. Those contributions took place in the context of clientistic, reciprocal, and less-structured exchange relationships.[35] Scandals and electoral reforms reduced their importance, however. Shoichiro Toyoda, chairman of Toyota and chairman of the Keidanren, stated, "In the future one hopes that public financing and donations from individuals will be sufficient to cover political parties' expenses, but we can't expect to reach that position overnight."[36]

Coalition Building

Coalition building often takes place through industry associations and peak associations that represent business interests on broad public issues. The principal peak organization is the Keidanren, which includes the 1,200 or so largest firms, both Japanese and foreign, plus the major trade associations. The other three principal peak organizations are the Nickering (Federation of Employers Association), the Japan Chamber of Commerce and Industry, and Keizai Doyukai (Japan Committee for Economic Development).[37] The principal business organization for political participation is the Keidanren, which advocates policies that support the general climate for business. It seldom supports particular industries or individual companies.[38] The Keidanren's approach is to attempt to build consensus on policies affecting the economy and business in general. It has supported deregulation and the opening of Japanese markets to imports as a means of improving economic efficiency, reducing Japan's trade surplus, and lessening the external pressure for market opening.

Because of the extensive set of long-term relationships among firms and between business and government in Japan, coalitions in Japan are less fluid and issue-specific

---

[34]Mason (1992) documents the difficulties encountered by firms such as Coca-Cola and Texas Instruments in entering the Japanese market in the early part of the post–World War II period.
[35]Foreign firms, particularly U.S. firms, have been more hesitant to make campaign contributions in light of the Lockheed scandal, considered in Chapter 23, which involved large, illegal contributions to the office of Prime Minister Tanaka and others.
[36]*Tokyo Business Today*, September 1994.
[37]See Lynn and McKeown (1988, pp. 78–81).
[38]The Keidanren does not deal with labor issues, which are the domain of the Nickering.

than in the United States. Thus, many of the interactions with the government take place through standing associations rather than ad hoc coalitions. In Japan, associations are numerous and politically active. Lynn and McKeown (1988) provide an analysis of industry associations in the steel and machine tool industries. The Japan Machine Tool Builders Association represented 112 companies, and the Japan Metal Forming Machine Builders Association represented another 115. The associations addressed issues of industrial standards and provided information on foreign markets and competitors. These associations were linked through a hierarchical network with other associations, including the Japan Machinery Federation, the Machine Tool and Related Products Committee, and the Japan Society for the Promotion of the Machinery Industry, which provided subsidies to machinery companies from funds raised through motorcycle and small car racing.[39]

The extent to which companies act on their own outside their industry associations and the Keidanren and whether their participation in *keiretsu* causes them to restrain the pursuit of their own interests is not well documented. Most companies, however, maintain their own relationships with bureaucrats in the relevant ministries and with important politicians rather than relying solely on the activities of the associations to which they belong.

Relationships with the Bureaucracy

In the context of Figure 2-2, the importance of nonmarket strategies is greater the greater the control of opportunities by government. Interactions with ministries and agencies are crucial for many companies because the government has been heavily involved in the economy. Extensive regulation and the administrative allocation of government resources such as public works contracts have made nonmarket strategies important. In addition, the bureaucracy has considerable discretion under existing laws, and it plays an important role in writing new legislation. Companies develop relationships with the bureaucracy and bureaucrats, and these relationships are reciprocal. Schaede (1998, pp. 165–166) indicates that administrative guidance represents the bulk of the regulation in industries. Moreover, "Administrative guidance is not transparent and often involves delicate conversations between ministry officials and firm management. Rules can be implemented or revoked at the discretion of the ministry in charge and without any prior notice."

Bureaucrats also seek close relationships with companies for their own purposes. Okimoto (1989, p. 158) wrote:

> Deputy division directors in MITI's vertical divisions have significant leeway to structure their relationships with corporate executives in ways that fulfill their notion of what their job should entail. Usually, there is a fairly well defined hierarchy of companies with which deputy directors must deal. The three deputy directors of the information industry divisions—Electronic Policy, Data Processing Promotion, and Industrial Electronics—are expected to establish close working relations with representatives from the big, blue-chip electronics corporations that dominate their fields—Hitachi, NEC, Toshiba, Mitsubishi Electronics, and Fujitsu. Working with industrial associations like the Electronics Industry Association of Japan (EIAJ) is also essential, especially when the association is strong or when there are too many large corporations for one or two MITI officials to handle.[40]

Ministries may also provide assistance to business through regulation and licensing. When the telecommunication industry was first opened to limited entry, the Public Highway Corporation encouraged a group of major companies, including Toyota,

---

[39]Lynn and McKeown (1988, pp. 71–73).
[40]Okimoto (1989, p. 158).

Mitsubishi, Mitsui & Company, and Sumitomo Corporation, to form a common carrier in the Tokyo-Nagoya-Osaka corridor. The company, Telway-Japan, was formed shortly before the filing deadline, and one purpose of the company was to compete with a joint venture formed by Daini Denden (DDI) and Motorola to provide cellular telephone service.[41] The Ministry of Posts and Telecommunications had the responsibility for deciding which territories Telway-Japan and the Daini Denden–Motorola joint venture could serve. Telway-Japan was allocated the territory constituting the largest potential market for cellular service. The resulting conflict between Motorola and the bureaucracy was a source of considerable discord between the United States and Japan in international trade negotiations.[42]

Lobbying and Points of Access

Lobbying is extensive in Japan and involves presenting information and representing interests before the bureaucracy, political parties, and the Diet. As shown in Figure 14-2, the policy formulation process begins before legislation is considered by the Diet or actions are taken by a ministry. It is thus essential that a firm or interest group be able to learn when an issue is being considered by a ministry or the policymaking apparatus of the governing parties. This requires developing relationships and points of access. Although there are many points of access, because of the close interactions among the governing parties' policymaking apparatus, the bureaucracy, *zoku,* and Diet committees, these points of access are not independent.

The appropriate points of access depend on the issue and the nature of the exchange relationship between business and government. An issue involving telecommunications necessarily involves the MIC and METI and their advisory committees. Policy committees of the governing parties will also be involved, as will the Diet committees for telecommunications and for commerce and industry. Access to the MIC may be provided both through its advisory committees and by *amakudari* bureaucrats who have maintained personal relationships with current vice ministers and bureau heads. Those high-ranking bureaucrats had been responsible for the careers of those in the junior cohorts who now run the ministry, so there can be a personal as well as a professional relationship. A number of *amakudari* bureaucrats hold positions in firms with which their former ministries had dealt.

The rise of the *zoku,* in terms of both expertise and political power, makes them an important point of access on many issues. Former prime minister Tanaka was the most important politician when NTT was privatized and the telecommunications industry was opened to competition, but he did not hold any formal position in the government other than his seat in the Diet—however, he headed both of the relevant *zoku.*

Access to political parties and members of the Diet is also important, particularly on issues requiring bureaucratic action, since parties can act as intermediaries between firms and ministries. The need for access had led many Japanese companies to make campaign contributions to parties and their leaders. Access is often facilitated by personal relationships between business executives and government officials.

Foreign firms have developed their capacity for lobbying the Japanese government and maintaining ties with the relevant ministries, the governing parties, and the Diet. AT&T hired a former U.S. trade negotiator to be its full-time lobbyist in Tokyo, and Nippon Motorola hired a former U.S. embassy official in Tokyo and a former congressional staffer as full-time lobbyists. Motorola retained former officials of METI and MIC as advisors.[43] These two ministries were the most important to the industries in which Motorola was engaged and were involved in the agreements granting the company access to the cellular telephone market.

---

[41]Harris (1989, p. 125).
[42]That discord is considered in more detail in Baron (1996).
[43]Motorola follows a similar strategy in the United States, where it employed a number of former government officials.

Information

Because legislative activity in Japan is often near completion when a bill is introduced in the Diet and because legislation is written within the bureaucracy and the government parties, advance information on potential legislative activity is essential for effective participation in the process. Similarly, since bureaucratic decisions are not made in public and regulations and other administrative practices are often not transparent, advance notice of possible bureaucratic action is important. Thus an important activity of business is gathering information about government activities, plans, and proposals. Many firms employ *amakudari* bureaucrats to provide information; others hire them as advisors. Schaede (1998) reported that 1,111 *amakudari* bureaucrats held positions in companies and many more were in public corporations and associations. *Amakudari* bureaucrats have by the time of their descent developed extensive personal communications networks called *jinmyaku* that can be valuable to their new employers or clients.

Johnson indicates the scope of the information that Japanese companies routinely develop about the government and its activities.[44]

> The potential lobbyist must know which ministry or ministries has jurisdiction over his or her problem and then find out everything it is possible to know about that organization, including its history, personnel cliques, post retirement patterns, scandals, and so forth. This is precisely the kind of information that any Japanese manufacturer or marketing organization compiles all the time. The major Japanese daily newspapers, for example, routinely print on page 2 details of personnel shifts within the ministries and agencies of the central government. It would be unheard of to read such information in the *New York Times* or the *Washington Post* on, say, the Department of Commerce, but in Tokyo it is important news. The Japanese press reports on who is in charge of what section throughout the Japanese executive branch because its readers need and want that information.

Government officials also need information, and firms are an important source of it. Homare Takenaka, managing director for external affairs of IBM Japan, explained: "If they think we have good intelligence and information, they rely on us. By doing this we can strengthen and expand our position. . . . I can call on director generals of ministries anytime. I know them personally."[45] Companies also participate on advisory committees for the purposes of obtaining information and influencing outcomes.

Corporate Nonmarket Styles

Some U.S. firms have adopted a strategy of acting aggressively, both in Japan and in the United States, to pressure the Japanese government to open its markets to their products. Other firms have adopted the Japanese style of patience both in markets and in their political and governmental interactions. Two U.S. semiconductor manufacturers, Texas Instruments and Motorola, opened production facilities in Japan, and they followed quite different nonmarket strategies. Texas Instruments, which has operated in Japan for over 30 years, maintained a low profile. In contrast, Motorola adopted a demonstrative style, using U.S. trade laws and political sentiment in Washington as levers to open Japanese markets for its telecommunications and semiconductor products. This caused resentment in Japan. Robert Orr, director of government relations for Motorola, explained: "We've got good friends in the U.S. government. And we have good friends in the Japanese government. That's the way it's played. There is resentment because they feel we ignited the trade issue, but it has been here a long, long, long, long time."

---

[44]See Johnson in Johnson, Tyson, and Zysman (1989, p. 231).
[45]*Japan Economic Journal*, May 19, 1990.

Johnson & Johnson has operated in a more traditional style. It had been unable to market Tylenol in Japan because the Ministry of Health, Labor, and Welfare (MHLW) restricted the dosage of acetaminophen, the active ingredient in Tylenol, to less than half the amount needed to make the pain reliever effective. Instead of taking aggressive action in Washington or Tokyo as Motorola had done, Johnson & Johnson adopted the Japanese style. President Masami Atarashi of Johnson & Johnson Japan attempted to persuade MHLW officials to increase the permitted dosage. He explained, "We believe in being an insider, wherever we are."[46] This approach can be very slow, particularly in a regulatory system known for keeping out many drugs available to consumers in other countries. Johnson & Johnson finally applied for formal approval in 1995, and after forming a partnership with a Japanese company to market the drug, Tylenol was approved and marketed in 2000, some 45 years after being introduced in the United States.

In choosing its strategy, a firm attempting to penetrate the Japanese market must determine whether it should pursue an aggressive strategy or adopt the Japanese style of patience. For a company such as Motorola that required government licenses to sell some of its products in Japan, patience may have been infeasible because of rapid technological change and the lengthy process required to gain access to the bureaucracy and to markets. The Part IV integrative case, *Toys 'R' Us and Globalization,* provides an opportunity to consider market opening strategies in the context of the market and nonmarket environments in Japan.

SUMMARY

The nonmarket environment in a country may be characterized in terms of issues, interests, institutions, and information. Culture and history are also important in shaping the pattern of social interactions and the behavior of institutions. Because of culture and the distinctive characteristics of the nonmarket environments in countries, nonmarket strategies must be tailored to the environment in a country. The framework of structured pluralism provides the foundation for both nonmarket analysis and strategy formulation.

Japan's parliamentary system of government was dominated by the LDP for decades, but scandals and defections resulted in a period of party reorganization, consolidation, and intensified competition. The LDP regained a majority in the lower house of the Diet and has governed with a coalition. The bureaucracy remained powerful and provided stability, but it was criticized for failing to deregulate the economy more quickly. Criticism of the bureaucracy led to political reform that reorganized several ministries and increased the power of the cabinet. The parliamentary system results in much of the legislative and policymaking work being done within the ministries and the party structure of the governing coalition. Consensus on policy is sought, although not always attained.

The bureaucracy has multiple roles as policymaker, regulator, and administrator. The ministries differ in the degree of politicization and power. One source of power is their expertise, often supported by a record of past successes. The bureaucracy attracts some of the most able Japanese college graduates, who enter and remain as a cohort until they retire. Many "descend" to positions in business, politics, or quasi-governmental organizations. Bureaucratic power is also due to regulatory authority, the allocation of public resources, and the use of administrative guidance. These activities often lack transparency. One aspect of governmental reform was to separate the implementation of policies from ministerial policymaking by creating Independent Administrative Institutions. The bureaucracy interacts with interests both directly and through a set of advisory committees that provide a mechanism for sharing information and developing consensus. Much of the interaction between interest groups and the bureaucracy takes place outside the view of the public.

---

[46]*Fortune,* September 11, 1989.

In Japan, complex networks of political exchange interconnect business and other interest groups with the three principal components of the government: the governing parties, the bureaucracy, and the Diet. The interaction between interests and the government may be understood in the framework of exchange. Reciprocal exchange, for example, involves support for the government in exchange for licensing, regulatory, and legislative policies that serve particular interests such as the construction and transportation industries. These interactions are both formal (party and ministerial advisory committees) and less formal (*zoku*). Some are visible, whereas others, such as the personal relationships between *amakudari* bureaucrats and those who remain in the ministry, are largely invisible. Participating effectively in this system requires understanding both the pattern of these relationships and Japan's history and culture. Understanding is not enough, however. Firms invest in networks and in personal relationships between their executives and the appropriate members of government.

The principal nonmarket strategies of firms in Japan are electoral, relationship building, lobbying, and coalition building. Electoral strategies have been important, but they have diminished in importance due to electoral reform and the public financing of elections. Lobbying focuses on the bureaucracy, the governing parties, and Diet members. Access is important, and firms develop relationships with government officials to provide that access. Peak organizations and trade associations are important in business-government relations, and most firms participate in these organizations.

In Japan legislative activity is largely over once a bill is introduced in the Diet. Moreover, much economic activity is regulated or subject to the administrative guidance by the ministries. Firms thus develop information about government ministries, Diet activities, and the governing parties' policy processes. Some engage the services of "advisors" or *amakudari* bureaucrats who know the organizational and decision-making structure of the ministries and have personal contacts with high-ranking bureaucrats.

-- C A S E S --

The Breakup of Nippon Telephone and Telegraph?

In 1990 the Japanese government considered breaking up Nippon Telephone and Telegraph (NTT) but postponed a decision until April 1996. During the ensuing 5 years much changed, yet much remained the same. The Ministry of Posts and Telecommunications (MPT) continued to press for breaking up NTT, and NTT continued to oppose a breakup. As 1996 approached, the political and economic situation remained complex and contentious.

Despite the "privatization" of NTT in 1985, the Ministry of Finance (MOF) still held 66 percent of NTT's shares. Several planned sales of shares by the MOF had been postponed because of the depressed price of NTT's shares. NTT continued to provide only domestic telecommunications services, and Kokusai Denshin Denwa (KDD) remained the country's dominant international carrier. NTT was prohibited by law from providing international telecommunications services, but it was allowed to invest overseas. NTT began investing offshore in 1992, but only 0.3 percent of its assets were outside Japan. NTT did not manufacture telecommunications equipment but instead relied on suppliers with which it maintained long-term relationships. NTT's principal suppliers were Fujitsu, Hitachi, NEC, and Oki, which were referred to as the "NTT family." NTT had begun to purchase from foreign suppliers, but the amounts were a much smaller percent of NTT's total equipment purchases compared with the equipment purchases from foreign suppliers by other Japanese telecommunications companies.

The Telecommunications Industry

On the surface, the Japanese telecommunications industry was structurally competitive with over 100 common carriers. In addition to NTT and KDD, there were three domestic long-distance carriers, two international carriers, 32 cellular companies, and 28 personal handheld system providers. As a result of the competition, NTT's long-distance market share had declined to 69 percent, but it still held 99 percent of the local service market and 80 percent of the total domestic telecommunications market. NTT practiced cross-subsidization with long-distance rates subsidizing local service, but it planned to reduce the current ¥340 charge for a 3-minute daytime long-distance call to ¥100 by the year 2000.

Most of its competitors were dependent on NTT's local network for access to customers, and some companies paid up to 50 percent of their revenues as access charges. Long-distance competitors such as DDI complained that interconnections with NTT required lengthy negotiations. DDI President Yusai Okuyama said, "We have to spend years on interconnection negotiations

[with NTT] and that has obstructed the speedy development of our business plan."[47] Jupiter TeleCommunications, a joint venture between Sumitomo Corporation and TeleCommunications International of the United States, sought access to NTT subscribers in its cable franchise area so that it could offer telephone and other services. If approved by NTT, Jupiter would then file for a license with the MPT. In the past NTT had refused to provide interconnections to cable companies.

As a virtual local service monopoly NTT's prices were high. The MPT reported that NTT's basic subscription rate for telephone service had risen by more than 15 percent during the past 10 years, and the initial subscription (hookup) charge of over $700 was four times that in the United Kingdom and 13 times the charge in France.[48] Moreover, subscribers had to purchase a long-term telephone bond that helped finance NTT's capital expenditures. NTT's access charges were sufficiently high that they limited entry.

The MPT maintained that not only did high access charges limit competition but that NTT also discriminated against competitors in interconnections and obtained commercially sensitive information on competitors through the negotiations on access and interconnection.

Regulation

The MPT had taken some steps to deregulate the long-distance, cellular, and CATV industries, and some politicians and economists believed that further deregulation would stimulate economic activity and create jobs. In 1994 the MPT allowed customers to own their own cellular terminals, which was credited with spurring growth in cellular telecommunications. This significantly reduced the market shares of existing carriers, including NTT and DDI.

Bureaucratic Influence

Critics of the MPT argued that it had allowed entry into the industry to give it more firms to regulate, more places to which its bureaucrats could descend, and more influence over the firms. These critics claimed that the MPT's push to break up NTT had the same motivation. As an example of the MPT's strategy for maintaining its influence and providing opportunities for *amakudari* bureaucrats, four members of NTT's board of directors were former MPT officials, including Shigeo Sawada, a former administrative vice minister of the MPT who joined NTT in 1990 as senior vice president. Eighteen

---

[47] *Financial Times*, August 7, 1996.
[48] *Financial Times*, August 7, 1996.

other former bureaucrats were in NTT-affiliated companies. As another example, the paging industry was divided into 32 regional operators, and according to a senior official at one Tokyo-based paging company, this division was "'only to give all the regional heads of the ministry places to enjoy their retired life.'"[49] Private companies such as the long-distance and cellular provider DDI also had *amakudari* bureaucrats. DDI president Okuyama was a former MPT administrative vice minister, and three other MPT officials were employed by DDI.

In 1994 the MPT had pushed for Sawada to be appointed president of NTT, but NTT opposed the appointment and supported Junichiro Miyazu, a career NTT employee. A stalemate resulted, and the current president, Masahi Kojima, remained in office. The MPT then turned its attention to preventing NTT from naming Kojima chairman and Miyazu president. The MPT enlisted the aid of the telecommunications *zoku,* members of the Diet who maintained an interest in telecommunications, in support of Sawada, but the financial community preferred Miyazu. Recognizing that Miyazu would likely become president, the MPT then sought to block Kojima from being appointed chairman. It blocked the appointment using a 1986 executive directive intended to restrict the influence of *amakudari* bureaucrats in special corporations, such as NTT. In 1996 an agreement was reached between NTT and its backers, the MPT and its backers, the telecommunications *zoku,* and politicians. In the agreement Sawada was appointed chairman, Miyazu was appointed president, and Kojima was named special advisor.[50]

The Government Coalition

After scandals resulted in the resignation of two prime ministers from the opposition parties in 1994, the government was formed by a coalition among the Liberal Democratic Party (LDP), the Social Democratic Party (SDP), and the small New Party Harbinger (Sakigake). To establish the coalition, the president of the SDP was given the position of prime minister. A poor performance in upper house elections and defections from the SDP, however, weakened the prime minister and resulted in a change in the government. Mr. Ryutaro Hashimoto, a long-standing member of the LDP, was elected head of the LDP and became prime minister in 1995. Hashimoto had entered politics at age 25 when he inherited his father's constituency and was elected to the Diet. He joined the Tanaka faction of the LDP and served as Minister of Finance and Minister of International Trade and Industry in previous governments. Hashimoto was popular with the Japanese public in part because he had stood up to the United States in trade negotiations. His popularity gave the LDP hope that it might return to power by winning a majority of the seats in the lower house in the April 1997 election. The prime minister could dissolve the Diet and call an early election, and the speculation was that he would do so.

The Minister of Posts and Telecommunication in Hashimoto's cabinet was Ichiro Hino, a member of the SDP. The SDP was backed by labor unions, including *Zen Dentsu,* which represented 185,000 NTT employees. *Zen Dentsu* believed that a breakup of NTT would result in a substantial loss of jobs. NTT had already reduced its employment from 314,000 in 1985 to 197,000 in 1994, although some of those job losses represented transfers to affiliated companies.

NTT's Strategy

NTT deployed an integrated strategy to avoid a breakup. In its market environment it announced in September 1995 that it planned to spin off its two software divisions. In the same month it announced that it would open its local service network to competitors. The high access charges, however, would prevent competitors from taking advantage of the opening. NTT subsequently announced that it would reduce its access fees. NTT also announced that it would eliminate 45,000 jobs over the next 5 years to improve its efficiency.[51]

In the nonmarket environment NTT used a representation strategy, rallying its suppliers and its union. Within the Keidanren, NTT's principal suppliers opposed a breakup, leading the Keidanren to take no position on the issue. *Zen Dentsu* used its relationships with the SDP to encourage it to oppose a breakup in the cabinet. NTT also argued that size was increasingly important in the global telecommunications industry and that a breakup would threaten its future international competitiveness.

Policy Analysis

A number of possible ways to break up NTT had been considered. One was to break it geographically into a set of regional companies, but as Japan is approximately the size of California, regional companies might not make economic sense. Another possibility was to break NTT vertically into a long-distance company and a local service company. A third possibility was to break it into a long-distance company and as many as 11 local service companies.

In late 1995 some policy analysts had come to believe that deregulating the telecommunications industry and allowing increased competition was more important than breaking up NTT. This, however, was contrary to the MPT's plans. Any substantial deregulation would thus have to come from the governing parties through new legislation.

---

[49]*Nikkei Weekly,* February 26, 1996.
[50]*Mainchi Daily News,* May 28, 1996.

[51]The *Nikkei Weekly* reported, however, that over half the employees would be loaned to NTT subsidiaries.

The Keidanren supported deregulation of the Japanese economy, and its Telecommunications Council studied the issue of the breakup of NTT. The council, however, chose not to issue a report due to internal disagreement with NTT's family of suppliers opposing a breakup and NTT's competitors and customers supporting a breakup. A Keidanren spokesperson stated that deregulation should take place before a breakup. The absence of Keidanren support for a breakup weakened the MPT's position.

The National Institute for Research Advancement also studied the issue and concluded that the AT&T breakup model was no longer valid and could weaken research and development and harm rural areas by reducing cross-subsidization. The Institute, however, did not make a recommendation.

The Decision-Making Process

In traditional fashion, the MPT issued a report in 1994 supporting greater competition in telecommunications. An Administrative Reform Council studied the issue and recommended a breakup, but did not specify how it should be done. That decision was referred to the Telecommunications Council, a deliberation council (advisory panel) of the MPT. Deliberation councils rely on the resources of the ministry and had been criticized as supporting the outcome the ministry wanted. The council was asked to make a recommendation regarding a breakup by early 1996.

At the end of February 1996, the Telecommunications Council recommended that by 1999 NTT be split into a long-distance carrier and two local service companies, one serving the western part of Japan including Osaka and one serving the eastern part including Tokyo.[52] In addition, the council recommended that NTT be allowed to provide international services, and KDD and International Digital Communications be allowed to provide domestic services. In an unusual failure of consensus, 3 of 22 members of the Telecommunications Council dissented, arguing that global competition required large companies.

NTT argued that the western region would be unprofitable because it would not serve the main business centers. It projected that the eastern region would have profits of ¥70 billion and the western region a deficit of ¥80 billion. The MPT countered with its own estimates. It forecasted a profit of ¥217.4 billion for the western region.

MITI had traditionally backed NTT because it believed that NTT was Japan's only realistic hope in the international telecommunications industry. MITI believed that preserving NTT's economies of scale and its investments in research and development was necessary to ensure its international competitiveness. Both MITI and the MOF, however, remained largely neutral in the current conflict. ■

Preparation Questions

1. How will the decision regarding breaking up NTT be made? That is, who will have influence in the decision making and why?
2. How effective is NTT's strategy likely to be?
3. What outcome do you predict and why?

[52]Ministry of Posts and Telecommunications, "The Status of Nippon Telegraph and Telephone Corporation: Toward the Creation of Dynamism in the Info-Communications Industry," February 29, 1996.

The Privatization of Japan Post

The postal service in Japan was much more than its 24,000 post offices and 270,000 employees. Japan Post was also the world's largest bank and largest provider of life insurance. Japan Post operated the postal savings system, which had deposits of $2 trillion in yucho savings accounts, much more than Japan's four largest banks and about half the total amount in savings accounts in Japan. In addition to the postal savings system Japan Post operated Kampo, which provided life insurance. Kampo received $150 billion in premiums in 2003. In total Japan Post held $3.2 trillion in assets, which represented 25 percent of Japan's household assets. Japan Post also held approximately 25 percent of the total outstanding government bonds.

The post office system was established during the Meiji period (1868–1912). The Postal Life Insurance Service began providing life insurance in 1916 to serve rural and poor parts of the country. Its successor, Kampo, had 40 percent of the market in Japan, which was the world's second largest, representing 22.8 percent of the world's life insurance market. Both the postal savings system and Kampo were obligated to provide universal service throughout Japan.

Economists complained that Japan Post funneled funds into quasi-government companies to fund public projects of questionable value. This distorted capital markets, resulting in economic inefficiency. The savings deposits received by Japan Post were funneled into the Fiscal Investment and Loan Program, which financed government-affiliated special corporations that provided public works projects. "The program has been criticized for using repayable postal savings for policy objectives like tax revenue, and for serving merely to perpetuate the franchises of politicians and bureaucrats, while accumulating latent delinquent assets."[53] *The International Herald Tribune* referred to the program as a "murky slush fund." The projects funded were important to the constituency exchange relationships of the Liberal Democratic Party.

The banking and insurance industries complained about unfair competition, since Japan Post was not subject to regulation. For example, it was not required to pay premiums to the government-backed Deposit Insurance Corporation. Kampo also benefited from large tax benefits as a government entity.

A survey by the *Nihon Keizai Shimbun* found 47 percent of respondents in favor of privatization and 34 percent opposed.

The Privatization Plan

The government was a coalition of the Liberal Democratic Party and the New Komeito party, which was backed by the Soka Gakkai Buddhist organization. Prime Minister Junichiro Koizumi had been postal minister in 1993 and became convinced that the postal system had to be privatized. He made privatization a core feature of his reform policy. He reshuffled his cabinet in 2003 and reportedly made support of privatization a condition for inclusion in the cabinet.

The privatization plan was to break Japan Post into four separate business entities: mail delivery, postal savings, insurance, and over-the-counter services. The split would occur in April 2007, and the entities operating the postal savings and the insurance services would be under private management at that time. The entities would be owned by a holding company, and the government would retain a one-third stake in the holding company even after the 10-year transition period was completed in 2017. In 2007 the preexisting Kampo insurance policies would be transferred to a new entity, the Public Successor Corporation. A remaining issue was whether any of the privatized companies should be broken up regionally. This would be left up to the management of the companies.

The privatization policy was to be formalized in a bill to be submitted to the Diet in the session commencing in January 2005. The Council on Economic and Fiscal Policy, chaired by the prime minister and located in the Cabinet Office, was responsible for developing the privatization policy. The Council issued its "Basic Policy on Postal Privatization," which was submitted for review and approval by the cabinet. To prepare the details for a bill to be submitted to the Diet, the government established the Preparatory Office for the Privatization of Postal Services, composed of members of the relevant ministries, agencies, and the Cabinet Office as well as private sector representatives.

As privatized companies, the savings bank and Kampo would be required to pay corporate profits taxes and deposit insurance premiums and would be required to meet reserve requirements rather than be supported by government guarantees. A privatized Kampo would be subject to the Insurance Business Law, although the government's Basic Policy mentioned "certain exemptions" during the 10-year transition period.

Interests

The interests supporting privatization had two objectives. The first was to make certain that the privatization process was not derailed. The second was to prevent Japan Post from using the time until 2007 to favorably position the entities to be privatized.

The Japanese Bankers Association argued that a privatized savings company should not offer fixed-rate savings instruments, and the Life Insurance Association of Japan argued that the privatized life insurance company should not be required to provide universal service. They were concerned that if universal service were required, which under the current law meant the same rates and prices throughout the country, the company would have to be subsidized to support loss-making services in some parts of the country. Yamato Transport Company, the largest parcel-delivery company, took out an advertisement in newspapers to protest the plan to require the privatized mail-delivery company to provide universal service. Yamato believed that a universal service mandate would require subsidies that would give the privatized company an unfair advantage.

With respect to the second objective, business interests wanted assurances that Japan Post would not use the time until 2007 to expand the scope of its services. Under the current law the postal savings system was prohibited from making loans, and Kampo could only provide life insurance. Kampo, however, had already begun offering a whole life insurance policy with a health care rider. Moreover, Japan Post had entered into an arrangement with Lawson Inc. to handle parcels delivered by Japan Post. Yamato Transport filed a lawsuit against Japan Post complaining that the arrangement could force it out of the parcel-delivery business. Yamato had a similar arrangement with Lawson, which it felt compelled to cancel as a result of the Japan Post-Lawson arrangement. Heizo Takenaka, Minister for Economic and Fiscal Policy and Minister for Privatization of Postal Services, commented, "The biggest message from the [Yamato] lawsuit is that Japan Post should be privatized

[53]*Financial Times* Information, July 1, 2004.

as speedily as possible. If it is privatized under the same terms as other businesses, problems like these would not take place."[54]

The American Council of Life Insurers (ACLI) prepared a study showing that Kampo had received over $20 billion of tax breaks during the past 10 years. Allen Smith, chairman of the privatization task force at the American Chamber of Commerce in Japan, said, "This is an opportunity to introduce market principles, and if done well could be very good for the Japanese economy. The big issue is, at what point will it come under the same regulations as applied to the private sector?"[55] Along with the ACLI, the U.S. Chamber of Commerce and the Life Insurance Association of Japan supported privatization of Kampo.

Since 1994 the United States and Japan had been holding bilateral discussions on the insurance industry. In 2004 the United States Trade Representative (USTR) initiated talks about the sale of life insurance by Kampo. Kampo was said to be offering new life insurance products to position itself favorably prior to the possible privatization. The USTR called on Japan to apply the same regulations to Kampo as applied to other insurance companies. The USTR also asked that no new postal services be offered until a level playing field had been established.

Masaharu Ikuta, president of Japan Post, argued that breaking up the system would lose the synergies among its services. He also said, "It may not make sense if (a new organizational plan) would weaken the services. It should be a great loss as (Japan Post) runs quite a few number of jobs. We want (the government) to bear these points in mind and make a plan under a certain time-frame."[56] The Ministry of Public Management, Home Affairs, Posts and Telecommunications agreed with Ikuta.

Japan Post also argued that it would be impossible to restructure its computer systems by April 2007. The government assigned a team of technical experts to evaluate whether the computer systems could be ready.

The workers at Japan Post were represented by two unions. The Japan Postal Workers Union represented 142,000 employees, and the All Japan Postal Labour Union represented 87,000 employees. In addition to its 270,000 employees, Japan Post had 100,000 temporary and part-time workers. Japan Post employees would no longer be public servants beginning with the privatization in 2007.

Some critics of privatization were concerned that universal service for postal savings and life insurance could be jeopardized by privatization. Economists also warned that interest rates could rise, slowing the growth in the economy, if Japan Post were privatized in a manner that required the sale of a substantial number of government bonds.

The Road to Privatization

To advance its privatization objectives, the Koizumi government had to go through a series of stages. The privatization policy required approval of the cabinet. The cabinet was composed of ministers from the LDP and its government partner the New Komeito party. Before seeking approval from the cabinet, Koizumi sought approval from the LDP, which could attempt to block the privatization policy in the cabinet. Opposition to privatization came from within the LDP.

The government decided to meet with both the LDP and the cabinet on the same day. In the morning the government went before the LDP and New Komeito Diet members to present its privatization policy. Two hundred and fifty of the 360 LDP members in the Diet signed a petition opposing privatization, and the members put "reservations" on any policy that they said should be taken into account in the privatization bill to be put before the Diet. The opponents in the LDP, however, did not attempt to block the plan in the cabinet. Referring to the customary practice of obtaining party approval before a bill could be submitted to the Diet, Tamisuke Watanuki, chair of the LDP's committee on postal business, said, "Without party procedures, no bills can be passed."[57] Koizumi was successful in obtaining cabinet approval in the afternoon. He said, "We are unable to win agreement with the party but we have finally reached cabinet approval."[58] He added, "This is the biggest reform since the Meiji Restoration. Although the party's approval was not obtained, it has great significance that the Cabinet approved it."[59] He said the government would "closely coordinate" with the party in drafting the bill to be submitted to the Diet.

Privatization was supported by the Democratic Party of Japan (DPJ), the largest opposition party. The challenge for the Koizumi government was how it could win the support of a majority of the LDP. The poor showing by the LDP and the success of the DPJ in the upper house elections in July provided an opportunity for the prime minister. Robert Feldman, chief economist of Morgan Stanley Japan, commented, "Koizumi has a strong opposition party that he can use to threaten the LDP."[60] ■

SOURCE: This case was prepared from public sources by Professor David P. Baron. Copyright © 2004 by David P. Baron. All rights reserved. Reprinted with permission.

---

[54]*Kyodo News International,* October 4, 2004. Takenaka had been responsible for ordering Japan's largest banks to cut their bad loans by 50 percent by March 2005.
[55]*Wall Street Journal,* September 13, 2004.
[56]*AFX Europe,* July 21, 2004.

---

[57]*Agence France Presse–English,* September 12, 2004.
[58]*Agence France Presse–English,* September 12, 2004.
[59]*Japan Economic Newswire,* September 10, 2004.
[60]*International Herald Tribune,* September 28, 2004.

Preparation Questions

1. Identify the interests that will attempt to influence the road to privatization.
2. Which institutions in the Japanese government will play a role on the road to privatization?

3. What strategy should a Japanese bank or insurance company adopt to influence the privatization plan?
4. What strategy should a U.S. bank or insurance company adopt to influence the privatization plan?

Uniqlo: Success Breeds Nonmarket Challenges

The Uniqlo brand burst onto the Japanese retail clothing scene in 1998 and was an instant success. By 2000 the Uniqlo chain had nearly 500 stores in Japan, with sales of $5 billion for its parent company, Fast Retailing. Its flagship items were fleece jackets for men and women, with sales of 8.5 million jackets in 2000. Uniqlo offered good quality clothing at attractive prices. Its fleece jackets sold for $16.50 compared to prices nearly three times as high at other retailers such as the Gap. Uniqlo sold 300 million items of clothing in Japan, an average of nearly three per person in the country. Its profit for the first half of 2001 was $600 million.

Uniqlo's success was as much due to its cachet as to its prices. Tadashi Yanai began Uniqlo with stores in Tokyo suburbs. By late 1998 he was ready to take the Uniqlo brand nationwide.[61] Launched with a stylish TV advertising campaign featuring pop singer Masayoshi Yamazaki, Yanai opened a store in Tokyo's Harajuku district, where Japanese fashion trends originate. Suddenly, Uniqlo's low-priced goods became chic and, as customers recognized the quality of the goods, sales skyrocketed.

In contrast to other Japanese retailers, Uniqlo's strategy was to design items in Japan and directly contract with factories in China for their production. In addition to low-cost production in China, Uniqlo bypassed the inefficient Japanese distribution system by supplying its stores directly. A number of other major retailers responded to Uniqlo's success by lowering their prices 25 to 30 percent, but their cost structure made it difficult for them to sustain the price cuts.

Yanai planned to take Uniqlo to Europe where he announced plans to open 50 stores in Great Britain. He explained the choice. "France is too conservative and the American market too competitive. Britain is quite conservative, like the Japanese. We both live on islands and are common-sense countries. We both like to be a bit different, but not too different."[62]

Uniqlo's growth contributed to a dramatic increase in imports from China, led by textiles and agricultural products. By 2000 Japan purchased more goods from China than from either Europe or the United States, and its trade deficit with China reached $25 billion. The impact on Japan's textile market was severe. Domestic production of textiles fell 31 percent from 1990 levels. Imports had surged 16.9 percent in 2000, and most of the growth was due to imports from China. The heart of Japan's textile industry was Ehime and Osaka prefectures, which were particularly hard hit.

In response to the surge in textile imports from China and other East Asian countries, the Japan Towel Industrial Association, with 457 domestic manufacturers, filed a petition with the Ministry of International Trade and Industry (MITI) asking the government to invoke a World Trade Organization safeguard provision allowing import restrictions for 3 years to give domestic manufacturers time to adjust to international competitive pressures. Association president Yoshihide Yoshihara said, "Compared with two years ago, imports have increased 34.5 percent and domestic production has decreased 25.9 percent. Towel-producing areas have been hard hit and jobs have been lost in them."[63] The market share of imported towels had reached 57.7 percent, and the association predicted that imports would increase to 70 percent by 2003. In the first half of 2000, textile imports from China increased 36 percent. Some Japanese commentators drew an analogy to the 1970s when U.S. textile manufacturers sought protection from lower-priced goods from Japan. In 2001 Japan was on the verge of taking the position it had so vigorously criticized.

The economic conditions in the Japanese textile industry were shared to a lesser extent by the Japanese economy. As of November 2000, consumer spending in Japan had fallen for 44 consecutive months. Consumer prices had fallen for over a year. Many Japanese companies followed Uniqlo's strategy of sourcing in China as a means of lowering costs so that they could cut prices to increase demand. For example, Yamaha Motor Company sourced parts in China and was able to reduce the price of a motorized bicycle by 30 percent. One observer commented, "There still are a lot of consumer durables with price gaps between domestic and overseas markets. Price decreases will spread into many other fields."[64]

Despite the filing by the Japan Towel Industrial Association, a number of towel manufacturers objected to

---

[61]Uniqlo is a combination of "unique" and "clothing."
[62]*Sunday Times*, February 4, 2001.

[63]*Daily Yomiuri*, February 18, 2001.
[64]*Daily Yomiuri*, August 7, 2001.

the petition. Seven towel manufacturers from Ehime Prefecture filed a petition opposing invoking the safeguard provision. The seven companies had already moved much of their sourcing of products to China because of competitive pressures. Their petition stated, "If the safeguard is imposed, firms that have made efforts to survive by moving their factories overseas will be critically damaged." The companies explained, "The petition to invoke the safeguard was decided by a majority vote (of the national association) that we did not support."[65] More Japanese firms were expected to move their production to other countries in an attempt to achieve competitiveness and avoid bankruptcy.

Opposition to invoking the safeguard provision also came from consumers. "Yoriko Inubushi, vice president of the Consumption Science Federation, said: 'Consumers want low-priced, high-quality goods. If the safeguard is imposed while domestic makers have not shown they are making an effort to meet demand, even consumers who advocate the importance of buying Japanese will not do so.'"[66]

Yoshihisa Kitai, chief economist for Shinsei Bank said, "I call it the Uniqlo effect. The import of textiles and vegetables and home appliances from the rest of Asia is rising rapidly. Therefore, manufacturers of textiles and farmers will inevitably have to go out of business because they can't compete."[67] Tadashi Yanai was fond of saying, "Those who can't swim should drown."[68]

The Liberal Democratic Party continued to be rocked by scandals, and Prime Minister Mori was expected to resign soon. The appeal by the textile companies to invoke the WTO safeguard provision put the LDP and MITI in a difficult position. In the past the LDP and MITI might have sided with the manufacturers, but with the LDP's fragile electoral support, the government was nervous about acting against the interests of consumers. The Japanese government hoped that China would voluntarily limit its exports to Japan.[69] ■

Preparation Questions

1. What are the causes of the surge in imports from China? Are imports from China and other East Asian countries likely to continue to grow?
2. What are the likely ramifications of invoking the safeguard provision?

3. What if anything should Uniqlo do in response to the strategy of the domestic manufacturers?

[65]*Daily Yomiuri,* March 10, 2001.
[66]*Daily Yomiuri,* February 18, 2001.

[67]*San Jose Mercury News,* March 17, 2001.
[68]*Scotsman,* January 3, 2001.
[69]*Daily Yomiuri,* February 21, 2001.

C H A P T E R
15

The Political Economy of the European Union

INTRODUCTION

The European Union (EU) has taken landmark steps toward economic and political integration. It has established a single market with half a billion consumers in 27 nations that allows the free movement of people, goods, services, and capital. It has also established a common currency and an independent central bank and has moved toward greater commonality in defense and foreign policy. The eventual breadth of the union remains open with other nations seeking to join, and the eventual depth of integration, particularly with respect to political union, remains unclear.

The European Union admitted Bulgaria and Romania in 2007, and official candidates for future entry are Croatia, Republic of Macedonia, and Turkey. Five other countries are potential candidates for entry. Norway was approved to join the Union, but in 1994 Norwegian voters rejected membership as they had done in 1972. The member states differ considerably with populations ranging from 436,000 to 82 million, a ratio of more than 10 to 1 in per capita income, and unemployment rates ranging from 2.9 to 10.5 percent in 2005. The EU has 23 languages. The 12 new countries that became members in 2004 and 2007 increased the differences among the member states. For example, the median corporate tax in the European Union was 33 percent, but the rate in Estonia was zero. The average price-level index in the 10 new members that entered in 2006 was 52 percent of that in the other 15 member states. The average wage and benefits of an autoworker in Denmark were €35 an hour, whereas the average in Bulgaria was only €2.10. Yet remarkable progress toward economic integration has been made, and the commitment to deeper integration remains strong in most of the member states.

This chapter considers the nonmarket environment in the European Union using the structured pluralism framework illustrated in Figure 14-1. The next section traces the history of the European Union and considers the two principal instruments for economic integration. The principal institutions are then considered along with the legislative procedures used by the European Union. The monetary union, fiscal harmonization, competition policy, state aid, market opening, and social democracy are then discussed. Issues and interests are considered, and these foundations are used to identify effective nonmarket strategies in the European Union.

THE EUROPEAN UNION

In the aftermath of World War II, Europeans recognized the need to increase trade and encourage political cooperation. In 1951 six nations—Belgium, France, Italy, Luxembourg, the Netherlands, and West Germany—signed the Treaty of Paris, which established the European Coal and Steel Community (ECSC). The ECSC's goal was to improve the efficiency of its member states' coal and steel industries through the reduction of trade barriers.

In 1957 those same nations signed the Treaty of Rome, which provided the basic framework for the European Union of today. The Treaty of Rome established the European Economic Community (EEC), or the common market, with the objectives of opening domestic markets to the members and rationalizing their industries.[1] The 1965 Treaty of Brussels represented an important step toward European integration by unifying the administration of the EEC, ECSC, and EURATOM. This provided an administrative structure upon which further steps toward economic and political integration could be built. The European Monetary System was established in 1979 to provide fixed, but adjustable, exchange rate bands for the currencies of the member states. In 1973 Denmark, Ireland, and the United Kingdom joined the EEC. Greece joined in 1981, Portugal and Spain in 1986, and Austria, Finland, and Sweden joined in 1995. The 2000 Treaty of Nice provided a road map for enlargement of the Union, and in 2004 the European Union admitted 10 new members: Cyprus, Latvia, Lithuania, the Czech Republic, Estonia, Hungary, Malta, Slovakia, Poland, and Slovenia, with Bulgaria and Romania joining in 2007.[2]

In addition to the broadening of the EU through the admission of new member states, the member states and their citizens faced the issue of the depth of political integration. Some supported a deeper union in which more authority would be transferred from the member states to the EU government. This could involve substantial changes in the institutions and the representation in those institutions. One possibility was a federal system such as the one in Germany or the United States. In contrast to those who sought a deeper union, a number of EU citizens began asking whether political union had already gone too far. This Euroskepticism stemmed from the view that once economic integration had been achieved, a deeper political union would provide little in the way of benefits.[3]

The two most recent major steps toward economic and political union have been the Single European Act and the Maastricht Treaty on European Union, considered next.[4]

The Single European Act

Economic growth in the common market was strong during the 1960s, but beginning in the 1970s and particularly in the early 1980s growth slowed markedly, unemployment rolls swelled to over 10 percent, and job creation came to a crawl. The slow growth, the high cost of labor, and the difficulties and costs involved in workforce reductions made many firms reluctant to hire. Europeans called their economic disease "Eurosclerosis" and worried about worsening competitiveness relative to Japan and the United States.

Many business leaders recognized that competitiveness was inhibited by a set of barriers that limited trade and increased costs. Progress in reducing many of the barriers had been slow because each state reserved the right to veto changes it believed were contrary to its interests. To document the potential gains from further market integration, the European Commission sponsored the Cecchini study, which concluded that the formation of a single market could increase GDP by 4.3 to 6.4 percent.[5]

The Single European Act (SEA), which took effect in 1987, addressed several impediments to trade and provided measures to facilitate access to national markets.[6] The SEA also increased the power of the EU government relative to the governments of the member states, particularly by limiting the use of the unanimity rule for decision making. The SEA mandated the realization of a single market by the beginning of 1993.

---

[1]The six nations also formed the European Atomic Energy Community (EURATOM).
[2]Cyprus is partitioned, and only the Greek portion of the island has become a member.
[3]See, for example, Alesina and Wacziarg (1999).
[4]The 1997 Treaty of Amsterdam strengthened the human rights provisions of the European Union, committed the Union to take steps to increase employment, adopted the objective of sustainable development, strengthened the Common Foreign and Security Policy, elevated the formal powers of the European Parliament, and prepared for institutional change when new members were admitted.
[5]See Cecchini et al. (1988) and Emerson et al. (1988).
[6]See Overturf (1986) for an analysis of the benefits from economic integration.

The program to realize market integration involved the removal of three types of barriers: physical, technical, and fiscal. The removal of physical barriers pertained to the movement of both goods and people, eliminating customs and other goods inspections, removing restrictions on the entry of people, and allowing individuals to work in any member state.

The European Union took two approaches—harmonization and mutual recognition—to the removal of internal barriers to trade. *Harmonization* refers to the development of a common set of policies for all member states. Because of the complexity of the bargaining, progress on technical issues such as product standards, product certification, and the licensing of professional services had become tediously slow as nationalistic considerations complicated negotiations. To avoid the roadblocks of the past, the principle of *mutual recognition,* first articulated by the European Court of Justice in the Cassis de Dijon case, was adopted.[7] The EU member states were able to agree on mutual recognition, whereas they had been unable to agree on a common set of standards. The principle of mutual recognition represented a major change in EU policy and increased the speed with which internal barriers were removed.

Fiscal harmonization pertains to tax policy, particularly value-added taxes (VAT), excise and profits taxes, government fiscal policy, and subsidization or "state aids." The member states differed substantially in their tax and other fiscal policies, and those differences distorted trade, the location of facilities, and the movement of people. For example, VAT rates were as high as 38 percent on some goods and as low as zero on others. Furthermore, some countries had multiple tiers of VAT rates, whereas others had a single rate. Progress on fiscal harmonization has been slow. One tax harmonization measure that was implemented abolished duty free sales for intra-EU travel, but the industry attempted to overturn the abolition, as considered in the chapter case, *Aldeasa and the EU Duty Free Abolition (A).*

With the entry of 12 new member states since 2004 the disparity in tax rates increased. The countries of Eastern Europe generally had low corporate tax rates, and several of them had reduced their tax rates prior to joining the EU. The average corporate tax rate of the 10 new entrants in 2004 was 21.3 percent, whereas the average for the 15 prior members was 31.3 percent. Tax harmonization was even farther in the future.

Harmonization is also the approach taken to the sensitive and important issues of public health, safety, and the environment. The approach was to reach agreement on a set of basic standards and then allow the individual member states to go beyond those standards as they chose.

The Maastricht Treaty

In 1992 the member states agreed to the Maastricht Treaty on European Union. The Treaty ran into immediate problems as the United Kingdom opted out of part of it, Denmark first rejected and then narrowly accepted it, and French voters only narrowly approved it.

The treaty established a timetable for a common European currency and an independent European Central Bank.[8] Twelve member states that had met targets on inflation rates, government budget deficits, and interest rates formed a monetary union with a common currency—the euro —and a European Central Bank. Denmark, Sweden, and the United Kingdom met the targets but opted not to join.

Political integration was considerably more difficult than monetary union, but some steps toward political union were taken. The member states entered into a protocol to establish a joint social policy. Nine of the member states agreed to establish a joint defense policy. Additional proposals included strengthening the European Parliament, establishing a European citizenship, and changing the unanimity rule still in effect for certain decisions. To advance the cause of political union, a constitutional

---

[7]In 1979 the court ruled that a German regulation on the alcohol content of liqueurs could not be used to block the sale of the French liqueur Cassis de Dijon.
[8]See Committee for the Study of Economic and Monetary Union (1989) and Goodman (1992).

convention was convened and developed a constitution, as considered in the next section, that was rejected by France and the Netherlands. The EU then repackaged most of the proposed constitution as the Treaty of Lisbon. Ratification began in 2008, but Irish voters rejected it.

THE INSTITUTIONS OF THE EUROPEAN UNION

The four principal institutions of the European Union are the European Commission, the Council of Ministers, the European Parliament, and the European Court of Justice. The following sections consider the institutions in more detail and the changes that would have resulted from the ratification of the EU constitution or the Treaty of Lisbon. Figure 15-1 highlights the roles of the three institutions involved in legislation and administration.

The European Commission

The European Commission, located in Brussels, is the executive and administrative body of the European Union. The commission administers EU policies and enforces the various treaties. It is responsible for monitoring the implementation of EU legislation and ensuring that the member states comply with EU law. The commission is responsible for trade negotiations and manages the EU budget. The commission is the only body with the power to initiate legislation. The European Parliament and the Council of Ministers, however, can ask the commission to review proposals and consider issues. The European Commission's role in initiating legislation and administering policies makes it a target for lobbying. Moreover, the commission is obligated to consult with interest groups and to notify the Council of Ministers and the parliament that it has done so. The commission has a relatively small staff (25,000), so it needs information and expertise, and its consultations with interest groups are a means of obtaining that information.

Each member state has one commissioner, who is obliged to serve the interests of the European Union and not those of their own countries. Commission terms are 5 years, and commissioners are nominated by the individual member states. The commissioners must be approved as a whole by the European Parliament, and the parliament can dismiss the commission on a vote of no confidence. In an unprecedented event in 1999 all the commissioners resigned under a threat from the European Parliament stemming from allegations of corruption and mismanagement. In 2004 the incoming

FIGURE 15-1 EU Legislative and Administrative Institutions

Approves, can censure

Appoints

Consults, advises, amends, vetoes

Commission (27 commissioners) DGs → Council of Ministers (27 member states) → Parliament (785 MEPs)

Commission:
- Serves EU, integrationist
- Main EU executive body (bureaucracy)
- Attempts to operate by consensus
- Initiates legislation
- DGs have well-specified jurisdictions
- Implements EU treaties

Council of Ministers:
- Executive and legislative functions
- Weighted voting; different rules for different decisions, unanimity for some decisions

Parliament:
- Directly elected by voters in member states
- Political groups (parties)
- Cannot initiate legislation but can amend and veto under co-decision procedure
- Committees are weak but are becoming more important

president of the commission withdrew his nominees for commissioners because of certain rejection by the parliament.

One commissioner serves as president and five as vice presidents, and the others have responsibility for one or more of the 22 Directorates-General (DGs). A DG is a bureau, with a particular policy or administrative jurisdiction. For example, one DG has responsibilities for economic and financial affairs, and the competition DG has responsibility for antitrust, mergers, and state aid. The commission also has several services.

The conflict between national and EU laws creates a tension within the community. EU law takes precedence over national law when a conflict arises, but not all national laws have been harmonized with EU law. In a number of cases member states have not complied with EU law, and the commission attempts to obtain compliance. In 2003 the commission initiated 1,552 infringement proceedings against member states for violating treaties or failing to implement directives. For example, the commission filed complaints against a number of member states for delays in implementing the Directive on Data Protection, as considered in the chapter case, *The European Union Data Protection Directive*.

The commission formally makes decisions by majority rule, but in practice it operates on a collegial basis, and no public reports of its deliberations or votes are issued. Conflict within the commission, however, can develop over policies, particularly those that have impacts across more than one DG. For example, the commissioner for industry proposed the elimination of price controls on pharmaceuticals as a means of encouraging firms to invest more in the development of innovative drugs. The commission, however, rejected the proposal in favor of asking the member states to bring their divergent pharmaceutical pricing policies into alignment.

The Council of Ministers

The Council of Ministers, based in Brussels, is the principal legislative body of the European Union.[9] In contrast to the commission, whose members are obliged to serve the European Union, council members are the individual member states. The council consists of one minister from each state, but the nations have different numbers of votes, based roughly on population, as indicated in Figure 15-2. The presidency rotates among the member states every 6 months, and which ministers belong to the council depends on the issue under consideration. On an issue involving economics and finance, the cognizant ministers of the member states meet as the Economic and Financial Affairs Council (ECOFIN). The council operates in private, but since 1995 its votes have been reported publicly. Twice a year, the heads of state or government of the member states meet as the European Council, which sets the general direction for the European Union.

FIGURE 15-2 Council of Ministers Voting Weights

France, Germany, Italy, United Kingdom	29
Poland, Spain	27
Romania	14
Netherlands	13
Belgium, Czech Republic, Greece, Hungary, Portugal	12
Austria, Bulgaria, Sweden	10
Denmark, Finland, Ireland, Lithuania, Slovakia	7
Cyprus, Estonia, Latvia, Luxembourg, Slovenia	4
Malta	3
Total	345

---

[9]See Hoscheit and Wessels (1988) and Nugent (2003) for an analysis of the Council of Ministers.

Associated with the council is the Committee of Permanent Representatives (COREPER), composed of ambassadors, or "permanent representatives," of the member states. COREPER represents the member states before the commission and serves as the secretariat of the Council of Ministers. It prepares the agenda, forms working parties, and negotiates informal agreements prior to council deliberations. Before the council considers proposals, COREPER appoints an ad hoc working party composed of government officials from the member states. Members of the commission may also participate. The working party gives its opinion on a legislative proposal to COREPER. If COREPER agrees with the opinion, it forwards the proposal to the council. COREPER is said to resolve 90 percent of the issues before they come to the council, leaving only the most politically sensitive issues for council deliberations.

Council decisions had been governed by a unanimity rule, which gave a veto to the member states. Because this created long delays on some issues, the SEA provided for decisions by majority rule. On most procedural matters the council acts under simple majority rule. Most of its substantive actions, however, require a "qualified" majority of 255 of the 345 votes. A qualified majority also requires approval by a majority of the member states, and a member state can request "verification," which requires approval by member states comprising at least 62 percent of the population of the European Union. The Treaty of Nice replaced unanimity with qualified majority on 27 treaty provisions, including negotiated agreements on trade in services and intellectual property protection. Decisions involving foreign and security policy, justice and home affairs, some aspects of fiscal policy, and enlargement of the community, however, require unanimity.

The European Union can take four types of actions, which differ in the extent to which they are binding on the member states.[10]

1. Regulations are legally binding on the member states and are enforced by the commission.
2. Directives are legally binding with respect to the result sought, but national governments are responsible for how the result is achieved.
3. Decisions are legally binding but pertain only to the parties identified in the decision.
4. Recommendations and opinions are not legally binding but may provide guidance and foretell future action on issues.

EU law becomes effective in a member state when that state accepts it as its law.

The Union operates under the principle of subsidiarity, meaning the intention to accomplish as much as possible at the level of the member states.[11] Article 35 of the Consolidated Treaty states that the Union can act "only if and in so far as the objectives of the proposed action cannot be sufficiently achieved by the Member States and can therefore, by reason of the scale or effects of the proposed action, be better achieved by the Community." This statement has been clarified by guidelines developed by the council. Any conflict over the application of the principle can be taken to the Court of Justice.

The European Parliament

The European Parliament (EP) has 785 members directly elected for 5-year terms under proportional representation by voters in the member states. Although the European Parliament's power has increased over time, the turnout in the elections has decreased over time. Parliament members organize by parties or political groupings. In 2008 the European People's Party (Christian Democrats) and the European Democrats held 288 seats and the Socialists Group held 215 seats. The EP meets in Brussels and Strasbourg.

As the only popularly elected institution in the European Union, the EP has powers of "democratic supervision."[12] The EP approves of and can dismiss the commission

---

[10]See Nugent (2003).
[11]The pledge to abide by the principle of subsidiarity was important in obtaining Denmark's support for the Maastricht Treaty.
[12]The term "democratic supervision" refers to the fact that the council is not popularly elected.

and can ask questions of commissioners in writing or during "Question Time" when the EP is in session. Through the co-decision procedure, the EP and the council share legislative authority. Parliament cannot initiate or enact laws but plays an important role in the legislative process. That role has expanded over time, and the SEA and the Maastricht Treaty gave it new legislative power, as described later in the chapter. Parliament also has budgetary authority.

The EP elects a president, who serves a 2 1/2-year term, and vice presidents from the other member states. It has 20 standing committees to which proposals are referred for consideration, and they are a focus of lobbying. Neither the committees nor the EP has the ability to delay a proposal, since action must be taken within a specified time period. The EP operates under simple majority rule.

Individual citizens and firms may petition the EP on issues arising from either EU actions or conflicts between EU law and national laws. Petitions are reviewed by a Petition Committee; if accepted for consideration, the Petition Committee evaluates the petition and may hold a hearing. Interest groups often work through their national representatives in the petition process.

The Court of Justice

The Court of Justice, located in Luxembourg, is the supreme judicial body of the Union and has the authority to overturn decisions that conflict with the EU treaties.[13] The court has one judge from each member state, with one judge elected as president for a 3-year term.[14] The Court makes decisions by majority vote in 13-judge chambers, and other cases are decided in three- and five-judge chambers. Dissenting opinions are not issued. The judges serve 6-year terms and are assisted by 8 advocates general who provide independent and impartial opinions. The court hears cases pertaining to the various treaties of the European Union and other cases involving disputes between the community's institutions. Some of the cases brought to the court involve complaints by the European Commission against the member states. Actions can also be brought directly to the court by individuals and legal entities of the member states. Although the court has the final word on EU law, treaties give the courts of the member states some responsibilities for implementing EU law. The court also hears cases from member states when the states' own courts are uncertain about EU law.[15] Because of the court's workload, the Council of Ministers, under the SEA, established the Court of First Instance (CFI). The CFI applies the law established by the Court of Justice, and its decisions may be appealed to the higher court.

The Court of Justice also hears appeals of commission decisions. For example, cases involving the competitive practices of firms are usually decided by the commission's DG for competition. Firms can appeal its decisions and the penalties assessed. As indicated later in the chapter, European airlines appealed the commission's decision to allow France to subsidize Air France, and Microsoft appealed a decision in a competition case.

The European Economic and Social Committee

The European Economic and Social Committee (EESC), based in Brussels, is an advisory body whose 344 members represent employees, employers, farmers, trades, and other interests. The EESC has six sections, or committees that provide forums to express opinions on commission proposals and suggest changes in them. Interest groups interact with the EESC through the representatives of their home countries in the relevant sections. The final opinions of the EESC can be important because they reflect the concerns of interest groups.

---

[13]See Nugent (2003).
[14]Europe also has a Council of Europe that has a European Court of Human Rights, which hears cases under the European Convention on Human Rights.
[15]A major difference between the United States and European countries results from the due process requirements of the U.S. Constitution. As discussed in Chapter 10, due process imposes a complex set of requirements on government processes intended to ensure individuals the right to participate in governmental decision-making processes. Unless provided for by specific legislation, the European Union and most European countries do not have the same requirements.

The EU Legislative Process

The European Union has three basic procedures—consultation, co-decision, and assent—for developing directives and regulations.[16] Under the consultation procedure that was used for nearly all important issues prior to the SEA, the European Commission, through one of its DGs, formulates a proposal that is sent to the Council of Ministers, which seeks opinions from both the EP and the EESC. The council weighs those opinions and returns the proposal to the commission for revision. The commission then sends the revised proposal to the council, which may amend, approve, or not act on it. If approved, the proposal becomes EU law, and the member states are required to abide by it.

The SEA established the assent procedure, which gives the EP a veto over council action. The assent procedure is used for decisions about admission of new member states, international agreements, and the structure of the European Central Bank.

The Maastricht Treaty established the co-decision procedure, and the scope of its use was expanded in the Treaty of Amsterdam and the Treaty of Nice. This procedure, as illustrated in Figure 15-3, gives the EP a greater role and more power relative to the commission and the council. This procedure begins as in the consultation procedure, but once the opinions of the EP and the EESC have been obtained, the Council of Ministers develops by qualified majority a "common position" on the proposal. It is then sent to the EP for a second reading. If the EP approves the proposal, it is enacted. If an absolute majority of the EP votes against the common position, it is defeated and the process ends. If the EP amends the common position, the council can accept the amendments, thereby enacting the proposal. If the council rejects the amendments, a conciliation committee composed of members of the council and the EP is formed. If they reach agreement, the amended proposal is enacted by qualified majority of the council and a simple majority of the Parliament at the third reading. If no agreement is reached, or if either the council or the Parliament fails to approve the amended proposal, the proposal fails.[17]

The co-decision procedure is said to be bicameral, since approval by both the council and Parliament is required. The procedure is not fully "democratic," however, because the popularly elected Parliament cannot enact laws itself. The co-decision procedure is thus best viewed as a legislative process in which both the Parliament and the council have a veto.

Economic and Monetary Union

The European Union's interest in a monetary union officially began in 1989 when the Council of Ministers endorsed a series of steps to realize an Economic and Monetary Union (EMU). The EMU commenced in 1998 with the formation of the European System of Central Banks and the European Central Bank (ECB) to conduct a single monetary policy for its members. In 1999 the euro became the common currency of the EMU, and euro notes and coins replaced national currencies in 2002.[18] The ECB is an independent central bank patterned after Germany's central bank (the Bundesbank). The primary objective of the ECB is "to maintain price stability."

The European Union estimated that the savings on transactions costs associated with currency exchange would be 0.4 percent of GDP. The euro has become an important global currency and could become a reserve currency. Some countries such as Italy saw another advantage in the EMU. It would serve as a commitment device that would provide price stability to which its governments had had difficulty committing.

---

[16]See Nugent (2003) and Hix (2005).
[17]The stages of the process each have timetables; for example, the conciliation committee has 6 weeks to reach an agreement.
[18]The European Union had a long history of coordinating exchange rate policies. In the 1970s European countries maintained the "snake" with fixed exchange rates, and subsequently a stable Deutschmark zone developed. The European Monetary System (EMS) was established to band exchange rates together. The EMS also used a weighted average of exchange rates, the ECU, that was a forerunner of the euro.

FIGURE 15-3   The European Union Co-Decision Legislative Procedure

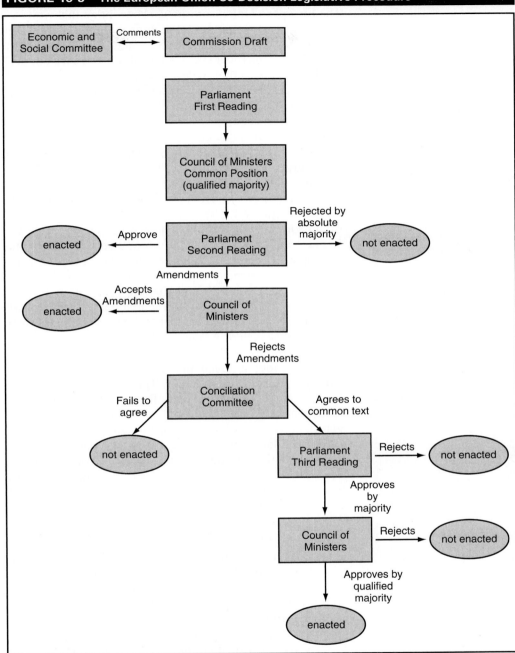

Not everyone shared the same enthusiasm for the EMU. Feldstein (1997, pp. 32–33) warned that the EMU may have costs that outweigh its benefits. He pointed to the loss of flexibility for a country to use discretionary monetary policy to offset temporary shocks to its economy. This could make it more difficult to reduce long-term unemployment.

One concern about monetary union was whether the member states would attempt to use the EMU for political purposes rather than price stability. The Treaty establishing the ECB stated that "without prejudice to the objective of price stability, the ECSB shall support the general economic policies in the Community. . . ." The ECB is independent of the governments of the member states, but some governments have sought to influence the policies of the ECB to stimulate economic growth and create jobs.

The EU Constitutional Treaty

The European Union convened a convention that wrote a treaty establishing a Constitution for Europe, intended to consolidate the seven EU treaties and revise the institutional structure of the Union. To take effect, the Constitutional Treaty had to be ratified by all member states, some of which used a popular referendum. Voters in both France and the Netherlands rejected it in 2005, reflecting a gulf between voters and political leaders. European political leaders repackaged the Constitutional Treaty as the Treaty of Lisbon, and France chose not to put the Treaty to a popular vote. Ireland, however, was required by its constitution to use a popular referendum, and in June 2008 Irish voters rejected the Treaty.

If the Treaty of Lisbon were adopted, it would formally recognize the Charter for Fundamental Rights, making human and civil rights enforceable by the European Union.[19] The Treaty would extend the co-decision procedure to cover 95 percent of EU lawmaking, so more legislation would require approval of both the Council of Ministers and the EP. Matters of taxation, social policy, and foreign and defense policy would continue to require unanimity. The Treaty would establish the positions of High Representative for Foreign Affairs and Security Policy and EU prosecutor for law enforcement. The Treaty would establish the European Council, composed of the heads of states of the member states, as a separate institution with a president with a 2 1/2-year term. The size of the EP would be capped at 750, and after 2014 the number of commissioners would be two-thirds of the number of member states.

The most contentious aspect of the Constitutional Treaty was the voting rule for the Council of Ministers. A qualified majority was specified as a double majority of countries constituting 55 percent of the member states and 65 percent of the population. To avoid a situation in which three large countries could stop an action, four countries were required for a blocking minority. The voting rule would not take effect until 2014.

The Treaty of Lisbon made the institutions more transparent and democratic, although the EP remained the only popularly elected body. The Council of Ministers' legislative proceedings were to be open to the public. Citizens were given the opportunity to initiate legislation by collecting 1 million signatures on a proposal inviting the Commission to initiate legislation. To strengthen the role of national governments, the Commission was required to review a legislative proposal if one-third of the national parliaments believed the proposal was not in accord with the principle of subsidiarity. The Treaty also declared that combating climate change and global warming was an objective of the EU.

Competition Policy

Competition policy includes EU policies involving the structure, conduct, and support of industries, including state aid. Antitrust policy is the centerpiece of competition policy, and this section addresses EU antitrust law and its administration. The member states also have their own competition laws. In 1998 France rejected Coca-Cola's planned acquisition of Orangina, after objections by PepsiCo and Orangina employees who feared layoffs.

The basic antitrust law of the European Union is found in Articles 81 and 82 of the Treaty Establishing the European Community, the principal components of which are presented in Figure 15-4.[20] The articles have two antecedents. The first is the Treaty of Rome goal of market integration. The second is U.S. antitrust law. Articles 81 and 82 correspond to Sections 1 and 2 of the Sherman Act, but EU antitrust law differs somewhat from U.S. law. Both aim at promoting competition, but EU law allows defenses, such as economic consequences, not explicitly provided for under U.S. law. Hence, EU law does not have per se offenses.

As with Section 1 of the Sherman Act, Article 81 refers to group activities that may limit competition or constitute a barrier to trade among member states. Much of the

---

[19]Ireland and the United Kingdom were allowed to opt out of the Charter because of their common law tradition.
[20]Article 82 is presented in its entirety.

FIGURE 15-4   European Union Antitrust Law: Articles 81 and 82 of the Treaty Establishing the European Community

Article 81:

(1) The following practices shall be prohibited as incompatible with the Common Market: all agreements between undertakings and all concerted practices which are liable to affect trade between Member States and which are designed to prevent, restrict or distort competition within the Common Market or which have this effect. This shall, in particular, include:

    (a) the direct or indirect fixing of purchase or selling prices or of any other trading conditions;

    (b) the limitation or control of production markets, technical development or investment;

    (c) market-sharing or the sharing of sources of supply;

    (d) the application of unequal conditions on parties undertaking equivalent engagements in commercial transactions, thereby placing them at a competitive disadvantage;

    (e) making the conclusion of a contract subject to the acceptance by the other party to the contract of additional obligations which, by their nature or according to commercial practice, have no connection with the subject of such contract.

(2) Any agreement or decisions prohibited pursuant to this article shall automatically be null and void.

(3) The provisions of paragraph (1) may, however, be declared inapplicable in the case of

    –any agreement or type of agreement between undertakings

    –any decision or type of agreement between undertakings

    –any concerted practice or type of concerted practice

which helps to improve the production or distribution of goods or to promote technical or economic progress, whilst allowing consumers a fair share of the resulting profit and which does not: (a) subject the concerns in question to any restrictions which are not indispensable to the achievement of the above objectives; (b) enable such concerns to eliminate competition in respect to a substantial part of the goods concerned.

Article 82:

Any improper exploitation by one or more undertakings of a dominant position within the Common Market or within a substantial part of it shall be deemed to be incompatible with the Common Market and shall be prohibited, in so far as trade between Member States could be affected by it. The following practices, in particular, shall be deemed to amount to improper exploitation:

    (a) the direct or indirect imposition of any unfair purchase or selling prices or of any other unfair trading conditions;

    (b) the limitation of production, markets or technical development to the prejudice of consumers;

    (c) the application of unequal conditions to parties undertaking equivalent engagements in commercial transactions, thereby placing them at a commercial disadvantage;

    (d) making the conclusion of a contract to the acceptance by the other party to the contract of additional obligations which by their nature or according to commercial practice have no connection with the subject of such contract.

text addresses vertical restraints, which were a concern at the time of establishment of the economic community because of the possibility that firms would use such arrangements in their channels of distribution to preserve national markets for themselves. Parts a, b, and c of Article 81, paragraph 1, pertain to vertical arrangements that might foreclose markets, and part d deals with price discrimination. Part e pertains to tying arrangements or reciprocal deals that might foreclose markets. The feature of Article 81 that distinguishes it most from Section 1 of the Sherman Act is the allowable defenses provided in paragraph 3. A firm may make the affirmative defense that an arrangement improves efficiency. The firm is obligated to use the least restrictive means to achieve that efficiency, and some of the efficiency gains must be passed on to consumers. The United States has adopted a similar perspective by considering whether a practice benefits consumers. Paragraph 3 virtually grants block exemptions for a variety of agreements—exclusive distributorships, exclusive purchase arrangements, patent licensing, motor vehicle distribution, specialization, research and development, franchises, and know-how licensing.

Article 82 deals with unilateral actions and differs from Section 2 of the Sherman Act. The article is not concerned with how a dominant position was obtained but rather with whether that position is abused. Its specific provisions apply to unfair practices, monopoly restriction of output, price discrimination, and tying.

Enforcement

Antitrust enforcement is by the DG for Competition, which investigates practices, initiates proceedings, serves as prosecutor, decides cases, and imposes fines. In contrast to the United States where antitrust cases are decided by judges or by an independent commission in the case of the Federal Trade Commission, the DG serves as both prosecutor and judge. The courts play no role unless there is an appeal of an action. Appeals are heard by the Court of First Instance and then by the Court of Justice if necessary. Private parties may file complaints with the European Commission, but private lawsuits are not permitted by Articles 81 and 82.[21] The DG is also required to consult with national competition officials before initiating proceedings. Those officials participate in the Advisory Committee on Restrictive Practices and Monopolies. In terms of remedies, the European Commission is limited to imposing fines and supervising conduct. Criminal penalties are not allowed. In 2004 the DG for Competition was given additional investigatory authority, and responsibility for certain merger approvals was devolved to the member states to allow the DG to concentrate on breaking up cartels. The commission has proposed that it be allowed to use structural remedies, such as ordering the divestiture of business units. The Microsoft example includes a range of remedies.

Fines of up to 10 percent of a company's sales are the principal enforcement instrument. In 2000 the commission imposed fines of €110 million on Archer Daniels Midland, two Japanese companies and one Korean company, for cartel price fixing of lysine used in animal foodstuffs. In 2001 the commission fined eight companies €855 million for cartel price fixing of vitamins. Roche Holding AG was fined €462 million as the ringleader of the price-fixing cartel.[22]

In 2004 the DG for Competition reached a settlement with Coca-Cola after a 5-year investigation. In member states in which its market share exceeds 40 percent and its sales are double those of the next largest company, Coca-Cola agreed to end restrictive practices, including offering large discounts on its popular brands in exchange for stocking its less popular brands. Coca-Cola also agreed to stop offering rebates for reserving shelf space as well as "target" and "growth" rebates. In addition, Coca-Cola agreed to make up to 20 percent of the space in its branded refrigerators available to competitors, including Pepsi, which had complained to the European Union about Coca-Cola's practices. The settlement avoided fines and years of appeals.

Mergers

The Treaty of Rome did not address mergers because they were viewed as a desirable means of enabling small-scale European firms to attain the scale needed to compete globally. In 1989 the Council of Ministers adopted a Merger Control Regulation, assigning the commission responsibility for reviewing large mergers, those in which the combined unit has sales of over €2.5 billion and the individual firms have sales of over €250 million.[23] Companies registered outside the European Union must submit a

---

[21]Private lawsuits may be filed under the antitrust laws of the member states.
[22]See Chapter 9 for U.S. actions against the cartel members.
[23]See Fishwick (1993) and Cini and McGowan (1998) for analyses of EU competition policy.

EXAMPLE

Microsoft and EU Competition Policy

Microsoft's competitive practices and dominance of the operating system and desktop software markets have been a concern of the DG for Competition for more than fifteen years. In 1991 the U.S. Department of Justice (DOJ) and the European Commission signed an agreement to cooperate on antitrust investigations. The DOJ and the commission, acting under a complaint from Novell, Inc., cooperated in an antitrust case against Microsoft with both agencies pressuring the company to enter into a consent decree to change its software licensing practices. At the end of the 1990s the DG for Competition prevented Microsoft from exercising joint control over the United Kingdom's Telewest Communications, in which Microsoft had invested $3 billion.

Sun Microsystems filed a complaint with the DG for Competition (and not with U.S. antitrust authorities) alleging that Microsoft withheld interface (API) information for connecting servers to PCs in a network. Sun hoped to benefit from a precedent in which the commission had ordered IBM to share certain interface information with Amdahl. A similar complaint was filed pertaining to interface information for Windows 2000. The commission combined these two cases and added new allegations about the bundling of Microsoft's music and video-streaming software with Windows XP. In 2003 a group of global telecommunications, electronics, and software companies joined the case as intervenors, alleging that Windows XP incorporated broader bundling, exclusion practices, and screen bias favoring Microsoft software.

After 5 years of investigation and several attempts to reach a settlement, in 2004 the DG for Competition found Microsoft guilty of abusing its dominant position in computer operating systems in violation of Articles 81 and 82. As remedies, the DG fined Microsoft €497 million and ordered it to offer a version of Windows without Media Player. The court also ordered Microsoft to disclose substantive portions of its Windows code to allow server manufacturers to develop software that works with Windows. The DG and Microsoft again attempted but failed to reach a settlement, and Microsoft appealed the decision to the European Court of First Instance and sought a suspension of the remedies order. The president of the Computer and Communications Industry Association (CCIA), which was among the intervenors, said, "Their history is to appeal everything so as to delay."[1]

Microsoft subsequently settled with Novell for $536 million and with the CCIA for an undisclosed amount. Microsoft had earlier settled with AOLTime-Warner and Sun Microsystems, leaving Real Networks as the only remaining intervenor. The Court of First Instance rejected Microsoft's appeals.

Microsoft took a number of steps to comply with the commission's judgment, but the commission concluded that the company had not adequately disclosed information on its server protocols. The commission announced that it would fine Microsoft €2 million a day until it complied, and in 2006 it fined the company €280.5 million. Microsoft lost its last appeal in 2007 and complied. In early 2008 the commission fined Microsoft an additional €899 million for its past failure to comply. Microsoft appealed the fine to the Court of First Instance.

---
[1]*New York Times,* October 2, 2004.

---

merger notification if they have sales in the European Union of €100 million. Merger review by the commission is based solely on the effect on competition. The member states have authority to review smaller mergers and can seek permission from the commission to conduct their own review of large mergers. If two-thirds of the revenues of each of two merging firms are from a single member state, that state rather than the commission has authority over the review. A country thus can allow the merger of two of its major companies.

The European Union has been active in the review of mergers, and its decisions have generally been consistent with those of the United States. In 2000 both the European Union and the United States blocked the merger of MCI (then WorldCom) and Sprint Communications. Also in 2000 the United States approved the merger of AOL and Time-Warner after requiring the companies to provide rival Internet access through Time-Warner's cable systems. The European Union also approved the $118 billion merger with the requirements that AOL TimeWarner scrap joint ventures with Bertelsmann AG, Vivendi SA, and EMI Group that threatened competition in the music business.

In 2001, however, the European Union blocked the merger of General Electric and Honeywell International after the United States and 15 other countries had approved it. The DG for Competition was concerned about General Electric's dominant position in aircraft leasing and the portfolio effect if combined with Honeywell's avionics business. Critics charged that the decision was intended to protect Airbus Industrie from stronger competition. General Electric and Honeywell dropped the merger, but the companies decided to appeal the decision to the European Court of Justice so that the case would not set a precedent for future acquisitions. The Court of First Instance rejected the General Electric appeal.

In 2003 the Court of First Instance overturned a DG for Competition decision to block the merger of two UK travel agencies. The court used unusually harsh language in its decision, stating that the DG had been guilty of "manifest error" and "exceeded the bounds of its discretion." The court added that the DG's analysis was "vitiated by errors" and that it was necessary to show a "direct and immediate effect" on creating or maintaining a dominant position. The DG subsequently announced that greater oversight and additional reviews, including a peer review panel, would be applied before making merger decisions.

State Aids and the Common Agriculture Policy

State aids are subsidies paid by member state governments to their industries or government-owned companies.[24] Compared with the United States and Japan, EU member states provide considerably more subsidization for their firms. In 2005 the EU member states provided €65 billion in state aids, with Germany providing €20 billion, France €10 billion, and Italy €6 billion. Much of the subsidization has gone to declining industries in an attempt to protect labor and capital.

The European Commission monitors state aids and, for example, directed Italy to obtain a refund for a subsidy given to Fiat and ordered France to stop the large-scale subsidization of Renault. Private parties can file complaints with the DG for Competition to stop state aid. For example, the European Banking Federation complained about German loan guarantees to state-owned savings banks and regional banks. The DG for Competition made 510 decisions in state aid cases in 2000—more than the number of antitrust and merger cases combined.

EU member states also provide subsidies to failing companies. In 2004 France provided a €2.2 billion bailout of Alstom, an engineering conglomerate, to avoid having the company broken up and the parts purchased by foreign companies. Such bailouts must be approved by the DG for Competition, which gave its approval to stem the declining prospects for a number of companies. France and Germany sought to create globally competitive industrial champions by consolidating firms in some industries. Germany began with the consolidation of its shipbuilding industry.

In addition to state aid to agriculture and fisheries, the EU's Common Agriculture Policy (CAP) provides subsidies to farmers totaling €43 billion in 2005. The European Union sought to rein in CAP and made some progress, although opposition from farmers and some member states remained intense. The CAP, along with agricultural subsidization in the United States and Japan, has been the source of considerable international trade tension, as considered in Chapter 18. CAP also complicated enlargement negotiations with applicant countries. France, for example, sought to avoid any diversion of payments from its farmers to the new EU members.

The Social Charter, Social Democracy, and Labor Markets

The European Union adopted a Social Charter as part of the Treaty Establishing the European Community. The charter provides a vision for the free circulation of labor and the rights to fair wages, improvement of living and working conditions; social security; free association and collective bargaining; vocational training and education;

---

[24]State aids are governed by Article 92 of the Treaty of Rome.

equal treatment for men and women; information; consultation and participation for workers; health protection and safety in the workplace; protection for children, adolescents, and the elderly; and protection of the disabled.[25] Translating the vision of the Social Charter into law has been marked by several disagreements between business and labor and by the reality of national policy differences.[26] This led to the practice of an open method of coordination for implementation. Many of the actions under the Social Charter have been directed at increasing employment.

The SEA and other EU laws reflect the objectives of empowering labor and protecting individuals from risk and hardship through extensive social programs.[27] The European Union requires works councils or a consultative process between management and workers, or "social partners" in the terminology of European Union. At the plant level in Germany, workers have both representation and participation rights.[28] Those rights are in the areas of personnel policy, working conditions, and information, such as required notification of business plans that affect workers. Works councils can effectively prohibit weekend and overtime work and have powers over dismissals and reassignments.[29] Works councils use their rights to influence management, and management thus has an interest in accommodating council interests. Management, however, controls most decision making.

Much of the European labor force is well educated and highly skilled, and labor costs in many EU member states are high. Workweeks are shorter and vacations longer in Europe than they are in the United States and Asia. The OECD reported that on average Americans worked 1,777 hours in 2003, whereas the French and Germans worked less than 1,400 hours and the Dutch 1,309 hours.[30] Edward Prescott, the 2004 Nobel laureate in economics, attributed the difference in hours worked between the United States and Europe to differences in the tax rates on income. During the 1970–1974 period the hours worked in France exceeded those in the United States, and tax increases in France and tax decreases in the United States led to the divergence, he argued.[31]

The short work hours led one German industrial relations manager to observe that "the German worker doesn't work very often, but when he does work, he works very, very hard."[32] Hard work was not enough, however, and the high labor costs led some German companies to move jobs to the new, low-wage-rate members of the EU. Some German unions began to accept longer work hours to retain jobs in Germany. In contrast, France reduced its workweek to 35 hours in 2000 in an effort to reduce its unemployment rate. By 2004 President Jacques Chirac said, "I feel it's been a brake on economic development and therefore a brake on overall employment."[33] President Nicholas Sarkozy said in 2008 that his government would scrap the 35-hour workweek.

With labor costs in the new EU member states far lower than those in the other member states, two threats faced the high-wage countries. One was that jobs could flow east to take advantage of both low wages and low taxes. This would increase unemployment and force wage concessions in the west. The other was that workers would flow west seeking higher wages. Anticipating this, the 15 existing EU member states reserved the right to restrict for up to 7 years the right of workers from the new member states to work in the west. Restrictions were imposed by several of the 15, including Austria, Denmark, Germany, the Netherlands, and the United Kingdom.

Economic growth in the Netherlands far outstripped that in other European countries during the 1990s, and by 2003 unemployment was less than 3 percent in contrast to over 9 percent in Germany and France. The economic performance of the Netherlands

---

[25]See Nugent (2003, pp. 313–315) and Pierson (1999).
[26]See Wise and Gibb (1993).
[27]See European Commission (1988).
[28]See Streeck (1984, Ch. 3).
[29]See Streeck (1984, Ch. 7).
[30]The hours worked in South Korea were 2,390, followed by Poland (1,984), Mexico (1,980), Czech Republic (1,882), Japan (1,825), and Greece (1,811). Source: OECD.
[31]*Wall Street Journal,* October 21, 2004.
[32]*New York Times,* January 25, 1985.
[33]*New York Times,* July 7, 2004.

was credited to moderate wage growth and labor market flexibility, including temporary and part-time work. In addition, the country cut unemployment benefits, which increased the incentives to find work. The country also shifted the burden of sick pay from the government to employers, which reduced significantly the number of employees calling in sick. Many of these reforms came under the leadership of a prime minister who was a former labor leader.

NONMARKET ISSUES

Nonmarket issues in the European Union may be categorized by the level at which they are addressed, the EU level versus that of a member state, and whether they are specific to an industry or to an individual firm. At the EU level, important issues include deeper political integration, the economic integration of the 12 new member states, the administration of competition policy, persistent high unemployment, further reforms of the common agriculture policy, trade policy, defense, harmonization of fiscal policies, the continued opening to competition of industries such as energy and financial services, and takeover policy. As an example, the governments of several member states held golden shares in companies, which in effect gave the governments a veto over any takeover attempt. This impeded the free flow of capital with the European Union. Some member states had voting rights caps that were intended to protect companies such as Volkswagen and the United Kingdom's BAA. The DG for Competition ordered Germany to revise the governance laws for Volkswagen including the majority of shareholders that had to approve major decisions such as closing a factory. Volkswagen had an 80 percent required majority, compared to 75 percent for other German companies, because the state of Lower Saxony held more than 20 percent of the shares of Volkswagen. The commission directed Germany to lower the majority to 75 percent, and Germany refused to do so. The commission sent a formal notice to Germany, which could take the issue to the Court of Justice.

At the national level the overall tax burden remains an issue. Countries including Denmark, France, and Sweden have a taxes-to-GDP ratio over 50 percent, compared to 31 percent in the United States and 33 percent in Japan. Citizens receive important services, such as health care, for the taxes, but many firms are concerned about the effect of taxes on global competitiveness. Moreover, as mentioned above, the tax rates in the 12 new member states are low, making them attractive locations for new plants and enterprises.

An important difference between the European Union and the United States is the nature of regulation. The European Union more readily uses what may be called "precautionary regulation" than does the United States. One example is the policy restricting the use of genetically modified organisms (GMOs) in food on the grounds that they might pose health risks. This approach generated a major trade conflict between the European Union and the United States, as considered in Chapter 18. The United States tends to regulate known, as opposed to unknown, hazards, and GMO foods are widely available in the United States and other countries.

Another difference is that the United States more frequently relies on voluntary approaches to regulation, as in the case of Internet privacy. The policies of the European Union and the United States diverge substantially on the protection of personally identifiable information on the Internet, as explored in more detail in the chapter case, *The European Union Data Protection Directive*. For example, Americans were amused by the woman who complained that Google's Street View showed her cat sitting in her apartment window.[34] In response Google voluntarily agreed to blur the faces of people visible in Street View. The EU's top data protection officer instead warned that Street View would have to comply with the data protection directive. Despite the strong EU and member state laws on data protection and privacy, in 2008 the news media revealed the Deutsche Telekom had hired a consultant to go over telephone records of journalists and its managers in an attempt to find the source of a leak of information to a magazine.

---

[34]See the Chapter 1 case, *The Nonmarket Environment of Google.*

Many Europeans are quite concerned about privacy, and these concerns have led to strong EU measures to protect personal information. These concerns range from information on credit card use to the use of cookies to track Internet site browsing. Some countries ban telephone marketing and unsolicited sales attempts by e-mail or fax. Germany and the Netherlands have strong national laws and enforcement agencies governing information. For example, in allowing Citibank to offer a credit card in Germany, the government obtained the right to supervise the data Citibank stores on cardholders. Inspectors from the Datenschutz regularly visited Citibank's Sioux Falls, South Dakota, data center "to make sure that the data are being handled according to [German] law."[35] American Express reached a similar agreement with several countries. An official with the Data Protection Agency of the Netherlands commented, "We are at the beginning of a new information society, and no one really knows the outcome. But privacy and trust are important parts of this society."[36]

At the EU level the Directive on Data Protection (95/46/EC) took effect in 1998 and required that a person grant explicit permission to a company before it could obtain personal information. In preparing its in-house telephone directory, General Motors had to obtain permission from each of its employees in the European Union to include their work telephone numbers, which were considered personal information. Individuals also have the right to inspect any files maintained and to correct any errors. Furthermore, an individual must be notified in advance if any personal information is to be sold. According to a spokesperson for Oracle, "Your business is essentially tubed until you get this resolved. It can be a life-or-death situation for some businesses."[37]

A number of the issues addressed by the European Union have major impacts on other countries. The Data Protection Directive has caused some countries to issue new data protection rules that satisfy the EU requirements for data transfers. In this sense the EU has been driving regulation not just among its member states but also around the world. This has generated concerns in other countries about regulations driven by extreme caution. The United States refused to change its policies in response to the Data Protection Directive and entered into negotiation with the EU, as considered in the chapter case, *The European Union Data Protection Directive.*

As another example, because of the health fears underlying the precautionary principle, the European Union faced the issue of what to do about existing materials and products that might pose health or safety risks. The commission embarked on a campaign to force the testing of 30,000 industrial chemicals either manufactured in or imported into the EU. The testing would be required even if there were no indication that there was any risk associated with the chemical. The chemical industry complained of the burden, and companies in the United States and other countries accused the EU of using regulation as a trade barrier. After intense lobbying the commission scaled back its proposed regulation, known as REACH (Registration, Evaluation, Authorization, and Restriction of Chemicals), and the Parliament approved it after considering a record 6,000 amendments. REACH created a new regulatory body, the European Chemicals Agency, to administer the regulation. Testing requirements would be phased in over 11 years beginning with chemicals considered "risky." Testing was to focus on safety, and for more heavily used chemicals on health as well. Some 1,500 chemicals viewed as "hazardous" are required to go through a new authorization process to stay on the market. Firms are responsible for assessing the safety of chemicals they use, including manufacturers and importers, producers or importers of articles containing the chemicals, distributors, and downstream users, so the responsibility falls broadly on the business community. Since the EU represents a large market for foreign firms, REACH in effect requires firms in other countries to know the chemicals used in their products and ultimately to comply with the testing and possible ban of the chemicals.

[35]*BusinessWeek,* November 2, 1998.
[36]*New York Times,* October 26, 1998.
[37]*San Jose Mercury News,* October 26, 1998.

The European Union and most of its member states have strong environmental regulations. As indicated in Chapter 1, the European Union and the European automobile industry agreed to voluntary CO_2 reduction goals, and the industry initially made substantial progress toward the goals in part because of the shift to diesel engines led by the lower price of diesel fuel. As demand shifted to larger vehicles, the industry quietly began to explore the possibility of revising the goals. The lack of progress, however, led the commission to impose mandatory reductions on the auto industry.

The European Union has been a leading advocate of reducing greenhouse gas emissions, and agreed to an aggressive Kyoto Protocol goal of reducing CO_2 emissions by 6 percent compared to 1990 levels. The EU had made considerable early progress because electric utilities had switched from coal to natural gas and the high price of energy had led to investments in efficiency. To meet its goal, the EU implemented a cap-and-trade system for controlling emissions from factories as discussed in Chapter 11, but in the first 3 years of operation emissions actually increased because member state governments, worried about the possible loss of jobs, issued too many permits. The EU then reduced the number of permits and broadened the coverage to include airlines, but whether the Kyoto goal would be realized was unclear.

At the level of the member states, issues affecting business include pharmaceutical approvals and price controls, tax policies to attract business, harmonization of financial services regulation, the convergence of products liability laws, Internet taxation, and the opening of government procurement to competition among the member states. Issues also pertain to individual firms, including the privatization of government-owned firms and the subsidization of firms through state aids. Many of the issues at the level of the member states involve the implementation of EU regulations and directives.

Many nonmarket issues are firm-specific and result from actions taken by activists. Activist groups, for example, protested a Benetton advertisement showing a bloody uniform of a fallen Croat soldier in the Yugoslav civil war. The ad was intended as a plea for peace, but Benetton was accused of exploiting the war. A German court banned Benetton ads, and the French minister for humanitarian affairs called for a boycott of Benetton and urged people to "pull [Benetton sweaters] off the people who are going to wear them."[38]

INTERESTS AND THEIR ORGANIZATION

Interests are pluralistic in the European Union as they are in the United States and other countries, but their organization is different, in part because the governments of the member states are parliamentary. Some firms are directly involved in issues at the EU level, and more are involved in the issues at the level of member states. For example, Philips Electronics worked for the creation of a center to conduct research on semiconductors. Much of the nonmarket activity at the EU level is conducted by peak associations that represent businesses within the member states.

Several European countries, such as Germany and Sweden and others to a lesser extent, have a strong corporatist organization in which interests are represented by national associations that interact directly, and often with formal sanction, with government. In a corporatist structure, unions and businesses have peak organizations that advise government and negotiate on policy. In Germany, for example, manufacturing enterprises, agricultural interests, service companies, and professionals are organized by law into "chambers," which exercise self-regulation authority over members and represent their members' interests before the government. The Federation of German Employers' Associations (BDA) is composed of 56 employer associations and represents business on social and labor issues. The Federation of German Industry (BDI), whose members are 39 national federations that include 40,000 businesses and 85 percent of German industry, is more active politically.[39] It provides expert testimony on

---

[38]See the Chapter 14 case *Benetton, Advertising Protests, and Franchising* in Baron (2000).
[39]A third, less active, peak organization is the Diet of German Industry and Commerce.

legislation, lobbies government institutions, and consults with government leaders. The peak business organizations cooperate both formally and informally. Informally, their leaders consult on issues, and formally the BDA and the BDI interact through organizations such as the Joint Committee of German Trade and Industry.

In many industries the national associations join to form EU-wide associations that implement nonmarket strategies directed at the EU institutions. The largest of these associations is the Union of Industrial and Employers Confederations of Europe (UNICE). The European Roundtable of Industrialists represents large companies in Brussels and in the member states. These peak associations take much of the nonmarket action that individual firms and ad hoc coalitions take in the United States. For example, the European Confederation of Retail Trade represents retail interests in the European Union, and CEFIC includes as members the national associations of chemical companies. A peak organization such as CEFIC represents relatively homogeneous interests, whereas the Confederation of Food and Drink Industries represents relatively heterogeneous interests including soft drinks, beer, beef, and cheese. CEFIC was active in the chapter case, *The European Union Carbon Tax.*

Foreign firms are organized in a similar manner. The EU Committee of the American Chamber of Commerce (Amcham) represents over 100 U.S. companies in Brussels and is highly regarded.[40] In addition, several U.S. associations formed the U.S. Industry Coordinating Group.[41] Some industry associations, such as the Pharmaceutical Research and Manufacturers Association, maintain offices in Brussels.

Much of the nonmarket action at the industry level has been conducted by EU-wide associations representing the industry associations in the member states. For example, the pharmaceutical industry had sought the decontrol of pharmaceutical prices, which have been kept low in countries such as France to relieve the government's health care budget. Issues involving the pharmaceutical industry are addressed by the European Federation of Pharmaceutical Industries' Associations. In some cases ad hoc groups of firms from various member states join together to seek support, as when Philips, Siemens, Thomson, and General Electric (UK) sought support for the European computer and semiconductor industries.

Unionization in the European Union is more extensive than in the United States, and unions are also organized in national federations and in EU-wide umbrella associations. For example, German unions typically are organized by industry and bargain with associations of employers in those industries. Seventeen German unions are members of the federation Deutscher Gewerkschaftsbund (DGB). The unions have considerable power because of the high rate of unionization and also because of their links to political parties, particularly socialist parties. In Germany the DGB exercises political power both through the political parties and through its interactions with the executive branch and the legislature. Many Social Democrat members of the Bundestag are union members.

Activists and NGOs are active in the European Union, particularly in northern Europe. Consumer groups such as Consumentenbond in the Netherlands are linked to consumer groups in other countries. Some interest groups, such as the Greens, have formed political parties. Green activists have vigorously opposed biotechnology and have had considerable success in slowing the growth of the industry. The Chapter 4 case, *Shell, Greenpeace, and Brent Spar,* concerns an activist protest in Europe against a company's actions.

NONMARKET STRATEGIES IN THE EUROPEAN UNION

The EU government and its institutions have evolved over time along with the relationships among the expanded member states and the Community. If the Treaty of Lisbon were eventually to be ratified, additional changes would take place. The nonmarket strategies for addressing issues in the European Union thus may continue to evolve.

---

[40]See, for example, Coen (1999).
[41]See Calingaert (1993).

Nonmarket strategies are implemented at the levels of the member states and the institutions of the European Union. To illustrate the multiple levels of nonmarket strategies, the European Union committed to achieving the goals established in the Kyoto Protocol on global climate change and worked for a cap-and-trade system (see Chapter 11) among the signatories. Within the EU, opposition occurred at both the EU and member state levels. A spokesperson for the Federation of German Industries said, "What we are against is the exaggerated ecological leadership which . . . the European Union wants to administer."[42] The commission was forced to delay the proposal because of complaints by pan-European associations and industry associations, such as those for autos and chemicals, concerned about the effect on their international competitiveness. The European Trading System (ETS) finally began in 2005. The opposition by business led the member states to issue more permits than needed, and in its first 3 years the ETS allowed emissions to increase. The United Kingdom had started a cap-and-trade system, and Blue Circle, a UK cement company owned by Lafarge Coppée of France, successfully lobbied to have its emissions goal stated in terms of CO_2 emissions per ton of cement produced, as opposed to an absolute cap. This allowed the company to expand its output.

The member states have parliamentary systems of government, but they differ considerably in terms of their institutions, their party organization, and the strength and organization of various interests. Van Schendelen (1993) presents an analysis of interests and lobbying in 12 EU countries, and the Part IV integrative case, *Toys 'Я' Us and Globalization,* considers strategies for individual countries. The focus here is on nonmarket activities and strategies at the EU level.[43]

In the terminology of Chapter 7, both representation and informational strategies are important in the European Union. Representation strategies are based on the constituency for each of the principal EU institutions, as indicated in Figure 15-5. For example, the constituency of the Council of Ministers is the member states, and hence representation strategies are implemented primarily through the member state governments. Because those governments are parliamentary and often controlled by coalitions, political parties are an important focus of these strategies. The national ministries are a locus of expertise and play important roles in how a member state votes in the Council of Ministers. The primary points of access to the council are COREPER and the working groups it forms to address issues.

Much of the nonmarket action in the European Union takes place behind the scenes, and most businesses avoid taking public action that might be subjected to criticism. In addition, because of the pervasive influence of government in many EU countries, firms seldom engage in open confrontation with government, as is more often the case in the United States. The chapter case, *Aldeasa and EU Duty Free Abolition (A),* provides an opportunity to consider whether a behind-the-scenes approach is sufficient or whether a more public nonmarket strategy is needed.

FIGURE 15-5 EU Institutions, Constituencies, and Access		
Institution	**Constituency**	**Access**
European Commission	EU-wide constituency—member states, citizens, interests	DGs, commissioners, staff
Council of Ministers	Member states	Member states, political parties, COREPER, working groups
European Parliament	Voters	Committees, political parties, members of Parliament
Economic and Social Committee	Interests	Representatives, Associations

---

[42]*Wall Street Journal,* July 13, 2001.
[43]Calingaert (1993) provides a description of the organization for nonmarket action at the EU level.

Lobbying is the principal political activity for implementing both representation and informational strategies in the European Union. A lobbyist's strategy is to demonstrate that the interests of a firm or industry are aligned with those of the person or office being lobbied. In the case of the European Union, those interests are a mixture of economic efficiency and social objectives at the EU level; sectoral interests in the case of agriculture, steel, or computers; and local interests in the case of some members of the EP and the Council of Ministers. EU officials face pressures from their home country constituents and from their mandate for economic and political integration.

Lobbyists are not required to register with the EU, but estimates put their number at over 15,000. In 2008 the EU adopted a code of conduct for lobbyists and established a voluntary registry. The European Parliament provides a one-year pass to its premises in exchange for a lobbyist signing a code of ethical behavior. The EU does not require disclosure of lobbying activity, the funds spent on hired lobbyists, or the policy issue on which the lobbyists work.

Former EU and national government officials have formed lobbying firms to represent interests. EU lobbyists have backgrounds similar to their counterparts in the United States. Firms hire former EU officials, trade negotiators, ambassadors, and former officials of national governments as lobbyists. Lobbying services are also provided by law firms and consultants. Firms have opened offices in Brussels to be close to the European Union and to track its activities. Managers frequently participate in lobbying along with heads of industry associations and peak organizations. In addition, in a number of countries business leaders have close personal relationships with government officials. In some countries, such as France, these relationships may have been formed through attendance at the same *grandes écoles*. In Germany top government officials consult with business leaders because of the status and strength of business in the country.[44]

Peak associations play a number of roles including the monitoring of government activities, the funneling of information and expertise from their members to the government, and lobbying. Lobbying, for example, is pervasive in German politics, but because of the omnipresence of associations it tends to be collective in its nature. Much of the political influence takes place through the executive branch and the interactions of high-ranking government officials, particularly bureaucrats, with the leaders of the peak associations. Seventy percent of the BDI's contacts were with the bureaucracy and only 5 percent with the Bundestag (parliament).[45] As a result of the SEA and the increasing importance of the EU government, German associations increased their presence and lobbying in Brussels.

Informational strategies center on the strategic provision of information to EU officeholders, and the nature and content of these strategies is the same as characterized in Chapter 7. The key to successful lobbying is the provision of information useful to the institutional officeholders. Successful lobbying requires an understanding of their interests, the relationship between policy alternatives and consequences, and the procedures and practices of EU institutions. Lobbying also takes place within each member state in attempts to convince politicians and bureaucrats of the importance of the interests affected. Figure 15-5 identifies the points of access.

The form that lobbying takes depends on the institution in question. The European Commission is perhaps the most important body because it is the agenda setter for legislation and also administers policies. Because the commission has a relatively small staff, it needs information and expertise for its legislative and regulatory actions. The commission stated, "The Commission has always been open to ideas from the outside world. It believes that openness is crucial for developing its polices. This dialogue has proved valuable to both the commission and interested outside parties. . . . The Commission will remain very accessible to the interest groups."[46] The commission has established a set of informal and formal consultation procedures, including the formation

---

[44]See Calingaert (1993).
[45]See Kohler-Koch (1998).
[46]europa.eu.int/secretariat/general/sgc/lobbies/approche/apercu_en.htm.

of advisory committees and policy forums. To provide voice to groups that would otherwise be underrepresented, the EU provides funding for NGOs to participate in political and policy-making processes.

The EU uses several thousand working groups and committees in writing and implementing legislation as part of its "comitology" procedures. These include advisory, management, regulation, and oversight committees. Some committees are composed solely of members of government, whereas others include representatives of business for their expertise. Interests direct their lobbying at these committees, particularly those that are involved in advising the commission on the implementation of policies.

The respect garnered by the American Chamber of Commerce (Amcham) in Brussels is due in part to the detailed information it provides on issues and its accurate representation of American concerns. As Coen (1999, p. 35) characterized the situation in the mid-1990s, "U.S. firms demonstrated to their European rivals the importance of direct, regular, and reliable representation at the European Commission . . . Amcham and its EU committee demonstrated the importance of both direct firm membership (at the collective European level) and the participation of senior executives with expertise in the policy debate. By adapting the organizational structure around 12 specialized technical committees on issues such as competition, trade, social affairs, and the environment, Amcham was able to complement the new European Commission's issue-based forums. . . ."

Interests interact with the commission directly through its DGs, but interests can also be represented by members of either the European Parliament or the Economic and Social Committee. Also, member governments intervene on behalf of interest groups in their own countries. The targets of lobbying are the commissioners and their cabinets. Because the DGs are the repositories of expertise and deal with the specifics of issues, access to members of the relevant DGs is important. Participation in working parties and advisory committees can be an important means of access as well as a source of information. The commission initiates legislation in the form of drafts that are circulated for comments before the legislative process begins (see Figure 15-3). Lobbying thus begins early in the process and is directed at the formulation of the initial draft as well as the subsequent legislative process. Affecting the agenda can be an effective means of laying a path to be followed with subsequent lobbying. Lobbyists are also active at the implementation stage, as the commission makes decisions and issues directives to implement legislation.

The Council of Ministers is the principal legislative institution, but it is difficult to influence directly because it operates in private. The principal route to influencing the council is through member state governments and their relevant ministries. National interests also are represented by a country's permanent representatives (COREPER) to the EU. COREPER is required by law to consult directly with interests, and industry and labor organizations maintain close contacts with it. COREPER is expected to resolve political issues on behalf of the council.

As a result of the Maastricht Treaty and the increased use of the co-decision legislative procedure, the EP has become more important as a result of its powers to amend and veto commission proposals. If the Treaty of Lisbon is eventually ratified, the scope of the EP's role will broaden. The EP's constituencies are voters and the political parties that represent them, and the principal points of access are the party organizations, individual members, and committees. The EP members are both issue oriented and concerned about the effects of issues on constituents. Members represent a variety of interests and may be willing to act as allies in advancing the interests of firms and industries. Although the EP has committees that formulate amendments, most of the lobbying takes place outside the formal committee structure. In addition, the party organization of the EP means that a path to influence is through the party system in the firm's home country. The attention given to lobbying the EP is smaller, but growing, than that given the commission, COREPER, and member state governments.

The custom in Europe has been to use peak organizations, such as UNICE and the Roundtable of European Industrialists, for political and other nonmarket actions. Issues involving the single market and international trade, however, are industry-specific but have differing imports on individual firms. Industry associations play a major role on such issues.[47] Also, coalitions are formed that cut across the lines of peak associations. These coalitions may include firms domiciled in different member states acting together on a trade issue or a firm and a union joining together to advance their joint interests.

As an example of an ad hoc coalition formed to address a specific issue, in 1996 the EP proposed amendments to a commission policy on the media industry. France, backed by socialist members of the EP, pushed for tighter quotas on the foreign content on television and multimedia outlets. According to one report, American companies produced 80 percent of the programming shown on European television. Opposition to the proposed amendments included not only American interests and private broadcasters, but also a broad set of other interests. Advertisers opposed the amendments because they would restrict advertising on home shopping channels. Retailers opposed the amendments because they would restrict the number of hours regular TV channels could devote to teleshopping. The prospect of quotas on Internet content led one Bertelsmann lobbyist to comment, "It's very silly what they want to do. It won't work in an Internet, online environment."[48] The chapter case, *The European Union Carbon Tax,* concerns another issue involving a broad set of interests.

Some firms undertake independent political action or form ad hoc coalitions to advance their agenda. Philips Electronics has been one of the most active. It was an early advocate of the creation of a single market and also worked to limit competition from outside the European Union. For example, it lobbied successfully for protection against Japanese compact disc systems. In addition to its extensive lobbying, Van Schendelen (1993) reports that Philips was successful in "parachuting" one of its technology experts into the DG responsible for subsidies for technology programs. Philips obtained R&D subsidies for 150 projects. Philips was also one of the principal forces behind the EU subsidies for the development of a European HDTV system, which ultimately was a failure. Working with the European Information Technology Roundtable, Philips also led the effort to obtain $4 billion for semiconductor research.

Philips Chairman Cornelis van der Klugt was personally active, lobbying in Brussels to obtain import protection for Philips. He argued that free trade with the European Union required "real reciprocity." To protect its VCR business, Philips pushed through the European Union a 30 percent levy on Japanese and South Korean VCRs. He worked to have the European Union investigate dumping charges against Asian producers of small televisions and compact disc players and to have semiconductors assembled by Japanese firms in Europe classified as imports so they would be subject to tariffs.[49] An antidumping complaint against six Japanese semiconductor manufacturers led to an agreement between the European Union and Japan that set a price floor on imported semiconductors. Van der Klugt defended his efforts: "It's not necessary for the Japanese to export unemployment to Europe. We have enough unemployment."[50] At the same time that he worked for protection, van der Klugt pushed the European Union to scrap its internal trade barriers as quickly as possible.

Nonmarket issues and strategies are often complicated by national concerns. Pharmaceuticals is far from a single market. Under the principle of subsidiarity the member states are responsible for health care and can institute their own price controls. The European Commission has expressed concern that very stringent price controls were driving pharmaceutical innovation out of the EU.[51] France, for example, required pharmaceutical companies to sign broad conventions that covered not only prices but also commitments to create jobs in France and to support state-owned research institutes.

---

[47]John and Schwarzer (2006) studied the lobbying of the European automobile industry.
[48]*Wall Street Journal,* February 12, 1996.
[49]Upon complaints by Philips and Bang & Olufsen of Denmark, the European Union imposed provisional duties of 6.4 to 40 percent on Japanese and South Korean compact disc players. Sony expressed little concern because it planned to supply three-quarters of its European demand from its plant in France.
[50]*New York Times,* June 4, 1989.
[51]European Commission press release, November 25, 1998.

EXAMPLE

Pronuptia and Franchising

In 1984 a German court invalidated a franchise agreement that required a German retailer, Pronuptia, to sell only the wedding dresses of its French franchiser and only in specific territories. The French franchiser appealed the decision to the Court of Justice. U.S. franchisers saw the decision as crucial to their use of U.S.-style franchise arrangements in the European Union. They launched a lobbying campaign directed at the European Commission, which planned to file an opinion on the case with the court. The lobbyist engaged by the U.S. franchisers conducted a "teach in" about U.S. franchising practices for officials of the DG for Competition. The commission subsequently argued before the court that the franchise restrictions were necessary to maintain product quality, among other things. In 1986 the court overruled the German court and upheld the rights of franchisers to restrict the actions of their franchisees on several dimensions.[1]

U.S. franchisers were still concerned that the franchising arrangements allowed by the court might be challenged under the antitrust provisions in Article 81. Some franchisers, including Pronuptia, sought and received exemptions from the commission. They also encouraged the commission to grant a broader exemption from antitrust rules for franchise arrangements. The U.S. interests, including McDonald's, Pizza Hut, Kentucky Fried Chicken, Midas Muffler, Coca-Cola, Holiday Inns, and others, were represented by the International Franchising Association (IFA), which was active in Brussels. The IFA met with a variety of officials including the competition commissioner, who was also lobbied when he visited the United States.

The lobbyist for the U.S. franchisers said, "The most important lessons we've learned so far are for American interests to get in early; in a European, not American, way; and demonstrate from the start that American interests are compatible with European interests." From the other side, an official with the DG for Competition said the IFA "made their points forcefully, but also gave us a lot of useful information about how the U.S. system works."[2]

U.S. franchisers obtained "96.5 percent" of what they sought, but they were prohibited from requiring franchisees to purchase one brand exclusively. A fast-food chain thus cannot force its franchisees to carry only one soft drink brand.

[1]*Pronuptia de Paris GmbH v. Pronuptia de Paris Irmgard Schillgalis* (case 161/84), January 28, 1986, Common Market Report (CCH) para. 14,245 (1986). See Rosenthal (1990) for a discussion of this case. Also see Hawk (1988).

[2]*Wall Street Journal,* May 17, 1989.

To hold down the cost of its national health care system, pharmaceutical prices were set at very low levels. This in part led the three largest French pharmaceutical companies to either merge or spin off their pharmaceutical operations into a jointly owned affiliate. The French Parliament also enacted a law that made pharmaceutical companies responsible for any costs above ceilings set by parliament for the national health service. Industry members challenged the new law in France and before the European Commission and the European Court of Justice.[52]

Specific nonmarket issues can also arise in the normal course of EU activities. An example of such an issue, a German court decision about wedding dresses that had important implications for franchising, is considered in the example.

Firms also employ judicial strategies in the European Union. A German environmental law favored reusable materials such as glass bottles over recyclable materials such as plastic and cans. Since glass bottles were much more costly to transport than other containers, beverage firms were effectively excluded from the German market. French mineral-water companies complained that it was prohibitively costly to collect and truck the empty bottles back to their springs for refilling. The 50-member packaging association Europen, whose members included Coca-Cola and Nestlé, successfully lobbied the commission to file a lawsuit against Germany. In 2004 the Court of Justice ruled that the German law discriminated against foreign companies.

[52]*Wall Street Journal,* December 7, 1998.

SUMMARY

The Single European Act represented a major step toward economic integration within the Union. It also increased the political power of the EU institutions relative to the governments of the member states. The Maastricht Treaty provided for a monetary union and for steps toward a political union. The European Union has also broadened with 10 additional countries joining the Union in 2004 and 2 others joining in 2007. The Maastricht Treaty increased the power of the European Parliament, which exercises democratic supervision.

The principal institutions of the European Union are the European Commission, the Council of Ministers, the European Parliament, and the Court of Justice. The Economic and Monetary Union established both an independent European Central Bank and a common currency among the participating states. Considerable progress has been made in eliminating internal barriers to trade, but several difficult issues, including fiscal harmonization, remain. Rigid labor markets, high wages and taxes, and the high costs of laying off workers have resulted in a high unemployment, but a strong economy reduced the rate to below 7 percent in 2008.

Interests take nonmarket action both individually and through associations and peak organizations, which play an important role at the EU level. The pattern of interest group activity and the nature of nonmarket action have evolved as firms, unions, and other organizations have adapted their strategies to institutional changes. The growth in lobbying is a sign of both the increased importance of the EU government and the stakes involved in its actions. Lobbying is the principal nonmarket strategy for influencing the EU institutions. Since much of the legislative and regulatory activity takes place outside the view of the public and prior to the formal procedures beginning, it is important to participate both early and continuously in the EU governmental processes.

Although the powers of the EU institutions have increased, the governments of the member states continue to be the focus of considerable nonmarket activity. Those governments are parliamentary but differ in their institutional structures and their politics. The organization of interests in a number of member states is corporatist with peak associations that represent interests and are active in nonmarket and governmental matters. Individual firms, however, also undertake their own nonmarket activities and form alliances with firms in other EU member states.

------------------------------------ C A S E S ------------------------------------
The European Union Carbon Tax

Whether and to what extent global warming was occurring remained the subject of considerable scientific uncertainty, disagreement, and debate during the early 1990s, but the scientific evidence increasingly supported the global warming hypothesis. The principal contributor to global warming was believed to be the burning of carbon-based fuels, principally coal, petroleum, and natural gas.

A European Union (EU) Joint Council of Energy and Environment Ministers declared in 1990 that the member states would by the year 2000 stabilize CO_2 emissions at the 1990 level. Because of projected economic growth, stabilization would require a reduction in emissions of approximately 10 percent from the unstabilized level. Some of the reductions required to stabilize emissions were anticipated to come from improved energy efficiency induced by the current prices of fossil fuels. These "no regrets" conservation measures were estimated to reduce emissions by 5.5 percent by 2000, leaving reductions of 5 percent to be accomplished by other measures. In October 1991 the European Commission issued a draft directive informing the member states of its plans to propose a variety of measures to reduce CO_2 emissions. These measures included R&D programs and a carbon/energy tax to achieve the remaining reduction of 5 percent. The proposed carbon/energy tax was intended to reduce carbon emissions by making fuels, particularly carbon-based fuels, more costly, thereby inducing conservation and the substitution of less carbon-intensive fuels.

The European Commission operated under collective responsibility but frequently deferred to the commissioner with policy jurisdiction if the issue was not controversial. This was not an uncontroversial issue. The lead commissions for this issue were DG XI (environment) and DG XVII (energy). Mr. Carlo Ripa di Meana, EU commissioner for the environment, pushed for a formal proposal by June 1992 in time for the Rio Earth Summit. Mr. Jacques Delors, president of the commission, also supported the tax and the leadership position it would give the European Union in Rio. Mr. Antonio Cardoso e Cunha, EU commissioner for energy, supported the taxes because they would promote energy efficiency.

The European Commission proposal involved specific (per unit) taxes that would impose half the burden on carbon-based fuels and the other half on energy. The commission estimated that the full tax would increase the price of natural gas for industry by 33 percent, hard coal by 60 percent, and gasoline by 6 percent.[53]

Because emissions of CO_2 were difficult to measure by source, the taxes would be applied to inputs rather than emissions. The proposed carbon tax would begin at $3 per barrel of oil and increase by $1 per year for the next 7 years, reaching $10 per barrel. (The $10 per barrel tax was equivalent to a tax of $75 per ton of carbon.) An equivalent tax would be applied to coal and natural gas. The energy tax would apply to all energy sources except renewable sources. The energy tax was included to satisfy environmentalists who opposed a pure carbon tax because it would provide incentives for the expansion of nuclear power. Countries such as Germany, Greece, and the United Kingdom, with carbon-intensive energy supplies, also favored an energy tax. Denmark and the Netherlands and two European Free Trade Association (EFTA) countries, Finland and Sweden, already had imposed a carbon tax.[54] Denmark's carbon tax averaged $16 per ton of carbon for individual consumption and $8 per ton for industry. Energy-intensive industries, however, could be granted an exemption of up to 100 percent of the tax. The Netherlands' carbon tax was $12.50 per ton. The tax in Sweden was $62 per ton of carbon, and in Finland the tax was $6.50 per ton.[55]

Neither Japan nor the United States had a carbon tax in 1992. The Japanese government argued that its regulations already set standards that were at least as strong as those the EU tax would achieve. Presidential candidate Bill Clinton had pledged during his campaign to address the global warming issue using efficient means, including taxes on carbon and/or energy. The Congressional Budget Office estimated that to stabilize CO_2 emissions a tax of $100 per ton of carbon would be required.[56] Representative Pete Stark (D-CA) introduced a bill to impose a tax of $15 per ton on coal, $3.25 per barrel of oil, and $0.40 per MCF of natural gas. The European Commission urged the member states to make every effort to ensure that other OECD countries, in particular Japan and the United States, adopted measures similar to its proposed carbon/energy tax.

The carbon/energy tax would affect production and consumption decisions throughout the European Union. It would also affect the competitiveness of EU businesses, particularly those that used energy-intensive technologies. Mr. Ripa di Meana, however, argued, "This is a chance to update European industry and

---

[53]The percentage increase for gasoline was low because gasoline was already heavily taxed.

[54]In 1995 Austria, Finland, and Sweden joined the European Union.
[55]See Poterba (1991, pp. 71–98).
[56]The United States had imposed a tax on CFCs as a means of speeding the elimination of their production. In addition to contributing to ozone depletion, CFCs were greenhouse gases and contributed to global warming.

make it a leader in a green-oriented market." To lessen the impact on the international competitiveness of European companies, the commission proposed to at least partially exempt from the tax those industries that had energy-intensive production processes.

The tax would ultimately be borne in large part by individuals and would have the greatest impact on those who intensively used energy, and particularly carbon-based fuels. Because lower-income individuals spent a higher portion of their income on energy, the tax would be regressive.

A carbon/energy tax also would generate substantial revenue for governments. For example, a tax of $100 per ton of carbon was estimated to generate revenue equal to 1.99 percent of GDP based on consumption in 1988. For France the revenue would be 1.28 percent of GDP, and for Germany and the United Kingdom it would be approximately 2.3 percent. The commission suggested that the carbon tax should be "fiscally neutral" for each country, although Mr. Ripa di Meana argued that a portion of the tax revenue should go to developing countries to prevent deforestation. Fiscal neutrality would require that any additional revenue generated by the tax be offset by fiscal incentives or reductions in other taxes. Because the individual member states rather than the European Union would receive the revenue from the tax, each member state would determine its own use of the revenue. Under EU law the member states would be responsible for the implementation of the tax.

The EU legislative process required that the imposition of a carbon/energy tax be decided under a unanimity rule. Some bargaining among the member states would likely be involved with compensation given to certain countries that otherwise would be substantially impacted by the tax. As part of its annual budget, the European Union provided grants of structural funds for economic development to countries and to regions within countries. In 1992 these funds were approximately 19 million ECUs ($25 billion). The budget and thus the amount and allocation of structural funds were decided by a qualified majority of the Council of Finance Ministers. In 1992 a qualified majority required 54 of the 76 votes. The number of votes for each member state is presented in Table 15-1.

In December 1991 the EU Joint Council of Environment and Energy Ministers unanimously endorsed the European Commission's draft directive. Denmark, Germany, Italy, Belgium, and the Netherlands came out clearly in favor of the proposal, whereas the lower-income southern countries led by Spain, along with Luxembourg, were concerned about how the abatement burden would be divided among the countries. The United Kingdom agreed in principle but was hesitant about the additional taxes. France, which generated much of its electricity from nuclear power, supported the proposed taxes but wanted to tilt the taxes more toward fossil fuels. Both endorsed the report. A few days later the EU

TABLE 15-1	Votes of Member States in the Council of Ministers, 1992
Member States	*Votes*
Belgium	5
Denmark	3
France	10
Germany	10
Greece	5
Ireland	3
Italy	10
Luxembourg	2
Netherlands	5
Portugal	5
Spain	8
United Kingdom	10
Total	76

finance ministers took note of the proposal and asked for a detailed study on the practical details of the tax.

The Economics of Emissions Control in the European Union

Before the European Commission presented its proposal for meeting the EU-wide stabilization target, it commissioned a study of the costs and benefits of CO_2 emissions reduction. Although emissions were to be stabilized by the year 2000, the Council of Ministers requested that the study analyze the effects in the year 2010, since the stabilization target was to hold indefinitely and some investments in energy conservation would take several years before they were fully implemented. Table 15-2 outlines the "base-case" scenario

TABLE 15-2	CO_2 Emissions (million tons) with No Further Abatement: 10 EU Countries	
	1988	*Projected, 2010*
Belgium	109	110
Denmark	61	60
France	374	370
Germany	718	677
Greece	84	127
Italy	399	489
Netherlands	146	165
Portugal	28	51
Spain	196	265
United Kingdom	561	505
Total	2,676	2.819

Source: Coherence (1991). "Cost-effectiveness analvsis of CO_2 reduction options." Synthesis report and country reports for the Commission of the European Communities, DG XII. May 1991.

that was predicted to occur in 2010 if no EU-wide emissions control took place. Column 1 of Table 15-2 presents 1988 CO_2 emissions for 10 EU countries for comparison purposes (Ireland and Luxembourg are omitted from the analysis because they had the lowest CO_2 emissions in the European Union and because important data were not available). Not surprisingly, the largest and wealthiest countries—France, Germany, Italy, and the United Kingdom—had the highest levels of CO_2 emissions in 1988. However, the projected growth in emissions for 1988 to 2010 exhibited a very different pattern. The lowest-income countries—Greece, Portugal, and Spain—were predicted, respectively, to emit 52, 82, and 35 percent more CO_2 by 2010 if no additional measures were taken, compared with decreases in emissions in France, Germany, and the United Kingdom. The declines were projected to result from increased energy efficiency.[57]

If emissions were to be stabilized in 2000 and beyond, the European Commission had to make a proposal that achieved a 143 million ton reduction in CO_2 by the year 2010. A uniform tax would induce efficient emissions control across countries by giving polluters in each country the incentive to abate up to the point at which the marginal cost of abatement equaled the emissions tax. As a result, the marginal cost of reducing pollution in any one country would equal the marginal cost of reducing pollution in every other country. The tax required to achieve the target reduction of 143 million tons of CO_2 was calculated by researchers to be approximately $75 per ton of carbon at an exchange rate of $1.30/ECU.[58]

Costs and Benefits of a Carbon/Energy Tax

The relative impact of a carbon tax would be greatest on the lower-income countries. The tax would reduce their growth rate in addition to imposing high costs of abatement. The countries that would be most severely affected were Greece, Italy, Portugal, and Spain. A reduction in CO_2 emissions by the European Union would constitute a public good, since all countries would benefit from the reductions. The benefits for individual EU member states would be roughly proportional to their populations.

The reactions to the proposed tax by industry were predictable. The trade association Euroelectric, representing the EU electricity industry, opposed the tax and argued for voluntary conservation measures. Electric power generators—Electrabel (Belgium), Endesa (Spain), PowerGen (United Kingdom), RWE (Germany), Scottish Power (United Kingdom), Union Fenosa (Spain), and VEAG (Germany)—pointed to the uncertain effects of the imposition of a tax and proposed a series of conservation measures as well as the export of energy-efficient technologies to Eastern Europe. In addition to the efforts of the coalition and the trade association, individual power generation companies lobbied to prevent the adoption of the tax.

The European Coal and Steel Council Consultative Committee also opposed the tax and argued for voluntary programs and payments to developing countries to stop deforestation. Opposition also developed within countries. For example, in France 14 major companies, including Electricité de France, Renault, Rhone Poulenc, Total, Elf Aquitaine, Pécincy, and Unisor Sacilor, organized "Business for the Environment" to oppose the tax. In exchange, the coalition offered help in cleaning up toxic waste sites.

Chemicals was one of the premier industries in Europe. The industry was energy intensive, and the petrochemical component of the industry used petroleum feedstocks. The global competitiveness of the industry thus would be significantly impacted by the proposed taxes. The industry estimated that the impact of the taxes when fully implemented would be $4.45 billion per year. The chemical industry pointed to the success of voluntary measures undertaken by individual companies. The managing director of Montedison Primary Chemicals stated that since 1974 the European chemicals industry had reduced by 35 percent the energy usage per unit of output and that another 15 percent reduction would be achieved by the year 2000.[59]

As was the case in many European industries, the chemical industry in each country was represented by an association that included most of the companies operating in that country. These national associations acted on behalf of their members within their countries. The associations in the individual countries were organized into the European Chemical Industry Council (CEFIC) that acted at the level of the European Union. As the importance of the EU governmental institutions had grown, individual companies had begun to take actions in addition to those of their national and pan-European associations. ■

---

[57]For example, CO_2 emissions in the United Kingdom in 1992 were below the emissions levels in 1972.

[58]See "Reaching a CO_2-Emission Limitation Agreement for the Community: Implications for Equity and Cost Effectiveness," *European Economy,* Special Edition No. 1, *The Economics of Limiting CO₂ Emissions,* Directorate-General for Economics and Financial Affairs, Commission of the European Communities, 1992.

[59]*The Economist,* May 9, 1992.

Preparation Questions

Economics

1. Identify the efficiency and distributive consequences of a carbon/energy tax.
2. What are the effects of a carbon tax for the global competitiveness of EU companies?

Government

1. What types of politics should be anticipated in the consideration of a carbon/energy tax in the European Union? Which EU institutions will be involved in the decision?
2. If structural funds could be provided to countries through the EU budget, what outcome would you expect? Assume for the purposes of this question that the European Union makes its decision on structural funds by a qualified majority of ECOFIN.

Nonmarket Strategy

1. As a European chemicals company dependent on petroleum feedstocks, what effects do you anticipate from the proposed carbon/energy tax?
2. What objectives and strategy should the company adopt to address the carbon/energy tax? How should that strategy be implemented? Which institutions should be targeted?

The European Union Data Protection Directive

Concerns about privacy led the European Union (EU) to harmonize the Internet privacy policies of its member states. The Directive on Data Protection, often referred to as the Privacy Directive, took effect in 1998 and prohibited the processing of personally identifiable information (PII) unless "the data subject has unambiguously given his consent" or the processing was necessary for the performance of a contract or government order.[60] Data could also be processed if it were in the vital interests of the individual, as in the case of a medical emergency. Individuals had the right to inspect any personal data maintained and to correct any errors. Furthermore, an individual had to be notified in advance if any personal information were to be transferred to a third party.

The Directive sought a "reasonable balance" between "the fundamental rights of the data subject, particularly the right to privacy" and "the business interest of the data controllers. . . ."[61] To implement and enforce the Directive, each member of the EU established a data protection (privacy) agency, and the privacy commissioners served as a continuing body to monitor progress on the Directive. The European activist group Privacy International said it was investigating the practices of 25 companies, including Microsoft and United Airlines, and planned to file lawsuits if it identified any violations of the EU directive.

The Directive also protected EU citizens from processors of information in other countries. Article 25 permitted data transfers only if the other country had an "adequate level of protection." The United States had no Internet privacy law or regulations to govern the Internet and relied on voluntary measures. Processing by U.S. companies of personal information on Europeans outside the European Union thus was problematic. Figure 15-6 summarizes features of data protection in

FIGURE 15-6 Data Protection Practices for Personally Identifiable Information (PII)	
EU Data Protection	*U.S. Practices*
• Strong notice	• Limited notice
• Strong opt in	• Opt out
• Access to PII	• Access not required
• Limited if any secondary use of data	• Secondary use allowed
• Data storage no longer than necessary for primary purpose; e.g., billing	• No limits on storage
• Privacy regulatory agency	• Self-regulation
• Notice if cookie deposited	• No notice of cookie
• Anonymous profiling (?)	• Anonymous profiling OK
• Security and data integrity	• Security and data integrity
• Privacy regulatory agency	

---

[60]Directive 95/46/EC of the European Parliament and Council.

[61]"Data Protection: Background Information," The European Commission, www.europa.eu.int.

the European Union and compares those features with the practice in the United States in 2001.

Critics of Article 25 argued that it was an unwarranted extraterritorial application of EU law. The U.S. National Business Coalition on E-Commerce and Privacy, which included such financial services companies as General Electric, Fidelity, and Aflac, in addition to Home Depot, Deere, and Seagrams, said, "The EU privacy principles that would effectively be imposed on American business . . . far exceed any privacy requirements that have ever been imposed in the U.S., thus raising a very real question of national sovereignty."[62] The European Union responded by stating that it had no interest in "exporting" its laws to other countries, but it also emphasized that it had to protect the privacy of its citizens and would block the transfer of information to countries with inadequate protection. It invited non-EU countries "to express their views." Jim Murray, director of the European Consumers' Organization, said, "We want anyone doing business with the EU to respect the rights that we have built up here."[63] The U.S. and EU governments initiated discussions about what U.S. policy would meet the adequacy standard.

The discussions had two tracks. The first was for nonfinancial institutions, and the second was for financial institutions. On the first track the Department of Commerce represented the United States, and the Commission represented the European Union. The European Parliament remained concerned that any agreement be operational before adequacy would be certified.

Financial institutions were treated separately because the United States had enacted the Financial Services Modernization Act, also known as the Gramm-Leach-Bliley Act, of 1999, which took effect in mid-2001. The act limited disclosure of nonpublic personal information to nonaffiliated third parties unless disclosure and opt-out requirements were met. In addition, the Fair Credit Reporting Act of 1970 restricted the reporting of personal information. The United States maintained that these laws provided adequate protection. An industry study by Ernst & Young commissioned by the Financial Services Coordinating Council estimated that full compliance with the Privacy Directive would cost U.S. consumers $16 billion a year in financial-services benefits. EU financial institutions supported the U.S. position.

The European Union viewed the Gramm-Leach-Bliley Act as inadequate. First, it did not provide individuals with access to their personal data. Second, the Act did not have an adequate enforcement mechanism. As a consequence of these shortcomings, the European Union sent privacy contracts to U.S. firms for them to sign. The financial services industry was dead set against the contracts, in part because they would be legally binding and therefore establish a liability for the improper handling of personal data. The European Parliament in particular wanted companies to be liable for violations of the Directive. The Parliament wanted "compensation for individual damage suffered as a result of possible violations . . ." The Parliament also stated that the commission should "draw up . . . standard contractual clauses that EU citizens could invoke in the courts of a third country."[64]

President George W. Bush personally announced that the United States rejected the privacy contracts, and he insisted that U.S. laws pertaining to financial institutions provided adequate protection. The Bush administration said that the contracts would "impose unduly burdensome requirements that are incompatible with real-world operations." The United States expressed a willingness to enter into discussions with the European Union on the issue, and asked the European Union to delay implementing the Directive. The European Union refused to do so.

In commenting on the difference in perspectives in Europe and the United States, Peter Swire and Robert Litan wrote, "It is roughly accurate to say that America does not have the general presumption that data should be used only for the purpose for which they were collected."[65] A spokesperson for TimeWarner in Brussels observed, "In Europe, people don't trust companies, they trust government. In the U.S., it's the opposite way around: Citizens must be protected from actions of the government."[66]

While establishing broad privacy rights, the EU Directive failed to address a number of issues. One was whether cookies and other devices could be used in the anonymous tracking of click-stream data. The Data Protection Working Party issued a draft report stating that "users must be informed before any cookie used in [online] profiling is placed" and that users have a right to object to the profiling.[67] Another was whether companies could internally transfer personnel information from the European Union to their offices in other countries. Microsoft had been fined $60,000 for obtaining information from its European employees using a Web site in the United States. Another issue was unsolicited e-mail used for marketing purposes. The European Parliament voted to allow each member state to decide whether to use an opt-out or an opt-in approach but required opt-out for inclusion of information in electronic directories. The commission had proposed a uniform approach to both issues. ■

---

[64]European Parliament, "Report on the Draft Commission Decision," A5–0177/2000, June 22, 2000.
[65]Swire and Litan (1998, p. 178).
[66]*BusinessWeek*, November 2, 1998.
[67]Data Protection Working Party (Article 29), "Privacy on the Internet—An Integrated EU Approach to On-line Data Protection," WP 37, November 21, 2000.

---

[62]*Wall Street Journal*, April 6, 2000. The financial services companies were concerned about their ability to use and sell information about customers.
[63]*San Jose Mercury News*, June 5, 2000.

Preparation Questions

1. Do the regulations in the European Union go too far in protecting PII? Do they limit the services businesses can provide?
2. Is protection in the United States for PII adequate? Is any protection needed beyond providing clear and conspicuous warning and an easy opt-out?
3. Is opt-out different from opt-in?

4. The United States and the European Union entered into negotiations to stipulate practices for the United States that would satisfy the European Union's "adequate protection" requirement. Predict the outcome of those negotiations for both tracks. Does the European Union or the United States have the stronger bargaining position?

Aldeasa and the EU Duty Free Abolition (A)

In 1985 the Single European Act paved the way for a complete integration of markets within the European Community by setting the stage for the free circulation of goods, capital, and people by January 1, 1993. One component of this drive toward economic integration was tax harmonization, especially on consumption taxes such as the value-added tax (VAT). Differences in tax rates across member states were considered important sources of distortions and impediments to full market integration, but most attempts by the European Commission to foster tax harmonization had been met with skepticism on the part of member states. One proposal that garnered support was to abolish duty free sales for intra-European travel.

In 1991 the European Union Council of Ministers (ECOFIN—Economy and Finance Ministers) decided under a unanimity rule to abolish duty free sales for travel within the European Union as part of a broader set of taxation and excise measures aimed at making the Single Market a reality. A lengthy transitional period, until June 30, 1999, was granted to allow duty free shop operators and suppliers to adapt to this drastic change in their nonmarket environment.

Aldeasa was a Spanish company whose core business was the operation of duty free shops in airports in Spain and abroad under exclusive concession contracts. At the end of 1995 Aldeasa ranked 11th by sales among the duty free operators in the world, with sales of $322 million and net profits of $35 million. As of November 1996, Aldeasa was still a state-owned company. The new conservative government elected in March 1996 announced that the company would be privatized, although no specific date was set. In July 1996 a new management team, headed by José Fernández Olano, was appointed by the Minister of Finance to design the privatization process and lead the company through it.

The Duty Free Industry

The origin of the duty free industry was the traditional exemption from local and national taxes granted to travelers on international routes, rooted in the concept of "international waters."[68] Over the last 50 years the bulk of duty free trade had progressively shifted from seaports to airports. At the end of 1995 there were 662 airports, 227 airlines, and 82 ferry lines operating duty free shops, with an unknown number of duty free shops in border zones. Over 650 million travelers walked into duty free shops in 1995.[69] Between 1990 and 1995 worldwide sales grew at an average rate of 6.5 percent and represented 2.7 percent of world exports. Airport stores accounted for 41.9 percent of total sales, followed by ferries (13.5 percent) and airlines (8.6 percent). Other channels (diplomatic stores, border shops, and free zones) represented the remaining 36 percent.

Goods sold in duty free shops were exempt only from certain duties and taxes. Those waived generally included the VAT, the luxury tax, local taxes, and import tariffs. In most countries duty free stores sold two different types of products: local products (tax free) and imported products (duty and tax free).[70] Price savings was not the only reason for duty free sales. In fact, in countries with relatively low taxes and import duties, many goods had higher prices at duty free stores than at local shops. This was because duty free retailers passed on to customers a portion of the higher operating costs they faced. Those costs resulted from special taxes on margins imposed on duty free retailers and the concession fees and rent paid to ports, airports, and customs offices for the right to operate the stores. Higher operating costs

---

[68]Since there was no national sovereignty on international waters, passengers and crew members on ships were entitled to purchase goods for personal use without being subject to customs. Thus "ship chandlers" (suppliers of goods to ships) became the first duty free merchants, and some of them still operate modern duty free stores at international airports and ports.

[69]"The Best 'n' Most Duty Free," 1996.

[70]The right to export tax-free products was granted to the passenger or traveler by the country of origin (and was normally unlimited), whereas the right to import duty free was granted by the country of destination and was subject to quantity and value limitations. Duty free shops thus were not concerned about quantity or value limitations, which were the responsibility of the traveler and the custom authorities at the destination. The exceptions to this rule were those stores where the "vendor control" system was applied. Under this system the store was responsible for enforcing the limitations.

also resulted from the use of more qualified labor (e.g., shop assistants fluent in several languages), longer hours associated with flight schedules, special passenger control systems required by the customs authorities, and costs associated with sales in different currencies.

Most passengers were "captive" customers; they had time to kill either at the airport or on a ferry or aircraft. They tended to have high purchasing power and were intrinsically more receptive to commercial offers associated with their travel experience. Duty free customers could be classified into two groups: business travelers, who had a higher disposable income but usually not much time to shop, and tourists, who saw the opportunity to buy in duty free shops as another component of their travel experience. In fact, passengers on charter flights spent more on average than those on regular flights. There were also two types of duty free products: heavily taxed products in the customer's country, such as perfumes or "socially disapproved" products like tobacco or alcoholic beverages; and gifts, such as watches, games, electronic items, and products associated with the local market (crafts, guides, local apparel and food, souvenirs). Many upscale products were heavily dependent on this channel.[71]

Passengers and retailers (whether airlines, ferries, or store operators) were not the only beneficiaries from duty free commercial activity. Owners of the facilities also extracted substantial revenue from the industry. For example, airports worldwide generated on average 19 percent of their total income in fees from retailers.[72] Moreover, as

the European airline industry was liberalized in the late 1980s and early 1990s, competition intensified. Carriers faced increasing pressures to cut costs to maintain competitive fares. In turn, they passed those pressures on to airport operators, and the landing fees charged by airports fell. In parallel, new airport facilities were required to cope with the rapid growth in traffic, so most airports had entered into ambitious investment plans. Many countries had decided to alleviate the burden on public sector budgets by privatizing airport facilities. As a result airport retailing and duty free stores in particular had become an essential source of income for airports, and many of them were expanding their commercial areas.

In 1995 private companies operated most duty free stores with concessions granted by airports or ferry lines. However, in a number of countries the duty free business was controlled, totally or partially, by state-owned companies or directly operated by state airports. For instance, whereas all duty free shops in the United States belonged to private groups, in Greece and Spain state-owned companies operated them. In some countries such as Portugal, Austria, Finland, Denmark, France and Japan, local airlines owned a stake in the duty free operator. In spite of this, the industry had experienced a profound transformation in its ownership structure. As the attractiveness of the sector became more evident, the number of companies involved increased. At the end of 1995 there were 1,550 companies operating duty free businesses. Table 15-3 presents the ranking of the 15 largest world operators by sales in 1995.[73]

TABLE 15-3   Major World Operators (1995)

Ranking	Company/Operator	Country	DF Sales (US$ m)	Market Share (%)
1	DFS	USA	2,800	13.7
2	Nuance	Switzerland	1,205	5.9
3	Gebr Heinemann	Germany	800	3.9
4	Weitnauer	Switzerland	744	3.6
5	Duty Free International	USA	515	2.5
6	Stena Line	Sweden	493	2.4
7	Alpha Retail Trading	UK	481	2.3
8	Silja Line	Finland	402	2.0
9	Aer Rianta	Ireland	355	1.7
10	Duty Free Philippines	Philippines	336	1.6
11	Aldeasa	Spain	322	1.6
12	Viking Line	Finland	314	1.5
13	King Power	Hong Kong/Thailand	314	1.5
14	Lotte Group	South Korea	307	1.5
15	Brasif	Brazil	306	1.5

Source: Santander Investment, The Best 'n' Most Duty Free, 1996

---

[71]For example, 75 percent of cognac sales in the European Union occurred in duty free stores.
[72]*The Future of Duty Free Retailing, Volume 1*, Financial Times Business Limited, 1998.

[73]Nuance and Weitnauer were Swiss companies, but a large share of their operations was in EU countries.

TABLE 15-4   Intra-EU Duty Free Sales by Channel and Product Category (1995)

Channel	Total Sales US$ bn	Intra-EU Sales US$ bn	% Sales at risk	Product	Total Sales US$ bn	Intra-EU Sales US$ bn	% Sales at risk
Airports	3.5	1.9	55	Wine & Spirits	1.7	1.2	71
Ferries	2.7	2.6	98	Perfumes	1.7	1.2	71
Airlines	1.0	0.6	57	Tobacco	1.3	1.1	85
				Others	2.5	1.5	60
EU	7.2	5.1	71	EU	7.2	5.1	71

Source: Santander Investment, The Best 'n' Most Duty Free, 1996
Source: European Travel Research Foundation, 1996

The Impact of Abolition

According to estimates from the European Travel Research Foundation, 71 percent of total duty free sales in airports, airlines, and ferries in the European Union in 1995 were intra-EU sales. This amounted to $5.1 billion and was the portion of sales that was at risk from the proposed abolition of intra-EU duty free sales. However, the potential impact differed across channels and products (Table 15-4). The estimated potential impact of the announced abolition by country is shown in Table 15-5. Scandinavian countries (Finland, Sweden, and Denmark), where ferry companies operated flour-

ishing duty free operations, would be potentially most adversely affected, together with Ireland and Luxembourg, with percentages at risk of over 80 percent.[74] The Netherlands and Italy would be the least impacted with percentages between 50 percent and 55 percent. An undetermined share of the sales would still take place after the abolition under a duty paid scheme essentially identical to that at ordinary retail outlets.

The European Union Decision

After the publication of the White Book on the European Single Market in 1985, the official position of the

TABLE 15-5   Intra-EU Duty Free Sales by Country (1995)

Sales by Channel	% Airports	% Airlines	% Ferries	Intra-EU Sales	Total Sales US$ m	Intra-EU Sales US$ m	% Sales at risk
Austria	80	20	0	Austria	67.2	37.6	56
Belgium	66	15	19	Belgium	179.4	132.5	74
Denmark	25	20	55	Denmark	740.4	590.9	80
Finland	9	4	86	Finland	924.2	829.2	90
France	68	8	24	France	613.0	359.3	59
Germany	48	24	28	Germany	808.8	528.7	65
Greece	75	7	18	Greece	181.7	139.5	77
Ireland	72	10	19	Ireland	168.2	143.3	85
Italy	86	12	2	Italy	314.1	169.0	54
Luxembourg	95	5	0	Luxembourg	15.2	13.9	91
Netherlands	86	15	0	Netherlands	389.1	195.0	50
Portugal	82	18	0	Portugal	75.8	49.0	65
Spain	81	17	2	Spain	331.1	201.3	61
Sweden	22	17	62	Sweden	485.0	429.2	88
United Kingdom	52	12	36	United Kingdom	1,919.5	1,309.9	68
EUROPEAN UNION	**51%**	**14%**	**35%**	**EUROPEAN UNION**	**7,212.7**	**5,128.3**	**71%**

Source: European Travel Research Foundation, 1996

---

[74]These were partly fueled by the weekend trips of young Scandinavians taking advantage of low prices to consume large quantities of alcohol, often without leaving the ferries for the duration of the weekend.

European Commission was that duty and tax-free sales for travelers within the European Community would end by January 1, 1993. The commission's basic argument was that tax-free shopping was not compatible with a single internal market. Also, duty free operators benefited from privileged locations and from "captive" customers, which gave them a natural competitive advantage vis-à-vis other retailers and other transport operators. The implicit subsidy also favored international air and sea travel operators over domestic route operators. Finally, within the retail industry the subsidy for duty free sales adversely affected ordinary retailers who did not benefit from the duty free status.

Some studies of duty free operations had shown that the tax advantage was reflected in higher retail margins and was not significantly passed on to consumers. This happened even in products subject to special consumption taxes (alcohol and tobacco), where the exemptions presented a greater potential for retail price reductions. The European Commission argued that the tax exemption was an indirect subsidy to duty free retailers rather than a subsidy to demand. Moreover, many of the goods sold in duty free shops were taxed, since goods priced at more than €90 were subject to taxes on the full value of the good.

In 1987 the European Commission, and most specifically its Directorate-General XXI (Taxation and Customs Union), in its role as initiator of legislation within the European Union, presented a proposal for a directive on fiscal measures needed to establish the internal market on January 1, 1993. The proposal did not mention specific measures regarding duty free and tax-free sales, so it raised doubts as to whether the creation of the Single Market implied the end of duty free sales. In 1990 Commissioner Scrivener made her position clear by answering a question at the European Parliament (EP). In her opinion, the exemption would automatically end on January 1, 1993, under the legal dispositions abolishing the concepts of import and export in intra-EU exchanges.

The commission's position was increasingly contested, especially by the International Duty Free Confederation (IDFC), created in 1988, which orchestrated an intense campaign aimed at maintaining the tax and duty free status. The IDFC argued that it would be impossible to achieve a completely integrated Single Market by December 31, 1992, since the drive toward the harmonization of indirect taxes had not gathered enough momentum. In June 1991 the European Parliament expressed its views on a projected directive concerning the "general framework for ownership and transport of products subjected to excise duties." One of the adopted amendments proposed postponing the abolition until December 31, 1995, to allow the industry to adapt and give time for the commission to prepare a detailed impact study.

In September the ECOFIN Council, after consulting with the European Parliament and the commission, decided to grant a transitional period to the duty free industry until June 30, 1999. The decision to grant such a long delay was received with surprise by some interested parties, for example, in the Parliament. It was difficult to know exactly what had happened in the council, but according to *The European* newspaper, Germany and Belgium stressed the contradiction between the Single Market and duty free sales.[75] In contrast, the British minister supported a 15-year exemption period, and Portugal defended an 8-year period. France remained neutral initially but finally supported postponement. A common view among commentators was that Ireland and Greece supported the longest possible delay; the Netherlands and Denmark supported Germany and Belgium; Spain supported Portugal; and Italy was aligned with France. The position of Luxembourg was not known.

The arrangement for VAT and excise duties, allowing for tax and duty free sales until June 30, 1999, was finally established in two separate directives (91/680/EEC of December 1991 and 92/12/EEC of February 1992). These directives set the rules for taxes and duties for intra-Community travelers after January 1, 1993. The legislation stipulated that member states may exempt from taxes and duties products sold in duty free stores located in ports or airports, in intra-Community flights and maritime routes, and in the two Eurotunnel terminals, until June 30, 1999. Although the commission's fiscal proposals had been adopted after the Single European Act, both directives were approved under the consultation procedure and adopted by the council under the unanimity rule (as required for all issues pertaining to tax harmonization). The same rule governed future amendments or changes in the decisions.

Aldeasa

Aldeasa was founded in 1974 by the Dirección General de Patrimonio del Estado (Patrimonio), a unit of the Spanish Ministry of Finance. The company was originally created to operate duty free shops in Spanish airports as well as customs warehouses and related logistical services. Like most companies owned by Patrimonio, Aldeasa operated as a monopolist under an exclusive concession granted by AENA (Aeropuertos Españoles y Navegación Aerea), another state-owned company that owned and operated all the airports in Spain. During the 1980s Aldeasa's duty free operations showed impressive growth, and the company opened duty free shops in virtually all the main tourist airports in Spain. In 1986 Spain became a member of the European Community. This caused a dramatic change in the company's regulatory environment, as Aldeasa's business became automatically subject to legislation and decisions adopted at the EU level.

[75]See *The European*, October 1995 supplement on duty free commerce.

After the European Commission initially proposed the abolition of intra-EU duty free sales with effect on January 1, 1993, Aldeasa started to implement a diversification strategy. The company created a Palaces and Museums division in 1990, operating souvenir shops located in museums, palaces, cathedrals, and other cultural or recreational sites. These shops were subject to the ordinary tax regime (duty paid as opposed to duty free). Aldeasa also created a Logistical Services division, where the company provided noncustoms warehousing, airport handling, and distribution. Simultaneously, it began expanding internationally, primarily in Latin America. In 1991 Aldeasa opened its first duty free shops outside Spain in the Dominican Republic. In 1993 the company won a contest to operate duty free shops at several airports in Peru. New concessions in Portugal, Chile (1995), Madeira, and Venezuela (1996) followed.

Other important changes in Aldeasa's operations came from its regulatory environment. Aside from abolition, new EU regulations impacted the company's business and forced it to react quickly to maintain its profitability. First, the implementation of the "vendor control" system in the European Union in 1993 had a direct negative effect on passengers' average spending at duty free shops and forced Aldeasa to reorganize its in-store operations, payment, and control technologies.[76] Second, the application of the Schengen agreements had a profound impact on the industry landscape. In the case of airports, passengers on EU-bound flights departing from airports located within the so-called "Schengen Zone" no longer had to go through passport control. In application of the new agreements, airports created two differentiated areas: Schengen and non-Schengen. This significantly altered passenger flows within airports, so Aldeasa had to relocate several stores or open new ones.

Despite the diversification initiatives, the Airports Division (duty free and duty paid shops, urban shops, and the wholesale business) still accounted for 89 percent of total sales and 96 percent of operating cash flow in 1995 (versus 95 and 90 percent, respectively, in 1990). Palaces and Museums contributed 5 percent to total sales and 2 percent to operating cash flow, whereas the Logistical Services Division contributed 6 and 2 percent, respectively. Fifty-six percent of Aldeasa's headcount, or 1,209 employees at the end of 1995, worked in the Airport Division. Revenues from this division had been growing since 1990 at a 17.6 percent compounded annual rate. Even after the implementation of vendor control in 1993, annual growth rates were well above 20 percent. The 67 duty free shops Aldeasa operated in

Spain were located in the 14 most important Spanish airports. Madrid (27 shops), Barcelona (12 shops), Málaga (9 shops), and Palma de Mallorca (6 shops) were the main locations. Madrid was ranked 10th in the world by duty free sales in 1995. Palma and Málaga, two of the most popular tourist destinations in Europe, were also among the top 20 airports.

The high growth was impressive considering that the number of passengers on international departure flights in airports where Aldeasa operated had risen at an annual rate of only 7.6 percent between 1990 and 1995. The 20.2 million passengers spent an average of $11.6 shopping at Aldeasa's duty free shops in 1995. The average was higher in the case of nontourist airports: $14 versus $10. The sales breakdown by product category was essentially similar to the industry average (Table 15-4), although there were some differences between tourist and nontourist airports. The company estimated that between 75 and 80 percent of its duty free sales in Spanish airports corresponded to passengers on intra-EU flights and were therefore at risk in 1999. Tobacco and alcoholic beverages were likely to be more sensitive to the abolition, since unlike perfumes and miscellaneous items, they were subject to excise duties in addition to ad-valorem taxes and would therefore register a higher price increase. The actual impact, however, ultimately depended on Aldeasa's marketing and pricing strategies.

Aldeasa could follow a volume strategy (maintain pre-abolition prices to protect sales volume, absorbing the taxes as a margin reduction) or a margin strategy (raise prices to pass the taxes on to customers). The company's gross margins were estimated to be around 25 percent for duty paid compared to 32 percent for duty free sales.

The exclusive concession agreement between Aldeasa and AENA, which acquired a 20 percent stake in Aldeasa in 1992, was due to expire in July 1999. Under this agreement, Aldeasa paid AENA an annual fee of approximately 25 percent of sales on average (the actual fee on sales was calculated by product and airport). AENA generated 30 percent of its total revenue from retailing fees, with 50 percent coming from the Aldeasa exclusive concession contract.

Privatization and Abolition

In November 1996 Fernández Olano, a friend of several Spanish cabinet members including the Finance Minister, had to preside over the privatization process. Investors and financial analysts regarded Aldeasa as a "jewel" among the state-owned companies. Indeed, it had always shown an extremely high and consistent profitability: a gross margin exceeding 30 percent of sales, an operating margin close to 15 percent of sales, and a net margin of approximately 10 percent of sales. Sales and operating profits had increased at an annual rate of approximately 20 percent, while net profits grew

---

[76]Under the vendor control system, compliance with the limits on duty free purchases (the so-called "duty free allowances") was controlled by the vendor as opposed to the country of destination. Passengers on intra-EU flights were allowed to purchase duty free goods up to certain limits (e.g., 1 liter of alcoholic beverages or 200 cigarettes). The limits did not apply to passengers on flights to destinations outside the European Union.

15 percent per year in the period 1990 to 1995. Aldeasa also had a healthy balance sheet, with a net cash position of ESP 2.218 million ($15 million) at the end of 1995. The main challenge facing the new management team came from the upcoming abolition of the intra-EU duty free sales in 1999. The success of the upcoming privatization and the future of the company were dependent on the company's market and nonmarket strategies. ■

SOURCE: This case was prepared for class use by Gonçalo Cadete, Antonio Varas, and Professor Romain Wacziarg. Copyright © 1999 by the Board of Trustees of the Leland Stanford Junior University. All rights reserved. Reproduced with permission.

Preparation Questions

1. What nonmarket objective, if any, should Aldeasa pursue? Which institutions should it target?
2. How are the institutional rules for enacting legislation within the European Union significant from Aldeasa's point of view? How do they affect the industry's chances of success in the nonmarket arena?
3. Formulate an integrated strategy for Aldeasa.
4. Evaluate the likelihood of success of the nonmarket component of your proposed strategy.
5. How are prospects for Aldeasa's privatization affected by the abolition of duty free for intra-EU travel? What conditions should Aldeasa seek in renegotiating its contract with AENA?

16

China: History, Culture, and Political Economy

INTRODUCTION

China is an ancient country that since 1978 has embarked on a remarkable economic path in which markets and foreign direct investment have been encouraged and economic reforms have been frequent if not always successful. Yet China remains a country under the domination of the Chinese Communist Party (CCP) with little popular participation in political activity and continuing restrictions on civil and human rights. The importance of a country with 1.3 billion people cannot be underestimated for both foreign businesses and governments, but the absence of democratic institutions and weak legal protections present challenges. Economic reforms have led thousands of companies to set up operations in China and, combined with the liberalization of business opportunities for Chinese citizens, have resulted in spectacular economic growth. Real growth in GDP has averaged 9 percent annually since the open-door policy began in 1978. The remnants of the planned economy era, however, posed a particular challenge for China as it attempted to make its state-owned enterprises (SOEs) more efficient while replacing the social services they had provided for workers and retirees. Economic growth was not led by the SOEs but by private enterprises and enterprises supported by provincial and village governments. Continued economic liberalization had to be accomplished while preserving the supremacy of the CCP.

In 2001 China joined the World Trade Organization, which brought both opportunity and new challenges. Membership provided additional access to foreign markets, but it also required China to open major industries to imports and foreign direct investment. This put additional pressure on SOEs and on the country to strengthen legal protections.

This chapter provides background on the history and culture of China and briefly characterizes the four I's with an emphasis on government institutions and business issues. The next section provides a historical background on China beginning with the pre-republican era and concluding with the current era. The following section considers Confucianism and its implications for business, society, and politics. The nonmarket environment is then discussed with an emphasis on the institutions of government. Business in China is considered with a focus on SOEs, foreign direct investment, and international trade. Several current issues, including human rights, piracy, corruption, product safety, energy and the environment, and workers' rights, are then considered. The chapter cases provide an opportunity to address particular managerial challenges in the context of China's political economy.

HISTORICAL BACKGROUND[1]

Pre-Republican

Ethnic Chinese, also known as Han people, originated in the Yellow River Valley in North-Central China. Organized rural society has existed in this region for over 10,000 years, and political control was typically divided by rival dynastic kingdoms. Invasion by barbarians resulted in centuries (c. 771–221 B.C.) of political fragmentation, during which much of China's most impressive philosophy was developed. Three important schools of Chinese philosophical thought emerged in this period: Daoism, Confucianism, and Legalism.[2] These laid the basis for much of China's future political thought and made the unification of China a paramount ideal. Confucianism, considered later in the chapter, had a profound impact on the organization of Chinese government, as it advocated the concept of government by meritocracy. This provided the intellectual foundation for the imperial bureaucracy.

Many historians regard the victory of the Qin kingdom after a period of prolonged conflicts known as the Warring States Period (403–221 B.C.) as the beginning of China's existence as a unified nation. The resulting state controlled an area roughly half the size of today's People's Republic of China. Technology played a central role in the Qin's success, as it had mastered iron-working in advance of most of its rivals. The Qin Dynasty played an important role in shaping the institutions and practices of imperial China. It eliminated the remnants of China's ancient feudal society and established the beginnings of a central bureaucracy based on Confucian principles. It also standardized the currency, weights, and measures; built some of China's first extensive irrigation projects; introduced a uniform system of writing; and consolidated many of the nation's defensive walls.

Bureaucracy in Imperial China

Despite the immense political changes made by the Qin, China's society and politics were dominated by regional aristocracies for almost another millennium. Each succeeding dynasty, however, expanded and strengthened the bureaucratic system, and by the Tang Dynasty (A.D. 618–907) the imperial bureaucracy was considered the preeminent political authority.[3]

Since the Early Han Dynasty (206 B.C.–A.D.8), membership in the bureaucracy was attained through highly competitive national examinations that in theory were open to all. The wealth, power, and prestige afforded by passing the examinations were so great that families often invested handsomely in educating their young men. Successful examinees spent their entire youth studying the Confucian classics in preparation for the examinations and often were in their mid-30s when they passed. The bureaucracy played an important role in ensuring social stability by preventing the rise of rival sources of political power while still permitting the accumulation of family wealth.[4]

Foreign Relations

Imperial China faced external military threats for much of its history. The Ming Dynasty (1368–1644) constructed the Great Wall of China to ward off northern barbarians, but it proved to be a military failure, as it could not stop a Manchurian invasion that resulted in the last dynasty, the Qing (1644–1911). In general, however, the pre-Ming Chinese welcomed foreign commerce. Trade with the Middle East and European nations flourished, and in the early 1400s a fleet of Chinese vessels successfully completed a trade and diplomatic mission to Africa. During the 15th century, however, Chinese leaders began to view foreign interactions with a peculiar contempt. Costly border wars and fiscal crises caused the Ming to pull back on their efforts to establish

---

[1]This section is based on a note prepared by Michael M. Ting under the supervision of Professor David P. Baron. Copyright © 1998 by the Board of Trustees of the Leland Stanford Junior University. All rights reserved. Reprinted with permission.
[2]See Pye (1978, pp. 32–59; 1985) for an introduction to the early Chinese schools of thought.
[3]See Shue (1988, pp. 84–85) and Moore (1966, p. 164).
[4]Fairbank (1992, pp. 179–182).

foreign relations and build a navy. Convinced that foreigners could offer little of value to China, conservative Confucian scholars of the period increasingly advocated xenophobic foreign policies.[5]

Notwithstanding the Qing's hostility, the British, led by the British East India Company, vigorously attempted to maintain trade ties in southern China. With the end of the Napoleonic Wars in 1815, England gradually increased its commercial interest in China. China's defeat in the Opium War at the hands of Britain's vastly superior military technology resulted in the 1842 Treaty of Nanjing. The terms of the treaty were widely regarded as humiliating to the Chinese, as they required massive reparations to Britain, the turnover of Hong Kong, and the opening of five coastal cities to British residents and commerce. Many of the Western powers also insisted on reciprocal "most favored nation" agreements that automatically granted to every foreign country the concessions made to any one country, thus hastening the pace and extent of economic concessions.

Collapse of Imperial China

The latter half of the 19th century was marked by numerous large-scale revolts that reflected the inability of the Qing to maintain domestic peace and contain foreign influence. The imperial bureaucracy was increasingly perceived as an incompetent and backwards institution, incapable of performing even its traditional duties of maintaining China's important waterways. As the 19th century drew to a close, internal calls for reform became increasingly prevalent, and the Qing initiated many ambitious reforms. They attempted to copy several Western-style government institutions and abolished the centuries-old examination system in 1905. Their drive toward modernization resulted in the outfitting of a Western-style military and plans for a new national rail network.

The Republican Era

By the first decade of the 20th century, local warlords had ascended to political prominence in China. Many raised their own armies, collected their own taxes, and showed questionable loyalty to the Qing. In addition, revolutionary societies and fraternities, many loosely organized into a group called the Revolutionary Alliance, were increasingly active in China's major urban centers. The Revolutionary Alliance, led by Dr. Sun Yat-sen, had relatively strong popular backing, but lacked an army. By early 1912, a large military faction led by former Qing general Yuan Shikai gained the upper hand, and the last Qing abdicated his throne in 1912.

While many credit Sun Yat-sen with the founding of the Republic of China in 1911, China at the time was hardly a coherent political entity. Yuan proved incapable of ruling China, as he insisted on central control over proposed modernizations but lacked substantial authority over local governments. He also actively attempted to undermine his Revolutionary Alliance allies, many of whom had organized themselves into the Guomindang (GMD), or Nationalist Party, under Sun.

Sun's death in 1925 cleared the way for the ascendancy of Chiang Kai-shek as the new GMD leader. Capitalizing on both the strength of his National Revolutionary Army and a wave of nationalist sentiment in the mid-1920s, Chiang launched military offensives in 1926 and 1928 that established a new capital in Nanjing and brought most of China under GMD rule. His sudden success convinced many that the GMD was China's best hope for modernizing its economy and political system. This hope proved to be illusory, however, as the Nanjing leaders lacked sufficient control over many regions to execute their policies. The GMD's support base was primarily urban, but since China's urban-industrial sector was still very small, its base and resources were limited.

The main unifying force for the GMD was the threat from the Chinese Communist Party formed in 1921. Chiang continually harassed the CCP and, in response, several communist uprisings took place, only to be crushed by GMD armies. The CCP did not recover until 1933, by which time it had transformed itself into a rural party largely independent of the international communist party. Headed by Mao Zedong, an early

---

[5]Fairbank (1992, pp. 138–140).

revolutionary leader who had carefully studied the rural economy, the CCP was once again strong enough to be of concern to the GMD. Chiang's continuous attacks drove the CCP to seek a new base, and in late 1934, 100,000 soldiers and party members began their famous Long March.

War and Civil War

In 1937 Japan invaded and Chinese armies were quickly routed by superior Japanese tactics and technology. Chinese resistance to Japan was highly fragmented in spite of the initial promise of a united front between the GMD and CCP. During the war and occupation, Mao was able to consolidate his leadership and develop his own distinctive brand of Marxism. As part of his program the CCP began to institute land reform in friendly areas, thus enlisting peasant support and swelling the ranks of CCP troops.

As World War II drew to a close, both sides prepared for a civil war. In 1945 the CCP was stronger than at any point in its history, but its army had little foreign support and was only half the size of Chiang's American-equipped army. American support, however, could not forestall the subsequent rout of the GMD in the 1946 to 1949 civil war. By mid-1949 the communist victory was nearly complete, and on October 1, 1949, Mao proclaimed the founding of the People's Republic of China.

As Chiang's losses mounted in 1948, he transferred the remains of the Republic of China to Taiwan, which as part of the Yalta agreements in World War II had been formally returned to the Republic of China after 50 years of Japanese colonization. The GMD instituted comprehensive land reform and compensated landlords with government bonds. With American economic aid it embarked on vigorous industrialization by attracting foreign investment and targeting export markets.[6]

The Communist Era

Although the communist victory had been complete, Mao and his followers still faced a daunting task that had eluded Chinese rulers for centuries: establishing a state with unquestioned control over the entire nation. The CCP's assumption of power took two distinct tracks. First, in the countryside, it sought to complete the process of land reform that had begun in Northern China earlier in the decade. Because peasants benefiting from land redistribution overwhelmingly outnumbered landlords, the process was quickly and enthusiastically embraced.[7] Second, in keeping with Marxist philosophy, the party sought to control all commerce, but again the magnitude of the task demanded considerable flexibility. Only the largest companies came under state control in the early years, and most urban professionals were allowed to continue working regardless of their political background. Meanwhile, governments at all levels gradually asserted control over prices, the banking system, and the allocation of various important goods.[8]

The end of the Korean War allowed policymakers to concentrate on their next task: the transformation of the Chinese economy into a socialist system. Following the early Soviet model, planners in Beijing hoped to stimulate the development of heavy industry by taxing the agricultural sector. They also believed that greater productivity could be best achieved by wiping out the remnants of capitalism and developing huge, self-contained production units in agriculture and industry.

A central feature of the First Five Year Plan was the collectivization of agriculture. Shortly after land reform was completed, the CCP began to organize peasant households into ever-larger cooperative associations. A similar process was under way in the industrial sector. State takeovers of large enterprises accelerated throughout the 1950s, until only the smallest street merchants were allowed to remain independent. With the aid of Soviet loans, CCP industrial policy emphasized sectors such as steel, petroleum, and chemicals at the expense of consumer goods. In addition to their economic importance, these enterprises also served a vital social role. Labor was furnished through the

---

[6]See Deyo (1987) and Haggard (1990) for a comparative perspective on Taiwanese industrial policy.
[7]Vogel (1980, pp. 91–124) discusses policy debates during the early years of land reform.
[8]See Naughton (2007, Ch.3) for an analysis of economic policies in this period.

danwei ("work unit") system, under which workers were permanently assigned to enterprises upon completing their education. The *danwei* provided its members with housing, child care, schooling, health care, shops, post offices, and other social services. It was also an instrument of social control. Because there was no welfare system, urban residents had no access to even the most basic social services outside of their *danwei*, and opportunities for changing enterprises were rare.

Convinced that China's lagging production could be blamed not on poor economic reasoning but on a lack of mobilization, the CCP unleashed a flurry of production efforts to spur the economy. Many of these projects launched in the Great Leap Forward in 1958 were at best ill conceived, and at worst destructive.[9] Agricultural cooperatives were rapidly combined into even larger county-size communes, but in 1959 poor weather highlighted the inefficiency of the communes. Production plummeted and China suffered a famine that claimed over 20 million lives through 1962.

The clear failure of the large communes prompted authority to devolve back to smaller production units, so that individual households were once again held responsible for meeting production quotas. More importantly, the government legalized private plots on which peasants were allowed to raise and market their own vegetables and animals while their communes produced grain. On a larger scale, leaders also began to question the Soviet-inspired strategy of developing heavy industry first.

Mao's allies—notably his wife Jiang Qing and army chief Lin Biao—insisted that China's problems were the result of insufficient dedication to the CCP's revolutionary principles. Mao's gambit to reassert power combined this message with his still considerable populist appeal in launching the Great Proletarian Cultural Revolution in 1966. Mao and Lin organized thousands of Red Guard units, consisting largely of fanatical students who were directed to purge their jurisdictions of the four "olds"—old ideas, old customs, old cultures, and old habits. Their campaigns destroyed many of China's most valuable cultural artifacts and degenerated into destructive excess and mob rule in the name of Mao. Finally, in 1967, the army stepped in to control the chaos, often by imposing martial law. The Cultural Revolution had decimated much of the party's organization, especially at the provincial and lower levels. It had also elevated the army's status within the party hierarchy.

As a result of the split of the Sino-Soviet alliance in 1958, successive American administrations expressed interest in renewing relations with China, and these efforts culminated in President Nixon's historic visit to China in 1972. As a result of improved relations, both nations gained a powerful ally against the Soviet Union.

The Reform Era

The deaths of Mao and foreign minister Zhou Enlai in 1976 led to Deng Xiaoping assuming the leadership of China. Deng's rise occurred during a period of tremendous foreign and domestic ferment. The United States formally switched its recognition of China from Taiwan to the People's Republic on January 1, 1979, after which Deng made historic visits to America and Japan. Inspired by the beginnings of political liberalization, many Chinese began to express their bitterness toward the communist party with large posters on various city walls, the most famous of which became known as the Democracy Wall in Beijing. The party, which was ready to commit itself to many reforms, had little intention of sharing its authority, and to emphasize its control, Deng consolidated power.

Deng's economic reforms were headlined by the "Four Modernizations"—agriculture, industry, defense, and science and technology.[10] Recognizing that China needed more exposure to Western products, ideas, and capital, Beijing lifted import restrictions in 1978 under its open-door policy. Four Special Economic Zones were opened in

---

[9]See the chapter case, *Wugang and the Reform of State-Owned Enterprises,* for a description of one of these projects.
[10]Naughton (2007, Ch.4) provides some detail on the economic policies of the reform era and the transition toward a market economy.

Southern China, where foreign investors could take advantage of low-wage labor and preferential tax rates. Small, household-run enterprises were once again legalized. Finally, larger enterprises such as agricultural production teams and many SOEs were subjected to a new fiscal regime under which some profits from above-quota production could be retained for the enterprise's use. This exposure to market forces resulted in a dramatic increase in nationwide investment in 1979 and 1980.[11]

A second, more intensive wave of reforms occurred between 1983 and 1985. In the agricultural sector, the government replaced mandatory grain purchases with a contracting system known as the Household Responsibility System, and prices for many goods were allowed to "float" to market levels. In the cities, SOEs were given increased discretion over their profits, and individual managers were made more accountable for their performance. Beijing also granted 14 additional coastal cities and Hainan Island Special Economic Zone status. The sudden changes and influx of wealth, however, created economic and social backlashes. Economic crime and corruption were rampant, and leaders often voiced concerns about excessive Western cultural influence.

Another period of retrenchment occurred in 1986, as restrictions were placed on investments and imports in an attempt to cool the economy. More ominously, however, large-scale social unrest had become evident throughout the country, and students and intellectuals grew increasingly disappointed that the nation's rapid economic change was not accompanied by changes in the authoritarian political system. For many students, Hu Yaobang personified many of the disappointments they faced. An outspoken progressive, Hu was forced to resign as party general secretary in January 1987 after other party leaders blamed him for not stopping student protests. His sudden death in 1989 set off a wave of nationwide student demonstrations, the most prominent of which attracted as many as a million demonstrators to Beijing's Tiananmen Square. For weeks the demonstrators and sympathetic civilians successfully resisted attempts to impose martial law, but in a move that was condemned worldwide, crack army units crushed the protests.

The repercussions of the Tiananmen massacre showed that China's efforts to join the world community were imposing constraints on the CCP and the government. China's desire for an international role commensurate with its growing economic strength had generated numerous frictions. Foremost among these were China's foreign economic relations. Both the United States, one of China's largest trading partners, and the GATT/World Trade Organization, which China hoped to join, insisted that China adhere more closely to international norms in its economy.

One foreign policy success was the 1984 agreement with the United Kingdom, returning Hong Kong to China in 1997. Under China's "One Country, Two Systems" policy, Hong Kong was to retain its autonomy, including a separate currency, for 50 years. Shortly before the return, the British government attempted to bolster the colony's legislative body as a popular institution, but Beijing ensured that only its own hand-picked representatives were permitted to sit. In 1999 Macao was returned to China by Portugal.

A potentially more serious sovereignty issue was the status of Taiwan. In their claims to sovereignty over both the mainland and Taiwan, both the CCP and GMD agreed that there was only a single Chinese nation. Because of their disparate political systems, however, movement toward reunification has been virtually nonexistent. Beijing originally proposed the One Country, Two Systems policy for Taiwan, but it was quickly rejected by the GMD government, which refused to unite with a communist regime. Beijing made clear that it would not tolerate a declaration of Taiwanese independence.

Domestic Reform in an Authoritarian Framework

Domestically, China resumed its economic reforms shortly after the furor over Tiananmen subsided. The 1990s saw the increasing autonomy of SOEs, reforms of the nation's financial system, as well as a fully convertible currency. The government also handled

---

[11]Harding (1987, p. 4).

the political transition of Deng's death in 1997 with few problems. The country, however, faced challenges that were as formidable as ever. One of the most urgent was the reform of over 300,000 obsolete SOEs. Few of these enterprises were profitable because they had functioned too long in the absence of competitive pressures. Many were hopelessly inefficient, saddled with old technology and employing up to 15 million excess workers nationwide. Moreover, these enterprises had accumulated combined debts approaching $120 billion (almost 20 percent of GDP), while absorbing most of China's domestic credit.[12] The problem was tightly linked with a crisis in the national banking system, whose long-standing practice of granting loans on the basis of political connections rather than commercial merit had resulted in high levels of bad debt. Transforming these enterprises into profitable entities would inevitably require the dismantling of the *danwei* system, but there was no social welfare system to replace it.

The economy continued to grow rapidly as a result of export growth and the growth of domestic demand. Beijing, however, also faced a host of long-term economic and political issues. The country's labor and housing markets required revamping. Corruption and cronyism were prevalent at all levels of government. The growing demand by an increasingly affluent population for energy and consumer goods was exacerbating China's already dire environmental problems. As SOEs were restructured, millions of workers lost their jobs, and they and millions of rural workers moved to the cities in search of work. Finally, the CCP faced the daunting task of addressing these issues without once again raising demands for political liberalization.

CONFUCIANISM AND SOCIAL EXPLANATIONS

An important factor in understanding Chinese social and economic organization is its rich cultural heritage. This section considers Confucianism, which has had a significant influence not only in China but also in several other Asian nations.[13] With its emphasis on hierarchy, deference, moral rectitude, and behavioral norms, Confucianism was well suited to the needs of social stability. Indeed, many historians have credited China's long existence as a unified nation to its Confucian heritage. Yet the attribution of highly complex social phenomena to a single body of philosophical work would be unwarranted. Over more than 2,000 years of development, a wide variety of theories have worked their way under the Confucian umbrella. Thus, the general framework of Confucian thought displays considerable flexibility. On the one hand, as Confucius might suggest, a degree of modesty is warranted in drawing conclusions about social and economic organization from this highly complex ethics system.[14] On the other hand, attempting to understand Chinese groups, organizations, and behavior without sensitivity to the Confucian heritage would be incomplete at best.

During the political turmoil following the fall of the Zhou Dynasty, Confucius (551–479 B.C.) recorded and organized the extant body of ethical thought and extended it by de-emphasizing religious aspects and instead giving priority to the human condition (De Bary, 1991). Under this humanistic reorientation, virtue figured prominently in personal and political affairs, and individuals were to possess virtue and follow rules of behavior just as emperors did. Thus, Confucius was responsible for initiating the central preoccupation of Chinese philosophical thought: moral self-cultivation (Ivanhoe, 1993).

---

[12]See Tomlinson (1997) for an example of the privatization of a state-owned enterprise.

[13]This section is adapted from a note prepared by Michael M. Ting under the supervision of Professor David P. Baron. Copyright © 1998 by the Board of Trustees of the Leland Stanford Junior University. All rights reserved. Reprinted with permission.

[14]Although the best exposition of Confucian thought is the *Analects,* over the centuries *Rujia* philosophers added dozens of major variations and extensions to this work. Zhu Xi grouped its existing strands into a two-tiered program of study that is regarded as the Confucian canon. First came the "Four Books": the *Analects, Mencius, Daxue (The Great Learning),* and *Zhongyong (Doctrine of Man).* Next were the "Five Classics": *Shujing (Book of History), Liji (Book of Rites), Shijing (Book of Odes), Spring and Autumn Annals,* and *Yijing (Book of Changes).* Thus, while Confucianism lacks a single, comprehensive statement, a commonly accepted body of tenets emerges from these works.

Perhaps the fundamental distinction between Confucianism and many Western systems of thought lies in its orientation toward the fundamental problem of social organization. As Yang (1959, p. 172) explained:

> Self-cultivation, the basic theme of Confucian ethics . . . did not seek a solution to social conflict in defining, limiting, and guaranteeing the rights and interests of the individual or in the balance of power and interests between individuals. It sought the solution from the self-sacrifice of the individual for the preservation of the group.

Confucianism links self-cultivation and social harmony through the development of group relations because it views the family as the ideal setting for moral self-cultivation. According to the Zhongyong, "Five Relationships" (*wu lun*) must be perfected before social harmony is achieved: father and son, husband and wife, sibling and sibling, friend and friend, and ruler and subject. Taking a pragmatic view of human nature, Confucius felt that most people could achieve perfection only in their intrafamily relationships. By extension, if virtue and harmony could be found most readily in family relationships, the process by which virtue is acquired must be present there as well (Schwartz, 1985, p. 99). As the individuals most responsible for this process, the leaders of such groups—family elders or bureaucrats—were accorded a high degree of deference and respect. Groups were therefore a vital part of the Confucian ethical system, as the individual goal of moral self-cultivation was in some sense an achievement of a larger group, be it a family or a nation.

The objectives of self-cultivation are two interrelated concepts: *ren,* or humanity, and *li,* or propriety. Loosely speaking, the former refers to one's internal discipline, whereas the latter concerns one's social relations. Confucius regarded *ren* as the more fundamental of the two concepts and considered it the ultimate object of moral self-cultivation. In its most abstract sense, the concept refers to the love of all human beings, and all people were thought to have an innate capacity for it.

Li is the external, or social, manifestation of *ren.* Although *li* is most commonly interpreted as "propriety," the term is also synonymous with "ceremony," "ritual," "decorum," and "good form," since it addresses all aspects of human behavior, including personal, familial, social, religious, and political conduct (Tu, 1979, pp. 20–21, 29). The Confucian tradition places a strong emphasis on behavioral minutiae because of its belief that self-cultivation is not a solitary endeavor, but rather occurs in a social context.

Confucian behavioral norms display a strongly particularistic, as opposed to universal, inclination. In contrast with ethics systems that require equal treatment of all individuals, Confucianism explicitly condoned behavior differentiated on the basis of social relationships. That is, differing standards could be applied to different social relationships, such as within a group to which a person belonged versus with regard to strangers. Appropriate behavior in a group could also differ depending on the person's position. For example, within a family a parent follows a particular form of proper behavior with regard to a child, whereas within a work group the same parent may be in the position of the "child" in relation to his or her employer.

The notion that appropriate behavior is specific to particular social relationships is largely attributable to the group foundations of moral self-cultivation, which forces numerous concessions out of necessity. Self-cultivation ideally encompasses relations with all people, but in practice most individuals can achieve only a limited degree of success in perfecting relationships. A family bond, for instance, creates opportunities for developing *ren* and *li* that may elude those outside the family. Thus, self-cultivation is seen as a process of gradual inclusion, beginning with the individual, then progressing to relations with family, nation, and the world. In this framework, universalism exists as an ideal, but discrimination and favoritism within groups should be expected because Confucians would find the notion of universalistic humanity incoherent without the prior achievement of harmony within smaller groups (Tu, 1979, p. 28).

Another feature of *li* in Confucian ethics is its distinctive conception of reciprocity. Many cultures have some variation of the Golden Rule: "Do unto others as you would have them do unto you." Beginning with the *Analects,* Confucians have devoted a great deal of attention to the idea of *shu,* or consideration. Confucius's classic statement of the rule is:

> Tzu-kung asked saying, Is there any single saying that one can act upon all day and every day? The Master said, Perhaps the saying about consideration: "Never do to others what you would not like them to do to you." (Analects 15.23)

Numerous variations and extensions on the Golden Rule exist in the Confucian canon. Taken together, they share the characteristic of emphasizing hierarchy. Nivison (1996, p. 73) constructs the following synthesis of the idealized version of *shu:*

> What I do to you, if I am in a superior position, should be what I would find it acceptable for you to do to me, if our positions were reversed. I should be kind, lenient, considerate. . . . What I do for you, if I am in an inferior position, should be what I would expect you to do for me, if our positions were reversed. I should be "loyal," and so should be strict with myself even when what I am doing might hurt me. . . .

Western variants of the Golden Rule typically make no allusions to the social position of the actors.

Confucianism does not include an independent notion of individual rights. As considered in Chapter 21, Western concepts of rights involve liberty, choice, and autonomy. These rights impose duties on others not to interfere with those rights. Chang (1998, p. 133) argues that "although the Confucians did not talk about 'human rights,' they maintained that people should treat each other as fellow human beings and help one another to live a good, human way of life. This idea is clearly comparable with the concept of 'human rights.'" Cheng (1998) explains the nature of rights in terms of the relationship between a person and a ruler and their duties within that relationship. A ruler, or government, has a duty to help develop virtue in subjects, and the "rights" of those subjects are to consideration by the ruler. Cheng (1998, p. 145) writes, "we can see how a Chinese might see his rights as his duties and define his own self in terms of his consciousness." That is, instead of independently identified rights, Confucianism focuses more on duties required by a relationship, and those duties give expectations of certain types of treatment for the others in the relationship.

Applications in Society, Politics, and Business
Political Institutions

The Confucian ideal of hierarchical relations within the family also extends to the political realm. Whereas family heads could exercise near-absolute authority over other family members, households were expected to defer to the state on nonhousehold matters. The promotion of one's self-interest in society was considered just as inappropriate as a child's selfishness before her parents (Pye, 1985). The analogy helped to justify the Confucians' advocacy of authoritarian rule by a meritocratic elite. It also identified some of the highest political priorities of the state: security, cohesion, loyalty, and stability. Confucius wrote extensively on the behavior expected of a ruler. The following passage touches on some important aspects of a ruler's behavior:

> The Master said, Govern the people by regulations, keep order among them by chastisements, and they will flee from you, and lose all self-respect. Govern them by moral force, keep order among them by ritual and they will keep their self-respect and come to you of their own accord. (Analects 2.3)

Confucius saw the ruler as a moral exemplar, but the primary purpose of governing by moral force was not divine reward but the moral development of the people. To achieve this, the ruler could use formal rules or coercion, but setting a virtuous example was both necessary and sufficient for improving society's moral character and inducing social harmony.

One of the most striking differences between Confucian and Western political thought is that the former does not conceive of a role for "civil society," or the collection of intermediate organizations between the family and state (Shils, 1996).[15] Because households were to show the same loyalty to the state that children showed to their parents, allegiance to other organizations had the potential for destabilizing society. Remarkably, imperial Chinese society mirrored these priorities for over two millennia, as merchants never achieved any substantial social status and social advancement was secured exclusively through advancement in the state bureaucracy (Pye, 1985, p. 57). The lack of recognition of legitimate interests outside the state and the deference expected of citizens also rendered Confucianism inconsistent with modern conceptions of democracy.

Firms and Bureaucracies

In more modern settings, Confucian paternalism may be seen in the context of other organizations, such as firms and bureaucracies (Abegglen and Stalk, 1985; Dollinger, 1988; Durlabhji, 1990; Taka, 1994). Because of the imperative of maintaining group harmony, decision making is typically achieved through consensus building. This process requires the cooperation of leaders and subordinates. Leaders must demonstrate decision-making ability commensurate with their position, treat subordinates fairly, and set a good example for all. Personal negotiation may be used to resolve disputes among peers. In return, subordinates are to recognize a leader's authoritarian prerogatives and subsume personal desires to the attainment of group goals. Little emphasis is placed on formal rules, and quiet suasion and deference are often sufficient for making decisions and maintaining organizational unity.

This familistic orientation can exert a powerful influence outside the boundaries of formal organizations. Informal personal ties in Chinese society are often referred to as *guanxi*. These relationships may be either vertical (e.g., between teacher and student) or horizontal (e.g., between residents of the same village). *Guanxi* ties create a form of diffuse reciprocity, allowing individuals to exchange favors even years after a formal relationship has been dissolved. Their importance in Chinese society should not be underestimated. Throughout history, decisions ranging from hiring to the sale of scarce goods have gone in favor of those possessing good *guanxi*. Such practices have persisted despite the increased bureaucratization of Chinese society during the communist era. Because these relationships are usually not reflected in formal laws, *guanxi* often makes Chinese organizational behavior appear nontransparent and at times resemble cronyism to outsiders. The strength of such ties in China frequently has frustrated Westerners, who are more accustomed to legally circumscribed contracts or quid pro quo arrangements (Pye, 1988).

The importance of *guanxi* is such that individuals must concern themselves with acquiring it. Some ties arise in the course of normal social interaction, for instance through school or family. Others require investment and must be cultivated directly through the giving of gifts and favors, for which an elaborate set of norms has evolved. Gift giving in China frequently serves the instrumental goal of initiating a relationship. Whereas gifts may sometimes be used to secure specific favors, the diffuse nature of *guanxi* requires that exchanges occur in private some time before the desired favor to avoid the public appearance of a quid pro quo (Yang, 1994, p. 144).

Confucianism's strong focus on group cohesion and solidarity has implications for other relationships. Because intragroup relations are so important, relationships of subordinates within a group with individuals outside the group are often frowned upon. Such relationships are the responsibility of the group leader, who may require the outsiders to acknowledge his or her moral authority (Pye, 1985, p. 63). As a result, outsiders hoping to influence a group must simultaneously respect the group leader's appearance

---

[15]Gold (1996) argues that large family networks serve as the functional equivalent of civil society.

of control while also exerting effort toward establishing trustworthiness and becoming more of an insider. The latter may entail a significant investment in the establishment of *guanxi* relationships prior to the execution of any significant interaction.

Business Relationships

Confucianism often has been linked with the development and operation of capitalism in China and other Asian countries.[16] In particular, the Chinese tendency toward small, family-owned businesses that operate within tight networks shows many traces of the Confucian heritage (Hamilton, 1996). The high status associated with public office, which required tremendous investment in education, and the traditional practice of dividing inheritances equally among children, mitigated the concentration of wealth in large firms.[17] Instead, wealthy merchant families would establish multiple small businesses that could be distributed evenly to the next generation. These multiple businesses relied on sometimes vast *guanxi* networks to conduct their affairs. The success of such businesses depended critically on the level of trust, and *guanxi*-based ties proved to be extremely successful in this regard.[18] Over the past century during which Chinese have migrated throughout the Pacific Rim, these ties have proven to be invaluable to the success of Chinese business communities throughout the region. In China's reform era, these ties have also been credited with aiding overseas Chinese who sought to do business in China.

Commercial and political success were closely linked in imperial China, as successful businessmen could more easily afford to invest in education, and bureaucrats used their political influence to favor family businesses. Thus, relationships between businesses and government traditionally have been close, often to the point of inappropriateness by Western standards. *Guanxi*-based influence networks remain pervasive throughout Asia, and while they can play an important role in facilitating business, today they are increasingly criticized for inducing favoritism, poor economic decisions by political institutions, and corruption. The state banking system in China, for instance, faced a bad debt crisis as a result of loans given on the basis of cronyism instead of merit.

Li (2004) described another purpose of *guanxi:*

> In China's relation-based system, personal connections are used to circumvent the legal and regulatory system to obtain public goods and to protect one's property rights when the legal system fails. The formal legal system in China tends to be opaque, unfair, and particularistic. This is the fundamental reason why circumventing laws and regulations by using personal connections is widely practiced in China and thus viewed as ethical by some investors as well as scholars. Furthermore, investors should realize that when they use *guanxi* to protect their interest, their local partners or competitors may use their *guanxi* to take advantage of the foreign investors—and very often the local partners and competitors tend to have stronger *guanxi.*

THE NONMARKET ENVIRONMENT AND THE FOUR I'S

The framework of structured pluralism illustrated in Figure 14-1 is relevant to China, but the importance of the components differs from that in other countries. With regard to culture and history, China has a long history as a relatively unified nation, but it has no democratic tradition. Instead, institutions have been dominated by the bureaucracy and in the postwar period by the CCP. Culturally, China has a rich tradition, and only one aspect of that culture, Confucianism, has been considered here. This section briefly considers the other components of the structured pluralism perspective, the four I's— issues, interests, institutions, and information—and pertains only to the current period.

---

[16]See Weidenbaum (1996).
[17]By contrast, "primogeniture," or the granting of the entire inheritance to the first son, was practiced in Japan, which encouraged the concentration of capital.
[18]See Redding (1996) for a discussion and comparison of trust networks in other cultures.

A host of contentious market and nonmarket issues faced business and government in China. Externally, the European Union and the United States criticized China's policy of pegging the yuan to the dollar at a low exchange rate. This kept its export prices low, and the prices of imports high, resulting in a huge trade surplus with the United States. The International Monetary Fund and the Group of 7 nations urged China to float the yuan. China pledged to act, but some observers believed that inclusion in the G-7 was China's price for floating or revaluing the yuan. In late 2004 China's central bank raised its lending rate for the first time in 9 years to slow inflation.

Internally, China had the problem of reforming or closing a large number of inefficient SOEs, as considered later in the chapter. Many of the SOEs had close ties to the CCP and the ministries that controlled them. China's inclusion in the World Trade Organization (WTO) resolved one issue, but compliance with WTO requirements was difficult. China had to address commercial piracy, quotas on imports, and restrictions on entry in many markets. A variety of human rights complaints had been lodged against China, ranging from the absence of civil rights to the enforcement of the one-child-per-family law to the working conditions in factories. Nonmarket issues stemmed from the weak protection of intellectual and other property rights in China and the widespread corruption stemming in part from the government's extensive involvement in and regulation of business.

Interests in China are pluralistic, but because of the domination of the CCP there is little interest group activity and collective nonmarket action is rare. Moreover, independent labor unions are not permitted. Instead, interests manifest themselves through client politics narrowly tailored to specific interests. This means that interests do not drive outcomes in the same manner as in a democracy such as Japan, the European Union, or the United States. The government, however, is sensitive to the possibility of popular unrest and attempts to anticipate problems. Riots and demonstrations break out in China as a result of local issues. For example, as inflation increased retirees protested that their pensions were not indexed to inflation. Farmers rioted against some local governments that had taken their land for development purposes without adequate compensation. The large population of migrant workers who had left the countryside to find work constituted a potential for unrest. Unrest and violent protests were not uncommon, particularly in China's rural areas and smaller cities.

Information is important in China in part because of the presence of a dominant political party and a hierarchical government. It also is important because government rules and regulations are not transparent and can be changed without due process or electoral sanction. This situation is exacerbated by the dominance by a closed political party of both business and the administration of laws. *Guanxi* relationships between business and government facilitate obtaining information, but this also makes it difficult for those who do not have *guanxi*. The chapter case, *Direct Selling in China*, illustrates some of these features.

The institutions in China are dominated by the CCP and include a strong and encompassing bureaucracy and a relatively weak legislature and judiciary. Despite the tight political control exercised by the CCP, China has devolved considerable authority to the provinces and local governments.

Institutions and Government

China's government is characterized by close ties between the CCP and state institutions. In practice a government body wields power to the extent that its leadership is influential within the CCP. The constitution of the PRC places the party in the highest position of authority and requires that government policies and civil liberties conform to its direction. As a result, the informal configuration of power within the party leadership is usually more informative than the government's organization charts for determining where policies are made.

Since the ascendance of Deng Xiaoping, three general trends have developed. First, political power has steadily devolved to local governments, thus shifting the locus of a considerable body of policymaking away from Beijing. Second, the relationship between party and state has been weakened by new restrictions on joint appointments in the leaderships of both bodies. This has been coupled with significant advances in administrative law and an increasing professionalization of the bureaucracy. Third, although their influence remains small, democratic procedures, such as elections to local People's Congresses that were once considered mere formalities, have become more important.

Party Organization

The CCP claims to represent the Chinese working people and is the highest source of political power in China. Moreover, the People's Liberation Army, which historically has been closely linked with the CCP, is sworn to defend the party rather than the state. In 2007 CCP membership stood at 73 million, or less than 6 percent of the population. At the local level, the party is represented in virtually all significant societal organizations, including townships, factories, and rural collectives. At higher levels, party organizations mirror the hierarchy of the national government. Decisions at all levels are made by a process known as democratic centralism, whereby party units may set their own policies in a democratic manner but may not contradict the directives of a higher level. This system of representation and centralization of authority guarantees significant party influence over potentially all aspects of political and economic activity.

National Party Congress

Nominally the highest authority of the CCP, Party Congresses meet every 5 years. The 17th Party Congress in 2007 had 2,217 delegates, elected from local party organizations, the central party, and the military. Because meetings are brief (usually a few days) and the number of delegates is large, the Congress usually does little more than rubber-stamp the decisions of its delegated bodies.

Central Committee

When the Party Congress is not in session, authority passes to the 198-member Central Committee, which convenes at least twice annually. The Central Committee is elected by the National Party Congress, but until 1987 ballots were not secret and the number of candidates did not exceed the number of seats. Members represent the central party, local party organizations, the government, and the military. The committee makes decisions by majority rule and has veto authority over many party decisions. Many of Deng's reforms catered to local governments to avoid a Central Committee veto.[19] The Central Committee also supervises many of the party's internal functions, such as propaganda and party organization.

Politburo

The Politburo is responsible for the ongoing administration of the party. This body meets regularly and makes decisions by majority rule. It holds a veto over many of the decisions of the Standing Committee and supervises the policy branches of the party organization (e.g., military, foreign affairs, finance). Much of the Politburo's authority comes from its personnel powers.

Standing Committee of the Politburo

In 2008 the Standing Committee consisted of nine members. This group handles the day-to-day affairs of the party and, like other CCP bodies, makes decisions by majority rule. Much of its leverage comes from its ability to convene Politburo meetings and set their agendas.[20]

The CCP and Policymaking

The prevalence of majority rule in CCP decision making may seem surprising, but in accordance with the principles of democratic centralism, the procedure is taken seriously. However, CCP decision making has an authoritarian character because delegated groups such as the Standing Committee of the Politburo exercise tremendous agenda control over their parent groups. The CCP's appointments process also contributes to

---

[19]Shirk (1993, Ch. 4).
[20]Christiansen and Rai (1996, pp. 110–111).

intraparty unity. Because career advancement within the party is typically achieved through patronage, intraparty factions tend to be highly cohesive.

As a given policy's importance increases, the number of veto bodies it must pass through also increases. For example, Five-Year Plans must be approved all the way down through the National Party Congress. Because the Congress and the Central Committee are composed of very diverse groups (including geographically based representatives), major policies must satisfy some particularistic interests.

Virtually all high-ranking party officials belong to an "entrance" *(kou)* that covers a major policy area. The most important *kou*s, such as Party Affairs and Military Affairs, are led by members of the Standing Committee of the Politburo, while other Politburo members lead less important or subordinate *kou*s. *Kou*s often form the basis of intraparty factions, and their members typically hold positions both within the party leadership as well as in the state institutions that carry out the policies associated with the *kou*.[21]

State Institutions
The Legislative Branch

The National People's Congress (NPC) is both the highest legislative body and formally the highest institution of the central state. One of its duties is the election of a premier, who serves as the PRC's head of state. The premier, however, has only limited formal authority. The PRC constitution grants the NPC authority to pass legislation and to appoint and remove most executive branch officials. Membership selection has a reciprocal character similar to that of the upper echelons of the CCP: The plenum elects a Standing Committee which in turn selects representatives to the plenum. The NPC's 3,000 delegates are elected to 5-year terms, but the plenum meets for only 2 weeks annually, leaving most day-to-day activities to the 150-member Standing Committee. Representation is both geographical and functional (or corporatist). Large social interests such as the People's Liberation Army, ethnic minority groups, and peasants, among others, are granted fixed proportions of representatives. Non-CCP members account for 20 to 30 percent of NPC delegates.

Historically, the divergence between the NPC's formal and actual powers has been large due to the domination by the CCP elite of all aspects of statecraft. Since the early 1980s, however, the NPC has with increasing frequency defeated or forced the rewriting of bills submitted by the State Council. Additionally, the NPC has established specialized committees, such as an environmental committee founded in 1990, that have given it some leverage in policy debates.[22] Public appreciation for this trend is evidenced by the increased volume of constituent letters written to NPC delegates.[23]

The Executive Branch

The four principal positions in the Chinese government are the general secretary of the CCP, the president of the country, the head of the Chinese Army, and the premier of the State Council. The first three positions are frequently held by the same person. Jiang Zemin held the positions into the early 2000s. In 2002 Hu Jintao replaced Jiang as head of the CCP and in 2003 replaced him as president. Jiang remained as chairman of the Central Military Commission, that is, head of the Chinese Army, a position he had held since the Tiananmen Square massacre. Hu replaced him as chairman of the Central Military Commission in 2004. The premier, or prime minister, is Wen Jiabao, whose current term extends until 2013.

China's paramount executive body is the State Council, which is headed by the premier and serves as China's cabinet. The State Council is composed of about 50 people, including the premier, several vice premiers, and ministers and vice ministers of all major ministries and commissions. Like most deliberative groups in Chinese government, much of the State Council's day-to-day responsibilities are delegated to a Standing

---

[21]See Lieberthal (1995).
[22]Christiansen and Rai (1996, pp. 106–107).
[23]See Pei (1997).

Committee. This committee consists of about 15 of the council's highest-ranking members and meets roughly every 2 weeks.

The State Council presides over dozens of commissions, which coordinate policies functionally across specific ministries. Commissions correspond roughly to departments in the U.S. executive branch; the National Defense Commission, for example, is analogous to the Department of Defense. Sometimes referred to as the "little State Council," the State Planning Commission (SPC) had been one of the most powerful commissions in the PRC. As its name suggests, the SPC was charged with overseeing China's vast planned economy. The magnitude of that task has resulted in SPC alumni being well represented in the Politburo. The decline of the planned sector relative to the private sector has reduced the SPC's authority, and the State Council's current formal delineation of its responsibilities reflects this. The SPC was merged with other economic agencies to form the National Development and Reform Commission in 2003. The commission has responsibility for economic performance, macroeconomic policies, finance, credit, and approves major capital construction projects, energy planning, industrial restructuring, and regional development.

Below the commissions stand the provinces and ministries. Each of the 22 provinces holds ministerial rank, as do some of China's largest cities (Beijing, Tianjin, Shanghai, and Chongqing). Ministries have more specific jurisdictions than commissions and often find themselves subject to oversight from many commissions. An important exception is the Ministry of Finance, which is the most powerful ministry and informally holds commission rank in the State Council hierarchy. Ministers are typically high-ranking party officials, and departments within ministries are staffed by contingents of party cadres to ensure compliance with CCP directives.

In 2008 China began the process of establishing five "super-ministries" to improve coordination and reduce interagency turf battles. The plan submitted to the National People's Congress would establish super-ministries for environmental protection, social services, housing and construction, transportation, and industry and information. In particular, this would elevate the importance of environmental protection in the bureaucratic hierarchy.

Each national-level commission or ministry is the head of a hierarchy, or *xitong,* of local offices that perform the same role for the corresponding local government. A *xitong* generally is under the informal control of a *kou.* A provincial government's Education Commission is therefore a branch of the State Education Commission. *Xitongs* are known for protecting institutional turf. Very little information is shared across hierarchies, and the incentives for vertical integration are strong. Many *xitongs* owned companies and operated colleges to satisfy funding and personnel needs. In response, the reform-era CCP leadership has become increasingly active in reorganizing and abolishing ministries, as well as strengthening interdepartmental professional organizations. For example, the Ministry of Power and Water Conservancy was broken up to fragment opposition to the Three Gorges Dam project.[24]

The Judicial Branch

China has no tradition of an independent judiciary, and its highest court, the Supreme People's Court, has long been little more than a reflection of the CCP. There is no judicial review process in China. Likewise, the Supreme People's Procurator has little ability to pursue cases on its own initiative. Nevertheless, the emphasis of Deng's reforms on a stable and predictable legal environment has resulted in a growing role for the national judiciary. Citizens have increasingly turned to the courts to resolve disputes.

Provincial and Local Governments

The governments and party organizations at the provincial, county, and city levels essentially mirror those at the national level. The highest state institution at each level is the People's Congress, a legislative body that has formal, but often weak, authority

---

[24]Christiansen and Rai (1996, pp. 111–114).

over the executive branch, the People's Government. Many representatives to People's Congresses are elected by popular vote at the county and township levels. The general devolution of fiscal authority to the provinces (as well as lower levels of the state hierarchy) has made local governments the locus of interest group activity.

Most provinces share their revenues with the central government according to a fixed formula that is renegotiated periodically. These formulas typically allow the provinces to keep a certain proportion of the earnings of provincial enterprises. Across China, lower levels of government also work under similar financial arrangements. As a result, local governments exercise a large amount of budget and taxation discretion and frequently are the locus of bargaining with private interests. Village governments, for example, can offer a prospective enterprise favorable tax treatment in exchange for taking on extra workers to alleviate local unemployment.[25]

BUSINESS: STATE-OWNED ENTERPRISES, FOREIGN DIRECT INVESTMENT, AND INTERNATIONAL TRADE

State-Owned Enterprises

The SOE is a unique entity that represents the single most important type of company in China in terms of employment, as well as in problems for the country. The SOEs are not the future of the Chinese economy, however, nor have they been responsible for China's growth in the reform era. Economic growth has been fueled on the demand side by both domestic and export demand and on the supply side by foreign direct investment and local companies formed by entrepreneurs and local governments. Strong economic growth has been essential for China, since growth absorbed the unemployed as SOEs were forced to improve their efficiency. China has privatized many of the SOEs, but the government still owns nearly 50 percent of all the companies listed on the Shanghai and Shenzhen stock exchanges. As of the end of 2001 there were 174,000 SOEs.

Most of China's largest firms are SOEs, and these enterprises employed over 48 million people in 2001. The number of industrial SOEs in 2004 was 31,750, compared to 4 times that number 10 years earlier. Correspondingly, other types of firms have steadily gained prominence in the economy.[26] Private enterprises have flourished in the reform era, although their role in industrial production remains relatively small. In between the SOEs and private enterprises are the urban collectives, which employed 33 million in 1994. Large urban collectives resemble SOEs in most respects, whereas small ones are run as local profit-sharing firms. Finally, joint ventures between SOEs and private or foreign firms are common. SOEs technically do not exist in rural areas, where private and collective firms have thrived in response to agricultural policy liberalization and a general lack of regulation. Although they tend to be individually quite small, town and village enterprises were estimated to employ 60 million in 1994, but employment declined after 1996 as household and private enterprises expanded.

The labor policies of the SOEs were the heart of the socialist economic system and gave SOEs a distinctive dual purpose. In addition to production, SOEs provided virtually all the major social services required by employees, their families, and retirees, including education, health care, and housing. Moreover, because many goods such as housing and food staples were rationed, workers could only receive necessities through enterprise-issued coupons. This set of services essentially served as China's social welfare system and became known as the "iron rice bowl." A major constraint on the Chinese government's willingness to take strong measures to reform SOEs has been the lack of social security and welfare systems for its citizens.

National plans promulgated by the State Planning Commission specified prices and production targets for national-level SOEs as well as for each province. In their rush to develop industry, planners set artificially low prices for inputs, including investment

---

[25]Christiansen and Rai (1996, pp. 232–233).
[26]See Lardy (1998) for an analysis of SOEs.

capital, and artificially high prices for outputs. In effect, agriculture subsidized industry, but instead of spurring industrial development, the subsidy became an entitlement to the SOEs.[27] As a result, SOEs were inefficient and had little incentive to invest and innovate. Moreover, the social welfare role of SOEs made it difficult for managers to dismiss poorly performing employees.

Since the late 1970s, SOE reform has been a constant priority for Chinese leaders. Managers have been given more authority to evaluate employees, and the emergence of the private sector has allowed many SOEs to shed some excess labor.[28] Enterprises were permitted to retain profits, which were taxed by the state. The deregulation of prices and increasing competition from private, foreign, and rural industries increasingly exposed SOEs to market discipline. Subsidies provided to SOEs accounted for 21 percent of China's budget in 1989, but by 1996 subsidies accounted for only 4 percent of the budget as the state reduced its support.

Despite these changes, much of the system, and its dual role and chronic inefficiencies, remained intact at the beginning of the new century. SOEs were still losing money, underutilizing capacity, and consuming much of the country's available capital. The Chinese government ceased using its budget to subsidize SOEs, but in its place the state-run banks made "policy loans" to many of the SOEs. These, however, were more in the form of subsidies than loans, and expectations were that the loans would never be repaid. These loans were in large part the cause of the financial difficulties of the state banks. The government planned to retain many of the larger and more competitive SOEs, but the remainder were to be sold, merged, privatized, or closed. The chapter case, *Wugang and the Reform of State-Owned Enterprises*, provides an example of the reform challenge.

Foreign Direct Investment

Joint Venture Policy

One cornerstone of Deng's liberalizations was the Central Committee's July 1979 decision to establish four Special Economic Zones (SEZs).[29] As a result of this liberalization, foreign direct investment (FDI) and joint ventures in the PRC skyrocketed, with over 100,000 in operation in the mid-1990s.[30] For example, in the chapter case, *Direct Selling in China*, Amway's plant in Guangzhou was a joint venture with a government development agency. Express companies such as UPS, FedEx, and DHL were required to have a Chinese partner.

Among the several forms of joint ventures, the most important is the equity joint venture (EJV). EJVs are limited liability companies in which the Chinese and foreign partners both manage day-to-day operations and divide the risk in direct proportion to their capital contributions to the project. Contractual (or cooperative) joint ventures (CJVs) divide risks by contract rather than by capital contribution. These arrangements permit greater flexibility for parties in allocating responsibilities. Such ventures are often riskier, however, because China's legal system is not well equipped to deal with contractual disputes between partners. CJVs were once quite popular but have declined in importance.

The third type is the wholly foreign-owned enterprise (WFOE). These give the foreign firm the greatest control and the greatest risk. The 1990 Law on Wholly Foreign-Owned Enterprises prohibited them from operating in markets such as media, insurance, and communications and restricted their activities in public utilities and real estate. Article 3 of the law permits WFOEs if they (1) are technologically advanced and (2) export most of their production. Large Western firms such as Motorola, 3M, and Shell entered China as WFOEs because they provided the best protection from being forced to share sensitive technology.[31] Beijing realized that the autonomy offered to

---

[27]Christiansen and Rai (1996, p. 199). This phenomenon was commonly known as "price scissors" or the "scissor's gap."
[28]See Groves et al. (1994, 1995) for studies of incentives and the managerial labor market in SOEs.
[29]Grub and Lin (1991, p. 65).
[30]See Urata (2001) for a study of European FDI in China.
[31]Grub and Lin (1991, Chs. 4–5, Appendix 3).

such enterprises was necessary for attracting export-oriented, high-technology firms that could help develop the Chinese economy, and as a result WFOEs have been the fastest-growing segment of FDI.

Foreign direct investment as a percent of GDP increased dramatically from 1 percent in 1991 to 6 percent in 1994, after which it declined to 3 percent in 2005.[32] This reflected the growth of the domestic economy. As China joined the WTO, FDI was over $60 billion in 2005. WTO membership required China to open its markets to foreign firms, although the opening was gradual. Major industries including banking, insurance, telecommunication, and agriculture remained to be opened.

International Trade Policy and WTO Membership

In the pre-reform era trade increased substantially, but trade policies remained essentially the same. All trade had to be approved by the Ministry of Foreign Economic Relations and Trade (MOFERT), and imported items were marketed directly by the cognizant state-owned firm. Deng's reforms and the open-door policy allowed China a wide range of international finance arrangements, including direct loans, export credits, and development assistance from foreign governments. In 1980 China joined the International Monetary Fund and World Bank, which gave it access to loans and other development aid.

Trade policy became one of the primary concerns of China's international relations in the 1990s. The PRC's application for membership in the WTO was a protracted and contentious issue. Many advanced industrialized nations, particularly the European Union and the United States, insisted that China open its markets further to foreign businesses as a condition for membership. Beijing resisted many market-opening initiatives because of worries about social instability caused by workers laid off by uncompetitive SOEs.

The United States is China's second-largest trading partner after Japan. The large U.S. trade deficit with China aroused animosity from some American policymakers and drew attention to PRC trade practices, including inadequate protection of intellectual property rights. Concerns over Chinese domestic policies and human rights abuses blocked WTO membership. After nearly 15 years of negotiations China was admitted to the WTO at the end of 2001.[33] During that period China made many domestic reforms to qualify for membership, and it was forced to make important changes in its foreign trade policies. It pledged to lower tariffs, reduce import quotas, open markets to imports, and open industries such as telecommunications and banking to FDI. In addition, companies, such as the express companies, were no longer required to operate through joint ventures with a Chinese company. China also agreed to reduce by 40 percent its tariffs, which averaged 15 percent. Foreign banks would be allowed to have wholly owned subsidiaries and branches and to accept deposits. China was also required to improve its legal system, which in the late 1990s had become independent of the other parts of the government.

Market opening resulted in continuing nonmarket issues at the level of industries as well as a set of societal-level problems. Domestic firms resisted the opening of their markets to imports and FDI. Retailers had been restricted to selling only products made in China, but as a result of WTO membership they were, after a transition period, allowed to sell imported goods. At the societal level reductions in tariffs on agricultural imports threatened farmers, and those imports were expected to increase the already high unemployment in rural provinces. More than 100 million migrant workers had moved to cities seeking employment, and millions more would follow. Coupled with the competitive pressures on SOEs, China faced the challenge of developing social welfare programs to meet the needs of the unemployed and those harmed by the reforms.

China began to train judges to handle trade cases and established a WTO Department to develop policies for implementing WTO requirements. The *Direct Selling in China* chapter case involves an opportunity to use WTO membership to overcome a directive barring the principal component of the direct sellers' business model.

---

[32]Naughton (2007, p. 404).
[33]Two days later Taiwan was admitted to the WTO.

Regulation

Regulation in China is established through the ministries and commissions and through agencies associated with the State Council. Many of the regulations pertain to the same issues as in more developed countries. An example is fuel economy standards. China's automobile market boomed in the 2000s and became the third largest in the world behind the United States and Japan. As incomes grew Chinese consumers bought larger vehicles, and SUVs became popular. Economic growth and increased driving made China more dependent on imported oil and also pushed up the price of oil. To address the dependence on foreign oil, China issued fuel economy standards.

The standards were developed over more than 2 years and did not involve public inputs, although Volkswagen, which had a quarter of the market in China, was consulted. The standards, which had been developed by the Automotive Technology and Research Center, were issued by the State Council. A fuel tax, which would be the most effective means of reducing fuel use, was considered but rejected because of concerns about public anger and increased inflation. Three basic types of fuel economy standards were used in other countries. The European Union had a voluntary program, Japan had standards for each model, and the United States had a corporate average system. China chose a weight-based system for automobiles, vans, and SUVs. The standards did not apply to pickup trucks, which were primarily used by business in China. The standards took effect in 2005 and increased in 2008.

CONTINUING ISSUES

Human Rights

The issue of human rights in China became internationalized in the 1990s. Foreign governments as well as human rights groups targeted China as a major abuser of human rights. International concern focused on four areas.[34] First, China's criminal justice system was said to allow arbitrary imposition of the death penalty, the torture of prisoners, detention without trial, and the use of prison labor in industrial production. Second, China was accused of persecution of ethnic (primarily Tibetan) and religious (primarily Christian) minorities. Third, Beijing had little tolerance for political dissidents and held many political prisoners. Finally, critics argued that the condition of Chinese women had deteriorated despite the advances in gender equality made during the communist era. Beijing often dismissed these complaints as interference in domestic affairs. The U.S. State Department's "Annual Country Reports on Human Rights Practices" identified specific abuses and discussed trends in their occurrence. The 2007 report dropped China from the list of 10 worst violators of human rights, but the report concluded that China's "overall human rights remained poor." The report pointed to "extrajudicial killings, torture and coerced confessions of prisoners, and the use of forced labor." The report also pointed to the censorship of the Internet and suppression of religious freedom in Tibet.

China censored the content on the Internet as well as blocking responses to searches on topics such as Tibet and the spiritual Falun Gong movement. Internet companies were not only subject to censorship, but they also could be required to turn over e-mails to the Chinese government. Yahoo! provided information to the government that led to the arrest and imprisonment of the journalist Shi Tao. Yahoo! was sharply criticized by human rights groups as well as members of the U.S. Congress. The chapter case, *Google in China*, concerns Google's entry into China and the associated censorship and human rights issues.

Several long-standing practices continued to provoke complaints and posed problems for companies. To control its population growth, China unofficially adopted a one-child-per-family policy with birth targets for each province. The average number of children per woman decreased from nearly six in 1970 to less than two in 2000.

---

[34]See Levine (1997) for a summary of human rights concerns in China.

Women who had more than one child were fined and in some cases a relative's house would be torn down as punishment. Forced sterilization was used in some cases. These measures were a continuing source of conflict between citizens and the government. Moreover, a survey by the National Population and Family Planning Commission found that prominent and wealthy Chinese generally had two children and 10 percent had three. The wealthy simply paid the fine. In a rural province the government revoked the membership in the CCP of 500 people, most of them government officials, who had violated the one-child-per-family policy. Beijing began studying population issues to determine if it would have enough workers to support an aging population. In 2008 China decided to continue its current policies for another decade. China increased the fine on wealthy people who had more than one child.

Some Chinese preferred male to female children. The national ratio of male to female births was 117 to 100 and was believed to be due to selective abortions made possible by advances in ultrasound technology. The one-child-per-family policy along with the preference for boys was blamed for both selective abortions and for female infanticide. The Chapter 22 case, *Advanced Technology Laboratories, Inc.,* addresses this issue in India.

In 1998 China signed the International Covenant on Civil and Political Rights and released the imprisoned leader of the Tiananmen Square democracy demonstrations. Although some elections have been held at the local level, the CCP has maintained itself as the sole political party in China. When a group of democracy supporters formed the China Democratic Party in November 1998, the government arrested party leaders, including three of the most prominent dissidents remaining in the country. The three were sentenced to between 11 and 13 years in prison. Some observers feared that since he had consolidated his political power, President Hu was beginning to suppress political criticism of the government and of social conditions in China. In 2007 China arrested Hu Jia, one of its most prominent human rights activists.

As the host of the 2008 summer Olympics, China was under a spotlight. Independence demonstrations in Tibet were suppressed by the Chinese police, which included the arrest of Tibetan monks. The traditional carrying of the Olympic flame from Greece to China was met by vigorous protests and demonstrations in many countries, including France. France also angered the Chinese government by awarding honorary citizenships to Hu Jia and the Dalai Lama. Popular antiforeign protests broke out in China against Western criticism of the country, including protests against the French retailer Carrefour. Chinese tourists stopped traveling to France, and the government unofficially told some travel agencies not to book tours to France. A spokesperson for China's Ministry of Foreign Affairs said, "France can do more to encourage and attract Chinese citizens to France."[35]

Despite the human rights abuses and political restrictions, Chinese citizens enjoyed greater freedoms than at any time since the communists gained control of the country. Much of the improvement resulted from growing economic prosperity that had given people the means to exercise more control over their lives. In addition, the accumulation of personal property led people to attempt to protect it, resulting in greater use of the courts. Moreover, with the widespread use of computers, faxes, and mobile telephones, information was more readily available and actions could be coordinated. This inevitably led to pressure for greater freedoms and a more responsive government, but democracy was not in the foreseeable future. In 2007 Premier Wen wrote that democracy was consistent with "socialism with Chinese characteristics," but he added, "We are still far away from advancing out of the primary stages of socialism. We must stick with the basic development guidelines of that stage for 100 years."[36]

Piracy of Intellectual Property

A major concern of firms has been the piracy of intellectual property ranging from pharmaceuticals to software to consumer goods. Copies of compact discs, videotapes, and

---

[35]*Wall Street Journal,* June 11, 2008.
[36]*Washington Post,* February 28, 2007.

books often appeared on Chinese street corners before they were available in stores in the United States. Even the CCP had been a victim of piracy. The party sponsored production of an anticorruption movie, and prior to its release pirated copies were being shown in Chinese state-owned cinemas.[37] The Chinese automaker Jonway UFO exported to Europe a copy of the RAV4, which Toyota had failed to patent in China. The U.S.-based Business Software Alliance estimated that in 2000, 91 percent of the software in China was pirated. In 2008 three music industry groups, two of which operated in China, called Baidu "the largest and most incorrigible purveyor of pirated music in China" and asked advertisers to punish Baidu. One reason it was difficult to stop the pirating of intellectual property was that local officials were said to support it. The pirating companies paid local taxes and more importantly provided badly needed jobs.

Chinese joint venture partners have set up competing companies with technology taken from their foreign partners.[38] Many foreign joint venture partners complained to their home countries and began to take their cases to China's courts. The earlier excerpt from Li about *guanxi* provides one perspective on the role of the courts in such matters. The example illustrates a case of piracy taken to the U.S. courts.

In some cases the piracy appeared to be legal. For example, patents on proprietary pharmaceutical formulas can receive administrative protection in China, but first an open and lengthy public comment period was required in which drug patents were available for inspection. Chinese pharmaceutical companies could inspect the patent filings and immediately file for permission to produce and market the drug. If the application was approved before the patent received administrative protection, the local company could sell its knockoff drug. For example, a Chinese pharmaceutical company received approval to produce Eli Lilly's Prozac before the patent had been protected. The company beat Eli Lilly to market with its drug. Eli Lilly sued in court, but lost at the lower court level. The deputy director of the Chinese company said, "Eli Lilly's effort

---

[37] *New York Times,* October 5, 2000.
[38] See *BusinessWeek,* October 6, 1997, for examples.

EXAMPLE

An Intellectual Property Challenge

Huawei Technologies, located in Shenzhen, was founded in 1988 and by 2004 had 22,000 employees and sales of over $4 billion. Huawei manufactured telecommunications equipment and had begun producing routers and servers. Huawei told customers that the commands for its router were similar to those for routers made by Cisco Systems, and Cisco believed that Huawei had copied its software. Cisco engineers found many lines of Huawei code identical to its code, including spelling errors and other Cisco glitches. Huawei's manual also included paragraphs copied from Cisco's manual.[1]

Cisco wrote to Huawei, which immediately withdrew its router from the U.S. market, but continued to sell it outside the United States. Cisco followed with a lawsuit alleging copyright violation. This was the first intellectual property lawsuit ever filed by Cisco, which commented, "We don't go around suing people."[2] Huawei stated in court filings that it had copied the code but stated that it was unintentional and had not believed it was copyrighted. A federal court issued a preliminary injunction against Huawei, ordering it to stop immediately "using, importing, exporting or selling" any software system using the Cisco code. A Huawei spokesperson stated, "Before Cisco initiated its legal action against Huawei, the company had already taken good-faith, voluntary action to proactively remove from the U.S. market the obsolete products outlined in the injunction." Huawei commented that the court order was immaterial because it was unenforceable outside the United States.

---

[1] Cisco also believed that Huawei had copied source code from its network operating system.

[2] *San Jose Mercury News,* January 24, 2003.

against us can't possibly lead to any positive result, as any resolution must have a legal basis. And everything we have done is in perfect conformity with the law."[39] China's patent office also overrode Pfizer's patent on Viagra.

Pressure from other countries has resulted in some progress on intellectual property protection, particularly as China prepared for entry into the WTO. Additional progress has occurred as a result of domestic rather than foreign pressure. As Chinese companies have grown and matured, many have developed their own brands and intellectual property. Between 2003 and 2007 the number of patents granted doubled, and trademark registrations increased by 60 percent. Chinese firms holding property rights face the same piracy risks as do foreign firms, and the number of patent infringement lawsuits filed in Chinese courts has doubled over this period. The Chinese government has encouraged the press to champion the lawsuits.[40]

Product Safety

Several widely publicized incidents in 2007 and 2008 involving the safety of products such as children's toys, food, and pharmaceuticals drew widespread news coverage and criticism. Some consumers avoided Chinese products, and politicians called for bans on imports. The Chapter 5 case, *Mattel, Inc: Crisis Management or Management Crisis*, considers incidents in which lead was found in the paint on children's toys. China initially was reactive but quickly shifted to trying to correct the problems.

Corruption

Corruption increased during the 1990s as economic activity grew. Transparency International ranked China tied for 72 among 179 countries in its 2007 corruption perception index. Citizens protested the corruption, and the evident corruption reached the point at which the CCP became concerned that it could undermine confidence in the government and the party.

Corruption was present at all levels of the government. For example, farmers protested that local governments took their land for industrial development. The farmers complained that the government paid too little, promised jobs that never materialized, and sold the land at a large profit. Local governments also took independently owned oil wells and paid only a fifth the value, according to the former owners. The Chinese central government sought to stop corruption, but uprooting it proved difficult.

The government launched an anticorruption drive that resulted in the bribery conviction of the head of the State Food and Drug Administration. He was executed in 2007. Over 20 people in and connected to the Shanghai government were convicted of corruption charges, including the head of the CCP in Shanghai. China established a National Bureau of Corruption to strengthen investigation and prosecution. The Bureau decided to establish a Web site where citizens could report corruption and identify corrupt officials. The site was deluged by citizens complaining about corruption, primarily of local government officials, and praising the Bureau for its apparent willingness to combat corruption.

Workers' Rights

Labor unions and human rights groups have been critical of working conditions in China and other countries that produce for the developed world. Labor unions complained because China denied "freedom of association," referring to the right to form a union that is independent of the government. NGOs and rights activists have pressured firms in the United States and Europe to ensure that the factories that supply their brands meet certain minimal labor standards.[41] These foreign firms have generally responded, having established codes and subjected factories to inspections. The apparel and footwear industries established the Fair Labor Association, considered in Chapter 23. Most factories in China, however, supply the domestic market or are in industries not covered by this monitoring.

---

[39]*Wall Street Journal*, March 25, 1998.
[40]*Economist*, April 12, 2008.
[41]See the Chapter 4 case, *Nike in Southeast Asia*.

Workers in China complained of harsh working conditions, unfair dismissals, failure to make severance payments, and failure to pay overtime. In 2007, parents of 400 children posted a letter on an Internet site describing how they had rescued 40 children who had been kidnapped and sold as slaves to work in brick kilns in Shanxi province. Local government officials, however, prevented the families from locating more of the children. Outrage broke out in China, and the government sent 35,000 police to the area to search 7,5000 workplaces. The police rescued and released nearly 1,000 workers, many of whom were dazed, bleeding, and exhausted. Pictures of the released men and boys added to the popular anger. This incident provided the final impetus for legislation to establish certain rights for workers.

The Labor Contract Law took effect in 2008 and provided for basic rights, although those rights are not as extensive as those found in Europe and the United States. The law was vigorously opposed by foreign corporations that argued that costs would rise substantially, making Chinese factories less competitive. The law went through three drafts and received 190,000 comments before being enacted.

The Labor Contract Law requires an employer to give a contract to a worker within one month of employment. The employer must also specify the nature of the job, working conditions, and compensation. Employees are also required to give 30 days notice if they intend to terminate employment, and the circumstances under which a worker can be let go are limited to factors such as poor performance or theft, or changing circumstances, such as the loss of a supply contract or financial distress. Severance pay is due upon termination. Employers are required to consult with the worker or a worker's representative before terminating employment. Wages must be at least the minimum wage for the municipality where the place of employment is located.

The impacts of the law were unclear with the Chinese government stating that costs would not be affected and business claiming that costs could increase as much as 40 percent. The cost would depend on how vigorously the government enforced the law. One effect of the law was to give individual workers the opportunity to stand up to their employers and take unresolved disputes to the courts.

Energy and the Environment

In 2007 China passed the United States to become the largest emitter of CO_2. Seventy percent of its energy demand is met by coal, and it has the third largest coal deposits in the world. For security purposes China has embarked on an energy conservation campaign to reduce its dependence on imported oil. In 2006 it introduced a "Save energy, cut emissions" campaign to reduce its energy use per unit of GDP by 20 percent over five years. The Beijing Olympics were the first to be carbon neutral.

China is not covered by the Kyoto Protocol, which will expire at the end of 2012, but it will be expected to participate in any post-Kyoto agreement. China has been a major beneficiary of the Kyoto Protocol because of the Clean Development Mechanism, or Kyoto mechanism, under which countries can invest in carbon reduction projects in developing countries in lieu of making reductions at home. China has received $5.4 billion, or nearly three-quarters of the total, mostly from European countries.[42]

China's principal environmental concerns have not been global warming but rather domestic pollution, including acid rain from burning coal to generate electricity. The State Environmental Protection Administration (SEPA) has become more aggressive in its enforcement and has begun to use its authority to reject investment projects that may have an adverse environmental impact. In advance of the Olympics China announced some progress in reducing pollutants. Scrubbers installed at coal-fired power plants helped reduce sulfur dioxide emissions by over 4 percent, and industries reduced their solid waste discharges by 8 percent. Emissions of organic pollutants into waterways were reduced by over 3 percent. Despite the progress on these dimensions SEPA reported that overall pollution in the country increased.

---

[42]*Economist*, June 7, 2008.

A recent phenomenon in China in 2007–2008 was citizen protests against planned construction projects. Using the Internet and cell phones for coordination, middle-class citizens protested the construction of a $5.5 billion ethanol plant in Sichuan Province. Thousands of protesters had shut down the construction of a chemical plant in Fujian Province, and protesters in Shanghai had stopped the extension of a rail line. The protesters complained that the projects were too close to population centers and the environmental reviews of the projects were inadequate. The protests were covered by the news media.

SUMMARY

China provides tremendous business opportunities yet poses a host of challenges, particularly in the nonmarket environment. China has no democratic tradition, and its Confucian heritage provides a degree of deference for hierarchical authority. It also has a long history as a unified nation and a willingness to assert and defend its independence. China has been building a modern economy with less dependence on foreign direct investment, yet with 1.3 billion people it faces a considerable challenge to create jobs and provide social services. Economic progress has enabled people to have better control over their lives and has generated pressure for political and economic liberalization. The Chinese Communist Party, however, continued to dominate government at every level. Political competition was not tolerated, and human rights were restricted. The government was not as responsive to human rights as in a Western democracy but was concerned about problems like the environment that were of increasing concern to citizens. The government was also sensitive to the possibility of popular dissent arising from economic dislocations and dissatisfaction with government performance, as in the case of corruption. Despite the limitations on rights, Chinese citizens enjoyed greater liberty than at any time in the postwar period.

The nonmarket environment was important not only because of the government and party involvement in business but also because of issues pertaining to human rights, intellectual property, and the environment. The nonmarket environment was structured by the hierarchical nature of government that persisted despite the devolution of authority to provincial and local governments. Since the government was not checked by opposition parties, elections, or interest or activist groups, some policies could be changed quickly, as in the case of environmental policy and the Labor Contract Law. The judicial system in China did not provide the protection available in other countries, but citizens were increasingly turning to the courts to resolve disputes and enforce rights.

The importance of *guanxi* networks, not only between companies but also between business and government, complicated strategies of those companies new to China. Joint ventures with domestic companies, most of which were enterprises owned by national, provincial, or local government units, could also provide the *guanxi* networks and access needed to address nonmarket issues. Joint ventures, however, posed their own set of problems, which led most entrants to China in recent years to establish wholly owned subsidiaries.

-- C A S E S --
Wugang and the Reform of State-Owned Enterprises

The Wuhan Iron and Steel Company, also known as Wugang, was typical of Chinese state-owned enterprises (SOEs) and the problems surrounding their reform. Located in the large industrial city of Wuhan nearly 400 miles up the Yangtze River from Shanghai, Wugang was the first of many massive ironworks built after the Chinese revolution. The $2 billion enterprise had many of the characteristics of a medium-size city. The facility occupied 6.5 square miles and employed 120,000 workers. Most of the employees, plus their families and 30,000 retirees, lived in company-provided housing. The company also operated 31 schools, three polytechnic institutes, three universities, and two hospitals.

Built with Soviet technology, Wugang opened in September 1958 at the beginning of Mao's "Great Leap Forward," a crash effort that was to have brought China's industrial output up to par with Western Europe. As a national-level SOE, all inputs and outputs were determined by economic plans. The State Planning Commission and Ministry of Metallurgical Industry specified its prices and production targets, and the Labor Administration Bureau assigned workers to the enterprise, most of whom were guaranteed by the *danwei* system to remain there for life. Like other national-level SOEs, Wugang played a crucial dual role in the socialist economy. In addition to industrial production, Wugang was the exclusive provider of housing, food, medicine, and other social services to its employees, their families, and retirees. This system, known as the "iron rice bowl," resulted in a high level of vertical integration within the enterprise.

The Chinese steel industry began with high expectations, but three factors combined to undermine its productivity during the 1960s and 1970s. First, the social welfare role of the enterprise robbed its management of labor flexibility. In the 1960s SOEs generally became overstaffed as central planners reacted to the oversupply of urban youths by assigning them to SOEs, and managers were unable to dismiss poorly performing employees. Second, in their rush to industrialize, planners had set artificially low prices for inputs and artificially high prices for outputs, effectively creating an industry-wide subsidy that led to inefficiency and weak incentives to invest and innovate. Individual plant managers also had little discretion in investments because profits were taxed at high rates and redistributed by government authorities.[43] Finally, the international isolation that China faced between 1960 and 1980 had cut off foreign investment,

technology, and expertise, as well as potential export markets.

By the end of the 1990s the steel industry employed 2 million workers and accounted for 3 percent of China's industrial output by value. Wugang was one of the nation's four largest steel companies, with an annual production capacity of 6 million tons. These four companies accounted for about a third of China's steel production in 1996.[44] After the Baoshan Iron and Steel Corporation (Baogang), Wugang was the second most profitable steel company in China, earning an $84 million profit in 1996. Although this was expected to drop to $24 million in 1997, Wugang's performance had been fairly good compared with most SOEs. By comparison, Angang, China's largest steel firm, was suffering huge losses. Wugang's primary asset was its specialization in high value-added products. The company manufactured extra-wide and heavy carbon structural plate, alloy structural plate, low-alloy high-strength plate, boiler and vessel plate, ship and offshore oil platform plate, and mould-making plate. It was also the only Chinese supplier of international-quality, cold rolled silicon steel sheets—a highly ductile type of plate. Its production processes had received certification from numerous international bodies, and its quality assurance system met ISO 9000 standards. Yet the company faced serious challenges.

Wugang's productivity, measured by tons of output per employee, was less than a fifth of those of the leading Asian firms.[45] Steel prices in China were declining, partially in response to imports from the former Soviet republics and South Korea, whose currency suffered a steep devaluation in 1997. At the same time, the cost of domestic inputs, such as energy and transportation, had risen substantially in 1997.

SOE Reform: National and Local Strategies

As China's economic reforms progressed in the 1990s, the leadership in Beijing realized that despite their valuable social welfare role, SOEs were increasingly becoming an obstacle to the creation of a modern economy. The SOE sector employed 100 million people and accounted for nearly half of China's industrial output in the early 1990s, yet few enterprises were profitable, and even successful SOEs were often hopelessly inefficient by international

---

[43]Because prices were centrally set, profits were in some sense illusory. A ministry in charge of an industry could redistribute funds from profitable to unprofitable enterprises, and it could also require expenditures on items not directly related to the enterprise's production (for instance, social services).

[44]These four companies each produced over 5 million tons per year. There were also 25 companies that produced between 1 and 5 million tons annually. Because many smaller companies were expected to close as a result of restructuring, the four largest SOEs were expected to account for 40 percent of total production by 2005. *South China Morning Post*, September 19, 1997, and *China Economic Review*, April 1998.

[45]*China Economic Review*, April 1998.

standards. Since the inception of market-based reforms in the 1970s, Beijing had cautiously increased the discretion of SOE managers while also increasing their exposure to market forces. However, party leaders at the Fifteenth Party Congress in September 1997 agreed that more radical reforms would be necessary to prevent the financial collapse of such a large part of the Chinese economy.

While the government did not specify many details, it intended to privatize the vast majority of the over 300,000 SOEs by selling shares in the companies. These changes were expected to affect over 10,000 of the 13,000 largest SOEs, but Beijing would continue to own and support many of the largest enterprises, such as Wugang. There were three principal reasons for continuing to support large SOEs. First, since privatization was expected to result in widespread plant closings and layoffs, Beijing wanted to avoid broad social unrest. Because of the SOE system, China had never developed a social welfare system, and despite a few pilot programs for worker retraining and social pensions, a comprehensive safety net was still years away. Second, Beijing hoped that its larger enterprises could duplicate the past success of large, government-favored industrial conglomerates such as the South Korean chaebol. This analogy proved worrisome as it had become increasingly evident that the chaebol were responsible in part for serious structural deficiencies in Korea's economy. Finally, the retention of some central control was necessary to placate conservatives within the Communist party.[46]

Unfortunately for Wugang's president, Liu Benren, continued government intervention deprived him of the autonomy to undertake cost-cutting methods that were commonly available to firms in other countries. Liu had little authority to reduce his vastly oversized labor force because the Wuhan city government would not permit the city's largest corporate employer to add to the growing unemployment problem. Like other official unemployment statistics across China, Wuhan's official unemployment rate was modest but unofficially was estimated to be as high as 26 percent. Many of the company's activities remained constrained by Beijing, even though in early 1998 steel was removed from the list of products subject to state-planned production targets. As part of the program adopted by the Fifteenth Party Congress, Beijing aided Wugang by facilitating its effort to go public and list its stock on domestic stock exchanges, but it also required the company to merge with smaller steel companies as a condition for doing so.[47] Wugang complied by announcing a merger with two smaller firms, the Daye Steel Group and the Ercheng Iron & Steel Group, in November 1997.[48] In 1998 it acquired the financially troubled Xiangfan Iron and Steel Group.

Liu was able to take some initiatives on his own to address Wugang's problems. For a number of years, he had pursued a foreign listing on the Hong Kong Stock Exchange. Despite the fact that the company was only listing its relatively profitable, cold rolled silicon steel unit, the offering was continually delayed due to the lack of investor interest in the weak Chinese steel market as well as to the Asian financial crisis.[49] The $200 million listing, underwritten by Merrill Lynch, was finally approved in February 1998 but postponed indefinitely 2 months later due to poor investor response.[50] Beijing was partly responsible for the failure. One reason for the lack of interest was a Chinese law prohibiting companies from pricing shares below the company's net asset value per share.[51]

Wugang's failure in the stock market had not prevented it from exploring other avenues. Liu had aggressively invested in new technology, adding billions of dollars worth of American and Austrian equipment since 1993. With the improved physical plant, the company hoped to increase capacity to 8 million tons by 2000 and expand sales to foreign markets, which accounted for 800,000 tons of its output in 1997. In March 1998 Wugang proposed a merger with Baogang in the hope of creating a single advanced, profitable entity that would reduce overproduction in the Chinese steel market.[52] The combined entity would have been one of the world's 10 largest steel firms, but concerns were raised about the efficiency gains from merging facilities 400 miles apart.[53]

Because of the economic crises in Asia and Russia, China was flooded with cheap steel imports. In response, Wugang initiated antidumping proceedings with the Ministry of Foreign Trade and Economic Cooperation against Russian silicon steel plate exporters.[54] The flood of imports along with overcapacity in China continued to drive steel prices down, and the government responded by banning the construction of any new steel plants until 2000.

Wugang also sought support from the government for more radical reforms. With the support of the State Council, it secured permission to pare its workforce and reduce its dependence on subsidiary workshops that were not part of its core steel business. These "ancillary companies" would be forced to seek outside customers and turn a profit independently of Wugang. Liu hoped that after this process was completed, Wugang would be a leaner, more focused company of only 27,000 employees.[55]

[46]*New York Times,* September 12, 1997, and *BusinessWeek,* September 29, 1997.
[47]*South China Morning Post,* September 19, 1997.
[48]*South China Morning Post,* November 26, 1997.

[49]*South China Morning Post,* October 21, 1997, and March 19, 1998.
[50]*South China Morning Post,* February 21, 1998.
[51]*South China Morning Post,* April 1, 1998.
[52]*New York Times,* March 12, 1998.
[53]*Wall Street Journal,* March 11, 1998.
[54]*South China Morning Post,* July 14, 1998.
[55]Employment across the industry was scheduled to drop to 500,000 by 2000 and 300,000 by 2005 with many reductions achieved through reorganizations. *China Economic Review,* April 1998.

This reorganization had helped some of the company's former subunits, such as the Metal Structures Company, which manufactured boilers and furnaces, to become profitable. However, in many cases it had only shifted the tension between social welfare and company efficiency from Wugang to its former subsidiaries.

Some analysts were cautiously optimistic about Wugang's long-term prospects. Part of the optimism, however, stemmed from the strong support the enterprise had received from Beijing. The favorable restructuring plan and technological investments were facilitated by Beijing's unwillingness to allow Wugang—considered one of China's most prestigious steel firms—to fail. It was a measure of the magnitude of the challenges faced by all SOEs that Wugang's viability seemed so uncertain despite this support. ■

SOURCE: This case was written by Michael Ting under the supervision of Professor David P. Baron based on public sources and in part on R. Tomlinson, "A Chinese Giant Forges a Capitalist Soul," *Fortune* (September 29, 1997), pp. 184–192. Copyright © 1998 by the Board of Trustees of the Leland Stanford Junior University. All rights reserved. Reproduced with permission.

Preparation Questions

1. What social and institutional factors limit Liu Benren's efforts to reform Wugang?
2. What should Wugang do about its social services responsibilities?
3. Should Liu Benren seek complete independence from the Chinese government?

Direct Selling in China

With over 1.2 billion people China represented an extremely attractive market for direct sellers such as Amway, Avon Products, Mary Kay Cosmetics, Sara Lee, and Tupperware. Also, in the 1990s the restructuring of state-owned enterprises had reduced workforces, providing an ample supply of people interested in becoming direct sellers, many of whom made door-to-door sales calls. With the Asian and Russian financial crises beginning in 1997 the supply of potential direct sales personnel increased further. In 1995 Amway opened a factory in Guangzhou and began sales in China. By 1997 it had 70,000 independent sales agents in China producing revenue of $178 million.[56] Avon's revenue in China was $75 million.

Companies such as Amway and Avon operated by enlisting independent sales agents who bought product from the company and sold it door-to-door. Amway used its standard business model in China with the exception that all other markets were supplied from U.S. plants. Its sales agents were compensated by their own sales and also were paid for the number of new sales agents they recruited. They also received a commission on the sales of those they recruited as well as those their recruits recruited. The companies operated distribution centers and provided training for their sales agents in both sales techniques and in the company's culture, which emphasized empowerment. Amway had a policy of buying back all unsold product, providing a full refund.

The success of U.S. direct sales companies led to a boom in home-grown direct sales companies selling everything from foot massagers to water beds to elixirs. By 1998 some 20 million Chinese were estimated to be working in direct selling.[57] It was said that 50,000 people had come to Wuhan seeking jobs selling Xingtian Company's foot massaging machine. Some of these companies operated pyramid and Ponzi schemes in which they profited by recruiting sellers and selling them products rather than making sure that products were being purchased by consumers. Other companies duped unsuspecting consumers. In a front-page article the *China Daily* said that these companies "have been behaving badly, getting involved in underworld crimes and preying on innocent people through their superstitions."

On April 21, 1998, the State Council published a directive banning all direct sales in the country. The directive stated, "Criminals have used direct selling to set up sects and cults, spread superstition and carry out illegal activities, affecting the country's social stability." The directive expressed concern about the massive sales meetings of direct sellers in which they clapped and chanted to build enthusiasm. The directive also stated that direct selling had attracted people, including teachers, members of the military, and officials of the Chinese Communist Party, who were legally prohibited from such sales activity. The *People's Daily,* the official newspaper of the Chinese Communist Party, justified the State Council's decision: "Due to immature market conditions, inadequate legislation and immature consumer psychology, direct sales have proved unsuitable for China and thus

---

[56]Amway had 667,000 independent sales representatives worldwide.

[57]In the United States 8.5 million people were engaged in direct selling.

must be resolutely banned." The newspaper also referred to "excessive hugging" at the mass sales meetings held by the direct selling companies.

The State Administration for Industry and Commerce, which was responsible for the distribution industry, asked local officials to enforce the ban and avoid civil disorder. Its director Wang Zhongfu said, "It's necessary to stop the operation of pyramid sales since it has begun to hurt social stability and economic development."[58] Government officials said that if the U.S. direct selling companies established normal retail shops they could stay.

This was not the first time China had addressed direct selling. In 1995 it had suspended all direct sales activity for several months over concerns about the "revival meeting atmosphere" used by some of the companies. Avon was forced to change its credo from "God first" to "Faith first."

Once the State Council had banned direct selling, many independent sales representatives were left with goods they could not sell. Protests occurred when they were unable to obtain refunds from companies. According to press reports, 10,000 disgruntled door-to-door salesmen came to the town of Zhangjiajie seeking refunds from a company that made foot massagers, but it had closed its doors. "'It has left me worse than bankrupt,' says Chen, an unemployed steelworker, who has been left with 60 mechanized foot massagers and, now barred from selling them, losses of roughly $4,830."[59] Riots broke out leaving four people dead and 100 injured.

The directive issued by the State Council came as U.S. Trade Representative Charlene Barshefsky was in Beijing making preparations for President Bill Clinton's upcoming state visit. In a news conference in Beijing she stated, "The ban has effectively shut down the legitimate operations of these and other U.S. companies in China. These companies have invested over $120 million in China and provide income to more than 2 million Chinese." She added, "It is a serious matter when the [Chinese] government simply bans the legitimate business of foreign-invested companies. . . . [the ban] goes well beyond China's legitimate need to pursue consumer protection." Wu Yi, China's minister for trade and foreign investment, told her that in addition to consumer protection concerns the direct selling companies were breaking the rule requiring them to sell only goods manufactured in China.

Steve Van Andel, chairman of Amway Asia Pacific, said, "We understand and respect the Chinese government's decision to take additional steps to protect consumers from illegal scams, which have become a more serious social problem in recent months. . . . We have invested over $100 million in China over the past five years and we continue to believe in the long-term business opportunities of this enormous market. . . . While management of Amway China has established strong government relations and is hopeful that discussions with government officials will be successful, it is too early to project the short-term and long-term impact of the directive on our business."[60] Amway and other direct sellers began to evaluate alternatives for restructuring the way they conducted their sales activities.

Richard Holwill, Amway's director of international relations, said, "We're frustrated that this sledgehammer approach gets rid of ours as well as the ones they're really trying to get rid of. 'Shut it down and sort it out later' seems to be the attitude."[61] Holwill also stated, "We don't want to be part of the problem, we want to be part of the solution."

Holwill served as co-chairman of the Asia Task Force of the U.S. Chamber of Commerce and discussed the ban in testimony before the House Ways and Means Committee in June during hearings on renewal of most favored nation status for China. China was also in the process of negotiating entry into the World Trade Organization (WTO). This involved negotiations with the European Union and the United States regarding specific reforms and market openings in China. ■

Preparation Questions

1. Why did China ban direct selling?
2. How might the U.S. direct sales companies restructure their sales activities to satisfy the concerns of the Chinese government? Should they establish retail stores?
3. Should U.S. direct marketers form a coalition or act independently to address this challenge?
4. Should the U.S. companies attempt to enlist the aid of the U.S. government?
5. What nonmarket strategy should the U.S. direct sellers in China adopt?

---

[58] China Business Information Network, May 12, 1998.
[59] *Financial Times,* May 5, 1998.
[60] Amway press release, April 21, 1998.
[61] *Los Angeles Times,* April 24, 1998.

Google in China

It's an imperfect world, we had to make an imperfect choice.

—Elliot Schrage, Google vice president for global communications and public affairs

Introduction

Using servers located in the United States, Google began offering a Chinese-language version of Google.com in 2000. The site, however, was frequently unavailable or slow because of censoring by the Chinese government. Google obtained a significant share of searches in China but lagged behind market leader Baidu.com. To achieve commercial success, Google concluded that it was imperative to host a Web site from within China. Given its motto, "Don't Be Evil," Google had to decide whether to operate from within China or to continue to rely on Google.com. If it decided to establish operations in China, the company had to decide how to deal with the censorship imposed by the Chinese government.

As a result of an extensive debate within the company, cofounder Serge Brin explained their decision: "We gradually came to the realization that we were hurting not just ourselves but the Chinese people."[62] Google decided to establish the site Google.cn, but without features that allowed users to provide content. To avoid putting individuals in jeopardy of being arrested, Google offered neither e-mail nor the ability to create blogs, since user-generated material could be seized by the Chinese government. This allowed Google to avoid putting individuals in jeopardy of being arrested. Because it would be required by Chinese law to censor search results associated with sensitive issues, Google decided to place a brief notice at the bottom of a search page when material had been censored, as it did in other countries such as France and Germany which banned the sale of Nazi items. Google planned to exercise self-censorship and developed a list of sensitive items by consulting with third parties and by studying the results of the Chinese government's Internet filtering. Senior policy counsel Andrew McLaughlin stated, "Google is mindful that governments around the world impose restriction on access to information. In order to operate from China, we have removed some content from the search results available on Google.cn, in response to local law, regulation or policy. While removing search results is inconsistent with Google's mission, providing no information (or a heavily degraded user experience that amounts to no information) is more inconsistent with our mission."[63]

Within a month of offering Google.cn, Google came under criticism from two government-run newspapers in China. The *Beijing News* criticized the company for not doing enough to block "harmful information." Referring to Google's practice of informing users when search results had been censored, the *China Business Times* wrote in an editorial, "Is it necessary for an enterprise that is operating within the borders of China to constantly tell your customers you are following domestic law?" Both publications claimed that Google was operating as an Internet content provider without a proper license.[64]

Reporters Without Borders, a Paris-based organization campaigning for freedom of expression, called the establishment of Google.cn "a black day for freedom of expression in China." It stated:

> The firm defends the rights of U.S. Internet users before the U.S. government, but fails to defend its Chinese users against theirs. United States companies are now bending to the same censorship rules as their Chinese competitors, but they continue to justify themselves by saying their presence has a long-term benefit. Yet the Internet in China is becoming more and more isolated from the outside world.[65]

Other activists demanded that Google publish its censorship blacklist in the United States.

Internet Censorship in China

According to the U.S. State Department, companies offering Internet services were "pressured to sign the Chinese government's 'Public Pledge on Self-Discipline for the Chinese Internet Industry.'" Under the agreement, they promised not to disseminate information that "breaks laws or spreads superstition or obscenity" or that "may jeopardize state security and disrupt social stability."[66] Providing Internet services required a license, which in turn required not circulating information that "damages the honor or interests of the state" or "disturbs the public order or destroys public stability. . . ."[67]

Censorship in China involved self-regulation by Internet companies as well as government actions. The government did not provide a list of objectionable subjects—instead companies inferred which topics were out of bounds by observing what the government censors removed. The State Council Information Office also convened weekly meetings with Internet service providers.

---

[62]*San Jose Mercury News*, March 3, 2006.
[63]*New York Times*, January 25, 2006.
[64]*Washington Post*, February 22, 2006. Google shared a license with a Chinese company, Ganji.com. This practice was common among foreign Internet firms.
[65]*New York Times*, January 25, 2006, op. cit.
[66]*BusinessWeek*, January 23, 2006.
[67]Clive Thompson, "Google's China Problem (and China's Google Problem)," *New York Times Magazine*, April 23, 2006.

An American executive explained, "It's known informally as the 'wind-blowing meeting'—in other words, which way is the wind blowing. They say: 'There's this party conference going on this week. There are some foreign dignitaries here on this trip.'"[68] Xin Ye, a founder of Sohu.com, a Chinese value-added Internet services firm, was asked how hard it was to navigate the censorship system. He said, "I'll tell you this, it's not more hard than dealing with Sarbanes and Oxley."[69]

Zhao Jing, a political blogger in China, "explained that he knew where the government drew the line. 'If you talk every day online and criticize the government, they don't care. Because it's just talk. But if you organize—even if it's just three or four people—that's what they crack down on. It's not speech; it's organizing.'"[70] In December 2005 Zhao called for a boycott of a newspaper because it had fired an editor. In response, the Chinese government asked Microsoft's MSN to close Zhao's blog and Microsoft complied.[71] Brooke Richardson of MSN said, "We only remove content if the order comes from the appropriate regulatory authority."[72]

Yahoo! and MSN, as well as other sites, complied with Chinese law as well as exercising self-censorship.[73] Robin Li, chairman of the Chinese search company Baidu.com, said, "We are trying to provide as much information as possible. But we need to obey Chinese law."[74] Baidu had reached an agreement that allowed the Chinese government to oversee its Web site and in exchange it avoided the disruptions of service and strict operating rules that plagued foreign Internet companies.[75]

In 2004 Yahoo! provided information to the Chinese government that led to the arrest of the journalist Shi Tao. Shi was subsequently sentenced to 10 years in prison for releasing state secrets on a foreign Web site. Shi had provided information by e-mail about a Communist party decision. Yahoo! general counsel Michael Callahan said the company regretted that action but had no alternative, since its Chinese employees could have been arrested on criminal charges for not providing the information to the government. Callahan also said that Chinese law prohibited disclosing how many times the company had provided information on users to the government.[76]

The agencies that regulated the Internet employed 30,000 people who monitored e-mail, Web sites, blogs, and chat rooms. Internet cafes were required to use software that stored data on all users. Anyone establishing a blog was required to register with the government. Telephone companies were required to incorporate software that censored text messaging.

A key part of the censorship system was the control by the government of all gateways into China. This allowed the censors to block undesired content on Web sites and restrict Internet search results. Referred to as the Great Firewall of China, routers at China's nine Internet gateways examined messages and search requests and were programmed to block or censor information. It was this firewall that made accessing Google.com slow or at times unavailable from China.

China also blocked certain news sites including the BBC News, Voice of America, Amnesty International, Human Rights in China, and Wikipedia, in addition to any information on the spiritual movement Falun Gong, which was banned in China. Search results on terms such as "Tiananmen Massacre," "Tibet," and "Dalai Lama" were also suppressed.

Censorship was also practiced elsewhere, including at universities. University computer systems and bulletin boards banned certain subjects such as politics, and student monitors directed chatroom conversations away from sensitive subjects to those that helped build a "harmonious society." Student monitor Hu Yingying said, "We don't control things, but we don't want bad or wrong things to appear on the Web sites. According to our social and educational systems, we should judge what is right and wrong. And as I'm a student cadre, I need to play a pioneering role among other students, to express my opinion, to make stronger my belief in Communism." Another student, Tang Guochao, said, "A bulletin board is like a family, and in a family, I want my room to be clean and well lighted, without dirty or dangerous things in it."[77]

The censorship system was in a technology race with those attempting to evade it. Bill Xia, who arrived in the United States as a student in the 1990s and subsequently founded Dynamic Internet Technology (DIT), developed software called FreeGate that masks the Web sites that users visit.[78] Companies such as DIT and UltraReach also used software to create new Web sites to elude the Chinese censors.[79] For Voice of America, for example, DIT established uncensored proxy sites that directed users to the real site. DIT and UltraReach sent millions of e-mails a day alerting users to the uncensored sites. The Chinese censors worked to shut down the proxy sites and were often able to close the sites within a

[68]Ibid.

[69]Ibid.

[70]Ibid.

[71]Microsoft's blogging servers are located in the United States. Clive Thompson, "Google's China Problem (and China's Google Problem)," *New York Times Magazine,* April 23, 2006.

[72]*BusinessWeek,* January 23, 2006, op. cit.

[73]Yahoo! lagged behind other Internet companies in China and in 2005 invested $1 billion for a 40 percent interest in the Chinese company Alibaba.com. Yahoo! then turned operating control of Yahoo! China over to Alibaba.com.

[74]*BusinessWeek,* January 23, 2006, op. cit. Baidu had a 46.5 percent share of Internet searches in China; Google was second with 26.9 percent. Google had a small stake in Baidu but sold it in June 2006.

[75]*New York Times,* September 17, 2006.

[76]*San Jose Mercury News,* February 20, 2006.

[77]*New York Times,* May 9, 2006.

[78]Human Rights in China and Radio Free Asia were also DIT clients.

[79]Both DIT and UltraReach were said to be connected to the Falun Gong movement. *San Jose Mercury News,* July 2, 2006.

few days. The companies then would develop new software to evade the censors.

The Chinese government sought to justify its practices. Liu Zhengrong, deputy director of the State Council Information Office's Internet Affairs Bureau, argued that China's efforts to keep out "harmful" and "illegal" information were similar to those in Western countries. He said, "If you study the main international practices in this regard you will find that China is basically in compliance. The main purposes and methods of implementing our laws are basically the same."[80] He observed that the *New York Times* and *Washington Post* Web sites deleted content that was illegal or in bad taste. He added, "Our practices are completely consistent with international practices." He continued, "Many of our practices we got from studying the U.S. experience."[81] He noted, "It is clear that any country's legal authorities closely monitor the spread of illegal information. We have noted that the U.S. is doing a good job on this front."[82]

Liu commented, "No one in China has been arrested simply because he or she said something on the Internet."[83] Reporters Without Borders claimed that 62 Chinese were in prison for "Posting on the Internet articles and criticism of the authorities."[84]

Despite the international criticism of Internet censorship in China, it was not clear that the Chinese people were concerned. Kai-Fu Lee, who headed operations for Google in China said, "People are actually quite free to talk about [democracy and human rights in China]. I don't think they care that much. I think people would say: 'Hey, U.S. democracy, *that's* a good form of government. Chinese government, good and stable, *that's* a good form of government. Whatever, as long as I get to go to my favorite Web site, see my friends, live happily.'"[85]

Ji Xiaoyin, a junior at Shanghai Normal University, commented, "I don't think anybody can possibly control any information in the Internet. If you're not allowed to talk here you just go to another place to talk, and there are countless places for your opinions. It's easy to bypass the firewalls, and anybody who spends a little time researching it can figure it out."[86]

Google's Perspective

In response to criticism that Google should lobby the Chinese government to change its censorship system, CEO Eric E. Schmidt said during a visit to China, "I think it's arrogant for us to walk into a country where we are just beginning operations and tell that country how to run itself." He also explained, "We had a choice to enter the country and follow the law. Or we had a choice not to enter the country." Earlier he had said, "We believe the decision that we made to follow the law in China was absolutely the right one."[87]

Speaking at an ethics conference on Internet search at Santa Clara University, Peter Norvig, director of research at Google, commented on the decision not to offer services such as e-mail and blogging in China. "We didn't want to be in a position to hand over users' information. . . . We thought that was just too dangerous. . . . We thought it was very important to keep our users out of jail."[88]

Norvig justified Google's policies in China. "Yes, it's important to get information about democracy and Falun Gong. They also want to know about outbreaks of bird flu. We thought it was more important to give them this information that they can use even if we have to compromise."[89]

Google continued to debate internally whether and how it should operate in China. It also hoped for guidance from the U.S. government and the industry. Norvig said, "We feel that the U.S. government can stand up and make stronger laws, and we feel that corporate America can get together and have stronger principles. We're supporting efforts on both those fronts. We feel we can't do it alone."[90]

Norvig disclosed that Google was not keeping search logs in China. "They don't have personally identifiable information but they do have IP addresses that are potentially identifiable with an individual."[91] That information was kept in the United States, and China could request that information through the U.S. State Department.

Political Pressure in the United States

In advance of congressional hearings on China and censorship, the State Department announced the creation of a Global Internet Task Force to decrease censorship and encourage change in other countries. Paula Dobriansky, undersecretary of state for democracy, human rights, and labor, said, "The Internet, especially, can be a liberating force. Topics once politically taboo can become freely discussed, and people can communicate anonymously. We must ensure it does not become a tool of repression."[92]

Representative Chris Smith (R-NJ), chairman of the House Subcommittee on Africa, Global Human Rights, and International Operations, introduced the Global Internet Freedom Act that would impose restrictions on U.S. companies operating in China. It included a code of

[80]*New York Times,* February, 15, 2006.
[81]*Wall Street Journal,* February 15, 2006.
[82]*New York Times,* February 15, 2006, op. cit.
[83]*San Jose Mercury News,* February 20, 2006, op. cit.
[84]*San Jose Mercury News,* July 2, 2006.
[85]Clive Thompson, op. cit.
[86]*New York Times,* May 9, 2006, op. cit.

[87]*New York Times,* April 13, 2006.
[88]*San Jose Mercury News,* March 1, 2006, and March 3, 2006, op. cit.
[89]*San Jose Mercury News,* March 1, 2006, op. cit.
[90]*San Jose Mercury News,* March 1, 2006, op. cit.
[91]*San Jose Mercury News,* March 3, 2006, op. cit.
[92]*San Jose Mercury News,* February 15, 2006, op. cit.

conduct, requiring that e-mail servers be located outside the country, and licensing requirements for the export of technologies that could be used for censorship. Smith held a hearing in which Cisco Systems, Google, Microsoft, and Yahoo! testified and were grilled by subcommittee members. Commenting on China's sophisticated censorship system, Smith said, "It's an active partnership with both the disinformation campaign and . . ., and the secret police in China are among the most brutal on the planet. I don't know if these companies understand that or they're naïve about it, whether they're witting or unwitting. But it's been a tragic collaboration. There are people in China being tortured courtesy of these corporations."[93] The bill was passed by the subcommittee and was sent to full committee for consideration.

Representative Tom Lantos (D-CA), leader of the Congressional Human Rights Caucus and a survivor of the Holocaust, said, "These captains of industry should have been developing new technologies to bypass the sickening censorship of government and repugnant barriers to the Internet. Instead, they enthusiastically volunteered for the censorship brigade."[94]

In congressional testimony Elliot Schrage, vice president of global communications and public affairs at Google, explained that China was an important market for the company. He said, "It would be disingenuous to say that we don't care about that because, of course, we do. We are a business with stockholders, and we want to prosper and grow in a highly competitive world. At the same time, acting ethically is a core value for our company, and an integral part of our business culture."[95]

Earlier in 2006 Google had refused to comply with a request from the U.S. government to provide information on Internet search requests.[96] The government had asked Google for a random sample of 1 million Web addresses

and a week's search requests with any information that could identify the user removed. The information was to be used for a study to show that Internet filters were not sufficient to prevent children from accessing pornographic Web sites. The Department of Justice sought the information to help revive the 1998 Child Online Protection Act, which had been blocked by the Supreme Court and sent to the Court of Appeals for reconsideration. Google strongly objected to the request on privacy grounds and refused to provide the information. The Department of Justice then took Google to court to force it to provide the information. In the court hearing the government substantially scaled back its request, and the judge ordered Google to provide 50,000 random Web addresses. The judge also ruled that providing the requested 50,000 random search queries could harm Google through a loss of goodwill among its users.[97]

In June Brin commented on the criticism Google had received. He said, "We felt that perhaps we could compromise our principles but provide ultimately more information for the Chinese and be a more effective service and perhaps make more of a difference. . . . Perhaps now the principled approach makes more sense."[98]

In July Amnesty International launched a campaign against Internet oppression, mentioning Sun Microsystems, Nortel, Cisco, Yahoo!, Google, and Microsoft. Amnesty stated, "Internet companies often claim to be ethically responsible—these pledges will highlight how their cooperation in repression risks making them complicit in human rights abuses and damages their credibility."[99] ■

SOURCE: This case was prepared from public sources by Professor David P. Baron. Copyright © 2006 by the Board of Trustees of the Leland Stanford Junior University. All rights reserved. Reprinted with permission.

Preparation Questions

1. What principles are relevant for Google's decision to enter China? Is censorship consistent with Google's core values? Should compromises be made?
2. Why does the Chinese government censor information so aggressively?
3. Should Google have entered China?
4. Given that Google decided to enter China, should it have offered e-mail and hosted blogs? Should it have restricted its offerings more than it actually did?

5. Are Google's practices sufficient? What else should it do?
6. Should Google lobby the Chinese government to change its censorship policies?
7. Should Google lobby the U.S. government to develop a policy to guide U.S. Internet companies in China?

---

[93]Ibid.
[94]*San Jose Mercury News,* February 19, 2006.
[95]*Wall Street Journal,* March 10, 2006.
[96]The government also sought similar data from AOL, Microsoft's MSN, and Yahoo!, all of which complied with the request.

[97]The judge also stated that the search queries could be within the scope of a subpoena. *San Francisco Chronicle,* March 18, 2006.
[98]*San Jose Mercury News,* June 7, 2006.
[99]Amnesty International, press release, July 20, 2006, www.amnesty.org.

17

Emerging Markets

INTRODUCTION

More than three-quarters of the world's population lives in emerging markets countries, and 90 percent of the world's population growth will be in these countries over the next thirty years. Per capita income is growing rapidly in China, India, and other countries with relatively open economies. Opportunities in many emerging market countries are very attractive to firms, and foreign direct investment has flowed to the relatively stable and lower-risk countries.

Yet more than half the people in the world still live on less than $2 a day. The informal sector plays an important role in many of these countries with estimates of over 40 percent of GDP accounted for by the informal sectors in Africa and Latin America. More than half the people live in nondemocratic countries, and some democratic countries such as Thailand are frequently at risk of a coup. Corruption plagues many emerging markets countries, and the rule of law is unevenly enforced. Refugees flow across borders in Africa, and civil wars rage in a number of countries. Cultural, ethnic, and religious conflict is present in many of these countries. Risk often accompanies opportunity.

Countries are distinctive, so making generalizations is difficult. Moreover, the principles of nonmarket strategy for operating in democracies cannot simply be transported to emerging markets, particularly for countries that are not democratic and where the rule of law is weak. This chapter focuses on opportunities in emerging market countries and the risks present in those countries that are not present in the established democracies of the developed world. The next section identifies sources of information available for evaluating a country, and the following sections address opportunities and risks. Nonmarket strategies for emerging markets are then considered.

COUNTRY ASSESSMENT

Opportunities for successful participation in an emerging markets economy depend not only on the characteristics of the particular markets in which a firm would participate but also on the characteristics of the country. The market environment may be different from that of the firm's home country, and the nonmarket environment can be even more different. Just as a firm entering an emerging markets economy will study in detail the demand and supply relations in the market, investigate competitors, and assess the labor market, the firm also needs to study the nonmarket environment. This includes understanding the government and its role in the market and nonmarket environments, the impact of corruption, divisions within the populace, freedoms, and risks associated with both the government and its policies.

The importance of these factors is indicated by the variety of assessment measures developed for countries and the growth of political risk consultancies. This section identifies several indexes useful in assessing conditions in a country. These indexes should not be viewed as conclusions about a country but instead should be viewed as indicating concerns that warrant further investigation.

Individual Freedoms

Freedom House, an independent, nonpartisan organization founded in 1941, supports the expansion of freedom in the world. The organization annually publishes an evaluation of the following freedoms for countries around the world: Political Rights with components Electoral Process, Political Pluralism and Participation, and the Functioning of Government and Civil Liberties with components Freedom of Expression and Belief, Associational and Organizational Rights, Rule of Law, and Personal Autonomy and Individual Rights. A large number of countries are identified as "Free," whereas at the bottom of the "Not Free" group are Burma, Cuba, Libya, North Korea, Sudan, Syria, Turkmenistan, and Uzbekistan.

Economic Freedom

Recognizing the relationship between economic prosperity and economic freedoms, the Heritage Foundation and the *Wall Street Journal* annually publish an Index of Economic Freedom based on 10 freedoms: business freedom, trade freedom, fiscal freedom, government size, monetary freedom, investment freedom, financial freedom, property rights, freedom from corruption, and labor freedom. The creators of the Index stated, "A systematic analysis of the 10 freedoms has demonstrated again this year that economic freedom is the key to creating an environment that allows a virtuous cycle of entrepreneurship, innovation, and sustained economic growth and development to flourish."[1] The 2008 Index covered 157 countries with Hong Kong and Singapore having the highest scores and Cuba and North Korea having the lowest.

Corruption

Corruption has a corrosive effect on a country and its people. It favors those in positions of influence and with resources to pay bribes and extend favors. It distorts economic activity and can substantially reduce GDP. A number of countries have hired private companies to run their ports so as to reduce corruption. Corruption is typically hard to observe, difficult to measure, and hard to eradicate. Several measures of the extent of corruption in a country are available, perhaps the best known of which is Transparency International's Corruption Perceptions Index (CPI).

Concerned by what he had observed from his position in the World Bank, Peter Eiger founded Transparency International (TI) in Berlin in 1993 as an NGO to lead in the curtailment of corruption.[2] In his introduction to TI's "Global Corruption Report 2001" he wrote:

> Corruption respects no national boundaries. It deepens poverty around the globe by distorting political, economic, and social life. Transparency International (TI) was born from the experience of people who witnessed first hand the real threat to human lives posed by corruption—and from its founders' frustration that nobody wanted to talk about it.

The instrument for TI's attack on corruption was the construction of a corruption index as a way of calling attention to the issue and putting pressure on countries. The CPI pertains to the corruption in a country or the demand side of corruption and is based on surveys asking people about their perceptions of corruption in a country.[3] For 2007 Denmark, Finland, and New Zealand headed the list, and Myanmar and Somalia were tied for last among the 180 countries.

---

[1] 2008 Index of Economic Freedom, "Executive Summary," p. 2.
[2] Transparency International now has chapters in 85 countries.
[3] According to its chairman, "Transparency International is not saying in this index that one country is more corrupt than another. We are reporting how business people, political analysts, and the general public around the globe perceive levels of corruption in different countries."

Political Risk

CountryWatch provides an index of political risk "based on criteria including stability, democratic accountability, and economic risk," where the last includes the transparency of regulation and the nonservicing of payments by the country, among other factors. The highest scores for 2007 were for Austria, Canada, Denmark, Finland, Luxembourg, Netherlands, Norway, Sweden, and Switzerland. The lowest score was for Iraq, followed by Lebanon, North Korea, Somalia, Sudan, and Zimbabwe.

Competitiveness

IMD of Switzerland conducts an assessment of the competitiveness of 55 countries covering economic performance, government efficiency, business efficiency, and infrastructure. For 2008 the leaders in overall competitiveness were the United States followed by Singapore, and Venezuela was last. The United States was first in economic performance and infrastructure, whereas Hong Kong and Singapore were first in government and business efficiency.

Culture

Culture can also be important, not only shaping the opportunities and risks in a country but also for the likelihood that a company can implement its market strategy. Lincoln Electric was renowned for its high productivity resulting from its piece-rate compensation system that provided strong individualized incentives to increase output. The company decided to expand overseas and selected a number of countries in which to make acquisitions and build plants. In some countries Lincoln Electric's system of individualized incentives clashed with local culture that was more collectivist in nature and hostile to individualized incentives. After a series of costly trial and error attempts to establish high-productivity plants, the company concluded that there were only two countries where its incentive approach worked—China and Poland.[4]

OPPORTUNITIES

Opportunities in emerging markets are of two basic types. The first is to use a country to export goods to better developed countries and markets. The extractive industries are the prime example, as are the factories in Asia that supply the apparel and footwear markets. This requires foreign markets to be open, which is generally the case in developed countries. The European Union, however, has placed a moratorium on products containing genetically modified organisms, which has restricted the opportunities for African farmers who seek the higher yields available with genetically modified seeds.

The second type is to recognize that the country may be a market for the firm's products, either immediately or in the not too distant future. McKinsey & Co. studied the marketplace in India and concluded that at the projected growth rates the middle class would increase from 50 million to 583 million people by 2025 and 291 million people would move from "desperate poverty to a more sustainable life. . . ."[5]

The attractiveness of the Indian retail market to Tesco PLC was due to the size and structure of retailing, in particular food retailing. The retail market in India had sales of $200 billion in 2005 and was growing rapidly with a projected market potential of $300 billion in 2010. The organized sector, consisting of establishments with 10 or more employees, accounted for only 3 percent of sales but was projected to account for 10 percent of sales by 2010. The unorganized sector consisted of nearly 11 million outlets, including kirana shops and other small stores, with only 4 percent having over 500 sq ft. of floor space.[6] Some 21 million people were employed in retailing. The restrictions on FDI in retailing meant that Tesco either had to stay out of

---

[4]See Siegel and Larson (2007).
[5]McKinsey Global Institute, "The 'Bird of Gold': The Rise of India's Consumer Market." May 2007.
[6]www.thehindubusinessline.com, June 1, 2006.

India

India is a country with 1.1 billion people and a rich cultural history. In contrast to China, India's population is relatively young, and its population growth rate is 1.38 percent a year. In the not too distant future India will overtake China as the most populous country in the world. Although India has experienced rapid economic growth over the past decade, one-quarter of the people lived on less than $1 a day.

After independence in 1947, the county established a vigorous democracy that has been uninterrupted since. The Constitution established a socialist system with political institutions based on the Westminster model from England. The country has 28 states with a degree of federalism, but the national government headed by the prime minister is paramount.

About 80 percent of the population is Hindu and 14 percent Muslim. India has had a caste system, and although discrimination based on caste was banned by the Constitution, the caste system remains a part of Indian culture. Considerable change has occurred in the implications of caste for individuals. An "untouchable" has been elected chief minister of the state of Uttar Pradesh, and another is head of the Supreme Court.

The country has been politically stable but faces lingering tensions between its Hindu and Muslim populations, a communist insurgency in the eastern states, and conflict with Pakistan over Kashmir. The CountryWatch Political Risk Index is 8, compared to a value of 9 for the United States. The Freedom House scores for political rights and civil liberties are 2 and 3, respectively, compared to 1 and 1 for the United States and 7 and 6 for China. Corruption has remained an issue in India. Transparency International ranked India tied with Brazil, China, Mexico, Peru, and Surinam for 72nd among 180 countries.

The country had adopted socialist economic policies intended to protect its domestic market. Controls were imposed on the domestic market, on foreign direct investment, and international trade. Trade policy was protectionist. Beginning in 1991 India began liberalizing its economic policies and has progressively adopted more free market policies. In particular Prime Minister Manmohan Singh has encouraged economic liberalization resulting in a spurt of economic growth. In terms of competitiveness India was 29th of 55 countries in the IMD Overall Competitiveness rankings, between 18th and 23rd for economic performance, government efficiency, and business efficiency. India was 49th in infrastructure, however.

Some of this economic liberalization has been required by membership in the World Trade Organization. For example, Indian patent law allowed patents on methods of production but not on products themselves. This allowed an Indian pharmaceutical company to produce a drug patented in Europe and the United States using a different production process. This spurred the development of a vigorous pharmaceutical industry in India with many companies producing generic versions of patented drugs. With the adoption of the TRIPS agreement for the protection of intellectual property, India was forced to change its patent system to conform with the type of intellectual property protection found in Europe and the United States. This changed the incentives for Indian pharmaceutical companies, and some began to develop their own proprietary drugs.

Despite the economic liberalization, restrictions remain in some sectors, such as retail. The Indian government had relaxed many of the restrictions on foreign direct investment (FDI), and FDI had increased from $8.28 billion in 2003 to $25.66 billion in 2006. FDI up to 51 percent was allowed in 35 high-priority industries, and most recently, FDI had been allowed in real estate. FDI was still banned in four industries: retail trading (with the exception of single-brand retailing), atomic energy, lottery business, and gambling and betting. The restrictions on retailing reflected the potential threat to small shops and stall retailers. Foreign retailers were banned from using FDI for direct sales to individuals, and multi-brand retailers were barred from owning and operating their own stores until at least 2009. Foreign retailers could make franchise arrangements, however, with local retailers, but India had few large retailers. The chapter case, *Tesco PLC in India?*, considers the issue of whether the largest retailer in the United Kingdom should enter the Indian market and if so, how it should do it, given the restrictions on FDI.

India or find a way to enter that would prepare the company for when the restrictions were relaxed.

A firm with superior know-how can also acquire a local firm supplying the domestic market and operate it more efficiently or better serve the market. Cemex began as a regional cement producer in Mexico and through internal growth and acquisitions became the third largest producer in the world. One aspect of its globalization strategy was to acquire inefficient producers in emerging markets where cement was sold as a branded product directly to consumers rather than in bulk to construction companies. In South America Cemex bought cement plants in Argentina, Columbia, and Venezuela. It improved the efficiency of the plants to lower their costs. In Venezuela it became the largest producer of cement and ready-mix concrete.

Hewlett-Packard's decision to source in Vietnam was in part motivated by the rapid income growth in a country with 100 million people, an increasing proportion of whom were potential customers. In addition, the government in a communist country is large and represents an important potential customer.

Few of the emerging markets countries share the strong opposition to genetically modified (GM) agriculture found in much of Europe. The opportunity to increase yields in the face of hunger and rising food prices has led to increased plantings of GM seeds. Africa welcomed GM seeds, except that the opportunities for export were restricted by opposition to GM foods in most of Europe.

Opportunity at the Bottom of the Pyramid?

C. K. Prahalad (2004) argued that companies had overlooked as customers the 4 billion people in the world who lived on less than $2 a day. Moreover, he argued that private companies could make a "fortune" serving these consumers, helping to bring them out of poverty. He further argued that multinational companies could play a leading role in selling to the poor, in particular because the poor wanted quality products. Prahalad presented a series of examples to illustrate his thesis. One of his most cited examples was a start-up company in India that made single-serve packages of shampoo that were said to be more affordable than conventional-size packages.

Karnani (2007) criticized all aspects of Prahalad's thesis, arguing that it was "logically flawed and inconsistent with the evidence." He examined the examples and concluded that most did not show profitability Moreover, he estimated that the market at the bottom of the pyramid was not that large and was costly to serve. He argued that the single-serve packages were not affordable, and moreover, no multinational company produced the packages. Hindustan Lever Limited did sell salt in small packages, but the salt sold for the same price per kilogram as in the larger packages. Moreover, the salt sold at nearly three times the price of unbranded salt. Whether there is a fortune in selling to the bottom of the pyramid remains an open question.

One example of serving the poor that has been successful is microfinance, as considered below. Banco Compartamos has been highly profitable serving the poor in Mexico, but it charges interest rates of 90 percent.[7] It, however, has helped hundreds of thousands of people to improve their lives.

Another company that has been highly successful in serving consumers in emerging markets is MTN Group, a provider of cellular telephone service and enhancements in Africa and the Middle East. Its customer base, however, pays on average $20 a month, which means that many customers are not at the bottom of the pyramid. The chapter case, *MTN Group Limited,* provides an opportunity to assess its business model and the opportunities and risks it faces.

River Blindness

The traditional business approach to addressing problems of poverty and illness involved voluntary donations to those in need. Merck developed a drug, Mectizan, for treating river blindness, which afflicts millions of people in developing countries. In 1987 Merck established a private-public partnership, the Mectizan Donation Program (MDP), to distribute the drug free to people in Africa where the disease was prevalent. The MDP now distributes the drug to 40 million people a year in 34 countries in Africa, Latin America, and Yemen. The MDP is complemented by a group of NGOs that support

---

[7]See the chapter case *Social Entrepreneurship: Banco Compartamos.*

and provide treatment for river blindness. The NGOs obtain 50–50 matching grants from Merck to fund their treatments.

Fair Trade

The fair trade movement was begun to improve the lives of poor farmers and workers trapped by market conditions. The movement can be understood as an approach to improving the well-being of poor farmers in developing countries by circumventing markets and coordinating market behavior. The fair trade system attempts to intervene directly on both the demand and the supply sides of the market by coordinating the flow of consumer revenue to participating producers. Coffee producers participating in the fair trade system are primarily organizations of small farmers that agree to meet certain production and environmental standards. Participating coffee brokers agree to pay a fixed, fair trade price, which exceeds the market price, so the income of coffee farmers is increased. The brokers charge a higher price for fair trade coffee, and retailers generally sell the coffee at a higher price. Fair Trade certification allows consumers to participate, and the fair trade movement monitors the system to ensure that the higher prices actually benefit farmers. Fair Trade labels are now available for coffee, tea, rice, bananas, mangoes, cocoa, sugar, honey, fruit juices, flowers, handicrafts, and soccer balls.[8]

Coffee production had been governed by the International Coffee Agreement (ICA), a cartel that established export quotas for the producing countries to maintain prices within a range referred to as the corset. The quotas were waived in times of shortage when prices could rise substantially. Growing opposition to cartels led to criticism of the ICA, which collapsed in 1989 when the United States withdrew from the agreement. The ICA was succeeded by the International Coffee Organization (ICO), but it was unable to limit production. Prices began to fall, and with the exception of two periods of high prices due to frost in Brazil, prices remained below the corset levels. After a small price increase in 1999 coffee prices fell by 50 percent over the following three years.

The price drop was due to increased supply and slow growth in demand. In particular, Vietnam had provided incentives for farmers to grow coffee, and the country quickly became the second-largest exporter after Brazil. Brazil also had increased production as a result of increased mechanization and shifting away from frost-prone regions. Demand growth was slowed by increased competition from soft drinks and the movement to natural fruit drinks, particularly in the United States. From 1970 to 2000 coffee consumption per capita fell from 36 gallons to 17 gallons annually in the United States, while soft drink consumption increased from 23 to 53 gallons per capita.[9] Coffee retailers attempted to increase sales by introducing specialty and flavored coffees. The latter increased the demand for low-quality coffee.

OxfamAmerica reported that 70 percent of coffee production was accounted for by small farmers, who were devastated by the price drop. Oxfam reported that in 1980 a coffee grower could purchase a Swiss Army knife with 4.171 kilograms of coffee, but by 2001, 10.464 kilograms were required. Oxfam estimated that 25 million coffee farmers were affected.

The Fair Trade System

The fair trade movement began in the Netherlands in 1988 with the introduction of Max Havelaar brand coffee, named after a 19th century Dutch novel depicting the exploitation of plantation workers in Dutch colonies. The objective of the movement was to protect small growers from fluctuating and falling prices. The movement grew in Europe and spread to the United States and other countries.

The fair trade coffee system paid farmers $1.26 a pound for their coffee or $1.41 for organic coffee. The market price for coffee in early 2004 was $0.65 a pound. To qualify for

---

[8]Fair Labeling Organizations International, www.fairtrade.net/sites/aboutflo/faq.html.
[9]Oxfam International, "Mugged: Poverty in Your Coffee Cup," 2002, p. 19.

the fair trade system farmers had to form a producer organization such as a democratically operated cooperative or association.[10] The production practices of the producer organization were then monitored to ensure compliance with the fair trade standards.

The fair trade system had two wings. One focused on the certification of coffee producers, the monitoring of coffee brokers, and enforcement to ensure that funds reached the producers. The other focused on building a demand for fair trade products, primarily in the consuming countries. The fair trade system was led by the Fairtrade Labeling Organizations (FLO), headquartered in Bonn, Germany. The FLO established FLO-Cert Ltd., which verified that the farmers benefited from the program.

The fair trade program in the United States was administered by TransFair USA, which tracked fair trade products from fair trade producers. TransFair was a member of the FLO. TransFair worked on the demand side of the market to increase the retail availability of fair trade coffee and other fair trade products. TransFair reported that 18.5 million pounds of fair trade coffee was sold in the United States in 2003 and projected 2004 sales at 29 million pounds. TransFair was financed by a 10 cents a pound fee paid by roasters for fair trade coffee as well as by grants from foundations.

In addition to TransFair and the FLO, NGOs worked to increase the availability of Fairtrade coffee. OxfamAmerica, Global Exchange, Co-Op America, and the Interfaith Fair Trade Initiative targeted coffee companies and retailers and sought to educate the public as well as coffee retailers. OxfamAmerica headed a private politics campaign to convince Procter & Gamble and Dunkin' Donuts to sell fair trade coffee. Adding to the direct pressure on the companies, the Center for Reflection, Education and Action (CREA) and Domini Social Investments registered shareholder resolutions for the P&G annual meeting, the first-ever shareholder resolution on fair trade. The U.S. Senate and House approved resolutions calling for support of coffee farmers in developing countries.

Dunkin' Donuts agreed to sell fair trade espresso in the spring of 2003. After 2 years of efforts by the NGOs, in September 2003 Procter & Gamble agreed to sell Fair Trade Certified coffee through its Millstone specialty division and over the Internet. Sister Ruth Rosenbaum of CREA praised P&G: "P&G's action is an excellent example of what can be accomplished through collaboration of shareholder activists and nonprofit organizations. It's a win-win for the world's small-scale coffee farmers, for the environment, and for P&G itself."[11]

Oxfam established a ratings system for the four largest coffee companies, assessing for the previous 12 months their actions to address the global coffee crisis. Procter & Gamble received a rating of 49 out of 100, Nestlé 43, Kraft 38, and Sara Lee 27. Phil Bloomer, the Make Trade Fair campaign director for Oxfam, said, "These companies continue to make massive profits while coffee farmers get poorer and poorer."[12]

Challenges

One concern with the fair trade concept was whether retailers would charge such a large price premium that demand would be suppressed. "'Supermarkets are taking advantage of the label to make more profit because they know that consumers are willing to pay a bit more because it is fair trade,' said Emily Daradaine, fruit-product manager" at the FLO.

At its 435 outlets Café Borders sold fair trade coffee for $16 a pound, whereas non–fair trade coffee was sold at $12 a pound. After an inquiry by a reporter for the *Wall Street Journal*, Café Borders said it would lower the price for a bag of fair trade coffee by 20 percent. At the online site of the United Kingdom's largest supermarket chain Tesco,

[10]"There are two sets of generic producer standards, one for small farmers and one for workers on plantations and in factories. The first set applies to smallholders organized in cooperatives or other organizations with a democratic, participative structure. The second set applies to organized workers, whose employers pay decent wages, guarantee the right to join trade unions, and provide good housing where relevant. On plantations and in factories, minimum health and safety as well as environmental standards must be complied with, and no child or forced labor may occur." Fairtrade Labeling Organizations International, www.fairtrade.net/sites/aboutflo/faq.html.
[11]OxfamAmerica, "Advocacy Groups and Shareholders Persuade Procter & Gamble to Offer Fair Trade Coffee," press release, September 15, 2003.
[12]OxfamAmerica, press release, December 9, 2003.

fair trade coffee sold at 46 percent more than non–fair trade coffee. Luuk Laurens Zonneveld, managing director of the FLO, said he was concerned about high retail margins because they would reduce the market share for fair trade products. He said some of the FLO's affiliates might "approach" the companies about their practices.[13]

Whole Foods Markets had declined to participate in the fair trade program because it believed that the system was unfair to family farms that did not qualify as a producer organization. Instead, Whole Foods started its own program, High Five for Farmers, under which it donated 5 percent of the price it paid for coffee to the farms that produced it.[14] Royal Ahold NV of the Netherlands also set up an alternative certification program. "'If you are a large supermarket brand or a large roaster, to buy all your products under the fair-trade conditions is just not economically possible,' said David Rosenberg, director of Utz Kapeh," the foundation Royal Ahold helped establish to certify coffee.[15]

The fair trade movement claimed that fair trade coffee was higher quality. Tadesse Meskala, who managed a farmers' coffee cooperative in Ethiopia, commented, "Better payments leads us to make sure the coffee is a better quality." Farmers "care for the coffee because people care for us. They pay us a fair price."[16] Starbucks, however, had delayed selling Fair Trade coffee because of concerns about its quality.

Ultimately, as the FLO stated, "The impact of Fair Trade in the end always depends on the goodwill and loyalty of the consumer."[17] Paul Rice, founder and chief executive of TransFair USA, said, "It is guilt-free coffee, but I would not call it that. I would call it feel-good coffee."[18] Bill Conerly of the National Center for Policy Analysis commented, "It's a feel-good program. I don't expect it to be a broad trend because people don't like to spend more money. I expect the impact to be trivial."[19] By the end of 2007 sales of fair trade products had reached $3.62 billion, and 632 producer organizations in 58 countries had been certified.

Microfinance

Microfinance has a long history, but the modern version is due to Muhammad Yunus, a Bangladesh economist, who in 1974 became concerned about the devastating poverty from which people were seemingly unable to escape. As he interviewed people he learned that many women made by hand small objects that they sold in local markets. Many borrowed in the morning from local lenders, purchased materials, made and sold the objects, and repaid the lender at the end of the day. The interest rates were usurious, leaving the women at best with a subsistence income and unable to improve their situation. He quickly identified 42 people in a similar situation and found that in total they needed only $27 a day in lending. Yunus began borrowing from a bank on his own account and lending to the people. The loan funds were used for agriculture, home business, and a variety of other purposes and made a large difference in the lives of the people. The borrowers repaid the loans, and Yunus established the Grameen Bank to expand the number of people served. By 2004 Grameen Bank had loaned over $4 billion and had 3.5 million current borrowers, 95 percent of whom were women. Grameen loaned to groups of five women, who were responsible for allocating the borrowings among themselves and for ensuring that the borrowings were repaid. Grameen reported a 99 percent repayment rate. By 2007 Grameen Bank had made loans to 5 million people and had assets of over a billion dollars. Yunus received the Nobel Peace Prize in 2006 for his work.

Yunus also developed an innovative approach to helping the poorest people— beggars. They could obtain a Grameen identity card that enabled them to borrow merchandise from stores and sell it door-to-door, with their borrowing financed by a loan from the bank. Yunus then turned to stationary beggars, many of whom were

[13]*Wall Street Journal,* June 8, 2004.
[14]*Wall Street Journal,* June 8, 2004.
[15]*Wall Street Journal,* June 8, 2004.
[16]*San Jose Mercury News,* April 28, 2004.
[17]www.fairtrade.net.
[18]*San Jose Mercury News,* April 28, 2004.
[19]*San Jose Mercury News,* April 28, 2004.

blind or missing a limb. Since they typically positioned themselves in strategic places, Grameen enabled them to sell drinks, food, and other objects from their places.

Inspired by the work of Yunus, thousands of other nonprofit microfinance institutions (MFIs) were formed. Most of these MFIs were subsidized by donors and provided low interest rates relative to the rates of local moneylenders. By 2006 microfinance customers were estimated at 133 million and were projected to increase to 175 million by 2015. These numbers were far below the number of people who could benefit from microfinance.

One means of reaching more of the poor was for-profit microfinance. Some entrepreneurs had started for-profit institutions, but the potential became clear in 2007 when Carlos Danel and Carlos Labarthe took Banco Compartamos public in an IPO valued at $1.53 billion. The bank had been started as a nonprofit in Mexico and received funding from NGOs and international development institutions such as the International Finance Corporation. The bank was converted to for-profit status in 2001 and expanded its customers from 60,000 to 839,000 in 2007. Banco Compartamos had profits of $81.5 million and a loan portfolio of $400 million with only 1.36 percent of its loans nonperforming.

The interest rates charged by the bank were in the 90 percent range, which was substantially less than the interest rates of local moneylenders. (Interest rates were generally much higher in Latin America than in Africa and Asia.) Yunus strongly criticized Banco Compartamos for its interest rates and argued that microfinance should be provided by nonprofit institutions. He said, "They're absolutely on the wrong track. Their priorities are screwed up. . . . Microcredit was created to fight the money lender, not to become the money lender."[20] Supporters of Banco Compartamos argued that for-profit status allowed the bank to raise capital and expand its services far more rapidly than it could as a nonprofit. Some participants in microfinance estimated that access to the capital markets could expand microfinance funding from $4 billion a year to $30 billion and serve 1 billion low-income customers.[21] The chapter case, *Social Entrepreneurship: Banco Compartamos,* provides an opportunity to consider these issues in more detail. The for-profit approach to microfinance can be contrasted with an innovative, nonprofit online microfinance approach pioneered by Kiva, as considered in the chapter case, *Social Entrepreneurship: Kiva.*

As an example of private-sector success and the risk present in some emerging markets, Equity Bank of Kenya began in 1984 as a mortgage lender, but was unable to become profitable. In 2004, under the leadership of CEO James Mwangi, the bank transformed itself into a savings and loan bank with an emphasis on microfinance.[22] The focus was on the 58 percent of Kenyans who lived on less than $2 a day, many of whom were women, who also constituted 70 percent of the illiterate in Kenya. By 2006 Equity Bank had 1 million customers with savings accounts, which after six months qualified the account holder for borrowing. Loans were from KSh 500 to KSh 50 million, and interest rates averaged 17.5 percent. To expand its coverage it had opened 42 branches by 2006 and planned to have 70 by 2008. Equity Bank sought to serve its customers with low fees and services tailored to their needs. In return, Equity Bank earned record revenues and profits and became the seventh largest for-profit bank in Kenya.

By 2008, however, Kenya was embroiled in turmoil, as described later in the chapter. The impact on Equity Bank was unclear.

Underdeveloped Markets and Business Groups

Often the set of markets on which a new firm depends for inputs is incomplete. In particular, domestic capital markets may be inadequate for the financing needed in emerging market economies. Over time this has led to the formation of business groups in a number of countries as a means of providing financing and diversifying risks. The companies in these groups are independent legal entities, but they are tied

[20]*BusinessWeek.* December 13, 2007.
[21]See Cull, Demirgüç-Kunt, and Morduch (2008).
[22]See the case "Equity Bank (A)," Case No. E260, Graduate School of Business, Stanford University, 2007.

together by cross shareholdings or familial ties. These groups have been said to be important to the development of the economy in many countries but also have been blamed for a failure of a country to reform and liberalize. Khanna and Yafeh (2007) surveyed the research on the performance and effects of business groups in emerging markets. They studied the data on business groups in Argentina, Brazil, Chile, India, Indonesia, Israel, South Korea, Mexico, Philippines, Taiwan, Thailand, and Turkey. In many cases the business groups were family controlled.[23] Khanna and Yafeh concluded that differences in structure, the industries covered by the groups, and the countries in which they operate meant that some groups were paragons and others parasites.

Business groups as well as individual companies have strong incentives to interact with government when it controls markets, lets contracts, and regulates business activity. Leuz and Oberholzer-Gee (2006) examined the performance of firms with and without relationships to the Suharto regime in Indonesia. Firms with strong political relationships relied less on global financial markets than did firms that had no political relationship. These political relationships increased the returns on those firms, but access to global financial market also increased returns. The higher returns for firms with political relationships were due to preferential financing, and those firms sought to avoid the global financial markets because of the greater transparency required and because it was more difficult to extract benefits from control of the firms when they were monitored by global lenders.

Relying on political relationships can also increase risk. The firms that relied on political connections underperformed during the Asian financial crisis and significantly underperformed once Suharto was gone and replaced by a new government hostile to the Suharto regime. Political relationships can become a liability when there is a regime change, and those relationships may be hard to reestablish with a new regime.

RISK ASSESSMENT

Risks in emerging markets can differ in magnitude and nature from those in developed countries.

- Risks are greater in magnitude in emerging markets. In 2007 Venezuelan president Hugo Chávez began to nationalize foreign businesses as a way of consolidating his power and realizing his vision of "21st century socialism." Nationalization is no longer an immediate risk in most developed countries.
- Foreign risks arise from a broader range of factors than do domestic risks. These include ethnic and religious differences, ideology, and class and income differences.
- Risks can depend on the country of origin.

In 2008 demonstrators in France disrupted the carrying of the Olympic torch to China as a protest against suppression in Tibet. France had also granted honorary citizenship to the Dalai Lama and to Hu Jia, a human rights activist in China. Chinese citizens were offended by the criticism and the honorary citizenship and launched protests against France. Many chose to demonstrate at the stores of Carrefour, the giant French retailer. Whether the protests affected sales is unclear, but it was clear that demonstrations against the company were because of its country of origin.

Experience is an important factor in assessing risks. Advice is available from a large industry of consultants, advisors, and ratings services. For example, the PRS Group, a political risk advisory company that provides 100 country reports monitoring risks to international business, assesses the following set of risks:

Turmoil
Equity restrictions
Operations restrictions

---

[23]Family-related business groups have been important to the success of the overseas Chinese in Southeast Asia.

Taxation discrimination
Repatriation restrictions
Exchange controls
Tariff barriers
Other import barriers
Payment delays
Fiscal and monetary expansion
Labor policies
Foreign debt
Investment restrictions
Trade restrictions
Domestic economic problems
International economic problems

Causes and Types of Risks

The immediate source of many risks is the weak rule of law in a country. This means that agreements and contracts may not be enforced, even if their terms are unambiguous. It can also mean that the law is not enforced impartially and that regulations can be applied in a discriminatory manner. Moreover, politics and political ties can override the rule of law. This section identifies a set of risks in emerging markets that differ from those in most developed countries.

Coups

Sudden changes can occur because of a military coup, as in Thailand. In 2006 the Thai military overthrew the elected regime of Prime Minister Thaksin Shinawatra, disbanded his political party, and reversed many of his policies. The military government forced Google to censor its searches because of YouTube postings objectionable to the government. The military pledged to allow elections in 2007, and Thaksin's supporters formed a new party backing him and his policies. The party was successful in the election and formed a new government that pledged it would reinstate Thaksin's policies.

Democratic Revolution

Venezuelans first elected President Hugo Chávez in 1998 and reelected him twice. In 2007 he embarked on a campaign to establish 21st century socialism and to consolidate and extend his power. He seized many companies owned by foreigners, including operators of oil fields and firms in the electricity and telecommunications industries. He nationalized a milk producer, sugar plantations, a cold storage and distribution company. He closed a television station that was critical of him. Despite skyrocketing oil prices, his policies worsened the economy, and he responded by nationalizing more companies. Because of a housing shortage he seized all the cement companies in the country, including the company owned by Cemex. In May 2008 he seized the Luxembourg-owned steel company Sidor and pledged to make it a "socialist company." The economy continued to weaken. To continue his program, Chávez attempted to change the constitution to eliminate the term limits that would prevent him from running for another term. In a referendum Venezuelan voters rejected the proposed change. To extend his influence in other countries, he financed rebels in neighboring Colombia, and sent an envoy to Argentina with $800,000 in cash intended for the Argentine presidential campaign. Customs officials found the cash in a suitcase.

Policy Risk

When the military took over in Thailand, it looked for policies that would be popular with citizens. One was to take on the global pharmaceutical companies. As discussed in Chapter 18, the TRIPS agreement as amended in the Doha Round negotiations allowed countries in a national emergency to issue a compulsory license for the importation or production of a patented drug to deal with the emergency. Thailand issued compulsory licenses for Merck's AIDS drug Efavirenz, Abbott Laboratories' AIDS drug Kaletra, and the Sanofi-Aventis' heart drug Plavix. Brazil followed by issuing a compulsory license for Efavirenz. The Chapter 18 case, *Compulsory Licensing, Thailand, and Abbott Laboratories,* considers the issue in more detail.

Regulatory Risk

Islamic finance has grown quickly since the Malaysian government issued the first Islamic bond in 2002. The most popular *sukuk,* or sharia-compliant bonds, structures in 2006 and 2007 were *musaraka,* a type of Islamic joint venture, and *mudaraba,* a form of trust financing.[24] In November 2007 the Islamic scholar Sheikh Muhammad Taqi Usmani stated that 85 percent of the *sukuk* being issued violated two principles of Islamic law. Usmani was the head of the religious board of the Accounting and Auditing Organization for Islamic Financial Institutions, based in Bahrain. No sizable international *sukuk* was issued during the next three months. The concerns were that the structures in effect had a guaranteed return, which is not in accord with Islam law, which calls for the sharing of risk and profit. Financial institutions participating in Islamic finance relied on Islamic scholars as advisors, but those scholars were frequently in disagreement. Islam does not have a hierarchical structure with a head who can make proclamations to resolve differing views and establish uniform religious policy.

Price Controls

In June 2008 Mexico approved a price freeze on 150 food products. The freeze was accepted by business and was intended to control inflation of food prices, which has traditionally been a powder keg for political protests in Latin America. At the same time Vietnam, the world's second largest exporter of rice, imposed a minimum export price of $800 a tonne. The price had risen from slightly over $300 a tonne in 2007 to a peak of $1,100 a tonne in 2008, before decreasing to $800. Given the action by Vietnam, $800 was likely to be the minimum price of rice until the next harvest was available.

India also felt the increase in food and energy prices. It initially banned the export of rice and some edible oils. Because of rising prices the government threatened to list steel as an "essential commodity," which would give it the authority to control output and distribution. This led the steel companies to enter into a voluntary agreement under which they cut the prices of steel used in the construction of homes.

Financial Restrictions

Emerging markets countries have imposed a variety of restrictions on foreign direct investment, foreign exchange transactions, and the repatriation of earnings. Some of these restrictions are temporary, but many are long lasting. India restricts foreign investment in telecommunications companies to 74 percent. Restrictions can also be imposed by developed countries. The European Union and the United States have imposed restrictions on financing of companies in the Sudan, and the United States has restrictions on doing business with Iran.

Nationalization and Seizures

During the 1960s and 1970s a number of countries expropriated the assets of firms, primarily foreign-owned firms. This discouraged investment in the countries and often led to mismanagement of the expropriated companies. By the late 1980s nationalizations and expropriations had largely ended—until Hugo Chávez began his campaign.

Political Megalomania

Zimbabwe was the breadbasket of Africa. In 2000 voters rejected a constitutional amendment that would allow the government to seize farmland, and President Mugabe then turned his supporters loose to seize the farmlands.[25] They took over the farms, most of which were owned by whites. Some of the whites resisted, but most fled the country. Agricultural output plummeted, and soon the country had been turned into an importer, rather than an exporter, of food. Mugabe continued with his disastrous

---

[24]*Financial Times,* June 19, 2008.
[25]Robert Mugabe was a national hero, having led the revolt that ended white rule in Rhodesia. He was elected president in 1980.

economic policies, including price controls, and conditions continued to worsen. Between 2000 and 2007 the economy contracted by 40 percent. Zimbabwe fell in the Heritage Foundation's index of economic freedoms to 155th of 157 countries, ahead only of Cuba and North Korea.

Political Corruption

Hunger gripped Zimbabwe, and the opposition went to the polls in 2008 in an attempt to defeat Mugabe in his reelection bid. Although the facts are not completely clear, many observers believed that Mugabe and his supporters engaged in voter fraud. Voters gave his opponent more votes but not a majority, forcing a runoff. Mugabe then began a campaign of intimidation in an attempt to secure the election. Mugabe pledged to stay in power even if he lost the runoff. His opponent withdrew from the election because it would not be fair. The violence continued, and world leaders pleaded with Mugabe to postpone the election, but he refused.[26] A boatload of weapons from China and destined for the Mugabe government was turned away by dock workers when it tried to unload in South Africa. Mozambique and other countries also refused to let the boat dock and eventually it returned to China with its cargo.

Ethnic and Religious Conflict

Kenya had a long record of stability since its independence in 1963. The country was led initially by Jomo Kenyatta, followed in 1978 by Daniel arap Moi after Kenyatta's death. Moi established a single-party state, and the economy deteriorated under his reign. International pressure including the holding up of international aid finally forced Moi to return the country to a multi-party system. In 2002, in the country's first democratic election, voters elected Mwai Kibaki, who embarked on economic reform that resulted in strong economic growth. Corruption scandals, however, tarnished the government and led the World Bank to suspend aid. In the election at the end of 2007 Kibaki was widely believed to have engaged in election fraud to obtain the highest vote share. The opposition protested, and Kibaki suppressed the protests, resulting in many deaths. The alleged election fraud gave rise to the first major ethnic conflict in Kenya. Kibaki was a Kikuyu, whereas his opponent was a Luo. The ethnic conflict threatened to paralyze the country, and Kenya's reputation for stability began to slip.

The Sudan has been racked by ethnic and religious conflict. The British had governed the northern, largely Islamic Arab, and the southern non-Arab, English-speaking region separately. The north was semi-arid land, whereas the south had more rainfall and had oil. Under pressure from the north the British consolidated the governance of the country. With independence in 1956 the president decided to make the country an Islamic state and impose sharia law throughout the country. Groups in the non-Arab south rebelled, and war broke out in 1983 that resulted in the deaths of nearly 2 million civilians. In 2003 drought caused the northern nomadic cattle herding tribes to move their cattle south in the western Darfur region. Rebel groups formed in Darfur citing oppression by the Arab government. The government then began a program that the United States called genocide. China was the principal supplier of weapons to the government.

As an example of religious risks YouTube was shut down in most of the world by a routing error by Pakistan. When a posting contained a trailer for an as-yet unreleased film by a Dutch lawmaker that was critical of Islam, Pakistan directed all YouTube traffic to a "black hole" where all content was discarded. A routing error, however, resulted in most of the world's access to YouTube to disappear for several hours. The Internet in many countries is censored on religious or other grounds.

Environmental Risks

Environmental risks center on both harm to the environment in an emerging markets country and the harm from cross-border externalities such as global climate change.

---

[26]Queen Elizabeth II revoked Mugabe's honorary knighthood as a "mark of revulsion" against his human rights abuses and his "abject disregard" for democracy.

Many countries are encouraging major development projects, some of which involve the construction of mines or the exploration for oil. The financing for major projects is now largely governed by the Equator Principles, which are a voluntary set of principles observed by major banks that have subscribed to the Principles. The Equator Principles applied to all projects of $50 million or more and categorized projects as A, B, or C (high, medium, and low) for their environmental or social impact. For A and B projects an Environmental Assessment was required, and the loan contracts from subscribing banks included a covenant stipulating that the borrower must comply with the Environmental Assessment. If a borrower did not fulfill its commitments, the bank could declare the loan in default.[27]

Another environmental risk centers on the successor to the Kyoto Protocol for controlling greenhouse gas emissions. Neither China nor India is subject to Kyoto goals, but both countries will be under pressure to participate in whatever agreement is negotiated to set goals for beyond 2012. India has done little with respect to greenhouse gas emissions. If it can meet its economic growth objective of 8 percent annually, it will need to increase its power generation by a factor of six.[28] India has said in the past that increased emissions were justified by the need to increase the standard of living of its people. That is, economic growth was an "overriding priority" as recognized by the Framework that gave rise to the Kyoto Protocol.

MANAGEMENT IN THE NONMARKET ENVIRONMENT

Operating in an emerging markets country requires an integrated strategy with a strong nonmarket component to shape opportunities and deal with risks. Management and strategy formulation in the nonmarket environment are based on the same conceptual frameworks developed earlier in the book with some exceptions. Some of the frameworks, such as legislative and electoral strategies, are not appropriate for countries with nondemocratic, authoritarian governments as found in many emerging markets countries. Frameworks such as identifying the issues, interests, institutions, and information in the nonmarket environment are broadly applicable. A second qualification is that in nondemocratic countries developing relations with influential members of government becomes more important because government is not bound by due process requirements and courts may not be present to discipline government officials and resolve disputes. In both democracies and nondemocracies, however, obtaining access to government officeholders, whether for the purpose of lobbying or using personal ties or political relationships, is necessary for success. Foreign firms may be at a disadvantage relative to domestic firms if there is mistrust of foreigners. In that case, the rationale for having local management and a domestic face are stronger. More generally, the stronger the rent chain in an emerging markets country, the more effective a nonmarket strategy is likely to be. One concern about personal relationships in emerging markets, however, is that they can become a locus for corruption, as in the Chapter 23 case *Complications in Mamera*.

Similarly, obtaining information about the agenda of regulators and administrators can be crucial to developing a successful strategy. This may require interacting with the media or others that interact directly with the public and government.

Another difference in nonmarket strategy between developed and emerging market countries is due to the nature and magnitude of risks, as discussed earlier in the chapter. For some risks such as those associated with currency fluctuations it may be sufficient simply to hedge the risk in the currency futures market. Similarly, insurance can be purchased for some risks, including the risk of seizure of a business. A firm can also borrow locally as a means of reducing its exposure. For other risks, strategies such as those developed earlier in this book can be useful. In some cases new strategies may be available. When Venezuela seized oil fields from ExxonMobil, the company filed lawsuits in Europe and the United States to freeze the financial assets of the country.

---

[27]The Principles are available at www.equator-principles.com.
[28]*Economist*, June 7, 2008.

For some risks it may be possible to draw upon an international institution or a home country government. For an issue involving international trade, the WTO is available, but it can only be accessed by governments. This requires working with the home country government. For other risks the home country may be able to intervene directly, although there is often a risk of backlash against foreign intervention. The Part IV integrative case, *Toys 'Я' Us and Globalization,* provides an opportunity to decide if the company should attempt to enlist the U.S. government to intervene on its behalf.

Henisz and Zellner (2008) propose a three-component approach to managing policy risk. The first is to understand the preferences of the actors in the market and nonmarket environments. The second is to have a structure analogous to that of the intelligence community that can provide information and assessments. The four I's provide a framework for identifying preferences and collecting information. The third is to influence the risk through collective action and coalitions. The strategy frameworks developed in earlier chapters provide guidance for doing so.

A useful perspective on risk management is risk reduction. This can involve working with NGOs and local stakeholders to reduce the likelihood that private politics against the firm will arise. This may involve formal interactions with stakeholders as is frequently done in the United States. A firm may also participate in industry associations to mitigate risk and may work on preparedness in the event that a risk materializes. In the event that a private politics campaign arises against a company, the crisis management approaches presented in Chapter 5 can be helpful.

SUMMARY

Much of the world's future rests with emerging markets countries that have over three-quarters of the world's population and an even larger share of population growth. More than half the people in these countries live in abject poverty. A number of countries have had very high growth rates that have helped bring more of their people out of poverty and create a middle class. Accompanying that growth are further demands on energy and greenhouse gas emissions.

Emerging markets present enormous opportunities not only to source products and extract raw materials but also to market to consumers with rising incomes. Most of these opportunities are analogous to those in developed countries at present or in their past. Some, however, such as microfinance and serving the consumption needs of the poor, involve more creative business models. Some opportunities are blocked by government restrictions, such as those on FDI in retailing in India. Others are accompanied by risks that can differ from those in developed countries in terms of their nature, breadth, and magnitude.

Managing in the nonmarket environment of emerging market economies is at least as great a challenge as in developed countries. Many of the same strategies are applicable, but some of the emerging market countries are not democracies, however, and others that are do not apply the rule of law consistently. This means that the strategies must be tailored to the specifics of the countries, their markets, and their nonmarket environments. For nondemocratic countries strategies for influencing outcomes on issues often involve the development of relationships with government officials. This provides a setting for corruption, and vigilance is required to make certain that managers and advisors do not succumb to temptation.

Some of the issues encountered in emerging markets are moral in nature and require additional frameworks to address them responsibly. Those frameworks are developed in Part V of the book, and Chapter 23 deals specifically with moral issues in international business with an emphasis on emerging markets. The Chapter 22 case, *Advanced Technologies Laboratories, Inc.,* and the Chapter 23 case, *De Beers and Conflict Diamonds,* are set in emerging markets countries. The Chapter 22 case, *Gilead Sciences (A): The Gilead Access Program for HIV Drugs,* concerns the company's attempts to make its HIV/AIDS drugs accessible in low income countries.

-- C A S E S --
Tesco PLC in India?

Introduction

India represented an attractive opportunity for retailers. With 1.1 billion people, more than half of whom are under 25 years of age, and a dearth of major retail chains the market in India presented tremendous opportunities for global retailers. The retail market had sales of $200 billion in 2005 and was growing rapidly with a projected market potential of $300 billion in 2010. The organized sector, consisting of establishments with 10 or more employees, accounted for only 3 percent of sales, but was projected to account for 10 percent of sales by 2010. The unorganized sector consisted of nearly 11 million outlets, including kirana shops and other small stores, with only 4 percent having over 500 sq ft. of retail space.[29] Some 21 million people were employed in retailing.

The booming economy and the absence of major retail chains provided opportunity to both domestic and foreign firms. The entry of foreign retailers, however, was limited by restrictions on foreign direct investment (FDI) in retailing. India had gradually been removing its restriction on FDI in other sectors but had not done so in retailing because of concerns about the fate of small retailers. Some restrictions had recently been relaxed as in the case of single-brand retailers, and removal of restrictions on FDI in retailing was inevitable. But when that would occur was unclear.

Most of the large industrial groups in India were scrambling to enter the retailing sector before the FDI restrictions were lifted and the global retailers could enter the market. In 2006 Reliance Industries, the largest business group in India, announced that it would invest $6 billion over 5 years to open 1,500 convenience stores and 1,000 hypermarkets. Chairman Mukesh Ambani said the strategy was to establish "a pan-India footprint of multi-format retail outlets" with large rural hubs to purchase produce and dairy products directly from farmers as part of its "field-to-fork" control of the supply chain.[30] This posed a substantial problem for the global retailers. They could enter the market now with constraints on their investments and hence on their organizational forms, or they could wait for further relaxations of the FDI regulations.

Tesco PLC was the largest retailer in the United Kingdom and accounted for £1 in every £7 spent on food. Tesco had begun selling nonfood items and had a successful Internet sales operation. In 1992 Tesco began diversifying internationally to take advantage of market opportunities. By 2005 over 50 percent of Tesco's floor space and over 20 percent of its sales were from outside the UK. Chairman Sir Terry Leahy said, "Our international

business is our biggest opportunity, both for growth and delivering returns."[31] In the year ending 2006 Tesco's revenue was £39.5 billion, and after-tax profit was £1.576 billion. Tesco's core purpose was "to create value for customers to earn their lifetime loyalty," and its strategy was based on six elements: be flexible, act local, keep focus, be multi-format, develop capability, and build brands.

FDI in India

As the Indian government relaxed restrictions, FDI had increased from $8.28 billion in 2003 to $25.66 billion in 2006. FDI up to 51 percent was allowed in 35 high-priority industries, and most recently, FDI had been allowed in real estate. FDI was still banned in four industries: retail trading (with the exception of single-brand retailing), atomic energy, lottery business, and gambling and betting. The restrictions on retailing reflected the potential threat to small shop and stall retailers. In contrast to India, Thailand, for example, had allowed global retailers to enter, and 7 of the top 10 global retailers operated there. China also allowed global retailers, including Carrefour, Wal-Mart, and 7-Eleven, to invest in the country.

FDI also was capped at "24 percent in the equity capital for units manufacturing items reserved for small scale industries." The small-scale industries restriction reflected the sensitivity of competition for small businesses in India and the priority given to growth in those businesses.[32]

Foreign retailers were banned from using FDI for direct sales to individuals, and multi-brand retailers were barred from owning and operating their own stores until at least 2009, and then only if the FDI restrictions were changed.

In lieu of FDI, foreign retailers could use franchise arrangements. International retailers, including Marks and Spencer, Shoprite Checkers, Reebok, Nike, Cartier, Woolworths (Australia), Debenhams, and McDonald's used franchising to operate in India.

FDI was unrestricted in wholesale operations that supplied registered retailers, but Metro Group, operator of Metro Cash-and-Carry GmbH wholesale stores for business customers, was the only firm to have entered the Indian market. Metro had begun operations in Bangalore, and in 2006 announced it would invest € 300 million to expand to 33 cities.

---

[29]www.thehindubusinessline.com, June 1, 2006.
[30]*Sunday Telegraph,* August 13, 2006.

[31]*The Independent,* October 4, 2006.
[32]"The present policy of encouraging growth of small scale industries is based on several promotional measures—one of these is reservation of products for exclusive manufacture in the small scale sector in areas where there is techno-economic jurisdiction for such an approach. Large/medium units can, however, manufacture such reserved items provided they undertake to export 50% or more of their production." www.smallindustryindia.com.

Beginning in 2006 single-brand retailers were allowed to use FDI up to 51 percent. For example, Lladro of Spain announced a joint venture with SPA Agencies to open Lladro India stores to sell its porcelain products. The French boutique retailer Fendi, owned by the Louis Vuitton and Moet Hennessey (LVMH) Group, announced a 51 percent joint venture with Fun Fashion India to establish a single-brand retail chain. The government approved the FDI, but even for a single-brand retailing venture added restrictions. The LVMH venture had proposed selling ballpoint pens, umbrellas, and cuff links, which were items reserved for small-scale industries and hence under the jurisdiction of the Ministry of Small-Scale Industries. The Ministry attached a rider to the approval of the FDI requiring LVMH to export at least 50 percent of any product manufactured in India. The government also imposed a requirement that if the joint venture sought to add another brand for sale it would have to obtain a new approval from the Foreign Investment Promotion Board (FIPB).[33]

Approval for FDI ventures was the responsibility of the FIPB. Approval for investments up to 51 percent in high priority industries was automatic upon application to the Reserve Bank of India.

In addition to restrictions on FDI, the organized retail sector faced a variety of regulations. The organized sector was prohibited from using hourly or part-time employees. The organized sector typically had lifetime employment, pension benefits, and union representation.

Retailers also faced differing regulations across the states, since the Shops and Establishments Acts, which regulated retailing, were implemented at the state level. For example, some states restricted certain types of promotions including prize offerings used to attract customers. Some states required retailers to close one day a week. Minimum wages also differed across the states.

Carrefour, the world's second largest retailer, had explored entering the Indian market but in 2004 announced, "We have postponed our plans for India. It is an important market and we hope to revisit it at a later date. We don't want to comment further." Carrefour had explored a franchise arrangement, but had rejected that route. The company was thought to want to retain direct control over operations.

Nonmarket Forces

Local merchants feared being driven out of business by major retailers, and they put nonmarket pressure on the governing Congress Party. Over 41 million people were unemployed in India, and the small retailers argued that many of those in retailing would lose their jobs if FDI restrictions were relaxed and foreign retailers entered. For example, "The West Bengal Minister in charge of Commerce and Industry, Mr. Nirupam Sen, has lauded the

city-based [Kolkata] Merchants' Chamber of Commerce (MCC) for 'categorically' expressing its reservations against free flow of foreign direct investment in the retail sector."[34] The MCC president argued that the state should not allow FDI where it had the potential to displace employment. Arvind Singhal, chairman of Tecknopak, a retail consultancy, said, "Shopkeepers are asking, 'is Reliance going to kill us?'" Jageshwar Prasad, who operated a vegetable shop and pavement stall, said, "It will affect us very much because [Reliance] will take both the rich and the poor customers with lower prices."[35] Montek Singh Ahluwalia, the deputy chairman of the government's Planning Commission, stated, "I do believe (that) the introduction of modern retailing is very crucial and overdue . . . (However) I want to emphasize one thing. FDI in retail is not in my view critical in the next few years to achieve 8.5 percent growth."[36]

Mohan Guruswamy, the head of the Center for Policy Alternatives, in Delhi said, "You can't stop the Chinese forever and you can't stop Wal-Mart forever, but you can take it in phases." Referring to the $28 billion in goods Wal-Mart bought in China, he said, "that pipeline is directly set up to come into India, and could be set to wipe out small industry."[37]

The Ministry of Commerce and Industry was responsible for initiating proposals for changes in FDI regulations. Referring to the FDI policy in the retail sector, the Minister of Commerce and Industry, Kamal Nath, stated, "We need a model that doesn't replace existing retailers."[38] Assocham, the Associated Chambers of Commerce and Industry of India, opposed the elimination of the regulations, but supported allowing 51 percent FDI.

Local retailers also used nonmarket strategies against foreign retailers. Retailers complained that Metro Cash & Carry was selling to retail customers in violation of its licensing conditions. The retailers were led by the Federation of Associations of Maharashtra state (FAM), which was "supported by the Karnataka and Tamil chambers of commerce at the state level and by the Confederation of India Industry at the national industry chamber level."[39] FAM renewed its criticism in 2003 when Metro launched a membership drive with loyalty cards. FAM claimed that the cards had been issued to groups not covered by its license. The communist newspaper, the People's Democracy, claimed that loyalty cards were being issued to employees of the groups and that Metro was "indulging in nothing but retail trade."[40] The Karnataka government, backed by the central

[33]*India Business Insight*, September 2, 2006.

[34]*Business Wire*, August 31, 2006.
[35]*Economist*, November 4, 2006.
[36]*Statesman (India)*, August 30, 2006.
[37]*San Francisco Chronicle*, November 25, 2006.
[38]*Economist*, November 4, 2006.
[39]Jayanthi Iyengar, "China, India Confront the Wal-Marts," Asia Times Online, www.atimes.com, 2004.
[40]Jayanthi Iyengar, "China, India Confront the Wal-Marts," Asia Times Online, www.atimes.com, 2004.

government, filed a writ petition against Metro in a Bangalore court. Muralidhara Rao, national convener of the Swadeshi Jagaran Manch, the nationalist wing of the Bharatiya Janata Party, criticized Metro in a speech to the Karnataka Chambers of Commerce and Industry. He said, "Our market is an asset [that should not be] sold to multinationals."[41]

Local merchants had also taken direct action. The Supreme Court of India had ordered the city of New Delhi to enforce its long-ignored zoning laws which required closing 40,000 illegal shops that lined roadways. An estimated 5,000 shopkeepers broke through police lines to protest at the city's assembly building.[42]

The Opportunity

A study by McKinsey & Co. and the Confederation of Indian Industry reported that a number of major international retailers, including Tesco, Kingfisher, Carrefour, and Ahold, were contemplating entering the Indian market. The report projected that the retail sector would reach $300 billion by 2010 if restrictions on FDI were relaxed. A study by AT Kearney concluded that India was the most attractive market for international retailers. It projected that sales in the organized sector would increase from $7 billion in 2006 to $21 billion in 2010. Technopak, a retail consultancy, estimated that the share of the organized sector would expand to 16–18 percent by 2010. This estimate depended on the strategies of the large global retailers.[43]

Modern retailing had begun to boom with the growth of shopping malls in metropolitan areas. Large domestic companies, such as Tata, RPG group, ITC, and HLL, had seized the opportunity in retailing and developed chains, primarily supermarkets. For example, the Tata group had the West Side chain, and Foodworld was owned by RPG.[44] Infiniti Retail of the Tata group announced an alliance with Woolworths to establish a retail chain, Croma, for consumer durables.[45] Woolworths owned the wholesale company in India that would supply the Croma stores. Pantaloon Retail and Spencer's were accelerating the expansion of their operations.

In 2006 Carrefour resumed exploring alternatives to enter the Indian market and was in discussions with the Landmark Group of Dubai.

Wal-Mart received approval from the government to set up an office in India to conduct market research. Spokesperson Amy Wyatt of Wal-Mart stated, "India is an emerging retail market in which we have a high interest. We continue to monitor the Indian government's policy on FDI and continue our market research."[46] Wal-Mart was rumored to be in discussions with DLF Universal, India's largest real estate developer. Wal-Mart said that its recent sale of its 85 German stores to Metro AG provided capital to invest in emerging markets. Wal-Mart had also sold its 16 stores in South Korea for $882 million.

Some Indian firms were actively seeking to partner with a foreign firm entering the retail sector. Bharti Enterprises had initiated discussions with Tesco and Wal-Mart about forming a venture. Sunil Mittal, chairman of the Bharti Group, said, "Government policy allows foreign equity in back-end wholesale and logistics and in real estate, so we'll do a joint venture with a foreign partner in those areas, and we will own the retail business 100 percent till the government allows FDI there, and then we'll do a joint venture there with our partner."[47] In late November 2006 Bharti and Wal-Mart announced that they would form a joint venture that would be responsible for logistics, supply-chain management, distribution, and wholesale operations, and Bharti would own the retail stores that sold directly to consumers.

In 2003 Tesco entered the markets in Japan and Turkey, and in 2004 it entered China and had 39 stores by 2006. In 2006 it decided to enter the U.S. market with a chain of convenience stores patterned after its successful Express format. India was the last remaining major market opportunity, and Tesco had to decide whether to enter the market, how to enter it, and when to do it. ■

Preparation Questions

1. How attractive are the opportunities given the FDI regulations in retailing?
2. Would it be better to delay entry until the FDI restrictions are eliminated?
3. What strategy should Tesco adopt for entering the Indian market?
4. Should Tesco adopt a nonmarket strategy to influence the pace of relaxation of FDI regulations in India? Should it implement the policy in India or through the European Union and the World Trade Organization?

[41]Jayanthi Iyengar, "China, India Confront the Wal-Marts," Asia Times Online, www.atimes.com, 2004. The Communist Party of India (Marxist) had the third largest number of seats in Parliament.
[42]San Francisco Chronicle, November 25, 2006.
[43]Economist, November 4, 2006.
[44]S. Majumder, "FDI in Retailing: India as a Supermarket," Business Line, September 17, 2002.
[45]Business Times Singapore, October 5, 2006.
[46]Press Trust of India, August 1, 2006.
[47]Economist, November 4, 2006.

Social Entrepreneurship: Banco Compartamos

In April 2007 Carlos Danel and Carlos Labarthe took Banco Compartamos public in an IPO that valued the bank at $1.53 billion. Compartamos had been formed in 1990 as a nongovernmental organization by Gente Nueva, a Catholic service organization, to aid the poor in rural areas of Chiapas and Oaxaca, Mexico. In 2001 the two Carloses took the organization private as an SOFOL, a non-deposit-taking financial services company. At that time Compartamos received capital from international development organizations, including ACCION International which provided $1 million for an 18 percent share, and the IFC, the private sector arm of the World Bank. The IFC also provided an initial loan and later provided a partial credit guarantee for a $47 million bond offering.[48]

In the IPO the executives of the bank received $150 million of the $450 million proceeds, and ACCION sold half its share for $135 million, which it invested in new initiatives to help the poor. In 2007 Compartamos had profits of $81.5 million and a loan portfolio of $400 million with only 1.36 percent of its loans nonperforming. Compartamos had become one of Mexico's most successful banks, with an average return on equity of 40 percent since becoming for-profit. Danel was named a Young Global Leader by the World Economic Forum.

Compartamos' business was microfinance. After taking the bank private, it increased its customers from 60,000 to 839,000 in 2007, and its goal for 2008 was 1 million customers.[49] The bank made loans without collateral to groups composed of friends and neighbors, 99 percent of whom were women.[50] The group then served to monitor the repayments by its members. For example, a group in Villa de Vázques met weekly to plan borrowings and repayments. Micaela Rivera and her mother Alejandra Abúndez had borrowed $3,550 for animal feed and supplies for their homemade cheese business, and another woman had borrowed to start and expand a small restaurant in her home.

Compartamos had 252 service centers in 27 Mexican states and hired over 1,000 new employees in 2006. Its mission statement read,

> Compartamos is a social company committed to the people. We generate development opportunities within the lowest economic segment, based on innovative and efficient models on a wide scale as well as transcending values that create external and internal culture, fulfilling permanent trusting relationships and contributing to a better world.

The interest rates charged by Compartamos were nearly 90 percent, 15 percent of which was a tax. The Mexican nonprofit social service organization Pro Mujer had interest rates only a little lower than those of Compartamos, but the interest rates were far higher than the average of 25 to 40 percent for microfinance in other countries. Compartamos reported that its interest rates had been reduced by 30 percentage points over the past 5 years as a result of efficiencies that were passed along to borrowers. Costs of operating in Mexico were high. For example, Compartamos agents collected payments on loans weekly, riding busses in rural areas to reach the borrowers. Compartamos employees also met with individual borrowing groups.

Labarthe explained the importance of being able to raise capital rather than relying on donations to fund lending, "It's marvelous to have one creditor, but it's marvelous to have one million creditors, and that's where we really start to change the face of opportunity."[51] Maria Otero of ACCION noted, "This is one strategy that doesn't remain small and beautiful."[52] The two Carloses argued that in a middle-income country like Mexico it was better to resort to the capital markets to raise funds than compete for donations. Compartamos' target customer base was the 14 million Mexican households without access to banking services.

The critics of Compartamos were vicious and vociferous.[53] Muhammad Yunus, the pioneer who started microfinance and received the 2006 Nobel Peace Prize, said, "They're absolutely on the wrong track. Their priorities are screwed up. When you discuss microcredit, don't bring Compartamos into it. Microcredit was created to fight the money lender, not to become the money lender."[54] Yunus also said, "A true microcredit organization must keep its interest rate as close to the cost of funds as possible. There is no justification for interest rates in the range of 100 percent. My own experience has convinced me that microcredit interest rates can be comfortably under the cost of funds plus 10 percent, or plus 15 percent at most."[55] Alex Counts, president of the Grameen Foundation, held that Compartamos' borrowers "were generating the profits but were excluded from them."[56]

Sam Daley-Harris, head of the Microcredit Summit Campaign, said, "Microfinance started in the 1970s with a focus on using this breakthrough to help end poverty. Now it is in great danger of being about how

---

[48]The IFC subsequently provided a $50 million financing package.
[49]Seguros Banamex began offering low-cost life insurance to Compartamos customers in 2006.
[50]The bank also began to make loans to individuals.

[51]*New York Times,* April 5, 2008.
[52]*New York Times,* April 5, 2008.
[53]MicroCredit.org hosted an online debate on Compartamos.
[54]*BusinessWeek,* December 13, 2007.
[55]PRNewswire, December 18, 2007.
[56]*New York Times,* April 5, 2008.

well the investors and the microfinance institutions are doing and not about ending poverty."[57] The microfinance industry group, Consultative Group to Assist the Poor, housed at the World Bank, estimated that 23.6 percent of Compartamos' interest went to profits and that the bank's return on assets was 45 percent compared to an average of 15 percent for Mexican banks. Charles Westerfield, a consultant and critic of Compartamos, said, "Not only are they making obscene profits off poor people, they are in danger of tarnishing the rest of the industry. Compartamos is the first but they won't be the last."[58]

Danel noted, "We don't only see ourselves as a specialist in microfinance but also as the builder of an industry."[59] Bob Patillo of the fund Gray Ghost observed, "This has got Wall Street's eye, London's eye, Geneva's eye—to have one out there to say that if all the dots got connected this can be quite profitable."[60]

Compartamos means "let's share" in Spanish. ■

SOURCE: This case was prepared by David P. Baron from public sources, including the article "Microloans, Big Profits," by Elizabeth Malkin, *New York Times,* April 5, 2008. Copyright © 2008 by the Board of Trustees of the Leland Stanford Junior University. All rights reserved. Reprinted with permission.

Preparation Questions

1. Why do the banks in Mexico not serve the poor?
2. What, if anything, are the advantages of Compartamos relative to traditional microfinance organizations that operate as described by Muhammad Yunus?
3. Are the critics of Compartamos right? Should the company lower its interest rates substantially?
4. Should more for-profit microfinance companies be formed? If you were to form such a company, what would you do differently?

---

[57]*New York Times,* April 5, 2008.
[58]*New York Times,* April 5, 2008.

[59]*New York Times,* April 5, 2008.
[60]*New York Times,* April 5, 2008.

Social Entrepreneurship: Kiva

Jessica Jackley moved to California in 2001 and began working for the Stanford Business School. In 2003 Muhammad Yunus, the Bangladesh economist who in 2006 would receive the Nobel Peace Prize, spoke at the school about an innovative program to provide loans to beggars who had been certified with a Grameen identify card. Jessica thought microfinance "was the coolest thing in the world."[61] Shortly thereafter she went to Kenya, Uganda, and Tanzania to interview recipients of microfinance loans. In 2004 her husband of a year, Mark Flannery, also went to Africa. He commented, "I liked the independent spirit of an informal economy. It's much more fun than formal economies. You could buy an entire business there for $500—*that* was exciting."[62]

The Flannerys began to discuss how they could contribute to microfinance, and an Internet approach seemed natural. In October 2005 they ran a pilot trial with eight Ugandan entrepreneurs, as borrowers were called. The Flannerys sent e-mail to their wedding guest list announcing the opportunity to lend, and over the weekend all eight were funded. They also sent out a press release that was posted on Daily Kos, and $10,000 was raised in one day. The first person-to-person micro-lending organization had been born.

At the time Jessica was enrolled in the Stanford MBA program, and Mark quit his job at Tivo to work full-time on Kiva. Mark explained, "We had no idea what we were getting into. Legally, it's a minefield."[63] For example, if they took funding over the Internet, would the financing arrangements be considered securities subject to regulation by the Securities and Exchange Commission? Jennifer was able to find legal assistance, and Kiva was established as a 501(c)(3) nonprofit organization.

A year later Kiva was featured in a 15-minute segment on PBS, and it was deluged with funds. The Flannerys also appeared on *Oprah* and other television programs, and Kiva was featured in Bill Clinton's book *Giving: How Each of Us Can Change the World.* Most loans were funded in less than a day. Kiva also introduced gift certificates, and sold $2.2 million of them over the 2007 Christmas holiday season.

Kiva recruited as president Premil Shah from PayPal, who obtained a commitment from the company to handle Kiva's transactions without charge. Shah had become interested in microfinance as an undergraduate at

---

[61]*Stanford Business,* November/December, 2007.
[62]*Stanford Business,* November/December, 2007.

[63]*Stanford Business,* November/December, 2007.

Stanford University and had worked in India for a micro-finance organization. Shah commented on the organization of Kiva, "We have all the complexity of being a Silicon Valley start-up that is growing real fast, coupled with the complexity of international financial transactions. It's a complicated model, with a lot of due diligence and screening required."[64]

Lenders received no interest on their loans, but their principal was repaid and lenders could take their funds or relend them to other borrowers. Most of the lenders reloaned their funds. Although lenders received no interest, Kiva hoped to be able to provide a small return to lenders in the near future. Interest payments would also help with the problem that ". . . some causes are more popular than others. Widows in Africa are almost always funded immediately, but men in Central America often have to wait longer. The Kiva team plans to experiment with higher interest rates on less popular causes to help attract funders."[65]

Kiva, which means "unity," "agreement," or "concord" in Swahili, matched lenders with entrepreneurs over the Internet. Fiona Ramsey of Kiva explained the role the organization played, "People are by nature generous and want to help others, but they want to do it in a way . . . where they can really see how they're making an impact on somebody's life. We all see [the philanthropic work that] Bill Gates and Oprah do, and we'd love to do that ourselves. But few of us can afford it." She added, "Right now, we can't offer a financial return on your investment. But we can offer you an emotional return."[66]

The matching of lenders and entrepreneurs took place on www.kiva.org, which not only provided the match but also established a personal link. Shah explained that people do not give to beggars on the street or charities over the telephone because of a lack of transparency. He said, "I don't know where that money's going to go. I don't know if it will be well used. So we back off on giving."[67] Through Kiva, lenders could see the persons to whom they were lending as well as descriptions of the use of the loans and learn about the differences the loans could make in their lives. Approximately 100 entrepreneurs were listed at any one time. Lenders chose how much and to whom to lend. Lenders received e-mail progress reports on the use of the loans, and entrepreneurs made monthly payments on the loans. Kiva later decided to limit to $25 the amount any one lender could lend to a single entrepreneur, so that more people had a chance to lend to the person.

Kiva did not select the entrepreneurs but instead relied on field partners—microfinance organizations

with people on the ground in various countries. Field partners identified and screened entrepreneurs, and funds were sent by Kiva to the field partner, who passed them on to the entrepreneur. The field partner administered the loans, collected the monthly payments, and remitted them to Kiva. In some cases the field partners visited borrowers on a daily basis by bicycle. Field partners set the interest rates on loans, which overall averaged 22 percent. The rates varied considerably from 4 percent to 50 percent. Rates in Latin America were the highest but were less than those charged by money lenders, which were as high as 100 percent. The interest payments were retained by the field partner to cover costs. As of the spring of 2008 Kiva had 96 field partners in 45 countries, although not all partners were active.

Loans were short term with most maturities between 6 and 12 months. Entrepreneurs could borrow again, and their credit histories were displayed on the Internet page next to their biography and planned use of the loan. In addition to a picture and information about the entrepreneur, the Internet page displayed information about the field partner, including its risk rating, total loans, time with Kiva, delinquency rate, and default rate.

On its Risk and Due Diligence page Kiva warned lenders about the potential risks associated with their lending. Risks were associated with the borrower, the field partner, and the country. Loans were made in countries such as Afghanistan and Iraq, which posed risks. Kiva's relations with field partners could also be subject to risk such as fraud or embezzlement, and each field partner was either active, paused, or closed. Entrepreneurs also posed risks ranging from uncontrolled events like a bad crop to diversion of the funds. Fiona Ramsey of Kiva observed, however, "We have a perception of the poor as a [poor] credit risk, but actually they're a very good credit risk. The poor are motivated to be successful. Usually, this is their only chance for a loan."[68]

As of the spring of 2008 Kiva had 27 employees and 250 volunteers, had funded loans of $27.2 million, and reported a repayment rate of 99.67 percent. Kiva's operating expenses were covered by donations by individuals and foundations. Lenders could donate 10 percent of their funds to Kiva for operating expenses, and those donations provided the bulk of its funding. Silicon Valley firms also assisted with operations.

The limits on Kiva's growth were not in obtaining funds but rather in identifying borrowers and maintaining integrity in the lending process. Field partners had difficulty expanding because their work required people on the ground to visit entrepreneurs and verify the needs of prospective borrowers, distribute funds,

[64]*Stanford Business,* November/December, 2007.
[65]*BusinessWeek,* July 31, 2006.
[66]*Los Angeles Times,* October 18, 2007.
[67]*Toronto Star,* June 14, 2007.
[68]*Wall Street Journal,* March 20, 2008.

and collect payments. Kiva monitored its field partners and gave them a rating of one to five stars. The maximum amount Kiva provided was $100,000 a month for a five-star partner and $10,000 a month for a one-star partner. Finding field partners was time consuming, requiring considerable due diligence and financial and reference checks. The objective was to find reputable and reliable partners, so as to maintain the integrity of the Kiva system. ■

Preparation Questions

1. What roles does the Internet play in the success of Kiva?
2. Identify the management challenges Kiva faces.
3. What are the limits to the growth of Kiva?
4. Are there additional roles or services that Kiva could provide to help the poor?
5. What potential threats does Kiva face?

MTN Group Limited

Introduction

In May 2008 MTN Group, a very successful South African wireless telephone company, began exclusive discussions with Reliance Communications Ltd., the second largest wireless company in India, regarding possible business combinations including a merger. The previous month discussions between MTN and Bharti Airtel Ltd., India's largest wireless company, had collapsed, reportedly because MTN balked at becoming a subsidiary of Bharti. MTN served 68 million customers in Africa and the Middle East and had a market capitalization of $32 billion.[69] Reliance Communications served 48 million customers and had a market capitalization of $26 billion. Reliance Chairman Anil Ambani said a combination "would provide investors, customers, and the people of both companies a unique and global platform for exponential growth."[70] The day of the announcement of the discussions the share prices of both companies fell by over 5 percent.

The two companies operated in different markets with Reliance Communications operating in India and MTN operating in 21 countries in Africa and the Middle East. The two companies had somewhat different strengths according to observers. MTN was experienced in entering new national markets and in efficiently building infrastructure. Reliance Communications was experienced in serving very poor customers in rural areas, and its average monthly revenue per subscriber was $8.80 a month. MTN's average customer spent less than $20 a month on wireless service, compared to $40–50 a month in Europe and the United States.

Regardless of whether MTN entered a combination with Reliance Communications, it had to deal with challenges in its ongoing operations and evaluate opportunities in emerging markets in which it was not yet present.

MTN Group Limited

MTN began in 1994 with the founding of the cellular telephone company M-Cell, which was 25 percent owned by MTN Holdings. Through internal growth and acquisitions the company grew rapidly from 800 employees in 1997 to 20,000 in 2008. In 2001 MTN acquired licenses in Nigeria and built a nationwide microwave transmission system. It continued its expansion in Africa with operations in Rwanda, Swaziland, Uganda, and Ghana. Cellular telephones were popular in Africa because of the lack of access to land-line telecommunications in many countries. In 2005 MTN paid $5.5 billion for Investcom LLC of Lebanon, which provided 21 million subscribers and entrance to the Middle East and North Africa.

In 2008 MTN had operations in the following countries: South Africa, Botswana, Ghana, Nigeria, Zambia, Cameroon, Ghana, Sudan, Uganda, Côte d'Ivoire, Benin, Syria, Afghanistan, Iran, Swaziland, Rwanda, Cyprus, Guinea-Bissau, Guinea-Conakry, Republic of Congo, and Yemen. The company was organized in three geographic regions: South and East Africa (SEA), West and Central Africa (WECA), and the Middle East and North Africa (MENA). In 2007 19 million of its subscribers and 43 percent of its revenues were in SEA, 28 million and 43 percent in WECA, and 14 million and 14 percent in MENA. MTN's EBITDA increased by 43 percent in 2007 resulting in an after tax profit of R11.9 ($1.6) billion on revenue of R73.1 ($9.7) billion. MTN's strongest growth was in South Africa and Nigeria. In its marketing MTN went to the people, using vans in rural areas and selling its prepaid phones at traffic lights.

---

[69]For comparison, the largest U.S. wireless company, AT&T Wireless, served 71.4 million customers.
[70]*Wall Street Journal,* May 27, 2008.

MTN provided mobile telephone service along with the following enhanced applications: Data Solutions, BlackBerry, International Roaming, Banking, EVD, Mobile TV, Me2U, and CallerTunes. MTN also had begun to invest in broadband in Nigeria and had acquired an Internet service provider in Cameroon.

One component of MTN's strategy was to build and rely on local talent in its operations in each country. Another component was to have local shareholder participation in its national operations, but MTN always maintained a controlling interest. In Uganda it had increased local shareholder participation to 5 percent and in Côte d'Ivoire to 40 percent.

MTN also embraced social responsibility. Mrs. Amina Oyagbola of the MTN Foundation explained, "Corporate Social Responsibility is an integral part of MTN's business strategy. As you know we set up the MTN Foundation to focus on implementing our CSR programmes. To date, MTN is the only organization in the telecom industry that sets aside a percentage of its earnings, annually to CSI (corporate social investment) initiatives in which the MTN executes."[71]

In 2007 MTN introduced "21 Days of Y'ello Care" in Nigeria and the other countries in which it operated. Its staff performed a wide variety of community services in addition to their work obligations. MTN Nigeria CEO Ahamad Farroukh also apologized for quality of service problems, "My firm assurance to you is that despite the infrastructural constraints we face, we remain firmly committed to ensuring that the quality of service on the network continues to improve. In the past nine months, we have embarked on one of the most aggressive network expansion programmes anywhere in the world. We are building dozens more of base station controllers, and several mobile switching centres."[72]

MTN also contributed R5 million for the relief efforts for refugees who had fled to South Africa from countries such as Zimbabwe. Some South Africans had attacked the refugees in the camps they had set up.

MTN was committed to sustainability, which for MTN meant:[73]

- Promoting ethical responsibility and sound corporate governance practices
- Providing a safe working environment in which the health of employees is protected and their opportunities for self-development are enhanced
- Promoting cultural diversity and equity in the workplace
- Minimising adverse environmental impacts
- Providing opportunities for social and economic development within the communities we operate

MTN was proud to have been chosen as the global sponsor of the 2010 FIFA World Cup to be held in South Africa.

Opportunities and Risks

Although the risks of operating in emerging markets were substantial, those markets provided tremendous opportunities. Market penetration of mobile telephones in Africa was 29 percent, 34 percent in India, 70 percent in the United States, and more than 90 percent in Europe. Because of poor transportation infrastructures and the low penetration rate of Internet service, banking transactions were now beginning to be conducted by cell phones in emerging markets countries. In South Africa many wireless customers use their handsets for even small transactions such as services and retail purchases. In much of Africa many people did not have bank accounts, but the opportunity to make transactions remotely by cell phone could lead them to open a bank account. Moreover, cell phones could be used to make payments on microfinance loans rather than requiring the lender or the borrower to make a physical trip.

One limit to growth in emerging markets was the price of a handset. The cheapest handset was made by Motorola and sold for $30, but with half the people in the world living on less than $2 a day even that price could be prohibitive. To reach rural customers some wireless companies had set up "telephone ladies" who rented their handsets, one customer at a time.

Entry into new markets required a license, and MTN both bid for licenses and acquired licenses from other parties. MTN faced competition from other wireless companies in Africa as well as companies from outside Africa. The largest wireless company in Africa was Orascom of Egypt with 71 million customers. Vodafone had a subsidiary in Egypt and operated in 8 countries in Africa, and Orange had investments in 13 African countries. Vodafone also owned Vodacom, a wireless company in South Africa.[74] U.S. firms had shown little recent interest in Africa. Robert Chaphe, who was CEO of MTN from 1995 to 2002, explained, "Many big U.S. telcos eventually lost interest in these markets: they were too small. Now U.S. telcos see more opportunity closer to home. After all, risk ratios are lower in Kansas than in Africa."[75]

In some countries a government-owned or regulated company provided fixed-line service and wireless service as well. Countries belonging to the World Trade Organization (WTO) were required to open their telecommunications industries and issuing a second license for wireless service was a straightforward way of meeting this obligation. For example, Saudi Arabia joined the WTO in 2005, and auctioned a second wireless license.

[71]*Africa News,* June 9, 2008.
[72]*Africa News,* June 9, 2008.
[73]www.mtn.com.

[74]*New York Times,* May 27, 2008.
[75]*New York Times,* May 27, 2008.

In 2007 it auctioned a third license for wireless service, as well as a license for fixed-line service.

MTN outbid Altech for Internet service provider Verizon Business in South Africa. MTN's competitors immediately complained about antitrust violations. Angus MacRobert, CEO of Internet Solutions, said, "We have seen how MTN operates around interconnection and mobile data and it is anticompetitive. This is going to intensify it."[76]

Wireless companies in South Africa were subject to reselling of airtime. The Competition Tribunal had scolded Vodacom for trying to eliminate resellers. MTN faced a decision on whether to block an acquisition bid by the Huge Group for reseller iTalk Cellular, which was 41 percent owned by MTN. MTN could do so by buying the remaining 59 percent. CEO Anton Potgieter of Huge said, "It's been such a game of poker that it's hard to know how hard MTN will try to push it, but I believe we have the moral and legal high ground."[77]

The regulatory systems in each of the countries in which it operated posed a variety of challenges. For example, MTN had experienced problems in repatriating funds from Ghana and Syria, and Benin had suspended the MTN network for 3 months in 2007. MTN described the regulatory environment:[78]

> Telecommunications is a regulated industry and MTN engages actively with governments and regulators in all the countries in which it operates. MTN respects the fact that the frequency spectrum is a natural and national resource, and that the management thereof is subject to much public scrutiny.
>
> MTN strives to participate fully in dialogue with governments and regulators on policy and legislative issues and frameworks. While we will lobby for fair treatment in the business interest, we respect the laws of countries in which we operate and the terms of our licence conditions. We endeavour to fulfill the terms of our license obligations, and to go the extra mile in facilitating universal access to communications services. We will not in any way compromise the national interest of countries where we do business. We also participate actively in industry forums that promote improved health and safety issues relating to mobile telephony.

A major problem for wireless companies operating in emerging markets was taxation. The billings systems of wireless companies provided an opportunity for countries to raise funds at little cost to the government by simply taxing wireless phone service and requiring the operator to remit the taxes to the government. Particularly in Africa where most countries were strapped for revenue, taxing wireless service was an opportunity too good to pass up. In addition to a value-added tax countries imposed special levies on wireless service. According to the GSM Association, an industry association, the tax on wireless service represented 47 percent of mobile phone service charges in the Congo, 35 percent in Ghana, 27 percent in South Africa, and 22 percent in Nigeria. Countries faced a tradeoff, however.[79] Wireless phones increased productivity and business activity, so a tax increase could reduce economic growth.[80]

Another challenge was to keep infrastructure costs low to be able to price to attract customers lower on the pyramid. Serving customers in a new country or expanding into new areas in a county required building infrastructure. In Nigeria MTN had not only to build base stations and transmission facilities but also its own power supplies. Some carriers had begun to experiment with new business models, such as franchising parts of the system. For example, Nokia Siemens Networks has been exploring a model in which a local entrepreneur or a village would own a base station and handle service and billings.

The Business Combination

One complication to a business combination with Reliance Communications was that billions of dollars of cash might have to be raised to complete the deal. U.S. banks were unlikely to be able to participate in the funding because of U.S. restrictions on facilitating business in Iran. MTN and its local partner Irancell had 6 million customers. Moreover, MTN had 2.1 million customers in the Sudan, and the European Union and the United States had imposed restrictions on companies doing business in that country. The United States also had financial restrictions on companies doing business in Syria, where MTN had 3.1 million customers.[81]

South Africa had regulations governing mergers. Any offer to purchase more than 35 percent of a company required the purchaser to make an open offer for the rest of the shares. India capped foreign direct investment in a telecommunications company at 74 percent, and a purchase of 15 percent of a company required an open offer for the remainder of the shares.[82] Ambani thus could obtain 34.9 percent of MTN, while retaining a share of Reliance Communications. The two companies were bargaining over the exchange of shares. During MTN's negotiations with Bharti, the Indian consumer group Telecom Watchdog had threatened to file a lawsuit to block their merger if a share swap was used in the transaction and violated the FDI restrictions.

[76]*Africa News,* June 6, 2008.
[77]*Africa News,* May 28, 2008.
[78]www.mtn.com.
[79]The GSM Association represented 750 wireless companies operating in 218 countries and territories and serving 82 percent of the world's users.
[80]*Economist,* May 29, 2008.
[81]*International Herald Tribune,* May 27, 2008.
[82]*Times* (London), June 10, 2008.

After discussions were underway between MTN and Reliance Communications, Reliance Industries LTD., whose chairman was Mukesh Ambani, the older brother of Anil, wrote to MTN stating that it had first rights of refusal on acquiring Reliance Communications. A spokesperson for MTN said, "We are aware that something is going on between the two brothers."[83] ■

Preparation Questions

1. Why has MTN been so successful?
2. Identify the risks MTN faces.
3. Why does MTN want local shareholders in the countries in which it operates? Why does it want to staff its operations with locals? Why is corporate social responsibility important to the company?
4. How should MTN deal with the risk of higher taxes on wireless service?

5. Suppose that a license were to be auctioned in Zimbabwe. Assess the opportunities and risks in that country.

---

[83]*New York Times,* June 14, 2008.

C H A P T E R

18

The Political Economy of International Trade Policy

INTRODUCTION

International trade policy is the result of economic and political forces. The principal economic force is the gains from trade, which provide the economic rationale for free trade. The principal political force is the benefits that firms, consumers, employees, and suppliers can obtain through favorable trade policies. The beneficiaries of those policies have incentives to adopt nonmarket strategies to protect and increase those benefits.

Since the Smoot-Hawley Act of 1930, which raised tariffs dramatically and contributed to the depth and duration of the Depression, the United States and other developed countries have supported reductions in tariffs and other barriers to international trade. In the aftermath of World War II, the reductions in trade barriers were largely the result of U.S. hegemony. As other countries recovered from the war and the U.S. share of international trade declined, the principal mechanism for reductions in trade barriers has been multilateral negotiations, most of which have been conducted in the context of the General Agreement on Tariffs and Trade (GATT). In 1995 the World Trade Organization (WTO) was established to encompass GATT and other multilateral agreements. The WTO also provided a continuing forum for addressing trade issues and resolving disputes among nations. In addition, a number of regional trade agreements, such as the North American Free Trade Agreement (NAFTA) and the treaties that established the single market in the European Union, have reduced barriers and increased trade. The United States and other countries also have concluded bilateral agreements to spur trade in services such as air transportation. The result has been a steady, if not uniform, reduction in trade barriers, and the resulting increase in international trade has been dramatic. The current Doha Round of multilateral trade negotiations, however, had stalled as a result of disagreement between developing and developed countries.

Trade policy consists of agreements among countries, domestic laws pertaining to international trade, and procedures for administering those laws and resolving disputes. International trade agreements are the result of bargaining among countries, but the positions from which countries bargain depend on domestic economic considerations and hence on domestic politics. The interactions between international trade policy and domestic politics are illustrated in Figure 18-1. The international negotiations, shown at the top of the figure, and the agreements reached, shown at the bottom, determine the rules of the game for the export and import practices of firms. The competition between imports and domestic production and the opportunities to trade in world markets provide incentives for interests—firms, employees, suppliers, and consumers—to seek support for exports and/or protection from imports. The opportunities to engage in domestic politics and the rights granted under domestic trade laws allow interests to affect trade policy directly by filing trade petitions as well as indirectly through the bargaining positions of their governments in bilateral

FIGURE 18-1   International Trade Policy Process

and multilateral negotiations. Trade policy thus depends not only on government actions but also on the market and nonmarket strategies of private interests. Conversely, international trade policy has important consequences for the market and nonmarket environments of business.

This chapter addresses the political economy of international trade policy, its connection to domestic politics, and the role of business and other interests in those politics. The perspective taken is that the system depicted in Figure 18-1 is animated by the incentives generated in domestic and international markets. Those incentives give rise to nonmarket strategies, implemented in both domestic and international institutional arenas, that shape trade policy. The next section considers the economics of international trade with an emphasis on competitive theory and strategic trade theory. Economic theory does not explain well many of the trade practices of countries, so the following section considers the political economy of international trade policy using the perspective developed in Chapter 6. The chapter also discusses the WTO and the agreements under its purview. The international trade policy of the United States is considered, including an analysis of the political economy of market opening and protectionism, including U.S. efforts to protect the steel industry. Current trade issues are considered, including the current Doha Round of WTO multilateral trade negotiations.

THE ECONOMICS OF INTERNATIONAL TRADE

Competitive Theory

The competitive theory of international trade is based on the *gains from trade*. Those gains are evident in the case of a country that cannot produce a product that its citizens wish to consume. Gains from trade are also evident when one country can produce a good more efficiently than another country, and the latter country can produce a different good more efficiently than can the former country. There are also gains from trade when one country is absolutely more efficient than the other in the production of both goods. That is, even though a country has an absolute disadvantage, gains from trade can be achieved if it produces the good for which it is relatively more efficient and the other country produces the good for which it is relatively more efficient. This result, known as the law of *comparative advantage,* provides the basic rationale for free trade—all countries, even those with an absolute disadvantage, can gain from trade.

The gains from trade can be demonstrated when two countries either determine the terms of their trade through bargaining or trade goods in a competitive market. Consider two countries, each of which can produce two goods, A and B. The production possibilities of each country are characterized by its resources and the technology it uses to produce the goods. To simplify the analysis, suppose that each country has one resource: 12 units of labor. Country I has a technology that requires 2 units of labor to produce 1 unit of A and 1 unit of labor to produce 1 unit of B. Country II can produce 1 unit of A with 1 unit of labor and 1 unit of B with 2 units of labor. These production possibilities are illustrated in Figure 18-2. As the figure illustrates, Country I is more efficient in the production of good B, and Country II is more efficient in the production of good A.

In the absence of trade, the consumption possibilities of each country are its own production possibilities. That is, Country I can produce and consume 12 units of B and none of A, 6 units of A and none of B, or any linear combination of those two outputs. Each country will produce and consume at the point on its production possibility frontier that yields the greatest aggregate well-being of its citizens. To be precise, suppose that the preferences of citizens in each country are identical and that their well-being is measured by the product of the quantities consumed of the two goods. For example, the goods could be bread and butter, and well-being is greatest when there is butter for each loaf of bread. The best combination of consumption is thus an equal amount of each good.

In the absence of trade, referred to as *autarky,* Country I can do no better than to produce and consume 3 units of A and 6 units of B. Analogously, under autarky Country II will produce and consume 6 units of A and 3 units of B. These autarky points are indicated in Figure 18-2 and correspond to levels of well-being of 18 for each country.

Trade benefits a country by allowing consumption to diverge from production. To illustrate this, Figure 18-3 presents the production and consumption possibilities of Countries I and II when they are able to trade. Gains from trade are possible because trade expands the consumption possibilities of each country beyond those of its own production. That is, both countries can benefit if Country I produces more of good B, for which it has an absolute advantage, and Country II produces more of good A, for which it has an absolute advantage. In this example, Country I will specialize in producing 12 units of good B and none of good A, whereas Country II will produce 12 units of A and none of B. Country I then will export 6 units of B and import 6 units of A. Country II's imports and exports will be the opposite of those of Country I. With the trades indicated in the figures, the resulting consumption in each country is 6 units of A and

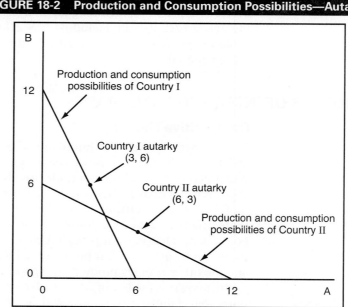

FIGURE 18-2   Production and Consumption Possibilities—Autarky

FIGURE 18-3   Production and Consumption Possibilities with Trade

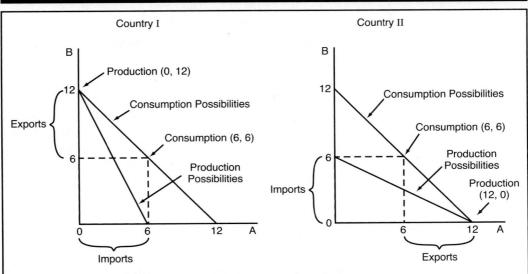

6 units of B. The well-being of each country is 36, so both are better off with trade.[1] Both countries gain from trade.

This example illustrates the gains from trade for the case in which Country I is more efficient (has an absolute advantage) in the production of good B and Country II is more efficient (has an absolute advantage) in the production of good A. Even if Country I is absolutely more efficient in the production of both goods, there are gains from trade. To illustrate this, suppose that Country I's technology is the same as above, but Country II's technology requires 3 units of labor to produce 1 unit of A and 4 units of labor to produce 1 unit of B. In the absence of trade, Country II would produce 2 units of A and 1.5 units of B for a level of well-being of 3. Both countries can gain, however, if, for example, Country II produces 4 units of A and no units of B and Country I produces 2 units of A and 8 units of B. Country II then can trade 2 units of A to Country I for 3 units of B.[2] The well-beings of the two countries are then 20 and 6, respectively, compared with 18 and 3 in the absence of trade. This gain is possible because Country II is relatively more efficient in the production of good A than is Country I. That is, the ratio of the number of units of labor required to produce a unit of A and a unit of B is $3 \div 4 = 0.75$ for Country II, whereas the corresponding ratio for Country I is $2 \div 1 = 2$. Country II thus has a comparative advantage in the production of A even though it has an absolute disadvantage in the production of both goods. Gains from trade thus result from comparative advantage.

Gains from trade are also present if there are differences in the relative prices of untraded factor inputs such as labor. That is, if one country has lower wage rates than another, gains can be achieved from trade. The high-wage country can gain by importing labor-intensive goods from the low-wage country and allocating its high-wage labor to the production of goods for which it has a comparative advantage. Consequently, a country such as the United States, with high labor costs, and a country such as China, with low labor costs, can gain by China producing labor-intensive textiles and apparel for export to the United States and the United States producing capital-intensive machinery for export to China. The United States, however, has for decades restricted textile and apparel imports to protect employment in its domestic industries. The gains

---

[1]This outcome is a competitive market equilibrium in the sense that each country, taking prices as given, produces the quantities of the two goods that maximize its well-being, and each country consumes the quantities it prefers given the prices for the goods. In this example, the price, or rate of exchange, is one unit of A for one unit of B. The value of imports thus equals the value of exports for each country.
[2]Other mutually beneficial trades are also possible. For example, Country II could trade 2 units of A for 2 units of B.

from trade thus are not sufficient to explain the trade policies of countries. That is, politics can intervene in international trade, as indicated in Figure 18-1. The political dimensions of international trade and trade policy are examined in more detail after a consideration of strategic trade theory.

Strategic Trade Theory

The theory of comparative advantage is based on the assumption of perfectly competitive markets. Information is assumed to be complete, consumers and producers act as price takers, goods are undifferentiated, and production is characterized by constant returns to scale or by decreasing returns to scale with costless entry and exit. From these assumptions, theories such as the law of comparative advantage demonstrate the gains from trade among open economies. The theory also implies that intervention by governments in perfectly competitive domestic or international markets will reduce aggregate well-being. Competitive theory thus provides a compelling rationale for free trade, and the role of government is thus to join in international efforts to reduce tariff and nontariff barriers to trade.

Economists have also considered whether a nation can gain from a strategic trade policy—that is, intervention to protect domestic industries, subsidize exports, or stimulate demand for domestic goods.[3] These interventions can be beneficial for a country only if one or more of the conditions for perfect competition is not satisfied. Theories of strategic trade policy thus are set in the context of imperfect competition.

As an example, consider the case of an undifferentiated good that is produced by only two firms, one domestic and the other foreign. Suppose they engage in Cournot competition where each firm chooses the quantity it will produce and both sell their quantities in the world market. Because there are only two firms, they each restrict output. Suppose one government subsidizes the production of its domestic firm, thus lowering that firm's marginal cost. This has two effects. First, the lower marginal cost induces the firm to expand its output. Second, as it expands its output, the foreign firm will react by reducing its output. This then allows the subsidized domestic firm to increase its output even more. This second effect is said to be strategic because the subsidization has altered the strategic relationship between the two firms by lowering the cost of one firm. In the new equilibrium, the subsidized firm makes greater profits than it did in the absence of the subsidy. Moreover, even taking into account the cost of the subsidy, subsidization can increase the aggregate well-being of the subsidizing country by expanding output.[4] The European subsidization of Airbus Industrie may be an example of this strategy. Although the subsidization of domestic firms in certain industries could increase well-being, it often does not. For example, the subsidization by the European Union of agricultural exports resulted in large reductions in well-being because agricultural markets generally satisfy the conditions for perfect competition.

The gains from strategic trade practices can turn to losses if other governments retaliate. If one country adopts a strategic trade policy, other countries can retaliate either by adopting the same policy or by taking measures to offset the effect of the other country's strategy. For example, the United States retaliated against the European Union's subsidization of agricultural exports with its own export subsidies, resulting in large losses to both.[5] Once both are subsidizing exports, they are in a dilemma, since neither has a unilateral incentive to stop the subsidization. To resolve the dilemma, countries negotiate agreements prohibiting such policies and establish institutions to enforce the agreements. This approach, represented by the WTO, is favored by most countries. Before considering international trade agreements, the nature of the politics of international trade is considered.

---

[3]For a nontechnical exposition of these theories, see Krugman (1986, 1990).
[4]Indeed, worldwide aggregate surplus is increased because the total quantity produced is greater than it would be without the subsidy. This results because the subsidization leads to a price that is closer to marginal cost. These conclusions, however, are not completely robust and may be reversed if firms compete in a manner different from that assumed in Cournot competition.
[5]The depressed commodity prices also harmed developing countries that produced the same crops.

THE POLITICAL ECONOMY OF INTERNATIONAL TRADE POLICY

The Dual Nature of the Politics of International Trade

As illustrated in Figure 18-1, the politics of international trade policy is driven by domestic politics, which arises from the interactions between international trade policy and the domestic economy. Trade policy has differentiated distributive consequences with some interests benefiting from trade liberalization and others harmed by it. Trade politics thus has two components—measures to liberalize trade and measures to support domestic interests harmed by liberalization.

According to the typology of political competition presented in Figure 6-2, the politics of international trade policy is at one level majoritarian. That is, everyone is affected by international trade. Because liberalized trade policy is beneficial in the aggregate, countries generally gain from multilateral reductions in tariff and nontariff barriers. The benefits, however, are often widely distributed, so preferences for trade liberalization may not be transformed into policy. In the United States, as in most countries, the politics of trade liberalization are basically entrepreneurial. In the United States, Congress has delegated the role of entrepreneur to the president. Congress is willing to delegate because the aggregate benefits of trade liberalization exceed the aggregate costs, and the benefits are sufficiently widely distributed that leadership must be exercised. Since the constituency of the president is the nation as a whole, as opposed to a congressional district or a state, presidents generally support trade liberalization.

The distributive consequences of a liberalized trade policy, however, are not uniform. Instead, liberalization has concentrated effects on particular interests, and those interests have an incentive to take nonmarket action to increase the benefits they receive or reduce the costs they bear.[6] In the case of trade policies that reduce domestic barriers to trade and thereby increase imports, the benefits typically are distributed broadly among consumers, whereas the costs are concentrated on import-competing industries. For example, in the United States steel companies and the United Steel Workers (USW) have been hurt by imports and have strong incentives to seek protection. Protectionism is thus characterized by client politics. In most countries, interests, including companies and unions, can seek protection and relief from injury due to imports. For example, countries have antidumping laws that allow domestic firms to petition to have duties placed on imports sold at "less than fair value."

The benefits from protection are concentrated on those interests that compete against imports, whereas the costs of protection are widely distributed among consumers and other users of the protected goods. Although consumers are harmed by these policies, the harm is typically small on a per capita basis, and hence consumers seldom take nonmarket action to oppose protection. Importers, however, are often harmed and have incentives to oppose protectionism. The steel companies and the USW sought protection from imports, but General Motors and Caterpillar opposed it because it would raise the price of the steel they use. Interest group politics can thus develop. Interest group politics can also result in political competition between import-competing industries and exporters as in the case of the ratification of broad trade liberalizations, such as NAFTA, that require reciprocity.

The politics of international trade policy is summarized in Figure 18-4. In the aggregate, trade policy is characterized by majoritarian politics. At a disaggregated level, the nature of the politics depends on the specific policy alternative in question. Export oriented trade liberalization and market opening are basically characterized by entrepreneurial politics. Client politics characterizes protectionism, since the benefits from supporting protectionism are concentrated and the costs are typically widely distributed. Protectionist policies may generate a response by importers, and reciprocity in market opening policies may generate a response by import-competing industries, so the number of interest groups involved can expand. The politics of protectionism and the politics of market opening thus can lead to interest group politics.

---

[6]Magee, Brock, and Young (1989) provide a theory of rent-seeking to explain aspects of international trade policy.

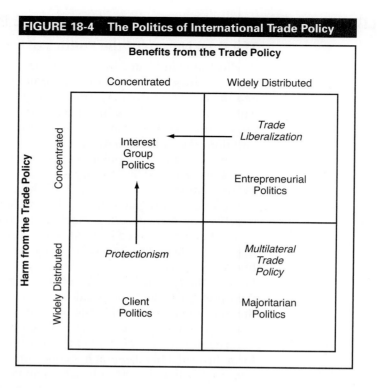

FIGURE 18-4 The Politics of International Trade Policy

Asymmetries in the Politics

Although trade policy liberalization creates opportunities for exporters and threats for import-competing industries, the domestic politics of international trade are asymmetric. The asymmetry is due to sunk resources and the rents on those resources. Consider the case of a firm that would construct a new plant dedicated to exports, provided that foreign barriers to trade were lowered. Its incentive to undertake nonmarket action to open the foreign market depends on the profit it can earn, which is given by the export revenue less the full cost of the resources required to produce the exports. In contrast, domestic firms faced with import competition typically have sunk resources. Because of sunk resources, the domestic firms earn rents. When there are sunk resources, the import-competing industry can have more to lose than the exporting industry has to gain, so in the short run the incentives for protection can be stronger than the incentives for market opening.

To illustrate this, consider the case of labor. Trade liberalization creates new jobs in exporting industries, but at the time at which the trade policy is chosen those new jobs are not yet identified, let alone occupied. Those jobs might be filled by many people, and hence the probability that any one person would obtain one of the jobs is small. The incentive for an individual to take nonmarket action thus is weak. As the managing director of one of the largest U.S. investment banks commented on organized labor's opposition to NAFTA, "The jobs that will be lost are identifiable; the jobs that will be created are as yet unidentified." Cisco Systems projected that its increased exports to Mexico would create 200 additional U.S. jobs at its suppliers, but who would hold those jobs was as yet unidentified. Thus, Cisco had clear incentives to support NAFTA, but those unidentified individuals who would hold the new jobs could not support it.

In contrast, workers in import-competing industries are often earning rents in their jobs; that is, their wages are higher than the wages they could obtain elsewhere. Rents are thus concentrated on identified individuals, and their incentives to oppose trade liberalization and seek protection from imports can be strong. This is the case for organized labor, where, for example, the wages of USW members are higher than the wages most of them would earn in other employment. Not surprisingly, the USW and similarly the United Automobile Workers have sought protection for the U.S. steel and auto industries, respectively, and have opposed liberalized trade. Organized labor vigorously, but unsuccessfully, opposed NAFTA and the Uruguay Round accord that established the WTO.

Global firms often have mixed incentives. As with any import-competing firm earning rents, a global firm would benefit from protection of its domestic market. A global firm also would benefit from opening foreign markets for its products. The simultaneous protection of domestic markets and the opening of foreign markets is not sustainable, however, since protectionism can generate retaliation by other countries and market opening may require reciprocity. Most global firms support liberalized trade because of the aggregate gains from trade and because liberalized trade creates opportunities to pursue their competitive advantages.

INTERNATIONAL TRADE AGREEMENTS

The World Trade Organization

At the conclusion of World War II, a group of countries led by the United States established the International Trade Organization (ITO). They hoped the ITO would allow them to avoid the disastrous trade policies that had contributed to the depression and the pressures for war. When the U.S. Senate failed to provide the two-thirds majority to ratify the organization's treaty, the ITO disbanded. However, a set of principles for international trade in goods had been drafted in conjunction with the ITO, and in 1948, 23 countries formalized those principles as the GATT. Seven subsequent rounds of multilateral trade negotiations among the signatories have resulted in major reductions in tariffs and nontariff barriers to trade.

The focus of international trade policy through the 1960s was on tariffs. Because tariffs limit the gains from trade, the United States and other countries sought in the Kennedy Round (1964–1967) of GATT negotiations to reduce tariffs on a more or less uniform basis among all signatories. The result was an average reduction of 36 percent in tariffs, and the volume of international trade increased substantially as a result.

After reducing tariffs to the point at which they no longer constituted a major barrier to trade, the focus of GATT turned in the Tokyo Round (1974–1979) to nontariff barriers to trade. Nontariff barriers were more complex and difficult to address and were often deeply rooted in both domestic politics and business practices that protected rents.[7] Trade in agricultural products, for example, had been distorted by a variety of policies such as import quotas, domestic subsidies, and export subsidies. Although the Tokyo Round focused on nontariff barriers, it also resulted in an average reduction of 34 percent in tariffs. As a result of the Tokyo Round agreements, the average tariff in developed countries was 6.3 percent. Thirty-two percent of U.S. imports were duty free, and the average duty on the rest was 5.5 percent.[8]

The Tokyo Round left several sectors, such as agriculture, unaddressed, and several others, such as services, became more salient. The Uruguay Round (1986–1993) was intended to improve GATT provisions on trade in goods and expand the multilateral trade agreements to include trade in services, agriculture, intellectual property protection, government procurement, and other issues. After nearly 8 years of negotiations an agreement was concluded that made major improvements in international trade policies and, in addition, reduced tariffs by 38 percent to an average of 3.9 percent in developed countries. To encompass this broader set of agreements, the WTO was established. The WTO agreements include GATT, GATS, TRIPS, dispute settlement, and trade policy reviews. The WTO also encompasses the Agricultural Agreement and an agreement on government procurement.

The WTO has 152 member countries and over 30 others, including Russia, are observers with the intention of becoming members. The WTO has three principal roles. First, it provides a system of agreements that helps trade move more freely. Second, it provides a forum for trade negotiations such as the telecommunications agreement concluded in 1997. Third, it provides a dispute settlement mechanism to resolve trade disputes in a timely manner.

---

[7]Grieco (1990) provides an analysis of the compliance with Tokyo Round nontariff barrier agreements.
[8]See Lande and VanGrasstek (1986, p. 4).

The central principle of the WTO agreements is embodied in the most favored nation (MFN) requirement that each signatory accord all other signatories the most favorable terms for trade provided to any country; that is, trade policies are to be nondiscriminatory.[9] A second principle is national treatment; that is, domestic and foreign goods are to be treated the same. For example, Canada imposed higher postage rates on U.S. magazines than for Canadian magazines, and a WTO dispute resolution panel held that the Canadian practice violated the national treatment principle.

GATT covers a variety of practices and policies governing trade in goods.[10] Article VI covers antidumping and countervailing duties and requires a finding of less than fair value sales or subsidization, respectively, and a finding of material injury. Article XI sets a framework for the elimination of quantitative restrictions on trade, but Article XVIII allows exceptions for balance of payments problems of developing countries. Article XIX allows for temporary safeguard relief from imports. Article XVI is the subsidies code, and Articles XX and XXI provide exceptions to the free trade provisions of the other articles. For example, a country may impose trade restrictions if they are required by national security considerations.[11]

General Agreement on Trade in Services (GATS)

U.S. service industries had complained that their international expansion was hindered by the protection many countries provided for their domestic industries. The effort to reduce barriers to trade in services was led by a number of CEOs, including James Robinson of American Express, who for years personally campaigned to open foreign markets. In 1982 the Coalition of Service Industries was formed and was successful in including trade in services in the Uruguay Round agenda.

The result was the General Agreement on Trade in Services (GATS), which covers all services and provides for MFN and national treatment. The agreement also requires countries to make transparent all regulations and conditions of service. Since the services markets of many countries were largely closed to foreign firms, GATS temporarily allowed countries not to apply MFN treatment.

Two services, telecommunications and finance, posed particular problems because of heavy regulation and the government ownership of firms. The Uruguay Round and GATS agreements were signed while negotiations on telecommunications and financial services continued. In 1997 over 68 countries agreed to open their telecommunications market to various degrees. The telecommunications agreement provided opportunities for telecommunications companies by requiring that countries grant licenses open to foreign firms, as in the Chapter 17 case, *MTN Group Limited*.

Later in 1997, 102 countries reached agreement to open banking, insurance, investments, and other financial services to international competition. Some countries, however, limited foreign ownership stakes in their financial services companies. GATS now covers all international trade in services.

Trade-Related Aspects of Intellectual Property Rights (TRIPS)

Intellectual property rights include copyrights, patents, trademarks, brand names and logos, industrial designs, semiconductor circuit designs, and trade secrets. Such rights allow individuals and firms to capture the benefits from their efforts to creating new concepts and products; infringement of these rights reduces the incentives to create.[12]

---

[9]Exceptions to the equal treatment principle include colonial preference arrangements in effect when GATT was established, preferences for developing countries, and certain multilateral agreements such as the Multi-Fiber Arrangement. The quotas established in the Multi-Fiber Arrangement were phased out, ending in 2005.

[10]Prior to 1995 GATT was not a single agreement but instead a set of agreements, each of which countries could choose to sign. For example, GATT included a subsidies code intended to limit the domestic subsidization of export industries, but the signatories were largely the members of the Organization for Economic Cooperation and Development (OECD), an association of industrial democracies.

[11]With the exception of Article II, the GATT articles have counterparts in U.S. trade law.

[12]See Chapter 12.

TRIPS provides broad protection and is included in the WTO dispute settlement system, allowing trade sanctions to be imposed in the event of violations. Because many countries had weak domestic laws for protecting intellectual property rights, developing countries were given 5 years to comply and the least developed countries were given 11 years.

Intellectual property is a contentious issue between developed and developing countries. Many developing countries believe that intellectual property rights allow companies to unfairly preclude their countries from obtaining important products such as pharmaceuticals that are priced beyond their means. TRIPS includes sections that allow a country to invoke compulsory licensing and to import generic versions of drugs in the event of a public health emergency. The chapter case, *Compulsory Licensing, Thailand, and Abbott Laboratories,* concerns the imposition of compulsory licenses by Thailand and the response by Abbott Laboratories. Drug pricing, compulsory licensing, and parallel imports are also considered in the Part V integrative case, *GlaxoSmithKline and AIDS Drugs Policy.*

As an example of the contentious nature of intellectual property rights, under the auspices of the World Intellectual Property Organization, a unit of the United Nations, a treaty providing protection for intellectual property was negotiated. Developing nations, however, refused to sign it, leaving fewer than 10 signatories.

Agriculture

Agriculture has been the sector with the greatest distortions in trade. An OECD report concluded that farm subsidies and import controls cost consumers and taxpayers $361 billion in 1999. The European Union accounted for the largest distortions, followed by the United States and Japan. The principal roadblock to an agreement on agricultural trade was the European Union's Common Agriculture Policy (CAP). CAP was intended to maintain farmers' incomes and did so by establishing prices high enough to yield a reasonable income for high-cost farms. The high prices, however, induced efficient farms to expand their output, resulting in huge crop surpluses, some of which were exported at subsidized prices. The European Union's export subsidization resulted in retaliatory subsidization of agricultural exports by the United States.

The Uruguay Round produced the Agricultural Agreement to reduce tariffs, domestic support, and export subsidies in agriculture. By 2000 developed countries were to reduce their tariffs by an average of 36 percent with a minimum reduction of 15 percent. Domestic support was to be reduced by 20 percent and export subsidies by 36 percent. The reductions required for developing countries were lower, and they were given until 2004 to comply. Because many countries used quotas to restrict imports, the agreement adopted a "tariffs only" policy in which quotas were replaced by equivalent tariffs, which were then subjected to the required reductions. The agreement on agriculture also addressed health and safety issues. It required that regulations be based on science and that they "be applied only to the extent necessary to protect human, animal, or plant life or health."

The Agricultural Agreement, however, left unresolved many issues. The European Union reformed CAP by decoupling the subsidies received by farmers from the amount they produced. A WTO trade policy review, however, concluded that "the reform of the Common Agricultural Policy (CAP) falls short of liberalizing EU's agriculture."[13] The United States has continued to subsidize its farmers.

Developing countries complained that the agricultural subsidies and protection provided by the European Union, Japan, United States, and other countries impeded their economic development in two ways. Domestic subsidies and import barriers reduced export opportunities for the developing countries, and export subsidies unfairly competed with their exports. NGOs such as Oxfam America called attention to the subsidies and lobbied for their elimination. Agriculture has been the main stumbling block to progress in the Doha Round of multilateral negotiations.

---

[13]WTO press release, October 27, 2004.

Government Procurement

The Uruguay Round negotiators reached a new Government Procurement Agreement (GPA) that extended the existing agreement to include construction and services and some procurement by subcentral governments and government-owned firms. The GPA is a "pluralateral" agreement among a subset of WTO countries. Developing countries were given special conditions. In a bilateral agreement with the European Union, the procurement of 15 U.S. states and seven major cities was opened to EU firms in exchange for opening the European Union's $28 billion heavy electric equipment market.

Antidumping, Countervailing Duties, and Safeguards

The Kennedy Round of GATT negotiations incorporated provisions in Article VI allowing domestic laws to include antidumping measures. From the perspective of economic theory, dumping occurs when a company sells a good at a price below the cost of producing it. As applied in international trade, however, antidumping pertains to sales at "less than fair value" that materially injure domestic industries. In response a duty on imports can be imposed to bring their price up to fair value. Antidumping provisions are thus intended to provide for "fair trade" rather than free or efficient trade. Antidumping provisions have been criticized as being protectionist because they can result in the imposition of duties on imports even when prices are above costs. Antidumping basically compares the domestic price of a product in the exporting country with the price in the importing country, so antidumping actually pertains to price discrimination rather than to dumping. In addition to a price less than fair value, the imports must cause material injury to domestic interests. The chapter case, *Cemex and Antidumping*, centers on this issue.

The Uruguay Round agreement standardized the procedures for calculating the dumping duty and for conducting investigations. It also imposed a 5-year sunset limit on any antidumping duty, unless ending the duty would result in imminent material injury.

Antidumping had been used almost exclusively by developed countries with the number of actions initiated averaging about 200 per year in the early 1990s.[14] The number of actions initiated by developed nations decreased to 120 in 1997. Developing countries have become active in using antidumping, and by 1997 they initiated more actions than developed countries. India became one of the largest users of antidumping, and China was the most frequent target. During the first half of 2004, 18 countries imposed 52 antidumping duties, with India, the European Union, and the United States imposing six each. The EU imposed duties in 44 antidumping and antisubsidy cases from 2005 to 2007, and China accounted for the largest number. Most antidumping cases do not result in disputes filed with the WTO. Despite the protectionist nature of antidumping, most countries prefer to retain the provisions as a safety valve to relieve pressure for broader protectionist measures.

Countervailing duties are allowed by the WTO agreements to offset the effects of subsidies provided by another country. These duties are subject to the same standards for antidumping duties. Special provisions are provided for developing countries.

Temporary safeguards against a surge in imports can be taken to avoid "serious injury" to a country. The United States invoked the safeguards provision to protect its steel industry, as indicated in the example presented later in the chapter.

Dispute Settlement

Under GATT, disputes between countries could be brought before a panel that investigated the matter and issued a recommendation. The recommendation became binding, however, only if all countries agreed to it, and countries including the United States frequently withheld their agreement. A major achievement of the Uruguay

---

[14]Bellis (1989) and Schuknecht (1992) provide analyses of the European Union's antidumping policies and procedures.

Round was to establish the WTO Dispute Settlement Body (DSB) to hear disputes and issue binding orders to resolve them.[15] The DSB encourages the parties to resolve disputes through negotiation and compromise; if that is unsuccessful, a country may request that a special panel be established to hear the dispute. The entire process, from the filing of the initial complaint to the issuance of a final report by the panel, is to be completed within 1 year, and any appeal is to be resolved in 3 months. Correction of a violation, however, can take considerable time.

If the DSB finds against a practice, the country is supposed to correct the fault.[16] Failure to comply can be brought to the attention of the DSB, which can authorize the petitioner to impose trade sanctions against the violator. Thus, countries need not change their laws or practices to comply with the decision of the DSB, but if they fail to do so, sanctions can be authorized by the WTO. The sanctions typically take the form of a suspension of previously granted trade concessions accorded to the violator. The violator is to accept the sanctions. The United States and other countries have generally complied with the decisions of the DSB.

The United States has been involved in more disputes than any other country. The United States has been the complainant in 90 and the respondent in 99 disputes filed with the WTO, followed by the European Union with 78 and 62, respectively. Thirty-one of the complaints by the United States were against EU, and 31 of the EU complaints were against the United States. Brazil has been the complainant in 23 and the respondent in 14 disputes.

Trade Disputes

The first case decided by the DSB involved a complaint by Venezuela, later joined by Brazil, that rules issued by the U.S. Environmental Protection Agency (EPA) for reformulated gasoline violated the WTO national treatment principle. The EPA had written its rules based on data that were readily available for U.S. refiners. Because foreign refiners had not kept the same data, the EPA required them to meet a more stringent standard. The DSB decided in favor of Venezuela, and the United States complied by rewriting the EPA rules to provide for national treatment.

Disputes typically center on specific protectionist practices. The European Union maintains a set of preferences for the overseas territories and former colonies of its member states. The United States and Latin American countries filed a complaint against EU rules for preferential treatment for bananas from the overseas territories and former colonies, particularly in Africa.[17] Banana exports from Honduras to the European Union fell by 90 percent as a result of the rule. The DSB decided against the European Union and rejected an appeal. The European Union then revised its rule under contentious internal bargaining, pitting Germany and other countries that opposed the preferences against France and other countries that favored them. The United States and Latin American countries, however, contended that the revised rule did little to remove the barriers to Latin American banana imports. The United States proposed that the new rule be taken to the WTO for an expedited DSB process, but the European Union refused. When the DSB failed to authorize sanctions by the required deadline, the United States announced 100 percent punitive tariffs on $500 million of imports of wine, cheese, and other products. The DSB subsequently reached a decision authorizing the United States to impose punitive tariffs on $191 million of imports. Finally, the United States and the European Union reached a settlement in which the United States lifted the punitive tariffs on July 1, 2001, and the European Union agreed to phase out the preferences over 5 years.

The largest case to date involved profits taxes on exports. In 1971 Congress allowed U.S. exporters to establish offshore foreign sales corporations through which the

---

[15]The DSB is not an organization, but instead is the General Council of the WTO. It is better thought of as a procedure for resolving disputes.
[16]A DSB finding can be overcome by a majority of the WTO members.
[17]The United States was a petitioner because Chiquita Brands and Dole Food Company export Latin American bananas to the European Union.

paper transactions on exports were funneled, saving U.S. exporters several billion dollars in profits taxes. The European Union filed a complaint against the U.S. practice, and the WTO ruled in favor of the European Union. Congress responded in 2000 by revoking the foreign sales corporation law and enacting a law that actually expanded the tax breaks by allowing additional U.S. exporters, such as Boeing and Caterpillar, to receive the tax breaks. The European Union was incensed and complained to the WTO that the United States had not complied with the initial ruling. The WTO agreed, and the United States appealed the ruling. The appeal was denied as expected, and the European Union was authorized to impose punitive tariffs on as much as $4 billion of imports from the United States. The European Union phased in the punitive tariffs, and Congress passed a bill that phased out the foreign sales corporation provision and granted other business tax breaks that were not trade distorting. The European Union complained about the phaseout but withdrew its punitive tariffs.

In addition to the foreign sales corporation case, the United States lost a series of DSB cases in the 2000s. The DSB ruled against temporary safeguards for steel, as considered in the example, subsidies for cotton production, and antidumping procedures.

The trade conflicts between the European Union and the United States continued as the United States filed a trade complaint claiming that the European Union provided billions of dollars of subsidies in the form of low-interest loans to Airbus Industrie. The European Union countered with a trade complaint claiming that the United States subsidized Boeing through military research and development grants. Negotiations to resolve the dispute collapsed.

A controversial case was brought by the United States against the European Union on its ban of beef from cattle treated with growth-enhancing hormones. The European ban did not violate the national treatment principle, because it applied to any hormone-treated beef, nor was it intended to protect European beef producers. Instead, the ban was enacted because of consumer health concerns about the beef. The DSB concluded that the European Union had no scientific basis for concluding that the hormone-treated beef might be a health hazard. The European Union, however, was given a period of time to conduct its own safety tests on the hormone-treated beef. After 2 years of inaction by the European Union, the WTO authorized the United States to impose 100 percent punitive tariffs on $117 million of imports of European goods. The European Union subsequently reviewed the scientific literature and concluded that the hormone-treated beef constituted a health risk because some hormone residue could cause cancer. The European Union then enacted new legislation banning six beef hormones. The United States replied that the review provided no new scientific evidence. A spokesperson for the office of the U.S. trade representative said, "The hormone levels they are concerned about—represent a tiny fraction of what occurs naturally in an egg or one glass of milk."[18]

The beef dispute was part of a broader U.S. complaint against the EU ban on imports of foods with genetically modified organisms (GMOs). In 1998 the European Union and the United States had agreed to an EU moratorium on new approvals of imports of GMO foods and animal feed. The European Union lifted the ban in 2003, replacing it with regulations requiring documentation of the genetic history with a comprehensive paper trail for all food imports. U.S. exporters of agricultural products claimed that it would be impossible to provide such documentation. The European Union had substituted a regulatory ban for its explicit ban, and agricultural exporters turned to the WTO. Since the EU ban on GMO foods was seen as a violation of the WTO agreements, Argentina, Canada, and the United States filed a trade complaint. The WTO ruled against the EU, and the EU did not appeal because it claimed that the approval process it had implemented after 2003 was compliant with the WTO ruling. The approval process was painstakingly slow from the perspective of the genetically modified foods industry.

---

[18]*Wall Street Journal,* November 9, 2004. The European Union took its evidence to the WTO in an attempt to have the sanctions lifted.

The ban and documentation requirement were based on the EU's "precautionary principle" under which temporary bans could be imposed on products that might pose risks. A member of the EU trade delegation explained that "in a democracy you have to take into account fears of the people, and the people in many European countries are concerned about genetically modified food."[19] In a case in which Monsanto claimed that Italy had illegally banned imports of GMO corn, the European Court of Justice upheld temporary bans under the precautionary principle "without having to wait until the reality and seriousness of risks become fully apparent, even if a full risk assessment becomes impossible because of the inadequate nature of scientific data available." The court, however, also said that the risks "must not be purely hypothetical or founded on mere suppositions which are not yet verified."[20] In 2008 only two GM crops were grown in the EU, and France filed a petition with the EU Commission to ban one, a corn that had been grown in Spain for over a decade. More trade complaints were likely.

The beef and GMO foods cases are important because they pertain to the question of whether countries can respond to consumer preferences whatever might be the basis for those preferences. Another example involves environmental protection. A U.S. law banned the sale of shrimp caught with nets from which sea turtles were unable to escape. The DSB upheld a complaint by India, Malaysia, Pakistan, and Thailand against the U.S. law on the grounds that the WTO agreements did not permit discrimination against products on the basis of how they were produced. Prior to the establishment of the WTO, a GATT panel had on the same grounds ruled against the U.S. Marine Mammal Protection Act ban of tuna caught in purse seine nets in which dolphins could become caught and drown. In the case of the dolphin decision, the United States withheld its consent and the panel decision did not take effect. Under the WTO DSB procedures, the sea turtle decision took effect. Environmental issues such as these and health issues such as the EU ban on hormone-treated beef and GMO foods spurred calls for a new round of WTO negotiations.

The Doha Round of WTO Negotiations

The Uruguay Round and follow-up agreements were generally successful, and the WTO dispute settlement process has been effective. Nevertheless, many trade issues remained unresolved. The members of the WTO had planned to adopt an agenda for a new round of multilateral trade negotiation at the 1999 Seattle ministerial meeting, but demonstrations by activist groups disrupted the meetings.[21] Finally, in 2001 after tense negotiations, particularly between developing and developed countries, the members agreed to a broad agenda for the Doha Round.[22]

Despite intense political pressure from the pharmaceutical industry, developing countries, led by India, received a pledge that TRIPS "does not and should not prevent Members from taking measures to protect public health." This would allow developing countries to violate pharmaceutical patents and produce or import generic drugs to protect public health without being subject to trade penalties. This is the subject of the chapter case, *Compulsory Licensing, Thailand, and Abbott Laboratories,* and plays a role in the Part V integrative case, *GlaxoSmithKline and AIDS Drugs Policy.*

Other issues added to the Doha agenda reflected the bargaining. Despite the opposition of France, the European Union agreed to negotiations on agricultural subsidies and market access. The European Union obtained a pledge to support sustainable development and for discussions on the relationship between trade and multilateral environmental agreements, but more specific environmental objectives were not specified. The United States agreed to negotiations on the clarification of antidumping procedures, much to the anger of U.S. industries that had used antidumping for protection from imports. The WTO members also agreed to reduce or eliminate tariffs on industrial

---

[19]*New York Times,* January 10, 2003.
[20]*Wall Street Journal,* September 9, 2003.
[21]See Prakash (2001) for an analysis of the Seattle meeting. The principal effect of the demonstrations in Seattle was to delay the next round of negotiations 2 years rather than to affect the agenda significantly.
[22]Esty (2001) analyzes the trade and environment issues.

goods. Activist groups failed to obtain commitments to labor protection due to objections by developing nations. The negotiations in the Doha Agenda were to pay special attention to the situations of developing countries. For example, developing countries were given until 2016 to bring their patent laws into accord with TRIPS.

Negotiations also were scheduled for the trade effects of competition (antitrust) policy, intellectual property protection under TRIPS, and services under GATS. The members also committed to a review of DSB procedures, discussions on rules pertaining to investments, and negotiations on transparency in government procurement.

Reaching agreement on the agenda for the Doha Round was hard, but making progress on substantive issues was far more difficult in several areas. The disagreements between the developing and developed countries were at the heart of the problem. Developing countries wanted the developed countries to bear the brunt of the costs of further trade liberalization. They sought reductions in U.S. agricultural subsidies, reductions in EU tariffs on agricultural products, and greater access to EU markets. For example, Brazil was the leader of the G22 block that had successfully filed trade complaints against EU sugar subsidiaries and U.S. cotton subsidies. The U.S. Congress, however, in an election year passed a $285 billion farm bill, which deputy secretary of agriculture Chuck Conner said increases "trade-distorting supports on 17 out of 25 of the commodities that we provide." [23] France complained that the rest of the EU was proposing too large a reduction in agricultural supports. In exchange for reducing agriculture supports, the developed countries sought reductions in industrial tariffs in developing countries and the opening of services in countries.[24] The developing countries rejected those demands. Although some progress had been made on agriculture, whether any significant agreement would result from the Doha Round remained uncertain.

Other Trade Agreements

A number of regional free trade agreements have been concluded, and those agreements have broadened the set of countries participating. The largest of these free trade areas are NAFTA and the Common Market of the European Union. In Latin America there are four regional trading areas: the Central American Common Market, the Andean Community, Caricom, and Mercosur. Mercosur members are Argentina, Brazil, Paraguay, Uruguay, and Venezuela, with Bolivia, Chile, Colombia, Ecuador, and Peru and Chile as associates. Mercosur and the European Union attempted to reach a free trade agreement, but negotiations broke down over the issue of trade in agriculture. In 1994 the 16 countries participating in the Asia-Pacific Economic Cooperation (APEC) forum agreed to work toward removing all barriers to trade by the year 2020. The developed countries in APEC established a goal of eliminating trade barriers by 2010. Progress has been slow.

In addition to WTO trade agreements, a large number of bilateral and multilateral agreements are in force. For example, in 2004 the United States concluded a free trade agreement with Chile, which already had such an agreement with Canada and the European Union. Also, the United States has worked to deregulate international air transportation, which had been governed by a cartel supported by countries with state-owned airlines. The U.S. strategy had been to negotiate bilateral agreements deregulating air fares and schedules with other countries. This increased competition and brought prices down, although restrictions remained in some markets because landing slots were limited.

U.S. TRADE POLICY

The Structure of U.S. Trade Policy

Article 1, Section 8 of the Constitution gives Congress the power "to regulate commerce with foreign nations" and to "lay and collect duties." In 1934 in the aftermath of the disastrous Smoot-Hawley tariff, Congress passed the Reciprocal Trade Agreement Act,

---

[23]*International Herald Tribune,* May 13, 2008.
[24]See the Chapter 17 case, *Tesco PLC in India?*

which delegated to the president the authority to negotiate trade agreements. The authority for U.S. trade negotiations has remained largely with the president. The Office of the U.S. Trade Representative (USTR), located in the Executive Office of the President, serves as the president's representative in trade negotiations. The United States has supported trade liberalization through the multilateral policies embodied in the WTO agreements, regional free trade agreements including NAFTA and APEC, and bilateral arrangements such as those promoting competition in international air transport.

In the late 1980s Congress began to assert its constitutional authority. The USTR is now required to consult with Congress on both trade policy and specific actions that implement that policy.[25] Being closer to constituents than the president, members of Congress have been concerned with protecting their constituents' interests. The result has been a series of amendments to the trade laws that make it easier for industries both to obtain protection and to initiate action to open foreign markets to their products. U.S. trade laws establish rights of private parties to initiate trade actions to further their own interests, so U.S. trade actions have both public and private initiation.

The politics of international trade takes place in four institutional arenas—cabinet departments, regulatory agencies, Congress, and the Office of the President. The administration of trade policy has been placed with executive branch agencies, primarily the Departments of the Treasury, State, and Commerce. The International Trade Agency (ITA) of the Department of Commerce and the International Trade Commission (ITC), an independent regulatory commission, have administrative responsibilities for certain sections of U.S. trade law. Cabinet departments participate in international trade policy, both administratively and politically, and regularly conduct policy research, provide congressional testimony, lobby for their policy objectives and the interests they represent, and interact with business in other countries.

U.S. Trade Law and Its Administration

The major components of U.S. trade law are embodied in the Trade Act of 1974 and the Tariff Act of 1930. The principal sections and their purposes are as follows:[26]

- Section 201 (temporary safeguards) provides for temporary relief for domestic industries seriously injured by increased imports; no unfair trade practice is required.
- Section 301 (presidential retaliation) provides for action against countries that restrict imports of U.S. goods or subsidize exports to the United States.
- Section 731 (antidumping) provides authority for the imposition of duties on goods imported to the United States at a price that is less than fair value (LTFV).
- Section 303 (countervailing duties) provides authority for the imposition of duties against countries that subsidize their domestic industries.
- Section 337 (intellectual property) allows retaliation against countries that violate U.S. patents, copyrights, or protected trade secrets.
- Trade Adjustment Assistance provides assistance for those injured by imports.

These laws establish rights that private interests may exercise either directly or indirectly through administrative channels. For example, firms, unions, and other interests may file antidumping petitions to initiate a complex administrative process that can result in duties assessed on imports. Antidumping and countervailing duty petitions are considered by the ITA and the ITC. In Section 201 and 301 cases, the president has final authority, as illustrated in the steel imports example in this chapter. Decisions by the ITC can be appealed to the U.S. Court of International Trade and the Court of Appeals (Federal Circuit), and many of the decisions are appealed. The chapter case, *Cemex and Antidumping,* provides details on the ITC and ITA administration of an antidumping case and considers a firm's market and nonmarket strategies for addressing a dumping complaint.

---

[25]See O'Halloran (1994) for a study of the development of U.S. policy and the choice of trade institutions.
[26]See Trebilcock and York (1990) for studies of the administration of trade laws in a number of countries.

The United States also imposes controls on the export to certain countries of sensitive items, including high-speed computers, encryption software, and computers with high-powered encryption software. These controls are mostly holdovers from the cold war, and high-tech firms have argued that the controls should be relaxed. The chapter case, *Sophis Networks and Encryption Export Controls (A),* involves one such issue.

THE POLITICAL ECONOMY OF PROTECTIONISM

Formal Policies

Although official U.S. trade policy has promoted free and fair trade, the client politics arising from import competition has been important since the 18th century. Protection may extend indefinitely, have a specified duration, or be extendable. Protection for coastal shipping has continued since 1789, but most of the recent protectionist measures are intended to be temporary to give an industry time to improve its competitiveness.

Protection applies to two kinds of conditions. The first involves a predatory trade practice, such as export subsidization or predatory dumping, where a foreign firm sells in the United States at a price below its cost. The second involves relative efficiency—when foreign firms have lower costs than U.S. firms and sell in the United States at prices above their costs yet below the prices of domestic goods. Economic efficiency requires allowing nonpredatory imports and calls for blocking predatory practices if they will lead to long-run inefficiency. The political process, however, has not drawn the same line as economists and instead focuses on fair trade and protection from injury.

Predatory and discriminatory trade practices are addressed by the antidumping provisions of Section 731 and countervailing duties under Section 303. From 1980 through 2006, 1,569 cases were filed, 70 percent of which were antidumping cases. The number of cases filed peaked in 2001 at 140 and declined thereafter, but increased again in 2007. Thirty-seven percent of the cases were decided for the complainant, 40 percent for the respondent, and 23 percent were terminated or suspended. Few of these cases involved predatory practices.

The duties in antidumping cases had been paid to the U.S. government, but in 2000 Congress enacted a provision, the Byrd Amendment, under which the duties were paid to the companies that were injured by the trade practice. The European Union and eight other countries filed a complaint with the WTO against the practice. The WTO ruled against the United States and authorized $150 million in duties on U.S. goods. The United States has not repealed the Byrd amendment.

The United States also established sector-specific retaliation mechanisms to respond to subsidization by other countries. A 1985 act provided for subsidization of exports of agricultural commodities through the Export Enhancement Program in retaliation for agriculture export subsidization by the European Union.[27] This retaliatory program was important in the Uruguay Round negotiations on trade in agriculture that resulted in an agreement to reduce export subsidies and other distortions to trade.

The relative inefficiency of domestic industries is addressed in four ways. First, those injured may be compensated under the Trade Adjustment Assistance Act, which is intended to help a domestic industry adjust by improving its efficiency. Trade adjustment assistance also compensates those, such as workers, who are injured, thereby reducing their political opposition to liberalized trade. The assistance is generally restricted to workers and has focused on retraining programs. Trade adjustment assistance has been provided sparingly because of concerns that it might become an entitlement for workers or used as a pork barrel program.

Second, safeguards relief can be granted under Section 201 in the form of temporary tariffs, import quotas, the suspension of previously granted trade concessions, or

---

[27]Although the program was directed at the European Union, it affected countries such as Australia that do not subsidize their agricultural exports. In response to complaints by Australia and other countries, the procedure for determining whether subsidies will be provided must include consideration of the effects on those countries.

trade adjustment assistance. Relief under Section 201 is infrequently requested and seldom granted. Relief for the steel industry, considered in the example, was the first Section 201 case in 17 years.

Third, relief is granted under Section 731 when a petitioner's dumping complaint is affirmed by the ITC and the ITA. A finding of dumping requires only that the imported good is sold at LTFV and that the petitioner has been materially injured by the imports. Antidumping thus is not restricted to predatory practices but instead can be used to protect domestic firms from imports.

Fourth, protection is provided by measures ranging from tariffs to voluntary agreements to limit imports. The United States imposes a 2.5 percent duty on passenger cars but imposes a 25 percent duty on light trucks. Textile and apparel exports to developed countries had been restricted by quotas specified in the Multi-Fiber Arrangement (MFA). The Uruguay Round accord eliminated the MFA and its quotas beginning in 2005. In anticipation of the end of the quotas, the U.S. textile and apparel industries sought protection from what was expected to be a huge increase in imports from China and India. U.S. manufacturers and textile unions petitioned the Bush administration for temporary safeguards protection under Section 201, and one week before the 2004 elections the president agreed to consider the petition.[28] Under a provision in the agreement allowing China to join the WTO, the United States imposed quotas on some clothing imports. Under pressure from both developed and developing countries, China announced that it would impose a tariff on its textile exports.

The Cost of Protectionism

Ultimately, the cost of protectionism is borne by consumers. Hufbauer and Elliott (1994) estimated that in 1990 special trade protection cost consumers over $70 billion, or approximately $280 per capita. U.S. producers were estimated to have captured approximately 45 percent of that amount as additional profits. Of the 21 cases of protection they studied, the annual cost per job saved ranged from $3,000 to $256,000, with an average of $54,000 for the 192,000 jobs saved by the protection. Over 152,000 of those jobs were in the apparel industry, and the cost to consumers per job was over $50,000 per year.

Although they bear the cost of protectionism, consumers are costly to organize, and individual consumers are unlikely to act politically on trade protection issues. Furthermore, organized consumer groups have largely been inactive in cases involving protection of domestic industries. This leaves the political arena open to domestic industries, with political opposition coming primarily from importers, U.S. exporters, and those in government who support free trade and economic efficiency. For example, in the Section 201 petition the U.S. textile manufacturers and unions were opposed by the United States Association of Importers of Textiles and Apparel.

Channels of Protection

Firms, labor unions, and industries can seek protection from imports through political and/or administrative channels. The political channel is through Congress and is directed either at specific legislation, such as a quota on sugar imports, or at the criteria used in the administrative channel. In addition to enacting new legislation, the political channel represents a threat that may strengthen the U.S. bargaining position with other countries. The protection obtained by an industry through the political channel depends on its ability to generate nonmarket pressure, as considered in Chapter 6, and on the pressure from opposing groups. Industries such as automobiles, steel, dairy farming, sugar, and textiles with large numbers of employees have been able to generate considerable nonmarket pressure.

The administrative channel involves regulatory and executive branch agencies and is accessed by a petition filed pursuant to the U.S. trade laws. Much of the administration of trade policy is delegated to the ITC, the ITA, and the president. In the chapter

---

[28]At the same time a group of the least-developed countries sought protection from the WTO for their domestic industries, which were expected to lose export markets to China.

EXAMPLE

Steel Imports and the Nonmarket Campaign

Overcapacity in the steel industry worldwide caused employment in the U.S. steel industry to drop by 325,000 during the 1980s, much of it at the hands of imported steel. Employment at Bethlehem Steel fell from 130,000 in the 1960s to 16,400 in 1998. To improve its competitiveness, the industry invested $50 billion in modernization and new technology. Despite the investment a number of inefficient plants were still in production, and the United States remained a high-cost producer. By the second half of the 1990s strong demand returned the U.S. industry to health, and prices and profits were up. The situation changed quickly, however, in 1997 as a result of the financial and economic crises in Asia and Russia and to a lesser extent in Latin America. Steel imports increased dramatically as foreign producers looked for markets for their excess capacity, and the robust U.S. economy with open markets was by far the most attractive opportunity. The imports drove prices down sharply and resulted in layoffs and the bankruptcy of one small steel company. The price of hot rolled steel fell by 18 percent in 1998 to the lowest level during the 1990s.

In response, the United Steel Workers (USW) and 12 leading steel producers joined in a broad client politics campaign to limit what they viewed as unfairly dumped steel. Curtis Barnette, CEO of Bethlehem Steel, said, "We're sometimes viewed as protectionist and rust belt in our thinking when we are a high-tech, low-cost, world-class industry. We believe in open markets. But when the rules are breached, they should be enforced."[1] Barnette was referring to U.S. laws against unfair competition resulting from dumping and the subsidization of foreign producers. To implement its nonmarket strategy the industry began the "Stand Up for Steel" campaign to bring the issue to the attention of the public, Congress, and the president.

Four producers of stainless steel and the USW also filed antidumping petitions against eight countries and countervailing duty petitions against Belgium, France, Italy, and South Korea for subsidizing their steel makers. Stainless sheet steel prices had fallen from $2,700 a metric ton in 1996 to $1,800 in 1998. Industry profits on stainless sheet steel fell from $466 million in 1995 to $141 million in 1997. The industry also filed antidumping and countervailing duty petitions against Brazil, Japan, and Russia for

dumping hot rolled steel and against Brazil for subsidizing its steel producers. With the downturn in the U.S. industry reflected in layoffs and lower prices and profits, the material injury standard was expected to be met.

In addition to pursuing its case in administrative channels, the industry pursued relief through political channels, deploying a nonmarket strategy intended to pressure the U.S. government to act. The industry lobbied Congress, and the House passed a nonbinding resolution calling for a ban on steel imports for a year. The industry also succeeded in inserting a provision in an appropriations bill requiring the Clinton administration to produce a plan for aiding the industry by January 5, 1999. Barnette and others lobbied in the Senate and convinced the Senate Steel Caucus to call on the administration to restrict imports.

The Stand Up for Steel campaign spent $3 million on a public advocacy campaign, including full-page newspaper advertisements presenting a letter calling on President Clinton to act.[2] George Becker, president of the USW, said, "We're fighting for the heartland of America. All the blood is gone from our industry; we can't bleed anymore."[3]

On the trade petitions the ITA found in favor of the steel industry and announced duties ranging from 3.44 percent to 67.68 percent. Overall, however, only about half the petitions were ultimately approved. The industry also sent a message to the president and the Democratic Party. In the 1997–1998 election cycle the USW and the steel companies provided $1.2 million in campaign contributions, most of which came from the USW, with over 80 percent going to Democrats. More importantly, the USW had been very effective in "get out the vote" efforts on behalf of Democrats. The president and vice president were not only concerned with rewarding their important political backers but also feared having unemployed steel workers when the 2000 elections arrived.

The campaign by the steel industry was not unopposed. Steel purchasers formed the Consuming Trade Action Coalition, which argued that any restraints on steel imports would result in higher prices for consumers. Both General Motors and Caterpillar criticized the antidumping and countervailing duty

---

[1] *New York Times,* December 10, 1998.

[2] *New York Times,* September 10, 1998.
[3] *New York Times,* December 10, 1998.

(Continued)

petitions. Caterpillar stated, "We strongly object to suggestions that steel trade should be subject to 'special' protection. The quotas used to protect the steel industry in each of the last four decades hurt American industries that use steel and rewarded foreign steel traders with a guaranteed share of a restricted market."[4]

Under the threat of action, Brazil and Russia agreed to quotas on imports of their steel products. The Clinton administration's report on the steel industry recommended that the administrative processes of U.S. trade law be accelerated, but the administration took no formal action under U.S. trade law. Some commentators believed that the failure to take action cost Vice President Gore the state of West Virginia and the election.

In 2001 President Bush ordered a review of the state of the steel industry. Employment in the industry had dropped from 800,000 in 1980 to 160,000 in 2001. Imports accounted for 27 percent of U.S. steel consumption, down from 30 percent during the Asian crisis, but prices for some steel products had fallen to their lowest levels in 20 years. In addition, 18 steel companies including LTV—one of the largest—had filed for bankruptcy.[5] The situation in the industry was due in part to the inefficiency of U.S. integrated steel producers, which had lost market share not only to imports but also to domestic mini mills. The market value of all U.S. steel producers was $10 billion, approximately 3 percent of the value of Microsoft.

As a result of its review the Bush administration took the rare action of filing a Section 201 petition for relief for the industry, the first such petition since 1985. The Emergency Committee for American Trade, a business organization that supported free trade, criticized the action.

Later in the year the ITC concluded that the industry had been "seriously injured" by imports in 12 product categories representing 74 percent of the imports under investigation.[6] The ITC recommended duties of from 5 to 40 percent on products representing 80 percent of imported steel. Hufbauer estimated that the cost to consumers for each steelworker job saved by the duties would be $326,000.[7]

The European Union and South Korea announced that they would file a complaint with the WTO if any new restrictions were imposed as a result of the Section 201 case. Pascal Lamy, the EU trade commissioner, said, "The cost of restructuring in the

U.S. steel sector should not be shifted to the rest of the world."[8]

The steel industry and the USW mounted an intense political campaign along with their allies in Congress. Under pressure the Bush administration imposed temporary 3-year tariffs on certain steel imports under Section 201. The ostensible purpose of the tariffs was to allow the steel companies to consolidate and improve their efficiency. The tariffs began at 30 percent and decreased to 24 percent the next year and to 18 percent in the third year. Developing countries were exempted, and the tariffs were primarily applied to industrialized countries and advanced developing countries. The Bush administration stated that the temporary tariffs were permitted under the WTO's safeguard provision, which allowed temporary relief in the event of a surge of imports.

Part of the assistance sought by the steel industry and USW was to cover the cost of health and pension benefits for 600,000 retired workers. The estimate of the cost over the next 10 years was more than $10 billion. The Bush administration refused to assume the pension obligations.

In response to the Section 201 action, the European Union took immediate action by filing two petitions with the WTO. First, it filed a complaint under the WTO dispute resolution process and identified U.S. imports to be targeted if the WTO ruled in its favor. Second, it filed a complaint that the United States had improperly imposed tariffs selectively under the "safeguards" procedures.

The direct effect of the tariffs on EU steel producers was small, since only 2.5 percent of EU production was affected. The principal concern was that low-cost steel that had been exported to the United States would now be diverted to the European Union, forcing prices down. The European Union announced that it would impose temporary tariffs on steel imports from any country that exceeded 2001 import levels. Canada also considered imposing temporary tariffs.

In late 2003 the WTO ruled that the U.S. tariffs were illegal and authorized punitive tariffs on $2.1 billion of U.S. exports to the European Union. In 2004 President Bush withdrew the safeguards tariffs. During the 2 years the tariffs were in effect, the U.S. steel industry consolidated and efficiency improved. As the tariffs were being withdrawn, U.S. demand for steel increased, raw material and energy costs increased, and the U.S. dollar fell, making steel imports more expensive. Steel prices in the United States rose sharply, and the industry returned to profitability.

---

[4]*New York Times,* December 10, 1998.
[5]Bethlehem filed for bankruptcy later in the year.
[6] The ITC found no serious injury in 17 product categories.
[7]*New York Times,* December 8, 2001.

[8]*New York Times,* June 7, 2001

case, *Cemex and Antidumping,* labor unions and U.S. cement producers filed an antidumping petition against Mexican cement imports. The administrative process imposes a series of gates through which a case must pass before relief is granted, and a petition may fail at any of several points in the process. In some cases, the threat of action is used to negotiate a voluntary settlement or suspension of the complaint. The steel imports example illustrates the use of both political and administrative channels.

THE POLITICAL ECONOMY OF MARKET OPENING

Market opening occurs through majoritarian policies such as those embodied in the WTO and NAFTA and through entrepreneurial politics, with the president attempting through multilateral and bilateral negotiations to reduce foreign tariff and nontariff barriers to trade. In some cases, market opening is characterized by client politics as interest groups pressure the government to take action to open specific foreign markets. This section considers the political economy of NAFTA and market opening under the threat of retaliation.

The North American Free Trade Agreement

The North American Free Trade Agreement established, subject to certain exceptions, free trade among Canada, Mexico, and the United States. NAFTA was an expansion of the United States–Canada Free Trade Agreement that had been in effect since 1988, and it adopted many of the features of that agreement. NAFTA is a free trade agreement and not a market integration agreement as is the Single Market Act in the European Union. The agreement thus does not cover the movement of people or the harmonization of domestic laws.

NAFTA provided for the elimination of tariff and nontariff barriers over a 10-year period, although some barriers were to be phased out over 15 years. To the extent that external trade barriers remained in effect, the elimination of trade barriers within North America gave foreign firms an incentive to locate operations in the NAFTA countries. Because of both market and nonmarket considerations, Japanese automobile manufacturers had incentives to shift light-truck production to North America. The principal market factor was the lower wages in Mexico. The principal nonmarket factor was to avoid the 25 percent U.S. tariff on imports from outside the NAFTA countries.

Despite the expected economic gains, political opposition to the agreement was strong in Canada and the United States. In the United States, opposition was led by organized labor, which feared the loss of jobs to Mexico, and by environmentalists. To overcome the opposition, the Bush administration, which negotiated the agreement, and the Clinton administration, which obtained congressional passage, made a number of deals and provided safeguards to obtain the needed votes. Nevertheless, 60 percent of the House Democrats voted against the agreement, and it passed as a result of strong Republican support.

The politics of NAFTA were similar to those of other trade liberalization measures. The weight of majoritarian interests was in favor of liberalized trade, and the opposition came from concentrated interests that were likely to be injured. Without concessions those interests and the client politics they generated might have defeated the agreement. Three types of measures were taken to reduce opposition. First, NAFTA included transition provisions for a gradual phaseout of trade barriers to give industries time to adjust. Moreover, to reduce opposition from agricultural interests that feared a flood of low-priced Mexican produce, NAFTA included safeguards that would take effect if there were large surges of imports that depressed agricultural prices.[29] Second, to obtain congressional votes, the Clinton administration made a number of side deals outside the trade area, including approval of public works

---

[29]In 2008 the last Mexican tariffs on corn, beans, milk, and sugar were eliminated under NAFTA. Mexican farmers took to the streets to protest the elimination and called for renegotiating NAFTA.

projects in members' districts. Third, side agreements were concluded to reduce the opposition of environmental groups concerned about higher pollution as production expanded in Mexico and of organized labor that feared that high-paying jobs would be lost to Mexico.

The elimination of tariff and nontariff barriers did not mean that trade disputes disappeared. NAFTA left domestic trade laws in place, so antidumping and counter-vailing duty cases continued. The Canada–U.S. bilateral free trade agreement had established a dispute settlement mechanism to avoid use of the courts. NAFTA incor-porated this feature by establishing a trilateral Trade Commission, composed of cabinet level officials, to hear complaints and resolve disputes on issues such as the ap-plication of antidumping laws. When the United States refused to allow Mexican trucks unrestricted access to U.S. roads, Mexico filed a complaint. A dispute settlement panel ruled in favor of Mexico, and fines could be imposed if the United States failed to grant access. The opposition in the United States was led by the Teamsters Union and by ac-tivists concerned that the United States did not have the safety inspection capacity to ensure that the trucks met U.S. safety standards. President Clinton refused to allow Mexican trucks into the United States, but President Bush announced that the United States would comply with the panel decision. Mexican trucks were finally allowed into the United States in 2007.

NAFTA established the Commission on Environmental Cooperation and the Commission on Labor Cooperation to monitor environmental and labor develop-ments, promote compliance, receive complaints, and resolve disputes.[30] The first peti-tion on environmental protection was filed in 1998 by local environmental groups in Mexico and the United States.[31] In 1998 the Canadian office of the USW filed a com-plaint against Mexico for failure to protect the rights of Mexican workers to choose which union represented them. The U.S. Department of Labor filed a supporting com-plaint to be addressed by the labor ministries of the three countries. To address envi-ronmental concerns, Mexico and the United States established the North American Development Bank to fund environmental projects along their 2,000 mile border.

Market Opening Under the Threat of Retaliation

The most effective means of addressing foreign barriers to trade is through negotia-tions, but countries, and particularly the United States, have used retaliation and its threat to provide leverage. In the 1980s the Semiconductor Industry Association filed a Section 301 petition to pry open the Japanese market to foreign-made semiconductors. Pressure from the United States and the threat of success in the administrative channel resulted in an agreement in which Japanese semiconductor manufacturers pledged not to sell in the United States at less than fair value, to open the Japanese market, and to increase the market share of foreign semiconductors to 20 percent.

More often, however, bilateral negotiations were lengthy and only moderately suc-cessful. Increasingly frustrated by what it viewed as inadequate action and by a process that placed much of the power in the hands of the president, Congress sought to in-crease its influence over both the relief and the retaliation processes. In 1988 Congress enacted the Omnibus Trade and Competitiveness Act, which established a mechanism for retaliation under a strengthened Section 301, referred to as Super 301.

Super 301 provided for mandatory sanctions against countries that engaged in un-fair trade practices that injured U.S. industries. The USTR prepared the National Trade Estimate Report (NTER) listing the countries with which the United States had a large trade deficit and the policies and practices that inhibited U.S. exports. The threat of mandatory retaliation under Super 301 contributed to an agreement under which Japan pledged to open its markets for wood products, communications satellites, and supercomputers.

---

[30]Rugman, Kirton, and Soloway (1999) present an analysis of the implications for corporate strategy of environmental regulation under NAFTA.
[31]Hufbauer et al. (2000) provide a review of the first 7 years of the effect of NAFTA on the environment.

Super 301 was sharply criticized by other countries, and both the European Union and Japan retaliated by issuing reports identifying U.S. tariff and nontariff barriers. Authorization for Super 301 expired at the end of 1990, but President Clinton issued an executive order reinstating a revised version of Super 301 under which sanctions were not mandatory. The rancor caused by Super 301 and the responses to it convinced most countries to pursue market opening through multilateral negotiations under the WTO.

The United States continues to issue the NTER and in 2008 put Thailand on the priority watchlist because of the compulsory licenses it had authorized. Fearing possible trade sanctions, Thailand prepared a plan for improving intellectual property protection and sought to convince the United States to take it off the priority watchlist. The chapter case, *Compulsory Licensing, Thailand, and Abbott Laboratories,* considers this issue from the perspective of a company whose patent has been violated by the compulsory license.

SUMMARY

The gains from trade and the law of comparative advantage provide a compelling rationale for free trade. Under certain conditions, however, a nation can benefit from a strategic trade policy that restricts imports or subsidizes exports. In such situations countries may be in a prisoners' dilemma in which each has an incentive to adopt a strategic trade policy, but all are worse off when they do so. International trade agreements are intended to avoid these dilemmas and allow gains from trade to be realized.

International trade policy is driven by economic incentives but governed by the politics that stem from those incentives. The politics of international trade are basically majoritarian, but because of rents associated with sunk resources, the politics of protectionism are often strong. Protectionism is characterized by client politics, whereas the politics of trade liberalization is entrepreneurial. Opposition to protectionism can develop from importers and their customers and from exporters concerned about retaliation by other countries. Interest group politics can be the result.

Multilateral trade liberalization policies are incorporated in the agreements that govern trade and dispute resolution. The WTO agreements cover trade in goods, services, and agricultural products and provide for intellectual property protection. Several regional free trade agreements, including NAFTA, the single market of the European Union, and Mercosur, have been established to eliminate internal barriers to trade.

The political economy of international trade is best understood by focusing on domestic politics and the negotiations among countries on trade policy. Trade negotiations reflect the desire to open foreign markets while avoiding injury to domestic interests. The political forces supporting protectionism are naturally strong because of the rents that accrue to sunk resources, but the long-run gains from trade are greater than the rents that would be dissipated by trade liberalization. In the United States the president usually advocates trade liberalization, and protectionism manifests itself primarily in Congress and administrative agencies.

Whereas the United States has generally supported free trade, it provides both administrative and political channels for relief of industries injured by imports. Because protectionism is costly to an economy, the administrative channel has been designed to provide easy access but to make relief relatively hard to obtain. Success for an industry seeking relief in the political channel requires an ability to generate nonmarket pressure, and this requires numbers, resources, and coverage of political districts.

The Part IV integrative case, *Toys 'R' Us and Globalization,* considers a firm that takes its domestic market strategy to other countries and encounters a variety of trade and other barriers.

------------------------------------ C A S E S ------------------------------------
Cemex and Antidumping

Lorenzo Zambrano was accustomed to making tough decisions. During his 6-year tenure as chief executive officer of Cementos Mexicanos, S.A. (Cemex), he had transformed Cemex from a small Mexican cement manufacturer to an industry superpower. In the fall of 1990, however, Zambrano faced perhaps his most difficult challenge. In August the U.S. International Trade Commission ruled that Cemex had unfairly depressed cement prices in the southern and southwestern United States by dumping cement and cement clinker. As a result, a duty of 58 percent was levied on all subsequent Cemex exports from Mexico into the region. The ruling threatened Cemex's expansion and its access to the lucrative U.S. market. Cemex needed a strategy to address the threat.

In early 1989 cement producers in the southern portion of the United States were concerned about the erosion of their domestic market share due to increased imports from Mexico. Imports of gray portland cement and cement clinker, two principal cement products, had been increasing steadily over the previous 5 years. At the same time the lackluster performance of the economy in the region, and in particular the depressed level of new construction, was reducing the demand for cement.

Historically, the cement industry was a very regionalized business with high overland transportation costs preventing the commodity from freely flowing between regional markets. This insulation helped cement producers ride out hard times in the highly cyclical industry. Throughout the 1980s, however, Mexican producers were able to transport their cement across the border and still remain competitive on price, sometimes undercutting domestic producers. The majority of Mexican cement imported into the United States came from one producer, Cemex.

U.S. cement companies in the South and Southwest realized that imports from Cemex and other Mexican companies presented a threat to their profitability and perhaps their survival. They believed that with high transportation costs, Mexican producers must be selling their cement at less than fair value, which would constitute dumping under Section 731 of U.S. trade law. Cement producers in Arizona, New Mexico, Texas, and Florida filed an antidumping petition claiming that Cemex and the Mexican cement industry were dumping cement and clinker in their markets.

The Mexican Cement Industry

Portland cement was used predominantly in the production of concrete, and cement clinker was the primary component in the production of portland cement. Demand for cement was cyclical and followed the general economic climate, demographic trends, and construction expenditures. In Mexico approximately 60 percent of cement expenditures were in residential construction, 20 percent in public works, and 20 percent in commercial construction.

A principal input to cement production was oil, with energy costs accounting for 40 to 50 percent of cement production expenses. Mexican cement firms had benefited from governmental policies. Mexico's vast oil resources allowed it to implement targeted domestic industrial policies, and in 1986 the government provided its domestic producers with oil for as little as $4 a barrel, compared with a weighted-average world price ranging from $14 to $16 a barrel.[32] In 1990, however, Mexican oil prices were raised to world levels.

The Mexican cement industry was dominated by Cemex, which by the early 1990s was the largest cement company in North America and the fourth largest in the world. By the end of 1991 its capacity had grown to 24 million tons, which was 63 percent of Mexican capacity. Cemex's primary Mexican competitor was Grupo Cementos Apasco, S.A. de C.V. (Apasco), which was 60 percent owned by Holderbank Financière Glarus Ltd. (Holderbank), a Swiss company that was the largest cement company in the world.[33] Apasco had 17 percent of the Mexican market in 1991. The next largest competitor was Cruz Azul, which had 13 percent of the market.

Part of Cemex's rapid growth had come through acquisitions. Cemex had spent nearly $1 billion on acquisitions acquiring Cementos Anahuac, then Mexico's third-largest cement producer, in 1987 and in 1989 acquiring Empresas Tolteca, Mexico's second-largest producer and Cemex's chief competitor. Geographic diversification in addition to locating plants close to major markets rationalized production. Cemex also spent $950 million on new plant and environmental control equipment. This made the plants more energy efficient, raised labor productivity, and added 4.8 million tons of new capacity. Another $330 million was spent to develop international operations, including U.S. distribution facilities in Arizona, Texas, and California. Cemex subsequently acquired for $1.8 billion the two largest Spanish cement producers, giving it a presence in the European Union.

In 1991 Cemex's sales were approximately $1.7 billion with exports accounting for 15 percent of the total. The combination of its plant modernization and capital expenditure programs and its management and engineering know-how had given Cemex very low costs. Cemex

------

[32]"Cement Makers Fight, Yet Buy from, Importers," *Business Marketing*, August 1986, and *Energy Statistics Sourcebook*, 1987.
[33]Holderbank subsequently changed its name to Holcim.

had outstanding plant management practices and had been able to reduce plant downtime substantially, which increased its effective capacity and reduced costs.

Cemex had high brand loyalty in Mexico. In most countries, cement was a commodity purchased primarily by industrial and commercial buyers. In Mexico, however, about 78 percent of cement sold was through retailers in bags under brand names. In 1991 Cemex's bagged cement was sold through 4,500 exclusive retail distributors. Cemex provided technical and marketing assistance to its dealers and maintained long-term relationships with them.

Cemex had several plants located close to the U.S. border. Cemex's headquarters in Monterrey was only 130 miles from Texas, and the rapid economic growth in Mexico along the U.S. border provided an attractive location for new cement plants. Since cement production involved economies of scale, large plants were desirable, leaving some capacity for exports to the United States.

The U.S. Cement Industry

As in Mexico, the U.S. industry was highly cyclical, depending on the general state of the economy and the construction industry in particular. Because of high overland transportation costs 95 percent of all gray portland cement shipments were made to customers located within 300 miles of the production site.

The U.S. industry was not nearly as concentrated as the Mexican industry. The leading U.S. cement producer in 1990 was Holnam, which was owned by Holderbank and had 11.8 percent of the domestic market.[34] Holnam was followed by Lafarge (6.7 percent), Southdown (6.1 percent), Lone Star Industries (5.5 percent), Ash Grove Cement (4.9 percent), and numerous other companies, at least five of which each had a domestic market share of over 3 percent. During the 1980s European companies began buying U.S. cement companies, and by 1989, 60 percent of the U.S. industry was owned by foreign companies. For example, Lafarge was owned by Lafarge Coppée of France, which was the world's second largest cement producer.

Cement imports accounted for 22 percent of the approximately 90 million tons of annual U.S. cement consumption, and imports had somewhat higher shares in the southern tier states. The Portland Cement Association estimated that in 1986 U.S. producers bought and resold approximately two-thirds of the cement imported into the country. The rationale provided by U.S. producers was that import prices were attractive, and since cement was a commodity, they were forced to serve their customers from the lowest-cost source.

The U.S. construction industry was weak at the end of the 1980s. The growth of the U.S. cement market was 1.3 percent in 1989 and 2.9 percent in 1990, whereas the growth rates of the Mexican cement market for the same years were 3.7 percent and 7.3 percent, respectively. In the southern and southwestern United States in particular, the success of Mexican cement importers contrasted sharply with the decline of local cement firms. In 1988, Mexican imports accounted for 14 percent of the Arizona–New Mexico–Texas market and 22 percent of the Florida market. In addition, since 1983 seven domestic cement plants had closed in the Arizona–New Mexico–Texas region and two had closed in Florida.

Domestic firms believed that Mexican firms were dumping cement in the United States by selling their exports at less than fair value (LTFV). The antidumping petitioners included two unions and eight companies, which formed the Ad Hoc Committee of AZ-NM-TX-FL Producers of Gray Portland Cement. The committee was led by Southdown, the largest U.S.-owned cement manufacturer. "Our investigation to date convinces us that the Mexicans' success in U.S. markets is due to dumping and not to any other factor," stated Clarence Comer, chief executive of Houston-based Southdown and chairman of the committee.[35]

The petitioners claimed that they had been materially injured by Mexican cement producers. The petition alleged that the dumping of cement depressed prices in the United States, caused investors to abandon the industry, and threatened their markets, production, and jobs. Comer summarized the allegation: "U.S. cement producers should not have to accept declining returns, declining employment, and declining capital investment. We should not have to cede U.S. markets and U.S. jobs to unfairly priced imports from Mexico. If we lose out to fair competition from Mexico, so be it."[36] Comer surmised that additional injury to the cement industry in the southern and southwestern United States was imminent. "Mexican producers continue to build export oriented capacity aimed at American markets."[37]

The petitioners identified two principal reasons the U.S. cement producers were vulnerable to imports from Mexico. First, because cement was a commodity, a small price change could result in large shifts in market shares. Thus, even a small price difference would cause a large loss of volume for domestic producers if they did not meet the lower import price. Second, cement imports displaced domestic production ton for ton because aggregate demand for cement was derived from the demand for construction, and cement represented a small share of construction costs. Consequently, the aggregate demand for cement did not vary appreciably with price, so lower prices did not create additional demand.[38]

---

[34]Holnam was formed by the merger of Dundee Cement and Ideal Basic, and in 2001 was renamed Holcim.

[35]"U.S. Cement Companies Charge Mexican Producers with Dumping Cement in U.S. Markets," *Business Wire*, September 27, 1989.
[36]Ibid.
[37]Ibid.
[38]Ibid.

A similar but unsuccessful antidumping petition had been filed in 1986 by all U.S. cement producers against Mexico, Colombia, Venezuela, France, Greece, Japan, South Korea, and Spain.[39] In that case, the International Trade Commission (ITC) determined that there was no material injury to the U.S. cement industry because it had begun its recovery from the recession. The 1989 case, however, was different in three key respects: the petition was more narrowly focused; demand for cement in Arizona, New Mexico, and Texas was depressed; and Mexican imports were rising while U.S. cement prices were falling.

U.S. Antidumping Law

The antidumping laws codified in Section 731 allowed either a private party or the International Trade Administration (ITA), an arm of the Department of Commerce (DOC), to file a petition for redress. The executive branch agencies charged with the administration of trade law in dumping cases were the ITC and the ITA. The ITC conducted a preliminary investigation to determine if there was a "reasonable indication" of material injury, or the threat of such injury, to the industry. Typically, the investigation covered the previous 3 years of activity. If no indication of injury were found, the petition was dismissed.

With a positive preliminary determination from the ITC, the ITA investigated whether there was a "reasonable likelihood" that imports were being sold at LTFV and calculated a preliminary estimate of the dumping margin. With an affirmative finding that a reasonable likelihood existed, the importer was required to make a cash deposit or post a bond or other security to guarantee the potential dumping liability. Upon concluding its investigation, the ITA announced its final determination of whether dumping was found. A positive finding included the final estimate of the dumping margin. A negative finding resulted in the petition being dismissed. Following an affirmative finding by the ITA, the ITC began the industry analysis stage. Here, the ITC investigated whether the imports in question caused or threatened to cause injury to the domestic industry. Unless the ITC found material injury, the case was dismissed. If the ITC found material injury, the case returned to the ITA for the negotiation of settlements and/or the imposition of duties.

The ITC and ITA Determinations

To find material injury or the threat of material injury, the ITC had to first determine the "like product" and the "domestic industry." The petitioners and respondents agreed that gray portland cement and cement clinker comprised a single like product. On November 8, 1989,

the ITC issued a unanimous affirmative preliminary determination in favor of the petitioners. The DOC then formally notified the Mexican cement producers that they had to submit to and fully cooperate with an administrative review if they wished to continue exporting to the United States. Questionnaires sent to Cemex requested general information on Cemex's strategy, production capacity, and number of plants. They also requested specific information on the Mexican and U.S. markets, including Cemex's costs, prices, pricing policies, market share, and customer information for the different markets.

The ITA concluded that Type II gray portland cement was the "like product" and that the bulk cement market was the relevant market for the basis of comparison. To test for dumping or the selling of a product at LTFV, the ITA considered the weighted-average price (for all the different plants from which U.S. sales were made) of the product as sold by the foreign firm to the first unrelated party in the importing country. This price was then compared with the price at which the same or a similar product was sold in the home country. Since data for the price comparisons were limited, the ITA "constructed" prices at the mill gate using an administrative provision in its procedures that subtracted transportation and other costs. The price comparison thus was of mill net prices, determined by taking the sale price and deducting all costs other than those incurred in the mill. Dumping would be found if the price at which a ton of cement left the mill to a U.S. customer was lower than the price at which a ton of cement left the mill to a Mexican customer. The dumping margin was then the average of all the margins for those comparison sales for which dumping was found. Figure 18-5 presents a sample calculation.

The ITA set the dumping margin for Cemex at 58.38 percent and for Apasco, Cementos Hidalgo, and all others at 53.26 percent, 3.69 percent, and 58.05 percent, respectively. Thus, if the ITC were to find injury, Cemex would be assessed a duty of 58 percent of the dollar value of each ton of cement leaving the mill for the U.S. market.

To determine whether there was "material injury" or the "threat of material injury" from imports of Mexican cement, the ITC assessed the effects of Mexican cement imports on U.S. prices, production, capacity, capacity utilization, shipments, inventories, employment, wages, financial performance, capital investments, and research and development expenditures. The data showed that from 1986 to 1989 the total quantity of cement shipped by U.S. producers had increased by 4.7 percent, but declining prices caused the total value to decrease by 3.7 percent. Capacity for cement and clinker production changed little, and capacity utilization decreased slightly. Additionally, the employment, wages, and hours worked of production workers fell by 19 percent, 13.8 percent, and 14 percent, respectively. Productivity rose by

---

[39]In contrast to shipping by land, shipping by sea is low cost.

FIGURE 18-5 Example of the Antidumping Margin

	Matched Pair of Sales in	
	Mexico	**United States**
Price	$85	$80
Transportation to terminal	10	30
Customs	0	2
Terminal and distribution	11	7
Other expenses	<u>12</u>	<u>10</u>
Mill net price	$52	$31
Dumping margin = 100 (52 − 31)/31 = 68 percent		

23 percent. The financial performance of southern tier producers deteriorated, as gross profit fell by 18.1 percent and operating income dropped by 36.7 percent. Some firms had curtailed planned investment. The data also indicated that the volume of Mexican imports had increased 24 percent.

In August 1990 the ITC issued an affirmative final determination in favor of the petitioners. To continue importing cement and clinker, Mexican importers were required to tender cash deposits to the U.S. Customs Service equal to the estimated dumping margins. For Cemex and Apasco, those margins were 58 percent and 53 percent of their mill net prices, respectively. The antidumping order had an unlimited duration, so the duties would remain in effect until the dumping ceased. The duties, however, were to be recalculated every year based on updated data. As a result of the duties, all the Mexican producers except Cemex left the U.S. market.

Cemex's Strategy

From the beginning of the process, Cemex complied fully with the requests for data. Cemex also opened its operations to the DOC as much as possible to expedite the administrative process and to demonstrate that the company was confident that it would prevail.

Cemex assigned the dumping issue top priority and created a new department to oversee the implementation of a multipronged strategy to address the issue. First, a U.S. law firm specializing in dumping cases was hired to provide advice. Second, Cemex sought to use the media in Mexico to build support and call the attention of the Mexican people to the alleged "unfair" treatment. Cemex also sought coverage from the U.S. media, including the *Wall Street Journal,* to educate the American people about Cemex and its overall strategy and performance both in Mexico and in the United States. Third, a presentation was made to the Mexican Commerce Department to demonstrate the importance of the petition and the effect it would have on Cemex and Mexico. The goal was to obtain the Mexican govern-

ment's support against the U.S. action. The Mexican government, however, was concerned about possibly jeopardizing the ongoing North American Free Trade Agreement (NAFTA) negotiations and decided not to pressure the U.S. DOC.

The opportunity for lobbying in Washington was limited because the issue was in the jurisdiction of regulatory rather than legislative institutions. As a result, little lobbying was done, although certain government leaders (including senators and governors in states where Cemex had operations) were contacted to explain the antidumping petition and Cemex's position.

Cemex believed that in reaching their conclusion that dumping had occurred the U.S. agencies had ignored Cemex's actual price and shipping costs. For example, Cemex sold its cement in the United States at market prices, but nearly a third of that went to the cost of transporting the cement from its plants south of the border. Zambrano noted that the ITC deducted the transportation costs and thus concluded there was dumping.[40]

Cemex argued that the antidumping petition was nothing more than an attempt by its competitors to halt its expansion in the United States. "Some of our competitors thought we were a rather weak neighbor," stated Zambrano. "And it just so happens that we grew, and they didn't like it."[41]

The ITC ruling had potentially devastating ramifications for Cemex's expansion drive into the U.S. market, and Zambrano implemented an integrated strategy, combining both market and nonmarket components. The market component consisted of a revamped short-term business strategy in response to the duty assessed. The nonmarket component focused on lowering the duty and reversing the ruling. It was designed to seek redress through three institutional arenas: administrative, judicial, and international.

---

[40]"Cement Wars," *Forbes,* October 1, 1990.
[41]Ibid.

Cemex's Market Strategy[42]

First, Zambrano decided to reduce substantially Cemex's exports to the United States. This was offset to some extent by growth in Cemex's home market, which had become much more attractive because Mexico initiated a number of public works projects that caused demand for cement to grow by about 10 percent.

Second, the 58 percent duty made shipments unprofitable in states where cement prices were low, so Zambrano withdrew completely from some U.S. states and focused only on those with higher prices. Cemex abandoned Florida outright after the ITC ruling and was content with breaking even in the higher-priced markets. Selling only in regions with high prices had the advantage of reducing the difference between U.S. and Mexican mill net prices, which would result in a lower dumping margin at the next annual review.

Third, Cemex maintained a substantial Type II (bulk) cement market in Mexico so that the ITA would compare the product sold in the U.S. market with the Mexican Type II (bulk) cement market. Cemex wanted to avoid the ITA concluding that the like product was its branded bagged cement in Mexico, which would substantially increase the dumping margin.

Cemex's Nonmarket Strategy

As part of its nonmarket strategy Cemex requested administrative reviews of the duty, and in the first review the petitioners alleged that Cemex had created a fictitious bulk market in its home country to reduce the duties. The ITA found that no fictitious market had been created, and as a result of Cemex's new market strategy of limiting exports to regions with high prices, the duty was reduced to 30.74 percent.

Zambrano also attempted to have the ITC's ruling reversed in judicial arenas. Cemex appealed the ITC determination of material injury to the U.S. Court of International Trade (CIT), arguing that the ITC had not followed proper procedures. The CIT rejected Cemex's argument, and Cemex appealed, using the same argument, to the U.S. Court of Appeals, but was also unsuccessful. Cemex also appealed to the CIT the duties imposed by the ITA, arguing that the ITA had followed neither statutory requirements nor precedents in determining the dumping margin. The CIT, however, ruled that the overall weight of precedent was in favor of the approach used in the Cemex case. The CIT upheld the dumping duty.

After failing in the U.S. judicial arenas, the Mexican government petitioned the General Agreement on Tariffs and Trade (GATT) requesting that a panel be established to review the antidumping dispute. In July 1992 the GATT panel found that the United States had improperly imposed duties on the Mexican cement industry and recommended that $30 million in duties already collected be returned. The order to refund duties was rarely made by GATT, so the decision was considered severe. The panel did not address whether the Mexican companies had sold at less than fair value. Rather, the panel concluded that the U.S. Department of Commerce had not verified that the ad hoc committee of petitioners that brought the action was sufficiently representative of the industry. The committee represented only 61.7 percent of all U.S. cement producers in the region, but under GATT antidumping rules, the petitioner in a regional dispute must represent all or almost all of the production in the region.

Since all GATT member nations had to adopt the panel's recommendation for it to take effect, any single member could effectively block action. Concluding that the basis for the GATT panel's determination was contrary to U.S. law, the United States withheld its approval and the duties and findings imposed under U.S. trade law remained in effect.

Frustrated by the U.S. rejection of the GATT panel's decision, Cemex faced four immediate problems. First, the antidumping duty remained in effect on Cemex's remaining exports to the United States, and the U.S. producers were sure to argue at each annual administrative review that the bulk cement market in Mexico was fictitious and that bagged rather than bulk cement was the relevant like product. This posed the threat of an even higher duty. Second, Cemex had some stranded assets in terminal and distribution facilities in the United States. Third, the reduction in exports to the United States left Cemex with excess capacity in Mexico. Fortunately, domestic demand for cement had grown somewhat. Fourth, Cemex had to decide what to do about the U.S. market.

U.S. demand continued to exceed domestic capacity, creating a demand for imports. Cemex could import cement from Spain, but this left the risk of another antidumping petition. Cemex could also directly invest in the United States by building new plants. This would meet some of the shortfall in domestic supply but would reduce the need for imports and Cemex continued to want to export to the United States. Cemex could also attempt to purchase existing capacity from a U.S. producer. This would be advantageous if Cemex were confident that it could operate the plants more efficiently than the seller. Purchasing capacity would not reduce the demand for imports, leaving export opportunities if the antidumping problem could somehow be resolved. ∎

SOURCE: This case was written by Justin Adams under the supervision of Professor David P. Baron. It draws upon two previous case studies, "Cemex and Mexican Cement Imports," by Darryl E. Walsh, and "Cemex vs. U.S. Sunbelt Competitors," by Juan Prestarno, as well as "Gray Portland Cement and Cement Clinker from Mexico," Determination of the ITC in Investigation No. 731–TA–461 (Preliminary) and (Final). Copyright © 1998 by the Board of Trustees of the Leland Stanford Junior University. All rights reserved. Reprinted with permission.

---

[42]Ibid.

Preparation Questions

1. Why might the price of cement be higher in Mexico than in the United States?
2. Is the dumping of cement likely to be harmful to the U.S. economy?
3. What was the motivation of the U.S. producers in filing the antidumping petition? Is this protectionism?
4. Evaluate Cemex's strategy for addressing the antidumping ruling. How well were its market and nonmarket components integrated?
5. After the United States withheld its approval of the GATT decision, what should Cemex do about the four problems?

Compulsory Licensing, Thailand, and Abbott Laboratories

TRIPS and Compulsory Licensing

The Trade Related Intellectual Property Rights (TRIPS) agreement negotiated in the Uruguay Round of multilateral trade negotiations was a major victory for the brand name pharmaceutical companies. Patent life was extended to 20 years in the United States, and countries participating in the World Trade Organization (WTO) agreed to bring their national patent law into conformity with the laws in the developed countries. This forced India, for example, to change its patent laws, preventing the Indian generic pharmaceutical companies from copying patented pharmaceuticals by using a different production process.

Article 31 of TRIPS, however, allowed for violation of a patent (compulsory licensing) without being specific about the reasons for the violation but also imposed certain requirements on governments. Under Article 31(f), entitled "Other Use Without Authorization of Right Holder," the country must first attempt to obtain a voluntary license under reasonable commercial terms. Pharmaceutical companies, however, typically do not license their patents, so Article 31 allowed countries to proceed in the cases of "national emergencies," "other circumstances of extreme urgency," or for "public noncommercial use" such as in research. If a compulsory license was issued, it normally was only for the domestic market, and a royalty (e.g., 5 percent) had to be paid to the patent holder.

Developing countries were unhappy with TRIPS, and when the Doha Round of WTO multilateral negotiations began, those countries insisted on more flexibility in interpreting Article 31. In 2001 the WTO ministers issued a Declaration on TRIPS and Public Health that supported actions by members to protect public health. In 2003 the General Council of the WTO allowed member countries to waive Article 31(f) under certain conditions to allow countries with no manufacturing capacity to import drugs made under a compulsory license. The Declaration stated that TRIPS should not prevent members from protecting public health and underscored "flexibilities" associated with compulsory licensing and parallel imports.[43] The General Council also extended to 2016 the deadline for least-developed countries to bring their laws regarding patent protection into compliance with TRIPS. Twenty-three developed countries pledged not to use the Declaration provisions, and 11 other countries said they would use the provisions only in the case of national emergencies or extremely urgent situations. Thailand was not one of those countries.

In 2005 the WTO added Article 31bis to TRIPS, which allows least developed countries to import a drug from another country for the treatment of HIV/AIDS, tuberculosis, and malaria epidemics. The article would go into effect if two-thirds of the WTO members ratified it. The European Union ratified the provision, bringing the number of members having approved it to 12. Rwanda was the first country to invoke the provision by arranging for the importation of an AIDS drug from Canada.

The pharmaceutical industry interpreted the language of Article 31 as applying to a health crisis such as virulent infectious flu or SARS. The industry knew, however, that the language was subject to interpretation. Compulsory licensing had been threatened but never invoked.

Brazil had threatened to invoke compulsory licensing in 2000 on three AIDS drugs, including one produced by Abbott Laboratories. The companies entered into negotiations with the Health Ministry, resulting in substantial price reductions, but compulsory licensing was not invoked. Brazil had a very successful national AIDS treatment program and had sought to reduce its cost by forcing down the prices of the drugs. The confrontation with the pharmaceutical companies was popular in Brazil, and its initiator, Health Minister Luiz Inacio Lula da Silva, subsequently was elected president of the country.

Pharmaceutical companies typically used a tiered-pricing system for their AIDS drugs. For developed countries prices were market based, whereas for the lowest income countries prices were at a major discount.

---

[43]The WTO allowed parallel imports, which were imports from a third country of a drug manufactured by a patent holder. A country that was paying a high price for a patented drug thus could import that drug from another country where it was sold at a discount.

Some companies priced at cost. Prices of AIDS drugs for the lowest-income countries had been reduced in response to pressure from governments and private politics initiated by activist organizations. For middle-income countries, such as Brazil, Mexico, and Thailand, the pharmaceutical companies priced at an intermediate level. Abbott Laboratories priced its AIDS drug Kaletra, a second-line AIDS drug used when first-line medications lost their effectiveness, at $7,000 a year in developed countries, $500 a year for the least developed countries, and $2,200 a year for low-income and low-middle income countries, which included Thailand. The World Bank categorized countries such as Thailand and Brazil as Upper Middle Income countries. The per capita gross national income of Thailand was $2,190 and Brazil was $2,760, whereas the per capita gross national income of the Least Developed Countries was $300 or less a year.[44]

Thailand and Abbott Laboratories

In 2004 Thailand introduced a national health care plan. In August 2006 a study funded by the World Bank and the health ministry estimated that compulsory licensing would save the government 100 billion baht through 2025.[45] In October 2006 a military coup in Thailand replaced the elected government. The military junta appointed Dr. Mongkol na Songkhla as Health Minister. He had been critical of pharmaceutical companies, and shortly after being appointed he launched a campaign to relieve the pharmaceutical burden on the national health care plan. On November 29, 2006 Dr. Mongkol sent a letter to Merck announcing that Thailand had invoked article 51 of its 1992 Patent Law that allowed the government to produce or import a generic version of Merck's patented AIDS drug Efavirenz, sold in Thailand under the name Stocrin. The government declared a public health emergency to justify importing the drug under TRIPS. Merck offered to reduce the price to avoid compulsory licensing, but Thailand went ahead and arranged for the supply of the drug from India.

In January 2007 Thailand notified Abbott and Sanofi-Aventis that compulsory licenses would be issued for Kaletra and Palvix, respectively. Thailand claimed that because of the price only about 40,000 of the 200,000 people who needed Plavix, a heart medicine, were receiving it. The government estimated that compulsory licensing would reduce the cost from $2 a pill to as low as 20 cents.[46]

In justifying its action, the Thai government issued a 96-page white paper in which Dr. Mongkol wrote, "The Thai ministry of public health views these decisions on the government use of patents as a form of social movement that aims at improving access to essential medicines and the health of the people. The public health interest is thus the main and final goal of this social movement. . . . We are convinced and committed to the view that Public Health interest and the life of the people must come before commercial interest."[47] Approximately 1 percent of the Thai population was estimated to have HIV/AIDS and less than 1 percent had chronic coronary disease.[48]

Dr. Mongkol also said, "We ask for the understanding of pharmaceutical companies. Much of our affected population cannot afford your drugs and we want people to have access to the medicines that they need. We are willing to negotiate with the companies if they are willing to give some discounts for the import of their originals."[49] "If they voluntarily reduce prices to let the poor people access to essential drugs, there is no need to do compulsory licensing. We are doing everything to help the poor people."[50]

The decision by the Thai government was endorsed by the Clinton Foundation, 22 U.S. senators, the World Health Organization, and UNAIDS, the United Nations agency responsible for coordinating AIDS care and prevention.

Compulsory licensing allowed a country to manufacture a patented drug, authorize a domestic company to produce it, or ask a pharmaceutical company in another country to supply the drug. Thailand planned to import a version of Efavirenz from India and pay for the Indian version of Efavirenz with funds from the Global Fund to Fight AIDS, Tuberculosis, and Malaria.[51] The Thai government decided to produce domestically its copy of Kaletra through its Government Procurement Organization (GPO), a state-owned company.

About 20 percent of the 500,000 people in Thailand living with HIV/AIDS were receiving treatment with a first-line antiretroviral drug produced by GPO, but an estimated 20,000 people had developed resistance to the drug. Those people would benefit from Kaletra. Another 60,000 patients could also benefit from Kaletra. Mongkol estimated that the cost of treating those patients could be reduced by two-thirds with compulsory licensing. The health ministry estimated that the country would save $24 million as a result of the three compulsory licenses.

---

[44]Source: World Bank, http://www.finfacts.com/biz10/globalworldincomepercapita.htm (October 26, 2006).

[45]*Straits Times,* January 31, 2007.

[46]Thailand entered into discussions with India for the supply of a copy of Plavix. Thailand asked for bids and M-cure was the lowest of the 4 bidders. The price was 1.01 baht per pill compared to 70 baht for the French-made Plavix.

[47]Inter Press Service/Global Information Network, March 21, 2007.

[48]The HIV/AIDS rate for the United States and Brazil was approximately 0.3 percent.

[49]Associated Press Worldstream, January 29, 2007.

[50]Agence France Presse, March 18, 2007.

[51]The Global Fund was an independent organization formed as a result of an initiative by United Nations Secretary General Kofi Annan. The Global Fund was funded by developed nations.

Abbott's Decision

Abbott reacted angrily to Thailand's action. It publicly objected and announced that it was withdrawing all pending applications for marketing new drugs in Thailand. Abbott withdrew applications for seven drugs: Aluvia, a version of Kaletra that required no refrigeration; a painkiller, Brufen; Abbotic, an antibiotic; a blood-clotting drug, Clivarine; Humira, an arthritis drug; Tarka, a high-blood-pressure medication; and a kidney disease drug, Zemplar.[52] Aluvia was particularly important because unlike Kaletra it did not require refrigeration, which was often not available to patients. "Without Aluvia in the arsenal of drugs to fight HIV/AIDS, Thailand will now have to maintain expensive cold storage for the drug, and poorer infected populations, who often cannot afford refrigeration, will continue to go without access to any form of Kaletra," said Dr. Homayoon Khanlou, AIDS Healthcare Foundation's director of global advocacy.[53]

Dirk Van Eeden, public affairs director of Abbott International, said, "Thailand has revoked the patent on our medicine, ignoring the patent system. Under these circumstances, we have elected not to introduce new medicines there."[54] He added, "Actions that don't respect patents make it difficult to justify bringing forward new medicines in Thailand."[55] Melissa Brotz, an Abbott spokeswoman, explained, "The Thai government has chosen to limit access to medicines by breaking patents and discouraging companies like Abbott from bringing new medicines forward there. This matter is about intellectual property and the integrity of the patent system."[56]

Bayer of Germany expressed support for Abbott. Arthur Higgins, head of Bayer's healthcare unit, said, "I fully support Abbott and I fully support the very strong stance the industry is taking. This is not the way forward. I do not believe it is in the long-term interest of the Thai people because Abbott has already said they will not bring any new products to the Thai market. This is what will happen."[57]

The Pharmaceutical Research & Manufacturers Association of Thailand, composed of 38 pharmaceutical companies mostly from Europe and the United States, warned that the government's move could discourage foreign investments. President Teera Chakajnarodom said, "Leading members of the association . . . have confirmed to me that their plans for further investment in Thailand will be put on hold pending a review of the foreign investment climate. They are concerned about continuing to invest in a country where the government cannot provide a basic guarantee for the safety of their assets. We fully appreciate the health challenges and financial constraints that the Ministry of Public Health faces. However, the best response to this situation is to engage constructively with industry to find a mutually agreeable solution."[58] Teera added, "We realize the problem of budget constraints of the Ministry of Public Health and we appreciate their efforts to provide better healthcare to patients. But compulsory licensing won't solve the problem. The best way is to negotiate."[59] Teera also said, "We don't want to see compulsory licenses used as a bargaining chip."[60] The Association said that Thailand was considering similar actions on 11 more AIDS, heart, and cancer drugs.

The International Federation of Pharmaceutical Manufacturers Associations said countries should initiate "direct discussions with the companies that invest, develop and market medicines to directly address key health challenges." President Harvey Bale added, "Compulsory licensing can be a route to commercial abuse and can put patients at risk."[61] The American Chamber of Commerce in Thailand said that compulsory licensing sends "a negative signal to foreign investors in Thailand regarding the government's commitment to transparency and support for intellectual property rights."[62]

Peter Mandelson, the trade commissioner of the European Union, wrote to the Thai government to protest the compulsory licensing of the Sanofi-Aventis drug. The European Parliament, however, disagreed and supported making HIV/AIDS and malaria drugs available in poor countries through breaking patents. The EU, however, did not define "poor," although the Commission of the European Union stated that it did not consider Thailand to be poor.

Reactions

Paul Cawthorne, head of Doctors Without Borders in Thailand, reacted to Abbott's decision to withdraw its new drug application, "I'm actually lost for words, if they really are going to do this. For me, it's just evil. It's appalling. If they really are going to do this, it reflects so badly on the multinational companies."[63] Cawthorne added, "It was the first time I have seen such a reaction from a drug company. If they think Thailand has broken a law, they should have challenged it in court instead of acting like a spoiled child."[64]

In May the Clinton Foundation announced that it had negotiated a major price reduction for generic second-line AIDS treatments. Making the announcement in Thailand accompanied by Dr. Mongkol, Bill Clinton commented, "Abbott has been almost alone in its hard-line position here over what I consider to be a life and death matter."[65]

[52]Associated Press Worldstream, March 21, 2007.
[53]PR Newswire US, March 14, 2007.
[54]Associated Press Financial Wire, March 14, 2007.
[55]*Financial Times,* March 14, 2007.
[56]Associated Press State and Local Wire, March 22, 2007.
[57]Reuters, March 15, 2007. Quoted in the *Nation* (Thailand), March 20, 2007.
[58]Associated Press Worldstream, January 25, 2007.
[59]*Christian Science Monitor,* January 31, 2007.
[60]*International Herald Tribune,* February 16, 2007.
[61]*Financial Times,* January 30, 2007.
[62]Associated Press Worldstream, January 31, 2007.
[63]*Wall Street Journal,* May 14, 2007.
[64]Associated Press Worldstream, March 21, 2007.
[65]*New York Times,* May 9, 2007.

Michael Weinstein, president of the AIDS Health-care Foundation, the largest U.S. AIDS health care and education organization, said, "This is a new low, and I am horrified that Abbott would deprive poor people in need of lifesaving medications, particularly for those living with HIV/AIDS, in a country as hard-hit by the epidemic as Thailand. . . . Abbott has the hubris to blacklist a courageous country like Thailand simply trying to do the right thing for its people. Astounding."[66] "What they did is synonymous with holding our patients hostage," said Kriengsak Vacharanukulki-eti, head of the Rural Doctors' Society. "It's not just a threat to Thai patients, it's a threat to patients in poor countries everywhere."[67]

"Abbott's move goes to show that they take no social responsibility and only care about maximum profit, especially since Thailand has not broken any laws or trade agreements," said Kamol Upakaew, an AIDS activist and former president of the Thai Network of People living with AIDS/HIV.[68]

Abbott was criticized in the United States by Christian Brothers Investment Services and 13 other religious investors. "We believe the company is overlooking risks that have a serious effect on brand, its relationships with patients, and ultimately, shareholder value."[69] The Interfaith Center on Corporate Responsibility (ICCR), which advised institutional investors such as universities, issued a report "Benchmarking AIDS: Evaluating Pharmaceutical Company Responses to the Public Health Crisis in Emerging Markets" in which it wrote, "there is an urgent clinical need for a number of products Abbott could provide including pediatric drugs, fixed dose combinations and low-cost generic versions of Kaletra. ICCR called on Abbott to ensure that its new, heat-stable version of Kaletra be registered, available and affordable in adult and pediatric formulations. ICCR continues to urge Abbott to bring its policies in line with these recommendations."[70]

Kannikar Kitjiwatchakul of Médecins Sans Frontières (MSF) Bangkok called for a local boycott of Abbott. Saree Aongsomwang of the Foundation for Consumers called for a global boycott. She said, "Since Abbott has challenged Thailand and shown it doesn't care about Thai consumers, please stop using any of its products. This act by Abbott is totally unacceptable. Please don't ignore this pressure against the government over stopping what really benefits the consumer."[71]

At the Eighth International Conference on AIDS in Asia and the Pacific attended by representatives of 70 countries, Prasada Rao, director of the UNAIDS regional support team, said, "Thailand has made a strong statement by invoking a compulsory license for the production of second-line antiretroviral drugs. It's the right

thing to do because we just can't provide those who need with only the first-line drugs because of the high cost. I urge countries in Asia and the Pacific region to use the WTO flexibilities to do more and show more commitment to AIDS responses."[72]

Relative to the importance of compulsory licensing, Thailand's savings of $24 million from compulsory licenses seemed small for a middle income country with 65 million people and a high growth rate of the economy. With no acute national health emergency the savings seemed a small reward for being the first country to invoke compulsory licensing of a pharmaceutical. Referring to Brazil's threat to use compulsory licensing, Tadataka Yamada, president of the Global Health Program of the Gates Foundation, observed, "Brazil is not Rwanda, which cannot afford to pay."[73] "Bruce Lehman, a lawyer who worked on the TRIPS accord in the Clinton administration, thinks it is cynical for middle-income countries 'to avoid paying their fair share of drug-discovery costs.' In doing so, he fears, they risk provoking a backlash from Americans who will, in effect, have to pay more as a result."[74] "Richard Epstein of the University of Chicago law school has observed that there is nothing to stop AIDS organizations or foreign governments from buying these products at a negotiated price and giving them away free. 'Charity can come from anywhere, not just drug companies,' he notes."[75]

A Change of Strategy

After discussions with the World Health Organization, Abbott agreed in April 2007 to reduce the price of Kaletra to $1,000 a year for several developing countries, including Thailand. The price in developed countries remained at $7,000.

The same month Abbott decided to change its strategy and negotiate with the Thai government. The company offered to resubmit its application for Aluvia and when approved sell it at $1,000 a year if Thailand would drop its plan to invoke compulsory licensing. Melissa Brotz of Abbott explained, "We are willing to have discussions to come to a solution, but we have not backed down on protecting intellectual property."[76] Abbott did not offer to reinstate the applications for the other six drugs. Miles D. White, Abbott CEO, explained the decision: "In this particular case, in the name of access for patients, we offered to resubmit Aluvia at our new price, which is lower than any generic, provided they wouldn't issue a compulsory license." He explained that the decision was the result of a "concern that compulsory licensing would be abused ever more widely, using HIV as an excuse."[77]

[66]Associated Press Financial Wire, March 14, 2007.
[67]Associated Press Worldstream, March 21, 2007.
[68]Associated Press Financial Wire, March 14, 2007.
[69]Associated Press State and Local Wire, March 22, 2007.
[70]PR Newswire US, March 22, 2007.
[71]Nation (Thailand), March 20, 2007.

[72]BBC Worldwide Monitoring, August 23, 2007.
[73]Economist, June 9, 2007.
[74]Economist, June 9, 2007.
[75]Economist, June 9, 2007.
[76]Wall Street Journal, April 24, 2007.
[77]Wall Street Journal, April 23, 2007.

The Thai government refused the offer, and Abbott did not resubmit the Aluvia application.[78] Yusuf Hamied, chairman of Cipla in India, which already produced a copy of Kaletra and was working on a copy of Aluvia, stated, "Let the multinationals go. We will supply whatever drugs the Thai or other governments may want."[79]

Michael Weinstein of the AIDS Healthcare Foundation supported Thailand's rejection of Abbott's offer, stating "Abbott took a huge hit from AIDS activists and advocates the world over when it first announced its drug blacklist against the people of Thailand last month, and the company bowed to pressure from activists by quickly announcing price cuts on its AIDS drugs in Thailand and 40 other low and lower middle-income countries. We fully support Thailand's right to exercise flexibility in promoting public health by issuing these compulsory licenses. We ask Abbott to immediately back off the 'quid pro quo' offer which holds Thai people in need of this lifesaving AIDS medicine hostage. We also question Abbott's real commitment to 'turning science into caring'—Abbott's hollow corporate slogan—when the company continues its blacklist on six other drugs in Thailand."[80]

Abbott's Response to Activists

The French AIDS activist group Act Up–Paris launched a cyber attack on Abbott's Web site which disrupted services, including its online sales. An Act Up–Paris member explained, "We use symbolic violence to call attention to real violence . . . ," such as against AIDS victims. Act Up–Paris responded to a call from a Thai patient advocacy group by setting up a link on its Web site that between 500 and 1,000 activists in 12 countries used in an International Day of Action to overload Abbott's Web site during a 4-hour period. The attack was launched on the evening before Abbott's annual meeting. Abbott wrote to the advocacy group and then filed a lawsuit in a French criminal court alleging that the group had violated two articles of French criminal law prohibiting disruption of a Web site and providing the means for others to do so.

Abbott characterized its lawsuit as "a principled action." A spokesperson explained, "We respect the right to protest and, while our organizations can disagree on various matters, it is important to convey those disagreements in a respectful, appropriate and lawful manner."[81] Michael Harrington, executive director of the Treatment Action Group in New York said, "It's the latest in a long line of miserable actions by Abbott."[82] Michael Weinstein said, "I've spoken to pharmaceutical industry executives who think that Abbott's position is a PR disaster for the industry."[83] Jerome Martin of Act Up–Paris said that the group would use the media attention and the trial to criticize Abbott's policy. He said, "We're going to use the forum they're offering us to talk about Thailand again and the horrible consequences their decision has had there."[84]

In July Abbott dropped its lawsuit after a discussion with Act Up–Paris at a conference in Australia. An Abbott spokesperson said she did not anticipate any further attacks, but Martin stated, "If we have to organize another net strike we will, because access to treatment is more important than information they have on their Web site."[85]

Brazil

Brazil decided to use compulsory licensing as a bargaining tactic. Brazil had a highly successful and acclaimed AIDS program that had brought the adult infection rate to the level of that in the United States. The program emphasized prevention and provided free drugs for those infected, but the cost of providing the drugs had doubled in the past 4 years. In May President Lula da Silva authorized Health Minister José Temporão to invoke compulsory licensing for Merck's drug Efavirenz, after negotiations over a price reduction broke down.[86] Brazil then began importing a substitute drug from India. Brazil was also attempting to negotiate lower prices for a number of other drugs. One was Abbott's Kaletra. ■

Preparation Questions

1. Evaluate Abbott's strategy regarding Thailand's compulsory licensing. Will it be successful?
2. What should Abbott do once Thailand rejected its offer?
3. What should Abbott do in Brazil?
4. What does this do for pharmaceutical companies' opportunities in rapidly growing lower and middle income countries?
5. How should the pharmaceutical industry deal with compulsory licensing?

---

[78]Sanofi-Aventis also offered a lower price for Plavix but also attached conditions. The Thai government rejected its offer.
[79]*Wall Street Journal,* April 24, 2007.
[80]*Biotech Business Week,* August 13, 2007.

[81]*Wall Street Journal,* June 18, 2007.
[82]*Wall Street Journal,* June 18, 2007. Abbott had infuriated AIDS activist groups in 2003 by increasing the price of Norvir by 400 percent to get patients to switch to Kaletra. (Datamonitor, June 20, 2007.) Both a Bristol-Myers Squibb and a GlaxoSmithKline drug needed a Norvir boost to be effective.
[83]*Wall Street Journal,* June 18, 2007.
[84]*Wall Street Journal,* June 18, 2007.
[85]*Wall Street Journal,* July 24, 2007.
[86]*Wall Street Journal,* July 5, 2007.

Sophis Networks and Encryption Export Controls (A)

On September 24, 1999, Joanne Mercer, vice president of Sophis Networks and head of the Security Products Division, faced a frustrating situation. She and the Government Affairs Group at Sophis Networks had spent the last 2½ years working closely with Congress and the Clinton administration to relax U.S. export restrictions on encryption products. Mercer had worked for passage of the Security and Freedom through Encryption Act (SAFE), but President Clinton had just pledged to veto it, and he announced his own legislative proposal. Sophis and other technology companies were dismayed by the proposal, which they believed would impair their competitiveness and cost them sales. The Clinton administration was concerned that the export of encryption products would impede the Federal Bureau of Investigation's (FBI) and the National Security Agency's (NSA) abilities to fight terrorists, spies, and criminals, who could conceal their plans using encryption products.

Encryption or cryptography is the science of designing code techniques that protect computer files and communications from eavesdroppers, hackers, spies, and other criminals. Encryption products allow employees confidential access to corporate data from remote locations using a public network. Encryption products protect medical records, corporate trade secrets, data on personal buying habits, air-traffic control centers, legal documents, credit histories, hospital databases, credit card transactions, and e-mail. Many companies, including Microsoft, Network Associates, Sun Microsystems, Lucent, Dell, IBM, Cisco Systems, and Sophis Networks, incorporated encryption and security technology into their products.

The United States restricted exports of encryption products and systems requiring encryption, allowing exports only of low-strength encryption products, whereas companies outside the U.S. could sell any type and strength of encryption products worldwide. The U.S. government worried that U.S. companies, including Sophis Networks, had sophisticated encryption products that were practically impenetrable, allowing terrorists and criminals to use encryption to conceal their activities. The export controls, however, meant lost sales for U.S. companies, since their customers outside the United States demanded products with the highest level of encryption available. Not only was encryption software affected by the controls, but more importantly, servers, computer systems, and other hardware systems incorporating encryption software were affected. A 1996 study estimated that the restrictions on encryption technology could cost the U.S. information industry $30 to $60 billion in sales by the year 2000 and cost 200,000 high-skill, high-wage jobs.[87]

Encryption

Cryptography dates back nearly 3,000 years to early Egypt. Between 50 and 60 B.C., Julius Caesar sent messages to Rome's distant forces using an encryption method that shifted and transposed the letters of their alphabet in a secret manner.[88] During the American Revolution, Benedict Arnold, arranging his betrayal of West Point, passed secret correspondence to the British using a code based on the legal classic, *Commentaries on the Laws of England*.[89] The use of cryptography flourished during World War II, and the United States succeeded in cracking the German "Ultra" codes and the Japanese "Purple" codes. In the postwar period cryptography increasingly involved computers to break codes, and the U.S. government began to view encryption as an important part of its national security system. The transfer of confidential data, messages, and information over communications networks and subsequently over the Internet dramatically increased the need for strong encryption products.

Cryptography involves making a "message incomprehensible to anyone who is not in possession of secret information needed to restore the message (ciphertext) to its normal plaintext form. The secret information is called the key, and its function is very similar to the function of a door key in a lock: it unlocks the message so that the recipient can read it."[90] Encryption converts a plain message to a secret message, and decryption is the process of converting the ciphertext back to its plaintext format.

Symmetric cryptography uses the same key for both encrypting and decrypting the coded message. To send a message about the time and location of a meeting at 3:25 P.M. on December 30, 2002, at the corner of 1st Avenue and 44th Street, the sender's message takes the following form:

Year	Date	Time	Street
2002	12 30	15 25	01 44

To encrypt the message, the sender and the receiver must agree on a key to transform the string of 14 digits into another string of 14 digits. Suppose the key was

64 25 83 09 76 23 55 12

The first agent would add the two strings and send the encrypted result:

84 27 95 39 91 48 56 56

which would then be decrypted using the same (symmetric) key.

---

[87]Computer Systems Policy Project (CSPP), *Perspectives on Security in the Information Age.* (Washington, DC: CSPP, January 1996), p. 10. The members of CSPP are the CEOs of Compaq, Dell, Hewlett-Packard, IBM, Intel, Lucent Technologies, NCR, SGI, Sun Microsystems, and Unisys.

[88]Kahn (1967, p. 83).
[89]Stender (1998).
[90]Diffie and Landau (1998, p. 13).

Symmetric cryptographic systems used in the mid-1990s usually involved an electronic machine that would encrypt and decrypt information by looking up data or letters in tables and adding them together using an arithmetic operation.[91] These systems, however, had an inherent vulnerability—finding a secure method to distribute the key among senders and receivers and protect it while in the custody of the recipients.

In the mid-1970s two Stanford University scientists, Whitfield Diffie and Martin Hellman, invented asymmetric encryption, or public key encryption, which sought to eliminate the symmetric key vulnerabilities. In public key encryption, the key used for encryption is different from the key used for decryption. Each person receives both a public and a private key.

1. A public key is used to encrypt a message that can only be decrypted using the mathematically linked private key. The public key is publicly available and can be transmitted and stored on unsecured networks, whereas the private key must be secured and is not transmitted. To send a message to person B, person A looks up in a directory B's public key and uses that to encrypt the message so that it can only be decrypted with B's private key.

2. To ensure that a particular encrypted message is genuine, A uses her private key at encryption time to create a digital signature attached to the message. B then uses A's public key and the message to verify A's signature.[92]

Although the public and private keys are mathematically related, it is difficult or computationally infeasible to derive one key from the other, thus making public key cryptography more secure than symmetric cryptography. The level of security provided by public key cryptography depends on the length (measured in "bits") of the public and private keys.[93] The more bits a key has, the more possible combinations a potential code-breaker would have to test and hence the stronger the encryption. For example, 56-bit symmetric encryption has 72,057,594,037,927,900 possible keys, and 128-bit symmetric encryption has 340,282,366,920,938,000,000,000,000,000,000,000,000 possible keys.

Everyday Uses of Cryptography

Many Web sites encrypt incoming and outgoing data so that consumers can securely use online banking, trading, and shopping. When consumers enter their credit card information on a Web site, the information and often the entire online session is encrypted. The Web server, or computer where the site's data are stored, receives the encrypted information and decrypts it, authenticates the card and the user (proves the user is who he or she claims to be), and authorizes the transaction. When investors trade securities online, they authenticate themselves (give the site access to their credentials) and obtain authorization. As their transaction begins, the data are encrypted.

E-mail security products automatically encrypt e-mail messages and attachments, authenticate senders, and verify that the contents have not changed in transit. Software such as Lotus Notes, Netscape's browser, and the Eudora e-mail program require encryption technology. Cryptography is also used to regulate satellite and cable television services. Cable companies use encryption technology to give consumers the regular and upgraded cable packages they order. They also use encryption with pay-per-view movies, which are decoded when the cable company sends a signal to the subscriber's cable box.[94]

Virtually all companies use encryption technology to protect their data from potential intruders. As end users, employees have user profiles, allowing them access to various authorized levels of company information. Encryption technology enables the authentication of machines (PCs, remote devices, and other hardware used to access corporate data) and users (individuals who must enter personal codes and passwords to gain entry).

Key Recovery

Key recovery is used to provide access to encrypted information, whether for intelligence or law enforcement purposes or merely because an encryption key was lost, forgotten, or misplaced. One key recovery method is escrowed encryption, where a trusted third party keeps "in escrow" part or all of a key. Government agencies such as the FBI could then recover the key when necessary. The FBI sought a "back door" into computer systems by requiring escrowed keys to be integrated into encryption and computer systems, giving it access to private information. However, giving the government access to private information (even through a trusted third party) raised privacy issues.[95] Sophis Networks had refused to include key recovery in its products.

When raw data or information was created and stored on a computer or device, they were in a form that could be accessed without a key. In the case of a message, this would be the case prior to the data being encrypted on the sender's machine or after it was decrypted on the receiver's machine. Companies such as Sophis Networks could pinpoint where the raw data was located on the

[91]Diffie and Landau (1998, p. 25).
[92]www.rsasecurity.com/rsalabs/faq/2-1-1.html.
[93]Levin (1999).

[94]RSA Security Laboratory. See www.rsasecurity.com. RSA Security is a leading cryptography supplier.
[95]For a more detailed description of key recovery, see RSA Security's Web site (www.rsasecurity.com). For additional details see www.rsasecurity.com/rsalabs/faq/7-12.html.

receiver's machine, providing three points at which to access the new data, similar to a "digital wiretap."

How Secure Is Encrypted Information?

Until the mid-1990s the U.S. government believed that 56-bit symmetric encryption was effectively impenetrable to even sophisticated data hackers. Then, in 1997 a team of technology professionals proved the government wrong. Granted a budget of approximately $1 million, the team cracked a 512-bit RSA Security asymmetric encryption code after 8 months of effort (roughly equivalent to 56-bit symmetric encryption).[96] In January 1999 the Electronic Frontier Foundation's "Deep Crack" computer won RSA Security's Challenge III by cracking a message encoded with 56-bit symmetric encryption in a record-breaking 22 hours and 15 minutes.

Experts now believe that hackers and technology specialists can break any code.[97] In 2000 RSA Security recommended 768-bit asymmetric encryption technology for personal use (80-bit symmetric encryption), 1024-bit asymmetric encryption for corporate use (128-bit symmetric encryption), and 2048-bit asymmetric encryption for highly sensitive information (256-bit symmetric encryption).[98]

The Encryption Policy Issue

In the late 1990s the Clinton administration created an Interagency Group to work on data security issues, including encryption. The White House Office of Science and Technology Policy and the National Security Council chaired the group. The Interagency Group included representatives of the Office of Management and Budget, FBI, Department of Justice, Department of Commerce, NSA, Department of Treasury, and Department of State. The administration argued that the proliferation of robust encryption products would make it easier for terrorists, spies, and criminals to conceal their activities and hence extremely difficult to gather intelligence, ensure national security, and enforce the law. The FBI and NSA cited the success of telephone wiretapping to support their argument. In addition to lawful wiretaps and searches, the government met its security objectives by clandestinely intercepting communications by criminals and terrorists. Each year wiretaps or electronic surveillance methods were responsible for the arrests of more than 2,000 people in the United States, of which approximately 20 percent resulted in conviction.[99]

The FBI and NSA generated concern in Congress and the Administration with accounts of terrorist attacks and global crime. These accounts were typically presented in closed briefings of congressional committees. In these closed briefings, technology companies and privacy advocates were prohibited from participating but could observe the proceedings. The observers were not allowed to provide any information on the content of the briefings to their organizations but were allowed to state whether anything discussed was important to their organizations. In support of continued export controls, the Interagency Group used a series of incidents to demonstrate their concern. The bombing of the World Trade Center by Ramzi Yousef was a case in point.[100] Yousef used over-the-counter encryption technology in his laptop computer, which took FBI experts more than a year to decipher. Once deciphered, the FBI discovered that among Yousef's terrorist projects was a plan to blow up 11 U.S. airliners in the Western Pacific in one day. A report by the National Strategy Information Center's Working Group on Organized Crime added to the Interagency Group's and the administration's concerns. Two researchers estimated that in at least 500 cases worldwide criminals had used encryption. The study reported that the use of encryption by criminals was growing at a rate of 50 to 100 percent a year. Despite this growth the NSA told the House National Security committee in a classified briefing that a "good percentage" of the intelligence it received was still unencrypted, said Representative Patrick Kennedy (D-RI), a member of the committee.[101]

Technology companies, consumer privacy advocates, and some members of Congress, however, viewed the issue quite differently. U.S. companies contended that since strong encryption technology was already available around the world to legitimate users, terrorists, and criminals alike, the encryption export controls were doomed to failure. A study by the George Washington University School of Engineering and Applied Science found good encryption programs available outside the United States on more than 800 Web sites.[102]

Moreover, the companies argued that due to export policy, they and the United States were rapidly losing their leadership position in encryption technology. The technology sector was also losing potential sales and thus jobs, in addition to spending large sums to alter their operations to satisfy the export controls. For example, Sophis Networks had to offer its servers three encryption systems—one for the open global market, one for the export-controlled segment of the global market, and one for the U.S. and Canadian markets. The companies also argued that the U.S. government was fighting a losing battle, since strong encryption was now being supplied by competitors in other countries.

[96]Asymmetric and symmetric encryption have different measurements. In general, asymmetric algorithms require longer keys to provide the same level of security as their symmetric key cousins.
[97]RSA Security Laboratory. See www.rsasecurity.com.
[98]RSA Security Laboratory. See www.rsasecurity.com.
[99]Jim Puzzanghera, "Encryption Dealt a Blow," *San Jose Mercury News*, September 10, 1998, p. C1.

[100]Levin (1999).
[101]C4I News, "HNSC Revises Encryption Bill," September 11, 1997.
[102]"Enemies of the State," *News World Communications*, September 13, 1999.

About 75 percent of the world's software was generated in the United States, but with the export controls on strong encryption products, U.S. companies had lost one-third of their market share in encryption software in 1998.[103]

Global customers preferred products and systems with strong encryption, but due to U.S. export restrictions, international customers were forced to purchase separate encryption devices and bolt them onto U.S. computer systems.[104] This was both expensive and clumsy and represented a competitive disadvantage for U.S. companies.[105] Brokat, a German company, provided strong encryption products for half the European Internet banking market and provided support for other forms of Internet commerce.[106] Analysts estimated that more than 500 non-U.S. encryption products were sold on the market by mid-1998, compared to only a handful in 1993.[107] "The U.S. really shot itself in the foot on this one," stated Stefan Roever, a managing partner at Brokat. Baltimore Technologies PLC, an Irish company selling encryption products, cited over 3,000 inquiries per day on its Web site. Siemens AG installed Baltimore's product at more than 500 corporate sites throughout Europe.[108] Microsoft claimed it had lost "hundreds of thousands" of potential users of its software. Consensus Development Corporation, which licensed encryption products to IBM, said it lost approximately 40 percent of new business leads because of U.S. encryption policy.[109]

U.S. software companies were also forced to alter their U.S. operations as a result of encryption export controls. For example, Netscape Communications continuously had to monitor its Internet site to prevent users from other countries from downloading the U.S. version of its browser, which featured 128-bit encryption.

Privacy advocates were also concerned about encryption policy. Information sent over the Internet passed through dozens of different computer systems on the way to its destination. A different system operator might manage each of these systems, and each system could be capable of capturing and storing the information. Furthermore, the online activities of Internet users could be monitored, both by their own service provider and by the system operator of any Web site they visited. Privacy advocates sought strong encryption products to protect the privacy of personal information and electronic transactions. They were particularly concerned that if communications and transactions over the Internet were subject to key recovery, the privacy of all Internet users would be jeopardized.

Evolution of U.S. Encryption Policy

During the postwar period, the Central Intelligence Agency (CIA) and the FBI became increasingly concerned about the evolution of encryption technology. The NSA took the lead in the development and creation of encryption technology, employing a majority of the encryption experts.[110]

With the advent of the information economy, private companies began to develop encryption technologies outside the reach of the NSA. The U.S. government became increasingly concerned and tried to control the proliferation of encryption technology through export controls and escrowed encryption keys. The government classified all encryption technologies as "munitions" and subjected them to the Arms Export Control Act (AECA) and the International Traffic in Arms Regulations (ITAR), administered by the U.S. Department of State. Placing encryption products under the jurisdictions of the AECA and ITAR reflected the government's perception of the significant national security risk of exported encryption products.

Export Controls

By the mid-1990s encryption policy had become more important to the Clinton administration and Congress. On November 15, 1996, the administration removed encryption technology from the Munitions List and transferred jurisdiction from the Department of State to the Department of Commerce. Encryption was designated as a dual-use commodity subject to the Export Administration regulations, and specific encryption technology export controls were established. Within the United States any strength encryption technology could be used, but exports of encryption products were restricted. Fifty-six-bit symmetric encryption software could be exported freely once a one-time inspection showed that the technology incorporated key recovery. Foreign banks and foreign subsidiaries of U.S. companies were granted exceptions to the key recovery provision. The administration's policy meant that the encryption exported was not really private, since a central administrator could turn keys over to law enforcement agencies when deemed necessary. Only "mass market software"

---

[103]"Safe Encryption Bill Re-Introduced," *TechWeb News*, February 25, 1999.

[104]International customers also were confused by U.S. government policy and concerned that so-called "back doors" had been built into U.S. systems to allow U.S. law enforcement access to private information.

[105]As of 1996, there were more than 300 companies that developed and exported cryptographic products from within the United States and more than 355 outside the United States. *Source:* Computer Systems Policy Project, *op. cit.*, p. 10.

[106]President's Export Council Subcommittee on Encryption (PECSENC), September 18, 1998. See 209.122.145.150 presidentsexportcouncil/pecsenc/iwgfind.htm.

[107]Kimberley A. Strassel, "U.S. Rules Boost Europe's Encryption—European Competitors Cash In on U.S. Export Limits," *Wall Street Journal*, July 7, 1998, p. B8.

[108]Ibid.

[109]Ibid.

[110]Levin (1999).

with 40-bit or lower strength encryption could be freely exported after a 15-day review process.[111]

An export license for any encryption product or technology required a cumbersome and confusing application process. "What's written or published is only about 40 percent of what you need to know from a regulatory standpoint, it's chaos," said Ken Bass, a partner at the Washington, D.C., law firm Venable, Baetjer, Howard & Civelletti. To receive export licenses for products incorporating strong encryption, multiple applications and extensive justifications were necessary: "You have to show a long-term relationship with the business partner and provide evidence, such as contracts."[112] Under the export rules, financial institutions received special permission to export strong 128-bit encryption technology but were restricted to encrypting only financial transactions and could not use the technology for general-purpose communication.

Technology companies and privacy advocates so strongly criticized this policy that the administration established a task force to reshape the policy. On September 16, 1998, the Clinton administration announced a new encryption export policy containing four important changes:

1. Elimination of key recovery for "mass market" 56-bit encryption and permission to export freely, except to the seven "terrorist" nations, after a one-time license exception[113]
2. Expansion of the definition of "financial institution" to include worldwide subsidiaries of U.S. firms, insurance companies, health and medical organizations (not including biochemical/pharmaceutical manufacturers), and online merchants
3. Continuation of the policy allowing key recovery products to be exported under a license exception
4. Provision for other export requests to be approved on a case-by-case basis

From the perspective of U.S. companies these changes were an improvement over earlier policies, but the new policy still did not allow the export of encryption stronger than 56-bit to individuals, companies, or government agencies in foreign countries, unless they were classified as a financial institution. Energy suppliers, telecommunications companies, the transportation industry, foreign governments, and human rights organizations were critical of the new policy.[114] Foreign governments were often the largest purchasers of strong encryption, but the U.S. government feared that some would use encryption technology to threaten U.S. national security.

As the complaints continued, members of Congress in 1997 introduced seven bills on encryption technology. No bill made it very far through the congressional process because the business, privacy, and national security concerns led to furious debates. One of these bills was SAFE.

The Security and Freedom Through Encryption Act

SAFE was introduced by Representative Bob Goodlatte (R-VA) and subsequently gained and lost momentum a number of times. The original intent of the bill was the full relaxation of encryption export controls with no key escrow requirement or bit limit. The bill received strong support from privacy advocates and technology companies alike. SAFE would

1. Permit the export of mass-market software and custom-designed software and hardware with encryption capabilities comparable to that already commercially available from foreign suppliers.
2. Impose stiff penalties for the use of encryption to commit or conceal a crime.
3. Allow U.S. companies to buy or sell any type of encryption within the United States and not require computer users to turn over copies of their keys to the U.S. government.

Because of its broad implications SAFE was referred to the House National Security (Armed Forces) Committee as well as to the International Relations, Intelligence, Judiciary, and Commerce committees. After the bill was reported, however, it stalled in the House Rules Committee as a result of opposition by the chair.

In 1999 SAFE was reintroduced by representatives Goodlatte and Zoe Lofgren (D-CA) with broader support and 258 co-sponsors. The bill was reported by the committees and given a rule by the Rules Committee, preparing it for floor consideration. Even though the Senate had not yet considered the bill, President Clinton declared he would veto it.

U.S. Encryption Policy in 1999: Continued Export Control

On September 16, 1999, the Clinton administration "announced a new approach to encryption."[115] The new

---

[111]Levin (1999, pp. 530–532).

[112]Ellen Messmer, "Navigating the World of Government Encryption Export Rules," *Network World,* May 18, 1998, p. 8.

[113]The seven terrorist nations were Cuba, Iran, Iraq, Libya, Sudan, Syria, and North Korea.

[114]In a number of countries human rights organizations were the most common targets of government surveillance, since some governments viewed these organizations as security risks (Levin, 1999, pp. 540–550).

[115]Statement released by the White House, "Administration Announces New Approach to Encryption," *U.S. Newswire,* September 16, 1999. In the same statement, Clinton transmitted to Congress the Cyberspace Electronic Security Act (CESA) to ensure that law enforcement agencies could access decrypted information, while protecting that information from inappropriate release. In addition, it authorized $80 million over 4 years for the FBI's technical support center, which would serve as a centralized technical resource for federal, state, and local law enforcement agencies for their use in responding to the increasing use of encryption by criminals.

strategy rested on three principles: "a one-time technical review of encryption products in advance of sale, a streamlined post-export reporting system, and a process that permits the government to review the exports of strong encryption to foreign government and military organizations and to nations of concern consistent with these principles, the government will significantly update and simplify export controls on encryption."[116] Under this new policy,

1. Any encryption commodity or software of any key length could be exported under license exception (i.e., without a license), after a technical review, to individuals, commercial firms, and other nongovernment end users in any country except for the seven state supporters of terrorism.
2. Any retail encryption commodities and software of any key length could be exported under license exception, after a technical review, to any end user in any country, except for the seven state supporters of terrorism.
3. Streamlined postexport reporting would provide government with an understanding of where strong encryption was being exported.
4. Sector definitions and country lists were eliminated.[117]

When privacy advocates, members of Congress, and technology companies read the details of Clinton's new approach to encryption, however, they were dismayed. For example, major customers of U.S. technology companies such as European telecommunications firms would be ineligible for unlicensed export sales because they were partly government-owned.[118] The new approach also continued to require an exporter to obtain permission to sell encryption products to foreign governments.

Sophis Networks Company Background

Sophis Networks' Security Products Division, which included approximately 200 employees worldwide, developed security and encryption software for businesses, generating over $100 million in product revenue in 1999. The division provided end-to-end security solutions for organizations such as brokerage companies with Internet businesses, companies giving their employees access to privileged information, and ASPs (application service providers) that hosted services for customers. Sophis Networks' principal activity was selling compatible and easily integrated security software technology to companies providing operating systems (e.g., Hewlett-Packard and Sun Microsystems). Its products helped companies authenti-

cate users (similar to an ATM card with a PIN), authorize user access to certain information (according to a predetermined "profile" of the individual seeking access), provide services (supply information), and encrypt information as it was transmitted over public or private networks.

During the 1990s an increasingly important component of Sophis Networks' business had become the sale of enterprise servers, desktop systems, and network computing software. The company's customers and their customers needed to send secure information over a corporate network or through the Internet.[119] Sophis Networks recognized that intruders could potentially gain access to this information if strong encryption were not incorporated into their systems. Moreover, as the Internet continued to grow as a communication and commerce medium, the issue of data privacy was becoming a top priority for companies, individuals, and governments. In a not-so-bold forecast, Sophis Networks predicted that effective encryption security would not only be in great demand in all sectors of U.S. society, but also worldwide. The challenge for Joanne Mercer, other product managers, and the government affairs office at Sophis Networks was to sell Sophis Networks' servers and systems with strong integrated encryption software freely both in the United States and worldwide.

Sophis Networks' Market Strategy

Because of the encryption export controls, companies such as Sophis Networks, Sun Microsystems, RSA Security, and Network Associates entered "into certain partnerships to build and foster [encryption] technologies and tried to anticipate the government regulations," according to Joanne Mercer. Network Associates acquired a Swiss computer company that developed a product at its Dutch subsidiary that was "functionally equivalent" to its Pretty Good Privacy encryption software. Network Associates customers outside the U.S. could purchase the Dutch software and expect it to be fully compatible with Network Associates' U.S. version. Because Network Associates had provided no assistance in the development of the encryption product, export laws were not infringed, according to Kelly Blough, director of government relations at Network Associates. "There is no contact between our developers here with any developers in Europe," Blough said. "We are confident that [the Department of Commerce] will uncover nothing that is not in compliance with U.S. law."[120]

Sun Microsystems developed a product through a Russian subsidiary in which it had a 10 percent stake.

[116]Ibid.
[117]Ibid.
[118]Bruce Scneier, "1999 Crypto: The Year in Review," *Cryptorhythms,* December 1999, p. 20.

[119]"Network Associates," *Interactive Week,* February 7, 2000, p. 35. Projections by International Data Corporation. The projections were (1) antivirus, $2.8 billion; (2) firewalls, $1.48 billion; and (3) encryption, $200 million.
[120]Matthew Nelson, "Network Associates Gets Around Export Laws," *Infoworld,* March 30, 1998, p. 58.

Sun's Network Security Products Group Manager, Humphrey Polanen, explained, "This is not being done to subvert export control laws but to deliver solutions to customers. We're doing this not to politicize encryption but to fulfill market demand."[121]

Sophis Networks formed similar partnerships with overseas companies. Joanne Mercer explained, "We did not do this with an intent to circumvent the government rules or to defraud in any way, shape, or form. It was a way for us to develop technology outside the United States for the world to use."

Many of the technology companies affected by encryption export controls continued to develop their encryption technology capabilities in the United States, since companies could sell encryption products freely in the United States. Sophis Networks maintained its tech-

nology development budgets because it retained hope that the administration would eventually relax the controls. The company built firewalls, encryption technologies, and authorization and authentication tools with the intention of exporting strong encryption products if the administration were to relax its policies.

Joanne Mercer leaned back in her chair in frustration and wondered what else she and Sophis Networks could do to influence administration policy on encryption exports controls. ■

SOURCE: This is an abridged version of a case written by Victoria Chang under the supervision of Professor David P. Baron as the basis for class discussion rather than to illustrate either effective or ineffective handling of an administrative situation. Copyright © 2000 by the Board of Trustees of the Leland Stanford Junior University. All rights reserved. Reproduced with permission.

Preparation Questions

1. Why has the U.S. government sought to restrict the export of strong encryption products? How serious are those concerns? What has been the nonmarket strategy of the FBI and NSA, and why has it been effective?

2. How serious are the controls for companies such as Sophis Networks?

3. Why have U.S. companies had only limited success in relaxing the controls? What should the companies have done differently?

4. If export controls were lifted, would U.S. companies likely be able to regain their former lead in encryption systems?

5. What should Sophis Networks do regarding President Clinton's threatened veto and the administration's revised export control policy?

---

[121]David Bank, "Sun Selling of Encryption to Skirt Policy," *Wall Street Journal,* May 19, 1997, pp. A3–A4 and Michael Kanellos, "Sun Signs Deal with Russian Company," *Computer Reseller News,* June 9, 1997, p. 68.

-------------------------------------- P A R T   I V --------------------------------------
Integrative Case
Toys 'Я' Us and Globalization

Charles Lazarus began his career working in his father's used bicycle shop. He subsequently started selling children's furniture out of the shop, and when customers kept asking if he carried toys, he added some toys in addition to the children's furniture. He soon recognized, however, that he was not getting any repeat business. "Furniture lasts forever," Lazarus pointed out. "But toys," he continued with a laugh, "toys are great because they have built-in obsolescence. Kids break them."[122]

Lazarus was intrigued by the success of self-service supermarkets and conceived the idea of selling toys in a similar manner. He opened his first Toys 'Я' Us store in 1957 using shopping carts, a large selection, and low prices. Because toy sales were highly seasonal, he advertised to build a year-round demand. To raise funds for expansion, in 1966 he sold the company to Interstate Stores, a retailing conglomerate, for $7.5 million. Lazarus retained operating control, and when Interstate went bankrupt, the court made him president. After selling off the Interstate assets, in 1978 he renamed the company Toys 'Я' Us and launched a rapid expansion program. Toy industry analysts had estimated that over the next 10 years industry-wide sales of toys by specialty retailers would increase to $2.4 billion. Over that period, the sales of Toys 'Я' Us alone increased by over tenfold, reaching $4 billion in 1989, including clothing sales at Kids 'Я' Us stores. Profits were $268 million. Because of his vision and the company's tremendous success, Lazarus was widely viewed as a retailing genius.

The Toys 'Я' Us market strategy was built on three principles: price, selection, and stock. The original idea was to sell at discount prices in stores with supermarket-style service and limited sales staff. It soon became clear that consumers wanted one-stop shopping, leading to larger stores, more varieties of items, and a broad range of goods including items such as disposable diapers. Toys 'Я' Us then began to stock an average of 18,000 items in its stores. The key, of course, as Lazarus explained, was "to pick the right toy at the right time—the toys that sell. We're very much like the fashion industry. Customer tastes are very fickle, and you have to move quickly when they change. Otherwise, you'll be out of business. It's that simple."[123] The third principle was to have the goods on hand, so Toys 'Я' Us operated a sophisticated inventory tracking and supply system designed to avoid stock-outs. The company used electronic point-of-purchase sales terminals in each store, which were linked to its central computers in its headquarters.

To supplement these principles, Toys 'Я' Us relied on advertising to get consumers to purchase toys year round, which both increased demand and reduced seasonality. It also provided a money-back guarantee policy under which a customer could return any item for any reason. In the United States, the location of stores was crucial. Toys 'Я' Us preferred locations with ample and adjacent parking so that customers could go out the door of the store and directly to their cars. Toys 'Я' Us also sought to keep its stores open 7 days a week, 365 days a year, where local ordinances permitted it. Toys 'Я' Us owned all its stores so as to maintain standardization and control.

Globalization

By 1984 Toys 'Я' Us operated 169 stores in over 40 states and had revenue of $1.3 billion and profits of $92 million. Although it operated only within the United States, it had developed a worldwide supply system, purchasing toys from around the world. East Asia represented the largest source of supply.

The company's initial international steps were cautious. It opened its first store outside the United States in Canada and then opened a store in England. Lazarus explained that "the Canadians seemed to be much like ourselves, and [our approach] seemed to work pretty well. And we went to England." Toys 'Я' Us continued to expand in Canada and the United Kingdom. Its other early international steps were serendipitous. Toys 'Я' Us had been approached by Jopie Ong, director of Singapore's Metro retail group, which wanted a franchise to open a store in Singapore. The Toys 'Я' Us policy was not to use franchisees, and hence it rejected the request. Ong persisted, however, and was eventually able to persuade the company to form a joint venture. Toys 'Я' Us–Metro opened its first Singapore store in 1984.

Its entry into Hong Kong was also serendipitous. Joseph Baczko, president of the Toys 'Я' Us international division, had met Victor Fung when they were both at Harvard. When Fung became chairman of Li & Fung Ltd., a Hong Kong trading company, the two companies were natural partners. The Toys 'Я' Us–Li & Fung joint venture was formed and opened a store in Hong Kong in 1985. The success of its stores in Singapore and Hong Kong led Toys 'Я' Us to develop a globalization strategy. Lazarus explained that the company was "interglobal." "Our registers in Hong Kong take eight currencies. They just punch in what kind of currency you're

---
[122]*Solutions*, March/April, 1988.
[123]*Solutions*, March/April, 1988.

giving them. It's a really international kind of thing. You have to see it to believe it." The company also preferred to hire locals as store and country managers.

Toys ' Я ' Us viewed opportunity in a country as stemming from a large population and high income. Those factors "combined with the lack of any dominant toy retail competition in Europe and Asia, afford Toys ' Я ' Us with an ideal climate for aggressive international expansion. "[124] As Lazarus put it, "We can go anywhere there are supermarkets and kids because we are, after all, a supermarket for kids."[125]

Each country posed different hurdles, however. Some were market based and others were nonmarket. Germany, Japan, and Sweden posed particular challenges.

Germany[126]

With one of the highest standards of living in the world, Germany offered considerable potential. Although Germany had a relatively open economy, a number of rules, regulations, and traditional relationships presented difficulties for foreign entrants. Entry into retailing, in particular, was more difficult than might have been expected.

Toys ' Я ' Us G.m.b.H. was formed in 1986, but as it attempted to enter the German market it encountered several hurdles. In contrast to the United States, a number of European countries had laws favoring employees over consumers. Germany protected employees in the retail trade by imposing strict rules on store-opening hours, except for gasoline stations and stores in railroad stations and airports. A federal law enacted in 1956 was intended to protect employees from having to work long hours, and it had continuing strong support from the 500,000-member union representing retail, banking, and insurance workers. Union members worked a 37.5-hour week. Many small retailers also supported the law, believing that extended hours would not increase sales enough to warrant the additional cost. Stores were required to close by 6:30 P.M. except on Thursday when they could remain open until 8:30 P.M. The 6:30 P.M. closing time gave employees little time to shop after work. Moreover, stores had to close by 2 P.M. on Saturday and were not allowed to open on Sunday.[127] In addition, in smaller towns many retailers closed at lunchtime.

Other federal laws also imposed hurdles. Not only were profits taxes the highest in Europe at 50 percent, but Germany also had regulations that were as strict as any in Europe, particularly in the retail sector. For example, German law prohibited discounts of more than 3 percent from previous prices except during certain restricted

periods. German antitrust law also restricted the use of loss leader pricing, and the Cartel Office could order price increases. German law also prohibited lifetime guarantees.

German labor laws made it difficult to dismiss an employee and gave rights to employees on some policy issues. For example, employees had a say in any legislative effort to revise the store opening laws. In addition, the worker participation requirements in Germany were foreign to an American company and reduced a company's flexibility. Wages and benefits were very high — German workers typically had 6 weeks of vacation a year and received a thirteenth month of salary as a bonus. German employees were well educated and highly productive, however.

Most German toy retail stores were small, family-owned shops, and many were located in city centers. These retailers were often active members of local organizations. As managing director Arnt Klöser of Toys ' Я ' Us G.m.b.H., who had been hired from a leading German department store chain, said, "When you ask a city for a construction permit, the first thing they do is ask the local chamber of commerce and retailers' association what they think of your idea. They always say the same thing: A toy store belongs in the city center, not the meadow on the edge of town."[128] To obtain store approval, Klöser's strategy was to try to convince the local toy retailers that the entry of Toys ' Я ' Us would actually benefit them by expanding the market.

German toy manufacturers opposed the entry of Toys ' Я ' Us because of concerns about the consequences for their current retail customers. To support local retailers, some manufacturers argued that a self-service retailer such as Toys ' Я ' Us could place children in danger. They said that customers needed the assistance of a Fachmann to provide expert advice. The German Toy Manufacturers Association complained about the Toys ' Я ' Us practice of selling such items as diapers, baby food, clothes, and sporting goods in addition to toys. Some manufacturers went further. The leading manufacturer of model trains, Gebruder Märklin, announced that it would not sell to Toys ' Я ' Us because doing so would damage its image.

Toys ' Я ' Us was willing to commit whatever resources were necessary to enter the German market, but it needed a strategy for dealing with the hurdles it faced.

Japan

By 1989 sales had reached $4 billion and net income was $238 million. The company operated nearly 500 Toys ' Я ' Us and over 100 Kids ' Я ' Us stores. Toys ' Я ' Us operated over 70 stores in countries other than the United States. However, the company had not yet entered the Japanese market.

---

[124]Toys ' Я ' Us, Annual Report, 1991, p. 7.
[125]*Solutions,* March/April, 1988.
[126]This section is based in part on an article in the *New York Times,* August 18, 1991, and on additional public sources.
[127]Stores could remain open until 4 P.M. on the first Saturday of every month and the four Saturdays before Christmas.

[128]*New York Times,* August 18, 1991.

The opportunities in Japan were substantial. The Japanese toy market was over $5.5 billion, and personal income was growing rapidly. Less than 5 percent of the $5 billion toy market was accounted for by imported toys, however. Domestic toy manufacturers had a lock on the distribution system that supplied the thousands of small toy stores that accounted for virtually all the toy sales in the country.

One estimate was that over 50 percent of all retail sales in Japan was accounted for by shops with one or two employees. Many of these "mom and pop" shops were owned by retirees. The aging of shopowners and their children's reluctance to take over the businesses resulted in a decline of 9.3 percent in the number of shops from 1982 to 1985 and a 7 percent decline from 1985 to 1988. In spite of the decline, over 1.4 million small shops remained in Japan. These shops represented an important component of the clientistic and reciprocal exchange relationships with the Liberal Democratic Party (LDP) and the bureaucracy. Local merchants also often played an important role in the *koenkai* of many Diet members.

These small shops were an important part of the fabric of Japanese society, but they were also the cap of a very inefficient distribution system. Japan had several more layers to its distribution system than most other countries and two to three times the number of small shops per capita. This increased costs and prices. The high prices provided an important profit opportunity for an efficient, large-scale retailer such as Toys 'Я' Us.

Charles Lazarus saw a potential for 100 stores in Japan and hoped to open the first Toys 'Я' Us store in Niigata, 160 miles north of Tokyo. Toys 'Я' Us planned to supply the stores directly, bypassing the Japanese distribution system. Approximately 80 percent of the merchandise sold in its Japanese stores would be the same as that sold in the other Toys 'Я' Us stores.

Toys 'Я' Us' market opportunities were controlled by government regulations. As Vice President Michael Goldstein explained, "A lot will depend on whether the Japanese government will relax [its] rules. We think we're going to expand the market there for toys. It'll be good for us, good for our suppliers and will be good for Japan in that we're going to bring a diversity of consumer products for Japanese children."

Entry into the Japanese market was complicated by a variety of factors. The structure of Japanese retailing persisted in part because of the Large-Scale Retail Store Law (LSRSL), which made it difficult to open a large store. Notice had to be given to the Small and Medium-Size Enterprises Agency (SMEA) of MITI to open a store larger than 1,500 square meters.[129] SMEA typically recommended postponing the opening as it sought the advice of a local large-scale retail council. Notice of any store larger

than 500 square meters also had to be given to the governor of the prefecture, which had authority similar to MITI's. Two laws enacted in 1977, the Coordinating Sphere of Activities Law and the Small and Medium-Size Business and Cooperative Law, strengthened the position of small enterprises by giving them a stronger voice in the local large-scale retail councils. Those councils sought the advice of the "commercial business arrangement committee," established by the local chamber of commerce. The committee's advice was often reflected in the decision of the governor or minister. Local councils played a role in setting not only store size but also store hours.[130] These laws and the local consultation process provided an opportunity for local merchants to oppose entry. As Tatsuki Kubo of McDonald's (Japan) explained, "It's a Japanese custom. If a big company wants to move into a local area, the people oppose it."[131]

These laws and the complex approval process did not preclude the opening of large stores, but they could result in long and often prohibitive delays. The laws placed no limit on the length of the consultation period, and there had been delays as long as 10 years. When faced with strong opposition some large-scale retailers had given up, whereas others had chosen to "negotiate" with the local store owners to overcome their opposition.

In spite of these restrictions, some supermarket and department store chains had expanded in Japan. Isao Nakauchi founded the Daiei chain in 1957; by 1988 Daiei had 181 outlets that sold clothing and other merchandise as well as groceries. Nakauchi complained that opening a new store took from 5 to 7 years and that 73 applications had to be filed for 26 permits under 12 laws.

Because of the size of their outlets, companies such as McDonald's and 7-Eleven were often unaffected by the LSRSL.[132] Indeed, McDonald's, led by President Den Fujita, had expanded rapidly and by 1989 had 675 restaurants in Japan. McDonald's Japan was skilled at dealing with the relevant bureaucracy and the local government units whose approval was needed to open a restaurant. McDonald's (Japan) also employed *amakudari* bureaucrats for their relationships with and knowledge of the ministries from which they had descended.[133]

In recent years, the approval process had been somewhat streamlined, and in some cases the delays had been reduced to as little as 2 years. Restrictions on store hours and expansion had also been eased. Rumors of the possible entry of Toys 'Я' Us, however, stirred concern in the retail industry. A toy wholesaler in Niigata

---

[129]Toys 'Я' Us stores were up to four times this size.

[130]Store hours and the number of employees permitted were regulated in the same manner.
[131]*Wall Street Journal*, February 7, 1990.
[132]McDonald's Company (Japan) Ltd. was a 50–50 joint venture of the U.S. McDonald's Corporation and Fujita & Company. 7-Eleven stores were owned by Ito Yokuda, a supermarket and department store chain, which licensed the 7-Eleven name.
[133]*Japan Economic Journal*, May 26, 1990.

commented, "This is not just a local problem; Toys 'Я' Us will have a big impact on the entire toy industry. We are opposed to their plan."[134] He said he would be meeting with other members of the industry to formulate a strategy against Toys 'Я' Us. Masao Sakurai, a toy retailer with eight shops in Niigata, predicted, "If Toys 'Я' Us comes in, Japanese shops will be wiped out."[135]

In 1989 MITI issued a report, "Vision of the Japanese Distribution Industry in the 1990s," which criticized the inefficiency in the distribution system and explored possible improvements. One possibility would be to limit the ability of local governments to impose restrictions that favored local retailers. As was frequently the case in Japan, MITI could make some changes through "administrative guidance," although it would have to obtain the consent of the Ministry of Local Autonomy.

The Toys 'Я' Us market strategy was to attempt to bypass the Japanese distribution system by opening large stores and supplying them directly. To implement this strategy, the company faced not only the problem of the LSRSL but also a host of local regulations on retailing. One strategy Toys 'Я' Us could adopt was to attempt to place the issue of retailing restrictions on the agenda of the ongoing U.S.–Japan trade negotiations. U.S. Trade Representative Carla Hills was believed to be sympathetic to this issue and might make Toys 'Я' Us a cause célèbre. Toys 'Я' Us also faced the difficult problem of finding store locations because the price of land in Japan had reached astronomical levels.

Sweden

Operating from its base in the United Kingdom, Toys 'Я' Us entered Sweden in September 1994, opening stores in Gothenberg, Malmo, and Skarholmen, a suburb of Stockholm.[136] In accord with its policies in other countries, the company required its 110 employees to sign the company handbook, which specified the work rules under which the company operated.

Unions were particularly strong in Sweden with over 90 percent of Swedish employees represented by a union. The Swedish model of labor relations had been an important factor in the country's long record of industrial peace. The Handelsanstalldas Forbund, the Retail Workers Union, had signed up a number of workers in Toys 'Я' Us stores and demanded that the company sign the standard nationwide collective labor agreement. The objective of the collective agreement was to allow organized labor to bring broad pressure on employers as a means of balancing corporate power. "'In all shops where we have members we want a collective agreement,' said Mr. Bjorn Sjoblom of Handelsanstalldas Forbund. 'This

is quite normal in Sweden. We have not had any problems before with other companies.'"[137]

Toys 'Я' Us refused to accept the collective agreement but remained willing to negotiate an agreement with the union. "'Toys 'Я' Us does not have any difficulty in accepting an agreement with the union, but considers itself to have the right to participate in negotiations to formulate a firm-adapted agreement,' Sten Yetraeus, attorney with the business law firm Lagerlof & Leman, explained. '[Accepting the collective agreement] would mean that we would be bound to a detailed book of regulations that is the product of many years of negotiations between the Retail Workers and the Retail Employers without us, '" Yetraeus added.[138] Frank Heskjer, the company's head for Scandinavia, said, "We get by without such agreements in other countries and we'll do the same in Sweden." Retail Workers Union chairman Kenth Pettersson said, "We haven't had a conflict like this for years. Signing collective agreements is a virtual formality these days."[139] The Retail Workers Union and its chairman were at the more militant end of the labor spectrum in Sweden.

A government commission failed in its efforts to mediate a settlement, and the first strike by the union in 20 years began. Toys 'Я' Us stated, "[Unions] have forced our employees to strike solely because we will not unconditionally sign a collective agreement." David Rurka, managing director of the company for the United Kingdom and Scandinavia, said, "The problem is the culture here. Many of our people don't want to strike. But they say they have fathers or other family members in unions who say they must support the union. The union has motivated the staff with fear and fear alone."[140]

The union provided the strikers with 100 percent pay and took out national advertisements asking the public to support the strike and boycott Toys 'Я' Us stores. The union not only picketed each of the stores but attempted to blockade the stores from supplies. It enlisted the aid of the Transport Workers, and truckers refused to cross the picket lines. The Seamen's Union forced the Swedish flagged carrier Tor Lines to refuse to carry goods from the distribution facility in the United Kingdom to Sweden. The Seamen's Union also announced that it would take actions against Stena Line, Lion Ferry, and SweFerry AB. A Seamen's Union spokesperson said, "A struggle like this is well known within our own union." The expanded actions by the union were in part the result of shoppers who crossed the picket lines to buy low-priced diapers that the union learned were being imported from Denmark. Other unions also announced sympathy measures of support for the Retail Workers Union. For example, the financial sector union refused to handle the Toys 'Я' Us daily receipts.

---

[134]*Wall Street Journal,* February 7, 1990.
[135]*Wall Street Journal,* February 7, 1990.
[136]Toys 'Я' Us became one of the few foreign retail chains operating in Sweden.
[137]*Financial Times,* May 11, 1995.
[138]*Dagens Nyheter,* May 10, 1995.
[139]*Reuter Business Report,* May 8, 1995.
[140]*Financial Times,* May 11, 1995.

Toys 'Я' Us paid a wage slightly higher than union members earned elsewhere and provided the same insurance. The principal concern, however, was job security. The employee handbook specified performance conditions that could lead to a firing, and one of the strikers explained, "You never felt really secure there, that you can stay." Therese Karlsson, who was let go by the company in Skarholmen during the provisional period, said, "Just prior to [being fired], management said that they were finished making cutbacks in personnel. Those of us who remained could feel secure, and a few were even promised permanent employment. Then they called me at home on a Saturday evening and told me 'you may leave.'"[141] Therese was one of the strikers on the picket line.

The conflict between Toys 'Я' Us and the union also involved other work rule issues. For example, the company handbook stated that employees were forbidden to "speak to or be interviewed by the mass media without special permission in advance from the managing director."[142] Gunnar Jonsson, manager of the Gothenberg store, explained, "Our rules about uniforms, searches at the end of the shift, about not talking to the media and so on do look hard on paper. But all stores demand a neat appearance from their staff, check purses and bags, and so on. Of course our employees may speak with the media—except when it has to do with the internal affairs of the company"[143] Fredrik Larsson, an employee since the store opened, commented, "In my personal opinion, the company's rules don't bother me. I don't see anything against a uniform, and the check that I have to undergo is not insulting, as I see it. After all, it's my own boss who does it. We know each other, and they do it mostly because they have to report to their manager that they have done it."[144]

In response to the strike Toys 'Я' Us halted its planned expansion in Sweden and speculated to the media that it might close its stores and leave the country. The company had planned 15 stores in Sweden employing 500 permanent and 1,000 seasonal workers.

As the strike continued, commentators viewed the conflict between Toys 'Я' Us and the union as a test for the Swedish model of collective bargaining in its new role as a member of the European Union. Peter Skogh, who managed the store in Malmo, said, "We are an international company coming into a new market. Of course we are trying to adapt to the conditions here. But Sweden, in order to survive, must also adapt to the European and international business climate."[145] "One self-employed mother who drove her four children past the pickets said, 'Swedish trade unions are inflexible and only interested in sticking to old principles. Sweden is sick to the back teeth of them.'"[146] Toys 'Я' Us began to receive expressions of support from other companies. ■

Preparation Questions

1. What is the Toys 'Я' Us market strategy?
2. In what kinds of national markets are its opportunities the most attractive? Which companies are its natural competitors? Are any of them global?
3. What nonmarket forces potentially impede the success of its market strategy?
4. What overall market and nonmarket strategies should Toys 'Я' Us develop, and how should those components be integrated?
5. What specific strategy should it adopt to gain entry to the Japanese market?
6. What specific strategy should it adopt to enter the German market successfully?
7. What should it do about the situation in Sweden?

[141]*Dagens Nyheter,* May 24, 1995.
[142]*Dagens Industri,* May 10, 1995.
[143]*Dagens Nyheter,* May 10, 1995.
[144]*Dagens Nyheter,* May 10, 1995.
[145]*Guardian,* May 13, 1995.
[146]*Guardian,* May 13, 1995.

C H A P T E R

19

Corporate Social Responsibility

INTRODUCTION

Corporate social responsibility has received increased attention from business, the public, and researchers. A recent survey by the Economist Intelligence Unit found that 47 percent of the firms responding agreed that corporate social responsibility (CSR) "is a necessary cost of doing business" and 47 percent agreed that it "gives us a distinctive position in the market." Only 4 percent of the respondents believed that corporate social responsibility was a "waste of time and money." The *Economist* observed, "It is almost unthinkable today for a big global corporation to be without [a CSR policy]."[1]

Many firms go beyond what is required by their market and nonmarket environments, and some explicitly attempt to serve directly the needs of their stakeholders or, more broadly, of society. For these firms, successful performance not only requires compliance with laws and regulations but also requires fulfilling broader responsibilities. Firms make charitable contributions, provide pharmaceuticals to those in need, respect and support human rights, exercise self-regulation, and take measures beyond those required by law to protect the environment and the safety of employees and customers. Firms vary considerably in the extent of these activities, however. The extent depends on their conceptions of corporate social responsibility and the role of business in society.

The previous chapters provide a basis for addressing issues in the market and nonmarket environments of business under the objective of maximizing shareholder value. The focus in those chapters was primarily on the nonmarket challenges directed at firms. In contrast, social responsibility focuses less on pressures and more on normative principles that identify duties based on conceptions of well-being, rights, and justice. These principles can require an objective broader than shareholder value maximization.

This part of the book thus adds another consideration—moral concerns—to management in the environment of business. As illustrated in Figure 19-1, formulating integrated strategies requires consideration of the market and nonmarket environments as well as attention to moral concerns and social responsibilities. This does not mean that the objective of shareholder value maximization is inappropriate; instead, it means that strategies and actions should be evaluated in terms of moral principles in addition to their effects on shareholder value.

This chapter examines the social responsibilities of business and provides a framework for reasoning about corporate social performance. The normative content of social responsibility is developed in the following chapters in terms of ethics systems and their application in management. Chapters 22 and 23 then address the implementation of ethics systems and conceptions of corporate social responsibility.

---

[1]*Economist*, January 17, 2008.

FIGURE 19-1 Integrated Strategy Framework

THE TRUST GAP

In interacting with the public or with stakeholders, it is useful to begin with caution. The public trust in large firms is low, and criticisms of business are often viewed with a degree of credibility that is not accorded to the communication of firms with the public. This may be due to the self-interested objectives of firms and a lack of confidence that competition in markets will serve society's interests. It may also be due to greater confidence among the public in the critics of firms, such as social activist organizations and NGOs. Their objectives are frequently viewed as better aligned with society's interests than are the objectives of firms.

In 2005 GlobeScan Inc. organized interviews with over 20,000 people in 20 countries to assess their degree of trust in society's institutions.[2] The question asked respondents was how much trust they had in the institutions to "operate in the best interests of our society." For 14 countries also surveyed in previous years, the surveys indicated an overall decrease in trust in all institutions.[3] More interesting is the ranking and ordinal scores of the five institutions covered:[4]

Institution	Scores
• NGOs	29
• United Nations	13
• Large local companies	2
• National governments	–9
• Global companies	–15

The apparent lack of trust in global companies stands in stark contrast to the trust in NGOs. To the extent that NGOs are critical of the conduct of business, as many are, firms are at a considerable disadvantage in communicating with the public. That is, the trust gap between NGOs and global firms gives the advantage to NGOs in most contexts involving communication with the public. Closing the trust gap through corporate social responsibility thus is a considerable challenge.

An individual firm may have earned a reputation for operating in a manner consistent with society's interests, but reputations can be fragile. Most of the public knows little about the conduct of the firm, and a reputation can be tarnished and trust dissipated

---

[2]www.globescan.com/news_archives/WEF_trust2005.html. The survey was conducted for the World Economic Forum.
[3]The countries were Argentina, Brazil, Canada, Germany, Great Britain, India, Indonesia, Italy, Nigeria, Russia, Spain, Turkey, and the USA. The only country with an increase in trust in institutions was Russia.
[4]The only countries with a positive trust in global companies were China, Indonesia, and India, whereas the only countries with a trust in government were Indonesia, Turkey, India, USA, and Argentina.

by the conduct of not only the firm but also other firms, particularly those in the same industry. Moreover, because of the trust gap, one criticism by an NGO or a media story about high executive compensation or backdating of stock options can negate several positive accomplishments by a firm. This means that management should have realistic expectations about building and sustaining a reputation and public trust.

WHAT IS CORPORATE SOCIAL RESPONSIBILITY?

Many conceptions of corporate social responsibility have been offered. This section considers one provided by Milton Friedman and another by the Business Roundtable. Friedman argues, based on economic theory and a conception of morality based on liberty, that the social responsibility of business is profit maximization. The Business Roundtable, based on a conception of obligation to stakeholders, provides a broader conception of the responsibilities of a firm, while leaving the specifics to management.

Milton Friedman's Profit Maximization

Markets and Resource Allocation

Adam Smith (1776) wrote that the surest way to achieve societal well-being was to place resources in the hands of individuals and allow them to transact in markets. Not only are markets the best means of allocating scarce resources to society's needs, but they are also a source of protection for consumers who can turn to other suppliers if they become dissatisfied with a product or service. Markets also allow decentralized decision making and, coupled with the protection of private property, encourage innovation. Smith concluded that it was better to rely on the profit incentives that private ownership provides than to rely on goodwill:

> It is not from the benevolence of the butcher, the brewer, or the baker, that we expect our dinner, but from their regard to their own self-interest. We address ourselves, not to their humanity but to their self-love, and never talk to them of their own necessities but of their advantages.

The corporate form is important in implementing this perspective because share ownership and the limited liability of owners allow ownership and management to be separated. This allows a person working in one field to provide capital for enterprises in other fields with the capital markets coordinating the allocation of capital between investors and business opportunities. Managers of an enterprise are then the agents of the owners—the providers of capital—and serve their interests by maximizing the value of the capital they provide. When markets are competitive, value maximization by firms results in economic efficiency and maximizes aggregate societal well-being.

From this perspective, the role of business in society is to generate well-being through economic efficiency. Private property, the corporate form, and markets are the principal institutions for organizing economic activity. Economic theory identifies the maximization of shareholder value—or long-term profit maximization—as the objective that provides the strongest incentives, and competition directs those incentives toward efficiency.

Corporate Social Responsibility

With this foundation Friedman's (1970) conception of corporate social responsibility is: "to conduct the business in accordance with [owners'] desires, which generally will be to make as much money as possible while conforming to the basic rules of society, both those embodied in law and those embodied in ethical custom." The objective of a corporation thus is the maximization of its profits, or shareholder value, subject to the constraints imposed by the rules of society. Friedman concludes that those who argue that a "corporate executive has a 'social responsibility'. . . must mean that he is to act in some way that is not in the interest of his employers"; that is, the shareholders. In maximizing its profits the firm is to respect both the law as considered in a later section and ethical custom as considered in Chapters 20 and 21.

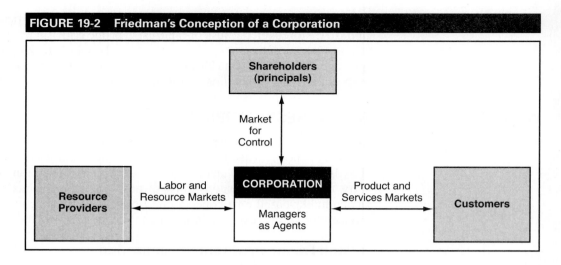

FIGURE 19-2 Friedman's Conception of a Corporation

He argues further that corporate executives who serve some social purpose are acting as civil servants by imposing taxes on shareholders and making expenditures that shareholders would not approve. They act as if "political mechanisms, not market mechanisms, are the appropriate way to determine the allocation of scarce resources to alternative uses." According to Friedman, that amounts to socialism rather than capitalism. Furthermore, calls for a broader social responsibility may, in Friedman's view, actually promote that which corporations should seek to avoid. That is, by calling for the adoption of objectives other than profit maximization, managers are advocating the use of a political process to direct the allocation of corporate resources. Friedman believes that these calls for social responsibility will weaken the free enterprise system and the well-being that flows from it.

From Friedman's perspective, a corporation is a voluntary association of individuals who have joined together for a mutual purpose. That purpose may be the generation of profits in which they will share or the achievement of some social or nonprofit objective. In the case of a for-profit corporation, shareholders have a property right to its assets and hence to the return on those assets. As indicated in Figure 19-2, shareholders are principals and the corporation is managed by agents—the managers—who are to operate it in the best interests of the principals. In an efficient capital market, shareholders will unanimously prefer that the firm be operated to maximize its market value. If one shareholder prefers to donate all his returns to charity and another prefers to spend all her returns on consumption, both will prefer that the firm be operated to make those returns as great as possible. If management does not maximize the value of the firm, the market for control will replace management through a takeover or proxy contest—if shareholders have not already done so.

From this perspective, the corporation engages in voluntary transactions with both resource providers and customers. As Figure 19-2 illustrates, labor and resource markets intermediate between resource providers and the corporation, and product and services markets intermediate between customers and the corporation. If markets are competitive, maximizing shareholder value is consistent with economic efficiency and yields the greatest aggregate well-being for society.

According to Friedman, then, the responsibility of managers, serving as agents of the owners of the firm, the principals, is to maximize profits (shareholder value) by engaging in free and open competition. In that competition, firms engage in voluntary exchanges with others, while abiding by the law and ethical custom.

The Role of Government

It is impossible to have a conception of the responsibilities of business without also having a conception of the responsibilities of government. In Friedman's view, government is to impose taxes and determine expenditures, and the judiciary is to mediate disputes and interpret the law. When there are market imperfections and private costs diverge from social costs, the role of governments is to assign clear entitlements and protect them with a property or liability rule, as called for by the Coase theorem considered in Chapters 11 and 12. Individuals then will internalize the social costs of their actions and reach socially efficient decisions through private bargaining. When transactions costs are high, the government may equate private and social costs through market-like mechanisms such as cap-and-trade systems for pollution control, as considered in Chapter 11. These functions are reserved for government, with its coercive powers limited by a system of checks and balances, individual rights, and the popular election of representatives. According to Friedman, a call for corporate social responsibility "amounts to an assertion that those who favor the taxes and expenditures in question have failed to persuade a majority of their fellow citizens to be of like mind and that they are seeking to attain by undemocratic procedures what they cannot attain by democratic procedures."

Friedman does not indicate whether and to what extent firms should participate in political processes to influence government policies. The natural extension of his perspective, however, is that political competition moves government toward social efficiency just as competition in markets drives firms toward social efficiency.[5]

Philosophical Underpinnings

Friedman holds his view of a corporation as a voluntary association of individuals that maximizes the value of their property not only because of economic efficiency considerations but also because it is consistent with a philosophy of individualism, liberty, and personal responsibility. From this perspective, society is a collection of individuals with differing interests who can be free only if they can act voluntarily. The role of government then is to protect private property and other rights. Since individual liberty and voluntary actions take priority over government direction, resource allocation is to take place through markets rather than through a political process.[6] In this philosophy, competition not only promotes efficiency but also allows people to protect themselves by providing alternatives in the marketplace. Friedman also identifies "the great virtue of private competitive enterprise—it forces people to be responsible for their own actions and makes it difficult for them to 'exploit' other people for either selfish or unselfish purposes. They can do good—but only at their own expense."

The Social Responsibility Label

A firm that maximizes shareholder value may directly benefit others. A value-maximizing firm may make philanthropic contributions because doing so strengthens the communities in which it operates, thereby helping it to attract and retain employees. A firm may institute worker participation programs to improve productivity by enhancing worker satisfaction. A firm may design high-quality products and inform consumers of their safety and performance features because doing so reduces liability costs and increases demand. According to Friedman, when such actions increase shareholder value, they should not be given the label of social responsibility. Those actions are simply another component of a strategy of profit maximization.

From Friedman's perspective a conception of CSR that differs from shareholder value maximization must be costly and can have only two interpretations—either a political process is to be used to make decisions or managers are to act as principals rather than as agents. In the former case he argues that political processes are to be reserved for government and not business. In the latter case, managers are determining who should bear the cost of social responsibility. When the markets in which the firm operates are competitive, the costs of social responsibility must ultimately be borne by

---

[5]See Becker (1983).

[6]See Friedman (1962, Chapter 8). The moral underpinnings of Friedman's conception of corporate responsibility as profit maximization are individual liberties similar to those of individualism. Lukes (1973) characterizes individualism as consisting of four elements: (1) accepting the intrinsic *moral worth* of individual human beings, (2) advocating the *autonomy* of individual thought and action, (3) acknowledging the existence and importance of individual *privacy,* and (4) expressing *self-development* or self-regulation as a desirable goal.

shareholders. The firm could then become the target of a takeover attempt by investors who would operate it to maximize its value. In principle, unless restricted, the market for control should drive the firm toward value maximization.

Understanding Friedman's Perspective[7]

The economic justification for Friedman's position is based on an environment in which citizens can both invest their funds in the capital markets and make personal gifts to social causes. Social causes can also be served by firms, and citizens can obtain satisfaction from corporate giving as well as from their personal giving. If shareholders as principals wish to support social goals, however, they can do so with the returns from their shareholdings rather than through the firm. If an entrepreneur starts a firm and makes it clear to investors that the firm will engage in social activities that may decrease profits, then investors will take this into account when determining how much they will pay for the shares of the firm. Any cost of the social activities then will be borne by the entrepreneur rather than subsequent investors. Since shareholders do not bear the cost when they anticipate the social activities, Friedman would have no objection to those actvities. The entrepreneur as the principal can operate the firm under any combination of financial and social objectives, provided that investors are informed in advance of those objectives. That is, Friedman's objection is not to CSR that is anticipated, since then shareholders do not bear the cost. Instead, Friedman's objection is to CSR that cannot be anticipated by investors.

The perspective that entrepreneurs rather than current shareholders choose the objectives of the firm and bear the cost of CSR was articulated by John Mackey (2005), CEO of Whole Foods, who wrote,

> I believe the entrepreneurs, not the current investors in a company's stock, have the right and responsibility to define the purpose of the company. It is the entrepreneurs who create a company, . . . and who negotiate the terms of trade with all of the voluntarily cooperating stakeholders—including the investors. At Whole Foods we "hired" our original investors. They didn't hire us.
>
> We first announced that we would donate 5 percent of the company's net profit to philanthropy when we drafted our mission statement. . . . Our policy . . . predates our IPO by seven years. All seven of the private investors at the time we created the policy voted for it when they served on our board of directors. . . . How can Whole Foods' philanthropy be "theft" from the current investors if the original owners of the company unanimously approved the policy and all subsequent investors made their investments after the policy was in effect and well publicized?

When costly social activities cannot be anticipated, Friedman views managers as imposing taxes on shareholders and spending the proceeds as they see fit. In doing so, he argues that managers become "in effect a public employee, a civil servant," and argues that if they are to play that role they should be chosen through a "political process." As indicated in the framework presented later in the chapter, a social entrepreneur can be willing to form a CSR firm at a financial loss because of either the good it does for others (altruism) or the personal satisfaction from providing that good (a warm glow). As an example of warm glow preferences, Paul Rice, founder and chief executive of TransFair USA, the U.S. fair trade coffee organization, said, "It is guilt-free coffee, but I would not call it that. I would call it feel-good coffee."[8]

The perspective of Friedman and Mackey that social policies of firms should be announced in advance so that investors can make informed choices about whether to invest in the firm may not be sufficient to sustain those policies. Friedman (1970) points to the discipline of the market for control, "Will not the stockholders fire [the manager]? (Either the present ones or those who take over when his actions in the name of social

---

[7]This section is based in part on Baron (2007).
[8]*San Jose Mercury News,* April 28, 2004.

responsibility have reduced the corporation's profit and the price of its stock.)" Even if the original shareholders supported CSR, the market for control could result in new shareholders taking over the firm, eliminating the costly CSR, and capturing the gain in market value. T. J. Rodgers (2005), CEO of Cypress Semiconductors, wrote, "Mackey spouts nonsense about how his company hired his original investors, not vice versa. If Whole Foods ever falls on persistent hard times—perhaps when the Luddites are no longer able to hold back the genetic food revolution using junk science and fear—he will quickly find out who has hired whom, as his investors fire him." To persist, CSR firms thus need insulation from the market for control. Social entrepreneurs may protect the firms they found with anti-takeover provisions, or socially responsible mutual funds can be formed to hold the shares of CSR firms. Socially responsible mutual funds can raise the share price of firms that engage in social activities, making a takeover less likely.

Corporate social activities may not be costly. Some are undertaken for strategic reasons because they will be rewarded by consumers, investors, or employees or other suppliers of inputs to the firm. This is discussed in more detail later in the section that presents a framework for corporate social performance and is only illustrated here. As an example of activities carried out under the banner of CSR that can also be motivated by strategic considerations, referring to days on which each store donates 5 percent of its sales to local charities, Mackey wrote, "While our stores select worthwhile organizations to support, they also tend to focus on groups that have large membership lists, which are contacted and encouraged to shop our store that day to support the organization. This usually brings hundreds of new or lapsed customers into our stores, many of whom then become regular shoppers. So a 5% Day not only allows us to support worthwhile causes, but is an excellent marketing strategy that has benefited Whole Foods investors immensely." Friedman would support such policies if they increase the profits of the firm, but he would see no reason to label the policies as CSR—unless that was an effective advertising term.

An entrepreneur seeking to pursue social objectives may be able to form a nonprofit firm to pursue those objectives. The Chapter 17 case, *Social Entrepreneurship: Kiva*, concerns an innovative microfinance enterprise organized as a nonprofit. In contrast, the Chapter 17 case, *Social Entrepreneurship: Banco Compartamos*, considers a microfinance enterprise organized as a for-profit firm.

COMPLIANCE WITH THE LAW

Any conception of the social responsibility of business must include compliance with just laws. Both civil and criminal laws apply to firms and their managers. Criminal prosecution can occur under the antitrust laws, securities and exchange laws (as with insider trading), certain environmental laws, and many others. Individual managers and corporations are also subject to fines and can be liable for damages under both statutory and common law. These laws proscribe actions that legislatures and/or the courts have held to be socially unacceptable.

Compliance with the law is a fundamental component of responsible management, yet in recent years the number and size of corporate scandals and incidents of wrongdoing have been alarming. A partial list from the current decade includes Adelphia Communications, AIG, Arthur Andersen, Citigroup, Computer Associates, Crédit Lyonnais, Enron, Global Crossing, HealthSouth, ImClone, Marsh and McLennan, Merrill Lynch, Metallgesellschaft, The New York Stock Exchange, Parmalat, Qwest Communications, Rite Aid, Shell Oil, Siemens, Sumitomo, Tyco, Vivendi, WorldCom, and Xerox. In addition, prominent executives including Jack Welch, former CEO of General Electric, were found to have received special treatment, and some such as Martha Stewart went to prison. *Fortune* (June 9, 2008) provided a rogue's gallery of corporate criminals: Conrad Black of Hollinger International, Bernard Ebbers of WorldCom, Andrew Fastow and Jeff Skilling of Enron, Dennis Kozlowski of Tyco, Sanjay Kumar of Computer Associates, John Rigas of Adelphia, Richard Scrushy of HealthSouth, and Sam Waksal of ImClone. The backdating of stock options by high-tech firms could lengthen the list. The chapter case, *Playing by the Rules?*, asks whether another name should be added to the list.

Some individual companies have been involved in a series of wrongdoings. Citigroup agreed to the following settlements:

- 2002: paid $215 million to settle Federal Trade Commission charges on subprime lending
- 2003: paid $400 million on Securities and Exchange Commission (SEC) charges of biased research
- 2003: paid $145 million on SEC and New York State charges involving Enron
- 2003: paid $325 million to settle New York State charges of biased research
- 2004: paid $70 million on Federal Reserve charges on subprime lending
- 2004: paid $2.58 billion to settle a class action lawsuit on its involvement in the WorldCom scandal

In mid-2004 Citigroup increased its reserve for "Enron and pending litigation" to $6.7 billion. Chairman Sandy Weill received a $29 million cash bonus for 2003. In addition, as considered in Chapter 14, Japan ordered Citigroup's private banking group to close because of violations of banking rules, and shortly thereafter Citigroup fired three of its highest-ranking officers. In 2007–2008 Citigroup was deeply involved in the subprime nortgage crisis and was subject to numerous lawsuits. The CEO brought in after the scandal in the early part of the decade was fired, and his replacement came under fire as the subprime mortgage crisis worsened.

Whether there have been more such incidents in recent years than in the past is unclear, but what is clear is that a substantial number of major companies have violated the law or entered into settlements to end legal complaints. Responsible management requires compliance with laws, yet a company's policing of the actions of its managers cannot be perfect. Some managers violate the law because of greed, some because they think they "can get away with it," some because they believe others are doing the same thing without reprimand, and others because they are pushing into gray areas where there is ambiguity in the law. Regardless of the source of the problem, a foundation of responsible management is compliance with the law and caution in areas where the law is ambiguous. Moreover, violations of the law by business can lead to more stringent regulation, such as the Sarbanes-Oxley corporate governance requirements considered later in the chapter.

In addition to proscribing actions, the law assigns certain duties to firms and managers. For example, the Americans with Disabilities Act assigns an extensive set of duties to firms to provide for the disabled in the workplace. Duties assigned by law are not always the limits of social responsibility, however. Duties also arise from moral considerations. The law thus is an essential guide for responsible management, but reliance solely on the law is rarely sufficient. The next section raises the issue of whether responsible management requires more than compliance with the law and serving the interests of shareholders.

STAKEHOLDER THEORY

The market perspective of Friedman leaves unresolved a number of issues about the role of business in society. First, market imperfections as considered in Chapters 9–12 can cause a divergence between private and social costs and can warrant a role for government regulation and antitrust policy. In some cases the divergence can be addressed through incentive-based regulation and the liability system that align—albeit imperfectly—private and social costs and direct economic activity toward efficiency even in the presence of market imperfections. Nevertheless, market imperfections can remain.

Second, the reliance on private ownership and markets to generate well-being is justified by the moral philosophy of utilitarianism, considered in Chapter 20. Other conceptions of morality, such as those based on rights and justice considerations, however, are also important. They may call for restrictions on the use of private property, the restructuring of incentives, and government intervention for purposes other than the correction of market imperfections. For example, principles of distributive justice may warrant the redistribution of wealth and income to those who are less advantaged, and basic rights may require that the fair equality of opportunity be assured in society. Third, just as markets can be imperfect, so too can government. Because government may be ineffective in correcting market imperfections, providing social justice, and assuring rights, some critics of Friedman argue that business has an affirmative duty to address societal needs unfulfilled by government.

A fourth concern results from agency problems. The corporate form involves a separation of ownership and management. This separation is essential for the efficient allocation of capital, but it also gives managers a degree of discretion to pursue interests other than those of owners.[9] The separation of ownership from management and the resulting managerial discretion means that Adam Smith's market capitalism—the reliance on markets to direct the allocation of resources—coexists with managerial capitalism—the reliance on managers for the allocation of resources.[10]

In principle, managerial capitalism could be more efficient than market capitalism. It allows the accumulation of resources through retained earnings and their allocation within the firm without having to incur the transactions costs of raising funds in the capital markets. It may also have advantages if management has information whose value would be dissipated if disclosed when raising capital. Managerial capitalism, however, can result in inefficiency when the incentives of management are not structured properly. For example, some firms cross-subsidize losses in one line of business with profits from another line of business. The more open are domestic and international markets, the stronger is competition, and the more active is the market for control, the greater are the pressures for efficiency, leaving less discretion to managers.

A firm interacts with a number of constituencies, including employees, suppliers, customers, the communities in which it operates, and the public in general.[11] To the extent that these constituents have an interest, or "stake," in their relationship with the firm, they are referred to as stakeholders.[12] Some stakes are protected by the law, as in the case of an employment contract or shareholder voting rights for approval of a merger. Most stakes, however, are protected by a relationship of mutual advantage with the firm. That is, a firm is attentive to the interests of stakeholders because it is advantageous to do so, and the stakeholders are attentive to the interests of the firm because they benefit from the relationship with it.

A stakeholder relationship centers on an exchange, as when an employee provides labor services to a firm in exchange for wages. Both parties presumably benefit from the continuation of the exchange relationship or else they would terminate it. Employees who have developed firm-specific human capital may earn a higher wage with their current employer than if they reentered the labor market. Similarly, the firm may have a stake in the relationship with employees to the extent that wages are less than the value of employees' contributions plus the costs of finding and training replacements. Both the firm and the employees then have incentives to take into account the interests of the other party in the relationship. Their stakes are voluntarily maintained through mutual advantage.

Does a firm have a responsibility to stakeholders other than to maintain the mutual advantage? Using an analogy to contract law (Chapter 12), an employee may have made reliance expenditures in the form of investing in firm-specific human capital that has little value to other prospective employers. Similarly, a supplier may change its workplace practices to satisfy the requirements of its customers. Responsibility in such cases is to create realistic expectations about the continuation of mutual advantage. It is those expectations that induce the firm-specific reliance investments by stakeholders. Those expectations may include how the firm will deal with the termination of the

[9]Berle and Means (1932) first called attention to the issue of the separation of ownership and control and to its implication. Fama and Jensen (1983) provide a contractual perspective on the issue.
[10]See Chandler (1977) and Chandler and Tedlow (1985).
[11]See Freeman (1984) for an examination of stakeholder concepts and business strategy and Pfeffer and Salancik (1978) and Thompson (1967) for organizational perspectives.
[12]Those with a direct economic stake in the relationship with the firm are sometimes referred to as primary stakeholders, whereas others such as the public without a direct economic stake are referred to as secondary stakeholders.

relationship. For example, the firm may compensate employees in the event of a plant closing and provide support to the community in which the plant was located. A firm thus has a responsibility to create and fulfill realistic expectations, and if it does not do so, it may have a further obligation to compensate stakeholders.[13]

Levi Strauss & Company had a strong commitment to its stakeholders and successfully sustained that commitment for decades. It also had continued to manufacture jeans in the United States, despite the high costs. When in 1997 it was forced by declining sales to lay off over 6,000 employees in the United States, the company was obligated by its principles to provide generous severance packages for the employees who lost their jobs and for the communities in which plants were closed. The cost to Levi Strauss was over $200 million. In 2002 it closed another eight plants at a cost of $113 million, and in 2003 it was forced to close its last plants in Canada and the United States, eliminating 21 percent of its workforce. Again, the company provided a generous severance package for those affected.

THE BUSINESS ROUNDTABLE STATEMENT ON SOCIAL RESPONSIBILITY

The Business Roundtable was founded to "examine public issues that affect the economy and develop positions which seek to reflect sound economic and social principles."[14] The Roundtable is composed of the CEOs of 150 major corporations, with combined employment of 10 million in the United States. In 1981 one of its task forces issued a "Statement on Corporate Responsibility." This statement reflects a constituency or stakeholder perspective and states that business is to "serve the public interest as well as private profit." The Roundtable stated that "some leading managers . . . believe that by giving enlightened consideration to balancing the legitimate claims of all its constituents, a corporation will best serve the interest of its shareholders."

The Roundtable's basic view of the firm is illustrated in Figure 19-3. The Roundtable identified seven constituencies: customers, employees, financiers, suppliers, communities, society at large, and shareholders. "Responsibility to all these constituencies in total constitutes responsibility to society, making the corporation both an economically and socially viable entity." The corporation thus is an entity whose existence depends on society's approval. That is, a corporation is a legal entity granted certain privileges, including limited liability, indefinite life, and special tax treatment such as depreciation allowances. In exchange for these privileges, the corporation has a responsibility to the society that granted them.

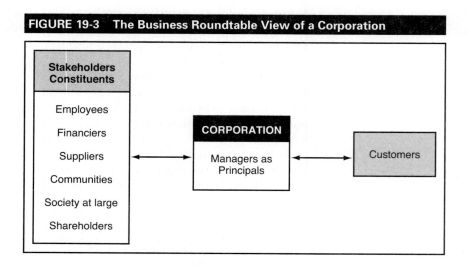

FIGURE 19-3   The Business Roundtable View of a Corporation

---

[13]Post, Preston, and Sachs (2002) and Jensen (2001) provide opposing views of the stakeholder perspective.
[14]See Business Roundtable (1981).

According to the Roundtable, customers have "a primary claim for corporate attention," so in Figure 19-3 they are represented separately as the providers of revenue for the firm. Shareholders also "have a special relationship to the corporation" but are viewed as "providers of risk capital" rather than as principals, as Friedman views them. The Roundtable goes further and criticizes institutional investors because "a high proportion of [shareholders] is made up of institutionally grouped and often unidentified short-term buyers most interested in near term gain. This has affected their role among business constituencies." Ownership of the firm is never mentioned in the Roundtable statement, which suggests that the corporation exists as a legal entity, and shareholders are simply providers of risk capital. In contrast to Friedman's perspective, the principals in the Roundtable's view are managers.

The objective of a corporation is not as clearly identified in the Roundtable statement as it is in Friedman's theory. Instead, managerial decision making involves "weighing the impacts of decisions and balancing different constituent interests. . . ." The statement adds, "The shareholder must receive a good return but the legitimate concerns of other constituencies also must have the appropriate attention." Although the term "good return" is not defined, this balancing is presumably different from shareholder value maximization. Management is to ensure that the corporation remains viable, but beyond a reasonable return on investment all constituents can have a claim to the resources and returns of the firm. The Roundtable statement intentionally provides little guidance about how a corporation makes trade-offs between the interests of various constituencies, since that is the responsibility of managers as principals.[15] As Vogel (1991, p. 114) noted, part of the "universal appeal of the concept of corporate social responsibility rests on the concept's ambiguity," allowing management to formulate its own vision of social responsibility.

The Roundtable argues that the legitimate concerns of constituents are to be taken into account, but it does not want those constituents to participate in managerial decision making. Although "[i]t is important that all sides be heard . . .", managers as principals are to give attention to constituents' interests and decide whether and how much to respond to those interests.

According to MacAvoy (1981), the Roundtable's concern for constituents "implies that the large corporation is a political entity subject to the votes of interest groups, rather than an economic organization subject to the market test for the efficient use of resources." He continued, "Political interests should not be served from corporate investment returns. If the stockholder wishes to support the local schools, or solutions to international problems, then he or she should do so with his or her own dividends." If managers operate their firms otherwise, they are acting as "politicians of the Roundtable," according to MacAvoy.

In a later statement "Corporate Governance and American Competitiveness," the Business Roundtable (1990, p. 5) stated, "It is important that all stakeholder interests be considered, but impossible to assure that all will be satisfied because competing claims may be mutually conflicting." In this statement, the Roundtable argued that corporate governance differs from political governance on several dimensions, including the speed and boldness with which businesses must act and the means through which shareholders can influence the course of management.

Discussion

Business leaders advocate CSR for a variety of reasons. Some argue that there are societal objectives that can be achieved only through corporate action. Business, for example, may be more efficient than government or educational institutions at training workers for certain jobs. Other business leaders call for restraint on the pursuit of profits and for self-regulation in the hope that it will forestall additional government regulation. These calls are viewed by some as a necessary response to pressures from the nonmarket environment, which if ignored could lead to more serious threats to the free enterprise system.

---

[15]The absence of specifics increased the support for the statement among members of the task force.

Some calls for CSR are directed to the public with the intent of increasing public support for business. Some who call for CSR believe that unless business uses at least the rhetoric of social responsibility, more onerous intervention by government will result.

Businesses thus advocate CSR for a variety of reasons, many of which are strategic. This has led skeptics to view as very limited what CSR can be expected to accomplish in meeting society's needs. Christian Aid, an agency of churches in the United Kingdom and Ireland, called "on the politicians to take responsibility for the ethical operation of companies rather than surrendering it to those from business peddling fine words and lofty sentiments."[16] In his evaluation of CSR, Vogel also sees its impact as limited. He states that "while the CSR movement has measurably improved the performance of some firms in some areas, its overall impact has been and will remain more modest than many of its advocates claim, or hope—or some of their critics fear." If business is to do more, he concludes, government will have to prescribe conduct.

Many businesses support a notion of CSR as voluntary self-regulation. At the Earth Summit in Rio de Janeiro in 1992 this perspective was challenged by a United Nations recommendation for international regulation of corporate behavior. The World Council for Sustainable Development, a coalition of businesses, opposed this recommendation and succeeded in obtaining endorsement for a manifesto of voluntary self-regulation. Similarly, in its definition of CSR the European Commission stated that businesses are to take into account the social and environmental consequences of their operations but on a voluntary basis.

CORPORATE SOCIAL RESPONSIBILITY AND CORPORATE SOCIAL PERFORMANCE

Corporate social responsibility focuses on the responsibility of a firm for social performance, but where does that responsibility come from? The perspective presented here is that the responsibility comes from a moral obligation; that is, the content of corporate social responsibility is found in moral principles. Corporate social responsibility thus arises from the combination of (1) an ethical failure that establishes a moral duty and (2) the assignment of that duty to the firm. The concept of a moral duty is developed in Chapters 20 and 21 from the perspectives of three foundational ethics systems—utilitarianism, moral rights, and justice—that correspond to basic moral intuitions. Some moral standards such as freedom of speech impose a duty on everyone to respect. In other cases the set of parties that can address an ethical failure may be small, and an approach to the assignment of duty requires identifying the party, such as a firm, government, or individuals, that is best positioned to address the failure. For example, some people view obesity as a social problem if not a moral problem. Is there a duty on a fast-food company such as McDonald's to address the obesity problem?[17] The party best positioned to deal with the obesity problem is clearly the individual, and government may be best positioned to provide information about obesity and its consequences. McDonald's, however, is well positioned to respond by broadening its menu items and providing more information about those items. Rather than address the assignment of duty in corporate social responsibility here, the broader concept of corporate social performance will be used.

In contrast to corporate social responsibility, corporate social performance need not be motivated by moral considerations but instead could be strategic or a response to the social pressure a firm faces. For example, McDonald's could broaden its menu items to include salads because an increasing number of consumers prefer salads. Similarly, McDonald's could offer salads because of criticism of its menu offerings, as depicted in the movie *Supersize Me*. Or it could offer salads because of pressure from lawsuits claiming it was liable for the obesity of its customers. Corporate social performance thus could be motivated by a number of considerations. The tuna and dolphins example illustrates the difference between social performance that is in response to social pressure and social performance that is morally motivated.

---

[16]Christian Aid, press release, January 21, 2004.
[17]See the Chapter 12 case, *Obesity and McLawsuits.*

EXAMPLE

Tuna and Dolphins

Environmental and animal rights groups protested the use of purse seine nets to catch yellow fin tuna in the Eastern Pacific fishery. In the Eastern Pacific, tuna swim underneath dolphins, and fishing boats cast their nets around the dolphins knowing that the tuna will be caught. Environmental groups estimated that more than 100,000 dolphins a year were being caught in the nets and drowned. However, August Felando, president of the American Tuna Boat Association in San Diego, argued that the 30-vessel U.S. fleet accounted for the deaths of only 12,643 dolphins in 1989, compared with the U.S. limit of 20,500 established by the Marine Mammal Protection Act of 1972. He added that the number had been decreasing because U.S. fishers had become skilled in freeing the dolphins from the nets. All U.S. tuna boats carried U.S. observers to monitor fishing practices. The United States also attempted to enforce its regulations on foreign boats, with 30 percent of foreign tuna boats, mostly from Latin America, also carrying U.S. observers.

H. J. Heinz, which owned StarKist Seafood Company, and other tuna companies had been under pressure for some time. The "save the dolphins" project had been working to convince tuna companies to change their practices and had led a national boycott of yellow fin tuna products. The Humane Society, Greenpeace, the Earth Island Institute, and the Dolphin Coalition were also pressuring the tuna companies. The key event in the campaign was a 1988 videotape taken by a biologist who had signed on as a crew member on a tuna boat. The videotape showed dolphins drowning in purse seine nets. The videotape was broadcast by the national television networks, and suddenly the public became involved. The Earth Island Institute, which had helped organize a boycott of StarKist, took out newspaper advertisements calling on Heinz to stop the "dolphin massacre." Consumers responded, schoolchildren boycotted tuna, and the boycott even found its way into movies such as *Lethal Weapon 2*. Politicians also became interested in the issue, introducing legislation to require "dolphin-unsafe" labels on cans containing tuna caught with purse seine nets.

On April 12, 1990, Heinz President Arthur O'Reilly announced that StarKist would purchase only "dolphin-safe" tuna and would no longer use tuna caught in purse seine nets.[1] StarKist planned to market its tuna under a "dolphin-safe" label. In an interview in the film *Where Have All the Dolphins Gone?*, O'Reilly said, "I think it would be a poor chief executive officer that was not attentive to his customers . . . because of the affection children have for Flipper . . . there was a growing barrage of criticism, well-orchestrated, which I think served to convey a growing sentiment among schoolchildren that the previous fishing methods were no longer acceptable." O'Reilly said that his children had asked him to stop killing dolphins.

In 1988 Hobee's restaurants, a popular and growing chain, switched from yellow fin to Tongol tuna, which is not caught in a manner that contributes to dolphin deaths. In early 1990 the 10 Hobee's restaurants in the San Francisco Bay area began a boycott of all tuna products. Hobee's replaced many of its tuna items with chicken, placed pamphlets on each table explaining its policy, and provided training to its servers so that they could provide more information on the subject if asked. Hobee's also began a boycott of all Heinz products, substituting other brands for such staples as Heinz ketchup. The boycott sent a signal to Heinz.[2]

This example illustrates the difference between responsibility and responsiveness to social pressure. Heinz's decision not to purchase tuna caught in purse seine nets was consistent with ethical consensus in the United States, but the decision was a response to the social pressure it faced. Heinz's motive appears to have been to reduce the actual and potential damage from a boycott and the effect on its brand. Heinz was well aware of the fishing practices in the Eastern Pacific and the number of dolphins being killed. The company also understood the widespread concern about the issue once the videotape was broadcast in March 1988. That Heinz took 2 years to change its policy and not until it had become a boycott target suggests that its action was in response to the social pressure it faced. In contrast, Hobee's restaurants did not act in response to pressure. Its motive was to protect dolphins, even if doing so reduced its profits. Hobee's actions reflected its conception of corporate social responsibility.

---

[1]Shortly thereafter, Bumble Bee Seafoods and Van Camp Seafood Company, producer of Chicken of the Sea brand tuna, announced that they would do likewise. Bumble Bee was owned by Unicord of Thailand, and Van Camp was owned by the Mam Trust of Indonesia.

[2]Hobee's lifted its ban on other Heinz products after the April 12 announcement, but it continued its boycott of StarKist tuna, awaiting implementation of Heinz's program.

A FRAMEWORK FOR CORPORATE SOCIAL PERFORMANCE

Terminology

The term *corporate social performance* (CSP) will be used to refer to social activities that satisfy two conditions. First, the social activities extend beyond the requirements of the law and regulations.[18] Second, the social activities involve the private provision of public goods or private redistribution. For example, the McDonald's project with Environmental Defense discussed in Chapter 11 reduced solid waste in the company's restaurants, which benefited the public by relieving a negative externality. Wal-Mart's corporate philanthropy also benefits the public and represents private redistribution from the company to local communities. CSR implies CSP, but CSP need not be morally motivated. Most of popular discussion as well as empirical analysis pertains to CSP, since identifying moral duties and their assignment is difficult.

From one perspective what matters is social performance and not the motivation for it. That is, if the objective is to serve society's needs, then actions and not motives matter. It should not matter whether a firm takes an action to maximize profits, avoid a challenge from an activist group, or fulfill a moral duty. If the objective is to predict the future behavior of firms, however, then motive matters. A firm that undertakes social activities only for strategic reasons or because of social pressure will act only when there is an opportunity for profits or when forced to act by its nonmarket environment. A firm motivated by moral principles can act in the absence of a profit opportunity or social pressure. From the perspective of anticipating when a firm will act, it is important to understand motive as well as market opportunities and social pressure.

The Setting

The framework for CSP begins with individuals who can allocate their resources among consumption goods, investments in the shares of firms that do and do not conduct social activities, and direct contributions to social causes.[19] Individuals have preferences for consumption and the financial return on their investments, and some may also have preferences for social causes. For example, in the United States contributions to charities in 2007 topped $300 billion, or approximately $1,100 a person.[20] Those contributions may be motivated by altruism for those whose lives are improved by the contributions or because the individual as a donor feels better about herself or himself because of the contribution. As an illustration of the latter type of preferences, in 2004 34 percent of the Prius purchasers stated that their primary reason for buying a Prius was that it "makes a statement about me." By 2007 that number had increased to 57 percent.[21] Prius purchaser Mary Gatch stated, "I felt like the Camry Hybrid was too subtle for the message I wanted to put out there. I wanted to have the biggest impact that I could, and the Prius puts out a clearer message."[22] Such preferences are referred to as "warm glow" preferences and pertain to the act of contributing to the social cause. Many actions by individuals are motivated by both altruism and warm glow preferences.

Individuals can also buy shares in firms that conduct social activities, but corporate social activities may be only an imperfect substitute for personal giving since, for example, the individual may not like all the social activities conducted by the firm.[23] Those

[18]The *Economist* survey found that 23 percent of the firms agreed that corporate social responsibility "is meaningless if it includes things that companies would do anyway" (*Economist,* January 17, 2008).
[19]The theory underlying the framework is presented in Baron (2007, 2008a, 2008b).
[20]Giving USA Foundation and Center on Philanthropy at Indiana University, June 25, 2008.
[21]The surveys were conducted by CNW Marketing Research.
[22]*New York Times,* July 4, 2007.
[23]One rationale for CSP in lieu of personal giving is that firms may have opportunities to make social improvements that are not available to individuals. Individuals, however, can contribute to NGOs that conduct social activities at the scale of a firm. Moreover, with the Internet the range of social activities in which an individual can participate has expanded enormously. Another rationale is that firms can provide social improvements more efficiently than can individuals or the nonprofit organizations to which they can give. Firms and most managers, however, typically have little experience or training in conducting social activities. One illustration of this is the eagerness of firms to partner with NGOs such as Environmental Defense and Conservation International on environmental practices and projects.

individuals who view the corporate social activities as a good substitute for personal giving would then hold shares of such firms, whereas other individuals who view those activities as a poor substitute for personal giving would instead purchase shares of firms without those activists and contribute personally to their preferred social causes. Firms thus attract an investor clientele corresponding to their social performance. Those clienteles could operate through socially responsible investment funds.

Motivations for CSP

CSP could have the following motivations:

- moral
- strategic
- social pressure
- managerial perquisites

Corporate social activities also can have costs. As the opening quotation from the *Economist* survey indicates, many companies view CSP as a "necessary cost of business." Social activities can be rewarded, and the strength of those rewards can depend on the motivation of the firm, although motivation is difficult to observe. Punishment can also result. Consumers may stop buying a product such as canned tuna; employees or communities may sue to block the closing of a plant; and consumer and environmental interest groups may intervene in regulatory proceedings. The motivations for CSP are considered first, followed by the possible rewards and punishments.

Moral Motivation

Social activities can be undertaken because of a moral concern for which the duty is assigned to the firm. The moral concern could be associated with the stakeholders of the firm, the environment, or the general public. The firm may voluntarily take actions to relieve global warming, support community activities, oppose corruption, and aid victims of natural disasters. Examples of such activities are presented in Chapters 22 and 23, and the moral foundations for the activities are considered in Chapters 20 and 21.

Strategic CSP

Corporate social activities could be undertaken for strategic reasons; that is, because the activities strengthen local community relations or improve employee morale and productivity. Wal-Mart is the largest corporate philanthropist, and most of its contributions are made at the local level with employees participating in the allocation of the contributions. Whole Foods' 5% Days are a similar example. Corporate social performance could also strengthen a brand as in the case of Starbucks and Whole Foods. Corporate social performance could make hiring of talented people easier. It could also attract a clientele of shareholders who value the social activities.

If social performance is rewarded, a firm could undertake social activities such as producing a green product, sourcing only from suppliers that respect worker rights, or meeting more stringent environmental standards than called for by regulations. If consumers will pay a premium for green products or for organic foods, a firm motivated by self-interest will supply those products regardless of its position on CSP. Similarly, if consumers prefer products produced from recycled materials or produced by a company with a reputation for environmentally friendly policies, a firm may find it profitable to develop such a policy. These policies can have nothing to do with social responsibility and everything to do with profit maximization. Strategic corporate social performance thus could be undertaken to maximize the profits of the firm and may have no moral motivation. Indeed, many companies argue that they engage in social activities when they make "business sense." One interpretation of business sense is that the activities increase profits.

CSP may also provide better access to government institutions and their officeholders. This may increase the effectiveness of lobbying and other nonmarket strategies, which can result in more favorable government policies or decisions. Responsible policies may also result in activists having greater trust in a firm. This may provide an opportunity to communicate with them on an emerging nonmarket issue in a less hostile context.

Social Pressure

A firm could also conduct social activities in response to social pressure from government or NGOs and social activists. Citigroup was under pressure from environmental NGOs, as considered in the Chapter 4 case, *Anatomy of a Corporate Campaign: Rainforest Action Network and Citigroup (A)(B),* and took the lead along with three other banks in establishing the Equator Principles with environmental and human rights standards for project finance, as considered in Chapter 11. This *responsive CSP* can be undertaken in the absence of any moral concerns and may or may not be rewarded by consumers, investors, or employees. Responsive CSP could relieve social pressure that affects financial performance directly.

Punishments could also result. Social pressure could have a direct effect on the financial performance of a firm if it causes consumers, investors, or employees to shun the firm. Social pressure could also damage the reputation of the firm or a brand, and it could also portend future problems arising from private or public politics, using the terminology of Chapter 4.

Social pressure can be applied to all firms as in the case of criticism of business for excessive executive compensation, but it is often targeted to individual firms or industries. Social activist organizations such as the Rainforest Action Network select targets for their campaigns, and government often focuses enforcement activities on particular firms or industries. Similarly, the threat of new legislation often focuses on particular industries, such as electric power, or on particular practices such as backdating stock options granted to executives. Social pressure stemming from private politics and public politics thus can be targeted to particular firms.

Targeting could focus on *worst offenders,* those firms with poor social performance, or it could focus on firms that are *soft targets* and more likely to bow to the social pressure. A firm could be a soft target because it has in the past conducted social activities or been responsive to social pressure or because it is financially weak or susceptible to brand or reputation damage. Argenti (2004, pp. 110–111) explained the decision by the activist group Global Exchange to target Starbucks to sell Fair Trade Coffee: "Truly socially responsible companies are actually more likely to be attacked by activist NGOs than those that are not. . . . Our interviews with Global Exchange suggested that Starbucks was a better target for the fair trade issue because of its emphasis on social responsibility, as opposed to a larger company without a socially responsible bent."

Managerial Perquisites

In contrast to strategic considerations and responsiveness to social pressure to conduct social activities, corporate social performance could be a perquisite for management in the sense that managers themselves have a preference for the social activities or receive a warm glow from the accolades of the advocates of broadened social performance. Corporate social activities could also be undertaken because management likes those activities, as mentioned earlier. This could be due to a personal preference for those activities, altruism for those whose lives are better as a result of the activities, a warm glow from having conducted the activities, or claiming credit for those activities. As a former employee of an investment bank commented, "the CEO liked birds, so we [the company] liked birds."

Rewards

CSP can be rewarded, although the reward may not exceed the cost. Rewards could come directly from investors, consumers, or employees or other inputs to production. Rewards could also be indirect through relieving social pressure that could arise from either private politics or public politics. CSP that responds to the interests of stakeholders or the demands of NGOs can also build support for the firm in the market and the nonmarket environments. Firms may develop loyal customers, suppliers, and local communities whose support they can call on if they need to expand their facilities or influence government policy.

Investor Rewards

Purchasing shares of a firm with CSP provides both a financial return and a social return, and that firm has a market value composed of the value of their financial return and the value of their social return. Costly social activities may not be fully valued in the capital market, so the market value of the firm could be less than if it eliminated the social activities. If the reward for those activities exceeds the cost, the market value could be higher. Investors thus may reward the firm for its social activities by holding its shares or may penalize a firm that engages in a business the investor dislikes. For example, Hong and Kacperczyk (2007) found that the market prices of sin stocks were depressed and concluded that investors shunned those stocks.

Consumer Rewards

Individuals could reward a firm in their roles as consumers. Consumers could prefer to buy a product from a firm that conducts social activities rather than from a firm that does not. That is, social activities could provide a form of product differentiation. Some consumers could prefer to purchase Timberline boots because of the company's commitment to social performance, and some consumers do not purchase gasoline from ExxonMobil because of the *Exxon Valdez* oil spill or the company's opposition to acting on global climate change.

Employee Rewards

Individuals as employees could also reward a firm through higher productivity motivated by the social activities of the firm. Alternatively, a firm that conducts social activities could attract higher ability employees or may be able to pay lower wages to its employees. Policies such as allowing employees to volunteer in community organizations on company time can improve employee morale and may be rewarded through higher productivity and lower turnover. Similarly, charitable contributions to local organizations can strengthen a community and improve employee satisfaction and morale as well as attract better employees. A firm that conducts social activities also could be included in the supply chain of a firm with a commitment to social performance. For example, a footwear company could restrict its sourcing to factories that meet its workplace standards.

Summary

The framework identifies relations among the financial and social performance of firms and social pressure from their nonmarket environment. A firm could be rewarded for its social performance by consumers, investors, or employees, but whether those rewards exceed the cost of social performance depends on the specifics of the market and nonmarket environments in which the firm operates. Its social performance could be morally motivated, but it also could be in response to social pressure, which itself could depress share prices. Social activities could also be undertaken as a perquisite for management, and if so, social performance should be greater the greater are the slack resources available to managers; for example, when financial performance is better. Social pressure results from private and public politics and is directed to selected firms and industries. The selection may be based on worst offenders or soft targets.

Empirical Research

Vogel (2005) assessed the literature and concluded that CSP has a small impact both on social issues and on corporate financial performance (CFP). Margolis and Walsh (2003) identified 127 empirical studies and 13 surveys focusing on the relation between CSP and CFP. Although a number of studies found no relation, they concluded that the overall weight of the studies showed a positive but weak correlation between the two components of corporate performance. Griffin and Mahon (1997), Mahon and Griffin (1999), Roman, Hayibor, and Agle (1999), and Orlitsky, Schmidt, and Rynes (2003) also examined and interpreted many of these studies. The overall conclusion from this literature is that although there are considerable differences among the studies in terms of methods, measurement, and findings, the weight of evidence supports a weak, positive correlation between CSP and CFP.

Research, however, has not established the direction of causation. That is, good CSP could cause good CFP, or good CFP could provide slack resources to spend on CSP. As the *Economist* put it, "whether profitable companies feel rich enough to splash out on CSR, or CSR brings profits."[24] Waddock and Graves (1997) evaluated the relationship between CSP and CFP and the direction of causation and concluded that good financial performance leads to good CSP. McGuire, Sundgren, and Schneeweis (1988) also suggest that "It may be more fruitful to consider financial performance as a variable causing social responsibility than the reverse." They and McGuire, Schneeweis, and Branch (1990) reach the same conclusion regarding causation as Waddock and Graves. Orlitsky, Schmidt, and Rynes conclude that causation runs in both directions: "Financially successful companies spend more [on CSR] because they can afford it, but CSP also helps them become a bit more successful [in CFP]."

Baron, Harjoto, and Jo (2008) conducted an empirical study of the relation between CFP, CSP, and social pressure and also examined the direction of causation between CSP and CFP. The study is based on financial and operational data, indices of CSP and social pressure from Kinder, Lydenberg, Domini Research & Analytics (KLD)'s Socrates database, as well as data on corporate governance. KLD is an independent research firm that compiles data on the social performance of firms. Its Socrates database is the most comprehensive and widely used data on social performance and includes social ratings data for more than 3,000 companies. KLD's "inclusive" social criteria contain strength ratings and concern ratings for community, diversity, employee relations, environment, governance, human rights, and product. The KLD strength ratings are an index of CSP, and the KLD concerns ratings are an index of social pressure. The KLD concerns include government actions such as regulatory enforcement actions, investigations, and fines, as well as private actions such as community protests and indigenous peoples relations. KLD also has "exclusionary" screens, such as alcohol, gambling, military, nuclear power, and tobacco, which are viewed as controversial lines of business. Only 3.3 percent of the firm-year observations have an exclusionary screen.

In the study, financial performance is measured by Tobin's Q, a standard measure used in economics and finance. Tobin's Q is the ratio of the market value of the firm divided by the capital invested in the firm. The capital invested is measured as total assets, and the market value is the value of all securities issued by the firm.

The empirical estimation involved three equations. One had Tobin's Q as the dependent variable representing the financial performance of the firm with independent variables CSP and social pressure as well as measures of operations (e.g., R&D ratio), financial structure, and capital market factors such as the percent of shares held by institutional investors and the number of analysts covering the firm. The second equation had CSP as the dependent variable and as independent variables had lagged financial performance and lagged social pressure, as well as the operational and market measures. The third equation had social pressure as the dependent variable and as independent variables had lagged financial performance, lagged CSP, and the KLD exclusionary variables as well as the operational and market controls. The equations were estimated (simultaneously) for 484 firms, most of which were in the S&P 500, for the 1996–2004 period as well as a broader sample with fewer years of data.

The estimations indicate the following. CFP is independent of CSP and is decreasing in social pressure. Thus, social pressure worsens the financial performance of the firm, whereas CSP has no significant relation to financial performance. That is, in comparing two firms one with low CSP and one with high CSP, the one with high CSP is no more likely to have better financial performance. This does not mean that there is no causal relationship between CSP and CFP for an individual firm; that is, consumers, investors, or employees sufficiently could reward firms for their CSP to offset the cost of those social activities.[25] Thus, firms could be choosing their CSP to maximize their market

---

[24]*Economist,* January 17, 2008.
[25]No data are available on the actual cost of the activities included as KLD strengths.

values, but looking across the population of firms in the study could reveal no statistically significant relation between CSP and CFP.

The results for the CSP equation provide no support for the perquisites hypothesis but support the responsive CSP hypothesis. That is, better CFP in the prior year does not lead to greater CSP. Thus, taking into account firm characteristics, CFP and CSP appear to be unrelated across the population of firms in the study. In contrast, CSP is also increasing in the social pressure from the prior year, implying that firms respond to that pressure by increasing their CSP. The data do not allow a test of whether social performance is morally motivated or strategically motivated, although if social performance were morally motivated, it should be independent of financial performance.

The results for the social pressure equation support the soft target hypothesis over the worst offenders hypothesis. That is, social pressure is increasing in the CSP from the prior year and is decreasing in CFP, suggesting as in the comment about Starbucks that social pressure may be directed at those firms that are vulnerable and more likely to respond than firms, such as ExxonMobil, that are tough targets and not likely to respond. Social pressure is also decreasing in CFP, indicating that firms that are financially weaker face greater social pressure, which is also consistent with the soft-target hypothesis. The estimation indicates that the component of social pressure with the larger effect on CFP and CSP comes from private rather than public politics.

Empirical studies such as the one reported here provide a picture of the landscape in which firms operate, but it does not provide a roadmap for an individual firm. From the perspective of an individual firm the challenge is to determine the relation between its CFP, its CSP, and the social pressure it encounters. This requires specific information on the possible rewards that it might receive for CSP and how the social pressure it faces depends on its CSP. The chapter case, *Wal-Mart: Nonmarket Pressure and Reputation Risk (B): A New Nonmarket Strategy,* provides an opportunity to consider a company under intense social pressure that must decide whether it should embark on a CSP program and if so how extensive it should be. In addition, it must assess the extent of any moral obligations it might have. These issues are also the subject of Chapters 20–23.

CORPORATE GOVERNANCE

Social Accountability

Accountability continues to be an issue for firms that adopt social responsibilities. Some firms experimented with independent "social audits" of their efforts, and some published those audits. The call for social audits faded in the 1980s as the impact of such reports was questioned, but in the mid-1990s they began to receive increased attention. As a result of public criticism the Body Shop decided to have an independent social audit as a means of quelling criticisms that its practices fell short of its pronouncements. This social audit is considered in Chapter 22.

Many firms now conduct their own assessments of social performance. Some of these assessments are comprehensive, and some focus on a specific issue such as the environment or employee safety. BP provided an extensive and detailed report on its greenhouse gas emissions, including a report on an independent audit of its individual facilities. Dow Chemical provides a detailed report on its environment, health, and safety performance.

In 2004 the Gap, Inc., issued its first social responsibility report.[26] Along with reporting on the company's charitable and volunteer activity and its corporate governance policies, the report provided a detailed summary of the findings by its 90-person compliance team that conducted 8,500 inspections of over 3,000 garment factories that supplied the company. The inspections focused on compliance with the Gap's standards for suppliers. As a result of the compliance inspections, 136 suppliers were terminated.

---

[26]Gap Inc., Social Responsibility Report, 2004, www.gapinc.com.

Many more suppliers were found to have deficiencies, and the Gap worked with them to correct the deficiencies. For example, between 10 and 25 percent of the factories in China, Saipan, and Taiwan were found to have used psychological coercion or verbal abuse. Half the factories in sub-Saharan Africa did not provide adequate safety equipment. The Gap also inspected 653 other garment factories that sought to supply the company and rejected 16 percent of them. The Reverend David Schilling of the Interfaith Center on Corporate Responsibility (ICCR) praised the report as a "major step forward."[27]

Social performance is not only self-assessed by firms but is also assessed through external monitoring and evaluation by activist and other groups. A number of "socially responsible" mutual funds have been established, which refuse to hold shares in cigarette companies, weapons manufacturers, or firms that damage the environment. KLD, for example, offers the Domini 400 Index. In 1994 Franklin Research & Development withdrew its highest rating for the Body Shop as a result of its evaluation of the company's social performance. Several independent organizations provide institutions, such as universities and pension funds, with evaluations of the social performance of firms. In preparing its social responsibility report, the Gap formed a public reporting working group with members from Domini Social Investments, the Calvert Group, the As You Sow Foundation, the Center for Reflection, Education and Action, and the ICCR. Organizations such as the ICCR provide evaluations of corporate policies on particular issues that are the subject of shareholder resolutions voted on at annual shareholder meetings.

Proponents of the stakeholder responsibility perspective, as articulated by the Business Roundtable, have argued for stakeholder representation on boards of directors to improve corporate social performance. Hillman, Keim, and Luce (2001) studied the relation between stakeholder directors and CSP.[28] Their statistical analysis revealed no aggregate relation between CSP and board representation, and when they disaggregated the components of CSP and types of board representatives, they also found little evidence of a relation. Even if an empirical relation had been found of a link between constituent representation and CSP, the direction of causality still would be unclear. As the authors noted, firms with poor CSP could be the ones that added constituent directors.

The Duties of Boards of Directors

Corporations are "managed under the direction" of a board of directors, and board members have fiduciary responsibilities. The legal obligations of directors generally fall into categories referred to as the *duty of loyalty* and the *duty of care*. The duty of loyalty pertains to conflicts of interest and requires that directors serve the interests of the corporation and its shareholders. According to Clark (1985, p. 73), "Case law on manager's fiduciary duty of care can fairly be read to say that the manager has an affirmative, open-ended duty to maximize the beneficiaries' wealth . . . " The duty of care requires directors to take care in their direction of the corporation under the "prudent person" standard and to make informed decisions. (Officers of the corporation have the same duty.) Directors are not expected to participate in the day-to-day management of the corporation.

The courts judge the discharge of the obligations of directors according to a common law standard referred to as the *business judgment rule*. Under this standard, actions taken by the board generally are not subject to judicial review if they are taken in accord with the duty of loyalty and the duty of care. The business judgment rule is based on the view that courts have no special expertise in second-guessing business decisions and that business decision making would be unduly hampered if it were subject to judicial review. Furthermore, the courts are likely to be less effective in monitoring managerial decisions than is the market for control.[29]

If directors do not exercise due care, they may be held liable. In *Smith v. Van Gorkom* (1985), 488 A.2d 858 (Del.), the Delaware Supreme Court held that the directors of Trans Union Corporation were grossly negligent, and hence not protected by the

---

[27]*Wall Street Journal*, May 12, 2000.
[28]Performance was measured using the same data used by Waddock and Graves.
[29]See Easterbrook and Fischel (1981).

business judgment rule, since they failed to independently value the firm in a leveraged buyout.[30] A subsequent case, *Hanson Trust PLC v. ML SCM Acquisition* (1986), 781 F.2d 264 (2nd Cir. 1986), established that being adequately informed is not sufficient to be protected by the business judgment rule. Directors must be well informed when they make decisions. Consequently, boards now seek the advice of independent experts in any valuation decision and in many other decisions as well. Reliance on experts is not sufficient, however, and directors are required to inquire into the content and quality of the reports given by management. The *Van Gorkom* and *Hanson* decisions caused the cost of directors and officers insurance to increase sharply. Most states responded by enacting statutes that allowed shareholders to limit the liability of directors and officers.

In addition to legal requirements, boards have a number of specific roles and functions. The Business Roundtable (1997, pp. 4–5) identified five principal functions of the board:

    i. Select, regularly evaluate and, if necessary, replace the chief executive officer, determine management compensation, and review succession planning.

    ii. Review and, where appropriate, approve the major strategies and financial and other objectives, and plans of the corporation.

    iii. Advise management on significant issues facing the corporation.

    iv. Oversee processes for evaluating the adequacy of internal controls, risk management, financial reporting and compliance, and satisfy itself as to the adequacy of such processes.

    v. Nominate directors and ensure that the structure and practices of the board provide for sound corporate governance.

The Roundtable also argued that board attention should focus on strategic decisions and the social impacts of corporate decisions, although it drew considerably narrower boundaries on social responsibility than did the task force statement on corporate social responsibility.

The Roundtable recommended a board composed of "a substantial majority of . . . outside (nonmanagement directors)" and recommended inclusion of more women and minorities on boards. The Roundtable also stated that "it is highly desirable for a board to have a central core of experienced business executives." Many corporations assign only nonmanagement directors to the audit, compensation, and nominating committees of their boards to ensure that the shareholders' interests are being served by management.

The duty of loyalty supports both Friedman's position and the strategic use of CSR. The business judgment rule, however, means that management and the board have a substantial range of discretion in deciding the extent of that responsibility. Concerns about managerial capitalism and the objectives that management pursues have resulted in direct pressure from institutional investors for a more independent and vigilant board of directors. The nation's largest fund, the California Public Employees' Retirement System (CalPERS), for example, pressures firms to have more independent boards and improve their financial performance. TIAA-CREF, a pension fund for teachers and professors, joined with CalPERS in seeking changes in boards of directors of companies such as Heinz, arguing that the board was not sufficiently independent. In 2004 CalPERS launched a campaign to withhold its vote for board members who were not sufficiently independent or who voted for auditors that also had consulting arrangements with the company.

Sarbanes-Oxley

In the wake of the Enron and WorldCom bankruptcies Congress enacted the Public Company Accounting Reform and Investor Protection Act, known as Sarbanes-Oxley after its congressional sponsors. The law requires a company to identify an independent "financial expert" on its board audit committee and requires the CEO and CFO to certify the firm's financial statements. If those statements are found not to meet the

---

[30]Corporations are incorporated under state law, and Delaware is the most popular state for incorporation.

standards in Sarbanes-Oxley, prison terms of up to 10 years and a fine of up to $1 million can be imposed. The law also prohibits audit firms from providing consulting services while conducting an audit. The law also established the independent Public Company Accounting Oversight Board as a watchdog over accounting firms. Penalties for destroying, falsifying, or altering records include prison terms of up to 20 years.[31] The National Association of Corporate Directors issued a report "Risk Oversight: Board Lessons for Turbulent Times" evaluating these board responsibilities.

Critics of Sarbanes-Oxley argued that it went too far. They worried that it would make it harder to recruit new board members, spur a rash of lawsuits, impose heavy costs for meeting documentation requirements for financial controls, and make firms risk averse. The first two concerns have not materialized, but firms, particularly small firms, have complained about the costs of documentation of their internal controls as required by Section 404.[32] The SEC has sought to lighten the administrative burden on small firms. Whether firms have become more risk averse remains unclear.

The Market for Control

The market for control disciplines management and directors to serve shareholder interests through mergers, acquisitions, hostile takeovers, proxy contests, and depressed market valuations.[33] However, many managers want to be insulated from the market for control, arguing that they are best able to chart the firm's course.[34] Investors often disagree and favor the discipline of the market to the discretion of management; that is, they prefer market capitalism to managerial capitalism. For example, through a series of acquisitions, United Airlines, which had renamed itself Allegis, had included in its system Hertz Rent-A-Car, Westin Hotels, and Hilton International. Pressure on the company for better financial performance caused its board of directors to replace the CEO. Under new management Allegis was broken up, with UAL, Inc., the surviving entity. In his letter to shareholders, the new chairman and CEO wrote, "My objective . . . has been . . . enhancing near-term stockholder values and the goal of permitting United Airlines to operate successfully and gain in value in the future in a very competitive environment. . . . We have determined to proceed immediately with the sale of all of our non-airline businesses—Hertz, Westin, and Hilton International—and to distribute the net proceeds from those sales to stockholders."[35]

Institutional investors are an increasingly important force in the market for control. During the 1970s and most of the 1980s, institutional investors were relatively passive and seldom attempted to influence the management of firms. Most institutions voted with management on proxy issues. With institutions now holding a majority of the shares of U.S. corporations, compared with slightly over 20 percent in 1970, institutional investors have been crucial in forcing management changes in companies such as General Motors and Eastman Kodak. Pension funds, such as CalPERS, have been concerned about the return on their investments and have increasingly opposed management on proxy challenges, anti-takeover charter amendments, and shareholder resolutions directed at forcing management to improve profitability. In addition, the Department of Labor has instructed pension fund managers to vote on proxy issues in the best interests of their beneficiaries.[36] In 1992 the Securities and Exchange Commission issued rules giving shareholders new powers, such as calling special meetings and maintaining confidentiality on proxy measures, which make it easier to take action against management. Although the market for control is active and limits the exercise of managerial capitalism, the imperfections in the market for control leave considerable discretion.

---

[31]The law also separated stock analysis from deal-making of financial services firms. Sarbanes-Oxley increased the maximum prison sentence for mail and wire fraud from 5 to 10 years.
[32]Both management and the external auditors are required to report on the firm's Internal Controls over Financial Reporting.
[33]See Weston, Chung, and Hoag (1990) for a comprehensive treatment of the market for control, Jensen (1988) for an analysis of the role of takeovers, and Tirole (2005) for insight into the market for control.
[34]See Coffee, Lowenstein, and Rose-Ackerman (1988).
[35]April 25, 1987, letter to Allegis Corporation stockholders from Frank A. Olson.
[36]The Department of Labor has regulatory authority under the Employee Retirement Income Security Act of 1974.

Under pressure from corporations and organized labor, Pennsylvania enacted an anti-takeover law intended to protect its firms and the jobs they provided in the state. This action provided evidence on both the market for control and managerial responses to the protection of firms and their management. A unique feature of the law was that it gave corporations a window during which they could opt out of one or more of the law's protective provisions. The capital market reaction occurred soon after the bill was introduced in the state legislature. The price of a market basket of 60 companies incorporated in Pennsylvania fell over 5 percent relative to the Standard & Poor's 500 index. As the likelihood increased that the bill would pass, the gap increased—when the state senate passed the bill, the gap was 6.9 percent.[37] Since some firms were expected to opt out of the law, the decrease in market value for those firms that were expected to choose the protection of the law was considerably greater than the average. The capital markets penalized those companies that protected management from the market for control.

SUMMARY

The role of business in society and the extent of its social responsibilities remain subjects of disagreement. The duties of care and loyalty and the business judgment rule leave considerable discretion to directors and management, but management is not free to rely on its personal preferences for charting the paths of the firms they control. Management and directors face continuing pressure for improved financial performance, which limits management's discretion to pursue social objectives. The chapter case, *The Collapse of Enron: Governance and Responsibility,* addresses the responsibilities of directors when management pushes the envelope of acceptable practices.

Corporate social responsibility is distinguished from corporate social performance by the presence of a moral duty assigned to the firm. CSP can be conducted for strategic as opposed to moral considerations, and can be rewarded by consumers, investors, or employees. CSP can also be a perquisite for management or can be undertaken in response to social pressure. Social pressure is directed at firms, as in the Wal-Mart chapter case, and can be directed at worst offenders or soft targets.

Many companies argue that corporate social performance and corporate finanacial performance can, and do, go hand in hand. Surveys of the empirical literature indicate that there is a positive but weak correlation between CSP and CFP, but the direction of causation remains an open question. The empirical study discussed earlier of the relations among social performance, financial performance, and social pressure found that greater CSP leads to better CFP, and CFP is decreasing in social pressure. Most firms both face social pressure and have positive CSP. CSP is responsive to social pressure and is increasing in CFP, suggesting that it may in part be a managerial perquisite. Social pressure is decreasing in CFP and increasing in CSP suggesting that soft targets are selected to receive social pressure. Social pressure is also greater for controversial lines of business.

Even Friedman's dictum to maximize profits is subject to the limits of the law and ethical custom, both of which leave a gray area between what is clearly responsible and what is clearly irresponsible. On such issues managers obtain guidance from two primary sources. The first is government, which proscribes as well as prescribes certain actions and provides incentives to adopt certain types of policies. The tax deductibility of philanthropic contributions and the tax advantages provided for hiring disadvantaged youths are examples of such incentives.[38] The second source of guidance is ethics. Ethics provides a basis for reasoning about and evaluating actions and policies. The content of social responsibility ultimately is found in these principles and their moral foundations. Moral foundations, however, do not always provide unambiguous prescriptions nor are the prescriptions provided by different ethics frameworks necessarily the same. The following chapters develop these frameworks and consider applications within the scope of the corporate social responsibility debate.

---

[37]See Karpoff and Malatesta (1989).
[38]Corporations can deduct charitable contributions up to 15 percent of their net income.

-- C A S E S --

The Collapse of Enron: Governance and Responsibility

In an interview with PBS in March 2001 when doubts were being raised about Enron, President and CEO Jeffrey Skilling said, "We are the good guys. We are on the side of the angels."

Addressing Jeffrey Skilling in a House hearing, Representative Edward J. Markey (D-MA), said, "You are employing the Sergeant Shultz defense of 'I see nothing. I hear nothing.'" (Sergeant Shultz was a character in the television series Hogan's Heroes.*)*

Representative James Greenwood (R-PA) referred to Enron CFO Andrew Fastow as the "Betty Crocker of cooked books."

Enron was a great business success soaring to a market capitalization in excess of $60 billion and ranking seventh on the *Fortune* 500 list. It was frequently voted one of the most admired companies and one of the best companies to work for. Enron also had a cutthroat corporate culture in which pushing the envelope was routine and failure led to departure.

The company built its success on natural gas pipelines, energy production, and an innovative energy trading business. Some of its investments were failures, however. One was the Dabhol electric power generation plant that was subject to contentious contract disagreements with the government of India. Enron decided to walk away from the contract in 2000. Enron also acquired Portland General Electric and attempted to grow its Internet unit into a nationwide fiber optics system. Enron acquired Wessex Water in the United Kingdom but failed in its attempt to develop it into a new line of business. Enron also invested in a broadband company that collapsed with the bursting of the telecom bubble.

Enron was creative in its financial arrangements, entering into numerous partnerships with a variety of entities. The purpose of some of the partnerships and their related-party transactions was to transfer certain assets, their associated borrowings, and their profits, or more often losses, to the partnership. This allowed Enron, with the approval of its auditor Arthur Andersen, to keep losses off its income statement and debt off its balance sheet. Many of the partnerships were organized by Enron executives, some of whom invested in them with guaranteed returns. Negotiations with the partnerships were thus not at arm's length, with Chief Financial Officer Andrew Fastow both representing Enron and participating through limited partnerships in deals with Enron. Fastow and several lower-level employees "were enriched, in the aggregate, by tens of millions of dollars they should never have received."[39]

The participation of the employees other than Fastow had not been approved by the chairman and CEO.

The partnerships allowed Enron to keep substantial losses off its financial statements. From the third quarter of 2000 through the third quarter of 2001 Enron reported a before-tax profit of $1.5 billion, but if certain partnerships referred to as Raptors had been consolidated into its financial statement, its earnings would have been $429 million. Although Enron stated that the partnerships protected the company from risk, the risk was actually borne by Enron through guarantees to the Raptors. As Enron's share price declined in 2001 the Raptors' ability to protect Enron's earnings disappeared. CEO Jeffrey Skilling resigned abruptly in August 2001, while proclaiming that Enron was in good health.

Under increasing pressure from its own failed investments, facing difficulty in obtaining financing, and under scrutiny from Wall Street, on October 16 Enron reported a third-quarter pre-tax loss of $710 million and subtracted $1.2 billion from shareholders' equity. One billion dollars of the write-down was due to the correction of "accounting errors," and $200 million was due to the termination of the Raptors. In November Enron restated its earnings back through 1997. The restatements of earnings included the consolidation of a number of partnerships that had been used to keep debt and earnings fluctuations off Enron's financial statements. Fastow was asked to leave the company on October 23, and the Securities and Exchange Commission began an investigation. Revelation of the hidden losses destroyed any remaining confidence in the company, and its share price continued its decline from its peak of $81.39 on January 25, 2001, to less than a dollar in December 2001. Enron filed for chapter 11 bankruptcy on December 2.[40] A flurry of class action and other lawsuits were filed against Enron and Andersen for securities fraud and other violations.

History of the Company

After stints as a corporate economist, assistant professor, Federal Power Commission staff member, and undersecretary of the Department of Interior, Kenneth Lay became vice president of Florida Gas and then of the Continental Group. He then became president and CEO of Transco, a Houston-based gas company, and then of Houston Natural Gas. In 1985 he arranged the merger of Houston Natural Gas and Internorth, and the merged companies subsequently became Enron.[41] Enron operated fixed assets in power generation and

---

[39]The Report of Investigation by the Special Investigative Committee of the Board of Directors of Enron Corp., February 1, 2002 [Special Report], p. 3.

[40]Subsequent to filing for bankruptcy Enron agreed to a merger with Dynergy, but Dynergy backed out of the agreement shortly thereafter.
[41]*New York Times*, February 3, 2002.

natural gas transmission and organized an energy trading market in which it traded electricity and natural gas. Enron also had a large merchant investment business in structured transactions in fixed assets and trading. Enron was an aggressive advocate of deregulating energy markets.

In 2000 Enron had sales of $101 billion and assets of $47.3 billion. Enron operated 30,000 miles of pipelines and 15,000 miles of fiber optic cable and had 19,000 employees in 2002.

Special Purpose Enterprises and Accounting Statements

A central component of Enron's strategy was to utilize subsidiaries and special purpose entities including partnerships for the funding and structuring of projects. Enron was estimated to have 3,000 partnerships and subsidiaries. It had over 140 subsidiaries in the Netherlands, where tax laws gave favorable treatment to holding companies with subsidiaries in other countries. The holding companies could loan funds to subsidiaries such as Enron Columbia Energy BV, and the interest on the loan was not taxable.

In partnerships named Marlin and Osprey, Enron formed an investment trust, lending its stock to the partnerships for use as collateral.[42] The partnership raised small amounts of outside equity and raised most of its funds by issuing debt with the Enron stock as collateral. The partnership then formed a joint venture with Enron in which Enron provided real assets to the joint venture in exchange for funds used to pay off debt on the assets. The debt in the joint venture did not appear on Enron's books, but if the joint venture were to fail or be unable to repay its debt obligations, Enron would have to provide shares to cover the debt payments. These partnerships were disclosed only in the fine print of Enron's annual report. In marketing such structured transactions Citigroup described one of the benefits as removing "certain items from 'plain view,' thus enhancing the appearance of the balance sheet."[43]

Enron used a variety of other means to keep debt off its books, one of which was a prepaid swap. For example, in December 2000 Enron signed a contract to deliver natural gas to Mahonia Ltd. over a 5-year period and simultaneously signed a contract with Stonehill Aegean Ltd. to purchase the gas to be delivered to Mahonia. In the deals Mahonia prepaid the fair value of the contract, while Enron's payment to Stonehill was to be spread over 5 years. This in effect gave Enron a loan of $330 million at a 7 percent interest rate, but the loan did not appear on Enron's balance sheet. Mahonia and Stonehill were affiliated companies linked to JPMorgan Chase, which structured the swap.[44] Citigroup reportedly loaned $2.4 billion to Enron through a series of prepaid swaps.[45]

Enron also established special purpose enterprises that participated in related-party transactions to keep certain assets and debt off its balance sheet and shield its earnings. Accounting for the enterprises was subject to generally accepted accounting principles. Enron could avoid having to consolidate these special purpose enterprises in its financial statements if they satisfied two conditions. One was that the enterprises were independently controlled, and the other was an SEC requirement that 3 percent of its assets be at risk; that is, outside equity of at least 3 percent was required.

Chewco

In 1993 Enron established a partnership named JEDI (Joint Energy Development Investments) with the California Public Employees' Retirement System (CalPERS) as the limited partner. JEDI initially invested in natural gas pipelines and was not consolidated in Enron's financial statements because Enron and CalPERS exercised joint control.

In 1997 CalPERS wanted out of JEDI, and Fastow established Chewco Investments LP to buy CalPERS's interest for $383 million.[46] Accounting rules would have required disclosure of the partnership if an Enron senior executive, such as Fastow, were to manage Chewco, so Fastow assigned Michael J. Kopper, who reported to Fastow, to manage Chewco. Disclosure was not required because of Kopper's rank.

Chewco was financed by a $240 million loan from Barclays Bank PLC, guaranteed by Enron, and by an advance of $132 million from JEDI. To keep Chewco off Enron's books, a minimum 3 percent equity investment, or $11.5 million, had to be invested. To provide the outside equity, Fastow and Kopper established Big River Funding as Chewco's limited partner, and Little River Funding was established to own Big River Funding. Kopper invested $125,000 of his own funds in the two entities and arranged to borrow the remaining $11.4 million "equity" from Barclays.[47] The credit document was written so that Barclays could treat it as a loan and Enron could treat it as equity for accounting purposes. For example, instead of referring to interest, the credit document referred to "yield." Barclays ultimately loaned only $6.8 million, so Chewco did not meet the SEC outside equity requirement.[48] Chewco thus was incorrectly kept off Enron's books with neither its debt nor its losses consolidated. Enron repurchased Chewco in March 2001, and Kopper and his partner Dodson

[42]*New York Times,* February 14, 2002.
[43]*New York Times,* February 14, 2002.
[44]*New York Times,* February 19, 2002.
[45]*New York Times,* February 17, 2002.
[46]Following a *Star Wars* theme, there were partnerships named JEDI, Obi 1, and Chewco, after Chewbacca.
[47]Shortly thereafter Kopper transferred his financial interests to his domestic partner, William Dodson.
[48]The remaining $6.6 million was funded from a distribution by JEDI from the sale of an energy company.

received $10.5 million for their investment. In November 2001 Enron disclosed Chewco when it revised its financial statements.

Enron also engaged in a variety of questionable accounting practices regarding revenue and income from JEDI and Chewco. For example, Chewco held 12 million shares of Enron stock, which were carried at fair value. As its stock appreciated, Enron recorded a share of the appreciation as its own income, which is contrary to generally accepted accounting principles. Moreover, as its stock price began to fall, Enron's $90 million share of the loss on the shares held by Chewco was not recorded as a decrease in income. Arthur Andersen approved both the recognition of appreciation as income and not recognizing the decrease in value as a reduction in income.

LJM Partnerships

In 1999 Fastow proposed establishing a partnership LJM Cayman LP (LJM1) for the ostensible purpose of hedging Enron's investment in Rhythms NetConnections by obtaining investments from outside investors.[49] Fastow would be the general partner, since, he explained, that would help attract outside investors. He said he would personally invest $1 million in LJM1. The proposal was approved by Lay, Skilling, and the board, which determined that Fastow serving as managing partner of LJM1 would not "adversely affect the interests of Enron." Such a determination was required by Enron's code of conduct.

Enron also sought to take advantage of the "embedded" value resulting from a forward contract with an investment bank to purchase Enron shares at a fixed price. Enron restructured the contract, releasing 3.4 million shares of its stock to be used as collateral. To "hedge" Enron's investment in Rhythms, LJM1 received these Enron shares in exchange for a note to pay $64 million to Enron. LJM1 then transferred the shares to a newly created limited partnership, Swap Sub, that gave Enron a put option on Enron's entire investment in Rhythms.[50] The put option entitled Enron to sell its Rhythms shares to Swap Sub at $54 per share in June 2004.[51] Enron had purchased its 5.4 million shares in Rhythms at $1.85 per share in March 1998, and when Rhythms went public in 1999 Enron's holding was valued at $300 million. This arrangement, however, did not provide a true hedge because if Enron's shares declined in value, Swap Sub would be unable to cover the put. In addition, Swap Sub did not have the required 3 percent equity investment. Arthur Andersen, which had not objected to the arrangement, concluded in October 2001 that it had made an error.

Enron began to unwind the hedging arrangement in the first quarter of 2000 in a series of complicated transactions. Five lower-level Enron employees plus Fastow formed a limited partnership, Southampton Place LP, to participate with LJM1 in the unwind. Within 2 months a $25,000 investment returned $4.5 million funneled into a "family foundation," whose limited partners were Fastow and the other five employees. Two of the five also invested $5,800 and received a return of $1 million in 2 months. These employees did not seek a determination from Lay and Skilling that their participation would not adversely affect the interests of Enron. The Report of the Special Committee established by the board in the wake of the collapse stated, "Enron employees involved in the partnerships were enriched, in the aggregate, by tens of millions of dollars they should never have received—Fastow by at least $30 million, Kopper by at least $10 million, two others by $1 million each. . . . " The Special Committee report concluded, "We have not seen any evidence that any of the employees, including Fastow, obtained approval from the chairman and CEO under the code of conduct to participate financially in the profits of an entity doing business with Enron. While every code violation is a matter to be taken seriously, these violations are particularly troubling."

LJM1 was also used to take certain assets off Enron's balance sheet and increase its current income. Enron had a 65 percent interest in a Brazilian company building a power plant that was "experiencing significant construction problems." Enron sold a portion of its interest to LJM1, leaving it no longer technically in control of the company and allowing Enron to take its investment in the company off its balance sheet. This also allowed Enron to mark-to-market the value of a gas supply contract an Enron unit had with the Brazilian company. This increased Enron's income for the second half of 1999 by $65 million.[52]

On Fastow's recommendation the board approved the establishment of a second (LJM2) partnership with Fastow as the general partner.[53] LJM2 raised $394 million primarily from 50 limited partners, including Merrill Lynch, JPMorgan Chase, and Citigroup. In addition, Fastow and other Enron employees invested in LJM2 through two limited partnerships, one of which, Big Doe, was managed by Kopper, and the other by Fastow himself. The LJM partnerships were in a gray area of accounting standards and were not consolidated with Enron's financial statements.

Raptors

Raptor was Enron's name for a partnership used to hedge its merchant investments portfolio in projects and companies. The Raptors were a result of the initial success

---

[49]Fastow named the LJM partnerships using the first letters of his wife's and children's names.
[50]Enron could not sell its shares in Rhythms before the end of 1999.
[51]PricewaterhouseCoopers reviewed the transactions and concurred that the arrangement was fair to the parties.

[52]Special Report, pp. 136–137.
[53]The LJM partnerships participated in 20 transactions with Enron.

of the Rhythms "hedge." Because its merchant investments were marked-to-market, changes in their value affected Enron's earnings on a quarterly basis. The first Raptor, named Talon, was established in April 2000. To provide the 3 percent equity required to keep Talon off Enron's balance sheet, LJM2 provided $30 million. LJM2 was guaranteed a payment of $41 million before Talon could engage in hedging. For accounting purposes the $41 million was treated as a return on LJM2's investment, leaving its $30 million to satisfy the 3 percent requirement. However, Enron, which contributed its shares to Talon, would keep 100 percent of its earnings. Talon's only assets were thus Enron's shares.

To pay LJM2 Enron signed a contract with Talon under which Enron paid $41 million in exchange for a put option, the right to sell Enron shares to Talon at a fixed price. Talon then paid the $41 million to LJM2, allowing Talon to begin operations. Enron and Talon then signed a contract under which Talon agreed to cover Enron's losses on certain investments in exchange for sharing in any appreciation of the investments. This protected Enron's income statement from losses on the merchant investments. The Raptor's ability to cover losses depended on the price of Enron shares, however. If Enron's share price were to decline to a $47 trigger, Talon would be unable to cover Enron's losses.

Four Raptors were used to keep $504 million of losses off Enron's books, but as its stock price fell, triggers were tripped that threatened their ability to protect Enron's reported earnings. Early in 2001 Enron restructured the Raptors to reestablish the façade that they were covering risks, but after the restructuring they were even more vulnerable. Within weeks of the restructuring Enron reported a profit of $425 million for the first quarter of 2001.

In referring to Talon the Board secretary wrote, "Does not transfer economic risk, but transfers P&L volatility."[54] The Board Special Committee stated, "Enron still bore virtually all of the economic risk. In effect, Enron was hedging risk with itself." The Special Committee concluded, "Especially after the restructuring, the Raptors were little more than a highly complex accounting construct that was destined to collapse."

As the Raptors were collapsing, Enron and Andersen accountants discovered that Enron's accounting for three of the Raptors was wrong. The shares Enron contributed to the Raptors had been treated as an increase in notes payable and a corresponding increase in shareholders' equity. This increased shareholders' equity by $1 billion during the first half of 2001. In October and November Enron restated its income and balance statements and consolidated the LJM partnerships.

In August Skilling abruptly resigned. After the resignation Sherron Watkins, an Enron vice president, wrote to CEO Kenneth Lay warning of the "inappropriateness" of some transactions. She wrote, "To the layman on the street it will look like we recognized funds flow of $800 million from merchant asset sales in 1999 by selling to a vehicle (Condor) that we capitalized with a promise of Enron stock in later years."[55] She also wrote, "I am incredibly nervous that we will implode in a wave of accounting scandals."[56]

As a result of Watkins's letter Enron asked its outside law firm Vinson & Elkins to prepare a report on its transactions. The report presented on October 15 concluded that nothing wrong had been done, although it noted that both Enron and Andersen agreed that the accounting had been "creative and aggressive." Although the law firm found nothing wrong, the report stated, "Within Enron, there appeared to be an air of secrecy regarding the LJM partnerships and suspicion that those Enron employees acting for LJM were receiving special or additional compensation."

Not everyone was fooled by Enron. A few analysts issued warnings, but most analysts followed the herd. In a conference call with analysts, Enron released its first quarter 2001 earnings and proclaimed the quarter a great success. One skeptical analyst asked why the company was issuing an income statement without the accompanying balance sheet and cash flow statement. Skilling brushed aside the question, mocking the analyst.

Citigroup, a major lender to Enron, decided to hedge some of its risk. Fifteen months before Enron's collapse and again in May 2001 Citigroup sold 5-year notes to investors who were guaranteed a return plus their principal unless Enron went bankrupt or failed to repay a loan. In those events the investors would be paid in Enron debt. This was the largest hedge Citigroup had ever taken against a company.

401(k) Plans and Deferred Compensation

Enron employees participated in 401(k) retirement plans, and most of them held Enron shares. The company matched employee contributions with equal contributions of Enron shares, and employees were prohibited from selling their shares until age 55.[57] Enron shares represented approximately 65 percent of the assets of the plans. During 2001 the company continued to tout its stock to employees as a good investment. Enron's collapse caused many employees to lose most of their retirement funds.

In addition to its 401(k) plans Enron had a deferred compensation plan under which managers could defer portions of their compensation. During 2001 before

---

[54]The reference to "P&L volatility" meant that the profit and loss effects would not appear on Enron's books.

[55]Later in congressional testimony she referred to the culture at Enron as "arrogant."

[56]See Watkins (2003) for her analysis of moral responsibility in the Enron episode.

[57]Contributions in stock and restrictions on when the shares could be sold were common features of corporate retirement plans.

Enron filed for bankruptcy a number of executives withdrew funds from their deferred compensation plans, but others, including executives who had already retired, did not do so. As a result of the bankruptcy filing, those participating in the plan became unsecured creditors of the firm with their compensation to be determined by the bankruptcy court. Allegations were made that current executives were able to withdraw funds from their deferred compensation plans and were paid their bonuses in November prior to the bankruptcy filing, while others were not allowed to do so.

During Enron's slide in 2001 Kenneth Lay sold $100 million in Enron shares, including $70.1 million sold back to the company. Sales in public markets had to be disclosed in the month following the sale, whereas sales back to a company did not have to be disclosed until the following year.

Days before filing for bankruptcy, Enron paid $100 million in retention bonuses to 600 key employees deemed essential to the continued operation of the company. Enron also laid off 4,500 employees, giving them severance pay of $4,500.

Political Contributions

Enron and its executives made substantial political contributions to members of Congress and state legislatures. Since 1989 it had given $5.7 million to members of Congress, with $2.0 million contributed in the 2000 election cycle. Approximately two-thirds went to Republicans. Approximately half the House and two-thirds of the Senate had received contributions from Enron executives. Enron also contributed substantially to state officeholders and parties. The company also lobbied intensely for the deregulation of energy markets and had participated in Vice President Richard Cheney's energy task force. Enron had also implemented a plan to cultivate a relationship with Vice President Al Gore during his presidential campaign.[58]

The contributions provided access in both Washington and state capitols for Enron's lobbying campaign. When it was collapsing, Enron executives sought relief from the Bush administration. Although he and President George W. Bush were well acquainted, Kenneth Lay went to the Secretaries of Commerce and Treasury, neither of whom contacted the president.[59] Secretary of Commerce Donald Evans rejected Lay's request for assistance. Evans commented on *Meet the Press*, "If I had stepped in, I think it would have been an egregious abuse of the office of Secretary of Commerce." Lay also called Secretary of Treasury Paul O'Neill and enlisted Robert Rubin, former Secretary of Treasury in the Clinton administration and currently a top executive at Citigroup, to call the Secretary urging assistance for Enron.[60] Secretary O'Neill rejected Enron's request.

Enron also attempted to lobby for deregulation with the Federal Energy Regulatory Commission headed by Pat Wood III, who had previously headed the Texas Public Utility Commission. Wood, however, was unresponsive to Enron and angered the company by imposing caps on wholesale prices of electricity in the West.

The Board of Directors

The Board of Directors was responsible for the performance of the company and had a fiduciary duty to shareholders. As Enron increased its use of related-party transactions, the board increased the control over those transactions and ordered annual reviews of all LJM transactions. The Special Committee (p. 12) concluded, however, "These controls as designed were not rigorous enough, and their implementation and oversight was inadequate at both the management and board levels." In addition, Enron's outside counsel "Vinson & Elkins should have brought a stronger, more objective and more critical voice to the disclosure process" (p. 26). Referring to Enron management and Arthur Andersen, outside director Robert K. Jaedicke, chairman of the Board Audit Committee, said in congressional testimony, "It now appears that none of them fulfilled their duty to [the board]. We do not manage the company. We do not do the auditing. We are not detectives … I am not confident as I sit here today that we would have gotten to the truth with any amount of questioning and discussion."[61]

Throughout the rise and fall of Enron the board apparently did not block the questionable transactions and financial arrangements that led to the collapse. The board maintained that it was unaware of some of the deals and that data were withheld from it. For example, Chewco was approved by the board during a telephone conference call without disclosure of the "equity" loan by Barclays to Chewco's limited partner. Kopper's management of Chewco was approved by Skilling, but Enron's code of conduct required it to be brought to the board.

After the announcement of its third-quarter 2001 loss, Enron named William Powers, dean of the University of Texas School of Law, to its Board of Directors. The board then appointed a Special Committee headed by Powers to produce a report on the collapse. The Special Committee concluded that the board had failed in "its oversight duties."

The Special Committee assigned much of the responsibility to Kenneth Lay in his role as a director. The report stated, "Lay approved the arrangements under which Enron permitted Fastow to engage in related-party transactions with Enron and authorized the Rhythms transaction and three of the Raptor vehicles. He bears significant responsibility for those flawed decisions, as well as for Enron's failure to implement sufficiently rigorous procedural controls to prevent the abuses that flowed from this inherent conflict of interest.

---

[58]*New York Times*, February 18, 2002.
[59]Lay had been chair of then–Governor Bush's business council.
[60]In 1999 Enron invited Rubin to join its board of directors, but he declined the offer.

[61]Six board members including Jaedicke resigned in March 2002.

In connection with the LJM transactions, the evidence we have examined suggests that Lay functioned almost entirely as a director, and less as a member of management. It appears that both he and Skilling agreed, and the board understood, that Skilling was the senior member of management responsible for the LJM relationship." In the initial congressional hearings on the collapse, five Enron executives, Lay, Fastow, Kopper, chief accounting officer Richard Causey, and chief risk officer Richard Buy, exercised their constitutional right under the Fifth Amendment to protection against self-incrimination.[62] Jeffrey Skilling testified but had difficulty recalling what had happened.

Arthur Andersen

Enron's auditor was Arthur Andersen, one of the big five accounting firms. Andersen also provided consulting services to the company. In 2000 Enron paid a total of $52 million to Andersen with approximately half for audit services. Enron paid $5.7 million to Andersen for nonaudit services provided to Chewco and the LJM partnerships.

Andersen issued no qualifications in its audit reports and apparently approved all transactions brought to it. Andersen claimed to be ignorant of most of the questionable partnership arrangements, however. Andersen indicated that it was not given access to data on Chewco, and if it had been it would have required a restatement of earnings.

Andersen CEO Joseph Berardino subsequently testified before Congress that it had questioned $51 million in earnings in 1997 and considered requiring adjustments in reported earnings. Andersen, however, decided that the adjustments were not "material" and did not require them. Berardino stated that the adjustments were "less than 8 percent" of normalized earnings. In November when Enron corrected its financial statements back to 1997, the $51 million adjustment was made. Berardino also stated that the Chewco/JEDI arrangements involved "possible illegal acts."

In October after the announcement of Enron's third-quarter loss and the write-down in its shareholders equity, Andersen's Houston office, which had the principal responsibility for the audits, began shredding documents associated with its audits.[63] The managing director said that he had consulted with a lawyer in Andersen's headquarters and had been advised to shred the documents. After the telephone conversation the lawyer had sent an e-mail reminding the Houston office that Andersen policy required the retention of certain audit documents and allowed the shredding of other documents. The managing director was subsequently fired. ■

SOURCE: This case was prepared by Professor David P. Baron from public sources including the Report of Investigation by the Special Investigative Committee of the Board of Directors of Enron Corp., February 1, 2002 [Special Report]. Copyright © 2002 by David P. Baron. All rights reserved. Reprinted with permission. This case was written in February 2002 when facts were still being revealed.

Preparation Questions

1. What factors led to the collapse of Enron?
2. Should Enron have used partnerships in the manner it did? What, if anything, is wrong with using partnerships such as the Raptors, Chewco, and the LJMs?
3. What responsibilities does the board of directors have in such situations? What responsibilities did and should Enron and its directors have for its employees' 401(k) plans?
4. Why did Arthur Andersen and Vinson & Elkins not conclude that there were problems with Enron's structuring of transactions?
5. Is there an inherent conflict of interest for an outside auditor that also provides other services to its client?
6. What, if anything, was wrong with Enron's political contributions and lobbying? What assistance did the contributions buy Enron when it was collapsing?
7. How much of its financial arrangements should Enron have disclosed?
8. What responsibilities does an audit firm have?

---

[62]Causey and Buy were fired in February 2002.

[63]The managing director of the Houston office asked the staff to work overtime so that the shredding would not delay service to other clients.

Wal-Mart: Nonmarket Pressure and Reputation Risk (B): A New Nonmarket Strategy[64]

In 2004 Wal-Mart decided to reduce the nonmarket pressure it faced by establishing a "gentler" image with respect to its competition. It decided not to threaten its competitors

aggressively with low price promotions during the holiday period, as it had done the previous year with toys. Instead of lowering its prices, Wal-Mart raised its prices slightly. Its competitors responded by cutting their prices and taking business away from Wal-Mart. Wal-Mart was forced to cut its prices in response. Wal-Mart reversed its strategy in

---

[64]See the Part I integrative case, *Wal-Mart: Nonmarket Pressure and Reputation Risk (A)*.

2005, announcing it would match its rivals' price discounts and offering door-busters on Black Friday, the Friday after Thanksgiving. "I would rather be accused of driving people out of business than getting fired because we don't have any sales," said CEO H. Lee Scott.[65]

To deal with the nonmarket pressures it faced, Wal-Mart established a war room at its Bentonville headquarters and staffed it with people with political experience, since many of the criticisms of the company were orchestrated by former political operatives. The company also established an Action Alley in Bentonville and one in Washington, D.C. to deal with breaking issues. Wal-Mart hired advisors including Michael Deaver, former advisor to President Reagan, and Leslie Dach, a former media consultant to Bill Clinton.[66] The company also hired Edelman, a public relations firm that had worked with activist groups.

To deal with grassroots critics, Wal-Mart opened eight community relations offices in various locations, including Chicago, Los Angeles, and New York where local opposition had blocked new store openings.

Wal-Mart began to respond to its critics. Scott began meeting with a number of critics including the Investor Responsibility Research Center (IRRC) and environmental and anti-sweatshop groups. To address the sweatshop criticism, Wal-Mart worked with Business for Social Responsibility and met with IRRC leaders. In addition, Scott met with members of Congress and the Congressional Black Caucus.

On January 13, 2005, Wal-Mart took out full-page advertisements in 100 newspapers nationwide explaining its wage and benefit policies and employment practices. In the ad Scott wrote, "When special-interest groups and critics spread misinformation about Wal-Mart, the public deserves the truth. Everyone is entitled to their own opinions about our company, but they are not entitled to make up their own facts."[67] The ad stated that Wal-Mart's average wage was nearly twice the minimum wage and reported that more than half its employees viewed benefits as important to their employment decisions. The company also stated, "Seventy-four percent of Wal-Mart's hourly associates work full-time. That's well above the 20-40 percent typically found in the retail industry." More than half its associates owned Wal-Mart stock through a profit-sharing/401(k) plan.

Earlier Wal-Mart had test marketed an ad explaining the company's policies. The company reported an average hourly wage of $10.37 an hour and stated that medical coverage was available to both full- and part-time employees. The ad also explained, "Many of our jobs are held by working 'retirees,' working spouses supplementing a family income and students working through school." A unique feature of the ad was pointing out the benefits consumers received. The ad cited a study by the Los Angeles Economic Development Corporation that concluded, "with the entry of Wal-Mart into Southern California, area consumers will save $3.7 billion annually, or $589 per household per year, once Wal-Mart reaches 20 percent market share in the region."[68]

In April 2005, Wal-Mart held its first-ever media conference. In response to criticism by Wal-Mart Watch, Scott reported that an internal company audit revealed that 7 percent of workers were on government health benefits prior to being hired, but two years later only 3 percent were still on government assistance.[69] Referring to the large number of people who applied for jobs at new Wal-Mart stores, Scott said, "It doesn't make sense that people would line up for jobs that are worse than they could get elsewhere, with fewer benefits and less opportunity."[70] Scott urged Congress to raise the minimum wage, and critics noted that that would harm Wal-Mart's competitors more than Wal-Mart itself.

Wal-Mart also ran ads in Asian languages on Chinese, Vietnamese, and Filipino television stations. It also ran a series of television ads in which minority and women associates told of their satisfaction working for Wal-Mart. Earlier Wal-Mart had agreed to sponsor PBS and NPR programs and began a $500,000 fellowship program for minority journalism students at nine universities. The company also sponsored "The Scholar," a reality series in which students competed for a full-ride college scholarship worth $300,000. Wal-Mart was woven into the plots of the shows.[71]

Wal-Mart began to work with Conservation International and the Natural Resources Defense Council on environmental initiatives. The company evaluated the packaging of products it sold and discovered that reducing packaging also reduced shipping costs. Wal-Mart also opened an Environmental Demonstration Store and planned to open another. The store used solar panels, wind turbines, burned the used oil from oil changes, and burned fat used to fry chickens.[72] It also had a computerized heating and cooling system and used low-mercury fluorescent lamps and electronic ballasts.

In 2005 Wal-Mart announced a $35 million, 10-year Acres for America program to offset the nearly 140,000 acres that its current stores occupied plus its planned

[65]Michael Barbaro, "Back to Basics at Wal-Mart: Spare No Rivals," *New York Times,* November 23, 2005.
[66]Michael Barbaro, "A New Weapon for Wal-Mart: A War Room," *New York Times,* November 1, 2005.
[67]"Wal-Mart Launches Nationwide Campaign to Set the Record Straight," press release, Wal-Mart, January 13, 2005, http://walmartstores.com/GlobalWMStoresWeb/navigate.do?catg=26&contId=4901 (May 23, 2006).

[68]*San Jose Mercury News,* September 23, 2005.
[69]Ann Zimmeran, "Wal-Mart Stores Defends Its Image, Wages and Benefits," *Wall Street Journal,* April 6, 2005.
[70]Steven Greenhouse, "Wal-Mart's Chief Calls Its Critics Unrealistic," *New York Times,* April 6, 2005.
[71]Stuart Elliott, "Wal-Mart's New Realm: Reality TV," *New York Times,* June 3, 2005.
[72]"Lee Scott on Why Wal-Mart Is Playing Nicer," *BusinessWeek,* October 3, 2005.

expansion over the next 10 years. The company formed a partnership with the Fish and Wildlife Foundation for the purchase of the acreage. The land would be available for hunting, fishing, and other outdoor activities and for sustainable logging.

In October 2005 Wal-Mart announced a major environmental initiative focused on reducing energy use. The initiative included improving the efficiency of energy use in its supercenters and other stores. It also pledged to improve the fuel efficiency of its huge truck fleet by 25 percent over three years and by 100 percent over 10 years. The company announced that it would invest $500 million annually to reduce its emissions of greenhouse gasses by 20 percent over 7 years. Wal-Mart also pledged to use its power to encourage its suppliers to be more energy efficient and to reduce their packaging. The initiative drew praise from Environmental Defense and the Sierra Club. A spokesperson for WakeUpWalMart.com, however, said, "It is a diversionary tactic. Wal-Mart understands that they have a growing public relations disaster on their hands."[73]

In 2005 Wal-Mart established a $25 million private equity fund to support businesses owned by women and minorities that could supply the company—approximately 8.5 percent of Wal-Mart's U.S. suppliers were women or minority owned. Spokeswoman Linda Blakely reported that women and minority-owned suppliers sold $3 billion of goods to the company compared to $2 million in the mid-1990s.[74] Blakely denied that the establishment of the fund was in response to the class-action lawsuit on behalf of 1.6 million current and past women employees or the lawsuit filed by two black truck drivers who claimed they had been denied jobs because of their race.

In November 2005, Wal-Mart went further and held a conference in which economists presented analyses of its economic impact. Wal-Mart presented its own study conducted by Global Insight.[75] The study concluded that between 1985 and 2004 Wal-Mart had lowered the Consumer Price Index by 3.1 percent, representing an annual savings of $2,329 for an average household. Wages were depressed by 2.2 percent, which was less than the decrease in the CPI. Benefits were not taken into account, however. The study concluded that Wal-Mart did not pay less than market wages, was more capital intensive than its competitors, and had efficient distribution and inventory control systems. The study reported that on net Wal-Mart had created 210,000 jobs. The other studies presented mixed findings, with one finding a similar impact on wages as in the Global Insight study. One study showed that Wal-Mart's entry into the grocery business reduced prices by 5 percent more than supermarkets would have reduced their prices in the absence of competition by Wal-Mart.

Wal-Mart also announced expanded health care benefits including reduced co-payments for generic drugs and extended its $11 a month health care coverage to at least half its employees. It also planned to open 50 clinics in its U.S. stores that would provide treatment for both customers and employees.

Wal-Mart decided to review its employment practices pertaining to diversity. It formed Business Resources Groups composed of women, African-Americans, Latinos, Asian-Americans, American Indians, gays, and disabled employees that met at Wal-Mart headquarters to provide advice.[76] The groups also provided advice on marketing.

In December 2005, "Working Families for Wal-Mart" was formed to counter the company's critics. Its Web site, www.forwalmart.com, stated that the organization was "standing up for Wal-Mart and helping it keep doing great things for families and communities." The site stated the organization was "committed to fostering open and honest dialogue with elected officials, opinion makers and community leaders that conveys the positive contributions of Wal-Mart to working families." The steering committee for the organization included religious leaders, community leaders, a former woman marine, and Pat Boone. Working Families for Wal-Mart was partly funded by Wal-Mart as well as supported by Taylor Gross, media operations coordinator for the Republicans in the 2000 elections.[77]

Working Families for Wal-Mart commissioned a survey by RT Strategies, a bipartisan firm. The survey found that:

- 71 percent of Americans believe Wal-Mart is good for consumers while 63 percent of union households hold the same belief.
- 58 percent of Americans and 54 percent of union households believe union leaders should make protecting union jobs a higher priority than attacking Wal-Mart.
- 60 percent of Americans say the campaign against Wal-Mart is not a good use of dues and 44 percent of union households agree.
- 54 percent of Americans and 42 percent of union households believe the campaign against Wal-Mart makes labor union leaders less relevant to solving the economic challenges facing working families today.

Critics of the survey noted that the "preface to some questions contrasted nonunion Wal-Mart's job growth with unionized General Motors' job losses."[78]

[73]Michael Barbaro and Felicity Barringer, "Wal-Mart to Seek Savings in Energy," *New York Times*, October 25, 2005.
[74]Michael Barbaro, "Wal-Mart to Start Equity Fund to Help Diversify Its Suppliers," *New York Times*, October 19, 2005.
[75]Global Insight was formed by the merger of DRI and Wharton Econometric Forecasting Associates.

[76]*San Jose Mercury News*, January 8, 2006.
[77]*Arkansas Democrat-Gazette*, December 22, 2005.
[78]Associated Press State & Local Wire, January 4, 2006.

To reduce opposition to its store openings in urban areas, Wal-Mart announced a policy to reduce the impact on small businesses. Scott said, "We see we can be better for communities than we have been in the past if we are willing to stretch ourselves and our resources."[79] Wal-Mart established jobs and opportunities zones in 50 cities in which it hoped to open stores and vowed to locate in areas that traditionally had been shunned by other retailers. Wal-Mart planned to help local businesses directly by placing advertisements for them in newspapers and on its in-store radio network. It also planned to provide coaching for local retailers and financial support for local chambers of commerce.

To reduce opposition from local banks to its industrial bank application in Utah, Wal-Mart pledged not to open any branch banks. The application was opposed by the Independent Community Bankers of America, the North Dakota Bankers Association, the American Bankers Association, and individual banks. Wal-Mart received support from the Salvation Army and the National Center for Missing and Exploited Children, both of which had traditionally been supported by the company.

Wal-Mart had refused to sell the Plan B contraceptive, also known as RU-486 or the morning-after pill, in its 3,700 pharmacies. When the state of Massachusetts ordered Wal-Mart to sell the pills, the company announced that it would do so in all states with the same requirement. Wal-Mart also announced a so-called conscientious objector policy in which a pharmacist could direct a customer to another pharmacist or pharmacy.

Wal-Mart announced a new position of senior director of stakeholder engagement and sought "an innovative, out-of-the box thinker" to "help pioneer a new model of how Wal-Mart works with outside stakeholders, resulting in fundamental changes in how the company does business."[80] Wal-Mart also announced a search for a person to conduct "opposition research" and oversee its "crisis communications program" and another for a person to "mobilize resources" during a "crisis situation."[81] ■

Preparation Questions

1. Evaluate the steps Wal-Mart has taken in developing a nonmarket strategy in response to the social pressure it faces.

2. What is Wal-Mart's motivation for its nonmarket strategy?

3. What else should Wal-Mart do, if anything?

---

[79]Michael Barbaro, "Wal-Mart Offers Aid to Rivals," *New York Times,* April 5, 2006.

[80]Aaron Bernstein, edited by Dan Beucke, "A Social Strategist for Wal-Mart," *BusinessWeek,* February 6, 2006.
[81]Michael Barbaro, "Wal-Mart Begins Quest for Generals in P.R. War," *New York Times,* March 30, 2006.

Playing by the Rules?

In the early 1990s the Federal Communications Commission (FCC) announced that it would begin auctioning licenses to use the radio spectrum. In 1993 Congress enacted a law to encourage the formation and success of businesses owned by minorities and women as well as small businesses and rural enterprises. The law provided set-asides for qualifying companies, preferences in bidding for federal contracts, and low-cost financing. In 1995 the Supreme Court ruled that the set-asides and preferences for minorities and women were discriminatory and imposed a stricter standard for conditions under which preferential treatment could be provided in federal contracting.[82] In response to the decision, the FCC dropped its preferences for women and minorities but not the preferences for small businesses and rural enterprises.

Qualifying small businesses and rural enterprises, referred to as designated entities, could receive preferential treatment of a variety of forms. Bid discounts of up to 45 percent could be provided to a designated entity. For example, Beta Communications, a designated entity, won three cellular telephone licenses in an FCC auction in 1999 with total bids of $17.2 million, but because of bid discounts provided under FCC rules, Beta paid only $12.9 million. Beta never provided cellular service, and a year later sold the licenses for $98 million. Beta was 50.1 percent owned by Alfred Angelo, an accountant in New Jersey, who invested $200,000 in the company formed for the purpose of bidding on the licenses.[83]

Victoria Kane, an aerobics instructor, formed Aer Force Communications, and her husband, Theodore Kane, a money manager in Rye, New York, invested in

---

[82]*Adarand Constructors v. Peña,* 515 U.S. 200 (1995).

[83]*Wall Street Journal,* December 27, 2005.

the company. Ms. Kane certified to the FCC that she was "acting alone, to manage the business and affairs" of Aer Force, which won five licenses for $18.9 million. The company received a 25 percent bid discount and low cost financing through the FCC. Aer Force subsequently sold the licenses in a deal worth $144 million.[84]

These two companies had one thing in common. Both were backed, usually with 49.9 percent ownership, by companies, including Lynch Interactive Corporation, and other entities controlled by Mario Gabelli, a money manager in Rye. Gabelli was chairman and CEO of Gamco Investors Inc. and managed $27 billion in assets. In 2005 his compensation at Gamco was $55 million, compared to $38 million in 2004. In addition to investing in the companies, Gabelli's companies loaned funds to the majority owners such as Angelo and Kane.

In addition to Beta Communications and Aer Force Communications, Gabelli backed firms with principals including "Trent Tucker, a Gabelli client and former New York Knicks basketball player with a graceful outside shot; . . . Nara Cadorin, an 82 year-old retired administrative assistant for a Gabelli associate; and Kathy Stafford of Moose, Wyoming, a property manager at one of his vacation homes."[85] Angelo had referred clients to Gabelli. Tucker stated that he had thought he was a passive owner, and Cadorin did not know whether the company of which she was president had a budget or employees. Gabelli-backed companies won 96 licenses in 8 auctions.[86] The head of another of the Gabelli-backed companies, Fortunet Wireless Communications L.P., did not know what a spectrum was nor what one did with it nor what FCC stood for.[87] Two of the principals of High Country Communications L.P. put no equity into the firm but instead borrowed from an associate of Gabelli.[88]

In addition to minority ownership and loans to the majority owners, some of the firms formed with Gabelli's backing may have had other contractual provisions with Gabelli enterprises. In the sale of its licenses Beta Communications paid to Gabelli enterprises "a $4 million commitment fee, a $10 million "special" fee, a second $2.75 million "special" fee and a $6 million finder's fee, in addition to a $14 million "investment banking services" fee. . . ."[89]

Lynch Interactive stated that it had "followed the spirit and letter of the law" and had relied on "highly qualified external counsel" in its 10 partnerships with small businesses that bid on FCC licenses. James Barker, an attorney who had helped establish the partnerships, had written a memo for his files in which he said he "had

warned Gabelli executives that Mr. Gabelli was 'seriously considering backing a [small business] venture' with Ms. Kane, who had 'business experience only as an aerobic dance instructor.'. . . While Ms. Kane's participation was 'not impermissible, the perceived lack of business experience might raise eyebrows and invite further investigation'. . . . [A]n executive of Lynch, the firm Mr. Gabelli leads, 'relayed similar concerns to Gabelli, but Gabelli was inclined to move forward anyway.'"[90]

In 2001 Russell Taylor, who had been a legal aide in a law firm, filed a civil fraud lawsuit against Gabelli under the False Claims Act, enacted after the Civil War to help the government recover monies from individuals who had defrauded the government. Taylor stood to gain 15 to 25 percent of any funds collected by the government. The lawsuit alleged that Gabelli had received $90 million in bid discounts and $70 million in financial benefits from low-cost federal financing. The False Claims Act allowed for treble damages, which could be as high as $480 million. Moreover, $206 million of profits from selling the licenses was potentially subject to recovery by the government.

In 2002 when the lawsuit was revealed, Gabelli "called the suit 'a form of legal extortion' seeking 'to extract money by assaulting the character and competence of minority and female entrepreneurs and small business people who did nothing wrong, and who were only seeking to participate in a process that the U.S. government was encouraging them to enter." Gabelli also said, "like Dracula, we believe this lawsuit can't survive the light of day."[91]

In the trial of the Taylor lawsuit Federal District Court judge Paul Crotty ruled that only the government could recover the $206 million profits. This caused the Department of Justice to enter the case in March 2006 on the side of the plaintiff to ensure that if Gabelli lost the lawsuit, some portion of the profits could be recovered. The Department of Justice stated, "the facts that go to the heart of the case are uniquely in the possession of the defendants themselves: namely, whether the designated entities that bid for the licenses were sham corporations created to hide from the FCC the control and financial involvement of Gabelli and the Lynch entities so that they could obtain licenses and use them as speculative investment vehicles to benefit themselves."[92]

A spokesperson for Lynch stated that all the information on the financing of the companies had been disclosed to the FCC and that having additional bidders had resulted in higher bids and greater revenue for the government. Lynch announced that it intended to bid in the upcoming August 2006 advanced wireless services auction of 1,122 licenses that was expected to generate $5-15 billion in revenue for the government. The FCC

[84]*Wall Street Journal*, December 27, 2005.
[85]*Wall Street Journal*, December 27, 2005.
[86]*Wall Street Journal*, December 27, 2005.
[87]RCR Wireless News, March 27, 2006.
[88]RCR Wireless News, March 27, 2006.
[89]*Wall Street Journal*, December 27, 2005.

[90]*Wall Street Journal*, December 27, 2005.
[91]*Wall Street Journal*, December 27, 2005.
[92]RCR Wireless News, March 27, 2006.

announced it would tighten its rules for small business discounts, financing, and the resale of licenses to avoid potential fraud.

In June "a proxy advisory group representing some of Gamco's big investors protested Gabelli's lofty pay."[93] In May Gabelli had reached a settlement with two initial investors in Gabelli Group Capital Partners that controls Gamco Investors. The investors claimed that they were prevented from selling their stakes at a fair market value. The settlement was valued at approximately $100 million.[94]

In July 2006 the Department of Justice and Mario Gabelli settled the civil fraud lawsuit with Gabelli paying to the government $130 million, with Taylor receiving $32.2 million of that amount. Gabelli also agreed to pay $8.7 million to the law firms representing Taylor.

Gabelli denied any wrongdoing and was not barred from future FCC auctions. FCC commissioner Jonathan Adelstein said, "Barring Mr. Gabelli from an upcoming auction would have been the best way to show we're serious about protecting the integrity of the program. We don't want this settlement to simply be a cost of doing business."[95]

Gabelli had earlier commented, "Look, lawsuits come and go. What I care about is making money for my investors."[96] ■

SOURCE: This case was prepared from public sources by David P. Baron. Copyright © 2006 by David P. Baron. All rights reserved. Reprinted with permission.

Preparation Questions

1. What, if anything, was wrong with forming firms to take advantage of the FCC rules as long as the letter of the rules was satisfied?
2. Profits of the Gabelli-backed small businesses were said to be $206 million, yet Gabelli settled the lawsuit for only $130 million. Does this prove that Gabelli's strategy was a good one? Was the settlement simply a cost of doing business?
3. Do you agree with Gabelli's comment at the end of the case?
4. Did Gabelli act responsibly?

---

[93] *Fortune,* June 26, 2006.
[94] *New York Times,* June 7, 2006.
[95] *Wall Street Journal,* July 14, 2006.
[96] *Fortune,* June 26, 2006.

Ethics Systems: Utilitarianism

INTRODUCTION

The content of corporate social responsibility is provided by ethics. This and the following chapter address the role of ethics in management and provide an introduction to three principal ethics systems. The objective is to increase moral sensitivity and provide frameworks for reasoning about issues based on ethics principles and moral standards. No single ethics framework encompasses all the moral intuitions of people, so it is important to consider issues from the perspectives of several systems. The ethics systems considered are utilitarianism, rights, and justice.[1] These systems correspond to basic ethical intuitions about the good and the right and are important guides to firms and managers in the evaluation of alternative courses of action.

Ethics and its application in management constitute a broad and deep subject. The approach taken here is to address the subject in a series of steps. This and the following chapter introduce the three ethics systems and evaluate nonmarket issues with moral concerns based on those systems. Chapters 22 and 23 focus on the implementation of these systems in domestic and international contexts, respectively. The chapter cases provide opportunities to reason from the perspectives of ethics systems and apply ethics principles and methods to managerial problems.

This chapter focuses on the nature of ethics in managerial contexts and on utilitarianism, a consequentialist ethics system that evaluates actions in terms of the well-being they yield. The next two sections consider the role of ethics in management and the distinction between ethics and other forms of managerial decision-making. The following sections address the relationship between ethics and self-interest, politics, and casuistry. The methodology of ethics and the relationship between ethics and moral and political philosophy are then considered. Utilitarianism, the principal consequentialist ethics system, is then introduced, including the distinction between act and rule utilitarianism. A framework for applying utilitarianism in competitive situations is presented, and the difficulties in its application are considered. Examples of utilitarian reasoning are presented, and those examples are then reconsidered in Chapter 21 from the perspectives of rights and justice.

THE MANAGERIAL ROLE OF ETHICS

Ethics has several managerial roles. As a normative approach, ethics provides principles for evaluating alternatives and formulating policies to take into account the interests, rights, and liberties of those affected by those policies. In the context of the framework for nonmarket analysis presented in Chapter 2 and Figure 2-5, ethics in its normative role is used in both the screening and choice stages. In the screening stage, ethics

---

[1]Confucianism is considered in Chapter 16.

provides the underpinnings for policies that guide managers in determining which alternatives should be screened out and which should be considered further. In the choice stage, ethics provides a basis for evaluating whether claims have moral standing and thus whether they are to be respected in the firm's decision making. Ethics also provides a basis both for assessing whether moral consensus is present and for justifying a firm's actions to stakeholders, government, and the public.

Ethics is also an important foundation for the positive analysis of nonmarket issues. Individuals, activists, interest groups, and government officeholders can be motivated by moral concerns about a firm's conduct. In the analysis stage of the framework in Figure 2-5, ethics contributes to the prediction of morally motivated nonmarket action. Managers must be sensitive to how the moral determinants of nonmarket action can affect the firm and shape its nonmarket environment. Because individuals have a range of ethical intuitions, it is important to view issues from the perspectives of several ethics systems. In its normative and positive roles, ethics thus provides a basis for analysis, decision making, and the formulation of strategies for addressing nonmarket issues and the nonmarket actions associated with them.

WHAT ETHICS IS AND IS NOT

Ethics is a systematic approach to moral judgments based on reason, analysis, synthesis, and reflection. Ethics addresses matters of importance to human well-being, autonomy, and liberty. Ethics is based on moral standards that are independent of the declarations of governments or other authoritative bodies. Moral standards are impartial, take precedence over self-interest, and are to apply to everyone; that is, they are to be universal.[2] Ethics thus is the discipline concerned with judgments based on moral standards and the reasoning therefrom.

Moral philosophers have proposed an array of ethics systems without arriving at consensus on a single system. On some issues, a decision alternative may be consistent with one ethics system and inconsistent with others. Random drug testing of employees may reduce social costs, and hence satisfy a utilitarian standard, yet it may violate an individual's right to privacy. Similarly, an absolute right to privacy could be unjust if it prevented drug testing of employees whose responsibilities include public safety.

The issues considered in this and subsequent chapters involve significant moral concerns not easily resolved through approaches that are independent of moral standards. The focus thus is not on simple temptation. There are many managerial situations in which an action is contrary to the law, a well-established company policy, or widely shared ethics principles, yet managers may be tempted to take the action because they, or the firm, may benefit from it. Since what is good or right is clearly evident in these situations, they have only limited interest from the perspective of ethics. Addressing the issue of temptation remains important, however. One responsibility of management is to develop procedures to reduce the temptation that often arises, for example, from how performance is compensated. Approaches to reducing temptation and guiding managers through situations in which temptation may arise are considered in Chapters 22 and 23. The Chapter 10 case, *Enron Power Marketing and the California Market,* considers a company that succumbs to the temptation to manipulate a market for electricity, and the chapter case, *Tax Shelters,* involves temptation.

The focus of ethics is not on issues involving direct mutual advantage. Such issues generally do not require ethics analysis. Every sale a firm makes benefits the firm and its customer. In the absence of external consequences, the transaction is generally free from moral objection. Mutual advantage may also control temptation. A consulting or investment services firm often has an opportunity to serve its own rather than its clients' interests. To attract future clients, however, the firm must maintain a reputation for effectively serving client interests. Honoring expectations in such cases can be explained by self-interest independently of moral standards. Serving client interests,

---

[2]Moral claims are distinguished from prudential claims, which are based on considerations of self-interest.

however, is not sufficient. Firms must assess whether client interests are consistent with ethics principles and the law, as illustrated by the chapter case, *Tax Shelters*.

PERSONAL AND BUSINESS ETHICS

Business ethics is the application of ethics principles to issues that arise in business. There is no separate discipline of business ethics. As opposed to personal ethics, where an individual is the principal in the sense of Chapter 19, business ethics pertains to situations in which individuals are in an organizational position and act as agents of the company and its owners.

Business ethics also differs from personal ethics because a manager has accepted the responsibilities associated with the position occupied. The set of issues faced also differs from those one encounters in one's personal life. In an organizational setting an individual may have duties, such as preventing sexual harassment by others or meeting fiduciary responsibilities, that may not be encountered in one's personal life. Moreover, in one's personal life an individual may focus on the virtuous life in an Aristotelian sense or a life of propriety in a Confucian sense. In an organization role, however, a manager must reason about situations in which virtue is not always present, conceptions of what is good or right differ among individuals, and interests are in conflict. Consequently, the focus here is on ethics systems as applied to moral issues that arise in an organizational context.

ETHICS AND PRIVATE INTERESTS

Ethical behavior enables society to realize the benefits from social interactions and allows individuals to rely on the word and conduct of others. Ethical behavior does not always make an individual or a firm better off, however. A policy of refusing to pay bribes to government officials can result in costly delays or the loss of sales in some countries. Furthermore, ethical behavior may not be self-evident to others and, even if it is, it may not be rewarded. Ethical behavior thus can conflict with profit objectives or with an individual's self-interest. That is, ethics principles prescribe behavior based on considerations that take precedence over self-interest. This is perhaps clearest in a utilitarian framework in which a person's own interests are given no greater consideration than the interests of any other person. Good ethics is thus not necessarily beneficial to an individual or profitable for a firm; however, good ethics is good for society and is a requirement of good management.

Although good ethics may not always be profitable, unethical behavior can result in substantial losses, as evidenced by the series of business scandals and violations of the law discussed in Chapter 19. Unethical actions by a firm can worsen the environment for all firms by causing the public to become suspicious of business and its motives. In the long run, harmony between business and society requires conduct consistent with the principles embodied in the social contract under which business operates. Business and its management thus are evaluated not only in terms of financial performance but also in terms of moral performance. The chapter case, *Pfizer and Celebrex*, and the Chapter 5 case, *Merck and Vioxx*, raise these issues.

ETHICS, POLITICS, AND CHANGE

Ethics involves an inquiry into whether a proposition has moral status. Propositions may be classified as claimed or granted. A granted proposition is one that has been established either by ethical consensus or by an authoritative body such as government. Claims often are made that a proposition has moral status. Frequently, these claims are intended to increase the likelihood that the proposition will be granted by government. For example, in some areas delivery services are plagued by robberies and threats to the safety of delivery personnel. As a result of reports from drivers concerned about their safety, a Federal Express district manager suspended after-dark pickups in Gary, Indiana. Similarly, a Domino's Pizza franchisee refused to

FIGURE 20-1 Ethics, Politics, and Change

deliver in certain high-risk areas in Miami. Consider the proposition that delivery services may not refuse to serve parts of their normal service area, even if the motive is to avoid possible harm to delivery personnel. One use of ethics is to determine whether such a proposition results in an injustice or a violation of rights. The use of ethics to establish the moral status of a proposition is illustrated by the horizontal arrows in Figure 20-1, which classifies propositions as claimed and granted and according to their moral status.[3]

Politics pertains to the vertical status of propositions in Figure 20-1. Most politics centers on private interests and is advanced in the absence of arguments about moral status, as illustrated by the three arrows in the left column of the figure. Some politics focuses on propositions with established moral status, as indicated by the arrow in the right column. The policies restricting deliveries were prohibited by the mayor of Gary and by a court order in Miami. San Francisco passed an ordinance making it illegal to refuse to deliver in parts of the regular service area of a restaurant.

Change can come from both ethics and politics. The Chapter 11 case, *Environmental Justice and Pollution Credits Trading Systems,* focuses on the ethics and politics of the proposition that less-advantaged persons, including minorities and women, are adversely affected by certain environmental protection policies, in this case a cap-and-trade system.

CASUISTRY

Ethics is principled reasoning and is distinguished from casuistry, which is an approach to moral practice that seeks to balance competing considerations by making exceptions to ethics principles in particular cases. Casuistry is an ancient approach that reemerged during the Reformation in the 16th century as the argument that different principles were applicable to different situations and in different roles. For example, a ruler might violate principles in an attempt to benefit his subjects. Casuistry was attacked by Pascal, who argued that although they may have been well intentioned, casuist methods were flawed and the results therefore questionable. Casuistry has been characterized as a false art of making exceptions in particular situations, resulting in the violation of underlying principles.[4] This approach is contrary to the ethics systems considered here, which are intended to apply universally. Thus, the familiar saying that "a diplomat is a person who lies abroad for the benefit of his country" may characterize politics but not ethics.

The following example illustrates casuist reasoning.

The casuist approach is dangerous precisely because it shortcuts the application of principles in favor of conceptions of responsibility that may be inconsistent with moral standards. Furthermore, those conceptions can be a disguise for the

---

[3]This figure was prepared by Keith Krehbiel.
[4]See Jonsen and Toulmin (1988) for a history of casuistry and for its defense as practical ethics.

EXAMPLE

Saving the Division

Leyden Corporation was a small manufacturer of household appliances, including blenders, food processors, mixers, and coffee makers. Competition had intensified in all its lines of business, particularly as companies in China had entered its markets. In 2006 Leyden incurred a loss of $6.4 million, and the first half of 2007 was worse. Leyden saw little opportunity to turn the situation around.

The most serious problem was with its line of blenders, which because of low-priced imports had experienced decreasing sales and was losing nearly $12 million a year. The blender division had done all it could to reduce costs, including freezing wage rates for the past year. If the profitability of the division could not be improved, Leyden's only alternative would be to close its plant. The general manager of the blender division formulated a plan that he believed would save the plant for a few years to buy time in the hope that something favorable, such as a change in exchange rates, might occur.

The general manager's plan involved cutting the quality of the blenders but marketing them as if they were the previous models. The plan was to use a lower-quality motor and cheaper internal materials, which together would reduce costs by nearly 14 percent. This would enable the plant to remain open, as long as volume could be maintained. Although the blenders would not be as durable, a consumer would have no way of knowing that at the time of purchase. To conceal the lower quality, the general manager proposed keeping the same model numbers, charging the same price, advertising and marketing the blenders as before, and making certain that the new blenders had the same external appearance as the current ones. The general manager was confident that neither retailers nor customers would soon detect the changes.

The general manager reasoned that the plan would benefit employees and shareholders, and Leyden could be said to have a social responsibility to both groups of stakeholders. Consumers would be worse off compared to their expectations, but employees were a more immediate constituency, and consumers would still be getting a serviceable blender. From the point of view of responsibility to stakeholders, the general manager decided to implement the plan.

The general manager's reasoning is an example of casuistry. That is, the reasoning proceeds from a concept of responsibility to the specifics of a case without reliance on principles. From a utilitarianism perspective, selling a lower-quality product as if it were a higher-quality product reduces aggregate well-being because some customers would be better off buying other blenders if they knew of the change. The plan also involves deception, which is difficult to support in any ethics system. Furthermore, it treats consumers as a means of saving the division. From a rights perspective, the company is not respecting their autonomy.

---

self-interest of the decision maker. Several factors indicate when casuistry is being practiced. It is often present in situations in which the action the manager wants to take is identified by self-interest, the firm's interest, or constituents' interests. Casuistry may be present when managers find themselves searching for a justification for the actions they wish to take based on self-interest. Casuistry may be present when a manager tries to rationalize around principles with the justification that constituents benefit. The chapter case, *Pfizer and Celebrex,* and the Chapter 21 case, *Consumer Awareness or Disease Mongering? GlaxoSmithKline and the Restless Legs Syndrome*, provide opportunities to assess the attraction of casuistry.

THE METHODOLOGY OF ETHICS

The methodology of ethics is illustrated in the left panel of Figure 20-2. It involves the identification of decision alternatives, evaluation of those alternatives in terms of ethics principles and moral standards, and choice based on those evaluations. Ethics analysis is to be applied early rather than late in the process. As illustrated in the right panel of Figure 20-2, ethics that serves only to explain decisions made on other bases is inappropriate. It encourages managers to choose actions that serve their and their firms' interests and then to search among the various ethics systems to find one that comes closest to justifying the already-chosen action. This does not mean that when

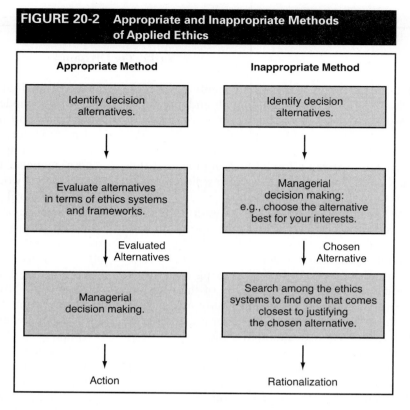

FIGURE 20-2 Appropriate and Inappropriate Methods of Applied Ethics

Appropriate Method	Inappropriate Method
Identify decision alternatives.	Identify decision alternatives.
↓	↓
Evaluate alternatives in terms of ethics systems and frameworks.	Managerial decision making: e.g., choose the alternative best for your interests.
↓ Evaluated Alternatives	↓ Chosen Alternative
Managerial decision making.	Search among the ethics systems to find one that comes closest to justifying the chosen alternative.
↓	↓
Action	Rationalization

correctly applied, ethics cannot be used to justify the action taken. That justification, however, should be consistent with the basis for the decision.

Figure 20-3 provides more detail on the methodology of ethics. The methodology begins with the identification of the facts about the issue, since if the facts are incorrectly understood, even a correct analysis can result in an inappropriate decision. Along with the facts, the moral concerns associated with the issue must be identified. They may involve concerns about well-being, rights and liberties, and fairness for those involved. Management also must identify alternatives for addressing the issue, and creativity should be used in generating alternatives.

FIGURE 20-3 Process of Ethics Analysis

Utilitarianism
Moral Rights
Justice

Ethics Principles and Moral Standards

Methods of Ethics Reasoning and Evaluation

Based on Principles
Logical
Systematic
Consistent
Reflective

Moral Concerns

Facts of the Issue

Analysis of Alternatives → Evaluations and Judgments → Decision Making, Implementation and Prediction

Experience and Reflection

Generating Alternatives

Once the facts have been discerned, moral concerns identified, and alternatives generated, ethics principles and moral standards are used to analyze the alternatives. Analysis involves reasoning that is logical, systematic, consistent, and reflective. The results of the analysis are judgments about whether the alternatives are consistent with ethics principles and moral standards. When ethics is directed at decision making, the final stage involves choice and implementation. When ethics is used for positive purposes, the final stage involves predicting whether objections to a decision are likely and whether nonmarket action can be expected. Finally, experience and reflection provide lessons for refining the methods of analysis and evaluation.

THE RELATIONSHIPS AMONG MORAL PHILOSOPHY, ETHICS, AND POLITICAL PHILOSOPHY

Figure 20-4 illustrates the relationship between moral philosophy and ethics. Moral philosophy is concerned with deducing moral principles and standards from axioms or self-evident principles. The self-evident principle that what matters is human well-being is the basis for utilitarianism. From that principle, the standard of maximizing aggregate well-being is deduced. The action that maximizes aggregate well-being then has moral standing because it yields the greatest good in terms of well-being. As considered in Chapter 21, Kant's categorical imperative provides a basis for deducing maxims to guide behavior, which in turn provide a basis for identifying individual rights. Choosing a social contract from an impartial position provides the basis for principles of justice as considered in Chapter 21.

As indicated in Figure 20-4, ethics is concerned with analysis and reasoning based on principles and standards. That reasoning may be directed at the design of society's institutions, such as the public education and justice systems, the identification of rights, and provisions for social justice. Analysis and reasoning may also be directed at determining which actions provide the greatest aggregate well-being or whether a right, such as a right to privacy, takes precedence over other considerations.

Political philosophy is related to ethics and moral philosophy but focuses on institutions to govern the interactions among individuals. Political philosophy naturally focuses on conceptions of the state, how the state should grant and limit liberties and ensure justice, and the extent to which markets or other institutions are used to organize economic activity.

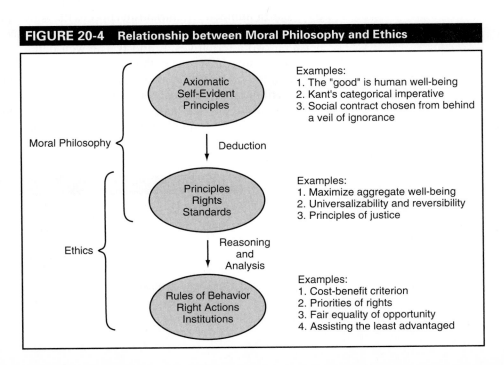

FIGURE 20-4   Relationship between Moral Philosophy and Ethics

Moral Philosophy

Axiomatic Self-Evident Principles

Examples:
1. The "good" is human well-being
2. Kant's categorical imperative
3. Social contract chosen from behind a veil of ignorance

↓ Deduction

Principles Rights Standards

Examples:
1. Maximize aggregate well-being
2. Universalizability and reversibility
3. Principles of justice

Ethics

↓ Reasoning and Analysis

Rules of Behavior Right Actions Institutions

Examples:
1. Cost-benefit criterion
2. Priorities of rights
3. Fair equality of opportunity
4. Assisting the least advantaged

Moral and political philosophies come together when they provide principles to govern the interactions among individuals. Utilitarianism provides a basis for a political philosophy in which the choice between private institutions, such as markets, and public institutions, such as government, is made according to which maximizes aggregate well-being.

UTILITARIANISM: A CONSEQUENTIALIST SYSTEM

Utilitarianism has a rich history with its origins in the work of Jeremy Bentham (1789), who argued for a calculus of pain and pleasure, and then of John Stuart Mill (1861). The moral standing of utilitarianism, however, is better understood in more recent expressions to which the criticisms applied to hedonism are less applicable. Utilitarianism is better understood as a particular form of a consequentialist moral philosophy.

In a consequentialist system, an action is moral if it produces better consequences than any other alternative. Utilitarianism is a consequentialist system with two particular features. First, consequences are to be evaluated in terms of the preferences of individuals, and second, those preferences are to be aggregated. Aggregation is required because an action may make some individuals better off and others worse off. The standard of human well-being and the need to consider the consequences for all persons correspond to fundamental ethical intuitions.

As an example, because of the oil crisis of 1973 the United States adopted a national speed limit of 55 miles per hour. As oil prices dropped and Americans increased their driving, the pressure for higher speed limits mounted. In 1995 Congress abolished the federal speed limit, and by 1998 all but one state had increased their speed limits. Many increased their speed limit to 70 or 75 on rural stretches of interstate highways. Data subsequently indicated that the higher speed limits increased fatalities and injuries. The higher speed limits also saved motorists and their passengers many hours of travel time. The overwhelming revealed preference among the states for higher speed limits suggests that the benefits from the time saved outweighed the safety costs. As one motorist said referring to the greater risks, "I'll take that trade-off."

Utilitarianism does not focus on the numbers of people who are better or worse off because of an action, nor is it equivalent to a vote among alternatives. If an action makes 100 people worse off by one unit each and makes one person better off by 101 units, the action should be taken. Utilitarianism also is not "the greatest good for the greatest number." That statement is ambiguous because, as the example indicates, one alternative could produce the greatest good yet another alternative could produce benefits for the greatest number. Utilitarianism chooses the action that yields the greatest good.

Table 20-1 illustrates the basic utilitarian approach. A decision maker is to choose between two alternatives, A and B. The well-being for each of the four members of society, measured in terms of their preferences or utilities for the consequences, is presented in the body of the table. The aggregate well-being is the sum of those utilities; that is, utilitarianism aggregates the utilities of the individuals. Alternative A yields an aggregate utility of 11, whereas action B yields a greater aggregate utility of 14. Utilitarianism identifies action B as the moral action, since it yields the greater good.

	Utility from Alternative	
Individual	*A*	*B*
1	3	3
2	3	5
3 (the decision maker)	3	2
4	2	4
aggregate utility	11	14

TABLE 20-1   Utilitarianism Example

Pure transfers among individuals have no effect on the utilitarianism calculus. If one firm signs a supply contract with another firm to provide a product, both firms presumably are better off as a result of the transaction. From a utilitarian perspective the transaction is morally right provided there are no associated externalities. Moreover, as long as both parties agree to the contract, the price at which the product is exchanged is irrelevant. That is, if the value of the product to the buyer is 20 and the cost to the supplier is 15, the transaction results in a net benefit of 5 regardless of whether the price is 19 or 16. The price paid is a pure transfer between the buyer and the seller, and the transfer nets to zero in the utilitarian calculus. In Table 20-1 if alternative B provided utility of 4 to individual 3 and 3 to individual 2, the conclusion that B is the right choice would remain.

Utilitarianism and Self-Interest

Utilitarianism is nearly the antithesis of self-interest because one's own interests are to be given no more consideration than those of any other person. That is, decisions are to be impartial. The interests considered thus are not just those of the decision maker but those of everyone affected by the action. In the Leyden Corporation example marketing the blenders as proposed would likely make customers worse off by more than the gain to the company and employees. In Table 20-1 individual 3 is worse off with action B than with A, but as a utilitarian decision maker, individual 3 has a moral duty to choose B over A. Note also that as utilitarians each of the four individuals would choose alternative B. That is, with utilitarianism there is unanimity about the moral action. Utilitarianism is also universalizable in the sense that as moral persons each would be willing to have everyone act in accord with the principle of maximizing aggregate well-being.

In the chapter case, *Pfizer and Celebrex,* Pfizer could not rule out the possibility that Celebrex might increase the risk of cardiovascular events such as heart attacks. Recognizing this, the company had the choice between marketing Celebrex only for patients at risk of stomach bleeding from over-the-counter pain relievers or marketing Celebrex more broadly. The latter would yield billions of dollars more in profits, and the company could concurrently conduct additional clinical tests on a possible link between Celebrex and cardiovascular problems. Pfizer chose to market Celebrex broadly with heavy direct-to-consumer advertising. The case focuses on whether Pfizer should withdraw Celebrex from the market once concerns were raised about the safety of Cox-2 inhibitors.

Aligning Self-Interest with Societal Well-Being

Utilitarianism coincides with self-interest only when societal consequences are aligned with private consequences. One role of government is to establish institutions that provide this alignment. When alignment has been achieved, individuals can evaluate actions in terms of the consequences for themselves rather than having to take into account the consequences for all others affected by an action.

Many of society's institutions are based on aligning the interests of firms and individuals with the aggregate interests of society. The institutions of private property and markets provide one means of alignment, since a voluntary transaction, such as a supply contract between two firms, makes both the buyer and seller better off. In the case of environmental protection, cap-and-trade systems align the interests of polluters and society, as considered in Chapter 11. The law of torts considered in Chapter 12 is an institution that assigns the social costs of accidents to individuals and firms, providing incentives to minimize the social costs of accidents. The Living Benefits example presented later in the chapter considers a market that arose in response to a demand for flexibility in the use of life insurance benefits.

When markets are competitive and institutions are in place that align self-interest with societal well-being, the maximization of profit by a firm results in the greatest aggregate societal well-being; that is, the greatest difference between societal benefits and societal costs. This alignment of private interests and societal interests provides a justification for Milton Friedman's view that the social responsibility of business is to maximize profits, as considered in Chapter 19.

Utilitarianism, Distribution, and Altruism

Utilitarianism aggregates individuals' well-being as evaluated in terms of their preferences, and every person's utility is given equal weight. In the example in Table 20-1 the distribution of utility is more equal with alternative A than with alternative B, but since utilitarianism is concerned with aggregate well-being, it does not matter how that utility is distributed across individuals. Alternative B yields the greater aggregate utility and hence is the moral choice.

Although utilitarianism gives equal weight to the utilities of all persons, this does not mean that redistribution is irrelevant. The transfer of a dollar from a rich person to a poor person can increase aggregate well-being if the poor person is made better off by more than the rich person is made worse off; that is, if the gain in the utility of the poor person is greater than the loss in the utility of the rich person. Utilitarianism thus evaluates redistribution as it does any other alternative—in terms of the aggregate utility of all persons. In the example of one firm supplying a product to another firm, the "marginal utilities" of the two firms are the same, so the price paid for the product does not affect the utilitarian conclusion that the transaction increases aggregate well-being.

Utilitarianism also takes into account altruism. If some individuals have altruistic preferences for the well-being of others, the well-being of those others receives consideration in the utility function of the altruist. For example, if a rich person has altruistic preferences for the well-being of the poor, the rich person has greater utility for alternatives that benefit the poor than for alternatives that do not, other things equal. The rich person's preferences for the well-being of the poor cannot be hypothetical, however. Instead, the rich person must be willing to act on those preferences by redistributing some of her wealth or contributing time to improving the well-being of the poor.

In evaluating two alternative government programs designed to benefit the poor, the preferences on which the rich person is willing to act are what is counted. Thus, a person concerned for the well-being of the poor is not able to assign a hypothetical or an arbitrary weight to their well-being. Similarly, a person cannot ascribe one's own altruism to others, that is, cannot assume that others are also altruistic. A person, however, may attempt to persuade others also to be altruistic or may engage in nonmarket action to have the government establish programs to provide benefits to the poor. If the resulting taxes reduce economic efficiency, the cost of that inefficiency must be taken into account in evaluating the programs to benefit the poor. Cost-benefit analysis incorporates these considerations.

Summary of the Components of Utilitarianism

Utilitarianism is a moral philosophy that holds that

- Moral good is judged in terms of consequences.
- Consequences are evaluated in terms of human well-being.
- Human well-being is evaluated in terms of individuals' preferences.
- The rightness of an action is judged by the aggregate well-being, or good, it yields.
- The morally justified action maximizes aggregate well-being.

Moreover, utilitarianism is the antithesis of self-interest, and the two are equivalent only if private and societal well-being are aligned.

UTILITARIAN DUTY AND THE CALABRESI AND MELAMED PRINCIPLES

One of the most difficult aspects of applying utilitarianism, or any other ethics system, is determining who has the duty to take a moral action. For example, if aggregate utility would be increased by transferring a dollar to a poor person, from whom should that dollar come? The answer is that it should come from the person or persons with the smallest decrease in utility from giving up the dollar. If there are many people who could contribute, each could give up some portion of the dollar if that would result in a smaller decrease in their aggregate utility.

The Calabresi and Melamed principles introduced in Chapter 12 provide a framework for reasoning about the assignment of duty. The principles are intended to identify which party is in the best position to determine whether the benefits of an action outweigh its costs and which party is in the best position to either act or induce others to take actions that yield benefits that exceed the costs. The party identified by those principles then has the duty to act.

For example, the appropriate level of safety to incorporate into a product depends on the safety features the manufacturer could incorporate and on the care the user of the product could take. To determine if the manufacturer or the user has the duty to add safety features or take care, respectively, the Calabresi and Melamed principles provide the following tests:

1. Assign the duty to the party—the manufacturer or the user—that can best achieve improvements in the difference between aggregate benefits and costs.
2. If it is not clear which party that is, the duty should be assigned to the party that is in the best position to assess the aggregate benefits and costs and then act on that assessment.
3. If that is unclear (and hence a mistake in the assignment of duty could be made), assign the duty to the party that can at the lowest cost induce the other party to take actions to improve the difference between aggregate benefits and aggregate costs in the event of a misassignment.

In the case of product safety the duty is usually assigned to the manufacturer who is better positioned than a consumer to assess aggregate costs and benefits and to reduce accidents through the incorporation of safety features. Moreover, the manufacturer is usually better positioned to induce the consumer through instructions and warnings to take care when the cost of that care is lower than the cost of adding additional safety features. Furthermore, a manufacturer may have a duty to anticipate carelessness and, in some situations, misuse of a product by a consumer. This assignment of duty is warranted when the manufacturer is better positioned to avoid the harm from carelessness and misuse through product design, the addition of safety features, and warnings to consumers. This does not mean that all potential harm from the use of the product should be eliminated, as in the case of a chain saw, since costs must be taken into account.

In identifying the locus of duty in situations not involving government institutions, the Calabresi and Melamed principles can be simplified to answering the question, "Which party is best positioned to act or to induce others to act to yield benefits that exceed the costs?" For example, in the Chapter 21 case, *Citigroup and Subprime Lending,* Citigroup acquired the Associates, a large subprime lender that had been accused of predatory lending. Citigroup could continue to market subprime loans aggressively and rely on customers to determine whether they wanted to borrow or it could attempt to restrict its lending to customers who would actually benefit from the loans. The Calabresi and Melamed principles ask whether Citigroup or a borrower is better positioned to assess whether the loans were beneficial or predatory. In the Chapter 2 case, *Exclusive Resorts: Entrepreneurial Positioning and Nonmarket Defense,* customers were wealthy and in all likelihood had personal lawyers, tax advisors, and financial planners, so there was no need for the company to assess whether they would benefit from membership with a fee of $350,000 plus annual assessments. In the Citigroup case, however, many of the borrowers were poor or elderly and could easily succumb to aggressive marketing, which in many cases would leave them worse off with a loan. The Calabresi and Melamed principles indicate that Citigroup is better positioned than are such borrowers to assess whether a subprime loan would be beneficial. Hence, the duty is on Citigroup to ensure that its subprime lending makes borrowers better off rather than exploiting them.

ACT AND RULE UTILITARIANISM

Utilitarianism may be applied in two forms, *act utilitarianism* and *rule utilitarianism*. The classical distinction between these two forms is considered in this section, and the following section considers an alternative form applicable to settings in which consequences are jointly determined by more than one party.[5]

Act utilitarianism focuses on the consequences of a particular action in a particular situation and prescribes the action that yields the greatest aggregate well-being for everyone affected by that action. Rule utilitarianism focuses on a general rule of behavior to be followed by all individuals in all similar situations. A moral rule is then the one that does best in terms of its consequences for everyone affected in those similar situations. An action is then moral if it is consistent with the moral rule appropriate for that type of situation. As an example of a rule, in the Chapter 18 case, *Compulsory Licensing, Thailand, and Abbott Laboratories,* and the Part V integrative case, *GlaxoSmithKline and AIDS Drugs Policy,* a candidate for a rule could be:

> *In the event of a public health emergency, a developing country may violate a patent and produce a life-preserving pharmaceutical under a compulsory license.*

The evaluation of this rule requires the specific information in the cases and only a brief analysis is presented here. The benefits flowing from the rule are measured in terms of lives saved. The costs are the production costs and the loss in well-being from the diminished incentives for pharmaceutical companies to conduct research and development when patents are not respected. In addition to aggregating the consequences, the rule must be compared to alternative rules such as having the pharmaceutical company provide the drug at preferential prices or developed countries purchase the drug and give it to the developing country. Further analysis is reserved for the cases.

Rule utilitarianism is viewed by its advocates as providing a set of rules for guiding the behavior of all individuals in society in a mutually advantageous manner. Act utilitarianism focuses on individual actions and does not explain what the overall consequences would be for society if everyone were to act in that manner.

To illustrate the substantive and methodological distinctions between act and rule utilitarianism, suppose that in a particular situation deceiving rather than dealing with a person honestly would yield benefits that exceed the costs. Under act utilitarianism, deception would be a morally justified action in this situation. If a general rule of behavior, however, were, "People may deceive others whenever they want to do so," relying on the word of others would be problematic. Aggregate well-being then would be lower because people would not be able to trust others. Thus, mutually advantageous reliance on the word of others would require costly enforcement mechanisms, such as explicit contracts. A rule such as "Always deal with people in an honest and forthright manner" would yield greater aggregate well-being if everyone followed the rule. This rule thus would have moral standing under rule utilitarianism.

Act utilitarianism also risks slipping into self-interest. Since act utilitarianism focuses on an individual's action in a specific situation rather than on general rules of behavior, individuals may be tempted to follow their self-interest. That is, the focus of act utilitarianism can place the decision maker on a slippery slope leading to evaluating actions based on self-interest rather than the consequences for all affected.

The weakness of rule utilitarianism, however, is precisely the strength of act utilitarianism. If deception in a particular situation X yields benefits that exceed the costs, the following modification of the rule would yield greater aggregate well-being: "Always deal with people in an honest and forthright manner except in situation X in which deception is permitted." Amending the rule to allow an exception in situation X improves the utilitarian calculus and hence yields a morally superior rule. Then, any exception that yields benefits in excess of its costs would also yield a morally superior rule. Rule utilitarianism then degenerates into act utilitarianism.[6]

---

[5]See Brandt (1959, 1979) for the classical distinction.
[6]See Lyons (1965).

The response of a rule utilitarian is that utilitarian methods are necessarily applied in an imperfect world in which some facts are missing, information is incomplete, and not all consequences can be foreseen, let alone evaluated. In such a world, it is better to evaluate general rules of behavior to guide individuals than to apply utilitarian methods separately to each action in each situation.[7] Rule utilitarianism encourages individuals to think about whether they would want everyone to follow the same rule of behavior in all similar situations. That is, rule utilitarianism encourages universalism. Rule utilitarianism thus is the preferred form of utilitarianism.

As an example, in the late 1980s American Airlines and United Airlines became concerned about the changes in medical standards adopted by the new federal air surgeon, an officer of the Federal Aviation Administration (FAA). The federal air surgeon had responsibility for granting medical waivers, referred to as "special issuances," that allowed reinstatement of pilots who had had their certification suspended. Under the new standards one pilot who had blacked out in the cockpit had been granted a special issuance, as had a pilot who had had bypass surgery. An airline was not required to put a pilot with a special issuance back in the cockpit, and American and United had kept their pilots grounded until receiving clearance from their own chief medical officers. The moral question was whether the airlines should take any action with regard to the new standards being followed by the federal air surgeon. Since the airlines could ground any of their pilots with special issuances that were questioned by their own medical officers, the airlines were not concerned about their own pilots. The broader concern was with general aviation pilots and other airlines that might not be aware of or concerned by the changes made by the federal air surgeon. American and United extrapolated from their own situations to the broader population of pilots and airlines; that is, they considered a general rule. They concluded based on reasoning analogous to the Calabresi and Melamed principles that they had a duty to make their concerns public. The airlines went to the FAA and to the congressional committee with oversight responsibility for the FAA, which held hearings leading to a review of the medical standards.

Jointly Determined Consequences

In many situations consequences are jointly determined by the actions of more than one person. In such a situation, a second form of act and rule utilitarianism is applicable.[8] As an example of such a situation, consider a firm seeking to sell telecommunication equipment to a government agency in a country in which corruption is known to be widespread. Suppose the firm believes that a competitor with inferior equipment is likely to be offering a bribe to the head of the agency. How should the firm reason about whether it should offer a matching bribe?

In act utilitarianism an individual chooses the action that maximizes aggregate well-being, taking the behavior of others as given. A matching bribe in this situation would increase aggregate well-being because the firm has superior equipment. In rule utilitarianism an individual chooses not only a rule for one's own action but also simultaneously for the actions of all individuals. In so doing the individual is choosing a rule of behavior to be followed by everyone, so the rule is universal. In addition, as utilitarians all persons would choose the same rule, since each person maximizes aggregate well-being. Each individual thus is choosing not only in an impartial manner but also chooses the same rule, so there is unanimity.[9] Bribery and the resulting corruption reduce aggregate well-being, so the moral rule is that neither firm is to offer a bribe. Bribery is considered in more detail in Chapter 23.

As a quantitative example, consider two individuals who each must decide whether to act honestly or dishonestly. Table 20-2 presents their utilities as a function of the actions each takes, where the first entry in each cell is the utility of individual 1

---

[7]See Hardin (1988).
[8]See Harsanyi (1982, p. 57) for this characterization and also Harsanyi (1977).
[9]As developed further in the next chapter, such a rule meets the two higher order moral standards—universalizability and unanimous impartial choice—that give it moral standing.

TABLE 20-2	Rule Utilitarianism and Joint Determination		
		Individual 2	
		Honest	Dishonest
Individual 1	Honest	10,7	2,8
	Dishonest	7,2	4,7

and the second is the utility of individual 2. Acting honestly is better for individual 1 if and only if individual 2 acts honestly, but acting dishonestly is better for 2 regardless of whether 1 acts honestly or dishonestly. With rule utilitarianism consider two alternative rules: (A) All act honestly and (B) All act dishonestly.[10] Rule A yields aggregate utility of 17, whereas rule B yields aggregate utility of 11. As rule utilitarians both individuals would choose rule A, so they are unanimous in their choice.

Act utilitarianism takes the other individual's action as given, so it is necessary to form expectations about which action the other individual is likely to take. In the example in Table 20-2 if individual 2 were to act dishonestly, as an act utilitarian individual 1 would act dishonestly, since that yields aggregate utility of 11 instead of 10. If 2 were to act honestly, 1 would act honestly. Individual 2 would reason in an identical manner, acting honestly if 1 were to act honestly, and acting dishonestly if 1 were to act dishonestly. Which actions would be taken thus depends on what the other individual can be expected to do. Suppose that 1 suspects that individual 2 might not be a utilitarian but instead might be self-interested. If 1 harbors such suspicions, the better action would be to act dishonestly. That is, if 2 were indeed self-interested, 2 would act dishonestly, since that is a dominant strategy; that is, acting dishonestly is better for 2 regardless of how 1 acts. If instead 2 were an act utilitarian but believed that 1 was suspicious and might believe that 2 was self-interested and act dishonestly, then 2 would act dishonestly. In this case incomplete information about what the other individual will do could easily cause act utilitarianism to degenerate into both being dishonest.[11] Rule utilitarianism thus is superior to act utilitarianism.

Decision Making in the Face of a Moral Transgression

Next consider the case in which individual 1 is a rule utilitarian and 2 is known to be self-interested and hence will act dishonestly. Is 1 morally justified in acting dishonestly? The answer at one level is no because the moral rule is for both to act honestly. It is 2 who is acting immorally. Under act utilitarianism 1 is morally right to act dishonestly, however, since doing so is justified by avoiding an even worse outcome. Rule utilitarianism, however, correctly indicates that the moral rule is for both to act honestly, so it is right for 1 to be honest. The moral obligation in such a case is to convince individual 2 to act honestly or more generally to initiate collective action to achieve a binding agreement for all to act honestly. In the case of bribery, the duty is on the firm, and all firms, to eliminate bribery and to reject extortion by government officials. This approach is considered in more detail in Chapter 23 in the case of bribery in international business, where the collective action occurred through the OECD. Chapter 23 also considers a policy of Cummins Inc. to address such situations.

UTILITARIANISM AND RIGHTS

Rights may be classified as intrinsic or instrumental. Intrinsic rights are to be respected because they have moral standing independently of the consequences they yield. Instrumental rights are to be respected because they lead to desirable consequences. Instrumental rights are justified in a consequentialist system, such as utilitarianism, when

---

[10]Note that there are other possible rules, such as, "Individual 1 is to act honestly and individual 2 dishonestly." The two rules A and B are considered because they are symmetric.
[11]Note that the situation in Table 20-2 is not a prisoners' dilemma.

in a wide variety of settings such rights improve well-being. Property rights are an example of instrumental rights in utilitarianism, since they facilitate beneficial economic transactions. Utilitarianism provides a means of evaluating instrumental rights but does not provide a basis for evaluating intrinsic rights, which must be justified by other considerations as identified in Chapter 21. The Chapter 21 case, *Genetic Testing in the Workplace,* includes issues of well-being and rights.

CRITICISMS OF UTILITARIANISM

Philosophical Criticisms

One criticism of consequentialist systems is that they do not give adequate attention to intrinsic rights and liberties, which are said to be fundamentally important. A related criticism is that consequentialist systems treat all things alike in their calculus. Thus, aspirations, wants, needs, liberties, and opportunities are relevant only with regard to their consequences. As Sen (1987, pp. 74–76) argues, however, consequences must remain an essential focus even of an ethics system that considers intrinsically important concepts.

Another concern with utilitarianism pertains to how duty is assigned when consequences are jointly determined or transgressions are possible. If there is only one person who can take the moral action, the assignment of duty is clear. In some cases, however, there may be several parties who could take the action, or the consequences could be jointly determined as in the example in Table 20-2.[12] One resolution is that the duty should be assigned to everyone who could take the action, but that leaves a collective choice problem that could be difficult to resolve. If there are costs associated with taking the action, the utilitarian resolution of the collective choice problem is that the person with the lowest cost of acting should be assigned the duty, as indicated previously. More generally, the assignment of duty can be based on the Calabresi and Melamed principles. In some cases the assignment may be either to a firm or to the government. For example, in the case of permanent layoffs, the duty to retrain laid-off employees could rest with the employer, the government, or the employees. The duty to retrain workers has been assigned primarily to government and the employees themselves, whereas many companies have assumed the responsibility for upgrading the education and skills of their current employees.

Assigning duty is also difficult when circumstances change. Most employers provide health, life, and disability insurance for their employees, but if an employee becomes permanently disabled and unable to work, which party has the responsibility for the worker? An increasing number of employers fire permanently disabled workers, frequently after a specified time period such as 6 months. A Mercer Human Resource Consulting study found that 51 percent of the companies surveyed fired employees on long-term disability.[13] Disability insurance payments continue after firing, but health care and life insurance benefits are no longer provided by the employers, which would impose a financial burden on the former employees. The employers argued that the fired workers were no longer employees, since they could not work. Moreover, the purpose of the disability insurance was to provide for the employee in the event of a disability, including providing funds to pay for health and life insurance. Who has the duty in such cases—the employer, the employee, or government?

Utilitarianism is also criticized for its focus solely on human well-being. Some critics claim that it should be expanded to include the well-being of other living creatures such as animals and trees and inanimate objects such as rocks and soil. For example, in the protection of nature what matters is not the pleasure that individuals obtain from an undisturbed mountain lake. Instead, the claim is that the well-being of the lake itself is to be taken into account. This is the subject of much disagreement, but if the claim were accepted, the approach to taking these broader considerations into effect would be similar to how altruism is taken into account, as considered earlier.

---

[12]See Hardin (1988).
[13]*Wall Street Journal,* July 14, 2003.

Interpersonal Comparisons of Utility

A fundamental problem with utilitarianism is the difficulty, if not the impossibility, of making interpersonal comparisons of utility. The preferences considered in the discipline of economics are ordinal in the sense that they indicate only how an individual orders one consequence relative to another. Those preferences do not reflect intensity. The Pareto criterion avoids interpersonal comparisons, since it requires only that an action make at least one person better off and no one worse off, both evaluated in terms of their own preferences. A rule that produces a Pareto improvement thus has a strong claim to moral standing in a consequentialist ethics system. When actions make some individuals better off and others worse off, however, interpersonal comparisons are necessary in applying utilitarianism. Interpersonal comparisons are problematic, though, unless some common measure of preference intensity can be devised.

In spite of the difficulties in making interpersonal comparisons of preferences, utilitarianism is regularly used to evaluate public policies by measuring benefits and costs in monetary units. Measurement may involve a direct estimate of how much individuals are willing to pay, or accept, for one consequence rather than another. Indirect estimates—using wage premiums to evaluate the cost of hazardous jobs such as high steel work or housing price differentials as a function of the distance from an airport to estimate the cost of noise pollution—are also possible. Because of the difficulties in making interpersonal comparisons, cost-benefit calculations are often only one of several considerations used in public policy analysis. These issues are also present in business decisions, as in the chapter case *Pricing the Norplant System.*

Identifying Costs and Benefits

A difficulty in the application of utilitarianism centers on whether well-being can be identified from observed actions; that is, from revealed preferences. If people choose to smoke or hang glide, actions that can reduce their life expectancy, is that a benefit or a cost? If preferences are revealed by actions, these choices presumably have benefits that outweigh the costs. In the case of smoking, however, addiction can mean that actions are not voluntary and hence do not reveal preferences.

Since utilitarianism considers the consequences for everyone, certain consequences net out. In the cap-and-trade systems for controlling sulfur dioxide emissions from power plants considered in Chapter 11, it did not matter from a social efficiency perspective whether the allowances were given free to power plants or were auctioned. Similarly, in Chapter 12 the focus of the analysis of the liability system was on efficiency—that is, which party could reduce accidents at lowest cost—rather than on the distributive consequences. It does matter, however, whether the FCC auctions licenses to use the radio spectrum rather than awarding them based on noneconomic criteria. An auction allocates the licenses to their highest valued use, which is consistent with utilitarianism. Auctions also redistribute wealth from broadcast companies to the government and hence to the public, but that redistribution may net to zero in the utilitarian calculus.

The Measurement Problem

Most applications of utilitarianism involve difficult measurement and estimation problems. Social costs and benefits typically are measured in monetary units based on the amount a person would accept in exchange for a beneficial consequence or would forego to avoid a harmful consequence. Consequences are thus measured in terms of their monetary equivalents. The methods of measuring monetary equivalents in cost-benefit analysis in the public sector serve as guides for utilitarian analysis. These methods are presented in Boardman et al. (2006).

Economists look at what individuals reveal through their actions rather than what they say. That is, rather than asking people how costly is noise pollution, economists estimate the price differentials of homes on airline flight paths.[14] Wage differentials are used to measure certain social costs. Are the wage premiums paid for dangerous construction work an appropriate measure of the social costs of the accidents and deaths associated with that work? One answer is that workers have chosen those jobs in exchange for higher wages, and those choices reveal their trade-off of wages for risk.

The Food and Drug Administration routinely uses an age-adjusted value of a life saved because the elderly have a shorter remaining life expectancy than do younger persons. When the Environmental Protection Agency (EPA) conducted a secondary analysis in which it reduced by 27 percent the estimated health benefits for a person over 70, activists labeled it "the senior citizen death discount." Private politics pressure led the EPA to stop using the measure.[15]

After an airline crash in 1989 safety activists led a movement to require the use of infant safety seats in aircraft. Children under the age of 2 years had been permitted to travel on airlines without tickets if they were held by a parent. Safety activists argued that parents should be required to purchase a ticket for the child and use an infant safety seat. The FAA conducted a cost-benefit analysis of the safety seat issue and concluded that requiring the use of safety seats would actually increase injuries and deaths. The FAA estimated that requiring infant safety seats would save one infant's life over a decade. Requiring infant safety seats, however, would increase the cost of air travel for families, which would cause some families to drive rather than fly. Since driving is considerably more dangerous than flying, deaths and injuries would increase. The FAA's estimate was nine additional highway fatalities, 52 serious injuries, and 2,300 minor injuries. The methods and conclusions of the FAA study were criticized on several dimensions, including the estimated cost increase for air travel for families. Others attacked the conclusion itself. Representative Jim Lightfoot (R-IA) stated, "What's your child worth? Is it worth the price of an airline ticket?"[16] The FAA began a rule-making procedure in 1998 but decided not to require safety seats despite pressure from the National Transportation Safety Board.

An alternative to a cost-benefit analysis in cases involving hazards is a cost-risk analysis or comparative risk analysis. Cost-risk analysis focuses on the costs required to reduce risks (e.g., to avoid the loss of a life) and compares the alternative in question with other alternatives. In evaluating the use of infant safety seats, the FAA estimated the lives that would be saved by the seats and the lives that would be lost because more families would drive rather than fly. The decision was then clear without attempting to value a child's life. In the chapter case, *Pricing the Norplant System,* instead of attempting to measure social benefits, Wyeth-Ayerst Laboratories examined the relative effectiveness of its product compared with others on the market. The Chapter 21 case, *Genetic Testing in the Workplace,* provides an opportunity to use cost-risk analysis.

The Information Problem

Another problem in the managerial application of utilitarianism is obtaining the information required to evaluate the consequences for all those affected, either directly or indirectly. In the case of an action that affects only the firm and its immediate stakeholders, the required information may be available. If the action affects others or if the effects are indirect, as when intermediated by markets or other institutions, or when consequences depend also on the actions of other parties, the information problem can be more serious. The information problem also is more serious in the application of rule utilitarianism because the rule is intended to be applicable to many decision makers and many similar situations. Obtaining information about those other situations can be difficult and requires assumptions.

One response to this information problem is extrapolation. If other firms are facing the same issue and if the situation of one firm is reasonably representative of the

---

[14]This approach takes into account the location decisions of people who have various tolerances for noise.
[15]The EPA uses a value of $6 million for prolonging a life.
[16]*Washington Post,* July 13, 1990.

others, a firm may extrapolate to the broader set of firms based on its own information. If the issue is a chronic health problem, such as carpal tunnel syndrome resulting from repetitive tasks, the experiences of most firms and their employees may be similar. On such issues, extrapolation may be straightforward. The example of American Airlines and United Airlines and the special issuances is one such case.

UTILITARIANISM IN APPLICATION

Categories of Situations

In applying utilitarianism it is useful to distinguish between two categories of situations. The first includes those in which institutions are in place to align the interests of the decision maker with societal well-being. The second includes those in which institutions are either not in place or only imperfectly align private and social interests.

In the first category, the interests of the firm and society are aligned, so the firm can act based on its own interests. If a firm makes a product that is hazardous when misused, and if misuse can be anticipated, the firm's decisions about safety features under a utilitarian standard can be made as considered in Chapter 12. The firm can maximize its profits and choose safety features based on their cost and the anticipated reductions in liability awards and legal costs. Even though these costs are not perfect measures of social costs, they represent the guidance of an institution, the law of torts that has evolved over time in response to the social cost of wrongs. The law of torts is an institution consistent with utilitarianism.

Similarly, if markets are competitive, a decision regarding closing a plant can be made on the basis of profitability. If the plant's costs are too high for it to be competitive, utilitarianism concludes that the resources used in that plant be reallocated to higher-valued uses. Furthermore, the government has established a set of institutions, such as unemployment insurance and job training programs, to deal with unemployment and reemployment. Decisions based on profitability then serve society's long-term interest in the efficient use of resources—although in some cases they do so only imperfectly. This does not mean, however, that the firm should not take measures to ease the transition for its former employees if it is best positioned to do so on some dimensions. It also does not mean that other ethics considerations such as rights and justice are not relevant.

The second category of situations includes those in which institutions are not in place to align the interests of the firm and society. In these situations, utilitarian analysis must be applied directly, as considered in the following section. Government agencies use cost-benefit analysis to provide information to policymakers. Firms may also use a cost-benefit analysis, as the chapter case, *Pricing the Norplant System,* indicates. These analyses may not be without controversy, however.

Methodology

The framework for the application of utilitarianism is illustrated in Figure 20-3. It begins with the identification of the facts of the situation and the moral concerns. As applied in the form of cost-benefit analysis, the analysis then involves the following steps:

1. Identify the alternatives—rules of behavior and actions.
2. For each alternative, identify the set of consequences for all persons and organizations affected.
3. Determine which of the consequences are social costs and which are social benefits.
4. Evaluate and estimate the social costs and social benefits.
5. Choose the action or rule that yields the greatest difference between social benefits and social costs.

The objective of a complete utilitarian analysis is to arrive at a decision in step 5. A more modest objective is to encourage managers to think broadly, rather than narrowly, about the consequences of actions. Even if a complete analysis cannot be conducted because, for example, of measurement and information problems, completing the first three steps can deepen the understanding of an issue and provide a sounder foundation for the application of ethical intuition and judgment. In particular, those steps encourage managers to consider the consequences of alternatives for all those affected.

To illustrate the analysis at this level, several examples are presented. These examples will also be considered in Chapter 21 from rights and justice perspectives.

EXAMPLE

Living Benefits[1]

Herman H. Silverman, a high school English teacher, started a part-time business called Beat the Grim Reaper International, Inc. Silverman's company—and rival upstarts—bought the beneficiary rights to the life insurance policies of the terminally ill, principally people with acquired immune deficiency syndrome (AIDS), but some cancer patients as well.[2] Silverman was sanguine about his new enterprise: "I don't think there's anything as guaranteed as this is in terms of getting a return."

The following examples clarify the contractual arrangements surrounding what have come to be known generically as living benefits or viatical settlements. One of Silverman's new competitors, Living Benefits, Inc., purchased a $100,000 insurance policy for $53,000 from a 34-year-old Boston real estate salesman with AIDS. For 65 cents on the dollar, the company also purchased a $250,000 policy from a 59-year-old San Diego man with cancer. As the new legal beneficiary, Living Benefits paid the premiums on the policies and would receive all the proceeds upon their deaths. In the meantime, the policyholders received $53,000 and $162,500, respectively, for use in their final years.

The benefits provided by these entrepreneurial enterprises did not go unnoticed by major public insurance companies. Robert Waldron, spokesman for the American Council of Life Insurance, said, "We recognize there's a desperate need. The high cost of dying just goes up every year." Indeed, the cost of prolonged illness frequently caused terminally ill individuals to stop their insurance premium payments before their deaths, causing their policies to lapse.[3] "As long as they're going soon anyway,"

added Silverman, "there's a service that I can provide for people who want to have their money right now." Living Benefits customers were favorably disposed toward the provision of these services. "I think it's a great idea," said the salesman from Boston. "It benefits the person who is suffering." Likewise, the San Diego man dying of cancer was spending some of the proceeds to build a new house for his wife. "It's like having your cake and eating it too," he said. "As far as I'm concerned, I'm going to keep living."

The process of contracting for living benefits was somewhat more complicated than these examples might suggest. Applicants for living benefits from Beat the Grim Reaper typically endured an 8-week information-gathering process that began with a four-page questionnaire. Next, the applicant's medical and insurance records were transmitted to Grim Reaper. Grim Reaper employed a staff of consulting physicians who met with the applicant's attending physicians to determine the applicant's life expectancy. Grim Reaper then offered the applicant a price for the policy. The price was based on the applicant's life expectancy, the face value of the policy, the premiums required to maintain an active policy, and interest rates. Upon receipt of a waiver signed by the beneficiary, the policy and the proceeds of the sale were placed in escrow. Shortly thereafter, funds were transferred to the applicant. Grim Reaper had a policy of offering its services only to those with a "pronounced financial need."

A range of objections—emotional and moral—were raised about the provision of living benefits. Some observers claimed that this growing industry was exploiting the impaired judgment of the terminally ill and, in the process, trampling on the rights of the would-be beneficiaries. The president of Living Benefits, Rob T. Worley, conceded that some public reactions were negative: "We've had a few people that say this is ghoulish." Mr. Waldron of the American Council of Life Insurance took the argument a step farther: "This gives a third party who's not family an economic interest in a policyholder's death. As a concept, that is dangerous."

---

[1] This example was written by Thomas Gilligan. Copyright © 1992 by Thomas Gilligan. All rights reserved. Reprinted with permission.
[2] AIDS advocacy groups had a well-developed national information network that informed members of the existence of such firms. Silverman also advertised the services of his company.
[3] A living-benefits spokesperson claimed that over 50 percent of those who died as a result of AIDS had let their life insurance policies lapse prior to death.

(Continued)

Nevertheless, living benefits arrangements were increasingly common, and major insurance companies began offering living benefits to their policyholders.

Consider the following rule:

Life insurance policies of the terminally ill can be bought and sold.

Sales of a life insurance policy by terminally ill policyholders are voluntary decisions, and the policyholders will sell their policies only if that makes them better off. Similarly, a company such as Living Benefits will purchase a policy only if doing so makes it better off. Consequently, a sale is a Pareto improvement—both parties are better off, so from the perspective of utilitarianism the rule is moral. Another way to look at the issue is that a market for such life insurance policies increases economic efficiency by giving parties an opportunity to trade.

The principal caveat to this analysis is that a company might exploit the terminally ill person. That person, however, would be protected by friends and by the beneficiaries, who could reject the offer in that case. Exploiting terminally ill persons by inducing them to sell their life insurance policies against their will would be immoral. A second caveat is that the beneficiaries could block a sale to preserve the amount they would otherwise be paid in the event of the policyholder's death. The beneficiaries would in this case be acting immorally. Utilitarianism requires the company to take steps to avoid both of these cases.

By 2008 there were 180 firms in the Life Insurance Settlement Association, and Goldman Sachs had begun participating in the market. Its objective was to bundle purchased life insurance policies into securities and sell the securities. Some referred to the securities as death bonds.

EXAMPLE

Integrity Tests

In 1988 a federal law took effect prohibiting the use of pre-hiring polygraph tests, which had been given to approximately 2 million current and prospective employees annually.[1] The law also placed certain restrictions on the use of polygraph tests for employees suspected of violating laws or company policies. In response to the ban on pre-hiring polygraph tests, employers began to use more extensive background checks and written "integrity tests."

Integrity tests are paper-and-pencil tests intended to identify individuals with desirable or undesirable traits.[2] Examples of questions on the tests include, "Do you think a person should be fired by a company if it is found that he helped the employees cheat the company out of overtime once in a while?" and "If you found $100 that was lost by a bank truck on the street yesterday, would you turn the money over to the bank, even though you knew for sure that there was no reward?"[3] Firms use these tests, along with information about an applicant's ability, education, and experience, to screen for integrity and potential loyalty to the firm. Some firms have found the tests useful in identifying individuals who might be a problem on the job.

From the perspective of costs and benefits, integrity tests can produce benefits to the extent that they help better match potential employees to the jobs in which they will be most productive. The tests may yield substantial benefits for some jobs and few benefits for others.

From the perspective of rule utilitarianism, the use of integrity tests is warranted if it better matches prospective employees to jobs. Integrity can be particularly important for jobs that involve security, as in defense industries; jobs that involve access to confidential information, such as that pertaining to clients; or jobs in which an employee is entrusted with resources, as with accountants, couriers, and bank tellers. Integrity tests may also be beneficial if they enable employers to select employees who are more likely to fit with the firm's culture. For these purposes, an integrity test may be one of several sources of information used in hiring decisions, alongside personal interviews and reference checks. Such tests can also be advantageous competitively. W. Thomas Van Etten, senior vice president of Sun Bank in Miami, commented on his bank's use of an integrity test, a background check, and urinalysis for prospective employees, "People with a substance-abuse or integrity problem are more likely to look for work with our competitors who don't take as close a look as we do."[4]

---

[1]Exemptions from the law were provided for security guards and jobs that involved health and safety. Pharmaceutical companies were also exempt, as was government.
[2]See Sackett and Harris (1984).
[3]The questions are from the Integrity Attitude Scale published by Reid Psychological Systems (*New York Times*, November 28, 1997).

[4]*New York Times*, October 1, 1989.

(Continued)

If integrity tests are used to better match potential employees to jobs, they pass the cost-benefit test and are morally good from the perspective of utilitarianism. Integrity tests, however, raise concerns about rights. Integrity tests may invade privacy if the questions are personal. The tests also raise concerns about arbitrary treatment to the extent to which the tests are imperfect measures and hence may misclassify individuals. Employers, however, have a right to hire whomever they prefer as long as they do not engage in illegal discrimination, and they may use relevant means in making hiring decisions. The tests also raise justice considerations because they may deny opportunity to those who, for whatever reason, do not perform well on such tests. Justice considerations may also be involved if the tests put at a disadvantage individuals with past experiences that cause them to perform poorly on the tests. In Chapter 21, integrity tests are reconsidered from rights and justice perspectives.

EXAMPLE

Life Insurance Screening for Preexisting Conditions

To determine eligibility for individual life insurance policies, the insurance industry uses medical examinations to screen for preexisting health problems such as a heart condition or a stroke.[1] Once people have a life-threatening condition, they have an incentive to purchase life insurance to provide for dependents and others. Screening is intended to prevent someone from purchasing a large policy once his or her health is impaired. This provides incentives for people to purchase life insurance ex ante, that is, before they have a life-threatening condition, rather than ex post, after they have such a condition.

The ethics issue is whether people with preexisting conditions should be screened and hence not included in the insurance in a pool with those with no preexisting conditions. The rule to be evaluated is:

Screening is permitted for preexisting conditions as a requirement for eligibility to purchase an individual life insurance policy.

If this rule were not followed, insurance companies would have to increase the price of insurance to cover the higher expected payments to the beneficiaries of those with preexisting conditions. The higher price would cause some individuals without preexisting conditions not to purchase insurance. This is an instance of adverse selection in which those with higher risks choose to buy life insurance, which increases the price of insurance and causes others who would have purchased insurance at the lower price not to do so.[2] If enough people with preexisting conditions were to buy life insurance, the price could ratchet up to the point at which those without preexisting conditions would drop out of the market. Those with preexisting conditions would then be alone in the pool, and the price would reflect solely the risks of their conditions.

Screening for preexisting conditions results in higher aggregate well-being because insurance would be available to those both with and without preexisting conditions. Utilitarian analysis thus supports a rule permitting screening for preexisting conditions. This analysis may be questioned from the perspective of ethics systems that take into account other considerations. Those considerations are addressed in Chapter 21.

---

[1] Group life insurance plans, such as those provided by an employer, do not require screening for preexisting conditions, but group policies are experience-related and premiums are adjusted annually. The cost of coverage for individuals with preexisting conditions is thus borne by the group members. In contrast, premiums for an individual life insurance policy are fixed at the time of purchase.

---

[2] Adverse selection is considered in Chapter 10.

EXAMPLE

Redlining

A significant problem in the insurance and banking industries arises from imperfect information about risks. The costs of investigating and assessing risks are often high, and risk assessment is itself imperfect. The collateral for a mortgage on a home or a commercial establishment serves as a means of reducing the risk to the lender, and the value of the collateral depends on property values in the area in which the property is located.

Insurance companies have similar difficulties assessing property and casualty risks on homes or

(Continued)

automobiles when the risks depend on location as well as on the precautions taken by owners. Even if an applicant takes every measure of care, the likelihood that an automobile will be stolen or vandalized is higher in some neighborhoods than in others. When prices are required to be uniform over broad geographic areas, policies written on high-risk areas can result in losses for insurance companies.

To deal with the costs of risk assessment and evaluation, some financial institutions and insurance companies identified high-risk regions of cities and refused to lend or write policies in those regions. This practice, referred to as redlining, might have been efficient, and hence ethical from a utilitarianism perspective, if the costs of risk and credit evaluation were high and the likelihood was high that a loan or policy application would be rejected because of the risks. That is, if the average cost of credit evaluation were high and demographic data indicated that most residents in an area would not purchase insurance or qualify for a policy or a mortgage, it could be efficient

for the insurance company or financial institution not to consider applications from the area.[1]

Although redlining could be ethical from the perspective of costs and benefits, it is unethical from other perspectives. Redlining is said to violate a fundamental right, since it denies opportunity to those who would qualify for loans or insurance but who do not have the opportunity to do so because they happen to reside in a redlined area. Redlining is also said to result in unjust de facto discrimination against minorities and the poor to the extent that they are overrepresented in high-risk areas. Rights and justice frameworks thus bring important considerations to bear on issues such as redlining and have resulted in laws prohibiting the practice. The redlining issue illustrates that a practice could be acceptable from the perspective of one ethics system but unacceptable from the perspective of another.

---

[1]Similar practices exist in a number of other industries, as indicated by the previous discussion of delivery services.

SUMMARY

Ethics is intended to provide mutually beneficial rules of behavior without requiring government regulation and enforcement. Some of those rules are incorporated into constitutions and statutes, but ethics extends beyond the law to provide guidance to people in their behavior and to firms in their formulation of policies.

Ethics standards are impartial and are to be applied universally, in contrast to casuistry, which holds that leaders may violate ethics standards to fulfill responsibilities to constituents. Ethics generally differs from self-interest, and utilitarianism holds that every individual's well-being is given equal weight.

Utilitarianism is a consequentialist system of ethics that defines the good in terms of human well-being and evaluates that well-being in terms of individuals' preferences. Utilitarianism then aggregates those preferences to obtain a measure of societal well-being. The right action is the one that yields the greatest well-being. Utilitarianism's practical usefulness is in providing a system for evaluating actions that make some individuals better off and others worse off.

Two forms of utilitarianism are act and rule utilitarianism. Act utilitarianism focuses on an individual action taking the actions of others as given. Rule utilitarianism focuses on rules that all individuals are to follow in similar situations. Act utilitarianism is criticized for allowing exceptions to general rules of behavior, which can then degenerate into self-interest. Rule utilitarianism seeks rules of behavior that apply universally to all individuals. When consequences are a function of the actions of more than one individual, rule utilitarianism considers the actions of all individuals simultaneously. The moral rule is the one that yields the greatest aggregate well-being when everyone follows that rule.

An applied form of utilitarianism is cost-benefit analysis that evaluates actions and rules in terms of the costs and benefits they generate. The application of utilitarianism, however, involves three basic problems: (1) determining what counts as a benefit or a cost, (2) making interpersonal comparisons, and (3) conducting analysis with imperfect information about consequences and preferences. Utilitarian principles are applied in the form of cost-benefit analysis, but often, critics say, that approach fails to account for other important considerations. For example, utilitarianism considers rights only in their instrumental role of producing well-being.

------------------------------------- C A S E S -------------------------------------

Pricing the Norplant System

Toward the end of the summer of 1993, Wyeth-Ayerst Laboratories, a unit of the American Home Products Corporation, was enjoying the continuing success of its contraceptive, the Norplant System. Introduced in 1991 in the United States, 1992 revenues from the Norplant System were $105 million, which exceeded initial projections by nearly 100 percent. Executives at Wyeth-Ayerst expected annual sales of the Norplant System to stabilize just below $165 million for the near term. Given the current hostile political and regulatory environment faced by the pharmaceutical industry, this success was indeed welcomed.

The Norplant System is a progestin (levonorgestrel) encased in six permeable polymer capsules (Silastic). The capsules, which are inserted in a woman's upper arm, continuously release the progestin into the bloodstream for 5 years. The progestin alters the chemical balance of a woman's own progesterone levels. This alteration prevents ovulation, decreases circulating sperm concentrations, and creates within the uterus an environment hostile for pregnancy.

The popularity of the Norplant System was not surprising. It exhibited several advantages over alternative forms of contraception. Clinical studies indicated that the Norplant System was a highly effective contraceptive method.[17] The average pregnancy rate for women using the system over the entire 5-year period was less than 1 percent, and the first-year pregnancy rate was less than 0.2 percent. In contrast, the first-year pregnancy rate was 3 percent for oral contraceptives and intrauterine devices (IUDs), 18 percent for diaphragms, and 0.4 percent for tubal ligation. The Norplant System also required no effort to use and was easily reversible. The Norplant System did, however, require surgical implantation and removal and provided no protection from sexually transmitted diseases. Clinical tests of the Norplant System were conducted on over 55,000 women in 46 countries prior to introduction in the United States.[18] The Norplant System had a strong record of safe use, having been used by 500,000 women worldwide for the past 20 years.

Pricing the Norplant System

The Norplant System was developed jointly by Wyeth-Ayerst and the Population Council, a nonprofit organization. In the development of the Norplant System, the Population Council received $10 million in grants from the federal government and private philanthropic organizations. The system used Wyeth-Ayerst's hormone levonorgestrel, which was licensed by Wyeth-Ayerst from its developer. Wyeth-Ayerst held the exclusive right to produce and distribute the Norplant System and could set its price. It paid the Population Council a royalty of no more than 5 percent of the sales price.

In its process of establishing a price for the Norplant System, Wyeth-Ayerst first conducted a study of the relative costs and benefits of alternative contraceptive methods. The direct costs to consumers included the financial costs of the contraceptive (i.e., average retail price), any additional costs related to the use of the contraceptive (i.e., fitting a diaphragm and spermicidal cream; inserting an IUD, insertion and removal of the Norplant System), additional physician follow-up visits (i.e., checkup and monitoring, recuperation, or development of side effects and complications), and the convenience and ease of use (i.e., the need to take oral contraceptives daily). The indirect costs included the need for medical treatment of the side effects resulting from contraceptive use (i.e., medical treatment of hypertension caused by oral contraceptives), the possibility of hospitalization due to side effects (i.e., cost of hospitalization for treatment of pelvic inflammatory disease), supplies used to treat side effects (i.e., the costs of the prescription and nonprescription drugs and supplies needed post vasectomy), the loss of productivity due to side effects (i.e., absenteeism during recuperation), and the costs of contraceptive failure (i.e., the medical costs of abortion or delivery). Certain indirect benefits (i.e., the fact that oral contraceptives reduced the risk of ovarian and endometrial cancers) were also considered. Based on these studies and using the actual average retail price of other contraceptive methods, Wyeth-Ayerst concluded that even at an initial price of $600, the annual expected costs of the Norplant System would be 5 percent less than the IUD, 31 percent less than oral contraceptives, and 50 percent less than diaphragms. The annual expected costs of the Norplant System at an initial price of $600 were, however, 8 percent higher than tubal ligation and 375 percent higher than vasectomy.

Apart from scientific studies on the relative benefits of the Norplant System, Wyeth-Ayerst also had to consider the market for contraceptive devices in the United States. Marketing studies indicated that women perceived a benefit from the Norplant System that justified high initial retail prices in the $400 to $600 range. The scientific and practical advantages of the Norplant System were evident to potential consumers.

Two important features of the market complicated Wyeth-Ayerst's pricing decision, however. First, a significant

---

[17]Population Council, *Norplant: A Summary of Scientific Data.* New York, January 1989.
[18]I. Sivin, "International Experience with Norplant® and Norplant®-2 Contraceptives." *Studies in Family Planning,* 1988: pp. 1981–1994.

percentage of all contraceptives were distributed through not-for-profit family planning clinics. These clinics financed their purchases of contraceptives and compensated their health professionals through grants from governments and philanthropic organizations. These clinics, which were usually strapped for funds, often enjoyed discounts from pharmaceutical manufacturers. For instance, Wyeth-Ayerst deeply discounted the price it charged these clinics for oral contraceptives. Such clinics would expect similar discounts on the Norplant System. Second, most contraceptives distributed in the United States were financed by third-party payers such as insurance companies, state, county, and city governments, and health maintenance organizations. In a world of rapidly escalating health care costs, these third-party payers were not simply price takers but, instead, engaged in tough negotiations with pharmaceutical companies to obtain as low as possible price on drugs. The discounted prices that some pharmaceutical companies offered family planning clinics were often used as targets in negotiations by third-party payers. Any discounts to family planning clinics would almost certainly be sought by medical insurers and government agencies.

The other consideration in the pricing of the Norplant System was cost. The actual costs of producing the Norplant System were quite small, less than $50 per unit including the insertion kit. An additional cost was the training of doctors and other health professionals in the insertion and use of the Norplant System. Wyeth-Ayerst estimated that these costs would be approximately $15 million annually. The other relevant cost was that of liability, since lawsuits followed from the use of virtually all contraceptive systems.

Under these circumstances Wyeth-Ayerst adopted a uniform price of $350 for the introduction of Norplant. This price included the six progestin capsules and the disposable kit required for insertion. The patient also had to pay a doctor for the insertion and removal of Norplant. No discounts were given to family planning clinics or third-party payers. Wyeth-Ayerst, however, helped establish and fund the Norplant Foundation to distribute the Norplant System free of charge to indigent patients.

Public Reaction to the Pricing of the Norplant System

Although commercial success of the Norplant System heartened Wyeth-Ayerst executives, public reaction to its pricing decision was not positive. Health professionals in family planning establishments criticized the pricing of the Norplant System on several grounds. Critics pointed to the $23 price per unit in bulk shipments of the Norplant System to developing countries (without the insertion kit) to highlight the glaring difference between the costs of production and average retail price of the Norplant System in the United States.[19] Critics charged that Wyeth-Ayerst was price-gouging American consumers. Whereas executives said that the success of the system indicated that it was priced fairly, critics countered that the pricing reflected the monopoly Wyeth-Ayerst enjoyed on the supply of the Norplant System.[20] This monopoly position was particularly troublesome for critics, who charged that the bulk of the development cost of the Norplant System had been provided by public funds through the activities of the Population Council.

Critics also charged Wyeth-Ayerst with betrayal and creating a "financial nightmare" for family planning clinics. Many family planning officials believed that they were instrumental in gaining approval for the Norplant System in the United States. However, as a result of Wyeth-Ayerst's pricing decision, they claimed, their budgets had been ruptured. For example, the director of a family planning unit in a major hospital said that shortly after the introduction of the Norplant System, 500 women applied for it. The costs of supplying the system to all these women would have been $175,000, but the clinic's yearly budget for all contraceptives was $20,000. "All of the income for Norplant goes right to the drug company," said Mr. Salo of Planned Parenthood in San Diego. "We don't charge a margin on it. We lose money on each patient that we serve because Medicaid doesn't reimburse the full cost. Staff members have had to forgo raises, and plans for outreach have been shelved as a result."

Critics were also concerned about the implications of Wyeth-Ayerst's pricing of the Norplant System for the pricing of other advances in women's health care products scheduled for introduction in the coming years. For example, Upjohn introduced a new contraceptive, Depo-Provera, which was priced much higher in the United States than it was overseas; and some were concerned about the pricing of RU-486, the so-called abortion pill, scheduled to begin clinical tests in the United States the following year. "Are we going to see RU-486 come into this country at a price that makes it no cheaper than getting a first trimester abortion?" asked Mr. Kring, vice chairman and treasurer of the Norplant Foundation. "It's a trend that scares me to death—that people are making huge profits in women's health care."

---

[19] Wyeth-Ayerst pointed out that these units were produced by a Danish manufacturer that held the exclusive right to distribute the Norplant System in certain African countries.

[20] Pharmaceutical prices generally involved a large markup above costs, since the prices of successful pharmaceuticals had to cover the research and development costs of both successful and unsuccessful attempts to discover new drugs. This also explained in part why prices of pharmaceuticals were higher in the United States and in other countries that have a pharmaceutical industry engaged in research and development than prices in countries that had no research and development–intensive pharmaceutical industry.

The pricing of the Norplant System also attracted the attention of lawmakers. Representative Ron Wyden (D-OR), a senior member of the Subcommittee on Health and the Environment of the House Energy and Commerce Committee, vowed to hold hearings on Wyeth-Ayerst's pricing decision. "You have a situation where clearly Americans are being charged more," said Representative Wyden. "We have a chance to expose these kinds of pricing practices and create a more competitive price."

The Assignment

The Executive Committee on Pricing for Wyeth-Ayerst hastily gathered for a meeting. The members were concerned with the public criticisms directed at the pricing of the Norplant System and about the unfolding nonmarket threats. The committee, composed of the top executives of Wyeth-Ayerst, knew that a good deal of their time over the coming months would be spent on this issue.

They were also concerned with a more general issue that had become increasingly important as the health industry came under closer public scrutiny. The issue revolved around the pricing of proprietary medicines. What factors or principles should guide the Pricing Committee's decisions? Up to this point, the Pricing Committee's primary consideration was the relative quality and costs of available substitutes. In the view of the committee, if Wyeth-Ayerst could provide a better product at or below the costs of existing medicines, everyone would be better off. This focus had led to the comparison of the Norplant System with oral contraceptives in determining the $350 price. But were other factors important as well? For instance, would the pricing of the Norplant System continue to be a nonmarket issue, or would the issue dissipate with time? Did Wyeth-Ayerst's responsibilities extend beyond providing a more effective contraceptive at a price below those of available substitutes? Should the fact that contraceptives were primarily a women's health care product have a bearing on the price it charged?

Should the fact that family planning clinics play an important role in the distribution of contraceptives to poor women be a factor? Should the fact that the Norplant System was deeply discounted in developing countries play a role in determining the prices charged in the United States? Should the fact that Wyeth-Ayerst discounts oral contraceptives to family planning clinics

impact the decision of whether to discount the Norplant System to the poor? What should Wyeth-Ayerst do with respect to the family planning clinics?

The Pricing Committee has asked you to provide specific criteria for pricing proprietary medicines and to apply them to the pricing of the Norplant System. That is, you are to come up with a number that you would have adopted for the price of the Norplant System if it had been your decision to make. The Pricing Committee has asked you for an oral and written presentation of clarity sufficient to implement your proposed criteria. To help your analysis, the committee has set the following set of parameters:

1. The variable costs of the Norplant System (including insertion kit) were $50 per unit. This figure included all production and delivery costs as well as the expected costs of products liability claims. This cost also included the royalties Wyeth-Ayerst paid the developer of levonorgestrel and the Population Council.

2. Wyeth-Ayerst employed 2,700 staff, executives, health care professionals, and salespeople, who educated health professionals on the insertion and use of the Norplant System. To this point, Wyeth-Ayerst had trained over 28,000 doctors on the use of the Norplant System. With benefits, the average annual cost per employee was roughly $65,000. The Norplant System was expected to generate nearly 6 percent of Wyeth-Ayerst's total revenues of $2.8 billion. If the total labor costs were amortized to each of Wyeth-Ayerst's products based on their contribution to revenues, nearly $11 million in annual labor costs would be assigned to the sale of the Norplant System.

3. Wyeth-Ayerst allocated approximately $5 million annually for the advertising and promotion of the Norplant System. ■

Tax Shelters

Financial services firms regularly designed financial instruments to benefit their clients, and one such instrument was a tax shelter. Many wealthy Americans sought ways to reduce their tax liability, so there was a natural demand for financial instruments to shelter income. For example, a person who sold a business and had a substantial capital gain would benefit from a financial loss that offset some portion of the capital gain. William C. Eacho and Donna Eacho sold their food distribution company in 1998, resulting in a large capital gain. The auditor for the Eachos' company was KPMG, the fourth largest public accounting firm. KPMG sold the Eachos a tax shelter that shielded $60 million in capital gains. The tax shelter, known as OPIS, was designed to generate paper losses, which to be deductible had to have economic substance. Otherwise, the IRS could disallow the deduction. The Eachos relied on the reputation of KPMG for the deductibility of the losses generated by the OPIS tax shelter.[21]

The economic boom in the 1990s and the technology bubble in 1999 and 2000 resulted in large wealth gains to many individuals, and KPMG developed a practice to mass-market tax shelters to them. "In 1997 KPMG established a Tax Innovation Center in Washington, with a dozen full-time staffers to develop shelters that could be widely marketed to multiple clients. The firm set up a telemarketing center in Fort Wayne, IN, to make cold calls to companies. KPMG hired about 60 veteran salespeople who worked on commissions as high as 6 percent of the tax-related revenue they brought in, according to former firm employees."[22] Other accounting firms also participated in the tax shelter business.

Sellers of tax shelters were required to register them with the Internal Revenue Service (IRS), and individuals using such tax shelters were required to report them on their individual tax returns. IRS regulations stated, "In certain cases, a tax shelter that does not expect to reduce the cumulative tax liability of any investor during the 5-year period ending after the date the investment is first offered for sale may be considered a 'projected income investment.' Such a tax shelter will not have to register, and thus not have to furnish a tax shelter registration number to investors, unless and until it ceases to be a projected income investment."[23] The IRS could challenge a tax shelter as abusive, disallow the deductions, and impose penalties.

In deciding whether to offer OPIS shelters, Gregg W. Ritchie of KPMG provided management with a risk analysis. He estimated an average fee of $360,000 for each shelter sold and potential penalties of $31,000 if the IRS took action. Ritchie wrote, "The rewards of a successful marketing of the OPIS product [and the competitive disadvantages which may result from registration] far exceeded the financial exposure to penalties that may arise."[24] He added, "Penalties would be no greater than $14,000 per $100,000 in KPMG fees, and as the size of the deal increases, our exposure to the penalties decreases as a percentage of our fees."[25] Richard Smith, head of the tax unit at KPMG, said the decision "was made based on an analysis of the law. It wasn't made on the basis of the size of the penalties" compared to the

fees.[26] OPIS was designed because of concerns expressed by partners about another tax shelter known as FLIP. Some partners expressed the view that KPMG was required to register FLIP with the IRS, and the firm discontinued the shelter. KPMG instead designed OPIS, which was a "watered down version" of FLIP. KPMG sold OPIS tax shelters to 111 individuals, generating fees of $28 million.

In total, KPMG designed several "tax solutions," four of which were mass-marketed. For example, Gary Winnick, former chairman of Global Crossing, purchased $161 million in tax-shelter losses in 1999 and 2000. The four tax shelters were named BLIPS (Bond Linked Issue Premium Structure), FLIP (Foreign Leveraged Investment Program), OPIS (Offshore Portfolio Investment Strategy), and SC2 (S Corporation Charitable Contribution Strategy). KPMG provided BLIPS shelters to 1,800 people. In total the four solutions sheltered over $11 billion in income, resulting in a tax savings of over $2.5 billion for KPMG clients.

An example of a tax solution was SC2, which generated $26 million in fees for KPMG. The SC2 shelters were referred to internally as S-CAPES. A KPMG senior tax official said in an e-mail, "I think the last thing we or a client would want is a letter in the files regarding a tax-planning strategy for which the acronym when pronounced sounds like we are saying 'escapes.'"[27]

The *Los Angeles Times* described the nature of an SC2 transaction. The objective was to change ordinary income into a capital gain at a time when capital gains were taxed at a lower rate than ordinary income. The tax solution involved forming an S corporation to receive the ordinary income, issuing new, nonvoting shares of the S corporation, and donating those shares to a tax-exempt entity. The income typically was allowed to accumulate in the S corporation. The income accruing to the shares held by the tax-exempt entity was not taxed, whereas the income accruing to the shares held by the original shareholders was taxed as ordinary income. After a few years sufficient to qualify as capital gains, the tax-exempt entity would sell the shares back to the S corporation, receiving a fee. The shareholders of the S corporation then paid the capital gains tax on the retained earnings associated with the donated shares. This generated a tax savings for the owners of the S corporation because of the difference between the tax rate on ordinary income and the capital gains tax rate. Such a tax solution required the participation of a tax-exempt entity. One such entity was the Los Angeles Fire and Police Pension System, known as L.A. Guns & Hoses, which completed 11 SC2 transactions netting $5.9 million with another 16 transactions not yet completed.

[21]*New York Times,* October 3, 2005.
[22]*Wall Street Journal,* February 25, 2004.
[23]IRS Form 8271, Rev. July 1998.
[24]*Wall Street Journal,* November 17, 2003.
[25]*Wall Street Journal,* November 17, 2003.

[26]*Wall Street Journal,* November 17, 2003.
[27]*Wall Street Journal,* April 2, 2004.

The KPMG tax shelters often involved bank loans to the clients to finance the transactions. Three banks in particular, UBS, Deutsche Bank AG, and HVB Group, provided loans to clients. The loans made were typically paper transactions with funds never leaving the bank.

In marketing the tax shelters KPMG issued letters of opinion stating that the transactions were legitimate and that clients were making the transactions for investment purposes or to diversify their portfolios. Jeffrey Eischeid, partner in charge of the Personal Financial Planning division, explained, "KPMG provided our clients with a 'more likely not' opinion as to their tax consequences. In other words, we informed our clients that based on the facts and actions they took, they would have a more likely than not or a greater than 50 percent chance of prevailing if the IRS challenged the transaction."[28] Opinion letters also stated that the loans had in-

vestment purposes and that clients had legitimate reasons for terminating the transactions. KPMG was advised by the outside law firm Brown & Wood.[29] KPMG tax officials decided to use client-lawyer privilege by routinely copying lawyers on memoranda and e-mail messages. Because of this practice KPMG had not registered the transactions with the IRS as tax shelters. A KPMG partner said referring to BLIPS, "My own recommendation is that we should be paid a lot of money here for our opinion since the transaction is clearly one that the IRS would view as falling squarely within the tax shelter orbit."[30] BLIPS were sold to at least 186 clients and were discontinued in 2000 when the IRS declared it as potentially abusive. ■

SOURCE: This case was prepared from public sources by David P. Baron. Copyright © 2006 by David P. Baron. Reprinted with permission.

Preparation Questions

1. Is there economic substance in the KPMG tax shelters? That is, from the perspective of utilitarianism, do the KPMG tax shelters increase, decrease, or leave unaffected aggregate well-being?
2. How strong were the incentives for KPMG to market tax shelters?
3. Financial services firms can easily stay years ahead of the IRS in innovative tax shelters. Should they clear their shelters in advance with the IRS? What level of certitude should a firm have before it markets a tax shelter? Was Ritchie's analysis sufficient?
4. What should KPMG tell its clients about any risks associated with the tax shelters it offered? Should

KPMG issue letters of opinion to its clients about the validity of the tax shelters?
5. If the four tax solutions are legal and produce allowable deductions, should KPMG market the shelters?
6. Should KPMG register the tax shelters with the IRS? Is this primarily a matter of a quantifiable risk?
7. Might KPMG or its partners be subject to criminal charges for tax evasion, aiding and abetting tax evasion, or obstruction of justice?
8. Should banks participate in the shelters? Are their loans shams?

---

[28]Testimony of Jeffrey Eischeid, Senate Permanent Subcommittee on Investigations, November 2003.

[29]Brown & Wood subsequently merged with Sidley Austin to form Sidley Austin Brown & Wood.
[30]*Wall Street Journal*, February 25, 2005.

Pfizer and Celebrex

On September 30, 2004, Merck withdrew from the market its Cox-2 inhibitor Vioxx because a clinical trial had found an increased risk of cardiac events such as strokes and heart attacks among patients taking the drug for over 18 months.[31] Commentators speculated that there could be problems with the entire class of Cox-2 inhibitors. Pfizer's Celebrex had become the best selling Cox-2 inhibitor with 21 million prescriptions written in 2003 and 2004, and sales were expected to reach $3.3 billion a year. The chemical formula for Celebrex was different from that of Vioxx, and none of the many studies

of Celebrex had shown evidence of increased risk of cardiac events. Pfizer began a brief advertising campaign telling the public and doctors that Celebrex was safe and was not associated with an increased risk of cardiac events. Pfizer considered beginning a clinical study to demonstrate that Celebrex did not cause adverse heart conditions and might even have beneficial effects.

Celebrex was discovered by Monsanto's Searle division, which was subsequently acquired by Pharmacia. In 2003 Pfizer acquired Pharmacia for $60 billion, in part because of Celebrex. Pfizer became the world's largest and most profitable pharmaceutical company. Celebrex's primary indication was for treating pain in patients subject to stomach bleeding, who could not

---

[31]See the chapter 5 case, *Merck and Vioxx,* for information on Cox-2 inhibitors and the withdrawal.

take over-the-counter pain relievers such as aspirin and ibuprofen. Celebrex, however, had been marketed with heavy direct-to-consumer advertising as a more general pain reliever with an emphasis on arthritis pain. Pfizer spent $71 million on Celebrex ads during the first 9 months of 2004. Ads featuring figure skating champion Dorothy Hamill and other middle-aged people were common on television. The purpose of the ads was to have patients ask their doctors for the drug by brand name, and the results confirmed the strategy.

Approximately 40 studies sponsored by the National Institutes of Health (NIH) were under way, ex-

ploring other applications for Celebrex. For example, a 5-year study on 2,000 patients was being conducted by the National Cancer Institute (NCI) to determine if high doses of Celebrex could prevent colon polyps and colorectal cancer. Three groups of clinical trial patients were given a placebo, 400 milligrams, and 800 milligrams of Celebrex. An earlier Pfizer study of patients taking 400 milligrams had shown no increase in cardiac events. The European Union had approved Pfizer's Cox-2 inhibitor Onsenal for treating intestinal polyps, and Pfizer planned to begin marketing the drug early in 2005. Onsenal used the same active ingredient celecoxib as Celebrex but was more potent. ■

Preparation Questions

1. Should Pfizer review the clinical studies in progress to determine if there is any new evidence on cardiac events?
2. Should Pfizer stop its direct-to-consumer advertising of Celebrex?

3. Should Pfizer withdraw Celebrex from the market as a precautionary measure?

The National Cancer Institute Study

As a result of the Vioxx withdrawal, the researchers conducting the cancer study for the NCI began a review of the patient trials in October. After 6 weeks of investigation the researchers had identified six patients with cardiac events in the placebo group, 15 in the 400 milligram group, and 20 in the 800 milligram group. The researchers presented their findings to a safety review panel of cardiologists on December 10. After reviewing the data, the panel was concerned. The NCI then informed the Food and Drug Administration (FDA), NIH, and Pfizer. The NIH notified the researchers conducting the other studies. The panel recommended that the NCI study be halted, and researchers did so. Pfizer learned of the results on Thursday, December 16, in a call from the NCI, and Pfizer CEO Henry McKinnell was called at his home at 7:00 P.M.

that evening. McKinnell immediately arranged a conference call with Pfizer's regulatory team for 8:00 P.M.[32] After the Vioxx withdrawal Pfizer had continued to market Celebrex to consumers and doctors. McKinnell had to decide what to do with Celebrex and how to present its decision to the FDA and the public. McKinnell and Pfizer had some experience with such issues. Shortly after it was marketed, patients taking both Viagra and angina medications reported cardiac events, including heart attacks.

Trial lawyers had scheduled a meeting for March 17 and 18, 2005, to plan their strategy for Vioxx, and Celebrex would certainly be added to their agenda. ■

Preparation Questions

1. Should Pfizer stop its direct-to-consumer advertising of Celebrex?
2. Should Pfizer stop its marketing of Celebrex to doctors?
3. Should Pfizer withdraw Celebrex from the market?
4. What should Pfizer be prepared to do when it informs the FDA of its decision?

5. How should Pfizer present its decision to patients, doctors, and the public?

[32]*Wall Street Journal,* December 20, 2004.

21

Ethics Systems: Rights and Justice

INTRODUCTION

Consequentialist ethics systems such as utilitarianism focus on the good and evaluate the good in terms of individuals' preferences for consequences. Rights established under a consequentialist system are instrumental, since their justification is in terms of the consequences they yield. Some moral philosophies hold instead that there are certain rights and liberties justified by considerations independent of their consequences. Basic liberties such as freedom of speech and rights such as equal opportunity are fundamental concepts that express considerations of freedom, autonomy, and basic equality. Other moral philosophies emphasize justice, which requires comparisons of the situations of individuals. For example, in the redlining example in Chapter 20, concerns were raised about the violation of a right to opportunity and an injustice to individuals who happened to live in a redlined area. This chapter considers ethics systems that emphasize considerations of rights and justice.

The following two sections consider classes of ethics systems and classes of rights, respectively. The following section introduces and critiques Kant's system of moral rules, which establishes intrinsic rights. An approach to rights analysis and to resolving conflicts among claimed rights is presented. An alternative—neoclassical liberalism— to Kant's system is then considered. Categories of justice theories are introduced with a focus on compensatory and distributive justice. Rawls's system of justice as fairness is presented, and his principles of justice are evaluated. The role of incentives in his system is identified and contrasted with utilitarianism and egalitarianism. The assignment of duty and the application of the justice principles are then considered. The chapter concludes with higher order principles used to evaluate ethics systems.

CLASSIFICATION OF ETHICS SYSTEMS

Ethics systems are classified as *teleological or deontological*. Teleological, or consequentialist, systems define the rightness of an action in terms of the good its consequences yield. Deontological ethics systems hold that moral right takes precedence over the good and can be evaluated by considerations independent of, or in addition to, consequences.[1] From a deontological perspective, the objective is to deduce from fundamental axioms a set of principles that have moral standing and then to identify rights and rules of behavior that correspond to those principles. Those rights and rules of behavior are intrinsic; that is, they are important in and of themselves. The principal deontological system considered here is Kant's theory of moral rules. Rawls's theory of justice brings together elements of deontological and consequentialist theories and prioritizes them.

---

[1]The root of deontology is *deon,* which means obligatory, to bind.

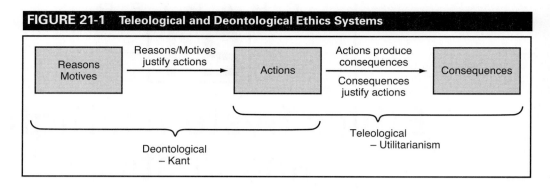

FIGURE 21-1 Teleological and Deontological Ethics Systems

As illustrated in Figure 21-1, both teleological and deontological systems are ultimately concerned with the evaluation of actions. Teleological systems approach this task by examining the relationship between actions and consequences. Deontological systems approach this task by examining the relationship between actions and the reasons or motives for taking those actions. In a teleological system, consequences are evaluated in terms of a value theory that is a part of the particular system. Utilitarianism, for example, uses a value theory based on individual preferences and their aggregation.

In deontological systems, the motive or reason for taking an action, or abiding by a principle, is required to have moral standing. A principle, for example, could be "respect each person's liberty by treating each person as he or she has freely consented to be treated." The reason to abide by the principle then is that individuals are willing to have everyone abide by it and are willing to have the principle applied to themselves.

Teleological and deontological systems are sufficiently different in their nature and structure that they do not necessarily yield the same evaluations of actions. Because no ethics system is immune to criticism, the objective here is not to decide which system is the most appropriate but instead to understand the guidance that each provides.

CLASSES OF RIGHTS

Rights may be derived from moral principles or may be established through political choice. Rights established by political choice often reflect moral principles. The U.S. Constitution identifies individual liberties, such as the freedom of speech, and rights of political participation. Rights are also established through legislation, such as the Civil Rights Act of 1964, which prohibits discrimination on the basis of race, color, religion, sex, or national origin. Legislation has also established entitlements, such as the right of the poor to receive medical care under Medicaid. Rights are also established by private agreements, such as contracts, that specify mutual obligations and expectations that are enforceable by the courts. Rights may also be established by implicit contracts such as those associated with the employment policies and practices of a firm.

Rights are often categorized as negative or positive. Reflecting the intellectual tradition at the time it was written, the U.S. Constitution primarily establishes negative rights that impose duties on people and the state not to interfere with the actions of a person. Freedom of speech and assembly are negative rights because they prohibit others from interfering with those activities. A property right is a negative right because others are prohibited from compelling the holder to take an action with respect to that property. In contrast, positive rights impose affirmative duties on others to take particular actions. For example, a person has a positive right to some level of public education, and that right imposes duties on others to pay the corresponding taxes. Some individuals argue that people should have positive "economic rights" to food, housing, and medical care. Others believe that positive rights such as economic rights have lower standing than negative rights because positive rights impose duties that necessarily limit the liberty and autonomy of others.

An important difference between rights established by the state and those based on moral principles is that the former can be publicly enforced, whereas for moral rights there is no enforcement mechanism other than individual sanction. Rights granted by the state or by private agreements are generally specific; if ambiguity exists, an authoritative body such as a court clarifies the right. As considered in Chapter 12, for example, the common law has established precedents for determining remedies for the breach of contracts.

Rights and entitlements evolve over time as a consequence of demographic change, changes in preferences, and technological developments. Rights may also evolve because of changing perceptions about the appropriate extent of liberties, the scope of justice, or the relative importance of various rights. Rights also evolve as a consequence of interest group pressures acting through the institutions of government and public sentiment.

The evolution of the rights of university students provides an example. In the 1960s many universities followed the principle of in loco parentis, under which the distribution of rights between the university and the student was analogous to that between a parent and a child. The distribution of rights has evolved to the point at which enrollment now carries with it a well-defined set of rights and access to quasi-judicial mechanisms intended to ensure fair treatment.

Rent control is an example of a right resulting from the collective action of interest groups. Rent control, such as on apartments, is a means of redistributing wealth from landlords to renters. If apartment renters have sufficient political power, they may be able to institute rent control as a means of benefiting themselves at the expense of landlords. Rent control on apartments also affects those people who would like to rent, since rent control decreases the incentives to build apartments and spurs the conversion of apartments to condominiums.

KANTIAN MAXIMS OR MORAL RULES

For Kant (1785, 1797) freedom and rationality are the foundations of a theory of morality. The expression of freedom is found in the concept of individual autonomy, and the requirement of rationality is found in the relationship between free will and maxims that govern actions. These maxims, or rules, are derived independently of their consequences by reasoning about the implications of freedom of the will. That is, maxims are evaluated based on the reasons or motives for them. The resulting maxims are thus impartial and universal—a person is to will universal rules. The purpose of the maxims is to allow individuals to judge their actions, and the actions of others, from the point of view of those maxims. As indicated in Figure 21-1, Kant's system is based on the motive, or mental disposition, and the reason for the action. Kant thus emphasizes the "right" over the "good."

Kant argued that because individuals are rational and each deduces maxims from a conception of freedom and autonomy that resides in everyone, all individuals will deduce the same maxims; that is, there will be unanimity. Reasoning in Kant's system is to be based on a fundamental axiom known as the *categorical imperative*.[2] The categorical imperative serves two basic functions. First, it provides a basis for determining maxims and moral rules. Second, it prescribes that individuals are to act in accord with those rules. Kant provides several formulations of the categorical imperative, but they basically hold that individuals are to be treated as autonomous beings, as ends rather than solely as means, and are to act based on a reason that each would will to be universal. Kant's basic formulation of the categorical imperative is:[3]

Act according to the maxim that you would will to be a universal rule.

According to Kant (1785, p. 39), "All rational beings stand under the law that each of them should treat himself and all others never merely as means but always at the

---

[2]The term *categorical* means that the imperative is not conditioned on any purpose other than the imperative itself. Kant (1785, p. 26) wrote, "It is not concerned with the matter of the action and its intended result, but rather with the form of the action and the principle from which it follows: what is essentially good in the action consists in the mental disposition, let the consequences be what they may."
[3]This formulation applies to a broad class of maxims including some that could be contemplated but never acted on, so the categorical imperative is sharpened to pertain to rules that could be acted on. That is, the maxims must have meaning.

EXAMPLE

Living Benefits

The Chapter 20 example "Living Benefits" focuses on the issue of whether it is right for companies to make viatical settlements; that is, to buy the life insurance policies of terminally ill policyholders at a substantial discount from the face value of the policy. The magnitude of the discount depends on the estimated life expectancy of the individual, the risk the company bears in holding the policy, the premiums it must pay to keep the policy in force, and the competitiveness of the market for such policies. To assess whether such a practice is moral from a rights perspective, consider the maxim, "People may make viatical settlements." The categorical imperative asks whether this maxim treats people as autonomous ends and never solely as means. The policyholders are treated as a means to a profit for the companies that buy the policies, but the policyholders also act autonomously in the sense that they can choose whether to sell their policies. That they have a free choice between holding and selling their policies means that they are treated as autonomous ends. As long as their capacity to choose is not impaired, living benefits satisfy this formulation of the categorical imperative.

The other formulation of the categorical imperative is whether one would will the maxim to be a universal rule. Since all individuals reason rationally from the same conception of freedom and autonomy, Kant would conclude that they would will it to be universal. This means that individuals do not consider their own personal circumstances and instead only the implications of freedom and autonomy.

---

same time as an end in himself." Morality for Kant then is the condition in which each individual can be an end, and ethics "is conceived as the law of one's own will. . . ." (1797, p. 47). This yields a second formulation of the categorical imperative:

Treat individuals always as autonomous ends, and so never solely as means.

This does not mean that a person cannot be treated as a means, for example, a means of production, but that person is also to be treated as an end with autonomy. An employee can thus be required to meet the standards for a particular job but has the right to quit or attempt to qualify for a better job.

The strength of Kant's conception of morality is that it focuses on motives or reasons for acting that are universal—apply to everyone—and thus are reversible—apply to oneself. The categorical imperative thus embodies two standards for the evaluation of maxims—*universalizability* and *reversibility*. Universalizability may be thought of as "Would I want everyone to behave according to that rule?" Reversibility may be thought of as "Would I want that rule applied to me?"[4] For example, if the rule under evaluation is "Discrimination based on height is not allowed," reversibility requires that I do not discriminate based on height. Universalizability requires that I would will a society in which no one discriminates on the basis of height. The third standard for evaluating a candidate for status as a maxim or moral rule is, "Does it treat people always as ends and never solely as means, respecting their autonomy?"

The Relationship between Maxims and Rights

Kant's system is expressed in terms of maxims, which individuals have a moral duty to respect. That duty establishes moral rights. Those moral rights are intrinsic, since they are derived from the categorical imperative and not from other considerations such as consequences. To illustrate the relationship between maxims, rights, and duties, consider the maxim, "A firm must sell its product to anyone who wants it, regardless of the price they are willing to pay."[5] This maxim violates the categorical imperative of treating individuals as autonomous ends, since the owners of the firm would be treated as means when forced to sell the product regardless of whether they wanted to do so.

---

[4]Reversibility is implied by universalizability, but it is useful to state it separately as a reminder.
[5]This example was suggested by Daniel Diermeier.

Consider next the maxim, "A firm must sell its product to anyone who is willing to pay the price set by the firm." This maxim satisfies the categorical imperative of treating everyone as autonomous and as ends. Hence, it is a moral rule. This rule then has implications for rights and duties. First, it establishes property rights as moral rights. Second, it establishes the right of the firm to set the price for its product. Third, it does not allow the firm to distinguish, or discriminate, among buyers based on any considerations other than their willingness to pay the price set by the firm. This establishes a right not to be discriminated against and a corresponding duty not to discriminate on irrelevant considerations in making sales.

Consider another maxim, "A firm must sell its product to anyone who is willing to pay the cost of producing it." This rule violates the categorical imperative by not treating the owners of the firm as autonomous ends, since they are compelled to sell at a particular price. The regulation of a natural monopoly by setting price equal to average cost thus would not be permitted in a Kantian system unless the owners of the firm were compensated sufficiently so that they would freely choose to sell at that price.

Rights consistent with Kant's system include the freedoms of speech and conscience, since otherwise a person would not be autonomous. Rights also include political equality and the right to vote. Kantian rights require the opportunity to exercise individual autonomy, which includes the right not to be discriminated against on dimensions irrelevant to those opportunities. The categorical imperative draws a line between a right to opportunity without discrimination and the claim that individuals should be provided with the means to pursue opportunity and hence that others have a duty to provide those means. That claim may treat the recipients as ends and respect their autonomy and freedom, but it does not so treat those who have the duty, since it uses them solely as means for serving others. Consequently, economic rights, such as rights to food or housing, are not consistent with Kant's ethics system. From this perspective, claims about economic rights are statements about political goals rather than moral rights.

There are thus few rather than many rights that follow from Kant's system. For example, Kant's system allows the voluntary provision of economic goods to individuals but does not compel anyone to provide those goods. In contrast, Rawls's system of justice, as considered later in the chapter, requires the fair equality of opportunity, which requires that individuals have the means to realize opportunities.

As an example of Kant's framework, consider the nature of the relationship between an employer and an employee. In the 19th century, the employment relationship was governed by the "at-will" legal doctrine derived from the theory of free contract under which either party was free to terminate the relationship whenever it chose. The Kantian right to be treated as an end rather than solely as a means suggests that even though both human beings and machines are factors of production, human beings differ from machines in that they are also to be treated as ends. The employer's right to free contract and to dismiss an employee at will thus may be limited by an employee's right to be discharged only for cause. The maxim thus is, "An employer may dismiss an employee based only on considerations relevant to his or her performance on the job." A corresponding duty is associated with any right, and in this case the duty is assigned to the employer. An employer thus cannot dismiss an employee for her political views but can dismiss a disabled employee who can no longer work.[6] What constitutes "relevant to his or her performance," however, remains a matter of disagreement; particularly as it pertains to issues such as the testing of employees, as in the chapter case *Genetic Testing in the Workplace.*[7]

Intrinsic and Instrumental Rights

Rights can be instrumental or intrinsic. Instrumental rights are to be respected because they contribute to achieving better consequences, by, for example, enabling individuals to pursue their interests. The right of free contract, that is, to enter into contracts, is intrinsic, but specific contract provisions are instrumental because they exist to facilitate mutually beneficial economic consequences by ensuring payment and the delivery of goods and

---

[6]See the discussion in Chapter 20.
[7]Kupfer (1993) provides an ethics analysis of genetic testing.

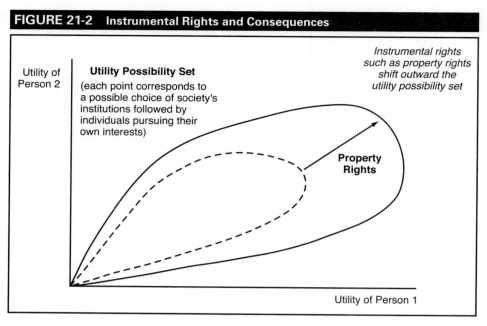

FIGURE 21-2   Instrumental Rights and Consequences

Utility of Person 2

Utility Possibility Set
(each point corresponds to
a possible choice of society's
institutions followed by
individuals pursuing their
own interests)

*Instrumental rights
such as property rights
shift outward the
utility possibility set*

**Property
Rights**

Utility of Person 1

services. Claims that individuals have economic rights to housing or food are claims about instrumental rights intended to improve their well-being.

Intrinsic rights are to be respected in and of themselves and do not require any justification in terms of consequences. Intrinsic rights are derived from fundamental moral concepts such as autonomy and liberty, as in Kant's system. Examples of intrinsic rights are freedom of speech, equal protection including equal opportunity, and certain aspects of privacy. Some rights, such as the right to contract, are intrinsic when viewed from the perspective of autonomy and liberty and instrumental when viewed in terms of the consequences they yield. These rights may be stated in constitutions and laws, but intrinsic rights are to be respected independently of formal institutions. Intrinsic rights are frequently negative rights in the sense that respecting autonomy precludes others from infringing that autonomy. Many claims are made about the extent and scope of intrinsic rights, and formal institutions are often relied on to resolve conflicting claims. The extent of a right to privacy in the employment relationship, for example, remains a subject of competing claims as indicated in the example.

To illustrate the distinction between instrumental and intrinsic rights, consider a consequentialist example presented in Figure 21-2 and Figure 21-3. These figures

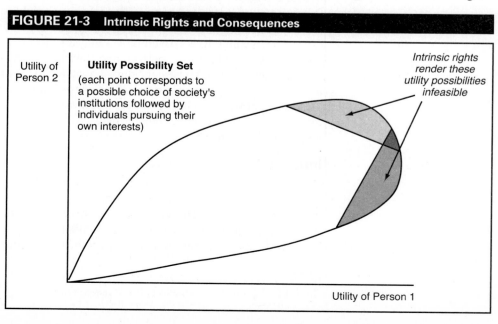

FIGURE 21-3   Intrinsic Rights and Consequences

Utility of Person 2

Utility Possibility Set
(each point corresponds to
a possible choice of society's
institutions followed by
individuals pursuing their
own interests)

*Intrinsic rights
render these
utility possibilities
infeasible*

Utility of Person 1

depict the possible combinations of utility, or well-being, for two individuals, 1 and 2, as a function of the activities in which they may engage, given society's institutions. That is, each point in the oblong shapes—the utility possibility sets—corresponds to the utilities the two individuals could attain if they acted to pursue their own interests, given the opportunities and incentives provided by a particular configuration of institutions. The institutions might correspond to various assignments of rights, the tax and transfer payment systems, the laws of torts and contracts, and public education. A point in the figure reflects the incentives provided by those particular institutions, so if the tax system dampens incentives for capital formation, aggregate output and the utility of both individuals could be lower than if stronger incentives were provided.

Instrumental rights affect the shape and size of the utility possibility set. For example, the dotted line might correspond to the set of institutions in communist countries such as the former Soviet Union and the nations of Eastern Europe under its control. The economies of those countries failed because the institutions of centralized state planning resulted in both insufficient capital formation and weak incentives for effort. As an instrumental right, a property right in which individuals keep the fruits of their labor provides stronger incentives for effort and capital formation and expands the utility possibility set, as illustrated in Figure 21-2. The privatization of companies in the former communist nations and in many other countries is one manifestation of this.

Intrinsic rights impose duties on individuals to respect those rights. Viewed from a Kantian perspective, property rights allow individuals to act as autonomous ends, and hence they have moral standing as intrinsic rights. In the context of Figure 21-2, the duty to respect those rights prevents moving from the larger to the smaller utility possibility set. Similarly, an intrinsic right to equal opportunity can expand the utility possibility set. An intrinsic right to equal opportunity, however, is not established in the Kantian system with reference to its effect on consequences but instead is established from the categorical imperative and the requirement of treating each person as autonomous with the opportunity to choose.

Other intrinsic rights may restrict the utility possibility set as illustrated in Figure 21-3. The claimed intrinsic right to privacy may limit the possible levels of utility attainable in a society. That is, intrinsic rights can constrain the set of available alternatives, and from a consequentialist perspective this can make at least some, and perhaps all, individuals worse off in terms of consequences. A right to privacy, for example, could be argued to prohibit genetic testing in the workplace, making it more difficult to move genetically susceptible individuals away from possible exposure to harmful chemicals.

The set of intrinsic rights established by Kant's ethics system is small and generally corresponds to negative rights that allow individuals to act as autonomous ends. The set of instrumental rights that enable people to pursue their interests is larger and may treat people solely as means with respect to an instrumental right. The right to some basic level of public education is one such right, and taxpayers are treated as a means. The set of rights established through political processes is larger still. That set includes measures such as rent control and the right to file an antidumping petition against imported goods. A right to file an international trade complaint is instrumental and is established by political authority.

Criticisms of Kantian Rights

The criticisms of Kant's ethics system include both those that pertain to deontological systems in general and those specific to his system. The fundamental criticism of deontological systems is that they fail to explain why a principle or right should be respected. When one attempts to do so, one is often led to justifying it in terms of the extent to which it protects or promotes human interests. For example, why is treating individuals as ends important if it is not to give them the opportunity to pursue their interests? Thus, critics contend that consequences rather than motives actually underlie the moral standing of these principles.

More specific criticisms of rights-based ethics systems are that they may not (1) identify sufficiently precisely where the corresponding duty lies, (2) indicate priority when one right conflicts with another, and (3) indicate when—if ever—it would be acceptable

---

EXAMPLE

Privacy

Privacy is important, but it remains controversial. In the employment relationship, for example, privacy pertains to issues such as whether employers can inspect the contents of an employee's locker, whether workplace surveillance of employees is permitted, whether supervisors can listen in on telephone order takers to determine how they handle customer calls, and whether employees can be tested for substance abuse.

A right to privacy is said to arise both from moral standards and from legal guarantees. In the Kantian framework an intrinsic right to privacy can be viewed as arising from the notion of freedom and autonomy. Freedom of conscience is restricted when privacy is violated. In this sense people are said to have a sphere in which their thoughts can remain private. The question is the extent to which this personal sphere extends beyond thoughts to behavior.

The notion of autonomy pertains to the size of the sphere, since a person can choose to allow others access to information about himself or herself. For example, in an employment relationship management generally has the right to supervise and monitor an employee's performance. This right can extend beyond actual performance to factors that could affect that performance. For example, many employers require drug tests of their employees, even though such tests primarily provide information about conduct outside the employment relationship. By accepting a job for which drug testing is required, individuals voluntarily sacrifice some of their personal sphere. Individuals thus can contract away some of their personal sphere. In that sense a right to privacy cannot be as important as inalienable rights such as speech and assembly. The intrinsic right in this example is a right not to be forced to accept or work in a job against one's will.

With regard to legal rights the U.S. Constitution does not mention privacy. The Fourth Amendment establishes a right "to be secure in their persons, houses, papers, and efforts, against searches and seizures . . ." but that right is generally held to apply to searches and seizures by government. Thus, in the private sector there is no constitutional prohibition against drug testing, but in the public sector in which government is an employer, employees have a right not to submit to drug tests unless they are in sensitive positions or are involved with public safety. The Supreme Court has concluded that other rights explicitly established by the Constitution imply that there is a right of privacy in a personal sphere.[1]

The extent of a right to privacy, or the size of the personal sphere, is difficult to identify. One has a right to the privacy of one's body and mind, but as the cases of drug tests and integrity tests indicate, that right can be limited in an employment relationship. One has a right to the privacy of certain behavior, but surveillance is not generally prohibited. One also has privacy rights with respect to information about one's self, but many parties, such as doctors, employers, governments, and others, have records of that personal information. As mentioned in Chapter 13 over 40 percent of the Internet users surveyed said they would exchange their personal data, such as name, address, and contact information, for a $100 gift certificate. The Chapter 13 case, *DoubleClick and Internet Privacy,* and the Chapter 15 case, *The European Union Data Protection Directive,* deal with the issue of data generated through Internet transactions and browsing. The chapter case, *Genetic Testing in the Workplace,* concerns another privacy issue.

---
[1]See *Griswold v. Connecticut,* 381 U.S. 479 (1965).

---

to violate a right. With respect to the first criticism, every right is accompanied by an associated duty, but who is to bear the burden of that duty is not always clear. Some negative rights, such as the right of free speech, impose a duty on everyone not to interfere with that speech. In the case of a claimed positive right, such as a right to medical care, however, the duty may fall on the individual, family, employer, or government. In such situations, legislation is often required to clarify where the duty lies. Legislation, however, reflects interests, and hence preferences and consequences.

A second criticism is that Kant's system does not clearly indicate whether or when one right has priority over another. The categorical imperative requires that individuals be treated as autonomous and so always as an end and never solely as a means. Kant's view was that there would be no conflict among the rights consistent with the categorical imperative. When a person, however, attempts to articulate the set of intrinsic rights, conflicts frequently appear. In such a case, Kant would argue that the person should reexamine those rights from the perspective of the categorical imperative, eliminating those inconsistent with it. In practice, this is difficult, and an approach to prioritizing rights, as presented in the later section "Conflicts Among Rights," is needed.

A third criticism centers on whether there are any circumstances in which it would be acceptable to violate a maxim or right. For example, if rights are in conflict, it may be necessary to violate one to respect another. A violation of a right for whatever reason is a moral wrong, but the seriousness of the violation must be considered. In the language of justice theory, the issue is when it is acceptable to violate one right to avoid a violation of a more important right. For example, paternalism is a wrong, but there may be circumstances, as considered in Chapter 22, in which it may be acceptable to take an action to benefit a person even though that action violates the person's autonomy.

In spite of these criticisms, individual rights are a fundamental component of our ethical intuition. Rights are embedded in constitutions, statutes, and moral understandings. The duties corresponding to legal and moral rights provide fundamental constraints on the actions of managers and on the policies of firms.

The practical difficulties with the application of rights-based ethics systems pertain to the evaluation of claims about rights, the priority of various rights, and the relationship between rights and other concerns such as well-being and justice. The next section addresses these issues in the context of applied rights analysis.

APPLIED RIGHTS ANALYSIS

In managerial decision making, rights have two effects. First, as illustrated in Figure 21-3, they rule out certain alternatives, such as those that would violate moral principles or constitutionally protected rights. Second, a right may impose an affirmative duty that requires a firm to take particular actions. The equal employment opportunity laws prohibit discrimination, whereas affirmative action regulations impose affirmative duties on employers to address the effects of past discrimination. The second effect is addressed later in the chapter in the context of equal employment opportunity, affirmative action, and the Americans with Disabilities Act. The focus here is on rights that rule out alternatives.

Claimed and Granted Rights

A granted right is established by moral consensus or by government and is accompanied by a clear assignment of the corresponding duty. If the duty has not been clearly assigned, moral consensus is absent, or government has not spoken, the right in question is said to be claimed. Individuals claim rights and make demands on others by asserting moral justifications, but others may view those claims as morally unjustified.

To illustrate the distinction between claims and grants and their moral standing, consider the issue of foods containing genetically modified organisms (GMO). A claim that a person has a right to ban imports of GMO foods neither has moral status nor is granted by government. A claim that a person has a right to have GMO food labeled as such may have moral standing because it enables persons to exercise their autonomy in their choice of foods. This right is not granted in the United States but is in the European Union. Even if there were moral consensus that GMO foods should be labeled, government need not play a role. Some grocers have policies of selling GMO-free foods, and some food manufacturers supply such products. A person then exercises autonomy by choosing where to shop.

Although it has no moral standing, people have a granted right through government to ban imports of GMO foods and to bear the sanctions authorized by the World Trade Organization (WTO), as in the case of the European Union as considered in Chapter 18. People have a granted right (in the United States a constitutional right to petition government) to lobby government to change WTO rules to require labeling or even the separation of GMO foods. The right to petition has moral standing as a form of free speech and as representation by people acting as autonomous ends.

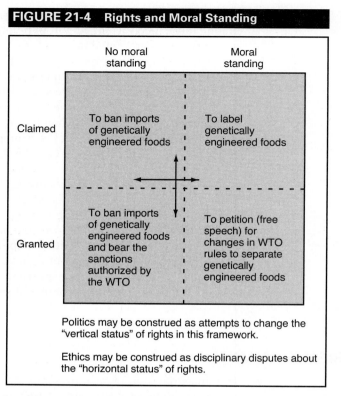

FIGURE 21-4   Rights and Moral Standing

	No moral standing	Moral standing
Claimed	To ban imports of genetically engineered foods	To label genetically engineered foods
Granted	To ban imports of genetically engineered foods and bear the sanctions authorized by the WTO	To petition (free speech) for changes in WTO rules to separate genetically engineered foods

Politics may be construed as attempts to change the "vertical status" of rights in this framework.

Ethics may be construed as disciplinary disputes about the "horizontal status" of rights.

Private and public policy regarding GMO foods involves both ethics and politics, as illustrated in Figure 21-4. Ethics pertains to the moral standing of claims. Politics involves efforts to turn claimed rights into granted rights.

To address nonmarket issues where rights are claimed, managers must evaluate contesting arguments. To illustrate the evaluation of a claimed right, consider the claim that the poor have, or should have, entitlements different from those of other people. In *Kadrmas v. Dickinson Public Schools,* 487 U.S. 450 (1988), the Supreme Court affirmed its 1973 ruling that the equal protection clause of the Constitution does not give special protection due to income. Plaintiff Kadrmas challenged a North Dakota law that allowed school districts to charge a fee for school bus service. The Dickinson School provided bus service for rural students, picking them up at their doors, but charged them $97 per year for the service. The Kadrmases' income was close to the "officially defined poverty level," and Kadrmas refused to pay the fee. The school bus then no longer stopped for Sarita Kadrmas. Since the Kadrmases lived 16 miles from the school, they had to incur an additional expense for Sarita's transportation. They sued, and the case reached the Supreme Court. For the majority in a 5-to-4 decision, Justice Sandra Day O'Connor wrote,

> The Constitution does not require that such [school bus] service be provided at all, and it is difficult to imagine why choosing to offer the service should entail a constitutional obligation to offer it for free .... We have previously rejected the suggestion that statutes having different effects on the wealthy and the poor should on that account alone be subjected to strict equal protection .... Nor have we accepted the proposition that education is a "fundamental right," like equality of the franchise, which should trigger strict government scrutiny when government interferes with an individual's access to it.[8]

The majority's opinion thus distinguishes the constitutional grant of equal protection under the law from the claim that because of income individuals should be relieved of certain economic burdens. Equal protection is a right consistent with the

[8]*United States Law Week,* (56), 6-21-88, 4777-4783, p. 4780.

EXAMPLE

Life Insurance Screening for Preexisting Conditions

The reasoning in the *Kadrmas* decision suggests that individuals have no granted right to life insurance nor to purchase insurance at a particular price. Insurance companies thus need not provide insurance to everyone or anyone. When individual life insurance is offered, however, screening for preexisting conditions is claimed to be discriminatory and an invasion of privacy. In most jurisdictions, an insurance company has a granted right to screen for preexisting conditions and to deny or at least limit coverage.[1] That right can be withdrawn or limited through politics and government action, but in the absence of restrictions most insurance companies screen for preexisting conditions based on utilitarian considerations as consid-

ered in Chapter 20. Claims about privacy and discrimination, however, warrant examination because if they have moral standing in this situation, legal and moral rights would be in conflict. Conflicts among rights are considered in the following section.

---

[1]The grant may extend considerably beyond screening. In 1990 a federal district court judge dismissed a lawsuit filed by an employee with AIDS who had charged that it was illegal for a firm that self-insured to limit medical coverage for AIDS. The judge held that the firm had complied with the requirements of the Employee Retirement Income Security Act (ERISA) by notifying employees that its medical plan could be revised on an annual basis. The Court of Appeals rejected the plaintiff's appeal, and in 1992 the Supreme Court let that decision stand.

Kantian system, whereas education and the economic right to free bus service are not. Managers must make similar judgments about claimed rights, and a method for the analysis of claims about rights is presented next.

A Methodology for Rights Analysis

Rights analysis has two principal components. The first is determining whether a claimed right has moral standing. The second is determining how conflicts among rights are to be resolved. The methodology of rights analysis is as follows:

1. Identify the rights claimed and their claimed moral bases.
2. Determine which claimed rights satisfy moral standards; for example, Kantian standards or a utilitarian standard that establishes instrumental rights.
3. If a claim is not morally justified, check whether it is established by government. If it is, it is granted and is to be respected. If not, the claim need not be respected.[9]
4. Identify the actions consistent with the protection or promotion of any morally justified rights.
5. Identify conflicts among rights. If there are none, those claimed rights with moral standing are to be respected.
6. If there are conflicts among rights with moral standing, investigate the importance of the interests those rights are intended to protect or promote.
7. Prioritize the rights based on the importance of those interests and determine the extent to which each is constrained by the others.
8. Choose the action that does best in terms of the priorities established.

The above example introduced in Chapter 20 illustrates the first four steps in the methodology.

CONFLICTS AMONG RIGHTS

Kant argued that the intrinsic rights established in accord with the categorical imperative do not conflict. When the set of rights is expanded to include instrumental rights and granted rights established by government through politics, however, rights can be in conflict. Those conflicts may mean that there is no action that respects all rights. This

---

[9]Claims should not be ignored, however, since they may motivate nonmarket action.

section presents an approach to steps 5, 6, and 7 in the applied rights methodology. The approach addresses conflicts by examining the interests the rights are intended to protect or promote and by prioritizing those rights based on the importance of those interests. This approach thus adds considerations of consequences to the evaluation of rights.

Rights and Interests

In the case of moral rights, or rights more generally, one approach to reasoning about, if not resolving, conflicts is to inquire into the importance of the rights by considering the interests they are intended to promote or protect. Rights established by deontological systems are intrinsic, however, and are justified independently of the interests to which they contribute. They thus have high standing. Nevertheless, the approach of inquiring into interests is a practical method for addressing conflicts in managerial applications and is consistent with ethical intuition.

To illustrate the inquiry into the interests a claimed right is intended to promote, in his dissent in *Kadrmas* Justice Thurgood Marshall stated his view of the constitutional basis for a right:

> The statute at issue here burdens a poor person's interest in an education. The extraordinary nature of this interest cannot be denied. By denying equal opportunity to exactly those who need it most, the law not only militates against the ability of each poor child to advance herself, but also increases the likelihood of the creation of a discrete and permanent underclass. Such a statute is difficult to reconcile with the framework of equality embodied in the Equal Protection Clause.
>
> As I have stated on prior occasions, proper analysis of equal protection claims depends . . . upon identifying and carefully analyzing the real interests at stake.[10]

Justice Marshall thus turned to the interests of the individual in attempting to determine the priority of the claimed right to free school bus service. Justice O'Connor, in contrast, focused on whether a right has been granted by the Constitution rather than on the interests affected.

Prioritization

The framework for analyzing conflicts among rights begins with an identification of a right, an assessment of whether it is claimed or granted, and its bases. The possible bases for a right are moral and legal, where the latter includes the Constitution, statutes, and contracts. A granted right is established by the state, by another individual or entity, or by moral consensus and has a clearly assigned duty. A claimed right either does not have a clearly assigned corresponding duty or has been established by neither a grant nor moral consensus.

The first four steps in the methodology presented earlier in the chapter identify rights and their status. Because moral and granted rights can be in conflict in managerial settings, they must be prioritized. Priorities are established by the institutions of society and by moral principles. The Constitution establishes certain priorities. For example, one has a right in one's home to prohibit others from trespassing for commercial purposes. However, one does not have the same right when its exercise denies others the opportunity to exercise their rights of free speech or religion. Consequently, home owners do not have the right to call on the state to prevent people from distributing religious materials on the sidewalk in front of their homes. Constitutional rights also take precedence over legislatively granted rights, particularly because many constitutional rights also have a moral justification. Rights that both are granted and have a moral basis have priority over claims that have a disputed moral basis. Intrinsic rights have priority over instrumental rights. More difficult are cases in which a granted right is in conflict with a claimed right.

To assess priorities in such a case, the interests those rights protect and promote are examined. Those interests may range from the opportunity to pursue one's own

---

[10]*California Reporter*, 829 (1987), p. 4782.

FIGURE 21-5 Applied Rights Analysis: Integrity Tests

			Addressing Conflicts		
Right	*Claimed/ Granted*	*Bases**	*Interests the Right Protects*	*Priority*	*Actions Consistent with the Right*
Privacy	Claimed	Moral	Liberty Human dignity	$2^\dagger, 3^\ddagger$	Limited use of tests
Free from arbitrary treatment	Claimed	Moral	Opportunity to qualify for jobs	1	Test verified; professional interpretation of results
To use test in hiring; (firm)	Granted	Moral/ Legal	Autonomy of employer Economic efficiency	$3^\dagger, 2^\ddagger$	Test where honesty is important to job performance

*moral, legal (constitutional, statutory, common law)
†for jobs where the efficiency interest is not compelling
‡for jobs where the efficiency interest is compelling

well-being to personal privacy, which has a moral basis in the right of conscience in a Kantian framework. The interests identified are intended to be fundamental, as in Justice Marshall's statement about the importance of education to opportunity. Once the interests have been identified, the rights that further those interests are to be assigned priority. At this point individuals may have differing assessments of priorities, but the assignment of priorities is intended to be impartial and based on the importance of the interest and not on the personal preferences of the person conducting the analysis. The final column in Figure 21-5 identifies actions that are consistent with a right.

The result of the analysis may be that there is no action that does not violate some right with legal or moral standing. Prioritization is then based on the seriousness of a violation. Given the assessment of priorities, the managerial task is to determine the extent to which a right should be limited to protect other rights and then to identify the actions that come closest to meeting the priorities. The chapter case, *Genetic Testing in the Workplace,* requires the prioritization of rights.

EXAMPLE

Integrity Tests

Integrity tests are currently legal under federal law and under the laws of at least 49 states, so the focus is on moral claims. The rights claimed are the prospective employees' right to privacy, their right not to be subject to arbitrary treatment as a consequence of an inaccurate test, and the employer's right to choose standards for hiring, as long as those standards do not discriminate on an illegal basis. Since these rights are in conflict, it is necessary to evaluate and prioritize them.

The right to privacy is granted by statute as it pertains to certain types of tests, such as polygraphs, but it is claimed as it pertains to integrity tests. Congress might in the future extend the right of privacy to integrity tests, but it has not yet done so. The right to be free from arbitrary treatment is based on the claim that the tests may misclassify individuals because of

inherent inaccuracies. The firm's right to use the tests in selecting among prospective employees, as long as it does not illegally discriminate, is granted and has both a moral and a legal basis. The moral basis derives from the autonomy of the employer (and employee) and the liberty to enter into contracts. The legal basis follows from property rights. The bases for the rights are indicated in Figure 21-5.

To investigate priorities, the interests the rights are intended to promote or protect must be identified. The claimed right to privacy is intended to promote liberty and protect human dignity. The claimed right to be free from arbitrary treatment protects the opportunity to qualify for jobs and positions. The employer's right to choose standards for hiring is, as an instrumental right, intended to promote economic

(Continued)

efficiency by allowing employers to match prospective employees to jobs.

In addressing the conflicts among these rights, intrinsic rights have priority, because in a deontological system the right takes precedence over the good. The right not to be subjected to arbitrary treatment seems important in this case. In the last column in Figure 21-5, the actions consistent with this right center on ensuring accuracy in testing. In 1991 the American Psychological Association issued a report concluding that "the preponderance of the evidence" indicates that integrity tests can be useful, but it expressed concerns about some of the tests, the claims made for them, and their use in the absence of supervision by a qualified psychologist. Given these concerns, the tests should be carefully evaluated and supervised by trained personnel. Furthermore, because of possible inaccuracies, passing an integrity test should not be a necessary condition for employment but could be one of several factors considered.

With respect to privacy, the fundamental issue is whether it is morally acceptable to base employment and job assignments on psychological considerations. Integrity and other forms of psychological tests are said to invade privacy by asking questions that are too personal and not closely linked to job requirements. Such questions might pertain to lifestyle and off-the-job activities. Privacy can be limited, however, when there is a compelling reason, and individuals can choose whether to accept a position that requires the sacrifice of a degree of privacy. Consequently, the claimed right to privacy can be limited when the employer has an important interest served by the integrity test.

The employer's right to use tests to select employees on nondiscriminatory grounds is intended to respect autonomy and promote the interest of economic efficiency. In a deontological framework, the former right may be limited if otherwise the liberties or rights of individuals would be restricted. Eco-nomic efficiency is clearly an important interest, but the right that promotes it is instrumental. Furthermore, deontological systems can require restrictions on that right to avoid infringing intrinsic rights, as illustrated in Figure 21-3. The actions consistent with this right to test thus might be to use the test depending on how important integrity and loyalty are for a particular position. A position such as security guard, bank teller, or purchasing agent might warrant an integrity test, whereas a custodial position might not.

Although there is ambiguity in the application of rights-based analysis in this case, the freedom from arbitrary treatment seems to have priority. The liberty and human dignity protected by a claimed right to privacy can be protected by not applying for a position for which an integrity test is required. This, however, would mean that opportunities are restricted by the tests. The interest that justifies the employer's use of an integrity test thus must be important to justify compromising the claimed right to privacy. For jobs in which integrity and loyalty are important to job performance, the employer's right to use the tests seems to have priority. For jobs in which integrity and loyalty are not important to job performance, the claimed right to privacy seems to have priority. Consequently, necessary conditions for the use of the tests is that they be reasonably accurate and administered by qualified individuals, that they be limited to jobs for which the tested traits are important to the interests of the firm, and that they be only one of several factors considered in employment decisions.[1] The chapter case, *Genetic Testing in the Workplace,* raises similar considerations about rights and their priorities.

---

[1]Dalton and Metzger (1993) reach a different conclusion based on concerns about the accuracy of the tests.

EQUAL EMPLOYMENT OPPORTUNITY

Equal employment opportunity is a principle supported by virtually all ethics systems. Its importance is supported by legal grants that provide for its public enforcement. Its legal manifestation is Title VII of the Civil Rights Act of 1964, which prohibits discrimination on the basis of "race, color, sex, religion, or national origin." Most states have similar laws applicable to businesses operating within their state.

Concerns about illegal discrimination in the employment relationship now focus less on intentional discrimination and more on employment practices and policies that, while appearing neutral with respect to an identifiable group, have a disparate impact on the members of that group. An employment policy that is neutral with respect to race, for example, has a disparate impact if the proportion of minorities hired is lower than the proportion of whites hired. Employers then must establish that the policy is required by business necessity—a bona fide occupational qualification (BFOQ). The concept of a disparate impact is broad and applies to hiring, promotion, and compensation. More subtly, it may also apply to grooming rules, physical requirements, language requirements, and information about an individual's past, such as an illness, criminal conviction, or past substance abuse. Other laws have applied the same principles to other attributes, including age, disability, and pregnancy.

Title VII is administered by the Equal Employment Opportunity Commission (EEOC), an independent administrative commission with five members appointed by the president. The EEOC can act on its own or in response to a complaint filed by an individual. In addition, the EEOC has rule-making authority over compliance with Title VII and may file suit in federal court if conciliation fails. An individual may also file suit in federal court once the EEOC has attempted to resolve the issue. Because most states have laws similar to Title VII, the EEOC allows state agencies to handle many of the cases.

The remedies available to the EEOC or a court under Title VII include injunctions and mandated changes in practices. A complainant may be awarded reinstatement, promotion, payment of back wages, attorney fees, or other awards. As an example, in 1996 Texaco settled a racial discrimination lawsuit for $176.1 million and agreed to establish an "equality and tolerance task force." Texaco also settled a complaint by the EEOC, allowing it to scrutinize Texaco's hiring and promotion policies for 5 years.

The EEOC has been concerned with discrimination on Wall Street. In 2001 it filed a sex-discrimination lawsuit against Morgan Stanley Dean Witter. Private lawsuits can also be filed. A group of women employees had filed a class action sex-discrimination lawsuit against Merrill Lynch, and a settlement was reached in 1998 in which the company agreed to change its practices and compensate some 900 employees. A small group of women were dissatisfied with the changes and with the pace at which individual settlements were being made. The women decided to take their complaints to the sky. They arranged to have aircraft tow banners reading "Merrill Lynch Discriminates Against Women" at events sponsored by Merrill, including golf tournaments, auto races, and vintage car shows.[11]

In 1993 Shoney's, Inc., agreed to a $105 million settlement in a case alleging discrimination against African Americans. Shoney's also agreed to institute an aggressive affirmative action program with a 10-year goal of 20 to 23 percent African American managers and assistant managers in its 754 company-owned restaurants. The Chapter 22 case, *Denny's and Customer Service,* addresses a discrimination case outside the employment relationship.

An employer has several defenses in a Title VII case. One is that of "business necessity," such as testing individuals for job-relevant skills. A second defense against a disparate impact charge is that of a BFOQ, but the EEOC and courts have interpreted this quite narrowly. A BFOQ defense pertains only to discrimination based on sex, religion, and national origin under Title VII and age under the Age Discrimination in Employment Act of 1967. Racial discrimination is never justified by a BFOQ. Third, seniority systems are not covered by Title VII, so a plaintiff must show intent of discrimination rather than a disparate impact. Seniority systems have been held to be protected against complaints under Title VII that they perpetuate the effects of discrimination.[12]

In addition to Title VII, the Civil Rights Act of 1866, codified as Section 1981 of Title 42 of the United States Code, provides protection against discrimination based on race. Section 1981 states that "all persons . . . have the same right to make and enforce contracts . . . as enjoyed by white persons." Since employment is viewed as a contract, Section 1981 covers the employment relationship. Protection from discrimination applies not only to minorities but to majorities as well. In *McDonald v. Santa Fe Trail Transportation Co.,* 427 U.S. 274 (1976), the Supreme Court held that Section 1981 protects whites from discrimination.

---

[11]*New York Times,* November 25, 2001.
[12]See *International Brotherhood of Teamsters v. United States,* 431 U.S. 324 (1977); *American Tobacco Company v. Patterson,* 452 U.S. 937 (1982); and *Firefighters Local Union No. 1784 and Memphis Fire Department v. Carl W. Stotts et al.,* 467 U.S. 561 (1984).

In 1968 the Supreme Court held that Congress enacted the Civil Rights Act of 1866 pursuant to the Thirteenth Amendment, which abolished slavery, rather than pursuant to the equal protection clause of the Fourteenth Amendment. This meant that the act applies not only to government actions but also to private actions. This considerably expanded the scope of application of Section 1981 and had a number of significant implications beyond those of Title VII. First, unlike Title VII, the act has no statute of limitations. Second, the act imposes no limit on the awards the courts may make, allowing both compensatory and punitive damages. Third, the act applies more broadly than Title VII, since it covers all employers whereas Title VII covers only those with at least 15 employees. Fourth, an individual can file a lawsuit directly without having to first go to the EEOC.[13]

Title VII bars discrimination in employment but is silent about how a finding of discrimination is to be made. In *Griggs v. Duke Power,* 401 U.S. 424 (1971), the Supreme Court held that an employment policy that is "fair in form, but discriminatory in operation" is in violation of Title VII. Duke Power had required a high school diploma for employment, but its policy had a disparate impact on African Americans, who were less likely than white applicants to have graduated from high school. Griggs also established that the burden of proof rests on the employee or the EEOC to show that the policy in question has a disparate impact on a protected class.[14]

The Bush administration and Congress negotiated a compromise resulting in the Civil Rights Act of 1991, which amended several civil rights laws and overturned several Supreme Court decisions. It reversed one Supreme Court decision by placing the burden on the employer to show that a practice was a business necessity. The act also allowed punitive damages for intentional discrimination on the basis of sex, religion, national origin, or disability.[15] The act also overturned a 1989 Supreme Court decision that had restricted Section 1981 to hiring decisions. Section 1981 as amended now covers hiring, working conditions, promotion, and termination.[16]

DISABILITIES AND RIGHTS

The Americans with Disabilities Act (ADA) of 1990 bans discrimination on the basis of disability in virtually all aspects of the employment relationship for employers with 15 or more employees. The ADA also requires that businesses, including retail stores and restaurants, provide "reasonable accommodations" for the disabled. Disability is broadly defined to include "a physical or mental impairment that substantially limits one or more of that person's major life activities." Substance abuse is not considered a disability, but a person who no longer abuses substances and has completed a rehabilitation program could be considered disabled. In the case of an employee fired for illegal drug use, the Supreme Court in 2003 upheld a Raytheon policy of refusing to rehire a person fired for misconduct.

AIDS is considered by the courts as a handicap under the 1973 Vocational Rehabilitation Act and hence represents a disability, but HIV may not be a disability if it does not limit a major life activity. Employers are required to provide reasonable accommodation for an employee's disability.

The ADA is enforced by the EEOC and by private litigation. In an unusual settlement Wal-Mart agreed to pay $427,500 to a disabilities advocacy organization and to broadcast two television commercials in which two deaf individuals, who had filed a

---

[13]In 2008 the Supreme Court broadened the applicability of the Civil Rights Act of 1866 by ruling that it protected a worker who was fired because he had complained that another worker had been fired because of her race (*CBOCS West, Inc. v. Humphries,* No. 06-1431).

[14]See also *McDonnell Douglas Corp. v. Green,* 411 U.S. 792 (1973) and *Texas Department of Community Affairs v. Burdine,* 447 U.S. 920 (1981).

[15]The Civil Rights Act of 1866 allowed punitive damages only for racial discrimination.

[16]The Supreme Court has clarified the requirements and procedures for filing complaints. The Court ruled against "stale claims," requiring that claims be filed within 180 days of the alleged act of discrimination. The Court also ruled that a claim could not be rejected because an employee had filled out the wrong form for the complaint.

lawsuit under the ADA, described their difficulties in obtaining employment and reasonable accommodation from Wal-Mart. Courts can award compensatory but not punitive damages.

The coverage of the ADA is still being determined and has been the subject of numerous lawsuits. One issue is what limiting "major life activities" means. Another is what constitutes a "reasonable accommodation." A number of cases have been appealed to the Supreme Court, which has substantially limited the ADA's coverage. The court ruled that an impairment that limited a person's ability to do a particular job was not a disability under the ADA, which applies only when the impairment affects "the variety of tasks central to most people's daily lives."[17] The court also held that a company did not have to hire a person with liver disease for a job in an oil refinery where the person would be exposed to chemicals that could worsen his condition.[18] The court also held that a company was not required to violate a seniority system[19] and that the ADA applied to foreign-flagged cruise ships that operate in the United States.[20] Although the courts have clarified the coverage of the ADA, considerable ambiguity remains.

NEOCLASSICAL LIBERALISM

Liberalism emphasizes the liberty of individuals and is concerned with the relationships between liberty and morality and between liberty and the state.[21] The former pertains to which rules or rights have moral standing, whereas the latter pertains to how individual liberty should be limited by the liberty of others and by the institutions individuals establish to govern their interactions. Liberal theory has a rich intellectual tradition including Hobbes (1651) and Locke (1690), but only a relatively recent version of that theory, that of Nozick (1974), is considered here. Nozick's theory is considered because it stakes out a position for a minimal state and because it provides a conception of rights and justice that is quite different from that of Kant and Rawls.

As with Kant, Nozick attempts to deduce principles that define the scope of autonomy and liberty and then from those principles derive a concept of justice. His starting point is the self-evident principle of requiring individuals' free consent to any restrictions that might be imposed on their personal liberty. Nozick derives his system based on the side constraint that "no moral balancing act can take place among us; there is no moral outweighing of one of our lives by others so as to lead to greater overall social good. There is no justified sacrifice of some of us for others" (p. 33). In Nozick's view, this side constraint ensures that individuals will be treated as ends—as the categorical imperative requires—and not as means. This is a stronger version of the categorical imperative than Kant employs, because Kant argues that individuals may be treated as means as long as they are also treated as ends.

Nozick recognizes that in the exercise of their own rights individuals could coerce or infringe the liberty of others. Individuals thus will form voluntary associations to protect their liberties. Such an association is one to which individuals freely consent, and it is the only entity allowed to use force to prevent violations of rights and liberties. That association may be viewed as a state, and the activities it is empowered to undertake have moral standing because they are the result of individuals exercising their autonomy. It thus satisfies the categorical imperative. Nozick concludes that the state would have minimal powers, limited to "protecting its citizens against violence, theft, and fraud, and to the enforcement of contracts . . . " (p. 26). Individuals thus have the negative right not to be coerced by others, and the state has the duty to enforce that right.

---

[17]*Toyota Motor Manufacturing, Kentucky Inc. V. Williams,* 534 U.S. 184, 122 S.Ct. 681 (2002).
[18]*Chevron U.S.A. v. Echazabal,* 536 U.S. 73, 122 S.Ct. 2045.
[19]*US Airways v. Barnett,* 535 U.S. 391, 122 S.Ct. 1516.
[20]*Spector et al. v. Norwegian Cruise Lines, Ltd.* (No.03-1388).
[21]The term *liberal* is generally used in the United States to refer to positions that are to the left on an ideological dimension in which individual responsibilities and limited government are on the right and collectivist responsibilities and larger government are on the left. In many countries, liberalism refers to positions on the right of this dimension, and that is its use here.

In Nozick's system the purpose of justice is to protect liberties. The fundamental principle of free consent provides his conception of distributive justice, which pertains to an individual's entitlements to goods and to the corresponding duties of others to satisfy those entitlements. Because any concept of distributive justice must be based on free consent, Nozick's conclusion is that what is just is whatever is the result of the voluntary actions of individuals. His maxim (p. 160) is expressed as, "From each as they choose, to each as they are chosen."

Nozick's theory has been criticized for its sole reliance on free consent. One line of criticism is based on the utilitarian perspective that actions should be evaluated in terms of their consequences. Another line of criticism is that his theory ignores, other than through what others choose to give them, the situation of those who are poorly off because of their initial endowments of abilities and resources. More importantly for applied purposes, Nozick's conception of a minimal state seems quite removed from modern society. It does, however, provide a basis for the justification and extension of liberties.

CATEGORIES OF JUSTICE THEORIES

Theories of justice add a comparative dimension to moral standards. Justice theories are concerned with how different individuals stand relative to each other on dimensions including, but not limited to, rights, liberties, and consequences. Rawls's theory of justice as fairness, for example, concludes that equality of moral and political rights is required but that economic rewards and burdens can be distributed unequally.

The three principal categories of justice theories are (1) distributive, (2) compensatory, and (3) retributive. Distributive justice is concerned with providing incentives to contribute to well-being in society and with providing a fair and just distribution of the rewards of those contributions. Compensatory justice is concerned with determining how individuals should be compensated for the harm done by others. Retributive justice is concerned with punishment for actions that are contrary to a moral rule or societal well-being. Retributive justice may be used to justify deterring harmful actions. Only distributive and compensatory justice are considered here.

Distributive Justice

Distributive justice is concerned with the distribution of the rewards and burdens of social interactions. A distributive standard is necessarily comparative, since it identifies how those rewards and burdens are assigned to individuals with particular attributes or in particular situations. Tax policy, for example, assigns the tax burden based on income, asset holdings, and consumption. Distributive justice is concerned with the question of which attributes are relevant for particular matters. Just as rights can rule out certain decision alternatives, as illustrated in Figure 21-3, justice principles can also rule out alternatives. Those principles can also impose duties to ensure that the distribution of rewards and burdens is just.

The basic comparative principle of distributive justice is that "Equals should be treated equally and unequals, unequally." Velasquez (1998, p. 105) elaborates by stating the principle,

> Individuals who are similar in all respects relevant to the kind of treatment in question should be given similar benefits and burdens, even if they are dissimilar in other irrelevant respects; and individuals who are dissimilar in a relevant respect ought to be treated dissimilarly, in proportion to their dissimilarity.

This principle implies that individuals should receive different pay if their productivity is different and should receive the same pay if their productivity is the same even though they differ in terms of irrelevant factors such as race or gender.

Distributive justice has a variety of conceptions. Egalitarianism requires the equal distribution of the rewards and burdens of society. This concept is typically rejected

TABLE 21-1	Distributive Justice: Utilitarianism, Egalitarianism, and Rawlsian Justice		
Individual	*Utilitarianism*	*Egalitarianism*	*Rawlsian Justice*
1	10	3	6
2	6	3	5
3	2	3	4
Aggregate utility	18	9	15

because an equal distribution of rewards would distort the incentives to produce those rewards. That is, at some point the more equally a society attempts to divide its pie the smaller the pie will be. Rawls's theory of justice concerns distributing the rewards and burdens of society in a manner that is fair yet gives attention to incentives to increase the size of the pie.

To illustrate the differences, consider the example in Table 21-1 of a three-person society in which individual 1 is more productive than individual 2 who is more productive than individual 3. The society has three possible systems of organizing the interactions of its members. A utilitarian system has the strongest incentives for individuals to use their abilities to pursue their interests, resulting in greater aggregate utility than the other systems. The distribution across individuals, however, is unequal due to the differences in productivity, as indicated in the utilitarianism column of the table. Compared with the utilitarian system, an egalitarian system redistributes aggregate utility equally among the three individuals. To accomplish this, incentives have to be distorted by, for example, taxing the more productive individuals and redistributing the proceeds to the less productive individuals. In the example this reduces aggregate utility from 18 to 9. In contrast, Rawls's theory of justice requires making the least advantaged individual, who in this society is individual 3, as well off as possible. In doing so Rawls seeks also to preserve incentives to the extent possible so that individuals can use their abilities to pursue their interests. This can also benefit the least advantaged individual through, for example, increased economic output. Aggregate utility is lower than that under utilitarianism, since incentives are distorted and there is redistribution in favor of individual 3. Aggregate utility is greater than under egalitarianism, however, since individuals have stronger incentives to pursue their interests and utilize their abilities.

Compensatory Justice

Compensatory justice is concerned with whether and how a person should be compensated for an injustice. Compensatory justice has fairness and restitution as its goals. If a person is injured, the institutions of society may be designed to compensate the person. The principal institutions through which compensation for accidents is provided are the liability, workers' compensation, and insurance systems. Compensation serves two objectives. First, it provides restitution for the injury. Second, it provides incentives to reduce injuries and their social costs by imposing the burden on the parties best placed to avoid accidents. If compensation is not well designed, however, it can result in a moral hazard problem that generates social costs by distorting the incentives to avoid accidents. In such a case, the benefits of compensation must be weighed against the distortions of economic incentives the compensation causes. For example, the provision of government-backed flood insurance results in more home building in flood-prone areas than would be warranted by economic efficiency considerations.

Because of past injustices from discrimination in hiring and promotion practices, the courts ruled that compensation was owed to minority group members as a class, rather than solely to the identifiable victims of discrimination. Rawls's principle of fair equality of opportunity provides a different justification for this ruling by focusing not on the nature of past injustices but on ensuring that all individuals have fair equality of opportunity. This requires not only the absence of discrimination, but also the fair opportunity for all to qualify for positions and pursue their interests. From this perspective, measures to ensure opportunities are warranted even if they extend beyond the set of actual victims of past discrimination.

Injustice

A general principle advanced in conceptions of justice is that an injustice is morally tolerated only if it is necessary to avoid a greater injustice. Such a principle requires an ordering of injustices. Gert (1988, pp. 110–111) offers a standard for when a violation of a moral rule is justified:

> A violation can be justified by providing reasons which would result in either some impartial rational persons advocating that that kind of violation be publicly allowed or less frequently, all impartial rational persons advocating that such a violation be publicly allowed.

Gert thus requires that the violator have reasons for the violation and that an impartial observer understand those reasons and be willing to have that form of violation publicly allowed.

An applied version of Gert's principle is the public disclosure test: "If I disclosed publicly that I had taken an action that violated a moral standard and explained my reasons for doing so, would the public understand and approve of my action?" One such explanation would be that a greater injustice was avoided. Since the public disclosure test is intended to be a hypothetical and reflective test for the person contemplating the action, it is important that the test not turn into a rationalization of a violation of a moral standard in the absence of a greater injustice. For this reason the public disclosure feature of the test is crucial. That is, others must agree that the injustice was warranted.

This principle is applied in Chapter 23 to the issue of whether avoiding a greater injustice justifies paying a bribe demanded as a condition for a sale. In the chapter case, *Genetic Testing in the Workplace,* a central issue is whether the injustice of the invasion of privacy through genetic testing is warranted to avoid the greater injustice of a person incurring serious physical harm from exposure to chemicals in the workplace.

RAWLS'S THEORY OF JUSTICE

The Framework for Justice as Fairness

Rawls (1971) provides a theory of distributive justice set in the tradition of the social contract theory of Locke (1690), Rousseau (1762), and Kant. Rawls argues for the priority of the right over the good, but he is less concerned with developing maxims for judging the reasons or motives that individuals have for their actions than with developing principles to guide the design of society's institutions. According to Rawls (1971, p. 7), "the primary subject of justice is . . . the way in which the major social institutions distribute fundamental rights and duties and determine the division of advantages from social cooperation . . . the legal protection of freedom of thought and liberty of conscience, competitive markets, private property in the means of production, and the monogamous family are examples of major social institutions."

Because any contemporaneous choice of principles by individuals would be based at least in part on who those individuals are and what roles they have in society, Rawls concludes that just principles are those that would be "chosen behind a veil of ignorance" from an "original position" in which one does not know one's personal characteristics and the place one will subsequently have in society. In this original position each individual is equal to every other individual, so the principles chosen will have moral standing, it is argued, because they will be deduced impartially where no one has an advantage.[22]

---

[22]One concern with deducing maxims in Kant's framework is that individuals, knowing their present positions in society, might not reason in an impartial manner. Kant argues that the sense of freedom and autonomy in everyone leads everyone to reason impartially and to will the same maxims, resulting in unanimity. Rawls seeks to ensure impartiality and unanimity through the device of the original position.

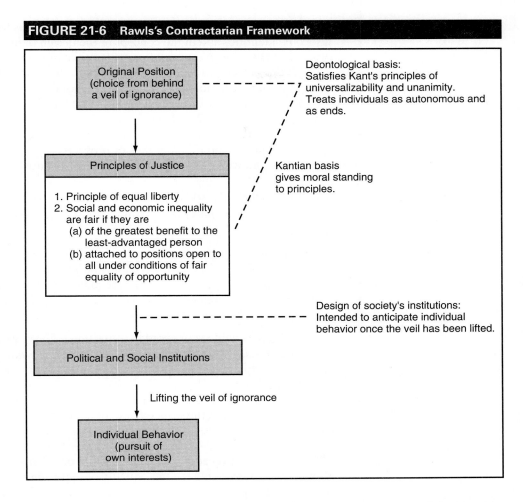

FIGURE 21-6   Rawls's Contractarian Framework

Rawls's contractarian method is illustrated in Figure 21-6. In the original position, individuals do not know which abilities they will have, which positions in society they will occupy, or what their tastes will be. What they do know is that there is a set of possible abilities, tastes, and positions they might be fortunate or unfortunate enough to have once the veil of ignorance has been lifted. They also know the laws of the natural sciences and the understandings gained from the social sciences, so they can anticipate the behavior that will result once society's institutions are in place and the veil has been lifted. In the original position all individuals are equal, and the principles they choose will apply to everyone and thus to themselves, so the original position satisfies the Kantian standards of universalizability and unanimity. From the original position, individuals will also treat people always as ends and never solely as means. Since Kant's categorical imperative is satisfied, the principles chosen in the original position will have moral standing, according to Rawls.[23] Those principles constitute the social contract.

Once the principles have been chosen, society's political and social institutions are to be designed based on those principles. Once those institutions are in place, the veil of ignorance is to be lifted, and individuals learn their abilities and tastes and may pursue whatever interests they have. An important feature of Rawls's theory is that it does not suppose that once the veil has been lifted people will necessarily behave according to a set of rules that take precedence over self-interest. Understanding that individuals may pursue their own interests, Rawls focuses on the role of institutions in guiding the pursuit of those interests in a mutually advantageous manner. The central task of Rawls's method then is to determine which principles and which institutions would be chosen in the original position.

---

[23]See Rawls (1980) for a further analysis of the Kantian construction.

The relevance of Rawls's system for management is found both in the principles of justice he identifies and in the concept of the design of institutions consistent with those principles. The principles provide a basis for reasoning about issues with moral dimensions. The choice of institutions corresponds to the formulation of policies to guide managers in dealing with nonmarket issues with moral dimensions. These policies are used in the screening stage of the framework for nonmarket analysis and strategy formulation introduced in Chapter 2 and summarized in Figure 2-5. In the case of integrity tests, for example, the principles provide a basis for reasoning about whether such tests involve an unjustified intrusion on the liberties of prospective employees, whether they distort opportunities, and whether they have desirable distributive consequences.

The Principles of Justice

Rawls argues that individuals would adopt two principles as a basis for justice as fairness.[24]

First: each person is to have an equal right to the most extensive basic liberty compatible with similar liberty for others.

Second: social and economic inequalities are to be arranged so that they are both (a) to the greatest benefit of the least advantaged and (b) attached to positions and offices open to all under conditions of fair equality of opportunity.[25]

The first principle is referred to as the *equal liberty* principle, part (a) of the second is the *difference principle,* and part (b) is the *fair equality of opportunity* principle. Rawls's principles can be thought of as incorporating both deontological considerations (in the form of liberty and opportunity) and consequentialist considerations of well-being (in terms of the benefit to the least advantaged).

Rawls argues that the principle of equal liberty has precedence over the fair equality of opportunity, which has precedence over the difference principle. By the first precedence, Rawls means "that liberty can be restricted only for the sake of liberty itself." The second precedence means that the difference principle is to be applied only after conditions ensuring the fair equality of opportunity are in place. In Rawls's system, no trade-off is permitted between basic liberties and social and economic conditions. Rawls thus concludes that society's institutions should be characterized by political equality but that social and economic inequalities can be tolerated as long as they are arranged in accord with the fair equality of opportunity and difference principles.

The equal liberty principle pertains to liberties such as the freedom of conscience and speech, the right to vote, the right to be eligible for office, freedom of assembly, freedom from arbitrary arrest, and the right to hold property. Such liberties can be limited only as necessary to maintain conditions of reasoned discourse and public order. For example, rules of recognition and procedure may be instituted to allow everyone to speak in a manner that allows that speech to be heard. With respect to political liberties, Rawls argues that there must be limits on "the scope of majority rule," such as limits like those in the Constitution and in the Bill of Rights.

Fair equality of opportunity is necessary to allow individuals to realize the worth of their liberty, and it requires that positions in society be open to all and that all individuals have a fair opportunity to qualify for those positions. When fair equality of opportunity has been assured, the difference principle requires that the least advantaged individuals be able to realize the worth of their liberty through the pursuit of their interests. The second principle thus is comparative and may require, for example, provisions for the disabled that provide them access to public facilities and to reasonable accommodations in the workplace. Rawls further argues that policies that improve the well-being of the least-advantaged individual would also improve the well-being of most, if not all, of the disadvantaged because their positions are "closely knit." Thus, a policy that benefits the least advantaged person also benefits other less advantaged persons.

---

[24]Rawls (2001) subsequently provided a restatement of his theory of justice as fairness.
[25]Rawls (1971, pp. 60, 83). He gives a more extensive statement of the principles on pages 302–303.

To apply the difference principle, Rawls faces the task of determining who are the least-advantaged persons. This involves making comparisons among individuals, but as indicated in the discussion of utilitarianism in Chapter 20, such interpersonal comparisons are problematic. Rawls attempts to avoid this problem by identifying a set of "primary goods" that all individuals require to be able to pursue their interests, whatever those interests might be. The primary goods are divided into broad categories—rights and liberties, opportunities and powers, and income and wealth. Rawls argues that an index of these primary goods be used to assess the well-being of individuals. This allows for interpersonal comparisons. The difference principle thus takes well-being into account.

The Role of Incentives

From Rawls's perspective, once the equal liberty and fair equality of opportunity principles are satisfied, the institutions of society allow one individual to be better off than another if that is necessary to make the least-advantaged person better off. This is illustrated in Table 21-1 where the Rawlsian choice results in lower aggregate utility than utilitarianism, but makes the least-advantaged person better off than under the other two systems. The Rawlsian choice also allows more-advantaged persons to pursue their interests resulting in greater aggregate well-being than with egalitarianism. Rawls, however, is concerned with the well-being of the least advantaged rather than aggregate well-being.

The role of incentives and the comparison between the utilitarian, egalitarian, and Rawlsian systems are illustrated in Figure 21-7, where the utility possibility set corresponds to societal institutions that satisfy the equal liberty and fair equality of opportunity principles. In the figure individual 1 is more advantaged than individual 2, since more of the alternatives result in a higher utility for 1 than for 2. Egalitarianism requires that the institutions be chosen to attain point A, which yields the greatest utility for each individual subject to the restriction that both are equally well-off. The difference principle states that it is just to move from A to B, even though individual 1 does relatively better than 2. It is just because the less advantaged person 2 is as well-off as possible at B. Rawls thus would choose institutions that provide incentives for economic efficiency to allow society to achieve B rather than A. Institutions that would allow C to be attained, however, would be unjust, since moving from B to C reduces the well-being of the less-advantaged person even though the well-being of 1 increases by more than the well-being of 2 decreases. A utilitarian system

FIGURE 21-7   Difference Principle, Utilitarianism, Egalitarianism

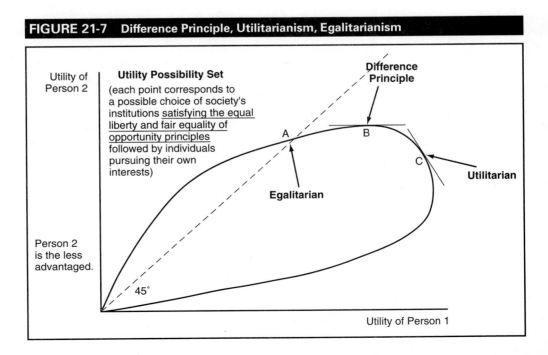

EXAMPLE

Living Benefits

Is the purchase of life insurance policies from the terminally ill, as considered in the Living Benefits example, consistent with Rawls's theory of justice? With respect to the principle of equal liberty, no liberties are infringed by the purchases, since a policyholder can freely choose to sell a policy or retain it.[1] Indeed, purchasing policies better enables the terminally ill to realize their liberties by providing funds for their use. Similarly, the purchases do not infringe the fair equal-

ity of opportunity, and if anything they expand the opportunities available to the terminally ill. The terminally ill can be regarded as the least advantaged, and allowing purchases of life insurance policies can make them better off. From a deontological perspective, the purchases allow the terminally ill to better realize the worth of their liberty, and from a consequentialist perspective the terminally ill can attain better consequences. The difference principle is thus satisfied. Under Rawls's theory the purchase of life insurance policies from the terminally ill is just and would be allowed in a choice in the original position from behind a veil of ignorance.

[1]As in the analysis of living benefits from the perspective of Kantian rights, the person must be competent to make a free choice.

---

that weights the well-being of each individual equally would choose institutions that result in point C.[26]

Rawls thus supports economic efficiency and the role of incentives and markets in attaining that efficiency. But his system of justice supports incentives and the market system only in so far as they benefit the least advantaged person. Economic efficiency and aggregate well-being thus can be sacrificed, through distortionary taxes and redistribution, for example, if doing so improves the situation of the least advantaged. The example above evaluates living benefits from the perspective of Rawls principles.

Duty in Rawls's Theory

The assignment of duty in Rawls's theory of justice is part of the choice of political and social institutions based on the principles of justice. Duty may be assigned to government, individuals, firms, or other organizations. All have a duty to respect and promote the basic liberties identified by the principle of equal liberty. The duty to ensure fair equality of opportunity is generally assigned to government and employers. Offices and positions are to be open to all, and employers may be assigned the duty to ensure that their employment practices provide all individuals with the opportunity to qualify for positions. The duty can extend further by requiring employers to take positive measures to ensure that employees have the means to qualify for better positions.

The duty to attend to the interests of the least advantaged under the difference principle should be assigned so that incentives are not distorted to the point that they jeopardize capital formation, investment, and the creation of jobs. That is, in the terminology of economics, incentives should be preserved so that society remains on the frontier of the utility possibility set in Figure 21-7. Thus, the party that is best positioned to attend to the interests of the least advantaged, and to do so efficiently, should be assigned the duty. That duty is often assigned to government when the means is a transfer of income to the least advantaged. Assigning the duty directly to individuals would violate the equal liberty principle, but individuals may through their voluntary choice contribute time and money to charitable and related activities to benefit the least advantaged. Firms as the property of owners may also contribute to such activities on the same grounds. Some duties to attend to the interests of the least advantaged are

---

[26]Rawls's difference principle requires that the choice of institutions be Pareto optimal. That is, any choice of institutions that yields a point in the interior of the utility possibility set in Figure 21-7 can be improved to make both individuals better off.

EXAMPLE

Clinical Trial Obligations

CV Therapeutics, a small biotechnology company, developed a new drug, ranolazine, for treating angina.[1] Because it had become increasingly difficult to recruit participants for clinical trials in the United States, pharmaceutical companies began conducting trials in Eastern Europe and Russia where people were eager for Western medicines. CV Technologies was completing its successful clinic trials in Russia, and CEO Dr. Louis G. Lange was concerned about whether the company had a continuing duty to those participants in the trials who had benefited from its drug.[2] In the United States companies typically continued to provide a drug for clinical trial participants until it was approved by the FDA for marketing. Also, many pharmaceutical companies had compassionate-use programs that made life-prolonging drugs available in poor countries. Ranolazine did not prolong life but improved the quality of life. Making it available for sale in Russia did not make economic sense, since few patients could afford it and obtaining approval and setting up a sales force would be prohibitively expensive for a company that did not yet have a product on the market. Providing the drug for free in a compassionate-use program

would also be very expensive. CV Therapeutics would have to train doctors in the use of the drug, set up a distribution system, and monitor use for any adverse side effects.

From the perspective of Kantian rights and Nozick's system, CV Therapeutics seems to have no duty to the clinical trial participants, as long as they were not promised that the drug would be provided after the trial was completed. The participants voluntarily entered into the trials and thus had acted as ends and exercised their autonomy. Given the infrastructure cost, providing the drug would likely not be warranted based on utilitarianism. From the perspective of Rawls's system basic liberties and the fair equality of opportunity principles seem not to be violated by not providing the drug, so is there a duty to provide it stemming from the difference principle? The Russian participants suffering from angina are certainly less advantaged, but providing the drug could result in an outcome in the interior of the utility possibility set in Figure 21-7. If providing drugs to trial participants were a general rule, the cost of conducting clinical trials overseas would be increased substantially, thus reducing the incentives for pharmaceutical R & D, particularly for start-ups and small companies. In that case any duty to provide the drug seems to rest with the Russian government or with private aid organizations.

---

[1]This example is based on an article in the *New York Times*, March 5, 2004, and other public sources.
[2]Ranolazine was approved for sale in the United States in 2006 under the brand name Remexa.

---

assigned to firms. For example, injured workers are compensated through the workers' compensation system funded by taxes on employers. The example on clinical trials provides another case.

On some matters, such as equal opportunity in employment, the duty naturally falls to the employer. Similarly, the duty to assure fair equality of opportunity and nondiscrimination in housing rests with landlords. But the duty to provide Rawls's primary goods, such as a minimum standard of living, so that individuals have a fair opportunity to realize the worth of their liberty, is a collective responsibility. As such, the assignment rests primarily with government.

Criticisms of Rawls's Theory

One form of criticism centers on whether all individuals in the original position would choose the same principles and, if so, whether they would choose Rawls's principles rather than some other principles.[27] For example, if the first principle is to take precedence over the second, then the "most extensive basic liberty compatible with similar liberty for others" could be viewed as implying the neoclassical liberalism principle of a minimal role for government. Rawls, however, concludes that the role of government is extensive.

---

[27]The same criticisms may be made about Kant's system. Brandt (1979) argues that individuals could choose a variety of different principles. Gauthier (1986) provides a moral theory that addresses the issue of compliance with the initial choice. Binmore (1994) provides a strategic theory with a framework similar to Rawls's.

Another criticism centers on Rawls's conclusion that in the original position, once liberties and equal opportunity have been assured, society would choose institutions that provide the maximum benefit to the least advantaged. Some critics have argued that this principle would not be chosen in the original position because the chance of any one person being the least disadvantaged is minuscule. Harsanyi (1982) argues that in the original position people would choose a principle corresponding to average rule utilitarianism, since that maximizes the expected well-being of each person when in the original position. Rawls's use of primary goods as a means of assessing the advantages of individuals is also subject to the same criticisms as is interpersonal comparisons of utility.

As with utilitarianism and rights theories, a conceptual and applied difficulty in justice theories pertains to how duty is to be assigned. The issues pertaining to basic liberties are similar to those previously addressed. The assignment of the burden of assuring fair equality of opportunity and improving the position of the least advantaged is similar to the assignment of duty considered in Chapter 20 in the context of utilitarianism. Affirmative action, considered in the example, is an institution that corresponds to these principles.

Nozick (1974) argues that any response to the least advantaged should rest with the free choice of individuals who may, if they so choose, contribute to the well-being of others. Private charity is one reflection of this principle.

Nozick also observes that Rawls's theory pertains to a "time slice" in which the allocation of rewards and burdens of society must necessarily be judged by "end results" and independently of history. That is, to apply the difference principle, the positions of people must be evaluated at a point in time, and Rawls does not inquire into how people came to be in those positions. Nozick argues that how individuals arrived at their current positions is important from a moral perspective. For example, if an injustice were done to a person in the past, it would be necessary to examine the subsequent chain of events to determine what compensation, if any, was warranted. If people had made voluntary choices that worked to their disadvantage, however, is there any duty to compensate them?

Nozick also argues that Rawls's system of justice is necessarily patterned according to characteristics of individuals or their situations, as required in the application of the difference principle. Whatever form of patterning is used, Nozick argues, must interfere with basic liberties.[28] This, he argues, means that no action can satisfy both Rawls's equal liberty principle and the difference principle.

Although Rawls's theory has been criticized on a variety of dimensions, it remains an important philosophical work and provides a useful framework for reasoning about managerial problems. His theory brings together several considerations, including liberties, opportunities, and well-being, that ethical intuition recognizes as important. It also provides a degree of prioritization that can be used in resolving conflicts. The Chapter 11 case, *Environmental Justice and Pollution Credits Trading Systems*, provides an opportunity to reason from Rawls's perspective about both managerial policies and one of society's institutions. The chapter cases, *Citigroup and Subprime Lending* and *Consumer Awareness or Disease Mongering? GlaxoSmithKline and the Restless Legs Syndrome*, raise justice concerns.

Applying the Principles of Justice

Although Rawls's system of justice is as much a political as a moral philosophy and is thus directed at the design of institutions more than at the evaluation of actions, it provides a set of considerations helpful to managers who must establish policies. Company policies are the managerial analogues of Rawls's institutions.

Because of its close relationship to Kantian rights, the application of Rawls's principle of equal liberty involves the same considerations found in rights analysis. This section thus focuses on fair equality of opportunity and the difference principle.

---

[28]See Nozick (1974, pp. 160–164).

EXAMPLE

Affirmative Action

Affirmative action is a conscious attempt to realize equal opportunity. It includes steps to remedy the effects of past discrimination and may involve preferential treatment for individuals in protected classes. The EEOC oversees affirmative action plans and issues guidelines for their design. Affirmative action requires that employers adopt recruiting policies that ensure that minorities and women are included in the pool of candidates and that all those who meet the qualifications, or are qualifiable, are given fair consideration. Over 10,000 firms, as well as universities and nonprofit organizations, are required to have quantitative affirmative action goals. Compliance may require changes in recruitment, hiring, or promotion policies, additional training programs, and the establishment of explicit goals. Affirmative action plans have been adopted more broadly than required by law and have become part of the social fabric of many companies.

Compensatory justice and fair equality of opportunity provide foundations for affirmative action. Compensatory justice is intended to compensate individuals for injustices and, in the context of affirmative action, applies to both individuals and protected classes. From this perspective, compensation for the actual victims of illegal discrimination is justified. Compensation may also be justified for classes, even though the individuals receiving the compensation have not themselves been the subjects of discrimination. The rationale for compensation for a class is that its members' "starting positions" have been adversely affected by past discrimination.[1] This is consistent with the principle of fair equality of opportunity, which holds that individuals are to have a fair chance to qualify for positions. If individuals are at a disadvantage because of their education, training, or other conditions important for qualification, justice considerations may call for providing them additional education or other means to pursue opportunities.

Affirmative action is not immune to criticism on ethics grounds. Criticism centers on who is to bear the burden of the compensation and how the opportunities of others are to be altered to provide opportunity to those who have been disadvantaged. One means of compensation that generates little opposition is providing additional education and training. Other means have resulted in reverse discrimination resulting from the preferential treatment given to others. Section 703(j) of Title VII of the Civil Rights Act of 1964 states: "Nothing contained in this title shall be interpreted to require any employer...to grant preferential treatment to any individual or to any group because of race, color, religion, sex, or national origin...."

An important attribute of many of the affirmative action programs that have withstood court scrutiny is that they are voluntarily agreed to. The court, however, may block a program that constitutes a permanent obstacle or barrier to those bearing the burden of an affirmative action program. In *Regents of University of California v. Bakke,* 438 U.S. 265, the Supreme Court struck down a voluntary policy that established a quota for minority admissions to a medical school because it precluded the admission of a qualified white male. In contrast, in *United Steelworkers of America v. Weber,* 443 U.S. 193 (1979), the court upheld a voluntary agreement between an employer and a union that established numerical goals for minority inclusion in a company training program. The court ruled that the agreement did not constitute discrimination against a white male with more seniority who was denied inclusion, since the goals were temporary and did not constitute an absolute barrier to his future inclusion in the program or to promotion.

In contrast to the language of Title VII, the federal government has had a variety of programs that explicitly took race or sex into account. These include minority preference programs for broadcasting licenses, small business loans, college scholarships, and highway construction and defense contracts. For example, federal law specified that 10 percent of the contract dollars on federally aided road projects be set aside for minorities. In 1988 Congress included women under the same program. On federal highway contracts a company qualified as "disadvantaged" was given up to a 10 percent price advantage over other firms.[2] When Adarand Construction lost a contract to a minority-owned firm even though it had the lowest bid, it sued the federal government, arguing that its right to equal protection under the Fifth Amendment had been violated. The Supreme Court in *Adarand Constructors v. Peña.* 515 U.S. 200 (1995) held in favor of Adarand, thereby forcing changes in federal set-aside programs.[3]

---

[2]That is, if a nondisadvantaged firm bids $109 on a supply contract and a disadvantaged firm bids $100 the contract is awarded to the disadvantaged firm at the bid of $109.

[3]In 2003 the Supreme Court refused to hear an appeal of a lower court decision upholding a Denver city ordinance requiring a prime contractor to explain why a minority subcontractor was not selected when it had made the lowest bid.

---

[1]Groarke (1990) offers a moral justification for compensation and restitution.

(Continued)

The courts had upheld minority preference programs when they served a compelling interest. As an example of a compelling interest, the Supreme Court in *Metro Broadcasting v. F.C.C.*, 110 SCt 2997 (1990), upheld an FCC policy that gave preference to minorities seeking to acquire a broadcasting license. The Court held that the FCC policy was important to the interest of providing a diversity of viewpoints and programming on the airways.[4] A federal appeals court, however, subsequently held that the *Adarand* decision implied a higher standard of scrutiny and concluded that the FCC policy was important but not compelling. Although the FCC policy was invalidated, many broadcasters vowed to continue following the FCC guidelines.[5] The Chapter 19 case, *Playing by the Rules?*, considers a preference program in the allocation of radio spectrum licenses.

Colleges and universities have affirmative action programs for student admissions, and in two 2003 decisions involving the University of Michigan, the Supreme Court clarified the legality of those programs. Relying on the *Bakke* decision, the court upheld a program of the Michigan Law School that considered minority applicants on an "individualized" basis.[6] The court, however, declared unconstitutional the university's affirmative action program for undergraduate admissions. That program automatically awarded 20 points on a 150-point admissions scale to African American, Hispanic, and Native American applicants. In a 6-to-3 decision the court held that the program was quota-like.[7]

Although court scrutiny of government affirmative action and preference programs continues, the affirmative action programs of most companies are likely to remain intact since they are by now a part of the fabric of those companies. The objectives of many of those programs are as yet unrealized, however.

In addition to issues pertaining to employees, affirmative action may be extended to other constituencies. Many firms have a considerable underrepresentation of minorities and women among their distributors, franchisees, and agents, and civil rights advocates have worked to extend affirmative action goals to these positions.

---

[4]See Spitzer (1991) for an analysis of the justifications for minority preference in broadcasting. In 1992 the U.S. Court of Appeals ruled that the FCC policy giving preference to women constituted illegal discrimination against men.
[5]In 1995 Congress repealed a law that gave a tax break to broadcasters that sold a station to a minority-owned firm.

[6]*Grutter v. Bollinger*, 539 U.S. 982, 124 S.Ct. 35.
[7]*Gratz v. Bollinger*, 539 U.S. 244, 123 S.Ct. 2411.

For firms, the principle of fair equality of opportunity is most directly applicable to policies associated with the employment relationship. As considered earlier in the chapter, Title VII of the Civil Rights Act of 1964 provides for equal opportunity by prohibiting discrimination in employment. Rawls's principle, however, goes beyond the prohibition of discrimination and requires the "fair equality" of opportunity. Fair equality requires not only that positions be open to all, but that individuals have the means to attempt to qualify for them. Justice Marshall's argument in the *Kadrmas* case is consistent with this principle. Affirmative action programs may be viewed as one application of this principle.

The difference principle is applicable once liberties and fair equality of opportunity have been assured. That principle calls for affirmative consideration of those who are the least advantaged or who would be put in such a position by policies or actions of a firm. As Rawls argues, the position of the least-advantaged person is closely linked to the positions of other less-advantaged persons. Consequently, responding to the situation of the least-advantaged person affects many less-advantaged persons. The difference principle provides a justification, for example, for special programs that make facilities accessible to the disabled and provide opportunities for the disadvantaged. It also provides a justification for policies that respond to the needs of laid-off employees and the communities in which they live.

The methodology for applying Rawls's framework involves the elimination of policy alternatives by using first the equal liberty principle and then the fair equality of opportunity principle. The remaining alternatives are then evaluated for fairness, and the choice among those remaining alternatives is based on the difference principle. The methodology may be summarized as follows:

EXAMPLE

Integrity Tests

Much of the rights analysis of integrity tests presented earlier in the chapter is relevant from the perspective of justice as well, so the focus here is on the difference principle and fair equality of opportunity. One concern with an integrity test is whether it puts those who are already disadvantaged at a further disadvantage. If they are already disadvantaged for a reason that would be revealed by the integrity test and would result in a "failure" on the test, an objection on justice grounds could be raised, provided the reason were not relevant to the job. Similarly, if the test systematically affected the opportunities of individuals with particular attributes that were irrelevant to job performance, the test would be unjust. Such concerns are reflected in laws in a number of states that prohibit employers from inquiring about criminal records of job applicants or about their lifestyles. Justice principles require that the tests not adversely affect individuals on irrelevant grounds, but otherwise the tests may be used if they enable the firm to improve its performance; that is, to stay on the frontier in Figure 21-7. The more compelling are the firm's interests and the more important are the tested traits for a particular job the more likely the tests are justified.

---

1. Identify the liberties and rights involved.
2. The principle of equal liberty: Evaluate alternative policies in terms of how extensive are the corresponding liberties and rights of individuals consistent with equal liberties and rights for all. Prioritize rights and liberties when conflicts arise. Eliminate alternatives that limit liberties for reasons other than assuring the liberties themselves.
3. The principle of fair equality of opportunity: Identify the opportunities associated with each remaining alternative, and evaluate those alternatives in terms of how extensive are the corresponding opportunities. Eliminate alternatives that unnecessarily limit opportunities.
4. For the remaining alternatives, evaluate their fairness implications for the pursuit of opportunities by those affected.
5. Choose among the remaining policies based on the difference principle by favoring policies that benefit the least advantaged even if those policies reduce aggregate well-being.
6. Identify which parties have which duties.

In this methodology a departure from equal liberty cannot be justified by greater advantage in social or economic matters for any individual. The two examples illustrate the analysis.

EXAMPLE

Redlining

Redlining, the practice of refusing to lend or write insurance policies in a designated geographic area, may be economically efficient if few of the people in the area are likely to qualify for a loan or insurance policy. That is, redlining could correspond to point C in Figure 21-7. Redlining, however, is inconsistent with Rawls's principles of justice. Redlining does not seem to violate the principle of equal liberty, but it may violate both the fair equality of opportunity principle and the difference principle. Redlining denies opportunity to people in a redlined area, and while it may not directly affect their ability to qualify for employment positions, it does restrict their opportunity to become a homeowner or to have an automobile insured. Redlining may also violate the difference principle, since redlined areas frequently are low-income areas that are often populated by disadvantaged people. Banning redlining then can result in point B in Figure 21-7.

Life Insurance Screening for Preexisting Conditions

If screening for preexisting conditions for life insurance is not a violation of the principle of equal liberty or the principle of fair equality of opportunity, it may conflict with the difference principle. Treatment of diseases such as AIDS can be very expensive, and to the extent that the cost is borne by the victim and the victim's family it can represent a heavy and in many cases insurmountable burden. To the extent that the cost of treatment substantially disadvantages some persons, the difference principle requires that institutions be de-

signed to relieve at least some of that burden. Rawls then asks to which institution the duty should be assigned. The institution of life insurance seems less appropriate than the use of public funds, since adverse selection by those with preexisting conditions could substantially reduce the efficiency of the life insurance system, resulting in a point in the interior of the utility possibility set in Figure 21-7. Screening for preexisting conditions thus seems consistent with Rawls's system with the duty assigned to government.

HIGHER ORDER STANDARDS FOR EVALUATING ETHICS SYSTEMS

The ethics systems based on utilitarian, rights, and justice considerations use two general standards for determining which principles or rules have moral standing. The first is universalizability (which implies reversibility). A principle or rule has moral standing if one would be willing to have everyone, including oneself, behave in accord with it. This standard, however, does not necessarily imply that everyone would choose the same set of principles or rules. The second standard is unanimous impartial choice as in Rawls's original position. The notion of reasoning about principles from the original position is important because ethics principles are to be impartial and not based on the actual position a person occupies in society.

Rule utilitarianism and the rules derived from it have moral standing because each individual chooses a rule to be followed by everyone and, since each individual is maximizing aggregate well-being, everyone would choose the same rule. That is, the principle of maximizing aggregate well-being is universalizable, since each individual would will that everyone abide by it. The principle also would be chosen unanimously from the original position, since everyone would choose the rule that yields the greatest well-being.

Rawls's principles of equal liberty and fair equality of opportunity meet both the standards of universalizability and unanimous choice from the original position. With respect to Rawls's difference principle individuals might be willing to have everyone abide by it, but it is not at all clear that in the original position everyone would choose the difference principle and not some other principle such as the utilitarian principle of maximizing aggregate well-being.

Kantian maxims meet both standards. The categorical imperative implies that maxims will be universal. The view that every individual is rational and deduces maxims from a conception of freedom and autonomy that resides in everyone means, according to Kant, that each will choose the same rule, so unanimity results. Kant's view of rationality and a common conception of freedom and autonomy serve as the original position, so reasoning and choice are impartial.

In business applications these two higher order standards provide a basis for evaluating alternative policies and provide guidance for managers in nonmarket analysis and strategy formulation. These standards are used in Chapter 22 to evaluate the principles developed by Levi Strauss & Co. and Cummins Inc. to guide their managers.

SUMMARY

Rights and justice are important concepts and correspond to fundamental ethical intuitions. Rights may be classified as intrinsic or instrumental. Intrinsic rights are justified independently of consequences by their consistency with conceptions of liberty and autonomy. Instrumental rights have moral standing because they lead to higher levels of well-being. Instrumental rights are an important component of teleological systems, which judge the good in terms of consequences. Intrinsic rights are a central component of deontological systems, which are based on considerations other than, or in addition to, consequences.

Kant's theory of moral rules is based on the categorical imperative, which holds that individuals are to be treated always as autonomous ends and never solely as means, and that rules of behavior are to be universal. Moral rules identify intrinsic rights of individuals and the corresponding duties to respect those rights. Intrinsic rights take precedence over considerations of well-being, but the ethical intuition that well-being is important remains strong.

Justice theories add an explicit comparative dimension to deontological systems. The three principal categories of justice theories are distributive, compensatory, and retributive. Distributive theories focus on the distribution of the rewards and burdens of social interactions. Compensatory theories are concerned with compensating for injustice. Retributive theories focus on punishment for moral wrongs. An injustice is a moral violation and is to be tolerated only if it is necessary to avoid a greater injustice.

Rawls provides a theory of justice as fairness that incorporates the Kantian framework and focuses on liberties, rights, and the comparative treatment of individuals. Rawls's theory prescribes that individuals are to be treated equally with respect to basic liberties but that individuals may be treated unequally in terms of rewards and burdens as long as the inequality satisfies conditions of fairness as embodied in the difference principle and the principle of fair equality of opportunity. Rawls argues that liberties have first priority, and when they are assured, the provision of fair equality of opportunity is required. The difference principle, which requires that institutions and policies be designed to benefit the least-advantaged person, is then applied.

Higher order standards are used to evaluate ethics systems and principles. One such standard is universalizability, which requires that an individual would will that everyone follow the rule or abide by the principle. The second standard is unanimity, which requires that everyone would impartially choose the same rule or principle. Reasoning about which rules and principles would be unanimously supported is intended to be based on Kant's conceptions of autonomy, freedom, and rationality and is to take place impartially as if from the original position.

Managers must make decisions in situations in which there are competing moral claims that require judgments about the effects of decisions on individuals, their rights, and their well-being. An understanding of ethics systems and sensitivity to the moral dimensions of issues are important for managers for several reasons. First, sensitivity to the ethics dimensions of issues and the use of ethics frameworks can help managers avoid wrongs that may otherwise result from a narrow focus on the firm's interests. Second, sensitivity to the moral concerns of others about the policies and practices of a firm can help management anticipate nonmarket actions and pressures. Third, managers will be more likely to make decisions that serve the long-run interests of society and ultimately of business itself. Fourth, the content of corporate social responsibility is found in ethics principles, as considered in the next chapter.

------------------------------------- C A S E S -------------------------------------
Genetic Testing in the Workplace

Companies and their employees have an important interest in reducing health risks in the workplace. One approach to doing so is to alter production processes and the workplace to reduce hazards. For some companies, this is quite expensive, and in some work situations it is impossible to eliminate all health risks. Another approach is to choose the workforce to minimize the risk. This may be done through evaluating workers' qualifications and experience and through subsequent training. It may also be done by determining workers' susceptibility to certain diseases that could result from exposure in the workplace. That susceptibility could be genetic.

Perhaps the first person to suggest the use of genetic information to improve workers' health was J. B. S. Haldane who in 1938 wrote,[29]

> The majority of potters do not die of bronchitis. It is quite possible that if we really understood the causation of this disease we should find out that only a fraction of potters are of a constitution which renders them liable to it. If so, we could eliminate potters' bronchitis by regulating entrants into the potters' industry who are congenitally disposed to it.

After the U.S. military found a susceptibility of soldiers with G-6-PD (glucose-6-phosphate dehydrogenase) deficiency to develop anemia, Stokinger and Mountain argued for the use of genetic testing for G-6-PD deficiency in workers who might be exposed to oxidants in the workplace: [30]

> Most important, the determination affords, for the first time, an opportunity to make a susceptibility evaluation during a job placement examination, and, thus, avoids placing a worker in exposures to which he is inordinately susceptible. This is preventive toxicology in the highest form; no previous single development in toxicology has opened such prospects for the medical supervision of workers.

In 1982 Representative Al Gore, chair of the House Subcommittee on Investigations and Oversight, warned that genetic testing had "the potential to serve as a marvelous tool to protect the health of workers or a terrible vehicle for invidious discrimination."[31]

Genetic testing to determine susceptibility to certain hazards can be done from a sample of blood or other bodily fluid. Such tests are generally quite accurate. Although they can be expensive, they offer a basis on which to select and assign workers to minimize the risks from exposure to certain health hazards and the possible tragedy of chronic or terminal diseases.

G-6-PD is an enzyme required for the stability of red blood cells. "Those with the deficiency are highly susceptible to having their red-blood-cell membranes destroyed by certain drugs or other oxidizing agents. It is especially a problem for blacks and some Mediterranean people."[32] The G-6-PD deficiency is carried by a sex-linked recessive gene, and approximately 100 million males worldwide are estimated to have the deficiency.

Another genetic test is for alpha-1-antitrypsin (AAT) deficiency, which results in susceptibility to respiratory irritants such as those found in many workplaces. Exposure to "dust and/or fumes" is one of the environmental risk factors and can result in lung and liver disease. [33] Approximately 100,000 Americans have severe AAT deficiency. AAT deficiency is a hereditary condition, and its most common abnormal gene originated in Scandinavia.[34] Treatment of the deficiency involves intravenous injections of AAT on a frequent basis.

Genetic testing can be used for either screening or monitoring purposes. In screening, genetic testing is used to select among job applicants for positions that may involve a potential health hazard. Screening can also be used in assigning current employees and new hires to jobs so as to minimize risks. Genetic testing can also be used to identify susceptible individuals who can take precautions to protect themselves or be moved to other jobs with less exposure to possible irritants such as oxidizing agents.

Genetic testing can also be used to monitor groups of employees over time to determine if they experience chromosome damage due to exposure in the workplace. This could be important for employees who work with oxidants, lead, beryllium, and other potentially toxic metals and chemicals. In addition to providing information that could be used to reduce risks, some companies believe that genetic testing could give them a degree of protection from liability if a worker chose to stay in a job after being notified that he or she was genetically susceptible to a disease that could be triggered by exposure in the workplace.

[29]Haldane, J. B. S. 1938. *Heredity and Politics*. New York, NY: Norton.
[30]Sokinger, H. E. and J. T. Mountain. 1963. "Test for Hypersusceptibility to Hemolytic Chemicals." *Archives of Environmental Health* 6: 57–64.
[31]Quoted in Brandt-Raul, Paul W. and Sherry I. Brandt-Rouf, 2004. "Genetic Testing in the Workplace: Ethical, Legal, and Social Implications." *Annual Review of Public Health* 25: 139–153.

[32]*Wall Street Journal*, February 24, 1986.
[33]The other environmental risk factors are personal smoking history, parental smoking history, and frequent lung infections. Robert A. Sandhaus, www.razziniusa.org/jan01/geneticprofiles.htm.
[34]The link between AAT and lung disease was made in Sweden. Robert A. Sandhaus, www.razziniusa.org/jan01/geneticprofiles.htm.

Many companies were hesitant to use genetic testing because of uncertainty about the relevant law. In 2002 the Burlington Northern Santa Fe Railway Company reached a settlement for $2.2 million with the Equal Employment Opportunity Commission (EEOC) of a lawsuit filed under the Americans with Disabilities Act. The company had tested without their knowledge 36 employees who complained of carpal tunnel syndrome to determine if they were genetically susceptible to the syndrome. The company did not acknowledge violating the law nor did the EEOC find that the company had violated the law. The case, however, served as a warning to companies.

Finally, in 2008 Congress enacted and the president signed the Genetic Information Nondiscrimination Act which defined as an unlawful employment practice:

1. to fail or refuse to hire, or to discharge, any employee, or otherwise to discriminate against any employee with respect to the compensation, terms, conditions, or privileges of employment of the employee, because of genetic information with respect to the employee; or
2. to limit, segregate, or classify the employees of the employer in any way that would deprive or tend to deprive any employee of employment

opportunities or otherwise adversely affect the status of the employee as an employee, because of genetic information with respect to the employee.

The act also made it illegal "to request, require, or purchase genetic information with respect to an employee or a family member of the employee except—

where (A) health or genetic services are offered by the employer, including such services offered as part of a wellness program; ... (5) where the information involved is used for genetic monitoring of the biological effects of toxic substances in the workplace, but only if (A) the employer provides written notice of the genetic monitoring to the employee; (B)(i) the employee provides prior, knowing, voluntary, and written authorization; or ..."

the information was required by federal or state law.

With the completion of the Human Genome Project the possibilities for more accurate and extensive genetic testing in the workplace were seemingly unlimited. ∎

SOURCE: Copyright © 1998 by the Board of Trustees of the Leland Stanford Junior University. Revised 2008. All rights reserved. Reprinted with permission.

Preparation Questions

1. Is genetic testing in the workplace warranted from a utilitarian perspective; that is, by the potential benefits it can yield? What ethics concerns does it involve?
2. Consider the use of genetic testing for screening job applicants, for assigning current employees to jobs, and for monitoring employees for genetic damage from exposure in the workplace. Which rights might be said to be violated by either the use or the prohibition of the use of genetic testing for these purposes? How would you prioritize those rights? Does the law accord with your assessment?
3. Who should be informed of the results of a genetic test? Is the use of genetic testing for monitoring more or less appropriate than its use for screening purposes?
4. Prepare a rights table as in Figure 21-5.
5. Design a wellness program for employees that includes an opportunity for an employee to have a genetic test and also provides the employer with an opportunity to use genetic information in screening and/or monitoring.
6. Organized labor and some activists oppose genetic testing on the grounds that the employer should ensure a safe workplace. Does an employer have a moral duty to reduce risks in the workplace to the point at which any qualified person regardless of

his or her susceptibility can safely occupy the position?
7. If an employee with full understanding of his or her genetic susceptibility chooses (because, for example, of higher pay) to work in an area in which exposure is possible, should the employer assign the employee to that job?
8. Consider the case of a company with a production process that requires the processing of a metal, such as beryllium, that can be toxic to workers with a particular genetic deficiency. The company has installed dust collection and ventilation equipment, and the workplace meets all government safety requirements by a substantial margin. Nevertheless, an individual with a particular genetic deficiency can develop chronic and serious long-term illnesses from exposure to the metal. At an annualized cost of $1 million the company could install additional equipment that would reduce by half the risk to an employee with the genetic deficiency, but illness could still occur. For jobs in the metals processing unit, the company could also screen job applicants for the genetic deficiency and not hire those who have the deficiency. The cost of the screening would be approximately 10 percent of the cost of the additional equipment and would reduce the risk of disease by 90 percent.

The company also has the alternative of replacing 80 percent of the workers in the metals processing unit with sophisticated and expensive robotic equipment at a net annualized cost of $3 million (net of the savings in labor costs). This would result in the layoff of 48 employees. What should the company do?

Citigroup and Subprime Lending

On September 6, 2000, Citigroup, Inc., announced an agreement to acquire Associates First Capital Corporation in an exchange of shares valued at $31.1 billion. The Associates was the largest publicly traded finance company with managed assets of $100 billion and shareholders equity of $10.4 billion. The Associates had 2,750 offices with approximately 1,000 in the United States and the rest in 13 other countries.[35] The Associates also did business through thousands of independent brokers. Citigroup had managed assets of $791 billion, shareholders equity of $51 billion, and operations in 100 countries. Citigroup chairman and CEO Sanford I. Weill said, "Our consumer finance operations are very well regarded. We are excited about the prospects for the combined operations." Keith W. Hughes, chairman and CEO of the Associates, said, "We are excited to be joining forces in this effort, contributing the energy and drive that has led the Associates to twenty-five consecutive years of record earnings."[36] Citigroup planned to merge the U.S. operations of the Associates into its CitiFinancial unit, which also provided consumer finance. Hughes would be the head of CitiFinancial and join Citigroup's board of directors as vice chairman.

The acquisition of the Associates brought Sandy Weill back to his roots. In 1986 he became CEO of a Baltimore finance company, Commercial Credit Corporation, that lent to working class families. He built the company through internal growth and acquisition and later merged The Travelers Group with Citicorp to form one of the largest financial institutions in the country. As a result of the merger Commercial Credit was succeeded by CitiFinancial, which in 2000 had $18.5 billion in loans and $390 million in profits. The Associates had profits of $409 million in the second quarter of 2000 and had 480,000 home equity loans outstanding. With the acquisition CitiFinancial would become the nation's largest finance company.

A major profit source for CitiFinancial and the Associates was subprime lending—lending to people who did not meet the customary credit requirements of banks. The growth of subprime lending during the 1990s had been spectacular, with lending increasing 13-fold between 1993 and 1999. Outstanding subprime loans were estimated at $150 billion in 1998. This lending had provided access to credit to many people who would not have qualified for prime loans because of their credit history. A study by Freddie Mac, however, estimated that perhaps one-third of subprime borrowers could have qualified for prime loans, and Freddie Mac chairman Franklin Raines believed that as many as half might be able to qualify. One study found that 35 percent of the subprime borrowers were over 55, and African Americans were twice as likely to borrow in the subprime market as in the prime market.

The growth in subprime lending was also driven by aggressive marketing by the subprime lenders. The lenders relied on both mass advertising and direct marketing. One form of subprime lending was home equity loans marketed to borrowers to consolidate their bills. *BusinessWeek* commented on an example of such a loan on the CitiFinancial Web site: "'I now can afford so much more than I thought possible,' says Spencer L. of Worcester, Mass. A sample worksheet shows that Spencer can take out a $20,000 home-equity loan to consolidate his bills, pay off credit cards, and reap $310.57 in 'monthly savings.' The fine print notes that Spencer will pay that back in 120 months at a 13.49 percent interest rate. But nowhere on the Web site does it say that it would cost $36,500 to pay off starting debts of $17,000."[37]

Subprime lending had generated vocal complaints from consumer and activist groups, which referred to it as predatory lending. Many of the people who borrowed in the subprime market were lower income, minority, and elderly, and consumer advocates claimed that they often did not understand the loans and what was bundled with them. Some of these critics referred to the Associates as a "rogue company."

A second aspect of subprime lending was single-premium life insurance sold along with a loan to pay off the principal in the case of the death of the borrower. The insurance premiums for several years were typically charged up front and added to the loan principal. Moreover, the insurance often covered not only the loan principal but the insurance premiums and the interest on the loan. Frequently, the insurance did not cover the entire period of the loan. Because the premiums were packed into the loan principal, the insurance was financed at the

---

[35]The Associates had been owned for a decade by the Ford Motor Company, which spun off the unit in 1998.
[36]Citigroup press release, September 6, 2000.

[37]*BusinessWeek*, March 19, 2001.

high interest rates on the loans. The resulting cost of single-premium life insurance was considerably higher than the cost of term life insurance. This single-premium life insurance was criticized by community activists and government officials because many borrowers did not understand that it was included in the loan principal. The Consumer Federation of America called this "the worst insurance rip-off" in America.

As an example of a complaint involving insurance, Benny and Linda Mackey of Chocowinity, North Carolina, had fallen behind on their $519 monthly mortgage payments, and refinanced their $37,117.76 mortgage with the Associates. The Associates added a $4,231 "loan discount" to their principal and also added $4,910.08 in life insurance premiums to the loan. At a 14.99 percent interest rate the Mackeys' monthly payment rose to $592. When they missed some payments, the Associates harassed them and threatened foreclosure, according to the Mackeys. The Mackeys filed a complaint with the state of North Carolina, and the Associates lowered their payments to $370 at a 9 percent interest rate. Alan Hirsch, a deputy attorney general of North Carolina, said that single-premium credit insurance was the most egregious practice, since "many borrowers don't understand it's been included in the loan." The attorney general of North Carolina had begun an investigation of the Associates in 1999 and subsequently filed a lawsuit against the company. The investigation focused on packing insurance premiums in the loan and financing it at high rates. North Carolina also enacted an antipredatory lending law.

Both the Associates and CitiFinancial sold single-premium life insurance. The Associates issued insurance through its subsidiary, Associates Corporation of North America, which over the past 5 years had collected $1.8 billion in insurance premiums and recorded earnings of $397.5 million.[38] Fannie Mae and Freddie Mac refused to buy first mortgages with single-premium credit insurance.

One of the principal critics of subprime lenders was ACORN (Association of Community Organizations for Reform Now). ACORN was an organization with 500 neighborhood chapters in 50 cities focusing on supporting low- and moderate-income families. It filed numerous lawsuits on behalf of people whom it viewed as victims. ACORN referred to subprime lending as "legalized robbery" and listed the following among the predatory lending tactics used by subprime lenders:[39]

- Charging excessive interest rates not justified by the risk involved
- Charging and financing excessive points and fees
- Packing loans with additional products like financial credit insurance or club memberships

- Charging extended prepayment penalties that trap people in high-interest-rate loans
- Financing single-premium credit insurance
- Misrepresenting the terms and conditions of loans
- Charging unfair and excessive late fees
- Refinancings, and especially repeated refinancings, that result in no benefit to the borrower
- Balloon payments and negative amortization schedules on high-cost loans
- Targeting high-cost loans to vulnerable borrowers, including the elderly, low-income, and minority families
- Using harassing and intimidating collection techniques

In particular, ACORN had criticized CitiFinancial and the Associates for sales of single-premium life insurance, high up-front fees, and high prepayment fees. ACORN had asked the companies to stop these practices.[40]

AARP (American Association of Retired Persons) also was concerned about predatory mortgage lending because many people over 50 were using subprime borrowing. AARP was studying subprime lending and was considering a campaign against it. A campaign would involve both public education and support for stringent state legislation to curtail abuses.

Regulation of subprime lending was loose, and the relevant agencies were considering whether tighter supervision was warranted. The relevant regulators were the Comptroller of the Currency, the Federal Reserve Board, the Federal Deposit Insurance Corporation, and the Office of Thrift Supervision.

One lever of the community activists had been taken away in 1999 when Congress passed banking reform legislation. The legislation eliminated a requirement that in approving bank acquisitions the Federal Reserve Board had to solicit and consider consumer opinions on how well the banks met the requirements of the 1977 Community Reinvestment Act (CRA). That Act required banks to loan in the communities in which their offices were located. The legislation eliminated this requirement in the case of the acquisition of financial companies that did not take deposits. Since the Associates did not take deposits, Citigroup was only required to provide information to federal regulators about CRA performance. Groups such as ACORN had regularly used the CRA requirement to scrutinize the banks' lending data and extract lending pledges from the banks.

When the acquisition was announced, Representative Stephanie Tubbs Jones (D-OH) said, "Citigroup needs to know there are members of the House banking committee—particularly the Congressional Black Caucus members—who are concerned about the merger and

[38]*New York Times,* October 22, 2000.
[39]ACORN, "Predatory Lending: A Growing Problem," www.acorn.org.

[40]ACORN also launched a campaign against Household Finance for what it called abusive and predatory practices.

they need to be concerned about our concerns." A North Carolina group had shown the Black Caucus a videotape of a man who had gone to an Associates office for a loan to buy groceries and over the next 10 years had been persuaded to refinance the loan 11 times, resulting in a $50,000 mortgage at an interest rate of 19 percent.[41]

The Associates had been named in approximately 700 lawsuits and had been fined $147,000 by the state of Georgia. The Department of Justice had filed a lawsuit against the Associates alleging that one of its credit card banks had violated fair lending laws in marketing credit cards to Hispanics.[42] The Federal Trade Commission (FTC) had initiated an investigation of the Associates in 1999 for allegations of deceptive marketing practices. Since 1998 the FTC had filed 14 lawsuits involving subprime lending, including complaints against the Associates. Citigroup was surprised by the intensity of the criticisms of its acquisition of the Associates and more generally of subprime lending. The allegations of predatory lending and deception were serious, and they

threatened a highly profitable business. In response to the criticisms William Street, a Citigroup attorney, said, "Citigroup is committed to improving . . . the compliance systems and operation systems and anything else they determine needs improving to meet their standards."[43]

In a letter to the Comptroller of the Currency, the Superintendent of the New York State Banking Department, and the Chairman of the Federal Deposit Insurance Corporation, the regulators that had to approve the acquisition, Sandy Weill stated, "We prize our long-standing reputation for service to customers and communities and we recognize that CitiFinancial's position as the soon-to-be largest consumer finance company in the U.S. gives it the opportunity to play an even more important and valuable role in communities in which it does business."[44] The motto on Citigroup's 1999 annual report was "Leading by Example." ■

SOURCE: This case was prepared from public sources by David P. Baron. Copyright © 2001 by David P. Baron. All rights reserved. Reprinted with permission.

Preparation Questions

1. Are there moral concerns associated with subprime lending? Are those moral concerns based on utilitarianism, rights, or justice considerations?

2. What should CitiFinancial do about single-premium life insurance?

3. What should CitiFinancial do about the other allegations of abuse?

4. Should Citigroup support the efforts of ACORN and AARP to weed out unscrupulous practices? Should it support tighter regulatory supervision of the subprime lending market?

5. What policies should Citigroup adopt for subprime lending?

[41]*Washington Post*, September 15, 2000.
[42]*Washington Post*, September 15, 2000.
[43]*Washington Post*, September 15, 2000.
[44]Citigroup, November 7, 2000.

Consumer Awareness or Disease Mongering? GlaxoSmithKline and the Restless Legs Syndrome

"The words 'It's frustrating,' shaped to look like a pair of legs, float across the screen. A voice intones: 'It's frustrating. Just when you're ready to relax, you feel the compelling urge to move.' Eventually, the legs morph into those of a woman draped lazily across a recliner."[45] "When I saw the ad, it pretty much described me to a tee. If that doesn't do it, then I'll talk to my doctor about trying something else," said Frank Stevens of Gillette, Wyoming.[46]

The advertisement was promoting GlaxoSmithKline's (GSK) drug Requip for the treatment of restless legs syndrome (RLS), a neurological condition causing an itchy, restless sensation in the legs. Requip (ropinirole) had earlier been approved for the treatment of

Parkinson's disease, and in 2005 it was approved for RLS with 2–4 milligrams doses versus 15 milligrams for Parkinson's disease.

In 2005 GSK spent $36 million to advertise Requip according to Nielsen Monitor-Plus. Sales increased by $50 million, or over 50 percent, in the United States. Worldwide, Requip was projected to have sales of over $500 million in 2006 with more than half accounted for by RLS.

GSK had begun an intensive promotional campaign for Requip prior to approval by the Food and Drug Administration. It began issuing press releases in 2003 referring to research presentations at an American Academy of Neurology conference. It then began advertising to doctors in medical journals and then turned to direct-to-consumer advertising. In 2003 it began developing consumer awareness of RLS with an advertising campaign stating a "new

[45]*Washington Post*, May 30, 2006.
[46]*Washington Post*, May 30, 2006.

survey reveals a common yet underrecognized disorder—restless legs syndrome—is keeping Americans awake at night."[47] The initial ads did not mention the drug but instead urged people to consult their physician. In preparation for the direct-to-consumers advertising campaign GSK had recruited sleep-disorder specialists to speak to doctors at hosted dinners at restaurants.[48]

GSK argued that its campaign was simply raising awareness of RLS. A GSK spokesperson said that it was "sharing medical information on a wide variety of conditions, including RLS, which is what we see as our mission."[49] John Winkelman of Harvard Medical School who treats sleep disorders said, "This was a disorder that was generally overlooked by most physicians and individuals."[50]

Others disagreed. "The argument the pharmaceutical industry is always making is that this is patient education—that this is an under-diagnosed condition and 'we're just trying to raise awareness,'" said Michael Wilkes of the University of California at Davis. 'If you're talking about something like hepatitis C or measles, that might be true. But if you're talking about toenail fungus or baldness or restless legs syndrome, I just don't buy it.'"[51]

Some accused drug companies of disease mongering.[52] Lisa M. Schwartz of the Veteran Affairs Outcomes Group and the Center for the Evaluative Clinical Sciences of the Dartmouth Medical School said, "We're increasingly turning normal people into patients. The ordinary experiences of life become a diagnosis, which makes healthy people feel like they're sick."[53]

"Researchers say it is surprisingly easy for patients to persuade doctors to prescribe medications, especially for unfamiliar conditions. Richard Kravitz of the University of California at Davis said of RLS, 'physicians don't know much about it and may be wanting to follow the path of least resistance and prescribe a medication for a condition that a patient might not have."[54]

Restless Legs Syndrome

Restless legs syndrome "is a neurological disorder characterized by an uncontrollable urge to move the legs, usually accompanied by unpleasant and sometimes painful sensations in the legs. RLS affects up to ten percent of the population worldwide aged between 30 and 79 years and around one-third of sufferers experience symptoms more than twice weekly causing moderate to severe distress. The motor-restlessness worsens during the evening and night causing difficulty initiating and maintaining sleep. The sleep disruption can lead to excessive daytime sleepiness and compromise work performance. RLS also has considerable impact on social activities that require immobility."[55]

GSK recognized the potential of Requip to treat RLS after doctors had begun to prescribe it for the disorder. Some doctors stated that RLS afflicted approximately 3 percent of people with symptoms at least twice a week, but GSK claimed that it affected up to 10 percent.[56] Steven Woloshin and Lisa Schwartz indicated that the 10 percent estimate was based on study responses to a single question rather than "the four standard criteria."[57] In a large-scale study only 7 percent reported all four criteria, and only 2.7 percent reported symptoms occurring sufficiently frequently that treatment might be appropriate.[58] Woloshin and Schwartz also argued that the 2.7 percent figure was likely too high because of selection bias.

Pharmaceutical companies regularly sought applications of their drugs beyond their primary indication. Use for new indications required approval by the Food and Drug Administration, and GSK had conducted the required clinical tests to establish the safety and efficacy of Requip for the treatment of RLS.[59] Similarly, Boehringer Ingelheim's pramipexole had been approved in 1997 for treatment of idiopathic Parkinson's disease, and the company sought approval for treatment of RLS. "Pramipexole was approved in April 2006 throughout the European Union for the symptomatic treatment of moderate to severe idiopathic restless legs syndrome and is also approved in Australia, Brazil, Mexico and others."[60] The lead investigators on an RLS research study concluded, "These studies provide evidence that supports the efficacy and safety of pramipexole for RLS across a range of symptoms which were sustained over time."[61] UCB SA of Belgium was also seeking approval for its Parkinson's drug for treating RLS.

The Restless Legs Syndrome Foundation

The Restless Legs Syndrome (RLS) Foundation, of Rochester, Minnesota, conducted research on and provided

[47] *BusinessWeek*, May 8, 2006.
[48] *Wall Street Journal*, October 26, 2006.
[49] *Wall Street Journal*, October 26, 2006.
[50] *Wall Street Journal*, October 26, 2006.
[51] *Washington Post*, May 30, 2006.
[52] Disease mongering was a term coined by Lynn Payer in a 1992 book *Disease-Mongers: How Doctors, Drug Companies, and Insurers Are Making You Feel Sick*. New York: John Wiley. See also R. Moynihan and A. Cassels. (2005) *Selling Sickness. How the World's Biggest Pharmaceutical Companies Are Turning Us All into Patients*. New York: Nation Books.
[53] *Washington Post*, May 30, 2006.
[54] *Washington Post*, May 30, 2006.
[55] "Boehringer Ingelheim's Pramipexole Can Provide Benefit of Improved Mood Disturbance for People with Restless Legs Syndrome," PR Newswire Europe, September 5, 2006.
[56] Phillips B., Young T., Finn L., Asher K., Hening W. A., et al. (2000). "Epidemiology of Restless Legs Symptoms in Adults." *Arch. Intern. Med.* 160:2137–2141.
[57] Woloshin, Steven and Lisa M. Schwartz. "Giving Legs to Restless Legs: A Case Study of How the Media Helps Make People Sick." *PLoS Medicine*, 3(4): e170 DOI, April 11, 2006.
[58] Allen R., Walters A., Montplaisir J., Hening W., Myers A., et al. (2005) "Restless Legs Syndrome Prevalence and Impact: REST General Population Study." *Arch. Intern. Med.* 165:1286–1292.
[59] There was no evidence to connect RLS and Parkinson's disease.
[60] "Boehringer Ingelheim's Pramipexole Can Provide Benefit of Improved Mood Disturbance for People with Restless Legs Syndrome," PR Newswire Europe, September 5, 2006.
[61] *Pain & Central Nervous System Week*, May 1, 2006.

education about RLS. The foundation organized support groups with over 2,500 people attending and also provided information at health fairs. Georgianna Bell, executive director of the RLS Foundation, said, "There's still people out there who have the condition and don't know they have it. It's a serious condition. Raising awareness is important. It can help a lot of people." The number of visits to the foundation's Web site nearly doubled to 4,500 a day after GSK's advertising campaign for Requip.

Robert H. Waterman, Jr., chair of the foundation, wrote in the 2005 annual report, "With our newfound visibility comes the realization that people living with RLS are a big audience. From relative obscurity, we have now become a market. We are a market for medications, a market for publications, a market for untested therapies, and a market for information, the bulk of which will be reliable and some of which will not. . . . Of all the major sources of information on RLS, our foundation aims to be the most consistently reliable, objective, unbiased, and science-based."

In 2005 the RLS Foundation received $578,000 in contributions, which represented over 40 percent of its total income. GlaxoSimthKline was the only Gold Corporate Partner contributing over $250,000.[62] In addition GlaxoSmithKline—USA was a Leader, contributing at least $10,000. The foundation also reported grants receivable of $300,000 in 2005. The grants "represent promises to give from pharmaceutical companies." Boehringer Ingelheim was also a Leader.

Disease Mongering?

Referring to the promotion of drugs for an underappreciated malady, "to a growing chorus of physicians and health-care specialists, the very idea of treating the risk of a risk is wrong. They have labeled the phenomenon 'disease-mongering,' defined as the corporate-sponsored creation or exaggeration of maladies for the purpose of selling more drugs."[63] Dr. Robert L. Klitxman of Columbia University said, "The problem is that mild cases are being made to seem more serious than they are." Dr. David Henry of the University of Newcastle in Australia stated, "Drug companies are playing off the desire we all have to get rid of things that bother us."[64]

Woloshin and Schwartz identified some of the costs of such promotions: "Helping sick people get treatment is a good thing. Convincing healthy people that they are sick is not. Sick people stand to benefit from treatment, but healthy people may only get hurt: They get labeled 'sick,' may become anxious about their condition, and, if they are treated, may experience side effects that over-

whelm any potential benefit."[65] They noted that "The market for treatment gets enlarged in two ways: by narrowing the definition of health so normal experiences get labeled as pathologic, and by expanding the definition of disease to include earlier, milder, and presymptomatic forms. . . . "[66]

The promotional campaigns of the pharmaceutical companies were often amplified by coverage in the media. Woloshin and Schwartz studied media coverage of RLS and found 33 articles on the syndrome, most of which exaggerated the prevalence and seriousness of the disease. *The Daily Telegraph* proclaimed, ". . . The condition sounds like a joke, but its consequences can be devastating. Driven to despair by years of sleepless nights, patients have become suicidal."[67] Many of the articles suggested that the symptoms should be treated, and half mentioned ropinirole, often with testimonials from patients who had used the drug. None of the articles suggested the possibility of overdiagnosis.

For a year in advance of approval of ropinirole in the United Kingdom GSK had advertised in doctors' magazines to promote awareness of RLS, which is also known as Ekbom's syndrome. The ads stated that the syndrome was serious and that sufferers should consult the Web site of the Ekbom Support Group. The Web site mentioned ropinirole as effective for the syndrome. GSK supported the Web site financially.

As a result of the advertising campaign a physician in the United Kingdom complained that GSK was advertising an unapproved drug.[68] "The Prescriptions Medicines Code of Practice Authority, set up by the Association of the British Pharmaceutical Industry, ruled that GSK broke the authority's rules by promoting an unlicensed drug. 'GSK was, in effect, directing patients to a Web site that contained misleading messages about the safety of ropinirole, which might indirectly encourage patients to ask their doctors to prescribe it,' the authority said."[69] The physician said, "The Ekbom Support Group was hijacked by GSK to promote restless legs syndrome and the GSK drug ropinirole. I am not saying some people do not experience pain and restless legs but claims on the Web site that it is a widespread and serious condition are disproportionate."[70] The head of the support group said that she had taken ropinirole for seven years and it was legitimate to tell others about it.

---

[62]GSK was the only corporate partner in 2005.
[63]*BusinessWeek*, May 8, 2006.
[64]*BusinessWeek*, May 8, 2006.

[65]The label on Requip noted nausea and dizziness as side effects. Woloshin and Schwartz report: "Nausea (40% in ropinirole group versus 8% in placebo group) and dizziness (11% versus 5%, respectively). Somnolence and fatigue (ostensibly, the real target of the drug) were also higher in the ropinirole versus the placebo group (12% versus 6%, 8% versus 4%, respectively)." Woloshin and Schwartz, op cit.
[66]Woloshin and Schwartz, op cit.
[67]*Daily Telegraph*, December 1, 2004.
[68]Ropinirole was not approved until April 2006.
[69]*Sunday Times*, August 6, 2006. The Prescription Medicines Code of Practice Authority was established by the Association of the British Pharmaceutical Industry.
[70]*Sunday Times*, August 6, 2006.

A spokesperson for GSK stated, "We realize that not every medicine is for every person. The labels contain important information about whether it's appropriate, and we're confident that doctors consulting with patients will assess their health-care issues and the risks and rewards and make an appropriate decision." [71]

GSK made drugs not only for RLS but also for social anxiety disorder and other criticized applications. ■

SOURCE: This case was prepared from public sources by David P. Baron. Copyright © 2006 by David P. Baron. All rights reserved. Reprinted with permission.

Preparation Questions

1. Did GSK act responsibly in seeking approval for Requip for the treatment of RLS?
2. Has GSK acted responsibly in promoting Requip? Should it have restricted its marketing to doctors? Should it have conducted a direct-to-consumers campaign? Has GSK violated any patient rights? Has it been fair to patients?
3. Should GSK continue to support the RLS Foundation to the extent it has been?
4. How should GSK deal with the criticism of its conduct?

[71] *BusinessWeek,* May 8, 2006.

C H A P T E R

22

Implementing Ethics Systems

INTRODUCTION

Corporate statements of social responsibility and codes of ethics have become commonplace. In addition, many companies have established the position of ethics officer, and membership in the Ethics and Compliance Officer Association increased from 12 in 1992 to 1,300 in 2007, including more than half of the *Fortune* 100 companies. Surveys by the Conference Board found that in 1987 only 21 percent of the members of boards of directors participated in creating codes of ethics; by 1998 the number had increased to 78 percent. Some codes and statements of responsibility are little more than public relations, whereas others reflect a strong corporate commitment to specific standards of conduct. That commitment increasingly involves not just policies but measurement and accountability. This chapter is concerned with the transformation of ethics principles and conceptions of social responsibility into management practice.

The framework for nonmarket analysis summarized in Figure 2-5 of Chapter 2 will be used to identify the roles of ethics in management. Ethics principles are used to screen out alternatives that are unacceptable on moral grounds, just as laws screen out alternatives. In the choice stage, ethics provides the basis for evaluating moral claims and assessing responsibilities. Because all employees are expected to abide by a firm's policies, those policies must be articulated in a manner that ensures that real people in real situations will be able to act in accord with them. In the wake of a series of scandals, Chuck Prince, the new CEO of Citigroup, said, "I never thought that you had to say to people, 'We want to grow aggressively—and don't forget not to break the law.'"[1] In addition to the use of ethics in the screening and choice stages of the framework, in the analysis stage ethics provides a basis for anticipating nonmarket action motivated by moral concerns. For example, in the Chapter 21 case, *Citigroup and Subprime Lending,* Citigroup failed to anticipate the morally motivated nonmarket action directed against its subprime lending business.

Implementation requires measures ranging from developing and supporting personal integrity to providing guidance for the types of situations likely to be encountered by employees. For example, Boeing uses a training program entitled "Questions of Integrity: The Boeing Ethics Challenge."[2] The program includes 54 situations that provide a basis for discussion among employees. All Boeing employees are required to have at least 1 hour of ethics training every year, and management receives at least 5 hours of training.

Implementation may involve compliance and audit programs capable of detecting violations and ensuring that standards are met. Compliance may involve institutional features such as an audit committee, an ombudsman, or a corporate ethics officer or

---

[1]*Fortune,* November 29, 2004.
[2]Boeing's "Ethics Challenge" can be found at http://active.boeing.com/companyoffices/ethicschallenge/cfm/intial/cfm.

department. Because structural approaches can be bureaucratic, less formal approaches emphasizing personal commitment and integrity are commonly used.

The Levi Strauss & Company example illustrates the basic approach to implementing the framework presented in Figure 2-5. The chapter next considers the role of ethics in assessing the moral determinants of nonmarket action. Tensions in the application of ethics principles, including paternalism and the extent to which self-restraint should be exercised in corporate political activity, are then considered. Corporate social responsibility is considered through examples of company programs. A number of issues pertaining to implementing ethics principles and social responsibilities are examined, including compliance and accountability. The chapter concludes with a consideration of sources of unethical behavior.

EXAMPLE

Levi Strauss & Company and Global Sourcing

Levi Strauss & Company is a privately owned firm that has integrated core values into its internal policies and earned a reputation for adherence to ethics principles and concern for the interests of its stakeholders.[1] In the 1980s the company made two important market decisions: to broaden its product lines, particularly into casual wear, and to expand internationally in both the markets in which it sells and in its sourcing of products.[2] The expansion of its markets and product lines, sales growth in the United States, and pressure for low-cost sources of supply resulted in a rapid expansion in the number of suppliers. Levi Strauss soon found that a high percentage of its garments was no longer being produced in its own facilities but instead was being produced by over 700 foreign suppliers.

The company became concerned about whether its suppliers met the safety and other standards it maintained in its own production facilities. In addition, it was concerned about possible damage to its brand name resulting from the conditions in its suppliers' facilities. The company had concerns pertaining to child labor, prison labor, plant safety, and environmental protection. The company also had concerns about the human rights conditions in several countries in which its suppliers were located. Its market strategy of expanding its markets and sourcing globally had generated a set of complex issues. Its challenge was how to bring its supplier relationships into congruence with its ethics principles and core values.

Levi Strauss formed a task force to develop two policies to guide its managers: one for suppliers and the other for determining in which countries it would do business. The former focused on working conditions in suppliers' factories and covered dimensions such as

safety, working hours, discrimination, child labor, dormitories for workers, and environmental protection. The latter focused on human rights concerns, political stability, the safety of company employees, and legal protection for trademarks and commercial interests.

These policies affected its market strategy in two ways. First, the company terminated its arrangements with suppliers in Burma because of widespread human rights violations in the country. Also due to human rights concerns, it decided to withdraw from China over several years. Not only did the China decision eliminate a low-cost, high-quality source of supply, it also precluded Levi Strauss from investing in its own facilities in China.[3] Second, the Terms of Engagement policy required inspections of suppliers' factories and possibly the termination of supply arrangements. The inspections were conducted by audit teams that regularly visited each supplier and provided a detailed assessment of the conditions at the supplier's facilities.

The process used by Levi Strauss to develop the guidelines can be interpreted through the framework of Figure 2-5. The top panel of Figure 22-1 represents the development of policies to guide its managers, and the bottom panel represents the application to two issues: (1) whether to source in Burma and (2) how to address a safety issue in suppliers' factories. Referring to the top panel, Levi Strauss developed policies pertaining to suppliers and countries and considered alternatives ranging from complete withdrawal from countries to requiring suppliers to meet U.S. building codes. Screening involved the application of fundamental ethics principles in addition to its business objectives. Analysis involved the application of its "principled reasoning approach," in which stakeholder interests were explicitly taken into account.

---

[1]The company had backed its principles with action. It was a leader in integrating its factories in the South in the 1950s, and during the Depression it kept employees on its payroll rather than laying them off. See Schoenberger (2000).
[2]This example is based on Baron (1995b).

[3]Levi Strauss returned to China in 1998.

(Continued)

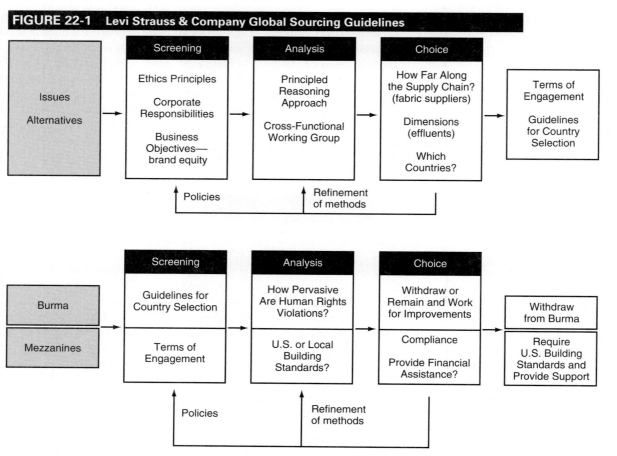

FIGURE 22-1 Levi Strauss & Company Global Sourcing Guidelines

The third stage involved developing recommendations and choosing among them. Choice included decisions about how broad the policies should be—should they cover effluents from washing operations—and how far down the supply chain they should go. Should the policies extend only to cutting and sewing operations or also to fabric producers? The results of this process were a Country Selection policy and a Terms of Engagement policy to guide managers in their decision-making about contractor practices and involvement in countries.

The bottom panel illustrates the application of the process to specific decisions about doing business in Burma and concerns about the safety of makeshift interior mezzanines used for storage in suppliers' factories in the Caribbean. The screening stage involved the application of the two policies, and analysis centered on the impact of alternatives on stakeholders as well as on specific concerns, such as how pervasive the human rights violations in Burma were and whether U.S. safety standards should be applied in the case of the mezzanines. Choices then were made between withdrawal and constructive engagement in the case of Burma and about who should pay for the safety improvements in the case of the mezzanines.

MORAL DETERMINANTS OF NONMARKET ACTION

Although nonmarket action is often motivated by self-interest, on many issues it is motivated by moral concerns.[3] A broad set of activists, advocacy groups, public interest centers, religious groups, civil rights organizations, community groups, and politicians use the language of morality to advance their causes, mobilize those sympathetic to their causes, and set social and political agendas. Managers must understand the source and strength of the moral determinants of nonmarket behavior and be able to assess the implications for the progress of issues in their life cycle. The task thus is to anticipate the types of issues on which morally based action is likely.

The first step involves assessing the range of moral concerns individuals may have about an issue. Since moral concerns are not the same as self-interest, individuals who

---

[3]See Chapter 6.

are not directly affected by an issue must be considered. These individuals may become aware of the issue through media coverage, as considered in Chapter 3. The activist and advocacy groups and the networks of NGOs and community groups considered in Chapter 4 are also an important source of information to the public and the media, and they often frame issues in moral terms.

The next step is to determine how members of the public are likely to evaluate an issue or company practice. To do so, managers should put themselves in the role of those in the firm's environment and evaluate the issue as they might. Since individuals use a variety of moral standards, managers should examine the issue from utilitarian, rights, and justice perspectives. The objective of this step is to identify the range of moral concerns that may be raised about an issue or practice.

The link between moral concerns and nonmarket action is mediated by the cost of taking individual and collective action. These costs are difficult to assess, but it is clear that there are some individuals who have a high degree of commitment and low costs of acting based on moral concerns. The likelihood of collective action thus is governed by the same factors considered in Chapter 6. The costs of nonmarket and collective action are lower when people with similar moral perspectives are already organized, as in the case of an advocacy group or a union as in the Chapter 4 case *Nike in Southeast Asia*. The impact increases with the number of concerned individuals; their resources in terms of dollars, time, and energy; and the effectiveness of the strategies they employ.

An important factor in collective action is the extent to which the initial actions of those motivated by moral concerns spark a responsive chord with the public or attract the attention of the media or politicians. In assessing this, it is useful to consider the claims and

---

EXAMPLE

Circle K's Health Care Policy

The Circle K Corporation operated gasoline service stations and convenience marts in the Midwest, South, and West. Circle K had high turnover in its predominantly low-skilled positions, and its health care costs had doubled over the past 2 years. Its costs were twice that of some of its competitors. The company self-insured, so it and its employees directly bore the costs of employee health care. To control its costs, the company decided to limit health care coverage for certain conditions. In a letter to employees the CEO explained,

> The company is concerned about certain personal lifestyle decisions regarding the use of alcohol, drugs, self-inflicted wounds, and sickness due to acquired immune deficiency syndrome. We believe that these personal lifestyle decisions could seriously impact other participants' health care costs. Employees who are proven to suffer illness and accidents that result from the use of alcohol, drugs, self-inflicted wounds and AIDS, proven not to be contracted from blood transfusion, will not be eligible to receive company health care coverage in those circumstances. . . .

Circle K had thoroughly researched the issue and was confident that its new policy was in accord with the relevant law.

The reaction to Circle K's policy was swift. Moral objections included whether Circle K was making judgments about the morality of its employees, whether the policy was discriminatory, and whether it was unjust to deny coverage to those who were most in need of it. The particular lightning rod was AIDS. AIDS activists and advocates were well organized and politically effective and were concerned that other companies might make similar changes in their health care policies. The activists brought the policy change to the attention of the public through the news media. AIDS had high societal significance and audience interest, so the news media provided extensive coverage. Circle K's CEO and its chairman were forced to defend the policy on national television. On the *Today* show Bryant Gumbel asked the chairman, "What is it you're trying to police here—is it health or morality?"[1] Facing intense social pressure, the company soon withdrew its new policy. The failure to assess how others might evaluate the policy and whether morally motivated nonmarket action might arise resulted in a debacle that tarnished the company.

[1] *Wall Street Journal*, August 18, 1988.

arguments made in attempting to attract broader public support. Even when motivation is based on self-interest, moral claims may be used to advance a cause, and the media is often responsive to its perception of the societal significance of such claims.

The final step is to predict the likely individual and collective action. This involves an assessment of how many people may act and how their moral concerns might affect the behavior of institutional officeholders. Little systematic evidence is available on how many individuals participate in nonmarket activity as a function of moral concerns, so experience is important to assessing morally motivated behavior. The Circle K example illustrates the impact of morally motivated action. The chapter case, *Advanced Technology Laboratories, Inc.,* provides another opportunity to consider the moral determinants of nonmarket action in the context of a company whose new hand-held ultrasound device could be used in the sex selection of fetuses.

THE CHALLENGE OF CORPORATE SOCIAL RESPONSIBILITY

The spread of codes of ethics and statements of social responsibility is due to two factors. The first is a belief by some firms that they should be accountable for conduct beyond profit maximization. The second is a defensive motivation intended to avoid private politics led by activists and other interest groups or to preempt public politics and additional government regulation. Regardless of the motivation, these codes and statements commit firms to particular standards of conduct. The focus in this section is on the first motivation and how the resulting standards are implemented.

The social responsibilities of business are identified by ethics principles and reasoning based on those principles. The reliance on principles, however, may not be sufficient to identify unambiguously the appropriate concept of corporate responsibility. Principles are stated generally, and translating them into rules of behavior and goals is challenging. Ethics systems are not sufficiently precise, for example, to determine how much corporations should contribute to charity. A system of justice might imply that some portion of profits be used for charitable purposes, whereas a rights-based system that emphasizes maximal liberty holds that the firm's owners as principals should choose whether and how much to contribute from their dividends or share price appreciation. On some issues the actions consistent with a utilitarian standard may differ from the actions consistent with rights or justice standards. From the perspective of utilitarianism, an integrity test is appropriate for a job if the benefits it yields are greater than its costs. An ethics system that holds that individuals have rights to privacy and freedom from arbitrary treatment, however, indicates that the use of the tests should be limited. The challenge for management is to formulate policies that respect these important considerations and resolve conflicts among them.

One frequently used approach to giving emphasis to corporate social responsibility is the "triple bottom line."[4] The triple bottom line is intended to measure corporate environmental, social, and financial performance. More importantly, it serves as a reminder to management and other employees that profits are not the only relevant measure of corporate performance. It also commits the firm to report on all three dimensions of performance. Much of this reporting could be done independently of the triple bottom line perspective, so the value of the triple bottom line may primarily be in terms of motivation and commitment.[5]

An important concern about the triple bottom line is whether the capital markets will actually reward environmental and social performance. And, if it is rewarded, is it because it helps reduce social pressure from private and public politics or because consumers, investors, and employees reward socially responsible behavior? As indicated in Chapter 18, the empirical literature is inconclusive on this question. The study by Baron, Harjoto, and Jo discussed in that chapter provides evidence that on average social performance may not be rewarded whereas social pressure is penalized.

---

[4]See Elkington (1997).
[5]Norman and MacDonald (2003) provide a scathing criticism of the triple bottom line concept.

Another approach to measuring corporate social performance is the balanced scorecard.[6] The balanced scorecard was proposed as a system for evaluating overall performance by assessing financial performance, customer relationships, internal company processes, and learning and growth. Some companies have extended it to include ethics and social performance. The balanced scorecard has been used to assess corporate performance, business unit performance, and the performance of individual managers. Compensation can then be based on the resulting scores.

As an example, in the late 1990s Citibank introduced a balanced scorecard that broadened performance evaluation to include five components: financial performance, customer/franchise performance, strategic cost management, risk management, and people management. Its incentive compensation system, including bonuses and stock options, was also broadened to include performance along these five dimensions. One objective was to build teamwork with a focus on the overall performance of the corporation and its businesses. Each of its five businesses—consumer banking, credit cards, private banking, corporate banking, and emerging markets—was evaluated in terms of these five measures. For the chairman and several other top executives, 100 percent of their variable compensation (bonus) was based on corporate scorecard performance. For the next group of 30 executives, 50 percent of their bonus was based on the corporate scorecard performance and 50 percent on individual scorecard performance. The balanced scorecard did not explicitly include corporate social responsibility, but compliance with the company's code of conduct was implicit in the evaluations. Given the scandals involving Citigroup listed in Chapter 19 and CEO Prince's comment earlier in the chapter, perhaps the code should have been explicitly included in the scorecard.

In a potentially important case affecting corporate communication and the reporting of social performance, Nike was the subject of a lawsuit alleging that in defending its practices pertaining to its overseas suppliers' factories it had provided false and misleading information about its corporate social responsibility (see the Chapter 4 case *Nike in Southeast Asia*). Nike argued that its statements were speech protected by the First Amendment, but the California Supreme Court ruled that the case could go to trial under state consumer fraud laws pertaining to commercial speech, which receives less protection than individual and political speech. The U.S. Supreme Court refused to hear Nike's appeal on technical rather than substantive grounds. Although Nike's position was backed by businesses and a group of 32 publishing and broadcast companies that filed a supporting brief, the company was in a dilemma. The only way it could get a Supreme Court ruling supporting corporate speech was to lose the case on trial, but it expected to win. Consequently, Nike decided to settle the case.[7] The California Supreme Court decision that such cases could be tried then remained in place.

Nike said that "the case had a chilling effect on Nike's ability to speak out on issues of public importance." In response to the settlement Nike announced that it would no longer issue its corporate social responsibility report and it would limit its "participation in public events and media engagement in California."[8] In 2005 Nike resumed issuing its corporate social responsibility report.

The implementation of social responsibility programs can also be thwarted by private politics. Under Warren Buffett's leadership Berkshire Hathaway allowed shareholders to designate $18 a share of their dividends to three charities of their choice. A woman who had become an independent sales agent for Berkshire's Pampered Chef company in part because the company's mission statement encouraged its employees to "develop their God-given talents," learned that some of the profits she would generate would be donated to Planned Parenthood and other pro-choice groups. She launched a private politics campaign over the Internet. Customers complained, some sales agents resigned, and Pampered Chef was pressured to the point that Berkshire ended the dividend contributions program. The company, which had frequently been targeted by pro-life groups, said it ended the program because it was hurting Pampered Chef and its employees.

---

[6]See Kaplan and Norton (1992).
[7]Nike also agreed to contribute $1.5 million to the Fair Labor Association (see Chapter 23) and continue its after-work educational programs in overseas suppliers' factories.
[8]Nike press release, "Kasky v. Nike," September 12, 2003. Nike also declined to release an updated version of the Chapter 4 case *Nike in Southeast Asia*.

The chapter case, *Gilead Sciences (A): The Gilead Access Program for HIV Drugs,* concerns a company committed to making its market-leading HIV drugs accessible to those who needed them throughout the world. The step from commitment to actually having the drugs reach HIV/AIDS victims in Africa and Asia, however, posed a considerable challenge. After the failure of its first attempt to provide access, the company needed a creative solution to the access problem.

CORPORATE SOCIAL RESPONSIBILITY AND ETHICS IN PRACTICE

Firms must put their conceptions of social responsibility into practice. This can involve the design of innovative programs, employee participation programs, or environmental projects. Individuals as well as firms can also implement their conception of social responsibility in organization forms other than for-profit corporations, as in the Chapter 17 case, *Social Entrepreneurship: Kiva,* and the South Shore Bank example in this chapter. Some company programs are specific to specific issues, as in the case of the Unocal example, whereas others involve broader programs. In three examples, BP was proactive in addressing nonmarket challenges; Wal-Mart acted soon after the nonmarket challenges began to spread; and Citigroup acted after a series of scandals had damaged its reputation.

EXAMPLE

Unocal Corporation and the Dirty Car Bounty

Air quality in the Los Angeles basin was among the worst in the nation, and stringent measures were being prepared to address the problem. Proposals included restricting driving and shutting down factories when air quality reached potentially hazardous levels. Some firms began to take steps on their own to address the problem.

Unocal announced a novel program in which it offered to pay $700 cash for 7,000 pre-1971 automobiles, which would then be scrapped.[1] The scrap value of the cars was estimated to be $10 to $20, and their market value was believed to be considerably lower than $700.[2] In addition, Unocal offered to provide free tune-ups for pre-1975 cars. The cost of the program was estimated to be nearly $10 million. Unocal Chairman and CEO Richard J. Stegemeier explained, "Sixty percent of smog comes from mobile sources, cars and trucks. Thirty percent is coming from pre-1975 automobiles. If you want to make a big impact in a hurry, this is by far the quickest and most cost-effective way."[3] Although the impact on air quality depended on which modes of transportation replaced the old cars, Unocal estimated that emissions of pollutants would be reduced by 6 million pounds a year.[4]

Within months, more than 10,000 car owners had applied to the program. Unocal also encouraged other companies to participate in the program. In July 1990 Ford announced that it would buy 1,000 old automobiles in the Los Angeles area and would offer the sellers an additional $700 rebate on the purchase of a new Ford.

The South Coast Air Resources Board, a state regulatory agency, subsequently adopted an old car scrap plan, which confirms that Unocal's innovation was a benefit to society. The program has been adopted elsewhere by private parties and by governments and has become a serious instrument in pollution control programs. A study by Dixon and Garber (2001) concluded that continuing to scrap old cars and light trucks "would improve air quality in the greater Los Angeles area at a reasonable cost."[5]

Unocal also benefited from the program. Goodwill was generated, and it earned emissions credits for reducing pollutants.[6] The program may also have relieved pressure on environmental issues. Nevertheless, the Unocal old car program probably made shareholders worse off, since it provided a public good with little likelihood of capturing benefits sufficient to cover its cost. That is, few consumers were likely to switch to Unocal gasoline because of the program. Unocal had identified an innovative alternative to more costly measures of reducing automobile emissions.

---

[1]The 7,000 represented approximately 1.7 percent of the old cars in the Los Angeles area.
[2]Because of the attractiveness of the offer and its desire to focus on the Los Angeles basin, Unocal restricted the offer to autos registered in the area for at least the prior 6 months.
[3]*New York Times,* April 27, 1990.
[4]Cars built before 1975, when catalytic converters were required on new automobiles, emitted 50 grams of carbon monoxide per mile driven on average, whereas post-1975 models emitted 20.7 grams per mile. Cars too old to have catalytic converters also emitted many more hydrocarbons and nitrogen oxides than newer models.

[5]See, however, the Chapter 11 case *Environmental Justice and Pollution Credits Trading Systems.*
[6]Unocal sought to build goodwill by producing television commercials showing the crushing of old automobiles under its program.

EXAMPLE

South Shore Bank and Community Development

In 1973 several corporations, foundations, and other organizations, including the Ford Foundation, Allstate Insurance, and the Episcopal Church, formed the ShoreBank Corporation to purchase the South Shore Bank in Chicago. The coalition's objective was for the bank to support community development by lending to small businesses and housing restoration groups. Over 90 percent of the residents in the local communities served were minorities, and the housing stock was primarily apartment buildings.

Working with neighborhood groups, by 2006 South Shore Bank had been involved in the rehabilitation of 52,000 affordable housing units and had loaned over $2.9 billion to 13,000 families and businesses. It also emphasized lending to small commercial establishments that might not qualify for regular bank loans. The bank had subsidiary banks in Chicago, Cleveland, Detroit, Ilwaco, Washington, and Portland, Oregon. It also had nonprofit affiliates in Chicago, Cleveland, Detroit, Ilwaco, and the Upper Peninsula of Michigan. Shore-Bank maintained a strong balance sheet, but its profitability was low. In 2006 it had total assets of $2.1 billion and its profits were a record $5.2 million.

ShoreBank was the inspiration for the federal government's Community Development Financial Institution (CDFI) program to support financing for people without access to conventional financing. The program, administered by the Treasury Department, provided subsidized financing and grants to CDFIs that financed housing and businesses in low-income areas. In 2005 the CDFI program financed the construction in rehabilitation of 27,000 affordable housing units. By 2007 the Treasury had provided grants of $864 million to support CDFIs, and the grants were matched by $16 billion in private sector investments.

The motivation for founding ShoreBank was primarily moral. In terms of performance the bank was not only successful in the communities in which it operated but it also was a model for other community development institutions. The initial funding of the bank was provided without expectation of a financial return, and all profits have been reinvested. The initial funders thus did not obtain a financial return, and their reward was a socially responsible investment that established a sustainable enterprise providing community development benefits.

EXAMPLE

BP and Social Responsibility

In the early 1990s BP developed an oil field in Colombia in an area in which Marxist guerillas were active. Some oil companies in the area made direct payments to the guerillas, but BP decided to back the government. BP paid $1.24 per barrel of oil produced to support the assignment of government troops to protect the oil field. It also made other payments to support the Colombian government. BP was widely criticized for its involvement and was accused of paying a war tax. The UK media provided extensive coverage of the situation, including a stinging television documentary. While BP defended its action, it was clearly hurt by the criticism.

At that time many businesses, and particularly those in the energy industries, had opposed taking strong measures to address global warming because of the costs that would be borne by industry and the public. In 1997 the chairman of Exxon expressed the view that costly actions should not be taken until the scientific evidence was more conclusive. BP reviewed the scientific evidence and the policy alternatives for addressing global warming and concluded that action was called for. Breaking ranks with the oil industry, CEO Lord Browne of Madingley (1997) stated in an address at Stanford University,

> The time to consider the policy dimensions of climate change is not when the link between greenhouse gases and climate change is conclusively proven—but when the possibility cannot be discounted and is taken seriously by the society of which we are part. We in BP have reached that point. It is an important moment for us. We must now focus on what can and what should be done not because we can be certain climate change is happening but because the possibility cannot be ignored.[1]

BP participated in the World Business Council on Sustainable Development, and Lord Browne and

[1]Browne, John, "Speech at Stanford University, 19 May 1997." *Review: The BP Quarterly Technology Magazine,* July/August, pp. 11–13.

(Continued)

other business leaders met with President Clinton to discuss measures to deal with global climate change. BP joined with Environmental Defense and other companies to develop an emissions trading system for greenhouse gases, as considered in Chapter 11. BP joined with the Nature Conservancy, American Electric Power, the U.S. and Bolivian governments, and a local conservation group to conserve a tropical forest in Bolivia. Flaring, the burning of natural gas released in conjunction with crude oil production, was a major source of carbon dioxide emissions, and BP, which had already dramatically reduced flaring in its Norwegian operations, pledged to eliminate all flaring. BP produced solar panels in Australia, Spain, and Saudi Arabia, and extended its commitment to solar power with a dozen plants in construction, including one in California. BP also served as the chair of the International Climate Change Partnership.

BP also decided to stop all nonmarket activity pertaining to opening the Arctic National Wildlife Refuge to oil exploration, although it did not pledge not to drill if the Refuge were opened.[2] BP stopped all corporate political contributions in the United States and elsewhere and, as considered in Chapter 23, refused to pay bribes in Russia.[3]

BP's commitment to corporate social responsibility included five components: ethical conduct; employees; relationships (customers and suppliers); health, safety, and environmental performance; and control and finance. To implement its policies and fulfill its commitments, it created a new staff function with seven regional directors to encourage commitments.

BP also reformulated its management performance contracts to include social and environmental performance including ethical conduct.[4]

BP's concept of corporate social responsibility did not go far enough for some activist groups. Greenpeace sought to end all oil exploration and launched protests against BP. Matthew Spencer of Greenpeace said that BP has "made a valiant attempt to put a green sheen on [its] organization. Inevitably, if you scratch the surface, you find an aggressive company looking for new oil reserves."[5]

BP subsequently decided to reposition, or in its own terminology, rebrand the company. It changed its name from British Petroleum to BP, adopted the slogan "Beyond Petroleum," and replaced its corporate symbol with a sunburst. It also launched a major public relations campaign promoting its new image at a cost estimated at $200 million. BP hoped that its rebranding and its substantive actions would be rewarded in the marketplace, but many observers remained skeptical.

BP's slogan "Beyond Petroleum" led some people to believe that the company was committed to switching from oil and gas to alternative sources of energy. Lord Browne was forced to clarify that BP's principal goal was "to create long-term—and I do stress long-term—shareholder value."[6] He also explained, "My view is that hydrocarbons will be the bulk of the energy supply for the next 30 to 50 years."[7] Skeptics wondered if BP's commitment to the environment was sustainable. As discussed in Chapter 1, BP had several serious violations of standards, including a refinery accident that killed 15 workers.

---

[2]BP was the largest producer on the north slope of Alaska.
[3]BP halted corporate soft money contributions in the United States, as had a number of major U.S. corporations, although its U.S. employees continued their contributions to a corporate PAC.

[4]See the case *British Petroleum (C): Social Responsibility* in Baron (2003c).
[5]*Wall Street Journal*, August 12, 1998.
[6]*Wall Street Journal*, November 25, 2004.
[7]*Fortune*, December 8, 2002.

EXAMPLE

Wal-Mart: Reputation and Stakeholder Management

Wal-Mart was criticized by activists, unions, and politicians for allegedly depressing wages, providing inadequate health insurance for its 1.2 million associates, opposing unions, driving small merchants out of business, and adversely affecting the sense of community in small towns. Wal-Mart had become part of America's culture and as such received increasing attention. Wal-Mart had regularly been in television's *King of the Hill* as Megalo-Mart, and began to appear elsewhere on television. "Every Mart" was the setting for a *Without a Trace* episode, *South Park* had an

episode on a "Wall-Mart" store coming to town, and the company was the butt of jokes on *The Daily Show*. Both CNBC and PBS's *Frontline* ran documentaries on the company.

Wal-Mart also experienced a host of labor incidents that generated criticism. In late 2003 Immigration and Customs agents raided several Wal-Mart stores, taking into custody 200 undocumented workers employed by custodial service companies that cleaned the stores. Some Wal-Mart employees were revealed to have been forced to punch out and

(Continued)

continue working, and some minors had worked too many hours. The media reported that in high-crime areas Wal-Mart had a policy of locking night shift employees in the building to prevent "shrinkage" from theft. In many cases there was no one with a key to unlock the doors in the case of an emergency, and employees had to call a store manager to have the doors unlocked.[1] Wal-Mart was criticized for refusing to sell some magazines and CDs and concealing parts of the covers of some magazines. Wal-Mart was also named in the largest-ever class action lawsuit on behalf of 1.6 million women alleging job discrimination in promotions.

Wal-Mart's strategy of entering urban markets and opening superstores that sold groceries directly threatened the Union of Food and Commercial Workers (UFCW). Because of growing competition from Wal-Mart, supermarket chains in Southern California demanded that their union employees pay a share of their health care costs. The UFCW struck, and after a lengthy strike an agreement was reached with the union members agreeing to share in the costs. The union then adopted a strategy of opposing the opening of Wal-Mart stores in urban areas. Backed by the California Labor Federation the California legislature passed a bill requiring an "economic impact" report for any new "superstore." Only Wal-Mart superstores would be affected. The governor vetoed the bill. In a public referendum, voters in Inglewood, California, rejected a proposed change in a zoning requirement to allow Wal-Mart to build a superstore. The nonmarket pressure not only damaged the company's reputation but also threatened its expansion strategy, as considered in the Chapter 7 case, *Wal-Mart and Its Urban Expansion Strategy.*

Wal-Mart belatedly recognized that it had focused on only one primary stakeholder—its customers. Wal-Mart CEO H. Lee Scott, Jr., observed, "What we have found is that there is a different group of stakeholders today that are important, and that is a person who's not familiar with Wal-Mart stores, they're not familiar with what we stand for. So their view of Wal-Mart stores is what they read in the newspaper and what they see on TV. We have decided it is important for us to reach out to that group."[2] Pointing to a change in direction, a spokesperson commented, "For too long, we thought that if we just focused on our customers then everything else would follow. We probably did not realize soon enough how important it was to work with the media. It is an acknowledgment that the media and others offer important venues for telling our story, and we need to continue to do a better job at that."[3] Wal-Mart had also ignored government and had not had a presence in Washington. Scott noted that Sam Walton "did not get involved in the political process; he prided himself on that."[4]

A spokeswoman for Wal-Mart explained, "The challenge to Wal-Mart is to change the way we do some things without changing who we are."[5] In 2004 Wal-Mart broadened its stakeholder focus and began to repair its tarnished reputation. It began a television and print advertising campaign featuring employees telling how happy they were working for Wal-Mart and how the company had provided opportunities for advancement. It sponsored PBS and NPR programs and began a $500,000 fellowship program for minority journalism students at nine universities. In California it took out full-page newspaper advertisements stating the facts with the introduction, "While we are always willing to consider constructive criticism, much of what has been said publicly about Wal-Mart in California is simply not true." Nationally, Wal-Mart took out full-page advertisements announcing its Teacher of the Year Program awards and stating that it would contribute $40 million to education in 2004. It also opened a Washington office to develop better relationships with the federal government. Wal-Mart also acted to deal with some of the community effects of its stores. It had closed hundreds of stores in the United States, with over 150 vacant. The company worked with local communities to find new businesses that could occupy the stores.

The Part I integrative case, *Wal-Mart: Nonmarket Pressure and Reputation Risk (A),* provides a broader look at the social pressure on the company, and the Chapter 19 case, *Wal-Mart: Nonmarket Pressure and Reputation Risk (B): A New Nonmarket Strategy,* considers the first step in the company's new environmental and corporate social responsibility programs.

---

[1]Emergency exits were not locked, but employees were told to use them only in a true emergency.
[2]*New York Times,* September 9, 2004.

[3]*New York Times,* September 9, 2004.
[4]*New York Times,* September 9, 2004.
[5]*New York Times,* September 9, 2004.

Statements of Commitment and Expectations

Many companies specifically identify the set of responsibilities they assume and state those responsibilities in a mission statement as both a form of commitment and an agenda for managerial action. One of the oldest of these statements is Johnson & Johnson's "Our Credo," first issued in 1948, which identifies a set of responsibilities

---

EXAMPLE

Citigroup: Responsibility Under Fire?

Citigroup was one of the most profitable companies in the world with 2003 net earnings of $18 billion, compared to $21.5 billion for ExxonMobil and $15 billion for General Electric. Earnings were up again in 2004. Yet Citigroup's involvement in a series of scandals had continued unabated, and some commentators argued its seeming inability to stop the scandals had depressed its stock price. In addition to the regulatory judgments, settlements of lawsuits, and remaining lawsuits discussed in Chapter 19, which could ultimately cost Citigroup $10 billion, new scandals arose. In London Citigroup traders had dumped $13.3 billion of European government bonds on the market and then repurchased the bonds at depressed prices. The whipsawing of the bond market violated unwritten financial services industry standards and led to an investigation by British and German regulators. In Japan irregularities in Citigroup's private banking operations were identified in 2001 by Japanese regulators, but by 2003 the private banking group had returned to the same practices. The Japanese government ordered Citigroup's private bank to close, and Citigroup did so and also voluntarily closed its trust bank. Several Citigroup bankers in Japan were fired, and CEO Prince publicly apologized in Japan.

Some commentators argued that the source of Citigroup's problems was a culture emphasizing strong earnings growth and aggressive internal competition for performance. Citigroup had a decentralized organizational structure with a matrix overlay.[1] Bonuses were tied to balanced scorecard grades, but financial and earnings performance dominated. High-powered incentives were used in trading, as was standard practice in the industry.

As the scandals began to unfold Citigroup hired a new chief financial officer from outside the company, and Prince instituted tighter financial controls. He transferred responsibility for compliance with Citigroup's code of conduct from the legal department to the bank's senior risk manager. Citigroup established a new Policy Compliance Assessment Group, and multiple compliance reports to the board of directors were required. Prince subsequently fired three of the most senior Citigroup executives, all of whom had had some oversight responsibility for private banking in Japan. In a message to employees, Prince said, "We have to have the moral compass to deliver those profits and growth responsibly and honestly. Citigroup's culture must be synonymous with integrity."[2] Prince attempted to embed the message in Citigroup's culture by requiring ethics training of all employees and promoting an internal "ethics hotline." All finance, accounting, treasury, tax, and investor relations professionals worldwide were required to sign Citigroup's code of ethics. Prince also planned to include additional qualitative questions in its balanced scorecard evaluation system.

Prince, however, commented, "We want to maintain that aggressive nature. We're not going to turn ourselves into a charity, we're not going to become, you know, a big, bureaucratic government institution."[3] One observer commented, "The constraint on Citi's growth is not its market size, nor its capital. It may well be that Citi can't achieve its growth ambitions because it cannot safeguard itself properly from regulatory and reputation risk."[4] The challenge for Citigroup was whether it could conduct its business with integrity and avoid nonmarket limits to its growth. With 300,000 employees operating in over 100 countries, the challenge was substantial.

Whether a result of culture or bad judgment, Citigroup was embroiled in a massive financial debacle in 2007–2008 requiring the write-off of $40 billion in subprime mortgage securities with more write-offs likely. CEO Chuck Prince was fired, and the bank faced lawsuits, investor outrage, and new regulations, and required a bailout from the government.

---

[1]See Baron and Besanko (2001) for an analysis of Citigroup's organization of its global corporate banking business.

[2]*BusinessWeek*, October 4, 2004.
[3]*New York Times*, November 7, 2004.
[4]*BusinessWeek*, October 4, 2004.

---

and forms the basis for the expectations of its constituents. Johnson & Johnson credited "Our Credo" for having guided its quick and successful actions in 1982 and 1986, when someone put cyanide in Tylenol capsules.

In accord with "Our Credo," Johnson & Johnson implemented a program to reduce its workplace injuries and accidents with the goal of an injury-free work environment. As a result of both capital expenditures and safety programs, the company reduced its

EXAMPLE

Johnson & Johnson's "Our Credo"

We believe our first responsibility is to the doctors, nurses, and patients, to mothers and fathers and all others who use our products and services. In meeting their needs everything we do must be of high quality. We must constantly strive to reduce our costs in order to maintain reasonable prices. Customers' orders must be serviced promptly and accurately. Our suppliers and distributors must have an opportunity to make a fair profit.

We are responsible to our employees, the men and women who work with us throughout the world. Everyone must be considered as an individual. We must respect their dignity and recognize their merit. They must have a sense of security in their jobs. Compensation must be fair and adequate, and working conditions clean, orderly and safe. We must be mindful of ways to help our employees fulfill their family responsibilities. Employees must feel free to make suggestions and complaints. There must be equal opportunity for employment, development and advancement for those qualified. We must provide competent management, and their actions must be just and ethical.

We are responsible to the communities in which we live and work and to the world community as well. We must be good citizens—support good works and charities and bear our fair share of taxes. We must encourage civic improvements and better health and education. We must maintain in good order the property we are privileged to use, protecting the environment and natural resources.

Our final responsibility is to our stockholders. Business must make a sound profit. We must experiment with new ideas. Research must be carried on, innovative programs developed and mistakes paid for. New equipment must be purchased, new facilities provided and new products launched. Reserves must be created to provide for adverse times. When we operate according to these principles, the stockholders should realize a fair return.

lost workday incidence rate from 1.81 in 1981 to 0.14 by 1989. The safety program established goals in the following areas: injury prevention and loss control, environmental surveillance and control, medical surveillance and examination, work-related injury and illness management, and disease intervention and associated employee assistance programs. In addition to complying with regulations, operating units were to "establish health and safety guidelines where Credo commitments, scientific principles or regulatory inadequacies dictate." The operating companies of Johnson & Johnson then evaluated and reported their safety records.

The safety program included a requirement that the head of the unit in which a serious, lost workday accident occurred file a report on the accident within 24 hours. The unit head then had to go to company headquarters to report in person to the operating board on the steps being taken to prevent similar accidents in the future. The purpose of the report was informational and was directed at measures that could be taken to reduce future accidents.

Core Principles and Their Evolution

Johnson & Johnson's "Our Credo" identifies commitments to a set of stakeholders and can be revised as the set of relevant issues it faces evolves. Revisions of guiding principles such as "Our Credo" are based on a set of core principles that provide consistency over time. The relationship between core principles and current policies and practices is illustrated in Figure 22-2.[9] The relationship is based on three components: organizational values, corporate objectives, and strategies and practices. Organizational values serve as the core principles that guide the strategies and practices of the company as it strives to achieve its objectives. Core principles can be viewed as unchanging. Organizational objectives are revised when necessary but only infrequently. Strategies and practices are revised frequently as a function of the salient issues in the market and nonmarket environments.

---

[9]This figure is due to Kirk Hanson.

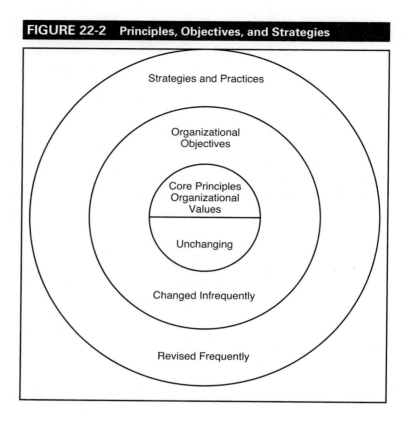

FIGURE 22-2 Principles, Objectives, and Strategies

Statements such as "Our Credo" serve as commitments to stakeholders and other constituents. They also communicate to employees a set of principles and values that they can follow in their jobs. The chapter case, *Denny's and Customer Service*, considers a company with serious allegations about racial discrimination that faced the challenge of developing a program for eliminating discrimination and changing its culture. Seven years later Advantica Restaurant Group, Inc., the company formed to operate Denny's, Coro's, and Carrows restaurants, was ranked first in *Fortune* magazine's "America's 50 Best Companies for Minorities."

The Body Shop and the Social Audit

By 1998 the Body Shop International PLC had grown from a single shop in Brighton, England, to over 1,500 stores in 47 countries. Founder Anita Roddick had propelled the growth of the Body Shop by positioning the company as an ethical and socially responsible merchandiser of cosmetics with environmentally friendly products and practices. The Body Shop developed a widely publicized Trade Not Aid program in which it sourced raw materials from indigenous peoples, purchasing, for example, blue corn from the Santa Ana Pueblo tribe in New Mexico and nuts from the Kayapo Indians in Brazil. In its promotional and public relations activities, the company highlighted these programs, along with other policies such as not testing its cosmetics on animals and pledging to "use our purchasing power to stop suppliers' animal testing." Roddick appeared in an American Express advertisement touting its program of buying ingredients from developing countries. These programs brought the Body Shop rapid growth, as consumers responded to its image and cachet. The economic and social success of the company made an international celebrity of Roddick, who used her podium to campaign for a variety of causes. To protest Shell Oil Company's failure to halt human rights abuses by the Nigerian government, she erected a large electronic sign reading STEER CLEAR OF SHELL—BOYCOTT NOW across from a Shell service station. The Body Shop also carried its campaigns into its stores.

In 1994 the Body Shop was criticized by a journalist in the magazine *Business Ethics*.[10] The criticism centered not on whether the Body Shop's record was better than that of other companies but instead on whether the company was living up to its lofty pronouncements. A company that had used its ethical and environmental policies to promote its business was held to meet a higher standard than other companies. The Body Shop and Roddick aggressively attacked their critics, but when the concerns did not subside, the company commissioned a social audit of its policies and accomplishments. The report concluded that "The Body Shop has been an important and powerful example to many other businesses and to consumers that it is possible to serve both social as well as economic goals. It has also pioneered many social innovations that have stimulated others to try similar efforts. The company's impact as an exemplary business, however, has at times been weakened by some of the behaviors noted in this report."[11]

The audit evaluated the Body Shop's social performance on the following dimensions: company values and mission; relations with shareholders, customers, employees, franchisees, suppliers, community, and trading with communities in need; concern for the environment; and contributions to social change. The audit gave high marks to the company's values, mission, and contributions to social change and the lowest mark to its reactions to criticisms. The audit also indicated several areas in which the company had not lived up to its proclamations. The company purchased only £2.25 million of supplies from communities in need, and the audit pointed to conflicts with its trading partners, including the Kayapo Indians. The report stated, "In this area more than any other, the company's performance lags behind what has been implied by its past promotions."

The Body Shop's financial performance began to slip as the cachet of retailing with a conscience faded and competition developed from other retailers using natural ingredients. Roddick was replaced as CEO by the board of directors in 1998, although she and her husband remained on the board of directors. In 2006 the Body Shop was acquired by L'Oréal.

Codes of Conduct

Ethics principles and corporate social responsibility commitments are implemented by individuals who may differ in their values, their ability to reason from ethics principles, and their moral fortitude. Firms therefore must provide guidance to their employees in the conduct of their duties. This guidance often is codified in a detailed set of procedures to which employees can refer when confronted with particular issues.[12] These codes include the requirements established by laws, prescriptions of behavior that go beyond the law, tests to determine whether an action should be taken, and, in some cases, principles from which the employee is to reason about a situation.

The Business Roundtable (1988, pp. 5–6) identified the topics covered by company codes of ethics and standards of conduct.

- Fundamental honesty and adherence to the law
- Product safety and quality
- Health and safety in the workplace
- Conflicts of interest
- Employment practices
- Fairness in selling/marketing practices
- Financial reporting
- Supplier relationships
- Pricing, billing, and contracting
- Trading in securities/using inside information
- Payments to obtain business/Foreign Corrupt Practices Act

---

[10]See Entine (1994).

[11]Kirk O. Hanson, "Social Evaluation: The Body Shop International 1995," The Body Shop International PLC, Watersmead, England, 1996.

[12]Williams (2000) addresses international codes of conduct.

- Acquiring and using information about others
- Security
- Political activities
- Protection of the environment
- Intellectual property/proprietary information

Competitive and Proprietary Information

Practices specified in a code of conduct are often directed at situations particular to the industries in which the firm operates. In industries characterized by a high level of research and development, rapid technological progress, and intense competition, market and competitor intelligence activities can be important. Procter & Gamble decided to expand in the hair care market by purchasing Clairol and introduced a new brand, Physique. A major competitor was Unilever PLC; its brands included Suave, Finesse, and Salon Selectives. P&G managers hired agents to obtain competitive intelligence on Unilever. The agents searched the trash of a Unilever office, obtaining 80 pages of confidential plans that they then gave to P&G. Searching the trash was not illegal, but it was prohibited by P&G's code of ethics. When top management of P&G learned about the espionage, P&G fired three of its managers and blew the whistle on itself. P&G notified Unilever that it had received the plans, and the two companies began negotiating a resolution of the issue. P&G agreed to pay $10 million to Unilever and submit to third-party audits to ensure that the confidential plans were not used.

In high-technology industries intellectual property is a crucial factor in competitive advantage. A temptation in such industries is to obtain information that may have intellectual property protection. Hewlett-Packard's policy on this issue was as follows:

> HP must be well informed of competitive developments and is entitled to review all pertinent public information concerning competitive products (e.g., published specifications and prices and trade journal articles). However, HP may not attempt through improper means to acquire a competitor's trade secrets or other proprietary or confidential information, including information as to facilities, manufacturing capacity, technical developments or customers. Improper means include industrial espionage, inducing a competitor's present or former personnel to disclose confidential information, and any other means that are not open and aboveboard. HP must not use consultants to acquire information by improper methods.[13]

Competitive situations may also involve the temptation to obtain business by demeaning competitors rather than by promoting the virtues of a firm's own products. Hewlett-Packard stated, "It is HP's policy to emphasize the quality of its products and to abstain from making disparaging comments or casting doubt on competitors or their products. If statements (oral or written) are made concerning a competitor or its products, they must be fair, factual and complete."

Principles and Reasoning

The content of company codes depends on the set of issues employees are likely to encounter and the approach the individual company takes. Cummins Inc. has long had a reputation for its corporate social responsibility, based on ethics constructs that provide both consistency and a basis from which employees can reason.

Cummins's basic principle is a version of the Golden Rule:

> For Cummins, ethics rests on a fundamental belief in people's dignity and decency. Our most basic ethical standard is to show respect for those whose lives

---

[13]Hewlett-Packard Corporation, "Standards of Business Conduct," Palo Alto, CA, 1989.

we affect and to treat them as we would expect them to treat us if our positions were reversed. This kind of respect implies that we must:

1. Obey the law.
2. Be honest—present the facts fairly and accurately.
3. Be fair—give everyone appropriate consideration.
4. Be concerned—care about how Cummins's actions affect others and try to make those effects as beneficial as possible.
5. Be courageous—treat others with respect even when it means losing business. It seldom does. Over the long haul, people trust and respect this kind of behavior and wish more of our institutions embodied it.

An application of Cummins's fundamental principle is presented in Chapter 23 in the context of questionable foreign payments. That application is important because it provides a basis from which employees can reason about a situation based on moral principles.

The implementation of Cummins's principles is to be guided by the following standards:

1. Cummins Engine Company, Inc., competes on a straight commercial basis; if something more is required, the Company is not interested.
2. Cummins employees do nothing in search of business that they should not reveal willingly and publicly to any other member of the Cummins family or to any government official in any land.
3. Cummins neither practices nor condones any activity that will not stand the most rigorous public ethical examination.
4. If an employee has any doubt about the appropriateness or morality of any act, it should not be done. If an employee believes that there is a conflict between what his or her supervisors expect and what corporate ethical standards require, the employee should raise the issue with the Corporate Responsibility Department. The Company is prepared to help any employee resolve a moral dilemma and to ensure that no employee is put at a career disadvantage because of his or her willingness to raise a question about a corporate practice or unwillingness to pursue a course of action which seems inappropriate or morally dubious.[14]

The fourth point is particularly important because it identifies what the employee is to do in case of doubt. It also places the burden on the company to protect employees in their fulfillment of their responsibility to raise concerns about its activities and practices.

TENSIONS IN THE IMPLEMENTATION OF ETHICS PRINCIPLES

Paternalism

A basic issue for management is when, if ever, a firm is justified in acting paternalistically by taking an action intended to benefit others but in so doing violating a moral standard. For example, should firms institute substance abuse programs and drug testing for their employees or encourage employees to vote for a particular candidate?

Paternalism refers to actions taken to benefit a person without that person's consent. In any ethics system emphasizing individual autonomy and liberty, consent is essential for an action or a rule to have moral standing. Paternalism is thus a moral wrong. Paternalism is also objectionable from a consequentialist perspective because it

---

[14]Cummins Practices, October 1, 1980.

denies individuals the opportunity to make choices that would further their interests. Gert (1988, pp. 286–287) provides a definition of paternalism:

> One is acting paternalistically toward a person if and only if . . . :
>
> 1. one's action benefits that person,
> 2. one's action involves violating a moral rule with regard to that person,
> 3. one's action does not have that person's past, present, or immediately forthcoming consent, and
> 4. that person is competent to give consent (simple or valid) to the violation.

Actions taken on behalf of others are often justified by claims that if those others had the information that the action taker has, consent would have been granted. According to Gert's definition, an action taken to benefit a person who has incomplete information about a situation is not paternalistic if the person would grant consent once the action has been explained and the information presented.

In some cases, it is easy to know whether consent would be granted. Firms take a variety of actions to benefit their stakeholders. A firm may bargain with HMOs over the price for health care services, and the firm's bargaining power can lower the cost to both employees and the firm. In such a case, it is in the interests of both employees and shareholders to have the firm represent them. Consent would surely be given.

In contrast, few companies endorse candidates for public office or try to influence how employees vote. Voting is an exercise of individual autonomy, and individuals have the fundamental right not to be coerced into associating with ideas, positions, or candidates with which they disagree. Consent by individuals to the endorsement of candidates by their employer likely would not be granted. Labor unions, however, regularly endorse candidates for office without the consent of their members. Labor unions differ from firms in an important dimension, however, since union members have the right to elect their leaders.

Nonmarket Action and Restraint

In the United States individuals, firms, interest groups, foreign governments, and others have broad granted rights to engage in nonmarket activity. Firms as well as other interests must decide whether and to what extent they should restrain themselves in the exercise of those rights.[15] On an issue such as the antitrust exemption sought by the soft drink industry, as discussed in Chapter 9, the right of bottlers to seek the exemption was clear, even if it would benefit the industry to the detriment of consumers. The issue then is when if ever a firm should restrain itself from pursuing its interests through nonmarket action.

In some cases, the nonmarket actions of business serve to uphold laws. The California constitution requires that a ballot proposition be limited to a single issue. When Proposition 105 was approved by the voters, the Chemical Specialties Manufacturers Association and the California Chamber of Commerce filed suit on the grounds that the proposition covered many different issues. The proposition pertained to the disclosure of toxic substances, apartheid, nursing home standards, the state election process, and protection for senior citizens against fraud. The court invalidated the proposition on the grounds that it was overly broad.

If a nonmarket alternative would result in a reduction in aggregate well-being, as is likely in the case of the antitrust exemption obtained by the soft drink industry, a utilitarian standard calls for restraint. More generally, utilitarianism views nonmarket rights as instrumental and calls for their exercise only to maximize aggregate well-being. Even when the exercise of nonmarket rights is based on self-interest, the nonmarket competition among interest groups may work in the direction of maximizing aggregate well-being. The intense nonmarket competition over the ratification of NAFTA is one such example.

---

[15]Reich (1998) offers a perspective on political restraint.

Pizza Hut's lobbying to retain the targeted jobs tax credit for the employment of low-income youths was considered in Chapter 8. Subsequently, the inspector general of the Department of Labor (1993) released the results of a study of the program's impact indicating that instead of enhancing the employment prospects of those taking the subsidized jobs, the jobs "often appeared to be one more low-skilled, low-wage job in a succession of similar jobs in a worker's employment history." The recipients of the $2,400 tax credit were primarily large corporations in the fast-food and retail industries that had high turnover in low-wage jobs. Furthermore, the companies surveyed reported that they would have hired 95 percent of the people even without the tax credit. The program, estimated to cost $282 million in 1994, was described in the study as the "most wasteful of all programs, the kind where the federal government gets involved when people would have done something anyway."[16]

In light of this study, should Pizza Hut support the program? Certainly, a company has the right to accept tax credits offered by the government and has the right to lobby the government in support of the tax credits with the objective of increasing its profits. The program was established without a test for whether those jobs would have been filled anyway and hence with the understanding that the tax credit would apply to such jobs. Pizza Hut was thus acting in accord with the law. Moreover, its support was consistent with the intent of the government, since the Clinton administration had proposed making the program permanent rather than requiring annual congressional authorizations.[17]

Lobbying and other nonmarket activity by business and interest groups have become integral components of the democratic process in a pluralistic society. In participating in this process firms not only represent the interests of their owners but also can give voice to stakeholders and others who would not otherwise participate in the process because of the costs of individual and collective action. Support for the tax credits by Pizza Hut gave voice to low-income youths who otherwise might not be represented in the process.

Lobbying is the strategic advocacy of a position, and as in a court of law most lobbyists advocate their side of an issue and rely on the opposition to present the other side. Lobbying and advocacy must be guided by principles, however, including avoiding false statements—for example, denying that tobacco is addictive.[18] This may require acting against the firm's immediate interests when warranted by ethical consensus. For example, once the National Academy of Sciences issued its report concluding that CFCs damage the ozone layer, DuPont announced that it would stop CFC production earlier than called for by the government. British Petroleum viewed the growing scientific evidence on global climate change as sufficient to warrant actions to reduce its CO_2 emissions and promote sustainable energy sources. Similarly, the coalition of Silicon Valley businesses that opposed Proposition 211, which would have made it easier for law firms to extract settlements from companies with volatile stock prices, acted in the interests of aggregate well-being by allowing more information to flow to the capital markets and by avoiding costly, frivolous lawsuits.

Since political rights are granted, the issue of political restraint often focuses on actions that may be deceptive. As an illustration of the types of actions that raise concerns, firms and interest groups frequently support grassroots organizations that lobby, support candidates for office, and campaign on public referenda. On the issue of fuel economy standards, in 1990 General Motors sponsored an organization called Nevadans for Fair Fuel Economy Standards, which generated 10,000 letters to Senator Richard Bryan (D-NV) opposing his bill to raise fuel economy standards. Senator Bryan accused the industry of conducting the letter-writing campaign "under false colors." GM spokesman William Noack defended the campaign as "a very straightforward, aboveboard educational program."[19] If Senator Bryan was correct in his assessment

---

[16]*Wall Street Journal,* August 24, 1993.
[17]The program can be viewed as pork.
[18]See Hamilton and Hoch (1997) and Weber (1996).
[19]*Wall Street Journal,* April 4, 1990.

that the letter writers were uninformed and did not understand the issue, the campaign was unjustified, since it treated the letter writers as means and not also as ends. More-over, such campaigns impose a negative externality in that they make it more difficult for informed letter writers to be heard.

SOURCES OF UNETHICAL BEHAVIOR

Unethical behavior has a number of sources; some are idiosyncratic to the particular individuals involved and others are functions of the managerial setting or the policies of the firm itself. Codes of conduct provide useful guidance, but alone they may be in-sufficient to prevent unethical behavior and promote ethical behavior. If the culture in the organization encourages or condones questionable behavior or if incentive systems place self-interest before all else, ethical behavior will primarily rest on the personal in-tegrity of employees. Personal integrity may be sufficient for most, but perhaps not all, employees, and for most, but perhaps not all, issues.[20]

Personal weakness and temptation can contribute to unethical behavior in busi-ness, as well as in other contexts. This includes situations in which an individual under-stands what is right but does not have the fortitude to take the right action, perhaps because it involves a degree of personal or career risk. In that case, the policies of the firm should be reexamined to lessen the personal risk associated with taking the right action. This may require revisions in incentive structures so that employees do not find themselves in positions in which their performance will be evaluated negatively as a re-sult, for example, of a lost sale that could have been obtained only through an unethi-cal act. Cummins's fourth standard is one means of addressing this problem.

The structure of both explicit and implicit incentives within a firm can be an impor-tant obstacle to ethical behavior. In 1990 Eastern Airlines and nine of its maintenance su-pervisors were indicted for failing to perform required maintenance and for falsifying maintenance records.[21] To improve its on-time performance, Eastern had instituted an incentive system for maintenance supervisors in which bonuses were paid for good on-time performance. Supervisors whose on-time and flight cancellation record was poor were transferred or in some cases fired. Not only did the supervisors face incentives and pressure from upper management, but the unions, which were incensed by layoffs and management's demands for wage reductions, often blocked supervisors' efforts to improve on-time performance. Under pressure from both sides, maintenance supervisors began to falsify records for maintenance that was not performed. The situation deterio-rated to the point at which some pilots refused to fly aircraft that had accumulated maintenance problems. Believing that the complaints were part of the unions' struggle with management, Eastern executives reportedly continued to pressure the supervisors.

Charges were brought against Sears for allegedly recommending unneeded repairs, such as brake repairs and front-wheel alignments, in its auto centers. Service advisors re-portedly recommended the repairs to earn higher commissions, and in settlements of charges in 41 states and 19 class action lawsuits, Sears agreed to eliminate commissions for its service advisors. After a corporate restructuring in 1993, the position of service advisor was eliminated and replaced by the position of service consultant, who was paid on a commission basis. The position of service consultant differed significantly from that of service advisor, however, because the consultants could not recommend repairs, whereas earlier the advisors had inspected cars and recommended repairs. Repairs were now recommended only by mechanics, who did not receive commissions. Because of its past problems, when its new system was announced, Sears received increased scrutiny by state attorneys general.

The problem of temptation can be exacerbated by several factors. First, if there is a belief that others are acting unethically or are succumbing to temptation, an individual

[20]See Sonnenfeld and Lawrence (1978) for an analysis of the causes of price fixing in the folding-carton industry.
[21]The FAA had frequently cited Eastern for maintenance, safety, and record-keeping violations and fined it $12 million between 1987 and 1989.

may have more difficulty resisting. This is particularly true if employees find themselves in a prisoners' dilemma in which each has a dominant strategy of succumbing to temptation. For example, if a partnership will go to the associate with the highest billings, the competing associates may be induced to take unwarranted actions. What is required is a promotion system that considers factors in addition to billings. Second, succumbing to temptation is more likely if the prevailing attitude in the firm involves either shortcutting ethics analysis, using principles only to justify actions taken on other bases, or practicing casuistry. For example, the balancing of responsibilities can induce managers to underemphasize rights and principles of justice in favor of lessening stakeholder pressure. Third, temptation may be exacerbated by an aggressive culture of earnings growth, as in the case of Enron, or may have been in the case in the Citigroup example. Fourth, temptation combined with greed can lead to unethical conduct. The Chapter 10 case, *Enron Power Marketing and the California Market,* provides an example, as does the Chapter 20 case *Tax Shelters*.

Unethical behavior can also result from too narrow a focus on the duties imposed by the law. The law identifies actions that an individual or firm must not take, but the set of lawful actions can be considerably larger than the set of ethical actions. Procter & Gamble's ethics standards prohibited espionage that was allowed by the law. The law provides only minimum restraints on behavior. Another source of unethical behavior is reliance on an ethics framework that gives insufficient attention to important considerations. Relying only on utilitarianism and ignoring intrinsic rights or justice considerations can result in conduct that violates ethics standards that some individuals hold to be important. For this reason, each of the three ethics systems considered in the previous two chapters should be considered in managerial decision making.

SUMMARY

A useful test in situations with moral dimensions is to assess whether an action can be explained both to others in the firm and to the public. This *public disclosure test* has two purposes. First, it forces the manager to articulate the reasons or basis for the action. This should involve an articulation of the reasoning used in arriving at the decision and should not be a search among ethics systems for arguments that come closest to justifying the action the manager prefers to take on other grounds. Second, it requires the manager to reflect on how others will evaluate the action. This does not mean that the action is subject to a vote among stakeholders. Instead, it focuses attention on the moral evaluations that others may have of the action.

Reliance on the personal integrity of employees is seldom sufficient to ensure ethical conduct, and employees should not be left to operate in an ethics vacuum. A commitment by top management is essential, and part of top management's responsibilities is to establish an environment in which ethical behavior is encouraged, supported, and rewarded. This requires formal and informal communication about exemplary conduct and leadership by deed as well as by word.

Statements of corporate responsibility and codes of conduct are useful guides for employees. These should identify principles, provide specific guidance for situations that are likely to be encountered, and indicate how to reason about situations and issues. A code should also indicate what an individual is to do when uncertain about whether an action is right. A compliance system is important in the implementation of ethics standards and should be designed to give top management confidence that unethical actions will be deterred or at least detected. A process that encourages and does not unduly punish self-disclosure can be an important component of a compliance system.

Temptation and pressure are principal causes of unethical behavior. Performance standards should be realistically attainable through means consistent with ethics principles. Incentive systems should be structured in a manner that encourages rather than hinders ethical conduct. In many firms, the selection, retention, and promotion of employees depend on the individual's integrity and record of conduct in addition to more traditional measures of performance.

-- C A S E S --
Denny's and Customer Service

Early on the morning of April 1, 1993, 21 members of the U.S. Secret Service arrived in Annapolis, Maryland, to prepare for President Bill Clinton's speech at the U.S. Naval Academy later that day. Before setting up security at the academy, the contingent, in full uniform, went to a local Denny's restaurant for breakfast. The group included six African American agents who sat at a table together, and an African American supervisor who, with the white agents, sat at other tables. After all the agents had ordered, the six black agents realized that the white agents and their supervisor had been served while they had not. Agent Robin Thompson went to ask the waitress about the order, and she said it was on its way. He then asked to talk with the manager and was told that the manager was on the phone. (White agents seated at other tables later reported that the waitress rolled her eyes after turning to leave the black agents' table.) After having waited an hour, the agents stood to leave, and only then, they said, were they offered a single tray of food. They refused the food because there was no time to eat. "We had to go to a Roy Rogers (a local fast-food restaurant) and eat in the van," said one of the African American agents.

Seven weeks after the incident, the six agents filed a lawsuit seeking unspecified monetary and punitive damages. The suit alleged that their civil rights had been violated because Denny's had denied them service because of their race. "It's a classic case of some kind of bias," Thompson said. The lawsuit immediately attracted nationwide media coverage. On the *CBS Evening News* Dan Rather summarized the incident by saying that the agents "put their lives on the line every day, but they can't get served at a Denny's."

Denny's, a unit of Flagstar, Inc., was a nationwide chain operating 1,487 restaurants throughout the United States. Flagstar was formed in 1989 when Coniston Partners headed a leveraged buyout of TW Services. In 1992 Kohlberg, Kravis, Roberts & Company paid $300 million for a 47 percent interest in the highly leveraged Flagstar. Approximately 70 percent of the Denny's restaurants were owned by Flagstar and the rest were owned by franchisees. In contrast to fast-food chains such as McDonald's and Burger King, Denny's operated sit-down restaurants, so when a restaurant became crowded, customers did not wait in lines but instead waited to be seated, order, and be served.

In response to the agents' charges, Flagstar ordered an investigation of the incident. After questioning employees at the restaurant the day after the lawsuit was filed, the company fired the manager of the restaurant for failure to report the episode. Flagstar officials also de-fended their employees' actions. Steve McManus, a senior vice president who had questioned employees at the Annapolis restaurant, said the delay in the agents' service was caused by the size of their party and the complexity of their orders, which caused a backlog in the kitchen. The black agents were most affected by the delay because their table was the last to order. He said, "It's a service issue, not a discriminatory issue." In response, the agents said a group of white customers entered the restaurant after them, ordered, and was served while the agents waited. Flagstar CEO Jerome J. Richardson said, "We had one cook, and either two or three servers to serve the entire restaurant. If they say they were discriminated against, I apologize. But in my opinion, there was not an intent to not serve black people."[22]

The Annapolis incident was neither the beginning nor the end of Denny's troubles. "It's 1993 and certain things should not be happening. I just cannot imagine them not wanting to serve those children," said Randy Shepard, director of the all-black Martin Luther King All Children's Choir of Virginia. Shepard was referring to a June 1993 incident in which 70 children and 54 adults were returning home by bus to Raleigh, North Carolina, after weekend performances in the Washington, D.C., area and were allegedly refused service at two Denny's restaurants. According to Shepard, the group first went to a Shoney's restaurant off Interstate 95 in Woodbridge, Virginia. "The manager there said he would be glad to accommodate us, but there was only 20 minutes before they closed, and service would take a long time," Shepard said. "He suggested we go to Denny's down the street." The three buses then stopped at a Denny's outside Dale City, Virginia, about 11:00 P.M. Shepard said he entered the restaurant and asked a manager if he could accommodate the group. "He said he couldn't accommodate us because he didn't have the staff and recommended a larger Denny's the next exit down." At the second Denny's, Shepard said the manager met him in the parking lot and also told him he could not accommodate the group. "Some of the children had gone in to use the bathroom, so I went to get them," Shepard said. He added that the restaurant did not seem full, and "they seemed like they had ample enough staff around, and it appeared they had already started clearing tables to serve us." Prince William County Supervisor John Jenkins, whose district included one of the two Denny's restaurants, commented: "I feel like they ought to close that chain down. They have an interstate service route and ought

---

to have enough help to serve those customers." Jenkins called for a county investigation of the incident.

Denny's officials and employees disputed many of Shepard's claims. "Our restaurant can't handle that kind of crowd—not with just two cooks and four servers. And I'm not prejudiced," said waitress Kimberly Marshall, who was white. However, her husband Dennis Marshall, an African American, said "If you're open for business, you can't say you can't serve that many people. It doesn't make sense to me."[23] Denny's officials said that the first restaurant was full, the second was half full, and the bus driver had "indicated the group outside was in a hurry." Furthermore, a company spokesman stated that "in both Denny's restaurants, we offered to serve the large group and indicated there would be a lengthy wait," but the group left before the restaurant could serve them. Denny's officials stated that they were not equipped to serve 130 people with a staff appropriate for the off-peak time of 11:00 P.M. The officials acknowledged that the manager at the first Denny's suggested that the group try the other restaurant, but added that "he offered to phone the other restaurant to make the arrangements." Coleman Sullivan, vice president of communications of Flagstar, said, "It was 11:00 P.M. on a Sunday, and our manager told this bus group it would take a while to serve them. There was no discrimination."[24]

Eighteen months before the Annapolis incident, the Department of Justice (DOJ) had initiated an investigation of the Denny's chain in response to complaints from African American customers in California. After the investigation substantiated allegations of bias, Denny's and the DOJ entered into negotiations to settle the complaints. The complainants also took other action. Their lawyers had earlier established a toll-free number to encourage others to report racist episodes so they could qualify a class action suit.[25] On March 24, 1993, a group of 32 African American customers filed a class action civil suit in San Jose alleging several discriminatory practices, including the following:

- A group of 18 African American college students was forced to pay a cover charge of $2 each and pay for their meals in advance at a Denny's restaurant in San Jose, California, while six white students acquainted with one of the African American students were seated at a nearby table and were not required to pay the cover charge or pay in advance for their meals. According to the company, several Denny's restaurants had in the past implemented a "late night policy" requiring all groups of 10 or more to prepay for meals after 10 P.M. as a "security measure" to thwart the

rising theft of meals, but the policy had "not been enforced in a discriminatory fashion."
- A racially mixed couple, Danny and Susan Thompson, took their three children to a Denny's restaurant in Vallejo, California, to celebrate their daughter Rachel's 13th birthday. According to the lawsuit, Denny's refused to serve Rachel their famous free birthday meal, despite the fact that she had both her baptismal certificate and school identification. "I felt violated, humiliated, and embarrassed, so we didn't eat there. I can't adequately describe the pain that you feel to see this happen to your child," Mrs. Thompson said.
- Denny's allegedly threatened or forcibly removed African American customers from several California restaurants.
- Denny's employed "a general policy of limiting black customers," using the term "blackout" to signal employees when too many blacks were in a restaurant. The suit also alleged that one district manager instructed store managers to "start cracking down and get rid of some of those blackouts." Some Denny's managers asked for prepayment of meals or told blacks that the restaurant would be closing soon.
- When an employee at a Denny's restaurant in San Jose, California, told a manager a customer's eggs needed to be recooked, he was told to "take it to the niggers, and if they have a complaint, tell them to come see me."

The class action lawsuit came only 5 months after a $105 million settlement of an employment discrimination suit against Shoney's, Inc., another leading national restaurant chain, which alleged that the company limited the number of African American employees at each location and restricted them to kitchen jobs by blackening the *o* in the word *Shoney's* on the job application to indicate an applicant was an African American. Lawyers for Saperstein, Mayeda, Larkin & Goldstein, the law firm that represented the plaintiffs in the Shoney's case and was currently negotiating for the plaintiffs in the Denny's suit, commented that the Denny's case might be more remarkable because it dealt with mistreatment of the most important element of any business, the customer. "These practices evoke the bald racism of the 1950s," the lawyers said in a statement. Former California Supreme Court Justice Cruz Reynoso, who had been recalled by California voters and was now a law professor at the University of California at Los Angeles, said he believed the Denny's case was the first "pattern and practice" racism case in the past 15 or 20 years involving a major public accommodation.

The service in a restaurant depended on a variety of factors, including Denny's policies, the practices of the

---

[23]*Washington Post,* June 7, 1993.
[24]*Fortune,* July 12, 1993.
[25]By early July, they had received over 1,000 calls.

restaurant managers, and the individual employees of the restaurant. The problem for Flagstar was twofold. First, although the company encouraged Denny's franchises to end practices that might be discriminatory, there was a limit to the control the company could exercise over the privately owned outlets. Second, the application of existing policies was problematic because policies intended to apply to all customers might instead be applied in a discriminatory fashion at individual locations by individual managers or employees.

While the negotiations with the DOJ were under way, Denny's addressed some of the issues by apologizing to customers, firing or transferring "bad-apple" employees, and creating a cultural diversity team. The "late night policy," which had been instituted to prevent diners from walking out without paying, was discontinued at all the chain's restaurants, both company owned and franchised. Mr. Richardson said, "The managers had problems with customers walking out on checks. Some required prepayment, which can be a problem when it's not applied to everyone."[26] In addition, Flagstar initiated meetings with civil rights groups.

Complicating the situation, Mr. Richardson, a former wide receiver for the Baltimore Colts who had started with a single hamburger restaurant in Spartansburg, South Carolina, had for 6 years been working to obtain one of the two National Football League franchises to be awarded in the fall of 1993. Denny's and Mr. Richardson had been criticized by the Reverend Jesse Jackson and his son, who headed the Rainbow Coalition. The younger Mr. Jackson had asked in a May 27 press release, "Are we seeing the beginning of a racist sports connection and pattern here?"[27] ■

SOURCE: This case was prepared from public sources by Abraham Wu under the supervision of Professor David P. Baron. Copyright © 1994 by the Board of Trustees of the Leland Stanford Junior University. All rights reserved. Reprinted with permission.

---

[26]*Fortune*, July 12, 1993.
[27]*Wall Street Journal*, July 1, 1993.

Preparation Questions

1. What were the causes of the individual incidents at the Denny's restaurants? Were they more than incidents of bad service? What might they reflect? How serious are they?
2. What responsibilities does Flagstar have with regard to the incidents?
3. What roles have the media and plaintiffs' attorneys played in this issue?
4. What should Flagstar do about these incidents and allegations? What should Flagstar do about the lawsuits?
5. What policies should it adopt for its customer service and its employees, and how should those policies be implemented? How should it deal with independently owned Denny's restaurants?

Gilead Sciences (A): The Gilead Access Program for HIV Drugs

In October 2001, Gilead Sciences received approval from the U.S. Food and Drug Administration for the commercial sale of Viread (chemical name: tenofovir disoproxil fumarate), a significant new drug for the treatment of HIV/AIDS. Viread proved to be an immediate success, increasing rapidly in sales and market share in the United States within its first year on the market. As Gilead made plans to take the drug global in early 2003, a high priority was to make the drug readily available to millions of people in the least developed nations, where the HIV virus was having its most devastating effects. Pricing and distribution were key considerations. Gilead did not have a distribution system in place in any of these countries, and the price charged in the United States would be prohibitive in the developing world. If it could solve these problems, Gilead was confident that Viread would make a major contribution to the treatment of AIDS throughout the world.

AIDS

Nearly 20 million people had died from AIDS by 2001, and about 40 million worldwide were infected with the HIV virus.[28] The daily death toll from AIDS was a staggering 8,500. Sub-Saharan Africa had been the hardest hit of all by AIDS with over 28 million people infected, which constituted more than 8 percent of the adult population. The incidence rate was as high as 30 to 40 percent in some countries. Primarily spread through unprotected heterosexual contact, the rapid spread of HIV had been

---

[28]The material in this section was originally published in "Note on AIDS and the Pharmaceutical Industry," GSB No. P-41, p. 3.

exacerbated by the high prevalence of other sexually transmitted diseases, which weakened the body's immune system. The inferior status of women, workforce intermigration and mobility, poverty, unemployment, and lack of care exacerbated the situation. Lack of knowledge about how HIV was spread, combined with an inadequate health infrastructure for testing and treatment, added to the crisis.

Education and precautions had limited the spread of HIV in North America and Western Europe, and the introduction of antiretroviral drugs in 1996 had made HIV/AIDS a treatable chronic disease. In poor countries neither individuals nor their governments could afford the drugs, leaving few of the victims able to access treatment.

Gilead Sciences: Early Days

Gilead Sciences was founded in 1987 with a mission of discovering new drugs that addressed significant unmet medical needs. The company's name was derived from a region of the ancient Middle East known for a balm with medicinal qualities, referred to in the Bible as "the balm of Gilead," and subsequently cited in Poe's "The Raven," Negro spirituals, and a Roald Dahl short story. Gilead Sciences was initially funded by prominent venture capital firms in the San Francisco Bay Area and had an initial public offering in 1992, which raised $86 million.

John Martin joined Gilead in 1990 as vice president for research and development, and shortly after joining the company he negotiated licensing of rights to a portfolio of nucleotides, several of which Gilead later developed into antiviral medicines for HIV, hepatitis and cytomegalovirus. Martin became president and CEO of the company in 1996. That same year, the company gained approval from the Food and Drug Administration (FDA) for its first commercial drug, Vistide (cidofovir injection), used in the treatment of cytomegalovirus retinitis in patients with AIDS. The product, however, did not gain widespread use, generating only $11.7 million in sales in its first full year and $6.1 million the following year.

Gilead's research and development pipeline proved increasingly fruitful, and the company successfully launched a string of new products. Tamiflu, approved in 1999, was a neuraminidase inhibitor for the treatment of influenza. Gilead co-developed the product with Hoffmann-La Roche, which held exclusive marketing rights and paid Gilead a royalty on sales.

The most successful of Gilead's early products was AmBisome, an antifungal agent that combated serious fungal infections and showed activity against visceral leishmaniasis, a parasitic infection. AmBisome achieved sales of $165 million in 2001, representing 86 percent of Gilead's total product sales that year. Despite the success of AmBisome and other products, Gilead had still not posted an operating profit since its founding.

Gilead's AIDS Drugs

Because the HIV virus is prone to mutation and eventual resistance to drugs, HIV/AIDS treatment typically consisted of three drugs used in combination, in what was called a drug cocktail. Drug cocktails included at least three agents that targeted the virus at two or more steps in its replication cycle. Nucleoside/nucleotide reverse transcriptase inhibitors (NRTIs) and non-nucleoside reverse transcriptase inhibitors (NNRTIs) both combat the HIV virus when it first enters the human cell. Protease inhibitors prevent the HIV virus from being successfully assembled and released from an infected cell.[29]

A major milestone in AIDS treatment therapy was reached in October 2001 when the FDA approved Gilead's breakthrough drug Viread as a first-line treatment for AIDS patients. This meant that the drug's use was not restricted to patients who had developed resistance to an initial treatment.

Viread was a significant improvement over existing drugs because it was the first NRTI based on a nucleotide analogue and not a nucleoside analogue. The body naturally converted nucleosides into nucleotides, and drugs based on nucleotide analogues allowed this conversion process to be skipped, resulting in less toxic build-up in the body. For AIDS patients, this meant that treatment with Viread would have a dramatically better side-effect profile and half-life in the body. Because of its once-a-day dosage and fewer side effects, patients were more likely to adhere to their treatment schedules, which improved their long-term health. Adherence to treatment schedules freed clinical space and resources for the treatment of new patients.

The director of research at the Community Research Initiative of New England and Harvard Vanguard Medical Associates praised the new drug, stating:

> Viread addresses many of the needs of people living with HIV today. The drug has demonstrated a significant antiviral response, even in patients who may no longer respond well to available therapies due to the development of viral resistance. . . . Viread is an important new option because it is powerful and convenient—it has a strong track record of safety in clinical studies, is well tolerated and is dosed as one tablet once a day. These are all important attributes for patients taking these types of drugs.[30]

In the pharmaceutical trade press, one pharmacist stated that he expected Viread "to be on all the formularies. There's no real secondary choice, there's no other option, and there's no generic."[31]

---

[29]"AIDS & HIV Antiretroviral Drug Treatment in Resource Poor Communities," AVERT, 2006.
[30]"FDA Approves Gilead's Anti-HIV Drug Viread," *Biotech Business,* vol. 14, issue 12, December 1, 2001.
[31]Kathy Hitchens, "HIV Treatment Advances with First Drug in a New Class," *Drug Topics,* November 19, 2001.

Viread was launched in the United States at a price of $4,135 for a treatment for a year.[32] A one-year supply cost approximately $475 to manufacture. After only one year on the market, Viread had become Gilead's largest product by revenue in 2002, achieving sales of $226 million. Largely because of Viread, Gilead reported its first operating profit.

Gilead also had several clinical studies under way for promising new drugs. One of these drugs, Emtriva, was a nucleoside reverse transcriptase inhibitor. Although not expected to be a significant therapeutic advancement like Viread, Emtriva (emtricitabine) was important as an extension of Gilead's AIDS drug franchise. If successful, Emtriva was to be included as one ingredient in a new combination pill, Truvada (emtricitabine and tenofovir disoproxil fumarate), also under development. Truvada was a once-a-day pill that included both Viread and Emtriva, helping to simplify the therapy regimen for AIDS patients by combining two of the three drugs in an AIDS drug cocktail into one pill. When approved by the FDA, Truvada was expected to result in greater regimen compliance by AIDS patients, a major concern of doctors who worried about patients skipping doses.

The Gilead Access Program

Gilead was motivated by the suffering of patients with HIV/AIDS and wanted its drugs to be available to those who needed them in the least developed countries. The challenge was to design an access program to accomplish this objective. Gilead would have to be sensitive to the diverse institutional environments of these countries. Gilead had a proven track record of success in the U.S., but the international situation, especially in developing nations, was more complicated.

International Institutions

No single governing body provided regulatory standards and oversight for pharmaceuticals. The World Health Organization (WHO), an agency of the United Nations, acted in a coordinating capacity by collecting and disseminating information on diseases and therapies to health ministries around the world. The WHO deliberated on global policies with regard to human health but did not have regulatory authority over countries. The WHO provided technical support for countries implementing treatment programs, including treatment guidelines, prequalification of medicines, and an essential medicines list. Since Gilead had not yet marketed Viread outside the United States and Europe, it was not included on the essential medicines list as either a first-line or second-line therapy.

Through its published treatment guidelines, the WHO recommended to health ministries best-practices in administering all aspects of a treatment program, including patient testing and monitoring, drug use, and education and prevention. Through its prequalification process, the WHO inspected and certified manufacturers for compliance with WHO Good Manufacturing Practices (GMP) which assured clinics that they were procuring medicines from suppliers that met WHO quality standards. In its essential medicines list, updated every two years, the WHO listed the medicines and vaccines that a clinic would need to serve its local patients.

National Institutions

A drug had to be registered in each country before it could be used. A company was not required to conduct additional trials to register the drug, but it was required to submit an application to the local ministry of health. In Africa, the registration process tended to be modeled after those of European countries, but the regulatory agencies were typically under-resourced. Approval could be quick in some countries but take two or three years in others. A drug could also be brought into a country while the registration application was pending through an import waiver. The import waiver could be requested either by local wholesalers or by the clinic prescribing the drug.

Funding

International organizations played an important role in funding drug purchases for clinical programs. The main source of funding in 2003 was the Global Fund to Fight AIDS, Tuberculosis, and Malaria. The Global Fund, a UN-related nonprofit organization, provided grant money directly to the health ministries of developing nations. Grants by the Global Fund averaged $1 billion per year and were collected from the pledges of 50 countries around the world, with the United States as the largest donor providing approximately 33 percent of total funds.[33]

In his 2003 State of the Union address, President George W. Bush asked Congress to allocate $15 billion over five years to fight AIDS in Africa and the Caribbean. The President's Emergency Plan for AIDS Relief (PEPFAR), when approved, would be the largest source of funding for AIDS treatment in the developing world. Unlike the Global Fund, whose grants were distributed to governments and health ministries through application, PEPFAR funds could be given directly to local clinics or health care organizations. The administrator of PEPFAR could actively seek recipients for funding. Governments and regional organizations that

---

[32]Gilead spokesperson cited in Tom Abate, "Gilead HIV Drug OK'd for Wide Use; Viread Allowed for Initial Therapy," *San Francisco Chronicle,* October 27, 2001, p. E1.

[33]"The Global Fund to Fight AIDS, Tuberculosis, and Malaria," AVERT, 2006, http://www.avert.org/global-fund.htm (October 19, 2006).

received funds directly from the U.S. government agencies were referred to as "prime" partners. Many prime partners redistributed funds to local clinics and organizations, referred to as "subpartners," to conduct AIDS treatment programs. Although drugs purchased with PEPFAR funds could be generics, clinics were required to purchase from manufacturers whose plants were FDA approved, which was a stricter quality standard than the WHO GMP.[34]

Intellectual Property

Patent protection allowed pharmaceutical companies to control drug pricing and distribution. Historically, the standards of patent and intellectual property protection varied widely around the world. The 1986–1994 Uruguay Round of multilateral trade negotiations resulted in the Agreement on Trade-Related Aspects of Intellectual Property Rights (TRIPS) which harmonized how these rights were protected by the members of the World Trade Organization. Under TRIPS, governments had to ensure that intellectual property rights were enforceable under their laws and that infringement penalties were sufficiently stringent to dissuade violations. TRIPS, however, provided for exceptions under Article 31, which allowed a government to supersede patent protection and force compulsory licensing of a product in the case of "national emergency or other circumstances of extreme urgency." In issuing a compulsory license, governments could grant to a third party the right to produce the patent-protected product domestically and, in some cases, to export it to a third country.[35] With a critical drug in the treatment of the AIDS epidemic, Gilead faced the threat of compulsory licensing for Viread if the product was not appropriately available or the price was too high.

In addition to the risk of compulsory licensing, Gilead faced the risk that its intellectual property rights would be violated by low-cost generic manufacturers, particularly those in India. Encouraged by India's lenient patent law regime, an extensive drug manufacturing industry had developed that was capable of reengineering advanced therapies for sale in India and other developing markets. With their advanced manufacturing techniques, these firms could copy Gilead's drugs and compete at very low prices. These firms also sold in the United States generic drugs produced in FDA-approved manufacturing facilities in India.

Another closely related risk was that drugs made available to poor countries at very low prices could be reimported into the U.S. market or sold in Europe, cannibalizing sales. Gilead decided to produce a white pill for developing nations that was easily differentiated from the blue version sold in the United States, Europe and other high-income regions of the world.[36]

Distribution

Distribution also posed a problem. In most developing countries, the company had no physical presence, local contacts, nor in-house expertise about potentially critical social and cultural forces. Furthermore, each country posed different regulatory challenges. The relevant political institutions varied widely across countries, so strategies that could work in Country A might not work in Country B. Similarly, the identities of key actors within a given regulatory body were usually unknown in advance and, once identified, were often uninformed about Viread (and medicines more generally), skeptical of drug companies, or corrupt. In some countries, government officials in the agencies that reviewed registration applications could demand payments. Failure to make such payments could result in significant delays in approval times. Also, drugs delivered to government agencies could be held up in customs or diverted from their intended recipients. Gilead risked similar problems from private distributors.

Public Perception

Gilead was developing its access program in a charged environment. AIDS activist groups, health care providers, and some governments were strong critics of pharmaceutical companies and their pricing and protection of intellectual property. Most pharmaceutical companies with HIV/AIDS drugs had been targeted by activists and criticized in the press for not doing more to make their drugs accessible. Although Gilead was trying to do the right thing, it had to consider how its efforts would be portrayed by the international organizations and AIDS activist groups that were watching carefully and critically.

The Outlook (2003)

In early 2003, CEO John Martin called 2002 "a remarkable year of transformation and achievements for Gilead." He was equally confident about the impact that Viread would have in treating AIDS patients around the world, stating: "With its efficacy, strong safety profile, and simple, one-tablet, once-daily dosing, Viread has an attractive profile to help address the HIV epidemic in developing parts of the world."[37] After only one year on the market, Viread was already the leading product for the treatment of HIV/AIDS in the United States. By offering the drug to the developing world at affordable

---

[34]"President's Emergency Plan for AIDS Relief (PEPFAR)," AVERT, 2006, http://www.avert.org/pepfar.htm (October 19, 2006).
[35]"Note on AIDS and the Pharmaceutical Industry," p. 7.

[36]Gilead believed that the risk of reimportation was lower for AIDS drugs than for other medicines because most AIDS drugs were paid for by state health services programs called AIDS Drug Assistance Programs (ADAP), which received funding from the U.S. government.
[37]"Q4 2002 Gilead Sciences Earnings Conference Call," Voxant FD (Fair Disclosure) Wire, January 20, 2003.

prices, Gilead was certain that the demand would be very high from governments, health ministries, international organizations, and local clinics that were eager to help the victims of AIDS.

Optimism notwithstanding, Gilead had to decide how best to resolve distribution and pricing issues. It could rely on third parties to implement the Access Program. Some pharmaceutical companies that were part of the Accelerated Access Initiative had used the Ireland-based advisory company Axios to design and manage their access programs.[38] Axios served as a strategic advisor in designing and implementing health care systems in developing nations. Axios consulted on market entry strategies, program design, identification of local part-

ners, implementation, and monitoring. Gilead believed Axios could greatly help its efforts to distribute to the developing world, since Gilead itself did not have any employees or partners in those countries. Reliance on Axios would represent a very significant outsourcing of the Access Program and require much less direct staffing and resource dedication on Gilead's part.

As part of its effort to make Viread available broadly, Gilead would have to develop a pricing strategy that was appropriate for each local market. Gilead had grouped the nations of the world into four tiers by per capita gross national income. The top tier included developed nations, and the second tier included upper-middle income nations with per capita gross national income at least that of Brazil ($3,000 per year). The third tier included lower-middle income nations (per capita GNI less than $3,000). The lowest tier included developing nations with GNI less than $825.

SOURCE: Brian Tayan, Professor David Baron and Professor Keith Krehbiel prepared this case as the basis for class discussion rather than to illustrate either effective or ineffective handling of an administrative situation. Copyright © 2007 by the Board of Trustees of the Leland Stanford Junior University. All rights reserved. Reprinted with permission.

---

[38]The Accelerated Access Initiative (AAI) was a cooperative effort between organizations such as UNAIDS, WHO, UNICEF, UNFPA, and the World Bank and pharmaceutical companies to broaden access to AIDS drugs. AAI was launched in May 2000 and the founding pharmaceutical companies included Boehringer Ingelheim, Bristol-Myers Squibb, F. Hoffman-La Roche, Glaxo Wellcome, and Merck & Co. See "Fostering Access to Treatment," Merck & Co., http://www.merck.com/cr/enabling_access/developing_world/hiv/hiv_access.html (November 30, 2006).

Preparation Questions

1. Does Gilead have responsibility to make its drug available to people who cannot afford it? How far does this responsibility extend? Does Gilead's responsibility extend to developing distribution networks and supervising the proper use of its drugs?

2. Is it wise to rely on Axios for distribution of Viread in Africa?

3. Should Gilead register Viread in each country or attempt to expedite the process by relying on import waivers?

4. Are the government agencies in the developing countries likely to expedite approval of the sale of Viread?

5. Are the media and AIDS activist groups likely to monitor and critique the success of the Gilead Access Program?

6. What, if anything, should Gilead attempt to accomplish with the WHO, and how successful is it likely to be?

7. In designing its Access Program with whom should Gilead work or consult?

8. How significant are the risks to Gilead's intellectual property rights for Viread, specifically those posed by compulsory licensing and Indian generic manufacturers?

9. How significant are the risks of drug reimportation and counterfeits? What strategy should Gilead develop to deal with these risks?

10. What other problems or obstacles not mentioned above should Gilead be worried about? How should Gilead mitigate them?

11. How should Gilead price Viread in each of the income tiers? Defend your pricing scheme based on strategic and/or moral principles.

Advanced Technology Laboratories, Inc.

Advanced Technology Laboratories, Inc. (ATL), with worldwide headquarters in Bothell, Washington, and European headquarters in Munich, Germany, was a leader in digital diagnostic ultrasound technology and equipment. "Ultrasound is a noninvasive technology that uses high frequency sound waves to image the body's soft tissues, organs and fetal anatomy and to dis-

play blood flow in real time."[39] ATL's ultrasound systems were used by cardiologists, radiologists, vascular surgeons, obstetricians, and gynecologists. Applications of ultrasound technology in gynecology included

---

[39]ATL Web site: www.atl.com.

diagnosis of ovarian cysts, endometrial hyperplasia, endometrium, and ovarian flow.

ATL ultrasound systems were sold in 100 countries to village clinics and world-renowned medical research centers. The worldwide ultrasound market was estimated at $2.5 billion. In 1996 ATL earned $21.8 million on sales of $419 million. Its competitors included such companies as General Electric and Siemens.

ATL's principal subsidiaries were located in OECD countries as well as in Argentina and India. In other countries ATL sold its systems through agents. Demand in the United States was sluggish, and ATL's worldwide competitors had introduced new products during the past 2 years. ATL looked to developing countries for growth.

The most attractive growth opportunities were in large countries with high growth rates of spending for medical care and health services. India, with a population of 800 million and a forecasted growth rate of 15 to 20 percent a year for medical devices, represented a particularly attractive market. ATL India, a joint venture with an Indian company that made low-end ultrasound instruments, was responsible for sales in India and Nepal. China, with a population of 1.2 billion, also represented an attractive market, and the installed base of ultrasound equipment was lower in China than in India. In 1997 ATL formed ATL China, where it had sold ultrasound systems since 1978. ATL also had a technology transfer agreement with the Shantou Institute of Ultrasonic Instruments.

In 1997 ATL introduced its HDI 1000 system, which replaced 50 percent of the hardware components with multitasking software, making digital ultrasound technology available at a substantially lower cost. ATL's Handheld Systems Business Division had also developed its FirstSight high-resolution digital imaging technology that would bring "highly portable, handheld ultrasound devices . . . to the examining table, the bedside and the field." ATL Chairman and CEO Dennis C. Fill said, "We believe that in the next few years these handheld ultrasound devices could have the same impact on patient care as the stethoscope and have the potential to create entirely new markets across many medical disciplines."[40]

In certain cultures some parents valued sons more than daughters. In the 1990s ultrasound devices became an effective means of allowing parents to engage in sex selection. Ultrasound was capable of identifying the sex of a fetus as early as 16 weeks, and local ultrasound clinics began to spring up throughout a number of Asian countries. A study by the Indian government revealed that for every 1,000 baby boys born, only 929 baby girls were born. A study reported that of the 8,000 abortions performed at one Bombay hospital, all but one were female fetuses.

One explanation for the preference for boys was given in a *CNN World News* story. "Sons are favored in India because it is they who are expected to carry on the family name and take care of the parents in their old age. Daughters are seen as a liability, and an expensive one at that. Families pay small fortunes in dowries to get their daughters married. . . . For those Indians too poor to afford tests, there is a grimmer option. Skakuntala admits to killing her newborn daughter several years ago. She already had two girls and didn't want another. 'We were poor,' she says. 'I put my sari over her face and she stopped breathing. It was the only thing to do.'"[41] CNN also reported that 25 percent of the girls born in India did not reach the age of 25, and in some families boys are given disproportionate shares of food, medical care, and education.

In 1994 India responded to the practice of using ultrasound to identify the sex and abort female fetuses by enacting the Pre-Natal Diagnostic Techniques (Regulation and Prevention of Misuses) Act. The law limited the use of ultrasound to women who were at high risk due to age or other factors and banned abortions of female fetuses identified by either amniocentesis or ultrasound. However, the use of ultrasound combined with abortion for purposes of sex selection continued unabated. According to the *New York Times,* "[f]or an investment amounting to a few thousand dollars, a mobile clinic operator can reap a small fortune from rural women, many of whom have never used a telephone or watched a television. Charges for the test can run as low as 150 rupees in poorer regions, about $5. . . . "[42] The same report noted that the law did not require registration of ultrasound machines, so it was virtually impossible to control their use in mobile clinics.

Gender selection was also practiced in several other Asian countries, including China. The natural ratio of boys to girls at birth worldwide was 105 to 100, but in China it was 114 to 100 and was considerably higher in some rural districts.[43] Chinese law prohibited gender selection through abortion, infanticide, and child abandonment.

Sex selection was widely criticized. The United Nations International Conference on Population and Development opposed sex selection. In the United States the President's Commission for the Study of Ethical Problems in Medicine and Biomedical and Behavioral Research strongly opposed the practice, as did the American College of Obstetricians and Gynecologists' Committee on Ethics. The Ethics Committee of the American Society for Reproductive Medicine argued that doctors should use "moral suasion" to convince couples to avoid sex selection.

[40]ATL Web site: www.atl.com.

[41]*CNN World News,* September 17, 1995.
[42]John F. Burns, *New York Times,* August 27, 1994, section 1, p. 5.
[43]The ratio in South Korea was 114 to 100 and in Taiwan it was 110 to 100.

In 1995 the Canadian minister of health ordered Canadian doctors to cease providing sex selection services for nonmedical purposes, and the British Columbia College of Physicians and Surgeons issued guidelines urging doctors and sonographers not to reveal the sex of fetuses. Vancouver, which had a substantial population of Asian-Canadians, was concerned about people going to the United States for fetal sex identification and returning to Canada for an abortion paid for by the government. Dr. Dalip Sandhu said, "I tell them it's a sin. But they're not here to ask for my opinion. They want the information. They don't get it from me. It doesn't mean it stops them."[44] Shashi Assanand, director of the Lower Mainland Multicultural Family Support Services Centre in Vancouver, blamed the dowry system. "Besides paying for a lavish wedding, the bride's family is expected to buy her a complete wardrobe and jewelry, as well as clothes and jewelry for the new son-in-law's family, with whom their daughter will be living. 'That's the minimum,' says Assanand. Those who can afford more are expected to give their new in-laws 'cash, furniture, appliances, a car and even property.'"[45]

Another group concerned with sex selection and women's issues was the Women's Environment and Development Organization (WEDO). WEDO and other women's groups were concerned about what was becoming known as the "missing women" of Asia.[46] ■

SOURCE: This case was written by Professors David P. Baron and Timothy J. Feddersen. Copyright © 1998 by the Board of Trustees of the Leland Stanford Junior University. All rights reserved. Reprinted with permission.

---

[44]*Chicago Tribune,* August 3, 1997.

[45]*Chicago Tribune,* August 3, 1997.
[46]See also *The Endangered Sex: Neglect of Female Children in Rural North India,* by Barbara Miller, 1981. Ithaca, NY: Cornell University Press.

Preparation Questions

1. Identify the moral concerns in using ultrasound for sex selection.
2. What possible reactions might ATL encounter on this issue?
3. Does ATL have any responsibility regarding the use of its products in sex selection?
4. Should ATL introduce its FirstSight handheld product in India?
5. Develop a strategy for ATL with respect to the issues discussed in the case. Be sure to include specific steps you would take to implement your strategy.

23

Ethics Issues in International Business

INTRODUCTION

Ethics issues abound within a country, but they take on added dimensions when a firm operates across national and cultural borders. Countries differ in the institutions that govern their political and economic activity as well as in their customs and culture. Countries also differ in their capacities to address issues of social and ethical concern. The capacities of many countries are limited by poverty, corruption, and political turmoil. Furthermore, their legal, health care, educational, and social services capabilities are often constrained by limited resources. World Bank (2004) data revealed that from 1980 to 2003 per capita real gross domestic product (GDP) in many countries in sub-Saharan Africa decreased from an already impoverished level. In 2007, per capita income was $281 a year in the Democratic Republic of the Congo, $333 in Burundi, and $334 in Liberia, compared to $75,595 in Luxembourg, $50,079 in Norway, and $43,968 in the United States. Life expectancy in 2007 was under 40 years in Swaziland and under 50 years in 17 African countries. In contrast, the life expectancy in China was 73 years, Mexico 76 years, and Japan 82 years.

In contrast to the differences among countries, ethics principles are intended to be universal. Applying those principles in international settings with such differences among countries, however, presents major challenges. Are the costs and benefits resulting from environmental protection in a low-income country the same as in a high-income country? Should a firm maintain the same safety and environmental standards in all countries? Should and do individuals in all countries have the same rights? Should practices that are morally unacceptable in one country be acceptable in other countries where they are legal? At a more general level, are the Western ethics systems considered in Chapters 20 and 21 applicable in countries that do not have the Western intellectual and moral traditions?

Rather than attempt to address the broad range of ethics issues that arises in international business, emphasis here is on five specific issues—culture and moral standards, human rights, operating in developing countries, company compliance programs, and questionable foreign payments made to secure sales. The next section considers international law and institutions, and the following section addresses the perspective of cultural relativism and contrasts it with the universalism perspective. Issues associated with operating in developing countries are then considered, including the development of private institutions to govern operating standards. The issues of corruption and questionable payments are then examined, and principles for reasoning about requests for payments are presented along with individual company and collective efforts to reduce bribery and corruption.

INTERNATIONAL LAW AND INSTITUTIONS

Interactions between nations and foreign firms are governed by the laws of the host nation and by international law. International law consists of national laws that pertain to foreign persons, entities, and other nations; intergovernmental treaties and agreements; rulings by international courts; and actions of international bodies such as the United Nations and the Organization of American States.[1]

National laws include laws pertaining to international trade, official boycotts such as that against Cuba, the Foreign Corrupt Practices Act (FCPA), and required government approval for the acquisition by a foreign firm of a U.S. firm essential to national defense. Treaties and agreements include the North American Free Trade Agreement, the International Monetary Fund, the treaties of the European Union, the Geneva Convention, the Kyoto Protocol on global climate change, reciprocal tax agreements, and accords on technical standards. International court rulings include those of the International Court of Justice, the World Court, the European Court of Justice, and the World Trade Organization's dispute resolution mechanism. Actions of international bodies include the United Nations' (UN) response to Iraq's invasion of Kuwait, the Law of the Sea, and the UN Convention on Contracts for the International Sale of Goods. Some international treaties meet with only modest support. The World Intellectual Property Organization treaty on copyright protection initially obtained few signatures, as developing countries refused to sign fearing that it would preclude them from having access to patented pharmaceuticals. By 2008, 65 countries had signed it.

International agreements also provide frameworks within which continuing problems can be addressed. The 1985 Vienna Convention for the Protection of the Ozone Layer provided a framework for addressing ozone depletion and global warming.[2] The 1987 Montreal Protocol on Substances That Deplete the Ozone Layer resulted from this framework and committed the signatories to reduce CFCs to 50 percent of 1986 consumption. This reduction was judged insufficient, and the 1989 Helsinki Declaration committed the parties to eliminate all CFC production as soon as possible and no later than 2000.

The international law pertaining to global climate change began with UN action in 1988 and the 1989 Hague Declaration calling for the establishment of the UN Framework Convention on Climate Change. The convention covered greenhouse gases not covered by the Montreal Protocol. The convention established a Conference of Nations as well as a secretariat and two advisory committees and committed the parties to concluding a more specific agreement by 1997. The result was the Kyoto Protocol on global climate change, which took effect in 2005.

International law differs from domestic law because sanctions may not be credible and enforcement is often left to individual nations. Some sanctions, such as the economic and military sanctions imposed on Iraq for the invasion of Kuwait, have been shown to be credible. Many elements of international law, however, are respected not because of enforcement powers but because of mutual interests in preserving those laws. For example, the Dispute Settlement Body (DSB) of the World Trade Organization (WTO) rules on trade disputes, but it has no real enforcement powers. It can only authorize a country to impose duties on imports of another country that refuses to halt a trade violation. WTO members have generally accepted the DSB decisions.

In 1789 the first U.S. Congress passed the Alien Tort Claims Act (ATCA) to protect U.S. diplomats abroad from attacks and U.S. ships from pirates. In the 1990s activists sought to use ATCA against U.S. corporations for alleged human rights violations abroad. In 1996, 12 refugees from Myanmar, formerly Burma, sued Unocal in the United States for alleged responsibility for murder, rape, forced labor, and torture. The actions were allegedly conducted by soldiers protecting a natural gas pipeline being built by Unocal subsidiaries, the French oil company Total, and the government of Myanmar.

In 2004 the Supreme Court limited the grounds on which lawsuits could be filed under ATCA, but allowed some cases involving serious human rights violations to go

---

[1]See Shaw (2003) for a treatment of international law.
[2]See Shaw (1997, pp. 610–614).

forward. A lawsuit against Unocal had been dismissed in federal court, but a California judge allowed the case to proceed. Unocal settled the case before it went to trial. In 2007 Yahoo! settled the case deriving from the arrest of a Chinese dissident discussed in Chapter 16. The application of ATCA created major uncertainties that would only be resolved by the Supreme Court.

Firms that operate internationally are subject to the laws of both their home country and their host countries, and at times those laws may be inconsistent. Moreover, practice and law are often in conflict, as in the case of questionable foreign payments. The FCPA prohibits practices that are not uncommon in some countries. Because of the demands for payments, a number of companies adopted codes of conduct that went beyond the requirements of the law. Increasing and persistent corruption and pressure from the United States and other countries resulted in an international agreement under the OECD to prohibit certain types of bribery.

Practices within a country pose both legal and ethical concerns. In some countries corruption is a fact (although not an inevitable fact) of life in many sectors of business activity.[3] In the mid-1980s Indonesia concluded that corruption and bribery in its ports were impeding economic growth by delaying imports and exports, at times for substantial periods. One report placed the amount of bribes at $200 million annually. To address the problem, the government ordered half the 13,000 employees in the Customs and Excise Service not to report to work. They continued to be paid their full wages, receive benefits, and even promotions, but they were not in a position to extract payments from importers and exporters.[4] A number of countries, including Indonesia, subsequently hired foreign firms to operate their customs services. The chapter case, *Complications in Marnera,* addresses management issues in a country with significant corruption.

CULTURAL RELATIVISM

In 1991 the Coalition for Justice in the Maquiladoras launched a campaign to improve conditions in the 2,000 U.S. plants (maquiladoras) located in the area near the U.S. border from Tijuana to Matamoros, Mexico. The coalition argued that although the firms met local standards in Mexico, they should meet the same health, safety, and environmental standards they met in the United States. "Moral behavior knows no borders. What would be wrong in the United States is wrong in Mexico," said Sister Susan Mika of the Interfaith Center on Corporate Responsibility (ICCR). Sister Mika expressed the view that moral standards are universal and that the standards in developed countries are the ones that should apply universally. The former is a rejection of cultural relativism, whereas the latter is a claim about particular standards.

Costs and benefits in the two countries differ, however, as is evident in the differences in per capita income. In 2001 the ICCR released a study of wages at maquiladoras. Reverend David Schilling said, "Our data show companies are nowhere paying a sustainable living wage."[5] Since wages and other costs differ, a utilitarianism or cost-benefit perspective could lead to different wage standards in Mexico and the United States. Differences also could be expected in terms of distributive justice as a result of the differences in standards of living between the countries.

Ethics, however, requires that firms, as well as individuals, not simply accept existing customs or prevailing practices in a country. Instead, firms and their managers are to evaluate issues of importance in terms of principles and standards that are universal.[6] Universal principles include respect for individual autonomy, improvements in aggregate well-being, and just actions regarding less-advantaged persons. Some cultural differences, such as in the institutions of political representation in

---

[3]See Palmier (1989) for examples.
[4]*Far Eastern Economic Review,* June 6, 1990.
[5]*Wall Street Journal,* June 28, 2001. The study was titled, "Making the Invisible Visible: A Study of the Purchasing Power of Mexican Maquila Workers," ICCR, New York.
[6]See Donaldson (1989, Ch. 2) and Freeman and Gilbert (1988, Ch. 2) for analyses and rejections of cultural relativism. Brandt (1959) provides an extended evaluation of ethical relativism.

democracies, are easily accepted. A democracy with a strong executive and a system of checks and balances, as in the United States, may be morally no better or worse than a parliamentary democracy. Some differences, such as the status of women under the Taliban in Afghanistan, however, are not so easily tolerated. Some differences, such as the suppression of political liberties and human rights in countries such as Myanmar and North Korea are not tolerated but are difficult to change.

In considering countries and cultures, Sen (1997) warned against generalizations that "hide more than they reveal." He advocated the simultaneous recognition of

- The significance of cultural variation
- The need to avoid cultural stereotypes and sweeping generalizations
- The importance of taking a dynamic rather than a static view of cultures
- The necessity of recognizing heterogeneity within given communities

In considering the relevance of differences in cultures and in the positions of peoples and nations in their development, it is useful to identify two concepts—*cultural relativism* and *cultural imperialism*—and to recognize that there is a considerable distance between the two. In its strongest version, cultural relativism holds that appropriate behavior in a country or culture is determined by its laws and customs.[7] That is, what is moral is defined by the customs within individual countries; when in Rome, do as the Romans do. If corruption is widespread in a country, then a firm should accept the functioning system and act as domestic firms do. At some level cultural differences and local practices surely are important, and it is clear that moral standards differ among cultures. Ethics principles, however, are to be universal rather than culturally determined.

Cultural imperialism in its strongest form means that in operating internationally a firm maintains the standards of its home country and judges others by those standards.[8] Cultural imperialism is surely not universally applicable, since the differences among cultures and countries are both important and difficult to ignore. Donaldson (1996) cites the instance of a U.S. company that caught one of its employees in China stealing and turned the employee over to the authorities—who had the employee executed.

Donaldson identifies two fundamental conflicts between universal principles and local customs and practices. The first is a "conflict of relative development," which requires firms to recognize that countries and their peoples may differ in their capabilities due to their stages of economic development. He advocates that the following question be asked about local practices:

> Would the practice be acceptable at home if my country were in a similar stage of economic development?

Levi Strauss & Company, for example, uses suppliers that pay the prevailing wage and employ children as young as 15, when that is consistent with host country laws. The likely answer to the question is that a firm is justified in paying the prevailing wage rate and legally hiring children. But, should it meet only local workplace safety standards? One answer is based on whether local safety standards are unreasonable to the point of jeopardizing a person's human dignity by failing to treat the person as an end as well as a means.

The second conflict is a "conflict of cultural tradition." In many cases, this conflict is more difficult to resolve. Donaldson (1996, p. 60) proposes,

> Managers should deem a practice permissible only if they can answer no to both of the following questions: Is it possible to conduct business successfully in the host country without undertaking the practice? And is the practice a violation of a core human value?

---

[7]See Bowie (1990).
[8]De George (1993) argues for an intermediate position in which the goal is not a set of ethics principles on which agreement is unlikely but rather is a set of international guidelines for business practice on which everyone can agree.

For example, the arbitrary firing of employees is unlikely to be necessary to operate successfully and is a violation of basic principles. A company thus would not be justified in acting in such a manner. Bribery, however, is sufficiently pervasive in some countries that it might be required at times to operate successfully. If it is not a violation of a core human value, a company could be justified in providing "facilitating payments" in certain circumstances, as indicated in the later section on questionable foreign payments. In considering whether it should do business in a country where the answer is persistently no to the first question and yes to the second question, Levi Strauss refused to do business in Myanmar.

Donaldson (1996, pp. 61–62) argues that three general principles should guide companies in their global business activity:

1. Respect for core human values (human dignity, respect for basic rights, and good citizenship), which determine the absolute moral threshold for all business activities
2. Respect for local traditions
3. The belief that context matters when deciding what is right and wrong

He also offers five guidelines for "ethical leadership": (1) Treat corporate values and formal standards of conduct as absolutes.[9] (2) Design and implement conditions of engagement for suppliers and customers. (3) Allow foreign business units to help formulate ethics standards and interpret ethics issues. (4) In host countries, support efforts to decrease institutional corruption. (5) Exercise moral imagination.

As an example of moral imagination, Levi Strauss faced a dilemma in Bangladesh. It learned that one of its suppliers was employing children younger than 14 years of age. The income earned by the children was important to their impoverished families, yet their working deprived them of the opportunity to attend school. Faced with this dilemma Levi Strauss convinced the supplier to pay the children their wages and benefits while they attended school and guarantee that they could return to their jobs once they completed their schooling.[10] Levi Strauss paid for their tuition, books, and school uniforms.

The chapter case, *De Beers and Conflict Diamonds,* provides an opportunity to design a mechanism that both can end the killings and atrocities financed by conflict diamonds in Africa and serve the interests of De Beers.

As indicated in Chapters 20 and 21, ethics frameworks can differ in terms of how the good and the right are conceived, as well as in their methods of analysis and their prescriptions. These differences, coupled with the differences among countries, suggest that at least some differences in practices and standards should be tolerated. Yet there are universal principles that are sufficiently important that firms should work toward their achievement. Donaldson (1989, pp. 81–86) proposes that respect for and promotion of rights should be universal and that all nations, firms, and individuals have a duty to respect a certain minimal set of rights. Those rights are the following:

1. Freedom of physical movement
2. Ownership of property
3. Freedom from torture
4. Fair trial
5. Nondiscriminatory treatment (freedom from discrimination on the basis of such characteristics as race and/or sex)
6. Physical security
7. Speech and association
8. Minimal education
9. Political participation
10. Subsistence

---

[9]For example, do not make exceptions to standards solely for the purpose of improving one's business prospects.
[10]See "Third-World Families at Work: Child Labor or Child Care?" *Harvard Business Review,* January–February, 1993.

Using a distinction suggested by Shue (1980), Donaldson argues that firms have a duty not to deprive individuals of any of these rights and an affirmative duty to help protect individuals from being deprived of any of the last six. He also argues that the rights to nondiscriminatory treatment, political participation, and ownership of property are subject to cultural interpretation. One might disagree about which rights should be included in these sets, but the concept that respect for and promotion of certain rights constitutes minimal acceptable behavior is important. The next section considers two companies' attempts to address human rights issues.

HUMAN RIGHTS AND JUSTICE

Some ethics issues arise not from the actions of individuals and firms, but instead from the policies of governments. Particularly in the case of countries that are not democracies, ethics concerns pertaining to human rights and justice can arise. In some countries, firms may be required to implement aspects of morally objectionable policies. For example, in China some firms have responsibility for enforcing aspects of the government's one-child-per-family law. Many people view this policy as violating basic human rights, such as those spelled out in the Universal Declaration of Human Rights proclaimed by the United Nations in 1948 and endorsed by many countries.

Because of concerns about human rights in the countries in which their suppliers were located, several firms, including Levi Strauss and Reebok, formulated human rights statements pertaining to their business partners. Reebok's "Human Rights Production Standards" covered the following subjects: nondiscrimination, working hours/overtime, fair wages, child labor, freedom of association, and a safe and healthy work environment. Reebok applied its standards at the level of its business partners.

Levi Strauss also developed guidelines for its business partners. In addition, the company applied its standards at the country level. It concluded that it should not do business with even an exemplary supplier if the policies of its home country resulted in pervasive violations of human rights.

To implement the guidelines, Levi Strauss established Country Assessment Guidelines and conducted an internal country review process that utilized information from a variety of public sources, such as the United Nations and the U.S. Department of State, as well as its own independent assessments. The review process led the company to withdraw immediately from Myanmar because of pervasive violations of human rights and to announce that it would withdraw over several years from China. The company also immediately canceled all contracts in China where prison labor was used, since the prisoners could have been convicted for political reasons. As the human rights conditions in China improved, the company reversed its decision in 1998.

Slave Labor in Saipan?

Shortly after Levi Strauss adopted its guidelines, they underwent their first challenge. The issue involved a supplier based in the U.S. Territory of Saipan that worked for a number of apparel firms, including Levi Strauss, Liz Claiborne, and Eddie Bauer. Levi Strauss learned that the supplier was in legal trouble, and one of its vice presidents met with the contractor in San Francisco. He asked blunt questions about the supplier's legal problems, but the supplier assured him that there were only routine problems and that he need not be concerned.

A few months later the NBC television affiliate in Washington, D.C., broadcast a story about the Saipan supplier, alleging that he was using Chinese workers as "slave labor" and that the merchandise they produced was mislabeled as "Made in the U.S.A." In fact, products produced in Saipan are required to carry that label. The slave labor allegation, however, was more serious. It centered on the common practice in Saipan of bringing young women from China to work in the factories for a few years and then returning them to China. The young women were eager to come because the wages were high compared with wages in China. The story also reported that the supplier was about to plead no contest to a felony charge of denying workers compensation totaling several million dollars.

A day after the story made the national news, Levi Strauss executives met to begin their own investigation of the Saipan facilities. A group of senior executives visited the factory and found it to be an excellent facility—better than some in the United States. The dormitories where the workers were housed were substandard, but Levi Strauss concluded that the allegations of slave labor were unwarranted. What was clear, however, was that the supplier had consistently misled Levi Strauss. The recently approved Global Sourcing Guidelines called for business partners to maintain standards consistent with the company's standards. Consequently, Levi Strauss canceled its contract with the Saipan supplier and paid several hundred thousand dollars in contract penalties to do so.

To Levi Strauss the Saipan incident indicated why guidelines were needed. In addition to protecting workers in some cases, the guidelines would protect the company's integrity and commercial success by preventing it from sourcing with suppliers with questionable practices.

OPERATING IN DEVELOPING COUNTRIES

In developing countries, institutions are not always present to provide guidance to firms and their managers. Also, issues are more complex when people do not have the means to protect their rights and advance their interests. Poverty, lack of education, and inadequate health care create situations in which individuals cannot be expected to make the same decisions that would be made in a developed country. Furthermore, their governments may not have the means to provide the needed information, guidance, or regulation found in developed countries.

In developed countries, for example, the liability system assigns the social cost of injuries to producers and consumers, creating incentives for care and the reduction of hazards. In addition, regulation establishes safety standards and requires information and warnings about hazards. If institutions are not present or function imperfectly in a developing country, business is without an important source of guidance. In such cases, the temptation may be to follow local practice. The consequences, however, may not be acceptable. Following local practice could lead to the exploitation of the ignorant and disadvantaged or the exposure of consumers or workers to serious hazards that they may not reasonably be able to avoid.

In such situations, ethics can provide guidance. To understand how a firm might reason in situations in which institutions are imperfect, consider the case of a safety decision about a product marketed in a developing country. Suppose that the product is safe under proper use but that misuse can result in injury. Also, suppose that many of the people who are likely to buy the product are impoverished and have a minimal formal education. There is no functioning liability system, and regulatory agencies are overburdened and cannot be expected to address the safety issue. The firm and its managers must provide their own guidance on appropriate action.

From the perspective of utilitarianism, the Calabresi and Melamed principles considered in Chapters 12 and 20 provide a basis for reasoning about the appropriate level of safety and how the product should be marketed. Those principles are intended to be applied in situations in which institutions are imperfect, entitlements and their protection are unclear, or transactions costs prohibit bargaining to resolve the issue. The principles first ask which party is best positioned to make a cost-benefit analysis of the product and its safety features. In a developed country, the answer is typically that the government is best placed to do so, as reflected in the institutions of liability and regulation. In the absence of those institutions, the responsibility falls on the firm and consumers. In a developing country, many consumers are poorly positioned to evaluate hazards and exercise proper care. The firm thus has the moral responsibility to make the evaluation.

The Calabresi and Melamed principles also ask which party is best positioned to induce others to take actions that will improve the difference between social benefits and social costs. Consumers are certainly not in that position. The firm may be able to induce consumers to use the product properly and can take steps through product design to reduce the hazards from anticipated misuse. The former, for example, might require instructions presented in pictures as well as in words. In addition, marketing might focus on those market segments in which the product is most likely to be used properly. Similarly, distribution of the product might be restricted to outlets where instruction in proper use can be given. In a number of countries, however, such measures may not be sufficient.

The firm then is faced with the prospect of anticipatable misuse. Depending on the product in question, design and safety features can be effective means of reducing hazards from misuse, but the institutions of liability and regulation are not present to provide information on which safety features to incorporate.[11] The firm then is left with the issue of determining if the social costs of an injury in Bangladesh are the same as in Germany. Compensation for injuries is not the same even among developed countries, and the disparity between developed and developing countries can be considerable. The Calabresi and Melamed principles are incapable of resolving this issue. Utilitarianism evaluates alternatives using the preferences of those affected, which suggests using the trade-offs made in the developing country as the guide for deciding on the safety features to incorporate to reduce the hazards from anticipatable misuse.

Donaldson (1989, p. 116) addressed the issue of risks in developing countries and proposed a modification of Rawls's second principle to guide decisions about risks. He argued that the "difference principle would need to be adjusted to include freedom from risk as one of the primary goods normally covered by the principle." From this perspective a basic level of safety should be assured for all individuals, which could mean that higher standards than those practiced in developing countries should be used.

Firms are also guided by principles of rights and justice. When misuse can be anticipated, marketing a product to those who are likely to misuse it may constitute deception. This would violate moral rules focusing on treating individuals as ends whose ability to choose should be developed rather than their ignorance exploited. Advertising is frequently viewed as a culprit in such situations. Activists have campaigned for over 30 years against the practices used in marketing infant formula in developing countries. Similarly, critics argue that the promotion and advertising of cigarettes in developing countries not only causes health problems but also leads to an economic burden on the poor.

AIDS AND DEVELOPING COUNTRIES

Many developing countries lack the means to provide basic services for their people. Many of these same countries, particularly those in sub-Saharan Africa, have also been devastated by the AIDS pandemic. Some 20 million people worldwide have died from AIDS, and 40 million people are HIV positive, nearly three-quarters of whom are in sub-Saharan Africa. In some African countries the incidence is nearly 30 percent. AIDS has led to sharp declines in life expectancy and negative economic growth, since AIDS strikes the most productive age group. This has worsened impoverishment and countries' abilities to address the pandemic.

The treatment of AIDS victims has been impeded by the high cost of AIDS drugs, all of which were under patent. Although there is no cure for AIDS, with a strict regimen of drugs AIDS has become a treatable chronic disease in developed countries. Those drugs, however, were priced high, with many costing $10,000 or more a year. With the per capita income in sub-Saharan Africa averaging $1.50 a day, AIDS drugs were beyond the means of almost every country.

With many countries unable to provide care for AIDS victims, developed countries belatedly began to provide funds for treatment and prevention programs.[12] The United Nations under the leadership of Secretary General Kofi Annan established the independent Global Fund to Fight AIDS, Tuberculosis and Malaria with $3 billion in funding financed by the developed countries. The United States pledged $3 billion a year for

---

[11]See the Chapter 12 case *California Space Heaters, Inc.*
[12]Private parties, and particularly the Gates Foundation, also funded care and prevention programs. Some, such as the AIDS Healthcare Foundation and Doctors Without Borders, directly provided medical care. The Gates Foundation emphasized prevention programs and has spent over $1 billion in Africa.

5 years for AIDS treatment and prevention programs in developing countries, including a pledge to provide one-third of the Global Fund on a matching basis. The contributions from many countries lagged, however. Moreover, the Global Fund initially was unable to find enough well-organized recipient programs to spend the money it had.

The UN goal was "3 by 5"; that is, to treat 3 million people with AIDS drugs by 2005. Given that only 200,000 were receiving AIDS drugs in 2002, with most of those in Brazil, the goal was not met. Contributions from the developed countries surged, however, reaching $10 billion in 2007, with 3 million people being treated. The number of AIDS related deaths declined from 3.9 million in 2001 to 2.1 million in 2007. The number of new infections also decreased from 3.2 million in 1998 to an estimated 2.5 million in 2007. Although progress was being made, the task ahead remained formidable.

Some countries such as Brazil threatened to use the "medical emergency" provisions of TRIPS to invoke compulsory licensing of AIDS drugs, and in 2007 Thailand did so, as considered in the Chapter 18 case, *Compulsory Licensing, Thailand, and Abbott Laboratories*. In addition, Indian pharmaceutical companies began to produce and export AIDS drugs under India's unique patent system.[13] The pharmaceutical companies argued vigorously that compulsory licensing weakened patent protection and diminished incentives to conduct research and development on AIDS drugs.[14]

Intense private and public politics were directed at pharmaceutical companies, and after several years they began to lower their prices under preferential pricing programs.

EXAMPLE

GlaxoSmithKline and Nonmarket Spillovers

For several years GlaxoSmithKline (GSK) had been under pressure from activists and the media for its pricing of AIDS drugs in the developing world, particularly in sub-Saharan Africa. Activists led by the AIDS Healthcare Foundation (AHF) deployed a multipronged nonmarket strategy against GSK. One prong was to lobby investors to pressure GSK to lower its prices for AIDS drugs and make them more widely available. One of AHF's objectives was to enlist the aid of CalPERS, one of the largest funds in the United States, which held nearly $1 billion in GSK shares.

In 2003 an opportunity to pressure GSK was provided by a new United Kingdom (UK) law requiring a shareholder advisory vote on new compensation packages for executives of UK companies. The UK law reflected growing European opposition to American-style compensation systems. European opposition to lucrative compensation packages resulted in pressure against Germany's Mannesmann AG and France's Vivendi Universal SA. Percy Barnevik, former CEO and chairman of ABB Ltd., was forced to return $54.4 million of his pension package. Opposition also appeared in the United Kingdom to compensation plans at Vodafone PLC, Prudential PLC, and Marconi PLC.

GSK was a UK company, but CEO Jean-Pierre Garnier and GSK's top management team worked out of Philadelphia. Garnier and GSK argued that American-style compensation was necessary to compete for management talent in global competition. The component of the compensation package that served as a lightning rod was a "golden parachute" for Garnier estimated to be worth $23.7 million. The compensation would be paid if Garnier lost his job due to an acquisition or resigned before 2007.

AIDS activists joined with British trade unions, including the union Amicus that represented GSK employees, to oppose the compensation package. AHF claimed that Garnier's golden parachute would buy AIDS treatment for 100,000 people. British mutual funds opposed the compensation package, and CalPERS joined in opposition. Sir Christopher Hogg, the non-executive chairman of GSK, wrote to shareholders telling them that American-style compensation was required to compete with American companies.

At GSK's annual meeting the 2.8 billion votes went 50.72 percent to 49.28 percent against the compensation plan with CalPERS among those that voted against it. In addition, 17.69 percent of the shares were voted against election of Garnier to the board.

The vote was advisory, but management could not ignore it. Sir Christopher said, "The board takes this very seriously."

---

[13]See Chapter 12. India was forced by World Trade Organization rules to change its patent law.
[14]See Vachani and Smith (2004) for a perspective on AIDS drugs pricing.

Even at cost, however, the drugs were not affordable. The Part V integrative case, *GlaxoSmithKline and AIDS Drugs Policy,* addresses the challenges faced by the early market leader in AIDS drugs in responding to the pandemic. The intensity of the private politics is illustrated in the preceding example.

Gilead Sciences, which produces the most effective first line drug, Viread, for treating HIV/AIDS, was committed to making its drug accessible throughout the developing world. It launched a major effort to make the drug available in Africa. After two years of work, however, only 35,000 patients in Africa were receiving Viread. The Chapter 22 case, *Gilead Sciences (A): The Gilead Access Program for HIV Drugs,* describes its efforts and seeks a more effective approach to making its drug available.

RESPONSIBILITY FOR WORKING CONDITIONS IN SUPPLIERS' FACTORIES

Sweatshops

In the 1990s concern developed about "sweatshops" in Asia and Latin America that supplied U.S. footwear and apparel companies. The issue was propelled by poignant stories of poverty and abuse; nonmarket action by labor unions, human rights groups, and activists; and pressure from the U.S. Department of Labor. The media provided extensive coverage of the issue and advocated higher workplace standards. The pressure reached a crescendo when abuses at a Nike supplier in Vietnam were reported.[15] (See the Chapter 4 case *Nike in Southeast Asia.*) Yet in many of the countries in which the factories in question were located, few concerns over the working conditions were expressed. Moreover, since demand in those industries had grown rapidly as factories in the United States closed, many of the overseas factories were modern, as Levi Strauss had found in Saipan. The fear of many workers in the overseas factories was that higher standards would increase costs, causing purchasers to look elsewhere for lower cost suppliers.

To improve practices in suppliers' factories, President Clinton appointed an 18-member White House Apparel Industry Partnership, which included Nike, Reebok, L.L. Bean, Liz Claiborne, unions, human rights groups, and activist and advocacy representatives.[16] The task force was charged with producing a code and an enforcement mechanism to achieve standards including a 60-hour workweek, a minimum employment age of 14, and wage guidelines. The task force, however, became embroiled in strong disagreements about implementation details.

The Union of Needletrade, Industrial, and Textile Employees (UNITE) and activists sought a majority on the governing board of any organization the partnership created to audit compliance with the standards. The companies were worried that the auditors of contractors' facilities would find that some met the standards and others did not, giving the former group a marketing and public relations advantage over the others. The companies were successful in having the board have an equal representation of companies and the other groups.

The other sources of disagreement proved to be more difficult, and the task force failed to reach an accord by the deadline. The two sides disagreed on the percentage of supplier facilities to be inspected each year, and the labor and human rights groups pressed for "living wages," rather than the prevailing wages, for suppliers' employees. The labor and human rights groups also sought a provision directed at China requiring that workers have the right to form independent unions and engage in collective bargaining. Such a requirement could force companies not to source products in China, since China did not allow independent unions. Some commentators suggested that the motivation behind these labor provisions was protection of union jobs in the United States.

With the partnership deadlocked a group of committee members, including Liz Claiborne, Nike, Reebok, and a number of human rights groups, reached an agreement

---

[15]One result was the 1997 enactment of the Sanders Amendment, which bans the import of foreign products produced with forced child labor.
[16]See Golodner (2000).

on standards and established a private governance organization, the Fair Labor Association (FLA), to ensure compliance. The standards included a 60-hour workweek, a ban on employing children under the age of 15 unless the country explicitly allowed 14-year-olds to work, independent monitoring of suppliers' factories, and a requirement to pay the maximum of the official minimum wage and the prevailing market wage. The U.S. Secretary of Labor praised the agreement: "It is workable for business and creates a credible system that will let consumers know the garments they buy are not produced by exploited workers."[17]

Two members of the partnership, UNITE and an activist group, rejected the agreement. They joined with other activist groups, including the United Students Against Sweatshops, and other labor unions to form the Worker Rights Consortium (WRC) to work for more aggressive monitoring and higher standards including a living wage. Both the FLA and the WRC recruited affiliated members, primarily colleges and universities concerned about their licenses for sports apparel, but the WRC had no companies as members.

Private Governance and Self-Regulation: The Fair Labor Association

The FLA was established in 1999 with many of the characteristics of a government institution. The FLA agreement specified representation, decision rights, standards, monitoring, certification, public reporting, and amendment procedures. In 2008 the FLA included 25 companies, and the companies and the labor/NGOs each had six board seats, with the 175 college and university affiliates also holding six board seats. The FLA has a detailed code of workplace standards, covering forced labor, child labor, harassment or abuse, nondiscrimination, health and safety, freedom of association and collective bargaining, wages and benefits, hours of work, and overtime compensation. The FLA code did not provide for a "living wage," as does the code for the WRC. A supermajority of two-thirds of the companies and two-thirds of the labor/NGOs was required to change the standards. This provided assurances to both sides that the standards would not be changed unless there was considerable consensus on both sides.

The FLA selected and certified independent third-party monitors to inspect a specified percentage of the factories each year, and the companies chose from the set for the inspections. The FLA has also specified detailed procedures (Monitoring Guidance and Compliance Benchmarks) for the inspections. During the initial 2 to 3 years, independent monitoring of at least 30 percent of the participating companies' applicable facilities was required. Subsequently, 5 percent of a company's suppliers' facilities were inspected annually. Inspections were unannounced, and the facilities inspected were chosen at random by the FLA staff based on prior compliance reports. Any finding of noncompliance by an independent monitor was posted on the FLA Web site. The FLA also had a Third-Party Complaint System that allowed any person or organization to report "any situation of serious noncompliance" for any FLA member company. The FLA then reviewed the complaint and investigated any verifiable violation of the code.

Company Responses

Nike went beyond the FLA standards by pledging not to hire anyone under the age of 18 in its footwear plants and to meet U.S. air quality standards in the workplace. CEO Phil Knight stated, "The Nike product has become synonymous with slave wages, forced overtime and arbitrary abuse. I truly believe the American consumer doesn't want to buy products made under abusive conditions."[18] In 1999 Nike began a reporting system, "Transparency 101," under which it publicly released the external monitoring reports conducted by PricewaterhouseCoopers on 53 North American factories. It also posted information on the factories' efforts to implement the action plans developed as a result

---

[17]*New York Times,* November 5, 1998.
[18]*New York Times,* May 13, 1998.

of the inspections. Nike also opened its contractors' facilities to student monitors and publicly released the reports on 32 contractors that produced college-licensed apparel. In 2005 in its corporate responsibility report Nike released the names of 700 of its suppliers and reviewed the problems remaining. In 2000 Phil Knight spoke at the United Nations about Nike's participation in the UN-sponsored Global Compact along with other companies and NGOs. The companies in the Global Compact pledged to meet global labor and environmental standards.

Nike embarked on an aggressive campaign to ensure that suppliers were complying fully with its code. It conducted its own monitoring of suppliers' factories in addition to the inspections by the FLA. When violations were found, Nike worked with the supplier to rectify the problem and in the case of recurrent violations it could terminate the supply arrangement. Its efforts were successful in improving working conditions, but the improvements stopped well short of its goals. Nike kept detailed records on its inspections, called M-Audits.

Nike turned over its factory inspection data to researchers at the Massachusetts Institute of Technology who sought to explain why some factories had better audit scores than others. Part of the difference appeared to be cultural. Factories in the Americas and the Europe, Middle East, and Africa regions performed significantly better than those in North Asia and South Asia. Locke, Qin, and Brause (2007) found that the two principal factors affecting compliance were the rule of law in the country and the number of employees in the factory.[19] Firms in countries in which the rule of law was stronger had significantly better performance, and larger factories had significantly worse performance. The authors also found that factories owned by citizens of the country had worse performance than those owned by foreigners. Overall, Nike's suppliers showed only modest improvement over time in their M-Audit scores: 2002 0.638, 2003 0.643, 2004 0.673.

Nike and other firms in the apparel and footwear industries, as well as the NGOs, concluded that compliance with codes was not sufficient to achieve workplace goals. Part of the problem rested with the factory owners and their supervisors, who were willing to violate the code to achieve more important goals such as meeting a delivery date. Nike recognized that it needed to identify the root causes of the problems in achieving compliance with its code. Some of the root cause rested with the factory owners and supervisors, who in some cases lacked respect for workers. Most of the suppliers had poor HR practices that made it difficult to respond to the rights of workers. Much of the root cause, however, was found to rest with Nike. Its purchasing agents, for example, would at times set unreasonable delivery schedules and not provide sufficient lead time. Moreover, purchasing made little attempt to smooth its orders over time. These failures forced factory supervisors to schedule excessive overtime and to pressure workers to be more productive, violating Nike's code.

Nike wrote in its 2005-6 Corporate Social Responsibility Report,

> Late design changes and poor forecasting by buyers pressure factory management who may already have done a poor job of production planning or have accepted orders beyond their capacity as a means of managing risk in a fluctuating market. . . . The pressure on the factory to deliver product on time seems to outweigh concerns about legal compliance, code compliance and general good work practices. . . . Many in local industry also are able to circumvent or ignore legal compliance standards, which may reflect a more generalized lack of clarity about or enforcement of the law.

Nike embarked on a process to move beyond compliance. "Nike has begun an extensive review of the company's own upstream business processes—such as product development, design, and commercialization—in order to identify potential drivers of excessive overtime among suppliers. All of this suggests that Nike is working

---

[19]The Rule of Law index used was from the World Bank's Worldwide Governance Indicator project.

on promoting greater integration of its labor compliance initiatives with core business processes."[20] In its 2005-6 Corporate Social Responsibility Report Nike stated,

> In Generation I we set standards. In Generation II we developed tools and methods to monitor those standards. Each generation was a stepping stone to the next and delivered vital learning and experience for all stakeholders. . . . Generation III is what we call responsible competitiveness. While monitoring continues to be a cornerstone of our approach, we are taking a broader, more holistic look at our supply chain, focusing on root cause identification and solutions that will drive systemic change.

INTERNATIONAL CODES

As illustrated by the Nike example, companies have developed their own codes of conduct for their global operations. In addition, industries such as the U.S. apparel and footwear industries and the worldwide chemical industry (Chapter 11) have developed codes. A number of broader attempts to establish global codes of conduct have also been undertaken to deal with human rights, labor conditions, the environment, and corruption.[21] The Global Reporting Initiative (GRI) goes further and has developed guidelines for sustainable reporting on the economic, environmental, and social performance of companies. Williams (2000) and the contributors to his volume review a variety of codes and include an appendix reproducing over 20 international codes. One of those codes is considered here.

In 1994 a group of business leaders and academics gathered to identify a set of transcultural values. The resulting Caux Round Table Principles for Business set forth both obligations and values derived from the Western concept of human dignity and the Japanese concept of *kyosei,* or acting for the common good.[22] According to the Caux Round Table, "*kyosei* means living and working together for the common good—enabling cooperation and mutual prosperity to coexist with healthy and fair competition. 'Human dignity' refers to the sacredness or value of each person as an end, not simply as a means to the fulfillment of others' purposes or even majority prescription." The concept of *kyosei* can be understood in the traditional eastern focus on groups beginning with the family and extending outward to the work unit and universe. The concept of human dignity is based on Kant's categorical imperative.

The Caux Principles include a set of general principles and a set of stakeholder principles identifying responsibilities to customers, employees, owners/investors, suppliers, competitors, and communities.[23] These responsibilities are similar to those espoused by the advocates of corporate social responsibility. The general principles, presented in Figure 23-1, represent an attempt to identify a set of values that can be respected across western and eastern cultures, and they have a strong communitarian flavor.

QUESTIONABLE FOREIGN PAYMENTS AND CORRUPTION

Corruption is costly both tangibly and intangibly. Corruption distorts economic activity, resulting in a substantial cost to an economy. Corruption also undermines trust and confidence in government. As international trade and foreign direct investment expanded, the opportunities for corruption increased and more firms were exposed to demands for payments or temptations to offer payments when they believed competitors were likely to be offering payments. Both countries and companies wanted to reduce corruption, and in the 1990s international efforts began. One important development was the establishment of Transparency International, an NGO formed to combat

---

[20]Locke, Qin, and Brause (2007, pp. 22–23).
[21]See Prakash and Hart (1999) for a broader focus on globalization and governance.
[22]See Skelly (1995) and Küng (1997, pp. 24–25).
[23]See Cavanagh (2000) and Goodpaster (2000) for background on and evaluation of the Caux Principles.

FIGURE 23-1 Caux Principles of Business

1. *The Responsibilities of Business: Beyond Shareholders Toward Stakeholders . . .* Businesses have a role to play in improving the lives of all their customers, employees, and shareholders by sharing with them the wealth they have created. . . .

2. *The Economic and Social Impact of Business: Toward Innovation, Justice, and World Community . . .* Business also should contribute to human rights, education, welfare, and vitalization of the countries in which they operate. Business should contribute to economic and social development not only in the countries in which they operate, but also in the world community at large, . . .

3. *Business Behavior: Beyond the Letter of the Law Toward a Spirit of Trust . . .* businesses should recognize that sincerity, candor, truthfulness, the keeping of promises, and transparency contribute not only to their own credibility and stability, but also to the smoothness and efficiency of business transactions, . . .

4. *Respect for Rules . . .* business should respect international and domestic rules. In addition, they should recognize that some behavior, although legal, may still have adverse consequences.

5. *Support for Multilateral Trade . . .* businesses should cooperate in efforts to promote the progressive and judicious liberalization of trade and to relax those domestic measures that unreasonably hinder global commerce, while giving due respect to national policy objectives.

6. *Respect for the Environment* A business should protect and, where possible, improve the environment, promote sustainable development, and prevent the wasteful use of natural resources.

7. *Avoidance of Illicit Operations* A business should not participate in or condone bribery, money laundering, or other corrupt practices: indeed, it should seek cooperation with others to eliminate them. . . .

Source: Caux Round Table.

corruption, considered in Chapter 17. Another development was the negotiation of an antibribery code under the auspices of the OECD. These developments are considered later in the chapter, after considering frameworks for evaluating the moral concerns about these questionable payments.

In a number of countries, the exchange of gifts and favors is customary, and in some cases favors may extend into the domain of unethical conduct. In a country in which small payments to low-level government employees are necessary to clear administrative hurdles, a firm may be justified in making the payments to avoid a greater injustice. When those payments are recurring and pervasive, however, the question is which is the greater injustice. A firm may decide to forgo sales if those sales necessitate a continuing violation of ethics principles.

When corruption is pervasive, a company may go further and decide to withdraw from a country. A Unilever executive explained the company's decision to leave Bulgaria: "It was impossible for us to do business without getting involved in corruption. So we took the logical step and accepted the consequences. That meant packing our bags."[24]

Questionable Payments and Ethics Principles

The disclosure in 1975 that the Lockheed Corporation had made payments of over $12 million to Japanese business executives and government officials to secure a sale of commercial aircraft led to revelations that over 450 U.S. companies had made similar payments totaling more than $300 million worldwide. The questionable foreign payments ranged from outright bribes to obtain sales to extortion payments made to customs officials to avoid delays in clearing imports. In response, Congress passed the FCPA.

---

[24]*Wall Street Journal,* February 16, 1999.

Some payments were made because firms, or their sales representatives, had reason to believe that competitors were offering payments to a customer. In an industry or a country in which such payments are customary, a firm may be unable unilaterally to change the practice, and the payments can be self-perpetuating.[25] This, however, does not provide a moral justification for the practice, and change can occur.[26]

In a situation in which payments are either demanded or likely to be required to obtain a sale, firms and their managers have two sources of guidance—one is ethics and the other is the law. Ethics is considered first, and then the law is presented and interpreted. Corporate codes of conduct are then considered. The ethics analysis focuses on bribery and the question of when, if ever, a firm is morally justified in paying a bribe.

A bribe is a payment to an individual in an organization intended to influence that person's exercise of his or her responsibilities; that is, a bribe is intended to corrupt the behavior of the recipient. Bribery is ethically objectionable on a number of grounds. From a utilitarian perspective, bribery distorts markets and reduces economic efficiency. That is, when bribes replace value and merit as the basis for decisions, competition cannot be as efficient. From a rights perspective, bribery distorts the fair opportunity to compete in markets. Furthermore, bribes induce the recipients to violate a duty to the principals who employ them.

More fundamentally, the bases for Kant's moral rules are violated. First, a rule under which bribes are allowed is not universalizable because there is little reason to believe that in the original position individuals would will economic competition in bribes rather than competition without bribes. Second, bribery is not reversible. A firm would not want its own purchasing agents to make their decisions based on the bribes they received.

With respect to justice, bribes paid to government officials undermine the impartiality of government and hence the equality of political rights. A bribe also exploits the position a person occupies in the recipient organization and distorts the fair equality of opportunity to qualify for the position. Furthermore, the recipient may receive too much, having done nothing to deserve it. Bribes would also not be expected to benefit the least advantaged persons, even indirectly.

The remaining issue is whether bribes are justified if there is a greater injustice that can be avoided. This issue is considered next in the context of the Lockheed case.

The Lockheed Case

The Lockheed case was described by Vice Chairman A. Carl Kotchian (1977), who authorized the payments in Japan. The $12 million payments in question represented less than 3 percent of the revenue on the L-1011 aircraft sold to All Nippon Airlines (ANA). The payments were made to the office of the prime minister, seven other politicians and government officials, and the president of ANA. The payments were not illegal under U.S. law at the time, and such payments were not unknown in the aircraft industry.[27] However, the payments were in violation of Japanese law. If Kotchian had been unsure of their legality in Japan, he could have contacted a Japanese lawyer or the commercial attaché at the U.S. embassy. Although it is customary in Japan to give gifts, an individual payment of $1.7 million cannot be viewed as a gift or as a routine political contribution.[28] Similarly, a payment of $50,000 per aircraft to the president of ANA could not be viewed as a part of the functioning system.

---

[25]Getz (2000) provides an overview and analysis of bribery and corruption.
[26]Klitgaard (1988) discusses the steps taken by the U.S. Army to overcome corruption in the construction and supply industries in Korea in the 1970s.
[27]Lockheed's subsequent legal problems in the United States were due to a failure to disclose the payments as required by U.S. law. See Hay and Gray (1981, pp. 134–138) for a discussion of some of the Lockheed payments. In 1982, the Boeing Company pleaded guilty and paid a $400,000 fine for 40 counts of failure to disclose to the Export-Import Bank that it had paid "irregular commissions" to agents involved in foreign sales. (The Export-Import Bank required such disclosure on any sales it financed.) In 1981 the McDonnell Douglas Corporation pleaded guilty to fraud and making false statements and paid fines of over $1.2 million.
[28]It might also be argued that the payments were justified because they were a part of the functioning system in the aircraft industry. This, however, is not a moral justification, even if the competition often involved payments.

Kotchian offered several justifications for making the payments. He argued that the payments were "worthwhile from Lockheed's standpoint" because "they would provide Lockheed workers with jobs, and thus redound to the benefit of their dependents, their communities, and stockholders of the corporation."[29] As considered in Chapter 20, this is casuist reasoning in that an unethical action is said to be justified by the benefits it provides to stakeholders. From a utilitarian perspective, the benefits to Lockheed's stakeholders are likely to be little different from the benefits to Boeing's or McDonnell Douglas's stakeholders if they were to obtain the sale. Furthermore, a market in which a competition in bribes takes place does not function as efficiently as when decisions are made on the basis of merit and value.

The ethics evaluation of this case depends on whether in the absence of payments ANA would have selected Lockheed aircraft. If ANA would have selected another aircraft supplier that did not offer a bribe, Lockheed's payments would be an explicit bribe, which cannot be ethically justified. To obtain the sale, Lockheed could have reduced the price of the aircraft, in which case the benefit would accrue to ANA and not to its officers and government officials.

A second possibility is that ANA would have purchased the L-1011 even if the payments were not made. The ethics issue then is whether Lockheed would be justified in making the payments, which, under this supposition, would be a response to extortion, as Kotchian claimed it was. He wrote: "From a purely ethical and moral standpoint I would have declined such a request [for payments]. However, in that case, I would most certainly have sacrificed commercial success."[30] Extortion involves the use of coercion to extract a payment. Such a payment would be morally justified in the case of ransom paid in a kidnapping, for example. The difference between a ransom payment and the payments that Lockheed made, however, is that if after the fact Lockheed had publicly revealed the payments, the public would have reacted quite differently than it would in the case of a ransom payment. The Lockheed payments thus do not pass Gert's injustice test (Chapter 21) or the public disclosure test discussed in Chapter 22. Gert's test for when an injustice is warranted to avoid a greater injustice requires that a rational observer would understand the reason for the action. That test would surely not be met. As for the public disclosure test, Lockheed would never have been able to justify the payments to the Japanese or American publics.

A third possibility is that the payments were required to match payments offered by other aircraft manufacturers. This situation is considered next.

A Utilitarian Analysis of Bribery

From a utilitarian perspective bribery is bad because it distorts economic activity away from producing the greatest well-being. To illustrate this, consider two companies, A and B, seeking a contract for a sale to country C. Suppose that company A's product is likely better for country C than is the product of company B and in the absence of bribes would likely be selected by C. If no bribes are offered, the expected utilities of A and B and country C are 4, 2, and 14, respectively, as presented in the upper left cell of Table 23-1. For example, suppose that the profit on the sale would be $6 million, and in the absence of bribery the likelihood that A would be selected is two-thirds and the

TABLE 23-1 Utilities of A, B, and C			
		Company B	
		Not Bribe	**Bribe**
Company A	**Not Bribe**	$(4, 2, 14)$	$(0, 5, 9)$
	Bribe	$(5, 0, 11)$	$(2, 1, 12)$

[29]Kotchian (1977, p. 12).
[30]Kotchian (1977, p. 12).

TABLE 23-2	Aggregate Utility		
		Company B	
		Not Bribe	**Bribe**
Company A	**Not Bribe**	20	14
	Bribe	16	15

likelihood that B would be selected is one-third. The expected profits for A and B then are 4 and 2, respectively.

Consider next the possibility that the government officials responsible for selecting the contract winner can be bribed. If one company offers a bribe and the other does not, suppose its probability of winning the contract becomes one. Bribery involves transactions costs because both parties must conceal the payments and take measures to justify the selection. Suppose that the utilities if A does not bribe and B does bribe are 0, 5, and 9, respectively.[31] Suppose also the utilities if A bribes and B does not are 5, 0, and 11. If both companies pay bribes, the likelihood that A would be selected is unchanged at two-thirds and the utilities are 2, 1, and 12.

Before considering the application of utilitarianism, suppose that the companies were self-interested. Inspection of Table 23-1 indicates that each company has a dominant strategy of paying a bribe. That is, if B were believed to be offering a bribe, then A is better off offering a bribe and obtaining a utility of 2 than not bribing and having a utility of 0. Similarly, if B were believed not to be offering a bribe, A is better off offering a bribe. Utilitarianism, however, requires that each company consider the aggregate utility of all three parties.

Under rule utilitarianism each of the three parties chooses actions for A and B simultaneously based on the greatest aggregate utility. The aggregate utilities are presented in Table 23-2. The moral rule thus is that neither A nor B bribes.

Suppose, however, that company B is not utilitarian but instead is purely self-interested. Since B has a dominant strategy, it will offer a bribe. Is a matching bribe ethically justified in this case? From the perspective of rule utilitarianism, the answer is no. As just demonstrated, the moral rule is that no bribes are offered, and hence B is acting immorally. From an act utilitarianism perspective, however, is aggregate utility higher if A offers a matching bribe? From Table 23-2, if B is offering a bribe, A should offer a bribe because that results in an aggregate utility of 15 compared with 14 if it does not offer a bribe.[32] Such reasoning can perpetuate bribery and is inappropriate.[32] This illustrates the weakness of act utilitarianism. Instead of offering the bribe, A could work for a collective agreement banning bribes.

Another test is whether a matching bribe is justified to avoid a greater injustice. The test provided in Chapter 21 is: "A violation of a moral rule [offering a bribe] can be justified by providing reasons which would result in either some impartial rational persons advocating that that kind of violation be publicly allowed, or less frequently, all impartial persons advocating that such a violation be publicly allowed." A more applied version of the test is: "If I disclosed publicly that I had taken the action, would the public understand and approve of my action?"

If a bribe were offered unilaterally, the public surely would not approve. If the payment represented extortion, the public might approve of it. The public, however, is more likely to demand that the extortion be stopped.

If one can show that the payment matches a payment that a competitor is offering, would the public approve? In some countries the answer might be yes. In the United States the FCPA requires the answer no. That is, pay no bribes but instead

---

[31]Recall that B's product is worse for C than is A's product, so C's utility if B is selected is lower than if A is selected. The well-being of the recipients of the bribes is included in the utility for C.

[32]The same question can be posed regarding whether B should offer a bribe if A is offering a bribe. The answer is no, since the aggregate utility with only A bribing is 16, whereas if both offer bribes, it is 15.

work to convince others not to offer or accept bribes. The OECD Anti-Bribery Convention reflects the success of such an approach.

A practical problem in applying the injustice standard is how to show that a competitor is offering a bribe. Both the offeror and the recipient have strong incentives to conceal it, which is one reason bribery is difficult to eradicate. More importantly, self-interest and the suspicion that a competitor may be offering a bribe may lead a company to offer a bribe. If both harbor such suspicions, the slippery slope can result in a competition in bribes. The chapter case, *Siemens: Anatomy of Bribery,* considers a company that engaged in widespread bribery.

Another reason not to pay bribes in situations in which there will be repeated encounters was given by an executive of a global company. He said, "If you pay once, you pay forever."

The Foreign Corrupt Practices Act

In the Lockheed case the payments were made both through an official agent, the Marubeni Trading Company, and a confidential consultant. In conducting business in foreign countries, it is often advisable to retain the services of a national who is familiar with the system in the country and has contacts that will, at a minimum, save time in arranging appointments and may help speed permits and contracts through the host country's institutional structure. These agents are often compensated on a fee or commission basis, and the disposition of those monies may be known only to agents. If a portion of the commissions might be passed on to influence the actions of customers or government officials, the firm may be contributing to a corrupt act. Ethically, the firm has an obligation to instruct its agent about which practices are acceptable and which are unacceptable. Moreover, the firm has a duty to monitor the activities of its agents. The FCPA addresses these issues, among others.[33]

The FCPA makes bribery of foreign officials, political parties, candidates for office, and public international organizations a criminal offense. It provides for a fine of up to $1 million for the company and up to $10,000 and imprisonment for not more than 5 years for an individual making a payment or offer covered by the act. It assigns the burden of knowing whether illegal payments are being made to the company and imposes detailed record-keeping requirements. Under the FCPA, it is unlawful to make any "offer, payment, promise to pay, or authorization of the payment of any money, or offer, gift, promise to give, or authorization of anything . . ." to influence a decision, omit a required action, or give "any improper advantage" to the company. The term foreign official "does not include any employee of a foreign government or any department, agency, or instrumentality thereof whose duties are essentially ministerial or clerical." The FCPA thus allows small "facilitating payments" to low-level government employees such as customs inspectors, if the payments do not influence a decision.

The use of agents, intermediaries, or third parties is also covered, and they are subject to both criminal and civil penalties. In its original language, the FCPA pertained to "any person, while knowing or having reason to know" about a payment for the purposes previously listed. This imposed a stringent duty on a company to know how fees paid to agents, intermediaries, and third parties were actually used. After the first few years of experience with the FCPA, a poll of 1,200 large businesses indicated that substantial sales had been lost in countries in which bribery was a common practice.[34] Although U.S. firms indicated that they supported the FCPA, 68 percent responded that the record-keeping burden should be reduced and that the law should be more specific about who in a foreign country can receive payments and for what purposes.

The Omnibus Trade and Competitiveness Act of 1988 amended the FCPA in several ways.[35] First, it altered the language about the use of third parties or intermediaries

---

[33]See Pastin and Hooker (1988) and Alpern (1988) for ethics analyses of the FCPA.
[34]*BusinessWeek,* September 19, 1983.
[35]The FCPA was also amended in the Anti-Bribery and Fair Competition Act of 1998 to bring it into accord with the OECD Convention considered later in the chapter. The preceding text includes these changes.

by eliminating the phrase "or having reason to know." Second, a payment to a foreign individual became illegal under the act if it was illegal in the foreign country. Third, if a payment were legal in the foreign country, the defendant in an action brought under the act could use that legality as a defense. Fourth, the language of the act was clarified to indicate that payments that secured performance of routine government actions, such as signing customs documents and unloading or loading cargoes, were not illegal. Fifth, the amendments provided firms with a number of affirmative defenses, including consistency with host country laws and legitimate business expenses.

The FCPA does not prohibit payments to private businesses. The bribery of private businesses, or private-to-private bribery, is believed to be less common than the bribery of government officials. In 2001, however, the Department of Justice obtained guilty pleas from major international construction companies, including ABB and Phillipp Holtzman, for kickbacks and the payment of bribes on U.S. Agency for International Development–financed water projects in Egypt. The companies met secretly to arrange for some of the companies to submit inflated bids and others not to bid at all on certain contracts. In exchange the companies received monetary payments from the winning bidder or the remaining bidders.[36]

Company Codes

Most firms have policies or codes to ensure compliance with the FCPA and international conventions and to clarify when foreign payments can be made and how they are to be accounted for. The three principal purposes of these codes are to provide guidance to employees, make it easier for them to say no to demands for payment, and ultimately discourage demands for payments.

The extent to which a firm encounters demands for payments depends on its lines of business, the countries in which it does business, and its organization. Some industries and some countries are characterized by a functioning system in which bribery and facilitating payments are not uncommon. A firm's lines of business and the countries in which it operates thus affect the scope of the problems it faces. That scope is also affected by the organizational structure of the firm. Firms can conduct their foreign business through a wholly owned subsidiary, a joint venture, a sales office that manages local dealers and distributors, or agents with whom the firm deals at arm's length. Controlling and monitoring payments generally become more difficult and making questionable payments becomes easier, the more independent is the business unit or agent.

Corruption in Russia is not uncommon, particularly in the oil industry. Demands for bribes were regularly made, and BP and Shell responded in quite different ways. Shell packed its bags and left the country. BP made a call to the chairman of Gazprom, the giant Russian natural gas producer, and complained about the demands for payments. Corruption in Russia is "organized," and the demands for payments stopped quickly. BP thanked the chairman and said to call if it could be any help. The son of the chairman subsequently attended a university in the United Kingdom at no expense.

Company codes typically state the principal features of the FCPA; require that the representatives of the firm know the local laws and the functioning system in the country; distinguish between gratuities, facilitating payments, and bribes; and specify record-keeping and reporting requirements. A code may also provide guidance for handling a request for a payment and indicate to whom an employee can turn if a payment's propriety is in question. Firms have also established audit procedures to detect illegal payments. In many firms, managers and sales representatives are required to pledge to abide by the FCPA and company guidelines.

Such policies not only provide guidance to managers and sales representatives, but they also establish a basis for a response when a government official or a customer demands a payment. A response that "company policy does not permit it" may, in some cases, lead to the demand being retracted. Furthermore, knowledge that the firm does

---

[36]*New York Times,* April 13, 2001.

not make such payments may eventually decrease the number of demands. For this to be effective, however, the firm must establish a reputation for not making payments.

BP has a policy of not paying bribes and also not making facilitating payments. CEO Lord Browne wrote to employees in 2002 stating, "We work within the law in every one of the 100 countries in which we operate and we work to our standards, which are often higher than the legal requirement. Those standards are universal in BP. We will not engage in bribery or corruption in any form including facilitating payments."[37]

As a result of the policy BP employees were held "hostage" in Russia, but gradually the requests for facilitating payments decreased. The demands resurfaced from time to time, and BP has been forced to add an extensive audit and control staff in Russia to detect whether payments have been made. Some employees have been fired for making payments. Lord Browne explained that BP ran "a high-cost operation in Russia."

BP also follows a policy of "publishing what you pay." That is, when contract payments such as royalties are made to foreign governments, the amounts and the recipients are made public. With this information, citizens in the country can hold government officials accountable for the disposition of the funds. Publish what you pay is now practiced by many companies in extractive industries. Thirty-seven large oil, gas, and mining companies participate along with countries in the Extractive Industries Transparency Initiative, which along with PWYP, a coalition of 300 NGOs, promotes publish what you pay.

Cummins's Practice

Cummins Inc.'s policy on questionable foreign payments is striking in its articulation of a principle for reasoning about whether a payment should be made in a particular instance. Cummins stated its "Primary Ethical Guide":

> The key element which distinguishes ethically unacceptable payments is the corruption of [a] relationship of trust. When a company pays an agent of a buyer in order to influence that agent's purchasing decision, and when that payment is not known to the buyer, the company corrupts a relationship of trust between buyer and agent. The buyer's expectation that his agent will act with only the buyer's interest in mind is betrayed. Similarly, when a company pays a government agent in order to influence that agent's official decisions, the company corrupts a relationship of trust between the public and that official. The corruption of such a relationship of trust not only violates fundamental principles of fair dealing but also hampers efficient economic development and undermines social cohesion.[38]

Cummins's guide meets both the Kantian standard and the standard of rule utilitarianism. It treats the buyer as an autonomous end, and the rule of not corrupting a relationship of trust is one that people would will to be universal. From the perspective of rule utilitarianism the guide supports efficiency by requiring competition to be on a commercial basis rather than on bribes.

Figure 23-2 displays the framework of this principle. In contrast to Kotchian's analysis, which focuses on the consequences to the firm from making the payment, Cummins's principle focuses on the buyer and its agent. That agent is in a relationship of trust with its principal—shareholders in the case of private firms and citizens in the case of a government agency. In this relationship, the agent is to serve the interests of the principal; accepting a bribe sacrifices the interests of the principal for the interests of the agent. Cummins applies this reasoning in the tests that an employee is to use in determining if a payment is acceptable. "Does this payment undermine a relationship of trust? What expectations does the principal have of his agent in the particular transaction at issue? Is the payment known to the principal or is it not?"

---

[37]Lord Browne of Madingley, "To Our Employees," August, 2002. In 2003 BP fired 165 people for violating the company's ethics standards.
[38]Cummins Practices, October 1, 1980.

FIGURE 23-2 Cummins Inc.: Questionable Foreign Payments and the Relationship of Trust

Payments are allowable only if three conditions are met:

a. The payment is required to induce the official to perform a routine act which he is already under a duty to perform . . .
b. The payment is consistent with local practice. If the payment is consistent with local practice, it is reasonable to assume that it is consistent with public expectations of official behavior, and
c. There is no reasonable alternative available for obtaining the official act or service at issue.

Although the phrase "reasonable alternative" is not precise, condition c requires the company to consider such possibilities as reducing the price or expediting delivery to obtain the sale. Reducing the price to make the sale, rather than paying a bribe, causes the benefit to go to the principal rather than the agent, which is consistent with the relationship of trust. The relevant test is the requirement that the Cummins employee determine whether the principal knows of the payment, since then the principal can determine where the benefit should reside.

In cases in which the employee is uncertain whether a payment is allowed, Cummins states, "Where there is a question as to the propriety of a particular payment in view of the foregoing standards, the payment should not be made." To encourage compliance, Cummins also assures that "no employee is put at a career disadvantage because of his or her willingness to raise a question about a corporate practice or unwillingness to pursue a course of action which seems inappropriate or morally dubious." Cummins also provides its version of the public disclosure test: "Cummins employees do nothing in search of business that they should not reveal willingly and publicly to any other member of the Cummins family or to any government official in any land."

In addition to providing principles on which to reason and standards for assessing when a payment is allowable, Cummins's standards go beyond the FCPA by prohibiting corrupt payments to private, as well as to public, buyers. Recognizing that in some countries payments that do not satisfy its standards could be necessary to do business, Cummins states that it will "accept the loss of business." If the pattern of questionable payments continues, Cummins states that it will bring the matter to the attention of the host government to determine how the government wants the matter to be handled. If the demands for payments persist, Cummins is prepared to forgo the business. The chapter case, *Complications in Marnera*, raises similar issues.

The OECD Anti-Bribery Convention

For over two decades the FCPA stood alone among the developed countries with its imposition of both criminal penalties and stringent requirements for reporting and monitoring. The United States estimated that its companies lost billions of dollars a year in sales because of bribes paid by companies from other countries. In France, Germany, and many other European countries, bribes and other payments to foreign officials were tax deductible if required to secure a sale. With the growth in foreign direct investment in developing countries and increased trade, the scale of corruption expanded, and more companies became concerned about the effect of corruption not only on business activity but also on the countries where the payments were made. Pressure from the United States and European countries and from organizations such as Transparency International led to negotiations within the OECD. The result was the 1997 Anti-Bribery Convention (Convention on Combating Bribery of Foreign Public Officials in International Business Transactions), signed by the 30 OECD member countries plus Argentina, Bulgaria, Czech Republic, Poland, and Turkey.

The Convention requires signatories to make the act of bribery and the making of other forms of illicit payments to foreign public officials a criminal offense, whether paid directly or indirectly "in order to obtain or retain business or other improper advantage in the conduct of international business."[39] Small "facilitation" payments that are not made "to obtain or retain business" are not viewed as an offense. A foreign public official is defined to include not only those holding elective or appointive office, but also officials of public agencies and public enterprises at least 50 percent owned by the government. The Convention also imposes record-keeping obligations on businesses so that payments can be identified. The Convention does not pertain to private-to-private bribery.

The bargaining on the Convention revealed the complexity of the issue. Since in many developing countries the government owns or controls companies, the United States argued and eventually was successful in including government-controlled companies under the Convention. The United States also successfully obtained inclusion of elected members of parliament in the category of government officials, over the objections of several European countries that allowed payments to their members of parliament provided the payments were not to influence votes. The United States lost, however, in its attempt to include payments to political parties and party officials as an offense.

The European Union enacted a Criminal Law Convention on Corruption in 1999 that made criminal offenses of active bribery and passive bribery (extortion) that gives any "undue advantage" of domestic and foreign public officials and of private sector personnel. The United States signed the OECD Convention in 2000 and changed its laws accordingly. Germany also enacted the Convention, which led in part to the prosecutions in the chapter case, *Siemens: Anatomy of Bribery.*

SUMMARY

Countries differ considerably in terms of their history, culture, resources, and institutions, yet fundamental ethics principles are intended to be universal rather than country specific. Cultural relativism, in which one relies solely on host country laws and practices, is inappropriate, and universal relativism, in which one applies the same principles everywhere, ignores relevant differences among countries. The principles underpinning utilitarianism, rights theories, and theories of justice remain useful guides for operating across borders. The application of these principles, however, leaves unresolved issues about trade-offs between costs and benefits, how duties to ensure rights are assigned, and how justice considerations are to be taken into account.

Guidance for managers is provided by international, host country, and home country law and by ethics principles. International law is important, yet its enforcement is often irregular and its application to moral issues is often limited to general, rather than specific, matters. Host country law is an important guide, and when those laws are

---

[39]The Convention pertains to "active corruption" committed by the offerer of a bribe rather than to "passive corruption" committed by the recipient of the bribe. Like the FCPA the Convention pertains to the supply side of bribery.

consistent with universal standards, they are to be respected. If they do not meet those standards, firms must develop policies guided by principles as well as law. Firms also must determine whether they will apply the same standards to their operations in all countries or adapt their policies and practices to the situation of each host country. This is a particular challenge in low-income countries that do not have the capacity to provide guidance through regulation or where people prefer economic growth over the safety and environmental standards of high-income countries.

The working conditions and human rights situation in the factories of overseas suppliers has raised moral concerns, and an innovative approach to addressing those concerns has been undertaken by individual companies and by the apparel and footwear industries. A multi-stakeholder approach has been institutionalized in the form of the Fair Labor Association, which provides for independent monitoring of factories and the public disclosure of results.

Bribery and other forms of corruption are common in some countries. The FCPA and the OECD Convention provide guidance, assign duties, and impose penalties for violations. However, laws can leave a variety of issues, such as payments to private companies, unaddressed. In such cases, principles in addition to host country practices can provide guidance. Utilitarianism concludes that bribery is morally wrong. Some managers argue that bribes are required because of extortion by government officials or bribes offered by competitors. In such cases, the injustice standard is applicable and requires that the manager ask whether, if it were publicly disclosed, the publics in the host and home country would agree that the payment should be made.

The approach of Cummins Inc. is useful for guiding managers in their reasoning about such issues, even if one does not reach the same conclusions the company reached. The approach involves a statement of principles, a method for reasoning from those principles to the specifics of a situation, standards that managers are to apply, and protection for individuals who raise corruption issues within the firm.

The range of ethics issues that arise in global operations is broader than those in a firm's home country, and in developing countries the institutions found in developed countries may be absent or may function imperfectly. Furthermore, the facts of the situations encountered internationally may be more difficult to discern. These factors complicate the application of ethics principles and leave managers with the challenge of formulating policies guided by a combination of law, ethics principles, and culture.

-- C A S E S --
Complications in Marnera

Pat Liu and her team of engineers from Bolton Engineering and Construction Company would be spending the next 6 months in Marnera while the government selected the contractor to develop a copper and gold mine in a remote part of the country. Development of the mine was likely to produce revenue of nearly $200 million over the next 7 years for Bolton. Bolton had just completed a successful mining project in a neighboring country, and Liu believed that the company was best qualified for the job because of that experience. The project in Marnera was particularly important because Bolton wanted to avoid laying off the engineers who had been working on the project in the neighboring country. Bolton had a modest local operation in Marnera, but Liu was the ranking Bolton official and would be in charge over the next 6 months. If Bolton were to win the contract, she would have responsibility for the mine project.

Upon arriving at the airport in Marnera, Liu and her team encountered an immediate problem. Each member of the team carried a top-of-the-line laptop computer, and in a traveling bag they had brought along three spares in case a computer were to develop problems due to the high humidity in Marnera. The customs official inspecting their bags expressed concern that Liu might try to sell the computers in Marnera. Selling the computers would violate import laws that required a license and customs duty for the sale of imported computers. Liu explained that the computers were for backup and would be used only by Bolton employees. The customs inspector remained concerned, however, and said that he would have to impound all their computers until either Bolton obtained a license and paid the customs duty or a hearing on the matter could be scheduled. The customs official said that he understood that they needed their computers and that the process of obtaining a license and paying the duty would take only a few weeks. A local Bolton employee who had met Liu and her party at the airport asked whether it would be possible for the customs inspector to take care of the matter if Bolton would entrust the customs fee to him. The customs official nodded. Needing the computers Liu decided to give the fee to the customs official, who stamped their customs declarations allowing the team and their computers to enter the country.

Shortly thereafter Liu encountered the tax system in Marnera. The tax laws were clear, but their interpretation and enforcement were different matters. For corporations the typical approach was for the National Tax Service (NTS) to send a company a bill for its taxes. The tax bill was an estimate based on previous years or on projections of what the company might earn. The tax bill was understood by those familiar with the system as an

invitation to negotiate with the NTS over the actual payment. Companies typically engaged the services of a licensed tax accountant or attorney to conduct the negotiations on their behalf. Bolton decided to seek the advice of a highly regarded and well-connected local attorney, who indicated that for a fee of 2 million richas he could take care of the matter and negotiate a quite reasonable tax bill. Liu expressed surprise at the size of the fee, and the attorney explained that much of the 2 million richas was for expenses that would be incurred during the negotiations with the NTS. The attorney said that this was the standard practice in Marnera and that the fee was tax deductible.

The attorney also explained to Liu that if she did not hire someone to handle the negotiations, Bolton would undoubtedly be assessed a final tax bill at least as high as the initial bill. He said that the NTS inspectors had a variety of means to increase tax bills, the easiest of which was to disqualify certain costs as nondeductible. Liu thanked the attorney for his advice and told him that she would get back to him within the week. Concerned about how the 2 million richas would be used, Liu decided to call the commercial attaché at the U.S. embassy whom she had met at a social event. The commercial attaché assured Liu that hiring an attorney to negotiate a company's tax bill was customary in Marnera. When Liu asked what the fee would be used for, the attaché avoided the question. Liu had to decide whether to hire the attorney or prepare Bolton's own tax statement.

In making final preparations for her presentation to the Ministry of Mining, Liu was surprised to learn from the managing director of Bolton's Marnera office that the bidding process had been changed. Instead of evaluating the bids directly, the Ministry would first select a preferred bidder based on its assessment of the technological capabilities of the bidders, costs, intangible factors, and their expressed willingness to utilize local suppliers. Then the Ministry would solicit final bids with the preferred bidder having the right to make the last bid—a right of first refusal. If the preferred bidder matched the highest bid of other contractors, it would be awarded the contract. If it did not match the highest bid, the selection process would be reopened.

One important factor in the cost of completing the project was the level of safety to provide for workers. Bolton could maintain U.S. safety standards and procedures or it could use the prevailing practices in Marnera. With U.S. safety standards and procedures, the pace of work would be slower, adding 5 percent to the cost of the project. Much of the work involved in bringing in roads, power, and water to the mine site, as well as the work on the mine itself, was hazardous, and accidents could be expected. Following the prevailing practices would result in more accidents, and in Marnera there was neither a system of workers' compensation nor a functioning liability system that would allow injured workers to sue for damages. Instead, the local custom was that if an employee were injured on the job and unable to work, that employee's job would be given to another family member so that the family would be supported. Two questions entered Liu's mind. First, what was the right decision regarding safety? Second, if the right decision were to use U.S. standards, would Bolton be at a competitive disadvantage relative to its competitors?

Before leaving for Marnera Liu had been warned that one of Bolton's European competitors would undoubtedly offer payments directly to the top officials at the Ministry of Mining. Such payments were prohibited by U.S. law and by the recently negotiated OECD Anti-Bribery Convention, and countries were to bring their domestic laws into harmony with the Convention.[40] A number of countries, however, still had laws that allowed their companies to make such payments if necessary to obtain business, and the payments were tax deductible. Some countries were expected to move slowly in changing their laws. Then, the matter of enforcement remained.

As a precaution Liu wondered if she should engage the services of the local attorney to represent the company before the Ministry. She was particularly concerned about the effect that losing the bid would have on the employees of Bolton, many of whom would lose their jobs if she failed to get this contract. "It would be unfair if we lose this contract to one of our rivals because of questionable payments," she thought.

Thinking ahead to the possibility of Bolton being selected as the preferred bidder, Liu wondered how high competitors might bid. She mused that it would be nice if they confined their aggressiveness to the competition for selection as the preferred bidder.

In anticipation of the competition for the mining project, the managing director of Bolton's Marnera operations had been developing a relationship with the vice minister of Mining. He had recently attended a reception at the vice minister's home and had brought his wife and children expensive gifts. The vice minister had mentioned that he was hoping to send his eldest child to a university in England, but the cost seemed prohibitive. ■

Preparation Questions

1. How should Liu reason about these situations from the perspective of utilitarianism? What other considerations are relevant?
2. Should Liu have made the payment to the customs official?
3. Should Liu engage the services of the tax attorney to deal with the tax matter?
4. Should Liu use U.S. safety standards?
5. What, if anything, should Liu do given the likelihood that a competitor would offer a payment to officials at the Ministry of Mining? Consider the issue from the perspectives of act and rule utilitarianism.
6. Should Liu help the vice minister send his child to England?
7. What should Liu do if Bolton is selected as the preferred bidder?

[40]The OECD had no legislative or enforcement authority, which was the responsibility of the member countries.

De Beers and Conflict Diamonds

For decades De Beers operated a cartel in the diamond industry in which it controlled nearly 80 percent of the distribution of rough diamonds.[41] De Beers also produced, primarily in South Africa, a large but decreasing share of the world's diamonds. The company founded by Cecile Rhodes and managed by the Oppenheimer family bought under long-term contracts the bulk of the world's diamonds from mining companies, maintained a large inventory, and sold rough diamonds in an orderly manner to maintain high prices. Distribution of the diamonds was through the Central Selling Organization in London, which sold in bulk to diamond cutters.[42] De Beers did not have retail operations.

This system worked well until 1990 when the production of diamonds increased and more began to leak into the market. The collapse of the Soviet Union and

[41]See Deborah Spar, *The Cooperative Edge: The Internal Politics of International Cartels*, Ithaca, NY: Cornell University Press, 1994, and Prakaj Ghemawat and Sonia Marciano, "De Beers at the Millennium," Case No. 9-706-518, Harvard Business School, February 5, 2007, for detailed information on De Beers and the diamond industry.

[42]Almost all diamond cutting was done in Amsterdam, Mumbai, New York, and Tel Aviv.

increased production there and production increases in Western Canada and elsewhere resulted in an increase in the supply of diamonds. Most diamond mining involved capital intensive shaft mining, but alluvial diamonds were found near the surface. Alluvial diamonds were easy to mine and became the source of funding for rebels and guerrillas in parts of Africa. The result was horrific civil wars, killings, torture, and mutilations. These diamonds become known as "conflict diamonds." Killings financed by conflict diamonds were most severe in Sierra Leone, Angola, and Liberia.

The world was incensed by the tragedy accompanying the conflict diamonds. The international diplomatic community and NGOs campaigned to end the killings, but it became clear that as long as conflict diamonds were available to finance the purchase of weapons the killings would continue. NGO activity increased during the 1990s led by Global Witness, which issued reports in 1998 and 1999, blaming companies as well as governments for the atrocities. The United Nations sanctioned the UNITA rebels in Angola and applied sanctions on the diamond trade in Angola and Sierra Leone, but conflict diamonds continued to find their way into the international markets.

De Beers continued its traditional policies during the 1990s but found that its stockpile of rough diamonds was skyrocketing as it bought excess diamonds. In 2000 it was forced to end its control of the diamond supply, focusing instead on the orderly distribution of diamonds. De Beers along with others in the industry was also worried that the image of diamonds could be tarnished. The high price of diamonds was in an important sense artificial, since diamonds had no intrinsic value.[43] De Beers began a consumer marketing campaign to enhance the image of diamonds as symbols of love and marriage and attempted to brand diamonds at retail.

The atrocities and killings in Africa had rallied an array of NGOs that concluded that the only way to stop the killings was to stop the flow of conflict diamonds. The NGOs pressured the United Nations, individual countries in the developed world, and the African countries to stop the flow of conflict diamonds. They also blamed the diamond companies for their role in buying the diamonds. Some of the NGOs began to label them "blood diamonds" and sought to persuade consumers not to buy diamonds. A movie entitled *Blood Diamond* was made, and rapper Kanye West released "Diamonds from Sierra Leone." The campaign posed a threat to the image that gave diamonds their value.

SOURCE: This case was based on public sources, including the paper by Virginia Haulfer, "The Kimberly Process, Club Goods, and Public Enforcement of a Private Regime." Working paper, University of Maryland College Park, 2007. Copyright © 2008 by David P. Baron. All rights reserved. Reprinted with permission.

Preparation Questions

1. How serious are the developments centering on conflict diamonds? To what extent is De Beers at risk? To what extent is De Beers responsible?
2. Identify the key actors in the case and their interests and objectives.
3. Is there a mechanism that can stop the supply of conflict diamonds, end the killings, and restore order to the market? Which parties should lead the development of this mechanism? How would the mechanism be enforced?
4. Are there ways to get around the mechanism?

---

[43]The industrial diamond market relied primarily on synthetic diamonds.

Siemens: Anatomy of Bribery

In November 2006, 200 German police officers raided the headquarters of Siemens AG, Europe's leading engineering company, seeking evidence pertaining to widespread bribery. The raid heightened attention to bribery issues, and at the January 2007 annual meeting CEO Klaus Kleinfeld said he was "shocked" and commented, "I can assure you that we are doing everything that we can to clear up these incidents completely." Supervisory board chairman Heinrich von Pierer said, "I am deeply distressed that these efforts were not successful enough."[44]

The raid followed extensive investigations of Siemens' activities that originated from a bank's internal scrutiny of accounts believed to be used for money laundering. The suspicions broadened, and the company initiated its own internal investigation. Siemens identified €420 million of suspicious transactions in its telecommunications unit and hired a private law firm to conduct an independent internal investigation. The law firm subsequently reported to the management board that it had identified €1.3 billion of suspicious payments since 1999. The law firm subsequently received "important . . . new information" that could implicate high-ranking executives. The possibility that the bribery investigation would identify high ranking officers caused

---

[44]*Wall Street Journal*, January 31, 2007.

the Siemens supervisory board to postpone the Entlastung or approval of the actions of the company's management board for the fiscal year 2007, seven of whom had resigned during the year.[45] The vote would have shielded the management board members from liability stemming from the ongoing bribery investigation.

Prior to 1999 German firms were allowed to deduct foreign bribes from their German taxes if those bribes were necessary to win business. Under pressure from the United States and other countries the Organization for Economic Cooperation and Development (OECD) adopted strong anti-bribery rules, including making bribes criminal offenses. The member states of the European Union endorsed the OECD agreement and enacted the rules as part of their national laws. The enacted OECD anti-bribery convention pertained only to bribery of public officials, and in 2002 Germany enacted an additional law extending the prohibition of bribes to employees of private firms as well as public officials.

With bribes illegal, companies took additional measures to hide their payments. Greater secrecy was required in the aftermath of September 11, as countries adopted stronger laws against money laundering. Despite the tougher laws, bribery continued as companies sought to secure foreign sales. Companies had used offshore accounts to transfer money, but once countries enacted new laws against money laundering, other routes were needed. One approach was to hire consulting companies to act on behalf of a company. For example, Siemens hired a consulting firm based in Monte Carlo and headed by Tonio Arcaini to assist in deals in the Middle East and Eastern Europe. In fiscal 2007 Siemens' auditor KPMG identified €100 million in questionable payments to more than a dozen consulting firms, including €14.5 million to Arcaini's firm. Siemens paid a total of €36.5 million to Arcaini between 2001 and 2006. Patrick Moulette, head of the anticorruption unit of the OECD observed, "It's much more difficult to detect bribery when funds are channeled through intermediaries. Today it seems this is a prevailing trend in international bribery schemes."[46]

In February 2007 CEO Kleinfeld said, "We are interested in getting to the facts, but getting to all the facts. We are talking about things that are important, that we can't take lightheartedly." In referring to obtaining change in the company's practices, he said, "You need a certain amount of time for adjustment. Don't get me wrong: this is not meant as an excuse." He added, "If you, in your mind, get it wrong and think, 'I just have to beat the competition,' you are fundamentally doing something wrong." He commented that he could make Siemens a model for corporate ethics and mused that someday this could make "a Harvard Business case on how you do it right."[47]

The German Court

The increased scrutiny of financial transactions after September 11 was directed at detecting money laundering used to finance terrorism. In 2003 LGT Group, the largest bank in Liechtenstein, noticed a flurry of money transfers in the account of Martha Overseas Corporation, based in Panama, and Eagle Invest & Finance AG, based in the British Virgin Islands. Martha Overseas was controlled by a Siemens telecommunications unit executive, Prodromos Mavridis, in Greece, and Eagle was controlled by another Siemens telecommunications unit executive, Reinhard Siekaczek, in Germany. After investigation LGT blocked a transaction by Siemens and notified authorities in Germany and Switzerland, as well as Siemens. Siekaczek subsequently alerted another executive, Michael Kutschenreuter, who said he then notified senior management. Swiss authorities froze €200 million of accounts suspected of belonging to Siemens.

In 2004 Kutschenreuter received a call from the Saudi Arabian consulting firm Beit Al Etisailat, a business partner of Siemens, demanding payment of $910 million for commissions on telecommunications contracts. Kutschenreuter said he reported the demand to Kleinfeld, then head of Siemens' telecommunications unit, and then CEO von Pierer. The management board subsequently approved a settlement of $50 million, according to testimony.

Three years of investigations by prosecutors in several countries revealed many more transfers involving a variety of offshore companies linked to Siemens. Prosecutors began to unravel a series of bribes associated with Siemens' telecommunications unit. In October 2007 a court in Munich ordered Siemens to pay €201 million after tracing €12 million in bribes paid to 77 government officials in Libya, Nigeria, and Russia.[48] The bribes were paid between 2001 and 2004 and were associated with Mr. Siekaczek.[49] The bribes were funneled through outside consulting contracts and Siemens executives. In testimony Siekaczek identified bribes in more than 12 countries, including Greece where payments were said to have been made to gain security systems contracts.[50] In August 2007 German prosecutors again searched the company's facilities in conjunction with

---

[45]The German corporate governance system included a two-tiered board arrangement. The management board was responsible for the management of the company. The supervisory board was responsible for overseeing the management board and approving major transactions. The supervisory board was composed of equal representation of shareholders and representatives of workers, including labor unions. A representative of workers was also a member of the management board.

[46]*Wall Street Journal*, April 20, 2007.

---

[47]*New York Times*, February 28, 2007.

[48]German law allowed a fine of only €1 million. The rest of the payment was for the profits earned as a result of the bribes.

[49]Siekaczek was indicted in 2007 for embezzling €24 million.

[50]*Wall Street Journal*, November 16, 2007.

alleged bribes in Serbia. Austria began an investigation into €60 million in suspicious payments.

In addition to the civil penalties and criminal charges against some former employees, Siemens risked being barred by countries from bidding on contracts. Nigeria announced that on "moral grounds" Siemens was not worthy of consideration for new contracts.

Bribery in Italy

In a separate case two Siemens employees went on trial in Darmstadt for paying €6 million to managers in the Italian company Enel to secure contracts for power generation equipment between 1999 and 2002. The two Siemens officials testified that the payments had been demanded by two managers conducting the bidding process and argued that the managers were not public officials because Enel was being privatized. One of the Siemens managers explained before the court the justification for paying the bribes, "The alternative would have been to turn down the project, which would have denied Siemens not only the business but also a foot in the door in the Italian market."[51] In May the court found the two Siemens managers guilty of breach of trust and bribery, ordered the company to forfeit €38 million in profits from the contract, and gave the managers suspended prison sentences. Siemens announced that it would appeal and stated, "The court's decision has no basis in law or in fact."

The Labor Scandal

In 2006 senior management was scheduled to receive 30 percent raises, and when the raises became public, complaints began to arise, particularly after the handset unit Siemens had sold to a Taiwanese firm went bankrupt. The pressure from workers and the public led the executives to forgo their raises and give the money to workers who had lost their jobs in the bankruptcy.[52]

In March 2007 German authorities in Nuremberg arrested Johannes Feldmayer, a member of Siemens' executive committee, in conjunction with a probe into questionable consulting contracts with the head of an independent union group, the Association of Independent Employees or AUB. The AUB was friendly to the company and offset some of the influence of IG Metall, the principal union representing Siemens employees. The head of AUB had been arrested in February for tax evasion in conjunction with the consulting contracts from Siemens.[53]

In December 2007 Siemens promoted Hannes Apitzsch to chief financial officer. Within a week the company revoked the appointment after a Siemens attorney was allowed to see a preliminary report of the prosecutor in Nuremberg in the AUB case.

Management Turnover

In April the supervisory board balked at approving the contract of Chairman von Pierer, who was under pressure as a result of the bribery revelations. He resigned and issued a statement, "Siemens has run into a difficult situation due to the in part apparent and in part alleged misconduct of a number of managers and employees. . . . I assume that electing a new chairman of the supervisory board will also make a contribution toward taking our company out of the headlines and bringing it back into calmer waters."[54] At the supervisory board meeting the following week the board did not renew CEO Kleinfeld's contract. Kleinfeld then announced he would leave the company when his contract expired in September.[55] He stated, "In times like these the company needs clarity about its leadership. I have therefore decided not to make myself available for an extension of my contract."[56] Within a week the top two executives at Siemens had stepped down.[57] In addition to the bribery allegations the resignations were also due to pressure from IG Metall, which held nearly half the seats on the supervisory board and was outraged by the questionable consulting contracts with AUB.

Siemens then hired Peter Loscher from Merck as CEO, the first outsider to head the company in its 160 year history. Gerhard Cromme, chairman of ThyssenKrupp, assumed the chairmanship of the supervisory board.

Other Developments

In January 2007 Siemens was fined €400 million by the European Union for price fixing on electric power switching equipment. Also in 2007 a Siemens subsidiary in the United States pleaded guilty and paid a $2.5 million fine for setting up a sham company with a minority firm to gain a $50 million medical equipment contract.[58]

The U.S. Securities and Exchange Commission (SEC) had begun an informal inquiry, and in April it upgraded the inquiry to a formal investigation. This gave the SEC the authority to issue subpoenas. The SEC had jurisdiction over Siemens because its shares were listed on the New York Stock Exchange. Siemens was also subject to the U.S. Foreign Corrupt Practices Act (FCPA), because it had sales of €22.9 billion and 104,000 employees in the United States. Peter von Blomberg, deputy chair of the German chapter of Transparency International, commented on the possible U.S. actions, "The potential fines are much bigger than what companies have been used to in Germany."[59] Daniel E. Karson,

[51]*New York Times*, March 14, 2007.
[52]*Wall Street Journal*, April 26, 2007.
[53]*Wall Street Journal*, March 28, 2007.
[54]*New York Times*, April 20, 2007.
[55]Kleinfeld became CEO of Alcoa, on whose board he had served.
[56]*New York Times*, April 26, 2007.
[57]The chief compliance officer also resigned after less than a year on the job.
[58]*Wall Street Journal*, April 26, 2007.
[59]*BusinessWeek*, November 26, 2007.

executive managing director of the investigative firm Kroll Associates, said, "The FCPA has now surpassed Sarbanes-Oxley for being at the nerve endings of corporate general counsels and executives."[60]

The Internal Investigation

After the November raid CEO Kleinfeld announced a "zero tolerance" for corruption. He hired Michael J. Hershman, a former Senate investigator for Watergate and a founder of Transparency International, to advise the audit committee of the supervisory board and assist in the development of a compliance system. Siemens tightened the requirements on consulting companies requiring an explanation for what the funds would be used for and requiring signatures of the senior executives and the chief compliance officer.[61] In December Kleinfeld hired the U.S. law firm Debevoise & Plimpton LLP to investigate possible wrongdoings.

Debevoise & Plimpton subsequently reported that it had identified €1.6 billion of suspicious payments of which €1.15 billion was in Siemens' telecommunications unit. Most of the rest was believed to be in the power generation unit. Prosecutors were subsequently reported to have found a €140 million slush fund in the health care unit. In January 2008 the company announced that it had found €80 million of suspicious payments in its power transmission unit.

To address employee suspicions about the internal investigations and the use of an American law firm, Siemens prepared a slide show entitled "Rumors vs. Facts." To encourage employees to cooperate in the company's investigation, Siemens established an amnesty program to encourage whistle-blowing on bribery. The amnesty program spurred the investigation and resulted in "significant new information and leads pertaining to individuals who in the past several years served on the managing board," according to a letter from Debevoise & Plimpton. Siemens extended the amnesty program through February 2008.

In January 2008 Debevoise & Plimpton wrote to the company that as a result of the amnesty program it had developed "very substantial leads" that could implicate management board members. Debevosie & Plimpton was investigating activities in 65 countries. The law firm also told the supervisory board that Siemens' long-time auditor, KPMG Germany, had not provided information to the audit committee in a timely manner.

Going Forward

In fiscal 2007 Siemens had sales of €87 billion, net income of €3.9 billion, 475,000 employees, and operations in 190 countries. During fiscal 2007 Siemens spent €347 million on outside advisors including Debevoise & Plimpton. Its stock price had increased by 37 in 2007. At the annual meeting in January 2008 CEO Loscher also heralded a surge in quarterly sales and profits and forecast strong sales and profits for 2008. He also said that Siemens would begin negotiations with the SEC and the U.S. Department of Justice on reaching "a comprehensive and fair settlement" of bribery allegations.

At the end of 2007 Siemens began a worldwide advertising campaign with planned expenditures of over €100 million for each of the next three years. The "Siemens answers" campaign emphasized the company's technological prowess. Siemens had dropped from the most respected company in Germany to number 10.

The trial of Mr. Siekaczek on 58 counts of breach of trust began in May 2008.

SOURCE: This case was prepared from public sources by Professor David P. Baron. Copyright © 2008 by the Board of Trustees of the Leland Stanford Junior University. David P. Baron. All rights reserved. Reprinted with permission.

Preparation Questions

1. What are the causes of the corruption problems within Siemens?
2. What is the likely scope of those problems?
3. How should Siemens clean up its problems?
4. Evaluate the justification given by the Siemens employee in the Italian case.
5. What principles should Siemens use to help its employees avoid bribery and corruption in the future?
6. What management systems should Siemens put in place to prevent bribery and corruption?

[60]*New York Times*, November 25, 2007.
[61]*Wall Street Journal*, April 20, 2007.

------------------------------------- P A R T   V -------------------------------------
Integrative Case
GlaxoSmithKline and AIDS Drugs Policy

In Africa GlaxoSmithKline (GSK) confronted the reality of the AIDS pandemic every day, and its decisions impacted thousands. There were no ready answers to the crisis, but everyone—governments, nongovernmental organizations, the media, shareholders, and others—had an opinion. GSK had to determine how to address the crisis while maintaining business viability in developing countries in the midst of the pressures swirling around it.

Throughout the late 1990s, the CEO of GSK, Stanford Graduate School of Business alumnus Dr. Jean-Pierre Garnier, was at the forefront of the controversy over antiretroviral drug pricing, patent protection, and drug access. Proactive in addressing critics, he was seen as the de facto spokesperson for the pharmaceutical industry in addressing these critical issues.

AZT Discovery: The Source of Hope and the Root of Controversy

The controversy traced back to 1987 when the FDA approved Burroughs Wellcome's compound, zidovudine, commonly known as AZT, as the first antiretroviral (ARV) drug for the treatment of the HIV virus. Burroughs Wellcome, expecting a small market and short life cycle for the drug and hoping to recoup development and clinical trial costs, announced that a year of the treatment would cost patients $8,000 to $10,000. This resulted in an avalanche of criticism for excessive corporate profiteering and united a number of disparate parties against Burroughs Wellcome. Activist groups, the media, and government officials led the charge.

The controversy was further fueled by the assertion of critics that its development was funded by government grants and therefore AZT should enter generic production immediately. In 1991 Barr Laboratories filed for FDA approval to produce a generic version of AZT. Burroughs Wellcome spent 5 years in court fighting to protect its patent, and in the end prevailed. The eventual commercial success of AZT increased the public outcry. Despite Burroughs Wellcome's initial belief that the market for the drug was quite small and its life cycle short due to anticipated new drugs, by 1993 AZT, marketed under the brand name Retrovir, was Burroughs Wellcome's number two product with cumulative sales of over $1 billion.

GlaxoSmithKline and AIDS Drugs

Because of the high costs and the risks of research and development, the pharmaceutical industry experienced a wave of mergers and acquisitions in the 1990s. In 1995 Glaxo acquired Burroughs Wellcome and AZT, making the company, now Glaxo Wellcome, the leader in AIDS therapy. Glaxo's own AIDS drug, lamivudine (3TC) was expected to soon be approved by the FDA, and the company hoped to combine 3TC with AZT into a dual-drug combination. During the merger process management carefully evaluated its strategy for AIDS therapies and considered abandoning the market altogether. There were significant risks involved in pursuing new research in the controversial AIDS area, as indicated by Burroughs Wellcome's AZT experience. Some of the company's executives worried that the new company would expose itself to more public inquiry and scrutiny if it continued to pursue a leadership position in AIDS drugs.

The company's competitors were proceeding with their own efforts to develop AIDS therapies. Advanced trials were underway for a new class of protease inhibitors that showed promise when combined with the older AIDS drugs. Concerned about these new offerings and convinced that the market for AIDS therapies would remain sustainable, Glaxo Wellcome decided to continue its AIDS research. In 1995 and 1996 the FDA approved four new AIDS drugs from Roche, Merck, Abbott Laboratories, and Agouron. In 1999 Glaxo Wellcome added to its AIDS portfolio with amprenavir.

In 2001 GlaxoSmithKline was formed by the merger of Glaxo Wellcome and SmithKline Beecham, becoming the world's second-largest pharmaceutical company. In 2002 GSK had net income of $6.941 billion on sales of $31.819 billion. Its return on equity was among the highest in the world. GSK was registered in the United Kingdom, but its top management was located in Philadelphia. GSK had been strategically pieced together through a number of mergers, combining the venerable pharmaceutical companies Glaxo, Wellcome, Burroughs, Beecham, and SmithKline & French and their drug portfolios, including some of the most successful AIDS therapies on the market.[62] In 2002 ARVs and AIDS drugs accounted for 7.9 percent of GSK's total revenues.

Commitment to Developing Countries

After the merger, GSK reaffirmed its corporate commitment to developing countries. For the past 20 years GSK, as one of the leading worldwide producers of vaccines, had offered vaccines to developing markets at preferential prices. As an indication of its continuing pledge to remain in the sub-Saharan Africa market, GSK maintained

------

[62]Rick Mullin, "Pharma M & A Declines, But Financing Picks Up," *Chemical Week*, March 20, 2002.

more registered patents in the countries of that region than any other pharmaceutical company, even though 90 percent of its revenues came from the larger markets of the United States and Europe. It also maintained a presence in a majority of markets in Africa and continued to serve both the public sector and the small emerging private sector. However, despite lowering prices to offer access to a wider population, GSK found that the local sub-Saharan African governments were either uninterested in or financially unable to provide these drugs to their citizens. With each successive drug price decrease, the private market participants benefited, but few additional drugs reached the community at large.

As corporate policy GSK did not sell its drugs below production cost even in sub-Saharan Africa. In February 2002 Garnier announced that GSK would "not profit" from AIDS drugs sold in the poorest countries, including those in sub-Saharan Africa.[63]

The AIDS Drug Pricing Controversy

There was no known cure for AIDS. Nonetheless, the introduction of ARVs as part of HIV clinical care made AIDS a more manageable chronic illness by achieving dramatic reductions in viral load (the level of the HIV virus in the blood), thereby arresting immune system damage. Typically, ARV-based treatment consisted of a "cocktail" of at least three drugs from the various classes of ARV drugs. This three-drug cocktail was called "Highly Active Antiretroviral Therapy" (HAART). Each class of anti-HIV drugs in a cocktail attacked the virus at a different stage of its replication in the human host lymphocyte cell. GSK combined AZT and Epivir to form Combivir, which became the company's largest selling ARV. Combivir was typically used in a combination with a protease inhibitor. As of June 2000 there were 14 FDA-approved HIV/AIDS drugs. GSK held patents on four of them.

The introduction of ARVs widened the discrepancy in the quality of AIDS care between rich and poor countries. In the United States HAART therapy led to a 70 percent decline in deaths attributable to HIV/AIDS. However, most of the 36 million people in the developing world living with HIV/AIDS did not benefit from the therapy. The World Health Organization (WHO) conservatively estimated that in 2002, 6 million people in developing countries were in need of life-sustaining ARV therapy. Yet, fewer than 250,000 had access to these therapies, and half of those were in one country, Brazil.

Pricing Pressure from Multiple Directions

As with other drugs the patents on the ARVs were owned by multinational pharmaceutical companies such as GSK, Bristol Myers Squibb, Pfizer, and Roche. Many observers argued that these patents resulted in high prices and kept needed drugs out of Africa and the rest of the developing world. Since most ARVs had been developed recently, the expiration of the patents would not occur soon. The patent for AZT would expire in 2005, but the patents on many other ARVs extended until 2014. As a result few observers expected AIDS drugs to reach the developing world during the height of the AIDS pandemic.

The first negotiations over global access to AIDS drugs began in Geneva in 1991 when 18 drug companies met with WHO representatives for a series of talks. A key topic in these discussions was the cost of new AIDS drugs—estimated to be $10,000 or more a year. The talks ended in 1993 with no resolution.

The major producers of AIDS drugs steadfastly opposed the idea of lowering prices in poor countries such as in sub-Saharan Africa. The industry maintained that the real obstacles to AIDS treatment in Africa and other low-income regions were not inflated drug prices but social, managerial, and political barriers, such as the absence of roads, shortages of doctors and nurses, the limited use of contraceptive devices, and the lack of resources to provide even basic health care to many citizens. They asserted that treatment should be borne by governments and society and not the companies per se. Moreover, the companies argued that on a continent where nearly half the population lived on less than a dollar a day, there was no price at which AIDS drugs could be commercially distributed to victims. In addition, the companies worried that without the proper infrastructure and health monitoring, the widespread use of AIDS drugs would result in an even more virulent strain of HIV that would be drug-resistant.[64]

GSK and the other pharmaceutical companies believed their pricing policies were justified by the high costs of research and development. Patents were essential to pricing successful drugs, and without patent protection, the economic model of the industry would fail, eliminating the incentive for future innovation in AIDS/HIV treatment. In the early 1990s the industry had lobbied the Clinton administration to extend domestic patent protection worldwide. These efforts were important in the creation of the Trade Related Aspects of Intellectual Property (TRIPS) agreement that was incorporated into the rules of the World Trade Organization (WTO) when it was formed in 1995. GSK and other drug companies were also concerned that if they agreed to price concessions for developing countries, they would face increased price pressures in their core U.S.

---

[63]"AHF Reports GlaxoSmithKline Head Vows to Make 'No Profit' on AIDS Drugs in Poor Countries; Advocates Ask for Public Disclosure of Costs," *Business Wire,* February 27, 2002.

[64]The distribution of ARVs and supervision of their use was crucial, since if a person did not follow a strict regimen of taking them every day, drug-resistant strains of HIV could develop. Moreover, if a patient stopped taking the ARVs for 2 weeks, resistance to the drug developed, and ARVs were then ineffective.

and European markets. Pressure could arise from the gray market importation of drugs from low-income countries or from activist campaigns that drew attention to the price differentials between developing countries and the U.S. and European markets.

The pressure on the industry continued for much of the 1990s, fueled by the unrelenting spread of HIV. Through agencies such as WHO and UNAIDS, the United Nations and its member countries exerted pressure on the pharmaceutical companies to reduce prices to improve access to drugs for HIV/AIDS victims. Activist groups like the AIDS Coalition to Unleash Power, or ACT UP! (which was formed in response to the initial launch price of AZT), Médecins sans Frontières, and the Consumer Project on Technology led protests and campaigns that charged the industry with profiteering from history's worst pandemic, using slogans like "Pfizer's Greed Kills," "Death Under Patent," and "GlaxoSmithKline! GlobalSerialKiller." These sentiments were exacerbated by the remarkable financial performance the drug industry experienced during this period. In 1999 the industry topped all three of *Fortune* magazine's measures of profitability and had one of the highest rates of return of any industry.

By the end of the decade public criticism had reached a crescendo. AIDS protestors badgered Vice President Gore's presidential campaign and chained themselves to desks in U.S. Trade Representative Charlene Barshefsky's office, demanding that the Clinton administration stop backing the industry against generic competitors. Activists became more aggressive and confrontational toward the drug companies, regularly taking actions such as storming into the offices of companies, including Pfizer and Bristol Myers, to disrupt their corporate events.

The media was also critical of drug companies and their handling of the AIDS drug pricing issue. Mainstream publications such as the *New York Times, Washington Post,* and the *Wall Street Journal* portrayed the pharmaceutical companies and their management as profit-centric and uncaring about the plight of poor countries. This public censure was echoed by journalists in both developed and developing countries and translated into antagonism against the drug companies and their pricing practices, domestically and internationally. The pharmaceutical industry had inadvertently become a primary recipient of the worldwide blame for the growing AIDS epidemic.

Preferential Pricing Begins

In late 1999 the industry responded to the mounting criticisms. Prompted by the senior management of GSK and Bristol-Myers Squibb, the International Federation of Pharmaceutical Manufacturers Associations organized a meeting to explore solutions to the issue. Six of the major companies participated in a conference call in

January 2000 at which executives at Glaxo and Bristol-Myers volunteered to draft a set of principles for an industry-led AIDS treatment initiative. After a series of talks and meetings, the companies agreed on a consensus draft to be presented to the United Nations agencies. By this time the original group of six companies had been reduced to five—Bristol-Myers Squibb, GlaxoSmithKline, Merck, Boehringer Ingelheim, and Roche. Pfizer had withdrawn, citing disagreement with the concept of preferential pricing.

Shortly after Pfizer's withdrawal, eight ACT UP! activists stormed the office of Pfizer CEO William Steere, Jr. They demanded that the company acquiesce to pressure from South African activists in the Treatment Action Campaign (TAC) and drop the price of fluconazole (diflucan) or issue a voluntary license for the importation of generic versions of the drug from a less expensive supplier. Fluconazole was effective in treating cryptococcal meningitis, the most common AIDS-related systemic fungal infection. Fluconazole was priced at $8.92 per pill in South Africa. In Thailand, where Pfizer did not have exclusive marketing rights, fluconazole cost only $0.29 per pill.[65] The average daily wage in South Africa in 1999 was about $7.00. The activists claimed that it was unacceptable for a corporation to maintain high prices while AIDS patients in poor countries were dying of treatable diseases. ACT UP! threatened to bring the issue to the attention of politicians and investors and claimed that Pfizer's actions were socially unconscionable. In April 2000 Pfizer announced that instead of lowering the price it would give away fluconazole to 3.6 million victims in South Africa. Two months later Pfizer extended the offer to 50 other less-developed countries.

Pfizer's initiative was applauded by advocacy groups. It immediately shifted the onus to the remaining five companies to follow Pfizer's lead. In particular, TAC called on GSK to make AZT available to pregnant women to reduce the risk of mother-to-child transmission. The five remaining pharmaceutical companies lobbied the U.N. agencies—UNAIDS, WHO, UNICEF, U.N. Development Program—and the World Bank to consider their proposed preferential pricing policy. Finally on May 11, 2000, the five companies and the United Nations issued a joint Statement of Intent for an Accelerating Access initiative as a basis for preferential pricing for HIV/AIDS medicines in developing countries. The concessions were to be made on a country-by-country basis and involved significant restrictions on the resale and use of the drugs. The industry and the United Nations publicly hailed the initiative as a major step forward. Still, critics remained unhappy and charged the drug companies with continuing to maintain high prices by offering discounts selectively. The critics were angry that the language of the initiative was vague and that none of

---

[65]*ACT UP!* Philadelphia/New York press release.

the drug companies, with the exception of GSK, had made firm commitments to exact price reductions.

In 2002 United Nations Secretary General Kofi Annan established the independent Global Fund to Fight AIDS, Tuberculosis and Malaria with $2.1 billion in funding to purchase AIDS drugs and conduct AIDS prevention programs in Africa. The funds came primarily from governments and the Gates Foundation. The Gates Foundation emphasized prevention programs over treatment of AIDS victims as the most cost effective means of addressing the AIDS pandemic.

Compulsory Licensing

Another issue confronting GSK was the decision of countries such as Thailand and Brazil to invoke compulsory licensing under TRIPS and either allow local manufacturers to produce ARVs based on patented formulas or import generic substitutes for the patented drugs. Although not directly affected by the decisions in Thailand and Brazil, GSK watched with great interest the unfolding of negotiations in both countries. Together with other major drug producers, GSK was a strong proponent of intellectual property protection and for many years had lobbied the U.S. government to support patent rights and the TRIPS agreement. However, at the end of 1999 the U.S. government reversed its stance and announced that it would not object to compulsory licensing in situations where a medical emergency justified it.

This represented a potentially serious threat to GSK's ability to protect its patented products from generic competitors in overseas markets. Management feared that many countries might follow the examples of Thailand and Brazil and use the opportunity to import or make cheap imitation drugs at the expense of patent holders. The decision by the U.S. government meant that foreign governments would not face trade sanctions if they used compulsory licensing.

In 1997 the South African parliament granted its Ministry of Health the power to permit parallel importation of drugs produced under license in another country. In February 1998, 39 major drug companies (including GSK), represented by the Pharmaceutical Manufacturers Association of South Africa (PMA), filed a lawsuit against the Government of South Africa to strike down the law on the grounds that it breached international trade agreements such as TRIPS and was unconstitutional, since it gave the health minister arbitrary power to ignore patent rights. The lawsuit and subsequent trial drew strong criticism from the media and advocacy groups, and in April 2001 after the trial had been under way for 6 weeks, the PMA withdrew its lawsuit.

On February 7, 2001, Cipla, an Indian generic drug manufacturer, offered to supply a triple-combination therapy for HIV/AIDS at $350 per patient per year to Médecins sans Frontières, an independent medical and humanitarian aid agency working in Africa. Cipla was able to manufacture these drugs under Indian patent law and export them at a fraction of the price at which the drugs were available from their primary manufacturers. It also offered to sell the therapy for $600 per patient per year to the governments of poor countries on the condition that the recipient governments provide the drugs for free to those with HIV/AIDS. The comparative cost of this regimen in developed nations was $10,000 to $15,000 annually. Cipla's offer put pressure on other pharmaceutical companies to reduce their prices. Cipla also began to produce AZT and by the end of 2002 was producing 10 of the 14 most widely used AIDS drugs. In May Merck announced that it would sell its AIDS drug Crixivan for $600 per patient per year and Stocrin for $500 per patient per year in the developing world. According to the company, it made no profit at these prices. Shortly thereafter, Boehringer Ingelheim, Bristol-Myers Squibb, and Abbott Laboratories followed with similar discount offers.

Preferential pricing and compulsory licensing posed another challenge to the patent holders of AIDS drugs. Corrupt officials could intercept AIDS drugs and smuggle them into European countries and the United States, where they could be sold at market prices. GSK sought to avoid this by providing the preferentially priced drugs directly to health care providers. Nevertheless, corruption and re-exportation posed a problem for its markets in developed countries.

Media Coverage

Extremely critical of the pharmaceutical industry on the drug pricing and access issue, the press had been relentless in its pressure on GSK. Beginning with Burroughs Wellcome's initial announcement of the price for AZT, the news media had successfully reframed HIV/AIDS drug pricing as a social justice and moral issue.

Even though GSK had lowered prices and negotiated with sub-Saharan Africa governments to provide the drugs to their citizens, the press reports continued to point to pricing as the primary barrier to drug access. In particular, the media in socially conscious Western countries faulted GSK and other pharmaceutical companies for not doing enough to ensure that those in sub-Saharan Africa had access to HIV/AIDS medicines. Initially, GSK was reactive in dealing with this pressure, often addressing questions and concerns with complex justifications about differential pricing and the specific positive steps that GSK had taken. Additionally, GSK was hesitant to fault publicly the governments that it had to work with on a regular basis.

Activist Groups

The activist groups were concerned about a broad range of issues, from HIV/AIDS itself to social justice, consumer rights, and humanitarian relief. The challenge for GSK lay in how to address the concerns of these often hostile groups without impairing its business objectives. The power and influence of the advocacy organizations could not be ignored. They were well organized, had access to funds, and possessed considerable leverage in shaping public opinion. Their campaigns drew considerable attention from the media and politicians and were effective in galvanizing support from the public for their cause. GSK management recognized this and was responsive to the major activist groups. Those groups, however, were generally distrustful of major corporations and continued to publicly pressure the drug companies to change their policies.

The AIDS Healthcare Foundation (AHF), an NGO that was the world's largest specialized provider of HIV medical care, launched a multipronged campaign against GSK. First, AHF sought to convince CalPERS, the California state retirement system, which held $1 billion of GSK's shares, to pressure the company to lower ARV prices. Second, AHF filed a lawsuit challenging GSK's patent on AZT, arguing that the research had been financed by public funds. Third, AHF filed a complaint against GSK in South Africa, where AHF operated a clinic, challenging GSK's pricing and other policies in South Africa. Fourth, it filed a false advertising lawsuit in California against GSK. Fifth, it organized protests and demonstrations against GSK.

GSK's Response

Social Responsibility Committee

Despite the commitment made to the Accelerating Access initiative in 2000, GSK continued to receive negative press coverage of its response to the AIDS crisis. The company faced unrelenting pressure to cut further its prices and extend its discounts to a broader group of countries and organizations. The intense public scrutiny in turn triggered concern among the company's shareholders about the reputational risks involved in failing to address the issue of access to needed medicines. GSK spent considerable time in discussions with its key institutional shareholders to address these concerns.

In response to the pressure GSK established a corporate social responsibility committee, chaired by Sir Richard Sykes, GSK's new nonexecutive chairman, to review the company's policies on access. Specifically, the committee was charged with crafting a policy response for GSK not only to HIV/AIDS but to the broader issue of access to drugs in the developing world. The committee would also advise the board of directors on issues of significance in the relationship between the company and society and would regularly review the company's policy on health care in the developing world.

On February 21, 2001, GSK announced that it would extend its preferential pricing offer for HIV/AIDS medicines beyond governments to include not-for-profit nongovernmental organizations (NGOs), such as international agencies, aid groups, and churches and charities that had facilities in place to appropriately monitor and treat patients. GSK also offered preferential prices on ARVs to employers in Africa that provided HIV/AIDS care and treatment directly to their employees through workplace clinics. Specifically, the price of Ziagen, which sold for $10.68 a day in the U.S. for the standard two-pill treatment, was reduced to $3.80 a day; Trizivir, a potent, triple-drug combination pill taken twice a day at a cost of $27.92 in the U.S. was priced at $6.60 in low-income countries; and Agenerase, a protease inhibitor that cost $18.50 a day for 16 pills in the U.S., was priced at $8.70 a day under the new preferential pricing plan. In addition to the AIDS drugs, GSK also reduced the price of its malarial pill Malarone from the U.S. list price of $52.71 for a full course of 12 tablets to $19.20 in the developing world.

Nonetheless, Garnier conceded that even with these steep discounts, the new prices would remain out of reach for most patients in the developing world. "We're not naive about the fact that compared to the means in these countries, everything is overpriced, even the generics," he said in an interview.

Corporate Policy: "Facing the Challenge"

One unexpected result of the criticism of GSK's policies concerning access to ARVs in sub-Saharan Africa was the impact on the morale of employees, shareholders, and partners. In an effort to reassure its internal constituents, in June 2001 GSK published "Facing the Challenge," a report articulating the company's product, pricing, and partnership commitments to increased access to medicines for patients in need in developing countries. Reshaping the role of GSK as a partner in the global fight against AIDS, the report was a turning point for the company and its stakeholders. Garnier said of GSK's new partner role:

> As a leading international research based pharmaceutical company, GlaxoSmithKline can make a real difference to health care in the developing world. We believe this is both an ethical imperative and key to business success. "Facing the Challenge" is a signal of our intention and commitment to making access to medicines a continued priority of our company. We are extending our preferential pricing offers to more products, to more countries and to more customer groups, in an effort to secure greater access for patients to treatment that is both appropriate and sustainable. Our activities will be undertaken together with organizations that have relevant specialized knowledge, such as governments, international agencies, charities and academic institutions. The pharmaceutical industry can play an important role, but it does not have the mandate, expertise or resources to deliver health care unilaterally to developing countries.

GSK's Challenge Going Forward

GSK faced an enormous challenge at the beginning of 2003. How could it address the continuing concerns raised by activists, the media, and governments, while simultaneously serving the interests of GSK stakeholders? How should social responsibility be balanced against generating profits? Should it go further than its current commitment and begin to deliver health care in the poorest countries? What should be the cost basis on which it prices its ARVs—for example, the marginal cost of producing the drugs or the average cost, taking into account its research and development costs? Should it make further reductions in its prices for its ARVs? How should GSK deal with the possibility of AIDS drugs supplied to Africa being diverted to Europe and the United States? Should GSK voluntarily license its ARVs to local drug producers in South Africa or other countries? Should it match Cipla's prices? How should it price its next AIDS drug currently in the pipeline? Should it continue to invest in research and development on drug therapies whose prices would likely be driven down by criticism from activists, governments, and the media or by patent infringements by companies in developing countries? GSK participated along with other pharmaceutical companies in TRIPS negotiations regarding compulsory licensing and parallel imports. What should GSK do to protect its intellectual property while providing access to drugs under patent for people and countries in need? More generally, what role should social concerns and societal pressure play in GSK's business strategy? And how could GSK better manage nonmarket considerations, both now and in the future? ∎

Preparation Questions

1. The European Union expressed concern about the availability of pharmaceuticals to poor countries. The Commission of the European Union held an annual meeting of its Health and TRIPS Issue Group on the subject of "Access to Essential Medicines." GSK was an active participant in the meetings, the next of which was scheduled for April 28, 2003. Garnier had agreed to attend the meeting and understood that he would be questioned about GSK's AIDS drugs policy. In the role of CEO Garnier, would you announce any changes in the company's policy? What defense would you give in support of either the current policy or the new policy you plan to announce?

2. What position should Garnier take on TRIPS and compulsory licensing?

References

Abegglen, James C., and George Stalk, Jr. (1985). *Kaisha, the Japanese Corporation.* New York: Basic Books.

Aggarwal, Vinod K. (Ed). (2001). *Winning in Asia, European Style.* New York: Palgrave.

Akerlof, George A. (1970). "The Market for 'Lemons': Qualitative Uncertainty and the Market Mechanism." *Quarterly Journal of Economics,* 84, 488–500.

Alesina, Alberto, and Romain Wacziarg. (1999). "Is Europe Going Too Far?" Carnegie-Rochester Conference on Public Policy (*Journal of Monetary Economics*), 51, 1–42.

Alpern, Kenneth D. (1988). "Moral Dimensions of the Foreign Corrupt Practices Act: Comments on Pastin and Hooker." In Donaldson and Werhane (1988), 54–59.

Alt, James A., and Kenneth Shepsle (Eds.). (1990). *Perspectives on Positive Political Economy.* Cambridge, UK: Cambridge University Press.

Aoki, Masahiko (Ed.). (1984). *The Economic Analysis of the Japanese Firm.* Amsterdam, The Netherlands: North Holland.

American Society of Newspaper Editors. (1999). "Examining Our Credibility: Examining Credibility, Explaining Ourselves." Reston, VA. www.asne.org.

Ansolabehere, Stephen, John de Figueiredo, and James M. Snyder. (2003). "Why Is There So Little Money in U.S. Politics?" *Journal of Economic Perspectives,* 17, 105–130.

Areeda, Phillip, and Herbert Hovenkamp. (2004). *Fundamentals of Antitrust Law.* New York: Aspen Law & Business.

Areeda, Phillip, and Louis Kaplow. (1997). *Antitrust Analysis: Problems, Text, and Cases* (5th ed.). New York: Aspen Publishers.

Areeda, Phillip, and Donald Turner. (1975, February). "Predatory Pricing and Related Practices under Section 2 of the Sherman Act." *Harvard Law Review,* 88, 697–733.

Argenti, Paul A. 2004. "Collaborating with Activists: How Starbucks Works with NGOs." *California Management Review,* 47, 91–116.

Arrow, Kenneth A. (1963). *Social Choice and Individual Values* (2d ed.). New York: Wiley.

Atsuyuki, Suzuta. (1978). "The Way of the Bureaucrat." *Japan Echo,* 5(3), 42–53. Reprinted in Okimoto and Rohlen (1988), 196–203.

Bach, David. (2004). "The Double Punch of Law and Technology: Fighting Music Piracy or Remaking Copyright in a Digital Age?" *Business and Politics,* 6: Article 3.

Baerwald, Hans H. (1974). *Japan's Parliament: An Introduction.* London, UK: Cambridge University Press.

Bagley, Constance E. (2002). *Managers and the Legal Environment: Strategies for the 21st Century* (4th ed.). St. Paul, MN: West Publishing.

Baker, Jonathan B. (1997). *Econometric Analysis in FTC v. Staples.* Washington, DC: Federal Trade Commission.

Banner, Stuart. (1998). "The Origin of the New York Stock Exchange, 1791–1860." *Journal of Legal Studies,* 27, 113–140.

Barker, Richard A. (1993). "An Evaluation of the Ethics Program at General Dynamics." *Journal of Business Ethics,* 12, 165–177.

Baron, David P. (1983). *The Export-Import Bank: An Economic Analysis.* New York: Academic Press.

_____. (1995a). "The Nonmarket Strategy System." *Sloan Management Review,* 37(Fall), 73–85.

_____. (1995b). "Integrated Strategy: Market and Nonmarket Components." *California Management Review,* 37(Winter), 47–65.

_____. (1996). *Business and Its Environment* (2d ed.). Upper Saddle River, NJ: Prentice Hall.

_____. (1997a). "Integrated Strategy in International Trade Disputes: The Kodak-Fujifilm Case." *Journal of Economics and Management Strategy,* 6(Summer), 291–346.

_____. (1997b). "Integrated Strategy, Trade Policy, and Global Competition." *California Management Review,* 39(Winter), 145–169.

_____. (1999). "Integrated Market and Nonmarket Strategies in Client and Interest Group Politics." *Business and Politics,* 1(April), 7–34.

_____. (2000). *Business and Its Environment* (3d ed.). Upper Saddle River, NJ: Prentice Hall.

_____. (2001). "Private Politics, Corporate Social Responsibility, and Integrated Strategy." *Journal of Economics & Management Strategy,* 10(Spring), 7–45.

_____. (2003a). "Private Politics." *Journal of Economics & Management Strategy,* 12, 31–66.

_____. (2003b). "Private Ordering on the Internet: The eBay Community of Traders." *Business and Politics,* 4, 245–274.

_____. (2003c). *Business and Its Environment* (4th ed.). Upper Saddle River, NJ: Prentice Hall.

_____. (2005). "Competing for the Public Through the News Media." *Journal of Economics and Management Strategy,* 14, 339–376.

_____. (2006). "Persistent Media Bias." *Journal of Public Economics,* 90, 1–36.

_____. (2007). "Corporate Social Responsibility and Social Entrepreneurship." *Journal of Economics and Management Strategy,* 16, 683–717.

_____. (2008a). "Managerial Contracting and Corporate Social Responsibility." *Journal of Public Economics,* 92, 268–288.

_____. (2008b). "A Positive Theory of Moral Management, Social Pressure, and Corporate Social Performance." *Journal of Economics and Management Strategy* (forthcoming).

Baron, David P., and David Besanko. (2001). "Strategy, Organization, and Incentives: Global Corporate Banking at Citibank." *Industrial and Corporate Change,* 10, 1–36.

Baron, David P., and Daniel Diermeier. (2007). "Strategic Activism and Nonmarket Strategy." *Journal of Economics and Management Strategy,* 16, 599–634.

Baron, David P., and John A. Ferejohn. (1989). "Bargaining in Legislatures." *American Political Science Review,* 83(December), 1181–1206.

Baron, David P., Maretno A. Harjoto, and Hoje Jo. (2008). "The Economics and Politics of Corporate Social Responsibility." Working paper, Stanford University.

Barone, Michael, and Richard E. Cohen. (2007). *The Almanac of American Politics 2008.* Washington, DC: National Journal.

Bartlett, Christopher A., and Sumantra Ghoshal. (1989). *Managing Across Borders: The Transnational Solution.* Boston, MA: Harvard Business School Press.

Baysinger, Barry D., Gerald D. Keim, and Carl P. Zeithaml. (1985). "An Empirical Evaluation of the Potential for Including Shareholders in Corporate Constituency Programs." *Academy of Management Journal,* 28, 180–200.

Becker, Gary S. (1983). "A Theory of Competition and Pressure Groups for Political Influence." *Quarterly Journal of Economics,* 98, 371–400.

Bellis, Jean-Francois. (1989). "The EEC Antidumping System." In Jackson and Vermulst, *Antidumping Laws and Practice: A Comparative Study,* 41–97.

Bentham, Jeremy. (1789). *An Introduction to the Principles of Morals and Legislation.* Reprint, Buffalo, NY: Prometheus Books (1988).

Berle, Adolph A., and Gardiner C. Means. (1932). "The Modern Corporation and Private Property." Reprint, Buffalo, NY: W. S. Wein (1982).

Bernstein, Marver H. (1955). *Regulation by Independent Commission.* Princeton, NJ: Princeton University Press.

Besanko, David, David Dranove, Mark Shanley, and Scott Schaefer. (2007). *The Economics of Strategy* (4th ed.). New York: Wiley.

Binmore, Kenneth M. (1994). *Game Theory and the Social Contract.* Cambridge, MA: MIT Press.

Black, Henry C. (1983). *Black's Law Dictionary* (abridged 5th ed.). St. Paul: West Publishing.

Boardman, Anthony E., David H. Greenberg, Aidan R. Vining, and David L. Weimer. (2006). *Cost-Benefit Analysis: Concepts and Practice* (4th ed.). Upper Saddle River, NJ: Prentice Hall.

Bouchoux, Deborah E. (2001). *Protecting Your Company's Intellectual Property.* New York: AMACOM.

Bowie, Norman E. (1990). "Business Ethics and Cultural Relativism." In Peter Madsen and Jay M. Shafritz (Eds.), *Essentials of Business Ethics,* 366–382. New York: Penguin Books.

Brady, David, and Craig Volden. (1998). *Revolving Gridlock.* Boulder, CO: Westview Press.

Brandt, Richard B. (1959). *Ethical Theory.* Upper Saddle River, NJ: Prentice Hall.

_____. (1979). *A Theory of the Good and the Right.* Oxford, UK: Clarendon Press.

Breyer, Stephen. (1982). *Regulation and Its Reform.* Cambridge, MA: Harvard University Press.

Brock, William A., and David S. Evans. (1986). *The Economics of Small Business.* New York: Holmes and Meyer.

Bronte, Stephen. (1982). *Japanese Finance: Markets and Institutions.* London, UK: Euromoney Publications.

Browne, John. (1997). "Speech at Stanford University, 19 May, 1997." *Review: The BP Quarterly Technology Magazine,* July/August, 11–13.

Budge, Ian, David Robertson, and Derek Hearl (Eds.). (1987). *Ideology, Strategy, and Party Change: Spatial Analyses of Post-War Election Programmes in Nineteen Democracies.* Cambridge, UK: Cambridge University Press.

Bulow, Jeremy, and Paul Klemperer. (1998). "The Tobacco Deal." *Brookings Papers on Economic Activity.* Washington DC: Brookings.

Business Roundtable. (1978). "The Role and Composition of the Board of Directors of the Large Publicly Owned Corporation." New York.

_____. (1981, October). "Statement on Corporate Responsibility." New York.

_____. (1988). "Corporate Ethics: A Prime Business Asset." New York.

_____. (1990). "Corporate Governance and American Competitiveness." New York.

_____. (1997, September). "Statement on Corporate Governance." New York.

Calabresi, Guido, and Douglas A. Melamed. (1972). "Property Rules, Liability Rules and Inalienability: One View of the Cathedral." *Harvard Law Review,* 85, 1089–1128.

Calingaert, Michael. (1993). "Government-Business Relations in the European Community." *California Management Review,* Winter, 118–133.

Campbell, Thomas J., Daniel P. Kessler, and George B. Shepherd. (1998). "The Link Between Liability Reforms and Productivity: Some Empirical Evidence." *Brookings Papers in Economic Activity: Microeconomics.* Washington, DC: Brookings.

Carp, Robert A., and Ronald Stidham. (2001). *The Federal Courts* (4th ed.). Washington, DC: CQ Press.

Cater, Douglass. (1959). *The Fourth Branch of Government.* Boston: Houghton Mifflin.

Cavanagh, Gerald F. (2000). "Executives' Code of Business Conduct: Prospects for the Caux Principles," in Williams (2000), 169–182.

CBS News. (1980). *60 Minutes Verbatim,* 149–153. New York: Arno Press.

Cecchini, Paolo, with Michel Catinat and Alexis Jacquemin. (1988). *The European Challenge 1992: The Benefits of a Single Market.* Aldershot, UK: Wildwood.

Chandler, Alfred D. (1977). *The Visible Hand.* Cambridge, MA: Harvard University Press.

Chandler, Alfred D., and Richard S. Tedlow. (1985). *The Coming of Managerial Capitalism: A Casebook on the History of American Economic Institutions.* Homewood, IL: Richard D. Irwin.

Chang, Wejen. (1998). "Confucian Theory of Norms and Human Rights." In Wm. Theodore de Bary and Tu Weiming, *Confucianism and Human Rights,* 117–141, New York: Columbia University Press.

Chavis, Larry, and Phillip Leslie. (2008). "Consumer Boycotts: The Impact of the Iraq War on French Wines." *Quantitative Marketing and Economics* (forthcoming).

Cheng, Chung-ying. (1998). "Transforming Confucian Virtues into Human Rights: A Study of Human Agency and Potency in Confucian Ethics." In Wm. Theodore de Bary and Tu Weiming, *Confucianism and Human Rights,* 142–153, New York: Columbia University Press.

Christiansen, Flemming, and Shirin M. Rai. (1996). *Chinese Politics and Society: An Introduction.* Upper Saddle River, NJ: Prentice Hall.

Cini, Michelle, and Lee McGowan. (1998). *Competition Policy in the European Union.* London, UK: Macmillan.

Clark, Robert C. (1985). "Agency Costs versus Fiduciary Duties." In John W. Pratt and Richard J. Zeckhauser (Eds.), *Principals and Agents: The Structure of Business,* 55–79. Boston, MA: Harvard Business School.

Clarkson, Kenneth W., and Timothy J. Muris (Eds.). (1981). *The Federal Trade Commission Since 1970.* Cambridge, UK: Cambridge University Press.

Cline, Robert J., and Thomas S. Neubig. (1999). "Masters of Complexity and Bearers of Great Burden: The Sales Tax System and Compliance Costs for Multistate Retailers." Technical Report, Ernst and Young Economics Consulting and Quantitative Analysis.

Coase, Ronald H. (1960). "The Problem of Social Cost." *The Journal of Law and Economics,* 3(October), 1–44.

Coen, David. (1999). "The Impact of U.S. Lobbying Practice on the European Business-Government Relationship." *California Management Review,* 41, 27–44.

Coffee, John C., Jr., Louis Lowenstein, and Susan Rose-Ackerman. (1988). *Knights, Raiders & Targets: The Impact of the Hostile Takeover.* New York: Oxford University Press.

Cohen, Henry. (1990, November). "Products Liability: A Legal Overview." Washington, DC: Congressional Research Service, Library of Congress.

Committee for the Study of Economic and Monetary Union. (1989). *Report of Economic and Monetary Union in the European Community.* Brussels, Belgium.

Condorcet, Marquis de. (1785). *Essai sur l'Application de l'Analyse à la Probabilité des Decisions Rendues a la Pluralité des Voix.* Reprint, New York: Chelsea, 1972.

Congressional Quarterly. (1994). *Federal Regulatory Directory* (7th ed.). Washington, DC: CQ Press.

_____. (1997). *Politics in America: The 104th Congress.* Washington, DC: CQ Press.

Cook, Timothy E. (1989). *Making Laws & Making News: Media Strategies in the U.S. House of Representatives.* Washington, DC: Brookings.

Cooter, Robert, and Thomas Ulen. (1997). *Law and Economics* (2d ed.). Reading, MA: Addison-Wesley.

_____. (2004). *Law and Economics,* (4th ed.) Boston: Addison-Wesley.

_____. (2007). *Law and Economics* (5th ed.). Boston: Addison-Wesley.

Cramton, Peter. (1997). "The FCC Spectrum Auctions: An Early Assessment." *Journal of Economics & Management Strategy,* 6(Fall), 431–495.

Cull, Robert, Asli Demirgüç-Kunt, and Jonathan Morduch. (2008). "Microfinance Meets the Market." World Bank Policy Research Working Paper No. 4630, World Bank, Washington, D.C.

Cummins Engine Company. (1980, October). Cummins Practice. Columbus, IN.

Curtis, Gerald L. (1975). "Big Business and Political Influence." In Ezra F. Vogel, *Modern Japanese Organization and Decision-Making,* 33–70. Berkeley: University of California Press.

_____. (1999). *The Logic of Japanese Politics: Leaders, Institutions, and the Limits of Change.* New York: Columbia University Press.

Cusamano, Michael A., and David B. Yoffie. (1998). *Competing on Internet Time: Lessons from Netscape and Its Battle with Microsoft.* New York: The Free Press.

Dalkir, Serdar, and Frederick R. Warren-Boulton. (1999). "Prices, Market Definition, and the Effects of Merger: Staples–Office Depot (1997)." In Kwoka and White (1999), 143–164.

Dalton, D., C. Daily, A. Ellstrand, and J. Johnson. (1998). "Meta-analytic Reviews of Board Composition, Leadership Structure, and Financial Performance." *Strategic Management Review,* 19, 269–290.

Dalton, Dan R., and Michael B. Metzger. (1993). "Integrity Testing for Personnel Selection: An Unsparing Perspective." *Journal of Business Ethics,* 12, 147–156.

Davidson, Wallace N., Dan L. Worrell, and Abuzar El-Jelly. (1995). "Influencing Managers to Change Unpopular Corporate Behavior Through Boycotts and Divestitures." *Business & Society,* 34(August), 171–196.

De Bary, William T. (1991). *The Trouble with Confucianism.* Cambridge, MA: Harvard University Press.

deFigueiredo, Rui J. P., Jr., and Geoff Edwards. (2007). "Does Private Money Buy Public Policy? Campaign Contributions and Regulatory Outcomes in Telecommunications." *Journal of Economics and Management Strategy,* 16, 547–576.

DeGeorge, Richard T. (1993). "International Business Ethics." *Business Ethics Quarterly,* 4, 1–9.

Delmas, Magali. (2000). "Barriers and Incentives to the Adoption of ISO 14001 in the United States." *Duke Environmental Law and Policy Forum,* Fall, 1–38.

_____. (2001). "Stakeholders and Competitive Advantage: The Case of ISO 14001." *Production and Operation Management,* 10, 343–358.

Department of Labor, Office of Inspector General. (1993). "Targeted Jobs Tax Credit Program," State of Alabama, October 1, 1990–September 30, 1991. Washington, DC.

Derthick, Martha, and Paul J. Quirk. (1985). *The Politics of Deregulation.* Washington, DC: Brookings.

_____. (1997). *Renewing Fast-Track Legislation.* Washington, DC: Institute for International Economics.

Destler, I. M., and Peter J. Balint. (1999). *The New Politics of American Trade: Trade, Labor, and the Environment.* Washington, DC: Institute for International Economics.

Deyo, Frederic C. (Ed.). (1987). *The Political Economy of the New Asian Industrialism.* Ithaca, NY: Cornell University Press.

Diffie, Whitfield, and Susan Landau. (1998). *Privacy on the Line: The Politics of Wiretapping and Encryption.* Cambridge, MA: MIT Press.

Dixit, Avinash, and Susan Skeath. (2004). *Games of Strategy* (2d ed.). New York: Norton.

Dixon, Lloyd, and Steven Garber. (2001). *Fighting Air Pollution in Southern California by Scrapping Old Vehicles.* Santa Monica, CA: RAND.

Doi, Takeo. (1988). "Dependency in Human Relationships." In Okimoto and Rohlen (1988), 20–25.

Dollinger, Marc J. (1988). "Confucian Ethics and Japanese Management Practices." *Journal of Business Ethics,* 7, 575–584.

Donaldson, Thomas. (1989). *The Ethics of International Business.* Oxford, UK: Oxford University Press.

_____. (1996). "Values in Tension: Ethics Away from Home." *Harvard Business Review,* September–October, 48–49, 52–56, 58, 60, 62.

Donaldson, Thomas, and Patricia H. Werhane. (1988). *Ethical Issues in Business: A Philosophical Approach* (3d ed.). Upper Saddle River, NJ: Prentice Hall.

Dornbusch, Rudiger, and James M. Poterba (Eds.). (1991). *Global Warming: Economic Policy Responses.* Cambridge, MA: MIT Press.

Durlabhji, Subhash. (1990). "The Influence of Confucianism and Zen on the Japanese Organization." *Akron Business and Economic Review,* 21(2), 31–45.

Duverger, Maurice. (1954). *Political Parties: Their Organization and Activity in the Modern State.* (Trans. Barbara and Robert North). New York: Wiley.

Easterbrook, Frank H., and Daniel R. Fischel. (1981). "The Proper Role of a Target's Management in Responding to a Tender Offer." *Harvard Law Review,* April, 1161–1204.

Edley, Christopher F., Jr. (1990). *Administrative Law.* New Haven, CT: Yale University Press.

Elkington, John. (1997). *Cannibals with Forks: The Triple Bottom Line of 21st Century Business.* Stony Creek, CT: New Society Publishers.

Ellerman, A. Denny, Paul L. Joskow, and David Harrison, Jr. (2003). "Emissions Trading in the U.S.: Experience, Lessons, and Considerations for Greenhouse Gases." Pew Center for Global Climate Change.

Ellickson, Robert C. (1991). *Order Without Law.* Cambridge, MA: Harvard University Press.

Elzinga, Kenneth G., and William Briet. (1976). *The Antitrust Penalties: A Study in Law and Economics.* New Haven, CT: Yale University Press.

Emerson, Michael, Michael Aujean, Michael Catinat, Phillippe Goybet, and Alexis Jacquemin. (1988). *The Economics of 1992.* Oxford, UK: Oxford University Press.

Entine, Jon. (1994). "Shattered Image: Is the Body Shop Too Good to Be True?" *Business Ethics.*

Epstein, David, and Sharyn O'Halloran. (1999). *Delegating Powers.* Cambridge, UK: Cambridge University Press.

Epstein, Edward Jay. (1973). *News from Nowhere.* New York: Random House.

_____. (1981). "The Selection of Reality." In Elie Abel (Ed.), *What's News,* 119–132, San Francisco: Institute for Contemporary Studies.

Epstein, Marc J., and Karen E. Schnietz. 2002. "Measuring the Cost of Environmental and Labor Protests to Globalization: An Event Study of the Failed 1999 Seattle WTO Talks." *The International Trade Journal,* XVI: 129–160.

Epstein, Richard A. (1980). *A Theory of Strict Liability.* San Francisco: Cato Institute.

Esty, Daniel C. (1994). *Greening the GATT: Trade, Environment, and the Future.* Washington, DC: Institute for International Economics.

_____. (2001). "Bridging the Trade-Environment Divide." *Journal of Economic Perspectives,* 15, 113–130.

European Commission. (1988). "Social Dimensions of the Internal Market." Commission Working Paper, SEC (88) 1148, Brussels, Belgium.

Evans, Fred J. (1987). *Managing the Media.* New York: Quorum Books.

Fairbank, John K. (1992). *China: A New History.* Cambridge, MA: Harvard University Press.

Fama, Eugene F., and Michael C. Jensen. (1983). "Separation of Ownership and Control." *Journal of Law & Economics,* 26(June), 301–325.

Federal Trade Commission. (1990). "The Hart-Scott-Rodino Antitrust Improvements Act of 1976." Washington, DC.

Feinstein, Alvan R. (1988). "Scientific Standards in Epidemiologic Studies of the Menace of Daily Life." *Science,* 242(December), 1257–1263.

Feldstein, Martin. (1997). "The Political Economy of the European Economic and Monetary Union: Political Sources of an Economic Liability." *Journal of Economic Perspectives,* 11(Fall), 23–42.

Fink, Steven. (2002). *Crisis Management: Planning for the Inevitable.* Authors Guild Backprint.com Edition: Lincoln, NE.

Fiorina, Morris P. (1989). *Congress: Keystone of the Washington Establishment* (2d ed.). New Haven, CT: Yale University Press.

Fiorino, Daniel J. (2006). *The New Environmental Regulation.* MIT Press; Cambridge, MA.

Fisher, Franklin M., John J. McGowan, and Joel E. Greenwood. (1983). *Folded, Spindled, and Mutilated: Economic Analysis of U.S. v. IBM.* Cambridge, MA: MIT Press.

Fishwick, Frank. (1993). *Making Sense of Competition Policy.* London, UK: Kogan Page.

Fowler, Linda L., and Ronald G. Shaiko. (1987). "The Grass Roots Connection: Environmental Activists and Senate Roll Calls." *American Journal of Political Science,* 31(August), 484–510.

Fox, J. Ronald. (1982). *Managing Business-Government Relations: Cases and Notes on Business-Government Problems.* Homewood, IL: Richard D. Irwin.

Francis, John. (1993). *The Politics of Regulation: A Comparative Perspective.* Oxford, UK: Blackwell.

Frank, Reuven. (1991). *Out of Thin Air: The Brief Wonderful Life of Network News.* New York: Simon & Schuster.

Franklin, Marc A., and Robert L. Rabin. (1996). *Cases and Materials on Tort Law and Alternatives* (6th ed.). Mineola, NY: Foundation Press.

Freeman, R. Edward. (1984). *Strategic Management: A Stakeholder Approach.* Boston: Pitman.

Freeman, R. Edward, and Daniel R. Gilbert, Jr. (1988). *Corporate Strategy and the Search for Ethics.* Upper Saddle River, NJ: Prentice Hall.

Friedman, Milton. (1962). *Capitalism and Freedom.* Chicago: University of Chicago Press.

_____. (1970, September 13). "The Social Responsibility of Business Is to Increase Its Profits." *New York Times Magazine,* 32–33, 122, 126.

Friedman, Monroe. (1985). "Consumer Boycotts in the United States, 1970–1980: Contemporary Events in Historical Perspective." *Journal of Consumer Affairs,* 19(Summer), 96–117.

_____. (1999). *Consumer Boycotts.* New York: Routledge.

Fukui, Haruhiro. (1970). *Party in Power.* Berkeley: University of California Press.

Gale, Jeffrey, and Rogene A. Buchholz. (1987). "The Political Pursuit of Competitive Advantage: What Business Can Gain from Government." In Marcus, Kaufman, and Beam (1987), 31–42.

Galvin, Robert W. (1992, October). *International Business and the Changing Nature of Global Competition.* Oxford, OH: Miami University.

Gauthier, David. (1986). *Morals by Agreement.* Oxford, UK: Clarendon Press.

Gavil, Andrew I., William E. Kovacic, and Jonathan B. Baker. (2008). *Antitrust Law in Perspective: Cases, Concepts and Problems in Competition Policy* (2d ed.). St. Paul, MN: Thomson/West.

_____. (2004). *Teacher's Update: Summer 2004,* to *Antitrust Law in Perspective.* St. Paul, MN: Thomson/West.

General Dynamics Corporation. "General Dynamics Standards of Business Ethics and Conduct." St. Louis, MO.

_____. "The Ethics Program 1985/1986." St. Louis, MO.

Gerlach, Michael L. (1992). *Alliance Capitalism: The Social Organization of Japanese Business.* Berkeley: University of California Press.

Gert, Bernard. (1988). *Morality: A New Justification of the Moral Rules.* New York: Oxford University Press.

Getz, Kathleen A. (2000). "International Instruments on Bribery and Corruption." In Williams (2000), 141–166.

Gibney, Frank (Ed.) (1998). *Unlocking the Bureaucrat's Kingdom: Deregulation and the Japanese Economy.* Washington, DC: Brookings.

Gilligan, Thomas W., and Keith Krehbiel. (1987). "Collective Decision-Making and Standing Committees: An Informational Rationale for Restrictive Amendment Procedures." *Journal of Law, Economics, and Organization,* 3(Fall), 287–335.

Gold, T. B. (1996). "Civil Society in Taiwan." In W. M. Tu (Ed.), *Confucian Traditions in East Asian Modernity.* Cambridge, MA: Harvard University Press.

Golodner, Linda F. (2000). "The Apparel Industry Code of Conduct: A Consumer Perspective on Social Responsibility." In Williams (2000), 241–252.

Goodman, John B. (1992). *Monetary Sovereignty: The Politics of Central Banking in Western Europe.* Ithaca, NY: Cornell University Press.

Goodpaster, Kenneth E. (2000). "The Caux Round Table Principles: Corporate Moral Reflection in a Global Business Environment." In Williams (2000), 183–208.

Goolsbee, Austan. (2000). "In a World Without Borders: The Impact of Taxes on Internet Commerce." *Quarterly Journal of Economics,* 115(2): 561–76.

Graber, Doris A. (Ed.) 2000. *Media Power in Politics.* Washington, DC: CQ Press.

Green, Edward, and Robert Porter. (1984). "Noncooperative Collusion under Imperfect Price Information." *Econometrica,* 52, 87–100.

Greenblat, Alan. (1998). "Growing Ranks of Cigarette Tax Critics Invigorate Big Tobacco's Lobbying Effort," *Congressional Quarterly Weekly Report,* May 16.

Greve, Michael S., and Fred L. Smith, Jr. (1992). *Environmental Politics: Public Costs, Private Politics.* New York: Praeger.

Grieco, Joseph. (1990). *Cooperation Among Nations.* Ithaca, NY: Cornell University Press.

Griffin, J.J., and J.F. Mahon. (1997). "The Corporate Social Performance and Corporate Financial Performance Debate: Twenty-Five Years of Incomparable Research." *Business and Society.* 36: 5–31.

Griffin, Kelley. (1987). *Ralph Nader Presents More Action for a Change.* New York: Dembner Books.

Groarke, Leo. (1990). "Affirmative Action as a Form of Restitution." *Journal of Business Ethics,* 9, 207–213.

Groseclose, Timothy. (1996). "An Examination of the Market for Favors and Votes in Congress." *Economic Inquiry,* 34(April), 1–21.

Groseclose, Timothy, and Jeff Milyo. (2005). "A Measure of Media Bias." *Quarterly Journal of Economics.* 120: 1191–1237.

Groseclose, Timothy, and James M. Snyder, Jr. (1996). "Buying Supermajorities." *American Political Science Review,* 90(June), 303–315.

Groves, Theodore, Yongmiao Hong, John McMillan, and Barry Naughton. (1994). "Autonomy and Incentives in Chinese State Enterprises." *Quarterly Journal of Economics,* 109 (February), 183–209.

_____. (1995). "China's Evolving Managerial Labor Market." *Journal of Political Economy,* 103(August), 873–892.

Grub, Phillip D., and Jian Hai Lin. (1991). *Foreign Direct Investment in China.* New York: Quorum Books.

Haggard, Stephen. (1990). *Pathways from the Periphery: The Politics of Growth in the Newly Industrializing Countries.* Ithaca, NY: Cornell University Press.

Hall, Richard L., and Frank W. Wayman. (1990). "Buying Time: Moneyed Interests and the Mobilization of Bias in Congressional Committees." *American Political Science Review,* 84, 707–820.

Hamilton, Gary G. (1996). "Overseas Chinese Capitalism." In W. M. Tu (Ed.), *Confucian Traditions in East Asian Modernity.* Cambridge, MA: Harvard University Press.

Hamilton, J. Brooke, III, and David Hoch. (1997). "Ethical Standards for Business Lobbying: Some Practical Suggestions." *Business Ethics Quarterly,* 7, 117–129.

Hamilton, James T. (1993). "Politics and Social Costs: Estimating the Impact of Collective Action on Hazardous Waste Facilities." *RAND Journal of Economics,* 24(Spring), 101–125.

_____. (1995). "Pollution as News: Media and Stock Market Reactions to the Toxics Release Inventory Data." *Journal of Environmental Economics & Management,* 28, 187–206.

_____. (1997). "Taxes, Torts, and the Toxics Release Inventory: Congressional Voting on Instruments to Control Pollution." *Economic Inquiry,* 35(October), 745–762.

_____. (1998). *Channeling Violence: The Economic Market for Violent Television Programming.* Princeton, NJ: Princeton University Press.

Hamilton, V. Lee, and Joseph Sanders. (1992). *Everyday Justice: Responsibility and the Individual in Japan and the United States.* New Haven, CT: Yale University Press.

Handler, Edward, and John R. Mulkern. (1982). *Business and Politics.* Lexington, MA: Lexington Books.

Hardin, Russell. (1982). *Collective Action,* Resources for the Future. Baltimore, MD: Johns Hopkins University Press.

_____. (1988). *Morality within the Limits of Reason.* Chicago, IL: University of Chicago Press.

Harding, Harry. (1987). *China's Second Revolution: Reform After Mao.* Washington, DC: Brookings.

Harris, Richard A., and Sidney M. Milkis. (1989). *The Politics of Regulatory Change: A Tale of Two Agencies.* Oxford, UK: Oxford University Press.

Harris, Robert G. (1989). "Telecommunications Policy in Japan: Lessons for the U.S." *California Management Review, 31*, 113–131.

Harsanyi, John C. (1982). "Morality and the Theory of Rational Behavior." In Sen and Williams (1982), 39–62.

_____. (1977). "Rule Utilitarianism and Decision Theory." *Erkenntnis, 11,* 25–53.

Haufler, Virginia. (2007). "The Kimberly Process, Club Goods, and Public Enforcement of a Private Regime?" Working paper, University of Maryland College Park.

Hawk, Barry E. (1988). "The American Antitrust Revolution: Lessons for the EEC?" *European Competition Law Review, 9,* 53–87.

Hay, Robert D., and Edmund R. Gray. (1981). *Business & Society: Cases and Text.* Cincinnati, OH: South-Western Publishing.

Heckathorn, Douglas D. and Steven M. Maser. (1990). "The Contractual Architecture of Public Policy: A Critical Reconstruction of Lowi's Typology." *Journal of Politics, 52,* 1101–1123.

Hendry, J.R. (2006). "Shareholder Influence Strategies: An Empirical Exploration." *Journal of Business Ethics.* 61: 79–99.

Henisz, Witold and Bennet A. Zelner. (2008). "Managing Policy Risk." Working paper, University of Pennsylvania.

Hewlett-Packard Company. (1984). "How to Deal with the Press." Palo Alto, CA.

_____. (1989). "Standards of Business Conduct." Palo Alto, CA.

Hillman, Amy J., Gerald D. Keim, and Rebecca A. Luce. (2001). "Board Composition and Stakeholder Performance: Do Stakeholder Directors Make a Difference." *Business & Society, 40,* 295–314.

Hirschman, Albert O. (1970). *Exit, Voice, and Loyalty.* Cambridge, MA: Harvard University Press.

Hix, Simon. (2005). The Political System of the European Union. Basingstoke: Macmillan/Palgrave.

Hobbes, Thomas. (1651). *Leviathan.* Edited by C. B. Macpherson. Reprint, London, UK: Pelican Books, 1968.

Holt, Charles A., and David T. Scheffman. (1989). "Strategic Business Behavior and Antitrust." In Larner and Meehan (1989), 39–82.

Hong, Harrison, and Marcin Kacperczyk. (2007). "The Price of Sin: The Effects of Social Norms on Markets." Working paper, Princeton University.

Hoscheit, J. M., and W. Wessels (Eds.). (1988). *The European Council 1974–1986: Evaluation and Prospects.* European Institute of Public Administration.

Huber, Peter, and Robert E. Litan (Eds.). (1991). *The Liability Maze: The Impact of Liability Law on Safety and Innovation.* Washington, DC: Brookings.

Hufbauer, Gary C., and Kimberly A. Elliott. (1994). *Measuring the Costs of Protection in the United States.* Washington, DC: Institute for International Economics.

Hufbauer, Gary C., Daniel C. Esty, Diana Orejas, Luis Rubio, and Jeffrey J. Schott. (2000). *NAFTA and the Environment: Seven Years Later.* Washington, DC: Institute for International Economics.

Huddleston, Jackson N. (1990). *Gaijan Kaisha: Running a Foreign Business in Japan.* Armonk, NY: M. E. Sharpe.

Ilinitch, Anne Y., Naomi S. Soderstrom, and Tom E. Thomas. (1998). "Measuring Corporate Environmental Performance." *Journal of Accounting and Public Policy, 17,* 383–408.

Inoguchi, Takashi, and Daniel I. Okimoto (Eds.). (1988). *The Political Economy of Japan: Volume 2, The Changing International Context.* Stanford, CA: Stanford University Press.

Investor Responsibility Research Center. (1993). "Voting by Institutional Investors on Corporate Governance Issues." Washington, DC.

Ito, Takatoshi. (1992). *The Japanese Economy.* Cambridge, MA: MIT Press.

Ivanhoe, Philip J. (1993). *Confucian Moral Self Cultivation.* New York: Peter Lang.

Iyengar, Shanto, and Donald R. Kinder. (1987). *News That Matters.* Chicago: University of Chicago Press.

Iyori, Hiroshi, and Akinori Uesuji. (1983). *The Antimonopoly Law in Japan.* New York: Federal Legal Publications.

Jackson, John H., and Edwin A. Vermulst. (1989). *Antidumping Laws and Practice.* Ann Arbor: University of Michigan Press.

Jensen, Michael J. (1988). "Takeovers: Their Causes and Consequences." *Journal of Economic Perspectives.* 2: 21–44.

_____. (2001). "Value Maximization, Stakeholder Theory, and the Corporate Objective Function." *Journal of Applied Corporate Finance.* 14: 8–21.

John, Stefanie, and Daniela Schwarzer. (2006). "Industrial Lobbying within the European Union: Actors, Strategies, and Trends in the Multi-Level System." American Institute for Contemporary German Studies, Johns Hopkins University.

Johnson, Chalmers. (1989). "MITI, MPT, and the Telecom Wars: How Japan Makes Policy for High Technology." In Johnson, Tyson, and Zysman (1989), 177–240.

Johnson, Chalmers, Laura D'Andrea Tyson, and John Zysman. (1989). *Politics and Productivity: The Real Story of Why Japan Works.* Cambridge, MA: Ballinger.

Jonsen, Albert R., and Stephen Toulmin. (1988). *The Abuse of Casuistry.* Berkeley: University of California Press.

Joskow, Paul L., and Richard Schmalensee. (1983). *Markets for Power: An Analysis of Electric Utility Deregulation.* Cambridge, MA: MIT Press.

_____. (1998). "The Political Economy of Market-Based Environmental Policy: The U.S. Acid Rain Program." *Journal of Law and Economics, 41*(April), 37–84.

Joskow, Paul L., Richard Schmalensee, and Elizabeth M. Bailey. (1998). "The Market for Sulfur Dioxide Emissions." *American Economic Review, 88*(September), 669–685.

Jury Verdict Research. (2001). *Personal Injury Valuation Handbook: Current Award Trends in Personal Injury, 2001 Edition.* LRP Publications.

Kahn, David. (1967). *The Codebreakers.* New York: Macmillan.

Kalt, Joseph P. (1981). *The Economics and Politics of Oil Price Regulation.* Cambridge, MA: MIT Press.

Kaplan, Robert, and David Norton. 1992. "The Balanced Scorecard—Measures That Drive Performance." *Harvard Business Review.*

Kant, Immanuel. (1785). *Ethical Philosophy, (a) Grounding for the Metaphysics of Morals; (1785) (b) The Metaphysical Principles of Virtue* (1797). Translation by James W. Ellington, introduction by Warner A. Wick. Indianapolis, IN: Hackett, 1983.

Karnani, Aneel. 2007. "Fortune at the Bottom of the Pyramid: A Mirage." Working paper, University of Michigan. *California Management Review* (forthcoming).

Karpoff, Jonathan M., and Paul H. Malatesta. (1989). "The Wealth Effects of Second-Generation State Take-Over Legislation." *Journal of Financial Economics,* 25, 291–322.

Keim, Gerald D. (1985). "Corporate Grassroots Programs in the 1980s." *California Management Review,* 28(Fall), 110–123.

Kerwin, Cornelius M. (1994). *Rulemaking: How Government Agencies Write Law and Make Policy.* Washington, DC: CQ Press.

_____. (2003). *Rulemaking: How Government Agencies Write Law and Make Policy* (3d ed.). Washington, DC: CQ Press.

Khanna, Tarun and Yishay Yafeh. (2007). "Business Groups in Emerging Markets: Paragons or Parasites." *Journal of Economic Literature,* 45, 331–372.

Kimmel, Lisa. (2008). "U.S. Tort Liability Index: 2008 Report." University of California—Berkeley, working paper.

King, Andrew A., and Michael J. Lenox. (2000). "Industry Self-Regulation without Sanctions: The Chemical Industry's Responsible Care Program." *Academy of Management Journal,* 43, 698–716.

_____. (2002). "Exploring the Locus of Profitable Pollution Reduction." *Management Science,* 48, 289–299.

King, Brayden G., and Sarah A. Soule. (2007). "Social Movements as Extra-institutional Entrepreneurs: The Effect of Protests on Stock Price Returns." *Administrative Science Quarterly.* 52: 413–442.

Klitgaard, Robert. (1988). *Controlling Corruption.* Berkeley: University of California Press.

Kneese, Alvin V., and Charles L. Schultze. (1975). *Pollution, Prices, and Public Policy.* Washington, DC: Brookings.

Kohler-Koch, Beate. (1998). *The Evolution and Transformation of European Governance.* Vienna: Institute for Advanced Studies.

Koku, Paul Sergius, Aigbe Akhigbe, and Thomas M. Springer. (1997). "The Financial Impact of Boycotts and Threats of Boycotts." *Journal of Business Research,* 40, 15–20.

Konar, Shameek, and Mark A. Cohen. (1997). "Information as Regulation: The Effect of Community Right to Know Laws on Toxic Emissions." *Journal of Environmental Economics & Management,* 32, 109–124.

Kotchian, A. Carl. (1977, July 9). "The Payoff: Lockheed's 70-Day Mission to Tokyo." *Saturday Review,* 5–12.

Krehbiel, Keith. (1991). *Information and Legislative Organization.* Ann Arbor: University of Michigan Press.

_____. (1996). "Institutional and Partisan Sources of Gridlock: A Theory of Divided and Unified Government." *Journal of Theoretical Politics,* 8, 7–40.

_____. (1998). *Pivotal Politics: A Theory of U.S. Lawmaking.* Chicago, IL: University of Chicago Press.

_____. (1999). "Pivotal Politics: A Refinement of Nonmarket Analysis for Voting Institutions." *Business and Politics,* 1(April).

Kreps, David M. (1990). "Corporate Culture and Economic Theory." In Alt and Shepsle (1990), 90–143.

Kreps, David M., and Robert Wilson. (1982). "Reputation and Imperfect Information." *Journal of Economic Theory,* 27, 253–279.

Kridel, Donald J., David E. M. Sappington, and Dennis L. Weisman. (1996). "The Effects of Incentive Regulation in the Telecommunications Industry: A Survey." *Journal of Regulatory Economics,* 9, 269–306.

Kroszner, Randall S., and Thomas Stratmann. (1998). "Interest Group Competition and the Organization of Congress: Theory and Evidence from Financial Services Political Action Committees." *American Economic Review,* 88(December), 1163–1187.

Krugman, Paul (Ed.). (1986). *Strategic Trade Policy and the New International Economics.* Cambridge, MA: MIT Press.

Krugman, Paul R. (1990). *Rethinking International Trade.* Cambridge, MA: MIT Press.

Küng, Hans. (1997). "A Global Ethic in an Age of Globalization." *Business Ethics Quarterly,* 7, 17–32.

Küng-Shankleman, Lucy. (2000). *Inside the BBC and CNN: Managing News Organizations.* London: Routledge.

Kupfer, Joseph. (1993). "The Ethics of Genetic Screening in the Workplace." *Business Ethics Quarterly,* 3, 17–25.

Kwoka, John E., Jr., and Lawrence J. White (Eds.). (1999). *The Antitrust Revolution: Economics, Competition, and Policy.* Oxford, UK: Oxford University Press.

Lake, Charles D., II. (1998). "Liberalizing Japan's Insurance Market." In Gibney (1998), 116–141.

Lande, Stephen L., and Craig Vangrasstek. (1986). *The Trade and Tariff Act of 1984: Trade Policy in the Reagan Administration.* Lexington, MA: Lexington Books.

Lardy, Nicholas R. 1998. *China's Unfinished Economic Revolution.* Washington, DC: Brookings.

Larner, Robert J., and James W. Meehan, Jr. (Eds.). (1989). *Economics and Antitrust Policy.* New York: Quorum.

Lenox, Michael, and Charles Eesley. (2008). "Private Environmental Activism and the Selection and Response of Firm Targets." *Journal of Economics and Strategy.* (forthcoming).

Leuz, Christian, and Felix Oberholzer-Gee. (2006). "Political Relationships, Global Financing, and Corporate Transparency: Evidence from Indonesia." *Journal of Financial Economics,* 81, 411–439.

Levin, Staci. (1999). "Who Are We Protecting? A Critical Evaluation of United States Encryption Technology Export Controls." *Law and Policy in International Business,* Spring, 529–552.

Levine, S. I. (1997). "The United States and China: Managing a Stormy Relationship." In W. A. Joseph (Ed.), *China Briefing 1995–1996.* Armonk, NY: M. E. Sharpe.

Li, Shaomin. (2004). "Why Is Property Right Protection Lacking in China?" *California Management Review,* 46: 99–115.

Lieberthal, Kenneth. (1995). *Governing China.* New York: Norton.

Littlejohn, Stephen E. (1986). "Competition and Cooperation: New Trends in Corporate Public Issue Identification and Resolution." *California Management Review,* 29(Fall), 109–123.

Locke, John. (1690). *The Works of John Locke.* Reprint, Westport, CT: Greenwood, 1989.

Locke, Richard M., Fei Qin, and Alberto Brause. (2007). "Does Monitoring Improve Labor Standards? Lessons from Nike." *Industrial and Labor Relations Review,* 61, 3–31.

Lord, Michael D. (2000). "Constituency-based Lobbying as Corporate Political Strategy: Testing an Agency Theory Perspective." *Business and Politics,* 2, 289–308.

Lowi, Theodore J. (1964). "American Business, Public Policy, Case-Studies, and Political Theory." *World Politics,* 16(July), 677–693.

Lukes, Steven. (1973). *Individualism.* Oxford, UK: Basil Blackwell.

Lynn, Leonard H., and Timothy J. McKeown. (1988). *Organizing Business: Trade Associations in America and Japan.* Washington, DC: American Enterprise Institute.

Lyon, Thomas P., and Eun-Hee Kim. (2007). "Greenhouse Gas Reductions or Greenwash? The DOE's 1605b Program." Working paper, University of Michigan.

Lyons, David. (1965). *The Forms and Limits of Utilitarianism.* Oxford, UK: Oxford University Press.

MacAvoy, Paul W. (1981, December 20). "The Business Lobby's Wrong Business." *The New York Times.*

Mackey, John. (2005). "Putting Customers Ahead of Investors." *Reason.* October.

Magat, Wesley A., Alan J. Krupnick, and Winston Harrington. (1986). *Rules in the Making: A Statistical Analysis of Regulatory Agency Behavior.* Washington, DC: Resources for the Future.

Magee, Stephen P., William A. Brock, and Leslie Young. (1989). *Black Hole Tariffs and Endogenous Policy Theory: Political Economy in General Equilibrium.* Cambridge, UK: Cambridge University Press.

Mahon, John F., and Jennifer J. Griffin. (1999). "Painting a Portrait." *Business & Society,* 38(March), 126–133.

Mahoney, Richard J., and Stephen E. Littlejohn. (1989). "Innovation on Trial: Punitive Damages Versus New Products." *Science,* 15(December), 1398.

Manheim, Jarol B. (2001). *The Death of a Thousand Cuts.* Mahwah, NJ: Lawrence Erlbaum.

Marcus, Alfred A., Allen M. Kaufman, and David R. Beam (Eds.). (1987). *Business Strategy and Public Policy.* New York: Quorum Books.

Margolis, Joshua D., and James P. Walsh. (2001). *People or Profits? The Search for a Link Between a Company's Social and Financial Performance.* Mahwah, NJ: Lawrence Erlbaum.

———. (2003). "Misery Loves Companies: Rethinking Social Initiatives by Business." *Administrative Sciences Quarterly.* 48: 268–305.

Mashaw, Jerry L., and Richard A. Merrill. (1985). *Administrative Law: The American Public Law System: Cases and Materials* (2d ed.). St. Paul, MN: West Publishing.

Mason, Mark. (1992). *Access Denied?: American Multinationals and Japan, 1899–1980.* Cambridge, MA: Harvard University Press.

Maxwell, John W., Thomas P. Lyon, and Steven C. Hackett. (2000). "Self-Regulation and Social Welfare: The Political Economy of Corporate Environmentalism." *Journal of Law & Economics,* 43(October), 583–617.

Mayhew, David. (1974). *Congress: The Electoral Connection.* New Haven, CT: Yale University Press.

McCraw, Thomas K. (Ed.). (1981). *Regulation in Perspective: Historical Essays.* Boston: Harvard Business School.

McCubbins, Mathew, Roger Noll, and Barry Weingast. (1987). "Administrative Procedures as Instruments of Political Control." *Journal of Law, Economics and Organizations,* 3, 243–277.

McDonald's Corporation—Environmental Defense Fund, Waste Reduction Task Force. (1991). "Final Report," April.

McGuire, J. B., T. Schneeweis, and B. Branch. (1990). "Perceptions of Firm Quality: A Cause or Result of Firm Performance." *Journal of Management,* 16, 167–180.

McGuire, Jean B., Alison Sundgren, and Thomas Schneeweis. (1988). "Corporate Social Responsibility and Firm Financial Performance." *Academy of Management Journal,* 31, 854–872.

McMillan, John. (1991). "DANGO: Japan's Price-Fixing Conspiracies." *Economics and Politics,* 3(November), 201–218.

McWilliams, Abagail, and Donald Siegel. (2001). "Corporate Social Responsibility: A Theory of the Firm Perspective." *Academy of Management Review,* 26, 117–127.

Milgrom, Paul, and John D. Roberts. (1982). "Limit Pricing and Entry under Incomplete Information." *Econometrica,* 50, 443–459.

Mill, John Stuart. (1859). *On Liberty.* Edited by David Spitz. New York: Norton. 1975.

———. (1861). "Utilitarianism." In Alan Ryan (Ed.), *Utilitarianism and Other Essays: J. S. Mill and Jeremy Bentham.* New York: Penguin Books, 1987.

Milyo, Jeffrey, David Primo, and Timothy Groseclose. (2000). "Corporate PAC Campaign Contributions in Perspective." *Business and Politics,* 2, 75–88.

Mitnick, Barry M. (1980). *The Political Economy of Regulation.* New York: Columbia University Press.

Moe, Terry M. (1980). *The Organization of Interests.* Chicago: University of Chicago Press.

———. (1985). "Congressional Control of the Bureaucracy: An Assessment of the Positive Theory of 'Congressional Dominance.'" Paper presented at the American Political Science Association annual meeting.

Moore, Barrington. (1966). *Social Origins of Dictatorship and Democracy.* Boston: Beacon Press.

Morduch, Jonathan. (1999). "The Microfinance Promise." *Journal of Economic Literature,* 37, 1569–1614.

Morishima, Michio. (1988). "Confucianism as a Basis for Capitalism." In Okimoto and Rohlen (1988), 36–38.

Mroczkowski, Thomas, and Masao Hanaoka. (1989). "Continuity and Change in Japanese Management." *California Management Review,* 31, 39–53.

Mundo, Philip A. (1992). *Interest Groups: Cases and Characteristics.* Chicago: Nelson-Hall Publishers.

Muramatsu, Michio, and Ellis S. Krauss. (1987). "The Conservative Policy Line and the Development of Patterned Pluralism." In Kozo Yamamura and Yasukichi Yasuba (Eds.), *The Political Economy of Japan: Volume I. The Domestic Transformation.* Stanford, CA: Stanford University Press.

Natural Resources Defense Council. (1989, February 27). "Intolerable Risk: Pesticides in Our Children's Food." Washington, DC.

Naughton, Barry. (2007). *The Chinese Economy: Transitions and Growth.* MIT Press: Cambridge, MA.

Newman, Edwin. (1984). "A Journalist's Responsibility." In Schumhl (1984), 19–38.

Nivison, David S. (1996). *The Ways of Confucianism.* Chicago: Open Court.

Noll, Roger G., and Bruce M. Owen. (1983). *The Political Economy of Deregulation: Interest Groups in the Regulatory Process.* Washington, DC: American Enterprise Institute.

Norman, Wayne, and Chris MacDonald. (2003). "Getting to the Bottom of 'Triple Bottom Line.'" *Business Ethics Quarterly.*

North, Douglass C. (1990). *Institutions, Institutional Change and Economic Performance.* Cambridge, UK: Cambridge University Press.

Nozick, Robert. (1974). *Anarchy, State, and Utopia.* New York: Basic Books.

Nugent, Neill. (2003). *The Government and Politics of the European Union* (5th ed.). Durham, NC: Duke University Press.

O'Halloran, Sharyn. (1994). *Politics, Process, and American Foreign Policy.* Ann Arbor: University of Michigan Press.

Okimoto, Daniel I. (1989). *Between MITI and the Market: Japanese Industrial Policy for High Technology.* Stanford, CA: Stanford University Press.

Okimoto, Daniel I., and Thomas P. Rohlen (Eds.). (1988). *Inside the Japanese System: Readings on Contemporary Society and Political Economy.* Stanford, CA: Stanford University Press.

Oleszek, Walter J. (2004). *Congressional Procedures and the Policy Process* (6th ed.). Washington, DC: CQ Press.

Olson, Mancur J. (1965). *The Logic of Collective Action.* Cambridge, MA: Harvard University Press.

Ordover, Janusz A., and Robert D. Willig. (1983). "The 1982 Department of Justice Merger Guidelines: An Economic Assessment." *California Law Review,* 71, 535–574.

Orlitsky, Marc, Frank L. Schmidt, and Sara L. Rynes. (2003). "Corporate Social and Financial Performance: A Meta-analysis." *Organization Studies,* 24, 403–411.

Ornstein, Norman J., Thomas E. Mann, and Michael J. Malbin. (2008). *Vital Statistics on Congress 2008.* Washington, DC: Brookings.

Oster, Sharon M. (1999). *Modern Competitive Analysis* (3d ed.). Oxford, UK: Oxford University Press.

Overturf, Stephen F. (1986). *The Economic Principles of European Integration.* New York: Praeger.

Owen, Bruce M., and Ronald Braeutigam. (1978). *The Regulation Game: Strategic Use of the Administrative Process.* Cambridge, MA: Balinger.

Paine, Lynn Sharp. (1994). "Managing for Organizational Integrity." *Harvard Business Review,* March–April, 106–117.

Palmier, Leslie. (1989). "Corruption in the West Pacific." *The Pacific Review,* 2(1), 23.

Pastin, Mark, and Michael Hooker. (1988). "Ethics and the Foreign Corrupt Practices Act." In Donaldson and Werhane (1988), 48–53.

Pearson, Margaret M. (1991). *Joint Ventures in the People's Republic of China.* Princeton, NJ: Princeton University Press.

Pei, M. (1997). "Racing Against Time: Institutional Decay and Renewal in China." In William A. Joseph (Ed.), *China Briefing 1995–1996,* Armonk, NY: M. E. Sharpe.

Peltzman, Sam. (1975). "The Effects of Automobile Safety Regulation." *Journal of Political Economy,* 83(August), 677–725.

_____. (1976). "Toward a More General Theory of Regulation." *Journal of Law and Economics,* 19, 211–240.

Peterson, Steven P., and George E. Hoffer. (1994). "The Impact of Airbag Adoption on Relative Personal Injury and Absolute Collision Insurance Claims." *Journal of Consumer Research,* 20(March), 657–662.

Pfeffer, Jeffrey, and Gerald Salancik. (1978). *The External Control of Organizations.* New York: Harper and Row.

Pierson, Paul. (1999). "Social Policy and European Integration." In Andrew Moravcsik (Ed.), *Centralization or Fragmentation: Europe Facing the Challenges of Deepening, Diversity, and Democracy.* New York: Council on Foreign Relations.

Polinsky, A. Mitchell. (2003). *An Introduction to Law and Economics* (3d ed.). New York: Aspen Publications.

Popoff, Frank P. (1992). "Going Beyond Pollution Prevention." In *Business: Championing the Global Environment,* Report Number 995, The Conference Board, New York.

Porter, Michael E. (1980). *Competitive Strategy: Techniques for Analyzing Industries and Competitions.* New York: Free Press.

_____. (1985). *Competitive Advantage.* New York: Free Press.

Porter, Michael E., and C. van der Linde. (1995). "Toward a New Conception of the Environment-Competitiveness Relationship." *Journal of Economic Perspectives,* 9, 97–118.

Posner, Richard A. (1974). "Theories of Economic Regulation." *Bell Journal of Economics,* 5(Autumn), 335–358.

_____. (1976). *Antitrust Law: An Economic Perspective.* Chicago: University of Chicago Press.

_____. (1981). *The Economics of Justice.* Cambridge, MA: Harvard University Press.

Post, James E., Lee F. Preston, and Sybille Sachs. (2002). "Managing the Extended Enterprise: The New Stakeholder View." *California Management Review.* 45: 6–28.

Poterba, James M. (1991). "Tax Policy to Combat Global Warming: On Designing a Carbon Tax." In Dornbusch and Poterba (1991), 71–98.

Potoski, Matthew, and Aseem Prakash. (2005). "Green Clubs and Voluntary Governance: ISO 14001 and Firms' Regulatory Compliance." *American Journal of Political Science.* (Forthcoming.)

Povich, Elaine S. (1996). *Partners and Adversaries.* Arlington, Va.: The Freedom Forum.

Prahalad, C.K. 2004. *The Fortune at the Bottom of the Pyramid: Eradicating Poverty through Profits.* Philadelphia: Wharton School Press.

Prahalad, C. K., and Gary Hamel. (1990). "The Core Competencies of the Corporation." *Harvard Business Review,* May–June, 79–91.

Prakash, Aseem. (2001). "Beyond Seattle: Globalization, the Nonmarket Environment, and Corporate Strategy." *Review of International Political Economy,* 8.

Prakash, Aseem, and Jeffrey A. Hart. (Eds.). (1999). *Globalization and Governance.* London, UK: Routledge.

President's Blue Ribbon Commission on Defense Management. (1986). "A Formula for Action." Washington, DC.

Priest, George L. (1977). "The Common Law Process and the Selection of Efficient Rules." *Journal of Legal Studies,* 6(January), 65–82.

Pruitt, S. W., and Monroe Friedman. (1986). "Determining the Effectiveness of Consumer Boycotts: A Stock Price Analysis of Their Impact on Corporate Targets." *Journal of Consumer Policy,* 9, 375–387.

Pruitt, S. W., K. C. John Wei, and Richard E. White. (1988). "The Impact of Union-Sponsored Boycotts on the Stock Prices of Target Firms." *Journal of Labor Research,* 9, 285–289.

Putnam, Todd. (1993). "Boycotts Are Busting Out All Over." *Business and Society Review,* 47–51.

Pye, Lucian W. (1978). *China: An Introduction.* Boston: Little, Brown.

_____. (1985). *Asian Power and Politics: The Cultural Dimensions of Authority.* Boston: Little, Brown.

_____. (1988). *The Mandarin and the Cadre: China's Political Cultures.* Ann Arbor: University of Michigan Press.

Quirk, Paul J. (1981). *Industry Influence in Federal Regulatory Agencies.* Princeton, NJ: Princeton University Press.

Rawls, John. (1971). *A Theory of Justice.* Cambridge, MA: Belknap Press.

_____. (1980). "Kantian Constructivism in Moral Theory." *The Journal of Philosophy,* 9(September), 515–572.

_____. (1993). *Political Liberalism.* New York: Columbia University Press.

_____. (2001). *Justice as Fairness: A Restatement,* edited by Erin Kelly. Harvard University Press: Cambridge, MA.

Redding, S. Gordon. (1996). "Societal Transformation and the Contribution of Authority Relations and Cooperative Norms in Overseas Chinese Business." In Wei-ming Tu (Ed.), *Confucian Traditions in East Asian Modernity.* Cambridge, MA: Harvard University Press.

Reed, Steven R. (1986). *Japanese Prefectures and Policymaking.* Pittsburgh, PA: University of Pittsburgh Press.

Reich, Robert B. (1998). "The New Meaning of Corporate Social Responsibility." *California Management Review,* 40(Winter), 8–17.

Reischauer, Edwin O. (1988). *The Japanese Today: Change and Continuity.* Cambridge, MA: Belknap Press.

Rehbein, K., S. Waddock, and S.B. Graves. (2004). "Understanding Shareholder Activism: Which Corporations are Targeted?" *Business and Society.* 43: 239–267.

Richards, Jonathon D. (1993). "Japan Fair Trade Commission Guidelines Concerning Distribution System and Business Practices: An Illustration of Why Antitrust Law Is a Weak Solution to U.S. Trade Problems with Japan." *Wisconsin Law Review,* 921–960.

Rodgers, T. J. (2005). "Put Profits First." *Reason.* October.

Roman, Ronald M., Sefa Hayibor, and Bradley R. Agle. (1999). "The Relationship Between Social and Financial Performance: Repainting a Portrait." *Business & Society,* 38(March): 109–125.

Rose, Nancy L. (1985). "The Incidence of Regulatory Rents in the Motor Carrier Industry." *RAND Journal of Economics,* 16(Autumn), 299–318.

_____. (1987). "Labor Rent Sharing and Regulation: Evidence from the Trucking Industry." *Journal of Political Economy,* 95, 1146–1178.

Rosenbaum, Walter A. (2007). *Environmental Politics and Policy* (7th ed.). Washington, DC: Congressional Quarterly.

Rosenthal, Douglas E. (1990). "Competition Policy." In Gary C. Hufbauer, *Europe 1992: An American Perspective,* 292–343. Washington, DC: Brookings.

Rousseau, Jean Jacques. (1762). *On the Social Contract.* Reprint, New York: Harper and Row, 1984.

Rubin, Paul H. (1983). *Business Firms and the Common Law: The Evolution of Efficient Rules.* New York: Praeger.

Rugman, Alan, John Kirton, and Julie Soloway. (1999). *Environmental Regulations and Corporate Strategy: A NAFTA Perspective.* Oxford, UK: Oxford University Press.

Sabato, Larry J. (1984). *PAC Power: Inside the World of Political Action Committees.* New York: Norton.

Sackett, P. R., and M. M. Harris. (1984). "Honesty Testing for Personnel Selection: A Review and Critique." *Personnel Psychology,* 37, 221–245.

Salisbury, Robert H. (1992). *Interests and Institutions.* Pittsburgh: University of Pittsburgh Press.

Saloner, Garth, Andrea Shepard, and Joel M. Podolny. (2001). *Strategic Management.* New York: Wiley.

Saloner, Garth, and A. Michael Spence. (2002). *Creating and Capturing Value: Perspectives and Cases on Electronic Commerce.* New York: Wiley.

Salop, Steven C., and Lawrence J. White. (1988). "Private Antitrust Litigation: An Introduction and Framework." In White (1988).

Sasser, Erika N., Aseem Prakash, Benjamin Cashore, and Graema Auld. (2006). "Direct Targeting as an NGO Political Strategy: Examining Private Authority Regimes in the Forestry Sector." *Business and Politics,* 8, Article 1.

Schaede, Ultike. (1998). "Bureaucrats in Business." In Gibney (1998), 160–170.

Schmalensee, Richard, Paul L. Joskow, A. Denny Ellerman, Juan Pablo Montero, and Elizabeth M. Bailey. (1998). "An Interim Evaluation of Sulfur Dioxide Emissions Trading." *Journal of Economic Perspectives,* 12(Summer), 53–68.

Schmidt, Benno C., Jr. (1981). "The First Amendment and the Press." In Elie Abel (Ed.), *What's News,* 57–80. San Francisco: Institute for Contemporary Studies.

Schmuhl, Robert (Ed.). (1984). *The Responsibilities of Journalism.* Notre Dame, IN: University of Notre Dame Press.

Schoenberger, Karl. (2000). *Levi's Children: Coming to Terms with Human Rights in the Global Marketplace.* New York: Grove Press.

Schuknecht, Ludger. (1992). *Trade Protection in the European Community.* Chur, Switzerland: Harwood Academic.

Schwartz, Benjamin I. (1985). *The World of Thought in Ancient China.* Cambridge, MA: Harvard University Press.

Sen, Amartya. (1987). *On Ethics & Economics.* Oxford, UK: Basil Blackwell.

_____. (1997). "Economics, Business Principles and Moral Sentiments." *Business Ethics Quarterly,* 7, 5–15.

Sen, Amartya, and Bernard Williams (Eds.). (1982). *Utilitarianism and Beyond.* Cambridge, UK: Cambridge University Press.

Shaffer, Brian, and Daniel T. Ostas. (2001). "Exploring the Political Economy of Consumer Legislation: The Development of Automobile Lemon Laws." *Business and Politics,* 3, 65–76.

Shapiro, Carl, and Hal R. Varian. (1999). *Information Rules: A Strategic Guide to the Network Economy.* Boston: Harvard University Press.

Shaw, Malcolm W. (1997). *International Law* (4th ed.). Cambridge, UK: Cambridge University Press.

_____. (2003). *International Law* (5th ed.). Cambridge, UK: Cambridge University Press.

Shepsle, Kenneth A., and Mark S. Bonchek. (1997). *Analyzing Politics: Rationality, Behavior, and Institutions.* New York: Norton.

Shils, Edward. (1996). "Reflections on Civil Society and Civility in the Chinese Intellectual Tradition." In Wei-ming Tu (Ed.), *Confucian Traditions in East Asian Modernity.* Cambridge, MA: Harvard University Press.

Shipper, Frank, and Marianne M. Jennings. (1984). *Business Strategy for the Political Arena.* Westport, CT: Quorum Books.

Shirk, Susan L. (1993). *The Political Logic of Economic Reform in China.* Berkeley: University of California Press.

Shue, Henry. (1980). *Basic Rights: Subsistence, Affluence, and U.S. Foreign Power.* Princeton, NJ: Princeton University Press.

Shue, Vivienne. (1988). *The Reach of the State.* Stanford, CA: Stanford University Press.

Shugart, William F., II. (1990). *Antitrust Policy and Interest-Group Politics.* New York: Quorum Books.

Siegel, Jordan and Barbara Zepp Larson. (2007). "Labor Market Institutions and Global Strategic Adaptation: Evidence from Lincoln Electric." Working paper, Harvard Business School, Boston, MA.

Sigman, Betsy Ann, and Susan-Kathryn McDonald. (1987). "The Issues Manager as Public Opinion and Policy Analyst." In Marcus, Kaufman, and Beam (1987), 164–194.

Skelly, Joe. (1995). "The Rise of International Ethics: The Caux Round Table Principles for Business." *Business Ethics,* March–April Supplement, 2–5.

Smith, Adam. (1776). *An Inquiry into the Nature and Causes of the Wealth of Nations.* Edited by R. H. Campbell and A. S. Skinner. Oxford, UK: Clarendon Press. 1995.

Snyder, James M., Jr. (1991). "On Buying Legislatures." *Economics and Politics,* 3(July), 93–109.

Sonnenfeld, Jeffrey, and Paul R. Lawrence. (1978). "Why Do Companies Succumb to Price Fixing?" *Harvard Business Review,* 56(July–August), 145–157.

Sood, Neeraj and Arkadipta Ghosh. (2007). "The Short and Long Run Effects of Daylight Saving Time on Fatal Automobile Crashes." *B.E. Journal of Economic Analysis & Policy,* 7, Article 11.

Spar, Deborah L., and Lane T. La Mure. (2003). "The Power of Activism: Assessing the Impact of NGOs on Global Business." *California Management Review,* 45: 78–101.

Sparrow, Batholomew H. (1999). *Uncertain Guardians: The News Media as a Political Institution.* Baltimore: Johns Hopkins University Press.

Spence, A. Michael. (1973). "Job Market Signaling." *Quarterly Journal of Economics,* 87, 355–374.

Spitzer, Matthew L. (1991). "Justifying Minority Preferences in Broadcasting." *Southern California Law Review,* 293, 334–336.

Spulber, Daniel F. (1989). *Regulation and Markets.* Cambridge, MA: MIT Press.

Stavins, Robert N. (1998). "What Can We Learn from the Grand Policy Experiment? Lessons from SO_2 Allowance Trading." *Economic Perspectives,* 12(Summer), 69–88.

Stender, Terrence. (1998). "Too Many Secrets: Challenges to the Control of Strong Crypto and the National Security Perspective." *Case Western Reserve Journal of International Law,* Winter, 287–337.

Stigler, George. (1971). "The Theory of Economic Regulation." *Bell Journal of Regulation,* 2(Spring), 3–21.

Streeck, Wolfgang. (1984). *Industrial Relations in West Germany.* New York: St. Martin's Press.

Swire, Peter P., and Robert E. Litan. (1998). *None of Your Business.* Washington, DC: Brookings.

Tachibanaki, Toshiaki. (1984). "Labor Mobility and Job Tenure." In Aoki (1984), 77–102.

Taka, Iwao. (1994). "Business Ethics: A Japanese View." *Business Ethics Quarterly,* 4, 53–78.

Teece, David J. (2000). *Managing Intellectual Capital.* Oxford, UK: Oxford University Press.

Temin, Peter, with Louis Galambos. (1987). *The Fall of the Bell System.* Cambridge, UK: Cambridge University Press.

Teoh, Slew Hong, Ivo Welch, and C. Paul Wazzan. (1999). "The Effect of Socially Activist Investment Policies on the Financial Markets: Evidence from the South African Boycott." *Journal of Business,* 72, 35–89.

Thompson, James. (1967). *Organizations in Action.* New York: McGraw-Hill.

Tirole, Jean. (2005). *The Theory of Corporate Finance.* Princeton, NJ: Princeton University Press.

Tomlinson, R. (1997). "A Chinese Giant Forges a Capitalist Soul." *Fortune* (September 29): 184–192.

Trebilcock, Michael J., and Robert C. York. (1990). *Fair Exchange: Reforming Trade Remedy Laws.* Toronto, Canada: C. D. Howe Institute.

Tu, Wei-ming. (1979). *Humanity and Self-Cultivation.* Berkeley: University of California Press.

Tyler, Lisa. (1997). "Liability Means Never Being Able to Say You're Sorry. Corporate Guilt, Legal Constraints, and Defensiveness in Corporate Communication." *Management Communication Quarterly,* 11, 51–73.

Uhlmann, Eric Luis, George Newman, Victoria Brescoll, Adam Galinsky, and Daniel Diermeier. (2008). "The Sound of Silence: Effects of an Engaged, Defensive, and No Comment Response to a Crisis on Corporate Reputation." Working paper, Northwestern University.

Ulmann, A. (1985). "Data in Search of a Theory: A Critical Examination of the Relationship Among Social Performance, Social Disclosure, and Economic Performance." *Academy of Management Review,* 10, 540–577.

Upham, Frank K. (1987). *Law and Social Change in Postwar Japan.* Cambridge, MA: Harvard University Press.

Urata, Shuijiro. (2001). "Europe's Trade and Foreign Direct Investment in Asia." In Aggarwal (2001), 31–58.

Vachani, Sushil and N. Craig Smith. (2004). "Socially Responsible Pricing: Lessons from the Pricing of AIDS Drugs in Developing Countries." *California Management Review,* 47, 117–144.

Van Schendelen, M. P. C. M. (1993). "The Netherlands: Lobby It Yourself." In M. P. C. M. Van Schendelen (Ed.), *National Public and Private EC Lobbying.* Hants, UK: Aldershot.

Van Wolferen, Karel. (1989). *The Enigma of Japanese Power.* New York: Alfred A. Knopf.

Vaughn, Jacqueline. (2007). *Environmental Politics: Domestic and Global Dimensions* (5th ed.). Belmont, CA; Wadsworth.

Velasquez, Manuel G. (1998). *Business Ethics: Concepts and Cases* (4th ed.). Upper Saddle River, NJ: Prentice Hall.

Viscusi, W. Kip. (1991). *Reforming Products Liability.* Cambridge, MA: Harvard University Press.

Viscusi, W. Kip, and Michael J. Moore. (1993). "Product Liability, Research and Development, and Innovation." *Journal of Political Economy,* 101, 161–184.

Viscusi, W. Kip, John M. Vernon, and Joseph E. Harrington, Jr. (2000). *Economics of Regulation and Antitrust* (3d ed.). Cambridge, MA: MIT Press.

Viscusi, W. Kip, John M. Vernon, and Joseph E. Harrington, Jr. (2005). *Economics of Regulation and Antitrust* (4th ed.). Cambridge, MA: MIT Press.

Vogel, David. (1978). *Lobbying the Corporation: Citizen Challenges to Business Authority.* New York: Basic Books.

_____. (1986). *National Styles of Regulation: Environmental Policy in Great Britain and the United States.* Ithaca, NY: Cornell University Press.

_____. (1991). "Business Ethics: New Perspectives on Old Problems." *California Business Review,* 33(Summer), 101–117.

Vogel, David. (2005). *Can Corporations Be Made Responsible? The Potential and Limits of Corporate Social Responsibility.* Washington, DC: Brookings.

Waddock, Sandra A., and Samuel B. Graves. (1997). "The Corporate Social Performance–Financial Performance Link." *Strategic Management Journal,* 18, 303–319.

Wartick, Steven L., and Robert E. Rude. (1986). "Issues Management: Corporate Fad or Corporate Function?" *California Management Review,* 29(Fall), 124–140.

Wasserstrom, Richard. (1978). "A Defense of Programs of Preferential Treatment." *National Forum: The Phi Kappa Phi Journal,* 58(Winter), 15–18.

Watkins, Sherron S. (2003). "Ethical Conflicts at Enron: Moral Responsibility in Corporate Capitalism." *California Management Review,* 45, 6–19.

Weaver, Suzanne. (1977). *Decision to Prosecute: Organization and Public Policy in the Antitrust Division.* Cambridge, MA: MIT Press.

Weber, Leonard J. (1996). "Citizenship and Democracy: The Ethics of Corporate Lobbying." *Business Ethics Quarterly,* 6(April), 253–259.

Weidenbaum, Murray L. (1996). "The Chinese Family Business Enterprise." *California Management Review*, 38(Summer), 141–156.

Weidenbaum, Murray L. (2004). *Business and Government in the Global Marketplace* (7th ed.). Upper Saddle River, NJ: Pearson Prentice Hall.

Weingast, Barry M., and Mark Moran. (1983). "Bureaucratic Discretion or Congressional Control? Regulatory Policymaking by the Federal Trade Commission." *Journal of Political Economy,* 91(October), 765–800.

Weston, J. Fred, Kwang S. Chung, and Susan E. Hoag. (1990). *Mergers, Restructuring, and Corporate Control.* Upper Saddle River, NJ: Prentice Hall.

White, Lawrence J. (Ed.). (1988). *Private Antitrust Litigation: New Evidence, New Learning.* Cambridge, MA: MIT Press.

White, Michelle J. (2004). "Asbestos and the Future of Mass Torts." Working Paper 10308, National Bureau of Economic Research, Cambridge, MA.

White, Matthew W. (1997). "Power Struggles: Explaining Deregulatory Reforms in Electricity Markets." *Brookings Papers on Economic Activity: Micro-economics,* 201–250.

Williams, Oliver F. (Ed.). (2000). *Global Codes of Conduct: An Idea Whose Time Has Come.* Notre Dame, IN: Notre Dame University Press.

Williamson, Oliver E. (1975). *Markets and Hierarchies: Analysis and Antitrust Implications.* New York: Free Press.

Wilson, James Q. (1980). *The Politics of Regulation.* New York: Basic Books.

_____. (1989). *Bureaucracy: What Government Agencies Do and Why They Do It.* New York: Basic Books.

Wilson, Robert. (2001). "Architecture of Power Markets." Working paper, Stanford University, Stanford, CA.

Wise, Mark, and Richard Gibb. (1993). *Single Market to Social Europe.* Essex, UK: Longman Scientific & Technical.

Wiseman, Alan. (2000). *The Internet Economy: Access, Taxes, and Market Structure.* Washington, DC: Brookings.

Wiseman, Alan E., and Jerry Ellig. (2004). "Market and Nonmarket Barriers to Internet Wine Sales: The Case of Virginia." *Business and Politics,* 6, Article 4.

Wolf, Charles, Jr. (1979). "A Theory of Nonmarket Failure." *Journal of Law and Economics,* 22(April), 107–139.

_____. (1988). *Markets or Governments.* Cambridge, MA: MIT Press.

World Bank. (2004). *World Development Indicators.* Washington, DC.

Wu, Abraham H. (1994). "Contributions, Lobbying, and Participation." Working paper, Stanford University, Stanford, CA.

Yang, C. K. (1959). *Chinese Communist Society: The Family and the Village.* Cambridge, MA: MIT Press.

Yang, M. M. (1994). *Gifts, Favors, and Banquets.* Ithaca, NY: Cornell University Press.

Yayama, Taro. (1998). "Who Has Obstructed Reform?" In Gibney (1998), 91–115.

Yoffie, David B. (1987). "Corporate Strategies for Political Action: A Rational Model." In Marcus, Kaufman, and Beam (1987).

_____. (1988a). "How an Industry Builds Political Advantage." *Harvard Business Review,* May–June, 82–89.

_____. (1988b). Motorola and Japan and Motorola and Japan: Supplements I, II, III, 0–388–057, 0–388–058, 9–388–059. Boston, MA: Harvard Business School.

Young, Louis H. (1978, September 21). "Business and the Media: The Failure to Understand How the Other Operates." Speech delivered at the ITT Key Issues Lecture Series, Columbia, Missouri.

Index

7-Eleven, 209, 616
60 Minutes (television program), 88–89
401(k) plans (Enron), 645–646

Abacus Direct, 428
Abacus Online, 428–431
Abatement, 343
ABB Ltd., 757, 767
Abbott, Herschel, 330
Abbott Laboratories, 133, 602–606, 778, 781
ABC, 74, 333
ABC Disney, 329
Abercrombie & Kent, 56
Abernathy, Kathleen, 326–327, 329, 333, 334
ABN Amro, 357
Abúndez, Alejandra, 567
Accelerated Access Initiative, 746
Access, 192, 225–226, 470, 500
Access to Capital Coalition, 215
ACCION International, 567
Accountability. *See* Social accountability
Accounting and Auditing Organization for Islamic Financial Institutions, 560
Accuracy, in news media, 76–77
Acid rain, cap-and-trade systems for, 345–346
ACORN, 98, 146
Acres for America, 648
Acrylamide, 22
Act Up–Paris, 133, 606
Act utilitarianism, 664–666
Action on Smoking and Health (ASH), 182
Actions, for environmental management and stability, 337–338
Activist organizations, 8–9, 101–103
GlaxoSmithKline case, 781–782
influence of, 91
interacting with, 103–107
See also specific organizations
Activist strategies, 96–101
Ad hoc coalitions, 235
Ad Hoc Committee of AZ-NM-TX-FL Producers of Gray Portland Cement, 598
Adams, Cathie, 245, 246
Adarand Constructors v. Peña, 707, 708
Adelphia Communications, 328
Adelstein, Jonathan, 326, 333, 652
Adjusted minimum tax (AMT), 213–214, 216
Administration, 14, 15
Administrative agencies. *See* Institutions; *specific administrative agencies*
Administrative institutions, responsiveness of, 205
Administrative law judge (ALJ), 350
Administrative Practices Act, 258
Administrative Procedures Act (APA), 306, 307
AdSense, 37, 38
Advanced Technologies Laboratories, Inc., 746–748
Advanced Technology Laboratories, ethics case, 746–748
Advantica Restaurant Group, Inc., 732
Adverse selection, 314

Advertising
children and, 22
direct-to-consumer, 40–41
tobacco politics and, 181, 182
Advisory Commission on Electronic Commerce, 248
Advisory committees, in Japan, 460
Advocacy groups, 8–9, 90–91
Advocacy journalism, 76–77
Advocacy science, 98, 354–355
Adware, 418
AENA, 514, 515
Aer Force Communications, 650–651
Affirmative action, 707–708
AFL-CIO, 147
Age Discrimination in Employment Act, 695
Agence France-Presse, 28
Agencies. *See* Regulatory agencies
Agenda-setting strategies, 201–202
Aggregate benefits, 155
Aggregate utility, 765
Agouron, 778
Agricultural Agreement, 583
Agriculture, international trade agreements and, 583
AIDS, 133, 192
Circle K and, 723
compulsory licensing case, 602–606
developing countries and, 756–758
Gilead Sciences case, 742–746
rights and, 696
AIDS Coalition to Unleash Power (ACT UP!), 780
AIDS drugs policy case, 778–783
AIDS Healthcare Foundation (AHF), 96, 606, 757, 782
Airbus, 164, 166, 170, 204, 494
Airline industry, price fixing case, 289–290
Airspace, 182
Alar, 67–68, 71, 72, 77, 81, 84
Alarmist media coverage, 77
Albertson's, 143, 147
Aldeasa, 511–516
Alfano, Deborah, 244
Alford, Harry, 372
Al-Hadithy, Nabil, 369
Alien Tort Claims Act (ATCA), 750–751
Allchin, James, 297
Allen, Doug, 330
Allergy and Asthma Network/Mothers of Asthmatics (AAN/MA), 255
Alliance for Community Media, 329
Alliance of Automobile Manufacturers, 5, 7, 11, 260–261
Allison, Michael, 420
All Japan Postal Labour Union, 478
Allmark, David, 137
All Nippon Airlines, 763–764
Allstate Insurance, 727
Alpac Corporation, 124
Alstom, 494
Altech, 572
Altruism, 662
Amakudari, 470, 471, 474–475
Amalgamated Clothing and Textile Workers Union, 359
Amazon.com, 28, 44
deregulation, 329

eBay database protection case, 433
Internet taxation, 251, 424
Ambani, Anil, 570, 572
Ambani, Mukesh, 564, 573
AMD, 273
America Online. *See* AOL
American Academy of Allergy, Asthma and Immunology, 254
American Academy of Neurology, 716
American Academy of Otolaryngology—Head and Neck Surgery, 254
American Academy of Pediatrics, 243, 319
American Airlines, 29, 235, 283, 665
American Association of Advertising Agencies, 182
American Association of Health Plans, 221
American Association of Nurserymen, 209
American Association of Retired Persons (AARP), 12, 174, 252, 715
American Bankers Association, 448
American Booksellers Association, 249
American Chamber of Commerce, 231–232, 499, 502
American Civil Liberties Union (ACLU), 329, 430, 431
American College of Obstetricians and Gynecologists' Committee on Ethics, 747
American Council of Life Insurers (ACLI), 478, 671
American Electric Power Company, 341, 347, 728
American Electronics Association, 249, 250, 251
American Express, 272, 497, 732
American Farm Bureau, 210
American Federation of State, County, and Municipal Employees (AFSCME), 195, 230
American Federation of Teachers (AFT), 230
American Feed Industry Association (AFIA), 84–85
American Furniture Manufacturers, 355
American Heart Association, 182
American Home Products Corporation, 19, 189, 675
American Honda Motor Company, 261
American Humane Association, 24
American Law Institute, 395
American League of Lobbyists, 229
American Lung Association, 182
American Medical Association (AMA), 18, 40
American Psychological Association (APA), 694
American Red Cross, 126, 382
American Resort Development Association (ARDA), 57
Americans for Democratic Action, 195
Americans for Nonsmokers' Rights, 182
Americans for Tax Reform, 248
American Society of Newspaper Editors (ASNE), 74, 76, 81
Americans with Disabilities Act (ADA), 22, 626, 689, 696–697, 713

eBay database protection case, 433
American Tort Reform Association, 398, 399
American Tuna Boat Association, 631
American Wholesalers Marketers Association, 182
American Wind Energy Association, 356
Ames, 292
Amnesty International, 104, 548
Amway, 543, 544
Amway Asia Pacific, 544
Analysis, of nonmarket issues, 50–52
Andean Community, 588
Anderson, Carolyn, 319
Angang, 541
Angel, Marcia, 401
Angelo, Alfred, 650
Animal Liberation Front (ALF), 24
Animal welfare, 23–24
Annan, Kofi, 756, 781
Antibiotics Coalition, 23
Anti-Bribery Convention, 770
Antidumping, 584, 597–602
Antiglobalization protests, 97
Anti-Monopoly Law (Japan), 462
Antitrust Division of the Department of Justice, 266, 272
Antitrust laws, 265–266
automobile industry, 7
compliance with, 286–287
enforcement of, 270–274
European Union, 490–491
exemptions, 269–270
Japan, 462
merger case, 290–293
Microsoft, 1, 4, 47, 294–301
price fixing case, 289–290
statutes, 267–269
Antitrust policy, 265–266, 287–288
Antitrust Procedures and Penalties Act, 271
Antitrust statutes, 265, 267–269
Antitrust thought, 274–280
Chicago school, 277–278
collusion and price fixing, 283–284
differences in, 280–286
mergers and merger guidelines, 284–286
new IO approach, 278–280
predatory pricing and entry deterrence, 282–283
structural approach, 275–277
vertical arrangements, 280–282
AOL, 25, 29, 84, 249
antitrust laws, 286
eBay database protection case, 433
Internet privacy, 430, 431
mergers, 493
online markets, 416
AOL Time Warner, 286, 335, 493
Aongsomwang, Saree, 605
Apitzsch, Hannes, 776
Apotex, 406–408
Apple Computer, 199, 297, 382, 416
Applied ethics, 658
Applied rights analysis, 689–690
Appropriability, 377, 378, 379
Apter, Andrea, 254
Arbitration, 386
Arby's, 24
Arcaini, Tonio, 775

Archer Daniels Midland, 272, 492
Arctic National Wildlife Refuge
    (ANWR), 728
Argentina, 559, 586, 588
Arms Export Control Act (AECA), 610
Armstrong, C. Michael, 248
Armstrong, Hannon, 349
Armstrong, Scott, 82
Arnold, Benedict, 607
Arthur Andersen, Enron and, 642,
    644, 645, 647
Ash Grove Cement, 598
Ashcroft, John, 332
Asia-Pacific Economic Cooperation
    (APEC), 588
Asner, Ed, 82, 118
Assanand, Sashi, 748
Assessment, of activist organizations,
    103–104
Assets, nonmarket, 192
Assocham, 565
Associates First Capital Corporation,
    714–716
Associates First Capital Group, 1
Association of American Publishers, 28
Association of Community
    Organizations for Reform
    Now (ACORN), 715
Association of Independent Employees
    (AUB), 776
Association of International Automo-
    bile Manufacturers, 260, 261
Association of Real Estate Licenses
    Law Officials (ARELLO), 57
Association of the British Pharmaceuti-
    cal Industry, 718
Association of Trial Lawyers, 398, 399
Assumption of risk, 396
Asymmetric information, 313–314
AT&T, 26, 27
    antitrust laws, 270, 278
    Citigroup and, 118
    deregulation, 320, 321, 326, 330
    Google and, 37, 38
    Internet privacy, 431
    Internet taxation case, 248
    Japan and, 470
    judicial actions, 238
    public advocacy, 237
Atarashi, Masami, 472
Atlantic Richfield, 232
AuctionRover, 433, 434
Auctions, deregulation of, 324–325
AuctionWeb, 433, 438
Audience interest perspective, 69, 70–72
Audits, in crisis management, 126
Auerbach, Alan, 214
Austin v. Michigan Chamber of
    Commerce, 187
Australia, 347, 420, 433
Authorization committees, 178
Authors Guild, 28
Automobile access, in India, 6
Automobile industry,
    fuel economy standards case, 259–263
    lemon laws, 188
    nonmarket environment of, 5–11
    positioning, 47
    safety regulations, 14–15
Aventis Pharmaceutical, 18, 252, 253,
    254, 257
Avoidance, in crisis management
    program, 126–127
Avon Products, 543
Axios, 746

BAA, 496
Babich, Josh, 62
Baczko, Jack, 614
BADvertising Institute, 182
Bahrain, 25, 560
Baidu.com, 30, 31, 537, 545, 546
Baker, Howard, Jr., 226, 256
Balance, in media coverage, 73
Bale, Harvey, 604

Ballmer, Steve, 31, 300
Baltimore Technologies PLC, 610
Banco Compartamos, 553, 557, 567–568
Banisar, David, 430
Bank of America, 338, 445, 446
Bankruptcy Abuse Prevention and
    Consumer Protection Act, 447
Banks, Louis, 70
Banzhaf, John, 20–21, 22, 408–409
Baogang, 541, 542
Barbecue Industry Association, 209
Barclays, 357, 643, 646
Bargaining, 376
Barker, James, 651
Barlow, David, 61, 64
Barnard, Neil, 21
Barnesandnoble.com, 250
Barnette, Curtis, 592
Barnevik, Percy, 757
Barns, Abraham, 358
Barrett, John, 62
Barriers to entry, 276, 277, 278
Barr Laboratories, 778
Barshefsky, Charlene, 544, 780
BASF, 271
Bass, Ken, 611
Battery safety and liability, 6
Bayer, 19
Baze, Christine, 244
BBBOnline, 431
Beard, Mike, 111
Beat the Grim Reaper International,
    Inc., 671
Becker, Daniel, 260
Becker, George, 592
Beit Al Etisailat, 775
Belgium, 28, 507, 514, 592
Bell, Georgianna, 718
BelleHavens, 56
Bell South, 322
Benda, Ernst, 110
Benfield, James A., 209, 210
Bennington College, 163
Benson, Martha, 114
Benson, Medea, 113
Bentham, Jeremy, 660
Bentley, Jeremy, 370, 371
Bentsen, Lloyd, 233
Berardino, Joseph, 647
Berk, Matthew, 421
Berkshire Hathaway, 725
Bernstein, Carl, 74
Bertelsmann AG, 286, 493
Best Buy, merger case (Staples–Office
    Depot), 291
Beta Communications, 650
Bethlehem Steel, 592
BEUC, 26
Bharti Airtel Ltd., 566, 570, 572
Bias, in news media, 76–77
BidBay, 45
Bidder's Edge, 45, 433, 434, 435, 437
Big Doe, 644
Big River Funding, 643
Billpoint, 440
Bills, 175–177
Biomaterials Access Assurance
    Act, 398
Bipartisan Campaign Reform Act, 229
Bisio, John, 217, 218
BJ's, 291
Black Women's Agenda, 113
Blackstone Group, 213, 214, 216
Blair, Jayson, 75
Blame avoidance, 179
Blank, Paul, 145
Bliley, Tom, 436
Bloomer, Phil, 555
Blough, Kelly, 612
Blue Circle, 500
Blue Cross of California, 18, 252,
    253, 255
Bluewater Network, 95, 98, 100
BMW of North America, 402

Boards of directors
    duties of, 638–639
    Enron, 646–647
Bocchini, Joseph A., 246
Bockstein, Mindy, 26
Bodnar, Andrew G., 407
Body Shop International PLC, 732–733
Boehner, John, 195, 196
Boehringer Ingelheim, 717, 718, 780, 781
Boeing, 764
    ethics and, 720
    nonmarket analysis, 155, 156, 162–171
    nonmarket strategies, 204
    trade disputes, 586
Bohannon, Mark, 251
Boies, David, 297
Boise Cascade, campaigns against, 91,
    92, 105, 106–107
Bolivia, 588, 728
Bolton Engineering and Construction
    Company, 772–773
Bondurant, Stuart, 401
Boofstin, Robert, 240
Book Search Library Project
    (Google), 28
Boone, Pat, 649
Borders.com, 250
Borys, Nicholas, 62
Boschwitz, Rudy, 230
Boucher, Rick, 263
Boycotts, 91–92, 94, 268
BP, 1, 726
    activist organizations and, 106
    activist targeting of, 99
    cap-and-trade systems, 344
    company codes, 767, 768
    corporate social responsibility,
        727–728
    crisis management, 121, 126, 127,
        129, 132–133
    emissions trading within, 348
    environmental protection issues, 361
    nonmarket action and restraint, 737
    nonmarket issue analysis, 51
    positioning, 45, 46, 48, 54
    reputation of, 49
BPAmoco, 95
BP Conservation program, 46
Bracy, Michael, 333
Brady, Jim, 28
Brazil, 19, 24, 30, 554, 588, 592, 593,
    603, 606
Breach of contract, 385–386
Brent Spar, 108–111
Breyer, Stephen, 237, 402
Bribery, 764–766, 774–777
Brin, Serge, 30, 420, 545, 548
Brink, Scott, 150
Brinton, Louise, 401
Bristol Myers, 189, 237, 780
Bristol-Myers Squibb, 20, 406–408,
    779, 780, 781
Britain, 519, 522, 561
British Airways, 135, 235, 273, 284,
    289–290
British Columbia College of Physicians
    and Surgeons, 747
British East India Company, 519
British Pharmaceutical Industry, 718
Broadband regulation case, 326–330
Brokat, 610
Bromberg, Lee, 27–28
Bromberg & Sustein, 27
Brook, Robert, 255
Brookins, Howard, Jr., 218
Brooks Eckerd Pharmacy, 148
Brotz, Melissa, 604, 605
Brower, David, 102
Brown, Jamie, 240
Brown, Mark, 218
Brown, Melvin, 144
Brown & Williamson Tobacco
    Corporation, 84
Brown & Wood, 679
Browne, Lord, 727–728

Browner, Carol, 97, 371
Brune, Michael, 95, 115, 363
Bryan, Richard, 737–738
Bubble program, 351
Buche, Tim, 319
Buchholz, Todd, 410
Buckley v. Valeo, 229
Buffalo Rock Company, 125
Buffalo Savings Bank, crisis manage-
    ment case, 134–135
Buffett, Warren, 215, 725
Bureaucracy
    China, 518, 526–527
    Japan, 469–470
    Nippon Telephone and Telegraph
        case, 474–475
Bureaucrats, in Japan, 459–460
Burger King, acrylamide, 22
Burke, Edmund, 66
Burlington Northern Santa Fe Railway
    Company, 713
Burroughs Wellcome, 778, 781
Bush, George H. W., 74, 180, 184, 308, 696
Bush, George W.
    automobile industry, 47
    campaign financing, 228
    Enron and, 646
    environmental politics, 356, 358
    executive authority, 179
    fuel economy standards case, 259, 260
    Kyoto Protocol, 347
    NAFTA, 595
    peak associations, 234
    pharmaceutical industry, 17, 20
    products liability politics, 399
    regulation, 326, 328
    regulatory rule making, 309
    steel imports, 593
    taxes, 214, 216
Business, nonmarket analysis for. See
    Nonmarket analysis (business)
Business characteristics, in Japan,
    466–467
Business Electronics Corp. v. Sharp
    Electronics Corp., 282, 287
Business environment, 2–3
    news media and, 68
Business Environmental Leadership
    Council, 46
Business ethics, 655. See also Interna-
    tional business ethics
Business–government interactions
    (Japan), 467–469
Business grassroots campaigns, 232
Business groups, in underdeveloped
    markets, 557–558
Business interactions, with news
    media, 78–81
Business judgment rule, 638
Business nonmarket action, criticisms
    of, 186–189
Business objectives, public interest
    versus, 186–187
Business relationships, in China, 527
Business Roundtable, 628–630, 639,
    733–734
Business Software Alliance (BSA),
    44, 537
Buy, Richard, 647
Byrd Amendment, 590

Cable, Stephen, 245
Cable Television Act, 318
Cadorin, Nara, 651
Café Borders, 555
Calabresi and Melamed principles,
    662–663
Cali, Len, 330
California Chamber of Commerce, 736
California electricity market case,
    330–332
California Institute of Technology, 351
California Labor Federation, 146, 729
California Proposition 105, 736
California Proposition 211, 737

California Public Utilities Commission (CPUC), 187, 324, 353
California Space Heaters, Inc., 404–406
Callahan, Michael, 546
CalPERS, 639, 640, 643, 757, 782
Calpine, 356
Camarillo, Lily, 371
Campaign contributions, 229–231
Campaign financing, myths and realities of, 228
Campaigns, 91–94
 grassroots and constituency, 231–233
 steel imports and, 592–593
Campbell, Jeff, 327
Canada
 automobile industry and, 7
 eBay database protection case, 433
 environmental activism in, 363
 international trade policy, 582
 Internet privacy, 420
 mad cow disease, 23
 NAFTA and, 594, 595
 Toys 'R' Us case, 614
 trade agreements, 588
 trade disputes, 586
 U.S. protectionism and, 593
 Wal-Mart crisis management case, 148
Canada Dry, 288
Cancer Research and Prevention Foundation, 243
Capacity constraints, in Chinese automobile industry, 8
Cap-and-trade systems, 344–346
Capital One, 449
Capital Research Center, 107
Capobianco, Fabrizio, 39
Capture theory, 316
Carbon dioxide emission regulations, 6, 10, 11, 58–61
Carbon tax case, 506–509
Cardoso e Cunha, Antonio, 506
Caricom, 588
Carlyle, Thomas, 66
Carlyle Group, 214, 215
Carney, James, 437
Carr, Janet, 24
Carrefour, 536, 558, 566
Carried interest taxation, 213–216
Carrows, 732
Carson, Rachel, 91
Carter, Jimmy, 288, 306–307, 308
Case, Steve, 249, 430
Casuistry, 656–657
Catalan Institute of Pharmacology, 141
Categorical imperative, 683
Catena Networks, 329
Caterpillar, 400, 579, 586, 592–593
Catlett, Jason, 430
Causey, Richard, 647
Caux principles of business, 762
Caux Round Table Principles for Business, 761, 762f
Cawthorne, Paul, 604
CBS, 74, 83, 84, 88–89, 333
CEFIC, 508
Celler-Kefauver Act, 284
Cellular Telecommunications Industry Association, 12, 27
Cemex, 191, 196–197
 antidumping case, 597–602
 emerging markets and, 552–553, 559
Censorship, in China, 545–548
Center for Auto Safety (CAS), 15, 86
Center for Business and Research, 424
Center for Community and Corporate Ethics, 145
Center for Democracy and Technology, 430, 431
Center for Digital Democracy, 26, 329, 335
Center for Environmental Leadership, 45–46
Center for Medical Consumers, 245
Center for Public Integrity, 222
Center for Responsive Politics, 47, 221

Center for Science in the Public Interest (CSPI), 21, 22, 23, 411
Center for Study of Responsive Law, 102
Center on Race, Poverty and the Environment, 371, 372
Centers for Disease Control and Prevention (CDC), 20, 409, 411–412
Centers for Disease Control and Prevention (CDC) Advisory Committee, 242–243, 244, 246
Centers for Medicare and Medicaid Services (CMS), 64
Central American Common Market, 588
Central Committee (China), 529
Central Intelligence Agency (CIA), 610
Central Selling Organization, 773
Cerebus Capital Management, 262
Cessna Aircraft, 398
Chafee, John H., 184
Chakajnaroom, Teera, 604
CHALPERS, 215
Chamber of Commerce. *See* U.S. Chamber of Commerce
Chambers, John, 326
Chambers, M. Susan, 149
Chan, Elisha, 136
Chan-Fishel, Michelle, 358
Change
 ethics and, 655–656
 nonmarket environment, 11–13
 nonmarket strategy and, 35–36
Chaphe, Robert, 571
Charter Communications, 328
Chase Card Services, 449
Chávez, Hugo, 559
Chavez, R. Martin, 332
Cheeseburger bill. *See* Personal Responsibility in Food Consumption Act
Chemical Specialties Manufacturers Association, 736
Cheney, Dick, 646
Chester, Jeff, 335
Chewco Investments LP, 643–644, 646, 647
Chiang Kai-shek, 519, 520
Chicago Climate Exchange, 344, 347
Chicago Federation of Labor, 217
Chicago school, 274, 275, 277–278, 280, 283–284
Chicago Workers' Rights Board, 217
Childhood Vaccine Act, 400
Child Online Protection Act, 29, 548
Children, advertising to, 22
Children's Online Privacy Protection Act, 421
Chile, 363, 588
Chin, Wendall, 144
China, 517
 antidumping measures and, 584
 automobile industry and, 6, 7, 8
 business, 532–535
 Confucianism and social explanations, 523–527
 direct selling case, 543–545
 emerging markets and, 561, 562, 565
 environmental global climate change and, 338
 foreign direct investment, 533–534
 global climate change and, 338
 Google, 30–31, 545–548
 historical background, 518–523
 human rights issues, 754
 international trade policy and WTO membership, 534
 Kyoto Protocol and, 346–347, 562
 Levi Strauss & Company, 721
 Mattel case, 135–140
 most favored nation status, 204
 Nike and, 112, 113
 nonmarket environment and four I's, 527–532
 nonmarket issues, 535–540
 protectionism, 591
 regulation, 535

 state-owned enterprises, 532–533, 541–543
 Uniqlo case, 479
 Wugang case, 541–543
China Automobile Deutschland, 8
China Democratic Party, 536
China Labor Watch, 138–139
Chinese Communist Party (CCP)
 Chinese history and, 517, 519–521, 522
 direct selling case, 543
 human rights issues, 536
 intellectual property issues, 537
 nonmarket environment, 527, 528, 529–530, 531
Chirac, Jacques, 204, 495
Chocolate Manufacturers Association, 209
Choi, Francis, 138
Choice. *See* Decision making
Christian Aid, 630
Chrysler, 8, 259, 260, 262
Ciba-Geigy, 286
Cigna Corporation, 221
Cipla, 606
Circle K, 723, 724
Cisco Systems
 antitrust laws, 286–287
 China and, 537, 548
 international trade policy, 580
 Internet taxation case, 251
 positioning, 47
 regulation, 326, 327, 329
Citibank, 50, 51–52
 corporate social responsibility, 725
 EU nonmarket issues, 497
 private politics and, 116, 118
Citicorp, 714
CitiFinancial, 714
Citigroup, 1, 726
 activist organizations and, 104, 105
 activist strategies, 96
 activist targeting of, 99–100
 boycotts against, 91
 Calabresi and Melamed principles, 663
 corporate social responsibility, 730
 credit card regulation case, 448
 crisis management, 127
 Enron and, 626, 643, 644, 645, 646
 environmental programs, 338
 environmental protection issues, 360
 Equator Principles, 357
 ethics and, 720
 Japan and, 461
 private politics case, 114–119
 subprime lending case, 714–716
Citizen journalism, 77–78
Citizens' Clearinghouse for Hazardous Waste, 362
City of Hope Medical Center (COH), 384
Civil Aeronautics Board (CAB), 15
Civil law, 375–376
Civil Rights Act (1866), 695–696
Civil Rights Act (1964), 371, 372, 682, 694, 695, 696, 707, 708
Civil Rights Act (1991), 696
Civil war, in China, 520
Claimed rights, 689–691
Clairol, 734
Claria Corporation, 418
Clark, Sarah, 144
Class action lawsuits, 12–13
Clayton, Kenneth, 448, 449
Clayton Act, 265, 267, 269, 270, 271, 288
Clean Air Act, 6, 133, 177, 309, 349–350
Clean Air Act Amendments (1977), 183
Clean Air Act Amendments (1990), 58, 235
 cap-and-trade systems, 345, 346
 distributive politics, 355
 Environmental Defense and, 362
 incentives, 351
Clean Air Northfield, 359
Clean Air Working Group, 235

Clean Development Mechanism (CDM) program, 348, 349
Cleaner and Greener Green Energy program, 345
Clean Water Act, 148, 354
Clear Channel Communication, 333
Cleland, Scott, 26
Cleveland Clinic, 141
Client politics, 160, 200, 205–206, 579, 580
Climate Exchange PLC, 348
Clinical trial obligations, 705
Clinton, Hillary, 215, 229
Clinton, William Jefferson, 13
 Abbott Laboratories, 604–605
 BP and, 728
 Btu tax, 352
 China and, 544
 encryption export controls case, 607, 610, 611
 EU carbon tax case, 506
 executive authority, 179
 health care reform, 93, 221, 237
 Internet privacy, 432
 Internet taxation, 250
 Kyoto Protocol, 346–347
 luxury tax repeal and, 184
 market opening, 596
 NAFTA, 594–595
 news media and, 74
 pollution credits trading systems case, 371, 372
 products liability politics, 398–399
 regulation, 308, 309, 318
 steel imports, 592, 593
 Superfund, 353
 sweatshops, 758
 vote recruitment by, 199
Clinton Climate Initiative, 349
Cloture, 175
Cloud, Doyle, 226
CNN, 77, 240, 747
Coalition Against Database Piracy (CADP), 434, 436
Coalition building, 233–236, 468–469
Coalition for Justice in the Maquiladoras, 751
Coalition nonmarket strategies, 192
Coalition of Affordable Quality Healthcare, 221
Coalition of Broadband Users and Innovators, 329
Coalition of Labor Union Women, 113
Coalition of Tri-Lakes Committees, 148
Coalition on Smoking OR Health, 182
Coalitions, consensus in, 235
Coase theorem, 340–343
Coastal Alliance for Aquaculture Reform, 100
Coble, Howard, 435
Coca-Cola Company
 antitrust laws, 288
 boycotts against, 91, 92
 European Union and, 490, 492, 504
 Greenpeace and, 102
 judicial actions, 238–239
Cohen, Ben, 411
Cohen, Jacqueline, 182
Cohen, Tod, 432
Collections of Information Antipiracy Act, 435–436
Collective action, 162, 173–174, 193
Collevecchio Declaration, 357
Collins, D. J., 28
Collins, Philip, 289
Collusion, 268, 283–284
 Chicago school, 277–278
 mergers and, 284–285
 structural approach, 276–277
Colombia, 559, 588
Columbia University, private politics at, 116–117, 118
Comcast, 317, 329
Comer, Clarence, 598
Command-and-control regulation, 340

Commercial Credit Corporation, 714
Commercial law, 376
Commission. *See* Regulatory commissions
Commission of the European Union, 19
Commission on Environmental Cooperation, 595
Commitment statements, 730–731
Committee of Permanent Representatives (COREPER), 486, 500, 502
Committees, in U.S. Congress, 177–178
Committee staffs, in U.S. Congress, 178
Committee to End Tax-Funded Abortions, 100
Common Agriculture Policy (CAP), 494, 583
Common Cause, 335
Common law, 375–376
Common Market of the European Union, 588
Common-Sense Consumption Act, 21, 411
Communication, in crisis management program, 129–132
Communications Decency Act (CDA), 44, 84
Communist era, in China, 520–521
Communities for a Better Environment, 370–371, 372
Community development, 439, 727
Community Development Financial Institution (CDFI), 727
Community Reinvestment Act (CRA), 106, 715
Community Research Initiative of New England, 743
Company codes, 767–768
Company resources, 759–761
Compaq, 249, 299
Comparative advantage, 575
Comparative damages, 397–398
Compassion Over Killing, 24
Compatibility, 415
Compensatory damages, 397
Compensatory justice, 699–700
Competition
    Chicago school, 277
    Exclusive Resorts, 56
    majority-building strategies and, 201
    nonmarket strategy and, 35–36
    pluralism of, 186
    political, 159–162
Competition policy, of European union, 490–494
Competitive advantage, of Envirotest Systems Corporation, 60
Competitive Enterprise Institute (CEI), 21
Competitive information, 734
Competitiveness, in emerging markets, 551
Competitive theory, 575–578
Complementary products, 415
Compliance, 286–287, 625–626
Comptroller of the Currency (OCC), 445, 446, 447, 715
Compulsory licensing, 781
CompuServe, 286
Computer and Communications Industry Association (CCIA), 28, 493
Computer City, 291
Computer Fraud and Abuse Act, 435
Concentration. *See* Industry concentration
Concerned Families for ATV Safety, 319
Conduct codes, 733–734
Conerly, Bill, 556
Confederation of Food and Drink Industries, 499
Confederation of India Industry, 565, 566
Conference Board, 720
Conference of Nations, 750
Conflict diamonds case, 773–774
Confucianism, 518, 523–527

Confucius, 523, 524, 525
Conglomerate merger, 268
Congo, 572
Congressional Black Caucus, 648
Congressional Support Group, 226
Congress Party (India), 565
Coniston, 740
Conner, Chuck, 588
Connolly, Sarah, 7
Consensus, in coalitions, 235
Consensus Development Corporation, 610
Consequential damages, 386
Conservation International (CI), 43, 45–46, 98, 104, 360, 648
Constituency campaigns, 231–233
Constituency connection, 179
Constituents, 178–179
Constitutional Treaty (EU), 490, 491
Consultative Group to Assist the Poor, 568
Consumentenbond, 499
Consumer Action, 431
Consumer and Investor Access to Information Act, 436
Consumer Electronics Association, 380
Consumer Federation of America (CFA), 138, 317, 329, 335, 420, 448, 715
Consumer Products Safety Commission (CPSC), 91, 309, 319
    California Space Heaters, Inc. case, 404
    crisis management and, 137, 138, 139
Consumer Protection Group, 429
Consumer rewards, for corporate social performance, 635
Consumer surplus, 310
Consumers Union, 333, 448
Consuming Trade Action Coalition, 592
Consumption Science Federation, 480
Continental Airlines, 283
Continental TV v. GTE Sylvania, 281–282, 287
Contractarian framework, 701
Contracts, 383–386
Contractual joint ventures (CJVs), 533
Contributory negligence, 396
Controls, on lobbying, 226–227
Cookies (Internet), 428, 431
CoolWebSearch, 418
Co-op America, 555
Cooper, Mark, 335
Coordinating Committee for Multilateral Export Controls (CoCom), 197, 198
Coordinating Sphere of Activities Law, 616
Copiepresse, 28
Copps, Michael, 326, 333, 334
Copyrights, 381–382, 433. *See also* Intellectual property
Core Financial Partners, 216
Core principles, 731–732
Cornell University, private politics at, 118
Coro's, 732
Coronado, Rodney, 24
Corporate Accountability Research Group, 102
Corporate Average Fuel Economy (CAFE), 259, 261
Corporate financial performance (CFP), 635, 636
Corporate governance, 637–641, 642–647
Corporate nonmarket styles (Japan), 471–472
Corporate social performance (CSP), 630–637
Corporate social responsibility (CSR), 8, 619
    BP, 727–728
    Business Roundtable statement on, 628–630

challenge of, 724–726
    Citigroup, 730
    corporate governance, 637–641, 642–647
    corporate social performance, 630–637
    Enron case, 642–647
    Federal Communications Commission case, 650–652
    GlaxoSmithKline case, 782
    Google, 30
    legal compliance, 625–626
    practice of, 726–735
    profit maximization and, 621–625
    stakeholder theory, 626–628
    summary, 641
    trust gap, 620–621
    Wal-Mart case, 647–650
Correction of a defect, 396
Corruption
    China, 538
    emerging markets, 550, 561
    international business ethics, 761–770
Corzine, Jon, 229
Costco, 148, 149
Cost-of-service regulation, 320–321
Costs
    business lobbying, 222
    media coverage, 73
    news media, 77
    nonmarket action, 156–158
    protectionism, 591
Cotton, Richard, 87
Council of Ministers (EU), 485–486, 500, 501, 502, 507, 511
Council on Economic and Fiscal Policy (Japan), 477
Countervailing duties, 584
Country assessment, 549–551
Country Assessment Guidelines, 754
CountryWatch, 551
Counts, Alex, 567
Coups, 559
Court of Justice (European Union), 487
Courts. *See* Judiciary; U.S. Supreme Court
Cowell, Lisa, 250
Cox, Christopher, 248
Cox Communications, 328
Crandall, Robert L., 235, 283
Cranston, Alan, 230
Credibility, 202–203, 224–225
Credit Card Accountability, Responsibility and Disclosure Act, 448
Credit Cardholders' Bill of Rights, 448
Credit cards, 51
Credit claiming, 179
Credit Lyonnais, 357
Credit Suisse, 348, 357
Criminal Law Convention on Corruption, 770
Crises, nature and causes of, 120–121
Crisis development, pattern of, 121–125, 126
Crisis management, 120
    Buffalo Savings Bank case, 134–135
    Mattel case, 135–140
    Merck case, 140–142
    summary, 133–134
    Wal-Mart case, 143–151
Crisis management program, components of, 125–133
Crisis preparedness, 127–128
Croma, 566
Cromme, Gerhard, 776
Cronk, Dennis R., 436
Crosby, Susan, 244
Cross-subsidization, 320
Cruz Azul, 597
Cryptography, 607
Cuisinart, 272
Cultural foundations, in Japan, 462–464
Cultural imperialism, 752
Cultural relativism, 751–754, 752

Culture, in emerging markets, 551
Cummings, Elijah, 139
Cummins Inc.
    corporate social responsibility, 734–735
    environmental management and stability case, 366–368
    questionable foreign payments guide of, 768–769
Customer service case, 740–742
CVS, 148
CV Therapeutics, 705
Cypress Semiconductors, 625

Dach, Leslie, 648
Daimler-Chrysler, 260, 366
Daini Denden (DDI), 470, 475
Dalai Lama, 536
Daley, Richard, 218
Daley-Harris, Sam, 567
Damages, in products liability cases, 397–398
Danel, Carlos, 557, 567, 568
Dango, 462
Daoism, 518
Darfur, 561
Daschle, Linda, 256
Daschle, Tom, 210, 327
Database protection case (eBay), 433–438
Data Protection Working Party, 510
Data Quality Act, 309
Data Retention Directive (EU), 26
DataTreasury Corporation, 431
Dateline (television program), 86–88, 194
Davenport, Chester, 58
Davidson, Alan, 239
Davies, Simon, 420
Davis, Gray, 250, 332
Dawson, Don, 146
Daye Steel Group, 542
Daylight Saving Time Coalition, 154, 156, 160, 206, 210, 233
Daylight saving time politics, 208–211
Deadweight loss (DWL), 310, 311
Dealing, exclusive, 268
Dean, Howard, 217
De Beers, 773–774
Debevoise & Plimpton LLP, 777
Debrowski, Thomas A., 136, 139
Decision making, 50
    moral transgressions and, 666
    nonmarket strategies, 205–206
    nonmarket strategy, 191–192
DeConcini, Dennis, 256
Defamation, 24, 83–84, 86–88
Defects, 395
Deferred compensation, at Enron, 645–646
Deficit Reduction Act, 171, 184
Delaney amendment, 354
DeLauro, Rosa, 21
Delegation, 306–307
Delisi, Dianne, 245
Dell, 39, 298
Delors, Jacques, 506
Delta Air Lines, 235
Demand-side increasing returns, 415, 416–417
Democracy, 66
Democratic Party of Japan (DPJ), 456, 478
Democratic revolutions, 559
Deng Xiaoping, 521, 528
Denier, Greg, 145
Denison, Richard, 362
Denmark
    environmental management and stability, 338
    EU carbon tax case, 506, 507
    EU duty free abolition and, 513
    EU nonmarket issues, 496
    McDonald's in, 24
    Shell case, 110

Denny's, 129, 130, 732, 740–742
Deontological ethics systems, 681, 682
Department of Justice, 741
Deregulation, 321–325
　California electricity market case, 330–332
　Telecommunications Act (1996), 326–330
Design defects, 395
D'Esposito, Steve, 109
Det Norske Veritas, 111
Deutsche Bank AG, 679
Deutscher Gewerkschaftsbund (DGB), 499
Deutsche Telekom, 496
Developing countries
　AIDS and, 756–758
　GlaxoSmithKline case, 778–779
　operations in, 755–756
　See also Emerging markets
Dickenson, Larry S., 204
Diet (Japan), 455–456, 464, 470, 478
Diffie, Whitfield, 608
Digene Corporation, 244
Digital Millennium Copyright Act (DMCA), 44, 435
Digital piracy, 379–380
Diners Club, 445
Dingell, John, 133, 181, 259, 260, 263
Directive on Data Protection (EU), 420, 497, 509–511
Directive on the Legal Protection of Databases, 437
Direct Marketing Association, 424
Direct Marketing Institute, 432
Direct selling case, 543–545
Direct-to-consumer advertising, 40–41
Dirty car bounty, 726
Disabilities, rights and, 696–697
Disclaimers, 396
Discovery credit cards, 272
Discretion, 306–307
Discrimination, 30, 150
Dispute resolution, 584–587
　eBay, 440
　news media, 81–85
Dispute Settlement Body (DSB), 585–587, 750
Distribution, altruism and, 662
Distribution channels, 194
Distributive consequences, 154, 165–166
Distributive justice, 698–699
Distributive politics, 355–356
Distributive politics spreadsheet, 158, 168, 169
Diversity, in automobile industry, 7
Dixon, Pam, 25, 420
DLC Management, 215
DLF Universal, 566
Dobriansky, Paula, 547
Dr. Miles Medical Co. v. John D. Park & Sons, 280
Doctors Without Borders, 604
Dodd, Christopher, 448
Dodson, William, 643–644
Doerfler, Katrina, 251
Doha Round, 583, 587–588
Dolan, Peter R., 407, 408
Dole, Elizabeth H., 210
Dole, Robert, 93, 164, 168, 170, 184
Domenici, Pete V., 262
Domestic reform, in China, 522–523
Domino's Pizza, 100, 656
Dongfeng Motor Corporation, 8
Dongguan Zhongxin Toner Powder Factory, 137
Dongxing New Energy Company, 137
Doniger, David, 259, 260
Dorgan, Byron, 250, 317, 335
DotOrg, 30
DoubleClick, 25–26, 31, 418, 422, 428–432
Douglass, Adele, 24
Dover, Michael, 648
Dow Chemical, 97, 361

Dow Corning Company, 401
Drea, Elizabeth, 218
Dreyer's Grand Ice Cream, 286
Driver's License Privacy Protection Act, 421
Drummond, David, 26, 31
Drunk driving, 7
Drury, Richard, 371
Due process, 306–307
Duke Power, 696
Dun & Bradstreet v. Greenmoss Builders, 83
Dunkin' Donuts, 555
DuPont, 12, 97, 360, 737
Durham-Humphrey Amendment, 253
Duties
　boards of directors, 638–639
　countervailing, 584
Duty
　justice and, 704–705
　utilitarian, 662–663
Duty free abolition case, 511–516
Duty of care, 638
Duty of loyalty, 638
Duty to warn, 395
Dynamic efficiency, 279, 280
Dynamic Internet Technology (DIT), 546
Dynegy, 323

Eacho, Donna, 677–679
Eacho, William C., 677–679
Eagle Invest & Finance AG, 775
Early Light Industrial Company, 138
Earth Island Institute (EII), 91, 102, 631
Earth Liberation Front (ELF), 24
Earthlink, 286, 329
Earth Proxy, 431
Eastern Airlines, 738
Eastern Railroad Conference v. Noerr Motor Freight, 187
Eastman Kodak, 278, 640
eBay
　coalitions and consensus, 235
　database protection case, 433–438
　integrated strategy, 44–45, 47
　international strategy, 37
　Internet privacy, 422, 432
　monopolies and, 269
　news media and, 84
　nonmarket issues, 413, 414
　online communities, 425, 438–444
　online markets and, 415–416, 417
Eckert, Robert A., 136, 137, 139
e-Commerce Coalition, 436
Economic and Monetary Union (EMU), 488–489
Economic efficiency, 277, 278
Economic freedom, emerging markets, 550
Economic policy, antitrust policy and, 265
Economic Recovery Tax Act (ERTA), 163, 165, 166, 170
Economics
　international trade policy, 575–578
　online markets, 414–417
EcoScrap, 370–371
EcoSecurities Ltd., 349
Ecuador, 588
Eddie Bauer, 754
Edelman, 648
Editors, 66
Edwards, Slivy, 58
E-Fairness Coalition, 250
Effective National Action to Control Tobacco (ENACT), 182
Effectiveness, of nonmarket action, 157–158
Eggart, Tim, 109
Egypt, 571
Eichorn, Tom, 371
Eiger, Peter, 550
Eighth Conference on AIDS in Asia and the Pacific, 605

Eizenstat, Stuart, 251
Ekbom Support Group, 718
Elanco Animal Health, 23
Election financing laws, 228–229
Electoral strategies, in Japan, 468
Electoral support, 227–231
Electoral system, in Japan, 456–458
Électricité de France, 79
Electricity market, in California, 330–332
Electric power, deregulation of, 323–324
Electric Power Development Company, 461
Electronic Communications Privacy Act, 421
Electronic Data Systems, 59
Electronic Frontier Foundation, 609
Electronic Industries Association, 199
Electronic Privacy Information Center (EPIC), 26, 420, 421, 429, 431
Eli Lilly & Co., 384, 537–538
Elise, Kimberly, 243
El Salvador, 82
Emergency Committee for American Trade, 593
Emergency Medical Treatment and Active Labor Act (EMTALA), 314–315
Emergency Planning and Community Right-to-Know Act, 97
Emerging markets, 549
　Banco Compartamos case, 567–568
　country assessment, 549–551
　Kiva case, 568–570
　MTN Group Limited case, 570–573
　nonmarket environment, management in, 562–563
　opportunities, 551–558
　risk assessment, 558–562
　summary, 563
　Tesco PLC case, 564–566
EMI Group, 493
EMILY'S List, 230
Emission trading systems, 346–348
Empirical research, on corporate social performance, 635–637
Employee rewards, for corporate social performance, 635
Empresa Tolteca, 597
Encryption export controls case, 607–613
Endangered Species Act, 309
Enel, 776
Energy Information Administration, 338–339
Energy issues, in China, 539–540
Energy Policy Act, 323
Energy services companies (ESCOs), 349
Enforceability, of contracts, 385
Enforcement, 14, 15, 29
Engineering controls, under EPA, 351
England, 614
Enirotest Systems Corporation, 58–61
Enron
　Citigroup and, 117, 118
　corporate social responsibility case, 642–647
　deregulation, 323
　ethics and, 654
　manipulation by, 188
Enron Columbia Energy BV, 643
Enron Energy Services, 331
Enron Power Marketing, Inc., 330–332
Entitlements, 389–391
Entrepreneurial politics, 160, 579, 580
Entrepreneurial positioning, 54–57
Entry deterrence, 282–283
Environmental Defense, 262
　BP and, 46, 728
　environmental protection issues, 360, 362, 364
　Equator Principles, 357, 358
　firm interactions with, 103, 104
　McDonald's and, 23, 98
　Wal-Mart and, 649

Environmental Demonstration Store, 360
Environmental issues
　China, 539–540
　Google, 30
　McDonald's and, 24
Environmental justice case, 370–373
Environmental management and stability, 337
　cap-and-trade systems, 344–346
　Cummins Inc. case, 366–368
　emission trading systems, 346–348
　Environmental Protection Agency, 349–353
　externalities, socially efficient control of, 340–343
　global climate change, 338, 346–348
　goals and actions, 337–338
　policy, 338–339, 349–353
　political economy of, 353–359
　pollution credits trading systems case, 370–373
　protection issues, 359–364
　regulation, 348–349, 366–370
　Samsung case, 368–370
　summary, 365
　tradeoffs, 339–340
　voluntary collective programs, 364–365
Environmental movement, automobile industry and, 7–8
Environmental politics, 183–184
Environmental Protection Agency (EPA), 5
　advocacy science and, 354
　automobile industry and, 6
　California Space Heaters, Inc. case, 404
　cap-and-trade systems, 345–346
　crisis management and, 136, 138, 148
　Cummins Inc. case, 367
　environmental policy, 349–353
　environmental politics, 183–184, 354, 358
　Envirotest Systems Corporation and, 58–59, 60, 61
　fuel economy standards case, 261
　pollution credits trading systems case, 370, 371, 372
　private and public politics, 95
　regulation, 304, 309, 310
　responsiveness of, 205
　restaurant industry, 22
　Samsung case, 369, 370
　trade disputes, 585
　utilitarianism and, 669
Environmental protection issues, 359–364
Environmental risks, in emerging markets, 561–562
Episcopal Church, 727
Epstein, Richard, 605
Equal employment opportunity, 694–696
Equal Employment Opportunity Commission (EEOC), 695, 696, 713
Equator Principles, 338, 357–358, 562
Equity Bank of Kenya, 557
Equity joint ventures (EJVs), 533
Ercheng Iron & Steel Group, 542
Ernst & Young, 17, 113, 114, 510
Escalation stage of crisis life cycle, 122–123
Escola v. Coca Cola Bottling Co., 394
eSolar, Inc., 30
Essential Information, 102
Esso, 46, 99
Ethics, 653
　casuistry, 656–657
　defining, 654–655
　managerial role of, 653–654
　methodology of, 657–659
　moral philosophy and political philosophy, 659–660
　Norplant System case, 675–677
　personal and business, 655

Pfizer case, 679–681
politics and change, 655–656
practice of, 726–735
private interests and, 655
summary, 674
tax shelters case, 677–679
See also International business ethics
Ethics analysis process, 658
Ethics and Compliance Officer Association, 720
Ethics Committee of the American Society for Reproductive Medicine, 747
Ethics in Government Act, 227
Ethics principles
nonmarket action and restraint, 736–738
paternalism and, 735–736
questionable payments and, 762–763
Ethics systems, 720–721
Advanced Technology Laboratories case, 746–748
classification of, 681–682
corporate social responsibility, challenge of, 724–726
Denny's customer service case, 740–742
Gilead Sciences case, 742–746
higher order standards for, 710
Levi Strauss and global sourcing, 721–722
nonmarket action, moral determinants of, 722–724
summary, 739
unethical behavior, sources of, 738–739
See also Justice; Rights; Utilitarianism
Ethnic conflicts, in emerging markets, 561
ETI, 59
EU-15, 347, 348
EURATOM, 482
European Agency for the Evaluation of Medicinal Products, 19, 242, 243
European Automobile Manufacturers Association, 6
European Banking Federation, 494
European Central Bank, 483
European Chemical Industry Council (CEFIC), 499, 508
European Chemicals Agency, 497
European Climate Exchange, 348
European Coal and Steel Community (ECSC), 481–482
European Coal and Steel Council Consultative Committee, 508
European Commission, 6, 26, 484–485, 493, 500, 501–502, 506, 507, 514, 630
European Confederation of Retail Trade, 499
European Council, 490
European Court of First Instance (CFI), 487, 492, 493, 494
European Court of Human Rights, 84
European Court of Justice, 750
European Economic and Social Committee (EESC), 487, 500
European Economic Community (EEC), 482
European Environment Agency (EEA), 347–348
European Federation of Pharmaceutical Industries' Associations, 499
European Information Technology Roundtable, 503
European Monetary System, 482
European Parliament (EP), 6, 201, 483, 486–487, 488, 490, 500, 502–503, 510
European Roundtable of Industrialists, 499
European System of Central Banks, 488
European Trading System (ETS), 347, 500
European Travel Research Foundation, 513

European Union
agenda setting, 201
antitrust laws, 286
applied rights analysis and, 689
bribery and, 770
cap-and-trade systems, 344
carbon dioxide emission regulations, 10
China and, 534
Constitutional Treaty, 490, 491
crisis management and, 139
database protection in, 437
Doha Round, 588
emissions trading in, 347–348
fuel economy regulation in, 6
GlaxoSmithKline case, 717
Google, 26
international law and, 750
international trade policy, 583, 584, 585
Internet privacy, 420, 423
Kyoto Protocol and, 347
legislative process, 488, 489
lobbying in, 37
McDonald's, 24
Microsoft antitrust case, 1, 4
pharmaceutical industry, 19
pivot voters and, 201
price fixing case, 289
privacy issues, 13
Single European Act, 12
trade agreements, 588
trade disputes, 585–587
U.S. protectionism and, 589
value-added tax, 251, 483, 511
European Union Committee of the American Chamber of Commerce (Amcham), 499
European Union political economy, 481–482
carbon tax case, 506–509
Directive on Data Protection case, 509–511
duty free abolition case, 511–516
institutions, 484–496
interests and their organization, 498–499
Maastricht Treaty, 483–484
nonmarket issues, 496–498
nonmarket strategies in, 499–504
Single European Act, 482–483
summary, 505
Evans, Daniel, 164, 170
Evans, Donald, 646
Excelon, 347
Exclusive dealing, 268
Exclusive Resorts, 54–57
Executive authority, 179
Executive branch, 179–180
access to, 225
China, 530–531
See also Institutions; Presidency; *specific U.S. presidents*
Executive Order 12291, 308
Exemptions, 269–270
Exon, J. James, 208, 210, 211
Expectations damages, 386
Expectations statements, 730–731
Export controls case, 607–613
Export-Import Bank (Eximbank), 154, 162, 164, 165, 166, 357
Export Trading Company Act, 270
Express warranties, 393
Externalities, 312
network, 415
socially efficient control of, 340–343
Extractive Industries Transparency Initiative, 768
Exxon, 350
crisis management, 121, 122–123, 124, 127, 131–132
environmental issues, 350
social responsibility and, 727
ExxonMobil, 46
activist targeting of, 98–99

corporate social responsibility, 730
emerging markets and, 562
public politics and, 95
reputation of, 49
Exxon Valdez oil spill, 4, 121, 122–123, 129, 131–132, 350

Fair Credit Reporting Act, 421, 510
Fair Labor Association (FLA), 91, 105, 150, 759–760
Fair Labor Standards Act, 309
Fairness
justice as, 700–702
news media, 73, 76–77
regulation, 316–317
Fairness Doctrine, 89
Fair trade, 554–556
Fair Trade Commission (Japan), 462
Fairtrade Labeling Organization (FLO), 555, 556
Fair trade laws, 271–272
Families USA, 17, 254–255
Family Leave Act, 320
Fannie Mae, 715
Fanning, Shawn, 380
Farroukh, Ahamad, 571
Fast-food industry, nonmarket environment of, 20–24
Fastow, Andrew, 642, 643, 644, 646, 647
Fast Retailing, 479
Fay, Christopher, 110–111
Featherstone, Lisa, 143
Federal Aviation Administration (FAA), 212, 665, 669
Federal Bureau of Investigation (FBI), 607, 608, 609, 610
Federal Communications Commission (FCC), 27, 210, 237
affirmative action and, 708
auctions, 324–325
broadband regulation case, 307, 322–323, 326–330
corporate social responsibility case, 650–652
Google, 38, 39
media ownership rules, 307, 310, 317, 332–336
utilitarianism and, 668
Federal Deposit Insurance Corporation (FDIC), 147, 447, 715
Federal Election Campaign Act (FECA), 228
Federal Election Commission (FEC), 228, 229
Federal Energy Regulatory Commission, 324, 330, 646
Federal Express, 656
ad hoc coalitions, 235
Environmental Defense and, 364
labor organization and, 212–213
lobbying, 226
Federal fuel taxes, 6
Federal judiciary, 180
Federal Register, 306
Federal Reserve Board, 447–448, 449, 715
Federal Trade Commission (FTC)
antitrust laws, 266, 270–271, 272, 274, 285–286, 287–288
Citigroup case, 716
eBay online communities case, 442
Google, 25, 26, 28
Internet privacy and, 421, 422, 431, 432
merger case, 290–291, 292, 293
news media and, 84
online communities and, 427
patents case, 407, 408
privacy regulations, 25, 26
responsiveness of, 205
restaurant industry, 20
Federal Trade Commission Act, 265, 267, 270, 288, 447, 448
Federal Water Pollution Control Act, 349
Federation of Associations of Maharashtra (FAM), 565

Federation of German Employers' Associations (BDA), 498–499
Federation of German Industry (BDI), 498–499, 500
FedEx Systems, 262
Feedback, positive, 416
Feinstein, Dianne, 332
Feist Publications, Inc. v. Rural Telephone Service Co., 44, 382, 433, 435
Felando, August, 631
Feldman, Robert, 478
Feldmayer, Johannes, 776
Fenton, David, 67–68
Fenton Communications, 67–68
Fernández Olano, José, 511, 515
Fiat, 494
Fifth Amendment, 304, 305, 306, 707
Figueroa, Liz, 420
Fill, Dennis C., 747
Fillippini, Tom, 55
Financial restrictions, in emerging markets, 560
Financial Services Agency (Japan), 461
Financial Services Coordinating Council, 510
Financial Services Modernization Act, 421, 510
Finland, 506, 513
Finnerman, John G., Jr., 449
Fiorina, Carly, 247
First Amendment, 70, 83, 84, 185, 186–187, 226, 229, 381
First Five Year Plan (China), 520
First-mover advantage, 97, 416–417
First National Bank of Boston v. Bellotti, 186–187
Fish and Wildlife Foundation, 649
Fisher, William, 436
Flagstar, Inc., 740, 741, 742
Flanagan, Brian, 409
Flannery, Mark, 568
Fleischer, Peter, 25, 27
Fleischer, Victor, 213, 215
FLO-Cert Ltd., 555
Flooz.com, 432
Focus, 226
Fonovisa, Inc. v. Cherry Auctions, Inc., 44
Food and Drug Administration (FDA), 5
crisis management and, 124–125, 129, 130, 133, 135, 136, 140, 141
Gilead Sciences case, 742, 743, 744, 745
GlaxoSmithKline cases, 716, 717, 778
lobbying and, 242, 243, 246
mad cow disease, 23
Molecular Insight Pharmaceuticals, 63–64, 65
patents case, 406
Pfizer case, 680
pharmaceutical industry, 17, 18, 19, 20, 40, 41, 42, 189
pharmaceutical politics and, 236
pharmaceutical switching case, 252–254, 255, 256, 257–258
preemption, 396, 397
regulation, 310, 318
restaurant industry, 22, 23
tobacco politics, 181
trade association lobbying and, 234
utilitarianism and, 669
Food, Drug, and Cosmetic Act, 253, 257–258
Food Marketing Institute (FMI), 182
Ford, Bill, 100
Ford, Wendell, 208, 209, 210, 211
Ford Foundation, 727
Ford Motor Company
activist targeting of, 100
Center for Environmental Leadership, 45–46
fuel economy standards case, 259, 260, 261

Ford Motor Company (continued)
Japan and, 464
nonmarket strategies, 204
private and public politics, 95
product liability, 8
recalls, 8
Foreign Corrupt Practices Act
(FCPA), 750, 751, 762, 765,
766–767, 769, 771, 776
Foreign direct investment (FDI)
China, 533–534
India, 552, 564–565
Foreign Investment Promotion Board
(India), 565
Foreign payments, questionable,
761–770
Foreign relations, of pre-Republican
China, 518–519
Forest and Biodiversity Conservation
Alliance, 104
Forest Ethics, 363
Forest Stewardship Council (FSC), 91,
98, 107
Fortunet Wireless Communications
L.P., 651
Fourteenth Amendment, 304, 305,
306, 696
Fourth Amendment, 688
"Fourth branch," 66. See also Journal-
ism; News media
Fourth International North Sea
Conference, 110
Fox, 74, 333
France, 494, 495
China and, 536
eBay cases, 433, 443
EU carbon tax case, 507, 508
EU duty free abolition and, 514
EU nonmarket issues, 496, 498
Google in, 28, 29
Greenpeace and, 102
lobbying in, 501
Mattel crisis management
case, 137
nonmarket strategy, 504
Shell case, 110
trade disputes, 585
U.S. protectionism and, 592
Yahoo!, 37
Franchisees, of McDonald's, 24
Franchisement, 193–194
Franchising, in European Union, 504
Frank, Barney, 448
Frank, Reuven, 74
Franke, Carter, 449
Franklin, Benjamin, 208
Franklin Research & Development, 638
Fraud prevention, by eBay, 441–442
Freddie Mac, 714
Free Press, 335
Free the Grapes, 161
Free the Planet, 102
Free trade agreements, 7, 11. See also
specific free trade agreements
Freedom, in emerging markets, 550
Freedom House, 550
Freedom Network, 417
Free-rider problem, 156–157, 158,
173–174
Frieberg, Steve, 448
Friedman, Milton, 621–625, 662
Friends of the Earth, 358
Frontline Wireless, 27
Fuel economy exception, 6
Fuel economy legislation, 5
Fuel economy regulation, 6
Fuel economy standards case,
259–263
Fuel taxes (federal), 6
Fuente, David, 290
Fujita, Den, 616
Fumento, Michael, 77
Funambol, 39
FutureGen Project, 347
Future of Music Coalition, 333

G-8, antiglobalization protests
against, 97
Gabelli, Mario, 651–652
Gabelli Group Capital Partners, 652
Gallahue, Bob, 62
Gallant, Paul, 30
Galloway, Ron, 145
Galson, Steven, 142
Galvin, Robert, 4
Gamco Investors Inc., 651
Ganley, Charles, 254
Gap Inc., 43, 107, 479, 637–638
Garnier, Jean-Pierre, 757, 778, 779,
782, 783
Gartner, Michael, 72–73, 82, 87
Gatch, Mary, 632
Gates, Bill, 294, 295, 297, 300, 414, 415,
424–425
Gates Foundation, 781
Gateway, 248
Gay and Lesbian Alliance Against
Defamation, 431
Gazprom, 767
GE Consumer Finance, 147
Genentech, 384
General Accounting Office (GAO),
249–250, 424, 445, 446, 447
General Agreement on Tariffs and
Trade (GATT), 574, 581, 582,
584, 601
General Agreement on Trade in
Services (GATS), 582
General Aviation Revitalization
Act, 398
General Electric (GE), 74
antitrust laws, 286
campaigns against, 91, 92, 94
corporate social responsibility, 730
European Union and, 494
General Motors (GM), 50
carbon dioxide emission regulations, 6
emerging markets and, 553
Envirotest Systems Corporation
and, 59
EU nonmarket issues, 497
fuel economy standards case, 259,
260, 261
international trade policy, 579
Internet privacy, 423
judicial actions, 238
market for control, 640
Nader, Ralph, 91
news media and, 82, 86–88
nonmarket action and restraint, 737
nonmarket analysis, 157
nonmarket strategies, 204
recalls, 8
safety regulations, 15
steel imports and, 592–593
General Services Administration
(GSA), 15
Generic activist strategies, 100–101
Generic nonmarket strategies, 196–204
Generic Pharmaceutical Industry
Association (GPIA), 236
Genetically modified organisms
(GMOs), 586–587, 689–690
Genetic Information Nondiscrimina-
tion Act, 713
Genetic testing in workplaces (case),
712–714
Geneva Convention, 750
Geneva Pharmaceuticals, 256
Genmar, 235
Gente Nueva, 567
Gephardt, Richard, 217
Gerard, Joe, 355
German, John, 261, 262
German Toy Manufacturers
Association, 615
Germany, 494, 495
eBay cases, 433, 443
EU carbon tax case, 507, 508
EU duty free abolition and, 514
EU nonmarket issues, 496, 498

interests, 498–499
Internet privacy, 420
lobbying in, 37, 501
nonmarket strategy, 504
pharmaceutical industry, 19
Pizza Hut in, 93
Shell in, 108, 109, 110
Siemens case, 775–776
Toys 'Я' Us case, 615
trade disputes, 585
Ghana, 570, 572
Gilding, Paul, 95
Gilead Sciences, 742–746, 758
Gillen, Michele, 86, 87
Gilmore, James, 248
Ginsburg, Ruth Bader, 381
Givens, Beth, 419
Glass-Steagal Act, 185
GlaxoSmithKline (GSK), 19, 40
international business ethics case,
778–783
lobbying case, 243, 244
nonmarket spillovers and, 757
private and public politics, 96
restless leg syndrome case, 716–719
Glaxo Wellcome, 778
Global Alliance, 760
Global Business Dialogue on Elec-
tronic Commerce, 249
Global climate change, 338, 346–348
Global Climate Coalition, 46
Global Crossing, 678
Global Exchange, 48, 99, 113, 555, 634
Global Finance Campaign, 114–119
Global Fund to Fight AIDS, Tuberculo-
sis and Malaria, 744, 756–757, 781
Global Health Program, 605
Global Internet Freedom Act,
547–548
Global Internet Task Force, 547
Globalization case (Toys 'Я' Us),
614–618. See also International
trade policy
Global market strategies, 36–37
Global Reporting Initiative, 761
Global sourcing, 721–722
Global Witness, 774
GlobeScan Inc., 620
Glover, Michael, 328
Gmail case, 419–421
Goals, for environmental management
and stability, 337–338
Golden Rule, 524–525
Goldman Sachs, 261, 332, 338, 672
Goldstein, Michael, 616
Goodlatte, Bob, 611
Goodman, Ellen, 242
Google, 1, 2
China case, 545–548
eBay database protection case, 434
EU nonmarket issues, 496
integrated strategy, 37, 38–39
nonmarket capabilities, 239–240
nonmarket environment of, 25–32
online markets, 416
privacy issues, 419–421
trade secrets, 383
Google Earth, 25, 30
Google Health, 29
Google News, 28
Gore, Al, 371, 372, 593, 646, 712, 780
Gorton, Slade, 164, 170, 208, 209, 211
Government, corporate social respon-
sibility and, 622–623
Government agencies. See Regulatory
agencies; specific agencies
Government allies, 226
Government arenas, nonmarket
strategies for. See Nonmarket
strategies (government arenas);
Nonmarket strategies implemen-
tation (government arenas)
Government–business interactions.
See Business–government
interactions

Government enforcement, of antitrust
laws, 270–272
Government imperfections, 315–316
Government institutions. See Institu-
tions; specific government
institutions
Government procurement, 584
Government Procurement Agreement
(GPA), 584
Government regulation. See Regulation
Graham, David, 142
Grameen Bank, 556
Grameen Foundation, 567
Gramm-Leach-Bliley Act, 185, 510
Grandin, Temple, 23
Granted rights, 689–691
Grassroots Action Information
Network, 234
Grassroots campaigns, 231–233
Great Leap Forward (China), 521
Greece, 508
Greed, Linda, 355
Green Corps, 116
Greenip, Janet, 245–246
Green Lights Programme (EU), 24
Greenman v. Yuba Power Products, 394
Greenmoss Builders, 83
Greenpeace, 24, 48, 102
activist strategy, 98, 101
BP and, 728
campaigns, 92
firm challenges against, 106
news media and, 67, 84
nonmarket analysis, 154
private politics case, 108–111
Greenwald, Robert, 145
Greenwood, James, 642
Griggs v. Duke Power, 696
Grokster, 379–380
Gross, Taylor, 649
Grossman, Andy, 145
Grouper Networks, 380
Grove, Andy, 247, 251, 432
Growth hormones, 23
Grubman, Jack, 118
Grupo Cementos Apasco, S.A. de C.V.
(Apasco), 597
GTE, 322
Guangzhou Automobile Corporation, 8
Guanxi, 526–527, 528
Guomindang (GMD), 519, 520, 522
Gurusawmy, Mohan, 565

Habitat for Humanity, 117
Hague Declaration, 750
Haldane, J. B. S., 712
Half.com, 438
Hallmark Cards, 14
Halvorson, Debbie, 246
Hamied, Yusuf, 606
Hamilton Test Systems, Inc., 58, 59
Hammermesh, Joshua, 62
Hand, Learned, 269
Handelsanstalldas Forbund, 617
Handler, Brad, 54
Handler, Brent, 54
Hannah, Daryl, 118
Hanson Trust PLC v. ML SCM
Acquisition, 639
Hard money, 229
Hardee's, 209
Harkin, Tom, 21
Harlan, Priscilla, 62
Harmonization, 483
Harrington, Michael, 606
Harris, William, 298
Hart-Scott-Rodino Antitrust
Improvements Act, 271, 290
Harvard Vanguard Medical
Associates, 743
Hasbro, 316
Hashimoto, Ryutaro, 475
Hastert, Dennis, 21, 411
Hatch, Orrin, 435
Hatch-Waxman Act, 63

Hate groups, 443
Hatteras Yachts, 182
Haupt, Richard M., 242, 246
Hausen, Harald zur, 242
Hausfeld, Michael, 289
Hayes, Randy, 118, 364
Heald v. Engler, 238
Health Benefits Coalition, 221
Health Care Reform Project, 93, 96
Health industry, lobbying by, 221, 222
Health Information National Trends
    Survey (HINTS), 246
Health issues
    news media and, 77
    restaurant industry, 20–24
    See also AIDS
Health maintenance organizations
    (HMOs), 221
Hearst Corporation, 271
Heesen, Mark, 215
Hellman, Martin, 608
Helsinki Declaration, 750
Henderson, Wade, 334–335
Henry, David, 718
Herfindahl-Hirschman index (HH),
    285, 292
Heritage Foundation, 262, 550
Herkstroeter, C.A.J., 108
Hershman, Michael J., 777
Hertz Rent-A-Car, 640
Heskjer, Fran, 617
Hewlett-Packard
    antitrust laws, 286, 287
    business grassroots campaigns, 232
    corporate social responsibility, 734
    emerging markets and, 553
    Internet taxation case, 247, 249
    media guidelines of, 80
    Microsoft antitrust case, 298
Higgins, Arthur, 604
High Country Communications L.P., 651
High Five for Farmers, 556
High Tech Broadband Coalition
    (HTBC), 329
Hillebrand, Gail, 448
Hilton international, 640
Hindrey, Leo, Jr., 215
Hindustan Lever Limited, 553
Hino, Ichiro, 475
Hirsch, Samuel, 408, 410
HIV drugs case, 742–746
Hjartarson, Jim, 329
H. J. Heinz, 631
HLL, 566
Hobee's, 631
Hoffmann-La Roche, 743
Hogg, Sir Christopher, 757
Hogue, Ilyse, 116, 117, 360
Holderbank Financière, Glaris Ltd.,
    597, 598
Holleyman, Robert, 328
Hollings, Ernest, 248
Hollings, Fritz, 326, 335
Holnam, 598
Holwill, Richard, 544
Holzle, Urs, 30
Home Depot
    campaigns against, 92
    Chicago public politics case, 218
    environmental activism at, 363–364
    environmental protection issues, 360
    nonmarket strategy, 191
    products liability politics, 399
    public politics and, 95
    strategy and negotiations, 105
Home Mortgage Disclosure Act
    (HMDA), 106
Honda, 8, 37, 259, 261, 262
Honduras, 585
Honeywell, 199, 286
Honeywell International, 494
Hong Kong, 519, 522, 614
Hong Li Da, 138
Hoofnagle, Chuck, 421
Horbaczewski, Henry, 437

Horizontal merger, 268
Horizontal practices, 268–269
Horizontal price fixing, 268
Horton, Chuck, 410
Household Responsibility System
    (China), 522
Huawei Technologies, 537
Huge Group, 572
Hughes, Keith W., 714
Hughes Aircraft, 86
Hu Jia, 536
Hu Jintao, 530, 536
Human Development Report
    (1999), 250
Human Genome Project, 713
Human rights
    automobile industry and, 7
    China, 30–31, 535–539
    justice and, 754–755
Human Rights Campaign, 7
Hume, Ellen, 72
Hundt, Reed, 27
Huntington Life Sciences, 107
Hustinx, Peter, 27
Huston, Allan S., 93
Hu Yaobang, 522
Hu Yingying, 546
HVB Group, 357, 679
Hyde, Henry, 250
Hynix Semiconductors, 238

IBM
    antitrust laws, 271, 278
    business grassroots campaigns, 232
    encryption export controls case, 610
    environmental protection issues, 360
    European Union and, 493
    Internet privacy, 431
    Internet taxation case, 249
    Microsoft antitrust case, 298
IBM Japan, 471
ICBA Bancard, 448
Identification stage of crisis life
    cycle, 122
IFC, 567
Ifshin, Adam, 215
IG Metall, 776
Ikuta, Masaharu, 478
Illinois Power Company, 88–89
IMD, 551, 552
Immune Deficiency Foundation, 92
Imperial China, 518–519
Implied warranties, 393
Imports, steel, 592–593
Incentives, 154
    environmental management and
        stability, 240
    EPA, 351–352
    justice and, 703–704
    property law, 377
Income redistribution, through regula-
    tion, 320
Independent Administrative Institu-
    tions (IAIs), 461
Independent Community Bankers of
    America, 147
Independent Service Organization
    (ISO), 331
Index of Economic Freedom, 550
India
    automobile access in, 6
    Kyoto Protocol and, 346–347, 562
    MTN Group Limited case, 570
    opportunities in, 551–552
    pharmaceutical industry, 19
    Tesco PLC case, 564–566
    trade disputes, 587
Indigenous peoples, 30
Individual freedoms, in emerging mar-
    kets, 550
Indonesia, Nike and, 112, 113
Industrial Bank of Japan (IBJ), 466
Industry concentration
    Chicago school, 277
    structural approach, 276

INFACT, 92
Infiniti Retail, 566
Information, 5, 10–11
    asymmetric, 313–314
    competitive and proprietary, 734
    daylight saving time politics, 210
    incentives and, 377
    Japan, 471
    news media and, 78
    relevance of, 224–225
    technical and political, 223–224
    utilitarianism and, 669–670
Informational strategies, 202–203
Information industries, 413–414
    database protection case (eBay),
        433–438
    Internet privacy, 417–423, 428–432
    Internet taxation issues, 423–425
    online communities, 425–427, 438–444
    online markets, economics of, 414–417
    summary, 427
Information Industry Association
    (IIA), 298
Information Technology Association
    of America (ITAA), 249
Injustice, 700
Installed base, 416
Institute of Medicine, 75
Institutional arenas, in nonmarket
    strategy, 191
Institutional change, 11, 12–13
Institutional officeholders
    nonmarket strategies targeting, 203
    political competition and, 162, 168, 170
    See also Access
Institutions, 5, 9–10
    China, 525–526, 528–530
    European Union, 484–496, 500
    Gilead Sciences case, 745
    international law and, 750–751
    Japan, 455–461
    nonmarket strategies and, 205–206
    political competition and, 162, 168, 170
Instrumental rights, 685–687
Insurance, 128, 440
Integrated strategy, 33, 37, 39, 40
    approaches to, 41–42
    eBay, 44–45
    Enirotest Systems Corporation
        case, 58–61
    Exclusive Resorts case, 54–57
    Google, 38–39
    Molecular Insight Pharmaceuticals
        case, 61–65
    nonmarket environment, 33–37
    nonmarket issues analysis frame-
        work, 50–52
    nonmarket positioning, 42–49
    nonmarket strategy function,
        organization of, 53
    pharmaceutical industry, 40–41
    summary, 53–54
Integrity tests, 672–673, 692, 693–694, 709
Intel, 27, 39
    antitrust laws, 270, 273, 287
    Internet privacy, 432
    Internet taxation case, 247
    Microsoft antitrust case, 294, 297, 298
    positioning, 47
    Project XL, 352
Intellectual property
    automobile industry and, 8
    China and, 536–538
    eBay, 44, 434
    Gilead Sciences case, 745
    Google, 27–28
    Molecular Insight Pharmaceuticals, 63
    pharmaceutical industry, 19
    TRIPS, 582–583
Intellectual property law, 377–383,
    406–408
Interagency Group, 609
Interbrand competition, 280
Interest group activity, 11, 12
Interest group formation, 14–15

Interest group politics, 160, 205–206,
    356, 579, 580
Interest groups, 8–9
    news media and, 67
    nonmarket analysis, 154–155
    See also specific groups
Interests, 5, 8–9
    Boeing, 167
    eBay database protection case, 435
    European Union, 498–499
    Japan, 454
    nonmarket analysis, 154–155
    nonmarket strategies and, 205–206
    rights and, 692
    tobacco politics, 181–182
Interfaith Center on Corporate
    Responsibility (ICCR), 605,
    638, 751
Interfaith Fairtrade initiative, 555
InterFit Health, 148
InterMedia Partners LP, 215
Internal Revenue Service (IRS), 216,
    421, 677–679
International business ethics, 749
    corruption and questionable foreign
        payments, 761–770
    cultural relativism, 751–754
    De Beers case, 773–774
    developing countries, 755–758
    GlaxoSmithKline case, 778–783
    human rights and justice, 754–755
    international codes, 761
    international law and institutions,
        750–751
    Marnera case, 772–773
    Siemens case, 774–777
    summary, 770–771
    working conditions in suppliers'
        factories, 758–761
International Climate Change Part-
    nership, 728
International codes, 761
International Coffee Agreement, 554
International Council of Shopping
    Centers, 249
International Court of Justice, 750
International Covenant on Civil and
    Political Rights, 536
International Duty Free Confedera-
    tion (IDFC), 514
International Federation of Pharma-
    ceutical Manufacturers Associa-
    tions, 604, 780
International Finance Corporation
    (IFC), 357
International Franchising Association
    (IFA), 504
International institutions. *See* Institu-
    tions; *specific international
    institutions*
International Labor Rights Fund, 150
International law, 750–751
International market strategies, 36–37
International Monetary Fund (IMF),
    97, 356, 534, 750
International Paper, 232
International Rivers Network, 102
International Trade Agency (ITA),
    589, 591, 599
International trade agreements,
    581–588
International Trade Commission (ITC),
    205, 589, 591, 593, 599, 600, 601
International Trade Organization
    (ITO), 581
International trade policy, 574–575
    Abbott Laboratories case, 602–606
    Cemex antidumping case, 597–602
    China, 534
    economics of, 575–578
    international trade agreements,
        581–588
    market opening, political economy
        of, 594–596
    political economy of, 579–581

International trade policy (continued)
  process, 575
  protectionism, political economy of, 590–594
  Sophis Networks case, 607–613
  summary, 596
  Toys 'Я' Us case, 614–618
  U.S. trade policy, 588–590
International Traffic in Arms Regulations (ITAR), 610
Internet
  citizen journalism on, 77–78
  crisis management and, 123
  digital piracy, 379–380
  online markets, economics of, 414–417
  regulation case, 326–330
  tax policy and, 423–425
Internet Crimes Group, 420
Internet Non-Discrimination Act, 247, 248, 250, 251
Internet online communities, 425–427, 438–444
Internet privacy, 25, 26, 417–423, 427, 428–432, 496–497
Internet Solutions, 572
Internet taxation case, 247–252
Internet Tax Fairness Coalition (ITFC), 249, 251
Internet Tax Freedom Act (ITFA), 248, 423
Interpretation, of news messages, 68–69
Interstate Commerce Act (1887), 265, 303, 310
Interstate Commerce Commission (ICC), 15, 303, 304
Intervention stage of crisis life cycle, 123
Interviews, with media, 79–80
Intrabrand competition, 280
Intrinsic rights, 685–687
Intuit Corporation, 298
Inubushi, Yoriko, 480
Investcom LLC, 570
Investor Responsibility Research Center (IRRC), 648
Investor rewards, for corporate social performance, 635
IO approach. See New IO approach
Irancell, 572
Ireland, 513
Ireland, Jay, 333
Iron triangles, 464
ISO 14001, 364
Issue identification, 14
Issues, 5–8. See also Nonmarket issues
iTalk Cellular, 572
Italy
  bribery in, 776
  EU carbon tax case, 507, 508
  EU duty free abolition and, 513
  trade disputes, 587
  U.S. protectionism and, 592
ITC, 566

Jackley, Jessica, 568
Jackson, Brooks, 73
Jackson, Henry, 164
Jackson, Jesse, 742
Jacobson, Michael F., 22
Jacobson, Walter, 84
Jaedicke, Robert K., 646
James, Charles A., 301
Japan, 503
  automobile industry and, 8
  eBay database protection case, 433
  EU agriculture policy and, 494
  EU carbon tax case, 506
  EU nonmarket issues, 496
  international trade policy, 583
  lobbying in, 37
  Pizza Hut in, 93
  representation strategy and, 197, 198, 199
  Toys 'Я' Us case, 615–617
  U.S. protectionism and, 592

Japanese Bankers Association, 477
Japan Highway Public Corporation, 461, 469–470
Japan Machine Tool Builders Association, 469
Japan Metal Forming Machine Builders Association, 469
Japan National Oil Corporation, 461
Japan political economy, 451–452
  bureaucracy, relationships with, 469–470
  business characteristics, 466–467
  business–government interactions, 467–469
  corporate nonmarket styles, 471–472
  cultural foundations, 462–464
  information, 471
  institutions, 455–461
  interests, 454
  issues, 452–454
  Japan Post privatization case, 476–479
  judicial system and antimonopoly law, 462
  lobbying and points of access, 470
  Nippon Telephone and Telegraph case, 474–476
  political exchange, 464–466
  summary, 472–473
  Uniqlo case, 479–480
Japan Postal Workers Union, 478
Japan Post privatization case, 476–479
Japan Towel Industrial Association, 479
Jarvis, Ron, 363, 364
JEDI, 643, 644, 647
Jenkins, John, 740–741
Jennings, John, 111
Jiang Zemin, 530
Jinmyaku, 471
Ji Xiaoyin, 547
Joepen, Horst, 431
Johnson, Bobby Jo, 125
Johnson, Laurie, 371
Johnson, Stephen L., 367
Johnson & Johnson
  credo of, 731
  crisis management, 121, 126, 127, 128, 131, 132
  institutional manipulation by, 189
  Japan and, 472
  trademarks, 382
Joint and several liability, 400–401
Joint Council of Energy and Environment Ministers, 506, 507
Jointly determined consequences, 665–666
Joint venture policy, in China, 533–534
Jones, Jim, 369
Jones, Stephanie Tubbs, 715
Jonsson, Gunnar, 618
Jonway UFO, 537
Jordan, Jim, 145
Journalism, 66
  citizen, 77–78
  news media and, 74–75
  standards versus judgments, 75
  See also News media
Journalists, 66, 79
JPMorgan Chase, 338, 449, 644
Judicial actions, 238–239
Judicial branch, in China, 531
Judicial politics, of environmental protection, 354
Judicial system, of Japan, 462
Judiciary
  appointments to, 180
  responsiveness of, 205
  See also U.S. Supreme Court; specific cases
JunkBusters, 430
Jupiter TeleCommunications, 474
Jurisline.com, 434
Jury Verdict Research, 397
Justice
  human rights and, 754–755
  principles of, 702–703, 706–710

Justice, Dwight, 139
Justice theories, 710–711
  categories of, 698–700
  Rawls, John, 700–710

Kadrmas, Sarita, 690
Kadrmas v. Dickinson Public Schools, 690–691, 692
Kahn, Alfred, 15
Kalin-Casey, Mary, 25
Kampo, 476, 477, 478
Kane, Theodore, 650–651
Kane, Victoria, 650–651
Kansas Alliance for U.S.-China Trade, 204
Kantian maxims, 683–689
Karlsson, Therese, 618
Karson, Daniel E., 776
Kassenbaum, Nancy, 93
KaZaA, 379, 380
Keating five, 230
Keidanren, 454, 468, 469, 475, 476
Keiretsu, 454, 463, 464, 466–467, 468, 469
Keller, Rick, 21, 411
Kelly, Craig, 289
Kelly, Jim, 367
Kennedy, Edward, 93, 143
Kennedy, Lisa, 257
Kennedy, Patrick, 609
Kennedy Round, 581, 584
Kenya, 561, 568
Kenyatta, John, 561
Kenzie, Ross, 134
Kerry, John, 216
Kessler, David, 124, 258, 401
Khalifa family (Bahrain), 25
Khanlou, Homayoon, 604
Kibaki, Mwai, 561
Killino, Jeffrey, 402
Kimmelman, Gene, 333–334, 335
Kinder, Lydenberg, Domini Research & Analytics (KLD), 636, 638
Kingsford Company, 209
Kinko's, 92, 104
Kiodex, 332
Kitani, Yoshihisa, 480
Kitjiwatchakul, Kannikar, 605
Kiva, 568–570
Kleiner Perkins Caufield & Byers, 215
Kleinfeld, Klaus, 774–777
Kline & Company, 368
Klitzman, Robert L., 718
Kmart, 291, 292
Knight, Douglas John, 125
Knight, Peter, 256
Knight, Phil, 66, 112, 113, 114, 759
Knight Foundation, 77
Koenkai, 456, 465
Kofinis, Chris, 145
Kogan, Richard J., 257
Kohl, Helmut, 110
Kohlberg, Kravis, Roberts & Company, 740
Koizumi, Junichiro, 477, 478
Kojima, Masahi, 475
Kokusai Denshin Denwa (KDD), 474, 476
Kollar-Kotelly, Colleen, 300, 301
Kongsberg Vaapenfabrik, 197, 199
Kopper, Michael J., 643–644, 646, 647
Kopperud, Steve, 84–85
Korea
  automobile industry and, 7, 11
  Nike and, 112, 114
Korean Air Lines, 289
Kotchian, A. Carl, 763–764
Kous, 530
KPMG, 677–679
KPMG Germany, 777
Kraft, 555
Kravis, Henry, 213
Kravitz, Lisa M., 717
Kravitz, Richard, 40–41
Kroc, Ray, 123

Kroger, 143
Kroll Associates, 777
Kronauge, James, 62
Kroszner, Randall S, 448
Krugman, Paul, 213
Krupp, Fred, 357, 362
Kubo, Tatsuko, 616
Kukuda, Yasuo, 455
Kuneva, Maglena, 139
Kutschenreuter, Michael, 775
Kuzak, Derrick M., 260
Kwak, Mary, 300
Kweder, Sandra, 142
Kyoto Protocol, 46, 338, 562
  cap-and-trade systems, 344
  China and, 539
  Clinton administration and, 346–347
  Environmental Defense and, 362
  European Union and, 347–348, 498
  international law and, 750
  Japan and, 453
Kyoto Treaty, 6

Labarthe, Carlos, 557, 567
Labor Contract Law (China), 539
Labor issues, in restaurant industry, 22
Labor markets, in European Union, 494–496
Labor organization, Federal Express and, 212–213
Labor Research Associates (LRA), 149
Labor unions
  automobile industry and, 7
  European Union, 499
  free-rider problem, 174
  grassroots campaigns, 231
  See also specific unions
Lacey, Frederick B., 408
Lafarge, 598
Lafarge Coppée, 500, 598
Lambert, Debra, 125
Lamy, Pascal, 593
Landmark Group, 566
Lands' End, 431
Lane, Barry, 371
Lange, Louis G., 705
Lantos, Tom, 548
Large-Scale Retail Store Law (Japan), 466, 616, 617
Larsson, Fredrik, 618
LaSorda, Tom, 8
Law, 374–375
  Anti-Monopoly Law (Japan), 462
  California Space Heaters, Inc. case, 404–406
  common law, 375–376
  contracts, 383–386
  entitlements, 389–391
  intellectual property law, 377–383, 406
  international, 750–751
  liability system, imperfections in, 399–402
  obesity and McLawsuits case, 408–412
  patents case, 406–408
  product safety problems, 387–389
  products liability case, 392–399
  property law, 376–377
  regulation versus liability, 391
  social efficiency, 387–389, 391–392
  summary, 403
  torts, 386–387
  U.S. trade, 589–590
  See also Antitrust law
Law of the Sea, 750
Lawson Inc., 477
Lawsuits, 98, 106
Lay, Kenneth, 642, 644, 645, 646, 647
Lazarus, Charles, 614–615, 616
Leadership Conference, 334
League of Conservation Voters, 195, 229, 356
Leahy, Sir Terry, 564

Lear, Norman, 335
Least-cost avoider, 388
Lederer, Bob, 209
Lee, Kai-fu, 547
Lee Der, 137
Legal compliance, 625–626
Legalism, 518
Legal recourse, to news media disputes, 83–84
Legal space, positioning in, 47
Legislation, 14, 15
  carried interest taxation, 214, 216
  daylight saving time, 208–209
  eBay database protection case, 435–436
  election financing, 228–229
  fuel efficiency standards, 260, 262–263
  informational strategies and, 203
  nonmarket strategy and, 192
  rights and, 682
  See also specific laws
Legislative arena, responsiveness of, 205
Legislative branch, in China, 530
Legislative process
  European Union, 488, 489
  Japan, 457–458
  U.S. Congress, 175–177
Legislators, 178–179
Legislature. See Institutions; U.S. Congress; specific laws
Lehman, Bruce, 605
Lemon laws, 188
Lentos, Tom, 31
Lents, James, 371
Leto, Joseph, 135
Levi Strauss & Company, 35, 36, 628, 721–722, 752–753, 754–755, 758
Levin, Andrew, 333
Levin, Carl, 259, 262, 448
Levin, Gerald M., 249
Levitan, Robert, 432
Lexis-Nexis, 430, 434
Lexus, 7
Leyden Corporation, 657
Leyden, Jochen, 110
LGT Group, 775
Li, 524
Li, Robin, 546
Liability
  crisis management and, 132
  products, 392–399
  regulation versus, 391
Liability rule, 342–343, 390
Liability system, imperfections in, 399–402
Li & Fung Ltd., 614
Libel, 83–84
Liberal Democratic Party (Japan), 455, 456, 457, 459, 461, 465, 475, 478, 616
Licensing, compulsory, 781
Lieberman, Ben, 262
Lieberman-Warner Climate Security Act, 338, 339, 356
Liecha, Harold, 218
Life Insurance Association of Japan, 477
Life insurance screening, 673, 691, 710
Life Insurance Settlement Association, 672
Lightfoot, Jim, 669
LimeWire, 380
Lin Biao, 521
Lincoln Electric, 551
Liquidated damages, 386
Litigation strategy, 98
Littlejohn, Gail, 436
Little River Funding, 643
Liu, Pat, 772–773
Liu Benren, 542
Liu Zhengrong, 547
Living benefits, 671–672, 704
Living Benefits, Inc., 671–672
Liz Claiborne, 754, 758
LJM Cayman LP, 644
LJM partnerships, 644, 645, 646, 647
Lladro, 565

L.L. Bean, 431, 758
Lloyd's of London, 440
Lobbying, 11, 220–222
  access, 225–226
  controls on, 226–227
  credibility and relevance of information, 224–225
  European Union, 501
  government allies, 226
  informational strategies, 202
  Japan, 470
  multidomestic market strategy and, 37
  nature of, 222–223
  technical and political information, 223–224
  timing and focus, 226
Lobbying Act (1946), 226–227
Lobbying case, 242–247
Lobbying Disclosure Act (1995), 227
Local governments, 191, 531–532
Locked in, 416
Lockheed Corporation, 762, 763–764, 766
Lofgren, Zoe, 611
Logue, William, 364
Lone Star Industries, 598
Long, Russell, 95
L'Oréal, 733
Lorfelder, Jochen, 110
Los Angeles Economic Development Corporation, 648
Los Angeles Fire and Police Pension System, 678
Loscher, Peter, 776–777
Loss, Ira A., 254, 258
Louis Vuitton, 29
Louis Vuitton and Moet Hennessey (LVMH) Group, 565
Lowell, Roger, 124, 125
Lowenstein, Doug, 213, 216
Lower Mainland Multicultural Family Support Services Centre, 748
Lowe's, 92, 218
LTV, 593
Lufthansa AG, 290
Lula da Silva, Luiz Inacio, 602, 606
Lustgarten, Karen, 242
Lutz, Robert, 261
Luxembourg, 507, 513
Luxury tax, repeal of, 184
Lynch, Elisa, 95
Lynch Interactive Corporation, 651

Maastricht Treaty, 483–484
MacArthur, Kelly Jo, 300
Mackey, Benny, 715
Mackey, John, 624, 625
Mackey, Linda, 715
MacPherson v. Buick Motor Company, 393
MacRobert, Angus, 572
Mad cow disease, 23
Maddox, Tom, 430
Magnuson, Keith, 362
Magnuson-Moss Warranty Act, 393, 396
Mahonia, 643
Major, John, 110
Majoritarian politics, 160, 356, 579, 580
Majority-building strategies, 199–202
Majority protection, 201
Major League Baseball, 270
Malaysia, 560, 587
Maloney, Carolyn B., 448
Managed Funds Association, 214, 216
Management
  corporate social performance, 634
  ethics and, 653–654
  integrated strategy and, 34
  Molecular Insight Pharmaceuticals, 62
  role of, 3
Managers, nonmarket strategies and, 189–194
Mandelson, Peter, 139, 604
Manipulation, in business nonmarket action, 188–189

Mankiw, Greg, 213
Mannesmann AG, 757
Manufacturing, by Molecular Insight Pharmaceuticals, 63
Mao Zedong, 519–520
Marconi PLC, 757
Marine Mammal Protection Act, 587, 631
Maritz, Paul, 297
Market capabilities, of Envirotest Systems Corporation, 59
Market environment, 1–2
  business, 2–3
  management, 3
  nonmarket environment and, 4
  summary, 16
Market for control, 640–641
Market forces, 13
Market imperfections, 310–316
Market opening, political economy of, 594–596
Market positioning, 55–56
Markets, resource allocation and, 621
Market strategy, 36–37
  Envirotest Systems Corporation, 59
  nonmarket positioning and, 43, 45–46
  nonmarket strategies and, 41–42
  See also Integrated strategy
Markey, Edward J., 208, 210, 211, 642
Märklin, Gebruder, 615
Marlin, 643
Marnera case, 772–773
Marquis Jet Partnership, 56
Marshall, Dennis, 741
Marshall, Kimberly, 741
Marshall, Thurgood, 187, 692, 693
Martha Overseas Corporation, 775
Martin, Jerome, 606
Martin, John, 743, 745
Martin, Kevin, 317, 326–327, 333, 334
Martin Luther King All Children's Choir of Virginia, 740
Marubeni Trading Company, 766
Mary Kay Cosmetics, 543
Mashboxx, 380
MasterCard, 272, 273, 274, 446
Matsushita, 416
Mattel, 45, 135–140, 316, 402
Maxims, Kantian, 683–689
May, Chandler, 257
Mazda, 464
Mazda North American Operations, 262
McCahill, Barry, 261
McCain, John, 181, 247, 248, 250, 335
McCaw Communications, 12
McConnell, Mitch, 195, 196
McCray, John, 62, 64
McCrery, Jim, 214
McCurdy, Dave, 260
McDonald's, 1, 2, 22
  activist organizations and, 103, 104–105
  campaigns against, 93, 96
  corporate social performance, 630
  crisis management, 123, 127–128
  Environmental Defense and, 362
  environmental issues, 362
  Greenpeace and, 102
  Japan and, 468, 616
  news media and, 84
  nonmarket environment of, 20–24
  obesity and McLawsuits case, 408–412
  regulation, 316
  strategy and negotiations, 104–105
McDonald v. Santa Fe Trail Transportation Co., 695
McDonnell Douglas, 164, 171, 764
M-Cell, 570
McGlynn, Margaret, 246
McGovern, James, 21, 411
McGraw, Ali, 118
McGreevy, Lisa, 214, 216
McGuire, Bill, 51
McGuire Act, 272
MCI, 238, 320, 321, 326, 330, 493

MCI-Worldcom, 249
McKinnell, Henry, 680
McKinsey & Co., 339, 551, 566
McLaughlin, Andrew, 30–31, 240, 545
McLawsuits case, 408–412
McLibel, 84
McManus, Steve, 740
McMenu bills, 411
McNealy, Scott, 300, 421
Mectizan Donation Program, 553
Medhome v. Riegel, 396
Media. See News media
Media Access Project, 329, 334, 335
Media coverage
  automobile industry, 8
  GlaxoSmithKline case, 781
Media interviews, 79–80
Median voter theorem, 195, 211
Media ownership rules (FCC), 317, 332–336
Media strategies, 78–79
Media vacuums, 79
Medicaid, 17, 18, 146, 245, 314–315
Medicare, 18, 20, 242
Medicines Control Agency (Germany), 19
Médecins sans Frontières, 781
Medstory, 29
Melchett, Lord Peter, 111
Menu Education and Labeling Act (MEAL), 21–22, 411
Mercedes-Benz, environmental regulations case, 366
Mercer, Joanne, 607, 612, 613
Mercer, William W., 289
Mercer Human Resource Consulting, 667
Merchants National Bank & Trust, 106
Merck
  compulsory licensing case, 603, 606
  crisis management case, 140–142
  emerging markets and, 553–554
  GlaxoSmithKline AIDS drugs policy case, 778, 780, 781
  lobbying case, 242, 243–244, 245, 246
  Siemens bribery case, 776
Mercosur, 588
Mergers
  case, 290–293
  conglomerate, 268
  EU competition policy and, 492–494
  horizontal, 268
  merger guidelines and, 284–286
Merkel, Angelika, 110
Merrill Lynch, 134, 644, 695
Meskala, Tadesse, 556
Messages (news), 68–69
Metro AG, 29
Metro Broadcasting v. F.C.C., 708
Metro Cash & Carry, 564, 565
Metro Group, 564, 565–566
Metzenbaum, Howard, 164
Mexican Cement Industry, 597–598
Mexico, 560, 594–595, 603. See also Cemex
Microcredit Summit Campaign, 567
Microfinance, 553, 556–557
Micron Technology, 238
Microsoft
  antitrust issues, 1, 4, 47, 270, 279, 283, 294–301
  China and, 546, 548
  copyrights, 382
  encryption export controls case, 610
  EU competition policy and, 493
  FCC and, 329
  Google and, 26, 28, 29, 39
  Internet privacy, 431
  Internet taxation case, 249
  online markets and, 414–415, 416, 417
  Yahoo! and, 31
Mika, Susan, 751
Mill, John Stuart, 660
Millennium Copyright Act, 29
Miller, Edward, 433

Miller, George, 218
Miller, J. Irwin, 367
Miller-Tydings Act, 272
Milliken & Company, 368
Milloy, Stephen, 22
Ministry of Commerce and Industry (India), 565
Ministry of Economy, Trade and Industry (Japan), 458–460, 466, 470, 476
Ministry of Finance (China), 531
Ministry of Finance (Japan), 453–454, 459–460, 461, 474, 476
Ministry of Health, Labor, and Welfare (Japan), 472
Ministry of Home Affairs (Japan), 466
Ministry of Information Industry (China), 31
Ministry of International Affairs and Communication (Japan), 459, 470
Ministry of International Trade and Industry (Japan), 197, 198
Ministry of Land, Infrastructure, and Transport (Japan), 465
Ministry of Posts and Telecommunications (Japan), 474, 475, 476
Ministry of Small-Scale Industries (India), 565
Minnesota Family Council, 245
Minnesota Medical Association, 246
Mirabella Estates, 56
Miramax Films, 92
Misener, Paul, 251
Mitchell, George J., 226
Mitsubishi Motors, 8, 464
Mitts, Emma, 148, 218
Mitusbishi Electric, boycott against, 92
Miyazu, Junichiro, 475
Mobilization, in grassroots and constituency campaigns, 231–232
Moi, Daniel arap, 561
Molecular Insight Pharmaceuticals, 42, 61–65
Monaghan, Thomas S., 100
Monoline banks, 446
Monopoly, 267, 268, 269, 310–312. *See also* Antitrust laws
Monsanto, 587, 679
Monsanto Co. v. Spray-Rite Service Co., 282, 287
Montgomery Ward, 292
Montreal Protocol on Substances That Deplete the Ozone Layer, 750
Moody, Krista, 245
Moore, Debbie, 148
Moral concerns, 11, 13, 50–51
    collective action, 162
    informational strategies and, 203
    nonmarket analysis, 154, 162
    See also Ethics
Moral determinants, of market action, 722–724
Moral hazard, 314–315
Moral motivation, for corporate social performance, 633
Moral philosophy, 659–660
Moral rules, 683–689
Moral standing, rights and, 690
Morgan Stanley Dean Witter, 695
Moroney, Dennis, 448
Morpheus, 379
Morris, Gillian, 368
Morris, Michael, 300
Most favored nation (MFN) status, for China, 204
Mothers Against Drunk Driving (MADD), 7, 14
Motion Picture Association of America, 380
Motivation, corporate social performance, 633–634
Motorola, 12, 470, 471, 472
Motor Vehicle Safety Act, 15
Moulette, Patrick, 775
MoveOn, 97

MoveOn.org, 145, 229, 230, 232, 335
Moynihan, Daniel Patrick, 14
Ms. Foundation for Women, 113
MSN, 29, 416, 546
MTN Foundation, 571
MTN Group Limited, 553, 570–573
MTN Holdings, 570
Mudaraba, 560
Mugabe, 560
Multidomestic market strategies, 36–37
Multi-Fiber Arrangement (MFA), 591
Multilateral trade policy, 579, 580
Multilevel lobbying, 224
Munn v. Illinois, 304, 310
Murdock, Rupert, 335
Murphy, Brian, 409
Musaraka, 560
Music downloads, on Google, 31
Mutual recognition, 483
Mwangi, James, 557
Myanmar, 754
Myers, Mark, 246

Nader, François, 254
Nader, Ralph, 14, 15, 91, 102
Nanotechnology regulation, 368–370
Nanya Technology, 238
Napoleonic Code, 376
Napster, 379
Nardelli, Robert, 399
Nath, Kamal, 565
National Academy of Sciences, 10–11, 12, 115, 737
National Ambient Air Quality Standards, 58
National Association for the Advancement of Colored People (NAACP), 371
National Association of Broadcasters, 210
National Association of Chain Drug Stores, 20
National Association of Clean Water Agencies (NACWA), 369
National Association of Convenience Stores, 147, 182
National Association of Corporate Directors, 640
National Association of Counties, 249
National Association of Home Builders (NAHB), 197
National Association of Manufacturers, 260
National Association of Realtors (NAR), 270, 436
National Association of Regulatory Utility Commissioners (NARUC), 309, 329
National Association of Securities Dealers, 118
National Bella Hess v. Department of Revenue of the State of Illinois, 247–248
National Black Chamber of Commerce, 372
National Bureau of Corruption (China), 538
National Cable Television Association (NCTA), 329
National Cancer Institute, 246, 680
National Candy Brokers Association, 209
National Cattlemen's Beef Association (NCBA), 23, 24
National Center for Policy Analysis, 556
National Center for Tobacco-Free Kids, 182
National Chamber Alliance for Politics, 234
National Community Pharmacist Association (NCPA), 20
National Confectioners Association, 209
National Conference of State Legislatures, 244

National Conference on Public Employee Retirement Systems (NCPERS), 215
National Consumers League, 254
National Council of State Legislators (NCSL), 249, 250
National Credit Union Administration, 447
National Development and Reform Commission (China), 8, 531
National Education Association (NEA), 145
National Federation of Independent Business (NFIB), 156, 157, 234, 320
National Federation of Teachers, 145
National Football League (NFL), 742
National Governors Association (NGA), 249, 250
National Grocers Association, 147, 182
National Highway Traffic Safety Administration (NHTSA), 6, 7, 8
    formation of, 15
    fuel economy standards case, 260, 261, 262
    General Motors and, 86
    regulation, 306–307
National Hispanic Media Coalition, 91
National Industrial Recovery Act, 306
National Institute for Research Advancement (Japan), 476
National Institutes of Health (NIH), 680
Nationalization, in emerging markets, 560
National Labor Relations Act (NLRA), 212
National Labor Relations Board (NLRB), 148
National League of Cities, 249
National Marine Manufacturers Association (NMMA), 184, 235
National Minority Automotive Advocacy Coalition (NMAAC), 7
National Network for Immunization Information, 246
National News Council, 89
National Organization for Women (NOW), 100, 113, 334–335
National Party Congress (China), 529, 530
National Population and Family Planning Commission (China), 536
National Restaurant Association, 22, 409
National Retail Federation (NRF), 249
National Rifle Association (NRA), 334, 335
National Safety Council, 210
National Security Agency (NSA), 607, 609, 610
National Small Business Association, 320
National Soft Drink Association, 288
National Tax Service (NTS), 772
National Telecommunications and Information Administration (NTIA), 329
National Tobacco Policy and Youth Smoking Reduction Act, 181
National Trade Estimate Report (NTER), 595, 596
National Transportation Safety Board (NTSB), 19, 669
National Vaccine Information Center, 246
National Venture Capital Association (NVCA), 215
Natural monopoly, 310–312
Natural Resources Defense Council (NRDC), 6, 8
    activist strategy, 97, 98
    environmental politics, 354, 355
    environmental protection issues, 360, 361
    fuel economy standards case, 259, 260
    news media and, 67–68, 71, 72, 83
    Project XL and, 352

Samsung case, 369
TRI and, 359
Wal-Mart and, 648
Nature Conservancy, 98, 104, 345, 363, 728
NatureServe, firm interactions with, 104
NBC, 74, 82, 86–88, 333
Nebbia v. New York, 304–305, 307
Nebergall, Mark, 249
Negligence, 393–394, 396
Neighbor to Neighbor, 82
Neoclassical liberalism, 697–698
Nestlé, 286, 504, 555
NetCoalition.com, 235, 435, 437
Netherlands, 495–496, 497
    emerging markets and, 554, 556
    Enron and, 643
    EU carbon tax case, 506, 57
    EU duty free abolition and, 513, 514
    fair trade movement, 554, 556
    Shell in, 108, 109, 110
NetPAC, 240
Netscape, 283, 297, 610
Netscape/AOL, 301
Network Advertising Initiative, 25, 430
Network Associates, 612
Network externalities, 415
Nevadans for Fair Fuel Economy Standards, 737
New IO approach, 275, 278–280, 282–283, 284
New Komeito Party (Japan), 455, 477, 478
Newman, Edwin, 70, 73
New Party Harbinger, 475
News Corporation, 74, 333, 335
News media, 66
    activist strategies, 97
    audience interest perspective, 69, 70–72
    balance and fairness, 73
    business interactions with, 78–81
    coverage and treatment theory, 69–73
    coverage costs, 73
    crisis management and, 125
    dispute resolution with, 81–85
    General Motors case, 86–88
    Illinois Power Company case, 88–89
    messages and their interpretation, 68–69
    nature of, 74–78
    newsworthiness, concept of, 72–73
    nonmarket issues and, 66–68
    societal significance perspective, 70–72
    summary, 85
News organizations, as businesses, 74
New Source Performance Standards (NSPS), 183–184, 345
Newsworthiness, concept of, 72–73
New Voices groups, 441
New York State Consumer Protection Board, 26
New York State Pension Funds, 31
New York Stock Exchange (NYSE), 776
New York Times v. Sullivan, 83, 84, 85
NextLevel Communications, 329
NGO Good Jobs First, 218
Nguyen, Thuyen, 113
Nielsen Monitor-Plus, 716
Nielson, Howard C., 208, 211
Nigeria, 570, 571, 572
Nike, 1, 2
    activist strategies, 96
    activist targeting of, 99
    boycotts against, 91
    corporate social responsibility, 725
    ethics issues, 758
    FLA and, 759–761
    news media and, 66
    nonmarket strategy, 36
    positioning, 43, 45
    private politics case, 112–114
    reputation of, 49

NIMBY movement, environmental politics and, 358–359
Nippon Motorola, 470
Nippon Telephone and Telegraph case, 474–476
Nissan
  fuel economy exception for, 6
  fuel economy standards case, 262
  lobbying by, 11
Nixon, Richard M., 181, 349
Noack, William, 737–738
Nocera, Barbara, 262
Nokia, 38
Nokia Siemens Networks, 572
Nongovernmental organizations (NGOs), 96–97, 620. *See also specific organizations*
Nonmarket action
  Boeing, 167
  business organization (Japan), 467–468
  criticisms of, 186–189
  free-rider problem and, 173–174
  moral determinants of, 722–724
  public politics and, 154
  responsible, 186–189
  restraint and, 736–738
Nonmarket agenda, of Boeing, 166
Nonmarket analysis, 153–154
  Boeing, 162–171
  collective action, moral determinants of, 162
  environmental politics and scrubbers, 183–184
  free-rider problem and nonmarket action, 173–174
  luxury tax repeal, 184
  nonmarket strategy and, 190
  political competition, nature of, 159–162
  public politics, 154–158
  summary, 171–172
  tobacco politics, 181–183
  U.S. Congress, 175–180
Nonmarket assets, 192
Nonmarket capabilities, 48–49, 60, 239–240
Nonmarket defense, 54–57
Nonmarket effectiveness, organizing for, 239
Nonmarket environment, 1–2
  analysis of, 5
  anticipation of change, 13
  automobile industry, 5–11
  business, 2–3
  change in, 11–13
  China, 527–532
  Google case, 25–32
  management, 3, 562–563
  market environment and, 5
  McDonald's case, 20–24
  nonmarket issue life cycle, 13–16
  pharmaceutical industry case, 17–20
  regulatory agencies, 307–310
  summary, 16
Nonmarket forces, India, 565–566
Nonmarket issue life cycle, 13–16, 36
Nonmarket issues
  analysis of, 50–52
  anticipation of, 80–81
  China, 535–540
  European Union, 496–498
  Japan, 452–454
  news coverage theory on, 70–71
  unanticipated, 81
  See also Information industries; News media
Nonmarket objectives, of Boeing, 166
Nonmarket portfolio, of PacifiCare, 221
Nonmarket positioning, 42–49, 55
Nonmarket pressure, 143–151, 647–650
Nonmarket spillovers, 757
Nonmarket strategy, 33–37
  Boeing, 170–171
  eBay database protection case, 435

Envirotest Systems Corporation, 60
European Union, 499–504
Japan, 468–469
market strategies and, 41–42
NTT, 475
organization of, 53
Wal-Mart case, 647–650
See also Integrated strategy
Nonmarket strategy (government arenas), 185–186
  carried interest taxation, 213–216
  choice of, 205–206
  daylight saving time politics, 208–211
  Federal Express and labor organization, 212–213
  formulation of, 189–194
  generic, 196–204
  institutions and interests, 205–206
  outcomes, understanding, 195–196
  responsible nonmarket action, 186–189
  summary, 206–207
  Wal-Mart's urban expansion strategy, 217–219
Nonmarket strategy implementation (government arenas), 220
  coalition building, 233–236
  electoral support, 227–231
  fuel economy standards case, 259–263
  grassroots and constituency campaigns, 231–233
  Internet taxation case, 247–252
  judicial actions, 238–239
  lobbying, 220–227, 242–247
  nonmarket capabilities, development of, 239–240
  nonmarket effectiveness, organizing for, 239
  pharmaceutical switching case, 252–258
  public advocacy, 237
  summary, 240–241
  testimony, 236–237
Nonmarket styles. *See* Corporate nonmarket styles
Nonmarket theory, 318–321
Nonpecuniary externality, 312
Nonprescription Drugs Advisory Committee, 253, 254
Norplant Foundation, 676
Norplant System, 675–677
Norquist, Grover, 248
Norris, Michael, 329
Norris-LaGuardia Act, 269
North American Free Trade Agreement (NAFTA), 6, 11, 12, 159
  Cemex and, 600
  international law and, 750
  international trade policy, 574, 579, 580, 588
  political economy of, 594–595
  vote recruiting and, 199
North, Douglass, 5
Northern Pacific Railroad v. U.S., 273, 274
NorthPoint Communications, 326
Northwest Airlines, 283
Norvig, Peter, 547
Norway, 110
Notice of Proposed Rule Making (NPRM), 306, 327, 332–333
Novartis, 286
Novell, Inc., 493

Obama, Barack, 216
Obesity, 20–24, 408–412
Obey, David R., 335
Objectives
  business objectives versus public interest, 186–187
  nonmarket strategy, 191
Occupational Safety and Health Administration (OSHA), 7, 91
O'Conner, Kevin, 428, 429

O'Connor, Sandra Day, 401–402, 690, 692
O'Donnell, William, 257
Odyssey Club, 56
OECD Anti-Bribery Convention, 766, 769–770, 773
Office Depot, merger case, 290–293
Officeholders. *See* Institutional officeholders
OfficeMax, 292
Office of Economic Analysis (OEA), 340
Office of Fair Trading (UK), 289
Office of Information and Regulatory Affairs (OIRA), 308, 309
Office of Management and Budget (OMB), 308
Office of Pesticide Programs, 369
Office of Thrift Supervision (OTS), 445, 447, 715
Offsets, 351
Ogilvy Government Relations, 214
Okrent, Daniel, 75–76
O'Leary, Michael, 289
Omidyar, Pierre, 433, 438
Omnibus Trade and Competitiveness Act, 595, 766
OnBank, 106
One-child-per-family policy (China), 535–536
O'Neill, Paul, 646
Online communities, 425–427, 438–444
Online markets, economics of, 414–417
Online Privacy Alliance, 429
Online Privacy Association, 433
OnSale, Inc., 442
Open Handset Alliance (OHA), 38
Open standards, 425
OPIS, 678
Opium War, 519
Opportunities
  emerging markets, 551–558, 566, 571–572
  Envirotest Systems Corporation, 58–59
  nonmarket strategy and, 34
Oracle, 298, 497
Orange, 571
Orangina, 490
Orascom, 571
O'Reilly, Arthur, 631
O'Reilly, Gavin, 28
Organization for Economic Cooperation and Development (OECD), 250–251, 357, 495, 751, 762, 769–770, 771, 775
Organization of American States, 750
Organizing costs, 156–157
O'Rourke, Dana, 136
Orphan Drug Act, 65
Orr, Robert, 471
Orszag, Peter R., 214
Osega, Mike, 366
Osprey, 643
Otero, Maria, 567
Ottawa Taxation Framework Conditions, 250–251
Outcomes, understanding, 195–196
Overstock.com, 424
Oxfam America, 555, 583
Oyagbola, Amina, 571

PACE, 328
PacifiCare, nonmarket portfolio of, 221
Pacific Gas & Electric, 232, 324, 353
Pacific Gas & Electric Co. v. Public Utilities Commission of California, 187
Pacific Stock Exchange, 351
Page, Larry, 30, 419
Pagrabs, Juris, 290
Pakistan, 29, 561, 587
Pampered Chef, 725
Pantaloon Retail, 566
Paraguay, 588

Parents Requesting Open Vaccine Education, 245
Parent Teacher Association (PTA), 14, 210
Parker, Dick, 111
Partnership to End Cervical Cancer, 244
Patents, 380–381, 406–408. *See also* Intellectual property
Paternalism, 735–736
Patient Bill of Rights, 221
Patillo, Bob, 568
Paulson, Hank, 214
Paxson Communications, 333
Paxton, Michael, 146
PayPal, 440
Peak associations, 233–234
Pearce, Harry, 87
Pecuniary externality, 312
Peer-to-peer systems, 379
Pelosi, Nancy, 195, 263
People for the Ethical Treatment of Animals (PETA), 23, 107
PepsiCo
  antitrust laws, 288
  crisis management, 124–125, 127, 129, 130, 133
  European Union and, 490
  judicial actions, 238–239
Per capita benefits, 156
Perfect 10, 29
Perfect competition, 277
Performance, Chicago school and, 277
Perrier. *See* Source Perrier S.A.
Perry, Rick, 245
Per se violations, 273–274
Personal ethics, 655
Personal injury lawsuits, 397–398
Personal Responsibility in Food Consumption Act, 21, 411
Personal staffs, in U.S. Congress, 178
Perspectives, changes in, 11, 12
Peru, 588
Pesterre, Pete, 86
Pettersson, Kenth, 617
Pew Charitable Trusts, 73
Pew Research Center, 77
Pew Trust, 46
Pfizer, 17, 18, 47, 257
  Celebrex case, 661, 679–680
  China and, 538
  ethics case, 679–681
  GlaxoSmithKline AIDS drugs policy case, 779, 780
  nonmarket strategy, 192
Pharmaceutical industry
  integrated strategy, 40–41
  lobbying case, 242–247
  manipulation in, 189
  Molecular Insight Pharmaceuticals, 42, 61–65
  nonmarket capabilities, 49
  nonmarket environment of, 17–20
  politics of, 236
  positioning, 46–47
  switching case, 252–258
Pharmaceutical Manufacturers Association (PMA), 233, 236, 781
Pharmaceutical Research and Manufacturers Association (PhRMA), 17, 18, 19, 41, 45, 47, 49, 234, 256, 499
Pharmaceutical Research & Manufacturing Association of Thailand, 604
Pharmacia, 679
Pharma Group, 257
Philanthropy, by Google, 30
Philips Electronics, 39, 498, 503
Phillip Holtzman, 767
Physicians Committee for Responsible Medicine, 411
Physicians for Social Responsibility, 92
Pickle, J. J., 162–171
Piracy. *See* Digital piracy; Intellectual property
Pirate Bay, 380

Pitofsky, Robert, 432
Pivotal voters, 200–201
Pizza Hut, 93, 96, 223, 226, 737
Planned Parenthood, 242, 676, 725
Platform for Privacy Preferences Protection, 431
Plavix case, 406–408
Plunkett, Travis, 448
Pluralism, 186, 452
Point Carbon, 347
Polenetsky, Jules, 25
Policy Affairs Research Committee (Japan), 457
Policy jurisdictions, 178
Policymaking, in China, 529–530
Policy risk, in emerging markets, 559–560
Politburo (China), 529, 530
Political action committees (PACs), 186, 188, 228–230
Political competition, nature of, 159–162
Political contributions, from Enron, 646
Political corruption, in emerging markets, 561
Political economy
  environmental management and stability, 353–359
  international trade policy, 579–581
  market opening, 594–596
  protectionism, 590–594
  regulation, 316–318, 319
  See also European Union political economy; International trade policy; Japan political economy
Political exchange, 464–466
Political information, 202, 223–224
Political institutions, in China, 525–526
Political megalomania, in emerging markets, 560–561
Political parties, 179, 456–457
Political philosophy, 659–660
Political recourse, to news media disputes, 84–85
Political reform, in Japan, 460
Political risk, in emerging markets, 551
Political space, positioning in, 46–47
Politics
  Boeing, 162–171
  daylight saving time, 208–211
  environmental, 183–184
  ethics and, 655–656
  products liability, 398–399
  tobacco, 181–183
  See also Nonmarket strategy (government arenas); Nonmarket strategy implementation (government arenas); Private politics; Public politics
Pollack, Ronald, 254–255
Pollution credits trading systems case, 370–373
Pope, Carl, 95, 145
Population Council, 675
Porras, Carlos, 372
Porsche, 262
Portland General Electric (PGE), 332
Portofino Club, 56
Portugal, 508, 514
Positioning
  entrepreneurial, 54–57
  nonmarket, 42–49
Positioning spaces, 46–47
Positive feedback, 416
Posner, Richard, 78, 299
Postal Life Insurance Service, 476
Potgieter, Anton, 572
Powell, Michael, 326, 330, 333
Powerex, 331
Power
  bureaucratic (Japan), 458–459
  business nonmarket action, 187–188
Powers, William, 646
Power Tree Carbon Company, 347
Prahalad, C. K., 553

Prasad, Jageshwar, 565
Precursor, 26
Predatory pricing, 282–283
Predictions, 50
Preemption, 318, 396–397
Preexisting conditions, screening for, 673, 691, 710
Pre-Natal Diagnostic Techniques (Regulation and Prevention of Misuses) Act, 747
Pre-Republican China, 518–519
Prescott, Edward, 495
Prescription Access Litigation Project, 19, 40
Prescription Medicines Code of Practice Authority, 718
Presidency, 179–180, 205. *See* Institutions; *specific U.S. presidents*
Presidential appointments, 179
President's Commission for the Study of Ethical Problems in Medicine and Biomedical and Behavioral Research, 747
President's Emergency Plan for AIDS Relief, 744–745
Price-Anderson Act, 400
Price controls, in emerging markets, 560
Price Costco, 291
Price discrimination, 268
Price fixing, 268, 283–284, 289–290
Price maintenance, resale, 268
PricewaterhouseCoopers, 759
Pricing
  AIDS drugs, 779–781
  Norplant System case, 675–677
  predatory, 282–283
Prince, Chuck, 720, 725, 730
Principles, reasoning and, 734–735
Prioritization, 692–693
Privacy
  European Union, 13
  Google, 25, 26–27
  Internet, 417–423, 427, 428–432
  See also Internet privacy
Privacy Act (1974), 421
Privacy International, 26, 420, 430
Privacy rights, 688
Privacyplace, 430
Privacy Rights Clearinghouse, 419, 431
PrivaSeek, 431
Private enforcement, of antitrust laws, 272–273
Private Equity Council, 213, 214, 215, 216
Private Escapes, 56, 57
Private governance, 759
Private interests, ethics and, 655
Private politics, 90–91
  activist organizations, 101–107
  activist strategies, 96–101
  campaigns, 91–94
  environmental protection, 356, 358–359
  Nike case, 112–114
  nonmarket strategy and, 35
  public politics versus, 95–96
  Rainforest Action Network and Citigroup case, 114–119
  Shell and Greenpeace case, 108–111
  summary, 107–108
Private recourse, to news media disputes, 81–82
Private Retreats, 56
Private vacation clubs, 54–57
Privatization, in Japan, 461, 476–479
Privity of contract, 393
Procedural due process, 306–307
Procter & Gamble
  business nonmarket action and, 189
  corporate social responsibility, 734
  crisis management, 123
  emerging markets and, 555
  ethics, 739
  news media and, 82

Product development, at Molecular Insight Pharmaceuticals, 64
Product liability, in automobile industry, 8
Product safety, 387–389, 538
Products liability law, 392–399
Product tampering, 125
Profit maximization, 621–625
Project XL, 351, 352
Pro Mujer, 567
Pronuptia, 504
Property law, 376–377
Property rule, 341, 390
Proposition 211 (California), 232
Proprietary information, 734
Proprietary standards, 415
Protection channels, 591, 594
Protectionism, 579, 580, 590–594
Provincial governments, 531–532
Proximate cause, 396
PRS Group, 558
Prudential PLC, 757
Public advocacy, 237
Public Citizen, 17, 18, 225, 254, 398
Public Company Accounting Oversight Board, 640
Public disclosure test, 739
Public goods, 313
Public Health Advocacy Institute of Boston, 409
Public interest, business objectives versus, 186–187
Public officeholders, nonmarket strategies targeting, 203. *See also* Institutional officeholders
Public policy, in eBay database protection case, 435
Public politics, 90, 95–96
  environmental protection, 356, 358
  nonmarket action in, 154–158
  See also Nonmarket strategy (government arenas); Nonmarket strategy implementation (government arenas)
Public sentiment, positioning for, 46
Public shaming, 96
Public Successor Corporation, 477
Puget Sound Electric, 331
Pulmonary-Allergy Drug Advisory Committee, 253
Punitive damages, 398
Pure Bioscience, 368
Pursglove, Kevin, 434

Qantas, 290
Qin Dynasty (China), 518
Qing Dynasty (China), 518–519
Quello, James, 327
Questionable foreign payments, 761–770
Quill v. North Dakota, 247–248
Qwest, 322

Rabobank, 357
Racketeer Influenced and Corrupt Organizations Act, 188
Railway Labor Act (RLA), 212
Rainbow Coalition, 742
Raines, Franklin, 714
Rainforest Action Network (RAN), 8, 9
  campaigns by, 92, 94
  corporate social performance and, 634
  Earth Island Institute and, 102
  environmental protection issues, 360
  Equator Principles, 357, 358
  firm challenges against, 106–107
  firm interactions with, 103, 104, 105
  first-mover advantage, 97
  Home Depot and, 363, 364
  private politics case, 94, 114–119
  public politics, 95
  target selection by, 99–100
Rainie, Harrison, 421
Rambus, Inc., 238
Ramsey, Fiona, 569

Rangel, Charles, 214, 216
Rao, Muralidhara, 566
Rao, Prasado, 605
Raptors, 644–645, 646
Rather, Dan, 88, 740
Rathke, Wade, 146
Rawl, Lawrence, 131
Rawls, John, 700–710
Raytheon, 696
RC2 Corporation, 135, 136, 138
REACH, 497
Read, Robert, 87
Read, Russell, 215
Reagan, Ronald, 166, 179, 180
  antitrust laws, 274, 278, 284
  regulation, 307, 308–309
Real Estate Roundtable, 215
RealNetwork, 296, 417, 430
Reason. *See* Rule of reason
Reasoner, Harry, 88
Reasoning, principles and, 734–735
Recalls, in automobile industry, 8
Reciprocal exchange, 464–466
Reciprocal Trade Agreement Act, 588–589
Recourse, to news media disputes, 81–85
Red Cross, 126, 382
Redistribution, through regulation, 320
Redlining, 673–674, 709
Reebok, 754, 758
Reed, Brian, 30
Reed Elsevier PLC, 434, 435, 436
Reform era, in China, 521–523
Refusals to deal, 268
Regents of University of California v. Bakke, 707, 708
Regional Clean Air Incentives Market (RECLAIM), 351–352
Regulation, 302–303
  China, 535
  command-and-control, 340
  constitutional basis for, 304–305
  credit card regulation case, 447–448
  Cummins Inc. case, 368
  delegation, rule-making, due process, and discretion, 306–307
  Enron Power Marketing, Inc. case, 330–332
  environmental management and stability, 348–349, 366–370
  explanations for, 310
  FCC and broadband regulation case, 326–330
  FCC media ownership rules, 332–336
  liability versus, 391
  market imperfections, 310–316
  nonmarket theory of, 318–321
  political economy of, 316–318, 319
  Samsung case, 368
  self-regulation, 429, 759
  summary, 325
  See also Deregulation
Regulatory agencies, 305–306, 307–310. *See also specific agencies*
Regulatory Analysis Review Group, 308
Regulatory change, periods of, 303–304
Regulatory commissions, 305–306
Regulatory Flexibility Act, 320
Regulatory Impact Analysis, 308
Regulatory institutions, responsiveness of, 205
Regulatory risk, in emerging markets, 560
Reid, Harry, 195, 216
Reilly, Thomas F., 300
Reinhardt, Uwe, 254
Relationships, with journalists, 79
Reliance, 383
Reliance Communications, 570, 572, 573
Reliance damages, 386
Reliance Industries LTD., 573
Religious conflicts, in emerging markets, 561

Remedies, for breach of contract, 385–386
Remote Sensing Technologies (RST), 59
Remuda Ranch, 24
Ren, 524
Renault, 494
Renewable Fuels, Consumer Protection, and Energy Efficiency Act, 260
Rensi, Ed, 362
Rent chain, 193–194
Rent-seeking theories, 316
Reporters Without Borders, 545, 547
Representation strategies, 196–199
Republican China, 519–520
Reputation, 48–49
  crisis management and, 126–127
  nonmarket strategy and, 192–193
  online communities, 426, 439
  Wal-Mart, 143–151, 647–650, 728–729
Resale price maintenance, 268
Research, on corporate social performance, 635–637
Resolution, in crisis management program, 132–133
Resolution stage of crisis life cycle, 123–124
Resource allocation, markets and, 621
Resources, for nonmarket action, 157–158
Response, in crisis management program, 129–132
Responsible Care programs, 364–365
Responsible nonmarket action, 186–189
Responsiveness, in nonmarket strategies, 205
Restaurant industry, nonmarket environment of, 20–24
Restless legs syndrome case, 716–719
Restless Legs Syndrome Foundation (RLS), 717–718
Restraint, 736–738
Retail Workers Union (Handelsanstalldas Forbund), 617
Retaliation, market opening and, 595–596
Reverse Auction, 442
Reversibility, 684
Revolutionary Alliance (China), 519
Revolutions, democratic, 559
Rewards, for corporate social performance, 634–635
Rexrodt, Guenther, 110
Reynoso, Cruz, 741
Rhodes, Cecile, 773
Rhone-Poulenc, 271
Rhythms NetConnections, 326, 644
Rice, Paul, 556, 624
Richardson, Brooke, 546
Richardson, Dawn, 245
Richardson, Jerome J., 740, 741
Rickard, Lisa A., 409
Riders, 212
Rightmire, Matthew, 437
Rights, 710–711
  applied rights analysis, 689–690
  Citigroup subprime lending case, 714–716
  classes of, 682–683
  conflicts among, 691–694
  disabilities and, 696–697
  equal employment opportunity, 694–696
  genetic testing in workplaces (case), 712–714
  GlaxoSmithKline restless leg syndrome case, 716–719
  Kantian maxims versus moral rules, 683–689
  neoclassical liberalism, 697–698
  utilitarianism and, 666–667
  See also Human rights; Workers' rights
Rio Earth Summit, 506, 630
Ripa di Meana, Carlo, 506, 507
Risk

emerging markets, 571–572
  strict liability and, 396
Risk assessment, for emerging markets, 558–562
Ritchie, Gregg W., 678
Rite-Aid, 148
Rivera, Micaela, 567
River Blindness, 553–554
R. J. Reynolds, 181
Robert Mondavi, 227
Roberts, Brian, 329
Roberts, John, 397
Roberts, Kenneth, 14
Robinson-Patman Act, 268, 271
Roche Holding AG, 271, 492, 778, 779, 780
Roddick, Anita, 732, 733
Rodgers, T. J., 625
Roe, David, 372
Roever, Stefan, 610
Röhm, Elizabeth, 243
Root cause analysis, 128–129
Rosenbaum, Ruth, 555
Rosenberg, David, 556
Rosenblum, Bruce, 214–215
Rosing, Wayne, 419, 420
Rosston, Gregory L., 39
Rotenberg, Marc, 25, 429, 430, 431
Royal Ahold NV, 556
Royal Bank of Scotland, 357
Royal Dutch/Shell Group. *See* Shell
RP Foundation Fighting Blindness, 154, 158, 160, 206, 209, 233
RPG Group, 566
RSA Security, 609, 612
RT Strategies, 649
Rubenstein, David M., 214
Rubin, Andy, 39
Rubin, Robert, 118, 646
Ruby Tuesday, Inc., 411
Ruckelshaus, William, 358
Ruckus Society, 102
Rule-making, 306–307, 309
Rule of reason, 273–274
Rules, moral, 683–689
Rules Committee, 175
Rule utilitarianism, 664–666
Rurka, David, 617
Russia, 347, 592, 593, 705, 728
Rwanda, 570
Rx Partners, 237
Ryan, Kevin, 432
Ryanair, 289

Sachs, Hari, 254
Safe Drinking Water and Toxic Enforcement Act, 22
Safeguards, in international trade agreements, 584
Safer, Morley, 88
Safety regulations and standards, in automobile industry, 7, 14–15
Safeway, 100, 125, 143
Saipan, slave labor in, 754–755
Sakurai, Masao, 617
Sakuri, Osamu, 467
Sales, of Molecular Insight Pharmaceuticals, 63
Sales tax, Internet and, 424
Salomon Smith Barney, 118
Sam's Club, 149
Samsung, 368–370
Sander, Nancy, 255
Sandhu, Dalip, 748
Sandoz, 286
Sangeorge, Robert, 111
Sanofi-Aventis, 406–408
Saperstein, Mayeda, Larkin & Goldstein, 741
Sara Lee, 543, 555
Sarandon, Susan, 118
Sarbanes-Oxley Act, 107, 639–640, 777
Sarkozy, Nicholas, 495
Sasich, Larry, 254

Sass, Jennifer, 368–369
Saudi Arabia, 571–572
Sawada, Shigeo, 474, 475
SBC, 322
Scalia, Antonin, 401–402
Schaeffer, Leonard D., 255
Schering-Plough, 18, 19, 40, 47, 222, 252, 253, 255–257
Schiemann, Dylan, 39
Schilling, David, 638, 751
Schlein, Ted, 215
Schmidt, Eric, 26, 28, 29, 31, 38, 547
Schmidt, Hans Chr., 24
Schondelmeyer, Stephen W., 255
Schrage, Elliot, 545, 548
Schueckler, Richard K., 135
Schumer, Charles, 139, 216
Schwartz, Lisa M., 717, 718
Schwartzman, Andrew, 334, 335
Schwarzman, Stephen A., 213
Science. *See* Advocacy science
Scientific Advisory Group on Cellular Telephone Research, 12
Scientific discovery, 11–12
Scott, H. Lee, 143, 144, 648, 729
Screening, 50
Scrubbers, environmental politics and, 183–184
Seamen's Union, 617
Sears, 738
SecureAssure, 431
Securities and Exchange Commission (SEC), 640, 642, 643, 775, 776
Security and Freedom through Encryption Act (SAFE), 607, 611
Sederholm, Pamela, 209
Sefl, Tracy, 145, 146
Seidenberg, Ivan G., 328
Seidman, Robert C., 252, 253, 254
Seizures, in emerging markets, 560
Self-cultivation, 523–524
Self-interest, 661–662
Self-regulation, 429, 759
Semiconductor Industry Association (SIA), 226, 595
Sen, Nirupam, 565
Sensenbrenner, James, 21, 411
Service Employees International Union (SEIU), 144, 145, 146, 215
  campaign contributions, 230
Sethi, S. Prakash, 136
Seven-Up, 288
SHAC, 107
Shaefer, Steven D., 256
Shah, Premil, 568–569
Shaming, 96–97
Shantou Institute of Ultrasonic Instruments, 747
Shapiro, Jonathan, 430
Shapiro, Paul, 24
Sharav, Vera Hassner, 246
Shareholder rights, 98
Sharper Image, 370
Shell
  activist organizations and, 103
  boycotts against, 91
  company codes, 767
  corporate social responsibility, 732
  environmental issues, 341–342
  private politics case, 94, 108–111
  public politics and, 95
Shendahl, 359
Shepard, Randy, 740
Sherman, Richard, 406
Sherman Antitrust Act, 265, 267
  enforcement of, 270, 272, 273, 274
  European Union and, 491
  Microsoft antitrust case, 294, 299, 300
  predatory pricing and entry deterrence, 283
  regulation, 310
Shinawatra, Thaksin, 559
Shinsei Bank, 480
Shi Tao, 535
Shoney's, 695, 740, 741

Shops and Establishments Acts (India), 565
ShoreBank Corporation, 727
Shu, 525
Shuhong, Zhang, 137
Sidor, 559
Siekaczek, Reinhard, 775, 777
Siemens AG, 610, 774–777
Sierra Club, 95, 103
  activist strategy, 98, 100
  crisis management and, 136
  environmental politics, 356
  environmental protection issues, 360
  fuel economy standards case, 260
  nonmarket analysis, 154, 156, 157, 158
  vote recruitment by, 199
  Wal-Mart and, 649
Sierra Student Coalition, 102
Sigma Delta Chi, 81
Silent Spring (Carson), 91
Silver, Jonathan, 216
Silver, Robert S., 407
Silverman, Herman H., 671
Singapore Airlines, 170
Singhal, Arvind, 565
Single European Act (SEA), 12, 482–483, 486, 488, 495
SitePen, 39
Sjoblom, Bjorn, 617
Skidmore, Janet, 246
Skilling, Jeffrey, 642, 644, 645, 646, 647
Skype, 27
Slave labor, in Saipan, 754–755
Small and Medium-Size Business and Cooperative Law (Japan), 616
Small and Medium-Size Enterprises Agency (Japan), 616
Small Business Administration, 154
Smith, Adam, 621, 627
Smith, Bradford, 26
Smith, Chris, 547
Smith, Gary, 319
Smith, Gordon, 213
Smith, Richard, 430, 678
Smith, Synthia, 125
Smith, Todd, 399
Smithfield Foods, 354
SmithKline Beecham, 778
Smith v. Van Gorkom, 638–639
Smoke*Screen, 182
Smoot-Hawley Act, 574
Snow, John W., 262
Social accountability, 637–638
Social audits, 732–733
Social Charter (EU), 494–496
Social costs, 389, 391–392
Social democracy, 494–496
Social Democratic Party (Japan), 475
Social efficiency
  environmental management and stability, 340–343
  law and, 387–389, 391–392
Social entrepreneurship cases, 567–570
Social explanations, 523–527
Social harmony, 524
Social policy, antitrust policy and, 265
Social pressure, 634
Social responsibility. *See* Corporate social responsibility
Social value, 342, 343
Societal significance perspective, 70–72
Societal well-being, 661–662
Société Générale, 121, 129
Society of Professional Journalists, 81
Soft Drink Interbrand Competition Act, 270, 288
Software and Information Industry Association, 251
Sohu.com, 546
Soka Gakkai Buddhist organization, 477

Songkhla, Mongkol na, 603
Sonny Bono Copyright Term Extension Act, 381
Sony, tipping, 416
Sony Corp. of America v. Universal City Studios, 379
Sophis Networks, 607–613
Source Perrier S.A., crisis management, 122–123
Sourcing, global, 721–722
South Africa, 571, 572
Southampton Place LP, 644
South Coast Air Resources Board, 726
Southdown, 598
Southern Baptist Convention, 91
Southern California Edison, 232, 324
Southern Wine and Spirits, 161
South Korea, 592, 593
Southland Corporation, 209
South Shore Bank, 727
Soviet Union, 197, 198
SPA Agencies, 565
Spain, 507, 508, 511–516
Special Economic Zones (China), 521–522, 533
Special interest groups, 8–9
Specialty Vehicle Institute of America (SVIA), 318–319
Specific performance, 386
Spectrum auction, 27, 37, 38–39
Spencer, Matthew, 728
Spencer's, 566
Spiegel, Robert J., 253, 255, 257
Spilker, Bert, 252, 257
Spitzer, Eliot, 118
Sporting Goods Manufacturers Association, 209
Sprint Communications, 321, 326, 330, 493
Spurlock, Morgan, 21
Spyware, 418
SquareTrade, 440
Stabenow, Debbie, 260
Stafford, Kathy, 651
Staffs, in U.S. Congress, 178
Stakeholder management, at Wal-Mart, 728–729
Stakeholder theory, 626–628
Standardization, 415
Standards setting, under EPA, 351
Standing Committee of Politburo (China), 529
Stanford Group Company, 30
Stanhill, William D., 215
Stanton, Michael, 260, 261
Staples, 104, 290–293
Starbucks, 43, 48, 99, 556, 633, 634
Stark, Pete, 506
Starkie-Alves, Anne, 139
StarKist Seafood Company, 631
StarKist Tuna, boycotts against, 91
State Administration for Industry and Commerce, 544
State Administration of Radio, Film, and Television (China), 31
State aid, in European union, 494
State Council (China), 530–531, 535, 543, 544
State Council Information Office (China), 545, 547
State Council of China, 6, 139
State Education Commission, 531
State Environmental Protection Administration (SEPA), 539
State Food and Drug Administration (China), 538
State government
   environmental policy initiatives, 353
   Internet taxation, 250, 423–424
   nonmarket strategy and, 191
   trade association lobbying and, 234
State institutions, in China, 530–531
"State of the News Media, The," 73, 76
State-owned enterprises (China), 517, 532–533, 541–543

State Planning Commission (China), 531, 532
Static efficiency, 279, 280
Statute of limitations, 396
Statute of repose, 396
Statutes, antitrust, 265, 267–269
Steel imports, 592–593
Steere, William, Jr., 780
Stegemeier, Richard J., 726
Stein, Sidney, 408
Steinhardt, Barry, 430
Stemberg, Thomas, 290
Step Up Women's Network, 243
Stevens, Frank, 716
Stevens, Ted, 335
Stinchfield, Patti, 246
Stonhill, 643
Strategic corporate social performance, 633
Strategic trade theory, 578
Strategy. *See* Nonmarket strategy
Streamcast, 379
Street, William, 716
Strict liability, 392–393, 394, 395–396
Structural approach (antitrust thought), 274, 275–277, 280
Structural pluralism, 452
Structured pluralism, 153–154
Student Environmental Action Coalition, 102
Students for Environmental and Economic Justice (SEEJ), 116–117
Students Transforming and Resisting Corporations, 102
Stupak, Bart, 135
Subprime lending case, 714–716
Subsidization, in European Union, 494. *See also* Cross-subsidization
Substantive due process, 307
Substitutes, 156
Sudan, 561
Sukuk, 560
Sullivan, Coleman, 741
Sumitomo Corporation, 474
Sumitomo Trust Bank, 467
Sun Bank, 672
Sun Electric Corporation, 59
Sun Microsystems, 232
   encryption export controls case, 612–613
   European Union and, 493
   Microsoft antitrust case, 295, 297, 298, 300, 301
Sun Yat-sen, 519
Super 301, 596–597
Super Size Me (documentary), 21
Superfund, 352–353, 359
Suppliers, in restaurant industry, 24
Suppliers' factories, working conditions in, 758–761
Supply side, in nonmarket analysis, 158, 167–168
Supreme People's Court (China), 531
Supreme People's Procurator (China), 531
Surui (indigenous tribe), 30
SustainAbility, Ltd., 107
Sustainable Forest Initiative (SFI), 107
Sustainable Forestry Institute (SFI), 98
SUV Owners of America, 261
Swap Sub, 644
Swaziland, 570
Sweatshops, 758–759
Sweden
   EU carbon tax case, 506
   EU duty free abolition and, 513
   EU nonmarket issues, 496
   interests, 498
   Internet privacy, 420
   Toys 'Я' Us case, 615, 617–618
Sweet, Robert W., 410
Swift Boat Veterans for Truth, 229
Swindle, Orson, 432
Swire, Peter, 510
Sykes, Sir Richard, 782

Syntex, 189
Syracuse Housing Partnership, 106
Syria, 572
Systems Control, Inc., 59

Taiwan, 112, 114, 520, 522
Takenaka, Heizo, 477–478
Talon, 645
Tandy/Radio Shack, 249
Tang Dynasty (China), 518
Tanzania, 568
Target
   Chicago public politics case, 218
   crisis management, 135, 136, 148
   merger case (Staples–Office Depot), 291
Target selection
   private politics, 98–100
   public officeholders, 203
Tariff Act (1930), 589
Tariffs, on automobile industry, 7
Tata, 566
Tauke, Thomas J., 27
Taxes
   carried interest, 213–216
   Internet, 247–252, 423–425
   luxury, 184
   value-added, 251, 483, 511
Tax Reduction and Reform Act (2007), 214
Tax shelters case, 677–679
Taylor, Russell, 651
Teamsters Union, 595
Technical information, 202, 223–224
Technological advancement, 11–12
Technology
   Molecular Insight Pharmaceuticals, 61–62
   privacy and, 418
   See also Internet
Technopak, 566
Telecom Watchdog, 572
Telecommunications Act (1996), 185, 322, 326, 332–333
Telecommunications industry
   deregulation of, 321–323
   Nippon Telephone and Telegraph case, 474–476
Telecommunications International, 474
Teleological ethics systems, 681, 682
Television news, 72–73, 76. *See also* News media
Telewest Communications, 493
Telway-Japan, 470
Tesco PLC, 551–552, 555–556, 564–566
Testimony, 236–237
Teva Pharmaceuticals, 256
Texaco, 695
Texas Eagle Forum, 245, 246
Texas Instruments, 471
Texas State Board of Education, 91–92
Thailand, 133, 559, 587, 596–606
Thai Network of People Living with AIDS/HIV, 605
Thirteenth Amendment, 696
Thompson, Danny, 741
Thompson, Robin, 740
Thompson, Susan, 741
Thomson Corporation, 434
ThyssenKrupp, 776
TIAA-CREF, 639
Tianya.cn, 31
Tibet, 558
Tides Foundation, 107
Tillinghast-Towers Perrin, 8
Tillman Act, 228
Timbers, The, 56
Timeshare industry, 57
Timing, 226
Tipping, 416–417
Tobacco politics, 181–183
Tobacco Resolution, 181
Tokyo Round, 581

Tolls, 29–30
Toomey, Mike, 245
Torts, 386–387
Toshiba Machine Company, 197–199
Toshiba, 232
Tower Group, 448
Toxic Substances Control Act (TSCA), 369
Toxics Release Inventory (TRI), 358–359
Toyoda, Shoichiro, 459, 468
Toyota, 1, 2
   antitrust thought, 280
   carbon dioxide emission regulations, 11
   China and, 537
   corporate social responsibility, 8
   diversity, 7
   environmental pressure on, 7–8
   fuel economy standards case, 261, 262
   intellectual property issues, 8
   Japan and, 459, 468
   media coverage of, 8
   products liability politics, 400
   recalls, 8
   UAW and, 7
   worker safety, 7
Toys 'R' Us, 199, 614–618
Tradable permits systems. *See* Cap-and-trade systems
Trade Act (1974), 589
Trade Adjustment Assistance Act, 590
Trade agreements. *See* International trade agreements
Trade associations, 234
Trade disputes, 585–587
Trade liberalization, 11, 579, 580. *See also* Free trade agreements; *specific free trade agreements*
Trademarks, 28–29, 382–383. *See also* Intellectual property
Tradenable, 440
Tradeoffs, 339–340
Trade policy. *See* International trade policy
Trade-Related Aspects of Intellectual Property Rights (TRIPS), 19, 582–583, 588, 602, 745, 757, 779, 781
Trade secrets, 382–383
Transaction costs, 343
Transfair USA, 555, 556
Transparency International (TI), 550, 761, 770, 776
Travelers Group, 714
Treatment Action Campaign (TAC), 780
Treatment Action Group, 606
Treaty Establishing the European Community, 490, 491
Treaty of Brussels, 482
Treaty of Lisbon, 484, 490, 502
Treaty of Nanjing, 519
Treaty of Paris, 481
Treaty of Rome, 482, 490
Treble damages, 273
Trial Lawyers Association, 8
Triplett, Earl, 124
Triplett, Mary, 124
Tri-TAC, 369
Tropical Forest Foundation, 363
Trust gap, 96–97, 620–621
TRUSTe, 421, 423, 431, 433
Truth in Lending Act, 447
Truth in Savings Act, 447
Tudou, 31
Tunney Act, 301
Tupperware, 543
TW Services, 740
Twenty-First Amendment, 161
Tying, 268
Tyson Foods, 227

UBS, 679
UCB SA, 257, 717

Uganda, 568, 570
Umbrella organizations. *See* Peak associations
UNAIDS, 780
Unanimous consent agreements (UCAs), 175
Underdeveloped markets, business groups in, 557–558
Understandings, changes in, 11, 12
Unethical behavior, sources of, 738–739
UNICEF, 780
Uniform Standards Coalition, 235
Uniform Time Act, 208
Unilateral nonmarket strategies, 192
Unilever PLC, 102, 734, 762
Union of Concerned Scientists, 11
Union of Food and Commercial Workers (UFCW), 144–145, 146, 147, 148, 729
Union of Industrial and Employers Confederations of Europe (UNICE), 499
Union of Needletrade, Industrial and Textile Employees (UNITE), 112, 758, 759
Unions. *See* Labor unions; *specific unions*
Uniqlo case, 479–480
UNITA, 774
United Airlines, 235, 640, 665
United Auto Workers (UAW), 7
  coalition building, 233
  fuel economy standards case, 259, 260, 262, 263
  international trade policy, 580
United Egg Producers (UEP), 23–24
United Food and Commercial Workers (UFCW), 217, 218
United Kingdom
  China and, 522
  eBay database protection case, 433
  emerging markets and, 564
  EU carbon tax case, 507, 508
  GlaxoSmithKline, 718
  Internet privacy, 420, 421
  McDonald's libel case, 84
  pharmaceutical industry, 19
  price fixing case, 289
  private politics case, 108–111
United Methodist Church, 92
United Mine Workers (UMW), 183
United Nations, 348, 349, 750, 754, 756–757, 760, 774, 781
United Nations Convention on Contracts for the International Sale of Goods, 750
United Nations Development Program, 780
United Nations Framework Convention on Climate Change, 750
United Nations International Conference on Population and Development, 747
United Online, 329
U.S. Agency for International Development (USAID), 767
U.S. Anti-Hacking Statute, 434
United States Association of Importers of Textiles and Apparel, 591
U.S. Chamber Institute for Legal Reform, 409, 410
U.S. Chamber of Commerce, 195, 215, 234, 372, 410
U.S. Climate Action Partnership, 338
U.S. Conference of Mayors, 249, 309, 372
U.S. Congress, 5, 9
  access to, 225
  automobile industry and, 6
  Boeing and, 164
  Doha Round, 588
  fuel economy standards, 259, 260, 262–263
  fuel efficiency standards, 260, 262–263

intellectual property law and, 377
Internet taxation case, 250
overview of, 154, 175–180
responsiveness of, 205
tobacco politics, 181
trade association lobbying and, 234
See also Legislation; Taxes; *specific laws, representatives, and senators*
U.S. Constitution, 175
  regulation and, 304–305, 306
  rights and, 682, 688
  See also specific amendments
U.S. Court of International Trade (CIT), 589, 601
U.S. Department of Agriculture (USDA), 5, 23, 24, 154, 182
U.S. Department of Commerce, 197, 205, 225, 226, 510
U.S. Department of Defense, 197
U.S. Department of Energy, 309, 347, 365, 367
U.S. Department of Health and Human Service, 409
U.S. Department of Justice, 350, 651, 767
  Antitrust Division, 266, 272
  antitrust laws, 270, 271, 272, 274, 278, 279, 285, 288
  Citigroup case, 716
  crisis management and, 148
  Denny's customer service case, 741
  European Union and, 493
  Google and, 29, 548
  Japan and, 462
  judicial actions, 238
  merger case, 290
  Microsoft and, 31, 294, 295, 298, 300
  price fixing case, 289
  responsiveness of, 205
U.S. Department of Labor, 149, 650, 737, 748
U.S. Department of State, 197, 754
U.S. Department of the Treasury, 225, 727
U.S. Department of Transportation, 208, 210, 238, 259
U.S. Green Building Council, 339–340
U.S. Green Lights program, 24
U.S. House of Representatives, 175
U.S. Industry Coordinating Group, 499
U.S. International Trade Commission, 597
U.S. National Business Coalition on E-Commerce and Privacy, 510
U.S. Naval Academy, 740
U.S. Navy, 163
U.S. Public Interest Research Group, 26, 102
U.S. Secret Service, 740
U.S. Senate, 175
U.S. Supreme Court
  appointments to, 180
  class action lawsuits and, 12
U.S. Surgeon General, 20, 409
U.S. trade policy, 588–590
U.S. Trade Representative (USTR), 205, 225, 478, 589, 595
U.S. v. Aluminum Co. of America, 269
U.S. v. Arnold Schwinn & Co., 280, 281
U.S. v. Harriss, 226–227
United Steel Workers (USW), 579, 580, 592, 593
United Steelworkers of America v. Weber, 707
United Students Against Sweatshops, 759
United Technologies Corporation, 58
Universal Declaration of Human Rights, 754
Universalizability, 684
Universal Music Group, 380
Universities, 11
University of California–Berkeley, 52
University of Tennessee, 249–250
Unocal Corporation, 726
Upakaew, Kamol, 605

Upjohn, 676
UPN, 333
Upsher-Smith Laboratories, 19
Upton, Fred, 260
Urban expansion strategy, of Wal-Mart, 217–219
Uruguay, 588
Uruguay Round, 581, 583, 584, 585, 587, 590, 591
USAir, 235
Usmani, Muhammad Taqi, 560
Utilitarian duty, 662–663
Utilitarianism, 660–661
  act and rule, 664–666
  application of, 670–674
  bribery and, 764–766
  criticisms of, 667–670
  distribution and altruism, 662
  rights and, 666–667
  self-interest and societal well-being, 661–662
  summary, 674
  utilitarian duty and the Calabresi and Melamed principles, 662–663
Utility, interpersonal comparisons of, 668
Utz Kapeh, 556

Vacharanukulki-eti, Kriengsak, 605
Vallese, Judy, 139
Value-added tax (VAT), 251, 483, 511–516
Value chain, 193, 194
Van Andel, Steve, 544
Van Eeden, Dirk, 604
Van Etten, W. Thomas, 672
Vegetarian Resource Group, 24
Venezuela, 559, 562, 588
Verispan LLC, 407
Verizon, 27, 37, 38, 39, 322, 328
Verizon Business, 572
Vermont Renewal, 245
Vertical arrangements, 280–282
Vertical integration, 268
Vertical practices, 268, 269
Veteran Affairs Outcomes Group, 717
Viacom, 74, 333
Victoria's Secret, 423
Video Privacy Protection Act, 421
Vienna Convention for the Protection of the Ozone Layer, 750
Vietnam, 112–113, 114, 560
Vietnam Labor Watch (VLW), 113
Viking Yacht, 184
Vinson and Elkins, 645
Virgin Atlantic Airways, price fixing by, 284, 289–290
Virtuoso, 56
Visa, 272, 273, 274, 446
Vista (operating system), 31
Vivendi SA, 286, 493
Vivendi Universal SA, 757
Vocational Rehabilitation Act, 696
Vodacom, 571, 572
Vodafone, 571, 757
Volkswagen, 366, 496
Voluntary collective programs, for environmental management and stability, 364–365
Von Blumberg, Peter, 776
Von Pierer, Heinrich, 774, 775, 776
Vote recruitment, 199–202
Vujovich, Christina M., 367

Wachholz, James, 62
Waggoner, Rick, 6, 157
Waitt, Thomas, 248
WakeUpWalMart.com, 145, 146, 147, 360, 649
Wako Koeki, 197
Waldron, Robert, 671
Wall, John C., 367
Wallace, Mike, 88
Wallerstein, Barry, 371
Wall Street Journal, 550

Wal-Mart, 1, 2, 726
  antitrust laws, 273
  corporate social performance, 632
  corporate social responsibility, 647–650, 728–729
  crisis management, 120, 127, 128, 143–151
  emerging markets and, 566
  environmental programs, 338
  environmental protection issues, 360
  Internet taxation case, 249, 250
  merger case (Staples–Office Depot), 291
  nonmarket capabilities of, 49
  rent chain and, 194
  reputation and stakeholder management, 49, 728–729
  rights and, 696–697
  urban expansion strategy, 217–219
Wal-Mart bill (Maryland), 147
Wal-Mart: The High Cost of Low Price (documentary), 145
Wal-Mart Watch, 146, 147, 648
Wal-Mart Workers Association, 146
Walsh, Willie, 289
Walt Disney Company, 74, 91, 249
Walter, Jim, 136, 138
Walton, Sam, 143
Walton Family Foundation, 146
Wang Zhongfu, 544
Warranties, 393
Warranty of merchantability, 393
Warring States Period (China), 518
Washington Analysis, 254
Waste reduction, by McDonald's, 362
Watanuki, Tamisuke, 478
Watchdog groups, 8–9, 90–91. *See also specific organizations*
Watergate affair, 74
Water Keeper Alliance, 354
Watkins, Sherron, 645
Watrman, Robert H., 718
WB, 333
WBBM (Chicago television station), 84
Weatherup, Craig A., 124, 125
Webb-Pomerene Act, 269–270
WebSideStory, 417
Webwasher.com, 431
Weeda, David F., 258
Weedfald, Peter, 368
Weill, Sandy, 100, 116, 118, 714, 716
Weinstein, Michael, 605, 606
Weintraub, Rachel, 138
WellPoint Health Networks, 18, 221, 252, 253, 254, 255, 256, 257
WellPoint Pharmacy Management, 255
Wendy's, 123
Wen Jiabao, 530, 536
Wessex Water, 642
West, Kanye, 774
Westco Oil Company, 370
Westerfield, Charles, 568
Westin Hotels, 640
WestLB, 357
Weston, Paul, 448
Westpac, 357
Weyerhauser, 92, 104, 105
Whaley, Soso, 21
WHDH-TV (Boston television station), 82
White, Miles D., 605
White House Apparel Industry Partnership, 758
White Spaces Coalition, 39
Whitman, Meg, 433, 435, 438
Whitt, Larry, 226
Whitt, Richard, 39
Whittle Shortline Railroad, 138
Whitworth, Mike, 138
Whole Foods Market, 286, 556, 624, 633
Wholly foreign-owned enterprise (WFOE), 531–532
Why Wal-Mart Works & Why That Makes Some People Crazy (Galloway), 145

Wilderness Society, 154
Wildfeuer, Christian, 296
Wild Oats Markets, 286
Wilkes, Michael, 717
Willett, Walter, 22
Williams, Simon, 289
Wilson-Lowi matrix, 159–160, 161, 162, 167, 190
Wine America, 161
Wine and Spirit Wholesalers of America, 161
Wine Institute (California), 161
Wingo, Scott, 434
Winkelman, John, 717
Winn-Dixie, 147
Winnick, Gary, 678
Winstar Communications, 328
Woicke, Peter, 357
Woloshin, Steven, 717, 718
Women in Government, 244
Women's Environment and Development Organization (WEDO), 748
Women's rights, in China, 535–536
Wong, Nicole, 26
Wood, Alastair, 254
Wood, Bob, 114
Wood, Pat, III, 646
Wood Purchasing Policy, 363
Woods, Willie E., Jr., 215
Woodward, Robert, 74
Woolard, Edgar S., Jr., 360
Woolworths, 566
Wootan, Margo, 21–22
Worker Rights Consortium, 759
Worker safety, in automobile industry, 7

Workers' rights, in China, 538–539
Working conditions, in suppliers' factories, 758–761
Working Families for Wal-Mart, 649
Workplace obesity, 22
World Intellectual Property Organization, 583
World Association of Newspapers, 28
World Bank, 356
  antiglobalization protests against, 97
  China and, 534
  emerging markets and, 561
  GlaxoSmithKline AIDS drugs policy case, 780
World Business Council on Sustainable Development, 727
WorldCom, 1, 330
World Council for Susatianable Development, 630
World Court, 750
World Health Organization (WHO), 409, 605, 744–745, 779, 780
World Intellectual Property Organization, 750
World Privacy Forum, 25, 420
World Trade Organization (WTO), 7, 9, 12, 750
  antiglobalization protests against, 97
  applied rights analysis and, 689
  China and, 204, 517, 528, 534
  compulsory licensing case, 602
  Dispute Settlement Body, 575–576
  Doha Round, 583, 587–588
  emerging markets and, 571

GlaxoSmithKline AIDS drugs policy case, 779
international trade agreements, 581–582
international trade policy, 574
Internet taxation, 248, 250, 251
pharmaceutical industry, 19
restaurant industry, 22
World War II, China and, 520
World Wildlife Fund, 104, 363
Worley, Rob T., 671
Wright, Robert, 87
Writers Guild of America, 335
Wu, Mae, 369
Wugang, 541–543
Wu Yi, 544
Wyatt, Amy, 566
Wyden, Ron, 248, 677
Wyeth-Ayerst Laboratories, 669, 675–677

Xia, Bill, 546
Xiangfan Iron and Steel Group, 542
Xingtian Company, 543
Xin Ye, 546
Xitongs, 531
XL Insurance, 128

Yahoo!
  China and, 535, 546, 548
  eBay database protection case, 433, 434, 437
  Google and, 27, 28, 29
  international strategy, 37
  Microsoft and, 31
  online markets, 416

Yamada, Tadataka, 605
Yamaha Motor Company, 479
Yamato Transport Company, 477
Yamoff, Seymour L., 82
Yanai, Tadashi, 479
Yang, Jerry, 31
Yetraeus, Sten, 617
Yi, Wu, 139
Yingling, Edward L., 448
Yoffie, David, 300
Yosihara, Yoshihide, 479
Youku, 31
Young, Andrew, 113
Young, Louis H., 70, 74
Yousef, Ramzi, 609
Yousif, Mahmoud al-, 25
YouTube, 8, 29–30, 31, 123, 137, 240, 561
Yuan Shikai, 519
Yuguang, Xie, 137
Yunus, Muhammad, 556, 567, 568

Zaibatsu, 466
Zambrano, Lorenzo, 597, 600, 601
Zayles, 292
Zen Dentsu, 475
Zero-Knowledge Systems, 417, 431
Zhao Jing, 546
Zhou Enlai, 521
Zimbabwe, 560–561
Zindler, Harald, 110
Zogby International, 146
Zoku, 456–457, 464, 470, 475
Zonneveld, Luuk Laurens, 556